THE OXFORD H

MARITIME
ARCHAEOLOGY

THE OXFORD HANDBOOK OF

MARITIME ARCHAEOLOGY

ALEXIS CATSAMBIS,
BEN FORD,
AND
DONNY L. HAMILTON

OXFORD
UNIVERSITY PRESS

OXFORD
UNIVERSITY PRESS

Oxford University Press is a department of the University of Oxford.
It furthers the University's objective of excellence in research, scholarship,
and education by publishing worldwide.

Oxford   New York
Auckland   Cape Town   Dar es Salaam   Hong Kong   Karachi
Kuala Lumpur   Madrid   Melbourne   Mexico City   Nairobi
New Delhi   Shanghai   Taipei   Toronto

With offices in
Argentina   Austria   Brazil   Chile   Czech Republic   France   Greece
Guatemala   Hungary   Italy   Japan   Poland   Portugal   Singapore
South Korea   Switzerland   Thailand   Turkey   Ukraine   Vietnam

Oxford is a registered trade mark of Oxford University Press
in the UK and certain other countries.

Published in the United States of America by
Oxford University Press
198 Madison Avenue, New York, NY 10016

© Oxford University Press 2011

First issued as an Oxford University Press paperback, 2014.

Library of Congress Cataloging-in-Publication Data
The Oxford handbook of maritime archaeology / edited by Alexis
Catsambis, Ben Ford, and Donny L. Hamilton.
p.   cm.
Includes bibliographical references and index.
ISBN 978-0-19-537517-6 (hardcover); 978-0-19-933600-5 (paperback)
1. Underwater archaeology—Handbooks, manuals, etc.
I. Catsambis, Alexis. II. Ford, Ben. III. Hamilton, Donny Leon.
IV. Title: Handbook of maritime archaeology.
CC77.U5O99   2011
930.1028′04—dc22   2010022350

To our significant others
for their patience
past, present, and future.

CONTENTS

....

PART VII GLOSSARY AND APPENDIX

PREFACE

....

ALEXIS CATSAMBIS,
BEN FORD,
AND
DONNY L. HAMILTON

Inquisitiveness is at the core of human nature. The same can be said for persistence in the face of overcoming boundaries, whether perceived or real. The sea is perhaps the greatest boundary that humankind has looked upon through most of history. This timeless relationship between humanity and the "wine-dark sea" is, therefore, inseparably linked with what it is to be human. It is the lasting physical traces of this effort to overcome the wet element that maritime archaeology attempts to illuminate. With this volume we hope to show the current state of this field, entering its sixth decade, now on firm footing and spreading its sails in all directions.

The *Oxford Handbook of Maritime Archaeology* coincides with a new period of development in a now confident and maturing field that seeks to expand its horizons into areas for which methods and concepts are only just being addressed. Exemplifying this current stage of advancement are new academic programs in maritime archaeology or related disciplines, an increasing number of academic and professional maritime archaeologists, an expanding scope of research, closer partnerships with sister fields, a growing emphasis on cultural resource management and public education, international conventions and symposia, and preservation of maritime heritage in deep or international waters. Maritime archaeology is now of worldwide scope. The research questions being asked are as varied and as interconnected as the researchers themselves and the following chapters written by the contributors of this volume. Growing out of single-site research, which has formed the basis of our field, the future now rests on synthesis– synthesis of geographically and chronologically diverse archaeological data; synthesis and evolution of concepts; synthesis of archaeological subdisciplines and maritime sciences; synthesis of regional cultural resource management strategies; and a synthesis of public initiatives for the preservation of our maritime cultural heritage. Understand, however, that synthesis does not mean conformity—the very opposite, in

fact: the more questions we ask, the more paths we follow, and the more collaborations we will embrace. As we press into deeper waters, both literally and conceptually, new discoveries will surely conceive new branches, which will follow their own
pace of growth and development.

The themes explored in this volume are by no means an all-encompassing
review of the field. This handbook was conceived as an overview of the state of the
art and science in maritime archaeology, as a benchmark in the development of the
field, and as a springboard for future research. However, only through an understanding of the work that has been accomplished can new and innovative techniques and questions be developed. The work that precedes this volume has led to
the establishment of maritime archaeology as a field in its own right—and it is on
this foundation that we build.

While principally concerned with submerged sites, the field now embraces the
full spectrum of past maritime culture, culture oriented toward and governed by its
interaction with the water. The term "maritime archaeology" was selected for the
title of this volume because it allows for the broadest interpretation of the field,
addressing components on either side of the waterline (e.g., shipwrecks to shipyards) and ethnographic components (e.g., maritime landscapes and maritime
communities). There are technical methods unique to maritime investigations
within the field of archaeology, most notably SCUBA and marine remote sensing,
but these techniques are not employed by all maritime archaeologists and are not
the sole hallmark of the discipline. Rather, what makes maritime archaeology largely
unique in the field of archaeology is its breadth of study.

Maritime archaeologists engage sites and questions that span human history,
as maritime peoples and communities, whether perennial or ephemeral, dynamic
or static, are all part of an enduring relationship with the sea that stems from a
time before modern humans walked the earth. A lack of regionalism also distinguishes the field. Vessels were often the vectors of cultural interactions, and maritime peoples the de facto ambassadors of cultural and technological diffusion.
Either through directed expansion, trade, war, and migration, or through serendipitous means such as exploration and accident, maritime cultures were so constantly in direct and indirect contact with other groups as to undermine the notion of region. The cross-cultural perspective engendered by these interregional
and pan-historical analyses is at the heart of effective anthropological and historical scholarship.

Through wide-ranging investigations, maritime archaeology has reached the
point where sufficient data have been gathered on so many aspects of the maritime
past that anthropological and historical questions can be addressed. The scientific
process of hypothesis forming, testing, and revising can begin to address questions
of past human culture. This development of data, method, and theory places maritime archaeology squarely within the realm of archaeology as a whole, allowing the
communication of ideas between subfields and the advancement of archaeology as
a science. The realization of a more holistic archaeology that accounts for life afloat
and ashore, trade routes and shipping lanes, the full range of resource procurement

strategies, and the cognitive correlates of life in the widest array of environments may be in the not-too-distant future.

In support of this matured, integrated maritime archaeology, the current handbook attempts to embrace the expansive diversity of the field, examining its various contemporary practices and forms, as well as regional approaches and the interdisciplinary nature of maritime archaeology. A wide range of archaeologists, including established authors synthesizing their wide experience and younger scholars drawing on recent research in public, private, and academic environments, have contributed to this volume. Each author speaks from his or her own experience and offers a unique perspective on the field, but all contributors were required to approach their topic from a broad and questioning perspective. Only by critically evaluating the current state of method and theory in maritime archaeology will the field continue to press forward in new and valuable directions. Furthermore, method and theory should be locked in a perpetually stimulating relationship, as the best archaeology pairs theory and practice. Consequently, theory is not segregated in a single section of the volume. Many of the authors include both interpretation and description in a single essay, increasing the usefulness of both.

As maritime archaeology grows in scope and integration, the ability of a single volume to capture all important facets of the discipline decreases. The fervent pace of research has not allowed for all areas, geographic or otherwise, to be represented to the preferred degree. At the same time, the increasing number of projects in areas not previously explored and in the middle-grounds between existing specialties has expanded the scope of the field so far that not every worthwhile topic could be covered in this volume without fear of reducing chapters to encyclopedic entries. In an attempt to circumscribe the scope of this handbook, we have adhered closely to the definition of maritime as "pertaining to the sea." Inland cultural heritage resources are covered only tangentially. There is no question, however, that such resources are a valid and important aspect of many maritime cultures, and the term "maritime" has often been comfortably applied to cultures operating exclusively on inland waters.

Furthermore, in an attempt to serve as wide a range of sophisticated interested parties as possible, this volume is intended to be not a collection of site-specific essays but rather a book of analytical and philosophical approaches that can be explored, tested, adhered to, or challenged. The focus is on established and emerging topics, regions, and methods that are instructive to the field as a whole. To that end, the handbook is organized into four main sections, prefaced with a retrospective and reflective introduction by George Bass (Part I) and summarized by the forward-looking concluding thoughts of Paula Martin (Part VI). Parts II through V are organized around the processes of maritime archaeology, ships and shipwrecks, maritime culture and life ashore, and maritime archaeology beyond the site.

The first section of the volume—Part II, "The Process"—follows the approaches applied to maritime archaeological projects, beginning with understanding ships, site formation processes, and framing one's work, through to postprocessing and long-term storage of archaeological data. Emphasizing shipwrecks and submerged sites, the section describes the process of locating, surveying, excavating, recording, conserving, analyzing, and synthesizing maritime archaeological sites and information. The authors of these essays address both established methods and emerging techniques while offering a critical review of the process of maritime archaeology. The goal of the section is to convey the present state of maritime archaeology and to expand on a set of best practices proposed by authorities in the field that can be applied to a wide range of sites.

Part III, "Ships and Shipwrecks," traces the regional evolution of ships and provides an international overview of shipwreck studies. In an attempt to address global variation in maritime archaeology, the section focuses both on lesser-studied areas and on traditional core regions of European and American nautical archaeology. The variety of adaptations to the water, which are dependent on technology, culture, and environment, are clearly visible in the wide array of shipwrecks that have been investigated. Each vessel type is unique to its period and region but is also indicative of global trends. The chapters in this section not only describe the vessels of a particular region or period, but trace their development, compare them to other vessels, and address larger questions of human adaptation to the marine environment. While recognizing that even this, the largest section of the volume, cannot be comprehensive, it is our hope that the broad coverage will encourage international and interregional collaborations to address topics of mutual interest.

Part IV, "Maritime Culture and Life Ashore," expands the scope of maritime archaeology beyond shipwrecks to include coastal sites and inundated terrestrial sites (both historic and prehistoric). These essays provide a wider context for past maritime cultures through a range of discussions. They consider how coastal or formerly coastal sites fit within the larger human maritime adaptation by answering questions pertaining to purpose, location, perception, and community. Maritime archaeology has traditionally been a subject of shipwreck studies, but in recent years the range of sites investigated and the types of research questions asked have grown significantly. Recognizing that the weight of current research remains with shipwreck studies, this section may be seen as a promise of where new (and not so new) fields of research are taking the discipline.

Finally, Part V, "Beyond the Site," extends the discussion past research proper and into the framework within which maritime archaeology frequently operates. Its main aim is to demonstrate the complex nature of the field as it interacts with government agencies, industry, other academic fields, economic interests, and multivocal publics. The importance of preserving underwater cultural heritage, the challenges faced in the realm of public policy, and the strong impact the public has on the field are among the aspects highlighted. Such issues have come to the forefront with the growth of cultural heritage management throughout the world, and a real-world model of one country's response to the challenge is presented, in hopes of providing inspiration for those parts of the world just beginning their journey. The pressing need to preserve cultural heritage is spurred on by increasing technological sophistication of commercial entities, whether aimed at salvage or trawling, that now have the ability to access and disturb sites previously protected through isolation. Fundamental to this section is the belief that archaeology that does not contribute to the public good, while preserving information for posterity, is of little value. Authors in this section clearly explain the current state of affairs and describe approaches to interpretation and protection that have succeeded and failed, as well as propose paths to be examined in the future.

And so, with respect to that which came before, and faith in the promise of what lies ahead, we hope this volume has done justice to the multifaceted art and science that is maritime archaeology. The work of establishing the field in many parts of the world is now done. What challenges us currently is to cast a wider net—geographically, chronologically, and conceptually—and make maritime archaeology, the study of mankind's long relationship with the sea, relevant to the humans of today.

ACKNOWLEDGMENTS

....

During the three years since Oxford University Press first proposed this volume to Donny Hamilton, a great number of people contributed to both forming the volume's overall concept and bringing it to fruition. The anonymous reviewers of the original handbook proposal helped the editors formulate a more comprehensive approach to the subject matter. Their thoughts were complemented by those of other scholars, many of whom eventually became contributors, who reviewed the overall scope and proposed list of topics. Several of the contributors were approached early on, and their input helped frame the volume's structure. Other informal but valuable advisers, such as John Hale, Dan Davis, and Mark Pollard, provided insights at various points throughout the process.

This handbook is a reflection of the determination of its contributing authors, their work, and that of their peers. Many of their thoughts, from formatting to author and topic selection, were adopted by the editors and deserve to be acknowledged. The support received from Oxford University Press and the liberties afforded to the editors allowed for all these valuable thoughts to be molded into the volume you now hold.

On the practical side, the always positive and effective staff of the Department of Anthropology at Texas A&M University and a number of talented graduate assistants were always there to tend to the numerous details involved in such an endeavor. We also wish to thank Texas A&M University Press for allowing us to reprint J. Richard Steffy's illustrated glossary, and all those institutions, publishers, artists, photographers, and scholars who endorsed the use of their work in this volume, as it is elevated by the many informative illustrations that reflect and convey the breadth of maritime archaeology. Indexing was performed by Robert Swanson.

—The Editors

An academic career, like life, is a circuitous journey, ending up where you never anticipated, much less planned. I never set out to be a historical or a nautical archaeologist doing conservation, but that is what I have been doing for the past 33 years, since joining the faculty of the Nautical Archaeology Program at Texas A&M University in 1978. This volume represents how far maritime archaeology has come. However, it could not have been compiled without the diligent, hard work of my two coeditors, Alexis Catsambis and Ben Ford, the best graduate students that I have had the privilege to work with. This volume stands as a testimony to them and all maritime archaeologists. It is also a tribute to a guy named Guy whom I met briefly once in Pecos, Texas, who told me when I was 18 that you can do anything you want to do. I believed him!

—Donny L. Hamilton

I acknowledge the love and support of Hilliary Creely, who patiently allowed me to sequester myself with a laptop weekend after weekend for the past several months. I also wish to thank the friends and colleagues who responded to the many technical questions that arose while editing; their wide knowledge base and willingness to help have improved this volume in countless ways. The Center for Maritime Archaeology and Conservation paid my salary for the first year of this project, allowing me to dedicate a substantial amount of time to the volume. Finally, compiling and editing a volume of this size and breadth is well beyond my individual abilities and I gratefully acknowledge the strengths and determination of my coeditors; without them this volume would not exist.

—Ben Ford

It is the unwavering encouragement of my wife, family, and close friends that has allowed me to commit my efforts to this volume. In large part, therefore, what my contribution has added to this endeavor is owed to the caring people around me. The support of a number of institutions—the Onassis Public Benefit Foundation, the Nautical Archaeology Program of Texas A&M University, the Institute of Nautical Archaeology, the Center for Maritime Archaeology & Conservation, the Naval History & Heritage Command, SEASPACE, and the Hellenic Professional Society of Texas—granted me the freedom to pursue this opportunity. I am most grateful for their backing. To all my tutors, colleagues, and friends who have mentored and led me through this exciting field, thank you. To the Clemson Conservation Center, the Hellenic Institute for the Preservation of Nautical Tradition, the Hellenic Institute of Ancient and Mediaeval Alexandrian Studies, the Institute for Exploration, the Hellenic Institute of Marine Archaeology, and the Greek Ephorate of Underwater Antiquities, my warm gratitude for your guidance. My name here appears due to the work of the great number of contributors that have made this volume what it is. Without the trust, generosity, and determination of my fellow editors, however, I would not be writing these words.

—Alexis Catsambis

Contributors

....

George F. Bass
Institute of Nautical Archaeology
Texas A&M University
United States of America

Kroum N. Batchvarov
Institute of Nautical Archaeology
United States of America

Vibeke Bischoff
The Viking Ship Museum in Roskilde
Denmark

Lucy Blue
Centre for Maritime Archaeology
University of Southampton
United Kingdom

Amy Borgens
Texas Historical Commission
United States of America

Deborah N. Carlson
Nautical Archaeology Program
Texas A&M University
United States of America

Filipe Castro
Nautical Archaeology Program
Texas A&M University
United States of America

Arthur B. Cohn
Lake Champlain Maritime Museum
United States of America

Kevin Crisman
Nautical Archaeology Program
Texas A&M University
United States of America

James P. Delgado
Office of National Marine Sanctuaries National Oceanic
and Atmospheric Administration
United States of America

Joanne M. Dennis
Lake Champlain Maritime Museum
United States of America

Francisco C. Domingues
Department of History
University of Lisbon
Portugal

Dolores Elkin
Underwater Archaeology Program (PROAS)
National Institute of Anthropology (INAPL)
National Research Council (CONICET)
Argentina

Anton Englert
The Viking Ship Museum in Roskilde
Denmark

Antony Firth
Wessex Archaeology
United Kingdom

Peter D. Fix
Center for Maritime Archaeology and Conservation
Texas A&M University
United States of America

Ben Ford
Department of Anthropology
Indiana University of Pennsylvania
United States of America

Richard Furuta
Center for the Study of Digital Libraries
Texas A&M University
United States of America

Aniruddh S. Gaur
Marine Archaeology Center
National Institute of Oceanography (CSIR)
India

Robert Gearhart
Atkins
United States of America

Donny L. Hamilton
Center for Maritime Archaeology and Conservation & Nautical Archaeology
    Program
Texas A&M University
United States of America

Fred Hocker
Vasa Museum
Sweden

Robert L. Hohlfelder
Department of History
University of Colorado at Boulder
United States of America

Yaacov Kahanov
Department of Maritime Civilizations
University of Haifa
Israel

Margaret Leshikar-Denton
Institute of Nautical Archaeology & Ships of Discovery
Cayman Islands

Pilar Luna Erreguerena
Underwater Archaeology Vice-Directorate
National Institute of Anthropology and History (INAH)
Mexico

Thijs J. Maarleveld
Maritime Archaeology Programme
University of Southern Denmark
Denmark

Colin Martin
University of St. Andrews
United Kingdom

Paula Martin
International Journal of Nautical Archaeology
United Kingdom

Michael McCarthy
Western Australian Museum
Australia

Carlos Monroy
Center for the Study of Digital Libraries
Texas A&M University
United States of America

Jason D. Moser
Florida State University
United States of America

Robert S. Neyland
Underwater Archaeology Branch
Naval History & Heritage Command
United States of America

Søren Nielsen
The Viking Ship Museum in Roskilde
Denmark

John P. Oleson
Department of Greek and Roman Studies
University of Victoria
Canada

Taras Pevny
Independent Scholar
United States of America

Mark E. Polzer
Institute of Nautical Archaeology & Nautical Archaeology Program
Texas A&M University
United States of America

Patrice Pomey
Centre Camille Jullian
Aix-Marseille Université & Centre National de la Recherche Scientifique
France

Rory Quinn
Centre for Maritime Archaeology
University of Ulster
Northern Ireland

Jesse Ransley
Centre for Maritime Archaeology
University of Southampton
United Kingdom

Morten Ravn
The Viking Ship Museum in Roskilde
Denmark

Nathan Richards
Program in Maritime Studies
East Carolina University
United States of America

Eric Rieth
Centre national de la recherche scientifique & Musée national de la marine
France

Susan Rose
Open University
United Kingdom

Timothy Runyan
Maritime Heritage Program, National Oceanic and Atmospheric
    Administration, and Coastal Resources Management Program,
East Carolina University
United States of America

Donald H. Sanders
Institute for the Visualization of History Inc.
United States of America

Randall J. Sasaki
Nautical Archaeology Program
Texas A&M University
United States of America

C. Wayne Smith
Center for Maritime Archaeology and Conservation & Nautical Archaeology
    Program
Texas A&M University
United States of America

Fredrik Søreide
Department of Archaeology and Religions Studies
Norwegian University of Science and Technology
Norway

Mark Staniforth
Department of Archaeology
Flinders University
Australia

J. Richard Steffy
In Memoriam

Michael C. Tuttle
Serapis Project
United States of America

Chris Underwood
Nautical Archaeology Society & Underwater Archaeology Program (PROAS)
National Institute of Anthropology
Argentina

Hans K. Van Tilburg
Office of National Marine Sanctuaries
National Oceanic and Atmospheric Administration
United States of America

Kamlesh H. Vora
Marine Archaeology Center
National Institute of Oceanography (CSIR)
India

Shelley Wachsmann
Nautical Archaeology Program
Texas A&M University
United States of America

Bruno E. J. S. Werz
African Institute for Marine and Underwater Research, Exploration and Education
   (AIMURE) & Department of Historical and Heritage Studies
University of Pretoria
South Africa

Christer Westerdahl
Department of Archaeology and Religious Studies
Norwegian University of Science and Technology
Norway

THE OXFORD HANDBOOK OF

MARITIME ARCHAEOLOGY

PART I

....

INTRODUCTION

....

THE DEVELOPMENT OF MARITIME ARCHAEOLOGY

GEORGE F. BASS

INTRODUCTION

THE importance of maritime cultures to the history of humankind is clear. Only by watercraft have some areas of our planet, from Australia to the smaller islands of the Earth's seas and oceans, been discovered, explored, settled, exploited, supplied, and defended. The myriad uses of watercraft include fishing and whaling, the transport of goods and people, warfare, exploration, and recreation. Watercraft require crews, usually drawn from the people living near the coasts. Additionally, watercraft require "homes," from simple sloping shores on which they may be beached to large and complex ports and harbors, the latter requiring specialized workers both for construction and later for utilization. These workers, in turn, as well as sailors, porters, merchants, and their families, require an infrastructure of support that includes at least temporary or permanent living quarters, suppliers of food and other essentials, land transport, maintenance installations including shipyards and chandleries, and financial, storage, and entertainment facilities.

The study of maritime cultures by means of archaeology is not the same as underwater archaeology. Although it may often use the general methods of underwater archaeology, maritime archaeology does not include the archaeology of sinkholes, like Little Salt Spring and Wakulla Springs in Florida, with their Paleo-Indian and paleontological remains, or the cenotes of the Yucatán Peninsula, with their Maya deposits, or the lake dwellings in Poland, Italy, Germany, Switzerland, and elsewhere. Indeed, an argument might be made that maritime archaeology does not include riverine archaeology, but that distinction is less clear, since a boat that leaves a sea to travel upriver stays the same boat, and how does one really distinguish riparian cultures from seashore cultures? Should there be any distinction between maritime and lacustrine archaeology, since there is so little difference between a small sea and a large lake?

In a sense, maritime archaeology is so new it is still defining itself. As this volume demonstrates, it has several branches. Coastal archaeology is the archaeology of those who simply lived in maritime zones, whether their sites are now on land, under water, or partly in both zones. Nautical archaeology is the archaeology of the *ship* (*naus* in Greek), whether the ship is on land, under water, partly on land and partly under water, or in some cases still afloat. It includes the archaeology not only of ships, but of all kinds of watercraft, from simple rafts, inflated skins, dugouts, kayaks, umiaks, and birch-bark canoes, to huge and complex modern freighters, tankers, passenger ships, and war vessels. Because the *naus* cannot be separated from its home, the study of ports and harbors and those who peopled them is usually considered part of nautical archaeology, just as it is part of the broader field of maritime archaeology (McCann et al. 1987; Raban 1985; Raban 1989; Raban and Holum 1996). Another developing specialization is the archaeology of aircraft, which may be included in nautical archaeology because aircraft are really ships of the sky.

The following chapters show that nautical archaeology remains the largest and best-known of the subdisciplines of maritime archaeology. A brief overview of its development should, therefore, be useful.

Development

What we today call nautical archaeology actually predates its perception as a separate branch of archaeology. In the nineteenth and twentieth centuries archaeologists routinely uncovered and studied Middle Kingdom boats in Egypt (de Morgan 1895: 81–83, with pls. XXIX–XXXI), part of a Roman ship dredged from a harbor at Marseille (Bass 1972: 81), the tenth-century Anglo-Saxon ship burial at Sutton Hoo in England (Bruce-Mitford et al. 1975–1983), various early vessels in Britain from the Bronze Age (Wright 1990) through the Roman period (Marsden 1994) and later (Marsden 1996), Viking ships in Scandinavia (Christensen 1972), and dugouts around the world (McGrail 2001: passim). These examples do not include the early, pre-SCUBA efforts of amateur archaeologists to examine sunken vessels. They range from the fifteenth-century breath-holding dives on two Roman vessels in Italy's Lake Nemi and the first use of a diving helmet in the following century on the same vessels (Ucelli 1950: 5–34), through the lowering of diving bells onto wrecks in Italy, Sweden, and the Caribbean as early as the sixteenth and seventeenth centuries, followed by eighteenth- and nineteenth-century explorations and salvage attempts by helmet divers on early wrecks in England (Broadwater 2002: 18, 23), to the 1935 raising, from Lake Champlain in the United States, of the intact colonial-period gunboat *Philadelphia*, now displayed at the Smithsonian Institution in Washington, DC (Bratten 2002).

Although the study of watercraft has continued on land in many places, as with the two Khufu ships in Egypt (Ward 2000: 45–68), parts of fifteenth-century BCE ships found in caves at a Pharaonic port near the Wadi Gawasis on the Egyptian Red Sea coast (Fattovich, Bard, and Ward 2007), dozens of ancient wrecks from the fifth century BCE to the fourth century CE at Pisa (Camilli and Setari 2006), Greek and Roman wrecks in Marseille (Pomey 1995), the Graveney boat in England (Fenwick 1978), and more than 30 Byzantine ships in a silted harbor at Constantinople (Kocabaş 2008), the branch of nautical archaeology that entails diving had its beginnings in the simple observation or collection of old things of antiquarian interest. There was nothing innately wrong with this at the time, for it satisfied the same craving for knowledge of the past that still attracts millions of people annually to visit the pyramids of Egypt, Pompeii, Machu Picchu, Angkor Vat, and Mount Vernon, or to view museum displays of the contents of King Tut's tomb, the Uluburun shipwreck, or the *Titanic*. Without this first stage, now unacceptable, scientific nautical archaeology would never have evolved.

By the nineteenth century, archaeologists like Augustus Pitt-Rivers in England, Heinrich Schliemann in Turkey, and Flinders Petrie in Egypt demonstrated how much more could be learned of the past by properly recorded stratigraphic excavations on land and the sequence dating of artifacts. Because helmeted sponge divers in cumbersome suits and lead-weighted shoes could not conduct such careful excavations, however, no one looked askance at their picking up artifacts from the floor of the Adriatic for personal and monastic collections. The early-twentieth-century discovery and salvage of classical bronzes by Greek sponge divers in the Mediterranean and Aegean Seas were even acclaimed by professional archaeologists, especially because on land such statues had rarely survived the scrap heap. Art historians knew only that the most highly prized classical Greek statues in the National Museum of Greece and in the Louvre came from the sea (Bass 1966: 74–85), as did the Roman statuary and pottery exhibited in Tunisia's Bardo Museum (Hellenkemper Salies 1994: 5–29). The salvage of these masterpieces, however, was not true archaeology.

All this changed in the 1940s when Frenchmen Jacques-Yves Cousteau and Emil Gagnan developed the Aqua-lung, a simple yet reliable self-contained underwater breathing apparatus, or SCUBA. By enhancing divers' mobility, this device allowed underwater excavators to work even more carefully than their terrestrial counterparts, a statement I can make with confidence from my own experiences both on land and under the sea; by floating just over a site and creating small currents with one or two fingers, a diver can remove sediment a few grains at a time, without the use of any scraping or digging tool.

Throughout the 1950s in the Mediterranean a number of noteworthy pioneering attempts to excavate Roman shipwrecks were made at places such as the Grand

Congloué, Cape Dramont, and Île du Levant in France, Mahdia off Tunisia, and Albenga in Italy (*Atti del II Congresso* 1961; du Plat Taylor 1965: 34–103). French and Italian divers adapted standard tools like airlifts to remove sediment and underwater television to allow archaeologists to follow the progress of work from the surface. Near the island of Spargi, north of Sardinia, Gianni Roghi developed a method of mapping by means of metal grids constructed over a wreck (Roghi 1958–1959, 1959, 1965). Still, underwater excavations lagged behind those on land because the archaeologists on these early projects did not dive; instead they stayed on deck and gratefully accepted the artifacts handed up to them by hired divers. None of the excavations were carried to completion.

This pioneering stage of shipwreck archaeology, controlled by SCUBA divers who at first often exaggerated the difficulties of diving in order to keep their monopoly on shipwrecks (Frost 1963: 13–18, 170–171, 254–259; Tailliez 1965: 91), was short-lived. As early as 1959 anthropology professor John Goggin, who dived in Florida's freshwaters, dismissed so-called archaeology by diving enthusiasts (Purdy 1991: 201–203), accurately stating that "it is far easier to teach diving to an archaeologist than archaeology to a diver!" (Goggin 1959–1960: 350).

In 1960, nautical archaeology exploded like a celestial nova, often at sites that had been identified in the previous decade. Scuttled Viking ships discovered by divers in Roskilde Fjord, Denmark, would soon be surrounded by a coffer dam to allow the site to be pumped dry and excavated by archaeologists like a terrestrial site (Crumlin-Pedersen and Olsen 2002: 23–41). A Bronze Age shipwreck at Cape Gelidonya, Turkey, was the first ancient wreck excavated in its entirety on the seabed, its excavation the first directed by a diving archaeologist (Bass 1967). In Sweden, the seventeenth-century warship *Vasa* was being raised from the depths of Stockholm harbor (Franzén 1962; Cederlund 2006: 12–290). That same year SCUBA divers began "whitewater archaeology" below rapids in Minnesota and Canada, where fur-traders' canoes had overturned, spilling out their cargoes (Wheeler et al. 1975); colonial bateaux came safely out of Lake George, New York, and were treated with polyethylene glycol (Inverarity 1964; Seborg 1964); and the first attempts were made to salvage the Civil War ironclad *Cairo* in Mississippi's Yazoo River (Bearss 1980).

The field was still so small that almost all directors of the projects just mentioned were able to meet in early 1963 in one room of the Minnesota Historical Society for an international conference on modern underwater archaeology (Holmquist and Wheeler 1964); sadly, word reached its participants that the prescient John Goggin, who was to have been a central figure, had died tragically young. In the half century since then, nautical archaeology has grown too vast for any one person to keep abreast of the major projects around the globe. Long gone are the days when virtually all practitioners knew one another on a first-name basis.

Diving archaeologists devoted the 1960s largely to overcoming some of the inherent problems of working at depth, especially on the deeper, usually better-preserved wrecks that require decompression dives, which limit the amount of time an excavator can spend on a site in any given day. Improving efficiency was critical.

Recognizing the importance of context, archaeologists devoted themselves to improving underwater mapping techniques, first using grids and photo towers (Bass and van Doorninck 1982: 8–31), then three-dimensional mapping by stereo-photography (Rosencrantz 1975), and finally photogrammetry from *Asherah*, the first commercially built American submersible (Bass and Rosencrantz 1977). Although all of those methods have been superseded by mapping with digital cameras and combinations of computer software (Green, Matthews, and Turanli 2002), the earlier techniques allowed Frederick van Doorninck to demonstrate for the first time that an ancient ship could be reconstructed on paper from its fragmentary seabed remains (Bass and van Doorninck 1982: 32–64, 87–120).

There could no longer be any excuse for conducting underwater excavations with lesser standards than those deemed acceptable on land. At the same time, technical improvements continued to be made (Bass 1968; Bass 1975: 147–167). Before the decade was over, plastic airlifts made of light and readily available irrigation pipes had replaced the heavy and cumbersome metal airlifts that had been used for nearly two decades. Safety improvements included the first use of oxygen for normal, twice-daily decompression periods, and the air-filled plastic dome situated on the seabed, dubbed the "underwater telephone booth," that served as a safety refuge in case of equipment failure. A submersible decompression chamber raised itself independently through the various stages of decompression during one 1967 project. The same year, in Turkey, sonar was shown to have the ability to locate ancient shipwrecks (Bass 1968: 417–423).

In the 1970s nautical archaeology truly came into its own. Its very name came into common use with the introduction of the *International Journal of Nautical Archaeology and Underwater Exploration* in 1972, although its publisher, the Council for Nautical Archaeology, had been around since 1964. The American Institute of Nautical Archaeology (now simply INA) borrowed the name from the journal when it was incorporated the year the journal began. About that time, the well-preserved classical Greek ship excavated off Kyrenia, Cyprus, demonstrated that a sunken and restored hull could be every bit as important as the salvaged ancient Mediterranean cargoes that earlier had dazzled both archaeologists and the public (S. W. Katzev 2005). Increasing attention was paid to the *naus*.

The same decade saw the global spread of underwater shipwreck excavations conducted to increasingly high standards, including those of a Roman shipwreck at the Madrague de Giens in France (Tchernia et al. 1978), a sixteenth-century Basque whaler at Red Bay in Canada (Grenier, Bernier, and Stevens 2007), the 1554 Spanish fleet sunk off Padre Island, Texas (Arnold and Weddle 1978), a Punic ship at Marsala in Sicily (Frost 1981), the seventeenth-century Portuguese frigate *Santo Antonio de Tanna* in Kenya (Piercy 2005), the fourteenth-century ship at Shinan-gun in Korea (Keith 1980), Spanish Armada wrecks in Ireland (Martin 1975), a classical Greek wreck in the Strait of Messina (Eiseman and Ridgway 1987), and Dutch East India Company ships off Australia (Green 1977).

In the 1970s, too, maritime and nautical archaeology became academic disciplines. The Leon Recanati Institute for Maritime Studies at the University of Haifa

(RIMS) was established in 1972, while the St. Andrews Institute of Maritime Archaeology was founded the following year. Although various courses on maritime or nautical archaeology had been taught around the world, in that decade there were now degree-granting programs, at the University of Haifa through its Department of Maritime Civilizations, followed by the Nautical Archaeology Program at Texas A&M University, and the Maritime Studies Program at East Carolina University. Maritime archaeology is today, with an increasing number of university programs and courses, a respected subject in which its earliest practitioners pass on what they learned by trial and error to increasingly better-educated generations of students. No longer can an archaeologist simply learn to dive, as half a century ago, and be considered competent to excavate an ancient ship. Today's graduate students can take seminars on preclassical, classical, medieval, postmedieval, and Far Eastern seafaring, learning the histories of naval warfare and of maritime commerce, sometimes studying paleography so they can conduct their own archival research. They learn to draw ships' lines and make half models and digital reconstructions in laboratory courses on the history and theory of wooden hull construction. They become familiar with the history of the politics of sea power and the principles of harbor design and construction. They increasingly become involved in the legal aspects of underwater archaeology. And they learn the methods of maritime conservation, often gaining practical experience in university, institute, or museum laboratories. Indeed, most graduate students serve apprenticeships on actual surveys and excavations and in laboratories.

Even in the subfield of nautical archaeology, there are various specializations. Just as any terrestrial excavation staff may include a numismatist, epigrapher, art historian, physical anthropologist, and palynologist, nautical excavations may include both those who study the vessels themselves—their hulls, rigging, ballast, anchors, and such—and those who only interpret vessels' contents, both cargoes and personal possessions. Even nondiving nautical archaeologists can be important members of the excavation team, as was J. Richard Steffy, a leading authority on ship reconstruction (Steffy 1994). The resultant collaborations among such specialists explain the multiple authorship of many excavation reports. In the same vein, should not those who study early and ancient ships by their representations and contemporary descriptions be considered nautical archaeologists (Basch 1987; Casson 1971; Needham 1971; Rougé 1966)? Both students of nautical archaeology and professional excavators would be hard pressed to work without the books of these and other scholars.

Many technical problems of shipwreck excavations have been solved since the first wreck was excavated in its entirety in 1960, but improvements are always welcome. Diving has become safer and more comfortable. Gauges allow divers to see how much compressed air remains in their tanks, buoyancy compensators increase diver safety, and fabric-lined wet suits no longer tear almost daily. Still, perfection of a flexible, one-atmosphere diving suit, being undertaken by Phil Nuytten in Canada, will allow excavators to work for hours instead of mere minutes at the depths that now limit bottom time (Symes 2005).

Conservation methods and treatments have been developed specifically for wet or waterlogged artifacts (Hamilton 1996). These methods are constantly being refined. Conservators have been experimenting with materials from sugar (Parrent 1983) to silicon oils (Smith 2003), for example, to find a better substance than polyethylene glycol for treating waterlogged wood.

Similarly, the technology of locating and excavating shipwreck sites is vastly improved by both remote sensing, with magnetometers and various kinds of sonar, and visual search from submersible vehicles, both human-occupied and remotely operated (Akal, Ballard, and Bass 2004; Bass 2004). Still, sonar of even higher resolution is needed so that one day searchers on the surface will be able to differentiate between sunken cargoes and seabed boulders.

The experimental archaeology of early ships has a long history, from the replica of the Gokstad ship that crossed the Atlantic for exhibition at the Chicago World's Fair of 1893, through a more recent replica of a *faering* (small boat propelled by two pairs of oars) found with the Gokstad ship (McGrail 1974) to the variously scaled sailing replicas of the fourth-century BCE Kyrenia ship (M. L. Katzev 1980: 44–45; M. L. Katzev 1991; Pomey 1997: 170–171) and the Lake Champlain Maritime Museum's replicas of the 1776 gunboat *Philadelphia* and the 1862 sailing canal boat *Lois McClure*. There are other authentic replicas, but some rather fanciful vessels built to retrace ancient routes are based on little archaeological evidence. Nevertheless, a less expensive method of testing the sailing qualities of excavated vessels is now at hand. Following on work done by the Germans on the Bremen Cog, Filipe Castro is using computer models to simulate stabilty conditions and sailing performance of archaeological reconstructions of various ships (Monroy, Castro, and Furuta in this volume).

CONTROVERSY AND PUBLICATION

This preface began with a discussion of the definition of maritime archaeology. Regardless of its precise definition, maritime archaeology will constantly evolve in both its aims and its techniques. The aims of the earliest nautical archaeologists, for instance, were originally the same as the aims of classical archaeologists, medieval archaeologists, and art historians, and this remains largely the case despite attempts to rid maritime archaeology of historical particularism—with a week-long symposium devoted solely to that purpose by those who believe that "archaeology is anthropology or it is nothing" (Gould 1983). Archaeologists of a different persuasion have never been so narrow as to claim that "archaeology is history or it is nothing," although the Bronze Age shipwreck excavated off Uluburun, Turkey, as just one example, has contributed greatly to the histories not only of ship construction, but also of trade, diet, metallurgy, metrology, glass, ceramics, religion, music, and literacy, involving such disparate fields as Homeric studies and Egyptology (Pulak 1998). No research design could have prepared the excavators for what they found.

Luckily, they were not restricted by one, for they simply wanted to learn everything possible from the site. The opposite approach has yet to prove its value (Gould 2000).

Another controversy in the aims of nautical archaeology is the debate over whether a shipwreck site should be excavated in its entirety rather than simply sampled. Proponents of the idea that it is wrong to excavate all of a shipwreck base that precept on accepted approaches to terrestrial sites. To excavate an entire terrestrial site to bedrock, whether a Bronze Age village or a sprawling Roman city, would be immoral. With new questions and better techniques, archaeologists of the future should be in a position to return to partially excavated sites for decades or centuries to come. Archaeologists at such sites, however, often excavate individual burials or dwellings in their entirety.

A shipwreck, being a coherent whole, is more like just one burial. It is hard to imagine an archaeologist excavating only part of a skeleton and leaving the rest. A concrete example is the eleventh-century shipwreck at Serçe Limanı, Turkey. At the end of the first excavation season, there was pressure to publish both scholarly and popular articles on the site. These publications are now embarrassing. Almost every conclusion was wrong. Because we had raised mainly the ship's Near Eastern cargo of glass vessels and glazed terra-cotta bowls during the initial campaign, I concluded that they were evidence of a Muslim merchant venture (Bass 1978). In the following campaign, however, we found the pork bones, lead seals with Christian images, fishing weights decorated with crosses and the name Jesus, and graffiti that proved the merchants on board were Hellenized Christian Bulgarians who lived on the north shore of the Sea of Marmara near Constantinople, which is slowly leading into even more detailed contributions to medieval history (Bass et al. 2004). This could be repeated for many excavated wrecks. Sampling wrecks can lead only to historical inaccuracies. The debate should be closed.

There should be no debate at all, however, about a serious problem facing all archaeologists, maritime or otherwise: the lack of thorough, scholarly publication of fieldwork. Sir John Boardman of the University of Oxford, who has carefully studied the situation, believes that "over the last fifty years, far less than 25 percent of material and results of professional archaeological excavations has been properly published, and the rest will never get beyond preliminary reports, if that (Boardman 2009: 109)." Others have estimated that 70% of excavations in the Near East is not published (Atwood 2007: 60; Owen 2009: 140–141), and perhaps 80% of all Italian archaeological material remains unpublished, with the record in Egypt perhaps no better (Stoddart and Malone 2001).

An unpublished shipwreck, no matter how meticulously and brilliantly excavated, is simply a looted wreck. That is why I stopped directing diving operations in 1985 and turned over the direction of the most exciting ancient shipwreck ever found, that at Uluburun, Turkey, to a younger colleague (Pulak 1998). I had seen the two excavation directors I assisted as a student in the 1950s die before publishing their decades of digging. My decision was proven correct when in 2009 the last of my publication obligations finally went to the printer (Bass et al. 2009). It takes years or decades to produce excavation reports that are more than simple catalogs, which is why some sites have not yet been completely published long after their excavation. It is a sad certainty, however, that far too many shipwreck excavations will never be published.

Still, it is encouraging to see the appearance of so many multivolume final reports, including, besides the volumes on Red Bay, the *Vasa*, and Serçe Limanı already referred to, the five-volume archaeology of the *Mary Rose* (including Jones 2003; Marsden 2003; Gardiner 2005), the final reports on the excavation of the fifth-century BCE Ma'agan Mikhael wreck in Israel (Linder and Kahanov 2003; Kahanov and Linder 2004), ships and boats of the North (including Crumlin-Pedersen 1997; Sørensen 2001; Crumlin-Pedersen and Trakadas 2003; and Lemée 2006), and the excavation reports coming out of Catalonia (including Nieto et al. 1989; Nieto and Puig 2001; Nieto and Raurich 1998), along with those on the Bremen Cog (Lahn 1992–2003) and on the vessels uncovered in the Dutch polders (Hocker and Vlierman 1996; McLaughlin-Neyland and Neyland 1993; Neyland and McLaughlin-Neyland 1996; Van de Moortel 1991). In addition, there are myriad single-volume reports, including those on the Archaic Greek shipwreck at Gela (Panvini 2001); a fishing boat from the time of Christ in the Sea of Galilee (Wachsmann 1990); a medieval boat in France (Rieth, Carriere-Desbois, and Serna 2001); the eighteenth-century *General Carleton*, lost in the Polish Baltic in 1785 (Ossowski 2008); and a Lake Champlain horse-powered ferry (Crisman and Cohn 1998).

ARCHAEOLOGY VS. TREASURE HUNTING

One of maritime archaeology's greatest challenges lies in educating the public about the purposes of archaeology and the difference between maritime archaeology and treasure hunting. There are still nations that grant permits to treasure hunters, sometimes with the naive belief, based on wild promises made by the treasure hunters, that nations will gain financially by cooperating in the search for treasure. Working with archaeologists, however, is usually of far greater national and financial benefit.

The *Vasa* Museum now attracts more than a million paying visitors annually, according to Marika Hedin, director of the museum, and Robert Olsson, Director General for Sweden's National Maritime Museums. This makes the museum 100% self-sufficient, other than for extraordinary costs of conservation and ongoing research. Approximately 25–30% of all international tourists who come to Sweden visit the *Vasa*. These foreign visitors contribute to the Swedish economy not only by museum entrance fees, but also by money spent simply getting to and from and staying in Stockholm. Similarly, according to Turkish government figures, the Bodrum Museum of Underwater Archaeology has become the most visited archaeological museum in Turkey, attracting a quarter of a million paying visitors every year. That should earn in ticket sales about $2 million annually for the Ministry of Culture, far more than the cost of staffing and maintaining the museum. Visitors to the Bodrum Museum, however, additionally pay for souvenirs, meals, taxis, and other things that help the Bodrum economy. Another example is provided by the United Kingdom, where the *Mary Rose*, according to maritime archaeologist Chris Dobbs (pers. comm. 2009) of the Mary Rose Trust, has attracted over 7.6 million paying visitors since its temporary museum opened in 1983. He says that this contributes significantly to the local economy and provides much of the funds required for the expensive process of conservation. An object of national pride, the purpose-built *Mary Rose* museum scheduled to open in 2012 will allow visitors from around the world to see the hull and contents of King Henry VIII's great warship *in one place*. This unity, common to all shipwreck museums, is as important for shipwrecked artifacts as for those found on land.

Treasure hunting does not equal archaeology in societal value largely because ships' contents are not usually kept together as permanent collections (would it not be regrettable for the public as well as Egyptologists had the contents of King Tut's tomb been auctioned off piecemeal rather than kept together for the enjoyment and education of millions of people around the world?). But there are other reasons as well. Treasure hunters must make a profit in order to repay the financial backers of their search and salvage operations. They do not have the luxury of time. Yet Institute of Nautical Archaeology excavators calculate that they spend far more money, energy, and time on post-excavation work than on the mapping and retrieval of their finds, spending on average two years on conservation, research, and publication for every month they dive. Treasure hunters, even those inclined to conserve the nonsalable items from their sites, cannot wait for decades to repay sponsors.

There are, of course, archaeological exceptions. Both cultural resources or heritage management archaeologists and those from academic institutions often face time constraints in collecting and publishing as much information as possible on sites that might otherwise be lost forever. An example is the work on an abandoned eighteenth-century British merchant frigate found under Manhattan's Water Street exactly where a large building was being constructed. It was not feasible to halt construction indefinitely, but it was stopped long enough for archaeologists to collect data and some of the physical remains (Riess 1987). More recently, Texas A&M University archaeologists, under contract with Okeanos Gas Gathering Company (OGGC), collected as much data as possible in two weeks from an early-nineteenth-century wreck 1,220 m deep in the Gulf of Mexico that OGGC had encountered during a survey for its Mardi Gras Pipeline System (Ford et al. 2008).

Despite such exceptions, and despite using accurate mapping techniques, raising and conserving some of the monetarily worthless materials from the seabed, and even hiring professional shipboard archaeologists to lend legitimacy to their work, treasure hunters are not practicing archaeology. The goals of treasure hunting and archaeology are in opposition. Archaeology does not stop when a site has been salvaged, no matter how completely. That is only the beginning. What treasure hunters would have spent years monitoring the chemical treatment of the disassembled Serçe Limanı hull, and additional years piecing together its thousands of wooden fragments in order to study and understand the hull and its place in the history of ship design and construction, as well as to display it for the public (Bass et al. 2004)? How many would have paid for a year-round conservation staff to spend decades looking for joins among between half a million and a million fragments of glass, and then having the resultant glass vessels cataloged and illustrated not only for museum display, but also for a 525-page volume on the largest collection of medieval Islamic glass in existence (Bass et al. 2009)? What treasure hunters would have spent the time learning to read Russian, Bulgarian, and Rumanian as diving archaeologist Frederick van Doorninck did at the conclusion of the excavation? Only by doing so could he determine the meaning of the graffiti he was finding on the amphoras, which in turn revealed remarkable details about the identity and commercial practices of their makers and owners, as he will reveal in the third volume of the Serçe Limanı report (van Doorninck, forthcoming).

There is, however, a gray area. Even to suggest it will draw instant and reflexive criticism, but the subject should be debated. Before continuing, therefore, I must make my credentials clear. I am the "balding Southerner" described by Karl Meyer in his seminal *The Plundered Past* as being a prime mover in the "revolt against the acquisitive tradition of major American art museums" (Meyer 1973: 73–75). Probably no professional archaeologist has been more outspoken against treasure hunting (Bass 1979a, 1981, 1983), by debating treasure hunters on national television, testifying before both House and Senate Committees as they considered bills to protect historic shipwrecks in American waters (Hearings 1986: 122–134; Hearings 1987: 154–179), and correcting some of the numerous falsehoods spread by and about treasure hunters, such as that they developed 90% of the equipment used in underwater excavation, that there is no need to excavate hull remains in the shallow Caribbean because they have been too badly damaged by storms and anyway there are accurate plans of early hulls in the Archives of the Indies in Seville, that archaeologists don't deal with monetarily valuable artifacts, that archaeologists don't go out and actually find wrecks, and other such nonsense (Bass 1985). However, I still must ask, which is worse: the professional archaeologist who carefully excavates a site and never publishes it, or the treasure hunter who spends millions of dollars searching 1,400 square miles of ocean in order to locate a nineteenth-century wreck more than a mile deep, salvages part of it, conserves that part, and publishes a book on the operation (Thompson 1998)? Would any archaeologist now or five hundred years from now spend that amount of money and effort to locate and excavate a vessel like many others of the same type that can be found in lesser depths? Is not saying that all vessels should be left alone like saying that all structures on land are sacrosanct because one day they will be antique? Old homes are demolished daily and replaced by more modern structures, just as old vessels are scrapped or sunk as artificial reefs. And one can know far more about the wreck just mentioned, the U.S. mail steamship *Central America*, than anyone will ever know about many wrecks excavated by professional archaeologists and never fully published. The *Central America*'s hull and machinery remain on the ocean bottom, on the slim chance that they will ever justify archaeological excavation, but clothing, written documents, ceramics, and glass were meticulously conserved, photographed, and published.

Perhaps a better example is the Spanish galleon *Nuestra Señora de la Concepción*, excavated off Saipan in the Northern Mariana Islands of the Pacific Ocean. Published both as a beautifully illustrated coffee-table book (Mathers and Shaw 1993) and in a 550-page excavation report (Mathers, Parker, and Copus 1990), its scattered cargo spread down a slope from near the surface to a depth of 60 m (c. 200 ft), so there was no hull to map and preserve. Rather than being auctioned off, the artifacts were sold as a collection to a Japanese company that promised to curate and display them for 40 years in a hotel as a tourist attraction and then donate the collection to the local government, but because the hotel was not built, the collection now simply belongs to the government (van Tilburg in this volume).

To be critical of treasure hunting, archaeologists must continue to make a better case to the public for their approach to shipwrecks, by doing a better job and not simply by chastising treasure hunters.

Lest treasure hunters take my comparison with archaeologists who do not publish out of context, it should be pointed out that INA archaeologists who have examined the known early ships of discovery and exploration of the New World—in the Bahamas, the Turks and Caicos, the Dominican Republic, and Mexico—have noted that the only postsinking damage suffered by the wrecks, once stabilized in the seabed, has been at the hands of misguided treasure hunters, and these ships are of inestimable historic and archaeological importance. The targets of treasure hunters are too often the most historically and archaeologically important wrecks. In general, treasure hunting simply is destructive of our search for knowledge of the past (Bass 1979b; Hall 2007).

Further, after spending years of expensive legal wrangling over ownership with states or the original insurers or owners of sunken vessels, it is a rare treasure hunter who actually makes any profit and repays investors (Pringle 2007).

Laypeople sometimes ask why it is necessary to keep duplicate artifacts together as permanent collections, out of sight in museum storerooms. The archaeologist will tell them why. With more advanced laboratory analyses, as well as new questions to be answered, teams of archaeologists work for months annually in the Bodrum Museum on artifacts raised nearly half a century earlier, often with startling results for history. Elsewhere artifacts are examined by the latest methods of dendrochronology, petrography, isotope analysis, radiocarbon dating, DNA studies, and dating by thermoluminescence. This is possible only because the collections remain intact. It is relatively simple to find and salvage antiques or antiquities. It is what happens to those antiques or antiquities later that makes their recovery part of archaeology.

In summation, because international admiralty laws often conflict with antiquities laws, maritime sites increasingly require new legal protections, both national and international. Because laws are created by people, education about maritime archaeology by means of publications, lectures, museum displays, and television programs is vital. The distinction between archaeology and treasure hunting is misunderstood by far too large a part of the population.

DEEPWATER ARCHAEOLOGY

Modern technology is opening the deeper parts of the world's seas and oceans to maritime archaeology, beyond the depths in which SCUBA divers can operate (McCann and Oleson 2004; Ballard 2008; Ford et al. 2008; Wachsmann in this volume). No deepwater wreck has yet been excavated in its entirety, but surely that day will come.

In the meantime, however, because most deepwater wrecks lie in international waters, they raise the question of where they and all their contents should go. For a while it was argued that archaeological finds from international waters should be returned to the land of cultural origin. The very first completely excavated wreck points to the absurdity of this notion. For nearly half a century archaeologists debated in academic publications whether the Bronze Age ship excavated at Cape Gelidonya was Greek or Proto-Phoenician in origin. But if the latter, should the finds from the ship go to Syria, Lebanon, or Israel? Recent, unpublished laboratory analyses—made possible only because the collection of artifacts has been kept together in the Bodrum Museum—have shown that neither hypothesis was correct, for the ship's metal cargo, ceramics, and anchor were all from the island of Cyprus.

A better and earlier example is the Uluburun shipwreck, with its cargo collected more than three millennia ago from what are today perhaps a dozen modern countries, from tropical Africa to Asia to northern Europe (Pulak 2008). Happily, it all stays together in one museum, the Bodrum Museum in Turkey, even though that is not near the sources of either the ship or its cargo, much of which has since been exhibited in museums in Germany (Yalçin, Pulak, and Slotta 2005) and the United States (Pulak 2008).

The problem is being partly resolved by countries bordering the Mediterranean that plan to extend their national boundaries out to 200 miles, leaving a relatively small part of that sea international (Kliot 1988: 209). This could protect many Mediterranean wrecks, but could also have the unfortunate result of keeping maritime archaeologists from northern Europe, America, Australia, and Asia from studying wrecks that could be more closely tied to their ancestry than to the modern peoples living around the Mediterranean who would control the wrecks. Three million Americans, for example, claim Greek descent according to the U.S. Department of State, and a third of a million Australians claim Greek ancestry. Why should they not have as much right to study an ancient Greek ship found nearly 200 miles off the North African coast as the modern inhabitants of the nearest nation?

The problem is exacerbated by wrecks lying in deep water that are now and always will be extranational. These wrecks are increasingly vulnerable to human disturbance. The partial but legal salvage that followed the discovery of the famed *Titanic* demonstrated even before the search for the *Central America* that vessels lying kilometers deep are no longer beyond the reach of either archaeologists or treasure salvors. The UNESCO Convention on the Protection of the Underwater

Cultural Heritage, already ratified by the minimum of 20 nations, is aimed at protecting such wrecks from destructive looters.

Because of the expense of excavating at great depth, however, perhaps a new model is needed. Early terrestrial excavations were funded by great museums that sent out expeditions to bring back antiquities, and although this is no longer a practice, the modern world is a richer and better place for encyclopedic museums like the Louvre, the British Museum, the Metropolitan Museum of Art, and the Berlin Museum (Cuno 2009). Would it not be sad if only visitors to Nigeria could ever see a Benin bronze? What if in order to see a single example of Chinese or Japanese porcelain one had to travel to China or Japan? Thus, if a Roman ship of unknown origin were found in the deep Atlantic Ocean, why should it not go to the British Museum, if that museum could afford its proper excavation? After all, London was once Roman. Why should not the half million Lebanese Americans have as much claim to enjoy a Phoenician wreck found in the Atlantic Ocean as the four million current inhabitants of Lebanon—both people now thoroughly mixed with more modern Arabs of non-Phoenician descent?

Nearly four decades ago, when urging that antiquities dealing in all countries be made illegal, except as approved by the governments in question, I also wrote: "For their part, the lands in which the only remnants of our most ancient past are to be found should take a realistic attitude toward sharing duplicate objects, offering frequent loan exhibits, and making vast basement stores readily available to scholars of all countries" (Editorial 1970). If nonpublishing archaeologists deserve criticism, so too do local museum directors who may often see artifacts as things to be locked away, out of sight, for safekeeping.

CONCLUSION

As these words are written, maritime archaeology is a mature discipline with well-trained practitioners around the world excavating, conserving, restoring, displaying, replicating, and, most importantly, publishing their sites (Delgado 1998). The future seems bright.

REFERENCES

Akal, T., R. D. Ballard, and G. F. Bass, eds. 2004. *The application of recent advances in underwater detection and survey techniques to underwater archeology*. Bodrum: Uluburun.

Arnold, J. Barto, III, and Robert S. Weddle. 1978. *The nautical archaeology of Padre Island: The Spanish shipwrecks of 1554*. New York: Academic Press.

Atti del II Congresso Internazionale di Archeologia Sottomarina, Albenga 1958. 1961.
   Bordighera: Istituto Internazionale di Studi Liguri.
Atwood, Roger. 2007. Publish or be punished: Israel cracks down on delinquent diggers.
   Archaeology 60 (2): 18, 60, 62.
Ballard, Robert D. 2008. *Archaeological oceanography.* Princeton, NJ: Princeton University
   Press.
Basch, Lucien. 1987. *Le museé imaginaire de la marine antique.* Athens: Institut Héllenique
   pour la Préservation de la Tradition Nautique.
Bass, George F. 1966. *Archaeology under water.* London: Thames & Hudson; New York:
   Frederick A. Praeger.
——. 1967. Cape Gelidonya: A Bronze Age shipwreck. *Transactions of the American
   Philosophical Society* 57 (8).
——. 1968. New tools for undersea archeology. *National Geographic* 134 (September):
   402–423.
——, ed. 1972. *A history of seafaring based on underwater archaeology.* London: Thames
   and Hudson; New York: Walker.
——. 1975. *Archaeology beneath the sea: A personal account.* New York: Walker.
——. 1978. Glass treasure from the Aegean. *National Geographic* 153 (June): 768–793.
——. 1979a. Treasure-hunting divers. *Journal of Field Archaeology* 6: 104–107.
——. 1979b. The men who stole the stars. *Sea History* 12 (Fall): 30.
——. 1981. Treasure-hunting vs. underwater archaeology [a letter coauthored with 10
   others]. *Journal of Field Archaeology* 8: 517.
——. 1983. Shipwrecks and treasure hunters. *Journal of Field Archaeology* 10: 389.
——. 1985. Archaeologists, sport divers, and treasure-hunters. *Journal of Field Archaeology*
   12: 256–258.
——. 2004. Wreck-hunting by *Carolyn,* a human-occupied submersible. *Sea Technology*
   45 (4): 59–64.
Bass, George F., Robert H. Brill, Berta Lledó, and Sheila D. Matthews. 2009. *Serçe Limanı,*
   vol. 2. *The glass of an eleventh-century shipwreck.* College Station: Texas A&M
   University Press.
Bass, George F., Sheila D. Matthews, J. Richard Steffy, and Frederick H. van Doorninck
   Jr. 2004. *Serçe Limanı: An eleventh-century shipwreck,* vol. 1. *The ship and
   its anchorage, crew, and passengers.* College Station: Texas A&M University
   Press.
Bass, George F., and Donald M. Rosencrantz. 1977. The *Asherah*—a pioneer in search of the
   past. In *Submersibles and their use in oceanography and ocean engineering,* ed. Richard
   A. Geyer, 335–351. Amsterdam: Elsevier.
Bass, George F., and Frederick H. van Doorninck Jr. 1982. *Yassi Ada,* vol. 1: *A seventh-century
   Byzantine shipwreck.* College Station: Texas A&M University Press.
Bearss, Edwin C. 1980. *Hardluck ironclad: The sinking and salvage of the* Cairo. Rev. ed.
   Baton Rouge: Louisiana State University Press.
Boardman, Sir John. 2009. Archaeologists, collectors, and museums. In *Whose culture?
   The promise of museums and the debate over antiquities,* ed. James Cuno, 107–124.
   Princeton, NJ: Princeton University Press.
Bratten, John R. 2002. *The gondola* Philadelphia *and the battle of Lake Champlain.* College
   Station: Texas A&M University Press.
Broadwater, John D. 2002. Timelines of underwater archeology. In *International handbook
   of underwater archaeology,* ed. Carol V. Ruppé and Janet F. Barstad, 17–24. New York:
   Kluwer Academic/Plenum.

Bruce-Mitford, Rupert, et al. 1975–1983. *The Sutton Hoo ship-burial*, 3 vols. London: British Museum.

Camilli, Andrea, and Elisabetta Setari. 2006. *Ancient shipwrecks of Pisa (Le navi antiche di Pisa)*. Milano: Electa.

Casson, Lionel. 1971. *Ships and seamanship in the ancient world*. Princeton, NJ: Princeton University Press.

Cederlund, Carl Olof, with Fred Hocker. 2006. *Vasa I: The archaeology of a Swedish warship of 1628*. Stockholm: Statens Maritima Museer.

Christensen, Arne Emil. 1972. Scandinavian ships from earliest times to the Vikings. In *A history of seafaring based on underwater archaeology*, ed. George F. Bass, 159–180: London: Thames and Hudson; New York: Walker.

Crisman, Kevin J., and Arthur B. Cohn. 1998. *When horses walked on water: Horse-powered ferries in nineteenth-century America*. Washington: Smithsonian Institution Press.

Crumlin-Pedersen, Ole. 1997. *Viking-age ships and shipbuilding in Hedeby/Haithabu and Schleswig*. Schleswig and Roskilde: Viking Ship Museum.

Crumlin-Pedersen, Ole, and Olaf Olsen, eds. 2002. *The Skuldelev ships I: Ships and boats of the North*, vol. 4.1. Roskilde: Viking Ship Museum.

Crumlin-Pedersen, Ole, and Athena Trakadas, eds. 2003. *Hjortspring: A pre-Roman iron-age warship in context*. Roskilde: Viking Ship Museum.

Cuno, James, ed. 2009. *Whose culture? The promise of museums and the debate over antiquities*. Princeton, NJ: Princeton University Press.

de Morgan, J. 1895. *Fouilles à Dahchour: Mars–juin 1894*. Vienna: Adolphe Holzhausen.

Delgado, James P. 1998. *Encyclopedia of underwater and maritime archaeology*. New Haven: Yale University Press.

du Plat Taylor, Joan, ed. 1965. *Marine archaeology*. London: Hutchinson.

Editorial [unsigned, by Glyn Daniel]. 1970. *Antiquity* 44: 89.

Eiseman, Cynthia Jones, and Brunilde Sismondo Ridgway. 1987. *The Porticello shipwreck: A Mediterranean merchant vessel of 415–385 B.C.* College Station: Texas A&M University Press.

Fattovich, R., K. Bard, and C. Ward. 2007. Sea port to punt: New evidence from Marsa Gawasis, Red Sea (Egypt). In *Natural resources and cultural connections of the Red Sea*, ed. J. Starkey, P. Starkey, and T. Wilkinson, 143–148. Oxford: BAR International Series 1661.

Fenwick, Valerie, ed. 1978. *The Graveney boat: A tenth-century find from Kent*. Oxford: BAR British Series 53.

Ford, B., A. Borgens, W. Bryant, D. Marshall, P. Hitchcock, C. Arias, and D. Hamilton. 2008. *Archaeological excavation of the Mardi Gras shipwreck (16GM01), Gulf of Mexico Continental Slope*. New Orleans: U.S. Department of the Interior Mineral Management Service.

Franzén, Anders. 1962. *The warship* Vasa: *Deep diving and marine archaeology in Stockholm*. Stockholm: Norstedt and Bonnier.

Frost, Honor. 1963. *Under the Mediterranean: Marine antiquities*. Englewood Cliffs, NJ: Prentice-Hall.

———. 1981. *Lilybaeum. Notizie degli scavi di antichità* 30 (1976): *Supplemento*. Rome: Accademia Nazionale dei Lincei.

Gardiner, Julie, with Michael J. Allen, eds. 2005. *Before the mast: Life and death aboard the Mary Rose*. Portsmouth: Mary Rose Trust.

Goggin, John M. 1959–1960. Underwater archaeology: Its nature and limitations. *American Antiquity* 25: 348–354.

Gould, Richard A., ed. 1983. *Shipwreck anthropology*. Albuquerque: University of New Mexico Press.

———. 2000. *Archaeology and the social history of ships*. Cambridge: Cambridge University Press.

Green, Jeremy N. 1977. *The loss of the Verenigde Oostindische Compagnie jacht* Vergulde Draeck, *western Australia 1656*. Oxford: British Archaeological Reports Supplementary Series 36(i).

Green, Jeremy, Sheila Matthews, and Tufan Turanli. 2002. Underwater archaeological surveying using PhotoModeler, VirtualMapper: Different applications for different problems. *International Journal of Nautical Archaeology* 31: 283–292.

Grenier, Robert, Marc-André Bernier, and Willis Stevens, eds. 2007. *The underwater archaeology of Red Bay: Basque shipbuilding and whaling in the 16th century*. 5 vols. Ottawa: Parks Canada.

Hall, Jerome. 2007. The Black Rhino. *Journal of Maritime Archaeology* 2 (2): 93–97.

Hamilton, Donny L. 1996. *Basic methods of conserving underwater archaeological material culture*. Washington, DC: U.S. Department of Defense.

Hearings before the Subcommittee on Oceanography of the Committee on Merchant Marine and Fisheries House of Representatives Ninety-Ninth Congress First Session on Abandoned Shipwreck Act (H.R. 3558) October 29, 1985, Serial No. 99-19. 1986. Washington, DC: U.S. Government Printing Office.

Hearings before the Subcommittee on Public Lands, National Parks and Forests of the Committee on Energy and Natural Resources United States Senate One Hundredth Congress First Session on S. 858 to Establish the Title of States in Certain Abandoned Shipwrecks, and for other purposes. September 29, 1987. 1987. Washington, DC: U.S. Government Printing Office.

Hellenkemper Salies, Gisela, et al. 1994. *Das Wrack: Der antike Schiffsfund von Mahdia*. 2 vols. Cologne: Rheinland-Verlag.

Hocker, Frederick M., and Karel Vlierman. 1996. *A small cog wrecked on the Zuiderzee in the early fifteenth century*. Lelystad: Nederlands Instituut voor Scheeps- en onderwater Archeologie.

Holmquist, June Drenning, and Ardis Hillman Wheeler, eds. 1964. *Diving into the past: Theories, techniques, and applications of underwater archaeology*. St. Paul: Minnesota Historical Society.

Inverarity, Robert Bruce. 1964. The conservation of wood from fresh water. In *Diving into the past*, ed. J. D. Holmquist and A. H. Wheeler, 68–70. St. Paul: Minnesota Historical Society.

Jones, Mark, ed. 2003. *For future generations: Conservation of a Tudor maritime collection*. Portsmouth: Mary Rose Trust.

Kahanov, Yaacov, and Elisha Linder. 2004. *The Ma'agan Mikhael ship: The recovery of a 2400-year-old merchantman*, vol. 2. Haifa: Israel Exploration Society.

Katzev, Michael L. 1980. Assessing a chance find near Kyrenia—a cargo from the age of Alexander: The study and conservation of an ancient hull. In Keith Muckelroy, ed., *Archeology under water: An atlas of the world's submerged sites*, 40–45. New York: McGraw-Hill.

———. 1991. The Kyrenia ship restored. In *The sea remembers*, ed. Peter Throckmorton, 55–59. New York: Smithmark.

Katzev, Susan Womer. 2005. Resurrecting an ancient Greek ship: Kyrenia, Cyprus. In *Beneath the seven seas*, ed. George Bass, 72–79. London and New York: Thames & Hudson.

Keith, Donald H. 1980. A fourteenth-century shipwreck at Sinan-gun. *Archaeology* 33 (2): 33–43.

Kliot, Nurit. 1988. Maritime boundaries in the Mediterranean: Aspects of cooperation and dispute. In *Maritime boundaries and ocean resources*, ed. Gerald Blake, 208–226. Lanham, MD: Rowman and Littlefield.

Kocabaş, Ufuk, ed. 2008. *The "old ships" of the "new gate,"* vol. 1. Istanbul: Ege Yayınları.

Lahn, Werner. 1992–2003. *Die Kogge von Bremen*. 2 vols. Hamburg: Ernst Kabel.

Lemée, Christian P. P. 2006. *The Renaissance shipwrecks from Christianshavn: An archaeological and architectural study of large carvel vessels in Danish waters, 1580–1640*. Roskilde: Viking Ship Museum.

Linder, Elisha, and Yaacov Kahanov. 2003. *The Ma'agan Mikhael ship: The recovery of a 2400-year-old merchantman*, vol. 1. Haifa: Israel Exploration Society.

Marsden, Peter. 1994. *Ships of the port of London: First to eleventh centuries CE*. London: English Heritage.

———. 1996. *Ships of the port of London: Twelfth to seventeenth centuries CE*. London: English Heritage.

———. 2003. *Sealed by time: The loss and recovery of the* Mary Rose. Portsmouth: Mary Rose Trust.

Martin, Colin. 1975. *Full fathom five: Wrecks of the Spanish Armada*. New York: Viking.

Mathers, William A., Henry S. Parker III, and Kathleen A. Copus, eds. 1990. *The recovery of the Manila galleon* Nuestra Señora de la Concepción. Sutton, VT: Pacific Sea Resources.

Mathers, William A., and Nancy Shaw. 1993. *Treasure of the* Concepción: *The archaeological recovery of a Spanish galleon*. Hong Kong: APA Publications.

McCann, Anna Marguerite, Joanne Bourgeois, Elaine K. Gazda, John Peter Oleson, and Elizabeth Lyding Will. 1987. *The Roman port and fishery of Cosa*. Princeton, NJ: Princeton University Press.

McCann, Anna Marguerite, and John Peter Oleson. 2004. *Deep-water shipwrecks off Skerki Bank: The 1997 survey*. Portsmouth, RI: Journal of Roman Archaeology Supplement.

McGrail, Seán. 1974. *The building and trials of the replica of an ancient boat: The Gokstad Faering. Part 1: Building the replica*; *Part 2: The sea trials*. Greenwich, England: National Maritime Museum.

———. 2001. *Boats of the world: From the Stone Age to medieval times*. Oxford: Oxford University Press.

McLaughlin-Neyland, Kathleen, and Bob Neyland. 1993. *Two prams wrecked on the Zuider Zee in the late eighteenth century*. Lelystad: Nederlands Instituut voor Scheeps- en onderwater Archeologie.

Meyer, Karl E. 1973. *The plundered past*. New York: Atheneum.

Muckelroy, Keith, ed. 1980. *Archeology under water: An atlas of the world's submerged sites*. New York: McGraw-Hill.

Needham, Joseph. 1971. *Science and civilisation in China*. Vol. 4, pt. 3: *Civil engineering and nautics*, with the collaboration of Wang Ling and Lu Gwei-Djen, 379–699. Cambridge: Cambridge University Press.

Neyland, Robert S., and Kathleen McLaughlin-Neyland. 1996. *A late sixteenth-century freighter from the Workumer Nieuwland Polder in Workum, Friesland*. Lelystad: Nederlands Instituut voor Scheeps- en onderwater Archeologie.

Nieto, Xavier, and Anna Maria Puig. 2001. *Excavacions arqueològiques subaquàtiques a Cala Culip 3. Culip IV: La terra sigillata decorada de la Graufesenque*. Girona: Museu d'Arqueologià de Catalunya.

Nieto, Xavier, and Xim Raurich, eds. 1998. *Excavacions arqueològiques subaquàtiques a Cala Culip 2. Culip VI*. Girona: Museu d'Arqueologià de Catalunya.

Nieto Prieto, Javier, et al. 1989. *Excavacions arqueològiques subaquatiques a Cala Culip 1*. Girona: Casa di Cultura.

Ossowski, Waldemar, ed. 2008. *The* General Carleton *shipwreck*, 1785 [in English and Polish]. Gdańsk: Polish Maritime Museum.

Owen, David I. 2009. Censoring knowledge: The case for the publication of unprovenanced cuneiform tablets. In *Whose culture? The promise of museums and the debate over antiquities*, ed. James Cuno, 125–142. Princeton, NJ: Princeton University Press.

Panvini, Rosalba. 2001. *The Archaic Greek ship at Gela*. Palermo: Salvatore Sciascia Editore.

Parrent, James M. 1983. The conservation of waterlogged wood using sucrose. MA thesis, Texas A&M University.

Piercy, Robin. 2005. The tragedy of the *Santo Antonio de Tanna*: Mombasa, Kenya. In *Beneath the seven seas*, ed. George F. Bass, 172–179. London: Thames & Hudson.

Pomey, Patrice. 1995. Les épaves grecques et romaines de la Place Jules-Verne à Marseille. *Comptes rendus des séances de l'année 1995 avril–juin de l'Académie des inscriptions et belles-lettres*, 459–482. Paris: Diffusion de Boccard.

———, ed. 1997. *La navigation dans l'antiquité*. Aix-en-Provence: Édisud.

Pringle, Heather. 2007. Profiteers on the high seas. *Archaeology* 60 (4): 20, 62, 64–65.

Pulak, Cemal. 1998. The Uluburun shipwreck: An overview. *International Journal of Nautical Archaeology* 27: 188–224.

———. 2008. The Uluburun shipwreck and Late Bronze Age trade. In *Beyond Babylon: Art, trade, and diplomacy in the second millennium B.C.*, ed. Joan Aruz, Kim Benzel, and Jean M. Evans, 288–385. New York: Metropolitan Museum of Art.

Purdy, Barbara A. 1991. *The art and archaeology of Florida's wetlands*. Boca Raton: CRC Press.

Raban, Avner, ed. 1985. *Harbour archaeology: Proceedings of the First International Workshop on Ancient Mediterranean Harbours, Caesarea Maritima, 24–28.6.83*. Oxford: British Archaeological Reports.

———. 1989. The harbours of Caesarea Maritima: Results of the Caesarea Ancient Harbour Excavation Project, 1980–1985. Oxford: BAR International Series.

Raban, Avner, and Kenneth G. Holum, eds. 1996. *Caesarea Maritima: A retrospective after two millennia*. Leiden: Brill.

Riess, Warren. 1987. The Ronson Ship: The study of an eighteenth century merchantman excavated in Manhattan, New York, in 1982. PhD diss., University of New Hampshire.

Rieth, Éric, Catherine Carriere-Desbois, and Virginie Serna. 2001. *L'épave de Port Berteau II (Charente-Maritime): Un caboteur fluvio-maritime du haut Moyen Âge et son contexte nautique*. Paris: La Maison des sciences de l'Homme.

Roghi, Gianni. 1958–1959. Note tecniche sul rilevamento e lo scavo della nave romana di Spargi. *Bollettino e atti* (Centro Italiano de Ricercatori Subacquei): 9–20.

———. 1959. La seconda campagna di scavi sotto marina sulla nave romana di Spargi (Sardegna). *Rivista di studi liguri* 25: 301–302.

———. 1965. Spargi. In *Marine archaeology*, ed. Joan du Plat Taylor, 103–118. London: Hutchinson.

Rosencrantz, Donald M. 1975. Underwater photography and photogrammetry. In *Photography in archaeological research*, ed. Elmer Harp Jr., 265–309. Albuquerque: University of New Mexico Press.

Rougé, Jean. 1966. *Recherches sur l'organisation du commerce maritime en Méditerranée sous l'empire romain*. Paris: SEVPEN.

Seborg, Ray M. 1964. Treating wood with polyethylene glycol. In *Diving into the past*, ed. J. D. Holmquist and A. H. Wheeler, 68–70. St. Paul: Minnesota Historical Society.

Smith, C. Wayne. 2003. *Archaeological conservation using polymers: Practical applications for organic artifact stabilization.* College Station: Texas A&M University Press.

Sørensen, Anne C. 2001. *Ladby: A Danish ship-grave from the Viking Age.* Roskilde: Viking Ship Museum.

Steffy, J. Richard. 1994. *Wooden ship building and the interpretation of shipwrecks.* College Station: Texas A&M University Press.

Stoddart, Simon, and Caroline Malone. 2001. Editorial. *Antiquity* 75: 233–240.

Symes, Gunild. 2005. Profile: Dr. Phil Nyutten. *X-Ray International Dive Magazine (X-Ray Mag)* 9: 69–74.

Tailliez, Philippe. 1965. Titan. In *Marine archaeology*, ed. Joan du Plat Taylor, 76–93. London: Hutchinson.

Tchernia, André, Patrice Pomey, H. Hesnard, et al. 1978. *L'épave romaine de la Madrague de Giens (Var), campagnes 1972–1975: Fouilles de l'Institut d'archéologie méditerranéene.* Paris: Éditions du Centre National de la Recherche Scientifique.

Thompson, Tommy. 1998. *America's lost treasure: A pictorial chronicle of the sinking and recovery of the United States Mail Steamship* Central America. New York: Atlantic Monthly Press.

Throckmorton, Peter, ed. 1991. *The sea remembers: Shipwrecks and archaeology.* New York: Smithmark.

Ucelli, Guido. 1950. *Le navi di Nemi.* Rome: Libreria dello Stato.

Van de Moortel, Aleydis. 1991. *A cog-like vessel from the Netherlands, Excavation Report 14.* Lelystad: Nederlands Instituut voor Scheeps- en onderwater Archeologie.

van Doorninck, Frederick H., Jr. Forthcoming. *Serçe Limanı*, vol. 3. *The ceramics, mercantile equipment, and historical context of an eleventh-century shipwreck.* College Station: Texas A&M University Press.

Wachsmann, Shelley. 1990. *The excavations of an ancient boat in the Sea of Galilee (Lake Kinneret).* Jerusalem: Antiqot English Series 19.

Ward, Cheryl A. 2000. *Sacred and secular: Ancient Egyptian ships and boats.* Philadelphia: University Museum, University of Pennsylvania.

Wheeler, Robert C., Walter A. Kenyon, Alan R. Woolworth, and Douglas A. Birk. 1975. *Voices from the rapids: An underwater search for fur trade artifacts 1960–73.* St. Paul: Minnesota Historical Society.

Wright, Edward. 1990. *The Ferriby boats: Seacraft of the Bronze Age.* London: Routledge.

Yalçin, Ünsal, Cemal Pulak, and Rainer Slotta, eds. 2005. *Das Schiff von Uluburun: Welthandel vor 3000 Jahren.* Bochum: Deutschen Bergbau-Museums.

PART II

THE PROCESS

CHAPTER 1

DEFINING A SHIP: ARCHITECTURE, FUNCTION, AND HUMAN SPACE

PATRICE POMEY

INTRODUCTION: DEFINING A SHIP

IN the field of archaeology, the study of a shipwreck is not simply a question of providing a description, however precise it may be, of the discovered remains. Rather, the study endeavors, through the understanding of these remains, to reconstitute the original ship and to interpret it within the framework of a well-defined historical context. This supposes that we can recognize (through these remains) the type of ship, with its technical and functional characteristics, and the use to which it was put within a given society. Thus, nautical archaeology, whose field of study is the ship itself, can claim to belong to the larger domain of maritime archaeology.

However, to arrive at this point, one must ask questions that are a function of the answers that one wishes to obtain in order to formulate a historical discourse. It is the a priori formulation of historical questions concerning each shipwreck that will lead to establishing an excavation strategy, then to defining the most appropriate methods in order to arrive at the anticipated results, and finally to choosing the techniques best adapted to the particular characteristics of each site.

Thus, the study of shipboard artifacts and cargo, of equipment and fittings, holds just as much importance as an analysis of the shape of the hull, its structure, and its assembly method. If these latter elements reveal the technical characteristics of the ship and its construction system, the former reveal the function and use. From the point of view of excavation strategy, the study of shipboard artifacts and cargo nearly always comes before it is possible to consider a structural analysis. Therefore, from the very beginning of any operation, one should be well aware of the importance of this data in any interpretation of the ship. This supposes an anticipation of the questions that will later arise during the study of the remains of the very hull of the ship. Likewise, the study of the structure will usually precede the more detailed study of the assembly, which will in turn reveal the sequences and processes of construction. Here, once again, one must know to anticipate the expected results in order to take into consideration the ensemble of data. It should be borne in mind that a ship constitutes a homogenous assemblage, of which all the elements, from the largest to the most minute, are very closely linked and yet only express their true role in their relation to the whole. Thus, the different fields of study, separated for obvious material reasons, will only be united and interpreted in an overall sense at the very end of the excavation.

Having presented these preliminary considerations, attention should now be turned to the different levels of analysis that will, at the end of the study, lead to a determination of the type of ship and its function.

Since the publication in 1978 of Keith Muckelroy's *Maritime Archaeology* there has been general agreement that a ship has a triple definition:

The ship is a machine. It is, however, a complex machine that floats and moves in a way that is both autonomous and controlled, and constitutes an architectural system coupled with a technical system.

The ship is an instrument adapted to a function. The instrument is designed to respond to precise needs arising from a political, economic, or military system. This instrument constitutes a functional system.

The ship is the living and working environment of a micro-society. It is, however, a closed society whose hierarchy, beliefs, rules, rhythms of life, and tools make up a particular social system.

Starting with the remains of a shipwreck, the study process will, through different levels of analysis, consist of reconstructing the original vessel as defined by the three aspects mentioned above, then retracing the entire operational process of its construction back to the initial architectural project as established between the builder and the commissioning agent (see Pomey and Rieth 2005; Steffy 1994).

The first of these aspects concerns the ship as machine, and that implies, first and foremost, an architectural structure, either simple or complex. Unlike a terrestrial architectural edifice, however, this structure must be able to float and move, in an autonomous and controlled way, from a point of departure to a point of arrival. The system is all the more complicated in that the movements are enacted within the interface of two elements, aquatic and aerial, that are themselves constantly in movement and submit the architectural structure to a tangle of complex forces that it must be able to resist. Thus, the choice of "architectural system" is decisive.

But the demands of mobility will add to the chosen architectural system a means of propulsion—pole, paddle, oar, sail, or different combinations—and steering devices—pole, paddle, oar, steering oar, quarter or axial rudder, directional sail— that transform the totality of the ship into a "technical system." In order to respond to these demands, the builder must, from the moment of conception of the ship and according to the stated needs of the commissioning agent (private or public), define an appropriate architectural system that is compatible with the required technical system.

The second aspect of the ship, that of an instrument adapted for a function, is so fundamental that it constitutes its very essence—its "raison d'être," as Muckelroy (1978) put it. Whatever the degree of elaboration or complexity, from the most basic boat to the most sophisticated ship, the construction of a vessel is never an act of chance. It is a response to a demand and to specific needs. These could be (a) economic, as in the transport of merchandise or persons, fishing activities, or the exploitation of marine resources; (b) military, as in the defense or attack of a territory or a city, seaborne combat, the policing and control of shipping lanes; or indeed (c) technical, as in towing, dredging, the maintenance of harbor basins, and the management of ports. And to these needs must be added the environmental constraints of the sailing area in which the vessel will perform its tasks: high seas or coastal waters, rivers or lakes, or even a sea-river combination. Clearly, these different functions and constraints influence the form of the hull, determine the means of propulsion, and dictate the specific fittings. In each case, the solution that is best adapted to the needs and most appropriate to requirements must be found. The final result is often a compromise between opposing demands.

In sum, the architectural and technical system that defines the ship-as-machine and the functional system that is the ship-as-instrument are tightly linked and come together in an inseparable fashion to determine the type of ship.

Lastly, the third aspect of the ship, a living and working environment, varies in importance as a precise function of the number of persons onboard and of their status (sailors or oarsmen, crew or passengers, civilian or soldiers, men or women), the length of stay onboard (long or short crossing, coastal or deep-sea navigation), the environmental conditions (open sea or inland navigation, climate and coastal morphology) and the nature of the work undertaken (transport, trade, warfare, fishing). It is obvious that the greater these parameters, the greater their influence on the organization of onboard life and space.

In all these cases, whenever the era and wherever the place, the construction of a ship and its employment, whatever its complexity, represents for the society that undertakes the endeavor a considerable effort in terms of savoir faire, technical means, supply, and development of materials. And in terms of social and political organization, it implies the conjunction, coordination, and application of the necessary means.

From a methodological point of view, the analysis of the ensemble of processes employed, from the conception of the ship to its use, can be broken down into a series of operations that constitute an "operational process" or an "operational chain." It is this operational process that one needs to explain in the study of the construction of the ship as machine, instrument, and living environment. At this stage of the analysis, one should distinguish the "conception" phase from the "realization" phase.

THE "CONCEPTION" PHASE

The preliminary phase of "conception"—aside from the decision to actually undertake the construction of a ship and the gathering of the required finances for such an undertaking—means fundamentally the definition of the architectural project. Depending on the degree of sophistication of the ship, this project will be more or less complex, but it must always define, on one hand, an architectural system (hull shape and structure), and, on the other hand, a technical system (means of propulsion and steering). Both systems must be appropriate to the needs of the ship's function and adapted to the sailing area, and moreover it must respect the outfitting and employment conditions according to the possibilities of the ship's owner.

When considering the concept of the architectural system, a general distinction is made between several basic architectural groups that have been defined largely through the analysis of ethnographic data (see Arnold 1995–1996; Greenhill 1976; Hornell 1946; McGrail 2001):

- Floats, whether natural or artificial (skin sacks, pottery, etc.), and rafts (reeds, papyrus, wood, etc.)
- Skin boats (kayaks, oumiaks, currachs, coracles, etc.)
- Bark boats (canoes, etc.)
- Log boats, simple (one single trunk), with outrigger or composite log boats (two or more trunks assembled side by side)
- Plank boats

In certain cases, these architectural groups, based on the nature of the material, the technique employed, and the physical principle of buoyancy—natural or artificial buoyancy (for example, displacement vessels)—can be combined. Such is the case, for example, of "extended log boats," halfway between the simple log boat and the plank boat, where the central trunk is generally split into several pieces to which other elements are attached. On the other hand, while the first categories evoke simple architectural principles, the last category—plank boats, which includes the most elaborate of vessels—can itself be subdivided into multiple construction principles representing different architectural concepts.

The builder must accomplish two fundamental operations within the definition of the architectural project. First, he must define a structure that on a mechanical level assures the buoyancy and the cohesion of the whole and that is capable of

resisting the complex mechanical forces the ship will be subjected to when in use—
Archimedes' principle of buoyancy, forces of gravity, propulsion and direction, and
so on. This is the "structural conception."

A great number of solutions are thus possible within these different architectural groups, and the choice depends above all on cultural and environmental
factors. At this level, the category of plank boats presents the widest range of possibilities, from the "extended log boat" to multipart vessels. These latter, characterized
by a multiplicity of frame timbers and planks, morphological diversity, and a variety
of assembly possibilities, represent a vast conceptual field. Recent research has led
to a distinction between ships that are built "bottom based"—that is, constructed
with a flat bottom and no keel—and those with a keel. The latter are generally for
seafaring, while the former are most often encountered in inland waters (Pomey
and Rieth 2005). However, within this grouping of ships built upon a keel, several
architectural concepts can once again be recognized according to the role played by
the axial framing, the transversal framing, and the hull planking, around which
the architectural structure is organized (see Basch 1972; Casson 1963; Crumlin-Pedersen
1991; Hasslöf 1963; McGrail 1998; Pomey 1988, 1998, 2004; Pomey and Rieth 2005;
Rieth 1998; Steffy 1994, 1995). Usually one is dealing with one of two: either the principal structural role is played by the axial framing and the hull planking, in the
case of a "shell structure concept," or it is played by the axial framing and the
transversal framing, in the case of a "frame structure concept" or "skeleton structure concept." Intermediary solutions are always possible with "mixed" concepts.

The second fundamental operation in the definition of the architectural project
is in determining the shape of the overall hull, or "hull shape conception." During
this operation, the functional aspect of the ship has a decisive influence. Thus, for a
cargo ship one would favor a full shape to increase carrying capacity and profitability, whereas for a warship one would look for a finer shape to improve speed and
maneuverability. The proportional ratios between the different basic dimensions
(length between perpendiculars, width at the main frame, depth of the hold) can
therefore be extremely variable from one type of vessel to another. Other important
characteristics, such as the main section, and the shape of the stempost and sternpost, must also be defined. All these parameters have a direct influence on the
behavior of the ship and its sailing capacities in relation to its particular function. In
addition, one should note that, depending on the ship's function and the chosen
technical system, specific fittings might be installed that could in certain cases have
a direct influence on form. For example, one need only think of what was required
to install 170 rowers on three levels, one above the other, in an ancient trireme. The
complexity of such an arrangement is still the source of debate to this day (Basch
1987; Morrison, Coates, and Rankov 2000).

This "hull shape concept" is also quite clearly and closely connected to the
"structural concept" and is treated separately here only because of the needs of this
article. It is obvious that the choice of the architectural structure has a direct influence on shape. As proof, we need only look at the log boat. More generally, the
architectural choice dictates the way in which the volume of the hull will be

determined once the reference dimensions are fixed. In the construction of bottom-based plank boats, this is dictated by the realization of the flat bottom itself. In a keel-based construction, this determination can lie in several alternatives. For example, it could be a "longitudinal" vision of the hull as defined by the placing of the axial framing and planking strakes in the case of a shell structure conception; one is then facing a "longitudinal" shape concept, also known as "plank orientated." Or it could be a "transversal" vision resting on the definition of the main frame and of certain sections as in the frame/skeleton structure conception; one is then facing a "transversal" or "frame-orientated" shape concept.

Having defined the "architectural system," one must complete it by defining the "technical system," which is also directly dependent on the functional aspect of the ship. Here again, this operation is strictly linked to those preceding and is not separated in actual practice.

According to the function of the vessel, one is often faced with a choice as to the means of propulsion. Thus, cargo vessels might favor sail propulsion, which, through its possibilities of expansion, can offer a great deal of power while allowing for a limited crew size. On the other hand, warships long favored, at least until the appearance of shipboard artillery in the sixteenth century, oar power, as developed with the galley, since it offered advantages in mobility, speed, and instant power. It is clear that the choice of propulsion system has a direct influence upon the form and proportions of the hull. Oar propulsion led to a lengthening of the hull in order to allow the positioning of more rowers on each side and thus to increase the power of propulsion. Besides, the increase in the length coefficient has a direct effect on the speed of a ship. However, a sail-propelled merchant ship is looking more for stability than rapidity and thus can have a fuller shape. One can therefore have totally different length coefficients (ratio of length to width), on the order of seven for ancient galleys and three for merchant vessels.

The last important point in defining the "technical system" is that of the steering devices. Here once more, according to the chosen architectural system, the shape of the hull, and the means of propulsion, the choice of steering gear can vary greatly in its principle, shape, and proportions. On very small vessels, the steering system may be part of the means of propulsion (pole, oar, paddle, etc.). However, it quickly becomes independent on bigger vessels. Despite an apparent uniformity due to a limited number of concepts, steering arrangements vary considerably in their shape and position as a function of numerous factors. Of these, the environmental factor, connected to the sailing area, is from this point of view decisive. So, for downstream river navigation an enlarged steering system is required to ensure efficiency.

Finally, the social dimension of the vessel as the living and working environment of a micro-society must be borne in mind in the architectural project. Work spaces and specific arrangements must be foreseen. Moreover, the larger the crew and the longer the period of life onboard, the more important the organization of accommodation and space. Consider, for example, the French 74-cannon ships-of-the-line of the 1780s that gained fame during the wars of the Revolution and Napoleonic period (Pomey and Rieth 2005: 19–20). Seven hundred seventy men lived aboard a ship that measured 56 m in length from stem to sternpost and roughly 14 m wide at the main frame. They were split among several rigidly hierarchical social groupings that involved officers, sailors, marines, sundry professions, and staff (apothecary, servants, etc.). All had to live and get along for several months in the limited and restricted space of the ship.

The "conception" phase, for which we have defined the general lines of the diverse, yet required, operations in determining the architectural project taking into account the different aspects of the ship, must then lead to a "realization" phase. This latter consists in the materialization in a shipyard of the previously defined architectural project. Several operations are necessary to achieve construction, and each one brings into play an operational process.

THE "REALIZATION" PHASE

The first operation of the "realization" phase is the acquisition of materials, which, until the industrial revolution of the mid-nineteenth century, primarily meant wood, although cloth, metals, ropes, coatings, paint, and so on were also necessary. Local resources and the possibilities of outside supply, as well as the level of technical development, all play a decisive role in the choice of materials. The contrast between northern European naval construction, which could count on only a relatively limited number of tree species, largely broad-leaved, and Mediterranean naval construction, which used a very large variety of broad-leaved and resinous species, presents a good reflection of the different resources on offer in the forests of the two regions. In addition, the acquisition of all these materials brings into play diverse operational processes. Thus, for example, in the case of wood, the choice of trees to fell as a function of their species, the morphological characteristics of each individual tree, and the different structural element that it could provide, then the felling, transport, and storage, all set in motion a series of operations that reveal the organizational system of the society that built the vessel. The use of dendrochronological and dendromorphological analyses with a view to identifying species, dates of felling, and provenance, as well as looking at the methods of cutting, have proven to be absolutely indispensable for today's study of nautical and maritime archaeology (Guibal and Pomey 2003, 2009).

The second important operation in this "realization" phase is the transformation of the raw material into worked pieces to be used in the vessel: planking, frames, pegs, nails, sails, ropes, anchors, and so on. To remain with wood, the way a log is cut and then the timber worked are both particularly revealing of the level of technical skill. Once again, the contrast between the northern regions, where splitting was the dominant technique, and the Mediterranean, where sawing was in use very early on, is a good illustration of the different practices. Their technological importance is illustrated by the fact that the introduction of sawing techniques into northern construction appears as a major historical event (Crumlin-Pedersen 2009).

The most fundamental and most complex operation of this "realization" phase is, of course, the construction on the stocks of the vessel itself. This "realization" phase takes place directly after the "conception" phase of the architectural project and is indeed the natural, practical extension of it. It must materialize, with the help of diverse processes or methods, the construction principles chosen for the structural and shape concept of the ship. Thus, the notion of construction "principles" is directly associated with the "conception" phase, whereas the notion of construction "processes" or "methods" corresponds to the "realization" phase (Pomey 1988, 2004).

These construction processes are in turn extremely varied and therefore particularly revealing of the technical skill of any given society. The complexity of the problem lies in the fact that the same construction principle can lead to several methods of realization depending on the period or place under consideration.

But before turning to examples that can illustrate the diversity of processes, one should emphasize that this distinction between phases of conception and realization, and the notions of construction principles and methods, while representing above all methodological considerations of analysis, do nevertheless correspond to a more or less visible reality. This separation is particularly evident in the modern era following the development, within the state arsenals of the great maritime powers, of the use of plans and hydrostatic calculations in the conception phase of the architectural project. It was perhaps thus, on a smaller scale, in certain ancient societies and for certain types of construction under the control of the state or the Crown (Pomey 2007). However, this separation is scarcely visible in so-called traditional constructions where the conception phase is not at all or just barely materialized—through, for example, molds—but remains essentially within the mind of the builder. In this case, on a concrete level, the phases of conception and of realization are practically simultaneous, and the vessel is gradually conceived as it is built, while nonetheless holding to a predetermined ship project. Some examples will allow us to better grasp the extent of these notions of conception principle and construction method.

The building of a simple log boat involves an architectural concept based on a well-defined construction principle that arises from the structure of a single tree trunk, whose natural size will impose certain limits of dimension. However, several construction processes can be employed within this construction principle. The simplest consists of digging into the trunk and extracting 85% to 90% of the interior matter, and of working the exterior until it forms a hull from a single tree. Depending on the section obtained by the cutting of the bottom and sides, and the position of the bottom relative to the pith of the tree, several varieties of form can be had (Arnold 1995–1996). Another procedure is to work the exterior and the extremities and then to hollow out the interior of the trunk as before. Thereafter, while one heats the wood, the sides are gently forced outward, expanding and modifying the natural shape of the trunk and creating new morphological possibilities (McGrail 1998; Nicolaisen and Damgård-Sørensen 1991). Thus, two construction processes, one by simple extraction (dugout), the other by extraction and expansion (expanded log boat), can be applied to the same principle of construction without in any way changing the architectural concept of the whole.

Another characteristic example that reveals the complexity of construction systems is provided by the shipyards of northern Holland in the sixteenth and seventeenth centuries (Hasslöf 1963; Pomey 1988, 2004; Rieth 1984). Here, merchantmen and men-of-war were built according to the frame structure concept that was usual for the period in large shipyards. Within the finished hull, the frame, homogenous throughout, played the fundamental structural role, while the planking nailed to the frame served as a covering. Nevertheless, most of the bottom of the hull was constructed following the shell-first method, using temporary cleats to hold the strakes in place. One can see that it would be difficult to qualify this type of construction without recourse to the notions of construction principles and methods. Within the architectural principle of "frame structure," the construction processes have involved a "plank-based and -orientated" method for a part of the form conception and of the realization of the hull. From the archaeological standpoint, a whole series of signs can reveal these different construction phases, as was shown by the excavation and study of the wrecks in Copenhagen port (Lemée 2006). It is certain that the interpretation of these signs is made easier by an analysis based on the distinction between the principles and the methods (Pomey 2004; see Pevny in this volume).

Within the framework of the study of ancient ship construction, the introduction of the idea of "active" or "passive" frames, according to which the framing does or does not play a role in determining the hull's shape (Basch 1972), represents an important contribution to the understanding of construction systems. It is all the more valuable within an analysis that takes into account the notions of construction principles and methods. If there is general agreement these days that ancient ship construction was fundamentally built on the plank-based and -orientated construction principle, as much for the form concept as for the architectural structure, it is nevertheless the case that excavations of shipwrecks, continually increasing in number, are uncovering a great diversity in construction processes. In this way, the introduction of one or more active frames fulfilling the role of a mold to guide and ease the placing of planking strakes, as seen on the fourth-century CE Roman wreck Yassi Ada II (van Doorninck 1976), would appear to be a construction process that fits into the basic plank-based and -orientated construction principle without actually calling it into question.

On the other hand, the use of battens supported by preerected frames to help in the fitting of other frames within a construction of the transversal framing principle is in itself just a construction process that does not contradict the fundamental principle. The study of the eleventh-century Serçe Limanı wreck (Steffy 2004) clearly demonstrates that the construction of this ship followed a transversal and not longitudinal concept and was based on an architectural structure employing homogenous framing, thus reflecting a conceptual change that occurred in ship construction.

A final example, provided by the seventh-century Byzantine wreck Yassi Ada I (Bass and van Doorninck 1982), shows how intermediary solutions can exist arising from a mixed conception and realization that in themselves, depending on the parts, spring from principles and processes of a different nature. In this ship, the lower section of the hull was built on the "plank-based and -orientated" principle following a shell-first process, while the upper section was constructed on the "transversal frame" principle using the frame-first process. In this case, we are truly confronted by a mixed-concept vessel having recourse to several construction processes during realization.

Tracing the Operational Process through Archaeology

The aim of any archaeological study of a shipwreck is, naturally, to discover the construction principles and methods that governed its conception and realization. In this way, it becomes possible to understand the architectural system as a whole and to fit the ship as machine into a precise historical context. Generally, the construction principles are grasped by studying the ensemble of the remains of the hull and, especially for keel-built boats, through the reciprocal relationship between the planking and the framing. In effect, whatever the construction processes employed, the construction principle is permanent and always appears in the final stage of realization. On the other hand, it is common for the construction processes to leave only the slightest of traces, since they generally correspond to temporary phases of construction. Most often they are found only by a detailed study of the hull. For example, the temporary assembly cleats or battens, once removed, leave only the marks of their nails. These clues that reveal the process can only be properly interpreted in the light of previously recognized construction principles (see Ravn et al.; Batchvarov; and Pevny, all in this volume).

Tracing the Technical System and the Function through Archaeology

The recognition of the technical system, composed of the means of propulsion and steering associated with an architectural system, lies essentially upon the identification of the necessary fitments for their use: the presence of thwarts, of tholepins or oar ports, of *apostis*, of oars, etc., for an oar-powered propulsion system; or the presence of mast step timbers or traces of their installation, of partners, of rigging elements, pulley blocks, brail rings, and so on, for a sail-powered propulsion system. The same applies for steering devices. Unfortunately, apart from the mast step and stern rudder, these systems are by design installed above the water line and for this reason are rarely or only very fragmentarily preserved. In the absence of these clues, it is necessary to look at the general characteristics of the wreck in order to determine its architectural and functional system and thus be able to deduce the technical system. The study of dimensions and proportions can prove decisive. In such a fashion, even in the absence of the remains of paddles (which was not in fact the case), the overall characteristics of the fourth-century CE war canoe from Hjortspring, at some 18 m in length, led one to consider a propulsion system based on paddlers. In fact, any other system would have been incompatible with the morphology and structure of the vessel (Crumlin-Pedersen and Trakadas 2003).

Identification of the function of the vessel proceeds from a general analysis of the whole, taking into account the architectural and technical characteristics that, as we have seen, are closely connected to its intended purpose. However, once again, this identification can be greatly simplified by the presence of remains directly linked to function, as, for example, elements of cargo for merchant ships or pieces of armament for warships. For example, the bronze ram discovered at Athlit on the Israeli coast attests with certainty the presence of an ancient war galley of a superior type (Casson and Steffy 1991). Likewise, cargoes of amphorae, which have the advantage of not being destroyed by the marine environment, are the surest evidence in identifying cargo vessel wrecks of the ancient Mediterranean, as exemplified by the Kyrenia and Madrague de Giens wrecks, to name but two of the most famous (Wylde-Swiny and Katzev 1973; Tchernia, Pomey, and Hesnard 1978) (Figure 1.1). This evidence is all the more useful given that the great diversity of ships attested by iconography makes the interpretation of remains more complicated. At the same time, nobody has yet definitely identified an ancient Mediterranean grain transporter, such as those celebrated ships of the *annona* that were responsible for the provisioning of Rome, because of the destruction of the cargo by seawater and the lack of known and distinctive characteristics. Nevertheless, we know that they were among the largest of vessels and took part in the most important commercial traffic of the ancient Mediterranean (Casson 1995; Pomey and Tchernia 1978; Tchernia 1997).

In the modern era, since the employment of shipboard cannon and the development of battery artillery, cannons seem to be the perfect clue for identifying a warship. Most often this is the case so long as one bears in mind that cargo vessels too were themselves often armed to defend against pirates and enemy powers. The example of the sixteenth-century wreck just off Villefranche-sur-Mer in France is a good illustration of this practice (Guérout, Reith, and Gassend 1989). Tentatively identified as the Genoese *nave Lomellina*, sunk in 1516, the wreck held cannons. In fact, the ship was working for the French Crown and engaged in campaigns and was transporting military material, including land artillery. It was these particular circumstances, confirmed by written archives, that resulted in cannon being found in the remains of a cargo vessel. This example also demonstrates that for the modern

Figure 1.1 Madrague de Giens shipwreck. General view of the hull and cargo of amphorae. Reproduced with the kind permission of Centre Camille Jullian, CNRS, Aix-en-Provence.

and contemporary periods especially, recourse to archival sources is fundamental in the search to identify a shipwreck (see Domingues in this volume). This type of research, however, goes beyond the framework of the present article.

With a lack of indisputable evidence, which is compounded when the remains are scarce, identification can become difficult and can lead to controversy. In this respect, the example of the Punic ships from Marsala is revealing. From 1971 to 1974 Honor Frost excavated the two wrecks. One consisted of the aft part of a ship with a prominently raked stern. The other was the fore part of another ship with a vertical stempost bearing two horizontal mounts. These mounts were designed to hold between them a piece of curved wood, interpreted as a ram, in the shape of an "elephant's tusk" (Frost 1981). Painted assembly marks in Punic letters left no doubt as to the origin of these vessels, the loss of which was dated to the middle of the third century BCE at the time of naval combat in the region related to the First Punic War. Assimilating the two neighboring wrecks into one type of ship and counting upon the presence of the ram, Frost proposed an identification consistent with a Punic war galley. This interpretation, however, was strongly opposed by Lionel Casson (1985) who, basing his argument on the fact that one of the wrecks bore lead sheathing, considered that this was incompatible with a war galley and therefore belonged to a cargo vessel. Whatever position one adopts regarding the argumentation put forward, this controversy raises two questions. The first concerns the assimilation of the two wrecks into one and the same type of vessel, and the second concerns the interpretation of the stempost as ram or as cutwater (Basch 1983). One can see that the interpretation of shipwrecks is not always a simple matter.

One might also mention the case of the fishing boat Fiumicino 5, discovered in 1960 in the port of Claudius at Ostia, Italy, whose identification was made obvious by the presence of an internal fish tank in the center of the hull (Boetto 2006) (Figure 1.2). But the identification of a wreck as a fishing boat is not always easy if the structures or specific fitments no longer exist. Thus, the wreck of the Archaic Greek boat from the second half of the sixth century BCE, Jules-Verne 9, discovered in 1993 in the ancient harbor of Marseille (France), could only be identified as a vessel used for fishing, and in this case coral fishing, thanks to the presence of small fragments of red coral that had fallen to the bottom of the hull and were then trapped within the waterproofing resin of the interior woodwork (Pomey 2000, 2003). Meanwhile, the Bon-Porté 1 wreck (France), which appeared to be the perfect "sister ship" of Jules-Verne 9, was instead used as a local transporter of small cargoes of amphorae (Joncheray 1976). Here we can see that the same or similar type of vessel, like these coastal craft (Jules-Verne 9 and Bon-Porté I), with mixed propulsion of sail and oar, could be used for different functions, either fishing or the local transport of goods or persons. However, in the absence of clues, like elements of cargo or the remains of fish, the distinction is not always obvious.

The excavations of the Place Jules-Verne at Marseille in 1993 brought to light a number of first- to second-century CE shipwrecks (Jules-Verne 3, 4, and 5) of a hitherto completely unknown type, characterized by the unusual presence of a shaft

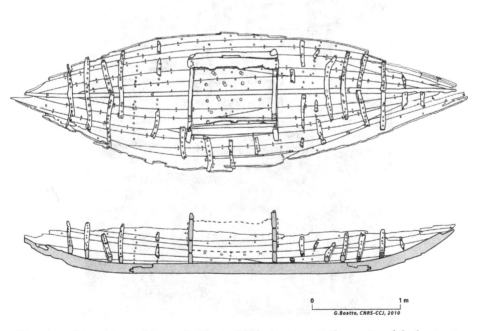

Figure 1.2 Fiumicino 5 shipwreck. The tanklike structure in the center of the boat was used to hold live fish. Reproduced with the kind permission of G. Boetto, Centre Camille Jullian, CNRS, Aix-en-Provence.

open to the sea deliberately created from the moment of construction in the center of the hull's structure (Figure 1.3). The flat-bottomed hull, the pronounced turn of the bilge, the numerous signs of repair undertaken around the edge of the hull and the existence of this central shaft all indicated that we were dealing with boats designed for a particular type of harbor work. At the same period, archaeological data tells us that the ancient harbor basin underwent some serious dredging, so it is possible that these boats were conceived specifically as dredgers, the central shaft being the site of some particular dredging mechanism (Pomey 1999).

Cross-referencing textual and iconographic documentation with archaeological data is often necessary when reflecting on the interpretation of a vessel. This is especially so when analyzing technical and functional systems whose characteristic elements have all too often disappeared from the wreck and yet are still present in iconographic documents. The case of the interpretation of the Fiumicino 1, 2, and 3

Figure 1.3 Jules-Verne 3 shipwreck. In the center of the wreck one can see in the bottom of the hull the open shaft that held some form of dredging equipment. Reproduced with the kind permission of Centre Camille Jullian, CNRS, Aix-en-Provence.

wrecks from the port of Claudius at Ostia is a fine example in this regard (Boetto 2008). The provisioning of Rome from its maritime port at the mouth of the Tiber, near Ostia, led to the creation of a system of river-seagoing boats, the *naves caudicariae*, that were used to haul merchandise from the main port to the city. This organization left written and iconographic records that, when compared with structural, morphological, and technical characteristics of the wrecks, led to an identification of them as being these very *naves caudicariae*. Without the possibility of consulting these written and iconographic records, the identification would have remained problematic. In general, we should remember that the great diversity of texts and iconography encompasses the variety of vessels and their usage of all times and in all places (see Basch 1987). This source is an indispensable tool for the understanding and identification of shipwrecks whether of oceangoing ships or small skiffs.

As for the vessel's aspect as the living and working environment of a microsociety, the study must essentially rely on an analysis of shipboard artifacts, diverse equipment (notably tools), and interior arrangements. We might mention here the Kyrenia wreck dating from the end of the fourth century BCE. The study of the distribution of material led to the reconstruction of a storage space at the fore of the vessel that held a water reserve and drinking cups, and to the aft a cabin with kitchen utensils and tableware. The presence of several series of four items of tableware (four cups, four plates, etc.) led to the understanding that the crew was composed of four sailors (Wylde-Swiny and Katzev 1973). Another example is provided by the detailed study of the shipboard artifacts recovered from the Byzantine wreck Yassi Ada I. Here, one was able to reconstruct the living space that was the ship's cabin (Figure 1.4) and recognize all the contents of the ship's carpenter's toolbox.

Figure 1.4 Yassi Ada I Byzantine shipwreck. Reconstruction of ship's cabin space with onboard kitchen, kitchen- and tableware, and daily objects (lamps, balance, etc.). Reproduced with the kind permission of the Bodrum Museum of Underwater Archaeology.

Moreover, the discovery of gold and silver coins and a balance engraved with the name of the *naukleros* (the ship's owner or his agent) *Georgios*, along with his counterweight and weights, came as evidence of the economic activity of the crew of this little coastal trader carrying a cargo of amphorae (Bass and van Doorninck 1982).

Once again, the cross-referencing of written texts describing shipboard life, iconography, and archaeological data proved to be indispensable in the study of the human space that makes up an aspect of the ship and the activities that happen within it.

Two Case Studies

Let us finish by looking at two particularly significant studies. The first concerns the Roman shipwreck of Madrague de Giens, sunk around 75–60 BCE off the French Mediterranean coast (Tchernia, Pomey, and Hesnard 1978). It was carrying a cargo of more than 6,000 wine amphorae stacked in three layers, on top of which was a large load of ceramics. This cargo indicates from the outset that we are dealing with a large Roman merchant ship. Nevertheless, the dimensions of the wreck would reconstitute a vessel roughly 40 m long by 9 m wide and 4.5 m deep, providing a length-to-beam coefficient of 4.4, which is easily greater than the usual coefficient of ancient merchant ships. The study of the hull soon confirmed that this was a large ship of a very particular type. It showed a sharp bottom with "wine glass" section and a prominent keel creating a large leeboard. The stem and stern displayed extended raking, and there was a reverse stempost in the shape of a ram. The structural study of the stempost showed that the ship was, in fact, equipped with a big cutwater that had nothing in common with a ram except the general shape. The presence, still in place, of the mast step timber with cavities corresponding to a main mast and a foremast, of the bilge pump well, and of various interior arrangements all completed the general characteristics of the ship's architectural system and suggested that this was a pure two-masted sailing ship. From these characteristics, it was possible to establish precise parallels with the iconography and to demonstrate the similarity, notably in the proportions between different parts and elements of the ship, between the Madrague de Giens wreck and ships on the great mosaic of the Ocean God in the baths of Themetra in Tunisia (Pomey 1982) (Figure 1.5). From there, it became possible to specify the type of ship, not just from the architectural angle but also from the point of its technical system, which could be entirely reconstituted. In sum, the Madrague de Giens vessel was a large merchantman of considerable tonnage—400 tons deadweight with a displacement of around 550 tons—and possessed two masts. The carefully shaped hull, characterized by a reverse stempost with cutwater, must have given this type of craft high-performance sailing qualities.

The second example comes from the Skuldelev wrecks near Roskilde in Denmark that were excavated by O. Crumlin-Pedersen in 1962 (Crumlin-Pedersen

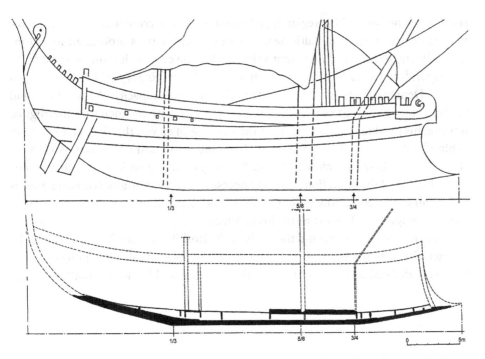

Figure 1.5 Comparison between the profile of the large ship of the Themetra baths mosaic (above) and the longitudinal section of the Madrague de Giens wreck (below) showing the similarity between the two vessels. Reproduced with the kind permission of M. Rival, Centre Camille Jullian, CNRS, Aix-en-Provence.

and Olsen 2002). The five Viking vessels, all built during the first half of the eleventh century, had been deliberately sunk in the mouth of Roskilde fjord sometime in the 1070s to create a barrier blocking direct access from the sea to the town of Roskilde. The study revealed the characteristics and origins of these different representative types (war, commerce, fishing) of Viking vessels in use at that period (Crumlin-Pedersen 2009). Of the two warships, the Skuldelev 2–4 belonged to the superior category of longships. A dendrochronological study established that the vessel was built in Ireland, in Dublin region, and that the keel had been cut from a tree felled in 1042. It measured some 30 m in length and was propelled by 60 rowers and a square sail of more than 100 m². It had probably been sent to Roskilde as part of a diplomatic mission aimed at expelling the Normans from England in order to reestablish Anglo-Saxon or Danish rule. The second warship, the Skuldelev 5, belonged to the same category of longships but was of more modest dimensions, reaching roughly 17 m in length and holding 26 rowers. Built in Denmark circa 1030, much repaired and with many reused planks, it is representative not of any royal or princely vessel but rather of those warships constructed and equipped by a local population for the defense of their land. The Skuldelev 1, conversely, was a cargo ship 16.50 m long and built, according to dendrochronology, circa 1030 on the west coast of Norway. Very seaworthy, equipped with a half-deck fore and aft and high sides, it belongs to the Norwegian type known as a *knarr*, constructed for commerce between Norway and the Baltic Sea. Its carrying capacity of around 20 to 25 tons makes it a medium-sized merchant ship. The Skuldelev 3, with rather elegant lines, corresponds to the category of coastal traders of the *byrding* type (Figure 1.6). It was built in Denmark, was some 14 m long with a carrying capacity of 4 to 5 tons, and probably met the needs of a Viking farmer traveling with his men to gatherings or ferrying his produce to market. Lastly, the simplest of all was the Skuldelev 6, a large fishing boat some 11 m long that came from the west coast of Norway. A detailed study of all of these craft allowed for the building of sailing replicas of each and thus an evaluation of the operational process necessary for their original construction, as well as an evaluation of the sailing qualities encountered during numerous experimental voyages (see Ravn et al. in this volume).

In sum, the interest behind the study of the Roskilde wrecks lies in revealing the characteristics that are proper to each of these boats from all three points of view that were defined at the beginning of this chapter, and in the evaluation of each

Figure 1.6 View of the *Roar Ege*—a sailing replica of the Skuldelev 3 wreck— under sail. Reproduced with the kind permission of the Viking Ship Museum, Roskilde.

vessel as an architectural, technical, functional, and social system. But to go beyond this exemplary study of nautical archaeology, the interpretation of the Skuldelev vessels gives rise to important historical considerations that confer upon the study of the ensemble a new dimension: that of marine archaeology in the service of the history of maritime societies.

CONCLUSION

In conclusion, the study of a ship, because of its complexity—most notably in understanding the construction principles and methods—requires different levels of analysis, and at the end of that study one should reconstitute the ship into the whole, in which its different aspects are tightly conjoined and indissoluble. It is only by adhering to this process that the researcher will be able to insert the ship into a well-determined context from the technical, functional, and social point of view, which will then confer upon it a true historic dimension.

ACKNOWLEDGMENTS

I would like to express my warmest thanks to Colin Clement for translating this article into English.

REFERENCES

Arnold, Béat. 1995–1996. *Pirogues monoxyles d'Europe centrale: Construction, typologie, évolution.* 2 vols. Archéologie Neuchâteloise, 20–21. Saint-Blaise: Office cantonal d'Archéologie de Neuchâtel.

Basch, Lucien. 1972. Ancient wrecks and the archaeology of ships. *International Journal of Nautical Archaeology* 1: 1–58.

———. 1983. When is a ram a ram? The case of the Punic ship. *Mariner's Mirror* 69: 129–142.

———. 1987. Le musée imaginaire de la marine antique. Athens: Institut Hellénique pour la Préservation de la Tradition Nautique.

Bass, George F., and Frederic H. van Doorninck Jr., eds. 1982. *Yassi Ada*, vol. 1: *A seventh-century Byzantine shipwreck.* College Station: Texas A&M University Press.

Boetto, Giulia. 2006. Roman techniques for the transport and conservation of fish: The case of the Fiumicino 5 wreck. In *Connected by the sea: Proceedings of the Xth International Symposium on Boat and Ship Archaeology, Roskilde, 2003,* ed. Lucy Blue, Frederic Hocker, and Anton Englert, 123–129. Oxford: Oxbow.

———. 2008. L'épave de l'Antiquité tardive *Fiumicino 1*: Analyse de la structure et étude fonctionnelle. *Archaeonautica* 15: 29–62.

Casson, Lionel. 1963. Ancient shipbuilding: New light on an old source. *Transactions of the American Philological Association* 44: 28–33.

———. 1985. Greek and Roman shipbuilding: New findings. *American Neptune* 45: 10–19.

———. 1995. Ships and seamanship in the ancient world. Baltimore: John Hopkins University Press.

Casson, Lionel, and Richard Steffy, eds.1991. *The Athlit Ram*. College Station: Texas A&M University Press.

Crumlin-Pedersen, Ole. 1991. Ship types and sizes CE 800–1400. In *Aspects of maritime Scandinavia CE 200–1200*, ed. Ole Crumlin-Pedersen, 69–82. Roskilde: Viking Ship Museum.

———. 2009. *Archaeology and the sea in Scandinavia and Britain*. Roskilde: Viking Ship Museum.

Crumlin-Pedersen, Ole, and Olaf Olsen, eds. 2002. *The Skuldelev ships I: Topography, archaeology, history, conservation and display*. Ships and Boats of the North 4-1. Roskilde: Viking Ship Museum.

Crumlin-Pedersen, Ole, and Athena Trakadas, eds. 2003. *Hjortspring: A pre-Roman iron-age warship in context*. Ships and Boats of the North 5. Roskilde: Viking Ship Museum.

Frost, Honor. 1981. *Lilybaeum (Marsala): The Punic ship; Final excavation report*. Notizie degli Scavi di Antiquità 30, 1976, sup. Rome: Academia Nazionale dei Lincei.

Greenhill, Basil. 1976. *Archaeology of the boat*. London: A&C Black.

Guérout, Max, Eric Rieth, and Jean-Marie Gassend. 1989. *Le navire génois de Villefranche: Un naufrage de 1516?* Archaeonautica 9. Paris: Centre National de la Recherche Scientifique.

Guibal, Frédéric, and Patrice Pomey. 2003. Timber supply and ancient naval architecture. In *Boats, ships and shipyards: Proceedings of the IXth International Symposium on Boat and Ship Archaeology, Venice 2000*, ed. Carlo Beltrame, 35–41. Oxford: Oxbow.

———. 2009. Ancient shipwrecks, naval architecture and dendrochronlogy in the western Mediterranean. In *Between the seas: Transfer and exchange in nautical technology; Proceedings of the XIth International Symposium on Boat and Ship Archaeology, Mainz 2006*, ed. Ronald Bockius, 219–226. Mainz: Römisch-Germanisches Zentralmuseum.

Hasslöf, Olav. 1963. Wrecks, archives and living tradition. *Mariner's Mirror* 49 (3): 162–177.

Hornell, James. 1946. *Water transport: Origin and early evolution*. Cambridge: Cambridge University Press.

Joncheray, Jean-Pierre. 1976. L'épave grecque, ou étrusque, de Bon Porté. *Cahiers d'Archéologie Subaquatiques* 5: 5–36.

Lemée, Christian. 2006. *The Renaissance shipwrecks from Christianshavn: An archaeological and architectural study of large carvel vessels in Danish waters, 1580–1640*. Ships and Boats of the North 6. Roskilde: Viking Ship Museum.

McGrail, Sean. 1998. *Ancient boats in NW Europe. The archaeology of water transport to CE 1500*. Harlow, England: Longman.

———. 2001. *Boats of the world from the Stone Age to medieval times*. Oxford: Oxford University Press.

Morrison, John S., J. F. Coates, and N. B. Rankov. 2000. *The Athenian trireme: The history and reconstruction of an ancient Greek warship*. Cambridge: Cambridge University Press.

Muckelroy, Keith. 1978. *Maritime archaeology.* Cambridge: Cambridge University Press.

Nicolaisen, Ida, and Tinna Damgård-Sørensen. 1991. *Building a logboat: An essay on the culture and history of a Bornean people.* Roskilde: Viking Ship Museum.

Pomey, Patrice. 1982. Le navire romain de la Madrague de Giens. *Comptes Rendus de l'Académie des Inscriptions et Belles Lettres,* Janvier–Mars: 133–154.

———. 1988. Principes et méthodes de construction en architecture navale antique. In *Navires et commerces de la Méditerranée antique: Hommage à Jean Rougé; Cahiers d'histoire* 33 (3–4): 397–412.

———. 1998. Conception et réalisation des navires dans l'Antiquité. In *Concevoir et construire les navires. De la trière au picoteux,* ed. Eric Rieth, 49–72. Technologie, Idéologie, Pratiques 13-1. Ramonville Saint-Agne: Erès.

———. 1999. Les épaves romaines de la place Jules-Verne à Marseille: des bateaux dragues? In *Tropis V: 5th International Symposium on Ship Construction in Antiquity, Nauplia 1993, proceedings,* ed. Harry Tzalas,: 321–328. Athens: Hellenic Institute for the Preservation of Nautical Tradition.

———. 2000. Un témoignage récent sur la pêche au corail à Marseille à l'époque archaïque. In *Corallo di ieri, corallo di oggi: Atti del Convegno di Ravello, 1996,* ed. Jean-Paul Morel, C. Rondi-Costanzo, and Daniela Ugolini, 37–39. Bari: Edipuglia.

———. 2003. Reconstruction of Marseilles 6th century BCE Greek ships. In *Boats, ships and shipyards: Proceedings of the IXth International Symposium on Boat and Ship Archaeology, Venice 2000,* ed. Carlo Beltrame, 57–65. Oxford: Oxbow.

———. 2004. Principles and methods of construction in ancient naval architecture. In *The philosophy of shipbuilding: Conceptual approaches to the study of wooden ships,* ed. Frederick M. Hocker and Cheryl A. Ward, 25–36. College Station: Texas A&M University Press.

———. 2007. On the use of design in ancient Mediterranean ship construction. In *Creating shapes in civil and naval architecture,* ed. Horst Nowacki and Wolfgang Lefèvre: 137–149. Max-Planck Institute for the History of Science, Preprint 338-1, Berlin.

Pomey, Patrice, and Eric Rieth. 2005. *L'archéologie navale.* Paris: Errance.

Pomey, Patrice, and André Tchernia. 1978. Le tonnage maximum des navires de commerce romains. *Archaeonautica* 2: 233–251.

Rieth, Eric. 1984. Principe de construction "charpente première" et procédés de construction "bordé premier" au XVIIe siècle. *Neptunia* 153: 21–31.

———, ed. 1998. *Concevoir et construire les navires. De la trière au picoteux.* Technologie, Idéologie, Pratiques 13-1. Ramonville Saint-Agne: Erès.

Steffy, J. Richard. 1994. *Wooden ship building and the interpretation of shipwrecks.* College Station: Texas A&M University Press.

———. 1995. Ancient scantlings: The projection and control of Mediterranean hull shapes. In *Tropis III: Third International Symposium on Ship Construction in Antiquity, Athens 1989, proceedings,* ed. Harry Tzalas, 417–428. Athens: Hellenic Institute for the Preservation of Nautical Tradition.

———. 2004. Construction and analysis of the vessel. In *Serçe Limanı: An eleventh-century shipwreck,* vol. 1: *The ship and its anchorage, crew and passengers,* ed. G. F. Bass, S. D. Matthews, J. R. Steffy, and F. H. van Doorninck Jr., 153–169. College Station: Texas A&M University Press.

Tchernia, André. 1997. Le commerce maritime dans la Méditerranée romaine. In *La navigation dans l'Antiquité,* ed. Patrice Pomey, 116–145. Aix-en-Provence: Edisud.

Tchernia, André, Patrice Pomey, and Antoinette Hesnard. 1978. *L'épave romaine de la Madrague de Giens (Var)*. Gallia sup. 34. Paris: Centre National de la Recherche Scientifique.

van Doorninck, Frederick H., Jr. 1976. The 4th century wreck at Yassi Ada: An interim report on the hull. *International Journal of Nautical Archaeology* 5 (2): 115–131.

Wylde-Swiny, Helena, and Mikael L. Katzev. 1973. The Kyrenia shipwreck: A fourth century B.C. Greek merchant ship. In *Marine archaeology*, ed. David Blackman, 339–355. Colston Paper 23, London: Butterworths.

CHAPTER 2

WRECK-SITE FORMATION PROCESSES

COLIN MARTIN

INTRODUCTION

UNLIKE an archaeological site on land, whose location usually reflects a positive choice by those who selected and occupied it, a ship is a mobile entity that can move freely over parts of the Earth's surface covered by water. Should it become a wreck, the placement of its remains is likely to be fortuitous, unintended, and very possibly far from its original provenance. The environmental settings within which ship-wrecks occur are thus matters of chance rather than choice, and seldom bear directly on their remains in terms of an original human intention to place them there.

In an absolute sense, therefore, it is primarily the wreck and not its physical context that is of consequence to nautical archaeologists. But unless they take account of the environment within which the remains lie, and seek to understand the complex mechanisms of destruction, dispersal, reordering, decay, and stabilization with which the relevant area of seafloor has reacted to the intrusion of a wreck, they will be unable to interpret the observed remains as archaeological phenomena. For this reason, a shipwreck cannot be separated from its environment; on the contrary, the two must be regarded as inextricably linked elements, which together constitute a single wreck-site formation.

No two wreck-site formations are the same, since the complex and interacting variables that constitute the environmental setting, the nature of the ship, and the circumstances of its loss will combine to create a set of attributes unique to each site. At one end of the scale a vessel may survive virtually intact, with its contents more or less complete and in situ, as for example the Swedish warship *Vasa*, which sank in Stockholm Harbor at the start of her maiden voyage in 1628 CE (Cederlund et al.

2006). At the other extreme, a ship may be so broken up and dispersed, and its component parts so reduced by anthropogenic, mechanical, chemical, and biological degradation, that it effectively ceases to exist.

In most cases, however, wreck-site formations lie somewhere between these extremes, and in reaching a state of balance with the environment they normally undergo three evolutionary phases. The first is a natural one with anthropogenic input, in which environmental factors conditioned by human behavior lead to the wrecking event (Gibbs 2006). The next phase is an unstable one with dynamic environmental input, as the ship's remains interact with and are in various ways transformed by their natural surroundings. Finally, there is a stable phase, in which the transformed remains of the wreck have become incorporated into a balanced environment. These phases are not necessarily clear-cut and may progress at different rates across a single site, while stable situations may revert to unstable ones, sometimes on a cyclical basis (Figure 2.1).

The dynamic phase begins with the event of shipwreck, the moment at which the organized entity represented by a vessel's structure, contents, and crew, together with its systems of propulsion, control, and management, begins an irreversible process of change in which it leaves the world of human artifice and reverts to nature. This phase may be extremely violent and short-lived, as when a ship strikes a reef in heavy seas and disintegrates in seconds. On the other hand it may, as in the case of a hull that has settled gently into a benign environment of soft sediments, continue for years or even centuries. In both cases, however, the dynamic phase is characterized by the wreck's status as an environmental anomaly. It is unstable, lacks integration with its surroundings, and is prone to further disintegration and dispersal by external influences. Some of its components, by virtue of their buoyancy, may relocate themselves within the wreck or float away. Tides, surges, currents, and wave action can induce water movement that may result in the breakup of structures and the transport elsewhere of their fabric and contents. Scour may create depressions or build up deposits that can influence the dispersal, destruction, or preservation of wreck material. These effects are determined by the geology, topography, and sediment regimes of the seabed on which the wreck lies (Quinn in this volume).

The chemical composition and physical properties of the water, particularly seawater—its temperature and the amount of dissolved oxygen it contains—will cause reactions of various kinds, especially to metals. Complex networks of electrolytic couplings between dissimilar metals, activated through seawater, will protect or corrode the metals according to their relative corrosion potentials (MacLeod 1995; Hamilton and Smith in this volume). Organic materials will be susceptible to the effects of water penetration, temperature, light, and biological attack. Seabed movement may cause mechanical degradation, while rockfalls, the laying down or shifting of sediments, and other processes of geomorphologic change may further influence the dynamic phase of a wreck site's evolution. Human activity, particularly salvage, dredging, and fishing, can also be regarded as extractive or scrambling processes (as can archaeological intervention). The deposition of unrelated material by

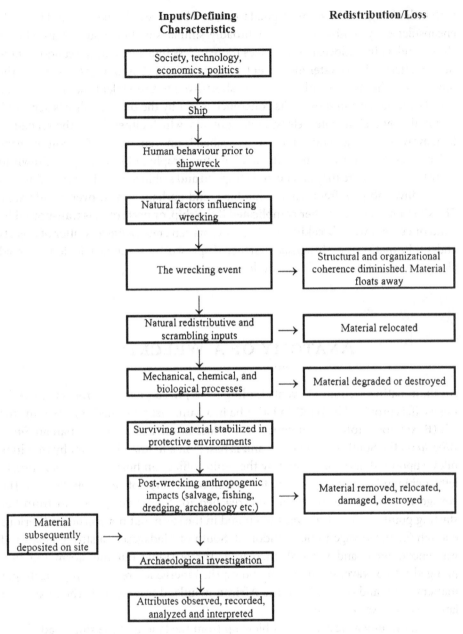

Figure 2.1 Wreck-site formation processes. Illustration by Colin Martin. Adapted from Muckelroy 1978: 158.

rubbish dumping, construction work, or the intrusion of a later wreck are other possibilities to be considered. Finally, sea-level change, geological upheaval, or land reclamation may in various ways affect the environment and hence the nature of a wreck-site formation.

Once the dynamic phase of a wreck's integration with the seabed is complete, a static or stabilized state will normally follow. This can happen quickly and perhaps with little change to the ship's original form, as when a vessel sinks into and is totally encapsulated by semi-fluid mud. A broadly similar situation may obtain when a ship founders in midocean and arrives more or less intact on a deep seafloor where there is effectively no water movement, oxygen, or light (Bascom 1976: 3–17). On the other hand, the dynamic phase may be short-lived but so violent that much of the vessel's substance and most of its coherence is lost by the time stability is achieved. The hull may disintegrate, releasing its contents, which either fall to the seabed or float away according to buoyancy. If the seabed is uneven, the distribution of heavy objects that fall to it may be influenced by topography; objects may be drawn to gully bottoms, where they can become trapped and stabilized. Such a formation will almost invariably be fragmentary, jumbled, and perhaps spread over a wide area. The situation may be further complicated if the ship, or parts of it, is transported by wind or current while breaking up. These events can create a linear scatter of objects and subformations, each perhaps farther dispersed by secondary actions, spread along the axis of the wreck's trail of destruction.

ANATOMY OF A WRECKING

An illuminating account of events leading to shipwreck, and the process of wrecking itself, is provided by Baptista Lavanha in a pamphlet published at Lisbon in 1597 CE (Boxer 2001: 106–186). It concerns the loss of the Portuguese Indiaman *Santo Alberto* on the South African coast and is based on a firsthand account by the ship's pilot, supported and augmented by the senior officer on board. The *Santo Alberto* left Cochin in January 1593, bound for Lisbon with a cargo of pepper and spices. The voyage was uneventful until the ship reached 10° S latitude, 3,000 km from her starting point. A small leak was then noted in the stern, but not considered serious enough for the voyage to be abandoned. South of Madagascar a strong headwind was encountered and the leak increased. While riding out the storm the ship plunged into a wave, springing the bowsprit. Emergency repairs temporarily put matters right, and on 21 March the African mainland was sighted. The next day a latitude of 32° was reached.

That evening a westerly wind blew up from the land and the ship headed seaward, but during the night, although the weather remained calm, the leak became much worse. Its source was located under a floor timber, where it could be reached only by cutting away part of the framing. This extreme measure brought temporary respite, but the weakened stern soon began to collapse under the external pressure of water. Before long 4 m of water filled the hold, and it was decided to jettison the cargo. The stern was put into the wind, and almost everything that could be removed from the main deck and spice hold was thrown over the side. The main hatch was then taken off, and a human chain began bailing with kegs to augment the pumps, while the chests in the lower hold, which could not be brought out whole because this would have disrupted pumping and bailing, were broken open and jettisoned. By the following night the water in the hold had been reduced to 2.75 m, but at this point the pumps became blocked with loose pepper, and the *Santo Alberto* was on the verge of foundering when, at dawn on 24 March, land was sighted.

Although almost everything movable had been thrown overboard, the hull had sunk to the level of the channels, and the two lower decks were under water. Even so, the ship still showed some response to her rudder. As land drew near and ship-wreck became inevitable the carpenters began to cut away the masts to reduce the risk of impact damage when the hull struck. The trailing rudder hit bottom first and was ripped away, and shortly afterward the ship ran aground north of the Umtata River, about 250 km south of modern Durban. As she struck, the shrouds were cut to jettison the masts, but some of the standing rigging failed to part and a tangle of masts and spars remained attached to the ship, pounding and ripping at the hull as the waves tossed them about. The top decks became detached from the two lower ones, leaving the bottom of the hull pinned to the seabed by its ballast. The now buoyant upper works, to which many survivors clung, drifted into the shore some 600 m away and grounded in the surf.

At nightfall the poop broke loose and was thrown up on the beach, where the survivors secured it with ropes. Shortly afterward the dislocated forecastle drifted athwart the poop, allowing more survivors to scramble ashore. Sometime later the lower part of the ship, including the keel (which was found to be rotten), was driven ashore, with several guns lodged inside it. When the survivors had salvaged every-thing that might be of use, they set fire to the vessel's remains and built a camp. Then they marched 725 km northward to Inhaca Bay, which most of them reached by 1 July, to be rescued eventually by a Portuguese ship.

The wreck-site formation trail left by the *Santo Alberto*'s misadventures (of which no trace has actually been found) stretches for some 2,800 km. The jettison-ing of cargo off Madagascar will have left a scatter of artifacts unassociated with ship's structure or fittings, while the complicated breakup sequence at the wreck site and subsequent deposition on shore of parts of the hull would probably be difficult to interpret from any archaeological evidence that may have survived. Traces may, however, be expected of the survivors' camp close to the wreck, while their journey northward to Inhaca might have left similar indications along the way.

The *Santo Alberto*'s story calls attention to an important consideration in the interpretation of wreck-site formations. A shipwreck is an essentially human event, caused by the failings and misjudgments that lie on the debit side of our species' unique qualities of forethought, ingenuity, collaboration, invention, and enterprise. As a phe-nomenon it should not therefore be analyzed in purely predictive or abstract terms.

It is human error that causes wrecks, and human cognition, resourcefulness, courage, and the instinct to survive that seeks to avoid them or mitigate their con-sequences. These factors may, in various ways, profoundly influence the course of formation processes generated by the various stages of a wrecking event, and conse-quently will affect the nature of the archaeological remains observed and interpreted on the seabed.

Without the actions of her crew the *Santo Alberto* would have foundered in the open sea, in a deepwater environment, where she would probably have become a discrete and well-preserved wreck-site. Right up to the end, a measure of control over her destiny was exercised by those on board. Even the eventual wrecking sequence might have been very different had an attempt not been made to cut away the masts, while the stern portion might have ended up elsewhere had steps not been taken to secure it on shore. Similarly, the sequential train of accidents that hindsight can show leading inexorably to disaster was triggered by human short-comings and not by immutable natural laws. We might level blame on the anony-mous caulker who failed to make a watertight joint where the fashion pieces met the stern, or perhaps more fairly we should question—as Baptista Lavanha did— the advisability of careening techniques that placed undue stresses on the hull when the grounded vessel was heeled over for caulking. We might criticize the *Santo Alberto*'s crew for cutting away a vital structural component to get at the leak, but since they had no other means of reaching it we might more profitably call to account the naval architects and shipwrights who designed and built her. And they, in turn, cannot be held responsible for the political and economic pressures that allowed the ship to remain in service for so long that her keel grew rotten, and that perhaps influenced the ship's officers in their decision to carry on with the voyage when the leak was first noticed. None of these factors is "rational" in a strictly scien-tific sense, but all influenced the processes leading to the *Santo Alberto*'s eventual wrecking and the way in which that event unfolded. It follows that human under-standing and intuition, guided and moderated by logic and objective science, are necessary elements in the investigation and interpretation of site formation pro-cesses associated with a shipwreck.

WRECK-SITE FORMATION THEORY

Nearly half a century ago classical shipwreck sites in the Mediterranean were char-acterized by Dumas (1962: 9–11, fig. 2) as partially buried mounds of amphorae that often pinned down elements of a vessel's lower structure. This configuration is cer-tainly common and widely seen in wrecks of other regions and periods when heavy cargoes or ballast are present in the lower hull. But it is an oversimplification to suggest, as was done during the discipline's early years, that these attributes apply to most partially coherent shipwreck sites.

The first systematic attempt to categorize shipwreck site formations and iden-tify the processual inputs involved was that proposed by Muckelroy (1975, 1978). His work was strongly influenced by contemporary research into formation processes on terrestrial sites, notably by Clarke (1968), who sought to codify the distortion, incomplete and unrepresentative survival of evidence, and bias inherent in archae-ological deposition and its interpretation. These difficulties are compounded by the selective character of archaeological excavation and by problems inherent in the recognition and interpretation of evidence, which varies between investigators. Clarke went on to identify and quantify the processes of change whereby an original cultural entity (habitation site, burial, etc.) metamorphoses within the environment to create the features and associations observed in the archaeological record. If these processes could be understood, Clarke reasoned, critical analysis might be applied to work backward, as it were, through the transformations to arrive at a better understanding of the investigated feature in its original form, in terms of physical attributes, cultural context, and the motives and behavioral characteristics that lay behind its creation.

Muckelroy applied these transformational theories to his analysis of wreck-site formation, taking into account the special characteristics of the maritime environment. In particular, he categorized a range of "extracting filters": processes that removed material from a wreck, including loss by flotation, in situ deterioration, and contemporary salvage. Material that remained on the site was subject to rearrangement by "scrambling devices," caused by the wrecking process and associated environmental factors. He tested these theories against a sample of 20 wreck sites investigated around the British Isles, quantifying them according to a set of variable attributes, including offshore fetch, wind, water movement, depth, slope, topography, and sediment composition. On the basis of this analysis he identified five general categories of wreck-site formation apparent in British waters (Muckelroy 1978: 164, table 5.2).

Class 1. Extensive structural remains with much organic material and many other objects, and coherent patterns of distribution.
Class 2. Elements of structure with some organic material and many other objects, and ordered patterns of distribution.
Class 3. Fragments of structure with some organic material and other objects, and scattered patterns of distribution.
Class 4. No structural remains and little organic material. Some other objects and scattered patterns of distribution.
Class 5. No structural remains and no organic material. Few other objects and disordered patterns of distribution.

Muckelroy's classification system and associated methodologies have since been widely followed, although his early death in 1980 precluded the development, expansion, and refinement of a theory rooted in wreck-site formation studies, by which he had hoped to characterize maritime archaeology as a core part of the mainstream discipline (this was the topic of the PhD he was working on at the time of his death). Unfortunately, no scholar of comparable stature has continued the study and analysis of wreck-site formation processes on a comprehensive basis, although Ferrari (1995), MacLeod (1995), Gregory (1995, 1996), Ward, Larcombe, and Veth (1999), O'Shea (2002), Quinn (2006), and Gibbs (2006) have addressed related topics. Gibbs in particular has emphasized the importance of cultural input, drawing attention to the growing literature on disaster response and its relevance to shipwreck events. The significance of this aspect is well illustrated by the *Santo Alberto* episode, described above. Gibbs (2006: 16, Fig. 2) has proposed an expanded and modified version of Muckelroy's much-cited flow diagram showing the processual evolution of a shipwreck (1978: 158, fig. 5.1), which incorporates the cultural element more fully. This shift of focus reflects a growing interest in behavioral archaeology, such as that articulated by Schiffer (1987, 1995), and in social archaeology, recently propounded in a maritime context by Gould (2000).

FIVE CASE STUDIES

We conclude with summary descriptions of five shipwreck sites, all except one of which has been investigated by the author. Between them they cover the range of Muckelroy's site-types. While not universally representative of the world's shipwrecks (they come from a single geographical area, the British Isles, and span a narrow date range, 1588–1728 CE), they illustrate aspects and general characteristics of formation processes that apply across regions and periods, although each demonstrates, as all shipwrecks do, its unique individuality. Each case study summarizes the formation processes identified on that site, and it is hoped that these examples will inform a more general understanding of the varied mechanisms involved. Space precludes discussion of the full evidence and the methodologies employed, for which readers are referred to the citations.

Kennemerland (Out Skerries, Shetland), Dutch East Indiaman, 1664

The *Kennemerland* (Figure 2.2) was on the first leg of an outward-bound voyage to Batavia, following the normal north-about route around the British Isles, when during a southerly gale on the night of 20 December 1664 she struck Stoura Stack at the entrance to the Out Skerries' natural harbor. The only survivors were three men stationed at the masthead, who were projected onto the stack. Much material was salvaged in the immediate aftermath by the islanders, and the extensive recovery operations that followed led to complex litigation. Further salvage work was conducted during the eighteenth century. These activities generated copious documentation, now preserved in Scottish archives. Further material concerning the ship and her cargo survives in Holland, while traditions about the wreck are still current on the Out Skerries.

The *Kennemerland*'s remains were discovered in 1971, and Muckelroy became involved with the project shortly afterward. He recognized that the wreck's character as a partially scattered site (Class 3 in his classification sequence) together with the extensive written sources relevant to the ship, her cargo, and the social structures

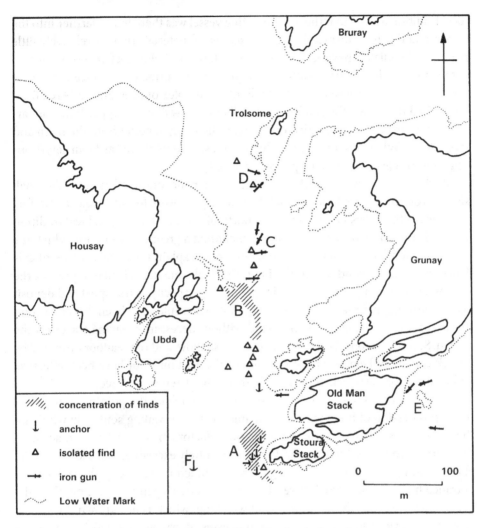

Figure 2.2 The *Kennemerland* site. For key to lettering see text.
Illustration by the author.

of those on board provided an opportunity to test evidence obtained from the site against known data concerning the vessel's prewrecking configuration. Five seasons of fieldwork followed, culminating in 1978. This work allowed him to apply his maturing ideas on systems description, extracting filters, scrambling devices, cluster analysis, and seabed movement mechanisms in a maritime context. These ideas were first articulated in an article (Muckelroy 1975), and later expanded in his seminal book (Muckelroy 1978).

The traditional location of the *Kennemerland*'s point of impact on Stoura Stack was confirmed by a concentration of lead ingots and thousands of bricks, seven anchors, and other material from the ballast (Area A in Figure 2.2). This was evidently where the ship struck, ripping open her bottom and spilling the contents.

Local tradition asserts that the disintegrating vessel was then driven farther into the harbor, and this is confirmed by a linear scatter of material. There is relatively little material immediately beyond the impact point, but a shallow reef area some 200 m to the north, where surf breaks in rough weather, attracted a concentration of remarkably well-preserved finds that fell into a complex of deep gullies (Area B). It is surmised that when the ship's bottom fell out, the wallowing upper hull was carried northward until it grounded on the reef, shedding material from the main and upper decks. What remained of the ship then resumed its shoreward journey, dropping four iron guns to mark its progress (Area C).

Archaeological evidence of the wreck's movement continued as far as the small islet of Trolsome, at the foot of which two more guns were found (Area D). No further trace of the wreck has been located north of this point, although local tradition asserts that much material came ashore, including a great deal of liquor, which the locals imbibed for several days. Two factors may explain the apparent lack of evidence for a trail beyond Trolsome. First, the Trolsome deposit may represent the final breakup of coherent pieces of ship, with their capacity to transport and deposit heavy items. Lighter material, such as liquor casks, would have been driven beyond this point toward the shore by the wind without necessarily leaving traces on the seabed. Second, beyond Trolsome the water is shallow, and the seafloor obscured by a thick canopy of kelp, so visual searches of the area may not have been effective, and evidence of the wreck, if present there, has not been recognized.

The basic dynamics of this wreck-site formation from the point of impact to a linear progression of breakup, driven mainly by the prevailing southerly wind, are thus relatively straightforward. However, other factors must be taken into account. The northward tidal set into the harbor is weak, rarely exceeding half a knot. On the ebb tide, however, the south-flowing current is much faster, and at the constricted entrance beside Stoura Stack it reaches three knots. Depending on how the tidal cycle synchronizes with the sequence of wrecking, which is not known, these currents may have influenced formation processes, carrying material in directions other than along the primary axis extending northward from Stoura Stack. This may explain the group of three guns to the east of Old Man Stack (Area E) and the isolated anchor beyond the mouth of the harbor (F) (Foster and Higgs 1973; Price and Muckelroy 1974, 1977, 1979; Muckelroy 1976; Dobbs and Price 1991).

Adelaar (Barra, Outer Hebrides), Dutch East Indiaman, 1728 CE

The *Adelaar* (Figure 2.3) struck an exposed reef while attempting to weather Greian Head, having become embayed on the northwest side of Barra during a strong northwesterly gale. There were no survivors, although much of the cargo, including a large consignment of specie, was subsequently salvaged. Like the *Kennemerland*, administrative documentation concerning the voyage and litigation over salvage generated an immense volume of paperwork. A contemporary

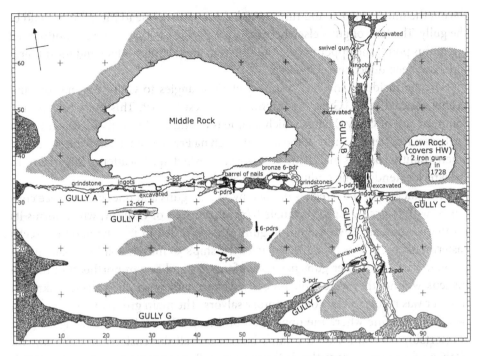

Figure 2.3 The *Adelaar* site. The hatched areas denote shallow water (3 m or less at low water). Illustration by the author.

shipyard model of a vessel of the same date and class survives in Holland. We thus possess much hard data, including a reliable three-dimensional template of the ship herself, against which to test the capacity of archaeological evidence to re-create, through the medium of formation process analysis, the reality of the vessel before it became a wreck.

It appears that the ship had approached Greian Head from the northeast, close-hauled on a track that would not quite clear the headland. She became lodged between the two easternmost rocks of a reef called Maolach Sgeir (the Cursed Reef), where her bottom fell out, depositing the ballast cargo of lead ingots and 60,000 bricks into a deep northward-running gully (Gully B in Figure 2.3). Many of the ingots lay where they fell, although only a few heavily abraded fragments of brick were noted at the bottom of deep fissures. The site is extremely dynamic, and the broad bottom of Gully B is filled with mobile pebbles rounded by constant water movement. It was concluded that most of the cargo of bricks, which documentary sources attest had been carried in the lower hold together with the ingots, had been ground to nothing by constant movement within this abrasive environment, so their almost total absence from the archaeological record is explained by postdepositional formation analysis.

No guns were present in Gully B apart from a small bronze swivel piece that would have been mounted on the stern upper works and may well have come loose during the initial impact, and three abraded iron guns close to the southern end of the gully. The lack of guns elsewhere in Gully B suggests that while the bottom fell out at this point, the upper part of the ship remained largely intact and must therefore have been deposited elsewhere.

On the inside of the reef, running at right angles to Gully B, a narrow and deeply fissured gully (Gully A) extends from west to east. This gully brushes the southern end of Gully B, after which its line is continued by Gully C, which 200 m farther on reaches the shore at the inlet of Sloch na Frange, or Creek of the Strangers, where tradition asserts that many bodies were washed up. A scatter of material from the wreck extends along Gully C into the Sloch.

The nucleus of the wreck is defined by 16 iron guns and one bronze piece contained within a 55 by 24 m rectangle lying on the axis of Gully A, which forms its northern boundary. Two more iron guns were recorded in 1728 lying on the reef's easternmost rock. This accounts for 19 of the ship's 36 muzzle-loading main armament, or 53%. Two other guns have been found 25 and 200 m northeast of the site nucleus, whither they were probably carried by secondary action, while an unknown number was recovered by contemporary salvors. The main group of guns may thus be taken to define where the upper hull broke up. The enclosing rectangle would comfortably accommodate the ship's known overall dimensions of 41 by 10.5 m, allowing for outspill from the disintegrating hull, suggesting that the main wreck deposition is reasonably coherent. Much of the cargo of domestic hardware and iron tools had also stabilized beneath the shingle of this gully, although no organic material has survived on this exposed and dynamic site.

From the above it may be deduced that after grounding between the two rocks and losing her bottom, the ship was carried over the reef by the wind and broaching seas, pivoting across Middle Rock until she lay broadside-on beyond its southern edge, stern toward the west. As the vessel was held against the reef by back-surge from the shore, a total breakup of the hull would have followed rapidly, depositing much of the armament and most of the cargo, including the specie, into Gully A. The treasure evidently remained concentrated and intact in its sealed boxes, facilitating its total recovery in 1728.

Isolated parts of the structure were carried to other locations, taking with them attached heavy objects, including guns, which eventually stabilized as subformations such as one identified near the entrance to Sloch na Frange. A final intriguing possibility has recently presented itself. Contemporary sources record that for several weeks after the wrecking, parts of the ship, as well as floating cargo and bodies, were thrown up on shores for many miles around. In recent years attention has been drawn to the remains of the lower hull of a large wooden ship that occasionally uncovers from the beach near high-water mark on the island of Fuday, 7 miles northeast of Greian Head. The surviving dimensions of this wreck (31.7 by 5.5 m), given its state of degradation and the loss of almost all its port side, are not inconsistent with those of the *Adelaar*. A recent survey has identified Dutch bricks similar to those found on the *Adelaar*, and the possibility that the remains may be those of the lower hull that became detached from the *Adelaar* during the first phase of the wrecking sequence, as suggested above, is currently being investigated (Prescott, Atkinson, and Liscoe 2008; Martin 1995, 2005).

La Trinidad Valencera (Kinnagoe Bay, Co. Donegal), Spanish Armada, 1588 CE

At 1,100 tons *La Trinidad Valencera* (Figure 2.4) was the Armada's fourth-largest ship. A Venetian merchant vessel built for the grain trade, she had been requisitioned by Spanish authorities in Sicily in 1587 to convey troops and war material to Lisbon for the projected Armada. On reaching Lisbon she was embargoed to take part in the campaign itself. The ship was heavily engaged in the fighting and sustained damage to her hull. During the retreat around the British Isles this damage drove her to seek refuge in Ireland, and her crew ran her aground in Kinnagoe Bay, North Donegal, where, two days later, she broke up and sank.

The wreck was found in 1971 and over the following 14 years was extensively surveyed and partially excavated. The main area of wreckage lies 150 m offshore on a flat, sandy seabed at a depth of 10 m, adjacent to a reef complex, which runs from the shore and rises to within 4 m of the surface close to the wreck. Here the ship evidently grounded. A visual survey supplemented by metal detector prospection indicated a spread of wreckage extending northward for more than 65 m from the reef, while wreckage spill among the rocks continued southward for at least another 30 m. This combined linear distribution accounts for nearly three times the ship's probable length, suggesting considerable dislocation and scatter. The visible wreckage included two anchors, five large spoked wooden gun carriage wheels reinforced with iron, three wooden axles from gun carriage assemblies, and five bronze guns, one of which lay in the broad sandy gully that runs through the reef. Several pieces of degraded structural timber were also observed within the reef complex.

Despite the scattered appearance of the site, it was felt likely that coherent parts of structure had stabilized in the sand, and to test this possibility a probe survey was conducted over a 30 × 60 m grid extending northward from the reef. This survey encountered no evidence of major structure, although three discrete deposits (A–C in Figure 2.4) of tightly packed organic material were located. A fourth such deposit (D) was subsequently identified just beyond the northeast corner of the grid.

Partial excavation based on the survey information confirmed that no articulated structure had survived, although disarticulated structural components were present in all four deposits of organic material. Deposit B also included four large gun carriage wheels. These deposits comprised a tightly packed matrix of organic debris, mainly wood splinters and fibers from textiles or cordage, within which well-preserved and often complete artifacts of wood, textile, and leather were randomly disposed. Together these comprised a full sampling of weaponry, military equipment, provisions, personal possessions, clothing, and ship-related material. Small quantities of metal were also present.

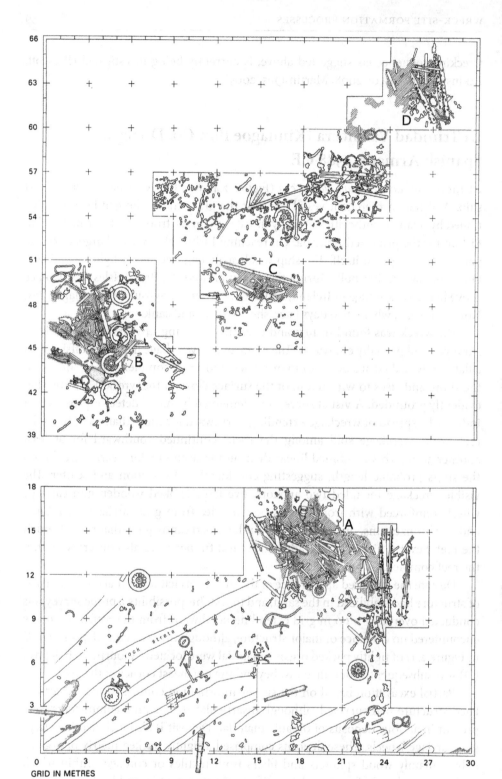

Figure 2.4 North (top) and south segments of the main wreck formation of *La Trinidad Valencera*, as excavated. Note that a 21 m gap separates the two segments. For key to lettering see text. Illustration by the author.

The organic deposits lay within shallow depressions filled with clean sediments through which ran lenticular bands of black sludge, identified as decayed seaweed. These characteristics suggest the nature of the formation process involved. It is evident that the flat sandy seafloor hereabouts is extremely stable and tends to restore itself quickly if disturbed by any anomaly. This was apparent during excavation, when trenches accumulated loose weed in even quite calm conditions. In more dynamic situations, mobile sand grains displaced on the flat surface naturally gravitate into any slight hollow until it has been leveled.

With these mechanisms in mind, a wreck-site formation sequence can be hypothesized. In seeking to run ashore, the *Trinidad Valencera* grounded bow-first on the reef, and, probably quite quickly (she was already leaking badly), her stern settled on the sand. It is known that the ship remained intact for about two days, allowing most of her crew to come ashore. She then broke apart, drowning the few still on board, apparently as a consequence of rough weather. The keel, with its extremities perched on the reef and flat seabed beyond, would have carried the weight of the mainmast on its unsupported central point, and it is likely that the hull fractured at this point. The bow end probably settled where it lay, precipitating deposit A and the material scattered among the reef, while the after part, driven by a southerly wind, was carried farther north to break up as a separate entity represented by deposits B, C, and D.

The depressions in which the organic deposits accumulated were probably caused by scour, followed by a reassertion of stability that filled in and protected their fragile contents with weed and sand. This scenario presupposes the existence of massive but temporary anomalies in the vicinities of the depressions. These anomalies can only have been parts of the disintegrating hull, which, while they stood proud of the seabed, would have induced scour in the lee of current and surge. It is significant that no identifiable pieces of ship structure are in any way joined to others, which suggests that the hull disintegrated completely and probably quite quickly. Examination of the surviving hull components has shown that they had been fastened exclusively with iron bolts, a Venetian construction technique adopted in the sixteenth century for the mass production of low-maintenance merchant ships designed for intensive but short working lives. Once the iron fastenings deteriorated, the whole structure would have fallen apart, and its individual components been destroyed or dispersed. This mechanism may explain the peculiar wreck-formation processes and archaeological survival characteristics noted on the *Trinidad Valencera* wreck site (Martin 1975, 1979).

Dartmouth (Rubha an Ridire, Sound of Mull), Fifth-Rate Warship, 1690 CE

The fifth-rate warship *Dartmouth* (Figure 2.5) was built at Portsmouth in 1655. She was 80 ft (24.4 m) on the keel and 25 ft (7.6 m) in beam, giving her a rated burden of 266 tons. She carried 32 guns, of which the largest were 9-pounders. *Dartmouth* was

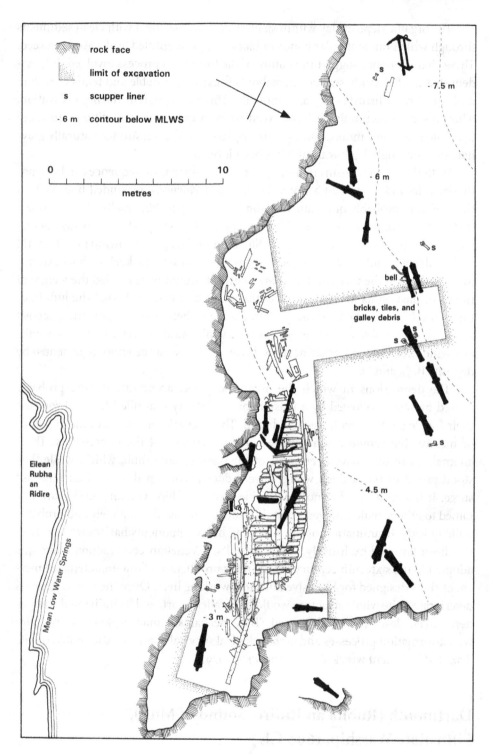

rock face

limit of excavation

s   scupper liner

- 6 m   contour below MLWS

0   10

metres

- 7.5 m

- 6 m

s

bell

bricks, tiles, and galley debris

s

s

s

- 4.5 m

Eilean Rubha an Ridire

Mean Low Water Springs

s

- 3 m

Figure 2.5 The *Dartmouth* site. Illustration by the author.

wrecked in 1690 near the Isle of Mull in Scotland's Inner Hebrides while engaged in anti-Jacobite operations following the accession of William and Mary.

The wreck was located off the small islet of Rudha an Ridire, close to the south-east entrance to the Sound of Mull. Local tradition asserts that *Dartmouth* had been anchored in Scallastle Bay, on the opposite side of the Sound, and had been blown onto her beam-ends in a gale before being driven stern-first to strike the island. There were only six survivors.

Dartmouth's remains were located in 1973 and partially excavated over the following two seasons. A run of some 13 m of articulated structure had survived, representing much of the after part of the lower starboard hull. Up to 3.5 m of framing was present on this side, extending from the remains of the keel.

The underside of the keel was heavily abraded, having ground itself into the seabed as the stern half of the ship rocked to and fro during the wrecking process. The trench thus formed created a trap for loose structural components and heavier artifacts that fell from the collapsing upper works. When the surviving structure stabilized it was heeled 15° to starboard, the lower timbers on that side encapsulated in a shallow depression excavated in the shingle by water displaced by the rocking hull. This configuration left the port side exposed above the seabed, where natural agencies soon demolished it.

Although the surviving section of the keel extends only 6 m from the aftermost part of the extant structure, a projection of its line encounters a rock outcrop at what would have been close to the midships point. This is also the forwardmost part of the surviving starboard structure. It seems likely that the ship broke hereabouts, separating the stabilized stern from its loose and more mobile forward partner.

This interpretation explains the line of guns and lead scupper-liners, which lie some 12 m from the projected line of the keel, running not quite parallel with it. This pattern suggests deposition from the main deck, such as would have occurred if the forward part of the hull rolled onto its side following separation from the stern. The linear run of scupper-liners, which would have been positioned along the waterway where the deck met the side of the ship, supports this hypothesis. So too does the deposit containing bricks, tiles, and galley debris, and the adjacent ship's bell, which would have been located on the upper part of the forecastle.

These observations suggest that this wreck-site formation, though superficially random and jumbled, retains a high level of cohesion. This was confirmed by Muckelroy (1978: 190–191) with a spatial analysis of finds categories and their distribution, which confirmed that the wreck's stern lay at its inshore end. It also indicated the arithmetical mean centers of particular activities aboard the ship, such as navigation and smoking (Martin 1978, 1998).

Swan (Duart Point, Mull), Cromwellian warship, 1653 CE

The small warship *Swan* (Figure 2.6) was lost off Duart Castle in the Sound of Mull, not far from the *Dartmouth* site. She had been part of a small flotilla sent to pacify the rebellious Western Isles during Cromwell's occupation of Scotland in the 1650s.

Figure 2.6 The *Swan* site. Illustration by the author.

The ship had been blown from her moorings during a gale and hit Duart Point before sliding down the rock face, where she settled on a shingle seabed, heeled toward the cliff at an angle of about 15°.

Located in 1979, the wreck was surveyed and partially excavated between 1992 and 2003 to mitigate erosion on the site. Two discrete mounds of stone ballast had held down and protected a substantial part of the lower hull, much of the port side from the bow to a point aft of amidships being preserved to the turn of the bilge. The beginning of an upward curve on the keel and keelson marked the forward extremity of these longitudinal components, while the still-articulated lower stern assembly was identified on the line of the keel projected aft. These findings suggested that much of the lower hull structure was substantially intact. The ship's estimated keel length of 60 ft (18.3 m) and beam of 25 ft (7.6 m) would give, by contemporary measurement, a burden of 150 tons.

The after part of the wreck, which lies mainly on the port side of the keel axis, comprises a tightly contained jumble of organic material that appears to derive largely from the upper stern structure. It includes paneling from the interior cabin, carvings from the exterior stern decoration, and a group of artifacts indicative of high rank within the social hierarchy of the ship. Framing associated with this deposit, and the sternpost's angle of heel to port, suggests that the aft section of the ship had twisted some 45° before the upper part of the structure broke away and collapsed onto its side.

From these observations the following sequence of formation processes may be hypothesized. The main input factor has been the current. On the ebb tide this flows from northwest to southeast along the axis of the wreck from bow to stern, reaching a speed of up to two knots. Toward the stern the current eddies in toward the shore. There is little movement on the flood tide.

During strong northwesterly winds (the prevailing direction) the tidal flow accumulates large quantities of suspended silt that are carried across the site, though they are not, under normal circumstances, deposited on it. When the wreck lay on the bottom, however, broken but still partially coherent, it represented a massive anomaly that attracted silt from the eddying current, particularly among the castle-works of the stern. The weight of sand accumulating within the interior caused the stern section to twist and eventually collapse onto its port side, sand and contents layering to encapsulate the jumbled remains of the aft interior as a stratified sequence within the seabed. The clearly defined aft boundary of the deposit reflects the angled set of the transom stern that had once retained it.

Forward of the stern the ship remained nearly upright, and under a combination of mechanical and biological processes it gradually fell apart, to be dispersed down-tide until only the lower part of the hull, pinned by the two mounds of stone ballast, stabilized on the seafloor. As the upper structure disintegrated, heavier items, including eight iron guns and an anchor, fell to the bottom.

The distribution of the guns is significant. Two lie beyond the bow and are probably a forward-firing pair. The amidships area is devoid of guns, and since it is known that the ship had auxiliary oar power, this space is likely to have been occupied by the rowing banks. What seem to be port and starboard pairs can be identified on the aft broadsides, while two small guns appear to have been mounted high in the stern, firing aft through the transom.

Though partially dislocated by a dynamic environment, and now stabilized within the seabed, this wreck demonstrates high levels of coherence, both structurally and in the distribution and survival characteristics of its contents. The archaeological interrogation of its remains, coupled with an appreciation of the formation processes involved, has allowed much of the ship's original organized complexity as a structural, operational, and social entity to be interpreted and quantified.

CONCLUSION

The investigation of a shipwreck involves an interactive study of its archaeological remains, viewed in the light of surviving documentary sources, naval architectural principles, and contemporary shipbuilding practice. This must be combined with an analysis of the environmental processes whereby the functioning ship was transformed into the often dislocated cohorts of evidence that survive in the seabed today. Understanding these natural processes in the context of the distinctively anthropogenic inputs we characterize as archaeology is an essential prerequisite to the interpretation of any shipwreck.

REFERENCES

Bascom, W. 1976. *Deep water, ancient wrecks: The treasure vault of the Mediterranean.* Newton Abbot: David & Charles.

Boxer, C. R., ed. and trans. 2001. *The tragic history of the sea*. Minneapolis: University of Minnesota Press.

Cederlund, C. O., with contributions by G. Hafström, F. Hocker, and P. Wendel. 2006. Vasa I: *The archaeology of a Swedish warship of 1628*. Stockholm: National Maritime Museums of Sweden.

Clarke, D. L. 1968. *Analytical archaeology*. London: Methuen.

Dobbs, C. T. C., and R. A. Price. 1991. The *Kennemerland* site: An interim report; The sixth and seventh seasons, 1984 and 1987, and the identification of five golf clubs. *International Journal of Nautical Archaeology* 20 (2): 111–122.

Dumas, F. 1962. *Deep-water archaeology*. Translated by H. Frost. London: Routledge and Kegan Paul.

Ferrari, B. 1995. Physical, biological and cultural factors influencing the formation, stabilisation and protection of archaeological deposits in U.K. coastal waters. PhD diss., University of St. Andrews.

Foster, W. A., and K. B. Higgs. 1973. The *Kennemerland*, 1971: An interim report. *International Journal of Nautical Archaeology* 2 (2): 291–300.

Gibbs, M. 2006. Cultural site formation processes in maritime archaeology. *International Journal of Nautical Archaeology* 35 (1): 4–19.

Gould, R. A. 2000. *Archaeology and the social history of ships*. Cambridge: Cambridge University Press.

Gregory, D. J. 1995. Experiments into the deterioration characteristics of material on the Duart Point wreck site: An interim report. *International Journal of Nautical Archaeology* 24 (1): 61–65.

———. 1996. Formation processes in marine archaeology, a study of chemical and biological deterioration. PhD diss., University of Leicester.

MacLeod, I. D. 1995. In situ corrosion studies on the Duart Point wreck, 1994. *International Journal of Nautical Archaeology* 24 (1): 53–59.

Martin, C. J. M. 1975. *Full fathom five: Wrecks of the Spanish Armada*. London: Hamish Hamilton.

———. 1978. The *Dartmouth*, a British frigate wrecked off Mull, 1690; 5: The ship. *International Journal of Nautical Archaeology* 7 (1): 29–58.

———. 1979. *La Trinidad Valencera*, an Armada invasion transport lost off Donegal: Interim site report. *International Journal of Nautical Archaeology* 8 (1): 13–38.

———. 1992. The Wreck of the Dutch East-Indiaman *Adelaar* off Barra in 1728. In *People and power in Scotland: Essays in honour of T. C. Smout*, ed. Roger Mason and Norman Macdougall, 145–169. Edinburgh: John Donald.

———. 1995. A Cromwellian warship off Duart Point, Mull: An interim report. *International Journal of Nautical Archaeology* 24 (1): 15–32.

———. 1998. *Dartmouth*: The archaeology and structural analysis of a small seventeenth century English warship. In *Excavating ships of war*, ed. Mensun Bound, 110–119. Oswestry: Anthony Nelson.

———. 2005. The *Adelaar*: A Dutch East Indiaman wrecked in 1728 off Barra, Outer Hebrides, Scotland. *International Journal of Nautical Archaeology* 34 (2): 179–210.

Muckelroy, K. 1975. A systematic approach to the investigation of scattered wreck sites. *International Journal of Nautical Archaeology* 4 (2): 173–190.

———. 1976. The integration of historical and archaeological data concerning an historic wreck site: The "Kennemerland." *World Archaeology* 7 (3): 280–290.

———. 1978. *Maritime archaeology*. Cambridge: Cambridge University Press.

O'Shea, J. M. 2002. The archaeology of scattered wreck-sites: Formation processes and shallow water archaeology in western Lake Huron. *International Journal of Nautical Archaeology* 31 (2): 211–227.

Prescott, R. G. W., D. Atkinson, and S. Liscoe. 2008. *Preliminary survey and assessment of a wreck on the island of Fuday, Barra, Western Isles.* Unpublished report for Historic Scotland by Headland Archaeology.

Price, R., and K. Muckelroy. 1974. The second season of work on the *Kennemerland* site, 1973. *International Journal of Nautical Archaeology* 3 (2): 257–268.

———. 1977. The *Kennemerland* site: The third and fourth seasons, 1974 and 1976. *International Journal of Nautical Archaeology* 6 (3): 187–218.

———. 1979. The *Kennemerland* site: The fifth season. *International Journal of Nautical Archaeology* 8 (4): 311–320.

Quinn, R. 2006. The role of scour in shipwreck site formation processes and the preservation of wreck-associated scour signatures in the sedimentary record: Evidence from the seabed and sub-surface data. *Journal of Archaeological Sciences* 33: 1419–1432.

Schiffer, M. B. 1987. *Formation processes of the archaeological record.* Albuquerque: University of New Mexico Press.

———. 1995. *Behavioral archaeology: First principles.* Salt Lake City: University of Utah Press.

Ward, I., P. Larcombe, and P. Veth. 1999. A new process-based model for wreck-site formation. *Journal of Archaeological Science* 26: 561–570.

CHAPTER 3

ACOUSTIC REMOTE SENSING IN MARITIME ARCHAEOLOGY

RORY QUINN

INTRODUCTION

IN the twenty-first century, acoustic (sonar) systems are routinely used for rapid, noninvasive surveys of the seafloor and subsurface. Indeed, bathymetric survey techniques have been employed in the marine sciences since at least the early part of the nineteenth century. Regrettably, the existing bathymetric charts for most parts of the world are Victorian in vintage, compiled from lead-line soundings and sextant positioning. These charts are therefore severely outdated in terms of spatial and temporal resolution and are unsuitable for marine research and stewardship. More importantly, due to the nature and size of archaeological artifacts and submerged sites, these charts are generally unsuitable for research as they are of such low resolution that they offer little functional use in archaeological investigations.

In the early part of the twentieth century, single-beam echo-sounders (SBES) replaced traditional lead-weighted lines as the primary bathymetric survey technique for civilian and military purposes (Lurton 2002). Between 1925 and 1927, the first large-scale scientific bathymetric survey was conducted by the German Atlantic Expedition on *RV Meteor* using SBES (Wüst and Defant 1936). In the early 1960s, side-scan sonar (SSS) was developed as a tool for regional-scale geological mapping, revolutionizing seafloor mapping in terms of spatial coverage and data resolution. The effectiveness of acoustic mapping evolved between the 1970s and the twenty-first century with the advent of multibeam echo-sounders (MBES) allied to powerful and affordable desktop computing facilities. In addition to modern bathymetric charts providing highly accurate depth information, the results from these acoustic surveys now routinely provide details of objects on the seabed and the geological and biological components therein. Modern seabed mapping therefore results from the integration of many different types of information, much of which is gathered acoustically (Lurton 2002).

Marine remote-sensing technology has been applied in maritime archaeology since the 1960s. Initially, remote sensing was primarily used as a tool in the search for submerged shipwreck sites and large-scale reconnaissance mapping investigations. More recently, with technological developments, emphasis of marine geo-archaeological research has moved away from pure prospection toward a fuller understanding of submerged landscapes and wrecks in terms of detailed site mapping, site formation processes, and site reconstructions.

The major advantages of acoustic mapping systems as applied to maritime archaeology are that they are rapid and noninvasive and capable of surveying large tracts of the seabed at very high resolution. Although acoustic systems will never completely replace diver surveys, they do provide baseline data at rates far exceeding those of experienced dive teams. Unfortunately, a full discussion of the theory behind the acquisition, processing, and interpretation of these data is beyond the scope and remit of this chapter. However, an excellent introduction to the principles and applications of underwater acoustics can be found in Lurton 2002.

Navigational Control and Positional Accuracy

To effectively map, interpret, integrate, and ground-truth remotely sensed acoustic data, tight navigational and positional control is essential in all phases of the investigation. To precisely locate the position of features and objects on the seabed, knowledge of the following three parameters is required: (1) the location of the survey vessel on the sea-surface, (2) the location of the sonar platform below the sea-surface, and (3) the portion of the seafloor that is being insonified (exposed to sonar energy) at any given time. This precise positional control is achieved through a combination of position fixing (latitude, longitude, and altitude above a reference datum), heading, speed, and attitude (heave, roll, pitch, yaw) information.

The minimum requirement for accurate navigation of a survey vessel is the Global Positioning System (GPS). Using the calculated distance and orbital position of satellites (a minimum of three is required for accuracy), the GPS receiver determines a position fix in degrees of latitude and longitude, conventionally to the WGS84 datum (World Geodetic System of 1984, the default datum for GPS units). This position can in turn be translated into any global or local metric coordinate system (e.g., UTM). Accuracy of GPS varies with satellite constellation geometry and receiver type, but an accuracy of ±5 m with an update rate of once per second is now common. To reduce positional errors to an acceptable level for high-resolution archaeological surveys (±1 m), differential GPS (DGPS) employs a land-based station to calculate the error in positioning and transmit the error to the shipboard receiver. Corrected data from the shipboard GPS unit is output to computer-based software packages for survey navigation and logging. Furthermore, for quantitative analysis of the seafloor and/or subsurface, it is essential to relate depth data to a static horizon, and therefore it is necessary to remove the effects of tidal variation over the survey period. Tidal corrections are achieved with reference to either a static tidal gauge or to modeled tidal predictions. For high-accuracy surveys the tidal curve should be recorded continuously at a site in close proximity (±1 km) to the survey site. Recently the technology of DGPS has been superseded by Real Time Kinematic (RTK) systems that use the characteristics of the signal carrying the GPS data from satellite to the receiver, to give x, y, and z values to an accuracy of ±1 cm. RTK-GPS also negates the requirement to set up a tide gauge, as tidal corrections can be derived from the z-component of the signal.

In many applications, the sonar platform (often referred to as the towfish) is towed by the ship, and its position determined in one of two ways—either by manual calculation or by using acoustic tracking techniques. "Layback" is the term used to define the horizontal distance between the towfish and the GPS antenna mounted on the survey vessel. It is important to remember that the sonar data is generated not at the survey vessel, but at the towfish. The layback correction can be calculated manually using Pythagoras' theorem, where the length of cable deployed corresponds to the hypotenuse and the depth of the towfish equates to one leg of the right-angled triangle. Alternatively, an acoustic beacon (transponder), operating at a set frequency, is attached to the towfish and interrogated by a ship-mounted hydrophone to accurately determine the position of the towed array.

Which portion of the seafloor is being insonified at any given time is addressed by measuring the motion of the ship or sonar platform using an Inertial Measurement Unit (IMU) or Motion Referencing Unit (MRU). This system uses a combination of accelerometers and angular rate sensors (gyroscopes) to track vessel movement, detecting the current acceleration and rate of change in attitude. These corrections are applied to remotely sensed data to correct for the effects of pitch, roll, and yaw on the survey vessel and/or towfish. In practice, as IMUs are expensive to purchase and/or hire and their mobilization is time-consuming, they are usually only used for MBES surveys, where these corrections are essential for high-quality data.

Brief Introduction to Ocean Acoustics

In order to effectively interpret acoustic data, it is essential to understand how these data are generated. Sonar systems function by transmitting acoustic pulses toward the seafloor and waiting for the returned energy to be received and processed by onboard computers. Once an acoustic pulse is transmitted by a survey instrument, it is at the mercy of the medium through which it propagates (the water column and sediment pile) and is no longer in the control of the surveyor or survey instrumentation. The interaction of the acoustic pulse with the water column, seafloor, and subsurface is not always straightforward and can influence the resulting acoustic data in many ways. In order to correctly interpret acoustic remote-sensing data, it is therefore essential to have some appreciation of underwater acoustics. Two factors must be considered: (1) interactions of the acoustic pulse with the water column, the seafloor, and the subsurface, and (2) mechanisms whereby the transmitted energy is returned to the instrument.

Sound is used to measure physical properties of the seafloor, the depth of the ocean, ocean temperature, and ocean currents, by transmitting an acoustic pulse into the water column and measuring the time taken for the pulse to travel back to the instrument. Sound velocity in water is dependent on temperature, salinity, and pressure. A typical value of sound velocity in saline water is 1,480 ms^{-1}. The value for freshwater is lower, as freshwater is less dense than saline water. Velocity depends primarily on temperature, less on pressure, and very little on salinity. All of the acoustic techniques described in this chapter are founded on the same basic principles of seismic reflection: each technique measures the time taken for an acoustic pulse to be transmitted from the survey instrument, travel through the water column (or sediment), reflect (or scatter) from a boundary, and travel back to the instrument.

The sonar transmits a fixed amount of energy into the water in the form of the acoustic pulse. As the pulse wavefront spreads in a spherical pattern, the intensity of the pulse falls with increasing distance (or range) from the source. The energy returning to the sonar is also affected by spherical spreading. As the acoustic pulse propagates through the water column and subsurface, some of the energy is simply absorbed by the medium due to frictional effects. In general terms, the higher the frequency of the transmitted pulse, the higher the absorption rate. Absorption is also stronger in saline water than in freshwater.

The transmitted acoustic pulse may be deflected as it propagates through the water column and subsurface. For example, it may encounter air bubbles, fish, suspended sediment, rough seafloors, subsurface targets, and so on. In each scenario, a proportion of the sound is scattered and reflected in various directions, including back toward the survey instrument. It is important to understand the differences between reflected energy and scattered energy. In general terms, echo-sounders and sub-bottom profilers rely on specular reflection, and side-scan sonar relies on scattered (diffuse) energy, to produce acoustic images of the seafloor and subsurface.

When the transmitted pulse reaches an obstacle in the water column, at the seafloor or in the subsurface, some portion of the acoustic pulse is reflected from the interface. The orientation of the reflecting medium with respect to the incident ray (measured as the angle of incidence, or grazing angle) is the most important factor in determining whether the reflected energy travels toward or away from the survey instrument.

As seismic reflection techniques (echo-sounders and sub-bottom profilers) rely on specular reflection, these sources conventionally transmit the acoustic pulse vertically downward and rely on the acoustic pulse being reflected vertically upward. The relative proportion of energy transmitted to each of these rays is determined by the contrast in acoustic impedance (Z) across the boundary, where acoustic impedance is equal to the velocity (V) of the medium multiplied by density (ρ):

$$Z = \rho V.$$

The strength of the reflection from the boundary between two materials (a measure of the proportion of energy returned toward the survey instrument) is governed by the reflection coefficient (K_R), where

$$K_R = \frac{Z_2 - Z_1}{Z_2 + Z_1}.$$

The polarity of the reflection coefficient is dependent on whether there is an increase (positive reflection) or decrease (negative reflection) in the acoustic impedance across the interface. In normal subsurface geological situations, values of K_R fall into the range of ±0.1 (Anstey 1981), with the majority of energy being transmitted. The reflection coefficient values for wood buried in unconsolidated marine sediments are generally large and negative (between −0.2 and −0.8; Quinn, Bull, and Dix 1997a). The magnitudes of these reflection coefficients indicate that acoustic instruments can readily image wooden artifacts and structures. Anstey (1981) states that values of K_R = ±0.3 are unusual in the earth because it is rare that such contrasting materials should be brought together. Clearly, however, in the realm of maritime archaeology, such high-order reflection coefficients are the norm rather than the exception.

Seismic reflection surveys account for more than 90% of the money spent worldwide on applied geophysics (Milsom 1996). The majority of these surveys are conducted by and for the hydrocarbon exploration industry in the search for oil and gas reserves. However, in the marine environment, seismic reflection techniques are employed in the form of bathymetric surveys and sub-bottom profiling surveys and, in a looser framework, in side-scan sonar surveys.

In side-scan sonar systems, the transducers transmit the acoustic pulse out to the side of the system, inclined at an angle toward the seafloor. The majority of the incident energy in this case is reflected away from the actual source. However, as the seafloor (and objects lying upon it) contain an inherent roughness, a proportion of the incident pulse is scattered by the roughness of the medium, and some of this scattered energy is "backscattered" (or diffused) toward the side-scan instrument. This backscattered sound is also known as reverberation. The intensity of the backscattered signal is a direct function of bottom roughness and angle of incidence. The rougher the bottom, the stronger the reverberation. However, roughness is a relative term and is dependent on the frequency (and, more importantly, the inherent wavelength) of the acoustic pulse.

To date, we have spoken in terms of time (or travel time), that is, the time taken for a pulse to be transmitted toward the seafloor and returned to the survey instrument. However, all measurement of depth or distance in marine acoustics depends on the conversion of time to depth and an assumption regarding the velocity of sound through sediment or water. The time taken for the acoustic wave to travel from the transducer to the reflecting boundary and back again is known as the two-way-travel-time (*twt*), which is related to depth (*d*) by the following equation:

$$d = \frac{V \times twt}{2}.$$

V is highly variable for different sediment types. As noted above, *V* for salt water is approximately 1,480 ms^{-1}. *V* varies between different sediment types and rocks. In general, hard rigid materials (rock, metal, wood) have relatively high compressional wave velocities, while soft plastic materials such as unconsolidated sediment have low compressional wave velocities. Furthermore, the general empirical rule applies that the compressional wave velocity increases in step with density in similar material types. For example, sediment generally becomes denser with depth of burial, hence their compressional wave velocity also increases with depth. In some shallow penetration applications, no differentiation is made between the velocity of sound in the water column and in the sediment pile. Instead, a constant value of 1,500 ms^{-1} is used for *V*. This is usually the same value used in side-scan sonar and bathymetric surveys.

The majority of users and manufacturers of acoustic instruments state that the resolution of acoustic systems is principally dependent on the frequency of the acoustic waves employed. This rule of thumb is misleading. It is naive to assume that higher-frequency acoustic systems always acquire higher-resolution acoustic data. In fact, the resolution and detection capability of acoustic instrumentation and resultant data is a complex issue, dependent on pulse lengths, beam angles, pulse rates, speed over ground, sample frequencies, and display mechanisms, to name a few (Quinn et al. 2005). It is therefore imperative that users of these data have some appreciation of underwater acoustics in order to carry out accurate and realistic geo-archaeological interpretations.

Some processed images derived from acoustic remote-sensing surveys are now of sufficient detail that they are interpretable by almost anyone, sometimes without much prior experience in remote-sensing interpretation. These types of images prove enormously beneficial in convincing resource managers and government bodies of the worth of this approach. Unfortunately however, many end-users of the acoustics tend to treat data as simple image data (often quoting the dreaded "wow factor"), without exploiting the inherent quantitative quality of the data. Given that acoustic remote sensors are designed to acquire quantitative data on geophysical properties of seafloor and subsurface materials, it is naive, uneconomical, and inefficient to treat these data purely as simple image (pictorial) data.

Profiling Methods

Single-Beam Echo-Sounders (SBES)

An essential component of all underwater investigations is the production of a detailed bathymetric (depth) chart. In maritime archaeology, bathymetric survey is a standard technique used in site investigations (Lawrence and Bates 2002; McNinch, Wells, and Trembanis 2006; Momber 1991; Momber and Geen 2000; Quinn 2006) and regional mapping initiatives (Quinn, Cooper, and Williams 2000). Inexpensive SBES are now commonplace, with many vessels equipped to conduct relatively unsophisticated but effective low-resolution bathymetric surveys. More sophisticated MBES are becoming increasingly common in archaeological investigations (see below), although relative cost remains a prohibitive factor.

Conventional echo-sounder systems consist of single hull-mounted or pole-mounted transducers that act as both an acoustic transmitter and receiver (transceiver). These systems transmit a single- or dual-frequency pulse, typically within the 50–300 kHz bandwidth. The frequency-dependent, vertical resolution of these systems can be as great as a few centimeters. Echo-sounders produce an acoustic pulse with a 30–45° cone angle, oriented vertically downward, concentrating the acoustic energy in a small circular area of the seabed (the radius of this circle is dependent on the water depth). The horizontal resolution of these systems is controlled by a combination of source frequency, cone angle, and water depth. For example, a 200 kHz echo-sounder with a 50° cone angle has a horizontal resolution of 0.14 m in a water depth of 20 m.

One major disadvantage of SBES systems is that the density of the survey grid controls the effective horizontal resolution of the survey. In a tidal environment, the maximum survey grid density achievable is on the order of 5 m. Therefore, the highest possible horizontal resolution for the bathymetric survey is ±5 m. Bathymetric data is conventionally represented as profiles, two-dimensional contour plots, or three-dimensional digital elevation models (DEMs). Regional-scale SBES surveys are conventionally designed with survey lines oriented perpendicular to the coast, as bathymetric variation is usually at a maximum in this direction. Site-specific SBES surveys are conventionally designed with survey lines oriented on a grid.

Sub-Bottom Profilers (SBP)

As many archaeological sites coincide with areas of high sedimentation, the partial or complete burial of structures, features, and artifacts is common (Figure 3.1). When nonmetallic artifacts, sites, and landscapes are buried, the only technique suitable for detecting them is sub-bottom (seismic) profiling (Bull, Quinn, and Dix 1998; Fitch, Thomson, and Gaffney 2005; Papatheodoru, Geraga, and Ferentinos 2005; Plets et al. 2007, in press; Quinn et al. 1997b, 1998, 2002a).

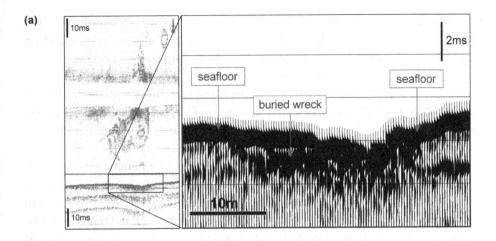

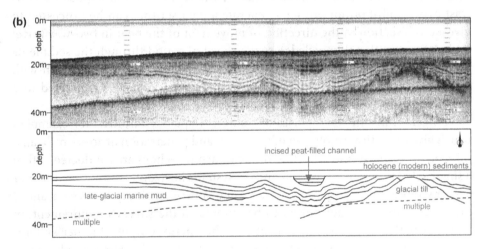

Figure 3.1 (a) Chirp sub-bottom profile acquired over the midships section of the *Invincible* (1797) wreck site, The Solent, United Kingdom. These data were acquired with a GeoAcoustics GeoChirp profiler using a 2–8kHz swept frequency source (Quinn et al. 1997) pulsing at 4 Hz. The chirp profile over the midships section images the buried oak wreck structure as a high-amplitude reflector with a measured reflection coefficient of −0.27; (b) Chirp profile illustrating the seismic stratigraphy of the postglacial and Holocene sequence in Belfast Lough, Ireland. These data were acquired by the CMA (University of Ulster) with an EdgeTech X-Star SB-216S using a 2–10 kHz swept frequency source pulsing at 4 Hz.

Two principal types of SBP exist: those that produce single frequency pulses (e.g., pingers, boomers, and sparkers) and those that produce swept frequency (wide-bandwidth) pulses (e.g., Chirp profilers). Single frequency systems suffer from a "penetration versus resolution" compromise, in that higher-frequency sources give better resolution but can penetrate only a short distance into the sediment, while lower-frequency systems penetrate farther but result in poorer resolution. The development of Chirp technology in the early 1990s addressed the classic trade-off between penetration and resolution by producing a swept frequency pulse capable of penetrating decameters into the seabed while still retaining decimeter resolution. It should be noted however, that the effectiveness of individual profiling systems is heavily dependent on the geological characteristics of the subsurface, with coarser sediments (sands and gravels) being harder to penetrate than fine-grained sediments (silts and clays).

All sub-bottom profilers employ acoustic sources that penetrate the seabed, reflect off boundaries or objects in the subsurface, and are detected by an acoustic receiver (or hydrophone) that is usually mounted in close proximity to the source. Reflections occur where there are differences in density and/or sound velocity across a boundary, that is, where an acoustic impedance contrast exists. Sub-bottom profilers generate a data set that can be processed to give a cross section in the direction of movement of the boat in two-way travel time. With additional knowledge of the speed of sound through the sediments (obtained from in situ measurements of core material or by comparison with standard empirically derived values), the time section can be converted to a depth section.

Pingers transmit short pulses of a single frequency (3.5 kHz, for example), which gives a vertical resolution of 0.3–0.5 m and penetration of 20–25 m. Transmission of the pulse and reception of the returning echoes are conducted within a single set of transceivers, optimizing the system's horizontal resolution. Boomer systems represent a single lower-frequency source, typically between 1 and 6 kHz. The boomer output pulse can be tailored to the survey's requirement, in terms of both the frequency content and the energy output. Boomer systems have a range of penetration of 50–100 m and a typical vertical resolution of 1.0 m. The bandwidth of Chirp systems is typically between 5 and 15 kHz, with a practical vertical resolution of 10–20 cm obtainable at penetration depths in excess of 30 m. To minimize attenuation and maximize resolution of the system, Chirp profilers are towed as close to the seabed as practical, typically 5–10 m above the bottom.

For artifact identification, Chirp systems currently represent the best available technology, not only because of their good resolution but because suitable postprocessing of this digital data allows some degree of material characterization of buried objects and materials (Bull, Quinn, and Dix 1998; Quinn, Bull, and Dix 1997a). For landscape reconstruction, the boomer system is most reliable, as it is capable of penetrating most sediment types found within the coastal zone and can thus guarantee some basic imagery of buried landscapes. However, in ideal circumstances both Chirp and boomer should be deployed on a survey to ensure both detailed imagery of any fine sedimentary cover and penetration to bedrock. Similar to SBES surveys, regional-scale seismic surveys are conventionally designed with track lines oriented perpendicular to shore, as stratigraphic variation is usually highest in this direction.

SWATH METHODS

Side-Scan Sonar

Side-scan sonar is a method of seabed imaging using narrow beams of acoustic energy transmitted out either side of the towfish and across the seabed (Fish and Carr 1990). Sound, scattered back from the seafloor and from submerged objects, is processed to provide laterally undistorted acoustic images of the seafloor in real time (Figure 3.2). The swath-width of side-scan sonars (i.e., the area of the seafloor surveyed in a single pass) is user-controlled, generally encompassing 10 times the water depth. For archaeological surveys, the angle at which the acoustic energy insonifies the target is important, as different grazing angles reveal different site characteristics. An effective way to alter this angle is to repeat survey lines encompassing the site at different towfish altitudes. Up to the early part of the twenty-first century, side-scan sonar was regarded as the workhorse of offshore survey, featuring heavily in archaeological investigations (Fish and Carr 1990; Sakellariou et al. 2007; Sonnenburg and Boyce 2008; Théorêt 1980; Ward and Ballard 2004). However, side-scan sonar is now slowly being replaced by the multibeam echo-sounder as the instrument of choice for archaeological investigations.

As with most acoustic instruments, side-scan systems are available in a variety of types, depth ratings, and operating frequencies. Standard systems are portable and suitable for deployment from inshore survey vessels, employing one of two industry-standard frequencies for imaging: 100 kHz and 500 kHz. In general terms, a 100 kHz operating frequency is chosen for regional surveys with swath widths in excess of 100 m per channel. Frequencies of 500 kHz are generally used where a higher resolution is required, such as for detailed shipwreck surveys. Very-high-frequency systems of up to 1 MHz give even better definition, but their effective range is limited to less than about 50 m. Modern systems provide resolution on a centimetric scale when operated under near-perfect survey conditions (Quinn et al. 2005).

Material properties of the substrate determine the acoustic response of the seafloor (Quinn et al. 2005). All materials have an inherent roughness—for example, coarse-grained material scatters more energy than fine-grained material due to the rougher interface presented to the acoustic pulse. Therefore, rock, gravel, wood, and metals scatter more energy than finer-grained sediments and will therefore be recorded as darker elements on the sonar record. Reflector shape, including seafloor gradient, also influences reflectivity and backscattering. Arguably the most important phenomenon on side-scan records for archaeological purposes is acoustic shadows, which provide a three-dimensional quality to what is essentially two-dimensional data. Acoustic shadows occur alongside objects that stand proud of, or are partially buried in, the seafloor. In side-scan sonar data, shadows can often indicate more about the target than the acoustic returns.

The majority of side-scan investigations follow a predetermined survey pattern, with lane spacing less than the swath width of the sonar, allowing for overlap between

(a)

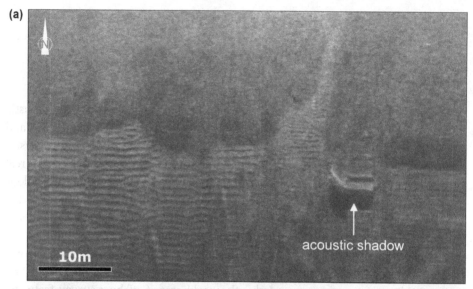

(b)

Figure 3.2 Side-scan sonar data from the (a) *Appin* (1913) and (b) *Oregon* (1945) wreck sites in Belfast Lough, Ireland. The sonar data were acquired using an EdgeTech 272-TD side-scan system operating at 500 kHz with a swath width of 150 m (Quinn et al. 2000). Side-scan data images the wrecks within their environmental context, allowing resource managers a valuable tool for site management strategies. For example, the remains of the hull of *Appin* are imaged lying among a field of bifurcating wave ripples, indicating that the long-term site evolution is influenced by its location within the wave base.

successive survey lines. This overlap allows for deviation off the survey line and also compensates for loss of resolution with range. Although data in the past was conventionally displayed on thermal film, modern systems allow for digital acquisition and geo-rectification. Individual geo-rectified side-scan lines are routinely compiled into mosaic views to provide large-area acoustic images at the original resolution.

Multibeam Echo-Sounders

Multibeam echo-sounders are a direct development of the SBES, but instead of estimating the depth of a single point on the seafloor directly beneath the transceiver, they estimate the depths of tens or hundreds of points within a swath orthogonal to the transceiver, ensuring high-density, high-resolution coverage (Momber and Geen 2000; Quinn 2006). MBES systems are therefore used to increase bottom coverage, with each of the narrow beams producing data at a resolution equivalent to that of a narrow SBES (Figure 3.3). MBES systems are usually mounted on the hull or on a remotely operated vehicle (ROV) but can be mounted on a towfish if required.

Two types of swath systems are commonly employed for bathymetric mapping—multibeam echo-sounders and interferometric sonars (also termed bathymetric side-scan sonar). Each of these systems has its own advantages and disadvantages. To put it simply, MBES systems offer higher-resolution bathymetric data with low-order backscatter data as a by-product, whereas interferometric systems offer lower-order bathymetric data and true side-scan. The more sophisticated MBES can simultaneously acquire depth and backscatter data for each point insonified on the seafloor. These data can then be used to derive charts of the seafloor showing relief and backscatter intensity, which can in turn be used to produce geological maps when ground-truthed using direct (grabs, cores) or indirect (video, stills) sampling methods. Despite their complexity and relative expense, MBES now dominate seafloor mapping.

MBES have many uses and are designed to operate in various water depths. System choice therefore depends on the water depth range to be surveyed. MBES systems are grouped into three main categories (Lurton 2002). Deepwater systems are designed for regional survey and operate in the frequency range of 12 kHz (deep ocean mapping) to 30 kHz (continental shelf investigations). The large size and weight of these MBES transceivers limits their installation to deep-sea vessels. Shallow-water systems typically operate at 100–200 kHz and are designed for hydrographic survey of the continental shelves. High-definition systems, operating between 300 and 500 kHz, are used for high-definition work and object detection (see Figure 3.3). Their small size and weight makes them ideal for small-vessel deployment and for mounting on ROVs.

Aspects of Data Acquisition, Processing, and Interpretation

The quality of remotely sensed data is affected by many factors, including towfish instability, positioning accuracy, weather, boat heave, and water column noise. To aid data interpretation, detailed and time-stamped field notes should be logged

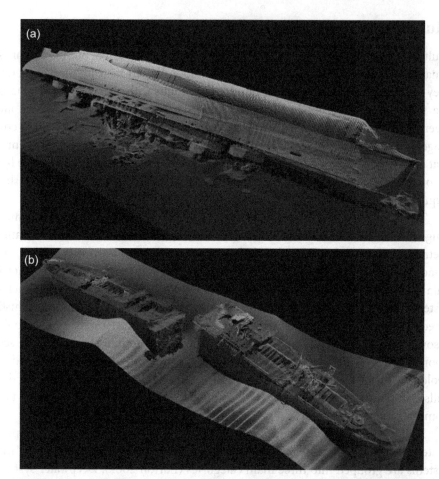

Figure 3.3 Multibeam echo-sounder data of (a) HMS *Royal Oak* and (b) the SS
Richard Montgomery (bottom) wreck sites. HMS *Royal Oak* was anchored at Scapa
Flow in Orkney, Scotland, when she became the first of five Royal Navy battleships
and battle cruisers sunk in World War II. She was torpedoed at anchor by the German
submarine *U-47* on 14 October 1939. HMS *Royal Oak* is a designated war grave and
now lies upside down in 30 m of water, with her hull 5 m beneath the surface. SS
Richard Montgomery was an American Liberty ship built during World War II and
subsequently wrecked in the Thames estuary (UK) in 1944 with around 1,500 tons of
explosives on board. The explosives continue to be a hazard to the area; time-lapse
MBES surveys are conducted over the site to assess change in the wreck and cargo.
These data were collected using a Reson 8125 operating at 455 kHz. Pulse rate was 5–7
Hz on the *Royal Oak* survey and 12–22 Hz on the *Richard Montgomery* survey. Data
acquired by ADUS for Salvage and Marine Operations, UK Ministry of Defence.

during survey. As the person interpreting the data has often not been involved in
the data acquisition phase, comprehensive survey logs can be of great benefit to the
interpreter. Simple things like "start of line" (SOL) and "end of line" (EOL) marks
should be recorded both on the data and in a field log to facilitate data processing.

Due to the large volume of data acquired in acoustic remote sensing surveys, systems of file naming should be logical and consistent. Files should be numbered sequentially to avoid ambiguity. For example, one of the easiest ways to name files is to use the date of survey followed by a letter. For example, the first navigation file recorded on 17 January 2008 could be called 170108a.dat; the second file recorded on the same day could be called 170108b.dat, and so on. Unfortunately, loss of remotely sensed data tends to be permanent. Backups are therefore essential. Originals and backups should be stored separately.

To the surveyor, "signal" is the portion of data that is required, and "noise" describes anything else that is recorded but is considered to contain no useful information. Good-quality data has a high signal-to-noise ratio (SNR). Because of this, much of the surveyors' efforts are dedicated to the need to improve the SNR of data. In the marine environment, noise is caused by such phenomena as vessel engine noise, wake from passing vessels, sea-surface chop, and in extreme cases by marine life. Survey procedures should be adapted to ensure that the best possible data is acquired. For example, a pulsing echo-sounder may cause regular interference on side-scan data. The easiest way of eliminating this interference is to turn off the echo-sounder. However, in shallow-water applications, the skipper may require a depth readout, so the echo-sounder cannot be switched off. In this case, interference may be limited by increasing the distance between the echo-sounder transducer and the side-scan towfish by towing on a longer cable length (Fish and Carr 1990).

Interpreters of remotely sensed data tend to concentrate on anomalies, that is, on appreciable differences between a constant or smoothly varying background and a very strong or "anomalous" signature. Archaeological anomalies take many forms. For example, a concentration of iron cannon in gullies on a bedrock substrate would give rise to a sharp magnetic anomaly but may not be imaged in a side-scan survey (see Gearhart in this volume for a discussion of magnetic anomalies). Conversely, a wooden vessel on a planar sand substrate may present a noticeable high-backscatter anomaly on side-scan data that would not be detected in a magnetometer survey.

The results from geophysical surveys can be presented in many formats, depending on data type and audience. The results of surveys along single traverses can be presented in profile form, where the horizontal scale is distance and the vertical scale is the quantity being measured: for example, the results of a single bathymetric transect would plot distance against depth. The results along grid-type surveys can be contoured and presented as two-dimensional or three-dimensional plots and surfaces: for instance, the results of a bathymetric survey could be contoured to provide a bathymetric chart of the area. The results of side-scan sonar surveys are usually presented as either acoustic snapshots (image data) or mosaics of the seafloor. Whatever method is used, it is important to present data in such a way that the target audience is addressed and data attributes are clear. Data should be presented to inform, not to impress.

The success of marine remote-sensing surveys is largely dependent upon the experience of the surveyors and interpreters. Although some research has focused on the acoustic signatures of anthropogenic materials submerged and buried in the marine environment (Bull, Quinn, and Dix 1998; Quinn, Bull, and Dix 1997a; Quinn et al. 2005), it remains a poorly understood subject. This often leads to the misinterpretation of acoustic archaeological data. The only satisfactory method presently available for quantifying marine archaeo-acoustic data is to physically ground-truth anomalies and ambiguous targets, either through diver, drop-down video, or ROV investigations. With the increase in predevelopment and research-oriented remote-sensing surveys, combined with initiatives to substantiate national, regional, or local cultural heritage registers, a rapid and accurate method for ground-truthing these data is essential (see, for example, Quinn et al. 2002b; Quinn et al. 2007).

APPLICATIONS TO SHIPWRECK ARCHAEOLOGY

In shipwreck studies, acoustic remote sensing has traditionally been used for reconnaissance surveys and for site relocation. More recently, with the advent of higher-resolution sonar systems, the focus in shipwreck studies has shifted toward site reconstruction and studies of site formation. Site formation processes at wreck sites are driven by some combination of chemical, biological, and physical processes, with physical processes initially dominant (Quinn 2006; Ward, Larcombe, and Veth 1999; see also C. Martin in this volume). Wreck sites act as open systems, with the exchange of material (sediment, water, organics, and inorganics) and energy (wave, tidal, storm) across system boundaries (Quinn 2006). Wrecks are therefore generally in a state of dynamic equilibrium with respect to the natural environment, characterized by negative disequilibrium, ultimately leading to wreck disintegration. Positive and negative feedbacks operate between physical, chemical, and biological processes in the water column, sediment pile, and the wreck as it disintegrates and interacts with the surrounding environment (Ward, Larcombe, and Veth 1999). Fundamental processes driving site formation therefore depend on the complex erosion (net sediment loss) and accretion (net sediment deposition) history of wreck sites. Furthermore, exposed parts of wreck structures tend to be affected by aerobic bacteria, wood-borers, and increased corrosion rates, while buried wreck components tend to be affected by anaerobic bacteria (Ward, Larcombe, and Veth 1999). Therefore, even major chemical and biological processes contributing to site formation are constrained by the physical processes of scour and deposition (Quinn 2006).

Acoustic methods can be used to elucidate and quantify these processes of site formation and aid our understanding of resultant wreck and artifact distributions. Acoustics can help to quantify sediment budgets at sites, provide information on hydrodynamics, quantify seabed movement, and play a primary role in recording artifact distributions. Examples of the application of acoustic techniques to site formation studies include the gravitational collapse of the *Santo Antonio de Tanna* (Quinn et al. 2007), scouring at the *Queen Anne's Revenge* (McNinch, Wells, and Trembanis 2006) and *Mary Rose* (Quinn et al. 1997b) wreck sites, and the storm-controlled redistribution of material and artifacts at the *Invincible* site (Quinn et al. 1998). Furthermore, repeat (time-lapse) side-scan sonar surveys have proven effective in quantifying change in a variety of studies, including at archaeological sites (Quinn 2006; Quinn et al. 1998).

An example of the successful implementation of the time-lapse technique to assessing change at a shipwreck site is illustrated with the case study of the Arklow Bank wreck, lying approximately 11 km off the east coast of Ireland (Quinn 2006). The wreck was discovered in 2002 during a side-scan sonar survey as part of an off-shore wind park development. Subsequent to relocation, repeat MBES surveys of the wreck site were conducted on 12 August and 23 August 2003 (Figure 3.4). The wreck stands proud of the seabed by up to 2 m at midships, with the wreck aligned approximately 60° to the dominant flow direction. The primary scour feature emanates from the eastern end of the vessel, with a maximum recorded depth of 16.3 m, approximately 3 m below mean bed level. Two accretionary ridges parallel the peak flow direction, one originating at midships and one at the western end of the wreck structure.

The results of the repeat MBES surveys were corrected for tidal variation and subsampled to generate corresponding spatial grids (0.05 m spatial resolution). These grids were subsequently subtracted to produce an accretion-erosion plot, displaying bed-level change after an 11-day period (Figure 3.4c). Migration of flow-perpendicular bifurcating ripples is characteristic of the site, indicating that live bed processes participate in site development. The most significant signatures developed in the accretion-erosion plot are the series of flow-parallel erosional "troughs" and the single accretionary "ridge" developed on the northeastern margin of the wreck. The amplitude of the accretionary ridge is in excess of 4 m, indicating the accumulation of at least 4 m of sediment at the midships section over an 11-day period, parallel to the dominant flow direction. This is equal to the deposition of 0.36 m per day, assuming a constant sedimentation rate. Other areas of sediment accumulation include the northwestern tip of the wreck and a mound on the southern margin of the structure, around the midship section. The series of erosional troughs form largely flow-parallel features, although the trough at the eastern side of the accretionary ridge converges with the ridge approximately 15 m from the wreck (Quinn 2006).

The results from the repeat MBES surveys highlight the extreme dynamic characteristics of some wreck sites, with gross bed-level change occurring rapidly over large areas. This result alone raises serious questions about the validity of many site formation models where "processes" are often generalized and averaged over periods of hundreds of years (Quinn 2006).

APPLICATIONS TO SUBMERGED LANDSCAPES

Much of the recent renewed interest in the archaeology of submerged coastlines stems from the increased resolving capability of acoustic methods and their role in locating, mapping, and reconstructing these environments (Figure 3.5; see also

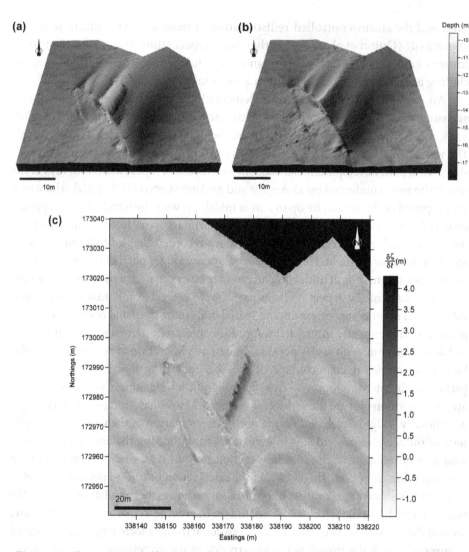

Figure 3.4 Composite graphic representing (a) three-dimensional terrain model of the Arklow Bank wreck site (Ireland) generated from multibeam data acquired on 12 August 2003; (b) three-dimensional terrain model of the wreck site generated from multibeam data acquired on 23 August 2003; and (c) three-dimensional accretion-erosion model produced by subtracting the results of the time-lapse surveys. The model shows areas of accretion in red and erosion in blue. The MBES data were acquired by Titan Environmental Surveys Ltd. using a GeoAcoustics GeoSwath system operating at 250 kHz with a beam angle of 1°, providing a theoretical vertical resolution of 0.0175 m.

Firth in this volume). The centimetric resolution of the acoustic remote-sensing techniques, allied to digital signal processing and analysis, allows for the interrogation of morphology of submerged landscapes and also of the materials that comprise the landscapes. For example, automated classification of backscatter data, signature analyses of seismic data and slope analysis of MBES data all find applications in submerged landscape studies.

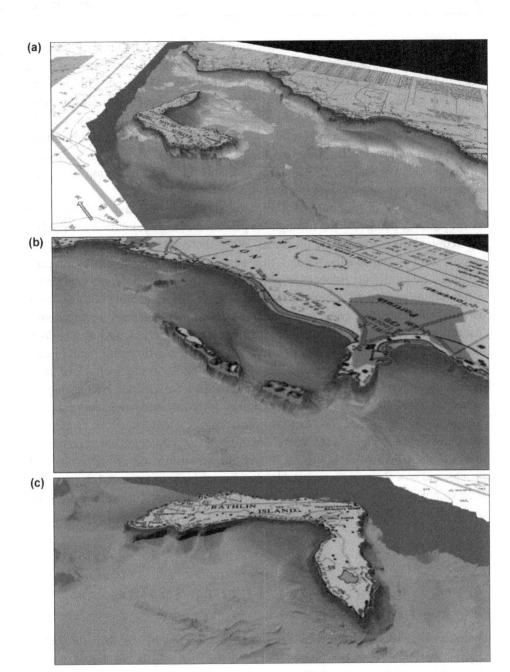

Figure 3.5 Paleo-geographic reconstructions of areas located off the northern coast of Ireland. These reconstructions are based on MBES data derived from the Joint Irish Bathymetric Survey (JIBS), co-coordinated by the Maritime and Coastguard Agency, the Irish Marine Institute, and the Northern Ireland Environment Agency. (a) Reconstruction of the northeastern coast of Ireland at a lowstand of –60 m; (b) Paleo-geographic reconstruction of The Skerries off Portrush (Co. Antrim), based on a lowstand of –30m identified by Kelley et al. (2006); and (c) Paleo-geographic reconstruction of Rathlin Island based on a lowstand of –30 m identified by Kelley et al. (2006).

Examples of the application of acoustic techniques to broad-scale studies of submerged landscapes include mapping the paleogeography of a submerged flood plain and archaeological sites through the fusion of SBES and SSS data (Sonnenburg and Boyce 2008), mapping of late Pleistocene and Holocene depositional systems on the Dogger Bank through the integration and visualization of 3D seismics (Fitch, Thomson, and Gaffney 2005), identifying the influence of climate and cultural activity on basin development in Lower Lough Erne using side-scan and Chirp seismic data (Lafferty, Quinn, and Breen 2006), and the characterization of buried inundated peat on seismic data (Plets et al. 2007).

Perhaps some of the most exciting developments in this area of research in recent years are being realized through the provision of high-resolution MBES data sets acquired over large geographic areas. When these data are integrated with the outputs from glacio-isostatic models, they allow research teams to produce nested regional- and local-scale paleogeographic reconstructions of submerged landscapes at resolutions previously unheard of (see Figure 3.5). The availability of these sonar data and the increasing cooperation between government agencies and academic institutions interested in seabed mapping, landscape evolution, and archaeology has spawned research networks dedicated to relocating, mapping, and understanding the evolution of these submerged landscapes. An example of one of these multidisciplinary research groups is the Submerged Landscapes Archaeological Network (SLAN; Bell, O'Sullivan, and Quinn 2006), comprising archaeologists and geoscientists from Europe and North America who use sonar data, numerical modeling, and archaeological theory to understand how the submerged coastal environments of the North Atlantic Rim facilitated the expansion and growth of its first peoples and how the evolving coastal landscape, marine resources, and climate may have stimulated social and cultural change across prehistoric times and into the medieval period (Bell, O'Sullivan, and Quinn 2008).

CURRENT AND FUTURE TRENDS

Undoubtedly, wreck and landscape remote-sensing surveys benefit from integrated approaches (Papatheodorou, Geraga, and Ferentinos 2005; Quinn et al. 1998, 2002a; Sonnenburg and Boyce 2008). To date, integrated surveys often meant using different acoustic systems to collect separate data sets, with the spatial integration of these data occurring in the postprocessing stage. However, the last few years have seen developments of multielement sonar platforms, which allow for the acquisition of true concurrent sonar data sets from one platform.

As outlined by Mayer (2006), the past few years have witnessed remarkable and simultaneous advances in sonar technology, positioning systems, and computer power that have revolutionized the imaging of the seafloor. Advances in the acquisition, processing, and visualization of these data will continue into the future, allied to further developments in digital acquisition, signal processing, and advanced visualization (see, for example, Plets et al. 2009). All of these developments are possible due to increasing power and decreasing costs of computers. Perhaps most importantly for maritime archaeology, every new phase of development in sonar technology brings an increase in sensors' resolving capability and therefore the ability to image smaller and smaller artifacts in greater detail.

REFERENCES

Anstey, N. A. 1981. *Signal characteristics and instrument specifications*. 2nd ed. Berlin: Gebruder Borntraeger.

Bell, T., A. O' Sullivan, and R. Quinn. 2006. Discovering ancient landscapes under the sea. *Archaeology Ireland* 20 (2): 12–17.

Bell, T., K. Westley, R. Plets, R. Quinn, and M. A. P. Renouf. 2008. Submerged archaeological landscapes—from ancient myth to new frontier. *Journal of Ocean Technology* 3 (4): 13–20.

Bull, J. M., R. Quinn, and J. K. Dix. 1998. Reflection coefficient calculation from marine high-resolution seismic reflection (Chirp) data and application to an archaeological case study. *Marine Geophysical Researches* 20: 1–11.

Delaporta, K., M. E. Jasinski, and F. Søreide. 2006. The Greek-Norwegian Deep-water Archaeological Survey. *International Journal of Nautical Archaeology* 35 (1): 79–87.

Fish, J. P., and A. H. Carr. 1990. *Sound underwater images: A guide to the generation and interpretation of side scan sonar data*. Orleans, MA: Lower Cape.

Fitch, S., K. Thomson, and V. Gaffney. 2005. Late Pleistocene and Holocene depositional systems and the palaeogeography of the Dogger Bank, North Sea. *Quaternary Research* 64: 185–196.

Kelley, J. T., J. A. G. Cooper, D. W. T. Jackson, D. F. Belknap, and R. Quinn. 2006. Sea-level change and inner shelf stratigraphy off northern Ireland. *Marine Geology* 232: 1–15.

Lafferty, B., R. Quinn, and C. Breen. 2006. A side-scan sonar and Chirp study of the natural and anthropogenic sedimentary record of Lower Lough Erne, NW Ireland. *Journal of Archaeological Science* 33: 756–766.

Lawrence, M. L., and C. R. Bates. 2002. Acoustic ground discrimination techniques for submerged archaeological site investigations. *Marine Technology Society Journal* 35: 65–73.

Lurton, X. 2002. *An introduction to underwater acoustics: Principles and applications*. Chichester, UK: Praxis.

Mayer, L. 2006. Frontiers in seafloor mapping and visualization. *Marine Geophysical Researches* 27 (1): 7–17.

McNinch, J. E., J. T. Wells, and A. C. Trembanis. 2006. Predicting the fate of artifacts in energetic, shallow marine environments: An approach to site management. *International Journal of Nautical Archaeology* 35 (2): 290–309.

Milsom, J. 1996. *Field geophysics*. Chichester, UK: Wiley.

Momber, G. 1991. Gorad Beuno: Investigation of an ancient fish-trap in Caernarvon Bay, N. Wales. *International Journal of Nautical Archaeology* 20: 95–109.

Momber, G., and M. Geen. 2000. The application of the Submetrix ISIS 100 swath bathymetry system to the management of underwater sites. *International Journal of Nautical Archaeology* 29 (1): 154–162.

Papatheodorou, G., M. Geraga, and G. Ferentinos. 2005. The Navarino Naval Battle Site, Greece—an integrated remote-sensing survey and a rational management approach. *International Journal of Nautical Archaeology* 34 (1): 95–109.

Plets, R., J. Dix, A. Bastos, and A. Best. 2007. Characterization of buried inundated peat on seismic (Chirp) data, inferred from core information. *Archaeological Prospection* 14 (4): 1–12.

Plets, R. M. K., J. K. Dix, J. R. Adams, J. M. Bull, T. J. Henstock, M. Gutowski, and A. I. Best. 2009. The use of a high-resolution 3D Chirp sub-bottom profiler for the reconstruction of the shallow water archaeological site of the Grace Dieu (1439), River Hamble, UK. *Journal of Archaeological Science* 36 (2): 408–418.

Quinn, R. 2006. The role of scour in shipwreck site formation processes and the preservation of wreck-associated scour signatures in the sedimentary record—evidence from seabed and sub-surface data. *Journal of Archaeological Science* 33: 1419–1432.

Quinn, R., J. R. Adams, J. K. Dix, and J. M. Bull. 1998. The *Invincible* (1758) site—an integrated geophysical assessment. *International Journal of Nautical Archaeology* 27 (3): 126–138.

Quinn, R., J. M. Bull, and J. K. Dix. 1997a. Imaging wooden artefacts using Chirp sources. *Archaeological Prospection* 4: 25–35.

Quinn, R., J. M. Bull, J. K. Dix, and J. R. Adams. 1997b. The *Mary Rose* site—geophysical evidence for palaeo-scour marks. *International Journal of Nautical Archaeology* 26 (1): 3–16.

Quinn, R., C. Breen, W. Forsythe, K. Barton, S. Rooney, and D. O' Hara. 2002a. Integrated geophysical surveys of the French frigate *La Surveillante* (1797), Bantry Bay, Co. Cork, Ireland. *Journal of Archaeological Science* 29: 413–422.

Quinn, R., J. A. G. Cooper, and B. Williams. 2000. Marine geophysical investigation of the inshore coastal waters of northern Ireland. *International Journal of Nautical Archaeology* 29 (2): 294–298.

Quinn., R., M. Dean, M. Lawrence, S. Liscoe, and D. Boland. 2005. Backscatter responses and resolution considerations in archaeological side-scan sonar surveys: A control experiment. *Journal of Archaeological Science* 32: 1252–1264.

Quinn, R., W. Forsythe, C. Breen, D. Boland, P. Lane, and A. Lali Omar. 2007. Process-based models for port evolution and wreck site formation at Mombasa, Kenya. *Journal of Archaeological Science* 34 (9): 1449–1460.

Quinn, R., W. Forsythe, C. Breen, M. Dean, M. Lawrence, and S. Liscoe. 2002b. Comparison of the Maritime Sites and Monuments Record with side-scan sonar and diver surveys: A case study from Rathlin Island, Ireland. *Geoarchaeology* 17 (5): 441–451.

Sakellariou, D., P. Georgiou, A. Mallios, V. Kapsimalis, D. Kourkoumelis, P. Micha, T. Theodoulou, and K. Dellaporta. 2007. Searching for ancient shipwrecks in the Aegean Sea: The discovery of Chios and Kythnos Hellenistic wrecks with the use of marine geological-geophysical methods. *International Journal of Nautical Archaeology* 36 (2): 365–381.

Sonnenburg, E. P., and J. I. Boyce. 2008. Data-fused digital bathymetry and side-scan sonar as a base for archaeological inventory of submerged landscapes in the Rideau Canal, Ontario, Canada. *Geoarchaeology* 23 (5): 654–674.

Théorêt, M. A. 1980. Side-scan sonar in Lake Champlain, Vermont, USA. *International Journal of Nautical Archaeology* 9 (1): 35–41.

Ward, C., and R. D. Ballard. 2004. Deep-water archaeological survey in the Black Sea: 2000 season. *International Journal of Nautical Archaeology* 33 (1): 2–13.

Ward, I. A. K., P. Larcombe, and P. Veth. 1999. A new process-based model for wreck site formation. *Journal of Archaeological Science* 26: 561–570.

Wüst, G., and A. Defant. 1936. *Deutsche Atlantische Expedition 1925–1927*. Band VI, Atlas: *Atlas zur Schichtung und Zirkulation des Atlantischen Ozeans*. Berlin: Verlag von Walther de Gruyter & Co.

CHAPTER 4

ARCHAEOLOGICAL INTERPRETATION OF MARINE MAGNETIC DATA

ROBERT GEARHART

INTRODUCTION

INTERPRETING remote-sensing data is certainly less glamorous than diving on a historic shipwreck, yet it is arguably one of the most important tasks of archaeologists working in submerged environments. Discovery of shipwrecks quite often depends on their detection by geophysical instruments and their recognition as shipwrecks by archaeologists interpreting that geophysical data. Researchers around the world rely on remote-sensing technologies to aid their search for historic shipwrecks of interest. In the United States, government agencies frequently require marine remote-sensing surveys as part of environmental permitting studies prior to construction projects. Long-term preservation of historic sites such as shipwrecks[1] is their ultimate goal. A shipwreck missed by a preconstruction archaeological survey is at increased risk of destruction both by the project that required the initial survey and by all subsequent projects that rely on that survey as a record of archaeological clearance.

Magnetometers have been integral to marine archaeological surveys for at least four decades and continue to remain essential for detection of buried shipwrecks. Burial is common in high-energy environments that have weakly consolidated seafloor sediments. Shipwrecks most susceptible to burial have wooden hulls and occur in environments where exposed wood is not preserved well underwater. Metal hulls survive exposure in such environments longer than wood and thus are more commonly discovered than wooden hulls. Burial disproportionately affects historic shipwrecks. For example, statistics of over 20,000 merchant vessels lost from 1876 through 1947 suggest that, in the United States, 57% of pre-1948 losses had wooden hulls and lacked machinery, while 36% had wooden hulls powered by machinery. Only 7% of shipwrecks predating 1948 had metal hulls (U.S. Treasury Department 1876–1899; U.S. Department of Commerce 1906–1947). By contrast, less than 5% of shipwrecks discovered by petroleum industry remote-sensing surveys conducted in the Gulf of Mexico for the Bureau of Ocean Energy Management, Regulation and Enforcement (BOEMRE) have been confirmed as having wooden hulls (U.S. Department of Interior 2007), and all of those are in deep water, where complete burial is unlikely. While the goal of the BOEMRE archaeological program is to protect potential archaeological sites, not to find and identify all shipwrecks, the small number of wooden hulls observed by side-scan sonar in the Gulf of Mexico, relative to the vast number of surveys completed there, demonstrates the importance of magnetometers to the discovery of buried historic shipwrecks.

Magnetometers are highly sensitive instruments, so detection of buried shipwrecks is usually an attainable objective provided that they contain ferromagnetic materials and that survey methods are adequate. Recognition of buried shipwrecks based on magnetometer data can be quite another matter. Only a tiny fraction of seafloor magnetic anomalies are associated with shipwrecks. The population of magnetic debris is many orders of magnitude larger than that of sunken vessels. Magnetic debris is defined here as any ferromagnetic object or group of such objects that is not part of a historic site or submerged vessel. Debris is the background noise against which a skilled interpreter must spot potential historic shipwrecks. The difficulty of discovering buried shipwrecks and the potential for mistakes increases in areas of high marine traffic, such as harbor mouths and inland waterways, where the density of magnetic debris can become quite high. Hands-on inspection of every buried anomaly source may not be an economic possibility, so researchers must trust their interpretive abilities. Consistent detection of buried shipwrecks, however, requires an objective methodology for interpretation of magnetic data that can be easily replicated by other researchers.

Historically, the main goal of magnetic interpretation has been to distinguish shipwrecks from debris, usually resulting in an archaeological assessment of each anomaly concerning its potential for historic significance. For decades, experienced archaeologists have relied on their professional judgment to interpret countless anomalies, classifying some as potential shipwrecks, but most as insignificant debris. Yet archaeologists have repeatedly struggled to characterize reliable differences between magnetic signatures of shipwrecks and debris, leading several (e.g., Murphy et al. 1981: 43; Pearson, Guevin, and Saltus 1991: 69; Watts 1986: 18) to conclude that it simply is not possible—that shipwrecks and debris cannot be differentiated with absolute certainty on the basis of their magnetic anomalies. Whether or not it is possible, the need for interpretation remains. So archaeologists continue to use their best judgment to interpret magnetic data with the same degree of uncertainty as 20 years ago. This uncertainty is reflected in their technical reports where criteria used to judge the significance of anomalies are often vague or unstated.

The past two decades have seen improvement in archaeologists' abilities to detect shipwreck anomalies. In the United States, this has come about largely through reductions in survey line spacing required by various state and federal agencies. But over that same period little progress has been made toward improving interpretation methods. One could argue that reduction of line spacing has placed pressure on data analysis to catch up with survey methodology. The increased number of debris anomalies detected at closer transect intervals has compounded the need for a more consistent and reliable method of differentiating shipwrecks from debris. Present methods for marine magnetic data interpretation are uncertain at best and scientifically unfounded at worst. Yet, in the United States at least, those responsible for historic preservation on submerged lands rely on archaeologists' interpretations of magnetic data when committing government funds to archaeological testing studies and when granting clearances for marine construction projects that could affect historic shipwrecks.

Magnetic data interpretation is not likely to improve on a broad scale unless archaeologists continue to debate relevant issues in an effort to build scientific consensus on the topic. Building a stronger scientific foundation for interpretations would require, at the very least, analysis of a broad collection of magnetic data for shipwrecks and debris. Achieving consistent results might be facilitated by development of a standardized methodology based on a common understanding of shipwreck magnetism and adaptable to specific research objectives. Adoption of standards certainly would require a renewed debate on the topic of data interpretation. This chapter is intended to rekindle that dialogue by encouraging fresh scientific perspectives on the topic while promoting the complementary goals of increased objectivity in marine magnetic interpretation and improved detection of historic shipwrecks.

Understanding the basic characteristics of magnetism and particularly the differences between induced and permanent magnetic fields is vitally important to archaeological interpretation of magnetic data, but many archaeologists have minimal academic training in the physical sciences. Thus, the following section provides social scientists with a basic, nonmathematical summary of magnetism relevant to archaeological interpretation. Readers already familiar with such topics might find the following discussion overly simplistic or needlessly detailed, depending on their perspectives, and may choose to skip this section.

MAGNETISM

The source of Earth's magnetic field can be envisioned as a huge dipole within the planet's core (Figure 4.1a). The dipole's negative "southern" pole corresponds to what is commonly referred to as Earth's Magnetic North Pole, and vice versa. The seemingly backward orientation of this imaginary magnet relative to Earth's magnetic poles is a common source of confusion. It is helpful to think of the north pole of a magnet as a north-seeking pole. The north-seeking pole of a compass needle, or of any other bar magnet, is designated by convention as having a positive charge. Since the positive end of a compass needle points northward and opposite charges attract one another, it follows that Earth's Magnetic North Pole must have a negative charge and is really the southern pole of Earth's magnetic dipole.

A magnetic dipole can be described in the simplest of terms by the magnitude and direction of its magnetic moment, which is a vector quantity pointing along the dipole's axis from its negative pole toward its positive pole (see Figure 4.1a). The magnetic field generated around a dipole source can be envisioned as lines of force emanating from the source's positive pole, initially in the direction of its magnetic moment, then traversing closed loops around the source, and finally reentering at its negative pole. The magnetic force directed along such lines is familiar as the cause of patterned iron filings in proximity to a bar magnet.

The magnetic sources of direct concern to archaeologists are ferromagnetic materials, principally those containing iron. Ferromagnetism is caused by the parallel alignment of atoms in such a way that unpaired electrons of each atom orbit the nucleus and spin in the same direction as those of neighboring atoms (Serway 1992: 852–854). The spinning and orbiting motion of each unpaired electron forms a tiny current loop, which in turn generates a magnetic dipole, or in essence an atom-sized bar magnet.

Magnetism resulting from an object's thermal history is called permanent, or remnant, magnetization. Iron atoms rotate freely and randomly when heated beyond their Curie temperature of 1,418°F (770°C) (Serway 1992: 559). As a ferromagnetic substance cools through its Curie temperature, the randomizing thermal energy of the atoms decreases below the strength of Earth's magnetic field. The positive pole of each atomic dipole is attracted to Earth's negative pole, and the object's magnetic moment aligns with Earth's magnetic field lines (see Figure 4.1a). Below this temperature, most atomic dipoles remain fixed in direction relative to one another, imbuing the object with a permanent magnetic moment. An object having permanent magnetism has fixed polarity, like a bar magnet, thus its magnetic moment changes direction when the object is moved.

Once an iron object has cooled below its Curie temperature, any subsequent movement of that object causes realignment of a small fraction of its atomic dipoles toward magnetic north. Such realignment induces a second much weaker magnetic dipole in the object. The magnetic moment of an induced dipole is not permanent and is always directed toward the Magnetic North Pole along Earth's field lines (see Figure 4.1a). An object's induced field may be less than one-tenth the strength of its permanent field (Breiner 1973: 9). The geometry of magnetic induction is illustrated in Figure 4.1b. Examples of induced anomalies over a spherical source, corresponding to various inclinations of Earth's magnetic field lines, are shown in Figure 4.1c.

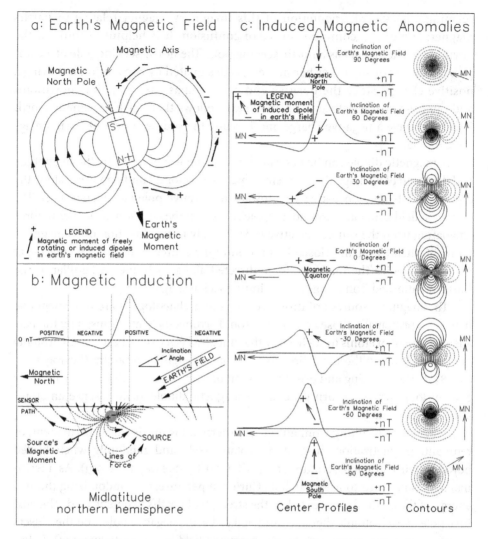

Figure 4.1 Characteristics of magnetism. Drawn by Robert Gearhart. Drawing c after Shekhtman 1999.

The ultimate goal of magnetic interpretation is to determine the sources of magnetic anomalies. Magnetic anomalies are local deviations in Earth's magnetic field. Many anomalies have a single ferromagnetic object as their source and thus have only one permanent magnetic field. Such anomalies are said to have simple sources. Other anomalies are caused by the magnetic interaction of two or more ferromagnetic objects. Anomalies caused by multiple objects are said to have complex sources, whether those objects are attached to one another or lying close enough so their magnetic fields interact. Examples of complex sources include shipwrecks and closely spaced accumulations of magnetic debris.

The polar orientation of an anomaly's magnetic contours is determined by the direction of its source's magnetic moment and by the magnetic hemisphere of the observer. In the northern magnetic hemisphere, an anomaly's magnetic moment points away from its maximum positive amplitude and toward its minimum negative amplitude, as detailed in Figure 4.1b. In Earth's southern magnetic hemisphere that pattern is reversed.

Every magnetic anomaly is the net result of its source's induced and permanent magnetic moments. The induced field, which always aligns with Earth's local field lines, is overshadowed by the stronger permanent field when an anomaly has a simple source. In such cases, the polar orientation of the magnetic anomaly will be determined by the magnetic moment of the source's permanent field. On the other hand, the induced field dominates observations over most complex sources. Each magnetic component of a shipwreck, or of any other complex source, has a unique permanent field that interacts with neighboring magnetic fields. As those permanent fields interact, they are reinforced by some of their neighbors, only to be canceled by others. The resultant magnetic field is a sum of all the vector forces occurring at every point in space occupied by the interacting fields. The net result of these interactions tends to be one of destructive interference, which minimizes the influence of permanent magnetization, leaving the normally weaker, induced magnetic field to dominate observations of a complex-source magnetic anomaly.

EVOLVING PERCEPTIONS OF SHIPWRECK ANOMALIES

Archaeologists have used magnetometers underwater since at least the mid-1960s (e.g., Breiner and MacNaughton 1965; Clausen 1966; Hall 1966), but until the advent of desktop contour-mapping software, most researchers based their magnetic interpretations on two-dimensional data profiles, commonly referred to as "strip charts." Strip charts showed researchers a cross-sectional view of magnetic anomalies, while plan view maps illustrated the horizontal relationships between strip chart anomalies. The term "anomaly" as used in early literature usually implied a magnetic deflection on a single strip chart.

Use of contour plots by marine archaeologists began by the mid-1970s and gradually found more common usage from the mid-1980s through the early 1990s. Today, contour maps or surface terrain models are used almost exclusively to illustrate archaeological magnetometer surveys. J. Barto Arnold and Carl Clausen were among the first archaeologists to illustrate marine magnetometer surveys as contour maps (Arnold 1974; Clausen and Arnold 1975). Based on their contoured magnetometer survey of the *San Esteban* (41KN10) and on earlier work by Clausen (1965, 1966), they concluded that the typical magnetic signature of a wood-hulled sailing vessel "will consist of a central area of magnetic distortion characterized by a number of intense and generally localized anomalies surrounded and, depending upon the depth and dispersion of the wreck in some instances, interspersed by scattered smaller magnetic disturbances" (Clausen and Arnold 1975: 78).

Digital data collection and contour mapping did not become standard procedure for marine archaeologists for several more years, and they were adopted only gradually. In the meantime, many researchers continued to interpret significance based on strip chart anomalies in the context of what was learned from the *San Esteban* and other verified shipwrecks. A common early criterion for potential archaeological significance of an anomaly was proximity to other anomalies. Anomaly clusters were viewed as potential shipwrecks, and isolated anomalies often were interpreted as debris. Arnold (1982: 56) stated that "the pattern of anomalies on adjoining survey tracks (spaced 50 m apart) is the key to identifying significant anomalies and distinguishing them from those far more numerous anomalies caused by isolated iron debris, which often show up on only one track."

A study of historic shipwrecks and magnetic anomalies in the Gulf of Mexico, conducted by Ervan Garrison et al. (1989: 2:223), summarized common archaeological perceptions of anomalies over shipwrecks and debris. The authors distilled observations by many archaeologists down to a list of several anomaly characteristics that they believed would allow one to confidently differentiate shipwrecks from modern ferromagnetic debris. Anomaly patterns of historic shipwrecks were said to include multiple amplitude peaks of differing magnitudes spread over an area greater than 10,000 m^2 (2.5 acres), gentle gradients, and a linear association with anomalies on adjacent transects. Debris anomalies were characterized as typically having single amplitude peaks covering an area of less than 10,000 m^2, steep gradients, and no alignment of anomalies on adjacent lines.

Many other archaeologists have attempted to characterize the differences between the anomalies of shipwrecks and debris. Several researchers have used the terms "multicomponent" or "complex" to describe a typical wreck anomaly, reminiscent of the fact that shipwreck anomalies, as observed on strip charts, often exhibit multiple dipoles as well as unpaired monopoles. In general, such efforts have added nuances to the basic perception of shipwreck anomalies, summarized by Garrison et al. (1989) above as relatively large features comprising multiple amplitude peaks.

The purpose here is not to exhaustively summarize earlier works, but to move beyond them. Even a casual review of recent archaeological survey reports will reveal that magnetic data interpretation has changed little over the past two decades or so. On the one hand, there remains a widely held belief that no anomaly can safely be written off as insignificant on the basis of magnetic data alone, while on the other hand, archaeologists recognize it is not always economically feasible for divers to investigate every anomaly. Archaeologists realize the need to prioritize anomalies regarding their potential for significance, yet they often do so based on personal experience rather than objective criteria.

Shipwreck Anomalies Today

Previous attempts to characterize magnetic signatures of shipwrecks and debris have been based on relatively few shipwreck examples illustrated in any single publication. What has been lacking is a sufficiently broad comparison of verified shipwreck anomalies recorded and illustrated in a consistent fashion. It is difficult to conduct meaningful comparisons between anomalies illustrated as strip charts and those reported as contour maps. It is even more problematic to analyze anomalies based on written descriptions of their characteristics. Technological innovations over the past two decades, including improved magnetometers, the creation of the Global Positioning System, compact portable computers, high-capacity data storage media, and a vast array of computer software, have facilitated a more expansive approach to characterization of shipwreck and debris magnetic signatures.

Over the past several years, the Cultural Resources Division of PBS&J (now Atkins) has assembled a collection of magnetic anomalies recorded over verified shipwrecks and debris sources in an effort to build a data set useful for the comparisons alluded to above. As of this writing, anomalies for 29 shipwrecks (Table 4.1) and numerous debris objects have been added to this data set.[2] A representative sample of anomaly contour maps, including 10 shipwrecks and 16 debris sources, is illustrated in Figure 4.2. The contour interval is 5 nanoTesla (nT). The sign of amplitude peaks is indicated by line style. Solid contour lines indicate positive amplitude, and dashed lines represent negative values. Anomalies sharing a common scale are grouped together. Arrows adjacent to anomalies indicate the approximate directions of their magnetic moments in the horizontal plane. The locations of hulls are indicated when known. Magnetic sources of the debris anomalies illustrated in Figure 4.2b are identified in Table 4.1.

The 29 shipwrecks in Table 4.1 encompass a wide variety of hull compositions, propulsion systems, ages, and depositional environments. Vessels of wood, iron, steel, and concrete are represented. Propulsion systems include sail, steam-driven paddlewheels and propellers, oil and diesel screws, and towed or pushed barges. These vessels range in age from the mid-sixteenth to the mid-twentieth century. Wreck environments range from high-energy to low-energy conditions, including harbor entrances, barrier-island surf zones, beaches, marsh, oyster reefs, open bay, and the Gulf of Mexico. These vessels variously stranded, foundered, experienced boiler explosions, burned, were partially demolished, and/or were salvaged. Several anomaly characteristics of shipwrecks and debris may be compared and contrasted from inspection of Table 4.1 and Figure 4.2.

Horizontal Dimensions

There is a broad range in the horizontal dimensions of shipwreck and debris anomalies.[3] Most debris anomalies shown in Figure 4.2b are not any larger than anomalies over wood-hulled sailing ships or wood-hulled steamboats. On the other hand, there is a 15-fold difference between the minimum anomaly width of the smallest

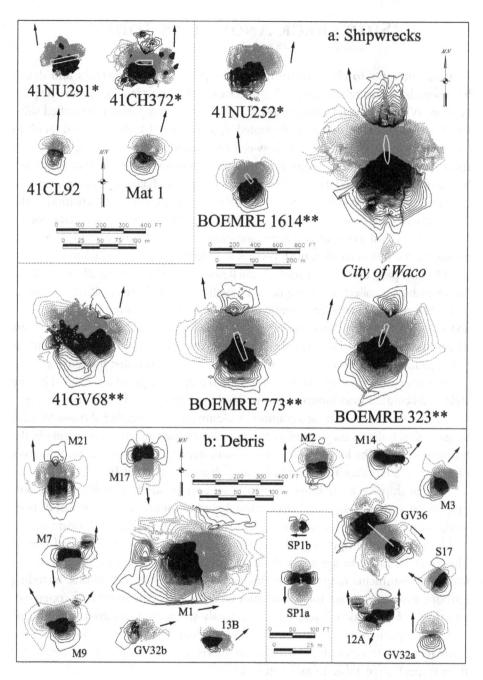

Figure 4.2 Magnetic anomalies of shipwrecks and debris. Drawn by Robert Gearhart
*Data reproduced with the kind permission of the U.S. Army Corps of Engineers,
Galveston District. ** Data reproduced with the kind permission of the BOEMRE, Gulf
of Mexico OCS Region.

Table 4.1 Anomalies of twenty-nine shipwrecks and sixteen debris sources

Shipwreck	Magnetic Moment Direction (deg)*	Min. Ampl. (nT)	Max. Ampl. (nT)	Min. Line Spacing** (m)	Date Lost, Hull Material, Propulsion, Dimensions (ft)
41CF125	7	−88	108	est. 20	Unknown, wood, sail, 88 × 20
41CL92	3	−113	78	22	e.19th-c., wood, sail, est. 50–70
Leaning Mast	15	−77	156	22	c. 1868, wood?, sail?, unknown
41NU291	−9	−1,333	3,358	23	1845, wood, steam, 125 × 18
41GV151	4	−839	509	25	1863, wood, steam, 213 × 34
Mat 1	14	−158	108	28	e.19th-c., wood, sail, est. 50–70
41CH372	1	−3,258	4,838	31	c. 1970, steel, diesel, 83 × 18
Perseverance	−11	−1,904	4,259	32	1856, wood, steam, unknown
41GV165	−10	−314	973	38	c. 1936, wood, unknown, 146 × 33
BOEMRE Site 344	−9	−267	396	41	1846, wood, steam, 161 × 23
Mary Conley***	8	−310	705	est. 41	1873, wood, steam, 137 × 28
41KN10***	−1	−95	125	45	1554, wood, sail, unknown
41JF65	−18	−1,893	4,123	est. 57	1864, wood, steam, 210 × 40
BOEMRE Site 1614	−7	−2,698	2,562	69	unknown, steel, barge, 89 × 30
41NU252	8	−403	653	72	1876, iron, steam, 234 × 33
BOEMRE Site 417	13	−2,757	4,726	80	1947, steel, diesel?, 165 × 47
41NU292	−10	−3,148	3,253	90	1920, wood, barge, 282 × 46
41GV143	26	−6,197	9,050	97	1865, wood, steam, 182 × 23

(continued)

Table 4.1 (*continued*)

Shipwreck	Magnetic Moment Direction (deg)*	Min. Ampl. (nT)	Max. Ampl. (nT)	Min. Line Spacing** (m)	Date Lost, Hull Material, Propulsion, Dimensions (ft)
41GV68	11	−2,425	3,170	109	1863, iron, steam, 210 × 34
BOEMRE Site 773	−8	−4,691	10,264	135	1954, steel, barge, 240 × 50
BOEMRE Site 15170	−15	−615	1,845	140	1924, steel, steam screw, 204 × 32
BOEMRE Site 432	−1	−4,100	11,700	140	1942, steel, diesel, 425 × 57
BOEMRE Site 323	13	−4,328	5,888	157	unknown, steel, diesel, 220 × 30
City of Waco	−9	−7,947	9,031	170	1875, iron, steam, 242
41GV102	21	−4,065	4,843	170	1922, concrete, diesel?, 421
BOEMRE Site 328	10	−5,625	30,425	330	1942, steel, diesel, 574 × 72
BOEMRE Site 15306	12	−341	347	—	unknown, steel, diesel?, 65 × 15
King Philip	—	−113	258	—	1878, wood, sail, 182 × 36
Reporter	—	−93	283	—	1902, wood, sail, 141 × 34

Debris (Figure 4.2b)

M21	Pipe; 41 × 2 ft	12A	1-inch braided cable; >30 ft
M17	Cable; >20 ft long	13B	42 × 2 ft pipe; 70 ft cable; 3 ft iron
M2	Pipe; 33 × 2 ft	GV32b	Cable of GV32a; east–west
M14	Pipe; 6 ft × 5 in	M9	Pipe frame; 41 × 15 ft
M3	Pipe; 6-inch diameter	M7	Pipe; 32 ft × 6 in
GV36	Pipe; 150 ft; position overlain	M1	7 dredge pipes; one vertical
S17	Pipe; 17 ft	SP1a	Cable; 4 ft; north–south orientation

Table 4.1 (*continued*)

Shipwreck	Magnetic Moment Direction (deg)*	Min. Ampl. (nT)	Max. Ampl. (nT)	Min. Line Spacing** (m)	Date Lost, Hull Material, Propulsion, Dimensions (ft)
GV32a		41 × 2 ft pipe; multiple cables		SP1b	Cable of SP1a; single coil

*Degrees variance from Magnetic North (negative = west; positive = east). **Minimum survey line interval (m) to guarantee detection on two adjacent transects. ***Not surveyed by PBS&J.

wood-hulled sailing vessel in Table 4.1 and that of the largest steel tanker, which is over 0.4 mile (0.64 km) across. Despite this fact, size does not seem a reliable indicator of a vessel's construction material or mode of propulsion for anomalies smaller than about 200 m across. Discovery of large shipwrecks is relatively easy, because their anomalies are detectable on several adjacent survey transects and their sheer size stands well above that of most debris concentrations. Very large wrecks also tend to have ferrous metal hulls that remain visible to sonar for a long time.

The smallest of shipwreck anomalies are the most difficult to detect and tend to correlate with the oldest wrecks in the data set. The smallest complete anomaly of a shipwreck in Table 4.1, 41CL92, is the wreck of an early-nineteenth-century sailing vessel. The portion of the site investigated by divers in 2004 measured roughly 23 by 52 ft (7 by 15.9 m). The site is characterized by a large collection of concreted artifacts, iron bar stock, and pig iron ballast. No intact hull remains have been found. Based on historic research and evidence from the artifact assemblage, the vessel could be the 67-foot New Orleans schooner *Hannah Elizabeth*, which sank in 1835, or the Mexican naval sloop *General Bustamante*, which sank in 1830 (Borgens 2004).

Recognizing potential small shipwrecks from magnetic data is complicated by the fact that debris produces anomalies in the same size range. Garrison et al. (1989: 2:223) characterized shipwreck anomalies as larger than 10,000 m²; however, that would exclude the smallest 15 shipwreck anomalies listed in Table 4.1, including all of the wood-hulled sailing vessels and all but one wood-hulled steamboat. Site 41CL92 covers an area of 1,580 m² (0.4 acre) out to the 5-nT contour. The largest shipwreck anomaly in Table 4.1, the tanker *Sheherazade* (MMS Site 328), is 180 times larger in area than the anomaly of 41CL92. It is apparent that in order to guarantee detection of shipwreck anomalies as small as 41CL92 on at least two adjacent transects, initial surveys must be conducted at intervals not exceeding 20 m. The state of Texas has recently mandated this interval for marine archaeological remote-sensing survey of waters within 3 nautical miles of the coast (Texas Administrative Code, Title 12, Part 2, Chapter 28), based in part on the research summarized in Table 4.1.

Amplitude

Amplitude appears of limited use for differentiating shipwrecks from debris, as substantial overlap exists between the ranges of shipwreck and debris anomaly amplitudes. Anomaly amplitude correlates reasonably well with type of hull material but poorly with either age or vessel size. The total peak-to-peak amplitude of shipwreck anomalies from Table 4.1 averages 270 nT for wood-hulled sailing vessels ($n = 6$); 5,020 nT for wood-hulled machine-powered vessels ($n = 7$); and 10,386 nT for iron- and steel-hulled vessels ($n = 12$). There is no overlap between anomaly amplitudes of wood-hulled sailing vessels and machine-powered wooden vessels represented in Table 4.1.

The anomaly amplitude of pre-1900 wrecks averages 3,766 nT, while post-1900 wrecks average 9,075 nT. The latter difference is accountable mainly by the prevalence of wooden hulls prior to 1900, but the overlap in amplitude range for the two periods is so great that this clearly is not a useful variable for assessing historic significance. There is a weak correlation between anomaly amplitude and vessel size, perhaps because amplitude depends so heavily on the distance between the sensor and the source. Even relatively small iron masses associated with wooden hulls can produce very large anomaly amplitude at close range.

Orientation

The magnetic moment direction of shipwreck anomalies differs in a consistent and predictable manner from a large percentage of simple-source debris anomalies. All of the shipwreck anomalies in Table 4.1 have magnetic moments typical of induced magnetic fields, whereas a high proportion of debris anomalies have magnetic moments indicative of permanent magnetic fields. Deviation from the northerly magnetic moment direction, common to all induced anomalies, has proven to be the single most powerful discriminator between simple-source anomalies and complex-source anomalies, including shipwrecks.

COMPLEX VERSUS SIMPLE ANOMALY SOURCES

The horizontal component of magnetic moment for the Table 4.1 shipwreck anomalies varies from magnetic north by an average of ±10° and does not exceed ±26°. In fact, the magnetic moment direction of most complex sources aligns closely with Earth's magnetic field. This tendency should increase in accordance with the number of magnetic components in the complex source and with the randomness of their orientations. As Sheldon Breiner (1973: 44) stated, "The more component parts an object has, the more these individual permanent magnetic moments tend to cancel, leaving only the induced magnetization." Conversely, the magnetic moment direction of simple sources is determined primarily by the orientation of the objects themselves.

The magnetic moment direction of most debris anomalies, shown in Figure 4.2b, do not follow the pattern typical of induced anomalies, indicating that they have simple sources dominated by permanent magnetism. Documenting the predominance of a source's permanent magnetism is all the evidence required to demonstrate that it is a simple source and therefore is unlikely to be a shipwreck. Knowing the precise orientation of a source or of its anomaly is unimportant to differentiating most simple sources from complex sources, including shipwrecks. It is sufficient to recognize that an anomaly's magnetic moment deviates substantially from the direction of magnetic north in order to eliminate it as a potential shipwreck anomaly. The only case in which the permanent anomaly of a simple source should resemble the induced anomaly of a complex source is when the magnetic moment of the simple source happens by chance to point roughly in the direction of magnetic north.

Certain complex-source debris anomalies actually behave as if they were caused by simple sources in that their magnetic moment does not point toward magnetic north. This occurs when the elements comprising a complex source are patterned in a nonrandom fashion. A good example is braided steel cable. When a single length of cable is arranged in a linear pattern or as a single coil (Figure 4.2b; anomalies SP1a and SP1b, respectively), it can behave as a simple source, even though its multiple strands technically qualify it as a complex source. This is presumed to occur as a result of the manufacturing process, such that all the strands share the same magnetic moment, thus reinforcing rather than canceling one another. But when cable is coiled in multiple loops or random tangles, it behaves as a complex source dominated by its induced anomaly. It is important to emphasize that this phenomenon is virtually impossible in a shipwreck site, as it would require a large percentage of a wreck's ferromagnetic components to have the same magnetic moment direction.

Reconciling Induced Shipwreck Anomalies with Earlier Observations

One might reasonably wonder how or whether the pattern of magnetic induction observed over so many verified shipwrecks agrees with descriptions of shipwreck anomalies by earlier researchers. Fortunately, the use of magnetic induction as an interpretive model does not preclude shipwrecks having complex, multicomponent anomalies with multiple dipoles and monopoles. Many intact shipwrecks have anomalies with more than one positive and one negative pole. Smaller amplitude peaks may be located north or south of the primary amplitude peaks. Five wreck anomalies in Figure 4.2a illustrate this characteristic. Such secondary amplitude peaks are not located over the main body of wreckage and might not indicate any buried materials whatsoever at their locations. The origin of secondary amplitude peaks is explained by Figure 4.1b.

A shipwreck anomaly can also exhibit multiple spatially discrete dipoles or monopoles if wreckage has scattered far enough from the main hull concentration that magnetic fields of some component parts no longer interact with their neighbors.

Such is likely the case for a vessel observed by the author that was damaged by explosions. The magnetic signature of USS *Westfield* (41GV151) consists of a large contiguous anomaly, centered over the main concentration of wreckage, surrounded by numerous discrete anomalies. The same pattern also may occur in high-energy environments or in cases of salvage. For example, the *San Esteban* was extensively salvaged by its Spanish owners and wrecked in an area subjected to repeated tropical storms. This site exhibited multiple small amplitude peaks centered on a prominent induced dipole (Clausen and Arnold 1975).

Finally, a shipwreck anomaly might have multiple dipoles or monopoles when the distance between the magnetometer sensor and the wreck is small. In close proximity to a shipwreck, localized amplitude peaks associated with large individual ferromagnetic components may contrast with the surrounding induced anomaly pattern of the shipwreck as a whole. The maximum distance at which such peaks are observed will vary according to the mass and orientation of their sources. This effect can be compounded when towing a magnetometer sensor without flotation in close proximity to a complex source. Large and sudden amplitude changes may occur as the sensor altitude fluctuates even slightly over the source in response to inevitable variations in tow speed.

Even an extreme example of a multicomponent shipwreck anomaly need not contradict the induced pattern described above for complex anomaly sources. The multiple dipoles and monopoles should be embedded in a broader underlying anomaly pattern reflecting the induced portion of a wreck's magnetic field. For example, the author conducted two surveys over the wreckage of USS *Westfield* (Figure 4.3), one at a sensor altitude of 10 ft (3 m) (Borgens et al. 2007) and another at a sensor altitude of 46 ft (14 m) (Gearhart et al. 2005). The anomaly produced 10 ft (3 m) above the wreck (Figure 4.3; gray contours) was extremely complex due to the presence of several large items, including a 9-inch Dahlgren cannon, portions of steam machinery, and several concentrations of ordnance at close range to the sensor. Yet underlying the local amplitude peaks associated with these objects was a broader induced anomaly pattern aligned with Earth's magnetic field. Most of the negative contours are situated north of positive contours. By comparison, the anomaly produced at 46 ft (14 m) (Figure 4.3; black contours) was a single, simple dipole aligned with Earth's field and with no hint of internal amplitude variations.

INTERPRETATION BASED ON
MAGNETIC INDUCTION

The study by Garrison et al. (1989) correctly predicted that shipwreck anomalies might be differentiated from debris based on the contrast between permanent and induced magnetization.

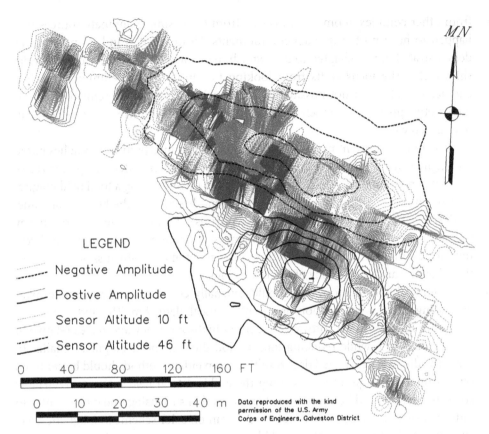

LEGEND

------- Negative Amplitude

——— Postive Amplitude

Sensor Altitude 10 ft

Sensor Altitude 46 ft

Data reproduced with the kind
permission of the U.S. Army
Corps of Engineers, Galveston District

Figure 4.3 Effects of sensor-source distance on shipwreck anomaly appearance (5-nT magnetic contours recorded over USS *Westfield*). Drawn by Robert Gearhart.

> The argument here would rely on the structural complexity of a shipwreck having a large or detectable inductive magnetization. Anomalies without this component could be classified as exclusively ferromagnetic features and by logical extension, debris. . . . this is an analytical approach that could improve the detection of and discrimination between classes of ferromagnetic materials and be used within the current methodology. (1989: 2:224)

Interpretation of anomalies based on the model of magnetic induction is a simple procedure that indeed fits quite well with the current method for processing and illustrating marine magnetic data from archaeological surveys (e.g., Gearhart 2002, 2004).

The goal of marine magnetic interpretation for decades has been to differentiate shipwrecks from debris. The interpretive method described here turns that idea upside down. The new goal is to differentiate debris from potential shipwrecks. The subtle change of wording makes a powerful difference in the possibilities. Those who argued that shipwrecks could not be differentiated from debris were correct in a sense, as there is still no proven interpretive method for separating shipwrecks from other complex anomaly sources or from those simple anomaly sources that happen to have northerly magnetic moments. However, it is indeed possible, as demonstrated in this chapter, to distinguish many debris anomalies from potential shipwrecks. The focus shifts from looking for shipwrecks to eliminating debris anomalies that could not possibly be shipwrecks. What should remain after this interpretive process is a much smaller list of potential shipwreck anomalies than one started with.

The most important parameter to consider when interpreting anomalies based on magnetic induction is the direction of magnetic moment. Measuring the precise magnetic moment direction of an anomaly is not possible using a total field magnetometer; however, estimating magnetic moment direction in the horizontal plane, as described above, will suffice for this purpose. Future refinement of survey methods could include direct measurement of anomaly magnetic moment direction, for example with a three-axis fluxgate magnetometer, which should improve the reliability and consistency of interpretations.

Prior to interpretation, one should diurnally correct the raw magnetometer data using either a base station or a mathematical algorithm. The author uses an algorithm in spreadsheet software to identify high-frequency anomalies relative to Earth's total field, while reducing long-period diurnal and geologic anomalies to zero. The diurnally corrected data resulting from either method should be centered on a common zero point representing the ambient total field intensity. Diurnally corrected data should be contoured at an interval of 5 nT using line type or color to indicate negative versus positive values. A common color scheme in magnetic literature uses red for positive values and blue for negative values. The location of every magnetic data point should be posted as an overlay on magnetic contours during analysis. This is essential when trying to determine whether an unidentified anomaly contradicts expectations for an induced magnetic field, because it allows one to visualize data gaps and thereby judge whether the contours are a reasonable representation of an anomaly's true shape.

Interpretation can proceed once the data have been prepared in the fashion described above. In practice, it is slow and unnecessary to measure the orientation of every anomaly to see which ones resemble the pattern expected for magnetic induction. Instead, it is quite effective to conduct analysis in a CAD or GIS environment by visually comparing an example of a verified shipwreck anomaly with each unidentified anomaly in one's data set (e.g., Gearhart 2004). The verified shipwreck anomaly selected for this purpose ideally should be representative of the smallest class of shipwreck anomalies, that of a wood-hulled sailing vessel, although the anomaly of a metal hull scaled to an appropriate small size would also work. Of course, if a researcher is searching only for a particular vessel of a larger size, the reference anomaly can be scaled up accordingly. The material of a hull and its contents affect an anomaly's size and amplitude more than its shape and orientation, as one can see from Figure 4.2 and Table 4.1. The reference anomaly also must represent a geographic location having a similar magnetic inclination as one's study area, as demonstrated in Figure 4.1c.

The anomaly chosen as one's model for interpretation should be used to create a digital image, such as a CAD cell, that can be overlain on unidentified anomalies, as described below. The author uses a contour map of 41CL92 (Figure 4.4) for this purpose, as it is the smallest complete anomaly in Table 4.1. Care must be taken to properly rotate and scale the model image to match the grid scale and orientation of the data set requiring interpretation.

Magnetic interpretation is as simple as juxtaposing the model anomaly with each unidentified anomaly in a data set. Unidentified anomalies of sufficient size that do not contradict the polarity of the model anomaly must be considered potential shipwrecks, and treated accordingly, until additional magnetic survey or ground-truthing disproves such interpretations. Unidentified anomalies that clearly could not resemble the model anomaly of a verified shipwreck, even if additional survey filled the data voids, can be classified as simple-source debris and removed from further consideration. It is helpful to track the progress of analysis in GIS or CAD by marking each anomaly as it is interpreted. This is especially helpful in magnetically busy areas and will ensure that no anomalies are excluded from analysis.

Several examples of this technique are illustrated in Figure 4.4. The anomalies illustrated in frames (a)–(i) of Figure 4.4 are based on a data set acquired over the wood-hulled sailing vessel designated as site 41CL92. The central anomaly (Figure 4.4e) was contoured using the entire 41CL92 data set and shows the locations of every magnetometer reading acquired over the site. The surrounding eight anomalies (frames [a]–[d] and [f]–[i]; black contours) were contoured from unique subsets of the 41CL92 data, sampled along the hypothetical survey transects shown, in order to illustrate how a site's magnetic appearance can vary based on survey orientation and chance. The anomaly in Figure 4.4j represents an unidentified anomaly that would be classified as debris based on this interpretive method. Each anomaly in Figure 4.4 is overlain on an image of the complete 41CL92 anomaly in order to demonstrate the technique for interpretation described above.

Contours of the sampled 41CL92 anomalies illustrate eight unique views of a verified shipwreck anomaly as it would appear when surveyed along various headings with a 30 m separation between transects. If any of the eight sampled 41CL92 anomalies were observed without prior knowledge of a shipwreck at this location, each might easily be misidentified as debris using another interpretive process. However, comparison with the 41CL92 anomaly requires that they be interpreted as potential shipwreck anomalies, because the distribution of their positive and negative amplitudes is consistent with that of a verified shipwreck anomaly of similar size. On the other hand, if the distribution of positive and negative amplitudes from any unidentified anomaly contradicts the polar orientation of a verified shipwreck anomaly, as demonstrated in Figure 4.4j, then the unidentified anomaly can be classified as debris and removed from further consideration. Substantial improvement in the confidence of interpretations can be achieved by a modest investment in conducting higher-resolution magnetometer surveys over ambiguous anomalies, such

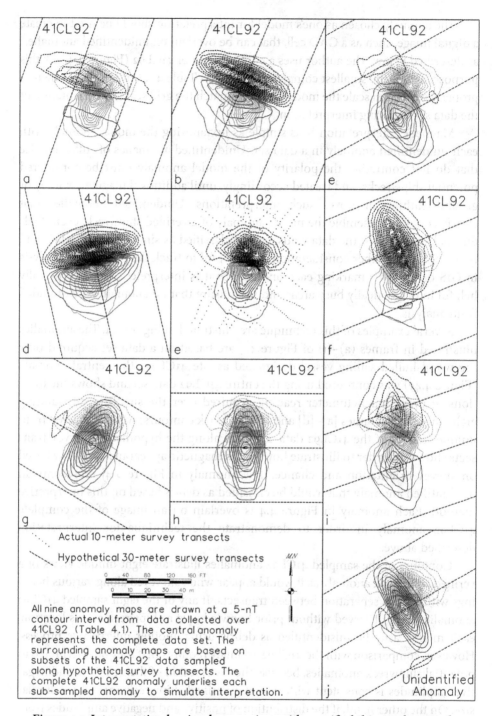

All nine anomaly maps are drawn at a 5-nT contour interval from data collected over 41CL92 (Table 4.1). The central anomaly represents the complete data set. The surrounding anomaly maps are based on subsets of the 41CL92 data sampled along hypothetical survey transects. The complete 41CL92 anomaly underlies each sub-sampled anomaly to simulate interpretation.

Figure 4.4 Interpretation by visual comparison with a verified shipwreck anomaly. Reproduced with the kind permission of Atkins.

as the bidirectional 10 by 10 m grid of the original 41CL92 survey (Figure 4.4e), prior to finalizing one's archaeological recommendations.

This method is not conducive to the interpretation of some anomalies. For example, extensive contiguous areas of anomalous magnetic readings can mask the presence of shipwreck anomalies, especially when the sensor-source distance is small. In magnetically busy areas, where individual anomalies cannot be viewed in isolation from their neighbors, differentiation of simple-source debris from potential shipwrecks may not be possible based on magnetometer data alone. Such areas must be judged based on other parameters: for example, the density of historic vessel traffic; historic waterfront development; navigation hazards such as reefs, bars, rocks, or shoals; and the prevalence of modern development that could reasonably account for the anomalies. A conservative treatment of such areas, in the absence of contrary evidence, would assume that a historic wreck might be present.

CONCLUSION

Magnetism is a predictable phenomenon that conforms to well-understood physical laws. Thus it should not be surprising that shipwreck and debris anomalies behave as predicted from the number and distribution of their ferromagnetic components. A simple debris source produces an anomaly dominated by its permanent magnetic field. As sources of increasing complexity are considered, the role of the induced magnetic field quickly overtakes that of permanent magnetic fields in determining the orientation of anomalies with respect to magnetic north. This tendency logically should increase in direct proportion both to the number and randomness of ferromagnetic objects comprising a complex source. Debris concentrations range in complexity from two to many interacting sources. On the high end of source complexity, shipwrecks and debris concentrations may produce indistinguishable anomalies.

It seems a reasonable assumption that orientations of debris on the seafloor should have a statistically random distribution. Since the magnetic moment direction of a simple source is independent of Earth's magnetic field direction, it follows that orientations of simple-source debris anomalies also should be random. Thus, it should be possible to distinguish most simple-source debris anomalies from shipwreck anomalies, which have north-pointing magnetic moments. Any anomaly with a magnetic moment deviating significantly from magnetic north is almost certainly not associated with a shipwreck. The greatest deviation from magnetic north observed in shipwreck anomalies from Table 4.1 is about 26°.

Assume for the sake of argument that by following the methods described above, all simple-source anomalies with magnetic moments varying from magnetic north by greater than ±45° could be differentiated successfully from most complex-source anomalies, including virtually all shipwreck anomalies. This would include all simple-source debris anomalies with magnetic moments pointing between 45° and 315° (magnetic), or three-fourths of the compass circle. Again assuming a random distribution of debris orientations, this would mean that 75% of all simple-source anomalies could be confidently excluded from further consideration. The primary limitation to achieving this level of success is survey line spacing. Experience suggests that decreasing survey line spacing from 30 m to 20 m, for example, greatly increases the percentage of anomalies that can be classified as insignificant using this method. Conducting even higher-resolution surveys over ambiguous anomalies further improves results with minimal expense.

It does not appear possible, at present, to differentiate between shipwreck anomalies and other complex-source anomalies. Depending on their size, many complex-source debris anomalies and something less than 25% of simple-source debris anomalies may bear sufficient resemblance to shipwreck anomalies that one must consider them as potential historic sites to be avoided or ground-truthed. Future research topics that might improve that situation include deployment of broad, multisensor arrays to economically reduce survey line spacing and to conduct high-resolution surveys over anomalies; analyzing magnetic gradients and kurtosis, or peak shape, of shipwreck and debris anomalies; routine use of a three-axis fluxgate magnetometer to accurately determine the magnetic moment direction of anomalies; and controlled experimental surveys designed to discover and quantify useful interpretive parameters. But for now, archaeologists must be content with distinguishing between possible shipwrecks and a large proportion of simple-source debris anomalies.

It seems that earlier researchers were correct, to varying degrees, in their assessments of shipwreck anomalies. It is true that when a shipwreck remains intact, what Keith Muckelroy (1978) would call a continuous wreck pattern, it produces a single contiguous anomaly, but when a wreck is widely dispersed, or discontinuous, it can produce multiple anomalies. It is equally true that a shipwreck can produce either a simple dipolar anomaly or a complex anomaly with multiple dipoles and monopoles, depending on one's observation distance (see Figure 4.3). And for now, at least, one cannot distinguish between the anomaly produced by a shipwreck and one produced by a similarly complex concentration of magnetic debris. But most importantly, none of these statements contradict the facts that shipwreck anomalies can be characterized by their induced magnetic fields and are distinguishable from a significant proportion of simple-source anomalies.

The data summarized in Table 4.1 have implications beyond interpretive methods, regarding how magnetometer surveys are designed. The range of horizontal dimensions for shipwreck anomalies is much broader than suggested by Garrison et al. (1989). Nearly half of all shipwreck anomalies, including most wooden vessels, cover an area smaller than 10,000 m² at the 5 nT contour. Thus, the dimensions of most anomalies of wood-hulled shipwrecks overlap the size range of many debris anomalies. These facts must be carefully considered when selecting line spacing for magnetometer surveys. The probability of detecting 41CL92, the smallest complete anomaly of a shipwreck from Table 4.1, on two adjacent survey lines at a level of 5 nT is 50% for lines spaced 50 m apart and 83% for a 30 m transect interval. Line spacing would need to tighten to 22 m or less to guarantee detection of this site on two adjacent lines.

Detection of historic shipwrecks is the highest priority of archaeological marine magnetic data interpretation, but there is undoubtedly room for improvement in the level and consistency of detection. Most importantly, the basis for assessing magnetic anomaly significance must be firmly rooted in empiricism in order to improve the objectivity of data interpretation. A fresh dialogue is needed between archaeologists from academia, business, and government to seek a common understanding of the issues and to agree on standards and guidelines that will guarantee a consistently high level of protection for historic shipwrecks.

NOTES

1. The ideas discussed in this chapter are based on research with shipwrecks but are also relevant to other types of archaeological sites, provided they contain magnetic materials.

2. All but two of these shipwreck anomalies were surveyed by PBS&J. Data from the *Mary Conley* was provided courtesy of the Texas Historical Commission, and data from the *San Esteban*, 41KN10, is based on a contour map of the site published by Clausen and Arnold (1975).

3. Figure 4.2a illustrates the six largest wreck anomalies at half the scale of all other anomalies in order to make them fit on the same page. Table 4.1 is sorted by minimum shipwreck anomaly width.

REFERENCES

Arnold, J. B., III. 1974. The archeological applications of computerized contour and perspective plotting. *Newsletter of Computer Archaeology* 10: 1–7.
———. 1982. *A Matagorda Bay magnetometer survey and site test excavation project*. Texas Antiquities Committee Publication 9. Austin: Texas Historical Commission.
Borgens, A. A. 2004. Analysis of the Pass Cavallo shipwreck assemblage, Matagorda Bay, Texas. MA thesis, Texas A&M University.
Borgens, A. A., D. Hudson, D. Jones, and R. Gearhart. 2007. *Marine remote-sensing survey of the proposed Texas City Dike groins and the additional close-order survey and archival investigation for the wreck of the USS* Westfield *for historic properties investigations, Texas City Channel improvements project, Galveston County, Galveston Bay, Texas*. Prepared for the U.S. Army Corps of Engineers, Galveston District, by PBS&J, Austin, TX.
Breiner, S. 1973. *Applications manual for portable magnetometers*. Sunnyvale, CA: Geometrics.

Breiner, S., and K. G. MacNaughton. 1965. The applications of magnetometers in underwater archeology. Paper presented at the Second Conference on Underwater Archeology, 15 April, Toronto.Clausen, C. J. 1965. *A 1715 Spanish treasure ship.* Contributions of the Florida State Museum, Social Sciences 12. University of Florida, Gainesville.

———. 1966. The proton magnetometer: Its use in plotting the distribution of ferrous components of a shipwreck site as an aid to archeological interpretation. *Florida Anthropologist* 19: 77–84.

Clausen, C. J., and J. B. Arnold III. 1975. Magnetic delineation of individual shipwreck sites: A new control technique. *Bulletin of the Texas Archeological Society* 46: 69–86.

Garrison, E. G., C. P. Giammona, F. J. Kelly, A. R. Tripp, and G. A. Wolff. 1989. *Historic shipwrecks and magnetic anomalies of the northern Gulf of Mexico: Reevaluation of archaeological resource management zone 1.* Vol. 2: *Technical narrative.* OCS Study, MMS 89-0024. U.S. Department of the Interior, Minerals Management Service, Gulf of Mexico OCS Region.

Gearhart, R. L., II. 2002. Technologies and strategies for locating submerged cultural resources in the Galveston District: Symposium contribution for *Current Issues in the Management of Submerged Cultural Resources in Texas.* Society for Historical Archaeology, 35th Conference on Historical and Underwater Archaeology, Mobile, AL.

———. 2004. Marine remote sensing: The next generation. Symposium presented at the Society for Historical Archaeology, 37th Conference on Historical and Underwater Archaeology, St. Louis, MO.

Gearhart, R. L., II, D. S. Jones, Jeffrey Enright, Jenna Enright, and T. Summerville. 2005. *Close-order remote-sensing survey of five anomalies and proposed channel modifications for historic properties investigations, Texas City Channel improvements, Galveston Bay, Texas.* Prepared for the U.S. Army Corps of Engineers, Galveston District, by PBS&J, Austin, TX.

Hall, E. T. 1966. The use of the proton magnetometer in underwater archaeology. *Archaeometry* 9: 32–44.

Muckelroy, K. 1978. *Maritime archaeology.* Cambridge: Cambridge University Press.

Murphy, L., A. R. Saltus Jr., T. S. Mistovich, B. H. Tew, and R. Walling. 1981. *Phase II identification and evaluation of submerged cultural resources in the Tombigbee River Multi-Resource District, Alabama and Mississippi.* Report of Investigations 17. Office of Archaeological Research, University of Alabama.

Pearson, C. E., B. L. Guevin, and A. R. Saltus Jr. 1991. *Remote-sensing survey of the Lower Pearl and West Pearl Rivers, Louisiana and Mississippi.* Prepared for the U.S. Army Corps of Engineers, Vicksburg District, by Coastal Environments, Inc., Baton Rouge, LA.

Serway, R. A. 1992. *Physics for scientists and engineers.* 3rd ed. Philadelphia: Saunders.

Shekhtman, R. 1999. *Magnetic dipole modeling applet.* Online at www.eos.ubc.ca/ubcgif/resources/magdipole/dipoleapp.html. Vancouver, BCE: Geophysical Inversion Facility, Department of Earth and Ocean Sciences, University of British Columbia. Accessed 23 January 2009.

U.S. Department of Commerce. 1906–1947. *Merchant Vessels of the United States* (formerly *Annual List of Merchant Vessels of the United States*). U.S. Department of Commerce, National Oceanic and Atmospheric Administration, National Ocean Service Bureau of Navigation. Washington, DC: Government Printing Office.

U.S. Department of the Interior. 2007. Archaeological Resource Information Database. New Orleans: Bureau of Ocean Energy Management, Regulation and Enforcement, Gulf of Mexico OCS Region.

U.S. Treasury Department. 1876–1899. *Life-Saving Service*. Annual Reports of the Operations of the United States Life-Saving Service. Washington, DC: Government Printing Office.

Watts, G. P., Jr. 1986. *An archaeological reconnaissance of proposed offshore borrow sites near Ocean City, Maryland*. Report submitted to Maryland Geological Survey by Tidewater Atlantic Research, Washington, NC.

CHAPTER 5

SEARCH AND DOCUMENTATION OF UNDERWATER ARCHAEOLOGICAL SITES

MICHAEL C. TUTTLE

INTRODUCTION

SURVEY, whether to establish baseline data or to define the spatial parameters of an individual site, is a scientific process and fundamental to archaeological data collection. Archaeology is an inherently destructive activity; it is the process of studying cultural material by disassembling it in situ. This process leaves an investigated area altered, sometimes with little or no trace of the original examined material remaining. Thus, prior to any disturbance or excavation of an archaeological site a thorough predisturbance examination should be conducted in order to provide information for the development of an effective excavation plan. The primary aim of survey is to collect data as efficiently and as accurately as possible. There are an array of methods and tools available to accomplish these goals. Data gathered during a survey will inform all following archeological endeavors.

A relatively young scientific discipline, underwater archaeology is still developing and maturing. Through its development, both potential benefits and problems have been encountered while conducting surveys in an aqueous environment

(Cleator 1973; Muckelroy 1978). Many of the tools used in underwater archaeological surveys were creatively adapted from other disciplines (e.g., hydrographic survey, oil exploration) to aid in data collection. Additionally, many of the newer technologies adapted have changed and are still changing rapidly due to the computerization and miniaturization. These changing technologies increase efficiency, which in turn facilitates the process of maritime archaeological surveys.

The levels of technology available for investigations are as variable as the objectives of surveys. For some basic-level investigations, the human eye, a pencil, and a map are all that is required to begin collecting meaningful data. The American Civil War ironclad USS *Cairo* was discovered in the 1950s by two men in a rowboat, armed only with a compass and historical data (Delgado 2001). Later in the decade, the Swedish warship *Vasa* (lost 1628 CE) was located by an amateur maritime historian with a homemade core sampler and a harbor chart (Burgess 1980). Today such simple techniques rarely produce dramatic results; rather, a survey may include numerous pieces of expensive remote-sensing gear, deployed from a large vessel far out at sea, integrated with computers utilizing the latest in navigation software while acquiring instantaneous positioning fixes from a collection of satellites orbiting Earth via a Global Positioning System (GPS). Numerous wreck sites continue to be discovered all over the world using these techniques. Low-tech or high-, through all levels of survey, two themes remain constant: accurate positioning and data recording.

MOTIVATION

A primary step in conducting any archaeological survey is deciding why a survey is required. What is the motivation? Is it to find a specific historic wreck site or submerged relict landforms, or to create an inventory of potential cultural resources in a particular area? Is the survey for research purposes, an educational exercise, or required by regulation? Where is the survey to be conducted: out at sea, near shore, or in a riverine or lacustrine setting? The answer to these questions, among other things, will determine how to proceed and which tools to use to attain optimum results.

COMPLETING A DESKTOP SURVEY

Prior to entering the field it makes good sense to complete desktop research, an in-office examination of pertinent available literature, in order to become familiar with the type of cultural material and environmental conditions that may be found in the area investigated and to develop a survey plan. Advance preparation in the office can save scarce time and resources in the field. Information available to a surveyor in the age of the Internet is almost limitless. Literature and documents may come from such august institutions as a nation's national archives or library to the local library down the street, from compiled shipwreck databases to general secondary histories of a region. Viewing maps and artwork or reviewing archaeological reports and historic newspapers may indicate the potential of cultural materials in an area. There is no excuse for going into the field without some prior information on the potential resources in the area of interest.

Prior to a survey of Orange Bay, St. Eustatius, Netherlands Antilles, in the 1980s, documentary evidence indicated that "yearly between two and four thousand ships were anchored in Orange Bay" (Nagelkerken 1988). Several suspected shipwreck sites were located as a result of the investigations. Archival evidence indicating a high traffic area corresponds to a potentially good place to conduct survey for historic resources compared to an area with little to no maritime commerce. Understanding an area's history and resource potential can aid in the interpretation of survey data. In addition to developing a cultural context for the area to be examined based on archival sources, one may also come across other forms of human activity that have impacted cultural material. Has the area been dredged, or has it been the site of a battle? One of these instances may remove cultural material, and the other may increase the likelihood of locating significant sites.

Another aspect of the present cultural environment is the legal structure for conducting archaeology. Many jurisdictions require permitting or notification to conduct work, whether for commercial, educational, or legally mandated purposes. Knowing the local regulations is a basic survey prerequisite. In 1964 Australia developed and implemented an act to protect historic shipwrecks; in time this legislation led to the Historic Shipwrecks Act of 1976 (Henderson 1986; Staniforth and Nash 2006; see Staniforth in this volume). In 1981, Muckelroy produced a small handbook, including legal actions, to take when finding a wreck in Britain. Each state in the United States is obligated to develop its own laws for submerged cultural heritage under the Abandoned Shipwreck Act of 1987. Many nations have institutes or government agencies to aid in the protection underwater resources, such as Mexico's Subdireccion de Arqueologia Subacuatica (SAS) (see Luna Erreguerena in this volume). International institutions such as the International Council on Monuments and Sites (ICOMOS) and United Nations Educational, Scientific, and Cultural Organization Convention on the Protection of the Underwater Cultural Heritage (UNESCO-CPUCH) (2001) are promoting and establishing guidelines and strategies for the protection of underwater cultural resources. There are regions with well-developed laws, regions developing standards and regulations, and areas where laws are yet to be determined. Wherever work is conducted, being ignorant of the local regulations is no excuse for potentially breaking the law, while being ignorant of mandated survey guidelines (such as the distance between remote-sensing survey lanes) could result in the need to repeat an entire survey.

In addition to understanding the cultural potential of a survey area, it is imperative to understand the physical environment. Rivers, lakes, cenotes, springs, near-shore areas, offshore areas, and reef and lagoons all have their own dynamic. For example, rivers in mountainous or hilly valleys generally stay within their banks, while rivers in plains or deltas can be highly sinuous and radically change course through the process of meandering. The implications for conducting underwater survey are immense: for instance, a river being surveyed may not follow the same course as it did when a shipwrecked vessel was lost, therefore survey time and resources may be wasted. The geomorphology of river systems are an extreme example, but illustrative of the importance of environmental considerations.

After the motivation for the survey has been settled, legal requirements are understood, and an initial investigation of pertinent archival materials has been consulted to create a historical and environmental context for the investigation, research can move into the "field." The fieldwork phase is often one of the most resource intensive and expensive tasks of any archaeological survey. Survey in an aquatic environment can multiply these expenses depending on logistics, equipment, and weather conditions. Therefore, for the efficient use of project resources, it is imperative prior to initiating fieldwork to consider the several factors that will go into completing a survey.

POSITIONING

There are numerous tools that can be used for determining a specific position. The most basic is the human eye. A site can be positioned by a transit, the visual alignment of two objects. The objects chosen for a transit should be permanent structures, and the more transits taken from a site, the better. Recording compass bearings of the transits adds another piece of data that increases the quality of the position. An observer need only record the transits information in a table. When drawn or overlaid on a map, one's position is where the transits intersect. A photograph or digital image of the transits is another way to record the position.

Other equipment used for positioning are surveyors' tools: theodolites, optical transits, and total stations. Each of these tools is used to measure horizontal and vertical angles of a distant object. A theodolite and optical transit work with simple optics. A total station incorporates the functions of a theodolite and transit and also has the capacity to determine distance measurements through a range-finding mechanism. Total stations have the capacity to record ranges of over a kilometer. Laser range finders can also serve as a modest tool adapted for positioning. Inexpensive, these handheld devices can also have a range of over a kilometer, and many have integrated compasses so that both range and bearing measurements can be taken. Taking observations from a benchmark or a datum, a target can be sighted in and plotted out or overlaid on a map or navigation chart. Range-finding devises have some limitations; for example, at their far ranges accuracy degrades and can be off by a number of meters.

While conducting near-shore survey from a vessel that is in constant motion, taking transits toward land might be impossible. Shore stations, on the other hand, composed of an individual with an instrument such as a theodolite or total station, can plot a vessel's course through the water. At least two shore stations are required to continually track the vessel; at a certain mark, called in via radio, the stations record the position of the vessel as an event. Positions interpolated between each event mark will provide the line of travel. At the end of a series of runs the events can be plotted to represent the track of the vessel.

Other than using visual methods, relying on angle measurements and time coordination, positioning can be accomplished by using radio waves. In the recent past, LORAN and mini-Ranger systems, shore-based radio beacons, were used for offshore applications to position a vessel at sea. Placed at known points, two beacons emit a signal at a predetermined time and frequency. A receiver on the survey vessel interrogates the time characteristics between the signals and determines a position.

Today, shore-based systems have been surpassed by Global Positioning System. Based on the same fundamentals as shore-based systems and radio signal time difference, GPS uses a constellation of satellites in Earth orbit that provide continuous, worldwide positioning (National Space-Based Positioning, Navigation, and Timing Coordination Office 2009). GPS receivers are relatively inexpensive and accurate and can be integrated with computers and navigation software to keep a continuous record of where a vessel is and has been. Due to ease of use, accuracy, low cost, and availability, GPS should be considered the positioning system of choice. Differential GPS (DGPS), although more complex and costly, should also be considered. There is some variability in the data signal received by a mobile unit, and one way to eliminate it is to set a base station over a known point and record the variations. By comparing the variation between the base station and a mobile unit, one can calibrate the signal, and the mobile position can be calculated with greater accuracy.

SWIM SEARCHES

In calm and clear waters, such as a small harbor, lagoon, or beach, a swim line survey can be completed. The area to be searched can be designated by buoys placed at known distances, and swimmers can complete survey transects by swimming between the buoys with just a mask, fins, and snorkel. The swimmers use slate (or Mylar attached to a clipboard) and pencil to record the data. The distance between transects will vary based on the water depth and visibility. There should always be some overlap; to ensure full coverage, swimmers should be able to observe over 100% of the width of a transect. The position of the buoys, the number of transects swum, and the direction the transects were swum in should be recorded and plotted on a map to create a record of the area examined.

Another variation on the swim line technique is the use range poles instead of buoys. Two poles set up on shore, one a distance behind the other, define a transect. A surface swimmer only needs to look up enough to keep the two range poles in line to complete a straight transect. Tides and current tend to push the swimmers, and they may find themselves swimming obliquely in order to perform a straight line. Swim line is an effective technique if there are several individuals available for survey.

If the water in an area is not clear enough for surface swimmers to see the sea-floor, the addition of SCUBA gear and a compass can overcome this impediment. With the use of SCUBA equipment, the surveyor can be in close proximity to the seafloor to make detailed observations. For good positioning the diver should take a compass bearing from the starting point to the end of the transect. While swim-ming along the seabed, the diver will have to be mindful to observe the bottom as well as a compass to stay on track. On reaching the desired end point, the diver moves to the next parallel transect and returns on reciprocal bearing ±180°. There are some factors that limit the effectiveness of this technique, such as current or tides that may prevent the diver from completing a straight transect.

If the waters to be surveyed are farther from land, where buoys, range poles, or compass navigation are of little to no use, towboarding may be the answer. This method is especially effective in reef environments where the waters are protected, clear, and shallow and the area to be covered is not wide. Required are a tow vessel (usually a small boat with outboard engines), a tow line, and a tow vehicle. Holding on to the tow vehicle, a rectangular or delta-shaped board with a tow-point attach-ment and handles, an observer is slowly pulled through the water. The observer being pulled by the boat just needs the simplest of equipment—mask, fins and snorkel—although SCUBA equipment can be useful in water that is turbid or deeper than bottom visibility allows.

A minimum of three individuals are required to safely conduct this technique: a boat pilot, someone to observe the swimmer and take notes, and the swimmer. Some form of positioning is needed to keep a record of the area that the vessel has traversed. Additionally, some form of communication system is required between the swimmer and observer to note when an object of interest is seen. Hand signals can be used to indicate the approximate location of a target for subsequent target identification.

PROBING

A simple and efficient method for examining subsurface features or defining the extent of a site is probing (Figure 5.1). This method can be employed both above and below water to determine the depth of burial of an object. A probe can be a simple

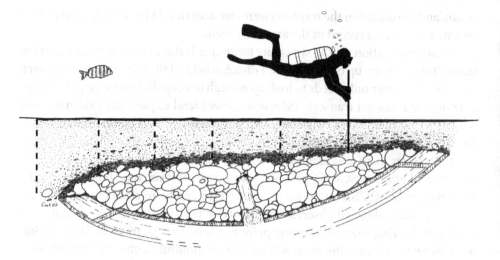

Figure 5.1 Diver probing beneath the seabed to determine the extent of a target.
Reproduced with the kind permission of Gregory Cook, Archaeology Institute,
University of West Florida.

rod that is manually inserted into the sediment. A point filed on one end and a grip
at the other make insertion and extraction easier. Another modification that greatly
increases the efficiency of a probe is a T-handle, a short section of material welded
to one end to form a "T." Iron round stock and rebar can be used for probes. Square
or rectangular bars may have the advantage of being slightly hardier, but they may
be more difficult to insert and extract.

There are some factors to consider in choosing a probe. Iron stock will have a
tendency to rust when used in salt water. Stainless steel will hold up better in salt
water but is more expensive. If probing is being done in conjunction with a metal
detector search, an iron probe may lead to some false readings, especially in low-
visibility conditions when the tools are in close proximity to each other. Thinner
stock has the tendency to bend and distort, while thicker stock is more robust but
takes more force to insert and extract. Probes can be any length, but ones longer
than 2 m (6 ft) will tend to bend or get distorted and are more difficult to handle.
Silts, sands, and clays are the best materials in which to use a probe. Pebbles, cobble,
and rocky areas are not recommended for probing, as the penetrating power is
inhibited by rock.

Another type of probe that is more complex but can attain quicker and deeper
penetration through denser material is a hydro-probe. Water sent through a small-
diameter pipe can easily cut through many materials. A small water pump, a hose,
some connectors, and pipe are all that is required for this useful tool. The water
pump can be set on land or deployed from a small craft, as long as there is access to
water via an intake hose. An outflow of 5–8 cm (2–3 in) can be reduced and coupled
to a hose, which should not be more than 5 cm (2 in) in diameter. The hose should be
plumbed into a valve that connects to a length of small-diameter pipe (approximately

1 cm [0.5 in]). The hose/valve/pipe interface should have a quick disconnect, such as a cam lock. If the probe becomes stuck, it is a simple procedure to de-cam the valve and direct a jet of water down around the pipe to dislodge it.

The probe should be of some robust material; copper, iron, or polyvinyl chloride (PVC). Each material has some advantages and disadvantages that must be taken into consideration based on the work environment. Copper tubing is light but expensive and may bend/break if too thin. Iron pipe is heavy and tends to rust, but is very robust and is easy to thread and connect to extending pieces. PVC is light and inexpensive but can crack and break after repeated bending, and the end can crack if it encounters hard surfaces too often. When the probe makes contact with material other than sediment, a distinct return should be felt, and the probe should cease to penetrate.

The water exiting the end of the probe drills a hole into the seabed, making for easy insertion. Usually the water flow returns up the outer sides of the piping, creating a wider hole and making extraction easy. On occasion, material may blow out of the probe hole and its color may change, possibly indicating a cultural material layer. Another advantage of the hydro-probe is that its weight is mostly supported by the water and the hose descending from the surface. Physical strain is decreased, so the diver can concentrate on collecting data.

While working a hydro-probe on land may be unwieldy, especially if long sections of pipe are used, its advantages deployed from a boat or underwater are well worth the trouble. If a diver is using a hydro-probe, some form of communication system should be developed between the surface and the diver. Simple tug signals on the hose or an accompanying down line may be adequate. Various through-water sonic devices are now available that allow for voice communication. If the diver is using surface supplied air through a helmet, hard-wire communications are very easy to integrate.

Communication will aid in directing the diver and keeping track of the work effort, position, number, and depth of each of probe location. A buoy may be dropped to the seabed and its coordinates taken by GPS or some other method. The diver can be directed to the buoy and probe in a regular pattern, straight lines, or radial or cruciform patterns. With slight modifications, the addition of a Venturi system or hydro-jet, the survey tool can be easily converted into an excavation tool.

Similar to a hydro-probe is an air-lance, which is based on the same general principles of displacing seabed materials but uses air rather than water. If a compressor or hookah system is utilized, an air-lance can be rigged up to a compressor port via a hose and valve system. The continuous flow of an air-lance may decrease pressure from a compressor. Using a valve to control the airflow, on for probing and off for withdrawing and moving to the next position, will conserve air. Also, the diver will be at less risk from vertigo if he or she is not totally ensconced in a whirl of bubbles. Like the hydro-probe, a compressor-based air-lance can easily be converted into a useful excavation tool, an air-dredge, by connecting the air line into long large-diameter pipe with a receptor for the air hose at one end.

REMOTE SENSING

Remote sensing is a very effective method to search for cultural material in a marine context. Though it is equipment- and technology-intensive and relatively expensive, this approach has many advantages. Sonic and magnetic gear interfaced with a computer and navigation system enables one to acquire data over large areas that can be analyzed quickly and efficiently. There are many commercially available remote-sensing tools and various software packages for integration, editing, and manipulation of data, as well as for the production of graphs and maps.

One of the most critical pieces of remote-sensing equipment is a GPS. A GPS unit will let researchers know where they are and have been with accuracies that were once unimaginable. Accurate positioning allows the surveyor to return to an exact point of interest in order to conduct further research on a target of interest. There are numerous GPS units on the market, as well as numerous types of navigation software that can create survey track lines for the vessel to follow. Acquiring accurate positioning data while in a dynamic environment—on a river or lake, for example, or out at sea—is fundamental to a successful survey.

Several types of remote-sensing equipment are based on the principles of sound (see Quinn in this volume). One simple yet very useful tool is a fathometer, which works by emitting sound energy from a transducer aimed at the seafloor. This thin, cone-shaped packet of energy continues through the water until it encounters a hard surface, the seafloor, or wreck material, and then bounces back to the transducer. Given that the speed of sound through water can be measured or estimated, the time it takes the fathometer to emit and receive the sound energy can be used to calculate depth.

Knowing the depth in a survey area will aid in determining whether SCUBA, mixed gas, or surface-supplied air should be used and what type of equipment may be deployed for subsequent investigations. In more adroit hands a fathometer may be used to locate underwater rises and gullies that could indicate a shipwreck site or submerged landscape features. Some skillful operators can also use a fathometer to find differences in seabed texture by interpreting the return.

Similar to a fathometer is a sub-bottom profiler; it works in the same manner, but when the sound energy hits the seafloor some is echoed back for an initial or first return, and some continues through the seabed sediments, hopefully to return an indication of what lies beneath. Sub-bottom profiler data can indicate gas pockets, pipelines, variable-density stratigraphy (potentially indicating past watercourses), prehistoric landforms, and buried wreck sites. McKee argues that sub-bottom profiler data recorded at the *Mary Rose* site indicated the wreck (McKee 1973). The data collected by a sub-bottom profiler comes from a relatively narrow swath, and its utility as a survey tool may be limited; it may, however, be a useful site assessment tool. Whether such data is beneficial to an intended project or survey is up to the researcher.

Another sonic devise that is widely used in survey is side-scan sonar (Figure 5.2). Side-scan sonar, like a simple fathometer, emits sonic energy from its transducers. However, the configuration of the emitted energy is much different. Rather than a thin cone of energy directed at the seafloor, a side-scan unit emits its energy down and out, in a wedge shape. The echo received by the transducer on a side-scan sonar is capable of producing near photographic-quality images of the seafloor and any material lying on its surface.

Side-scan sonar units can emit sound energy in various frequencies and res-olutions, making them very adaptable tools for lower-resolution, wider-coverage surveys, as well as for higher-resolution, narrower-coverage surveys. During a broad-area survey, large swaths of seafloor (50 to 100+ m per channel) can be covered at a lower resolution, making for efficient use of resources. A refined, higher-resolution survey with tighter transect spacing (10–20 m per channel) can provide a more detailed look at a target or aid in locating harder-to-detect targets. The desired resolution, based on the type of target under investigation and environ-mental parameters, will aid in determining the swath width to use.

A tool similar in purpose and function to a side-scan sonar is a multibeam echo sounder, a more expensive and sophisticated option. The basic principles of emit-ting sound energy and receiving the echo return are the same for side-scan sonar and multibeam echo sounders; however, a multibeam unit can create a three-dimensional representation of the area that is surveyed by calculating x, y, and z

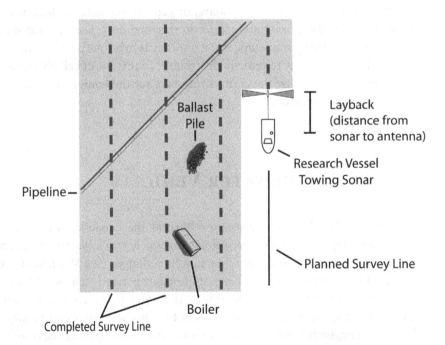

Figure 5.2 Remote-sensing survey ensuring full coverage of seabed. Reproduced with the kind permission of Gregory Cook, Archaeology Institute, University of West Florida.

coordinates from the returned signal. These sonic devices are discussed in more detail in the preceding chapter (Quinn), but their utility for survey cannot be overlooked and must be mentioned.

Other remote-sensing tools depend on another physical phenomenon: magnetism. Both a magnetometer and a metal detector use the principles of magnetism to locate ferrous or metallic objects. For broad-area survey applications a magnetometer is a more useful tool. Based on identifying disturbances, or anomalies, in the Earth's magnetic field, a magnetometer can be used to detect shipwrecks or ferrous artifacts at a fair distance (although usually not as far as a broad-area side-scan sonar survey). A metal detector is based on creating a magnetic field around a coil, thereby indentifying metal objects within the artificial field. This tool is useful for pinpointing the position of buried material, or material that is hard to recognize on the surface, but is not well suited for general survey. Gearhart (in this volume) discusses both the tools that function based on magnetic properties and the interpretation of related data.

Remote-sensing tools are usually towed behind the survey vessel. To ensure the highest-quality data, the distance between the antenna, which is receiving GPS signals, and the sensors, which are collecting data, should be noted. The distance is known as layback and has three components: fore/aft, left/right, and up/down. Most navigation software packages have applications to account for layback, thereby increasing the accuracy of survey data.

The capacity to conduct in-field analysis of remote-sensing data is crucial to the success of a survey. A review of data may indicate that there were navigation errors or some other problem that created holidays, or gaps, in the data. If there is any problem with one of the numerous connections, computers, sensors, software, weather, or any of the other parameters, and it only needs to be one problem, on-site diagnosis may be the only way to remedy the trouble. In this age of cell phones and instant communication, having the contact numbers for the equipment technical support groups is also important.

Underwater Vehicles

An underwater archaeological site may be beyond the capabilities of human divers, but several types of underwater vehicle can safely reach beyond where an archaeological diver can go, and can often stay there longer (see Wachsmann in this volume). One class of such vehicles, remotely operated vehicles (ROVs), includes tethered remotely controlled robots deployed from a surface vessel. ROVs can range in size from a microwave oven to a bus, and their complexity is limited only by a suggested use. Armed with cameras, sonar, grab arms, or other scientific equipment, ROVs can be effective, although expensive, data collectors. ROVs were used in the investigations of the *Titanic* (Ballard and Crean 1988) and, more recently, even in excavations such as the Ormen Lange Project (see Søreide in this volume).

A tool similar to an ROV that seems almost out of the space age but is becoming less expensive and more available for underwater archaeology is an autonomous underwater vehicle (AUV). Just as the name indicates, an AUV is a small submersible with its own power and locomotion source, an internal guidance mechanism that can complete a survey of a large area or individual target with preprogrammed coordinates, and a host of remote-sensing equipment. All that is required for an AUV survey is a proper launch platform and a crew to launch and retrieve it. Technical support teams are also often needed for more complex vehicles. Data collected from an AUV can be downloaded and analyzed immediately.

A recent survey conducted in 2005 by a joint Greek and American team off the island of Chios utilized an AUV that was less than 2 m long to investigate two ancient shipwreck sites, one at 70 m and the other at 36–42 m deep. In approximately nine hours of active data collection, the AUV collected side-scan sonar images and over 7,000 digital images for photomosaics and used chemical sensors to examine the environment of the deeper site. The remote-sensing data collection, integrated with precision positioning, created a data set that was comparable to any diver survey (Foley et al. 2009). The ability to collect high-quality data in a relatively rapid manner without the expense or danger of placing a diver at such depth makes such new and technically intensive methods quite useful. While the expense of the technology may be out of reach at present, costs are falling.

While ROVs and AUVs can extend the range of archaeological survey to places where people may never get, the submersible is another tool that will keep humans involved. In the mid-1960s, during the nascent stages of underwater archaeology, George Bass speculated on the utility of submersibles to underwater archaeology (Bass 1966). Today that speculation has become a reality, as manned submersibles have been deployed on multiple archaeological projects (Green 2004). Submersibles require a team of specialized technicians and a platform from which to work, and they may be out of the reach of most survey budgets; their potential, however, is now being tapped.

PREDISTURBANCE SITE SURVEY

Once a general survey has located acoustic targets, magnetic anomalies, or other areas of interest, a predisturbance site survey of the targets may be conducted. If positioning and survey data were properly acquired during a general search, there should be no trouble returning to the site(s) of interest. For a traditional survey, the water in which the work is to be conducted cannot be beyond the divers' capabilities in terms of depth, clarity, or turbulence. SCUBA or hookah-based diving can take place in waters with low visibility (0 to 1 m [0 to 3 ft]); but for many, surface-supplied air (SSA) helmet systems that support communications make for a safer and more comfortable work atmosphere.

Just as with general survey, accurate positioning during a predisturbance investigation is critical. One of the easiest ways to establish positioning is by setting a baseline from which to take measurements. In general it is best to set a baseline along the longitudinal axis of a target and off to one side. The baseline should be straight, with no bends around objects, and should not bow or drift in the current. Additionally, the baseline should be marked or graduated in some way—by a measuring tape attached to hardy line, for example—so that it can act as a measuring tool. Both ends of the baseline should extend well past observable material and be buoyed, at least initially, to obtain positioning points either by shooting them in from shore or taking GPS coordinates. In some environments, such as rocky coasts, reefs, or other high-relief areas, it may be impossible to establish a straight baseline from which to work. Establishing a network of datums along or around the site from which to take measurements will work as well. Underwater measurements can easily be recorded using a slate (or Mylar attached to a clipboard) and a pencil.

There are many ways to initially record a site prior to excavation; sketching, offset measurement, trilateration, griding, photographic or digital imaging, and so on. If drawing and sketching are the main components of the recording procedure, two- or three-dimensional representations are both options. Again, this process is dependent on the training, resources, material, environmental conditions, and time that the archaeologists have at their disposal. In clear, calm waters an underwater theodolite set up over a known point and measurements taken with a tape can be used with confidence. Simple geometry is all that is needed to plot the recorded points. In deeper or darker waters, where time or visibility may be a constraint, there are other options.

One of the least time-consuming underwater recording methods is offset measuring. A diver simply measures perpendicularly (90°) off the baseline, recording when the first material is encountered, the type and extent of that material, and when the material is no longer observable or extends beneath the seabed. Continuing along the baseline at regular intervals (e.g., 1 m or 3 ft), a diver can quickly assess the extent of the site. Individual objects of interest can be plotted as well. If there are two divers, one can hold the zero end of the tape while the other measures for quicker work.

Offset recordation was considered the method of choice for the recent predisturbance survey of the suspected remains of HMS *Serapis* (Figure 5.3). Overall resource limitations for the project and non-decompression diving limits to 23 m (75 ft) restricted the time available for site recordation. However, the information recovered—size of the site, areas of concretion, cannon, anchor, and hull remains, and so forth—will be used to plan future excavation activities.

The offset method has some limitations, such as the need to ensure perpendicular transects from the baseline. "Eyeballing it" is fine to gain a sense of a site; the closer to the baseline, the smaller the potential errors. However, at distances where

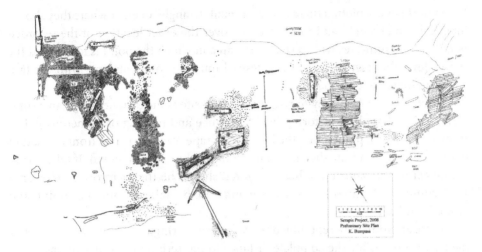

Figure 5.3 Offset recordation of the suspected remains of the HMS *Serapis*. Reproduced with the kind permission of Kelly Bumpass, Greg Cook, and the Serapis Project.

the baseline cannot be seen, the potential error in angle of measurement increases. This can be mitigated if the diver takes a bearing down the baseline with an underwater compass. Knowing the bearing of the baseline, the surveyor can take the bearing of the measuring tape during recording to verify that it is ±90° to the baseline measurement. Another limitation is if material extends above the seabed. The measuring tape may become caught or snagged, and the elevation of the material will add an error in the distance measured if the zero end of the tape is attached at seabed level. This error can be reduced by raising the zero end of the tape either with another diver or a tall rod.

Related to offset measuring, and generally considered more accurate but more time-consuming, is trilateration. For two-dimensional trilateration, at least two measurements of an unknown point need to be taken from two known points. Using datums or a baseline, measuring a point to two known points creates three legs of a triangle that are of known lengths. These measurements are recorded systematically for later plotting and mapping. In this manner several measurements can be efficiently taken. For three-dimensional trilateration, measurements to at least three known points are required, and at least one known point should be at a different elevation than the others. In processing trilateration measurements, two possible points in space may be plotted out, each point a mirror of itself off the baseline or between datums. With good note-taking, perhaps a sketch, and common sense, all measurements should be taken to one side of the baseline to create an outline view of the site.

If time is of little concern, or superseded by a need for accuracy, three measurements to a point can be attempted. Actually, numerous measurements can be taken, but with more measurements there is also an increased possibility of error.

When the lines are plotted there may be a small "triangle" of error where they should intercept, which could add to uncertainty over the exact location of the recorded point but also indicates with certainty the area in which the point is located. At the survey level the degree of accuracy desired must be commensurate with the task (Bowens 2009; Green 2004).

Another form of survey measurement for a site is the distance-angle measurement. This is based on factoring in the distance and bearing of numerous points from a datum or a point along the baseline. A tape measure is run from the datum out to an object, and the distance and a compass bearing are noted. If taken from the object to the datum, the bearing noted should be the reciprocal: ±180° on a 360° compass. Numerous measurements can be taken from one point and plotted out later.

There are some inherent difficulties when measuring with a tape underwater. If the tape is not visible the complete distance to the zero point, it may be caught or hung on material, drooping, bowing in the current, and so on, all of which are sources of error. A single diver with a tape pegged at the datum, or two divers working one tape, can work efficiently. The data collected can be hand-plotted or entered into a computer to obtain a visual representation of the survey. Some mathematical modeling has been developed to aid in plotting out survey data to increase its accuracy, while others use trilateration and advanced photogrammetric techniques to calculate points in three-dimensional space.

Another potential source of error is introduced by using a compass to determine bearings down the baseline or along the line of measurement. A high-quality compass is required, but even with the best compass unseen errors due to magnetism can skew the data. If one is working in an area with cannon or anchors, or on an iron vessel or other area of high magnetics, the utility of a compass will diminish.

In clear, no-current or low-current water, the above methods are generally quick and efficient ways to record material on the seabed. In lower visibility, in current sufficient to make long tape pulls inaccurate, or when the requirement for accuracy is higher, creating a stable grid over the site is an option. The position of the grid can be recorded by extending it out from a baseline or by buoying the corners and recording them with GPS. The legs of a grid framework should be solidly established into the seabed so that there is no movement if divers rest on or inadvertently bump the framework while doing their duties. There are several advantages to working within a grid system, and they have to do with control and accuracy.

A grid should be made from a hardy material; metal piping, connectors, and hardware are preferable to plastic. Although some metals will rust, they should not sag, which introduces errors if vertical measurements are taken from the grid. The framework will create a plane above the work area that archaeologists can use as a stable platform to do their recording. Areas directly under each grid square can be subdivided and recorded individually. Later, the individual drawings of each area can be merged to create a single image of the entire site.

Erecting a grid over a site allows for the efficient collection of three-dimensional data. Creating a flat, horizontal surface is easy with the aid of a bubble or carpenter's level. Once a grid is set up, quick checks with the level on the cross-pieces are all that is needed to create this surface. Measuring down to material on the seabed from the horizontal plane is easily accomplished. A grid system can also be useful during underwater photography or digital imaging. Additionally, if excavation is to follow a survey, the expense and energy of establishing a grid system is well worth the investment (Bass 1972).

There are, however, some inherent difficulties with a grid system. The main, perhaps most obvious issue is that there is a rigid framework in the work area. It can be bumped or knocked out of kilter by a clumsy diver. Additionally, the framework may inhibit ease of access to the material being examined. Therefore, consideration of the size of grid is important. Also working through a grid introduces a perception error called parallax. If either an archaeologist's eyes or a camera lens moves or changes position in the process of recording an object through a grid, it may create an apparent shift in the position of the object being recorded.

Underwater photography and digital imaging are methods for rapidly and accurately creating a representation of a site. Underwater photography is not necessarily easy; there are problems with perspective and parallax that must be addressed if high-quality photo recordation is to be accomplished (Green 2004, UNESCO 1972). Photomosaics, or combinations of numerous overlapping and adjacent images of portions of a site, can create an overall representation of a site or area. Photomosaics are in their own way detailed maps. In-the-field film photography can be a labor-intensive process requiring a darkroom and film processing. If it is to be used, it is wise to develop film as rapidly as possible to ensure that the pictures do indeed develop and contain the required information. Film photography is becoming an obsolete art, however, as digital imaging provides many advantages over film photography.

Ease of use and lower costs are the primary benefits of digital photography. Images can be downloaded immediately to a computer and manipulated with common software to highlight, shade, or darken for the desired result. There are no film or developing costs, nor must time be dedicated to the developing process. Photomosaics may be rapidly created (Figure 5.4), and any errors or bad images can

Figure 5.4 Mosaic composed of nine digital images that cross the suspected HMS *Serapis* site. Reproduced with the kind permission of Michael Krivor, Norine Carroll, and the Serapis Project.

be immediately reshot. However, with digital data, data management and storage become of primary importance in order to avoid loss of data and to ensure that it can be properly retrieved.

In addition to creating a visual image of a site underwater, imaging may also be useful for site analysis. Using various techniques to analyze images, measurements of a site and associated artifacts can be obtained. Photogrammetry, for example, can be accomplished by taking an image that contains a calibrated two-dimensional object, such as a cross or square, or three-dimensional cube. The object can then provide the data that allow for measurements to be taken from within the image. Additionally, stereophotography can be accomplished through a system of two cameras aligned so that their optical axes are parallel when taking an image. Three-dimensional information can be obtained using this technique (Green 2004).

Artifacts

A survey or pre-excavation investigation is generally conducted to obtain information on what type of cultural material may be found in an area or to document a particular site thoroughly, whether in preparation for an excavation or for long-term management purposes. Surveys tend to be noninvasive and usually do not disturb cultural material. In general, it is not wise to remove artifacts from their in situ context if an excavation plan has not been developed, even if artifacts appear randomly scattered on the seafloor. Additionally, survey-level projects rarely include plans for conservation and curation of artifacts, which can be expensive and time-consuming, particularly when dealing with material that originates from a submerged environment. Ceramics, glass, metals, and wood all react differently in seawater, can rapidly deteriorate when removed from it, and must be treated appropriately to prevent or limit degradation (see Hamilton and Smith in this volume; Pearson 1987). There are, however, some instances in which removing finds is an acceptable practice.

Assuming a conservation or redeposition plan is in place, surface collection is a suitable method of survey that provides information on the temporal and cultural context of a site. Removal of surface finds for imaging, measuring, drawing, or analysis can provide researchers with valuable clues, insights, and information. Returning recorded materials back to the site, assuming their long-term preservation is not under threat, is a wise approach. Permanent collection of artifacts is usually avoided at the survey level of investigation unless there is an overriding imperative, such as fear of looting, but artifact sampling will significantly contribute to a site's identification and long-term management plan. Material that has been in a marine environment and reached equilibrium with the ambient surroundings should not be collected if provisions for conservation and curation have not been established.

CONCLUSION

There are numerous methods and techniques for completing an underwater archaeological survey, including some that have not been addressed here. Additional methods, techniques, and survey situations are described by other authors (e.g., Bowens 2009; Marx 1990; Peterson 1965; Ruppe and Barstad 2002). The tools and techniques noted give an idea of the simplicity or complexity for underwater archaeological endeavors. Enterprising archaeologists should be able to adapt off-the-shelf tools to tackle problems that present themselves during any fieldwork campaign. How best to position and record data should be an underlying theme in choosing methods and equipment for a project. Continued developments in technology, positioning, and remote sensing appear to offer new ways to move underwater archaeology forward.

With an area survey complete or a predisturbance survey conducted, the next step in the archaeological process is excavation (see Underwood in this volume).

REFERENCES

Ballard, R., and P. Crean. 1988. *Exploring the* Titanic. New York: Scholastic.

Bass, G. 1966. *Archaeology under water.* New York: Frederick A. Praeger.

———. 1972. *A history of seafaring based on underwater archaeology.* New York: Walker and Company.

Bowens, A., ed. 2009. *Underwater archaeology: The NAS guide to principles and practice.* 2nd ed. Malden, MA: Blackwell.

Burgess, R. 1980. *Man 12,000 years under the sea: A story of underwater archaeology.* New York: Dodd, Mead & Company.

Cleator, P. 1973. *Underwater archaeology.* New York: St. Martin's.

Delgado, J. 2001. *Lost warships: An archaeological tour of war at sea.* London: Conway Maritime Press.

Foley, B. P., et al. 2009. The 2005 Chios Ancient Shipwreck Survey: New methods for underwater archaeology. *Hesperia: The Journal of the American School of Classical Studies at Athens* 78: 269–305.

Green, J. 2004. *Maritime archaeology: A technical handbook.* 2nd ed. San Diego: Elsevier Academic.

Henderson, G. 1986. *Maritime archaeology in Australia.* Nedlands, Western Australia: University of Western Australia Press.

Marx, R. 1990. *The underwater dig: Introduction to maritime archaeology.* 2nd ed. Houston, TX: Gulf Publishing.

McKee, A. 1973. *King Henry VIII's* Mary Rose. London: Butler & Tanner.

Muckelroy, K. 1978. *Maritime archaeology*. Cambridge: Cambridge University Press.

———. 1981. *Discovering a historic wreck*. Basildon, England: National Maritime Museum.

Nagelkerken, W. 1988. Test excavations on shipwrecks in St. Eustatius. In *Underwater archaeology proceedings for Historical Archaeology Conference*, ed. James P. Delgado, 105–107. Ann Arbor: Braun-Brumfield.

National Space-Based Positioning, Navigation, and Timing Coordination Office. 2009. *Global Positioning System*. Online at www.gps.gov. 25 November.

Pearson, C. 1987. *Conservation of marine archaeological objects*. London: Butterworths.

Peterson, M. 1965. *History under the sea: A handbook for underwater exploration*. Washington, DC: Smithsonian Institution.

Ruppe, C. V., and J. Barstad, eds. 2002. *International handbook of underwater archaeology*. New York: Kluwer Academic/Plenum.

Staniforth, M., and M. Nash, eds. 2006. *Maritime archaeology: Australian approaches*. New York: Springer.

UNESCO. 1972. *Underwater archaeology: A nascent discipline*. Lausanne: Imprimeries Réunies.

———. 1981. *Protection of the underwater heritage*. Genève: Impremeries Populaire.

———. 2001. The UNESCO Convention on the Protection of the Underwater Cultural Heritage. http://unesdoc.unesco.org/images/0015/001528/152883E.pdf/.

CHAPTER 6

EXCAVATION PLANNING AND LOGISTICS: THE HMS *SWIFT* PROJECT

CHRIS UNDERWOOD

INTRODUCTION

WHILE maritime archaeology projects differ in character, their organization and planning share many components. Common to all projects should be a clear set of aims and objectives laid out within a project or research design, the scope of which is outlined in Rule 9 in the Annex to the UNESCO Convention on the Protection of Underwater Cultural Heritage (2001). Adequate planning and the provision of appropriate logistical support should aim to ensure that the project is carried out safely, completed according to a predetermined timetable, and within budget.

To illustrate these components this chapter will outline the planning and logistical support required for the excavation of sloop of war HMS *Swift* (1770) and, where relevant, make additional general comments regarding excavation planning and logistics. It is our intention that those involved in, or considering planning, their own projects, large or small, will use the factors outlined below as a reference and be able to more effectively develop their project plan.

HISTORICAL BACKGROUND

HMS *Swift* left Port Egmont on the Falkland/Malvinas Islands in early March 1770, following Admiralty Orders (ADM 1/5304:3) to carry out surveys of the islands and coast in the region. Shortly into the mission, gale-force winds (ADM1/5304; Gower 1803) drove the vessel close to the Patagonian coast. Seeking shelter, the *Swift* headed for the estuary of Port Desire (now Puerto Deseado), a harbor already known to some of the crew. Close to the entrance of the *ria* (estuary) she ran aground, but was soon refloated. Court martial accounts are unclear as to what extent damage was sustained during this first incident. Out of control, the ship drifted farther up the estuary and grounded again on an unchartered rock covered by the high tide. This second stranding resulted in the total loss of the vessel, and three of the ship's complement perished—two private marines and the cook. Facing a desperate situation, with few supplies, the ship's master and six seamen rowed in an open boat over 480 km (300 miles) back to the islands to seek help. A month later, all of the remaining members of the crew were rescued by HMS *Favourite*, also based on the islands at the time (see Elkin in this volume).

Discovery

The wreck lay undisturbed until 1982, when it was discovered by a local group of young, enthusiastic SCUBA divers. The seed of the idea for their search was sewn by Patrick Gower, a descendent of Erasmus Gower, first lieutenant of the HMS *Swift*. Gower had visited Puerto Deseado in 1975, bringing along his predecessor's diary, which accurately described the loss of the vessel, but much to his surprise he found that nobody in the town was aware of the loss, much less knew where the wreck was located. The discovery of *Swift* subsequently acted as a catalyst for the early development of maritime archaeology in Argentina and continues to be one of the most important underwater archaeological projects in the country.

Previous Investigations

Artifacts were recovered by the local divers, who were then followed by the Underwater Archeology Working Group (GTPS), although these groups did not include a trained archaeologist. GTPS was created (Libonatti 1986) following a series of seminars on underwater archaeology between 1983 and 1985 organized by ICOMOS (International Committee on Monuments and Sites). One of the group's aims was to experiment with underwater archaeological techniques on several sites, including *Swift*. Between 1987 and 1989 the GTPS/ICOMOS group carried out four field seasons, during which approximately 80 objects were recovered (Elkin 2002).

Current Research

In 1997 an interdisciplinary team, Programa de Arqueología Subacuática (PROAS) of the National Institute of Anthropology (INAPL), Buenos Aires, Argentina, was commissioned by the provincial government of Santa Cruz to develop research aims for a new stage of work. For the first time, the investigating team included a trained archaeologist and specialists in naval architecture and marine biology. Under this new direction, a number of research themes were developed (Elkin 1997). These included the examination of: (1) the role of the ship within the geopolitical context of the South Atlantic at that time (Dellino-Musgrave 2007); (2) the ship's design, construction, and subsequent alterations; (3) the social hierarchy and other aspects of life on board as reflected by the material culture; (4) evidence of technological change that characterized the eighteenth century; and (5) site formation processes (Elkin et al. 2007). A further theme has been added to take account of the unexpected discovery of the skeletal remains of one of the two private marines lost with the ship, which were discovered in 2005 and subsequently recovered in 2006 (Barrientos et al. 2007).

PLANNING

The main considerations, aside from the specific archaeological aims, objectives, methodologies, and artifact conservation, include safety, accommodation, transport (air, land, and water), size, composition, and experience of the team, equipment requirements and maintenance (diving and archaeological), and funding, as well as other things that sometimes may not seem so obvious, such as allowing time for media and local public events, which can have significant benefits in promoting community involvement, goodwill, and support for the project.

One of the fundamental issues in the planning of all of PROAS's projects is taking into account the significant distances between Buenos Aires and other parts of the country. Puerto Deseado is situated over 2,090 km (1,300 miles) south of Buenos Aires. The planning of an underwater excavation is further complicated by the specialized nature of the diving and excavation equipment, which requires support that is not readily available in most coastal locations. Should equipment break down or be left behind, the solution is unlikely to be a visit to the local dive or hardware store to find a replacement. The nearest dive store stocking anything beyond the basics is over 483 km (300 miles) north, in Puerto Madryn, one of the main centers of recreational diving in Argentina, or alternatively Rio Gallegos, which is almost 724 km (450 miles) to the south.

Aside from the lack of specialized equipment, locally the sourcing of even more mundane materials can be a problem, and such materials are likely to be more expensive. Due to this factor, virtually everything required for the project, as well as replacement gear, is sourced in Buenos Aires and transported south. Consequently, the transportation of project personnel, as well as the heavy and bulky equipment necessary to carry out even a small excavation field season, becomes an issue, particularly when the project budget is relatively constrained.

Administrative Considerations

An important factor in the continuity of the project is maintaining relationships with the three levels of Argentine administration (federal, provincial, and municipal), each of which has a role in enabling the project. All are involved to some extent with providing permissions, funding, or administrative support in one form or another. It is essential that all necessary permits are received well in advance of the beginning of the fieldwork. This whole process involves a significant amount of time. Aside from the official process, it is also important to coordinate the timing of the project with the director of the Brozoski Museum, the local base of operations. The museum provides space for administration, the high-pressure diving air compressor, and changing and drying facilities. An open area at the rear of the museum is used for the cleaning of dive equipment.

Funding

Since PROAS's involvement in 1997, fieldwork has been intermittent, partly due to the sporadic nature of funding, but also to prevent the limited conservation capability and storage area from becoming inundated with finds. Several field campaigns have been devoted to hull surveys and environmental monitoring rather than to excavation.

Most of the funding for the project comes from government sources. The Ministry of Science and Technology and the Ministry of Culture cover staff salaries, the municipal administration of Puerto Deseado contributes to the costs of accommodation and consumables such as fuel, and there is a considerable gift-in-kind contribution made by the local community. In 2008, PROAS received a grant covering two field campaigns from Argentina's National Research Council and also a project grant from the National Geographic Society, with some additional support from the British Embassy. Valuable nonmonetary support is provided locally, such as a berth in the harbor for the project boat, towage, loan of equipment, and occasional emergency repairs of equipment.

The estimated budget for a typical three-week field season, excluding salaries, flights, and additional local transportation, is US$12,000. This sum covers, accommodation, and food, honorariums for the nonstaff members of the team, routine preproject equipment-servicing costs, spares for and replacement of diving and archaeological equipment, consumables such as fuel for the boat and water pump, freight of equipment, transfers to and from the airport to Puerto Deseado, local repairs, incidentals, and so on. The cost of the postseason report, written by the salaried members, is absorbed in staff time, with much of the scientific analysis done in collaborative exchanges with academic institutions, at minimal cost. The municipality is responsible for the costs of the storage and conservation of the recovered artifacts. An estimate of these considerable costs would normally need to be factored into the project budget. A realistic estimate of them is somewhat dependent on an assessment of the type and quantity of artifacts that could be found during the excavation. This is not always easy, but it can be attempted based on the known physical characteristics of the site and to what extent salvage or other human or environmental factors have resulted in the loss of archaeological material. Comparison with the recovered material on sites in relatively similar environmental conditions will also provide a guide to expected discoveries and related conservation budgets. Relative to the *Swift*, the upstanding hull is evidence that the environmental conditions are conducive to preservation, combined with the knowledge that there has been relatively little human impact on the site since the sinking and that previously recovered finds are normally in good condition—indicators that new finds can be expected in a range of categories, including organics, glassware, ceramics, and mainly nonferrous metal objects. Although a definitive figure is not available for the costs of conservation and curation, based on most excavations, the figure will match and likely significantly exceed the costs of the fieldwork. The provision of adequate conservation and storage facilities will therefore define the limits of the archaeological aims and objectives. Recognizing the level of the museum's resources, the *Swift*'s archaeological excavation objectives are therefore limited to small concise areas aimed at answering specific research objectives outlined above. Failure to take this important factor into account will almost certainly lead to excavated material languishing in storage, unconserved, for longer than is justifiable.

Accommodations and Catering

An important but sometimes underestimated component in the organization of field projects is the matter of where the team will rest, eat, and sleep, not to mention where archaeological logs, diaries, and so on will be completed. The phrase "An army marches on its stomach" can equally be applied to archaeological projects, particularly those where temperatures and conditions are unduly cold. A typical day in the field, especially when diving in cold conditions, is quite long and arduous. It is therefore essential that the team is adequately fed and accommodated. Although to camp is an option that should not be discounted and may in some cases be the only option, in less than ideal conditions, the team's performance will be affected as time passes. It has to be borne in mind that factors affecting the participants' physical well-being will gradually have an impact on daily performance and even exacerbate the possibility of accident. Archaeological standards may also suffer.

Transportation

The prime objectives of transportation are to get all equipment and personnel to the project location on schedule and, once on site, to be able to access the site, either from the shore or by water transport. With regard to this specific project, there are several components: moving the archaeological team and equipment to and from Buenos Aires; local transportation from the Brozoski Museum to the port's maintenance facility; and the water transport to the diving platform. For reasons of operational convenience as well as to reduce the freighting costs of equipment, the larger and heavier components, such as the diving cylinders, the diving weights, the inflatable boat, the outboard engine, the high-pressure air compressor used to charge the diving cylinders, and the excavation equipment, remain in Puerto Deseado between field seasons. Should the need arise to run a project elsewhere, additional diving equipment can be sourced in Buenos Aires or Puerto Madryn, the main diving centers. Only personal diving equipment and that which requires maintenance is routinely brought back to Buenos Aires.

Despite this arrangement, a significant amount of diving and archaeological equipment, as well as supplies and personal items, need to be transported. Until recently, airlines have been sympathetic to requests for the carriage of project equipment that exceeds the normal baggage allowance, but recently normal baggage limits are much more strictly enforced. Most of the remaining diving equipment and archaeological materials is sent by road transport from Buenos Aires to Puerto Deseado, which takes two days. On arrival, the shipment is stored in the Brozoski Museum.

Personnel fly to the closest domestic airport, Comodoro Rivadavia, 290 km (180 miles) north of Deseado, with the final leg of the journey being completed by road. Consequently, most of the first day is lost in traveling.

Locally, the team is dependent on the Prefectura (coast guard) for the transportation of personnel and equipment from the museum to the harbor, with the project's own boat being used as a ferry from the berth to the dive platform, a routine that is carried out daily.

THE WRECK SITE OF HMS *SWIFT*

The wreck site, located at Lat. 47° 45′ 12″ S / Long. 65° 54′ 57″ W (Figure 6.1), is approximately 45 m (148 ft) offshore of the commercial port facilities, adjacent to the rock on which the ship foundered, now somewhat closer to shore than in 1770 due to recent land reclamation. It lies between the end of the commercial quay and the port's maintenance facility. To the south side of the site is a secondary channel that leads out to the *ria* and from there on to the open sea.

Figure 6.1 Site location. The site of HMS *Swift* is in the harbor of Puerto Deseado.
Reproduced with the kind permission of PROAS, Underwater Archaeology Program,
National Institute of Anthropology, Argentina.

The location has a number of important advantages over more exposed or
remote coastal locations: a smaller/simpler platform suffices; minimal transfer time
from berth to site is needed; relatively sheltered water reduces the number of days
lost to bad weather; and importantly, in the event of an accident, medical services
are relatively close.

Description

The wreck of HMS *Swift* lies on an 8° slope, heeled over to port at an angle of 58°
(Elkin et al. 2007). Many of the starboard frames rise 2.75 m (9 ft) above the seabed,
although the keel remains buried, as are the port frames (Figure 6.2). The main deck
is broken in various places along the length of the ship, and most of what was originally above it, such as the masts, has either disappeared or is no longer in place.
Despite the partial structural collapse, a diver can, even in low visibility, move from
bow to stern following either the starboard side structure or the line of the main
deck. Due to the position of the hull, many artifacts originally located on the starboard side, such as the main armament, now lie on the port side of the wreck. In
addition, part of the capstan and two anchor stocks can also be seen, partially
hidden or camouflaged under sediment and biofouling. Smaller artifacts of various
materials, mainly glass, ceramic, various metals, stone, and wood, are sometimes
found partially exposed. Artifacts determined to be at significant risk are recorded
and recovered, with the remaining ones lying outside the excavation areas normally

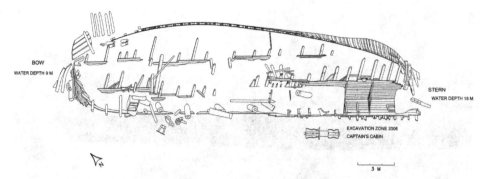

Figure 6.2 HMS *Swift* excavation zone. Reproduced with the kind permission
of PROAS, Underwater Archaeology Program, National Institute of Anthropology,
Argentina.

reburied and left in situ. Artifacts that have remained covered by the fine-grained
silt have survived in remarkably good condition.

Site Characteristics and Their Impact on Diving Operations

Depth, visibility, temperature (underwater and surface), and tidal flow all affect the
way in which the work is organized and the time required to achieve the project
aims and objectives. However, while any or all of them, in combination, may be
limiting factors, they should not be used as excuses for poor archaeological standards. Solutions can be found to most problems. It just may take longer and cost
more to achieve acceptable results. Although the site is in relatively shallow water, it
is cold and dark, and unpredictable strong currents that can result in diver disorien-
tation often sweep through the three-dimensional structure. Additional complicating factors are boat traffic that is sometimes close to the site; marine animals; and
environmental factors, such as the kelps, that may affect how diving is conducted.

Depth

The bow lies in 10 m (33 ft) at mean spring tide, with the stern in no more than 18 m
(60 ft) (Elkin et al. 2007). The seabed continues to gradually slope away from the
stern toward the open area of the *ria* and is characterized by the dominance of fine-
fraction sediments ranging from clay to fine sands overlying a pebble bottom.
Although the depth of the wreck site makes it ideal for the use of enriched air
(nitrox), it is not commonly available in Argentina.

Underwater Visibility

Poor underwater visibility can seriously limit the achievement of good archaeological results. On the site of the *Swift*, visibility ranges from an almost lack of visibility
during or after storms, as heavy rains wash sediments off the land, to dark but relatively clear 4 m (13 ft) water during neap tides combined with periods of calm dry

weather. The average visibility is around 1 m (3 ft 3 in). Light levels vary significantly depending on the depth, surface light, and sea conditions. There are numerous artificial lighting solutions, whether handheld or head-mounted, or more sophisticated solutions, such as using surface-powered floodlights. Handheld torches and video lamps are used on the project; in addition, a strobe light is placed on the access point to the excavation zone to help divers find their way. Although they are not always used on the site, strobe lights or light sticks attached to divers' equipment can also help them to maintain contact with their buddies in poor conditions.

Water and Surface Temperatures

A cold diver is less efficient than a warm one and is also potentially less able to deal with an incident, so it is important to use appropriate equipment to keep divers reasonably comfortable for the full duration of a dive. Seawater temperatures during the Patagonian summer (21 December to 21 March) vary between 8° and 13° Celsius (46° –55° Fahrenheit), with winter temperatures reaching a low of 4° C (39° F), although no diving on the site is actually carried out during this period. As underwater excavators are likely to remain quite still for relatively long periods during a dive, they tend not to generate much heat and therefore will tend to get cold more quickly. Dry suits are the norm, although some of the region's archaeological divers choose to use wet suits made from 4/10 inch (10 mm) smooth-skin neoprene. These wet suits provide sufficient insulation from cold, are much less expensive, and are easier to repair, a factor to be taken into consideration in more remote locations.

Air temperatures during the same period range between 6.5° and 23° C (44°–73° F), but can change dramatically within these extremes. Higher surface temperatures can also cause a fully kitted diver waiting to dive to become very uncomfortable, potentially even hyperthermic, so it is important to coordinate dive times and handovers to reduce this possibility. Maintaining adequate supplies of fresh water will help avoid dehydration.

Tidal Factors

A tidal amplitude of 4 m (13 ft) during mean spring tides generates strong tidal currents that can reach 2 knots on the site and are even stronger in the *ria*. The strongest currents tend to flow on the ebb tide, sweeping the wreck from bow to stern. The timing of the dive periods is also variable due to the natural topography and harbor construction in and around the area. This factor often leads to the need to arrive on site early and wait until diving conditions improve. Depending on the time within the lunar tidal cycle, a diving window of around 4–6 hours coinciding with the beginning of the ebb tide usually provides the best visibility. This tidal window is the main factor that governs the start time for each diving day.

Although there is some natural shelter from the currents provided by the ship's structure, this is not the case when entering or leaving the site. To help divers, there is a line from the diving platform (a small pontoon described below) to the excavation zone. The down-line from the pontoon is attached to a seabed sinker marked with a strobe light placed a few meters outside the structure (to avoid damage to the site), and from there a ground line runs to the grid.

Marine Life

The *ria* is a natural habitat for many species of fauna, including shark (*Heptranchias* sp., *Galeorhinus galeus*, and *Scyliorhinus canicula*) and the Southern sea lion (*Otaria flavescens*). Although sharks have not been seen on the site, sea lions are a regular visitor. While seemingly not posing a direct threat to the diver, they are inquisitive and can become excited in their desire to "play," to the point that on some occasions it is impossible to continue to work, at which point dives have to be terminated. The possibility of such events becomes part of the project planning.

In addition, planning needs to account for the large loose kelps (*Macrocystis pyrifera*), often more than 6 m (20 ft) in length, with holdfasts up to 1 m (3 ft 3 in) in diameter. They drift down the *ria* and accumulate around the site and the pontoon. They are remarkably durable and in the very poor underwater conditions pose a potential entrapment hazard for the diver. On the surface, they accumulate around the diving platform, and if not regularly removed they would significantly increase the drag on the pontoon's mooring, raising the risk of a mooring line failure.

PERSONNEL

A major component in the planning and ultimate success of any underwater archaeological project, particularly an excavation, is the experience of the team. It is essential that the team as a whole is qualified and competent to carry out the full range of project tasks. Aside from the archaeological tasks, provision should also be made for those tasks that are similar to those often found in a commercial context, such as the laying or moving of moorings, the lifting or moving heavier artifacts (such as cannon or anchors), the construction of grids, etc., all of which become more difficult in poor underwater conditions. If these tasks are anticipated, either the archaeological team will need experience or training in doing them, or additional team members will be necessary.

Archaeological Experience

PROAS's archaeological field team normally consists of six diving members at any one time: three staff members from the Institute of Anthropology in Buenos Aires, plus other archaeologists who, although they are not part of the Institute's staff, routinely take part in PROAS's projects. Many of the team members have been involved with the project for over 10 years. This level of experience on the site is a major factor in the planning of individual dives and in the subsequent archaeological interpretation of results.

Colleagues from other Latin American countries also occasionally take part in the project, which forms part of an informal initiative to provide project experience and help maintain and develop field skills across the region. There are also several overseas archaeologists associated with the project who provide expertise on specific issues, such as physical site protection methods, and long-term site protection should further port development pose a threat to the site's integrity.

Although the project should not be considered a training project, a number of archaeology students have also had the opportunity to take part. They are permitted to excavate only under the direct supervision of one of the more experienced team members, an important consideration in ensuring that excavation standards are maintained to the highest possible level.

The archaeological team is also accompanied by a documentary filmmaker, who has been recording the progress of the project for the past three years. Occasionally one or two local divers help with nonarchaeological tasks, such as being a dive buddy to one of the archaeological team during routine dives, helping with the backfilling process at the end of the field season, and assisting with mooring operations associated with the diving platform (discussed below).

Diving Qualifications and Experience

Following a review of Argentina's diving regulations, a professional "scientific diver" qualification has been introduced, the criteria for which have been developed in association with PROAS and other Argentine scientific groups (Prefectura Naval Argentina 2008). This qualification will in effect supersede the variety of amateur and other professional diving qualifications currently held by team members. Along with the new scientific diver regulations, a more stringent and regular medical requirement has been introduced, in line with the domestic commercial diver requirements and the practices of other countries. It is also important to ensure that personal insurance for all team members covers personal accidents, including recompression treatments and possible air transfers to the decompression chamber, and that there is third-party insurance to cover accidents involving other members of the team and the public.

Prior to arrival in Puerto Deseado, the Prefectura (coast guard), the competent authority for the administration of safety matters and policing of Argentina's coastal zone, must receive notification of the intended diving operations, including a list of all project diving members and an outline of the planned field campaign—dates, times, and so forth—but excluding archaeological details. On arrival in Puerto Deseado, diving credentials are registered and approved by the authority. Only after this step can diving begin.

In planning the diving operations and selecting the team it is important to understand that the level of archaeological and diving experience required on one site will not automatically be the same as that on another. The level of experience required will vary depending on the site characteristics and the tasks scheduled to be carried out. Also, possession of what appears to be an appropriate level of diving qualification and requisite numbers of dives logged should be viewed only as indicators of competence, not as a guarantee. Those responsible for safety (see below) should not take anything for granted. An assessment of each team member's experience should include the number of dives in similar environments, how recently they were done, experience in the range of intended tasks, and whether similar diving equipment was used. When there is any doubt about the competency or fitness of an individual, checkout dives and additional training should be considered.

Any additional skills training for anticipated new tasks should be completed before the project. It is also advisable to consider workup dives to try out new or repaired equipment, or to generally refresh skills (e.g., good buoyancy control). Avoiding contact with sensitive archaeological areas is no less important than avoiding landing on a coral reef; the only difference is that coral can potentially regenerate itself. It is therefore good practice to acquire and practice these skills prior to the project, rather than during it. Being completely at ease and in control are major factors in successfully completing any task.

Developing a Project Safety Policy

A safety policy that covers all aspects of the project, marine and terrestrial, must be an intrinsic part of all project designs. Over recent years, safety has become a major concern for anyone involved in running a project due to a marked change in attitudes, which have moved from an acceptance of personal responsibility to a desire to establish liability and obtain compensation. While acting as project safety officer has always been a heavy responsibility, this new culture makes it even more so and as such should not be accepted lightly.

Dive Safety Officer and Documentation

One of the primary tasks is to identify all hazards or risks associated with the project. Once the scope of the risks has been identified, actions should be taken to minimize the possibility of hazards affecting the project team, and procedures should be developed to be followed in the event on an incident, such as a casualty evacuation plan. It is important that a project member has responsibility for all safety-related matters, perhaps on a day-to-day basis, or even shared, as long as all concerned are competent to carry out the role. These fundamental principles should apply to all projects, large or small.

On larger projects, the roles of safety officer or dive supervisor should be separate from that of the archaeological director or principal investigator to ensure that conflicting interests do not interfere with the decision-making process and that the necessary attention is directed toward team safety. Consideration should also be given to creating a project-specific code of operations that everyone associated with the project is given, accepts, and ideally signs, confirming adherence. Even on a small project such as the excavation of *Swift*, it is essential that someone with the appropriate experience is responsible for dive supervision. The person responsible for safety has the ultimate say over all factors of the operation relating to safety of team members. On the *Swift* project the role of dive supervisor is shared, allowing everyone to dive; the responsibility for the supervision of individual dives is noted in the daily dive log. On a larger project it is good practice to keep a daily operational log that is complementary to, but separate from, the archaeological daily diary that records aspects relating to the diving operation. This record should include the date, site, names of the team and of visitors, name(s) and times of responsibility of the dive supervisor(s), time of arrival and departure from the site, time of the start and end of the dive operation, weather conditions, high- or low-water times, tidal amplitude, and any significant event occurring during the operation (HSE 1997). There should also be regular reassessment of the identified risks and daily equipment checks to ensure, as far as is possible, that all equipment is in good condition and is functioning properly. It is recommended that a written checklist be completed daily by a competent person and signed by the dive supervisor. On arrival in Puerto Deseado the local hospital is informed about the diving timetable and an emergency casualty evacuation plan is agreed on. Emergency telephone numbers and VHF radio channels are checked and noted on the dive safety log, including the contact number of the closest decompression chamber.

One potential but undesirable possibility is the influence of peer pressure: pressure on team members to dive, irrespective of diving conditions, competence, or personal well-being. New team members, perhaps wanting to demonstrate their value to the project, may be affected more than others by peer pressure. The situation can sometimes be difficult to recognize, so it must be made clear during safety briefings that no one is obliged to dive, that pressure will not be applied on anyone to do so, and that any dive must be aborted if the diver feels ill at ease. Everyone also has a responsibility not to ignore factors that may affect their diving fitness, such as seasickness, tiredness, anxiety, alcohol or substance abuse, illness, or injury. By ignoring such things, divers can potentially place themselves and others at risk. The dive safety officer must be prepared to intervene should there be good reason to doubt that someone is either fit to dive or competent to carry out a specific task.

Daily Safety Procedures

On board the diving platform there are first-aid and O_2 kits, and VHF radios for routine and emergency communication with the Prefectura. In addition, team members have personal cellular phones. These represent an informal backup, but their performance in remote locations or far from shore should not be taken for granted. The Diving A flag is flown for the duration of the operation. Several members of the team also have first-aid and oxygen-administration training; there should always be someone on the diving platform able to render first aid. In addition to the diving cylinders routinely required for the day's diving, extra cylinders are also available on the pontoon for emergency use. Before commencement and on completion of diving, the Prefectura is notified by radio with a prearranged call sign. They are responsible for notifying the team of any shipping movements that will necessitate the temporary cessation of diving and of imminent bad weather that would lead to the closure of the port, during which time all diving and shipping movements are restricted.

Emergencies

In the event of an accident, the Prefectura is responsible for the incident's management and for coordinating the movement of a casualty from the diving platform to the hospital. This is a local arrangement and one that is not necessarily typical of all sites. It is crucial that procedures be established with the appropriate authorities before the operation commences and that they be periodically reviewed to ensure that the plan remains up-to-date and, where changes have been made, that relevant people have been informed. Although there is a small but well-equipped local hospital that can deal with accident and emergency injuries, the nearest hyperbaric-chamber is in Puerto Madryn, a 966 km (600 mile) round trip for the rescue helicopter or light aircraft—if one is available, which, given Patagonia's size, cannot always be guaranteed. Consequently, the daily diving regime has to be conservative and accident prevention paramount.

EXCAVATING AT HMS *SWIFT*

Preparing for Project Operations

As most of the bulkier project equipment remains in Puerto Deseado between field seasons, it cannot be prepared in advance of arrival on location. Therefore the pre-departure preparations in Buenos Aires focus on repairing and servicing personal diving equipment; identifying and purchasing key spares, such as filters, compressor lubricants, torch batteries and chargers, O-rings, fin straps, and buckles; acquiring spares for the boat and motor; and organizing or purchasing archaeological paperwork, daily log sheets, measuring tapes, underwater drawing boards, pencils, erasers, finds and environmental sample containers, cameras, photographic scales, archaeological recording tools, calipers and additional items for samples, self-sealing finds bags, permanent markers, finds tags, and so on.

Once in Puerto Deseado, the team divides into two groups. One organizes and prepares the paperwork and associated archaeological materials, while the other prepares the boat, the outboard engine, the high-pressure compressor, and the water pump that powers the water dredge (detailed below). Individuals are responsible for the preparation of their personal equipment.

The inflatable boat is reassembled, the outboard motor's fuel system is cleaned, ignition plugs are routinely replaced, moving parts are lubricated, and the necessary fuel is secured. The engine is briefly run before being attached to the boat transom. The water pump for the water dredge is stripped down, cleaned, and lubricated, and the spark plug is replaced. Before deployment on site, the components (dredge, hose, and water pump) are connected and tried out on the foreshore.

The diving air compressor is the heart of any diving operation; without it the project would come to an abrupt halt. To reduce the possibility of mechanical failure, the manufacturer's servicing and operating recommendations are strictly followed, and only personnel familiar with its operation are allowed to operate it. If in the unlikely, but possible, event that a spare part is required, it may be necessary to import it, as few specialized parts are available in the country. This is not only expensive but also time-consuming, as imports are normally routed through Buenos Aires. As a fallback position there are other small-capacity compressors in the town, but the daily project requirement would place a heavy burden on them. For many mechanical parts it is customary to replicate them locally, but this pragmatic innovative solution does not extend to more sophisticated equipment, such as the compressor.

Diving Operations

Before diving operations are under way, the team meets to discuss the specific archaeological aims of the day. Once agreed on, the tasks are scheduled into a preferred order, and dive pairings are decided. Depending on progress and diving conditions, the original plan may be amended, but there is a significant benefit in developing the plan in the relative comfort of the museum before the distractions of preparing diving equipment commence.

All diving is carried out in pairs using SCUBA equipment, comprising a single 100 ft³ (3,000 psi) capacity tank, a buoyancy compensator, and a regulator with an alternative air supply, plus the usual ancillaries. The U.S. Navy Standard Air Table is used as the basis of the diving, and all dives are recorded: times in and out, cylinder contents in and out, length of dive, and responsible supervisor are all noted on a daily dive log sheet. In the case of the HMS *Swift* site, only occasionally is there more than one pair of divers in the water, mainly due to the limitations of the size of the excavation area. However, should there be more than one area being excavated, or the need to do other tasks such as video or photographic recording or hull survey, and where the underwater conditions are suitable, it is sensible to utilize the available dive time and undertake tasks simultaneously. It is important that the separate diving pairs not get in each other's way and that the appropriate levels of safety are planned.

During an average day, depending on the tidal window it is normal for the team to complete 10 or 12 dives (five or six diving pairs) per day. While the use of dive computers or dive timers is routine, they are only used as a backup to the agreed-upon procedure based on the dive tables and the instructions of the dive safety officer. Each pair carries out their first dive of usually between 45–55 minutes, depending on the depth of the area being excavated, with a surface interval of a minimum of 1.5 hours before doing a second, usually shorter, dive. Prior to all dives each diver carries out routine checks to ensure that the equipment is functioning properly (Figure 6.3).

All tasks require a level of concentration. Some, including excavation, can become totally absorbing, to the point that awareness of one's surroundings diminishes. When underwater, this can have consequences that can place the excavator at increased risk. The main danger is that the diver may fail to regularly monitor dive times and dive tank contents. The consequences can be serious, including going beyond the planned dive time, incurring unplanned decompression, or perhaps even running out of air. Sharing air with a companion is an option, but as buddy pairs are on the same profile with the same equipment it is possible that they will run out of air more or less simultaneously. Given the strong tidal conditions, combined with harbor constructions, large moored vessels, and surface traffic, a free ascent to the surface is not a risk-free option. A secondary independent breathing supply would reduce this factor, but it is not a common practice in Latin America. Diver/surface/diver communications would enable a supervisor to monitor dive durations and remind the diver to check air contents, as well as to advise him or her when to stop work and surface. Archaeological instructions from an archaeological supervisor can also be provided, without interrupting the dive. However, this equipment remains on the team's wish list.

Figure 6.3 Pre-dive equipment checks. Reproduced with the kind permission of PROAS, Underwater Archaeology Program, National Institute of Anthropology, Argentina.

Part of the daily routine is to take and remove all equipment except diving weight-belts from the diving platform. Although it would be more efficient to leave more equipment on the platform, the risk of losing it through bad weather, collision, or theft is considered too high. This daily routine continues for six days; the seventh day is a rest day.

Dive Platform

The dive platform is a steel pontoon provided to the project at minimal cost by a local towage company; it allows for a working area of 5 m by 4 m (16 ft by 13 ft). A reasonably large boat would be required to create a similar working space, the potential charter of which would have a significant impact on the project's overall budget. Although the platform lacks shelter or other conveniences, they are only a short boat ride away, so it is adequate for the needs of the project. It is held in position by four moorings strategically placed to enable it to be moved as close as possible to the excavation area. Two moorings would suffice, but four is preferred due to the lack of shelter from the strong winds and currents that can create rough sea conditions. Three of the moorings are cylindrical concrete blocks with metal rings cast into the concrete; the fourth, which forms the bow mooring point, is a metal strong point drilled and securely cemented to the rock adjacent to the site. Irrespective of the time between field seasons, it is important to inspect the moorings, shackles, and mooring ropes for any defect prior to securing the diving platform. It is also important not to cut corners with the mooring system, as the breakage of a single component will lead to a sudden repositioning, possibly causing excavation equipment to be dragged through the site, causing damage and potentially putting divers at risk. It also necessary, sometimes daily, to remove large quantities of kelp that accumulate around the moorings; the kelp makes access to the down-line more difficult and puts additional strain on the mooring components.

The main site marker buoy remains permanently in place, but those that normally mark the moorings are removed between field seasons. Their positions are known, but it still requires a dive to relocate and mark them. Once they are found, inspected, and moved if required, and their positions are buoyed, the pontoon is towed into position. The team's small inflatable is inadequate for this purpose, so a local tug company provides the service free of charge, an example of the support the project receives from the local community. The only downside to this arrangement is that the timing of the operation is beyond the team's control.

Excavation

Preparation of the Excavation Area

The excavation areas are divided into 2 m by 2.m (6 ft 3 in by 6 ft 3 in) sections that conveniently fit between decks. The grid also provides a means of supporting the excavators above sensitive archaeological areas, but it should be noted that if the grid is used as a reference for surveying it may be disturbed by a diver involved in excavation, which will affect the accuracy levels of the measurements. The grid is made from stainless steel and has adjustable legs that enable it to be leveled over the excavation area.

Excavation Equipment

Although the *Swift* project uses a water dredge, otherwise known as an induction dredge (Figures 6.4 and 6.5), it is also useful to consider the airlift (Figure 6.6), as together they are the tools most frequently used when excavating underwater archaeological sites. Ultimately, choosing which to use will depend on the site characteristics, the size of the diving platform, the experience and training of the excavators, and to some extent on a personal preference for one or other of the tools. Both utilize suction to carry away the spoil from the excavation area, but as their names imply, one is powered by air and the other by water; they also differ insofar as the water dredge lies horizontally when in use, whereas the airlift is almost vertical when being operated. They can both be constructed from plastic or metal, ideally lightweight for ease of setup on site, and the suggested diameter of the equipment for archaeological purposes is 10 cm (4 in), although larger diameters can be useful for quickly removing backfill. They can be purchased from specialist equipment suppliers or, alternatively, can be constructed from components found in home construction stores, but advisably using a proven design.

The *Swift* project's single water dredge is powered by a relatively small 5-horsepower, 200-gallons-per-minute water pump, a decision based on the limitations of space on the project's diving platform and the need for portability, but it should be noted that much larger pumps are available that can power numerous dredges when required.

WATER DREDGE

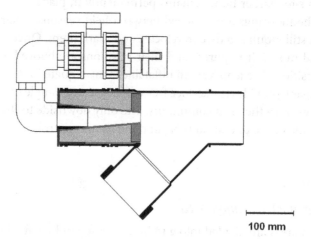

100 mm

Figure 6.4 Water dredge. Reproduced with the kind permission
of Charles Pochin from a design by Pochin & Adams.

Figure 6.5 Water dredge equipment, including the dredge, discharge pipe, 5 hp gas water pump, inlet pipe, and lay-flat hose. Photograph by Chris Underwood.

Figure 6.6 Airlift nozzle. Photograph by Chris Underwood.

The amount of suction depends mainly on the pump's flow rate, but it is also affected by the pump's head pressure, leakages through joints or small tears in the delivery hoses, the diameter and position of the dredge-jet, the diameter of the dredge, and the angle and length of exhaust pipe. The pump supplies water to the tool via a flexible hose connecting the pump and dredge; this can be either lay-flat hose, commonly used by firefighters, or a more inflexible tubular hose. Lay-flat hoses have the advantage of occupying less space in a small boat, but they tend to be more prone to damage than the more rigid alternative.

The 7.5 cm (3 in) diameter inlet/outlet pump used on the project produces enough suction for the single dredge to remove fine silt, sand, mud, broken shell, and light gravel along the horizontally positioned 4 m (13 ft) long discharge pipe that carries the spoil off the ship's structure. Larger material such as pebbles and stones can gradually accumulate along the discharge pipe, particularly if it is quite long, eventually reducing or stopping the suction completely. The dredge-head has a coupling for the water supply hose, and an on/off valve, an important safety feature that is discussed below. At the rear of the dredge-head there is a compatible fitting for attaching the exhaust section, which can be in sections if necessary to facilitate easier transportation and storage. A flexible extension to the working end of the dredge is used to provide greater mobility around the excavation area, bearing in mind that the on/off water control valve should always be accessible to the excavator.

Airlift

The airlift is also a simple device, consisting of a length of hollow pipe, typically about 2–3 m (6–10 ft) long (although it can be longer depending on water depth) and a 30 mm diameter (1.25 in) air supply hose that connects to a coupling on the airlift to the low-pressure air compressor located on the surface. Suction is created at the working end by the expanding air rising up the body after it enters the airlift. Even the lower-capacity compressors, more usually found powering tools on a construction site, will deliver approximately 190 cfm (5.38m³/min) of air between 102–175 psig (7–12 bars), which is sufficient power for two airlifts to be used simultaneously. The disadvantage is that the machine is quite large and heavy, needing rather more space on the diving platform than the small water pump used on the *Swift* project. The rate of airflow from the compressor is the main factor that determines power, but leakages through loose joints, excessive length, small tears or porosity in the delivery hoses, and greater water depth can also reduce the power.

Setting Up the Excavation Equipment

Water-Dredge

The water pump used on the *Swift* project is placed on the corner of the pontoon closest to the site to reduce the length of supply hose to the dredge on the seabed, to avoid unnecessarily increasing the water-drag on the hose. Normally, the hose spans about twice the water depth, but this depends on factors such as tidal amplitude, strength of current, and the distance from the platform to the excavation area. It is advisable to place the pump close to the water-level to reduce the head pressure, which will affect performance. The pump inlet draws water toward it, but in so doing it can suck in seaweed or other floating debris that can accumulate and block the pump inlet, resulting in a partial or sometimes total loss of suction. Although the water inlet itself is protected by a filter, placing the inlet in a secondary container such as a bucket can help protect the inlet and reduce this problem, but it is recommended that the inlet be periodically inspected and any material removed as necessary.

The dredge is placed and fixed adjacent to the excavation area, with the long exhaust or discharge pipe positioned horizontally and with the end outside the ship's structure and ideally downstream to avoid fine material from drifting back over the excavator, which would reduce visibility. If the exhaust is inclined too high, heavier material will begin to accumulate inside and will eventually reduce suction, leading to a blockage. A dredge constructed from plastic materials can be more or less neutrally buoyant, so it may require securing to the seabed or site by weights or lines. It is also useful to place a small buoy or container tied toward the end of the exhaust, the contents adjusted so as to keep it level, or slightly declined to help material move away. This will keep the exhaust off the seabed and minimize the stirring up of loose sediment. Care has to be taken to keep the exhaust away from potentially sensitive archaeological material. Less-well-designed equipment may have an imbalance of pressure between the inlet and outlet of the dredge, causing it to move forward or backward. Minor imbalances can be overcome by reducing/increasing water flow, or by attaching the dredge to weights placed on the seabed. Excessive lengths of supply hose will also have similar effects, particularly where there is strong tidal flow. Without a tether this movement can tire the diver and also make the dredge harder to control, potentially having a negative impact on archaeological standards. A tether will reduce the mobility, but this can be easily overcome by attaching a 2–3 m (6.5–10 ft) flexible extension to the mouth of the dredge-head. This will enable the excavator to move around the excavation zone much more easily, but care has to be taken not to allow the extension to drag through archaeologically sensitive material.

Airlift

The position of the compressor on the diving platform depends mainly on the length of available hose, but it is always good practice to minimize trip hazards on the diving platform, so consideration should be given to placing the compressor outlets convenient to the side of the platform nearest to the site. Avoid excessive lengths of hose in the water, as this will cause water drag. Because it is of a smaller diameter the air delivery hose is not quite so affected; nonetheless, it is advisable to anchor the airlift to the seabed, or, where several airlifts are being used, consider the use of a distribution manifold.

Effect of Tidal Flow

Placeing the long water-dredge exhaust downstream of the tidal flow will prevent spoil from drifting back toward the excavation area. However, if the schedule includes working the ebb and flood tides, and spoil drifting back over the excavation area becomes a real problem in maintaining visibility, the only options are to change the position of the exhaust, which can be time-consuming, or perhaps install a second dredge lying in the opposite direction.

Airlift spoil rises up the body of the lift and will tend to follow the tidal flow. Depending on the strength of this flow, fine deposits will travel well away from the site, creating spoil heaps, but heavier material will tend to fall back on top of the excavator or just behind. In some cases, this could be into another excavation area. If the water flow slows or stops, such as during slack-water periods, most of the excavated material will tend to fall back on the excavator. Fixing a tether to angle the exhaust helps, but this reduces mobility and may well not solve the problem entirely. If the problem cannot be resolved, then either different tasks should be undertaken or the excavation should be temporarily terminated until conditions improve.

Technique

The primary function of the airlift and water-dredge is to remove excavated spoil from the excavation area in a controlled way, analogous to the wheelbarrow or bucket commonly used on a terrestrial archaeological site. Underwater excavators have an advantage over their terrestrial colleagues in that moving the spoil from the site to the spoil heap is, by comparison, automated. The most sensitive excavation tool is the hand (Figure 6.7), preferably one without a glove, but this may be impractical

Figure 6.7 The hand is the most sensitive excavation tool. Reproduced with the kind permission of Uriel Sokolowicz, ODYSSEUS Producciones.

due to low water temperatures or the hardness of the seabed. Some excavators, even in cold water, will cut off the fingertip of at least one finger of their glove to provide additional sensitivity. When excavating delicate material it is often necessary to use a single finger to painstakingly separate an artifact from its surrounding sediment. Some types of glove, particularly "dry" gloves, do not readily lend themselves to excavation, no matter how warm they may make the hands.

Where it is not feasible to use the hand, other appropriate tools should be selected: for example, a 10 cm (4 in) trowel is often used on harder substrates, and a soft-haired brush can be used for cleaning an artifact prior to photography or drawing. Hand-fanning is also a very common and effective method of excavating loose material. Gentle movement of the hand from side to side will dislodge fine material, with the loose material being sucked toward the dredge or airlift. This technique is also very effective for cleaning artifacts or structures prior to recording. Over-vigorous hand-fanning is likely to result in clouds of silt, reducing the excavator's visibility. Whatever tool is selected, the utmost care should be taken to avoid damage to archaeological material.

On no account should these suction excavation tools be used as the primary means of excavating archaeological material. This would inevitably result in individual components of fragile artifacts being separated, while organic materials would almost certainly be damaged, if not lost completely, and contextual information will be lost as well.

Good excavation technique should prevent the dredge or airlift from becoming blocked. A piece or cross of wire (or other suitable material) placed at the mouth will prevent larger objects from entering the equipment, but this will not necessarily prevent the mouth from becoming blocked if a large object is allowed to completely cover the working end. It is also advisable to place a trap of some form over the discharge pipe. A net sack is tied over the exhaust end of the dredge on the HMS *Swift* project, allowing the fine silts that characterize the site to easily pass through the mesh but trapping small finds inadvertently missed by an excavator. The net sack is removed each day and inspected, in part to aid in maintaining provenience information for any artifacts that were accidentally recovered.

Safety Considerations

One needs training and experience to become a competent archaeological excavator and to be aware of and therefore avoid the associated dangers when using the airlift or water dredge. The main risks to the excavator are entrapment caused by the lines used to anchor the equipment and from loose diving equipment, or even a hand, being sucked into the working end of the tool, if the tool is particularly powerful. One particularly serious eventuality is the second-stage regulator of the alternative air supply becoming trapped in the dredge. The suction can rapidly deplete the contents of a diving tank, as if the regulator was on maximum free-flow, with potentially dangerous consequences for the diver. All personal extraneous diving equipment, especially hoses for gauges and alternative air supply, must be positioned so as to minimize this risk while still remaining accessible. Care should also be taken to prevent large loose pieces of spoil or even archaeological material entering the dredge, to prevent damage and to avoid the consequences of blocking the tool. While this possibility is common to both tools, the significant difference is that if an airlift becomes blocked it will become buoyant and rapidly rise toward the surface, perhaps carrying the excavator with it. A tether will reduce the risk, but anchors also somewhat reduce the mobility of the tool. For both tools, an on/off valve in easy reach of the diver is essential. Quarter-turn valves are quicker and easier to operate than wheel valves, particularly if the diver is wearing thick neoprene gloves or mittens.

Artifact Recovery and Inventory

All artifact recoveries are planned taking into account the need to ensure that an object has been first recorded in situ (sketch, survey, video, photography). There is an agreed-upon recovery method based on the artifact's physical condition, material, dimensions, and weight; packaging materials that will be required underwater and on the surface to prevent damage during the recovery and transportation to the museum; and the personnel required to carry out the plan. The museum's conservation staff are consulted to ensure that they are fully prepared to receive the artifact(s). A recovery operation can be a relatively simple affair, or rather more complex when recovering larger artifacts such as cannon, anchors, or even ship structures that may require specialist lifting equipment, but the decision-making process should be more or less the same. The timing of the artifact recovery normally coincides with slack water or shortly before or after; a little water movement can be helpful in maintaining underwater visibility. Typically an appropriate container for the object—generally one with a lid and lined with protective foam—is prepared in advance. If the container is quite large, the foam will increase its buoyancy, so compensatory weights are attached to the container, making the diver's task easier.

As there are a relatively small number of artifacts recovered during a typical season, the labeling is normally carried out by placing an identification tag in the receptacle prior to the recovery of the artifact to the surface. In the event that there are more numerous objects of a similar category, or where it is deemed better to dismantle an artifact comprising numerous components prior to recovery, such as a stave-built container, it is advisable to label in a sequence that will aid subsequent recording and reconstruction.

First-Aid Conservation

Whereas on some projects the archaeological team is responsible for carrying out first-aid stabilization and cleaning, this is not the case on the *Swift* project. The archaeological team is responsible for the archaeological material from the seabed to the conservation facilities in the Brozoski Museum, where the museum staff takes over, although it is often the case that museum staff will be present on the diving platform to receive the artifacts as soon as they arrive on the surface. Initial cleaning, finds stabilization, and first-aid conservation are part of the museum's role, along with assistance in handling material during any postexcavation archaeological recording or sampling carried out in the museum by the archaeological team. The complete archaeological collection is held in the museum's conservation and storage facilities. A conservator contracted by the municipal government is responsible for the conservation and subsequent monitoring of the archaeological collection.

Demobilization and Site Management

Closing the Excavation Area

On completion of the excavation of a particular area or at the end of each field season the exposed area is covered, but the method varies depending on whether the area has been finished or further excavation is planned. In 2006, the excavation in the captain's cabin in the stern of HMS *Swift* was completed. The decision was made to replicate a site protection method successfully used on sites in the Netherlands (Manders, pers. comm. 2006). The first stage was to recover the grid to the surface and move the water dredge away from the excavation area, but not to the surface. The exposed area was then covered by a mesh fabric held in place by sandbags to provide an interface between the ship's structure and the backfill. The exhaust of the water dredge was then positioned to enable spoil to be replaced into the area. A number of dives were required to fill the zone. Finally, a second mesh was loosely placed over the area, again affixed to the structure, rather like the fly sheet of a camping tent. It was intended that the mesh would act as a sediment trap, gradually accumulating material beneath it. During subsequent seasons, inspections have revealed that the method has been quite successful, to the extent that the "free" net is no longer visible.

If researchers plan to return to an area to continue the excavation, the exposed area is covered, ensuring that any partially exposed archaeological material is either recovered or reburied and then protected by a mesh held in place by sandbags, but the active backfilling process is not done. The mesh provides an interface that enables rapid removal of any naturally accumulated backfill without running the risk of inadvertently disturbing or damaging unexcavated archaeological material.

PROJECT OUTREACH

During each field season, at least one public presentation is held in the Brozoski Museum to describe the progress of research resulting from previous seasons and to outline the aims and objectives of the current work. These presentations are an opportunity to recognize the site's discoverers and early investigators, as well as to publicly thank the local community for their significant contribution to the project. The museum staff prepares a display of the latest discoveries and provides access to the laboratory to allow visitors to see the conservation of the objects that will enhance the museum's display.

Individuals who have helped in some way are invited to come out to the diving platform to experience the project firsthand. Those that dive, including some members of the original amateur team, are taken on site tours. Local radio and TV interviews are also a part of the project routine, and although they can interrupt the working day, such opportunities are rarely if ever turned down. Maintaining a close connection with the local community, who consider *Swift* to be part of their heritage, is an important aspect of the project.

A natural extension to the periodic interview or broadcast is to consider maintaining a blog or online "journal" that follows the progress of the project. Such journals can give daily updates and potentially be live. While there are local technical issues, due mainly to the town's relative isolation, and while admittedly a lack of relevant skills in the team may currently prevent the utilization of this method of outreach, there is no doubt that it will play an increasingly important role in the future and should be considered an option where feasible.

Conclusion

In planning all field-based research projects it is important to understand the relationship between the aims and objectives and the resources required to fulfill them. If they are too ambitious, it may be very difficult to successfully complete them. Inevitably, an archaeologically intrusive project is more complicated than a nonintrusive survey, given the additional components of excavation, finds handling, conservation, and protection of the excavated areas, and all that these phases require in terms of equipment, personnel, and expertise. The HMS *Swift* project is no exception.

Because of the benign nature of the sinking and advantageous environmental conditions, large parts of the hull and contents survive in excellent condition, although the exposed structural elements are clearly slowly deteriorating. As has already been seen from the array of finds recovered since 1982, the potential for recovering a significant percentage of what was lost with the vessel in 1770 remains high. It would therefore be tempting to undertake a full excavation at some point, if not in the immediate future. However, to do so would inundate the current conservation and storage facility, which does not now have, and is not soon likely to have, the capacity to deal with large amounts of additional material. The current archaeological team would also not be able to cope with the resultant backlog of research. Therefore, the project themes are wisely restricted to those that are achievable within the human, physical, and financial resources currently available, retaining a degree of flexibility to enable unexpected discoveries, such as the human remains.

The site is not under imminent threat from harbor development, although this remains a possibility; and some archaeological sites are threatened by looting, but this is not the case with *Swift*. Apart from its legal protection, the site is located in a controlled area of the port. More importantly, it is acknowledged by the local population as a very significant part of their local heritage, and as such they play an active role in the site's protection. The team continues to monitor the situation and is taking steps to understand the options for physically protecting the site. Until any of the above factors change, the project remains committed to studying HMS *Swift* while preserving as much of the site as possible for future researchers, a key objective of current archaeological thinking.

REFERENCES

Anonymous. 1770. ADM 5304. *Court Martial to the HMS* Swift. Public Record Office, London.

Barrientos, G., M. Béguelin, V. Bernal, M. Del Papa, S. García Guraieb, G. Ghidini, P. González, and D. Elkin. 2007. *Estudio bioarqueológico del esqueleto recuperado en la corbeta británica del siglo XVIII HMS* Swift *(Puerto Deseado, Santa Cruz)*. Octavas Jornadas Nacionales de Antropología Biológica, Salta, 1–5 October 2007. Ms. on file, Buenos Aires, Argentina: Instituto Nacional de Antropología.

Dellino-Musgrave, V. 2007. *Maritime archaeology and social relations: British actions in the Southern Hemisphere*. Springer Series in Underwater Archaeology. College Station, TX: Institute of Nautical Archaeology.

Elkin, D. 1997. *Proyecto Arqueologico H.M.S.* Swift: *Research project presented to the government of the Province of Santa Cruz, Argentina*. Buenos Aires: Instituto Nacional de Antropologia.

———. 2002. Water: A new field in Argentinian archaeology. In *International handbook of underwater archaeology*, ed. Carol V. Ruppé and Janet F. Barstad, 313–332. New York: Kluwer Academic/Plenum.

———. 2003. Arqueología marítima y patrimonio cultural subacuático en Argentina: El trabajo actual desarrollado por el Instituto Nacional de Antropología y Pensamiento Latinoamericano. *Protección del Patrimonio Cultural Subacuático en América Latina y el Caribe 26–33* UNESCO—Oficina regional de Cultura para América Latina y el Caribe, La Habana.

Elkin, D., A. Argüeso, R. Bastida, V. Dellino-Musgrave, M. Grosso, C. Murray, and D. Vainstub. 2007. Archeological research on HMS *Swift*: A British sloop-of-war lost off Patagonia, Southern Argentina, in 1770. *International Journal of Nautical Archaeology* 36 (1): 32–58.

Gower, E., 1803. An Account of the Loss of His Majesty's Sloop Swift, in Port Desire, on the Coast of Patagonia, on the 13th March, 1770. London.

Health and Safety Executive. 1997. Scientific and archaeological diving projects: The Diving at Work Regulations 1997, Approved Code of Practice and Guidance—L107. N.p.: HSE Books.

Libonatti, F. 1986. Arquelogia subacuatica. In *ICOMOS Argentina—Boletin* 3 (January): 1–2.
     Buenos Aires: Instituto Nacional de Antropologia.
Prefectura Naval Argentina. 2008. Ordenanza No. 408 (DPSN), Tomo 5, Regimen del
     Personal de la Marina Mercante.
UNESCO. 2001. The UNESCO Convention on the Protection of the Underwater Cultural
     Heritage. http://unesdoc.unesco.org/images/0015/001528/152883E.pdf/.

CHAPTER 7

SHIP RECONSTRUCTION, DOCUMENTATION, AND IN SITU RECORDING

YAACOV KAHANOV

INTRODUCTION

THE process of excavating, documenting, analyzing, and reconstructing the original form and construction of a shipwreck is different in each case, although the general principles are common. This chapter presents two different projects, carried out between 1985 and 2009, that demonstrate shallow-water excavation methods and the treatment of shipwrecks. The Maʻagan Mikhael shipwreck is a single-site project, a chance discovery resulting from local sand movement. The site was excavated, and the hull was dismantled underwater, retrieved, conserved, and reassembled in a museum. It was recorded and studied both underwater and on land. On the other hand, the lagoon at Dor (Tantura) contains about 25 shipwrecks, 10 of which have been thoroughly excavated. Some were naturally exposed; others were located through water-jet probe surveys. The Dor shipwrecks were recorded underwater, and only a limited number of components and finds were retrieved for analysis on land. The different approaches of these two projects are described in detail below.

The Ma'agan Mikhael Shipwreck

The Ma'agan Mikhael ship excavation was a project of the Leon Recanati Institute for Maritime Studies at the University of Haifa, directed by Elisha Linder. A detailed account of the project is presented in Linder and Kahanov 2003 and Kahanov and Linder 2004. The ship was discovered in 1985, 70 m off the shoreline of Kibbutz Ma'agan Mikhael, at a water depth of 1.5 m, and buried under 1.5 m of sand. It was found perpendicular to the coastline, bow pointing to the shore. The ship seems to have been new when it sank. Three seasons of excavations were carried out during 1988 and 1989, under the guidance of field director J. Rosloff. Researchers from the Leon Recanati Institute for Maritime Studies at the University of Haifa took part, together with Israeli and foreign experts, advisers, and volunteers. The excavated shipwreck has been conserved and is now exhibited at the Hecht Museum of the University of Haifa (Figure 7.1).

The original vessel was a small sailing merchantman, approximately 14.4 m long, with a displacement of 22.9 tons. A significant portion of the wooden hull of the ship—11.15 m long, 3.11 m wide, and 1.5 m deep—was preserved. The following parts of the hull survived: the entire keel, the false keel, the stem, the sternpost and a section of its upper extension, remains of planks on the starboard side up to the twelfth strake, and, on the port side, up to the seventh strake, two knees (one at the bow and the other at the stern), parts of all of the 14 full frames, parts of futtocks and top timbers, a central stringer resembling a keelson, the mast step, two mast partners, two mast supports, fragments of carlings, and four vertical stanchions (Kahanov 2003a).

Figure 7.1 The Ma'agan Mikhael Ship at the Hecht Museum, University of Haifa. Reproduced with the kind permission of Itamar Grinberg.

Among the finds were remains of 70 pottery items, decorative wooden arti-facts, carpenter's tools, a whetstone, food remnants, ropes, a lead ingot, a one-armed wooden anchor, and 12.5 tons of stones of several types. The ship was dated to about 400 BCE by radiocarbon dating and ceramic analyses (Artzy and Lyon 2003). The origin of the ship and the ports of call of her last voyage have not been fully determined. The stones came from Euboea and Cyprus. Most of the pottery came from Cyprus and/or the Levant, with a few items from East Greece (Asia Minor). Food remains were from the vicinity of Samos; the lead, from Lavrion; the copper, from which the nails had been made, from Cyprus; and pollen, from late-summer blooming plants growing in the coastal region where the ship was discov-ered. The ropes were made of various plants, some growing on the Israeli coast and others not found locally. Thirteen tree species, all common in the eastern Mediter-ranean basin, were used in the hull and accessories (Liphschitz 2004). This infor-mation is only partly helpful in determining the origin of the ship or her ports of call, since at least some of the materials and objects may have been brought by another vessel to the place where they were loaded, or were collected by the ship along her route.

The remains of 11 technologically similar vessels have been found in the Mediterranean: Giglio, Pabuç Burnu, Bon Porté, Cala Sant Vicenç, Jules-Verne 9, Jules-Verne 7, Villeneuve-Bargemon 1 (César 1), Grand Ribaud F, Gela 1, and Gela 2. Sewing was used in the construction of all of the hulls of these vessels. Except for Gela 1 and 2, which were dated to the fifth century BCE, all date to the sixth century BCE. Another comparable wreck is the Kyrenia ship, dating to the beginning of the third century BCE, in which sewing was identified only in ceiling planks in secondary use. Comparison of these wrecks led to important advances in the study of ship construction of the period (Kahanov and Pomey 2004).

Measuring, Recording, and Documentation

The underwater recording of the Ma'agan Mikhael shipwreck was based on direct manual measurements from fixed datum points, using measuring tapes. Depth was recorded by plumb lines. The exact three-dimensional position of the cargo stones was not recorded during the excavations, which made it difficult to determine their original order. Normal wood-graphite pencils were used for writing notes underwater on Mylar taped to plastic slates. Slates or Mylar can be printed with a reference grid, scales, or other aids.

Precise recording of the locations of all items in three dimensions, their distribution and context, is vital for the correct analysis of the finds, their purpose and use, and their implications for analysis of the ship. The relative positions between the finds and the hull components help in identifying finds and hull timbers. Fixed markers, such as datum points outside or inside the shipwreck, as well as reference points, are essential in identifying different items, whether hull components or finds.

The Maʻagan Mikhael shipwreck was abundantly photographed under and above water on color and black-and-white film, both stills and video. All finds were photographed and drawn on land. Hull timbers were cleaned, and all sides were recorded for their main features: contours, main dimensions, nail remains, sewing holes, and the like. After conservation they were recorded in minute detail, to the level of tree grain, knots, tapered pegs, and nails. Recording after conservation may perhaps seem strange and wrong: however, as all timbers were waterlogged and very soft and fragile, only very few could be recorded in detail before conservation. This approach prevented considerable damage to the timbers. As for accuracy, all data were compared to preconservation recording. It should be noted that the tree species of the majority of the timbers was also determined after conservation. Both detailed drawings and species identification were found to be successful.

Although this approach was appropriate under the circumstances, analysis of tree species should be done before conservation if possible, after identifying and marking the hull components while still underwater. Detailed recording should be considered according to the condition of specific timbers, conservation facilities, recording equipment, and the project management. Considering the condition of the wood of the Maʻagan Mikhael shipwreck, and documentation tools available at that time, drawing of the main features before conservation and detailed hand drawing after conservation was found to be a good compromise.

As it was intended to dismantle the hull underwater and retrieve it from the seabed in pieces, all timbers were marked before dismantling underwater. The purpose of this recording was not for measuring the hull shape, but rather to enable the reconstruction and identification of the precise location of each timber. Dymo tape was used for tagging. These tape tags were attached to the timbers with hypodermic needles prior to recovery. Every component was tagged at several points, with parallel recording of each point on a sketch of the hull. Both the Dymo tapes and the needles survived sea conditions, the rinsing of salts from the wood with freshwater before conservation, and the entire conservation process, and proved invaluable during the reassembly. Their only disadvantage was their small size, which made them difficult to read in photographs. The type of needles should be considered in every specific case, depending on their dimensions and the timber characteristics. Sometimes stainless nails may be a better solution, promising better survival. When a tape or marker is attached with two pins, the correct pin must be noted as the reference point.

A general view of the hull in situ during the progress of excavation, recording components, documentation, and study of minute details above water, enabled the researchers to understand, among other things, the construction sequence of the hull. For example, the hull was sewn at its extremities. Several sewing holes were found penetrating through planking tenons, which showed that sewing had been done after the installation of the tenon-joints of the planking. Frames were located over knees, covering sewing holes, which indicates that frames were installed after sewing, and consequently after planking. The sequence was confirmed in a few instances where copper nails connecting frames to planks penetrated through existing tenons and tapered pegs. This sequence of construction is evidence of shell-first construction. The tapered pegs which locked the tenons were generally driven from the inside; however, after a close examination some pegs were found to have been driven from the outside. Following this it was suggested that port side strake 2 was installed before starboard side strake 2 (Jabour 2004: 123; Kahanov, 2003a, 2004b).

Following the in situ documentation, and thorough study above water, the sequence of construction has been determined to have been as follows: The stem and sternposts were scarfed to the keel. The keel had no rabbets or chamfers for the garboards. The strakes were connected to the keel, to the stem and sternpost, and to each other by mortise-and-tenon joints, locked by tapered pegs. After the planking was completed, the knees were nailed to the keel and endposts, and the planks were sewn at bow and stern to the keel, knees, and endposts. Then the preassembled frames were nailed to the planking by double-clenched copper nails. Frames rested on the keel and the knees, but were not connected to them. Each frame consisted of a floor timber with one futtock on each side, hook-scarfed together. Most of the hull was made of softwood, *Pinus brutia*. The tenons and their pegs, the false keel, and the anchor were made of hardwood, mostly *Quercus* sp. (Liphschitz 2004).

Conservation of the Wood

The wood appeared to be in good, almost new, condition, without wear or barnacles, and with only limited teredo attack in the uppermost parts of the remains. However, as the wood had decayed and its cells had filled with seawater, it was extremely fragile and required very careful handling at all stages. The hull was dismantled underwater and retrieved in sections. The keel was retrieved intact, in a 10 m long tank. The timbers were transferred to the conservation laboratory of the Leon Recanati Institute for Maritime Studies at the University of Haifa (Kahanov 1997, 2004a).

The retrieved wood was waterlogged, with a moisture content of 709% on dry basis. The first stage of the conservation was desalination of the wood. While there appears to be no accepted procedure for desalination, measurements taken during the process showed that after the water was fully replaced seven times at two-weekly intervals, an acceptable level of chlorides was achieved.

For the conservation, 100% polyethylene glycol (PEG) 3350 was chosen. Dry PEG powder was added to the tanks with no pretreatment, at a rate of 1% per week, with the solution being gradually heated to 60°C. The progress of impregnation was monitored by several simple laboratory procedures. As soon as measurements confirmed that the wood had been well impregnated, it was retrieved from the tanks.

The decision to stop the conservation process, remove the wood from the tanks, and dry it, is a critical one that must be made soon after conservation is completed. As this step is irreversible, conservators are tempted to continue the conservation longer than necessary. However, the chemical characteristics of PEG change with time, and it may rapidly degrade to a material of lower molecular weight that barely

solidifies. Other unforeseen circumstances, such as malfunctioning of the conservation system, may also occur, causing damage. Lastly, the financial aspect must be
taken into consideration. All these factors should be fully considered in order to
encourage the conservator to stop the process as soon as it is finished.

The conservation of the keel, the largest timber, took 2 years of desalination and
4.5 years of PEG impregnation. The pine components of the hull were successfully
impregnated, whereas the oak components reacted differently, sometimes poorly;
the worst example being the collapse of the false keel. Shrinkage monitoring showed
that an average 2.8% volume shrinkage had occurred a few months after the end of
the conservation. However, no additional shrinkage could be measured 12 years
after the treatment. The conserved timbers were heavier than the original wood,
and the color was dark. Correct handling of timbers at the time of extraction from
the PEG improves the color. Wiping it with a sponge dampened with water at a later
stage can lighten it further.

Over the many years from excavation to exhibition, the wood was vulnerable to
damage by environmental effects, technical mishaps, and the interference of experts,
researchers, students, and visitors. Despite these concerns, the only noteworthy
"damage" to this archaeological find was the original underwater dismantling of the
hull for retrieval.

Reassembly of the Hull

Archaeological accuracy and research accessibility were the two main guiding
principles of the reassembly of the hull, undertaken shortly after completion of the
conservation treatment. The keel and endposts were placed first on temporary
adjustable scaffolding, followed by the garboard and subsequent strakes. Longitudinal
wooden battens supported the outside of the planking. The battens were connected
to transverse supports by adjustable slides. The supports, made of medium-density
fiberboard (MDF), followed the original shape of the frames, but about 15 cm outside the hull. The battens, usually one per strake, followed the lines of the hull from
stem to sternpost. They provided support for the planking, compensating for the
lack of strength of the planks and the now dysfunctional mortise-and-tenon joints.
Timbers were not connected to each other; the upper planking was supported
mainly on the planking below. Frames rested on the planking, and other internal
components on the frames and keel. The ship was reassembled shell-first, the
planking being adjusted to conform to other features. In particular, the frames provided accurate information regarding the original hull form. Component matching,
locations of frame-plank nails, mortises, tenons and pegs, sewing holes, rabbet settings, and so forth indicated the exact locations of timbers and the precision of the
reassembly. During the excavation, retrieval, and conservation, some timbers,
mainly in the bow and stern, lost their original artificially bent three-dimensional
shape. These timbers were softened by reheating to 60°C in PEG and reshaped.
For the purpose of reshaping the planks, molds made of plywood sheathed with

polyethylene on the outside were constructed on the scaffold over the bow and the stern areas. The form of the molds was based on the shape of the extant frames, with a smooth continuation to match existing strakes (Votruba 2004).

Following a generous donation, a permanent cradle for the ship was constructed. Steel frames that followed the shape of the original frames, now only 7 cm outside the extant timbers, were installed. Adjustable screwed metal struts were set on the metal frames, and longitudinal metal battens supported the strakes (see Figure 7.1). Relative adjustments between adjacent components resulted in a maximum accumulated variance in three dimensions of less than 1 cm.

In addition to the research on the ship and its exhibition, the reassembly was an opportunity to learn about relationships between associated features. The placement of two important pieces found separated from the hull was a direct result of such analysis. The first was the foremost section of the port fourth strake, providing evidence of the highest location of sewing found in the hull remains. The second was the only remaining piece of the second wale, now reliably located. At the final stage of placing the keel on its permanent support, it was found that the keel was slightly tapered along its length: sided 11.2 cm at the stern and 10.4 cm at the bow, and molded 16.5 cm at the stern and 14.2 cm at the bow. A final crucial cross-check based on the mast partner (a transverse beam) and its supporting vertical stanchion confirmed the accuracy of the reassembly.

The hull was assembled and dismantled three times, and the fourth reassembly achieved a match to the original archaeological find of the hull remains as recorded in situ. The gaps that remained in the reassembled hull matched the accuracy of the carpentry of the original ship.

Lessons Learned

Prior to the excavation of a waterlogged hull, the subsequent phases of the process— the retrieval of the wood, and its conservation, restoration, and exhibition—should be considered, as these have major implications for the following stages. For example, retrieval of timbers from the sea and their removal to the laboratory should take into account the dimensions of the holding tanks and conservation facilities. Marking or sampling timbers can be done differently, depending on whether the intention is to conserve the wood and exhibit it, or to leave it sandbagged underwater or in storage for scientific purposes only. However, when faced with similar excavation conditions, the complexity of conservation must not deter excavation itself, as a functional conservation system can be installed with a reasonable amount of effort and expense.

During the stage when the conserved timbers were taken out of the tanks, and during the few minutes when they were still hot and soft, it was possible to extract various components of the hull, such as treenails and tenons, from their original locations. This made it possible to examine many parts in detail and relate them to the locations in which they were originally found. The PEG conservation treatment is to some extent reversible. A piece of treated wood can be reheated and softened in PEG at 60°C for reshaping, removal of excess PEG, and the revealing of previously unseen details.

PEG tends to decompose above 60°C, emitting formaldehyde, which is a health hazard. Therefore, regulations stipulating maximum concentrations for short time exposure and continuous working conditions must be adhered to, necessitating installation of ventilation equipment, detection instruments, and continuous air monitoring.

A number of areas were identified during the conservation process that, in hindsight, could have been improved upon.

The conservation process itself could have been reduced by at least two years if the desalination phase had been shortened from two years to one, and if each stage of the keel conservation had been shortened by six months. With additional cuts, the entire conservation would have taken a little over four years rather than seven (Kahanov 1997: 327, 2004a: 204).

Using flexible trays that tended to bend under the weight of the timbers resulted in cracks in the wood. The trays were made from poultry cages and were connected by metal screws prone to rust, which endangered the function of the trays. Later the screws were replaced, but this, and the (minimal) damage to the waterlogged wood, could have been avoided. Plastic material, vulnerable to high (over 60°C) temperature, was incorporated in the construction of the tanks. Alternative materials should have been employed.

Situations involving a limited number of conservation tanks and the inability to sort the wood according to species and dimensions require the longest impregnation time, adapted to the timber least responsive to conservation. Each species, considering its condition, should receive the most suitable treatment separately, as far as possible. Although the heating elements were made of stainless steel coated with PTFE (Teflon), they corroded, disintegrated, and apparently caused degradation of the PEG in the keel tank. The air sparge mixing system became clogged when the PEG concentration in the solution reached 80%. An alternative mixing system should have been employed. Solidification of PEG was encountered in the corners and on the bottom of the tanks. Systems should be planned to avoid this problem. Controlled evaporation of the solution was used, mainly in the first stages, in order to decrease the conservation fluid level, to be compensated by adding PEG. This decision was based on the assumption that only water evaporates, and not the PEG. This was found to be incorrect, as PEG drops were observed on the ceiling of the conservation room.

The evaluation of the impregnation was also done by sampling the wood. A few samples were taken from places that are visible to visitors to the museum. Samples should have been taken from areas that are out of sight.

Reconstruction of the Original Ship

One of the main objectives of recording the excavated shipwreck was to provide a basis for reconstructing the ship, as far as is feasible, from the archaeological findings. Based on the archaeological remains of the Ma'agan Mikhael ship, two reconstructions of the hull lines were suggested. Later, with additional evidence from contemporary shipwrecks of similar vessels, iconography, and making computer and physical models, a third, more comprehensive, reconstruction, including the planking pattern, was proposed in an attempt to complete the picture (Ben Zeev et al. 2009).

Building a full-scale replica would be the final stage in the process. This would verify the results of the theoretical studies and provide much practical information on the seagoing characteristics of the original ship.

The Dor (Tantura) Lagoon Shipwrecks

The lagoon is located on the Mediterranean coast of Israel, 30 km south of Haifa, a few hundred meters south of Tel Dor. It is a shallow anchorage protected by four small islands. The lagoon is partially sheltered and can be used as a protected anchorage up to maximum Beaufort 4 sea conditions. In the lagoon there is a navigational channel, through which a strong south-setting current can develop. The prevailing winds during the day are from the west: southwest in the morning, west about midday, and northwest during the afternoon; at night there is a light easterly breeze. Maneuvering inside the lagoon is tricky, even with local knowledge. It was, and remains so, unsafe for vessels seeking refuge in a storm. Perhaps some of the sunken ships became nuclei for sand accumulation, creating shallows. Wood remains of about 25 shipwrecks have been found in the lagoon. Some have not been excavated, some only consisted of a few surviving finds, and 10 have been thoroughly excavated (Kingsley and Raveh 1996; Wachsmann and Kahanov 1997; Wachsmann, Kahanov, and Hall 1997) (Figure 7.2).

Shipwrecks are naturally exposed by seasonal sand movements, or discovered by systematic surveys. As the lagoon is shallow and contaminated with junk (e.g., used car batteries, torn fishing nets, net sinkers, ropes, fenders, and used tires), the use of advanced survey equipment is limited, if not impossible. The lagoon had been surveyed at times since the 1960s, but systematic excavations were only begun in 1983–1984 and have been carried out regularly from 1994. The Underwater Exploration Society of Israel, and later the Leon Recanati Institute (then the Center) for Maritime Studies at the University of Haifa (RIMS), surveyed the lagoon and excavated sporadically from 1962, and from 1983 with the Nautical Archaeology Society of Great Britain (NAS). Since 1979, S. Wachsmann and K. Raveh of the Israel Antiquities Authority joined in the work. The latter continued with S. Kingsley of the Center of Nautical and Regional Archaeology Dor (CONRAD) until 1993. The majority of discovered shipwrecks are described in Kingsley and Raveh 1996. They are identified by the prefix Dor Wreck: for example, Dor Wreck 3 (Dor C) or Dor Wreck 2 (Dor B or DW2). Between 1994 and 1996, a combined expedition

Figure 7.2 Dor lagoon, showing locations of shipwreck sites. Reproduced with the kind
permission of Itamar Grinberg, Alon Tako, M. L. Sneh, Survey Ltd. Haifa.

headed by S. Wachsmann of the Institute of Nautical Archaeology (INA) at Texas
A&M University and the RIMS surveyed the lagoon by water-jet probes and excavated several shipwrecks. These shipwrecks are indicated by the name Tantura: for
example, Tantura A (Wachsmann and Kahanov 1997; Wachsmann, Kahanov and
Hall 1997). Since 1998, annual underwater expeditions have been directed by the
author, with the participation of the NAS headed by C. Brandon, and with K. Raveh
from the local Aqua Dora Diving Center. Shipwrecks discovered after the year 2000
are identified by the year of discovery (e.g., Dor 2001/1). Thus, shipwreck names are
inconsistent and appear with different prefixes: Dor Wreck, Tantura, or the year of
discovery. The main shipwrecks referred to in this article are identified in Table 7.1
(and see Figure 7.2).

The majority of the shipwrecks are oriented northwest–southeast. All were
found in shallow water, from less than 0.5 m (Dor 2002/2, Dor 2004) to about 2.5 m
(Dor C and Tantura E). They were all buried under a sand layer about 1 m thick.

The methods of locating the wreck sites and mapping the area have improved
over the years. Initially, bearings were taken, relying on conspicuous objects on land
and compass readings. The large number of sites, their close proximity, and mainly
the sand layer covering them, led to the need for precise positioning. Several
methods are now used in addition to taking bearings and distances, such as differential GPS. However, the most frequently used and most reliable method is to attach buoys to specific points in the wreck site and locate their positions by a professional surveyor. Using this method, the wreck site can be located precisely, which is
necessary for subsequent excavations.

Table 7.1 Shipwrecks excavated at Dor/Tantura lagoon as discussed in this article (in chronological order)

Shipwreck	Date (CE)	Period	Description	References
Tantura A	5th–6th cent.	Byzantine	small coaster	Kahanov 2001; Kahanov et al. 2004; Wachsmann and Kahanov 1997
Dor 2001/1	early 6th cent.	Byzantine	medium-sized coaster	Kahanov and Mor 2006; Kahanov and Mor 2009; Mor and Kahanov 2006;
Dor D	5th–7th cent.	Byzantine–early Islamic	several badly preserved planks	Kahanov 2003b; Kahanov and Royal 2001; Kingsley and Raveh 1996; Royal and Kahanov 2005
Tantura F	mid-7th–end 8th cent.	early Islamic	medium-sized coaster	Barkai 2009; Barkai and Kahanov 2007
Tantura E	7th–9th cent.	late Byzantine–early Islamic	badly preserved coaster	Kahanov et al. 2008, Royal and Kahanov 2000; Planer 2007; Wachsmann and Kahanov 1997
Tantura B	9th cent.	Islamic–Abbasid	large/long ship	Kahanov 2000; Kahanov et al. 2004; Wachsmann et al. 1997
DW2	circa 1800	late Ottoman	coaster	Kahanov and Yovel 2001; Yovel 2004, 2005
Dor 2002/2	circa 1800	late Ottoman	well-built vessel	Cvikel and Kahanov 2007; Cvikel et al. 2008
Dor C	late 19th cent.	late Ottoman	coaster	Bowens 2001; Kahanov et al. 2008

Byzantine period: CE 324–638, early Islamic period: CE 638–1099, Ottoman period: CE 1517–1917.

The excavations used underwater dredgers, operated by seawater at high pressure supplied from a pump installed on a boat. Generally two sites were excavated in parallel, with two dredgers on each site. However, up to three sites with six dredgers have been operated simultaneously. During excavation, metal frames were installed above the wrecks for supporting divers, protecting the finds, and as a reference for recording.

Dating is based on ^{14}C analysis (by the Weizmann Institute for Science, Rehovot, Israel), typology of ceramics, Accelerator Mass Spectrometry (AMS) tests of organic materials (by the Institute for Particle Physics, ETA, Zurich, Switzerland), and dendrochronology, including wiggle-matching tests (by the Cornell Tree-Ring Laboratory, Ithaca, New York). In only three wrecks were artifacts indisputably found in situ (Tantura B, Tantura F, and Dor C). In some sites (DW2 and Dor 2002/2), finds were probably in situ, but this cannot be proved. In other shipwrecks, a large amount of intrusive mixed ceramics from late Roman, Byzantine, and early Islamic periods have been found. In a few instances, Persian and late Ottoman period ceramics were found in the same layer (Royal and Kahanov 2005: 309; Sibella 1995: 16). For radiocarbon dating, wood was sampled from outer tree rings, as close to the bark as possible. Where available, short-living organic materials were tested. In the majority of the shipwrecks, all components were sampled for tree species identification by N. Liphschitz of Tel Aviv University. Petrographic analyses of ceramics were made or supervised by Y. Goren of Tel Aviv University.

Wood remains of shipwrecks have been dated to the Roman, Byzantine, Islamic, and late Ottoman periods. Wood remains of ships' accessories and some items of unidentified origin and purpose are dated as far back as the ninth century BCE. Evidence for maritime activities in the lagoon, such as pottery that was raised during excavation and surveys, but cannot be considered as in situ, has been dated to the second millennium BCE (Kingsley and Raveh 1996: 46; Sibella 1995).

ANALYSIS

Shallow-Water Excavation

The Israeli coastline is generally sandy, with a gentle gradient. Most shipwrecks so far discovered are within a few score meters of the shoreline, and in water a few meters deep. In Dor/Tantura lagoon, diving is easy, in warm water with good visibility. Sea conditions make for suitable working conditions in May–June and September–November, when the sea is relatively calm. However, the occasional periods of rough seas (usually not more than two or three days) cause difficulty because of wave action affecting the stability of divers, possible damage to exposed timbers, and sand being washed into the excavation area. Waterlogged wood is only slightly heavier than seawater and may require securing in position or temporary covering during rough weather. Full coverage (with sandbags) is required to protect the site, particularly the wood, after completing an excavation season. The lagoon is an excellent location for study and training in underwater archaeology. However, out of the lagoon, conditions are different. Shallow water also implies working in the surf zone, where divers, boats, digging facilities, and archaeological equipment are subject to interference by even small changes in weather, waves, and wind. Proper archaeology—delicate excavation, recording, measuring, and photographing—becomes tricky and complicated and must be done fast, professionally, and efficiently.

Two exceptionally shallow projects were Dor 2002/2 and Dor 2004. Dor 2002/2 was found a few meters from the shoreline. The maximum depth of the wreck was 1.5 m, with waves washing the excavation site, which was also influenced by the

30 cm tide. As a result dredgers could be installed and operated only with difficulty, and divers found themselves disturbed by the sea. As it was on the seashore, it could not be excavated as a land or wet-land site. Similarly, Dor 2004 was found in shallow water and included a large stone weighing about 800 kg with a hole, resembling a very large stone anchor, with a timber underneath. The timber was dated by radio-carbon analysis to about the ninth century BCE. Because of sand movements the shoreline moved: the site disappeared under the beach, then reappeared in the sea after 18 months. Later it was found about 20 m inland. The site was dug by a mechanical backhoe, which caused seawater to fill the trench. This facilitated exca-vating the site as an underwater excavation. However, this method was unsatisfac-tory. Nevertheless, researchers intend to excavate the site further in the future, per-haps when it is again in the sea.

Recording

Generally, shipwrecks in Dor lagoon are studied underwater. Timbers are tagged, mainly by Dymo tags fixed by hypodermic needles or stainless steel nails, depend-ing on timber hardness. The Dymo tapes are of several colors, assisting in the iden-tification of different features and sides.

A thin, level baseline with a measuring tape is stretched above the longitudinal axis (the keel) of the wreck, or close to it. Transverse level lines are laid in selected places for cross-section recording. Direct measurements are made on every available component. Generally, several measurements are taken for each timber at about 20 cm intervals along its length, and duplicate measurements are later averaged. Mea-surements are made using tapes, plumb lines, carpenter's levels, rulers, and (plastic) calipers, and recorded in pencil on Mylar sheets. All measurements are repeated at least twice and checked to within a 5 mm margin of error; although most are gener-ally accurate to within 1 mm. In measuring a series of components such as frame width (sided) and spacing, a measuring tape is used for recording distances from a base point rather than those of each component and spaces between them separately, to avoid accumulated error. Recording includes writing a general description of com-ponents, drawing each component and noting how each fits into the adjacent section of hull, and describing wood characteristics and fastener details. Finds are recorded, photographed with attached tags, and retrieved to tap-water holding containers.

The Direct Survey Method (DSM or WEB) computer software program (Rule 1989) is employed. This method can solve three-dimensional positions of specific points marked on the wreck site with high precision, while the diver only has to measure straight lines. Data can be easily input soon after collection. Unsatisfactory results are highlighted by the software, so specific measurements can be rechecked. Photographs of each WEB point, close-up and from a distance, are helpful in post-excavation analysis of the wreck site.

Photography and video are extensively used. Photomosaics made in water less than 3 m deep without using a leveled, fixed frame placed at adjustable intervals are less accurate than those made in deeper water or on land. Panoramic photographs

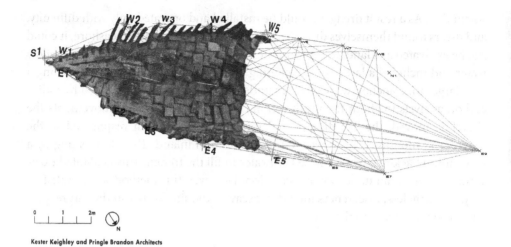

Kester Keighley and Pringle Brandon Architects

Figure 7.3 Combined photomosaic and WEB measurements of Dor C. Reproduced with
the kind permission of Chris Brandon and Kester Keighley.

are even less useful, as they distort the image, and so their scientific value is limited
(Figure 7.3).

Later, on land, all details of retrieved wood components and finds are recorded.
This stage can be done by hand—the method preferred by this author, considering
the scientific, teaching, and research aspects. However, other modern tools, such as
FaroArm and laser scanning, are also used in recording (see Ravn et al. in this
volume). These require proper facilities and trained and experienced personnel,
and while appreciating their advantages, their drawbacks must be acknowledged.
The site plan, the ship as a whole, sections of the hull, and individual timbers are
drawn to scale, combining the above methods.

Retrieval

Whether to retrieve a wreck from the seabed whole as an intact find, or to dismantle
it into its individual components, has long been a dilemma. The archaeological
aspects favor the treatment of the intact object. In addition to the basic ethical value
of not causing damage, conserving an archaeological find as a single entity enables
researchers to avoid, at least partially, the task of reassembly.

Retrieval after dismantling confers the following advantages:

1. Study of construction details is more effective when dealing with
   disassembled timbers, as the archaeological evidence is more accessible
   and of a higher quality.
2. Smaller facilities are required for individual components than for an intact
   find.
3. The volume of a conservation tank or space, the necessary conservation systems,
   and the consumption of materials and utilities are several times smaller.

4. Conservation of a wooden hull that contains different tree species in different states of preservation requires a more elaborate and longer process, whereas conservation of timbers of the same species together is shorter for the majority of the timbers, and more easily monitored and controlled.

Both approaches have been employed in excavating shipwrecks in Israel. The Ma'agan Mikhael ship was completely dismantled underwater and retrieved for analysis and conservation, a relatively long and expensive operation, justified by the uniqueness of the find. During the excavation, retrieval, and conservation, many timbers lost their original artificially bent three-dimensional shapes. These pieces had to undergo a shape restoration process, which can be avoided when a shipwreck is retrieved as a whole.

On the other hand, only selected components and sections of the Dor wrecks were retrieved for further analysis on land, depending on their value as sources of information on construction. These timbers were generally keel scarfs, endposts, or a special frame or plank. Some wrecks were left entirely in situ after recording. Archaeological finds other than wood were generally recorded underwater, after which they were removed for detailed documentation, study, conservation, and exhibition or storage on land.

A larger-scale operation was the retrieval of a 2 m section of the hull of Dor 2001/1 (Figure 7.4). It included sections of the keel, the false keel, the central longitudinal timber, stringers, frames, planks up to the second wale, and ceiling planks. The timbers composing this section were transferred to the conservation facilities of the Leon Recanati Institute, where they were examined free of underwater constraints. High-resolution information was extracted and recorded by direct measurements, hand drawings, and photographs. Timbers were traced, including all details, such as nails and holes, tool marks, and staining and marking.

There is a need to avoid, on the one hand, the great expense of retrieving and conserving the ship intact in one unit, and on the other, the damage caused in dismantling it completely. Maybe the golden mean is to dismantle it into several major sections, keeping the problematic areas intact, and thereby avoiding the restoration difficulties.

Figure 7.4 Photomosaic of Dor 2001/1. Reproduced with the kind permission of Stephen Breitstein.

Wood

The origin of ships' timbers was not necessarily near the place of construction. Wood was traded and transported, and shipyards built vessels from imported timbers. Nevertheless, much can be concluded by the identification of the tree species of every component. In Dor 2001/1 the existence of some frames of *Ziziphus spina Christi* and *Tamarix (X5)*, which are different from the rest of the species used for frames, may indicate a local repair.

DW2 was apparently built of old, poor-quality timbers (Figure 7.5). Dor 2002/2 is different: state or government involvement can be deduced from the good quality of the timbers and the high standard of their carpentry and construction. These two examples, and also Dor C, represent two different types of vessels. DW2 and Dor C were merchant coasters, apparently schooners, while Dor 2002/2 was perhaps an auxiliary naval vessel that played a part in the operations of Napoleon Bonaparte in 1799.

Transition in Construction

The expression "transition in construction" refers to basic changes in the principles of ship design and methods of construction. Instead of viewing a ship longitudinally and building it based on a shell of strakes joined together, which is termed "shell-first" or "strake-based," the concept changed to that of a construction based on transverse frames, termed "frame-based" or "skeleton-first." The transition was a process that lasted about a thousand years, mainly during the first millennium CE. Until recently it was widely accepted that the first archaeologically excavated ship whose construction was purely frame-based was the Serçe Limanı "Glass Wreck," dated to 1025 CE (Steffy 1994: 83–85; Steffy 2004: 153–169). However, the Byzantine and Islamic period shipwrecks at Dor lagoon have provided evidence that the completion of the transition in ship construction

Figure 7.5 Top view of DW2. Reproduced with the kind permission of Kitty and Chris Brandon.

occurred earlier. Both Tantura A and Dor 2001/1 show a complete transition about 500 years earlier than Serçe Limanı. There is no doubt that these hulls were built on frames, as is further supported by the Islamic period shipwrecks Tantura B, Tantura E, and Tantura F. However, evidence from the Byzantine harbor at Yenikapı (in Istanbul, Turkey), dated to between the fifth and eleventh centuries CE, indicates the parallel existence of another tradition: a comprehensive process of transition of hulls using plank edge-joints, which means at least partially based on shell of strakes, in a systematic process lasting until the eleventh century CE (Kocabaş and Kocabaş 2008: and see pp. 102, 164, 168, Yenikapı (YK) 15 and YK 17 "built with skeleton-first technique"; Pulak 2007). Thus, questions regarding the transition still exist; apparently it was not a linear process. Perhaps local construction traditions in separate regions developed in parallel. For example, a Nilotic/Egyptian construction tradition for Dor 2001/1 has been suggested by Rieth (2008) and Basch (2008).

In the transition, and parallel to the disappearance of plank edge-joints, frames became the basis for the shape and strength of hulls. Still, however, there is no significant tendency toward increasing frame dimensions or reducing room and space. Another aspect of this question is the fact that the sequence of construction of many hulls was a mixture of strake-based and frame-based. Frames were nailed to the keel, but in the Dor wrecks not all frames crossing the keel were actually nailed to it. Similarly, in the Serçe Limanı ship, not all of the frames were connected to the keel before planking (Steffy 2004: 157–161). Thus, in hulls which are completely frame-based, not all frames need to be in place before planking is fitted. McGrail (2008: 624–627) has suggested the terms "frame first" and "framing first" to differentiate between the two methods: "frame first" describes ships where the entire framework was fashioned and fastened to the keel and endposts before any planking was connected, and "framing first" describes those where a framework of keel, endposts and selected frames was first set up and fastened together, then planking was fastened, then more framing, then more planking, and so on. In the latter method not all frames were nailed to the keel. Regardless of the terminology, before planks were nailed to the entire framework or to several preexisting frames, there must have been a method to give the frames their proper shapes—mathematical, geometrical, or practical—based on years of experience, rules of thumb, and control by eye, battens, or other methods.

Tantura A, Dor 2001/1, and Tantura F raise the question of whether the existence of a keelson is essential in defining a frame-based or skeleton-first hull. Dor 2001/1 and Tantura F have only short central longitudinal timbers, not found in Tantura A. At first glance it seems, by definition, that a keelson is a necessary component of a skeleton. Although these hulls do not have keelsons, they are clearly built on frames. It seems that other elements, such as the keel and false keel, chine strake, wales, stringers, long ceiling planks nailed to frames, foot-wales, clamps, and perhaps additional elements that did not survive, contributed to the longitudinal integrity of the hull.

Dor Anchorage

The shipwrecks and finds in the lagoon are evidence of its being an active anchorage for about four millennia. As maneuvering in the lagoon requires skilled handling and local knowledge, it was only entered for a specific purpose. This supports the evidence for the existence of a community at Dor. As the background information and historical and archaeological sources about Dor in the Islamic period, especially concerning maritime activities, are sparse, this is significant. These wrecks indicate that Dor and the nearby area were populated, had trading connections, and were on commercial sailing routes in the Islamic period.

SUMMARY

The underwater archaeological projects of shipwrecks described above summarize the techniques employed in studying the construction of the Ma'agan Mikhael ship, and some of the advances of this discipline since the resumption of thorough research into the shipwrecks in Dor lagoon. The research employs the latest analytical techniques. However, real "hands on wood" analysis, although it is "low-tech," is still relevant. Research continues to provide new evidence about ship construction in antiquity and seamanship in the ancient world. A shipwreck has physical, social, and historical connections with its place of construction, its sailing routes, and the site of its wrecking, and its cargo gives information on trading of the period. The detailed study of the finds supplements the information on both the ship and its context. An additional significant benefit is the teaching and training of new generations of scholars.

REFERENCES

Artzy, Michal, and J. Lyon. 2003. The ceramics. In *The Ma'agan Mikhael ship: The recovery of a 2400-year-old merchantman, final report, volume 1*, ed. Eve Black, 183–202. Jerusalem: Israel Exploration Society and University of Haifa.

Barkai, Ofra. 2009. The Tantura F shipwreck. In *Between the seas: Transfer and exchange in nautical technology: Proceedings of the Eleventh International Symposium on Boat and Ship Archaeology, Mainz 2006*, ed. Ronald Bockius, 25–31. Mainz: Römisch-Germanischen Zentralmuseums.

Barkai, Ofra, and Yaacov Kahanov. 2007. The Tantura F shipwreck, Israel. *International Journal of Nautical Archaeology* 36 (1): 21–31.

Basch, Lucien. 2008. Recherche d'une généalogie. *Archaeologia Maritima Mediterranea* 5: 69–81.

Ben Zeev, Adina, Yaacov Kahanov, John Tresman, and Michal Artzy. 2009. *The Ma'agan Mikhael ship, volume 3: A reconstruction of the hull.* Jerusalem: Israel Exploration Society, Leon Recanati Institute for Maritime Studies, University of Haifa.

Bowens, Amanda. 2001. A late 19th century wreck from Tantura Lagoon (Dor C). *RIMS News, University of Haifa, Leon Recanati Institute for Maritime Studies* 28: 12–14.

Cvikel, Deborah, and Yaacov Kahanov. 2007. The Dor 2002/2 shipwreck. *Archaeologia Maritima Mediterranea* 3: 79–98.

Cvikel, Deborah, Yaacov Kahanov, Haim Goren, Elisabetta Boaretto, and Kurt Raveh. 2008. Napoleon Bonaparte's adventure in Tantura Lagoon: Historical and archaeological evidence. *Israel Exploration Journal* 58 (2): 199–219.

Jabour, Iscandar. 2004. Tapered pegs. In *The Ma'agan Mikhael ship: The recovery of a 2400-year-old merchantman, final report, volume 2,* ed. John Tresman, 117–132. Jerusalem: Israel Exploration Society and University of Haifa.

Kahanov, Yaacov. 1997. Wood conservation of the Ma'agan Mikhael shipwreck. *International Journal of Nautical Archaeology* 26 (4): 316–329.

———. 2000. The Tantura B shipwreck, Tantura Lagoon, Israel: Preliminary hull construction report. In *Down the river to the sea: Eighth International Symposium on Boat and Ship Archaeology, Gdańsk, 1997,* ed. Jerzy Litwin, 151–154. Gdańsk: Polish Maritime Museum.

———. 2001. A Byzantine shipwreck (Tantura A) in the Tantura Lagoon, Israel: Hull construction report. In *Tropis VI: Proceedings of the 6th International Symposium on Ship Construction in Antiquity, Lamia 1996,* ed. Harry Tzalas, 265–271. Athens: Hellenic Institute for the Preservation of Nautical Tradition.

———. 2003a. The hull. In *The Ma'agan Mikhael ship: The recovery of a 2400-year-old merchantman, final report, volume 1,* ed. Eve Black, 53–129. Jerusalem: Israel Exploration Society and University of Haifa.

———. 2003b. Dor D wreck, Tantura Lagoon, Israel. In *Boats, ships and shipyards: Proceedings of the Ninth International Symposium on Boat and Ship Archaeology, Venice 2000,* ed. Carlo Beltrame, 49–56. Oxford: Oxbow.

———. 2004a. Conservation. In *The Ma'agan Mikhael ship: The recovery of a 2400-year-old merchantman, final report, volume 2,* ed. John Tresman, 195–206. Jerusalem: Israel Exploration Society and University of Haifa.

———. 2004b. The sewing of the ship. In *The Ma'agan Mikhael ship: The recovery of a 2400-year-old merchantman, final report, volume 2,* ed. John Tresman, 3–79. Jerusalem: Israel Exploration Society and University of Haifa.

Kahanov, Yaacov, Deborah Cvikel, Amir Wielinski, and Eyal Israeli. 2008. Dor underwater excavation—report of the 2008 season. *RIMS News, University of Haifa, Leon Recanati Institute for Maritime Studies* 34: 15–18.

Kahanov, Yaacov, and Elisha Linder. 2004. *The Ma'agan Mikhael ship: The recovery of a 2400-year-old merchantman, final report, volume 2,* ed. John Tresman. Jerusalem: Israel Exploration Society and University of Haifa.

Kahanov, Yaacov, and Hadas Mor. 2006. The Dor 2001/1 wreck, Dor/Tantura Lagoon, Israel: Preliminary report. In *Connected by the sea: Proceedings of the Tenth International Symposium on Boat and Ship Archaeology, Roskilde 2003,* ed. Lucy Blue, Fred Hocker, and Anton Englert, 84–88. Oxford: Oxbow.

———. 2009. Dor 2001/1: Updated information and the retrieval of a section of the shipwreck. In *Between the seas: Transfer and exchange in nautical technology; Proceedings of the Eleventh International Symposium on Boat and Ship Archaeology, Mainz 2006,* ed. Ronald Bockius, 17–24. Mainz: Römisch-Germanischen Zentralmuseums.

Kahanov, Yaacov, and Patrice Pomey. 2004. The Greek sewn shipbuilding tradition and the
    Ma'agan Mikhael ship: A comparison with Mediterranean parallels from the sixth to
    the fourth centuries BCE. *Mariner's Mirror* 90 (1): 6–28.
Kahanov, Yaacov, and Jeffrey G. Royal. 2001. Analysis of hull remains of the Dor D vessel,
    Tantura Lagoon, Israel. *International Journal of Nautical Archaeology* 30 (2): 257–265.
Kahanov, Yaacov, Jeffrey G. Royal, and Jerome L. Hall. 2004. The Tantura wrecks and
    ancient Mediterranean shipbuilding. In *The philosophy of shipbuilding*, ed. Frederick
    M. Hocker and Cheryl A. Ward, 113–127. College Station: Texas A&M University Press.
Kahanov, Yaacov, and Idit Yovel. 2001. Dor DW2—a preliminary report. *RIMS News,
    University of Haifa, Leon Recanati Institute for Maritime Studies* 28: 10–12.
Kingsley, Sean A., and Kurt Raveh. 1996. *The ancient harbour and anchorage at Dor, Israel:
    Results of the underwater surveys, 1976–1991*. Oxford: Tempus Reparatum, BAR
    International Series 626.
Kocabaş, Işil Ö., and Ufuk Kocabaş. 2008. Technological and constructional features of
    Yenikapı shipwrecks: A preliminary evaluation. In *The "Old Ships" of the "New Gate" 1*,
    ed. Ufuk Kocabaş, 97–186. Istanbul: Yayınları.
Linder, Elisha, and Yaacov Kahanov. 2003. *The Ma'agan Mikhael ship: The recovery of a
    2400-year-old merchantman, final report, volume 1*, ed. Eve Black. Jerusalem: Israel
    Exploration Society and University of Haifa.
Liphschitz, Nili. 2004. Dendroarchaeological investigations. In *The Ma'agan Mikhael ship:
    The recovery of a 2400-year-old merchantman, final report, volume 2*, ed. John Tresman,
    156–163. Jerusalem: Israel Exploration Society and University of Haifa.
McGrail, Seán. 2008. Sea transport, part 1: Ships and navigation. In *The Oxford handbook
    of engineering and technology in the classical world*, ed. John P. Oleson, 606–637. New
    York: Oxford University Press.
Mor, Hadas, and Yaacov Kahanov. 2006. The Dor 2001/1 shipwreck, Israel—a summary of
    the excavation. *International Journal of Nautical Archaeology* 35 (2): 274–289.
Planer, Dror. 2007. Tantura E—Dor Lagoon, 2007. *RIMS News, University of Haifa, Leon
    Recanati Institute for Maritime Studies* 33: 19–20.
Pulak, Cemal. 2007. Yenikapı batıkları: Fırtınanın armağani (The wrecks of Yenikapı: The
    gift of storm). *Arkeoatlas* 6: 129–141.
Rieth, Eric. 2008. Géométrie des forms de carène et construction "sur membrure premiere"
    (Veme–XIIeme siècles): Une autre approche de l'histoire de l'architecture naval
    Méditerranéenne au moyen âge. *Archaeologia Maritima Mediterranea* 5: 45–68.
Royal, Jeffrey G., and Yaacov Kahanov. 2000. An Arab-period merchant vessel at Tantura
    Lagoon, Israel (Trench 9). *International Journal of Nautical Archaeology* 29 (1):
    151–153.
———. 2005. New dating and contextual evidence for the fragmentary timber remains
    located in the Dor D site, Israel. *International Journal of Nautical Archaeology* 34 (2):
    308–313.
Rule, Nick. 1989. The Direct Survey Method (DSM) of underwater survey, and its
    application underwater. *International Journal of Nautical Archaeology* 18 (2): 157–162.
Sibella, Patricia. 1995. The ceramics. *INA Quarterly* 22 (2): 13–16.
Steffy, Richard J. 1994. *Wooden shipbuilding and the interpretation of shipwrecks*. College
    Station: Texas A&M University Press.
———. 2004. Construction and analysis of the vessel. In *Serçe Limani: An eleventh-century
    shipwreck, volume 1: The ship and its anchorage, crew and passengers*, ed. George F.
    Bass, Sheila D. Matthews, and Richard J. Steffy, 153–169. College Station: Texas A&M
    University Press.

Votruba, Gregory F. 2004. Reassembly of the hull. In *The Ma'agan Mikhael ship: The recovery of a 2400-year-old merchantman, final report, volume 2*, ed. John Tresman, 211–220. Jerusalem: Israel Exploration Society and University of Haifa.

Wachsmann, Shelley, and Yaacov Kahanov. 1997. Shipwreck fall: The INA/CMS joint expedition to Tantura Lagoon, Israel. *INA Quarterly* 24 (1): 3–18.

Wachsmann, Shelley, Yaacov Kahanov, and Jerome L. Hall. 1997. The Tantura B shipwreck: The 1996 INA/CMS joint expedition to Tantura Lagoon. *INA Quarterly* 24 (4): 3–15.

Yovel, Idit. 2004. The DW2 wreck and its finds as historical evidence for coastal trade in South Syria and Israel in the seventeenth and eighteenth centuries. MA thesis, University of Haifa: (Hebrew with English abstract).

———. 2005. The DW2 wreck and its finds as historical evidence for coastal trade in South Syria and Israel in the 17th and 18th centuries. *RIMS News, University of Haifa, Leon Recanati Institute for Maritime Studies* 31: 19–20.

CHAPTER 8

SHIPS ON LAND

JAMES P. DELGADO

INTRODUCTION

SOME of the earliest discoveries of the remains of ships came in the nineteenth century and the early twentieth century CE from sites once underwater and subsequently covered by land as a result of either natural or artificial landfill. These seemingly dry but frequently "wet" sites, often encapsulated by water-saturated mud, have yielded incredibly well-preserved discoveries. In the twenty-first century, archaeologists are seeing an increased number of sites and a growing sense that "buried ships" provide unique opportunities in nautical archaeology. At the same time, modern nautical and maritime archaeologists are also realizing that a more holistic view of maritime sites on land provides opportunities to assess the growth and decline of ports, port-related infrastructure and technology, and activities such as fishing, as well as broader perspectives on maritime activity and maritime cultural landscapes in now land-filled port sites. This has particularly been the case in Istanbul with the Yenikapı site (third to tenth century CE), in London (second to sixteenth centuries CE), in Pisa (first century BCE to fourth century CE), in New York (seventeenth to nineteenth centuries CE) and in San Francisco (1849–1907 CE).

One class of "buried ships" comprises vessels deliberately interred as ship burials. These include riverine funerary craft associated with Egyptian royal burials, notably the Dashur boats and the Khufu (Cheops) ship at Giza (Lipke 1984). Other famous examples include the seventh-century CE Saxon ship burial at Sutton Hoo, Suffolk, England, and Viking ship burials, notably the ninth-century CE Oseberg, Gokstad, and Tune ships, excavated in Norway in the late nineteenth and early twentieth centuries (McGrail 1987; Christensen, Ingstad, and Myhre 1993). Other examples include the tenth-century Ladby ship in Denmark, as well as several hundred boat burials, nearly all of them unexcavated, throughout Scandinavia (McGrail 1987; Sørensen 2001). In 2004, "metal detecting enthusiasts" in Yorkshire, England, discovered a likely Viking boat burial, one of several known or probable boat burials in the United Kingdom (there are four known Viking ship or boat burials in Scotland, for example, and in the Orkneys) in addition to the Sutton Hoo ship (McGrail 1987, Owen, and Dalland 1999).

Another type of buried site is represented by beached shipwrecks. These vessels, either as largely intact entities or as dispersed components of ships broken against the shore, are buried in wet sand and sediments in the intertidal zones of beaches. While some are visible to varying degrees, others are completely buried and are visible only when seasonal beach erosion, storm-induced erosion, or dredging exposes them (Delgado 1998). Among the more famous examples of this type of buried ship is *Amsterdam*, a Dutch East Indiaman that stranded on the foreshore of Bulverhythe, near Hastings, England, on 26 January 1749. The vessel settled approximately 8.5 m into the sand, leaving only frame tops exposed on the beach surface, outlining the wreck site at low tide for centuries (Marsden 1974a).

The largest quantity of sites, however, exists in rural and urban areas where marshes, sea-level change, river channel shifts, siltation, or deliberate land-filling or drainage (notably, in the case of the polders in the Netherlands, where substantially well-preserved ships, most from postmedieval contexts, have been discovered and excavated) have buried ships. In one case, a Roman vessel from the first century CE was found, carbonized and upside down, but intact, in the volcanic flow at the former beach of the Roman city of Herculaneum, destroyed along with Pompeii in 79 CE (Steffy 1985).

Sea-level changes have covered former bays, river courses, ports, and harbors. This includes former anchorages and ports of ancient cities, such as Troy, where the Bronze Age port now lies beneath modern fields, and Greek and Roman port cities such as Miletus and Ephesus. While still unassessed and still unexcavated, the former port areas of sites such as these will likely yield significant evidence of maritime activity, including the remains of vessels. The potential of such sites has been demonstrated by discoveries in Italy, France, the United Kingdom, the Netherlands, Sweden, Turkey, Argentina, the United States, Canada, China, and New Zealand. What follows is a discussion of a variety of sites. It should be noted that this listing is intended to be illustrative, not comprehensive.

Buried Ships from Antiquity to the Late Roman Period

In 1992, workers constructing a road near the present-day shores of Dover encountered the well-preserved buried remains of a middle Bronze Age plank boat built circa 1400–1300 BCE. The Dover Boat, as it became known, was excavated by the

Canterbury Archaeological Trust, raised, and subsequently conserved. The vessel was a well-used and repaired craft, perhaps an oceangoing vessel, that measured 2.32 m wide and over 9.35 m long. The Dover Boat is a contemporary of the Ferriby Boats F1, F2, and F3, all dating to c. 1300 BCE, which were found in an intertidal clay deposit on the north shore of the Humber estuary in East Yorkshire, England, and excavated in 1937 by E. V. and C. W. Wright. In addition to these craft, a large number of Bronze Age and later log boats have been discovered and excavated from former riverine areas in the United Kingdom since the nineteenth century, many in the area around the Humber (Wright 1990).

The first-century BCE Comacchio Wreck is a ship over 21 m long and 5.62 m wide that stranded and wrecked in beach sediments near an ancient river mouth and was subsequently buried. Reclamation of the area between 1919 and 1922 left the shipwreck site out of water but buried in wet mud until dredging struck it in 1980. Initial excavation in 1981, and final excavation and recovery between 1986 and 1989, recovered the hull and a cargo of boxwood logs, amphorae carrying foodstuffs, and 102 lead ingots from Spanish mines. Due to the high level of preservation in its environment, the buried wreck also yielded clothing, leather goods, tools belonging to the ship's carpenter, a boat bailer, sheaves, and an iron anchor (Berti 1990).

The buried remains of part of a ship dating to the late third to early fourth century CE were discovered during construction of the County Hall on the south bank of the Thames, London, in 1910. The find and recovery of the County Hall Ship generated much media attention thanks to its buried yet accessible context. The wreck was discovered 6.55 m beneath the street level, and 91.44 m east of the retaining wall between the Westminster and Hungerford bridges. After decades of display, and decay because the timbers were not conserved, the County Hall Ship was dismantled and removed from exhibit at the London Museum in 1978. Archaeologist Peter Marsden conducted significant research and reconstructed the vessel on paper, generating new plans and a scale model of the ship. Marsden's work demonstrated that what had survived was 13 m by 5.5 m of the midships portion of a Mediterranean-type vessel 19.1 m long. Built of oak that demonstrated tree ring patterns compatible with southeastern England, Marsden surmised that the County Hall Ship may have been constructed by an English shipwright familiar with Mediterranean construction methods. Dendrochronological evidence and other factors suggest a probable construction date of 300 CE (Marsden 1974b).

Another UK find, an early-fourth-century CE vessel uncovered from a former river channel at Barland's Farm, near Gwent, Wales, was made in late 1993. The oak-built vessel was represented at the site by the bow, lower hull, and one side of the 9.7 m long, 2.6 m wide craft. The well-preserved hull remains provided a detailed look at Romano-Celtic shipbuilding tradition, with sewn planking, massive and closely spaced frames, and treenails and iron nails used to fasten planks to the frames (Nayling and McGrail 2004).

A Roman wreck dating from the fifth century CE emerged from fill that covered the former shoreline of Ravenna, Italy, in late 1998. Known as the Parco di Teodorico Wreck, these remains were buried 8.5 m below the modern land level in sand. An accidental encounter during construction cut off the vessel's stern, but the craft was estimated to have been 9 m in length and approximately 3.1 m wide. The wreck was excavated and recovered by the Soprintendenza per I Beni Archeologici dell'Emilia Romagna under the direction of Maria Grazia Maioli (Medas 2004).

More substantial remains, including multiple wrecks and materials from associated maritime activities, have come to light when ancient ports or harbors have been excavated. The Claudian harbor of Rome, built in 42 CE by the emperor Claudius, outside the city between the harbor of Ostia and the banks of the Tiber River, came to light in 1957 at Fiumicino during construction of the Leonardo Da Vinci International Airport. Excavation disclosed substantial remains of a mole, with wooden caissons utilized in its construction, concrete jetties, the ruins of several structures, a cistern, and a variety of finds in the silted-in harbor basin, including the remains of five vessels (Boetto 1999a, 1999b, 2000). These were discovered between 1958 and 1965 abutting the mole in what had been a backwater area of the harbor and most likely a graveyard of abandoned and unusable ships (see also Richards in this volume). Vessel timbers exhibited signs of preburial carbonization and wood-boring marine organisms.

The five wrecks, Fiumicino 1–5, dated from the late second to early fifth centuries CE. All were cargo-carrying vessels with the exception of Fiumicino 5, a second-century CE small fishing boat with a central compartment to keep fish alive in a "wet well." One vessel, Fiumicino 4, was a small oceangoing craft, while the remaining three hulls, Fiumicino 1, 2, and 3, were examples of *naves caudicaria*, or wide, flat-bottomed craft used to transport cargoes upriver. The remains of the five vessels, as well as other maritime finds recovered from the harbor basin, are displayed in the Museum of the Roman Ships (Museo delle Navi), which opened at the site of the excavations in 1979.

Another group of Roman wrecks, discovered 7.5 m below street level in November 1981 during waterfront construction of a new hotel one block away from the modern bank of the Rhine in Mainz, Germany, was exposed and recovered in a three-month excavation, stored until 1992, and then conserved and reassembled after study. The Mainz ships are now displayed with full-scale re-creations in the Museum for Ancient Shipping (Museum für Antike Schiffahrt) of the Römisch-Germanisches Zentralmuseummuseum in Mainz. Known as Mainz 1, 2, 3, 4, and 5, these vessels are late Roman military craft of the late third to fourth centuries CE, employed on the Rhine at a time when the river was the frontier of Rome and Germania Magna (post 260 CE).

Four of the craft (Mainz 1, 2, 4, and 5) were troop transports, while Mainz 3 was apparently a riverine patrol boat. The transports ranged between 17 and 21 m in length, with a midships beam of little more than 2.7 m, and a depth of 90 cm. The craft, as reconstructed, were both rowed and sailed, apparently by the 24 to 32 soldiers in each boat. Mainz 3 is a smaller, more compact craft, 18 m in length, with a 4.8 m breath and a 1.3 m depth. It is believed that the vessels were abandoned and sank after 402 CE, when Germanic invasions forced the Romans to abandon the Rhine frontier and the garrison outpost where the fleet was moored (Pferderhirt 1994; Bockius 1996).

In Marseille, excavation for construction has uncovered wrecks since 1864, when a 17 m by 7 m Roman coastal cargo vessel of the second to third centuries CE was unearthed. The oldest wrecks, two Archaic Greek ships from the sixth century BCE, were unearthed along with the remains of Roman waterfront warehouses, piers, fragments of a fourth-century CE Roman wreck, and three Roman wrecks from the first and second centuries CE, during the construction of a subterranean parking garage at the Place Jules-Verne (Pomey and Hesnard 1994: 110–115; Pomey 1995, 2003). The vessels are curated at the Musée d'Histoire de Marseille.

The remains of the two Archaic Greek vessels, Jules-Verne 7 and Jules-Verne 9, have been extensively studied and reconstructed. Jules-Verne 7, as recovered, was a distorted and broken hull measuring over 14 m in length and 4 m in width. A more or less complete reconstruction using models and drawings showed that it was a small, sailing coastal merchant vessel 15.65 m long, with a beam of 3.8 m, a depth of 1.7 m, and a displacement weight of about 15 tons (Pomey 2003: 63). Jules-Verne 9, less well preserved, with a section of the bottom of the hull measuring some 5 m long and 1.4 m wide, was sufficiently preserved to warrant its reconstruction as a "light and fast ship devoted to oar-propelled coastal fishing and sailing" that was 9.5 m long, with a beam of 1.88 m, a depth of 0.75 m, and a 3-ton displacement (Pomey 2003: 63–64).

Excavation of a tunnel on the waterfront of Olbia, Sardinia, in 1999–2001 exposed the silted-over remains of the ancient waterfront, with finds ranging from wooden jetties, ceramics, ship fittings, carpenter's tools, rough and partially worked wood, and two masts that suggested the presence of a Roman period shipyard, to 16 vessels in varying degrees of preservation dating from the first century to the fourteenth century CE. Ten of the Olbia ships were dated to the fifth century and were discovered lying parallel to each other, suggesting a single, catastrophic loss event, which the excavators believe to be deliberate, suggesting as a possibility the political instability of the period and Vandal raids (D'Oriano and Riccardi 1999).

In 1998, construction in Pisa, Italy, near the San Rossore railway station encountered the land-filled former harbor of Pisa known as the Porto delle Conche (Port of the Basins). Reports vary from between 39 to 41 vessels encountered, but it is likely that eight individual keels were included in the count (Colombini et. al. 2009). A now vanished channel of the Arno River had connected the harbor to both the river and the sea. A variety of well-preserved remains, including harbor infrastructure such as wharves, dating from the Etruscan period (tenth century BCE) to the late Roman period (fifth century CE) were excavated, along with 16 buried ships (dating from the first century BCE to the fourth century CE) by the Cooperativa Indagione Documentazione Ricerca Archeologica under the direction of Stefano Bruni. The initial find of 10 vessels, 8 of which were more or less intact, came from a 100 m by 45 m area. The San Rossore shipwrecks, as they were initially known (they are now known as the Navi Antichi di Pisa), were covered by sediments and evidenced four catastrophic floods in antiquity that led not only to their loss but also the siltation and burial of the harbor. In total, the finds document maritime activity and various ship types involved in the thousand-year span between the development of the riverine harbor by the Etruscans and its subsequent use by the Romans (Bruni and Abbado 2000).

Many of the craft appear to have been small coastal freighters (*onerariae*). For example, three of the first craft excavated fit this type. The first to be discovered, half of a craft originally some 16 m or more in length, was missing its bow and stern and was devoid of cargo. It dates to the second century CE. The second ship, Ship B, was a smaller craft; approximately 5 m of its starboard hull survived, along with oarsmen's seats, frames, and a portion of the port side. A basket, leather sandal, and wooden winch with line still attached were found with the ship. It has been dated to the late second to early first century BCE. Ship D, dated to the second century CE, was found essentially intact and upside down. It is 13.93 m long and 6 m broad (Bruni and Abbado 2000).

The vessels and the harbor area included a large array of material culture relating to the ships and their use: for example, fishing equipment, anchors, baskets, rigging, cargo (including amphorae still packed with their contents), and, in one vessel, the skeleton of a drowned sailor and his dog. The Museum of the Antique Ships of Pisa (Il Cantiere delle Navi Antiche di Pisa) is the central point for the conservation, study, and interpretation of the ships. A number of the ships were encapsulated in fiberglass at the time of excavation to await further study and conservation (Bruni and Abbado 2000).

In 2004, excavation for the subway in Naples discovered the former waterfront and the Port of Neapolis near the Piazza Municipio. Construction work was preceded by archaeological investigation by the Soprintendenza per i Beni Archeologici delle Province di Napoli e Carcerta. Structures that lined the shore of antiquity included a pier, 23 m long and 4.5 m wide, with two associated wrecks that appear to have been abandoned close by it and another that wrecked, perhaps by smashing into the pier. The pier and the ships were found at a stratigraphic layer dated to the late first century CE. The three vessels were designated Naples A, B, and C, and after excavation they were lifted intact for conservation, analysis, and eventual display.

Ships A and C had both been abandoned and contained no cargo, although associated cultural material, including wicker baskets, needles for mending fishing nets, leather bags, and lines and blocks, were found in association with them. Ship B, wrecked next to the pier, was carrying a cargo of limestone. Ship A, an 11.7 m long, 3.2 m broad vessel, was an *onerariae*, or small to mid-range coastal trader, as was Ship B, which measured 9 m long and 2 m broad. Ship C was a *horeia*, a heavily built vessel used to unload and move cargo around the port. The remains of Ship C measured 13.2 m by 3.7 m (Capretti et al. 2008).

BURIED SHIPS FROM THE BYZANTINE PERIOD

One of the better-known Byzantine period ships discovered in a buried context came from a reclaimed Sicilian marsh. The Pantano Longarini wreck was discovered during the winter of 1963–1964 when mechanical excavation of drainage channels

600 m from the modern shoreline struck and exposed the well-preserved vessel, which dates to the seventh century CE. While half of the hull was destroyed before the antiquity of the craft was determined—including the bow, which disappeared before archaeologists arrived—excavation of the remaining 9.1 m of the wreck by Peter Throckmorton and Gerhard Kapitan documented its construction and determined that it was a massively framed and strongly constructed craft most likely built either in southern Italy or Greece between 600 and 650 CE. A transitional ship in that it no longer represented the sleeker double-ended craft of antiquity but rather had a pronounced stern with a transom, it was built heavily, relying on its framing for strength. The Pantano Longarini ship is often cited as significant because of the extensive nature of its remains, preserved by burial. Reconstruction of the vessel suggests that it was originally 23.20 m long at the keel and that it was capable of carrying up to 300 tons of cargo (Throckmorton and Throckmorton 1973).

In 2004, during construction of the Marmaray rail line, the undersea tunnel that will link Istanbul's Asian and European shores, a rich and diverse archaeological site was discovered in the district of Yenikapı. The wide array of finds from the site spans eight millennia, from the Neolithic period to the late Ottoman. Although the excavation is still in progress at the time of this writing (2009), archaeologists have thus far discovered at least 34 shipwrecks and numerous loose ship timbers associated with the Byzantine *Portus Theodosiacus,* or Harbor of Theodosius. This harbor, probably built in the late fourth century CE, may have been the largest harbor of the ancient Byzantine capital (Mango 1986: 121; Müller-Wiener 1994: 9). Located at the mouth of the Lykos River on the city's Propontid shore, the harbor seems to have been associated with the grain trade, based on the proximity of large granaries; it was also likely used in the importation of building materials during the city's early expansion in the fourth and fifth centuries (Magdalino 2001: 211–212; Mango 1986: 121). The harbor enclosure was fortified with a single wall and towers, remnants of which can be seen today (Tsangadas 1980: 56–57). A breakwater on the south side of the harbor promoted gradual siltation, which reduced the depth and area of the harbor over several centuries; after 1000 CE, it was likely accessible only to shallow-draft vessels. The latest stage of activity is represented by dock pilings at the site, many of which were driven through earlier shipwrecks. Cross sections of these pilings were used to construct a dendrochronological sequence ranging from c. 1248 to c. 1445 CE, showing that the latest extensions or repairs to the docks occurred only a few years before the Ottoman conquest. By this time, the reduced harbor was likely used only by small fishing boats (Kuniholm, Griggs, and Newton 2007: 381–383). In his account of Constantinople in the 1540s, Petrus Gyllius indicates that the area of the Theodosian harbor was completely filled in, with the land used for vegetable gardens (Gilles 2008: xx, 2001).

Although the earliest evidence of a vessel at the site is a fragment of planking that dates from the fourth to fifth centuries CE, the 34 extant shipwrecks at the site date from the seventh to early eleventh centuries CE, making the wrecks at Yenikapı the largest assemblage of ships ever discovered from the early to middle Byzantine periods. The shipwrecks are in an excellent state of preservation due to the rapid deposition of sediments. The Yenikapı wrecks include several types of vessels not hitherto documented archaeologically, most importantly at least four Byzantine *galea* or rowed warships. The large number of vessels from the late tenth or early eleventh century suggests a catastrophic event, such as a sizable storm, and the subsequent rapid burial of the remains.

Initial excavation of the wrecks was carried out by the Istanbul Archaeological Museums under the direction of Ismail Karamut and Metin Gökçay, while in situ recording and dismantling were carried out by an international team from the Institute of Nautical Archaeology (INA) at Texas A&M University and a Turkish team from Istanbul University's Conservation Department. The INA team excavated eight of the shipwrecks between 2005 and 2008 under the direction of Cemal Pulak and Sheila Matthews. These include two *galea* (YK 2 and YK 4) dating to the late tenth or early eleventh centuries, and six merchant craft dating from the seventh to eleventh centuries (YK 1, YK 5, YK 11, YK 14, YK 23, and YK 24). Istanbul Archaeological Museums have reported on 10 of the 22 ships excavated under the direction of Sait Başaran and Ufuk Kocabaş (Kocabaş 2008). Nine of the 10 are merchant craft, and the tenth is a *galea*. The wrecks excavated by Başaran and Kocabaş and noted here are those with the field designations YK 3, YK 6, YK 7, YK 8, YK 9, YK 12, YK 15, YK 16, YK17, and YK 18.

The majority of the ships found at Yenikapı may be grouped into one of two categories. Most are merchant vessels (or roundships); this category includes some possible variants, such as fishing vessels and stone carriers. The rowed vessels (or galleys) comprise the second category on the site and are easily distinguished by their long and slender hull shape as well as the survival of oar ports in the hull of one wreck. Based on ship iconography of the period, all of the merchant ships were likely rigged with a single lateen sail (Pulak 2007: 211). The galleys would have also had lateen sails rigged on one or two masts, but unfortunately almost no archaeological evidence for the masts or rigging of the galleys survived (Pryor 2006: 127–128, 140–142, 157–159). Because excavations are continuing at the time of this writing, an exhaustive catalog of ships at the site will not be presented here. The following is an overview of the two principal categories, merchant vessels and rowed vessels, using specific ships as examples.

The merchant vessels or roundships include ships that range from the seventh century CE to the late tenth or early eleventh century CE. The original sizes of these vessels varied greatly: some measured less than 9 or 10 m long, others as large as 20 m. These differences in size likely represent differences in function (ranging from fishing boats to merchant vessels to stone carriers). The majority of the roundships appear to have been 10–15 m in length and 3–5 m in beam. Most of the roundships were built with oak (usually Turkey oak, or *Quercus cerris*), although pine, sycamore, elm, and other wood species were also utilized (Pulak and Liphschitz forthcoming; Pulak 2007: 208). These ships appear to have been built with a mixed building method, utilizing a shell-based technique involving edge fasteners up to the waterline, and a skeleton-based system without edge fasteners above the waterline. The chronological range and number of merchant vessels found at Yenikapı show a clear evolution of the Byzantine shipbuilding tradition over time, including changes in the edge fastening of planks and perhaps the eventual abandonment of the edge-fastening technique as well as changes in the framing patterns and types of frame fasteners used in the ships' hulls.

An excellent example of a merchant vessel is YK 1, a small ship, around 12 m long, dating to the late tenth or early eleventh century. This was the first shipwreck found on the site and the first to be fully recorded. Unusually, the side of the ship was preserved from the turn of the bilge to the bulwark rail. During the life of the ship, several additional strakes were added to the hull to increase its freeboard and cargo capacity (Pulak 2007: 209). The vessel apparently capsized, with the surviving portion of the hull pinned under the cargo, which was then quickly covered with sand and thereby preserved. Two iron anchors and a large coil of rope were found in the bow of YK 1. One of only two ships on the site found with cargo, YK 1 was preserved along with several dozen Ganos-type amphoras, produced on the island of Ganos in the Sea of Marmara in the tenth and eleventh centuries, and used for transporting wine or olive oil (Vroom 2005: 95). Other objects recovered from the wreck include coins, glass bracelets, metal objects, and a range of wooden objects, such as combs, spoons, a bowl, fragments of a cylindrical wooden container, and rigging toggles. A second smaller ship (YK 12, originally 8.5 m long) dating to the ninth century was found with a cargo of similar amphoras as well as a ceramic brazier for onboard cooking, a reed basket still containing cherry pits, and other objects (Kocabaş 2008: 112–123).

Other vessels were used to carry building supplies. For example, YK 17 was the well-preserved starboard side of another larger cargo vessel still loaded with 56 stone blocks measuring roughly 25 cm by 30 cm by 45 cm and weighing 647 kg total. Dating to the eighth or ninth century CE, YK 17 was iron fastened and had two wales and thick planking, which might be expected if the craft was a stone carrier. The remains were 8.20 m long and 2.03 m wide, although the originally the vessel was probably 18 m long, or perhaps more (Kocabaş 2008). A similarly large cargo vessel, YK 3, dating to the tenth to eleventh centuries CE, contained roof tile fragments and mortar that may represent the remains of its last cargo. The vessel's remains, comprising the starboard side from the wale to the keel, are 9.12 m long and 2.28 m wide. The vessel's original dimensions were probably close to 18 m by 6 m (Kocabaş 2008).

The second category comprises the long, rowed vessels or galleys (*galea*) (Figure 8.1). These finds are notable in that they are the first Byzantine warships discovered. In contrast to the range of ships of the merchant vessel category, all four galleys appear to be roughly contemporary (tenth to early eleventh centuries CE). They are also notably uniform in design and in materials used; two of the galleys were built with the same species of pine, *Pinus nigra*, and with frames almost entirely of Oriental plane, *Platanus orientalis* (Pulak and Liphschitz forthcoming; Pulak 2007: 214). This standardization in design suggests that they may have been built in a state-run shipyard and indicates a concern for speed and lightness that is not apparent in the roundships. Their size and design suggests

Figure 8.1 Yenikapı *galea* during excavation in 2006. Photograph
by James P. Delgado.

that the ships were probably light, multipurpose war galleys, approximately 30 m
long, designed for reconnaissance, running messages, supporting the larger
dromons, and warfare (Pulak 2007: 215).

As analysis and, ultimately, reconstruction of the Yenikapı ships continues over
the next decade, much more will be learned from this unique site. Istanbul Archaeological Museums mounted a preliminary display of the finds in 2008, and plans for
a permanent museum on the site to display the conserved and reconstructed vessels
are in the design stages.

Buried Ships from the Medieval
Period to the Sixteenth Century CE

A serendipitous discovery of buried ships came through the expansion of the existing Viking Ship Museum at Roskilde, Denmark. In 1996–1997 this museum, which
housed the remains of cofferdam-excavated Viking ships discovered earlier, undertook an expansion project during which workers discovered the old shoreline, now
filled in, and nine vessels from the Viking period through the early Middle Ages, or
roughly from 1025 to 1336 CE. The oldest vessel, a Viking warship, was 36 m long
and 3.5 m broad and carried an estimated crew of 78 (Croome 2006).

As previously noted, the excavation of a tunnel on the waterfront of Olbia,
Sardinia, in 1999–2001 exposed the silted-over remains of the ancient waterfront,
which included 16 vessels in varying degrees of preservation dating from the first
century CE to the fourteenth. The Roman period wrecks were covered with silt as the
harbor began to fill in late antiquity, and the medieval port therefore lay a slight
distance from the ancient shoreline. The excavation also revealed five medieval
period wrecks. One sank as a result of a shipboard fire, two were abandoned and left
to fall apart, and two were deliberately scuttled, perhaps as a breakwater. One of the
Olbia medieval vessels was a long, sleek craft 12 m in length and 2.5 m in breadth. The
wrecks were covered by landfill, including gravel and stones, in the thirteenth and
fourteenth centuries CE. A range of medieval period ceramics and glass, including
Pisan and Liguran goblets, Sicilian pottery, and Islamic glass and ceramics, attested
to the thriving nature of trade in the medieval port (D'Oriano and Riccardi 1999).

On Stockholm's Helgeandsholmen Island, excavations in 1978–1980 for a new
parking garage for the Swedish parliament (Riksdagshuset), which was then being
renovated, revealed a major complex of finds, including burials, the remains of the
1530 CE city wall, and 11 ship and boat hulls within an 8,000 m² excavation, resulting
in the largest and most comprehensive excavations yet undertaken in Stockholm.
The project was popular with the media and the public, and the excavation was soon
dubbed Riksgropen (the National Hole). The excavations documented the development of Stockholm from the mid-thirteenth century CE through the modern era
(Varenius 1985). The site is now an archaeological park and museum, and the conservation and analysis of the hulls is ongoing in 2009. One of the finds, Boat V, was
built sometime between 1316 and 1350 CE. A small, narrow craft, it carried eight
pairs of oars and had slightly elevated decks fore and aft. It has been suggested that
it was a personnel carrier, perhaps a guard or patrol ship on the Stockholm archipelago or on Lake Mälalren. Another find, Boat X, is described as a 10 m long "peas-
ant-built cargo sailing vessel" of the period (Hattendorf and Unger 2003).

A fifteenth-century wreck was discovered and excavated in Newport, South
Wales, in 2002. Known as the Newport Ship, it was located in landfill in central
Newport, on the banks of the River Usk, and is more than 25 m long. Tree ring
dating suggests that the timber used to build it was felled between 1465 and 1466 CE,

but the hull, which shows evidence of hard use and heavy repair, may have been decades old when sunk or abandoned. The encapsulation of the hull sealed and preserved a wide array of artifacts that indicated it was an armed merchantman that had traded with Portugal. Among the artifacts were Portuguese ceramics, coins, large lumps of cork, leather shoes, cordage, rigging tackle, barrel staves, woolen clothing, wooden bowls, stone cannon shot, and a complete archer's leather wrist guard, lined and decorated with a heart and a tooled Latin inscription (Hunter 1999; Roberts 2003).

Eight buried ships were excavated in 1996–1997 by Christian P. P. Lemée at the site of the engine works of the Burmeister & Wain Shipyard, built on landfill over the former harbor of Grønnegaard in Copenhagen, Denmark. Six of the vessels dated to between 1585 and 1640 CE, and five of these were large carvel-built ships, making this a unique assemblage of Renaissance period shipbuilding. The site was established as a private mercantile harbor for the city of Christianshavn in the fifteenth century CE. Excavation showed that two of the hulls, B&W 1 and B&W 2, had been purposely scuttled to serve as the foundations for a careening wharf between 1624 and 1636 CE; subsequently, in the mid-eighteenth century, another vessel, B&W 5, was also scuttled by the wharf to support a large crane. One of the focuses of Lemée's work was the four-century history of the site as an industrial shipbuilding facility (Lemée 2006).

The major focus of the research, however, was on the vessels themselves. Time and construction constraints required that the fieldwork be completed quickly, and none of the hulls was preserved except through documentation, which included Total Station measurement and dissection of selected wrecks through chain-saw extraction of 2 by 4 m sections for analysis. Lemée analyzed four wrecks, then reconstructed B&W 4 and B&W 5. The vessels were all built in the Dutch shell-based tradition, and most were built in Holland (Lemée 2006).

B&W 1, a carvel-built vessel, 26 m long and 6 m wide, was built in or around Hoorn circa 1584 CE. The vessel was rebuilt and lengthened by 7.7 m circa 1608 CE with wood from Denmark. This type of vessel, not before seen archaeologically, was a *verlanger*, the "lengthened ship" mentioned in Dutch treatises. It was partially dismantled and scuttled for the careening wharf in the early seventeenth century (Lemée 2006). **B&W 2,** another carvel-built ship of circa 1606 CE, built possibly near Amsterdam and subsequently rebuilt in Denmark between 1618–1622 CE, was approximately 27 m long and 7.5 m wide. Like B&W 1, it was scuttled in place between 1624 and 1636 CE for the careening wharf's foundation. Historical sources indicate that the wreck is one of three possible ships—*David, København,* or *Elephanten*—that sailed from Copenhagen in 1618 on the first Danish voyage to the East Indies and returned in 1622. Two of the ships were, according to the documentary record, scuttled as foundations (Lemée 2006).

B&W 3 was a small clinker-built vessel, built around 1606 CE, probably in Denmark. Fragmentary remains of the vessel survived, and it was likely an accidental sinking at the site in the early seventeenth century (Lemée 2006). **B&W 4** was another probable accidental loss at the site. Built between 1585 and 1590 CE, the hull was carvel-planked, about 15 m long and 5 m wide. Lemée (2006) suggests that it was likely a smak, a small coastal trader or ferry built in the Netherlands or Friesland and employed both there and in the southern Baltic.

B&W 5, a *fluit* built either in the Netherlands or in a Dutch-influenced area, was an older vessel scuttled near the careening wharf around 1750 CE. Built around 1635, this carvel-planked ship was rebuilt around 1644. It was a 32 m long and 8 m wide ship that had seen much use and many repairs when it was finally partially dismantled and scuttled (Lemée 2006).

B&W 6 was represented by fragments and was originally a clinker-built ship of the mid-seventeenth to mid-eighteenth century CE. B&W 7, in turn, comprised the remains of a circa 1588 CE carvel-built vessel. Both hulls were too fragmentary for adequate reconstruction or more detailed analysis (Lemée 2006). The last hull, B&W 8, was a small 4.5 m long carvel-built boat dating to about 1738 CE that had either sunk or been abandoned by a revetment and subsequently buried (Lemée 2006).

Finally, a tremendous number of wrecks lost on the former Zuyder Zee in the Netherlands, now reclaimed land known as the polders (or the Ijsselmeer), have been excavated. As of 1997, some 435 wrecks had been recovered from the polders, most ranging in date from the thirteenth to the nineteenth centuries CE. The types of craft range from late medieval cogs to later clinker- and carvel-built ships of the fifteenth and sixteenth centuries to coastal barges, eighteenth-century inland freighters known as *prams*, fishing vessels, and oceangoing ships (Hutchinson 1994; Maarleveld and van Ginkel 1990; Van Der Heide n.d.). The wrecks of the polders often include well-preserved upper works and cargo, making the former Zuyder Zee one of the greatest repositories not only of fairly well-intact examples of northern European shipbuilding from the past five centuries but also of maritime trade and activities in the region.

On average, a new ship find per year is made, and the polders constitute what is probably the single largest collection of ships found on "dry" land. It is also the most extensive archaeological collection of medieval and postmedieval wrecks found to date in Europe. The wet conditions of burial in mud have resulted in a high degree of preservation on these sites, and in some cases, crashed aircraft from the Second World War recovered from the polders have yielded preserved bodies, uniforms, and paper. Ongoing archaeological work in the polders is conducted by the Netherlands Institute of Ship and Underwater Archaeology (NISA), formerly known as the Centre for Ship Archaeology, in Lelystad. NISA has excavated 350 of the 435 known wrecks in the polders.

BURIED SHIPS FROM THE SEVENTEENTH TO NINETEENTH CENTURIES CE

While the polders wrecks are the greatest known archaeological collection of medieval and postmedieval wrecks in Europe to have come from a buried context on land, other areas also possess significant numbers of buried ships from this "modern" period of history. These include buried ships in London and in other port cities. Notable work on buried ships has also taken place in America, particularly in New York and San Francisco, both of which have large tracts of reclaimed land that buries former port areas.

Other American examples of buried ships include river steamers wrecked and subsequently buried "beneath the corn field" as the rivers changed courses and former channels silted in to become dry land. Two steamboats have been excavated from this context in the United States—*Bertrand* and *Arabia*. *Bertrand*, built in 1864 and wrecked in 1865 while running up the Missouri River to the Montana gold fields with cargo and settlers' goods, was rediscovered and excavated under U.S. government supervision in the DeSoto Wildlife Refuge (Nebraska) in 1969 (Petsche 1974). *Arabia*, built in 1853 and wrecked in 1856, was excavated by amateur archaeologists in a Kansas field along the former alignment of the Missouri River in 1988–1989. Burial in wet mud resulted in an outstanding level of preservation for both steamers: there were intact cases, barrels, and crates of goods, including tools, firearms, clothing, boots, hats, bottled foods, liquor, ceramics, hardware, textiles, and personal items. The artifacts from *Bertrand* are preserved and displayed as an assemblage at the De Soto Wildlife Refuge, which is operated by the U.S. Fish and Wildlife Service. The *Arabia* excavation ended in the recovery of nearly 100 tons of artifacts, including the boilers, paddlewheels, and the stern of the steamboat, all now displayed in a private museum (Hawley 1995).

The oldest ship recovered in America from a buried context was found in New York and dates to the earliest years of the city's establishment as the Dutch trading outpost of Nieuw Amsterdam. In 1916, workers digging a subway tunnel near the southern end of Manhattan Island encountered the charred remains of ship's bow and artifacts including trade beads, clay pipes, a cannon ball, chain, a double-headed axe, and blue-and-white ceramic shards. A 2.6 m section of the hull was removed to allow construction to proceed. Historians surmised that the remains were those of the Dutch ship *Tyjger*, which burned off Nieuw Amsterdam in 1613 CE. The hull remains were studied by J. Richard Steffy, who concluded that the vessel was a seventeenth-century craft (Steffy 1994).

Substantial remains of another buried ship in New York were found in 1982, when construction on Water Street, several blocks from the present waterfront, discovered the well-preserved remains of an early-eighteenth-century vessel buried several meters below street level. Known as the Water Street Ship, or the Ronson Ship, the nearly complete 25 m long hull had been abandoned on the site sometime prior to 1750 CE, sunk in place, and filled with rubble to support a wharf, and in succeeding years it was buried as landfill reclaimed the waterfront (Cantwell and Wall 2001). Research by archaeologist Warren Reiss concluded that the vessel was a Virginia- or Carolinas-built Chesapeake trader constructed between 1710 and 1720 (Riess 1987; Steffy 1994).

During the fall and winter of 1984–1985, excavation for the Quebec Museum of Civilization in Quebec City discovered the remains of three substantially intact bateaux. The excavation of the bateaux, the recording of three of the boats, and the recovery of portions of two additional vessels were all accomplished under the supervision of archaeologist Daniel LaRoche. The Quebec bateaux were found close together, on the buried former bank of the St. Lawrence River, beneath the foundation of a quay and a house built between 1751 and 1752 CE. The five craft, all in deteriorated condition, were apparently abandoned on the site prior to 1751 and subsequently buried. The conserved craft are displayed in situ, where they were found, in the Quebec Museum of Civilization (Delgado 1998). Similarly, more than 60 buried bateaux were discovered in 1983 during excavation for a new building complex in downtown Richmond, Virginia. Known as the James River bateaux, these craft were abandoned in the former Great Basin of the James River between 1800 and 1880. An archaeological project documented the remains of the boats and completely excavated one (Delgado 1998).

Construction workers encountered a late-seventeenth- to early-eighteenth-century wreck with four iron cannon, two olive jars, and preserved cordage during excavation for an apartment building alongside the Rio Plata in Buenos Aires, Argentina, at the site of the landfilled Puerto Madero, in December 2008. The Puerto Madero ship was buried beneath 7 m of fill. The vessel was excavated by a team led by the city's director of archaeology, Marcelo Weissel, and there are plans to recover it for eventual display.

The largest collection of modern era buried ships (as opposed to small craft) known to exist in an archaeological context within a specific port context are a group of more than 40 vessels lying beneath San Francisco's Financial District, which covers the land-filled harbor of the city's original waterfront. The vessels all date to the California Gold Rush (1848–1857 CE) except one nineteenth-century ship buried as a derelict hulk around 1907. The original waterfront of 1848 was a shallow, muddy inlet known as Yerba Buena Cove. The rapid influx of ships and capital during the Gold Rush, when more than 500 vessels arrived in less than a year (1849), induced the rapid redevelopment of the cove. Within a space of two years the formerly open water was subdivided by piers and wharves, buildings had been constructed on pilings, and more than 200 ships had been converted into floating warehouses or were being used as offices and hotels (Delgado 2009).

The San Francisco waterfront burned in May 1851 and was quickly filled over. Subsequent fill through the early twentieth century significantly altered the original shoreline, extending it by several city blocks and covering Yerba Buena Cove under 10+ m of fill. The former waterfront, with a number of ships, lay encapsulated in that fill. Excavation for building foundations and basements during the late nineteenth through mid-twentieth century encountered the remains of ships and ship timbers. The first archaeological excavation of a buried ship in San Francisco was in May 1978, when construction workers discovered the 1835 ship *Niantic* under 5.35 m of fill near the Transamerica Pyramid building. The bow of the ship lay under an adjacent lot, but 25 m of the hull was exposed by construction. A hasty emergency rescue dig by the San Francisco Maritime Museum recovered thousands of artifacts stored inside the ship between 1849 and 1851, when it was a "storeship" or warehouse before burning and sinking in May 1851. In 2001, a second storeship with a large and diverse supply of goods, the 1840 ship *General Harrison*, was excavated by Allen Pastron, James Delgado, and Rhonda Robichaud (Figure 8.2). Pastron and Delgado, along with James Allan, also excavated a series of waterfront sites that include wharves, buildings, and maritime infrastructure, and they have assessed and partly reconstructed the "instant city" and port of 1849–1857 (Delgado 2009).

In June 1978, excavation for a sewer line trenched through the hull of the whaler *Lydia* on the waterfront. The 1840-built vessel, laid up as a derelict and buried by landfill in 1907, was documented by archaeologist Allen Pastron and historian Roger Olmsted and reconstructed by naval architectural historian Raymond Aker (Delgado 2009). In late 1979 and early 1980, the same team conducted a test excavation on the more intact hull of the 1827 ship *William Gray*, which was used as a floating warehouse before being scuttled after 1854 to serve as a breakwater and dock. The excavation exposed the forecastle deck and part of the bow of the intact vessel, which was documented and then reburied (Delgado 2009). Another intact vessel, the ship *Rome*, was encountered in 1994 during the boring of a subway tunnel at the foot of Market Street, and was documented by archaeologist James Allan. In 2005, Allan, working with James Delgado, also excavated and documented the stern of the bark *Candace*, built in 1818 and partially broken up and scuttled in 1857. The stern was recovered and awaits display at the new San Francisco History Museum (Delgado 2009).

Figure 8.2 The September 2001 excavation of the 1840 ship *General Harrison*,
which burned and sank in 1851 and was subsequently buried in landfill.
Photograph by James P. Delgado.

CONCLUSION

As this brief overview demonstrates, a significant body of work has been accomplished, and there is tremendous ongoing potential for nautical and maritime archaeology with "dry-land" sites and buried ships, including ports, harbor facilities, and cargoes from all periods of history. As an archaeologist who has worked on both sunken and buried ships for over 30 years and visited a number of excavated vessels recovered from land excavations, I would like to make a few observations. The level of preservation in these sites is usually exceptional, and often much better than one finds in underwater excavations. The examples cited in this overview include a number of stunning sites, including vessels of considerable antiquity where the only detailed evidence we have for vessel construction in those times comes from ships recovered from land. This includes every known example of logboats and early watercraft as far back as 6000 BCE. The finds at Yenikapı have provided a new understanding of Byzantine shipbuilding that cannot be overemphasized. Future excavations on land will recover additional and significant vessels and greatly add to our knowledge of shipbuilding as well as of the history and development of ports. From port infrastructure to derelict vessels, and lost and discarded cargoes in port contexts, land excavations on reclaimed land also offer a unique opportunity to archaeologically assess ports from antiquity up to the modern era. While excavation underwater will continue to provide access to shipwrecked cargoes within the context of the vessel itself, excavations on land offer the same potential, as a number of the polders wrecks contained cargoes. It has been observed by some prescient nautical archaeologists that the new frontiers of nautical archaeology lie both at great depth and beneath parking lots and fields that cover former waterfronts. I concur with them and encourage further work on the latter.

ACKNOWLEDGMENTS

I gratefully acknowledge the help of Rebecca Ingram and Michael Jones in completing the Yenikapı portion of this chapter.

REFERENCES

Benvenuti, M. 2006. Late-Holocene catastrophic floods in the terminal Arno River (Pisa, Central Italy) from the story of a Roman riverine harbour. *Holocene* 16 (6): 863–876.
Berti, F. 1990. *Fortuna maris: La nave romana di Comacchio.* Bologna: Nuova Alfa.

Bettazzi, F., G. Giachi, S. Staccioli, and S. Chimichi. 2003. Chemical characterisation of wood of Roman ships brought to light in the recently discovered ancient harbour of Pisa (Tuscany, Italy). *Holzforschung* 57 (4): 373–376.

Bockius, Ronald. 1996. *Die spätrömischen Schiffswracks aus Mainz: Schiffsarchäologisch-technikgeschichtliche Untersuchung spätantiker Schiffsfunde vom nördlichen Oberrhein.* Mainz: Verlag des Römisch-Germanischen Zentralmuseums.

Boetto, G. 1999a. Le navi di Fiumicino: Un contributo alla ricostruzione della topografia del porto di Claudio e della geomorfologia costiera. *Meded* 58: 41.

———. 1999b. New technological and historical observations on the Fiumicino I wreck from Portus Claudius (Fiumicino, Rome). In *Down the river to the sea: Proceedings of the Eighth International Symposium on Boat and Ship Archaeology,* ed. J. Litwin, 99–102. Oxford: Oxbow.

———. 2000. The late Roman Fiumicino 1 wreck: Reconstructing the hull. In *Boats, ships and shipyards: Proceedings of the Ninth International Symposium on Boat and Ship Archaeology,* ed. C. Beltrame, 66–70. Oxford: Oxbow.

Bruni, S., and M. Abbado. 2000. *Le navi antiche di Pisa: Ad un anno dall'inizio delle ricerche.* Firenze: Polistampa.

Cantwell, Anne-Marie, and Diana diZerega Wall. 2001. *Unearthing Gotham: The archaeology of New York City.* New Haven: Yale University Press.

Capretti, C., N. Macchioni, B. Pizzo, G. Galotta, G. Giachi, and D. Giampaola. 2008. Characterization of waterlogged archaeological wood: The Three Roman ships found in Naples (Italy). *Archaeometry* 50 (5): 855–876.

Christensen, A. E., A. S. Ingstad, and B. Myhre. 1993. *Oseberg Dronningens Grav.* Oslo: Schibsted.

Colombini, M. P., J. J. Lucejko, F. Modugno, M. Orlandi, E.-L. Tolppa, and L. Zoia. 2009. A multi-analytical study of degradation of lignin in archaeological waterlogged wood. *Talanta* 80 (1): 61–70.

Croome, A. 2006. The Viking Ship Museum at Roskilde: Expansion uncovers nine more early ships and advances experimental ocean-sailing plans. *International Journal of Nautical Archaeology* 28 (4): 382–393.

D'Oriano, R., and E. Riccardi. 1999. A lost fleet of ships in the Port of Olbia. In *Encyclopedia of underwater archaeology: Barbarian seas; Late Rome to Islam,* ed. S. Kingsley, 89–95. London: Periplus.

Delgado, J. P., ed. 1998. *Encyclopedia of maritime and underwater archaeology.* New Haven: Yale University Press.

———. 2009. *Gold rush port: The maritime archaeology of the San Francisco waterfront.* Berkeley and Los Angeles: University of California Press.

Gilles, P. 2008. *Pierre Gilles' Constantinople.* Translated by K. Byrd. New York: Italica Press.

Hattendorf, John B., and Richard W. Unger. 2003. *War at sea in the Middle Ages and Renaissance.* Woodbridge and Rochester, NY: Boydell Press.

Hawley, D. 1995. *The treasures of the Steamboat Arabia.* Kansas City: Arabia Steamboat Museum.

Hunter, K. 1999. The discovery and lifting of the Newport Ship. *Conservation News* 82: 16–18.

Hutchinson, G. 1994. *Medieval ships and shipping.* London: Leicester University Press.

Kocabaş, U. 2008. *The "old ships" of the "new gate," Yenikapi'nin Eski Gemileri.* Istanbul: Zero Productions.

Kuniholm, P. J., C. B. Griggs, and M. W. Newton. 2007. Evidence for early timber trade in the Mediterranean. In *Byzantina mediterranea: Festschrift für Johannes Koder zum 65.*

Geburtstag, ed. K. Belke, E. Kislinger, A. Külzer, and A. Stassinopoulou, 365–386. Wien: Böhlau Verlag.

Lemée, C. P. P. 2006. *Renaissance shipwrecks from Christianshavn: An archaeological and architectural study of large cargo vessels in Danish waters, 1580–1640.* Roskilde: Viking Ship Museum in collaboration with the National Museum of Denmark.

Lipke, P. 1984. *The royal ship of Cheops.* Archaeological Series No. 9, Bar International Series 225. Greenwich: National Maritime Museum.

Maarleveld, T. J., and E. J. van Ginkel. 1990. *Archeologie under water: Het verleden van een varend volk.* Amsterdam: Muelenhoff.

Magdalino, P. 2001. The maritime neighbourhoods of Constantinople: Commercial and residential functions, sixth to twelfth centuries. *Dumbarton Oaks Papers* 54: 209–226.

Mango, C. 1986. The development of Constantinople as an urban centre. In *The 17th International Byzantine Congress: Major papers,* 117–136. New Rochelle: Aristide D. Caratzas.

Marsden, P. 1974a. *The wreck of the Amsterdam.* New York: Stein and Day.

———. 1974b. The County Hall Ship. *International Journal of Nautical Archaeology and Underwater Exploration* 3 (1): 55–65.

———. 1994. *Ships of the port of London: First to eleventh centuries A.D.* London: English Heritage.

McGrail, S. 1987. *Ancient boats in N.W. Europe.* London: Longman.

Medas, S. 2003. The 5th-century A.D. wreck at the Parco di Teodorico. In *Encyclopedia of underwater archaeology: Barbarian seas; Late Rome to Islam,* ed. S. Kingsley, 86–88. London: Periplus.

Müller-Wiener, W. 1994. *Die Häfen von Byzantion–Konstantinupolis–Istanbul.* Tübingen: Ernst Wasmuth Verlag.

Nayling, N., and S. McGrail 2004. *The Barland's Farm Romano-Celtic boat: CBA Research Report 138.* Walmgate, York: Council for British Archaeology.

Owen, O., and M. Dalland 1999. *Scar: A Viking boat burial on Sanday, Orkney.* East Linton: Tuckwell Press and Historic Scotland.

Pecchioni, E., E. Cantisani, P. Pallecchi, F. Fratini, A. Buccianti, E. Pandeli, S. Rescic, and S. Conticelli. 2007. Characterization of the amphorae, stone ballast and stowage materials of the ships from the archaeological site of Pisa-San Rossore, Italy: Inferences on their provenance and possible trading routes. *Archaeometry* 49 (1): 1–22.

Petsche, J. E. 1974. *Steamboat Bertrand: History, excavation, and architecture.* Washington, DC: U.S. Government Printing Office.

Pferderhirt, B. 1994. *Das Museum für antike Schifffahrt: Ein Forschungsbericht des Römisch-Germanischen Zentralmuseums.* Mainz: Römisch-Germanisches Zentralmuseum.

Pomey, P. 1994. Les épaves grecques et romaines de la Place Jules-Verne Marseille. In *Comptes rendus des siècles de l'anne 1995* (avril–juin), 459–484. Paris: Académie des Inscription & Belles-Lettres.

———. 2003. Reconstruction of Marseilles 6th century BCE Greek ships. In *Boats, ships and shipyards: Proceedings of the Ninth International Symposium on Boat and Ship Archaeology, 2000,* ed. C. Beltrame, 57–65. Oxford: Oxbow.

Pomey, P., and A. Hesnard. 1994. Marseille Place Jules-Verne. In *Bilan scientifique de la région Provence-Alpes-Côte d'Azur 1993,* Ministère de la Culture, 110–115. Aix-en-Provence: Direction Régionale des Affaires Culturales.

Pryor, J. H. 2006. *The age of the dromon: The Byzantine navy ca. 500–1204.* Leiden: Brill.

Pulak, C. 2007. Yenikapı Bizans batıkları. In *Gün Işığında: İstanbul'un 8000 yılı. Marmaray, Metro, ve Sultanahmet kazıları,* 202–215. Istanbul: Vehbi Koç Vakfı.

Pulak, C., and N. Liphschitz. Forthcoming. *Skyllis, the Journal of the German Society for the Promotion of Underwater Archaeology*.

Riess, R. 1987. The Ronson Ship: The study of an eighteenth century merchantman excavated in Manhattan, New York, in 1982. PhD diss. University of New Hampshire.

Roberts, O. T. P. 2003. Llong Casnewydd: The Newport Ship; A personal view. *International Journal of Nautical Archaeology* 33 (1): 158–163.

Sørensen, A. C. 2001. *Ladby: A Danish ship-grave from the Viking age.* Roskilde: Viking Ship Museum.

Steffy, J. R. 1985. The Herculaneum Boat: Preliminary notes on hull details. *American Journal of Archaeology* 89 (3): 519–521.

———. 1994. *Wooden ship building and the interpretation of shipwrecks.* College Station: Texas A&M University Press.

Throckmorton, P., and J. Throckmorton. 1973. The Roman wreck at Pantano Longarini. *International Journal of Nautical Archaeology* 2: 243–266.

Tsangadas, B. C. P. 1980. *The fortifications and defense of Constantinople.* New York: Columbia University Press.

Van Der Heide, G. D. (n.d.). *Archeological investigations on new land.* The Hague: W. A. Ruysch.

Varenius, B. 1985. Medieval ships from the centre of Stockholm. In *Postmedieval boat and ship archaeology,* ed. C. O. Cederlund. Stockholm: Swedish National Maritime Museum.

Varoqueaux, C. 1970. L'épave du Musée des Docks à Marseille. *Etudes Classiques* 3: 28–50.

Vroom, J. 2005. *Byzantine to modern pottery in the Aegean.* Utrecht: Parnassus Press.

Wright, E. V. 1990. *The Ferriby Boats: Seacraft of the Bronze Age.* London: Routledge.

CHAPTER 9

DEEP-SUBMERGENCE ARCHAEOLOGY

SHELLEY WACHSMANN

INTRODUCTION

COASTAL waters represent the greatest danger to ships and seafarers, despite the persistence of a modern myth that has ancient mariners hugging the shore for safety (Davis 2000, 2009; Pomey 1997: 18–35; Wachsmann 1998: 295–301).[1] It is precisely here, at the intersection of water and shore, that ships are most commonly lost. It is doubtful that this fact was lost on ancient seafarers.

The open sea represents relative safety for a ship caught in a storm, for the vessel can attempt to outrun the weather. Ships can be overwhelmed by stormy conditions, but their survival rate in the open sea remains far more favorable, and most ships that come to grief do so within several hundred meters of a coastal obstruction (see, e.g., Acts 27:27–32). Apart from the dangers inherent in a lee shore, the perils of shore-based piracy in antiquity gave further incentive to avoid near-shore sailing (de Souza 1999; Ormerod 1987; Wachsmann 1998: 320–321). Thus, even long-haul coastal sailing had good reason to remain well out to sea, although probably staying in sight of land. Amphoras and other antiquities recovered from the depths in coastal waters by trawler nets presumably derive primarily from ships that sank along such sea lanes. Israel's Mediterranean coast is a good example of this phenomenon (Barag 1963; Gophna 2002; Safrai 1960; Zemer 1978). Other amphora would have reached the bottom as jetsam from passing ships (i.e., Spiess and Orzech 1981; Wachsmann et al. 2009).

Sailing over open water to and from islands located in the Mediterranean and its ancillary seas was already well established by the Neolithic period and in some cases possibly much earlier (Strasser et al. 2010). Much of the evidence for this traffic derives from visitations to, and colonization of, islands (General: Cherry 1981, 1990; Cyprus: Simmons 1991, 2007: 232–263; the Aegean: Broodbank 2000; Broodbank and Strasser 1991; Davis 1992; Tzalas 1995; Tzamtzis 1990). Obsidian obtained on Melos and recovered from Mesolithic levels at Franchthi Cave, located in the southern Peloponnese, could only have arrived by means of water transport and is at present the earliest evidence for seafaring in the Mediterranean (Tzalas 1995: 459–462). The fact that Mesolithic sailor-prospectors reached Melos intimates that they also had a wide-ranging knowledge of other islands. The present seeming lack of Mesolithic remains on Mediterranean islands may be the result of global sea-level changes: most coastal sites dating to that era are now underwater and presumably covered with thick sediments (Broodbank 2000: 116; Firth in this volume).

Routes crossing the open Mediterranean required a sail of several days out of sight of land (Figure 9.1). One such route ran from Crete to Egypt and may have been in use by the end of the third millennium BCE (Pritchard 1969: 416; Vercoutter 1956: 420–421; Wachsmann 1998: 297–299).

Minoan fresco fragments from Tell el Daba (ancient Avaris) indicate extensive contact with Crete in the mid-second millennium, as does the appearance of Minoan emissaries depicted in Theban tombs as bringing their goods to Egypt during the reigns of Hatshepsut and Thutmose III (Bietak 1992, 1995; Bietak, Marinatos, and Palyvou 2000; Bietak et al. 2007; Vercoutter 1956; Wachsmann 1987). Vercoutter (1956: 51–53, 56–57, 81, 87–88, 91–92) notes that the Egyptians

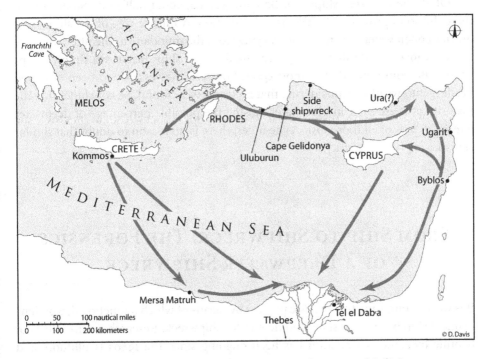

Figure 9.1 Documented Bronze Age sea routes in the eastern Mediterranean.
Data provided by the author. Illustration by D. Davis.

consistently identified these strangers with the "west" and that this strongly implies that the Minoans reached Egypt by sailing straight across the Mediterranean from Crete. Homer (*Od.* 14:252–258; 17:426) mentions this blue-water route twice and notes that it took five days. Classical sources describe the voyage as taking three to four days (Casson 1995: 287 n. 75).

Another documented Bronze Age Mediterranean open-water route stretched from Cyprus to Egypt. In the fourteenth century BCE, Rib-Addi, the embattled and loquacious king of Byblos, describes sending the Egyptian envoy Amanmasha from his court to Egypt in this roundabout manner, apparently to prevent the capture of the vessel by enemy ships patrolling the Syro-Canaanite coast (Wachsmann 1986). A geological survey of the Eratosthenes Seamount, which lies astride the Cyprus-Egypt route, raised granite and basalt rock samples that have been identified as ships' ballast (Krasheninnikov et al. 1994: 118, 125 fig. 6.11: a–c, 126, 128; Mart and Robertson 1998: 702–703).

In 1976 the marine geologist Willard Bascom published a challenge to exploration. In a groundbreaking book published decades before its time, entitled *Deep Water, Ancient Ships*, he laid out a fascinating argument for the survival of shipwrecks of historical and archaeological significance in the depths of the Mediterranean and Black Seas. Based on his study of records kept by Lloyds of London during the mid-nineteenth century, he argued that not only might shipwrecks survive in better condition at great depths than in shallow waters, but also that they might be numerous (Bascom 1976: 71–84).

Of all the recorded ships that Bascom studied, about half sank. Some 80% of these did so in proximity to a coastal obstruction. A further 10% of the ships went down in open water, due to causes varying from the mundane to the utterly bizarre (Bascom 1976: 73–76; Regan 1993). The final 10% of ships lost at sea simply disappeared. Bascom notes that in most cases, however, the vessels had been observed heading into weather. Considering that no traces were found, he concludes that the majority of these sank in blue water, raising the possible percentage of deepwater wrecks to 20% of all those lost. As he notes, there is no reason to doubt that similar statistics apply to antiquity.

FROM SHIP TO SHIPWRECK: THE FORENSICS OF A DEEPWATER SHIPWRECK

It is worth pondering the forensic process by means of which a functional, wooden-planked ship becomes a stabilized deepwater shipwreck. Research on the effects of benthic biogenic degradation has been ongoing since the 1960s (Cullimore and Johnson 2008; Herdendorf, Thompson, and Evans 1995: 62–78, 159–163; Muraoka 1964, 1965, 1966a, 1966b, 1966c, 1967, 1969, 1970).

A vessel that sinks in deep water will not suffer damage by storms, waves, surges, strong currents, or the agencies of ancient salvagers, all of which have contributed to the scrambling, loss of artifacts, and outright destruction of so many shallow-water shipwrecks (Casson 1995: 252 n. 108, 370 n. 45; Frost 1968; Muckelroy 1978: 157–214; Pomey 1997: 42–43; Stewart 1999; Tchernia 1978; Martin in this volume). Rather, ships sinking in deep water will undergo a much gentler transition.

Changes may have occurred even before the vessel slipped beneath the waves. Marine borers and waterlogging may have already weakened the vessel's timbers (Herdendorf, Thompson, and Evans 1995: 100, 159–161). Rigging, masts, and sails may have been cut away during storms or in the aftermath of battles; cargoes may have been cast overboard in an attempt to lighten the vessel (see, e.g., Jonah 1:5; Acts 27:18). The discovery at Skerkie Bank near Sicily, and off Chrisi (Gadaranoussi) Island south of Crete, of lines of discarded amphoras represents the archaeological reality of a commonly described phenomenon (Ballard et al. 2000: 1594, 1595 fig. 2, 1607, 1617–1618; Foley and Ballard 2004; Wachsmann et al. 2009: 148, 149 fig. 2). If the ship sank as a result of a storm, items may have shifted greatly as the ship ran before the storm. Additionally, the manner in which the vessel slipped below the waves—upright, listing, capsized, bow or stern first—could result in the displacement of items.

The cargo-stowing abilities of the ancients must not be underestimated, however. Amphoras were designed, and constantly evolved, specifically for a nautical environment. Such cargoes would have been well secured and perhaps roped down through their handles, and cushioned with sufficient dunnage to protect from stormy weather (Pomey and Tchernia 1978; Rival, Hesnard, and Bernard-Maugiron 1988). Thus, the well-aligned rows of amphoras commonly seen on the wrecks of ancient merchantmen do not preclude these vessels having experienced severe weather prior to sinking.

Most wooden-planked ships that now exist at great depths must have reached the sea bottom in a more or less intact condition (Muckelroy 1978: 150, 166). The natural buoyancy alone of a wooden hull will result in her floating, unless she is carried down by her contents (ballast, cargo, cannon, etc.). Indeed, numerous reports exist of ancient warships—lacking cargo and only lightly ballasted—remaining afloat and being captured and towed away by the victors after they "sank" (Casson 1995: 82; Morrison and Williams 1968: 34–35, pls. 6: e, 7: a [Geom. 32, 38]; Wachsmann 1998: 167 fig. 8.5, 171 fig. 8.14). If, however, during the wrecking event a wooden-planked ship broke up and spilled her contents in deep water, only a debris field might remain on the seabottom to mark the event.

As a cargo ship sank in deep water, sealed amphora containing air-pockets would implode, perhaps forcing their sealing bungs inside (Bass 1986: 278 ill. 8). Light unattached objects not trapped between deck(s) and hull would float back to the sea surface as flotsam. Heavier items that fell free of the ship would sink at their own velocities and might come to rest at some distance from the shipwreck. In some cases these processes will have formed a visible debris trail (if not covered by subsequent sedimentation), which may aid in locating the wreck (Ballard 2008b: 97–104).

Anchors that had been deployed to keep the ship from broaching during a storm would hang below the ship during the descent and, depending on the speed of the current, might end up beneath the ship or at some distance from it (Acts 27:17, 29, 40). This may explain the location of a lead anchor stock found some 20 m from the main grouping of the Skerkie B shipwreck and the distance that a stone bow anchor lies from the Tanit ship's cargo spread (Ballard et al. 2000: 1599, 1600 fig. 5, 2002: 154 fig. 3; McCann and Oleson 2004c: 128 fig. 7.1, 131 fig. 7.3, 150, 151 figs. 7.44–45).

As the ship sank, she would have reached a terminal velocity based on her overall density and drag. RMS *Titanic*, for example, is estimated to have reached a terminal velocity of 25–30 mph (about 40–48 kmh) when she hit the seabed at a depth of 3,795 m (Uchupi, Ballard, and Lange 1988–1989: 59). Similarly, a study of the copper-clad SS *Central America* led to the estimate that it had taken the ship about 18 minutes from the time that she sank beneath the waves till her collision with the seabed, some 2,200 m below. The vessel's impact velocity is calculated at 7.3 kmh (Herdendorf, Thompson, and Evans 1995: 64).

In deep water, a sinking ship will tend to right herself and, therefore, will normally impact the seabed more or less on an even keel (R. D. Ballard, pers. comm.; Ballard et al. 2000: 1616). Just before the ship hits the bottom, if it consists of unconsolidated sediments, the pressure wave beneath the hull will blow a crater in the seabed sediment (J. Morris, pers. comm.). Craters, which are presumably relics of this phenomenon, have been recorded by means of microbathymetry on the late-eighth-century BCE Phoenician shipwrecks Tanit and Elissa, found at a depth of 400 m off the Mediterranean coast of Egypt (Ballard et al. 2002: 155 fig. 4, 157 fig. 6; Singh, Whitcomb et al. 2000: 156 fig. 4, 157 fig. 5). The force of the vessel's impact on the seabed may result in weakening, or even cracking the hull open. At the very least it is an additional opportunity for items to shift, particularly if the vessel hits the seabed bow or stern first.

Most of the Mediterranean's deep seabed consists of unconsolidated sediments. When landing on such a bottom, lower parts of the hull would be forced into the bottom by the kinetic energy of the collision. This would also raise a cloud of displaced sediment, some of which would sink back onto the ship, beginning the process of burying at least the lower parts of the hull.

Over time, additional sediments will continue to filter down onto the shipwreck. Currents may scour sediments away from some parts of the wreck (or from artifacts) or cause them to accumulate in other areas (Ballard et al. 2000: 1616–1618; Herdendorf, Thompson, and Evans 1995: 70 fig. 69, 77 fig. 76). If the rate of sedimentation is high, the wreck may be buried entirely, making it nearly impossible to locate and study with present technology.

Parts of the ship's hull that remain exposed in the water column undergo a gentle disintegration as the result of two primary phenomena: marine borers and the waterlogging of her timbers. All of the timbers' water-soluble components—starches, organic acids, and sugars—leach out (Grattan 1987). Bacteria, and to a lesser degree fungi, subsequently consume the cellulose (Herdendorf, Thompson, and Evans 1995: 80–82; Kohlmeyer 1969; Wessel 1969). Eventually, even lignin, the skeletal part of the wood cell walls, disintegrates. Wood-boring organisms, mainly deepwater boring mollusks (family Pholadidae), aid and abet this process by tunneling into the wood. As most of the biological activity takes place in the first meter above the seabed, the hull will disintegrate first in the area nearest to the seabed, so that if one could observe the process in time-lapse photography, the hull would seem to disappear into the seafloor (Muraoka 1970: ii, 5–6, 12 table 3). As these processes continue, the actual percentage of wood in a timber diminishes until nothing remains but the calcareous mollusk burrows (Herdendorf, Thompson, and Evans 1995: 98, 100, 154, 155 fig. 136, 156 figs. 137–138, 157). As there is a deficiency of calcium carbonate at depth, even these burrows will eventually disappear, having dissolved into the surrounding water column (Morse and Berner 1972).

Although the degradation of the wood will be a gradual process, cataclysmic events will occur as portions of the hull weaken and fall off in sections. These sections of hull will be buried under collapsing cargo and equipment, or remain exposed on the seabed and rapidly disintegrate (Herdendorf, Thompson, and Evans 1995: 65, 156 fig. 138).

No longer constrained by the hull, cargo will disperse accordingly. Items carried on deck or in castles will come to rest on top of, or next to, the contents stored in the hull (e.g., Tanit and Elissa wrecks: Ballard et al. 2002: 154 fig. 3 [upper right], 158 figs. 7.1–3, 159 fig. 8, 160 figs. 9.1–3, 7–10, 161; SS *Central America*: Herdendorf, Thompson, and Evans 1995: 65). If the ship lists only slightly and if the amphoras are tightly packed, they might simply "lean" to one side. Whether lying horizontally or vertically, open amphoras can fill up, acting as sediment traps as current-borne particles that enter their mouths decelerate and settle out inside them (J. K. Hall, pers. comm.).

As with shallow-water shipwrecks, in normal conditions the preservation of the hull, and of other organic items aboard, will be limited to those portions buried in the anoxic sediment soon after the sinking. In other words, the lower portions of a deepwater hull might be expected to survive in a manner analogous to those of better-preserved shallow-water shipwrecks that sink into soft sediments away from surface turbulence (Bascom 1976: 105–118).

Timbers recovered from Roman period Skerkie Bank shipwrecks demonstrate that wood from antiquity can survive at depth if rapidly buried in the sediment (Bascom 1976: 105–118; McCann 1994b: 11 fig. 9, 12 figss 10–11, 13; McCann and Oleson 2004c: 150–151, 152 figs. 7.46–48; McCann and Oleson 2004d: 87, 88 figs. 4.63:a–b, 64; Piechota and Giangrande 2004: 201). The situation in the anoxic levels of the Black Sea and in very cold waters, such as the Baltic Sea, is exceptional at preserving timbers even in the water column, as seen on the Sinop D shipwreck in the former sea and an intact seventeenth-century Dutch *fluit* and other, more recent wrecks in the latter (Sinop D: Ballard et al. 2001: 619–621; Coleman, Ballard, and Gregory 2003: 1288 fig. 3; Davis 2008: 79–82; Ward and Ballard 2004: 6–12; Ward and Horlings 2008: 160–165; Baltic: Hagberg et al. 2007; Rönnby 2008).

As copper and its alloys tend to retard the attack of marine borers on shipwrecks, a cargo of copper ingots similar to the lading of the Uluburun shipwreck, or a bronze ram, might be expected to aid in the preservation of nearby timbers (Herdendorf, Thompson, and Evans 1995: 66; Pulak 1999b: 212; Uchupi, Ballard, and Lange 1988–1989: 57). If left unburied by sediment, organic cargoes, which may have comprised a considerable percentage of a ship's total cargo, will be consumed and disintegrate, becoming "invisible" and leaving areas of the wreck site seemingly empty. This is the most likely explanation for the gaps noted between clusters of artifacts on the Skerkie D shipwreck (Ballard et al. 2000: 1603 fig. 7, 1608–1609; McCann and Oleson 2004d: 53). Eventually, however, the wreck will reach a state of equilibrium, with the upper works gone and the buried remains securely interred.

Subsequently, the wreck will be affected solely by geological phenomena or human interventions. Many shipwrecks now lie buried beneath meters of sediment and at present are invisible and unattainable with even the most advanced technology. Human intervention can cause devastating damage to shipwrecks even in deep water. While treasure hunters are the most conspicuous despoilers, other more mundane human enterprises can destroy deepwater shipwrecks inadvertently and are just as damaging and infinitely more common. Trawlers represent by far the most serious anthropogenic threat to deepwater shipwrecks; additional dangers to shipwreck may result from the laying of pipelines or cables, the construction of deepwater facilities for power plants, and even the anchor drag of large ships (Gibbins 1991: 167 n. 1; Hiney 2002: cover, 2–12; Smith, Banks, and Banks 2007; Stewart 1999).

Deep-Submergence Archaeology

Until the last few decades, the archaeological investigation of shipwrecks has been largely limited to those located in depths achievable by diving archaeologists (Bass 1976a: 111–123, 169–184; Delgado 1997; Gibbins 1991: 166–167; Long 1987, 1988, 1998; Pomey 1997: 44). More recently, a number of archaeologically and historically significant shipwrecks lying at depth have been located and studied to various degrees (e.g., Skerkie Bank: McCann and Freed 1994; McCann and Oleson 2004a; the Tanit and Elissa wrecks: Ballard et al. 2002; Stager 2003; Chios: Foley 2008; Foley et al. 2009; Sakellariou et al. 2007: 365–373, 379–380; Egadi Islands (off Sicily): Anonymous 2009; Royal 2008; Ventotene (Italy): Flynn 2009; Black Sea: Davis 2008; Ward and Horlings 2008; Trondheim Harbor: Søreide 2000; Norwegian Sea: Søreide et al. 2006; modern shipwrecks: Ballard 2008b; Ballard and Archbold 1987; Bryant and Hamilton 2007; Church and Warren 2008; Church et al. 2002, 2003, 2004; Ford et al. 2009; Ford, Borgens, and Hitchcock 2010; Jourdan 2009; Warren, Church, and Davey 2004).

Deep-submergence archaeology (DSA), the term given here to the archaeological study of cultural resources beyond the limits of traditional diving, may also contribute to our understanding of the distant human past, when much of the

Earth's water was locked in ice sheets, causing the ocean system to drop signifi-
cantly. Human habitation sites may exist in areas that are now in deep water
(Coleman 2008a, 2008b; Coleman and McBride 2008; Faught and Flemming 2008;
Largent 2009, 2010; Ryan et al. 1997; Ryan and Pitman 1998; Firth in this volume).

Of course, each nautical archaeologist could generate a list of shipwrecks at
great depths worthy of study based on their own research interests. For scholars
interested in seafaring of the early Mediterranean, shipwrecks supplying a relatively
complete picture of a vessel and her contents remain rare prior to the sixth century
BCE, and hull remains are even scarcer. The Uluburun ship, dating to the last quarter of the thirteenth century BCE, carried a rich cargo and remained sufficiently
intact to recover parts of her hull, which indicate that her builders used an already
remarkably developed form of pegged mortise-and-tenon joinery to edge-join the
hull planking (Fitzgerald 1996; Pulak 1999a, 1999b; Steffy 1994: 36–37). Dated about
a century later, the more poorly preserved Cape Gelidonya shipwreck may have
broken up during the sinking event; but the hull remains, though they consist of
only a few wood fragments, are sufficient to indicate that her builders also used a
similar form of construction (Bass 1967: 45, 48 figs. 45–46, 49 fig. 48, 50 fig. 51; Pulak
1999b: 214, 219–220, 232 table 1, 237 fig. 6; Wachsmann 1989: 192, 1998: 217, 218 fig.
10.3). Other Bronze Age "shipwrecks" are in truth better described as cargo scatters,
or materials derived from nearby land sites, and contribute nothing to our understanding of ancient ship construction (Dokos: Papathanassopoulos, Vichos, and
Lolos 1995; Vichos and Papathanassopoulos 1996; Sheytan Deresi: Bass 1976b; Catsambis 2008; Margariti 1998; Cape Iria: Phelps, Lolos, and Vichos 1999; Vichos 1999;
Vichos and Lolos 1997; Pseira: Bonn-Muller 2009; Hadjidaki and Betancourt 2005–
2006). Valuable though these sites may be in terms of archaeological data, they
cannot be considered coherent shipwrecks.

Subsequently, the record of relatively intact hulls only picks up again in the
seventh century BCE. From this time, we have a series of vessels: Mazarrone (circa
seventh century BCE, Aizpurua and Méndez 1996; Negueruela 2000a: 182–184;
Negueruela 2000b), Bon-Porté and Pabuç Burnu (late sixth century BCE, Bass,
Carlson, and Polzer 2006: 139; Bound 1985, 1991; Greene and Polzer 2004; Polzer
2004, 2005, in press), Place Jules Verne–9 and Place Jules Verne–7 (last quarter sixth
century BCE, Pomey 1997: 90–93), and Gela (circa 500 BCE, Freschi 1991, 1996).
Additionally, an intriguing Phoenician wreck dating to the late seventh or early
sixth centuries BCE is currently under excavation at Bajo de la Campana, Spain, and
one may hope for hull survival at this site also (Mas 1985; Polzer 2007, 2008, 2009;
Polzer and Reyes 2007; Roldán Bernal, Miñano Domínguez, and Martín Camino
1991; Roldán Bernal, Martín Camino, and Pérez Bonet 1995). Thus, regarding ancient
Mediterranean shipwrecks, virtually any vessel predating the seventh century BCE
discovered in deep water would be of sufficient archaeological and historical significance to make her worthy of study.

These considerations put into perspective the remarkable discovery of not one,
but two late-eighth-century BCE Phoenician shipwrecks found in deep water by
the crew of the NR-1 off the northern coast of Egypt in 1997 and subsequently stud-

ied by Ballard and Stager in 1999 (Ballard et al. 2002; Gore 2001: 91–93; Stager 2003). Dating to about the time when Homer is believed to have written his epics, not only are these vessels exceptional in being the first Levantine Phoenician ship-wrecks found, but they also date to a century for which we have no other recorded shipwrecks.

Deep-submergence archaeology is indeed more costly than a conventional ship-wreck excavation, but there are significant trade-offs. A variety of factors—daylight hours, decompression, and cold, to list but a few—limit conventional shipwreck exca-vations. On the other hand, DSA is a round-the-clock operation, with control teams working in shifts. Once a remotely operated vehicle (ROV) reaches the seabottom, barring truly inclement weather or the unexpected, work can continue uninterrupted on a 24-hour work schedule (Figure 9.2). Additionally, an ROV or an autonomous underwater vehicle (AUV) can carry out site recording, which takes up an extraordi-nary amount of total bottom-time on any conventional underwater excavation, far more effectively than archaeological divers (Figure 9.3) (Ballard et al. 2000: 1602, 2002: 154; Foley et al. 2009; Singh, Pizzaro et al. 2000; Warren and Church 2003; Warren, Church, and Westrick 2008; Yoerger et al. 2007).

Some might argue that no ship in deep water should be touched until all the appropriate excavation tools have been developed. However, technology does not develop on its own: it is purpose-driven and can be improved upon only by initi-ating actual work. Additionally, this approach leaves the deep seas open to treasure hunters, while excluding nautical archaeologists, which is clearly an unacceptable

Figure 9.2 This MaxRover class remotely operated vehicle (ROV), owned by Greece's Hellenic Centre for Marine Research (HCMR), has been used effectively for checking anomalies and for other archaeological purposes. It is rated to 2,000 m.
Photograph by the author.

Figure 9.3 Recovery of Woods Hole's Autonomous Benthic Explorer (ABE)
Autonomous Underwater Vehicle (AUV). Reproduced with kind permission
of the WHOI/ABE Group.

situation. Given present realities, by not expanding into these new areas, the archaeological community would be harming its own interests.

Archaeologists have lagged behind treasure hunters in the race to develop and
carry out strategies for excavating shipwrecks at depth (e.g., SS *Central America*:
Herdendorf, Thompson, and Evans 1995; Kinder 1998; Thompson 1998; wreck identified as the *Buen Jesus y Nuestra Señora del Rosario*: Moore 1997; the Black Swan
wreck: Colapinto 2008). Treasure-hunting groups have developed their own technologies for retrieving and raising artifacts from the deep-sea floor. As tools for exploring and exploiting the deep seas continue to develop rapidly, and become
cheaper to purchase and operate, treasure-hunting initiatives will continue to expand
aggressively into the deep sea. These regions are appealing, as deep waters to a large
degree are synonymous with international waters and, therefore, at present at least,
lie largely beyond the reach of governmental controls and restrictions (Elia 2000;
Irion 2002; Irion, Ball, and Horrell 2008; McCann and Oleson 2004b: 23–24; O'Keef
1999). Unless something is done to change this trend, we stand the danger of losing
the final frontier of archaeology (Colapinto 2008; Goodheart 1999; Koerner 1999).

At the risk of stating the obvious, the archaeological excavation of a shipwreck
at depth is a highly complex affair, requiring diverse areas of expertise. The role of
the archaeologist within this multidimensional operation requires a paradigm shift.
In conventional excavations, be they terrestrial or marine, the principal investigator
normally bears the overall responsibility for the entire expedition. The new paradigm, however, calls for a somewhat different approach—one in which the archaeologists are the specialists brought to the site by the oceanographers. A good analogy
may be the relationship between submariners and "spooks" in naval intelligence-
gathering missions (Sontag, Drew, and Lawrence-Drew 1999). Just as is not the role
of the intelligence gatherers to drive submarines, similarly, running technical

aspects of the project should not be the responsibility of the archaeologists. Rather, their responsibility must be focused on, and limited to, the archaeology.

The totality of archaeological exploration at great depths—discovering, recording, excavating, and recovering—requires function-specific tools. Deep Submergence Archaeological Excavations (DSAE), however, takes advantage of a remarkable existent toolkit, designed for a variety of oceanographic purposes other than the study of ancient shipwrecks. Truly, we would not be considering DSAE at all were it not for such advances as side-scan sonar, bottom-penetrating sonar, Differential Global Positioning System (DGPS), dynamic positioning, fiber optics, high-definition video, ROVs, and a host of other technologies (Coleman and Ballard 2008; Newman, Gregory, and Howland 2008).

Viewed from this perspective, missing technologies remain challenging yet relatively minor problems. Deepwater archaeological survey is already at an advanced stage. Through experience and experimentation, strategies for locating shipwrecks in deep water have developed considerably in recent years (Ballard 2008a, 2008b; Herdendorf, Thompson, and Evans 1995: 46–52; Jourdan 2009; Sakellariou 2007–2008; Sakellariou et al. 2007).

What *is* lacking at present is a comprehensive methodology for deepwater excavation. In addition, it seems to me that the most important element to bring with us in approaching wrecks at depth is a sincere and intense sense of humility. We are poised to reach back to human treasures that have not been seen since they sank. In such a situation it is important to remember that just because a technical ability exists, it does not necessarily have to be used. The ultimate goal of DSAE will be to develop the technologies and the skills that will permit expeditions to excavate and safely raise the contents and hull of an entire ship for conservation, study, and display. The technological toolkit to accomplish this remains years away, if not decades. Yet the future ability to reach this goal should dictate present steps.

For the purpose of this discussion, let us imagine a deepwater shipwreck of unique archaeological/historical significance to make it a worthwhile candidate for excavation. This wreck lies on a flat abyssal plain of negligible gradient consisting of unconsolidated sediments. A significant portion of the hull survives buried in the sediment beneath the wreck's inorganic contents. These may include anchors, amphoras, pithoi, ingots, stone blocks, pillars, ballast, and the like. Embedded in this matrix are numerous smaller artifacts, down to the size of a bead. That these minute artifacts are hardly a theoretical concern is demonstrated by the thousands of beads found scattered throughout the Uluburun shipwreck (Ingram 2005; Pulak 1997: 245).

A shipwreck must be considered a complex artifact rather than a habitation site (Muckelroy 1978: 215–225). For that reason, most nautical archaeologists will prefer to excavate an entire shipwreck. At this pioneering stage, however, it would be premature to excavate an entire deepwater shipwreck. Rather, by excavating several controlled archaeological sections, an expedition will be able to address the most pertinent questions raised by a shipwreck: the date, the source(s) of the cargo, the last itinerary, the cultural identity of the vessel's home port, and the construction techniques used in the building of the hull.

If we lack a vessel's ethnic identity, it is difficult to evaluate a ship's historical significance. Yet one of the most perplexing problems that arise in the archaeology of ancient ships remains the identification of a vessel's homeport. Cargoes are of little value in determining a homeport, as a ship can carry a cargo loaded at any port. A Late Bronze Age vessel loaded to the caprails with Mycenaean Greek stirrup jars, for example, might have traded them at the last port of call for a cargo of Syro-Canaanite copper-oxhide ingots from the home port (Bass 1967: 165). For Mediterranean Bronze and Iron Age ships there are several indicators that, taken together, might help determine ethnic identity, including personal items belonging to the crew and passengers, balance-pan weight sets, cultic items, and stone anchors or killick stones (Bachhuber 2006; Bass 1967: 163–167; Pulak 1996, 1998, 2008: 300–302; Wachsmann 1998: 211–212, 2000: 815–820). With the notable exception of the anchors, most of these items normally would have been located at the stern, which traditionally served as the crew's quarters.

As hulls narrow at their extremities, resulting in structural changes, the best location to learn about the vessel's construction is found amidships. Excavators should take advantage, however, of any locations where hull remains might be reached with minimal excavation as, for example, areas covered only by stone anchors, or a layer of ballast stones.

Prior to excavation, an accurate site plan must be generated. Advanced solutions have been developed for this purpose (Ballard 1993; Ballard et al. 2000; Foley et al. 2009; Mindell et al. 2004; Singh, Adams et al. 2000; Singh, Romans et al. 2000, 2008; Singh, Howland, and Pizarro 2004; Whitcomb, Yoerger, and Singh 1999a, 1999b; Whitcomb et al. 1999).

The very nature of photomosaics precludes their use for accurate measurements (Bass 1982: 21–22; Singh, Adams, et al. 2000: 321–322). Accurate site plans can be generated from the optical data by means of stereophotogrammetry, a method that has been in use for many years in shallow-water excavations (Bass 1976a: 96–97, 103–106, 1982: 24–26). For this purpose, the merging of microbathymetric maps with optical data may be the solution (Singh, Whitcomb et al. 2000; Singh, Roman et al. 2000; Mindell et al. 2004).

In an ideal world, archaeologists could get a virtual "sneak peak" into a ship-wreck before the onset of excavation to permit them to formulate the best excavation strategy. A prototype high-frequency, narrow-beam sub-bottom profiler designed for this purpose was first deployed on *Jason* during the 1999 survey of the Tanit and Elissa wrecks (Mindell and Bingham 2001). Further refinement of such a device, and a better understanding of the data it generates, could significantly enhance predisturbance examination.

DSAE requires creative robotic solutions to handle a bewildering assortment of situations and artifacts that may vary considerably in size, weight, volume, brittleness, and structural strength. Solutions to raising many types of artifacts already exist.

Any artifact that is moved in the context of excavation must first receive some form of firmly secured identification (Wachsmann 2007–2008: 137 fig. 6). Repeat optical recording of a depot has been employed to record the few artifacts that might be moved and stored during an archaeological survey of a wreck (Singh, Adams et al. 2000: 326 fig. 6). An excavation, however, will generate too many displaced objects to depend solely on this manner of recording. Additionally, pottery on deep shipwrecks undergoes stress resulting from benthic processes not normally encountered in ceramics from shallower wrecks (Ballard et al. 2000: 1614–1616; Piechota 1994; Piechota and Giangrande 2004: 196–197, 2008). Thus, the fragility of these artifacts also must be taken into consideration when stockpiling them: an artifact might shatter even during the most careful handling.

The process of excavation favors a method of stabilizing the ROV on site, and several versions of frameworks or railing have been developed for this purpose (Alfsen 2006; Coleman, Ballard, and Gregory 2003: 1289, 1290 fig. 9; Søreide 2000; Søreide, Jasiinski, and Sperre 2006: 11–12; Webster 2008: 57 figs. 4.18–19).

Two distinct actions compose controlled underwater excavation: the gentle raising of sediment into the water column without harming or moving the artifacts embedded in it, and the transportation of the sediment off-site. To transport off-site the large quantities of sediment generated by the excavation, a Venturi dredge is the tool of choice: it is commonly used on conventional underwater excavations in water too shallow to allow for an airlift (Breitstein 2003: 12 fig. 5 and n. 8, 14 fig. 7; Dean et al. 1992: 211–213, 310–312). The dredge's task is not to excavate into the sediments, but rather to act as a slurry conveyer belt to transport sediments off-site after they have been raised into the water column by other methods. The slightest disturbances of these unconsolidated sediments—the movement of an amphora, for example—raises clouds of fine silt that remain suspended in the water until it settles out and/or is transported off-site by the current (Ballard et al. 2000: 1607). This phenomenon lowers visibility to the degree that work must often cease. Thus, in a low-velocity current this problem alone can result in a significant drop in on-site productivity. Solutions have been developed to solve this problem (Herdendorf, Thompson, and Evans 1995: 54). The most recent of these is the "snuffler" excavation tool, which sucks up the suspended silt as it is being excavated (Figure 9.4; Coleman, Ballard, and Gregory 2003: 1289–1290; Webster 2008: 49–55).

A diving archaeologist has three-dimensional vision and tactile sense. Two forward-facing cameras on the ROV *Nemo* generated a three-dimensional image that, upon transmission to an optically polarized monitor, created a three-dimensional display (Herdendorf, Thompson, and Evans 1995: 57–58). Similarly, the ROV *Hercules* allows the pilot the option of force feedback manipulation (B. Buxton, pers. comm.).

Cases may arise when it might be preferable to raise a group of small artifacts in their in situ spatial arrangement. Thus, on the SS *Central America*, *Nemo* raised gold coins in their original stacking position by placing an open-bottomed aluminum mold with a form-fitting skirt of soft material over the selected feature and then injecting the mold with liquid silicon (Herdendorf, Thompson, and Evans 1995: 53–54, 58 figs. 49–50, 59 fig. 51). For larger items, ROVs can employ simple yet remarkably dexterous tools like those developed for *Jason*, nicknamed the "Cowcatcher" and

Figure 9.4 The ROV's left robotic arm holds the "snuffler" in place to collect suspended sediment as the right robotic arm gently brushes away sediment clinging to timbers on the Sinop D shipwreck, Black Sea. Reproduced with kind permission of the Institute for Exploration and University of Rhode Island Center for Ocean Exploration and Archaeological Oceanography, URI Graduate School of Oceanography.

"Deep Spank" (McCann 1994a: 97, color figs. 12, 27; Webster 2008: 58, 58 fig. 4.20–21). These can be deployed safely to retrieve a wide range of artifacts varying in size and weight, from an amphora to an oil lamp. A hydraulic suction cup may be used to safely raise medium-sized artifacts, up to the size of an amphora, while an interchangeable tool set for use with an ROV's robotic arm adds additional functionality (Wachsmann 2007–2008: 139 fig. 8; Webster 2008: 55, 56 figs. 4.15–17, 57).

A highly controlled system is required to raise particularly heavy items without damaging them or their immediate surroundings. Prior to the excavation of the SS *Central America*, *Nemo* raised the ship's bell, weighing 125 kilograms (Herdendorf, Thompson, and Evans 1995: 51, 52 fig. 38, 53 fig. 39). How this procedure affected the surrounding hull is not reported. Bronze Age anchors may weigh up to half a ton (Wachsmann 1998: 255–293). Heavy metal items, such as copper ingots, might concrete together to a degree that it would be preferable to raise them as a consolidated unit, rather than individually. During the excavation of the Cape Gelidonya shipwreck, the archaeologists removed a group of concreted oxhide ingots as a single lump and then separated them on land (Bass 1967: 28 figs. 11–12, 29 figs. 13–16). Excavators might find anchors or ingots stored in the hull, separated from the hull planking only by a thin layer of dunnage and/or ballast stones; even in a shipwreck with minimal hull preservation, such items may be expected to have pressed the portion of the hull beneath them into the sediment, and thus preserved it, as in the case of the Uluburun shipwreck (Pulak 1998: 212 fig. 24, 1999b: 212). Thought should also be given to the potential need to strengthen badly corroded artifacts prior to retrieval (Peachey 1990).

Paleoethnobotanical materials uncovered during an excavation can contain valuable clues to shipboard life and ghost cargoes (Uluburun: Haldane 1990, 1993; Pulak 2008: 295–296; Madrague de Giens: Tchernia et al. 1978: 112–118; Skerkie Bank: Beck, Stewart, and Stout 1994; Ward 2004; Tantura Lagoon: Bryant 1995; Wachsmann and Kahanov 1997: 14; Wachsmann, Kahanov, and Hall 1997: 11; Yassıada: Bryant and Murry 1982; Bozburun: Gorham 2000a, 2000b; the *Betsy*: Weinstein 1992; Mardi Gras: Ford et al. 2009: 164–173). Additionally, discolored patches of sediment, which have been noted on both shallow- and deepwater wrecks, may indicate decomposed materials and should be retrieved for study (Ballard et al. 2000: 1612; McCann and Oleson 2004e: 101; Pulak 1989: 6–7). DNA information may also be collected remotely (Foley et al. 2009).

Wood—be it hull timbers, dunnage, or firewood—may survive beneath cargo and gear. Branches used for onboard firewood and other purposes that would have been cut close in time to the ship's loss are particularly valuable for dendrochronological study (Kuniholm 1997; Kuniholm et al. 1996; Pomey 1998; Pulak 1998: 213–214). Leather products also tend to escape attack by benthic organisms, presumably due to the tannic acids used in their curing process (Ballard and Archbold 1987: 207, 218; Herdendorf, Thompson, and Evans 1995: 163 fig. 146, 164 fig. 147, 165 figs. 150–151).

Lowly bilge mud may be one of the most valuable sources for learning about a ship's history. Composed of detritus collecting primarily amidships, it may contain information on shipboard life hidden in a potpourri of spilled cargoes, garbage, and coprolites containing pollen, phytoliths, fungi, and a collection of other plant remains. Bilge mud stands out quite clearly on a shipwreck buried in sand (Wachsmann and Kahanov 1997: 14 fig. 16). It might be difficult to identify it in benthic sediment, so care should be taken to collect all the sediment in the areas where it tends to collect (along the keel/keel-plank and wedged between frames and planking). Control core samples must be retrieved from the seafloor around a shipwreck during the predisturbance survey to ensure against contamination (Davis 2008: 76, 77 fig. 7; Wachsmann 2007–2008: 141 fig. 10; Webster 2008: 46–49). Artifacts may be retrieved to the surface by means of an "elevator," a device designed to raise items without requiring the ROV to break surface (Figure 9.5; Ballard 1993: 1680 fig. 4, 1683, 1998: 38; Bowen et al. 2000; Ford et al. 2009: 22–23; Webster 2008: 44–45). As excavation proceeds, the hull should be kept cradled in its outer sedimentary matrix, as the timbers will not have sufficient structural strength to support their own weight. Robotically applied polysulfide molds could be used to record hull structure underwater (Murdock and Daley 1981, 1982).

To learn even more about the construction of the hull, consideration should be given to raising a section across it in the manner carried out on the Madrague de Giens shipwreck (Pomey 1978: 76–80 figs. 10–11, pl. XXVIII: 2). Robotically raising a hull-section intact from great depth might be considered the single most complex task to be accomplished at the present stage of technological development. It is important to emphasize that such a project on a deepwater shipwreck of

Figure 9.5 An elevator with artifacts in its containers rising from the sea. Reproduced with kind permission of the Institute for Exploration and University of Rhode Island Center for Ocean Exploration and Archaeological Oceanography, URI Graduate School of Oceanography.

archaeological/historical significance should be attempted only after careful consideration and only following much experimentation on a "sacrificial" wreck of *relatively* negligible significance. Due to the structural weakness of waterlogged wood, the safest retrieval method for this envisioned section might be to encase it prior to retrieval (Wachsmann 2007–2008: 139, 142, 144).

At the end of any excavation that reveals ship's timbers and other organic materials, the excavated section of the hull must be reburied to ensure that exposed timbers do not fall prey to benthic organisms and that cargo does not shift due to currents. One method used successfully on shallow-water shipwrecks is to cover the timbers with a layer of synthetic sandbags (Breitstein 2003: 16 fig. 10, 17 fig. 12, 18 fig. 13; Grenier, Bernier, and Stevens 2007: 149–152). An ROV could deploy beanbag-sized sacks complete with Velcro tabs that cause them to "coagulate" on contact with each other. These bags could be filled with copper pellets to further repel marine borer larvae.

PUBLICATION

The results from the archaeological project must be presented in a final scientific excavation report, and disseminated to the general public as well. Given the highly digital nature of DSAE, which depends on electronic recording, such an excavation would be ideally positioned to take the lead in examining the many exciting possibilities in employing electronic media before the general archaeo-logical community. Directions for this potential include, but are not limited to, the following possibilities:

- Color photographs are prohibitively expensive to publish in most scientific reports. By using electronic media or a Web site, however, an archaeological report could include an almost unlimited number of color images.
- A selection of the most significant artifacts raised could be recorded as three-dimensional computer-generated models for a "virtual" museum. The user could manipulate an architect's avatar as if the artifact itself were held in the hand (Wachsmann, in press).
- Three-dimensional constructs of the excavation area could demonstrate to the viewer the general lay of the land and the spatial relationships between artifacts in situ (e.g., VIZ-Tantura). Taking this one step further, clicking on an artifact would take the viewer to information about it. Alternately, the viewer could call up site plans displaying the spatial relationships of differing types of artifacts.
- Footage of the excavation process can be provided via streaming video from a Web site to purchasers of the publication, or to create documentary movies (Aig and Haywood 2008). Well-indexed video would permit the reader to call up the materials regarding the discovery and find location of any given artifact. When translated into a virtual reality format, it would allow the user to experience the excavation.

All of the above possibilities—and there are others, such as site-specific role-playing games for children and live Web sites—can be served up in popular formats for the general public and for educational purposes, contributing to the cultural awareness of DSA's value (Corbin and Smith 2008; Hall 2008). The possibilities are confined only by the limits of our imagination.

ACKNOWLEDGMENTS

I have received much welcome help in preparing this article and wish to thank the follow-ing persons for kindly giving of their time, knowledge, and experience: Robert D. Ballard, Bridget Buxton, Carlos Cabrera, Alexis Catsambis, Dwight Coleman, Dan Davis, John Hall, Jeff Morris, Mark Polzer, Cemal Pulak, Hanumaunt Singh, the late J. Richard (Dick) Steffy, Louis Whitcom, and Dana Yoerger. Special thanks to the Institute for Exploration and the University of Rhode Island Center for Ocean Exploration and Archaeological Oceanography, URI Graduate School of Oceanography, and Woods Hole Oceanographic Institution (WHOI) for permission to use here photos from their expeditions and of their equipment.

NOTES

1. This article is an updated and condensed version of Wachsmann (2007–2008). It includes references to deep-submergence salvage operations from shipwrecks of archaeological and historical significance carried out by organizations for commercial gain. These are discussed here because they contain important information regarding documented benthic site formation processes on wooden-planked ships and other issues related to this discussion. These references do not condone the salvage of such shipwrecks for commercial profit, a practice that I believe to be antithetically opposed to the preservation and the understanding of the past.

REFERENCES

Aig, D., and K. Haywood. 2008. Through the sea snow: The central role of videography in the Deep Gulf Wrecks Mission. *International Journal of Historical Archaeology* 12 (2): 133–145.

Aizpurua, C. G.-G., and J. L. S. Méndez. 1996. Extracción y tratamientos del barco Fenicio (Barco I) de la Playa de la Isla (Puerto de Mazarrón, Mazarrón). In *Cuadernos de Arqueología Marítima 4*, 217–225. Cartagena: Museo Nacional de Arqueología Marítima.

Alfsen, M. 2006. Digging deep: Revolutionary technology takes archaeologist to new depths. *Archaeology* 59 (3): 28–33.

Anonymous. 2009. *Levanzo I wreck 2006, RPM Nautical.* Online at www.rpmnautical.org/levanzowreck.htm. Accessed 23 December 2009.

Bachhuber, C. 2006. Aegean interest on the Uluburun Ship. *American Journal of Archaeology* 110: 345–363.

Ballard, R. D. 1993. The MEDEA/JASON Remotely Operated Vehicle System. *Deep-Sea Research* I 40 (8): 1673–1687.

———. 1998. High-tech search for Roman shipwrecks. *National Geographic* 193 (4): 32–41.

———. 2008a. Seaching for ancient shipwrecks in the deep sea. In *Archaeological Oceanography*, ed. R. D. Ballard, 131–147. Princeton, NJ: Princeton University Press.

———. 2008b. The search for contemporary shipwrecks in the deep sea: Lessons learned. In *Archaeological Oceanography*, ed. R. D. Ballard, 95–127. Princeton, NJ: Princeton University Press.

Ballard, R. D., and R. Archbold. 1987. *The discovery of the Titanic.* New York: Warner/Madison Press.

Ballard, R. D., F. T. Hiebert, D. F. Coleman, C. Ward, J. S. Smith, K. Willis, B. Foley, K. Croff, C. Major, and F. Torre. 2001. Deepwater archaeology of the Black Sea: The 2000 season at Sinop, Turkey. *American Journal of Archaeology* 105 (4): 607–623.

Ballard, R. D., A. M. McCann, et al. 2000. The discovery of ancient history in the deep sea using advanced deep submergence technology. *Deep-Sea Research* I 47: 1591–1620.

Ballard, R. D., L. Stager, D. Master, D. Yoerger, D. Mindell, L. L. Whitcomb, H. Singh, and D. Piechota. 2002. Iron age shipwrecks in deep water off Ashkelon, Israel. *American Journal of Archaeology* 106: 151–168.

Barag, D. 1963. A survey of pottery recovered from the sea off the coast of Israel. *Israel Exploration Journal* 13: 13–19, pl. 5.

Bascom, W. 1976. *Deep water, ancient ships: The treasure vault of the Mediterranean.* Garden City: Doubleday & Company.

Bass, G. F. 1976a. *Archaeology beneath the sea.* New York: Harper Colophon Books.

———. 1976b. Sheytan Deresi: Preliminary report. *International Journal of Nautical Archaeology* 5: 293–303.

———. 1982. The excavation. In *Yassi Ada I* (Nautical Archaeology Series 1), ed. G. F. Bass and F. H. van Doorninck Jr., 8–31. College Station: Texas A&M Press.

———. 1986. A Bronze Age shipwreck at Ulu Burun (Kaş): 1984 campaign. *American Journal of Archaeology* 90: 269–296, pl. 17.

Bass, G. F., ed. 1967. *Cape Gelidonya: A Bronze Age shipwreck. Transactions of the American Philosophical Society,* n.s. 57:8. Philadelphia: American Philosophical Society.

Bass, G. F., D. N. Carlson, and M. E. Polzer. 2006. A brief history of ships' hulls and anchors as revealed along the Turkish coast by the Institute of Nautical Archaeology. In *Studies in honor of Hayat Erkanal: Cultural reflections,* ed. B. Avunç, 138–144. Ankara: Homer Kitabevi.

Beck, C. W., D. R. Stewart, and E. C. Stout. 1994. Appendix D: Analysis of naval stores from the Late-Roman ship. In *Deep water archaeology: A Late-Roman ship from Carthage and an ancient trade route near Skerki Bank off northwest Sicily,* ed. A. M. McCann and J. Freed, 109–121. Ann Arbor: Journal of Roman Archaeology, Supplemental Series 13.

Bietak, M. 1992. Minoan wall-paintings unearthed at ancient Avaris. *Egyptian Archaeology* 2: 26–38.

———. 1995. Connections between Egypt and the Minoan world: New results from Tell el-Dab'a/Avaris. In *Egypt, the Aegean and the Levant: Interconnections in the second millennium BCE,* ed. W. V. Davies and L. Schofield, 19–28, pls. 1–4, 14–17. London: British Museum Press.

Bietak, M., N. Marinatos, and C. Palyvou. 2000. The Maze Tableau from Tell el Dab'a. In *Proceedings of the First International Symposium, the Wall Paintings of Thera (Thera, Hellas, 30 August–4 September 1997),* vol. 1, ed. S. Sherratt, 77–90. Athens: Thera Foundation.

Bietak, M., N. Marinatos, C. Palivou, and A. Brysbaert. 2007. *Taureador scenes in Tell El-Dab'a (Avaris) and Knossos: Denkschriften der Gesamtakademie* Bd. 43. Vienna: ÖAW, Verlag der Österreichischen Akademie der Wissenschaften.

Bonn-Muller, E. 2009. First Minoan shipwreck. *Archaeology* 63 (1): 44–47.

Bound, M. 1985. Early observations on the construction of a preclassical wreck, at Campese Bay, Island of Giglio. In *Sewn plank boats: Archaeological and ethnographic papers presented to a conference at Greenwich, November 1984, BARIS 276,* ed. S. McGrail and E. Kentley, 49–65. Oxford: BAR.

———. 1991. The Giglio wreck, a wreck of the Archaic period (c. 600 BCE) off the Tuscan Island of Giglio: An account of its discovery and excavation; A review of the main finds. *ENALIA Supplement* 1: 5–36.

Bowen, M. F., P. J. Bernard, D. E. Gleason, and L. L.Whitcomb. 2000. *Elevators—autonomous transporters for deep sea benthic sample recovery.* Woods Hole, MA: Woods Hole Oceanographic Institution.

Breitstein, S. 2003. Logistic and operational aspects of the excavation. In *The Ma'agan Mikhael ship: The recovery of a 2400-year-old merchantman,* vol. 1, ed. E. Linder and Y. Kahanov, 8–23. Jerusalem: Israel Exploration Society and University of Haifa.

Broodbank, C. 2000. *The island archaeology of the early Cyclades.* Cambridge: Cambridge University Press.

Broodbank, C., and T. F. Strasser. 1991. Migrant farmers and the neolithic colonization of Crete. *Antiquity* 65: 233–245.

Bryant, B., and D. Hamilton. 2007. Deep-water excavation: Unlocking the secrets of the Mardi Gras shipwreck. *Geoconnections* 18–21.

Bryant, V. M., Jr. 1995. Preliminary pollen analysis of sediments collected from Tantura Lagoon. *INA Quarterly* 22 (2): 18–19.

Bryant, V. M., Jr., and R. E. Murry Jr. 1982. Appendix E: Preliminary analysis of amphora contents. In *Yassi Ada I* (Nautical Archaeology Series 1), ed. G. F. Bass and F. H. van Doorninck Jr., 327–331. College Station: Texas A&M Press.

Casson, L. 1995. *Ships and seamanship in the ancient world*. Reprint with addenda and corrigenda. Baltimore: Johns Hopkins University Press.

Catsambis, A. 2008. The Bronze Age shipwreck at Sheytan Deresi. MA thesis, Texas A&M University.

Cherry, J. F. 1981. Pattern and process in the earliest colonization of the Mediterranean islands. *Proceedings of the Prehistoric Society* 47: 41–68.

———. 1990. The first colonization of the Mediterranean islands: A review of recent research. *Journal of Mediterranean Archaeology* 3: 145–221.

Church, R. A., L. Landry, D. J. Warren, and J. S. Smith. 2003. *Underwater Intervention 2003: The SS Alcoa Puritan: Deepwater discovery and investigation; Underwater intervention proceedings*. New Orleans, LA (February).

Church, R. A., and D. J. Warren. 2008. The 2004 Deepwrecks Project: Analysis of World War II era shipwrecks in the Gulf of Mexico. *International Journal of Historical Archaeology* 12 (2): 82–102.

Church, R. A., D. J. Warren, A. W. Hill, and J. S. Smith. 2002. *The discovery of U-166: Rewriting history with new technology*. Offshore Technology Conference Proceedings No. OTC 14136, Houston, TX (May).

Church, R. A., D. J. Warren, J. B. Weirich, and D. Ball. 2004. *Underwater Intervention 2004: Return to the U-166: Working together to meet the challenge of deepwater archaeology; Underwater intervention proceedings*. New Orleans, LA (February).

Colapinto, J. 2008. Secrets of the deep: The dispute over what may be the biggest sunken treasure ever found. *New Yorker* (April 7): 44–55.

Coleman, D. F. 2008a. Archaeological and geological oceanography of inundated coastal landscapes: An introduction. In *Archaeological oceanography*, ed. R. D. Ballard, 177–199. Princeton, NJ: Princeton University Press.

———. 2008b. Sinkholes in Lake Huron and the possibility for early human occupation on the submerged Great Lakes Shelf. In *Archaeological oceanography*, ed. R. D. Ballard, 224–245. Princeton, NJ: Princeton University Press.

Coleman, D. F., and R. D. Ballard. 2008. Oceanographic methods for underwater archaeological surveys. In *Archaeological oceanography*, ed. R. D. Ballard, 3–14. Princeton, NJ: Princeton University Press.

Coleman, D. F., R. D. Ballard, and T. Gregory. 2003. Marine archaeological exploration of the Black Sea. *Oceans 2003: Proceedings* 3 (22–26): 1287–1291.

Coleman, D. F., and K. McBride. 2008. Underwater prehistoric archaeological potential on the southern New England continental shelf off Block Island. In *Archaeological oceanography*, ed. R. D. Ballard, 200–223. Princeton, NJ: Princeton University Press.

Corbin, A., and S. O. Smith. 2008. After the fanfare: Education, the lasting legacy. *International Journal of Historical Archaeology* 12 (2): 157–180.

Cullimore, D. R., and L. A. Johnson. 2008. Microbiology of concretions, sediments and mechanisms influencing the preservation of submerged archaeological artifacts. *International Journal of Historical Archaeology* 12 (2): 120–132.

Davis, D. 2000. Navigation in the ancient eastern Mediterranean. MA thesis, Texas A&M University.

————. 2008. Exploration and excavation of two deepwater wrecks in the Black Sea. In *The study of ancient territories: Chersonesos and South Italy: 2006-2007 Annual Report*, ed. Anonymous, 73–82. Austin: Institute of Classical Archaeology, University of Texas at Austin.

————. 2009. Commercial navigation in the Greek and Roman world. PhD diss., University of Texas at Austin.

Davis, J. L. 1992. Review of the Aegean prehistory I: The islands of the Aegean. *American Journal of Archaeology* 96: 699–756.

de Souza, P. 1999. *Piracy in the Graeco-Roman world.* Cambridge: Cambridge University Press.

Dean, M., B. Ferrari, I. Oxley, M. Redknap, and K. Wilson, eds. 1992. *Archaeology underwater: The NAS guide to principles and practice.* Dorchester: Nautical Archaeology Society.

Delgado, J. P. 1997. Deep water sites. In *The British Museum encyclopedia of underwater and maritime archaeology*, ed. J. P. Delgado, 126–128. London: British Museum Press.

Elia, R. J. 2000. US protection of underwater cultural heritage beyond the territorial sea: Problems and prospects. *International Journal of Nautical Archaeology* 29: 43–56.

Faught, M. K., and N. Flemming. 2008. Submerged prehistoric sites: "Needles in haystacks" for CRMs and industry. *Sea Technology* 49 (10): 37–38, 40–42.

Fitzgerald, M. A. 1996. Continuing study of the Uluburun shipwreck: Laboratory research and analysis. *INA Quarterly* 23 (1): 7–9.

Flynn, D. 2009. Archaeologists find graveyard of sunken Roman ships. *Yahoo News*, 23 July. Online at http://news.yahoo.com/s/nm/20090723/sc_nm/us_italy_shipwrecks.

Foley, B. 2008. Greek deepwater survey. In *Nautical archaeology, 2006-2007 seasons*, ed. J. Delgado. *American Journal of Archaeology* 112: 331–333.

Foley, B. P., and R. D. Ballard. 2004. Amphora alleys I and II. In *Deep-water shipwrecks off Skerki Bank: The 1997 survey (Journal of Roman Archaeology, Supplemental Series 58)*, ed. A. M. McCann and J. P. Oleson, 183–194. Portsmouth: Journal of Roman Archaeology.

Foley, B. P., K. Dellaporta, D. Sakellariou, et al. 2009. The 2005 Chios ancient shipwreck survey: New methods for underwater archaeology. *Hesperia* 78: 269–305.

Ford, B., A. Borgens, W. Bryant, D. Marshall, P. Hitchcock, C. Arias, and D. Hamilton. 2009. *Archaeological excavation of the Mardi Gras shipwreck (16GM01), Gulf of Mexico Continental Slope.* OCS Report MMS 2008-037. U.S. Department of the Interior, Minerals Management Service, New Orleans, LA.

Ford, B., A. Borgens, and P. Hitchcock. 2010. The "Mardi Gras" shipwreck: Results of a deep-water excavation, Gulf of Mexico, USA. *International Journal of Nautical Archaeology* 39: 76–98.

Freschi, A. 1991. Note tecniche sul relitto greco arcaico di Gela. In *IV rassegna di archeologica subaquea: IV premio Franco Papò: Atti (Gardini Naxos 13–15 ottobre 1989)*, ed. P. Gianfrotta, 201–210. Messina: Edizioni P&M Associati.

————. 1996. The sewn plank boat of Gela in Sicily: Preliminary observations about construction of hull. In *Tropis IV: Fourth International Symposium on Ship Construction in Antiquity (Athens, 28–31 August 1991)*, ed. H. E. Tzalas, 187. Athens: Hellenic Institute for the Preservation of Nautical Tradition.

Frost, F. J. 1968. Scyllias: Diving in antiquity. *Greece and Rome*, 2nd ser. 15: 180–185.

Gibbins, D. 1991. Archaeology in deep water–a preliminary view. *International Journal of Nautical Archaeology* 20: 163–168.

Goodheart, A. 1999. Into the depths of history: With robots exploring the bounty of shipwrecks on the ocean floor, we're faced with the issue of whether to take it or leave it. *Preservation* 51 (1): 36–45.

Gophna, R. 2002. Elusive anchorage points along the Israel littoral and the Egyptian-Canaanite maritime route during the Early Bronze Age I. In *Egypt and the Levant: Interrelations from the fourth through the third millennia BCE*, ed. E. C. van den Brink and T. E. Levy, 418–421. London: Continuum.

Gore, R. 2001. Ancient Ashkelon: Ancient city of the sea. *National Geographic* 199 (1): 66–93.

Gorham, L. D. 2000a. The archaeobotany of the Bozburun shipwreck. PhD diss., Texas A&M University.

——. 2000b. Grapes, wine, and olives: Commodities and other cargo of the Bozburun Byzantine shipwreck. *INA Quarterly* 27 (1): 11–17.

Grattan, D. W. 1987. Waterlogged wood. In *Conservation of marine archaeological objects*, ed. C. Pearson, 55–67. London: Butterworths.

Greene, E. S., and M. E. Polzer. 2004. Evidence for a 6th-century lifeboat and its anchor? *INA Quarterly* 31 (3, Fall): 12–18.

Grenier, R., M.-A. Bernier, and W. Stevens, eds. 2007. *The underwater archaeology of Red Bay: Basque shipbuilding and whaling in the 16th century.* Vol. 1. Ottawa: Parks Canada.

Hadjidaki, E., and P. Betancourt. 2005–2006. A Minoan shipwreck off Pseira Island, East Crete, preliminary report. *Eulimene* 6–7: 79–96.

Hagberg, B., J. Dahm, and C. Douglas. 2007. *Shipwrecks of the Baltic.* Stockholm: Prisma.

Haldane, C. 1990. Shipwrecked plant remains. *Biblical Archaeologist* 53 (1): 55–60.

——. 1993. Direct evidence for organic cargoes in the Late Bronze Age. *World Archaeology* 24: 348–360.

Hall, A. W. 2008. Looking over the archaeologists' shoulders: Web-based public outreach in the Deep Wrecks Project. *International Journal of Historical Archaeology* 12 (2): 146–156.

Herdendorf, C. E., T. Thompson, and R. D. Evans. 1995. Science on a deep-ocean shipwreck. *Ohio Journal of Science* 95 (1): 4–224.

Hiney, J. 2002. Pipeline to history. *Texas Shores* (Fall): cover, 2–19.

Homer. *The Odyssey* (abbreviated *Od.*).

Ingram, R. S. 2005. Faience and glass beads from the Late Bronze Age shipwreck at Uluburun. MA thesis, Texas A&M University.

Irion, J. B. 2002. *Cultural resource management of shipwrecks on the Gulf of Mexico outer continental slope.* Second MIT Conference on Technology, Archaeology, and the Deep Sea, Boston, MA (April).

Irion, J. B., D. Ball, and C. E. Horrell. 2008. The US government's role in deepwater archaeology: The Deep Gulf Wrecks Project. *International Journal of Historical Archaeology* 12 (2): 75–81.

Jourdan, D. W. 2009. *Never forgotten: The search for and discovery of Israel's lost submarine DAKAR.* Annapolis: Naval Institute Press.

Kinder, G. 1998. *Ship of gold in the deep blue sea.* New York: Atlantic Monthly Press.

Koerner, B. I. 1999. The race for riches: Under the sea, treasure hunters and scientists battle for history's bounty. *U.S. News and World Report* 127 (13, 4 October): 44–50.

Kohlmeyer, J. 1969. Deterioration of wood by marine fungi in the deep sea. In *Symposium on Materials Performance and the Deep Sea (1969)*, ed. Anonymous, 20–30. Philadelphia: American Society for Testing and Materials.

Krasheninnikov, V. A., G. B. Undenstev, V. I. Mouraviov, and J. K. Hall. 1994. Geological structure of Eratosthenes seamount. In *Geological structure of the northeastern*

Mediterranean (Cruise 5 of the research vessel "Akadmik Nikolaj Strakhov"), ed.
     V. A. Krasheninnikov and J. K. Hall, 113–130. Jerusalem: Historical Publications, Hall.
Kuniholm, P. I. 1997. Aegean Dendrochronology Project, December 1997 progress report.
     Ithaca: Malcolm and Carolyn Weiner Laboratory for Aegean and Near Eastern
     Dendrochronology.
Kuniholm, P. I., B. Kromer, S. Manning, M. Newton, C. Latini, and M. Bruce. 1996.
     Anatolian tree rings and the absolute chronology of the eastern Mediterranean,
     2220–718 B.C. Nature 381: 780–783.
Largent, F. 2009. Putting muscle into coastal-entry research. Mammoth Trumpet 24 (3):
     cover, 1, 8–11, 19.
———. 2010. Finding traces of early hunters beneath the Great Lakes. Mammoth Trumpet
     25 (1): 4–7, 20.
Long, L. 1987. L'épave antique Bénat 4: Expertise archéologique d'un talus d'amphores à
     grand profondeur. Cahiers d'archéologie subaquatique 6: 99–108.
———. 1988. L'épave antique des basses de Can (Var): Nouvelle expertise archéologique à
     l'aide d'un sous-marine. Cahiers d'archéologie subaquatique 7: 5–20.
———. 1998. L'archéologie sous-marine à grande porfondeur: Fiction ou réalité. In Archeo-
     logia subacquea: Come opera l'archeologo storie dalle acque (VIII Ciclo di Lezioni sulla
     Ricerca applicata in Archeologica Certosa di Pontignano, Siena, 9–15 Dicembre 1996), ed.
     G. Volpe, 341–379. Firenze: Edizioni All'Insegna del Giglio.
Margariti, R. E. 1998. The Sheytan Deresi wreck and the Minoan connection in the eastern
     Aegean. MA thesis, Texas A&M University.
Mart, Y., and H. F. Robertson. 1998. Eratosthenes Seamount: An oceanographic yardstick
     recording the late Mesozoic-Tertiary geological history of the eastern Mediterranean.
     Proceedings of the Ocean Drilling Program, Scientific Results 160: 701–708.
Mas, J. 1985. El polígono submarino de Cabo de Palos: Sus aportaciones al estudio del
     tráfico marítimo antiguo. In Arqueología Submarina: VI Congreso Internacional de
     Arqueología Submarina, Cartagena 1982, ed. Museo y Centro Nacionales de Investiga-
     ciones Arqueológicas Submarinas, 153–171. Madrid: Ministerio de Cultura, Dirección
     General de Bellas Artes y Archivos, Subdirección General de Arqueología y Etnografía.
McCann, A. M. 1994a. The technology. In Deep water archaeology: A Late-Roman ship
     from Carthage and an ancient trade route near Skerki Bank off northwest Sicily, ed.
     A. M. McCann and J. Freed, 92–98. Ann Arbor: Journal of Roman Archaeology,
     Supplemental Series 13.
———. 1994b. The Late-Roman ship and the non-ceramic finds. In Deep water archaeology:
     A Late-Roman ship from Carthage and an ancient trade route near Skerki Bank off
     northwest Sicily, ed. A. M. McCann and J. Freed, 11–20. Ann Arbor: Journal of Roman
     Archaeology, Supplemental Series 13.
McCann, A. M., and J. Freed, eds. 1994. Deep water archaeology: A Late-Roman ship from
     Carthage and an ancient trade route near Skerki Bank off northwest Sicily. Ann Arbor:
     Journal of Roman Archaeology, Supplemental Series 13.
McCann, A. M., and J. P. Oleson, eds. 2004a. Deep-water shipwrecks off Skerki Bank: The
     1997 survey. Portsmouth: Journal of Roman Archaeology, Supplemental Series 58.
McCann, A. M., and J. P. Oleson. 2004b. Introduction: The genesis and significance of the
     1997 survey. In Deep-water shipwrecks off Skerki Bank: The 1997 survey, ed. A. M.
     McCann and J. P. Oleson, 15–24. Portsmouth: Journal of Roman Archaeology,
     Supplemental Series 58.
McCann, A. M., and J. P. Oleson. 2004c. Wreck B (last quarter of the 1st c. A.D.). In Deep-
     water shipwrecks off Skerki Bank: The 1997 survey, ed. A. M. McCann and J. P. Oleson,
     128–153. Portsmouth: Journal of Roman Archaeology, Supplemental Series 58.

McCann, A. M., and J. P. Oleson. 2004d. Wreck D (c. 80–50 B.C.). In *Deep-water shipwrecks off Skerki Bank: The 1997 survey*, ed. A. M. McCann and J. P. Oleson, 40–89. Portsmouth: Journal of Roman Archaeology, Supplemental Series 58.

McCann, A. M., and J. P. Oleson. 2004e. Wreck F (Mid-1st c. A.D.). In *Deep-water shipwrecks off Skerki Bank: The 1997 survey*, ed. A. M. McCann and J. P. Oleson, 90–117. Portsmouth: Journal of Roman Archaeology, Supplemental Series 58.

Mindell, D. A., and B. Bingham. 2001. A high-frequency, narrow-beam sub-bottom profiler for archaeological applications. *Oceans, 2001. MTS/IEEE Conference and Exhibition* 4: 2115–2123.

Mindell, D. A., H. Singh, D. R. Yoerger, L. Whitcomb, and J. Howland. 2004. Precision mapping and imaging of underwater sites at Skerki Bank using robotic vehicles. In *Deep-water shipwrecks off Skerki Bank: The 1997 survey*, ed. A. M. McCann and J. P. Oleson, 25–39. Portsmouth: Journal of Roman Archaeology, Supplemental Series 58.

Moore, D. 1997. Seahawk. In *British Museum encyclopedia of underwater and maritime archaeology*, ed. J. P. Delgado, 363–364. London: British Museum Press.

Morrison, J. S., and R. T. Williams. 1968. *Greek oared ships: 900–322 B.C.* Cambridge: Cambridge University Press.

Morse, J. W., and R. A. Berner. 1972. Dissolution kinetics of calcium carbonate in sea water: II. A kinetic origin for the lysocline. *American Journal of Science* 272: 840–851.

Muckelroy, K. 1978. *Maritime archaeology.* London: Cambridge University Press.

Muraoka, J. S. 1964. *Deep-ocean biodeterioration of materials. Part 1. Four months at 5,640 feet.* Ft. Belvoir, VA: Defense Technical Information Center.

———. 1965. *Deep-ocean biodeterioration of materials. Part 2. Six months at 2,340 feet.* Ft. Belvoir, VA: Defense Technical Information Center.

———. 1966a. *Deep-ocean biodeterioration of materials. Part 3. Three years at 5,300 feet.* Ft. Belvoir, VA: Defense Technical Information Center.

———. 1966b. *Deep-ocean biodeterioration of materials. Part 4. One year at 6,800 feet.* Ft. Belvoir, VA: Defense Technical Information Center.

———. 1966c. *Deep-ocean biodeterioration of materials. Part 5. Two years at 5,640 feet.* Ft. Belvoir, VA: Defense Technical Information Center.

———. 1967. *Deep-ocean biodeterioration of materials. Part 6. One year at 2,370 feet.* Ft. Belvoir, VA: Defense Technical Information Center.

———. 1969. Effect of deep-ocean environment on plastics. In *Symposium on materials performance and the deep sea (1969): Materials performance and the deep sea*, ed. Anonymous, 5–19. Philadelphia: American Society for Testing and Materials.

———. 1970. *Deep-ocean biodeterioration of materials—six months at 6,000 feet.* Ft. Belvoir, VA: Defense Technical Information Center.

Murdock, L. D., and T. Daley. 1981. Polysulfide rubber and its application for recording archaeological ship features in a marine environment. *International Journal of Nautical Archaeology* 10: 337–342.

———. 1982. Progress report on the use of FMC polysulfide rubber compounds for recording archaeological ships' features in a marine environment. *International Journal of Nautical Archaeology* 11 (4): 349–352.

Negueruela, I. 2000a. Managing the maritime heritage: The National Maritime Archaeological Museum and National Centre for Underwater Research, Cartagena, Spain. *International Journal of Nautical Archaeology* 29: 179–198.

———. 2000b. Protection of shipwrecks: The experience of the Spanish Maritime Archaeological Museum. In *Underwater archaeology and coastal management (Coastal Management Sourcebooks 2)*, ed. M. H. Mostafa, N. Grimal, and D. Nakashima, 111–116. Paris: UNESCO.

Newman, J. B., T. S. Gregory, and J. Howland. 2008. The development of towed optical and acoustical vehicle systems and remotely operated vehicles in support of archaeological oceanography. In *Archaeological oceanography*, ed. R. D. Ballard, 15–29. Princeton, NJ: Princeton University Press.

O'Keef, P. J. 1999. International waters. In *Legal protection of the underwater cultural heritage: National and international perspectives*, ed. S. Droomgoole. London: Kluwer Law International.

Ormerod, H. [1924] 1987. *Piracy in the ancient world: An essay on Mediterranean history.* Liverpool: Dorset.

Papathanassopoulos, G., Y. Vichos, and Y. Lolos. 1995. Dokos: 1991 campaign. *Enalia Annual 1991* (English edition) 3: 17–37.

Peachey, C. 1990. Taking conservation underwater at Ulu Burun. *INA Newsletter* 17 (3): 10–13.

Phelps, W., Y. Lolos, and Y. Vichos, eds. 1999. *The Point Iria wreck: Interconnections in the Mediterranean ca. 1200 BCE (Proceedings of the International Conference, Island of Spetses, 19 September 1998).* Athens: Hellenic Institute of Marine Archeology.

Piechota, D. 1994. Appendix B: Laboratory conservation. In *Deep water archaeology: A Late-Roman ship from Carthage and an ancient trade route near Skerki Bank off northwest Sicily*, ed. A. M. McCann and J. Freed, 103–107. Ann Arbor: Journal of Roman Archaeology, Supplemental Series 13.

Piechota, D., and C. Giangrande. 2004. Conservation of archaeological finds. In *Deep-water shipwrecks off Skerki Bank: The 1997 survey*, ed. A. M. McCann and J. P. Oleson, 195–201. Portsmouth: Journal of Roman Archaeology, Supplemental Series 58.

———. 2008. Conservation of archaeological finds from deep-water wreck sites. In *Archaeological oceanography*, ed. R. D. Ballard, 65–91. Princeton, NJ: Princeton University Press.

Polzer, M. E. 2004. An Archaic laced hull in the Aegean: The 2003 excavation and study of the Pabuç Burnu Ship remains. *INA Quarterly* 31 (3 Fall): 3–11.

———. 2005. Hull remains from the Archaic shipwreck at Pabuç Burnu, Turkey: Signs of shifting technology? In *AIA 106th Annual Meeting Abstracts.* Vol. 28, ed. Anonymous, 165. Boston: Archaeological Institute of America.

———. 2007. INA fieldwork: In Spain. *INA Quarterly* 34 (3): 13.

———. 2008. Phoenician rising: Excavation of the Bajo de la Campana site begins. *INA Annual* 5–10.

———. 2009. Hard rocks, heavy metals: A report from Bajo de la Campana. *INA Quarterly* 36 (3): 10.

———. In press. Laced hull remains from the 6th-century B.C. shipwreck at Pabuç Burnu, Turkey. In *Tropis IX: Proceedings of the 9th International Symposium on Ship Construction in Antiquity (Agia Napa, Cyprus 25–30 August)*, ed. H. Tzalas. Athens: Hellenic Institute for the Preservation of Ship Construction in Antiquity.

Polzer, M. E., and P. Reyes. 2007. Phoenicians in the West: The ancient shipwreck site of Bajo de la Campana, Spain. *INA Annual:* 57–61.

Pomey, P. 1978. La coque. In *L'épave romaine de la Madrague de Giens (Var) (Campagnes 1972–1975): Fouilles de l'Institute d'archéologie méditerranéenne* 34, ed. A. Tchernia, P. Pomey, and A. Hesnard, 75–99, pls. XXVI-XLI. Paris: Editions du CNRS.

———. 1981. L'épave de Bon-Porté et les bateaux cousus de Méditerranée. *Mariner's Mirror* 67: 225–243.

———, ed. 1997. *La navigation dans l'antiquité.* Aix-en-Provence: Édisud.

————. 1998. Dendrochronologie et dendromorphologie. In *Archeologia subacquea: Come opera l'archeologo: Storie di acque*, ed. G. Volpe, 432–446. Quaderni del Dipartimento di archeologia e storia delle arti, Sezione archeologica, Università di Siena, 44. Firenze: Edizione all'insegna del giglio, 1998.

Pomey, P., and A. Tchernia. 1978. La disposition du chargement. In *L'épave romaine de la Madrague de Giens (Var) (Campagnes 1972–1975): Fouilles de l'Institute d'archéologie méditerranéenne* 34, ed. A. Tchernia, P. Pomey, and A. Hesnard, 19–27. Paris: Éditions du CNRS.

Pritchard, J. B., ed. 1969. *Ancient Near Eastern texts relating to the Old Testament.* Princeton, NJ: Princeton University Press.

Pulak, C. M. 1989. Ulu Burun: 1989 excavation campaign. *INA Newsletter* 16 (4): cover, 4–10.

————. 1996. Analysis of the weight assemblages from the Late Bronze Age shipwrecks at Uluburun and Cape Gelidonya, Turkey. PhD diss., Texas A&M University.

————. 1997. The Uluburun shipwreck. In *Res maritimae: Cyprus and the Eastern Mediterranean from prehistory to late antiquity: Proceedings of the Second International Symposium "Cities on the Sea" (Nicosia, Cyprus, 18–22 October 1994)*, Cyprus American Archaeological Research Institute Monograph Series, vol. 1, ed. S. Swiny, R. L. Hohlfelder, and H. W. Swiny, 233–262. Atlanta: Scholars Press.

————. 1998. The Uluburun shipwreck: An overview. *International Journal of Nautical Archaeology* 27: 188–224.

————. 1999a. Hull construction of the Late Bronze Age shipwreck at Uluburun. *INA Quarterly* 26 (4): 16–21.

————. 1999b. The Late Bronze Age shipwreck at Uluburun: Aspects of hull construction. In *The Point Iria wreck: Interconnections in the Mediterranean ca. 1200 BCE (Proceedings of the International Conference, Island of Spetses, 19 September 1998)*, ed. W. Phelps, Y. Lolos, and Y. Vichos, 209–238. Athens: Hellenic Institute of Marine Archaeology.

————. 2008. The Uluburun shipwreck and Late Bronze Age trade. In *Beyond Babylon: Art, trade, and diplomacy in the second millennium B.C.*, ed. J. Aruz, K. Benzel, and J. M. Evans, 288–305, artifact catalog: 306–310, 313–321, 324–333, 336–348, 350–358, 366–370, 372–378, 382–385. New York: Metropolitan Museum of Art.

Regan, G. 1993. *The Past Times book of naval blunders.* London: Guinness.

Rival, M., A. Hesnard, and M. Bernard-Maugiron. 1988. III: Le navire; 2: Quelques hypothèses de restitution. In *L'épave romaine Grand Ribaud D (Hyères, Var). (Archaeonautica 8)*, ed. A. Hesnard, M.-B. Carre, M. Rival et al., 127–142. Paris: Éditions du Centre national de la recherche scientifique.

Roldán Bernal, B., M. Martín Camino, and A. Pérez Bonet. 1995. El yacimiento submarino del Bajo de la Campana (Cartagena, Murcia): Catálogo y estudio de los materiales arqueológicos. *Cuadernos de Arqueología Marítima* 3: 11–61.

Roldán Bernal, B., A. Miñano Domínguez, and M. Martín Camino. 1991. El yacimiento arqueológico subacuático de "El Bajo de la Campana." *Congreso Nacional de Arqueología* 21: 965–974.

Rönnby, J. 2008. The ghost ship: Current state of research and project plan for maritime archaeological exploration, Nov. 2008. Unpublished ms.

Rose, J. I., 2010. New Light on Human Prehistory in the Arabo-Persian Gulf Oasis. *Current Anthropology* 51: 849–883.

Royal, J. 2008. Warship Ram discovered . . . An ancient naval battle revealed? *INA Quarterly* 35 (2): 6.

Ryan, W. B. F., and W. C. Pitman III. 1998. *Noah's flood: The new scientific discoveries about the event that changed history.* New York: Simon & Schuster.

Ryan, W. B. F., W. C. Pitman III, C. O. Major, K. Shimkus, V. Moskalenko, G. A. Jones,
    P. Dimitrov, N. Gorür, M. Sakinç, and H. Yüce. 1997. An abrupt drowning of the Black
    Sea Shelf. *Marine Geology* 138: 119–126.
Safrai, B. 1960. *Al Kadim v-Yam (On jars and sea)*. Kibbutz Saar. (In Hebrew.)
Sakellariou, D. 2007–2008. Rocks, wrecks or waste? Integration of sub-bottom profiling
    and side scan sonar data in deep water archaeological research: Site formation and
    interpretation of geophysical recordings. *Skyllis (Deutsche Gesellschaft zur Förderung
    der Unterwasserarchäeologie e. V.)* 8 (1–2): 154–168.
Sakellariou, D., P. Georgiou, A. Mallios, V. Kapsimalis, D. Kourkoumelis, P. Micha,
    T. Theodoulou, and K. Dellaporta. 2007. Searching for ancient shipwrecks in the
    Aegean Sea: The discovery of Chios and Kythnos Hellenistic wrecks with the use of
    marine gelogical geophysical methods. *International Journal of Nautical Archaeology*
    36: 365–381.
Simmons, A. H. 1991. Humans, island colonization and Pleiestocene extinctions in the
    Mediterranean: The view from Akrotiri Aetokremnos, Cyprus. *Antiquity* 65: 857–869.
———. 2007. *The Neolithic revolution in the Near East: Transforming the human landscape.*
    Tucson: University of Arizona Press.
Singh, H., J. Adams, D. Mindell, and B. Foley. 2000. Imaging for underwater archaeology.
    American Journal of Field Archaeology 27 (3): 319–328.
Singh, H., J. Howland, and O. Pizarro. 2004. Large area photomosaicking underwater. *IEEE
    Journal of Oceanic Engineering* 29 (3): 872–886.
Singh, H., O. Pizarro, A. Duester, and J. C. Howland. 2000. Optical imaging from the ABE
    AUV: Designed to provide quantitative stereo and photomosaics of the seafloor. *Sea
    Technology* 27 (4): 39–43.
Singh, H., C. Roman, O. Pizzaro, B. Foley, R. Eustice, and A. Can. 2008. High-resolution
    optical imaging for deep-water archaeology. In *Archaeological oceanography*, ed.
    R. D. Ballard, 30–40. Princeton: Princeton University Press.
Singh, H., C. Roman, L. Whitcomb, and D. Yoerger. 2000. Advances in fusion of high
    resolution underwater optical and acoustic data. In *Proceedings of the 2000
    International Symposium on Underwater Technology (May 2000)*, 206–211. Tokyo:
    Institute of Electrical and Electronics Engineers.
Singh, H., L. L. Whitcomb, D. Yoerger, and O. Pizarro. 2000. Microbathymetric mapping
    from underwater vehicles in the deep ocean. *Computer Vision and Image
    Understanding* 79 (1): 143–161.
Smith, C. J., A. C. Banks, and K.-N. Papadopoulou. 2007. Improving the quantitative
    estimation of trawling impacts from sidescan-sonar and underwater-video imagery.
    ICES Journal of Marine Science 64: 1692–1701.
Sontag, S., C. Drew, and A. Lawrence-Drew. 1999. *Blind man's bluff: The untold story of
    American submarine espionage.* New York: Harper.
Søreide, F. 2000. Technical communication: Cost-effective deep water archaeology;
    Preliminary investigations in Trondheim Harbour. *International Journal of Nautical
    Archaeology* 29 (2): 284–293.
Søreide, F., M. E. Jasiinski, and T. O. Sperre. 2006. Unique new technology enables
    archaeology in the deep sea: An exploration into how to excavate a shipwreck in 170
    meters' depth. *Sea Technology* 47 (10): 10–13.
Spiess, F. N., and J. K. Orzech. 1981. Location of ancient amphorae in the deep waters
    of the eastern Mediterranean Sea by the deep tow vehicle. In *In the realms of gold:
    Proceedings of the 10th Confererence on Underwater Archaeology (Fathom Eight*

Special Publications, No. 1), ed. W. A. Cockrell, 149–159. San Marino: Fathom Eight.

Stager, L. E. 2003. Phoenician shipwrecks in the deep sea. In *PLOES . . . Sea Routes . . . Interconnections in the Mediterranean 16th–6th c. BCE (Proceedings of the International Symposium Held at Rethymnon, Crete, September 29th–October 2nd 2002)*, ed. N. C. Stampolidis and V. Karageorghis, 233–247. Athens: University of Crete/A. G. Leventis Foundation.

Steffy, J. R. 1994. *Wooden ship building and the interpretation of shipwrecks*. College Station: Texas A&M Press.

Stewart, D. J. 1999. Formation processes affecting submerged archaeological sites: An overview. *Geoarchaeology* 14: 565–587.

Strasser, T. F., E. Panagopoulou, C. N. Runnels, P. M. Murray, N. Thompson, P. Karkanas, F. W. McCoy, K. W. Wegmann. 2010. Stone Age seafaring in the Mediterranean: Evidence from the Plakias region for Lower Paleolithic and Mesolithic habitation of Crete. *Hesperia* 79: 145–190.

Tchernia, A. 1978. Les vrinatores. In *L'épave romaine de la Madrague de Giens (Var) (Campagnes 1972–1975): Fouilles de l'Institute d'archéologie méditerranéenne (Gallia suppl. 34*, ed. A. Tchernia, P. Pomey, and A. Hesnard, 29–31. Paris: Éditions du CNRS.

Tchernia, A., P. Pomey, and A. Hesnard. 1978. *L'épave romaine de la Madrague de Giens (Var) (Campagnes 1972–1975): Fouilles de l'Institute d'archéologie méditerranéenne (Gallia suppl. 34)*. Paris: Éditions du CNRS.

Thompson, T. 1998. *America's lost treasure*. New York: Atlantic Monthly Press.

Tzalas, H. E. 1995. On the obsidian trail: With a papyrus craft in the Cyclades. In *Tropis III: Third International Symposium on Ship Construction in Antiquity (Athens, 24–27 August 1989)*, ed. H. E. Tzalas, 441–469. Athens: Hellenic Institute for the Preservation of Nautical Tradition.

Tzamtzis, A. I. 1990. "Papyrella": Remote descendant of a middle Stone Age craft? In *Tropis II: Second International Symposium on Ship Construction in Antiquity (Delphi 27–29 August 1987)*, ed. H. E. Tzalas, 329–332. Athens: Hellenic Institute for the Preservation of Nautical Tradition.

Uchupi, E., R. D. Ballard, and W. N. Lange. 1988–1989. New evidence about Titanic's final moments: Resting in pieces. *Oceanus* 31/4: 53–60.

Vercoutter, J. 1956. *L'Égypt et le monde égéen préhellénique*. Biblioteque d'étude 22. Cairo: Institut francais d'archeologie orientale.

Vichos, Y. 1999. The Point Iria wreck: The nautical dimension. In *The Point Iria wreck: Interconnections in the Mediterranean ca. 1200 BCE (Proceedings of the International Conference, Island of Spetses, 19 September 1998)*, ed. W. Phelps, Y. Lolos, and Y. Vichos, 77–98. Athens: Hellenic Institute of Marine Archeology.

Vichos, Y., and Y. Lolos. 1997. The Cypro-Minoan wreck at Point Iria in the Argolic Gulf: First thoughts on the origin and nature of the vessel. In *Res maritimae: Cyprus and the eastern Mediterranean from prehistory to late antiquity; Proceedings of the Second International Symposium "Cities on the Sea" (Nicosia, Cyprus, October 18–22, 1994)*. Cyprus American Archaeological Research Institute Monograph Series, vol. 1, ed. S. Swiny, R. L. Hohlfelder, and H. W. Swiny, 321–337. Atlanta: Scholars Press.

Vichos, Y., and G. Papathanassopoulos. 1996. The excavation of an Early Bronze Age cargo at Dokos: The first two campaign seasons (1989–1990). In *Tropis IV: Fourth International*

Symposium on Ship Construction in Antiquity (Athens, 28–31 August 1991), ed. H. E.
     Tzalas, 519–538. Athens: Hellenic Institute for the Preservation of Nautical Tradition.
VIZ-Tantura. *Shipwreck, Tantura Harbor, Israel: The Institute for the Visualization of
     History.* Online at www.vizin.org/projects/master.htm#tantura/html/tantura.htm.
     Accessed 23 December 2009.
Wachsmann, S. 1986. Is Cyprus ancient Alashiya? New evidence from an Egyptian tablet.
     Biblical Archaeologist 49 (1): 37–40.
——. 1987. *Aegeans in the Theban tombs.* Orientalia Lovaniensia Analecta 20. Leuven:
     Uitgeverij Peters.
——. 1989. Seagoing ships and seamanship in the Late Bronze Age Levant. PhD diss.,
     Hebrew University, Jerusalem.
——. 1998. *Seagoing ships and seamanship in the Bronze Age Levant.* College Station:
     Texas A&M University Press and Chatham Press.
——. 2000. Some notes on Mediterranean seafaring during the second millennium B.C.
     In *Proceedings of the First International Symposium: The Wall Paintings of Thera (Thera,
     Hellas, 30 August–4 September 1997)*, vol. 2, ed. S. Sherratt, 803–824. Athens: Thera
     Foundation.
——. 2007–2008. Deep submergence archaeology: The final frontier. *Skyllis (Deutsche
     Gesellschaft zur Förderung der Unterwasserarchäeologie e.V.) (Proceedings of In
     Poseidons Reich XII)* 8 (1–2): 130–154.
——. In press. *The Gurob ship-cart model and its Mediterranean context.* College Station:
     Texas A&M University Press.
Wachsmann, S., and Y. Kahanov. 1997. Shipwreck fall: The 1995 INA/CMS Joint Expedition
     to Tantura Lagoon, Israel. *INA Quarterly* 24/1: cover, 3–18.
Wachsmann, S., Y. Kahanov, and J. Hall. 1997. The Tantura B shipwreck: The 1997 INA/
     CMS Joint Expedition to Tantura Lagoon. *INA Quarterly* 24 (4): cover, 3–15.
Wachsmann, S., et al. 2009. The Danaos Project, 2008: Reconstructing the Crete to Egypt
     route. In *Proceedings of the 9th Hellenic Symposium on Oceanography and Fisheries,
     May 13–16, 2009, Patras, Greece*, vol. 1, 146–151. Athens: Association of Employees of
     the Hellenic Centre for Marine Research.
Ward, C. 2004. Appendix A: Archaeobotanical remains. In *Deep-water Shipwrecks off
     Skerki Bank: The 1997 survey*, ed. A. M. McCann and J. P. Oleson, 211–213. Portsmouth:
     Journal of Roman Archaeology, Supplemental Series Number 58.
Ward, C., and R. D. Ballard. 2004. Deep-water archaeological survey in the Black Sea: 2000
     season. *International Journal of Nautical Archaeology* 33: 2–13.
Ward, C., and R. L. Horlings. 2008. The remote exploration and archaeological survey of
     four Byzantine ships in the Black Sea. In *Archaeological oceanography*, ed.
     R. D. Ballard, 148–173. Princeton, NJ: Princeton University Press.
Warren, D. J., and R. A. Church. 2003. New technology, the AUV and the potential in
     oilfield maritime archaeology. In *Proceedings: Twenty-First Annual Gulf of Mexico
     Information Transfer Meeting, January 2002.* OCS Study MMS 2003-05, 101–104. New
     Orleans, LA. U.S. Department of the Interior Minerals Management Service, Gulf of
     Mexico OCS Region.
Warren, D., R. Church, and R. Davey. 2004. Discovering HMS *Ark Royal. Hydro
     International* 8 (7 September): 26–29.
Warren, D., R. Church, and R. Westrick. 2008. Using AUVs to investigate shipwrecks:
     Deepwater archaeology in the Gulf. *Sea Technology* 49 (10): 15–16, 18.
Webster, S. 2008. The development of excavation technology for remotely operated
     vehicles. In *Archaeological oceanography*, ed. R. D. Ballard, 41–64. Princeton, NJ:
     Princeton University Press.

Weinstein, E. N. 1992. The recovery and analysis of paleoethnobotanical remains from an eighteenth century shipwreck. PhD diss., Texas A&M University.

Wessel, C. J. 1969. The information background in the field of biological deterioration of nonmetallic materials. In *Symposium on Materials Performance and the Deep Sea (1969)*, ed. Anonymous, 131–141. Philadelphia: American Society for Testing and Materials.

Whitcomb, L., D. Yoerger, and H. Singh. 1999a. Advances in Doppler-based navigation of underwater robotic vehicles. In *Proceedings of the 1999 IEEE International Conference on Robotics and Automation 1*, 399–406. Piscataway: IEEE Press.

———. 1999b. Combined Doppler/LBL based navigation of underwater vehicles. In *Proceedings of the 11th International Symposium on Unmanned Untethered Submersible Technology (UUST99), 22–25 August 1999, Durham, NH*, 1–7.

Whitcomb, L., D. Yoerger, H. Singh, and J. Howland. 1999. Advances in underwater robot vehicles for deep ocean exploration: Navigation, control, and survey operations. In *Robotics research 9: Proceedings of the Ninth International Symposium of Robotics Research (ISRR '99), 9–12 October 1999, Snowbird, UT*, 1–12.

Yoerger, D. R., M. Jakuba, A. M. Bradley, and B. Bingham. 2007. Techniques for deep sea near bottom survey using an autonomous underwater vehicle. *International Journal of Robotics Research* 26: 41–54.

Zemer, A. 1978. *Storage jars in ancient sea trade*. Rev. ed. Haifa: National Maritime Museum Foundation.

CHAPTER 10

RECENT ADVANCES IN POST-EXCAVATION DOCUMENTATION, RECONSTRUCTION, AND EXPERIMENTAL MARITIME ARCHAEOLOGY

MORTEN RAVN, VIBEKE BISCHOFF, ANTON ENGLERT, AND SØREN NIELSEN

INTRODUCTION

WITHIN the context of experimental maritime archaeology, post-excavation documentation of ship-finds serves as the first step toward building an authentic reconstruction of a vessel in order to evaluate its practical use and cultural significance in the past.

Experimental maritime archaeology is multidisciplinary by nature. The combined knowledge of academics, craftsmen, and sailors provides ideal conditions for the reconstruction process. Issues and discussions are often different whether they take place at universities, at boatbuilding sites, or at sea. Members of a reconstruction team are obliged to contribute their own professional skills and to share their multifaceted knowledge in order to produce relevant results (Damgård-Sørensen et al. 2003: 48; Nielsen 2006: 20).

Being a relatively new branch within the field of archaeology, the theory of experimental maritime archaeology is still under debate. Should the methodology be based on the principles of natural sciences, whereby a hypothesis is formed and tested and the results are published (Coates et al. 1995: 294–295), or should the methodology focus on a research plan establishing the scientific potentials of the find (Crumlin-Pedersen 1995: 305)? Another pivot of debate is the interrelation between the tacit knowledge of craftsmanship and the evidence and methods of archaeology. Can one really build a vessel of a certain tradition without belonging to this tradition (Eldjarn 2008; Eldjarn and Sæther 2006)? How can one integrate the tacit knowledge and ancient and present tradition of craftsmanship into the process of archaeological reconstruction (Andersen et al. 2005; Bischoff 2007: 40; Planke 02)?

The terminology used in experimental maritime archaeology has also been subject to discussion (Fenwick 1993; Goodburn 1993; Marsden 1993; Westerdahl 1992, 1993). Which is the right term to use: "replica," "copy," "reconstruction," or "floating hypothesis"? At the Viking Ship Museum in Roskilde, the term "reconstruction" has been chosen following closely the meaning of the verb "reconstruct": "build up a complete structure or description of something of which one has only a few parts or only partial evidence" (*Oxford Advanced Learner's Dictionary of Current English* 1980; see also Marsden 1993: 207).

The path from wreck to reconstruction begins with the detailed documentation of hull remains and progresses to the building of a reconstruction scale model. This model provides the base for the inner-edge lines and torso drawings (lines drawings with the preserved parts drawn in), as well as the subsequent reconstruction of the parts missing from the hull. Then workshop drawings can be made, laying the groundwork for the building of a full-scale reconstruction, ready to be tested under sea conditions.

POST-EXCAVATION DOCUMENTATION

In naval architecture a ship is built according to its intended design. By contrast, archaeologists working with shipwrecks are left with fragments of the results of this original design. It is therefore necessary to describe the former design as accurately as possible. "Reverse naval architecture"—a term coined by Ole Crumlin-Pedersen—describes the process of clarifying the form, function, and construction of an excavated vessel, while also documenting its date, its origin, and the material used in its construction (Lemée 2006: 97). All elements of post-excavation documentation and reconstruction are focused on reaching this goal.

The initial methods used to document ship timbers were developed in the early 1960s (namely with the Skuldelev Ships [Crumlin-Pedersen 2002], the Bremen Cog [Lahn 1992], and the *Vasa* [Cederlund 2006]). In Roskilde, the Skuldelev Ships' individual elements were recorded in full-scale drawings using the principles of projection by eye (Crumlin-Pedersen 2002: 53–56). The waterlogged parts were recorded by placing transparent polyester sheets on glass set above the artifact; waterproof pens with different line thicknesses and colors were then used to draw their outlines and features. Full documentation of ship timbers rested on the combined use of these drawings and photographs as well as recording and excavation notes. This process was used with success for more than 40 years, until digital documentation took over.

A project conducted by the National Museum of Denmark's Centre for Maritime Archaeology (1993–2003) introduced to the field of archaeology the practice of three-dimensional documentation of ship timbers. After initial trials with various devices (Hocker 2000: 27–30; Holm 1998: 31), a Faro Sterling 10-ft Arm digitizer was purchased in 2000 (Hocker 2003: 1) (Figure 10.1).

Figure 10.1 The Faro Sterling 10-foot Arm, operated by Ivan Conrad Hansen. Photo by Werner Karrasch. Reproduced with the kind permission of the Viking Ship Museum.

Three-dimensional digital documentation not only increases the accuracy of the recording of ship timbers, but also allows for the storage of geometrical information in three dimensions. In addition, one can view the entire digitized object three-dimensionally on a monitor (Hocker 2003: 2). A digitizer forces the skilled user to "read" and interpret the artifact during the very documentation process. The standards for this archaeological interpretation are best defined in seamless collaboration between those conducting the documentation and those building the reconstruction.

Through the use of a FaroArm, the edges and details of artifacts are documented manually by tracing features with a probe connected to the end of a digitizing arm. The probe's exact position is located by spherical trigonometry, and when activated, the probe records its position as x, y, and z coordinates. Many different types of probe tips can be used with a FaroArm, and these can be changed during a recording session, although each new probe must be calibrated using the proprietary software program Cam2measure (Hocker 2003: 5–6).

In order to view and edit the data being captured with the FaroArm, a three-dimensional drawing program is needed (Figure 10.2). Rhinoceros software is a good choice and is furthermore ideal as a tool for modeling wooden ships (Hocker 2003: 7). Rhinoceros is designed for Windows platforms and based on NURBS (Non-Uniform Rational Bézier-Spline) geometry (McNeel and Associates 2002: 4, 500). This means that the program allows free-form, three-dimensional drawings to be created following the rules for parametric curves invented by the French engineer Pierre Etienne Bézier (1910–1999). In vector graphics, Bézier's rules are characterized by the possibility to transform a curve using control points on the curve; the more complex the curves, the higher the degree of curvature.

The information that can be retrieved from an artifact varies. In general, one should look for the original edges of the worked timber, limits of original edges, edges damaged during construction or use, cracks, lands (plank overlap in clinker-built vessels), the position of pith, direction of wood fibers, the pattern of the medullary rays, sapwood, caulking grooves, inlaid or driven caulking material, molds, traces of rivets and additional nails, treenails, rivet holes and plugged holes, wear, tool marks, and traces of repair. In addition to these details, cross sections of the artifact should be made, and registration tags, control points used for reorientation, and text and symbols should be noted.

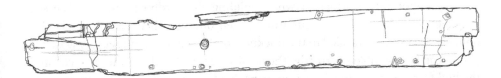

Figure 10.2 Plank X 109 from the Amager Strand wreck, Copenhagen. The plank is drawn using the FaroArm digitizer and the Rhinoceros drawing software program. Drawing by Morten Ravn. Reproduced with the kind permission of the Viking Ship Museum.

It is advisable to use a checklist when recording with a FaroArm. The checklist can be designed as a layer system in Rhinoceros. Alpha-numerical prefixed layers can be deleted or added without destroying the general order of the checklist (Jones 2009). Each layer should have its own color so that the layers can be visually differentiated. By following the layer system from top to bottom, the data can be systematically recorded, and the user of the FaroArm is less likely to overlook important details during documentation. It is important to stress that the contents of the layer system should be considered before beginning a new project, and the alpha-numerical prefixes and the color system should remain unchanged.

Beside the Viking Ship Museum in Roskilde, several other centers of research use digital documentation. The Norwegian Maritime Museum in Oslo, the Yenikapı Shipwrecks Project, the Newport Medieval Ship Project, and the Drogheda Boat Project are using digitizers and layer-based drawing programs following closely the above-mentioned procedure for documenting archaeological ship timbers. Other researchers have used three-dimensional laser scanners to document entire ship hulls, namely the Swedish flagship *Vasa*, the Confederate submarine *HL Hunley* (DeVine 2002), the Dutch East Indiaman *Batavia* (Duivenvoorde 2005: 3–6), and the Norwegian grave ship of Oseberg (Bischoff 2007: 36–40; Paasche et al. 2007: 9–14). Furthermore, at the Nautical Archaeology Program at Texas A&M University two-dimensional drawings have been transformed into three-dimensional digital drawings, which have led to virtual reconstructions (Catsambis 2006: 12–15; Sasaki 2005: 16–21).

BUILDING A SCALE MODEL AND GENERATING DRAWINGS

In order to determine the shape and construction of a hull, a reconstruction model is built in a suitable material and scale (e.g., cardboard and at 1:10 scale). First, freehand or digitizer-generated drawings of the documented ship timbers are printed on paper at the desired scale. These drawings show, among other things, the outline of the planks, their cross sections, nail holes, treenail holes, cracks, lands, and scarfs, all very important information when building the cardboard model. The scale drawings of each element are cut around their outlines, then each image is glued onto cardboard that is scaled to the thickness of the ship elements, ensuring that the planks can be assembled correctly. The planks are then fitted together to reconstruct the hull form, and in situ excavation plans, field notes, and photographs are useful to assist in this process. The cardboard planks are connected to each other with pins placed in the nail holes that originally held the planks together. The frames are fixed in the model so the treenail holes in these and in the planks line up as they would have in the original ship.

Through the creation of a three-dimensional physical model of the preserved parts of ship timbers, a reliable hull form can be established. As the hull form is also a coherent structure, one cannot make alterations in one dimension without influencing changes in other dimensions. If a large percentage of the ship is preserved, the model will present a reasonably precise image of the original ship.

Ship-finds are seldom complete, and in most cases, large parts of the hull are missing. There will always be room for a certain degree of interpretation when reconstructing archaeological ship-finds, and in many cases is it up to the reconstruction expert to interpret the material as much as possible in order to develop a realistic idea of the former hull form. The curvature of the keel (rocker) might be more or less straight, the bow more or less lifted, the sides more or less raised. However, if one wishes to build a full-scale physical reconstruction, all possibilities cannot be left open, and informed and educated decisions have to be made in this step of the process. Therefore, the lines not preserved are determined on the basis of the wreck's preserved lines and hull form, as well as through comparisons to other contemporary vessels or those of the same type and size. Relevant iconographic material and written sources can also be consulted. If this work is done thoroughly, it will lead to an impression of the former vessel's approximate shape and size.

After the physical cardboard model is completed, its dimensions are recorded. This is done with the use of a digitizer such as the FaroArm (Figure 10.3), and these dimensions are transformed into an inner-edge lines drawing. The inner-edge lines

Figure 10.3 The reconstruction model of the Oseberg ship was recorded digitally so that drawings could be made. The ship model was built in order to reevaluate its hull form. Photograph by Werner Karrasch. Reproduced with the kind permission of the Viking Ship Museum.

drawing describes the lines of the upper inner-edges of all strakes in a hull. Cross sections of the reconstructed hull are defined as stations, and the upper inner-edge of every plank in this cross section is recorded.

Based on the inner-edge lines drawing, a torso drawing of the hull (showing all the preserved parts) is made. A torso drawing is important in order to document the degree of completeness of the original vessel and the authenticity of the reconstruction. In addition, a plank-expansion drawing, generated from the documentation drawings that show the character of the planks; their shape, width, length, and thickness; the bevel of the overlap; and framing distance, is important in order to provide a good overview of the preserved planks. Finally, if possible, a reconstruction drawing of the whole ship, complete with rigging, is made.

In 1999, the NMF Ship software program was developed in order to improve reconstruction and analysis of clinker-built historic ships. Naval engineer Kenn Jensen developed the program at the Centre for Maritime Archaeology at the National Museum of Denmark (NMF) and the Department of Naval Architecture and Offshore Engineering (ISH) at the Technical University of Denmark (Jensen 1999). The program is used for the rendering of a hull form as well as for calculating its performance data and statistical measurements.

NMF Ship is divided into input and results sections. In the input section, the geometry of the inner hull is defined (Jensen 1999: 12). The input requirements are primarily based on data from clinker-built ships, where the basic data source is an inner-edge lines drawing. However, the software can also handle other related hull construction types, such as cogs, which are partly carvel-built and partly clinker-built. In the results section, the calculated data are presented. The calculations are specifically adapted to the characteristics of ancient clinker-built ships.

After the inner geometry is measured on the model or the drawing, the data are entered into NMF Ship, and transferred to another ship-design software program, I-ship. I-ship was developed at the Department of Naval Architecture and Offshore Engineering (ISH), Technical University of Denmark (DTU), in collaboration with the Danish Maritime Institute (DMI). With this program it is possible to define the geometry of the ship — both the outer and the inner dimensions. A simple digital wire-frame model, in which the separate curves are connected at joining points, demonstrates the form of the hull (Bischoff and Jensen 2001: 204–208). In I-ship the inner geometry is corrected by use of the graphical user interface and thereafter returned to NMF Ship.

As the later calculations and drawings of the vessel are to be made on the basis of the outer hull lines, it is necessary to transform the inner dimensions into outer dimensions. On the basis of the recorded thickness of the strakes, the width of the overlap and the width of the keel, the outer hull is determined and set into NMF Ship (Jensen 1999: 15). After any last corrections and minor modifications of the geometry, the definition of the hull geometry has been completed. Then the digital wireframe file is ready for further processing in NMF Ship, where the desired calculation and drawing data are generated. Finally, an AutoCAD script file containing a drawing is generated in NMF Ship (Bischoff and Jensen 2001: 204).

If a solid three-dimensional model is needed for presentation or for use in a hydrodynamic laboratory tank test, the data from I-ship can be exported as an IGES (Initial Graphics Exchange Specification) file and imported into Rhinoceros. Rhinoceros, in addition to its application described above, is suitable for making a surface model of the hull, which will make it possible for a milling machine to produce a solid model. The aim of this work is to make hydrodynamic measurements in order to generate data regarding the seaworthiness and sailing capacity of the original vessel prior to building a full-scale reconstruction.

Often a wooden presentation model is built. This model's purpose is twofold: first, it provides a solid foundation prior to building a full-scale reconstruction, since here all details and measurements have been worked through in practice; second, it is an important part of the public presentation of the ship-find (Bischoff and Jensen 2001: 209).

FULL-SCALE PHYSICAL RECONSTRUCTION

Since the first full-scale reconstruction of a Viking ship, the Gokstad ship reconstruction *Viking* (Andersen 1895), many similar projects have been conducted. Most of them are what we today call reenactment projects. Some reconstructed vessels, however, are soundly based on the scientific methodology mentioned above. In 1984 an international "ship replica seminar" was held in Roskilde, focusing on all scientifically conducted reconstructions, replicas, reproductions, and re-creations (Crumlin-Pedersen et al. 1986). Today, the International Symposium on Boat and Ship Archaeology (ISBSA) serves as a forum for the presentation of new reconstruction projects and their results. The proceedings of this triennial meeting are usually published by the latest host institution in time for the next symposium. A complete table of contents of all previous volumes is available on www.isbsa.org.

By building a full-scale reconstruction it is possible to address questions regarding the knowledge of the ancient boatbuilders, the relationship between natural resources and boatbuilding, the man-hours required in the building process, and the tools used. When the physical reconstruction is launched, the vessel's seaworthiness and performance can be studied. Building full-scale reconstructions is a component of the experimental analysis of archaeologically recorded shipwrecks. The methodology discussed here, within the framework of experimental archaeology, provides information that may otherwise not be apparent from the archaeological artifacts studied (Crumlin-Pedersen 2003: 1).

To ensure that the reconstruction is as authentic as possible, it is important to build on the information gained during the documentation of the ship-find and the building of the scale model. The inner-edge lines drawing and the wooden presentation model are the starting points for a full-scale reconstruction. Inner-edge lines drawings sometimes have to be altered due to the fact that oak planks do not behave in exactly the same way as the material used in the scale model. Furthermore, it is important to examine the original wooden artifacts and digitized drawings of these so as to clarify the position of pith, the direction of wood fibers, and the pattern of the medullary rays. Relevant archaeological, iconographic, and ethnographical material as well as written sources should also be consulted in order to identify comparable finds and uses (Nielsen 2006: 17–18).

A reliable reconstruction is highly dependent on how much experience the boatbuilders have using the tools and techniques that were applied when the original vessel was built (Figure 10.4). The more modern boatbuilders are familiar with earlier techniques and tools, the better the chance of choosing the same solutions as historic and prehistoric boatbuilders. Furthermore, the ability to evaluate the original purpose of the vessel, with regard to its function and area served, is desirable (Nielsen 2006: 17).

Before the building process begins, basic rules have to be determined: the reconstructed ship should be built to the same size and with the same hull form as the original vessel. The reconstructed ship should be built of the same materials and with the same tools and techniques as the original ship. In some cases modern tools can be applied, but if they are used, care should be taken so that their use does not affect the quality or appearance of the ship. Furthermore, the places where these modern tools are used, and the reasons for their use, should be documented.

If a reconstruction project is to be scientifically useful, the parts of the reconstruction that are based on archaeological evidence and those that are based on

Figure 10.4 Boatbuilder Ture M. Møller working on a frame part for the Skuldelev 1 reconstruction, *Ottar*, using a copy of a Viking Age axe found in Sæbø Ulvik in Norway. Photograph by Werner Karrasch. Reproduced with the kind permission of the Viking Ship Museum.

educated suppositions should be documented. This documentation consists of reports, drawings, photographs, and video recordings and is an integral component of published reports of the project.

The main objective when building a full-scale physical reconstruction is to gain an understanding of the original vessel's design, function, and qualities and to relate this to the society in which it was built. A ship-find reflects, among other things, craftsmanship traditions, design comprehension, and aesthetics, and the building of a full-scale reconstruction can contribute greatly to the enhancement of this knowledge (Damgård-Sørensen 2006: 4).

The building process involves many different kinds of specialists besides boatbuilders. Blacksmiths, rope makers, weavers, sail makers, painters, tar-burners, charcoal-burners, and craftsmen who extract iron, fell and transport timber, and make flax and wool are needed (Bill et al. 2007: 51; Nielsen 2006: 20). In the process of the full-scale reconstruction all of these crafts are examined, as are the various craftsmen's tools. The tool marks recorded on archaeological artifacts, archaeological finds of tools, and iconographical depictions of the use of tools help determine which tools were used when the original ship was built. In some cases the documentation of tool marks made during the reconstruction process can lead to the recognition of tool marks on the original ship timbers.

By recording the amount of man-hours invested during the various steps of the building process using authentic tools and techniques, it is possible to estimate the effort put into the building process in historic or prehistoric times. This information can also provide valuable insight into the organizational structure of past societies.

Another important aspect of the full-scale reconstruction of ship-finds is its function in creating public awareness. The process and final product of reconstruction provides an ideal form of presenting archaeological research. People can identify and interact with the experimental results, and more than once, public response has led to new and valuable questions regarding the material and its interpretation.

SAILING TRIALS WITH RECONSTRUCTED SHIP-FINDS

Sailing trials have become an important component of the experimental analysis of ship-finds. A wholesale approach to archaeological reconstruction includes the experimental use of the reconstructed artifact under realistic conditions. The repeated practical use of the vessel in question makes it possible to investigate and interpret the use of the original craft and its significance for the society that relied on it. Ideally, the experiment ends when the reconstructed vessel is deemed beyond repair after many seasons at sea. Sometimes, today as well as in the past, vessels are lost at sea. The full-scale reconstruction of the Oseberg ship, *Dronningen*, built in 1987,

sank on the first test trial under sail in 1988 (Carver 1995), and the reconstruction of
Skuldelev 1, *Saga Siglar*, built in 1983, was lost in 1992 off Catalonia after her circumnavigation of the world in 1984–1986 (Thorseth 1988, 1993). Other reconstructed
ships endure many seasons at sea, like the Skuldelev 3 reconstruction *Roar Ege*,
launched in Roskilde in 1984, and thus over time need numerous repairs (Andersen
et al. 1997; Annual Reports from the Viking Ship Museum in Roskilde 2001, 2003,
2004, 2006, 2007). Traces of wear and usage can be related to the original ship-find
and give new clues about the use of the original vessel. If parts of the reconstructed
vessel are proven inaccurate during sailing trials, the original artifacts and the doc-
umentation-toward-reconstruction process should be reexamined. This can lead to
improved versions, as in the case of the ship-find Skuldelev 1. Its first reconstruction, *Saga Siglar*, was built by traditional boatbuilders advised by archaeologists
(Thorseth 1988). The experiences gained during the building of *Saga Siglar* and her
circumnavigation of the world in 1984–1986, as well as a reexamination of the original find and its tool marks, enabled the specialized boatbuilders of the Viking Ship
Museum in Roskilde to built a new and improved reconstruction, *Ottar*, in 2000
(Nielsen 2000a: 34–35, 2000b: 18–21).

Sailing and rowing trials lead to a profound understanding of ancient seamanship and other essential operational and logistical aspects. In practice, sailing experiments comprise two supplementary methods: standardized trials (i.e., short daily
trials from the same shore base), and longer trial voyages over greater stretches of
water. The combined results of standardized sailing and rowing trials and the systematic documentation of these provide essential empirical data for a better understanding of the use of vessels in the past.

Standardized sailing and rowing trials and the use of advanced measuring devices in these trials illustrate the sailing and rowing properties of a specific vessel
within chosen parameters. After the launch of a new reconstruction, standardized
trials can help to improve and assess the performance of the hull, rudder, rig, and
trial crew. Once the sailing performance of vessel and crew are considered to be
representative of past levels and use, this method makes it possible to compare the
vessel's properties to those of other tested vessels, based on absolute data.

Despite the unalterable nature of wind and sea, standardized trials can be carried out under circumstances that come close to preferred or laboratory conditions.
A suitable trial theater under minimal influence of currents may be chosen, where
the reconstructed vessel can be exposed to open, undisturbed onshore winds and
wave motion on some days, and to land winds with a relatively calm sea on other
days (Vinner 1986).

Experience has shown that it is better to sail numerous trials over short distances
rather than a few trials over long distances. In that way, many different maneuvers
with respect to course, propulsion, and trim can be carried out and documented
within the same state of wind and sea. This trial scenario applies to rowed vessels and
sailing craft alike. A wide range of instruments can be employed to collect absolute
data: log, GPS, wind indicator, stopwatch, inclinometer, and scales, to name a few. The
resulting data are, for example: speed through water, ground track, speed over ground,

velocity made good, wind direction, wind speed (apparent and true), duration of maneuvers, heeling angle, weight and trim of hull, and notations on rigging, ship's equipment, ballast, and the amount and distribution of cargo and crew.

A typical example for the results of standardized sailing trials can be seen in a polar diagram (Figure 10.5) published by Max Vinner in the monograph *Roar Ege* on the reconstruction of the Danish Viking ship-find Skuldelev 3 (Andersen et al. 1997: 262). Standardized trials also make it possible to compare vessels of different types, as well as time periods: two reconstructed ship-finds of the eleventh century (Skuldelev 1 [*Saga Siglar*] and Skuldelev 3 [*Roar Ege*]), one traditional working boat with single square rig of the late nineteenth century (*Rana*), and one modern racing yacht (X-99 with and without spinnaker) are shown in Figure 5. The diagram shows the velocity made good (VMG) of these vessels at

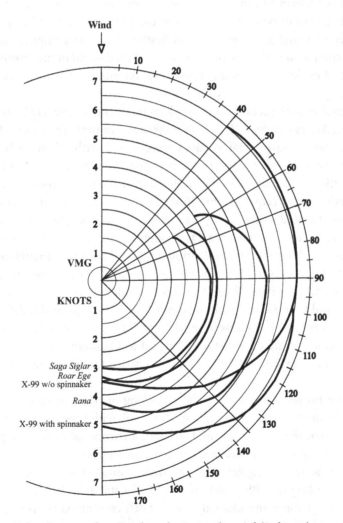

Figure 10.5 Polar diagram showing the velocity made good (in knots) at various angles to the wind of certain historical, traditional, and modern sailing vessels. Reproduced with the kind permission of Andersen et al. (1997: 262).

various angles to the wind. It demonstrates that the single-square-rigged boats, with their shallow draft, share a modest windward performance. At the same time, the modern Bermuda-rigged racer cannot outrun a 900-year-old design on the dead run without pulling the spinnaker. Clearly, this kind of sailing experiment is a valuable tool for exploring the history of naval architecture in relation to ship types. However, in order to relate a certain vessel type to its former use and its former function within a society, a second, complementary method should be applied: the trial voyage.

Trial voyages are real voyages at sea or in inland waters, carried out in the same nautical environment that the original vessel sailed, under conditions known from the time of original use, and with a minimum of modern aids. Enabling a variety of valuable and often unpredictable observations, trial voyages provide an authentic insight into the length of time and the precautions required to carry out a certain voyage with a certain type of vessel under the experienced weather pattern. The performance of vessel and crew delivers firsthand data and physical experiences that can be compared with historical sources and used to aid in the interpretation of archaeological evidence for nautical activities like goods exchange, naval warfare, and fishing.

Trial voyages with reconstructions of ancient vessels have a long and popular history (e.g., Andersen 1895; Heyerdahl 1948; Severin 1978; Thorseth 1988; Vinner 1995). Some well-known trial voyages were sailed with "floating hypotheses" rather than authentic reconstructions. It is therefore necessary to identify and define conditions of authenticity for trial voyages. The following points may serve as an extensive list of requirements (Englert 2006): (1) a faithful reconstruction of a well-documented shipwreck, (2) a voyage through waters similar to those of the ship's original operational area, (3) no engine use, (4) no external help except in an emergency, (5) no use of navigational methods or instruments unknown at the time, (6) no fixed schedule, (7) use of natural harbors rather than modern harbor facilities, (8) personal hygiene without modern comfort, (9) use of authentic clothing, and (10) use of authentic provisions. One may find it difficult, if not impossible, to meet all of these requirements at the same time. It is essential, however, to concentrate on some of these and to maintain them. In any circumstance there must be sufficient equipment on board to ensure the life and health of the crew.

There are no set standards for the recording of trial voyages. Minimum recording equipment is composed of, first, a logbook with times, positions, observations on weather, ship, and crew, and, second, a chronometer for dating logbook entries. In the absence of a steering compass, a compass is needed for recording wind directions (e.g., Englert and Ossowski 2009). Under ideal conditions, automatic recording of GPS positions and wind data, as well as photo and video recordings, supplement the manual record. Such conditions were met when *Sea Stallion from Glendalough* (Figure 10.6), a reconstruction of the late Viking Age longship Skuldelev 2, sailed from Roskilde to Dublin and back, circumnavigating Britain counterclockwise (www.vikingshipmuseum.dk).

Figure 10.6 The reconstruction of the late Viking Age longship Skuldelev 2, *Sea Stallion from Glendalough*, plowing the Irish Sea with one reef taken in. Photo by Werner Karrasch. Reproduced with the kind permission of the Viking Ship Museum.

RECENT ADVANCES AND FUTURE PERSPECTIVES

At the turn of the twenty-first century, the hand-drawn recording of archaeological ship timbers is being replaced by digital recording. The goal is to develop documentation methods that are accurate and efficient in recording artifacts as objectively as possible.

Three-dimensional documentation of ship timbers has been integrated slightly differently at the various centers of research. This is mainly caused by the character of the artifacts to be documented, but also by individual preferences and traditions at research institutions influence the documentation methods. However, collaboration between research institutions is emerging. In 2007 a working group was established in order to develop common standards for digital documentation and to share experiences with new features relevant for three-dimensional documentation and reconstruction: FRAUG (FaroArm-Rhino Archaeology Users Group). As of this writing (in 2009), the group consists of the Vasa Museum, the Norwegian Maritime Museum, the Newport Medieval Ship Project, the Drogheda Boat Project, the Yenikapı Shipwrecks Project, and the Viking Ship Museum in Roskilde.

Digitalization is a clear trend among the emerging methods in post-excavation documentation and reconstruction. Direct Digital Manufacturing (DDM) of the three-dimensional documentation drawings may replace the cardboard planks and frames of the reconstruction scale model. Future computer technology may even allow a reconstruction to be made in virtual reality, which then could be projected into the physical world in the form of holograms, primarily for public presentation.

When reconstructing archaeological ship-finds, working with all the preserved parts interlocked in a coherent three-dimensional model is crucial in order to reconstruct the hull form, since alterations in one dimension will affect the other dimensions. Specialized computer software programs such as I-ship and NMF Ship improve the understanding of the find by generating hydrostatic data and three-dimensional lines drawings of the reconstructed ship. The use of tank tests allows us to investigate various aspects of the vessel's performance and seaworthiness prior to building a full-scale reconstruction.

From the early attempts to build full-scale reconstructions of archaeological ship-finds until today, many advances have been made. The building and sailing of reconstructed vessels has become an important component of the experimental analysis of ship-finds. The building process provides knowledge of the many different specialized trades involved in boat- and shipbuilding, and the reconstructed vessel can serve as a living source of information regarding the maritime knowledge and needs of past societies.

Sailing trials and trial voyages are an empirical way of reconstructing the transport conditions of the past. One could argue that any aspect of ancient transport could just as well be theoretically calculated and debated from the writing desk, and from dry, indoor reconstruction work. This may be true to a certain extent, but without the practical experiment, crucial aspects like the flexibility of a complex hull, the vulnerability of the rudder system, the seaworthiness and speed of the vessel, the real travel speed of a voyage within a certain weather pattern, logistical limitations, and the physical and nautical abilities required from the crew would not come to light.

REFERENCES

Andersen, Erik, Ole Crumlin-Pedersen, Søren Vadstrup, and Max Vinner. 1997. *Roar Ege: Skuldelev 3 skibet som arkæologisk eksperiment*. Roskilde: Viking Ship Museum.

Andersen, Erik, Tinna Damgård-Sørensen, and Søren Nielsen. 2005. Skuldelevskibene. Rekonstruktion af arkæologiske skibsfund. *Kysten* 2005 (2): 10–13.

Andersen, Magnus. 1895. *Vikingefærden: En illustreret Beskrivelse af "Vikings" Reise i 1893*. Kristiania, Norway: Author.

Annual Reports from the Viking Ship Museum in Roskilde. 2001, 2003, 2004, 2006, and 2007. Online at www.vikingeskibsmuseet.dk/index.php?id=1342&L=1. Accessed 3 June 2009.

Bill, Jan, Søren Nielsen, Erik Andersen, and Tinna Damgård-Sørensen. 2007. *Welcome on board! The Sea Stallion from Glendalough*. Roskilde: Viking Ship Museum.

Bischoff, Vibeke. 2007. Gåden Osebergskibet. *Kysten* 2007 (3): 36–40.

Bischoff, Vibeke, and Kenn Jensen. 2001. Ladby II: The ship. In *Ladby: A Danish ship-grave from the Viking Age; Ships and boats of the North 3*, ed. Anne C. Sørensen, 181–245. Roskilde: Viking Ship Museum.

Carver, Martin. 1995. On—and off—the Edda. In *Shipshape: Essays for Ole Crumlin-Pedersen on the occasion of his 60th anniversary February 24th 1995*, ed. Olaf Olsen, Jan Skamby Madsen, and Flemming Rieck, 305–312. Roskilde: Viking Ship Museum.

Catsambis, Alexis. 2006. Reconstructing vessels: From two-dimensional drawings to three-dimensional models. *INA Quarterly* 33 (3): 12–15.

Cederlund, Carl Oluf. 2006. Vasa I: *The archaeology of a Swedish warship 1628*. Ed. Fred Hocker. Stockholm: National Maritime Museums of Sweden.

Coates, John, Sean McGrail, David Brown, Edwin Gifford, Gerald Grainge, Basil Greenhill, Peter Marsden, Boris Rankov, Colin Tipping, and Edward Wright. 1995. Experimental boat and ship archaeology: Principles and methods. *International Journal of Nautical Archaeology* 24 (4): 293–301.

Crumlin-Pedersen, Ole. 1995. Experimental archaeology and ships—bridging the arts and the sciences. *International Journal of Nautical Archaeology* 24 (4): 303–306.

———. 2002. Post-excavation documentation. In *The Skuldelev Ships I: Topography, archaeology, history, conservation and display; Ships and boats of the North 4.1*, ed. Ole Crumlin-Pedersen, 53–56. Roskilde: Viking Ship Museum.

———. 2003. Experimental archaeology and ships—principles, problems and examples. In *Connected by the sea: Proceedings of the Tenth International Symposium on Boat and Ship Archaeology, Roskilde 2003*, ed. Lucy Blue, Fred Hocker, and Anton Englert, 1–7. Oxford: Oxbow.

Crumlin-Pedersen, Ole, and Max Vinner. 1986. *Sailing into the past: The International Ship Replica Seminar, Roskilde 1984*. Roskilde: Viking Ship Museum.

Damgård-Sørensen, Tinna. 2006. *Project: Thoroughbred of the Sea; The trial voyage to Dublin: Research plan*. Roskilde: Viking Ship Museum. Online at www.vikingeskibsmuseet.dk/uploads/media/Fuldblodpaahavet_Forskningsplan_nov2006_UK.pdf. Accessed 9 December 2008.

Damgård-Sørensen, Tinna, Søren Nielsen, and Erik Andersen. 2003. Fuldblod på havet. In *Beretning fra toogtyvende tværfaglige vikingesymposium*, ed. Niels Lund, 5–50. Aarhus: Forlaget Hikuin and Aarhus Universitet.

DeVine, Doug. 2002. Mapping the CSS *Hunley*. *Professional Surveyor* 22 (3): 6–16.

Duivenvoorde, Wendy van. 2005. Capturing curves and timber with a laser scanner: Digital imaging of *Batavia*. *INA Quarterly* 32 (3): 3–6.

Eldjarn, Gunnar. 2008. Båtbygging og båtbygging fru Blom. *Kysten* 2008 (5): 32–33.

Eldjarn, Gunnar, and Arne-Terje Sæther. 2006. Krefter mellom seil og skrog. In *Klink og seil—Festskrift til Arne Emil Christensen*, ed. Torstein Arisholm, Knut Paasche, and Trine Lise Wahl, 205–213. Oslo: Norsk Sjøfartsmuseum and Kulturhistorisk Museum Universitetet i Oslo.

Englert, Anton. 2006. Trial voyages as a method of experimental archaeology: The aspect of speed. In *Connected by the sea: Proceedings of the Tenth International Symposium on Boat and Ship Archaeology, Roskilde 2003*, ed. Lucy Blue, Fred Hocker, and Anton Englert, 35–42. Oxford: Oxbow Books.

Englert, Anton, and Waldemar Ossowski. 2009. Sailing in Wulfstan's wake: The 2004 trial voyage Hedeby-Gdańsk with the Skuldelev 1-reconstruction, *Ottar*. In *Wulfstan's voyage: The Baltic Sea region in the early Viking Age as seen from shipboard*, ed. Anton Englert and Athena Trakadas, 257–270. Roskilde: Viking Ship Museum.

Fenwick, Valerie. 1993. The replication debate. *International Journal of Nautical Archaeology* 22 (3): 197.

Goodburn, D. M. 1993. Some further thoughts on reconstructions, replicas, and simulations of ancient boats and ships. *International Journal of Nautical Archaeology* 22 (3): 199–203.

Heyerdahl, Thor. 1948. *Kon-Tiki ekspedisjonen*. Oslo: Gyldendal.

Hocker, Fred. 2000. New tools—for maritime archaeology. *Maritime Archaeology Newsletter from Roskilde, Denmark* 14: 27–30.

———. 2003. *Three-dimensional documentation of ship timbers using FaroArm, Handbook v. 2.0*. Roskilde: Nationalmuseets Marinarkæologiske Forskningscenter. Unpublished report.

Holm, Jørgen. 1998. New recording methods for ship-finds. *Maritime Archaeology Newsletter from Roskilde, Denmark* 10: 30–31.

Hornby, A. S., A. P. Cowie, and A. C. Gimson, eds. 1980. *Oxford Advanced Learner's Dictionary of Current English*. Berlin: Cornelsen and Oxford University Press.

Jensen, Kenn. 1999. Documentation and analysis of ancient ships. PhD diss., Centre for Maritime Archaeology and Department of Naval Architecture and Offshore Engineering, Technical University of Denmark.

Jones, Toby. 2009. *The Newport medieval ship: Timber recording manual; Digital recording of ship timbers using a FaroArm 3D Digitiser, Faro Arm Laser Line Probe and Rhinoceros 3D software*. Unpublished report, Newport Medieval Ship Project.

Lahn, Werner. 1992. *Die Kogge von Bremen, band 1*. Hamburg: Ernst Kabel Verlag.

Lemée, Christian. 2006. Reverse naval architecture. In *The Renaissance shipwrecks from Christianshavn: An archaeological and architectural study of large carvel vessels in Danish waters, 1580–1640; Ships and boats of the North 6*, ed. Ole Crumlin-Pedersen, 97–98. Roskilde: Viking Ship Museum.

Marsden, Peter. 1993. Replica versus reconstruction. *International Journal of Nautical Archaeology* 22 (3): 206–207.

McGrail, Sean. 1992. Replicas, reconstructions and floating hypotheses. *International Journal of Nautical Archaeology* 21 (4): 353–355.

McNeel, Robert, & Associates. 2002. *Rhinoceros®. NURBS modeling for Windows: Version 3.0; User's Guide*. Seattle, Washington: Robert McNeel & Associates

Nielsen, Søren. 2000a. *Maritime Archaeology Newsletter from Roskilde, Denmark* 13: 34–35.

——— 2000b. The Skuldelev 1 replica launched. *Maritime Archaeology Newsletter from Roskilde, Denmark* 15: 18–21.

———. 2006. Experimental archaeology at the Viking Ship in Roskilde. In *Connected by the sea: Proceedings of the Tenth International Symposium on Boat and Ship Archaeology, Roskilde 2003*, ed. Lucy Blue, Fred Hocker, and Anton Englert, 16–20. Oxford: Oxbow Books.

Paasche, Knut, Geir Røvik, and Vibeke Bischoff. 2007. *Rekonstruksjon av Osebergskipets form*. Kulturhistorisk Museum, Vikingeskibsmuseet i Roskilde and Stiftelsen Nytt Osebergskip. Unpublished report.

Planke, Terje. 2002. Hva' båten er et svar på. *Kysten* 2002 (5): 12–15.

Sasaki, Randall. 2005. Methods for recording timbers in three dimensions. *INA Quarterly* 32 (3): 16–21.

Severin, Tim. 1978. *The Brendan voyage*. London: Hutchinson.

Thorseth, Ragnar. 1988. Saga Siglar—*Århundrets seilas jorda rundt*. Ålesund: Nordvest Forlag.

———. 1993. Saga Siglar's *Forlis: Vikingenes seilaser*. Ålesund: Nordvest Forlag AS.

Vinner, Max. 1986. Recording the trial run. In *Sailing into the past: The International Ship Replica Seminar; Roskilde 1984*, ed. Ole Crumlin-Pedersen and Max Vinner, 220–225. Roskilde: Viking Ship Museum.

———. 1995. A Viking-ship off Cape Farewell 1984. In *Shipshape: Essays for Ole Crumlin Pedersen on the occasion of his 60th anniversary February 24th 1995*, ed. Olaf Olsen, Jan Skamby Madsen, and Flemming Rieck, 289–304. Roskilde: Viking Ship Museum.

Westerdahl, Christer. 1992. Review of Welsh, Frank, 1988, *Building the trireme*. *International Journal of Nautical Archaeology* 21 (1): 84–85.

———. 1993. The trireme—an experimental form? *International Journal of Nautical Archaeology* 22 (3): 205–207.

CHAPTER 11

SHIPWRECK RECONSTRUCTION BASED ON THE ARCHAEOLOGICAL RECORD: MEDITERRANEAN WHOLE-MOLDING AND THE KITTEN WRECK CASE STUDY

KROUM N. BATCHVAROV

INTRODUCTION

IN the early 1980s Bulgarian archaeologists of the Centre for Underwater Archaeology (CUA) discovered the remains of a postmedieval ship in the southern Bay of Kitten (Figure 11.1). Over three seasons, Dr. Kalin Porozhanov directed a limited excavation of the site, which came to an abrupt halt when an Early Bronze Age settlement was discovered beneath the ship. The need for the construction of a marina on top of the settlement and the lack of nautical archaeologists in Bulgaria led the excavators to rebury the wreck and concentrate their efforts on the settlement (Porozhanov 2000). In 2000, a joint Institute of Nautical Archaeology–Centre for Underwater Archaeology team returned to the wreck to inaugurate a full excavation of the site (Batchvarov 2003: 306).

Figure 11.1 Site location at Kitten, Bulgaria. Drawing by the author.

DESCRIPTION OF THE HULL

The Kitten shipwreck is the first, and so far only, example of a postmedieval ship from the Black Sea to have been excavated and recorded, and for this reason, no exact parallels for this wreck have been published. However, Mediterranean examples of vessels featuring similar construction to that observed on the Kitten ship do exist; they include the Culip VI wreck of the early fourteenth century (Catalonia, Spain), the Yassiada sixteenth-/seventeenth-century wreck (Turkey), and the Sardineaux wreck (France) of the latter seventeenth century (Joncheray 1988; Rieth 1998a, 1998b). The Kitten vessel is the largest, latest, and best-preserved of the group.

A description of the hull remains has been published by the author (Batchvarov 2003; Batchvarov 2009), but a brief review is offered here. The articulated hull remains have a length of 19 m, a width of approximately 5 m, and a depth in hold of nearly 3 m. The port side of the ship is almost completely missing above the wrongheads, the outer ends of the floor timbers. The starboard side amidships is preserved almost to the height of breadth. The bow is eroded down to the level of the keelson, but not broken up, while the stern is torn to pieces, especially on the port side. Fortunately, the lower portion of the sternpost was discovered, and its recovery aided greatly in the reconstruction of the vessel. The keel is made of a single timber, with no evidence of a scarf, although it could not be directly observed in its entirety. Its estimated length is 16.86 m. The scantlings of the keel could be deduced from the scantlings of the sternpost and the stem. At the gripe the stem measured 17 cm sided by 27 cm molded, and at the sternpost the keel measures 16.7 cm by 17 cm. It appears that it did not taper in sided dimensions for its length. Although in the bow and the stern evidence for a rabbet was discovered, it is not certain that the rabbet was continuous throughout the length. The wrecks from Culip VI, Sardineaux, and Yassiada did not have a rabbet in the central sections of their hulls (Joncheray 1988; Rieth 1998a; Pulak, pers. comm.).

On the starboard external side of the hull, the third plank from the keel was found to be a longitudinal timber with a thickness of 9.6 cm and width of 14.5 cm. This timber is notched to fit over the frames, to which it was fastened with spikes. The length of the notches averaged 21 cm, which is about equal to the sided dimensions of a floor timber and its associated futtock. Remains of an identical timber were also found to port of the keel. These timbers may have supported the lower end of the stem (Figure 11.2). It was not possible to trace them farther aft, because of the solid wall of timber that the framing formed. Drawings published by the French Admiral Edmond Paris illustrate a Turkish coaster from the Black Sea that had similar bilge wales extending throughout the length of the vessel (Paris 1999: 103). On the Kitten shipwreck, these timbers were paralleled on the inside—at least in the visible part of the hull—by the bilge stringers, which are also notched over the frames. Thus, the heavier outer timbers probably continued throughout the length of the vessel. Joncheray (1988: 45–47, figure 21) reports two broadly similar timbers from the Sardineaux wreck, though their morphology is not identical to that of the Kitten timbers. The Contarina I wreck, from the Po delta in Italy, usually dated to the fourteenth century, also features similar bilge wales (Bonino 1978: 14, figure 4).

The stem of the Kitten ship is eroded almost down to the level of the keelson, but the surviving part of the stem is sufficient to suggest that it was heavily raked forward and had scantlings of 17 cm sided and 27 cm molded. The rabbet is 10.5 cm wide by 2.5 cm deep. The stem is simply butted into the keel without a scarf. No trace survives of a knee or apron. Although some remains of the stem were discovered on Culip VI, it is not clear how it attached to the keel, but it appears that a flat scarf was used. On the Sardineaux wreck, the connection between the stem and keel is a flat scarf, fastened with spikes (Joncheray 1988: 42–44). The forward part of the sixteenth-century Yassiada keel is broken, so it is not clear how the missing stem was attached to the keel, but there are some traces remaining on the upper face that may be remains of a flat scarf. The stem was supported by an apron, a small piece of which survives (Pulak, pers. comm.). The late-sixteenth- or early-seventeenth-century wreck from Rondinara, France, likewise had its stem butted into the keel rather than scarfed (Villie 1988: 142–143).

The sternpost, a naturally grown knee, survives in better condition than the stem. It has a length of over 2 m and includes the lower part of the post, in remarkably good condition, with the lower pintle. The sternpost, like the stem, was not scarfed but simply butted to the keel. The surface of the butt is original and shows the half-round notch left by drilling for a waterstop. The thickness of the timber is almost uniform, varying between 16 and 16.7 cm. The depth of throat is 48 cm. The rabbet is cut to a 3 cm width and a 2 cm depth. The pintle is now bent out of shape, but extends to its original length of 2.27 meters. It tapers throughout its length and

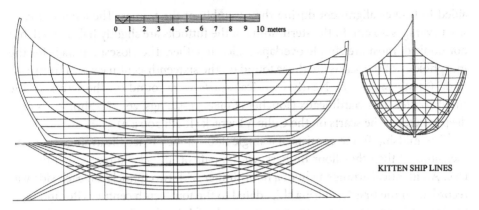

Figure 11.2 Reconstructed lines of the Kitten Ship. Drawing by the author.

appears to have originally been bent slightly to port, which would have eased the hanging of the rudder and is typical for double-ended vessels in the region. Two metal cheeks support the pintle on the sides of the sternpost and are held in place by forelock bolts driven from opposite directions. The plates are 3 cm thick by 9 cm wide and 59 cm long. The pintle lies on top of a long forelock bolt that penetrates the sternpost and extends over 30 cm from the inner edge, but the end is broken off and now missing. The long pintle proves that the vessel had a round sharp stern, similar to the sixteenth-century Ottoman wreck from Yassiada. This type of stern was generally popular among traditional lateen-rigged craft in the Mediterranean world at least until the nineteenth century. Usually, sternposts with long pintles are curved, but there are some exceptions, as evidenced by Jouve's and Baugean's drawings (Joncheray 1988: figs. 30, 31, 32, 39; Harland 2000). The sternpost of the sixteenth-century Yassiada ship is very poorly preserved, and the heel does not survive. It appears that a flat scarf, strengthened by an inner post, attached it to the keel. A concretion containing the pintle was cast and analyzed, and, although not identical to the pintle of the Kitten ship, it is similar (Pulak, pers. comm.). A concreted pintle was also discovered on the wreck from Sardineaux. It was supported and secured to the now missing sternpost with a strap bent into a U shape. Three holes in each side match holes on the opposite side. Joncheray (1988: 62–64, figures 37–38) believed that the sides were riveted through the hull.

The frames of the Kitten vessel consist of a floor, two futtocks, and two top-timbers. Their scantlings vary, but most average 12 cm sided by 11.5–13 cm molded. Instead of deadwood, the shipwright used deep-grown Y-shaped crooks for floor timbers in the bow and the stern of the vessel. Cant frames were not used in the construction of the ship.

All timbers within a bend (i.e., those timbers that constitute a full frame) are longitudinally fastened. In the bow, the futtocks simply overlap the floors and are secured with a single nail. In the central part of the hull, extending over half the length of keel, the floors and the futtocks are hook-scarfed. The hooks are shallow, 1.5 cm to 2 cm deep, and, as the port side broke off exactly at the scarfs, they could not have added materially to the strength of the frames. However, they would have aided in timber alignment during the assembly of the frames. The length of each scarf averages 40 cm. In the stern, some of the futtocks are slightly half-lapped, but not hooked; most are simple overlaps nailed together. The closest parallels for the morphology of the scarfs are those found on the sixteenth-century vessel from Yassiada (Steffy 1994: 137). Nearly identical scarfs were found on the wreck of the small coaster from Sardineaux (Joncheray 1988: 51–54, figs. 26–28). Similar, though deeper-cut, are the scarfs on the Culip VI wreck (Rieth 2003: 9).

The midship frame consists of a single floor timber, twice the average sided dimensions of the other floor timbers, with a pair of futtocks hook-scarfed to each face. An identical arrangement of a floor timber with two futtocks on each side was recorded on the first Contarina ship, dated to the fourteenth century (Bonino 1978: 14, figure 4), and the sixteenth-century wreck of *Lomellina* from Villefranche-sur-Mer, France (Guerot and Rieth 1995: 43, 49, n. 3). The Culip VI wreck had two midship floor timbers, one of which had the port and starboard scarfs cut on opposite sides of the wrongheads (Rieth 1998b: 206, figure 2). The Yassiada ship had two floor timbers with single futtocks attached to each wronghead. The forward bend had the futtocks fastened to the forward side of the floor timber, and the aft bend had them facing the stern of the vessel. The same arrangement is also observable on the Sardineaux wreck (Joncheray 1988: 52, figure 26).

In the central section of the hull, filling timbers are driven between the futtocks, thus forming a solid timber wall. The filling timbers extend only down to the turn of the bilge. Their scantlings conform to the spaces between the futtocks and vary accordingly. The lower ends taper toward the external planking, while the upper ends are cut diagonally, thus conforming to the heels of the top-timbers. No evidence was found for fastening of the filling timbers to the frames, but only to the stringers and, presumably, the planking. They must have been added before the attachment of the stringers, for otherwise it would have been very hard, if not impossible, to install them.

The keelson is a single timber of about 15 m in length and tapering in section from 46 cm sided by 19 cm molded amidships, to 19 cm by 15 cm in the bow. It is even narrower in the stern. The keelson is notched over every floor to a depth of about 3 cm. No fastening pattern is clearly identifiable; however, two or three concretions in the forward third of the keelson may be remains of bolts or spikes. Likely the keelson was also fastened with treenails, which tend to be hard to identify in the poor visibility and limited light conditions that were encountered during excavation. In comparison with Western shipbuilding traditions, the keelson is lightly fastened, but this evidently did not weaken this part of the hull, as it was not displaced in the wrecking process.

Amidships, two 5.15 m long sister-keelsons run parallel and adjacent to the keelson to which they are spiked. Like the keelson itself, they are notched over the floors. The sister-keelsons are supported transversally by two sets of buttresses, which lie on top of floor timbers. Immediately forward of the sister-keelsons, a shallow square mortise is cut into the keelson, which is surrounded by a square imprint, probably caused by the pressure from a stanchion. The only surviving maststep is located between the sister-keelsons. The maststep has a length of 70 cm and is cut through the keelson, ending just forward of the midship frame. The excessive length of the mortise suggests that there must have been a wedging system to hold the mast heel in position, which does not survive. A very close parallel for this maststep is the one found on the Boccalama galley in the Venetian Lagoon (M. Bondioli 2003, pers. comm.).

The scarfs of the floor timbers and the futtocks are reinforced with heavy bilge stringers, consisting of three pieces fitted together with long diagonal scarfs. No evidence was found that the pieces were fastened together. The timbers are deeply notched over the frames, to which they are spiked. The bilge stringer is partially covered by two thinner, but still massive strakes. Forward, the outer strake butts into a timber with a nearly square section, which forms the continuation of the strake toward the bow of the vessel. Originally, it probably reached the stem or a breasthook that no longer survives. Dovetail mortises were clearly observable on its outer upper surface, and some still contained the dovetails of filling pieces that fitted between the futtocks and covered the ends of the wrongheads. Aft, the outer of the two footwaling strakes is crenelated and notched around the futtocks, with dovetail-jointed filling pieces between the frames. This arrangement is very similar to the one recorded on the Cattewater wreck (Steffy 1994: 133) and on a medieval wreck from Tantura Lagoon, Israel (Kahanov, Royal, and Hall 2004: 118, fig. 8.9). It is popularly associated with the Iberian or Atlantic tradition of shipbuilding (Oertling 2004: 133, fig. 9.5). Evidently, this association needs to be extended to include Mediterranean and Black Sea shipbuilding as well.

The surviving part of the starboard side of the vessel has four more stringers fastened to it. They differ in scantlings and form two groups—narrow and thick, or wide and thin. The scantlings of the first group vary in dimensions from 15 to 20 cm by 8 cm, and those of the second are consistent at 20 cm by 4 cm. The stringers are fastened to every frame timber they cross, with two nails driven at an angle to each other. Most of the stringers were built of at least two planks scarfed together with simple flat diagonal scarfs. It is notable that contrary to generally accepted conventions, the scarfing of adjacent stringers was not spread out, but is concentrated in the same area of the vessel. This ought to have caused a weakening of the construction, but no evidence for such effect was identified on the wreck. The uppermost surviving stringer is thin, and as no evidence for attachment of deck beams was observed on the surviving stringers, there must have been at least one more stringer—the beam clamp—which has not survived.

Transversal ceiling, well preserved for the entire length of the ship, covers the bottom up to the turn of the bilge. The ceiling planks are the same thickness as the exterior planks (3.5 cm) and are also made of oak. Interestingly, they are nailed in place and their inner edges are level with the *upper* edge of the keelson. The inner edges are nailed to ledges nailed to the sides of the keelson. The outer edges of the planks are nailed to the bilge stringer and butt into the inner footwaling strake. A round opening of approximately 20 cm diameter that most likely contained a pump is cut in one of the starboard planks located between the transversal buttresses. At the time of excavation, the pump opening was covered with a square softwood plank. From the marking on the plank, it seems probable that it was in place at the time of sinking of the vessel and the pump was missing. The nailing of the ceiling planks makes it impossible to reach the bilges and inspect limber holes routing the water to the pump. The bottom ceiling planks, the footwaling, and the filling boards between the futtocks completely seal off the bottom of the vessel from the hold.

One nearly complete deck beam was found. The extant length is 6.04 m, but evidently it was about a meter longer originally. One face of the beam is very heavily eroded, and no original surface is preserved, but the better-preserved face has a shallow indentation approximately 50 cm wide and less than 2 cm deep at the peak of the camber. The indentation is more visible at the upper part of the beam than at the lower, which suggests that the pressure that caused it was applied at an angle. On both sides of it, deeply cut notches are preserved that probably supported carlings. Another notch is cut into the lower face of the beam, in the middle of the indentation. It appears to have been the mortise for the tenon of a supporting stanchion. The preserved end of the beam shows remains of a dovetail joint, which secured it to a now missing beam clamp. The location of the beam and its purpose can also be reconstructed from the position of the stanchion notch on the keelson. As only one such mortise was found, it is likely that the corresponding notch on the beam was directly above it. The indentation on the beam was likely caused by pressure from the mast, and the two carlings around it would have formed the sides of the mast partners.

RECONSTRUCTION OF THE KITTEN SHIP

The lines of the Kitten vessel were reconstructed from the archaeological evidence, traditional proportions, iconography, and limited comparative material from vernacular boats (Batchvarov 2009: 109–168). For the calculation of proportions in order to compare them with available sources, the length of keel is taken to be the length of the imprint the keel would make on the ground, known in seventeenth-century English sources as "thread length." Thus, the gripe of the stem and the hook of the sternpost are included in the measurement (Batchvarov 2009: 112). Table 11.1 supplies typical hull proportions based on surviving Venetian shipbuilding treatises for Mediterranean craft and the limited number of archaeological finds for which the necessary data exists. The dimensions of the one recovered deck beam provided the molded breadth of the Kitten ship to within a few centimeters and enabled the author to calculate the keel length-to-beam ratio. Table 11.1 demonstrates that this ratio for contemporary Mediterranean vessels can vary between 2.3 and 3.2. The ratio for the Kitten ship, at 2.5, falls in the midrange of values and suggests that the listed proportions are also relevant for this Black Sea vessel.

Little survives to guide the researcher in establishing the bow and stern rakes of the Kitten ship. Two floor timbers found in the bow area provided some assistance

Table 11.1 Comparison of proportions of Mediterranean vessels and the Kitten ship

Source	LOA	LKL	Beam	Depth	Floor Length	LOA/B	LKL/B	B/D	B/Floor
Culip VI (reconstructed)	16.35	c.11	4.11	1.94	n/a	4	2.7	2.1	n/a
Contarina I (1300)	20.98	16.5	5.2	n/a	2.63	4.03	3.2	n/a	2
Nave Latina, c. 1410	27.5	20.7	8.28?	n/a	3.1	3.32	2.5	n/a	2.7
Nave Quadra, c. 1410	33.06	22.62	9.22	4.52	3.93	3.58	2.5	2	2.4
Contarina II (1550)	20.5	14.55	6.3	n/a	1.67	3.25	2.3	n/a	3.8
Timbotta's 250-botte nave	n/a	20.88	7.13	2.96	2.96	n/a	2.9	2.4	2.4
Pre Teodoro Nave (1550)	24.9	17.4	8	4	2.44	3.1	2.8	2	3.3
Pre Teodoro Galleon (1550)	47.15	34.8	13.05	5.92	3.83	3.6	2.7	2.2	3.4
Kitten shipwreck c. 1800	23?	16.86	7.46	3.56	2.4	3.1	2.3	2.1	3.1
Tartane, c. 1800	13.5	10?	4.21	1.99	n/a	3.2	2.4	2.1	n/a

All measurements are in meters.

in the form of bevel angles of the lower faces, which helped to reconstruct a plausible fair curve for the lower stem, as high as waterline 5 (Figures 11.2 and 11.3). The curve of the upper stem, however, is conjectural and based on iconographic evidence (Batchvarov 2009: 116; Müller-Wiener 1994: plate 20; Ovcharov 1992; Tzamtzis 1972: 53–174), personal observations of the general shape of stems on traditional Black Sea boats, and especially the proportions derived from the two Turkish coasters published by Edmond Paris (1999: plates 103, 109).

The preservation of the sternpost was more extensive than that of the bow, so a higher confidence can be placed in its reconstruction. The rake and height proportions were calculated from Admiral Paris's drawings and compared to the values provided by Damianidis (Batchvarov 2009: 118; Damianidis 1989: table 6; Paris 1999). The general shape is based on the archaeological material and iconographic evidence (Ovcharov 1992).

A goniometer, an angle-measuring device (Cozzi 1998), was used to record 11 sections across the vessel. In addition, every futtock of the forward half of the ship was recorded in the same way. The lines plan was drawn from this data, as was the reconstructed profile of the ship. The extensive preservation of a coherent structure permitted the calculation of the likely displacement and a partial hydrostatical analysis from which an idea of the likely performance of the Kitten ship can be developed.

The calculations were based on the assumption that the normal load waterline of the vessel was between waterline 5 and waterline 6 (see Figure 11.2). The estimate

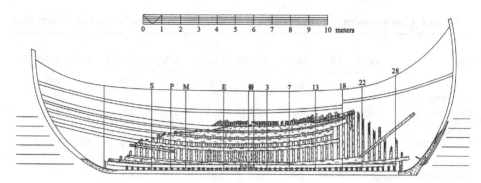

Figure 11.3 Longitudinal section of the hull, showing the extent of hull preservation.
Drawing by the author.

was reached by determining that the end of the rudder pintle probably reached about waterline 6, as on double-ended vessels pintles usually protruded above the water. Displacement and all other calculations, however, were carried out for both possible load waterlines, 5 and 6. Using the trapezoidal rule, the volumetric displacement for waterline 5 was determined to be 114.43 m³, giving a weight displacement of 117.3 metric tons (Steffy 1994: 251–252). At load waterline 6, the respective values would be 158.327 m³ and 162.3 metric tons. It must be noted that these displacement values are approximations, as the volumes of the keel, stem, sternpost, and rudder were ignored for lack of information needed to calculate them. Thus, it can be estimated that the Kitten ship displaced at light load about 117 tons and at full load about 160 tons.

The ratio of the actual underwater volume of the hull to that of a block with dimensions equal to the waterline length, maximum beam, and depth of hull, is known as the block coefficient. The higher a block coefficient is, the higher the resistance of the hull and, consequently, the slower the vessel is. As with the displacement, the block coefficient of the Kitten ship was calculated for both waterlines 5 and 6, but it was found that the two barely differed. For waterline 5, the block coefficient is 0.39, and for waterline 6, 0.4. For comparison, the ratio varies between 0.25 and 0.50 for modern small craft. Sailing yachts usually have a block coefficient of 0.35 to 0.45. Thus, the value for the Kitten ship is relatively low, which means that the hull had low resistance. In practical terms, a low-resistance hull requires less "power" to be driven through the water, and thus a modest rig would have been sufficient for the operation of the Kitten vessel.

The prismatic coefficient describes the distribution of hull volume (whether the ends are fine or full) by comparing the vessel's underwater volume to a prism with length equal to the length of the waterline and cross section equal to the largest hull cross section. Higher values indicate fuller ends. In modern yacht design, values of 0.50 to 0.56 are considered acceptable. The prismatic coefficients for waterlines 5 and 6 were found to be, respectively, 0.56 and 0.57. In both cases, the value falls in the higher end of accepted values, indicating that the ends of the vessel were full, at least in comparison to a modern yacht. Higher values are advantageous in vessels intended to sail in stronger wind conditions, though, in the case of the Kitten ship, they probably reveal an attempt to maximize carrying capacity rather than reflect weather conditions.

The coefficient of the waterline plane is a ratio between the area of the load waterline and a rectangle as long as the vessel's waterline and as wide as the beam. It illustrates the fullness of the hull, and as the waterline plane contributes to hull stability, the coefficient gives some indication of that as well. In modern small craft the values range between 0.65 and 0.80, or even higher. The lower end of the range represents fine-ended sailboats. The Kitten ship had values of 0.62 when loaded to the fifth waterline, and 0.61 when loaded to the sixth waterline. A waterline plane coefficient of 0.61–0.62 is on the low end of the now usual design range and may be explained by the double-ended shape of the hull, for which finer ends than on square-sterned vessels are characteristic. The somewhat low value of the coefficient indicates that under sail the ship may have been tender and prone to heeling. It is likely that the ship was lateen- or settee-rigged, and the tender hull would have been compensated by the rig's ability to spill wind rather than endangering the vessel.

The midship section coefficient, which compares the actual area of the midship section to a rectangle with sides equal to the waterline beam amidships, and the maximum depth was also calculated. The coefficient indicates the fullness of the section and varies between 0.40 and 0.80 or higher for modern small craft. For the Kitten ship, the value (for both waterlines) is 0.71, which demonstrates that the vessel had full sections, consistent with its cargo-carrying purpose.

The calculation of the wetted surface is a close approximation of the vessel as built because sufficient hull remains make the reconstruction of the underwater hull highly probable. If the vessel floated at or near waterline 5, the wetted surface would have been about 111.85 square meters. For waterline 6, wetted surface would have risen to 128.9 square meters. At the low speeds at which the Kitten ship was sailed, most of the hull's resistance would have been frictional resistance, which is directly related to the wetted surface. The ratio between the sail and the wetted surface area is more informative for the speed potential of a sailing vessel, but this calculation unfortunately cannot be made for the Kitten ship, as the rig's reconstruction is based more on comparative material than on archaeological data (Batchvarov 2009: 170–200). Another potentially informative but very approximate calculation is that of the weight of the ship. Based on the reconstruction, it can be estimated that the ship, without its rig and empty, weighed between 25 and 35 metric tons, thus leaving a payload of 120–130 tons.

WHOLE-MOLDING AND THE KITTEN SHIP

Having calculated the beam, and with the documented surviving archaeological record, it was possible to reconstruct the midship frame of the vessel (Batchvarov 2009: 123–124) (Figure 11.4). Analysis of the angle measurements for the 11 recorded sections (S, P, M, E, the midship frame, 3, 7, 13, 18, 22, and 28: see Figure 11.3) suggested that the frames were cut to the same pattern. An experiment with a mold cut to the shape of the midship frame and compared to the other recorded sections confirmed this finding. This was clear evidence that the hull was designed using a single mold, adjusted along the length of the vessel for the narrowing of the hull. This system of design, known as whole-molding, is a method of shipbuilding in which the vessel's shape is based on incremental modifications of the midship frame. Different versions of this system were used around the Mediterranean and along the Atlantic coast to northern Europe, including the British Isles (Batchvarov 2009: 122; Damianidis 1989; Bellabarba 1993; Sarsfield 1984).

Based on his analysis of the Culip VI wreck from Catalonia (Spain), Eric Rieth (1998b: 206) suggested that hook scarfs are characteristic of the Mediterranean shipbuilding tradition, a position accepted by Hocker and McManamon (2006: 7). Rieth concluded that hook scarfs are a diagnostic feature for the use of whole-molding. The Culip VI wreck is so far the earliest evidence reported for this type of scarf in association with whole-molding (Rieth 1998.b). Discovering the same characteristic in the framing of the Kitten vessel suggested that the shape of this ship was also developed by whole-molding.

In surviving Venetian shipbuilding treatises the guides for the incremental modifications to the midship frame required by this design process are known as *partisoni* (Hocker and McManamon 2006: 1). The physical process of shaping the hull through molds and *partisoni* was very clearly explained and illustrated by Joseph Furtenbach (1629) in his *Architectura Navalis*. The starting point for all

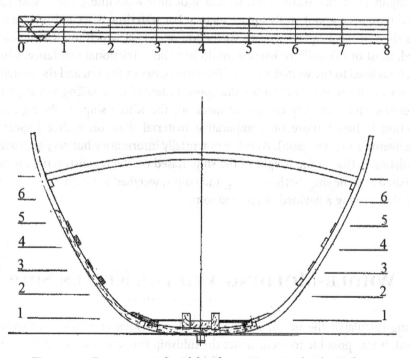

Figure 11.4 Reconstructed midship frame. Drawing by the author.

variations of whole-molding is the shape of the midship frame, which was trans-ferred to patterns or molds used to shape the rest of the frames. In the classical Venetian system, four *partisoni* were used: the narrowing of the floor, the rising of the floor, the narrowing of the breadth, and the rising of the breadth (Hocker and McManamon 2006: 6). Other variants of the method spread throughout the Medi-terranean (Marzari 1998: 187). The variations usually differed in the number of pre-determined frames, the number of *partisoni* used, and the exact technique (geometrical or arithmetic mechanical aids) of producing their increments. The *partisoni* determined the positions of the points at which the different pieces of the mold overlapped (surmarks), thus forming narrower and sharper mutations of the midship frame. The *partisoni* were a function of the number of frames that had to be designed prior to erection on the keel (Marzari 1998: 187).

In whole-molding's most basic form, a vessel can be built with a single prede-signed frame, the midship bend, and use of ribbands bent around it and termi-nating at the stem and sternpost to determine the shape of the other frames. Although a fair shape can be achieved in this way, the available volume of such a vessel would be limited. This problem was resolved through the use of "tail frames," which pushed the useful volume of the hull into the ends of the ship. It is generally accepted that this method predicted the shapes of the frames between the tail frames and the midship frame, but the ends of the vessel still had to be framed by spiling the timbers to ribbands (Hocker and McManamon 2006: 2). In contrast, almost all frames of the fourteenth-century Culip VI wreck were molded, as evidenced by the carpenter's marks, and all of them had hook scarfs (Rieth 2003: 9). Only three frames, placed on top of the stem, do not bear carpenter's marks and therefore were likely spiled to ribbands. These three frames are also the only ones that did not have hook scarfs. This implies that predetermined frames were always scarfed in this shipbuilding tradition, probably because the scarfs aided in aligning the timbers within the bend. Brad Loewen (1998: 214) quotes Joao Baptista Lavanha's treatise from Portugal and the Spaniard M. de Aroztegui's Shipbuilding Ordinances of 1618 as also identifying mortised frames with molded frames. Thus, on the sixteenth-century Ottoman wreck from Yassiada it is likely that all frames were molded, as all surviving timbers bear hook scarfs (Pulak, pers. comm.). The same seems to be the case with the seventeenth-century wreck from Sardineaux, although its incomplete preservation leaves some room for uncertainty. In the Kitten ship, the chronologi-cally latest example in the group, half of the frames, a total of 27, bear hook scarfs and thus can be considered predesigned. From the recording of the hull sections, it is evident that in both extremities of the hull, the rising beyond the last scarfed frame was more marked, as was the narrowing. Thus, the last scarfed frames were assumed to be the tail frames, as they also delineated the central portion of the vessel, a feature typical for Mediterranean practice (Batchvarov 2009: 145–149; Damianidis 1998).

Having established that all futtocks of the vessel were cut to the same pattern, that the frames in the central portion of the vessel likely had predetermined shapes, and that some form of whole-molding was used in constructing the ship, an attempt was made to determine the method of controlling the incremental modifications to the midship frame used to derive the rest of the frames. By fitting a pattern of the midship frame to the other recorded frames, particularly to those with hook scarfs, it was easy to determine both the rising and the narrowing of the floor timbers. Thus, the range of two *partisoni* could be established, and it remained to determine the geometrical aid used to design the increments of change. The limitations of hull survival did not permit the same to be done for the *partisoni* of the breadth.

Knowing the maximum narrowing and rising of the floor timbers at the last scarfed frames fore and aft, an attempt was made to find the geometrical aid—a *mezzaluna, mezzarola,* or incremental triangle—that would produce divisions corresponding to the recorded values. Although working solutions were found for both rising and narrowing of the floor timbers, the lack of identified surmarks does not permit one to positively state that one of these methods was indeed utilized in developing the sections of the hull, but only that such a method was *most probably* used.

To determine the narrowing and rising, the presumed tail frames—M forward and 13 aft of midships—were redrawn on separate Mylar sheets, and the common pattern (the mold), cut to the shape of the midship frame, was slid into place until it faired with the recorded shape of the respective section. Along the drawn center-line, the rising of the mold/pattern above the base of the midship frame was measured. The narrowing was measured along the protruding part of the floor mold from the centerline. Although the narrowing was noticeable, the rising was significantly less so. Bellabarba (1993: 280) commented that following the traditional Venetian methods, the rising should not begin with the midship frame. This was found to be the case on the Kitten vessel. The rising is supposed to be less than the narrowing (also observed on the Kitten ship) and be greater aft than forward (Bellabarba 1993: 280), in order to achieve a clean and narrow run of the ship for good steering.

Because the maximum narrowing or rising at the tail frames and the narrowing and rising at intermediate stations between the midship frame and the tail frames were known, experiments were undertaken to find the geometrical aid that would produce increments that would fit the measured values for frames E and 7.

As this was a trial-and-error process, *mezzalunas* and *mezzarolas* were constructed to cover all of the most likely scenarios. The *mezzaluna* is a half circle, with a diameter equal to the total narrowing or rising of the frames. The two quarter circles are each divided into as many equal parts as the number of frames over which the narrowing/rising has to be achieved. The divisions on the quarters are connected with lines parallel to the diameter that divide the 90° radius into segments. These segments are the incremental narrowings and risings of the respective frames (Furtenbach 1629: 30). The *mezzaluna* is arguably the best-known geometrical aid, and instructions on its use are frequent in contemporary literature on ship design. A drawing of a *mezzaluna* can be found in the mid-fifteenth-century Zorzi da Modon (Trombetta) manuscript (Anderson 1925: 154). Furtenbach (1629: 33), too, describes it and offers instructions on its construction (Figure 11.5).

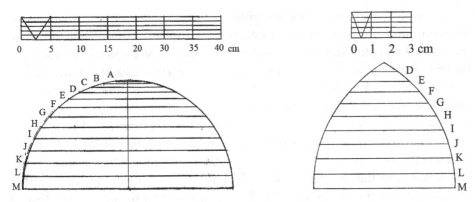

Figure 11.5 *Mezzaluna* and *mezzarola* from the archaeological evidence of the Kitten ship. Drawing by the author.

The *mezzarola*, another geometrical aid, is similarly constructed but so far does not appear to have been reported outside the Aegean (Damianidis 1998: 222). A *mezzarola* is constructed by drawing a line equal in length to the maximum narrowing or rising. From each end an arc is struck, with the two arcs crossing above the line. Each of them is divided into as many equal parts as the number of frames over which the modifications need to be applied. Straight lines, parallel to the base, connect the respective points on each arc. These lines are the incremental modifications to be applied for the respective frames. Damianidis (1998: 230) determined that compared to the *mezzaluna*, the *mezzarola* produces lines that are slightly fuller, but otherwise similar.

A variation on the *mezzarola* is the triangle. A base is drawn equal to the narrowing or rising. With a compass, two small arcs are drawn with as large a radius as possible. The arcs cross above the line, creating a point that marks the apex of a triangle. Each of the sides is divided into as many equal parts as the number of frames. The respective points are connected with lines parallel to the baseline, and these lines are equal to the narrowing or rising of the respective frame. Furtenbach (1629: 45–49) also employs the triangle and a direct derivative, a trapezoid, for determining the rising in the bow of his galley and for the deck line both fore and aft.

The experiment with the Kitten ship began with constructing four *mezzalunas* for the narrowing and rising of the floors before and abaft the midship frame. There are 13 scarfed frames forward of the master frame and the same number aft for a total, including the midship bend of timbers, of 27 scarfed and, presumably, predesigned frames. The fore and aft narrowings differed very little from each other (less than 1 cm), and it is most probable that the shipwright originally used the same increments for both, thereby using the same gauge. The *mezzaluna* was constructed on the basis of 13 frames. The intermediate sections fit surprisingly well, and the other increments also produced results that do not contradict the reconstructed lines. Thus, it is very probable that the incremental narrowing of the floor timbers was controlled with a *mezzaluna*, using all 13 frames from the master to the tail frame.

Attempts to make the rising, insignificant in the middle part of the hull, fit dimensions produced by a *mezzaluna* were unsuccessful, even though attempts were made based on 13-frame, 10-frame, and even 7-frame divisions, to take into account the probability that at least some of the frames immediately adjacent to the midship section would not have had any rising. None of these attempts produced increments fitting the recorded values for frames E and 7. A 10-frame *mezzarola* was the only one that fit the risings for these two sections (E and 7). It appears that the shipwright was familiar with more than one geometrical aid for producing *partisoni*. It should be noted that the same result for the rising could probably be achieved with the use of a batten or by the hanging of a string as a guide. Until the emergence of further evidence, the most that can be said is that a *mezzaluna* for the narrowing, divided into 13 parts corresponding to the number of scarfed frames on either side of the master frame, and a *mezzarola* with 10 divisions, leaving the 3 frames fore and aft of the master with no rising, produce results that best match the recorded evidence.

Although we have assumed that the whole-molding of the hull was limited to the scarfed frames only, there is no technical reason why the rest of the hull could not have been molded too. In fact, it is possible that this was at least partially the case, as the recorded shape of the futtocks forward of tail frame M are identical to those within the middle section of the hull. However, given the much more haphazard way in which the frames are assembled outside the tail frames, it is likely that a less structured approach to their shaping was followed. It can be suggested that ribbands may have guided the narrowing and rising of the frames in the extremities of the hull but that their actual shape was cut according to the same mold used for the central part of the vessel.

CONCLUSION

Based on the archaeological evidence of the wrecks from Catalonia, Yassiada, Sardineaux, and Kitten, it appears that a common tradition of whole-molding existed in southern and southeastern Europe at least as early as the fourteenth century. Experiments with determining the method of controlling the shape of the vessel suggested that the Kitten shipwreck is indeed a late example showing further development of this old shipbuilding tradition, some of whose elements may have been in place in the eastern Mediterranean region as early as the building of the Bozburun ship in about 874 CE (possibly built not too far from the launching place of the Kitten ship itself) (Batchvarov 2009: 161–165; Harpster 2005; Hocker and McManamon 2006: 1).

The reconstructed method of controlling the shape of the Kitten vessel fits well with the tradition recorded in documents of the Italian Renaissance. It is evident that the master shipwright was conversant with whole-molding techniques similar to those described in the extant treatises and observed on the Culip VI wreck. It appears likely that he was aware of the slightly different characteristics of the curves produced with a *mezzaluna* and a *mezzarola*, and may have utilized both of them to produce the rising and narrowing of the Kitten ship frames.

The use of different geometrical aids demonstrates the flexibility of whole-molding as a ship-design tool. The broad similarities observed between such wrecks as the fourteenth-century Culip VI, the sixteenth-century Yassiada, the seventeenth-century Sardineaux, and the late-eighteenth-/early-nineteenth-century Kitten vessel are evidence that a common Mediterranean and Black Sea tradition of whole-molding and ship construction existed during the postmedieval period. The hook scarfs between floor timbers and futtocks are an easily observable and diagnostic mark of this tradition. It would appear that the fall of Constantinople to the Ottoman Turks in 1453 CE came about at a time when this shipbuilding practice had already established itself along the western shore of the Black Sea, and that sea's subsequent transformation into an internal lake for the Ottoman Empire helped preserve the practice later in this region than anywhere else in the Mediterranean world. The archaeological evidence suggests that Black Sea shipbuilding was conceptually and essentially part of the Mediterranean shipbuilding tradition, demonstrating that until the Ottoman conquest the maritime culture of the Black Sea was an extension of the Mediterranean seafaring world.

REFERENCES

Anderson, R. C. 1925. Italian naval architecture about 1445. *Mariner's Mirror* 11 (2): 135–163.

Batchvarov, K. N. 2003. A Black Sea merchantman. In *Connected by the sea: Proceedings of the Tenth International Symposium on Boat and Ship Archaeology, Roskilde 2003*, ed. Lucy Blue, Fred Hocker, and Anton Englert, 306–311. Oxford: Oxbow.

———. 2009. The Kitten shipwreck: The archaeology and reconstruction of a Black Sea merchantman. PhD diss., Texas A&M University.

Bellabarba, S. 1993. The ancient methods of designing hulls. *Mariner's Mirror* 79 (3): 274–292.

Bonino, M. 1978. Lateen-rigged medieval ships: New evidence from wrecks in the Po Delta (Italy) and notes on pictorial and other documents. *International Journal of Nautical Archaeology* 7 (1): 9–28.

Cozzi, J. 1998. The goniometer: An improved device for recording submerged shipwreck timbers. *International Journal of Nautical Archaeology* 27 (1): 64–80.

Damianidis, K.A. 1989. Vernacular boats and boatbuilding in Greece. PhD diss., St. Andrews University.

———. 1998. Methods used to control the form of vessels in the Greek traditional boatyards. In *Concevoir et construire les navires*, ed. Eric Rieth, 217–244. Paris: Eres.

Furtenbach, J. 1629. *Architectura Navalis*. Ulm.

Guerot, M., and E. Rieth. 1995. The wreck of the *Lomellina* at Villefranche sur Mer. In *Archaeology of ships of war*, ed. M. Bound, 38–49. London: Anthony Nelson.

Harland, J. 2000. *Ships and seamanship: The maritime prints of J. J. Baugean*. London: Chatham.

Harpster, M. 2005. A re-assembly and reconstruction of the 9th-century CE vessel wrecked off the coast of Bozburun, Turkey. PhD diss., Texas A&M University.

Hocker, F., and J. McManamon. 2006. Medieval shipbuilding in the Mediterranean and the written culture at Venice. *Mediterranean Historical Review* 21 (1): 1–37.

Joncheray, J.-P. 1988. Un navire de commerce de la fin du XVII siècle, l'épave des Sardineaux. *Cahiers d'Archeologie Subaquatique* 7: 22–67.

Kahanov, Y., Jeffrey Royal, and Jerome Hall. 2004. The Tantura wrecks and ancient Mediterranean shipbuilding. In *The philosophy of shipbuilding*, ed. F. Hocker and C. Ward, 113–128. College Station: Texas A&M University Press.

Loewen, B. 1998. The morticed frames of the XVIth century Atlantic ships and the "Madeiras da Conta" of Renaissance texts. *Archaeonautica* 14: 213–222.

Marzari, M. 1998. Evolution of shipbuilding techniques and methodologies in Adriatic and Tyrrhenian traditional shipyards. In *Concevoir et construire les navires*, ed. E. Rieth, 181–215. Paris: Eres.

Müller-Wiener, W. 1994. *Die Haefen von Byzantion, Konstantinupolis, Istanbul*. Tübingen: E. Wasmuth.

Oertling, T. J. 2004. Characteristics of fifteenth- and sixteenth-century Iberian ships. In *The philosophy of shipbuilding*, ed. F. Hocker and Cheryl Ward, 129–136. College Station: Texas A&M University Press.

Ovcharov, N. 1992. *Ships and shipping in the Black Sea, 14th–19th centuries*. Sofia: St. Clement of Ochrida University Press.

Paris, E. 1999. *Souvenirs de marine conservés*. Paris: Musée National de la Marine.

Porozhanov, K. 2000. The sunken ship near Urdoviza: Preliminary notes. *Archaeologia Bulgarica* 4 (3): 92–95.

Rieth, E. 1998a. L'arquitectura naval. In *Excavations arquelogiques subquatiques a Cala Culip 2; Culip VI*, ed. E. Rieth, 115–189. Girona: Generalitat de Catalunya.

———. 1998b. L'épave du caboteur de Culip VI. *Archaeonautica* 14: 205–212.

———. 2003. First archaeological evidence of the Mediterranean moulding ship design method, the example of the Culip VI wreck: Spain, XIIth–XIVth c. In *Shipbuilding practice and ship design methods from the Renaissance to the 18th century*, Max-Planck Institut für Wissenschaftsgeschichte Preprint 245, ed. H. Nowacki and M. Valleriani, 9–16. Berlin: Max-Planck Institut für Wissenschaftsgeschichte.

Sarsfield, J. P. 1984. Mediterranean whole moulding. *Mariner's Mirror* 70 (1): 86–88.

Steffy, J. R. 1994. *Wooden shipbuilding and the interpretation of shipwrecks*. College Station: Texas A&M University Press.

Tzamtzis, A. I. 1972. *Ships, ports and sailors*. In *The Greek merchant marine*, ed. S. A. Papadopoulos, 53–174. Athens: National Bank of Greece.

Villie, P. 1988. La Rondinara: Épave d'un caboteur du XVI/XVI siecle I. *Cahiers d'Archeologie Subaquatique* 7: 137–157.

CHAPTER 12

HISTORIC NAVAL ARCHITECTURE PRACTICES AS A GUIDE TO SHIPWRECK RECONSTRUCTION: THE *LA BELLE* EXAMPLE

TARAS PEVNY

INTRODUCTION

RENÉ-ROBERT Cavelier Sieur de La Salle sailed from La Rochelle, France, in July 1684 with four vessels, hoping to found a French colony near the mouth of the Mississippi River. The expedition was a failure, and *La Belle* (built in 1684), the last of his ships, sank during February 1686 within what is today Matagorda Bay, Texas. After more than three centuries on the bottom of the bay, the lower hull and partial cargo of *La Belle* were discovered in 1995 and excavated within a dry cofferdam during 1996 and 1997 under the direction of the Texas Historical Commission (Bruseth and Turner 2005). The hull was documented, disassembled, and transported to the Conservation Research Laboratory at Texas A&M University, where it was subjected to additional recording and reassembled in order to conserve it as a unit. Based on the extant remains, some of which retained carpenter's marks (surmarks), it was possible to not only reconstruct the hull but also understand several aspects of the design and construction process.

Studying the design of *La Belle* was to a great extent a circular process—much like a design spiral in modern naval architecture. The discovery of new information, whether in the process of the reconstruction of the archaeological remains or from documentary research, necessitated a reexamination and/or a reworking of earlier recordings, preliminary reconstructions, and working hypotheses. This process ultimately spiraled toward the method that I believe was used to design *La Belle*. It is beyond the scope of a single chapter to fully discuss the entire design process for a ship. Consequently, here I will focus on the longitudinal timbers— the keel, sternpost, and stem. While not a complete reconstruction, these are sufficient to explain the value of understanding the design process in reconstructing a shipwreck.

For each step in the process I will attempt to answer the following question: what would the designer have to know or do to take the next step in the design of the hull? I will endeavor to adhere to the progressive logic of the design sequence. I followed the same approach in originally working out the design method in order not to be biased by the fact that I was starting with the end result of the design process—the surviving articulated timber remains. It is dangerous to search for combinations of curves that fit archaeological remains without trying to explain how the original designer would have generated and used these curves.

A *devis* is a list of what the shipwrights considered the fundamental measurements that defined the design of the hull, and we are lucky enough to have this document for *La Belle* (Bruseth and Turner 2005: 66–67, 69). Early on in the study of the remains of *La Belle* it became obvious that while some archaeological measurements are exactly the same as those in the *devis*, others are only close, and some are completely different. The work presented in this chapter is part of the design study of the "archaeological" *La Belle*; discrepancies with the *devis* will be identified, and an attempt will be made to explain the reason for these discrepancies. Various possibilities will be considered and discussed. Are the differences simply a question of terminology? Were the measurements listed taken off the completed hull or off a plan? If they were taken off the hull, then at what point in the construction were they recorded? Are they design measurements, capacity measurements, or a combination of the two? If the measurements are off a plan, then was the design altered during construction? Many of the dimensions in the *devis* relate to parts of the hull that are not preserved. In order to use them in the overall reconstruction of the hull, we had to identify and understand these discrepancies.

In this presentation I will try to provide supportive or at least comparative evidence for every design step from surviving French drafts and written source material relating to shipbuilding or hull design. In general there is very little historical material directly relating to the design of a small vessel like *La Belle*. Most known drafts, regulations, and treatises relate to the design and construction of much larger vessels. However, as will become apparent, the design and construction of *La Belle* does indeed reflect that of larger ships on a small scale—in many ways *La Belle* is a little "big ship."

LENGTH AND DETAILS OF THE KEEL

A keel length of 45 ft (14.62 m; measurements reported in the *devis* are given in French feet [*pied du roi*] of 1668–1840 and converted to metric based on Ross 1983: 77) is the first measurement listed in the *devis*. Although the stern end of the keel is degraded, the archaeological remains definitively show that the original length of the combined keel timbers was at least 45.5 ft (14.78 m; Figure 12.1). Although the two measurements are fairly close and the discrepancy could be attributed to such reasons as a lack of skill, an intentional deviation on the parts of the shipwrights, or an inherent inaccuracy in wooden shipbuilding or shipwreck archaeology, it turns out that there is a specific explanation for the "extra" 0.5 ft (16.24 cm). Since several of *La Belle*'s basic measurements are derived from the keel length, and establishing this length is the first and simplest step in the design process, it is fundamental to the entire reconstruction.

The preserved keel is composed of two timbers joined by a 3 ft 4 in (1.08 m) scarf. Over most of its length the keel is 6 in (16.24 cm) sided (wide) and 8 in (21.7 cm) molded (high). The forward piece of the keel, which includes part of the lower curve of the stem, is known in French as the *brion* or *ringeot*. In his partial translation of Blaise Ollivier's dictionary (1736), David Roberts (1992: 357) uses the term "forefoot" for *brion*. In other shipbuilding traditions the forefoot was usually a separate piece attached to the forwardmost end of the keel. A hybrid forefoot-keel timber is common in French wooden shipbuilding, and it is depicted in various drafts and drawings, for example in the 1670 *Album de Colbert* (*Album de Colbert* 1670: Plate 2), the 1680 Tourville/Pangalo draft (Boudriot 1998: 50–51), and the late-1680s Langeron/Salicon draft (Boudriot 1998: 61). In this study, when the general term "keel" is used it is meant to include the straight part of the forefoot. Ollivier (1736) states that "the length of the forefoot is not fixed, for it is always made as long as the timber will allow" (Roberts 1992: 357). Since the bottom of the forefoot is eroded, the curve of the forefoot has to be projected downward to an extended baseline in order to reconstruct the forward corner for measuring. In Figure 12.1 the

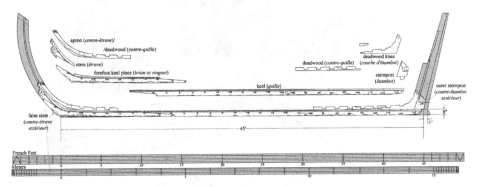

Figure 12.1 The centerline timbers of the longitudinal profile of *La Belle*. The gray parts are reconstructed. Illustration by the author.

reconstructed parts are shown in gray. The straight part of *La Belle*'s forefoot is 14 ft 1.5 in long (4.59 m); this is almost a third of the overall keel length.

Although the lower part of the sternpost is preserved with its tenon, the keel is degraded in the area of the mortise that this tenon would have fit into (Figure 12.2). The length of the keel from the aft end of the sternpost to its forwardmost point is 45.07 ft (14.64 m). Although this is about 0.75 in (2 cm) greater than 45 ft (14.62 m), there is little doubt that the shipwrights laid out this length as 45 ft (14.62 m). Therefore, taken between these points, the archaeological measurement and that of the *devis* are the same; however, there is evidence that the keel extended past the aft side of the stern-post. The lower parts of an outer sternpost (or false post) survive. The significantly degraded remains of the outer sternpost are composed of several small pieces. At the level of the keel the main piece extends aft approximately 4.5 in (12.2 cm). Behind this piece there was an additional timber/plank 1.5 in (4.1 cm) thick. There seems to have been yet another block of wood inserted higher up just below the rudder support (the gudgeon). For simplicity, in Figure 12.1 and other reconstruction drawings all these pieces are represented as a single timber. In Figure 12.2 the port garboard, the lowest hull plank, is shown extending beyond the aft end of the sternpost by approximately 6 in (16.24 cm). The garboard overlaps both the sternpost and the outer sternpost remains. The preserved length of the garboard and the outer sternpost assembly sup-ports the addition of another 6 in (16.24 cm) to the length of the top of the keel.

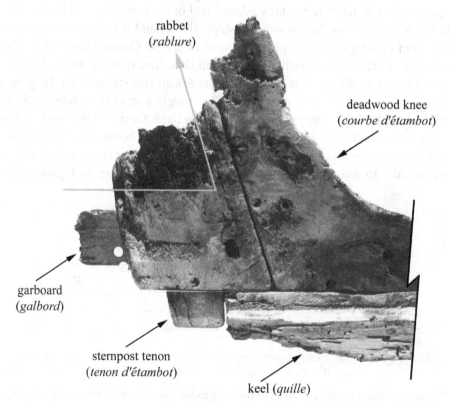

rabbet
(*rablure*)

deadwood knee
(*courbe d'étambot*)

garboard
(*galbord*)

sternpost tenon
(*tenon d'étambot*)

keel (*quille*)

Figure 12.2 The components of *La Belle*'s sternpost assembly. Illustration by the author.

The overlapping of an inset garboard and sometimes the next plank higher over the sternpost is a common feature of French shipbuilding at the time. The planks above these would fit into a notch, the rabbet, cut into the forward port and starboard edges of the sternpost. This is exactly the arrangement depicted in the drawings from the *Album de Colbert* (1670). In these drawings the keel extends beyond the aft end of the sternpost to include the outer sternpost. In addition, the aft end of the keel is angled, thus its bottom face extends even farther than the top. This extension of the keel at the stern is known as the skeg. Its purpose is to protect the forward corner of the rudder and the seam between it and the sternpost.

Therefore, the combined straight length of *La Belle*'s keel timbers was 45.5 ft (14.78 m) on its top face and probably longer along its bottom. However, this is not a discrepancy with the *devis*, because for the purposes of design the French shipwrights only considered the length to the aft side of the sternpost—the tread of the keel. This accounts for the *devis*'s specific phrasing: "Longueur de quille portant sur terre." Where this length should be measured is clearly stated by Blaise Ollivier in his 1736 dictionary: .... "the length of the keel [is] measured in a straight line from the angle of the forefoot to the angle of the keel with the sternpost. ... It should not be confused with the effective length of the keel which exceeds the other by the full width of the false post and the bearding of the skeg" (Roberts 1992: 362). Writing around 50 years after *La Belle* was built, Ollivier also states: "The tread of the keel was formerly considered as the principal dimension of a ship and it was on this dimension that all the other dimensions were regulated, whereas today we take the length from the stem to post" (Roberts 1992: 362).

Another prominent feature of *La Belle*'s keel is the frame position labels carved along its port side. There are 30 preserved frames on *La Belle* (Figure 12.3). The widest frame is the midship frame, and there are 12 frames forward and 17 frames aft. Midships is labeled with a star that represents the starting point for the rest of the labeling. The frames forward and aft are numbered sequentially with Roman numerals,

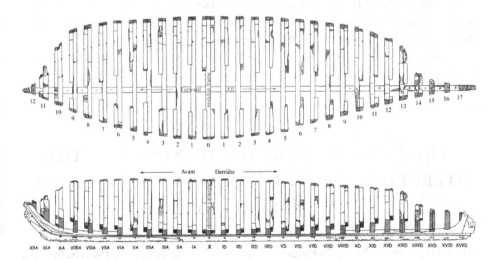

Figure 12.3 The logic underlying the labeling of the frame positions on the port side of *La Belle*'s keel. Illustration by the author.

starting from midships. In addition, these numbers are accompanied with a letter designating forward or aft in French, A for *avant* (forward) and D for *derrière* (aft). Thus the frames forward of midships are labeled XIIA, XIA, XA, VIIIA, . . . IA up to the midships star and the frames aft are labeled ID, IID, IIID, . . . XVIID. These labels were definitely carved when the two pieces of the keel were already joined, because the label IIIA is carved across the seam of the scarf between the forefoot and the aft part of the keel. Label XIIA is actually on a completely separate timber, the stem timber that is scarfed to the forward end of the forefoot. These labels are consistently the same size and fairly neatly carved from XIIA to VIID, but beginning with VIIID the numbers get larger and/or a little sloppier. One can speculate that the shipwright carved these toward the end of a day or handed the job over to someone else. Another interesting aspect of these labels is that all the numbers are additive—4 is IIII and not IV, 9 is VIIII and not IX, 14 is XIIII and not XIV.

Above these numbers, a feature of the keel that could not be added by the ship-wright until the frame spacing and for that matter the frame shapes were deter-mined, is the rabbet. As was mentioned earlier, the rabbet is a groove cut into the centerline timbers (keel, stem, and sternpost) into which the lower edge of the gar-board and the ends of all the planks (hood ends) are fitted. Its shape varies from a sideways V to an upright L depending at what angle the planks join into the center-line timbers. The rabbet along the central section of the keel is set down from the top of the keel a little more than 1 in (2.7 cm). The rabbet starts to change in shape toward the bow between frames 5 and 6 forward and toward the stern between frames 8 and 9 aft. This change is due to the pinching of the hull shape at the ends of the vessel, which forces the garboard plank to twist more toward the vertical. At approximately frames 9 forward and 12 aft the rabbet's upper line—the bearding line—crosses onto the deadwood timbers as the rabbet rotates toward an upright L orientation. The forward and aft deadwoods are timbers that sit on top of the keel to raise its height in the areas where the hull shape narrows. On *La Belle* the stern deadwood is scarfed to a deadwood knee that reinforces the unions of the keel with the sternpost. In the bow the deadwood is usually scarfed to a separate timber—the apron or inner stem—that reinforces the joint between the keel and the stem. On *La Belle* the apron and forward deadwood are one timber.

The Length between the Stem and the Sternpost and the Rakes of the Stem and Sternpost

The *devis* provides three other measurements that relate directly to the length of the vessel. The total length between the stem and sternpost is given as 51 ft (16.57 m), the rake of the stem as 4.5 ft (1.46 m), and the rake of the sternpost as 1.5 ft (48.7 cm).

Thus the stated total length equals the length of the keel plus the two rakes (45 + 4.5 + 1.5 = 51). The listed rake of 4.5 ft (1.46 m) is one-tenth of the given keel length. In turn, the sternpost rake of 1.5 ft (48.7 cm) is one-third the stem rake. Although the ratios may vary, deriving the sternpost rake from the stem rake that itself was determined by a ratio to keel length is a common procedure for the period; for example, the 1673 regulations generate rakes in this fashion (Boudriot 1993: 16–17). Based on the terminology used and the measurements given in the *devis*, the rakes should be the horizontal distances from the ends of the design keel length (at the 45 foot points A or C and B or D in Figure 12.4) to vertical lines at the outside of the endposts— lines dropped to the baseline from points F and M'. Lemineur (2000: 107) interpreted the *devis'* measurements this way in his reconstruction of *La Belle*'s longitudinal profile with the exception of incorporating the outer sternpost into all the measurements. The 45 ft (14.62 m) design length of the keel was archaeologically confirmed, so these mathematical ratios are valid; however, the reconstructed archaeological rakes to the outside of the endposts do not correspond to the numbers given. The timber remains provide conclusive evidence that the distance between the outside of the endposts was greater than the listed 51 ft (16.57 m).

Although only a little less than 2 ft (0.65 m) of the sternpost survive, it is a straight timber, therefore its lines can be extended with confidence. Extending the preserved lines of the sternpost results in an archaeological rake measurement to the outer face of the sternpost of 3 ft (0.97 m), twice as large as that given in the *devis* and two-thirds vs. one-third the listed stem rake (Figure 12.4). The rake of the outer sternpost is 2.5 ft (0.81 m) plus 2.5 in (6.8 cm) or 2.7 ft (87.7 cm). So according to the common usage of the terms in the *devis*, the rake in the stern and thus the length between posts given do not coincide with the archaeological evidence. However, if the horizontal measurement of 1.5 ft (48.7 cm) is extended from the aft side of the outer sternpost (point B' in Figure 12.4), a vertical line raised at this point (I) intersects the sternpost rabbet at point J, which is at the height listed in the *devis* for the wing transom—9 ft 4 in (3.03 m). Interpreted this way, the listed rake measurement is for the horizontal projection of the rabbet; this is also a possibility for the rake of the archaeological stem.

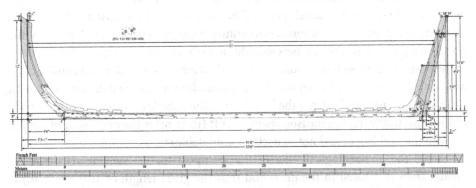

Figure 12.4 The design measurements for *La Belle*'s longitudinal profile. Illustration by the author.

The stem is curved, therefore reconstructing its complete shape is more difficult. The stem is preserved only a little farther up than the top of the forefoot. The stem timber that is scarfed to the forefoot extends the preserved curve to a total vertical height from the bottom of the keel of 4.25 ft (1.38 m). This height is only about a third of the original stem height, but there is enough preservation to project these curves upward with some confidence. Preliminary projections indicated that the stem rake measurement of 4.5 ft (1.46 m) fell at the rabbet and not at the outside of the stem (distance from C to C' in Figure 12.4). In order to conform to the measurements in the *devis* in terms of design, 51 ft (16.57 m), or 51 ft 6 in (16.73 m), would have to be the length between rabbets, also known as the length between perpendiculars (Steffy 1994: 253).

There are several difficulties with concluding that *La Belle's devis* measurements relate to the length between rabbets. In the seventeenth-century French regulations, treatises, and *devis* accompanying drafts, rakes and lengths are given to the outside of the posts. Length between rabbets did not come into common use until the eighteenth century, and in that century there were several ways in which the length between rabbets was defined. Which definition was used varied both over time and from shipyard to shipyard (Boudriot 1993: 50; 1986: 19). Jean Boudriot, an expert on shipbuilding of this period, writes that the length between rabbets could be "taken from rabbet to rabbet on the gundeck—at the height of the breadth—at the load waterline—from the perpendicular of the stem to the rabbet of the post at the wing transom" (Boudriot 1993: 50). Ollivier, in the 1730s, already makes reference to the length between rabbets along the gundeck and along the waterline (Roberts 1992: 132, 362). In addition, he specifically describes the method of measuring from the rabbet of the wing transom height that I believe is most applicable to *La Belle*: "The length from the rabbet of the stem to the rabbet of the sternpost is measured from the rabbet of the stem at the point of the greatest projection of this timber to the rabbet of the sternpost at the level of the wing transom" (Roberts 1992: 362). Specifically referring to the length between rabbets at the waterline, Ollivier notes that "recently some Builders have come to consider it as the principal dimension of ships in place of the length from the outside of the stem to the outside of the post which hitherto has been taken for the first dimension" (Roberts 1992: 362). This statement does not mean that the concept of length between rabbets was first developed at this time. In fact, in almost all of the drafts from the last quarter of the seventeenth century there are vertical lines depicted at the horizontal projection of the rabbets in addition to the lines at the outboard projections of the posts. Thus these lines would have been laid out during design and construction and could have been used to lay out the rakes. In addition, the "first dimension" for *La Belle* was the length of keel, not the length from the outside of the stem to the outside of the post; therefore, the measurement of 51 ft (16.57 m) is the end result of adding rakes to the keel length and not in itself an immutable starting point.

Since the archaeological rake of the sternpost to the "outside" is definitely greater than that listed in the *devis* and thus the given length of 51 ft (16.57 m) is certainly too short, the design of the end posts was examined in greater detail in order to understand these discrepancies with the *devis* before simply accepting them as "mistakes." A careful study and reconstruction of the design of the end posts supports the hypothesis that these measurements were in fact used to lay out the rakes relative to the rabbets.

THE STEM

At the time of *La Belle*'s construction and continuing through the eighteenth century, stems in French ship design were designed using arcs of circles. A single radius arc was commonly used to draw the outboard curve of the stem from its top to bottom. As a result, the forefoot in these vessels had a distinct corner at the union of the stem curve with the bottom of the keel (point C in Figure 12.4). The inner curves of the stem and the curves of the rabbet were also commonly designed using single radius arcs, although in the case of *La Belle* the corners where these curves join the corresponding lines from the keel are rounded. Only in the case of the inner curve of the apron would an additional arc be introduced to design the lower part of this curve. Given the simplicity of the methods used to draw the stems, with sufficient archaeological preservation it is possible to determine the centers of the circles used in the original design.

There are several ways of finding the center of the circle when part of its arc is preserved; these methods are important because they provide a way to determine the centers used by the shipwrights that is independent of determining the historical method they used to find these centers or relying on any documentary measurements. Additionally, these techniques give the ship reconstructor a way to extend the curves of the hull that is less prejudicial than simply deciding "what looks right." Although only a third of *La Belle*'s original stem survives, its curves are well preserved. As a result, it was possible both to determine that *La Belle*'s stem was indeed designed using circular arcs and to identify their specific radii and center points.

The preferred method utilizes the geometric theorem that a perpendicular bisector of a chord passes through the center of the circle. A chord is a straight line draw between two points on the circumference of a circle. The part of the circle between these two points is the arc subtended by this chord. A perpendicular line drawn through the midpoint of this chord will pass through the center of the circle that the arc is part of. The intersection point of the perpendicular bisectors of two or more chords is the center of the circle.

The geometric way to construct a perpendicular bisector utilizes arcs of circles and does not require any measuring of lengths or angles. In Figure 12.5a points 1 and 2 were chosen on the outer curve of the stem. These points are toward the ends of the well-preserved part of the surviving arc of the stem. Using point 1 as a center, arcs are drawn from 3 to 3′ and 5 to 5′. These small arcs do not have to be of any particular length. In fact, it should be kept in mind that they are part of one circle. For clarity I have depicted only the parts of the circle in the regions of intersection. Using the same radius but point 2 as the center, small arcs are drawn from 4 to 4' and 6 to 6'. A line passing through the intersections of arc 3–3' with 4–4' and arc 5–5' with 6–6' is the perpendicular bisector of the chord between points 1 and 2. This bisector also divides the arc between points 1 and 2 in half at point 7. The chord is omitted from this figure for clarity, and drawing it is unnecessary for finding the center. A radius of any length can be used for this construction; however, the longer the radius, the less distinct the points of intersection become. On the other hand, the closer the points of intersection to the chord, the harder it is to accurately project the bisector. The reconstructor consequently has to strike a comfortable balance. The same procedure was used to construct the perpendicular bisectors of the chords between points 1 and 7, and 7 and 2. The three perpendicular bisectors intersect at point G, which is the center of the circle presumably used by the shipwright to draw the outer curve of the stem.

Figure 12.5a has been cleaned up for illustrative purposes and is at a small scale. Originally, this work was conducted at a 1:10 scale multiple times using several radii

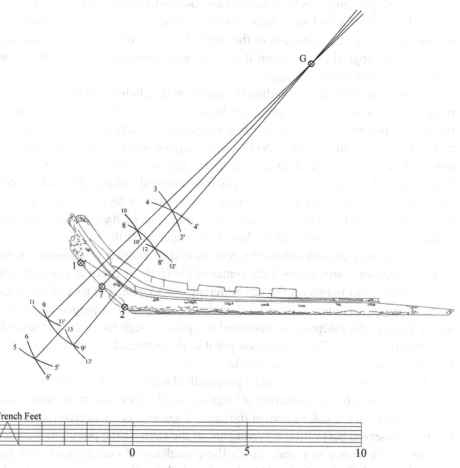

French Feet

Figure 12.5a Method of finding the center of the outer curve of *La Belle*'s stem using the perpendicular bisector of the chord method. Illustration by the author.

and various different end points in order to be certain of the location of the original center. This method is quite sensitive, and any misplacement of the compass or mis-judgment of the intersection points results in the bisectors being a little off from the center. Furthermore, any variation in the archaeological curve resulting from original shaping of the timber by the shipwrights, the deterioration of the timber over time, or inaccuracy in the archaeological recording results in the bisectors being a little off center. Multiple trials at a large scale greatly increase the reliability of the result.

In Figure 12.5b the center determined above, point G, was used to draw an arc from point C to point F; the reconstructed curve superimposes exactly on the ar-chaeologically preserved curve of the stem. This reconstruction of the outer stem curve confirms that the rake in the bow is larger than the 4.5 ft (1.46 m) listed in the *devis*. Thus it is certain that in both the bow and the stern the archaeological rakes to the outside of the posts are greater than the measurements given in the *devis* and that the length of 51 ft (16.57 m) cannot represent the length from the outside of the stem to the outside of the sternpost.

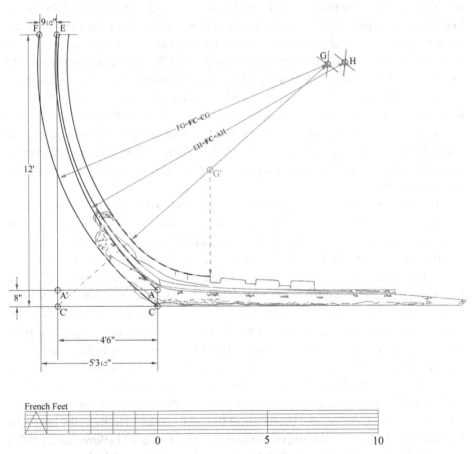

Figure 12.5b Reconstruction of the stem's original design superimposed on the archaeological recording of the stem. The stem height is taken from the bottom of the keel and the rake measurement to the rabbet. Illustration by the author.

The question that must be addressed next is whether the rake measurements in the *devis* are simply wrong or, rather, represent differently defined distances. In order to answer this question, it is to not only necessary to reconstruct the other arcs, but also to determine how the original designer generated them. Uncovering the original designer's method would substantiate whether any centers determined by the methods above were actually utilized in designing *La Belle*.

The center for the arc of the rabbet line, point H, was determined to be a different point than center point G for the outer curve of the stem (Figure 12.5b). When the arc for the rabbet line was drawn using point H as the center, it superimposed perfectly on the archaeologically preserved arc except in the corner where this curve is filleted to join the rabbet line of the keel. When the main curve of the rabbet line is extended farther down, it intersects with point A, which was defined above in the discussion of the keel. At its upper end the rake of this curve falls in the area of 4.5 ft (1.46 m). In fact, it crosses the vertical line at 4.5 ft (1.46 m) in two places, one of which is labeled in Figure 12.5b as point E.

Although points F and E are shown in Figure 12.5b, it is necessary to describe how they were determined. The radii used to draw the outer stem arc and the rabbet line arc are directly related to the locations of these points. These two arcs have the same length radius, and this is not a coincidence. Using this radius, an arc swung from point C intersects the outer stem arc at point F. The distance from point F to the bottom of the keel is 12 ft (3.9 m). This is very significant, because the height of the stem in the *devis* is listed as 12 ft (3.9 m). Point E is also at 12 ft (3.9 m) above the bottom of the keel at the listed rake of 4.5 ft (1.46 m). Thus the diagonal distance FC not only equals FG and CG but also EH and AH. What is important to keep in mind is that the original designer had to establish the length of these radii and determine the centers G and H. His starting measurements were the height of the stem with the desired rake.

The above investigation indicates that the height of the stem given in the *devis* as 12 ft (3.9 m) (distance from C' to E) includes the 8 in (21.7 cm) molded dimension of the keel (distance A to C). Dassié (1695) states that the stem height should be one-fourth of the keel length. In *La Belle's* case 1/4 the keel length is 11 ft 3 in (3.65 m). At 12 ft (3.9 m), the stem is longer. If the keel height of 8 in (21.6 cm) is subtracted from the 12 ft (3.9 m), the height of the stem above the keel is 11 ft 4 in (3.68 m). Although this is close to the one-fourth keel length, this could just be a coincidence. The available documentary sources show that the height of the stem could be taken from either the top or the bottom of the keel. Dassié (1695: 73) states in his treatise that this height should be taken from the bottom of the keel. In the *devis* that accompanies the 1686 Chaille draft, the stem height is also given from the bottom of the keel (Boudriot 1998: 60; 1993: 26–27). In other drafts, such as the 1680 Tourville/Pangalo and the 1697 Cochois, the height of the stem is measured from the top of the keel (Boudriot 1998: 70). It is important to clarify this because I believe that *La Belle's* sternpost height, unlike its stem height, is given from the top of the keel.

Concluding that the rake measurement is for the projection of the rabbet and the stem height is from the bottom of the keel, a plausible sequence of steps for the original design of the stem was reconstructed. A 12 ft (3.9 m) perpendicular (C'–E) at point C' 4.5 ft (1.46 m) from point C was raised. Before being able to draw the outside curve of the stem, the molded dimension beyond the rabbet must be added (E to F). In Duhamel du Monceau's (1758: 164) treatise from the mid-eighteenth century the length of the hull is given between rabbets; he confirms that a necessary step in the sequence of drawing the stem curve is to establish how much the stem projects to the outside of the rabbet. For *La Belle* this distance, E to F, was determined to be 9.5 in (25.7 cm). This gives a rake of 5 ft 3.5 in (1.72 m) to the outer face of the stem. There is enough flexibility in the reconstruction that I now believe that a distance of 10 in (27.1 cm) was laid off by the designer, resulting in a rake to the outer face of the stem of 5 ft 4 in (1.73 m).

I must add that Duhamel du Monceau (1758: 170) states that the distance to the outside of the stem from the rabbet must be laid off prior to marking the actual rake of the stem. This is slightly different than in the case of *La Belle* because in Duhamel du Monceau's treatise the rake of the stem is subtracted from the overall length to establish the forward end of the keel. The rake itself is given as one-tenth of the length between rabbets. The rake measurement is therefore subtracted from the point established for the outside of the stem. The keel length is no longer the starting dimension in this process; its length is a consequence of the stated procedures. By contrast, *La Belle*'s rake is one-tenth of the already established keel length. Despite these differences, Duhamel du Monceau's description for drawing the stem proved very useful for reconstructing the curves of *La Belle*'s stem and its rabbet.

Although writing more than 60 years apart, Duhamel du Monceau (1758: 166–167) and Dassié (1695: 73–74) present the same basic instructions for drawing the outer curve of the stem. They say to open a compass to a distance that equals the height of the stem and then to draw two small arcs with the top of the stem and the forward bottom corner of the keel as their centers. The point where they intersect serves as the center for the stem arc. In both Dassié's (1695: 73–74) and Duhamel du Monceau's (1758: 165–167) treatises the stem height is laid off from the bottom of the keel. However, when finding the center for the stem arc they both state to use the stem height from the top of the keel. In the course of my research, I reconstructed the methods of drawing the stem arcs for most of the available seventeenth-century drafts. The prevalent method of determining the radius for the outer stem arc was to take the vertical height of the stem either from the top or the bottom of the keel, although using the top of the keel is more common. In most cases the inner curve of the stem has a slightly shorter radius and a different center; as a result the curves are not concentric, and the stem widens toward its top. The curve of the rabbet is usually concentric with either the outer or inner curve, although in most cases it is concentric with the inner curve.

La Belle's stem seems to have been designed using the same general approach; however, the archaeological evidence supports the use of a diagonal distance, not the vertical height for the radius of the outer stem arc. Unlike the diagonal distance, the shorter vertical heights simply do not result in arcs that superimpose well on the archaeological arc of the stem. Initially this lack of exact parallels cast some doubt on the reconstruction; however, in the anonymous galley treatise from 1691 the diagonal distance from the bottom to the top of the stem is used for the radius, just like in *La Belle* (Fennis 1983: 5–6). Thus, I propose that *La Belle*'s original designer established point G at the intersection of two arcs of radius CF swung from points F and C (Figure 12.5b).

The same center G was used to draw the inboard curve of the stem and the apron using shorter radii. These design curves also flowed into the archaeological curves perfectly. While the very bottom of the inner curve of the stem seems to have been filleted, an additional arc was used to draw the lower part of the inner curve of the apron. While G' is the most probable center for this second arc, I am less certain how it was originally established. It is possible that the designer drew a construction line from G to C' and established the center at the intersection of this diagonal with a vertical at frame 9 forward. In addition to the apron inboard of the stem, to the outside of the stem there would have been an outer or false stem (gripe). Only a small and much-eroded piece of it was preserved; it was originally about 2 to 2.5 in (6.77 cm) molded (Figure 12.1).

The reconstruction of the curve of the rabbet confirms that this was most likely the method used to draw *La Belle*'s stem. To draw the stem rabbet, Duhamel du Monceau (1758: 167) says to use the same radius as for drawing the stem curve. The bottom design point for *La Belle*'s rabbet is point A, 8 in (21.7 cm) up from the bottom end point of the keel (point C) (Figure 12.5b). Since *La Belle*'s keel increases in molded dimension forward, this point falls on the face of the forefoot. If the keel was the same height throughout its length, this point would have been situated at the top of the keel. From this point and a point at the top of the rabbet height, two arcs were swung of the same radius as the original stem arc (CF) to establish the center for the rabbet arc (point H) (Figure 12.5b). The resulting arc completely coincides with the preserved curve of the rabbet line. Using the same center and a shorter radius, I was able to draw the middle line of the rabbet, which also coincides with the archaeological evidence. Since they do not share a common center, the stem arcs and the rabbet arcs are not concentric. Duhamel du Monceau (1758: 167) gives this as one of the characteristics of the stem rabbet. This lack of concentricity is evident in the archaeologically preserved curves.

Finally, the top of the stem is trimmed to the angle of the bowsprit, which rests on top of the stem. The outboard curve could also be extended to achieve the same result; in that case the tip of the stem would be higher than the listed stem height. Although both are possibilities, it seems that in most of the drafts with accompanying lists of dimensions the stem height includes the tip. In terms of the design of the rabbet, the angling of the top of the stem is a secondary step that does not affect the procedure described above. This is illustrated in Duhamel du Monceau's treatise (1758: Plate V), where the bowsprit is dotted in over the untrimmed stem design. On *La Belle* when the top of the stem timber is finally trimmed during the cutting of the timber to shape, point E at the top rabbet ceases to exist in reality (Figure 12.4).

In laying out the shape s of the timbers and in the process of raising them for assembly of the hull, shipwrights use temporary fastenings for such purposes as anchoring strings for measuring, drawing, and aligning, and for attaching various temporary supports. Toward the end of the reassembly of the hull remains, several small square holes filled with wooden plugs on both sides of the forefoot were observed. Although it is quite probable that some or all of these were used to nail on braces to keep the keel plumb and in alignment, several of them lined up on the baseline that would have been necessary to lay out the rabbet for the stem.

THE STERNPOST

In order to reconstruct the complete sternpost and confirm the relevance of a 1.5 ft (48.7 cm) rake measurement to the archaeological *La Belle*'s remains, it is necessary to rely on some of the other measurements in the *devis*. The *devis* lists the height of the sternpost as 11 ft 6 in (3.74 m); the height of the floor line in the stern as 5 ft 6 in (1.79 m); and the height of the maximum beam line in the stern as 9 ft 4 in (3.03 m) (Figure 12.4).

The description that accompanies the 1680 Tourville/Pangalo draft states that the maximum beam line in the stern starts at the level of the wing transom or transom beam (Boudriot 1998: 51). Describing the sternpost rabbet, Ollivier (1736) writes: "On either side of the sternpost a rabbet is cut to receive the hooding ends of the planking of the bottom and some of the planks of the stern. This rabbet extends only as far as the wing transom" (Roberts 1992: 365).

Although the rabbet extends to the wing transom on the sternpost, above the height of the floor line (5.5 ft; 1.79 m) it receives the ends of transverse planks of the transom. The longitudinal hull planks end on the fashion pieces, which are basically an aftermost set of framing timbers that define the shape of the transom. The bottoms of the fashion pieces sit on top of the deadwood knee or its inner sternpost extension (Figure 12.1). The corner where the lower ends of the fashion pieces join into the sternpost is known as the tuck. The bottom 9 in (24.4 cm) of the port and starboard faces of the sternpost and outer sternpost are completely inset to allow for the complete overlap of the lowest plank(s).

If the logic used for setting up the rake is the same in the stern as in the bow, the rake measurement in the stern should correspond to the height of the wing transom. Before ascertaining whether this is the case, it is necessary to determine from what point to measure the given heights in the stern. As was discussed above, Dassié (1695: 73) says to take the height of the stem from the bottom of the keel; on the other hand, for the sternpost he says to lay off the height from the top of the keel. In the 1686 Chaille draft *devis* the stem height is also given from the bottom of the keel, while the sternpost height is measured from the top of the keel (Boudriot 1998: 60; 1993: 26–27). In the 1680 Tourville/Pangalo draft the bottom line of the keel is not even depicted along the full length of the vessel; only in the bow, where the complete forefoot is drawn, is the bottom of the keel indicated. However, in this case the heights of the stem and sternpost are given from the top of the keel (Boudriot 1998: 108). After taking these examples into consideration and trying various arrangements, it appears that in *La Belle's devis* the sternpost height, the height of the transom beam, and the height of the floor line are given from the top of the keel. In fact, other than for the stem height, the top of the keel serves as the baseline for all of *La Belle's* design.

As was discussed above, the end of the keel in the stern at point B′ is 6 in (16.24 cm) farther aft than the aft side of the sternpost at point B. B′ corresponds to the aft side of the outer sternpost (Figure 12.4). Point I is 1.5 ft (48.7 cm)—the listed stern rake—from the back of the keel at point B′. A perpendicular raised at point I intersects the projected line of the rabbet at point J, which is 9 ft 4 in (3.03 m) above the top of the keel. The given height for the transom beam in the *devis* is 9 ft 4 in (3.03 m). Taken from the back of the sternpost at point B, the rake to point I equals 2 ft (0.65 m). Thus, only if the shipwright laid off the stern rake measurement from the back of the outer sternpost do the *devis's* bow and the stern rake measurements correspond to distances to the rabbet in the proposed reconstruction. I believe this is a reasonable conclusion given the sum total of the evidence.

In order to draw all the sternpost and outer sternpost lines, several molded dimensions have to be determined. In the archaeological remains the distance from the aft side of the sternpost to a line projected down from the rabbet is 1 ft (32.48 cm) (KB). The actual width of the rabbet is 3 in (8.1 cm) (KK′), and the outer sternpost assembly is 6 in (16.24 cm) at its base (BB′). At the level of the transom beam the width of the rabbet stays the same (LJ) and the other two widths are reduced by half, to 6 in (16.24 cm) (JM) and 3 in (8.1 cm) (MN), respectively. Lines from the corresponding points at the base of the sternpost are then extended through these points to draw the top of the sternpost (L′M′N′) at a vertical height of 11.5 ft (3.74 m) above the top of the keel.

An Alternative Explanation for the Discrepancies with the *Devis*

The length between the bow and the stern in the *devis* is given as 51 ft (16.57 m), which equals the length of the keel plus the two rake measurements. On the archaeological *La Belle* due to the additional 6 in (16.24 cm) of the outer sternpost the length between rabbets equals 51.5 ft (16.73 m). The archaeologically reconstructed length of the vessel from the outside of the stem to the outside of the sternpost is 53.5 ft (17.38 m) (Figure 12.4). For reference, in Figure 12.4 a 51 ft (16.57 m) line is drawn in where it fits between the 4.5 ft (1.46 m) stem rake line and the inner line of the sternpost. In the stern this point is 1.5 ft (48.7 cm) aft of point B on the sternpost—the given stern rake measurement. This line is 8.5 ft (2.76 m) above the top of the keel. Approximately another 9 in (24.4 cm) lower, the 1.5 ft (48.7 cm) line crosses the reconstructed sternpost rabbet. At midships the underside of the deck beam is at a height of 7.5 ft (2.44 m), and when the thickness of the beam and deck planking is added, the total height for the deck level is about 8 ft (2.6 m). Glenn Grieco, in building two models of La Belle, proposed that several of the *devis* measurements could represent internal measurements taken off the constructed hull (2003: 53, 55). Grieco proposed (2003: 55) that 51 ft (16.57 m) represents the length from "the rabbet of the stem to the rabbet of the sternpost at about the height of deck." This is a reasonable alternative explanation for the *devis*'s measurements; it conforms well to the longitudinal profile reconstructed in this study. However, the rationale of the reconstructed design sequence in Figure 12.4 is supported by the facts that the stem rake is one-tenth the length of the keel, the sternpost rake is one-third of the stem rake, and the interrelationship between these rake measurements and the heights listed in the *devis* in laying out the archaeologically documented shapes of the endposts. Given how the length between rabbets is defined in this design sequence, a close correspondence to length on deck is not surprising.

The designer had to derive and lay out the required measurements in some fashion; this must be considered in any design study based on archaeological remains. For example, the *devis* provides several measurements that relate to designing the deck at midships, none of which correspond to the height determined for the 51 ft (16.57 m) length on deck between rabbets. Similarly, 51 ft (16.57 m) is approximately the distance between the outside of the stem and sternpost at the given 5.5 ft (1.79 m) height of the tuck. Without a substantiated explanation of how the overall length and rake measurements were used by the designer in relation to this height, this "coincidence" should be noted and analyzed, but cannot be presented as reflecting a contemporaneous design procedure.

CONCLUSION

The timbers composing the longitudinal centerline of the hull are three-dimensional, but their design is developed on a two-dimensional flat plane. In relation to the development of the curvature of the lower hull, the longitudinal timbers discussed above define the general limits of the hull in profile. In terms of construction, the hull extends a little farther in the stern and the bow, and includes the counter, rudder, and head structures. And none of this even touches on the arrangement and shape of the frames that define the breadth of the vessel. Clearly, this method of reconstruction is an involved and time-consuming process. The benefits reward the investment, however, and create a fuller understanding of the historical design process than is attainable through reliance on the archaeological record or historical documents alone.

Through the extended example of *La Belle*'s longitudinal timbers I have attempted to show how a late-seventeenth-century French shipbuilder would have conceived of and designed the hull of a ship. The details of similar reconstructions will vary with the period under study, the type and preservation of the archaeological remains, and the quantity, quality, and availability of relevant historical texts. What is important, however, is that the recursive relationship this approach develops between the archaeological remains and the historical record creates stronger and potentially more accurate reconstructions of ancient hulls. This level of accuracy is increasingly important as nautical archaeologists begin to explore the sailing characteristics of these vessels using computer simulations (Monroy, Castro, and Furuta in this volume). Furthermore, this approach advances the anthropological aspects of maritime archaeology by exploring the decision-making processes of shipbuilders and placing them in the wider context of contemporary mathematics and science (Rieth in this volume).

REFERENCES

Album de Colbert. 1670 [1988]. Facsimile, transcription, translation. Nice: Éditions Oméga.

Anonymous. 1691 [1983]. *Un manuel de construction des Galères*, annotated transcription, J. Fennis. Amsterdam: APA Holland University Press.

Boudriot, Jean. 1986. *The seventy-four gun ship: A practical treatise on the art of naval architecture*. Vol. 1, *Hull construction*. Translated by D. H. Roberts. Annapolis: Naval Institute Press.

———. 1993. *The history of the French frigate 1650–1850*. Translated by D. H. Roberts. Rotherfield: Jean Boudriot Publications.

———. 1998. *Le vaisseau trois-ponts du Chevalier de Tourville: Précédé de mélanges sur l'architecture navale française au XVIe*. Paris: ANCRE.

———, ed. 2000. *Cavelier de La Salle, l'expédition de 1684: La Belle*. Paris: ANCRE.

Bruseth, James E., and Toni S. Turner. 2005. *From a watery grave: The discovery and excavation of La Salle's shipwreck, La Belle*. College Station: Texas A&M University Press.

Dassié, F. 1695 [1994]. *L'architecture navale*. Facsimile of the 2nd ed. (1695). Sanremo: PHAROS.

Duhamel du Monceau, H.-L. 1758 [1970]. *Élemens de l'architecure navale, ou Traité pratique de la construction des vaisseaux*. Facsimile of the 2nd ed. (1758). Grenoble: Éditions des 4 Seigneurs.

Fennis, Jan, ed. 1983. *Un manuel de construction des galères: Édition annotée des manuscripts SH 132 A 134 (1691)*. Amsterdam: APA Holland University Press.

Grieco, Glenn. 2003. Modeling *La Belle*: A reconstruction of a seventeenth-century light frigate. MA thesis, Texas A&M University.

Lemineur, Jean Claude. 2000. Restitution volumetrique de la coque. In *Cavelier de La Salle, l'expédition de 1684, La Belle*, ed. J. Boudriot. Paris: Ancre.

Roberts, David H. 1992. *18th century shipbuilding: Remarks on the navies of the English and the Dutch from observations made at their dockyards in 1737 by Blaise Ollivier, master shipwright of the King of France*. Rotherfield: Jean Boudriot Publications.

Ross, Lester A. 1983. *Archaeological metrology: English, French, American and Canadian systems of weights and measures for North American historical archaeology*. Ottawa: National Historic Parks and Sites Branch, Parks Canada, Environment Canada.

Steffy, J. Richard. 1994. *Wooden ship building and the interpretation of shipwrecks*. College Station: Texas A&M University Press.

CHAPTER 13

THE ARCHAEOLOGICAL ROLE OF CONSERVATION IN MARITIME ARCHAEOLOGY

DONNY L. HAMILTON AND C. WAYNE SMITH

INTRODUCTION

MARITIME archaeology is the one field of archaeology that is completely tied to the conservation laboratory. Without the efforts of trained laboratory personnel, underwater field excavations would be for naught; indeed, the success of every underwater project—whether maritime, nautical, freshwater, or saltwater—is dependent on properly treating recovered artifacts so that they can be studied and eventually displayed in a museum in order to tell the story behind an excavation. The emphasis of this chapter is not to describe the numerous techniques and procedures by which the recovered material culture is treated, but to emphasize the archaeological role of the conservation laboratory. Readers interested in conservation techniques can consult any number of published conservation sources, which will lead to an even larger array of articles addressing specific problems (Cronyn 1990; Dowman 1970; Hamilton 1973, 1976, 1996, 2010; Pearson 1987; Plenderleith and Torraca 1968; Plenderleith and Werner 1971; Rodgers 2006; Singley 1988). Of these, only Hamilton and Pearson concentrate on the conservation problems of the array of material recovered from maritime or nautical archaeology sites; however, the basic techniques discussed in the other references are applicable in many instances. A thorough overview of the more standardized conservation treatments can be found on the Internet at http://nautarch.tamu.edu/crl/conservationmanual/ (Hamilton 2010), which also contains an extensive conservation bibliography.

Presented here, with specific examples from various underwater archaeology projects, are conservation case studies where the archaeological role of the conservation laboratory is emphasized, for it is there that much of the actual archaeology is done. In the course of discussing the case studies some of the applied conservation techniques are addressed.

THE 1554 PLATE FLEET

On 9 April 1554, four Spanish ships—*San Esteban, Santa Maria de Yciar, Espíritu Santo,* and *San Andrés*—departed Vera Cruz for Spain, only to wreck on Padre Island 20 days later. *San Andrés* made it to Havana, but it was so badly damaged that the cargo was off-loaded onto another ship (Arnold 1978: 326–327; Weddle 1978: 19–35; see Borgens in this volume). In 1967, the wreck sites were rediscovered by a treasure-hunting venture, Platoro Ltd. of Gary, Indiana, and a salvage operation was started. However, following an injunction filed by the state of Texas, the newly created Texas Antiquities Committee took over the excavation of the ships under the direction of Carl Clausen and subsequently J. Barto Arnold III. This move made the 1554 Spanish Plate Fleet one of the first shipwreck sites in the United States to be excavated by professional archaeologists (Arnold and Weddle 1978; Olds 1976). It also established nautical archaeology in Texas and brought the cultural resources in the extensive tidelands of Texas under the control of the Texas Antiquities Committee.

The array of material recovered in the earlier salvage operation was confiscated and put under the custody of the Texas Archeological Research Laboratory (TARL) with a directive to "study, describe, photograph, and analyze" all the artifacts (Olds 1976: 3). In 1973 this led to the establishment of the Antiquities Conservation Facility (ACF) at TARL, the first archaeological conservation laboratory in the state. Donny Hamilton, at the time a graduate student at the University of Texas at Austin, was hired to run the laboratory. All of the materials recovered by the Texas Antiquities Committee were sent to the Antiquities Conservation Facility for conservation. Since the conservation laboratory was established within the oldest archaeological research laboratory in the state of Texas, existing documentation and excavation standards were employed to recover as much archaeological data as possible from the material during treatment. The conservation processes, the basic philosophy of shipwreck conservation, and many of the standards were developed at the Antiquities Conservation Facility (Hamilton 1976). ACF is no longer in operation, the principles established there continue in the procedures of the Conservation Research Laboratory (CRL) of the Center for Maritime Archaeology and Conservation (CMAC) at Texas A&M University, which was created by Donny Hamilton in 1978. Presently, CRL is one of the oldest continuously operating and largest conservation laboratories in the United States. It is responsible for conserving the artifacts recovered by CMAC projects and conserves artifacts on a contract basis for legitimate archaeological excavations on land or underwater across the United States, as well as various countries in the Caribbean (Hamilton 2009).

The Texas Antiquities Committee concentrated on the excavation of *San Esteban*, but most if not all of the material recovered by Platoro Ltd. was from *Espíritu Santo*. In later years, additional material was recovered from *Santa Maria de Yciar*. During the excavation of *San Esteban*, the diving archaeologists often complained that despite their careful mapping of the recovered material, they never knew what was contained in the metal concretions that delineated the shipwreck, as most were heavily encrusted with marine growth. Other than a large section of the stern end of the keel, relatively little of the wooden hull remained, but the alignment and extent of the ship was revealed by the distribution of the concreted material—anchors, large gun, swivel guns, and iron fasteners. The hold was marked by 10 or so large concretions. Interestingly, three of the concretions were broken, unemployable anchors. Two were fragmented at midshank, with the two sections lashed together, and another had one arm broken off. There was also a wrought iron swivel gun with its rat-tail handle broken off and apparently tied alongside its barrel. For whatever reason, these large broken iron pieces were being retained, possibly to be repaired at some future date or to be used as permanent ballast. Four other functioning anchors were found. One was recovered from what is believed to be the stern, the second was out from the bow end of the ship, and two more were from the central hold area, one stacked on top of the other.

As shown on the site map (see Arnold 1978: 210–211), all of the encrustations are just outlines, with no details on what they contained. Some of them can be identified by their shape, but many cannot, and there is no indication of the hundreds of other objects, such as coins, tools, fasteners, and even cockroaches and cockroach egg cases, concreted along with the large iron pieces. All of the material tells the story of the shipwreck, and it was in the conservation laboratory that this story was revealed and the full array of associated material was determined. Throughout the conservation process, the artifact catalog system used in the field was maintained. In the process, all of the details within the outlined encrustations were filled in. And, of course, all of this material was properly documented, analyzed, and conserved.

To demonstrate the methods employed to process the encrusted material, commonly referred to as either encrustations or conglomerates, the two stacked anchors found in the hold (Artifact No. 156) are described. As is the case with all of the encrustations, the first order of business was to fill out a conservation record card that contained all of the references to the photographs, the radiographs, all of the artifacts recovered from the encrustation, and detailed conservation records on each of those artifacts. A photograph looking straight down on the top surface of encrustation No. 156 was taken, using a second-story walkway that allowed conservators to get high enough for an overhead perspective (Figure 13.1a). When possible, a radiograph was also taken of encrustations, but for an artifact as large as No. 156, this was not feasible.

Using a mixture of hammers and chisels, along with small pneumatic chisels (Chicago Pneumatic Air Scribes) for more detailed work, the secrets of the huge

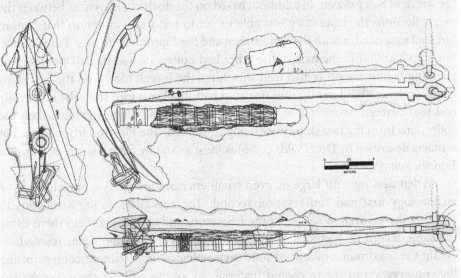

Figure 13.1 (a) Large anchor encrustation, 1554 Plate Fleet; (b) Final drawing of stacked anchors encrustation, 1554 Plate Fleet. Reproduced with the kind permission of the Texas Historical Commission, Austin.

encrustation were revealed (Figure 13.1b). Clearly, two typical sixteenth-century Spanish anchors were stacked, one on top of the other, arms on top of arms. Lying alongside, tucked in at the juncture of the arms and the shank, was an upside-down bombardetta lashed with rope to the remnants of its wooden undercarriage. A breech block, possibly for the bombardetta, a swivel gun breech block, and an iron chain were also contained in the encrustation. Smaller objects included a brass buckle, glass fragments, obsidian blades, olive pits, potsherds, a brass sheath for a straight pin, and even cockroach exoskeletons preserved in the encrustation, and cockroach egg cases under the rope lashing the gun to the carriage (Arnold 1978: 305–322). Other cockroach exoskeletons were found in separate concretions, validating the earliest evidence we have for the exchange of cockroaches between the Old and New Worlds (Durden 1978: 407–416).

Once all of the metal artifacts were removed from the encrustation and documented, they underwent a long electrolytic reduction treatment that lasted over a year to reduce the outer corrosion products and remove all chlorides to prevent subsequent corrosion. After electrolysis, the artifacts went through intensive rinsing in heated deionized water, followed by three coats of tannic acid to make them more corrosion resistant and darken the color of the iron. The final step was to immerse them into microcrystalline wax to boil off any remaining water and seal off the conserved iron with a water vapor–impervious barrier of wax (Hamilton 1978). The waterlogged wood was treated with polyethylene glycol. See Hamilton 1976 and 2010 for details on electrolytic cleaning of metal artifacts recovered from a marine environment.

Only through the data provided by the conservation laboratory on the artifacts contained in the concretions was the archaeologist able to tell the complete story of the wreck of San Esteban. In addition, based on the distinct differences between the two collections the laboratory was able to put to rest the assumption that Platoro Ltd. had excavated at both the San Esteban and the Espíritu Santo sites. For instance, one ship had flint in the ballast, the other had none; one had lead strips along the planking seams, the other had lead sheathing; the breech blocks on the two ships were constructed differently; and one ship had small cast iron shot, the other only had lead-covered wrought iron shot. These differences became obvious when the collections from the two ships were being conserved. The Platoro Ltd. collection of artifacts described by Doris Olds (1976) is most assuredly from a single site, that of Espíritu Santo.

When dealing with large or even small encrustations, the approach must be archaeology first and conservation second. The encrustations are analogous to bringing the excavation square to the laboratory and excavating them there using the same recording methods used in the field. With this approach, researchers obtain the maximum amount of solid archaeological data without compromising the conservation of the recovered material. All of the artifacts conserved by the Antiquities Conservation Facility are displayed and curated by the Corpus Christi Museum of Science and History in Corpus Christi, Texas, the state's marine archaeology repository.

LA BELLE, 1686

On 24 July 1684, the famous French explorer René-Robert Cavelier Sieur de La Salle, the discoverer of the mouth of the Mississippi River, left La Rochelle, France, to establish a fort and a colony at its mouth, thereby securing France's claim to Louisiana and all of the land drained by the formidable river. La Salle sailed with a fleet of four ships: *Le Joly*, a naval gunship; *L' Aimable*, a private merchant ship; *La Belle*, a barque longue; and *Saint François*, a small ketch. The fleet contained supplies and 300 colonists (Bruseth and Turner 2005: 20–21; see Pevny in this volume). Before arriving, *Saint François* was captured by Spanish pirates off Hispaniola. The three remaining ships sailed toward the Mississippi River, but missed it and ended up some 800 km (500 miles) west, at the entry into Matagorda Bay, Texas, on 17 January 1685. The small *La Belle* easily made the entry over the sandbar into the bay. *L' Aimable*, the main supply ship for the colony, ran aground trying to get into the bay, and *Le Joly* returned to France with 120 of the colonists who had had a change of heart after seeing what was confronting them in the New World. La Salle was left with 180 persons to build and man Fort St. Louis, a short distance from the bay. Over the next two years, La Salle made a number of trips to the west and east to look for the Mississippi River and explore the territory. Two years later, in January 1686, the lone remaining ship, *La Belle*, ran aground on the sand peninsula separating Matagorda Bay from the open Gulf of Mexico. Now the colonists were stranded in a new and hostile world. Desperate, on 12 January 1687 La Salle and 16 of his men set off to seek help from Canada; only 20 survivors were left to defend Fort St. Louis. In March 1687, La Salle was killed by one his own men near present-day Navasota, Texas. Only 6 of the 16 men accompanying La Salle eventually made it to Canada (Bruseth and Turner 2005: 29). Most of the settlers left at the fort were killed by American Indians. The colonization attempt failed, with only a few survivors. An excellent overview of the *La Belle* shipwreck history and excavation is presented on the Web site of Texas Beyond History (2008).

   La Belle lay undiscovered, but not forgotten, in the murky waters of Matagorda Bay until she was rediscovered in 1995 by J. Barto Arnold III, Texas's state marine archaeologist. A limited investigation was undertaken in June 1995, and the recovered artifacts, including one brass gun, were sent to the Corpus Christi Museum of Science and History for conservation. A plan was devised to excavate *La Belle* by constructing a doughnut-shaped cofferdam around the ship and draining the water from the interior, making the excavation more or less a dry-land excavation. The operation started in August 1997. As soon as the last inches of water were pumped out, a layer of encompassing mud with protruding objects lay exposed. Once the muddy layer was removed, it became apparent that the site of *La Belle* was quite different from most shipwrecks, for there lay a well-preserved, intact shipwreck, all of its contents sealed in an anaerobic, organic-preserving environment. The final eight months of the excavation were directed by Dr. James Bruseth of the Texas Historical Commission. All of the artifacts from *La Belle* conserved by CRL are being displayed, or will be displayed, at one of the eight regional Texas museums in the La Salle's Odyssey Trail collaboration of museums, which includes Bob Bullock State History Museum in Austin, Corpus Christi Museum of Science and History in Corpus Christi, Texas Maritime Museum in Rockport, Texana Museum in Edna, Calhoun County Museum in Port Lavaca, Museum of the Coastal Bend in Victoria, Matagorda County Museum in Bay City, and La Petit Belle Palacios Area Historical Museum in Palacios (Texas Beyond History 2008). Artifacts not on display are curated at the Corpus Christi Museum of Science and History.

The preservation and array of cultural material was amazing. In Figure 13.2, two archaeologists are leaning on the frames and planking of the port side of the ship. To the right can be seen two of three boxes containing muskets, which proved to be a conservation nightmare that is still ongoing. Toward the center, several wood barrels on their sides are visible. To the left under the meter square is a jumble of barrel staves and other wood parts. Just to the right front corner of the grid can be seen the end of a wood chest with a handle on the end. This chest came to be known as the "mystery chest," since all six sides were intact, hiding the contents from view. This wood chest and its contents, along with a boxwood nocturnal, exemplify some of the archaeological and conservation techniques used to process the array of artifacts found on *La Belle*.

Figure 13.2 Chest in situ in hold of *La Belle*. Reproduced with the kind permission of the Texas Historical Commission, Austin.

Conservation of a Wood Chest

The chest, shown in situ on the ship in Figure 13.3a, was roughly 64.8 cm (25.5 in) long, 33 cm (13 in) wide, and 34.5 cm (13.5 in) tall, and weighed in excess of 136 kg (300 lbs). The chest, its contents, the conservation of the artifacts, and their analysis was adopted as an MA thesis by Michael West (2005). A preliminary report and the thesis itself are accessible on the Internet (West and Hamilton 2004). Prior to its conservation, the chest was stored in an aquarium of filtered tap water that was changed regularly to reduce the salt level in the wood resulting from its long submersion in seawater. Once the chest was opened, a 5% sodium sesquicarbonate storage solution (pH apx. 9.7) was used in order to prevent corrosion of the iron artifacts as they became exposed. When the chest was not being worked on, it was totally submerged in a storage vat. Fabric straps were placed around the chest so it could be lifted from the vat with a forklift and set on boards that were laid across the vat. This allowed the conservator to have 360° access to the box and keep everything wet (Figure 13.3a). The storage solution was changed regularly in order to remove the accumulated debris as the chest was mechanically cleaned. The pH of the sodium sesquicarbonate solution was kept high enough to prevent the iron from corroding, but not so high as to degrade the wood.

X-rays of the wood revealed that the box had been nailed and hinged and that a lock was once located on the front side. The position of the lock allowed us to correctly orient the box in its proper upright position. Upon delivery and during storage in the laboratory, it was upside down. Now the solid internal matrix of the chest could be excavated from the top down, after the six wooden side boards were removed.

Once the top was lifted off, a number of wooden handles and a bow saw could be seen. All were heavily concreted from the iron present and the mineral load of the seawater. The concreted material was chipped away where possible. This concretion, along with the high weight of the chest, indicated the presence of a large number of iron artifacts, and indeed, this proved to be the case. Although the iron objects could be seen, the metallic iron was gone, leaving a partial mold along with corrosion products of the artifacts. If present, the original artifacts were in extremely fragile condition, making it difficult to keep them from crumbling. It became clear that little to no actual iron remained in the objects due to the extensive corrosion they had undergone during their submarine deterioration. However, they had not deteriorated enough to become hollow molds that are relatively easy to cast. Therefore, for most of these artifacts a method for preserving their shape had to be developed in order to prevent their total destruction as they were removed from the chest. This was complicated by the fact that one could not work from all sides at once on any given artifact, as many other artifacts were lying below, next to, and occasionally intertwined with the one being examined.

The method devised to save them was multi-stepped. First, an artifact had to be uncovered as safely as possible, taking into account both its fragility and that of the artifacts around it. A clay wall was then built around the artifact, and a thin layer of

Figure 13.3 (a) Conservator working on *La Belle* chest; (b) Array of conserved artifacts from *La Belle* chest. Reproduced with the kind permission of the Center for Maritime Archaeology and Conservation, Texas A&M University, and the Texas Historical Commission, Austin.

RTV silicone rubber was laid over the object. Several layers of marine epoxy-soaked carbon-fiber cloth sheets were then immediately placed atop the RTV. A day or two later, when both the RTV and the epoxy had set, the artifact could be carefully wedged out of the chest. The RTV preserved the exact surface of the artifact, while the epoxy-soaked carbon-fiber sheets preserved the shape. This technique worked very well for keeping the curvature of the adze blades and other complex shapes that would be difficult to reconstruct from fragmented pieces. It was also imperative in helping to reconstruct those iron items that were already so far deteriorated that they did not survive removal from the chest. Once an artifact was removed, along with the silicone rubber layer with the carbon-fiber backing supporting it, the conservator could then go in from the back side and make an epoxy cast of the void left by the corroded iron of each artifact. The iron parts of each of the hafted tools in the box were cast in epoxy around the original wood handles. The wood handles were treated with silicone oil (Klosowski et al. 2000).

As a group, the organic artifacts, such as the handles of the tools and even four drumsticks, were well preserved. Some of the wood had originally been sanded, and the smoothness of these surfaces was generally retained. Rope and twine found in the chest were in poor condition, but sections of textile (possibly canvas or sail-cloth) used to wrap several drawknife blades were extracted and still retained much of their strength.

Several other non-iron metallic objects were also inside the chest, and these objects generally were found in pristine condition. The brass was still as shiny as it must have been the day the ship sank. The lead and pewter objects were still strong, with smooth, clean surfaces. Designs on the brass hilt pieces and a maker's mark on a pewter fork could not have been better preserved. In large part this was due to the amount of surrounding iron that, as it degraded, contributed electrons to the other, more noble surrounding metals. The encasing iron concretion also helped save these other metals by forming a barrier against any circulating salt water.

Periodically, throughout the examination process, the chest was X-rayed; however, no usable radiographs were obtained until the layers of artifacts in the chest had been reduced. For most of the process, the thickness and density of the chest was too great for any discernible image to be seen on the radiographs. As the final layers were reached, the remaining pewter, lead, and brass items could clearly be seen. Only in the last layer, however, could the wood and iron artifacts be faintly discerned. This was due to the multiple, overlapping layers of artifacts, the extensive corrosion the iron artifacts had undergone, and a sheet of unidentified metal placed across the bottom of the chest that created a barrier between the artifacts and the X-ray film.

After their removal from the chest the various artifacts were treated according to their material composition. The brass items underwent electrolytic reduction (ER), as did the pewter fork. Lead was chemically cleaned and then sealed with microcrystalline wax. No iron objects were strong enough to undergo electrolytic reduction, so all were cast in epoxy from the concretion molds. Figure 13.3b illustrates all of the working iron portions of the tools cast in epoxy to replace the corroded metal. Organic artifacts (wood, rope, twine, cloth, and fur) were dehydrated and conserved with silicone oil. While relatively expensive, silicone oil produces much better results than polyethylene glycol, rosin, or other methods such as freeze drying, commonly employed to conserve waterlogged wood.

A brass artifact at the top of the chest, the first artifact to be removed, posed a mystery until it was determined to be a chape used to protect the tip of a scabbard for a sword. After this, however, continuing work revealed an array of carpentry tools: a cooper's heading saw, three drawknives, three adzes, a hewing hatchet, two gimlets, an augur with six spare bits, a cooper's axe, a cold chisel, two gouges, and a carpenter's square. A number of these tools, perhaps all, were specifically for cask-making, a specialized job performed by a cooper. In fact, many of the implements are comparable to those belonging to a French wine-cask cooper (West 2005: 101).

Originally tenderly dubbed the "mystery chest," it lived up to its name by the additional and unusual associated artifacts it produced. Two sickles used for agricultural clearing or harvesting were recovered, along with four drumsticks (only two of which form a mated pair), a pair of brass navigational dividers, a sounding lead with the rope still attached, and a large seven-tined fishing spear. The oddness of these items discovered together in one cache was compounded by finding most of the component parts of a small sword hilt, as well as a well-preserved pewter fork, and three locks (one triangular, and two with a more traditional padlock shape).

Identifying marks are always of interest to archaeologists for both dating and ownership purposes. Only two items in the box had ownership initials etched onto their surfaces. A small gimlet had a "WF" mark, and the pewter fork had either an "OT" or "LO" as the owner; the same fork carried an interesting maker's mark consisting of a pair of clasped hands beneath a crown, with the word "FIN" beneath and the name "M CARDIN" above. This fork was identified as belonging to a pewterer, Michel Cardin, of La Rochelle, France (West 2005: 52).

The chest contained what appeared to be a hodgepodge of artifacts, or at minimum an eclectic assortment of tools and implements from a variety of skills. The chest may well reflect the history of the shipwreck site. In France it may have started off containing the tools of a craftsman, such as a cooper, and through the hectic days leading to the demise of the colony may have come to be filled with a varied collection of scrounged objects. Agricultural, woodworking, and even locksmith implements stand out. What is significant in the conservation of the box is the importance of the time-consuming process of casting each of the corroded iron artifacts with epoxy and the successful treatment of the accompanying wood handles and other organic material found packed together in the box. Without the work of the conservation laboratory, none of this would have survived, except for the nonferrous metal artifacts.

Conservation of a Nocturnal

A unique English-made nocturnal/planisphere with a maximum length of 23.8 cm and a main plate diameter of 13 cm was found on *La Belle*. The nocturnal consisted of three boxwood plates: the main plate with the handle, and two dials held to the main plate with a brass bolt and nut. Nocturnals are navigational devices used to determine time at night by sighting on the North Star and aligning the long arm plate with the two brightest stars in the Big Dipper and the other dial with either Ursa Major in the Big Dipper or Ursa Minor in the Little Dipper. The English were noted for making the best nocturnals and commonly used boxwood. This nocturnal is known to be British in origin, since all of the months and the zodiac names are in English. It is unique in that on the back of the main plate there is a detailed planisphere. The conservation of the nocturnal was conducted by Helen Dewolf (2010), chief conservator of the Conservation Research Laboratory, and was analyzed as part of an MA thesis by Lois Swanick (2005).

When the nocturnal was received in the laboratory, it was heavily concreted, especially on the back side, and most of the intricate details were obliterated with iron corrosion products from adjacent artifacts and with marine concretion (Figure 13.4a). From the onset, the intent of the conservation was to stabilize the waterlogged boxwood by a process that would assure absolute minimum shrinkage, reveal the markings, and allow the plates to rotate smoothly. Additionally, it was intended that the treating chemicals would not have any short- or long-term adverse affects on any part of the nocturnal and that the artifact would have lasting stability. First, all of the marine and iron concretion covering the device had to be removed. Over a series of weeks, Helen Dewolf chemically softened and mechanically removed the gross encrustations that coated the surfaces of the nocturnal and delicately extricated the concretions between the plates. Before recovery, the iron corrosion products between the main plate and the second plate expanded, cracking the plate, as can be seen in Figure 13.4b. Fine beading needles and strips of Mylar were used to remove any corrosion or concretion remaining between the plates. In some areas this required using cotton swabs to brush the concretion with dilute hydrochloric acid, wiping it off, and mechanically scraping with dental picks and other similar tools. At all times, care had to be taken not to scratch or otherwise mar the wood. At this stage, no attempt was made to remove all of the debris in the minute stamped letters and numbers. This was done during the final stages of the treatment.

The conservation technique that the conservators deemed would offer the best result for treating this rare navigational instrument was the silicone oil process (Smith 2003). They were reassured by the successes achieved on an array of wooden artifacts from La Belle (Smith 2010). The treatment involves three steps: dehydration, impregnation with silicone oil, and catalyzation. The first step was to remove all water from the wood by moving it through a series of ethanol and water baths (increasing the ethanol to water ratio in 25% increments), then into a series of ethanol baths, and then into a series of acetone baths until the wood was saturated with acetone and all the water had been removed. In the second step, the acetone-saturated wood was placed into a silicone oil solution with up to 20% methyltrimethoxysilane cross linker (MTMS). Once the silicone oil/MTMS mixture completely penetrated the wood, it was removed, and all of the excess silicone oil was allowed to drain off. Impregnating the wood with silicone oil at this stage loosened the adhesion of the concretion to the wood. In the case of the nocturnal, this process loosened the grime inside the stamped letters. The surfaces of the plates were then cleaned with MTMS. This made the remaining concretion more visible, and a fine hypodermic needle, as well as a very pointed scalpel blade, were used under a

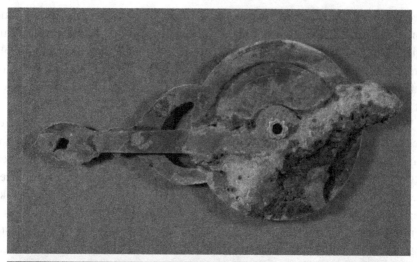

Figure 13.4 (a) *La Belle* nocturnal before conservation; (b) *La Belle* nocturnal after conservation. Reproduced with the kind permission of the Center for Maritime Archaeology and Conservation, Texas A&M University, and the Texas Historical Commission, Austin.

binocular microscope to remove the residual concretion in the grooves, in the fine lines, and inside the stamped letters and numbers.

Once the mechanical and chemical pre- and post-conservation steps were completed, the third and final step was to catalyze the silicone oil in the device. This was done by placing the silicone-saturated nocturnal in a sealed plastic bag with a small dish containing 5 mm of dibutyl tin diacetate (DBTDA), the catalyst that locks the silicone oil chains that have bonded to the wood cells. The catalyst has a working time of 24 hours and was changed daily for 10 days to completely catalyze the polymer in the wood.

Following treatment, the three plates rotate on each other, all of the marking details are clear and crisp, and there is reasonable assurance that the treatment will be long-lasting and stable. There was minimal shrinkage, if any, to the wood. Not only were the letters and numbers readily visible (Figure 13.4b), but it could be seen that the planisphere on the back of the main plate was made specifically for the owner with vernacular names of the constellations used by the pilot who owned the instrument. The conservation regimen was successful. In our experience with conserving waterlogged wood, we know of no other techniques that could have achieved the same degree of success and could have satisfied all the requirements we set out before starting treatment, especially the requirement for long-term stability. Clearly, silicone is another tool in the never-ending process of developing new conservation treatments for challenging and significant artifacts. It is not a solution for all cases, but it is another option in the arsenal of the artifact conservator that should be given consideration. Additional information on silicone oil and polymerization techniques can be found in C. W. Smith 2003 and 2010.

The Mardi Gras Shipwreck, Early Nineteenth Century

To a much greater extent than ever before, the future of underwater archaeology lies in the excavation of shipwrecks in deep water (see Wachsmann in this volume). As with all shipwreck archaeology, it is a continuing race against treasure hunters. It has only been in the last few years that the first ventures into deep waters began, one of the most recent being the Mardi Gras Shipwreck Project conducted by the Department of Oceanography and the Center for Maritime Archaeology and Conservation at Texas A&M University, in conjunction with Okeanos Gas Gathering Company and the Minerals Management Service, in May–June 2007. To a large degree, and throughout the project, it was a continuous learning process that concentrated on how to use the available technology to maintain archaeological controls, and in particular a remotely operated vehicle (ROV) 1,220 m (4,000 ft) below the ship and more than 50 km (31 miles) out in the Gulf of Mexico. Despite the constraints, an interesting array of artifacts including earthenware, stoneware, navigational devices, glass liquor bottles, sand glasses, a telescope, an octant, compasses, lead shot, cannon balls, organic material, and even a cast iron stove were recovered (Ford et al. 2008, 2010; Hamilton 2007). All of the artifacts were successfully conserved at the Conservation Research Laboratory and, as a group, date the shipwreck to 1808–1820 (Ford, Borgens, and Hitchcock 2010: 76). The only large encrusted objects brought to the surface were a 6 lb cannon and a large concretion located at the stern of the shipwreck.

The encrustation was slightly over 1.5 m per side and about 1 m tall, weighing at least 1,000 lb. On delivery to the conservation laboratory, it was placed in an upright

position on a fiberglass grating with fiber straps in a large vat. Overhead there was a
chain hoist that allowed one to lift the encrustation out of the water-filled vat and place
it on support boards spanning the vat (Figure 13.5a). This arrangement also enabled

Figure 13.5 (a) Large stern encrustation from Mardi Gras shipwreck; (b) Hull remains
in Mardi Gras encrustation with barrel and box on ceiling planking. Reproduced with
the kind permission of the Center for Maritime Archaeology and Conservation, Texas
A&M University.

the conservators to circle the encrustation as they started mechanically cleaning the marine concretion off with pneumatic chisels and standard hammers and chisels.

During the field excavation, very few hull remains were ever visible, making it difficult to arrive at meaningful data to identify the construction of the ship. The stern encrustation, however, was expected to potentially provide some construction data. Now it was up to the conservator to archaeologically excavate the concretion and see what data it contained. During the mechanical cleaning process, a large number of cannonballs, lead shot, and gunflints were recovered from the encrustation, along with a bar shot. Beginning in the field, it was noted that there was something large concreted near the center of the encrustation, and a possible box toward one corner.

As the work progressed, two yellow pine frames with white pine ceiling and outer planking were exposed (Ford, Borgens, and Hitchcock 2010: 82). Breaking through the top of the ceiling plank was the lower half of a wood barrel, filled with miscellaneous scrap iron. It is obvious that the heavy barrel broke through the ceiling planking during the wrecking process, leaving the barrel tilted at an angle (Figure 13.5). With this information it could be determined that the two frames were set at an acute angle to each other, suggesting that they represented cant frames at the stern of the vessel. The small size of the frames, 3.5 in (8.9 cm) sided and 4.5 in (11.4 cm) molded, suggests a slightly smaller-than-average vessel, like the ones that were commonly built in the Gulf of Mexico (Ford, Borgens, and Hitchcock 2010: 83). The encrustation with all of the iron corrosion products preserved the wood in this area of the ship. The box located just in the back of the barrel contained an assortment of wood handles for wood-working chisels, bits, a cooper's knife, and a couple of unidentified tools—all useful for routine ship maintenance requiring cutting and drilling. Even a few stray coffee beans were found. The careful mechanical cleaning and recording of all of the associated material, as well as the conservation of the artifacts, provided data on the hull construction and shipboard life that was not available from any other source.

All of the metal artifacts originating from the stern encrustation were conserved by electrolytic reduction cleaning; some of the organic artifacts, as well as the glass bottles, were stabilized with silicone oil. Conservation treatments currently were completed during the summer of 2010. All material is curated and displayed at the Louisiana State Museum in New Orleans.

SUMMARY

The preceding four conservation case studies of a large encrustation with two anchors from the 1554 Spanish Plate Fleet off Padre Island, the mystery chest and the nocturnal from the 1686 wreck of La Belle in Matagorda Bay, and the stern encrustation from the early 1800s Mardi Gras deepwater shipwreck in the Gulf of Mexico, demonstrate the array of basic archaeological data provided by the conservation laboratory. Similar accounts could be presented for all CRL conservation projects. With the conservation of encrusted artifacts from shipwrecks, or any marine site, even sunken buildings such as at Port Royal, Jamaica, comes the responsibility to record and provide this archaeological data, as well as conserve the artifacts. Especially important, all recovered artifacts from each of these three projects that were conserved—as should be the case for all archaeological conservation projects—are being displayed and properly curated. If this is not done, then the archaeological project will suffer. Approaching conservation with this archaeological perspective has been part of the senior author's perspective ever since he became involved with conserving the artifacts from the 1554 Plate Fleet in 1973 and continues to this day. Many see the authors primarily as conservators, but we see ourselves as archaeologists who happen to do conservation.

When an underwater site is excavated, the project directors take on the responsibility to properly conserve the recovered material and to pursue archaeological data collection into the laboratory. Each encrustation should be viewed as bringing the excavation unit back to the laboratory to be excavated using the same recording and artifact numbering system used in the field. Every conservation laboratory processing archaeological material must have an archaeological perspective along with a conservation ethic. However, it must always be kept in mind that, realistically, all too often the conservator has only one chance to conserve some of the material. The concept of reversibility is an important factor in any conservation procedure, for artifacts often have to be retreated. However, many iron artifacts cannot be satisfactorily conserved a second time around, so it is important that they be treated as well as possible the first time. Perhaps the concept of *re-treatability* is a more important conservation concept than the concept of *reversibility* when evaluating a treatment like silicone oil, which technically is not reversible. However, an artifact can be re-treated successfully with silicone oil a second time, or more, if it is deemed necessary in the future. Archaeological conservators must always be open to trying new conservation treatments to expand conservation science. By this process, both conservation and archaeology will advance.

REFERENCES

Arnold, J. Barto, III. 1978. Archaeological research. In *The nautical archaeology of Padre Island: The Spanish shipwrecks of 1554*, ed. J. Barto Arnold III and Robert Weddle, 181–327. New York: Academic Press.
Arnold, J. Barto, III, and Robert Weddle, eds. 1978. *The nautical archaeology of Padre Island: The Spanish shipwrecks of 1554*. New York: Academic Press.
Bruseth, James E., and Toni S. Turner. 2005. *From a watery grave: The discovery and excavation of La Salle's Shipwreck*, La Belle. College Station: Texas A&M University Press.
Cronyn, J. M. 1990. *The elements of archaeological conservation*. London: Routledge.
Dewolf, Helen C. 2010. Conservation of a composite navigation device. *CMAC News and Reports* 2: 12–15.
Dowman, E. A. 1970. *Conservation in field archaeology*. London: Methuen.

Durden, Christopher. 1978. Fossil cockroaches from a 1554 Spanish shipwreck. In *The nautical archaeology of Padre Island: The Spanish shipwrecks of 1554*, ed. J. Barto Arnold III and Robert Weddle, 407–416. New York: Academic Press.

Ford, Ben, Amy Borgens, William Bryant, Dawn Marshall, Peter Hitchcock, Ceasar Arias, and Donny Hamilton. 2008. *Archaeological Excavation of the Mardi Gras Shipwreck (16GM01), Gulf of Mexico Continental Slope*. New Orleans: OCS Report, MMS 2008-037, U.S. Department of the Interior, Minerals Management Service, Gulf of Mexico OCS Region. Online at www.gomr.mms.gov/PDFs/2008/2008-037.pdf.

Ford, Ben, Amy Borgens, and Peter Hitchcock. 2010. The "Mardi Gras" shipwreck: Results of a deep-water excavation, Gulf of Mexico, USA. *International Journal of Nautical Archaeology* 39 (1): 76–98.

Hamilton, Donny L. 1973. Electrolytic cleaning of metal articles recovered from the sea. In *Science Diving International: Proceedings of the 3rd Scientific Symposium of CMAS, 8–9th October 1973*, ed. N.C. Flemming, 96–104. London: British Sub Aqua Club.

———. 1976. *Conservation of metal objects from underwater sites: A study in methods*. Texas Memorial Museum Miscellaneous Papers No. 4, Texas Antiquities Committee Publication No. 1. Austin: Texas Antiquities Committee.

———. 1978. Conservation procedures utilized for the sixteenth-century Spanish shipwreck materials. In *The nautical archaeology of Padre Island: The Spanish shipwrecks of 1554*, ed. J. Barto Arnold III and Robert Weddle, 417–439. New York: Academic Press.

———. 1996. *Basic methods of conserving underwater archaeological material culture*. Washington, DC: U.S. Department of Defense, Legacy Resource Management Program.

———. 2007. *Mardi Gras Project: Ongoing Work*. Center for Maritime Archaeology and Conservation, Texas A&M University. Online at http://nautarch.tamu.edu/mardigras/ongoing work/. Accessed 1 October 2010.

———. 2009. *Contract conservation*. Center for Maritime Archaeology and Conservation, Texas A&M University. Online at http://nautarch.tamu.edu/CRL/services/. Accessed 1 October 2010.

———. 2010. *Methods of conserving underwater archaeological material culture: Conservation files; ANTH 605*. Conservation of Cultural Resources I. Nautical Archaeology Program, Texas A&M University. Rev. 1 March 2010. Online at http://nautarch.tamu.edu/class/ANTH605. Accessed 1 March 2010.

Klosowski, Jerome Melvin, Charles Wayne Smith, and Donny Leon Hamilton. 2000. A method of conserving waterlogged materials, United States Patent No. 6,020,027, issued 1 February 2000. Assignee: Dow Corning Corporation.

Olds, Doris L. 1976. *Texas legacy from the Gulf: A report on sixteenth century shipwreck; Materials recovered from the Texas tidelands*. Austin: Texas Memorial Museum. Pearson, C., ed. 1987. *Conservation of marine archaeological objects*. London: Butterworths.

Plenderleith, H. J., and G. Torraca. 1968. The conservation of metals in the tropics. In *The conservation of cultural property: Museum and monuments*, 237–249. Paris: UNESCO.

Plenderleith, H. J., and A. E. A. Werner. 1971. *The conservation of antiquities and works of art*. Rev. ed. London: Oxford University Press.

Rodgers, Bradley A. 2006. *The archaeologist's manual for conservation: A guide to non-toxic minimal intervention artifact stabilization*. New York: Kluwer Academic/Plenum.

Singley, Katherine. 1988. *The conservation of archaeological artifacts from freshwater environment*. Southhaven: Lake Michigan Maritime Museum.

Smith, C. Wayne. 2003. *Archaeological conservation using polymers: Practical applications for organic artifact stabilization*. College Station: Texas A&M University Press.

————. 2010. *Archaeological Preservation Research Laboratory*. Nautical Archaeology
Program, Texas A&M University. Rev. 1 March 2010. Online at http://nautarch.tamu.
edu/aprl/reports.shtm. Accessed 1 March 2010.

Swanick, Lois. 2005. An analysis of navigational instruments in the age of exploration: 15th
century to mid-17th century. MA thesis, Texas A&M University.

Texas Beyond History. 2008. La Belle *Shipwreck*. University of Texas at Austin. Online at
www.texasbeyondhistory.net/belle/index.html. Accessed 16 October 2010.

Weddle, Robert. 1978. History. In *The nautical archaeology of Padre Island: The Spanish
shipwrecks of 1554*, ed. J. Barto Arnold III and Robert Weddle, 1–180. New York:
Academic Press.

West, Michael Carl. 2005. An intact chest from the 1686 French shipwreck *La Belle*,
Matagorda Bay, Texas: Artifacts from the La Salle colonization expedition to the
spanish Sea. MA thesis, Texas A&M University.

West, Michael C., and Donny L. Hamilton. 2004. Conservation of closed wooden containers—a chest from *La Belle*. Conservation Research Laboratory Research Report No. 5.
Online at http://nautarch.tamu.edu/crl/Report5/chest.htm. Accessed 3 September 2010.

CHAPTER 14

VIRTUAL RECONSTRUCTION OF MARITIME SITES AND ARTIFACTS

DONALD H. SANDERS

> Once a treasure is lost, so is the chance to study, analyze, or simply appreciate its impact on society. Through digital means, however, culturally significant sites can be preserved by committing them to computer memory, so these wonders of the past can be enjoyed by generations in the future. . . . Virtual cultural heritage also makes it possible to conserve and interpret an area, building, or object in ways that were previously inconceivable through photographs or other techniques.
>
> —Moltenbrey 2001

INTRODUCTION

Virtual-reality-based reconstructions of archaeological and other heritage sites and their accompanying artifacts have been created and used since the early 1990s as a way to supplement and enhance traditional methods of understanding the past. Global growth in the application of such new media techniques has given rise to the (relatively) new field of virtual heritage (e.g., www.virtualheritage.net; Addison

2000; Jacobson and Holden 2007; Sanders 2008). Computer graphics software and display hardware have improved significantly over the past 15 years, and the ease of realizing the benefits of virtual heritage techniques for documenting, analyzing, visualizing, and disseminating cultural information are now being recognized by maritime archaeologists (although a prescient call for the use of virtual reality for nautical sites was issued early on; Hill 1994).

Virtual heritage professionals work with the knowledge that interactive computer graphics technologies can (1) envision the past so precisely and completely that archaeologists are able to ask new questions about the existing data that often leads to new and unforeseen insights, sometimes challenging traditional interpretations that have been based on 2D, static visualizations; (2) re-create excavated sites that are difficult to visit, have been covered over, or are no longer accessible at all; and (3) offer a more engaging, participatory, and exciting means of understanding and teaching complex situations (such as cargo arrangements, shipwreck scenarios, or trim conditions). Each of these advantages of virtual reality offers benefits to the documentation, preservation, and conservation of our global cultural heritage.

Practitioners of virtual heritage are acutely aware that the adjective "virtual" has become diluted, as, for example, in virtual libraries, virtual tours, and virtual museums, and even in publications (e.g., Watts and Knoerl 2007), where "virtual" is often simply a substitute for "digital" or "online." "Virtual" has lost its original sense pertaining to computer simulations of real or imaginary places offering visitors the ability to move around in those places, whether ships, blood vessels, or universes. Virtual heritage practitioners are eager to maintain the distinction. Thus, for the purposes of the following discussion, "virtual reconstructions" will have the broadly accepted specific meaning of interactive three-dimensional (3D) computer visualizations that provide the viewer with self-directed freedom of movement and first-person navigation—in and around spaces and manipulating objects—that mimic real-world experience. Therefore, virtual heritage does not include uploading photographs to a Web site, digitizing books about antiquity, or building online electronic versions of collections of objects, even if they have clickable links and animated graphics.

History taught from a series of static, disconnected, black-and-white images has been the norm for more than a century and has been adequate to stimulate the imaginations of generations of devotees for understanding the past. The technology now exists to examine a reconstructed past in 3D and even real-time (4D), and developing this methodology is a direction that promises significant benefits to maritime archaeology. The focus of this chapter, with examples from current projects, is the usefulness of virtual reality environments in dramatically altering how the results of maritime research are visualized and, hence, interpreted.

A discussion about the value of virtual reality for maritime archaeology falls within the larger debate in archaeology (and other disciplines) about the benefits, difficulties, and stability of digital data. The discourse within the broader discipline of archaeology has ensued since the 1980s, when experimentation with 3D modeling techniques for studying ancient sites began (Sanders 1999). Perceived drawbacks regarding costs, distribution methods, long-term access, data integrity, standards, transparency, and accuracy have often caused the discipline to lose sight of virtual reality's advantages over traditional analysis and visualization methods (Madov 2002; Paley and Sanders 2004; Sanders 1997, 2001, 2002; Sanders and Gay 1996). That debate is not under review here, except to argue in favor of expanding the use of virtual re-creations because of the increased efficiency, effectiveness, and insight gained from their implementation (if handled in a responsible and professional manner following established professional guidelines and standards; Fernie and Richards 2003 and the London Charter 2009, for example).

The integration of virtual reality into archaeological research began in the early 1990s (with projects nearly simultaneously constructed by English Heritage in collaboration with Intel Corporation [Stonehenge]; Carnegie Mellon University [an imaginary Egyptian temple]; the group that eventually became Learning Sites, Inc. [the Fortress at Buhen]; the American Institute of Archaeology in collaboration with the Studio for Creative Inquiry, Carnegie Mellon University [theater complex and Temple of Isis, Pompeii], and artist Benjamin Britton [Caves at Lascaux]). These early virtual worlds could be viewed only on very expensive hardware running equally high-end and complex software, sometimes reaching $1 million per system. Over the years, virtual reality has become a staple means of visualization in many fields, a platform for testing new hypotheses, and a medium that allows unique understanding of things far beyond what is possible with physical techniques alone. Display hardware has also evolved to the point where virtual reality (in its broadest definition) can now be enjoyed on typical laptop or desktop computers rather than exclusively on special machinery found only in university laboratories. Thus, the experience of virtual reality and access to interactive computer graphics, as well as widespread availability of software to create virtual environments, means that re-creations of cultural heritage sites and artifacts can be globally enjoyed in classrooms, museums, excavations, research labs, and living rooms, much the way photography eventually infiltrated those same domains in the late nineteenth century, after decades of wrestling with cumbersome equipment, untrustworthy results, and resistance from the history profession (which utilized some of the same arguments levied against the use of virtual reality by archaeologists; for complaints about photography during its early use by archaeologists, see, for example, Dorrell 1994: 1–7; Lemagny and Rouillé 1987: 54–55,277n; Meyers 1997: 331–333).

CURRENT METHODS

How maritime sites and artifacts are traditionally depicted is instructive as a basis of comparison with new media techniques. Generally, and in a very similar vein to archaeology in general, journal articles, excavation reports, and even maritime archaeology Web sites have relied on drawings, photographs, charts, and dive sheets to inform the reader and researcher about the finds and to illustrate particular points. The vast majority of these images are in black-and-white and represent only a tiny sampling of all of the visual data collected about a site.

A dependence on paper-based reports and 2D images (such as photographs, drawings, and charts) has been basic to archaeology since the profession's inception in the late eighteenth century, and continues to be the mainstay of maritime archaeology publications. Typically, these contain long descriptions of the site in question, the excavation and its finds, and only as many pictures as printing costs or manuscript lengths permit. Ship or timber drawings unquestionably repeat the plans, sections, and elevations in use since archaeology's origins. While some projects are using GIS mapping methods, the issue of 3D modeling rarely is mentioned. Even projects that take advantage of the Internet to post excavation information seldom use their Web presence to its full potential for providing 3D images of a site and its remains. The most comprehensive publications, presented as lengthy expositions, often carry but a few grayscale images and line drawings, which necessarily present only selected portions of the whole story; only single-viewpoint static samplings of ship remains, artifacts, or excavation methods. (Note the irony of this present chapter detailing, in 2D on paper, the advantages of moving beyond 2D paper-bound media.)

Today's emphasis on quantitative methods of analysis and explanations of cultural totality demands more information. Trying to understand site formation processes or stratigraphic or cultural complexity requires not just more data but innovative methods of assimilating and displaying the additional material. Virtual reality and associated interactive technologies can eliminate many shortcomings associated with traditional excavation reporting.

EMERGING METHODS

The following descriptions of computer-based methods can still be considered "emerging" because in maritime archaeology their use is relatively recent, when compared to the use of digital visualizations in archaeology as a whole, and especially when compared to other humanities disciplines (neither maritime sites nor the particular problems associated with recovering or reconstructing underwater remains are mentioned in many recent virtual heritage compendia—e.g., Fernie and Richards 2003; Virtual Systems and Multimedia [VSMM]; International Symposium on Virtual Reality, Archaeology, and Cultural Heritage [VAST]; Computer Applictions in Archaeology [CAA] conference proceedings; Posluschny, Lambers, and Herzog 2008 is a rare exception).

Before a real-time virtual world can be explored, a 3D computer model must be created. These models can be built using specialty modeling software (such as

Maya, 3DStudioMax, Blender, or Rhinoceros), using the modules in game engines (such as Ogre, C4, or Unreal), or using CAD (Computer Aided Design) packages (such as AutoCAD, TurboCAD, or SolidWorks). Models usually are constructed from precise drawings, general sketches, a series of raw dimensions, 3D scanned data, or photographs, or by starting from scratch using simple primitives and "drawing" in the computer. Often, 2D images or sets of dimensions are converted into 3D models (as solids, editable polygons, or meshes with unique x, y, and z coordinates for each point) with faces that are "textured," that is, overlain or mapped with images, colors, or shading to make the surfaces appear to simulate reality. Inside the software packages, the models can be rotated and zoomed so that each side or detail can be inspected for accuracy, precision, and quality of the texture. Cameras and lights are added to the scene. Cameras act as surrogate eyes inside the model, and lights provide shadows and general illumination so that the results are visible when rendered to any of various output formats. At any stage during the construction process, test images can be produced (from any viewpoint or distance) to gauge the integrity of the model, look for errors or omissions, and send to colleagues or experts for comment.

Software that specializes in 3D modeling offers great flexibility and utility to maritime archaeologists for quick, yet highly precise and detailed, visualizations of artifacts, timbers, ships, and sites. Modeling packages range from those that are easy to use and have quick-to-see results, to those that are rather complex and difficult to learn but ultimately provide stunning visuals. Display methods, such as immersive visualization walls, Web sites, game environments, and Earth viewers, offer a full range of options for disseminating the results. Their disadvantages, for the purposes of virtual reality, lie primarily in the variance to which they can output to stable and useful interactive graphics file formats. Some can output to standards like VRML (Virtual Reality Modeling Language), others only to proprietary viewers or file formats that restrict their mass appeal or the ability of an entire discipline to access the results easily and at minimal cost.

Once a 3D computer model has been built, there are several output formats available for viewing the results, such as animations, QTVR (QuickTime Virtual Reality) panoramas, virtual reality simulators, and online perpetual game environments. The output of choice depends on the goals for using the resulting images, the audience, and the display hardware and software.

Animations (such as flyovers of a site model or flythroughs of ship interiors) are similar to short films or cartoons, in that they are composed of a sequence of individual stills stitched together fast enough so that the result appears to be a seamless movie. There is no user interaction; the viewing experience is passive.

QTVR was developed by Apple to simulate the viewing experience of true virtual reality. QTVR panoramas, sometimes referred to as photobubbles, are in essence a series of 2D images pasted onto the inside of a sphere, cube, or cylinder and viewed with special software from Apple. The results make it appear as though the viewer can move through a 3D space, but the viewer is really stuck at the center point of the sphere or cube and provided with zoom and rotate capabilities that together simulate movement. Linked bubbles allow users to jump from space to space. QTVR can also be used to create object models that spin single artifacts around. There is some user interaction, but no real-time navigation or freedom to explore a space, because no 3D geometry has been input.

Game environments generally rely on proprietary game engine software to drive the interaction and provide real-time navigation through spaces that can range from nearly limitless to small and confined. The software permits avatars (virtual characters, often imbued with quite lifelike movement, speech, and interactions), rapid movement, internal and external links to information or virtual objects, sound, and worlds that are increasingly more realistic through the use of physics engines that enable features such as momentum when an object is kicked, random swinging of trees and bushes, real-time footprints, and moving water. These worlds are full of interactivity and are capable of hosting conversations among avatars; the precision and accuracy of the models and textures do not yet quite approach the detail needed for scholarly research or publication, but the results are fun and engaging.

Virtual reality is a simulation of physical reality offering the viewer real-time movement through a true 3D space and interactivity with the objects, virtual characters, or hyperlinks in the virtual environment, which can be further enhanced with 3D sound, lighting, and touch. The software available for creating virtual worlds include VRML; X3D (a new and extended version of VRML); proprietary software from manufacturers such as Adobe (Adobe3D and Flash 3D), Virtools, and EonReality; games like 2ndLife; and options from the serious games industry, a branch of education that uses games engines, role playing, and other computer-game strategies to teach.

Virtual reality can be enjoyed using many types of displays, such as:

- Cave Automated Virtual Environments (CAVEs), introduced by the Electronic Visualization Laboratory at the University of Illinois in 1992. CAVEs are composed of one or more walls, sometimes also with ceiling and floor, onto which are projected stereo images from computers mounted behind the surfaces, and tracking devices that move the scene as viewers move. The projection systems create totally immersive surroundings that make viewers feel they are moving in a virtual world without being physically linked to a hardware device
- Desktop or laptop computers (using Web browser plugins such as VRML, Flash, Eon, or Virtools viewers)
- Earth viewers (such as Google Earth, which displays 3D models created with SketchUp)
- Virtual-reality-capable tables or semi-immersive large flat or panoramic curved systems (such as the ImmersaDesk or TouchTable, and videowalls, powerwalls, immersion domes, or reality theaters)
- Autostereo computer screens that do not require any special headgear or glasses

At the same time, 3D modeling is now widely used for investigating various aspects of maritime sites and artifacts. For example:

- The remains of the Newport Ship, a mid-fifteenth-century clinker-built merchantman discovered in Newport, Wales, UK, have been scanned with a FaroArm 3D digitizer to create a 3D blueprint of each timber for conservation (Newport Ship 2010; Jones 2005; Toby Jones, Curator, Newport Medieval Ship Project, pers. e-mail comm. 2008).
- The timbers of the Viking ship Roskilde I, excavated in the harbor of Roskilde, Denmark, were scanned FaroArm 3D digitizer as a more accurate, cost-effective, and efficient means of understanding the ship's original design (Posluschny, Lambers, and Herzog 2008).
- The many shipwreck projects undertaken by the Woods Hole Oceanographic Institution, Massachusetts, U.S., in collaboration with maritime archaeologists and archaeological organizations around the world, use multibeam sonar to create accurate bathymetric maps and 3D site models (Foley 2010a, 2010b).
- The Confederate States of America commerce raider CSS *Alabama*, sunk in 1864 off the coast of Cherbourg, France, has been documented with digital images to produce a full 3D visualization of the exposed wreckage and a georeferenced site mosiac (DoD 2004; U.S. Navy 2009).
- The Late Bronze Age ship and cargo remains of the wreck discovered at Uluburun, Turkey, have been modeled to test assumptions about cargo arrangements and hull design (in 2003; Cemal Pulak, pers. e-mail comm. 2008). This is one of many projects of the nautical archaeology program at Texas A&M University making use of 3D modeling technologies for visualizing the complexities of ancient and historical ship construction (e.g., Catsambis 2006; Kocabas 2008).
- The last remaining extreme clipper ship, *Cutty Sark* (presently under conservation in Greenwich, England), is undergoing repair based on laser scans, 3D solids modeling, and finite element analysis (a computational mechanics numerical technique that can be used to simulate on a computer the structural behavior of the ship subject to different loads) that allow researchers to visualize critical areas and understand the stresses in each component during the restoration process (Jim Solomon, Buro Happold Ltd., London, pers. e-mail comm. 2008; Stoyan Stoyanov, University of Greenwich, pers. e-mail comm. 2008; Cooke 2008; Cutty Sark 2005; Redfern 2004).
- The 3D visualization of the Confederate combat submarine *H. L. Hunley*, found buried off the coast of Charleston, South Carolina, U.S., is based on data from laser scans and X-ray and computerized tomography imaging of sediment cores (www.hunley.org/index.asp; session papers presented by Maria Jacobsen and Michael Scafuri, the Friends of Hunley, Charleston, South Carolina, at the 2007 Computer Applications and Quantitative Methods in Archaeology annual meetings in Berlin).

Only those projects in which the computer models have been exported into an environment allowing self-directed movement (VR) are detailed here.

CASE STUDIES

Underwater archaeologists operate under excavation circumstances that present problems quite distinct from those encountered by terrestrial archaeologists. For example, it is difficult and impractical to revisit an underwater site after excavation, whether by the investigators, by their colleagues, or by an interested public; it is difficult to obtain good color images of wreck remains or associated artifacts due to the water, particles in the water, and limited natural light; and it is difficult to appreciate the entire site from a distance. Interactive 3D computer graphics offer useful alternatives and provide unique advantages for producing studiable depictions of underwater sites.

In addition to elucidating underwater sites, numerous current maritime archaeology projects are using virtual reality to understand ship construction and to reconstruct past maritime cultural contexts. The case studies below show how virtual reality becomes valuable for the four components of archaeology: documentation, research/analysis/hypothesis testing, teaching, and publication (data dissemination).

The Pepper Wreck

Filipe Vieira de Castro and colleagues at Texas A&M University are using virtual reality to study the Portuguese Indiaman that sank at the mouth of the Tagus River, Portugal, in September 1606, nicknamed the Pepper Wreck due to the amount of pepper found in its hull (Castro, Fonseca, and Wells 2009; Castro 2008, 2005; Monroy, Castro, and Furuta in this volume). Researchers are trying to understand how the interior space of this ship was used and occupied and to propose a plausible configuration for the cargo storage, which will be tested in terms of the fully loaded ship's intact stability. The result is intended as a theory of what constituted an early-seventeenth-century Portuguese *nau*. Only further archaeological investigations will tell whether this is an accurate theoretical model or not.

Researchers completed a 3D reconstruction of the ship in Maya, with textures created in Photoshop. The site was modeled using 3DEM (a freely available software product of Visualization Software LLC with the ability to merge multiple digital elevation models to provide detailed overhead maps, 3D renders, and flyovers of large surface areas) and Terragen (Planeside Software) for the environmental context of the model. The finished environment was exported to a low-cost, PC-based, 180°, multiscreen, CAVE-like system using tools developed at TAMU (Figure 14.1). The

Figure 14.1 View of the virtual *nau* on the CAVE walls at Texas A&M University.
Reproduced with the kind permission of Audrey Wells.

results have been used for in-house research to demonstrate the capabilities of the immersive virtual reality system and will eventually be available for teaching (Wells 2008; Audrey Wells, pers. comm. 2008).

Thus, complex scenes and environments that are much too difficult to understand and research using conventional 2D image techniques can be imagined, visualized, and studied interactively as if in a first-person experience with immersive computer graphics. When compared to video and QTVR panoramas, CAVEs require specialized equipment, software, and space, but they provide experiences that are much closer to reality, such as enabling users to walk through a seventeenth-century ship or virtually examine a reconstructed artifact. The resulting environment dramatically improves the ability to understand the complexities of cargo distribution, spatial relationships, and nuances of rigging, trim, and deck space allocation that cannot be appreciated any other way.

Doggerland, North Sea, Submerged Landscapes

The area now encompassed by the North Sea, between England and Europe, was, during the Mesolithic (c. 10,000–7,500 years before present), a habitable and fertile stretch of land. As oil and other natural resource explorations in the North Sea continue to expand, marine archaeologists see that vital evidence of this once key part of the European cultural landscape is disappearing (see Firth in this volume). Researchers at the University of Birmingham have been working with 3D seismic data to assess the historical viability of the region for human activity by creating interactive 3D models of the undersea terrain (Gaffney, Thomson, and Fitch 2007; Fitch, Gaffney, and Thomson 2007).

The Birmingham team is using a visualization powerwall (multiscreen, rear-projection, high-resolution display system) with head-tracking capability to display all of the models (and accompanying 3D Geographic Information Systems [GIS] data). The active stereo display has improved the team's understanding of the data, while also allowing the public to walk around in the models. The powerwall system is used for teaching because it gets students engaged.

Given the inaccessibility of the region and the vast scale of the data, few archaeologists and fewer members of the public will ever be able to experience the actual marine environment. Only through interactive 3D graphics can the information be adequately processed, viewed, and interpreted, and then appreciated by audiences not used to visualizing traditional GIS datasets. The availability of such information will transform how we interpret traditional terrestrial data by studying how and to what extent past communities interacted. The study of marine prehistoric landscapes is still in its infancy, but the data currently available are sufficient to warrant that future interpretations of the early British Mesolithic include the archaeology of the North Sea region (Simon Fitch, Marine Geophysics and Palaeolandscape Manager, Institute of Archaeology and Antiquity, University of Birmingham, pers. comm. 2008).

Shotton River Corridor of the North Sea

University of Wolverhampton researchers led by Eugene Ch'ng are expanding on the Birmingham studies of the North Sea to create an enhanced virtual environment, one that incorporates environmental models and biological systems (artificial life, or ALife). The approach is being used to research the Shotton River submerged landscape, an ancient Mesolithic era habitation site currently under the North Sea. The goal is to visualize a Mesolithic landscape with accurately arrayed vegetation positioned according to expert opinions from geologists, archaeologists, and environmentalists, and introduced using software-based artificial life properties and algorithms. Ch'ng hopes that by simulating localized and dispersed growth patterns, reproduction, adaptation, and competition, it will be possible to obtain a credible interpretation of the landscape in order to determine settlement patterns of the ancient inhabitants (Ch'ng and Stone 2006). The results of the modeling and simulation are visualized using associated VR technologies (such as VRML, Adobe Director Shockwave, Worldviz Vizard with immersive displays, and the CryTek CryEngine, a 3D games engine). Eventually, other organisms (arthropods and animals) will be added.

The combination of VR and ALife to investigate re-creations of ancient maritime settlements and growth of natural landscapes is crucially beneficial for regions inaccessible in time and space. Immersive 3D visualization technologies have already proved themselves advantageous for the interpretation of complex issues related to the Mesolithic landscape. There is work in progress using artificial life algorithms to describe vegetation behaviors in relation to growth limits and environmental influences in Mesolithic settings (Ch'ng, Stone, and Arvanitis 2004;

Eugene Ch'ng, School of Computing and Information Technology, University of Wolverhampton, pers. comm. 2008).

The Tantura Lagoon Shipwrecks

A group of ninth- to tenth-century CE Arab coastal trading vessels wrecked during storms while navigating their way into the harbor of the ancient settlement at Tel Dor, Israel. They were excavated in very shallow water just off the coast in Tantura lagoon from 1994 to 1996 by the Institute for Nautical Archaeology and Haifa University's Center for Maritime Studies, under the codirection of Shelley Wachsmann and Yaakov Kahanov (Wachsmann, Kahanov, and Hall 1997; Wachsmann and Kahanov 1997).

The Tantura team collaborated with the Institute for the Visualization of History (VIZIN) to develop something more informative and visually comprehensive than a traditional site publication. The objective was a publication that would allow readers the closest thing possible to an actual experience of viewing a shipwreck. Wachsmann recognized (pers. comm. 2006) that this approach helps the reader comprehend the site in a tangible way that cannot be reproduced in 2D. The entire modeling process allowed the excavators to revisit the site again in 3D, that is, from all angles; in turn, this led them to reevaluate their own recollections of the site, which had been based on photographs and sketch plans that could not adequately replicate the wrecks in all their complexity. The process challenged presumptions about how excavators remember a site; and if the excavators have troubles, how are other researchers supposed to understand the details and nuances of a wreck site that they cannot visit in person? Interactive 3D computer graphics can create the closest thing we have to replicating excavation contexts, which is especially crucial for sites that are inaccessible, lost, too expensive or difficult to reach, or too fragile or fragmentary for general visitation.

The Kyrenia Shipwreck

Around 300 BCE, a small Greek cargo ship sank off the north coast of Cyprus, near Kyrenia. It was excavated from 1967 to 1969 (M. L. Katzev 1974, 1969; S. W. Katzev and M. L. Katzev 1974; Steffy 1994: 42–58) and fully documented by 1974, including traditional site plans, a vast array of color and black-and-white photographs, and standard inventory catalog cards for the hundreds of artifacts. It is unusual in shipwreck archaeology to have such an old ship survive so completely, with so much of its cargo still nicely arrayed among the surviving hull timbers. After many years of analyzing the cargo, the crew's belongings, and ship's timbers, questions remained. Could there be clues here to determine not only the original arrangement of the contents, but also what happened to the ship when it crashed into the seabed, breaking apart and scattering its cargo?

The typical transport amphora had a long tapering base, making it unable to stand up by itself—it had to be secured onboard ship so as not to rattle around and break during transit. No one is quite sure how this was done; however, given the vast number of unbroken amphoras at this and other wreck sites, ancient sailors clearly had solutions that worked. Archaeologists can only speculate as to what they were. The excavation team realized that such issues could not be adequately addressed by traditional archaeological interpretive or visualization methods.

VIZIN modeled the Kyrenia hull and cargo in their as-discovered state (Figure 14.2) and will virtually fold the broken hull back together to form the ship just before it hit bottom to see how the objects might arrange themselves. A second, and parallel, process will be to model a digital version of the whole as-built ship, place objects as archaeologists believe they were loaded, and then virtually sink the ship. The final stages of hull collapse will be fast-forwarded to see where the items end up when the ship hits the seabed. In this way, modelers can change the starting positions of the cargo each time they simulate the sinking until the objects end up matching their as-found positions. An animation showing this process of sinking, striking the bottom, and hull decay and collapse will eventually become a teaching tool accessible on the Internet and on a DVD accompanying the final publication. Many more hypotheses about ancient seafaring can be tested this way than through the use of traditional media.

The Gurob Ship Model

This next example relates to maritime archaeology tangentially, only in that the model is of a ship model. In 1920, Flinders Petrie assigned two of his assistants to excavate Gurob, a site he had first examined three decades earlier, located on the

Figure 14.2 Rendering showing the cargo scattered across the broken hull of the Kyrenia ship; image from the VIZIN virtual reality model of the wreck site. Reproduced with the kind permission of the Institute for the Visualization of History Inc.

western edge of the desert south of Lahun, Egypt. Tomb 611 yielded fragments of a remarkable little wooden boat, which is now located in a drawer at the Petrie Museum of Egyptian Archaeology. The Gurob model is exceptional in being one of only two known nonroyal ship models from the New Kingdom. Its importance lies in the fact that it most likely represents very early evidence of the importation into Egypt of the Dionysiac cult, possibly introduced there by the so-called Sea Peoples during the end of Bronze Age upheavals that shook the eastern Mediterranean around 1200 BCE (Shelley Wachsmann, pers. comms. 2006–2007). This conclusion could only have been reached after determining what the Gurob ship actually looked like; after all, it survived in dozens of disconnected small pieces.

Wachsmann asked VIZIN to help him test his theories about the fragments' original arrangement and color, determine their original attachments or use, and provide the readers of his recent book (Wachsmann 2013) with a new ability to examine this remarkable artifact in ways a museum would never allow with the real thing. In the virtual realm, much that is not possible in the real world can be achieved, investigated, and changed. The interactive Gurob VRML models (to become available on a DVD and on VIZIN's Web site) will offer readers a radical approach to studying ancient artifacts: the VR files allow researchers not only to change the configuration of the ship model in real time, but also to click on sections of the ship model and link to the entire master photo inventory so users can test their own hypotheses against the actual data in the book (Figure 14.3).

The many advantages of interactive 3D graphics over a conventional publication and its standard array of images are apparent. How else could an author convey all of the possible ways the pieces might have fitted together? How else could

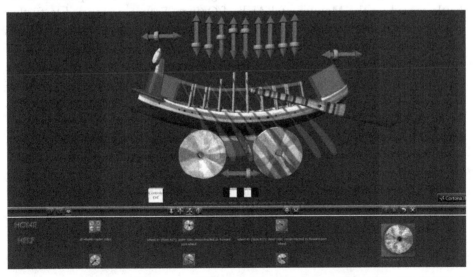

Figure 14.3 Screen grab from one of the virtual reality re-creations of the Gurob ship model; this one shows how users can manipulate elements of the model and link to accompanying images for detailed study. Reproduced with the kind permission of the Institute for the Visualization of History Inc.

publishers print so many high-resolution color images? How else could researchers examine the fragments so closely? An additional advantage of interactive computer graphics became evident during the research process, as the artifact is stored in a museum quite distant from Wachsmann's office: constant travel to view the object and ponder the function of its various components was out of the question. Interactive 3D models overcame these obstacles to research, analysis, and publication.

Actium and the Athlit Ram

In 31 BCE, Mark Antony and Cleopatra fought Octavian in what became the crucial naval battle in a war for control of the entire ancient Roman world. The two fleets clashed along the western coast of Greece; a nearby cape called Actium gave the battle its name. Two years after the battle, Octavian built a victory monument on the heights overlooking the waters where the battle had been waged. The monument has a stone podium, into one side of which masons cut specially shaped sockets to hold bronze ramming prows cut off of Antony and Cleopatra's sunken ships. The cuttings in the podium wall represent the negative shape of the backs of the projecting rams. Each socket is unique in its size and shape, reflecting the dimensions of the actual rams at their point of contact with the wall.

VIZIN, working with William M. Murray (2007, 1997), began this project by modeling the Athlit Ram. Discovered in 1980 off the coast of Israel, near Athlit, this was the first ancient bronze ram to be discovered and is one of the best preserved (Steffy 1994: 59–62). Then the monument and its sockets were modeled. The computer model of the Athlit Ram was then warped in 3DStudioMax, keeping its proportions intact, until it fit into one of the largest sockets (No. 4). Depictions of the battle carved on the Monumental Arch of Orange, France, were used to further refine the shape of the virtual ram, which could be further tweaked using fragments of sculptural stone and bronze rams found at sites from Rome to Actium.

While modeling the first ram and its socket, the team began to appreciate the challenges that faced the builders of the monument when attempting to fit the enormous rams into their sockets, and the problems faced by the artisans who designed the rams and by the founders who cast them. The models of the rams will allow researchers to examine the accuracy of claims made by various ancient writers regarding the size and composition of the warring fleets, since at Actium there is a representative sample of the rams, and thus the size of the ships, actually used in battle. Working backward from a single artifact, the team could build a large historical picture and educate archaeologists about the nature of ancient naval construction and warfare.

VENUS

VENUS (Virtual ExploratioN of Underwater Sites; VENUS 2008) is a European consortium founded in 2006 that aims to provide scientific methodologies and technological tools for the virtual exploration of deepwater archaeological sites, to establish a guide of best practices, and to show by example how virtual reality can benefit the study of deepwater and other inaccessible underwater and coastal sites. The first VENUS project (two more have followed) focused on several maritime sites known from amphora scatters discovered in 1989 from Pianosa, an island off the coast of Tuscany, Italy. The sites were mapped by divers and ROVs in 2006 using multibeam sonar, color photography, and calibrated photogrammetry. Artifact locations were marked, and examples of amphoras dating from the first century BCE to the third century CE were retrieved. Blender was used to create 3D models of a typical set of amphoras, and then the data was exported to VRML for online viewing and further research. Although the process of documenting sites and artifacts evolves, there is now a stable, widely accessible, and globally recognized intractive means of displaying the information from that process so a wide audience can appreciate the finds, the complexity of archaeological sites, and their significance to history.

East Carolina University Program in Maritime Studies

Professors and students at the East Carolina University Program in Maritime Studies have been experimenting with various 3D modeling packages (such as SurfaceWorks, PhotoModeler, and Rhinoceros), photogrammetry techniques, and their related interactive computer graphics output formats (VRML and IVS 3D) for understanding ship construction, sailing characteristics of historic vessels, and teaching maritime history around the world (including *Lady Washington*, American Civil War ironclads, and the seventeenth-century warship *Vasa*; Richards et al. 2006; Nathan Richards, Program in Maritime Studies, East Carolina University, pers. comm. 2008). Both excavation data and archival images are being used during the digital reconstruction process. All in-progress and completed models as part of coursework and field schools will be made available on the university Web site (ECU 2010). In addition, the interactive files have been ported for teaching purposes to the university's visualization wall, a 6.4 m by 1.8 m rear-projection display system used for immersive virtual reality content that, besides ships, includes the study of coastal environments, erosion, flooding, storm surges, and disaster response (RENCI 2010). Showing virtual reality on such a display has proven a remarkable adjunct for campus education and public outreach.

Interactive 3D computer graphics are important for maritime archaeology because the combination of modeling packages, interactive graphic output formats, and large immersive display options provides a unique opportunity for students, teachers, and the general public to investigate the many aspects of historic ships, their construction and sculptural details, and their lifespan.

WreckSight Software

Advanced Underwater Surveys Ltd. (ADUS 2009) is the commercial arm that evolved from collaborative research activities at two academic institutions in

Scotland, the Universities of St. Andrews and Dundee. Those activities emerged
from the recognition that many historic shipwrecks are posing environmental hazards, particularly if they contain unstable munitions or ocean contaminants. The
ADUS team utilized high-resolution multibeam sonar technology to create accurate 3D point clouds of a group of shipwrecks in situ and their local bathymetry. The
data were imported into Maya to create digital flyovers of the sites, as the basis for
more comprehensive interactive research and outreach packages (Flack and Rowland 2006). One result of the project is the WreckSight interactive 3D software
package (WreckSight 2009), which includes VR visualizations of eight wrecks from
the Scapa Flow region off the northern tip of Scotland. The package provides users
with 3D models, animations, multiple viewpoints, measurement tools, and many
more features. The results present to specialists and nonspecialists alike complex
visualizations of seabed hazards, modern ship construction, and large underwater
sites impossible to comprehend through traditional media.

Virtual Ship Project

An ambitious virtual reality project is unfolding in the Netherlands. The goal is to
build a VR model of the seventeenth-century ship described in great detail by
Amsterdam Lord Mayor Nicolaes Witsen (Witsen 1671). Users will be able to walk
through the model of the ship and remove, rotate, and examine every part of its
construction, then click on any item to access additional information about its
name, dimensions, research data, and relevant bibliography. Viewers will also be
presented with a short film demonstrating how and in what order the ship was constructed. A wiki (a Web site designed so multiple users can collaboratively edit and
comment on the content) will be added to the online interactives so that archaeologists can add information about related Dutch ships found all over the world. Thus,
an expanding knowledge bank could be generated. The package will be geared not
only to archaeologists but also to historians, shiplovers, model-builders, and anyone
interested in the Dutch Golden Age. A team of museum specialists, a ship design
and engineering studio with 3D modeling expertise, and games builders are formulating their options (Ab Hoving, Rijksmuseum, pers. comm. 2008) so that a vast
dynamic compendium of current and future information, discussion, and analysis
can be turned into a global exercise in cooperation and understanding for the benefit of all involved in maritime archaeology.

CONCLUSION: THE FUTURE

Computer modeling, simulation, and virtual reality visualizations have become an
important part of the maritime archaeologist's interpretive skill set. The increasing
use of interactive 3D computer graphics technologies for the study, teaching, and
dissemination of maritime archaeological information follows their acceptance by

the broader discipline of virtual heritage. The advantages for understanding history and its remains interactively and in three dimensions are that they provide not only new research tools but also the ability to ask new types of questions that inevitably lead to new insight into how the past actually happened, and they do so in ways that are more effective and efficient than traditional paper-based 2D images.

Currently, interactive visualizations are being used by maritime archaeologists for ship reconstructions, wreck re-creations, cargo configuration research, ancient seabed terrain analysis and interpretation, hypothesis testing, contextual simulations, and manipulation of individual objects in context or as adjunct links to other images. As demonstrated in allied humanities and scientific disciplines, interactive 3D graphics can help to dramatically expand our knowledge of the past, whether for maritime sites or heritage studies in general (e.g., the vast virtual reality and education bibliography produced by the Virtual Reality and Education Laboratory at East Carolina University [Pantelidis 2009] and the extensive virtual heritage projects of the Institute for the Visualization of History [VIZIN 2010], Learning Sites Inc. [Learning Sites 2010], the Foundation of the Hellenic World [FHW 2010], the Via Flaminia project [Flaminia 2010], and the virtual Herculaneum experience [MAV 2010]). The study of the past no longer needs to rely on the technologies of the past.

The imagery in virtual environments can be stunning, believable, and beguiling, and users of all backgrounds need to be reminded that what they are seeing is a simulation. Not only should users critically appraise the results, but purveyors of virtual maritime worlds also should provide users with markers and linked information explaining what elements in the virtual world are based on evidence and what are conjectural. The need for transparency in disseminating virtual ancient worlds has been recognized by the virtual heritage community. The London Charter (2009) has been drafted to address these issues in order to (1) provide a benchmark widely accepted by stakeholders; (2) promote intellectual and technical rigor; (3) ensure that 3D modeling processes and visualizations can be properly understood and evaluated by users; (4) enable such visualizations to contribute authoritatively to the study, interpretation, and management of cultural heritage assets; (5) ensure that access and sustainability strategies are determined and applied; and (6) provide a robust basis on which communities of good practice can be built.

As digital technologies advance, so too will the opportunities to explore underwater sites in ways that will continue to enhance our abilities to understand and teach maritime history. Given the pace of change in computer technologies, what may seem outrageously far-fetched today could become commonplace in less time than it would take to explain it. Many exciting things are already in development that have maritime virtual heritage applications:

- 3D autostereoscopic monitors: These enable users to see interactive 3D stereo worlds without the use of headsets or glasses; screens up to 107 cm already exist, displaying images that are amazingly convincing, jumping virtually 30–60 cm out in front of the screen (Phillips Electronics, NewSight, or Dimension Technologies).

- Projection holography: While the *Star Trek* holodeck is not yet attainable, the ability to project 3D holographic images onto a table with no visible means of supporting display has been demonstrated; larger, more sophisticated, color-rich, and animated environments are coming soon (e.g., HoloVizio).
- Cloud computing: Distributed online software suites (e.g., Google Chrome) that are specifically devised to harness the power of multiple and otherwise disconnected computers around the world could all work toward a single task, such as rendering a single visualization or displaying detailed virtual maritime worlds.
- Semantic networks: These are linked information sources offering real-time, natural-language, multilingual search and retrieval capabilities across images and complex text.
- The Immersive Education Media Grid: A group at Boston College is developing an open and extensible platform with a universal translator for the major yet very different interactive real-time environments of Croquet, Wonderland, 2ndLife, and VRML; the Grid will bring high-level standards and a single interface to the diverse approaches to online virtual communities (Grid 2010).
- Computer Vision: The juncture of computer processing and high-resolution cameras produces new tools for the automatic and continuous extraction of 3D data about archaeological and heritage sites, landscapes, and excavation activities using hundreds of small, inexpensive devices to capture and process still and video images, thus mitigating the need for hand-measuring, surveying, or even expensive laser scanners.

Extrapolating from current trends and projects, it is not difficult to imagine that soon we will have location-aware wearable computers linked to a 3D-based semantic Internet with the capability of projection-holographic imagery of distant, hard-to-access, or lost maritime sites. This could become the personal virtual time machine. Please use it wisely.

REFERENCES

Addison, A. C. 2000. Emerging trends in virtual heritage. *IEEE Multimedia* 7 (2): 22–25.

ADUS. 2009. Online at www.adus-uk.com/index.html. Accessed 2 February 2010.

Castro, Filipe. 2005. *The Pepper Wreck: A Portuguese Indiaman at the mouth of the Tagus River*. College Station: Texas A&M University Press.

———. 2008. Virtual nau. Online at http://nautarch.tamu.edu/shiplab/Index-virtualnau.htm. Accessed 29 January 2010.

Castro, Filipe, Nuno Fonseca, and Audrey Wells. Forthcoming (2009). Outfitting the Pepper Wreck. *Historical Archaeology*.

Catsambis, Alexis. 2006. Reconstructing vessels: From two-dimensional drawings to three-dimensional models. *INA Quarterly* 33 (1): 12–15.

Ch'ng, Eugene, and Robert J. Stone. 2006. Enhancing virtual reality with artificial life: Reconstructing a flooded European Mesolithic landscape. *Presence: Teleoperators and Virtual Environments* 15 (3): 341–352.

Ch'ng, Eugene, Robert J. Stone, and T. N. Arvanitis. 2004. The Shotton River and Mesolithic dwellings: Re-creating the past from geo-seismic data sources. In *The 5th International Symposium on Virtual Reality, Archaeology and Cultural Heritage, VAST04: Interdisciplinarity or "the best of both worlds": The grand challenge for cultural heritage informatics in the 21st century,* ed. N. S. Y. Chrysanthou, K. Cain, and F. Niccolucci, 125–133. Brussels: Eurographics Association.

Cooke, Matthew. 2008. IT helps to save the *Cutty Sark.* Online at www.bbc.co.uk/london/content/articles/2008/03/11/greenwich_cutty_university_feature.shtml. Accessed 1 February 2010.

Cutty Sark. 2005. Online at www.cuttysark.org.uk/index.cfm. Accessed 1 February 2010.

DoD. 2004. Archaeological investigation and remote operated vehicle documentation: Confederate commerce raider CSS *Alabama*—2002. Washington, DC: Department of Defense Legacy Resource Management Program (Project 02-109). Online at https://www.denix.osd.mil/portal/page/portal/content/environment/CR/ArchaeologicalRe-sources/UnderwaterArchaeology/02-109_ARCHAEOLOGICAL-INVESTIGA-TION_0.PDF. Accessed 29 January 2010.

Dorrell, Peter G. 1994. *Photography in archaeology and conservation.* 2nd ed. Cambridge: Cambridge University Press.

ECU. 2010. Online at www.ecu.edu/maritime/projects. Accessed 2 February 2010.

Fernie, Kate, and Julian D. Richards. 2003. *Creating and using virtual reality: A guide for the arts and humanities.* Oxford: Oxbow.

FHW. 2010. Foundation of the Hellenic world. Online at www.fhw.gr/fhw/index.php?lg=2. Accessed 2 February 2010.

Fitch, Simon, Vince Gaffney, and Ken Thomson. 2007. In sight of Doggerland: From speculative survey to landscape exploration. *Internet Archaeology* 22. http://intarch.ac.uk/journal/issue22/3/toc.html.

Flack, Steve, and Chris Rowland. 2006. Visualising the invisible: Visualising historic shipwrecks. *Computer Graphics* 40 (3). Online at www.siggraph.org/publications/newsletter/volume-40-number-3/visualising-the-invisible-visualising-historic-ship-wrecks-1. Accessed 2 February 2010.

Flaminia. 2010. Virtual museum of the ancient Via Flaminia. Online at www.vhlab.itabc.cnr.it/flaminia/. Accessed 2 February 2010.

Foley, Brendan. 2010a. Archaeology and technology in the Deep Sea. Rev. January 11, 2010. Online at www.whoi.edu/sbl/liteSite.do?litesiteid=2740&articleId=4364. 28 January 2010.

———. 2010b. 2005 SeaBED AUV survey of classical Greek wreck. Rev. 10 January 2010. Online at www.whoi.edu/sbl/liteSite.do?litesiteid=2740&articleId=5698. Accessed 28 January 2010.

Foley, Brendan, et al. 2009. The 2005 Chios Ancient Shipwreck Survey: New methods for underwater archaeology. *Hesperia* 78 (2): 269–305. Also online at www.whoi.edu/cms/files/2009_Foley_et_al_Hesperia_56523.pdf. Accessed 28 January 2010.

Gaffney, Vincent, Kenneth Thomson, and Simon Fitch, eds. 2007. *Mapping Doggerland: The Mesolithic landscapes of the southern North Sea.* Oxford: Archaeopress.

Greene, Elizabeth S., Mark L. Lawall, and Mark E. Polzer. 2008. Inconspicuous consumption: The sixth-century BCE shipwreck at Pabuc Burnu, Turkey. *American Journal of Archaeology* 112 (4): 685–711.

Grid. 2010. Grid Institute. Online at http://immersiveeducation.org/. Accessed 2 February 2010.

Hill, Roger W. 1994. A dynamic context recording and modelling system for archaeology. *International Journal of Nautical Archaeology* 23 (2): 141–145.

Jacobsen, Jeffrey, and Lynn Holden. 2007. Virtual heritage: Living in the past. *Techne* 10 (3, Spring): 55–61.

Jones, Toby. 2005. Recording the Newport Ship: Using three-dimensional digital recording techniques with a late medieval clinker-built merchantman. *INA Quarterly* 32 (3): 12–15.

Katzev, Michael L. 1969. The Kyrenia shipwreck. *Expedition* (Winter): 55–57.

———. 1974. Cyprus Ship discovery. *Illustrated London News* (June): 69–72.

Katzev, Susan W., and Michael L. Katzev. 1974. Last harbor for the oldest ship. *National Geographic* 146 (5): 618–625.

Kocabas, Ufuk, ed. 2008. *The old ships of the new gate / Yenikapı'nin Eski Gemileri*. Istanbul: Ege Yayinlari.

Learning Sites. 2010. Learning Sites Inc. Online at www.learningsites.com. Accessed 2 February 2010.

Lemagny, Jean-Claude, and André Rouillé, eds. 1987. *A history of photography: Social and cultural perspectives*, trans. Janet Lloyd. Cambridge: Cambridge University Press.

Lin, Shih-Han Samuel. 2003. Lading of the Late Bronze Age ship at Uluburun. MA thesis, Texas A&M University.

London Charter. 2009. The London Charter for the Computer-Based Visualisation of Cultural Heritage. Online at www.londoncharter.org. Accessed 2 February 2010.

Madov, Natasha. 2002. Como era há 2000 anos. *Veja*, 15 May 1751: 67–68. http://www2.uol.com.br/veja/idade/exclusivo/150502/p_067.html.

MAV. 2010. Museo Archeologico Virtuale. Online at www.museomav.com. Accessed 2 February 2010.

Meyers, Eric, ed. 1997. *The Oxford encyclopedia of archaeology in the Near East*. Oxford: Oxford University Press.

Moltenbrey, Karen. 2001. Preserving the past. *Computer Graphics World* 24 (9): 24–30.

Murray, William M. 1997. The Actium Project. Online at http://luna.cas.usf.edu/~murray/actium/brochure.html. Accessed 2 February 2010.

———. 2007. Recovering rams from the Battle of Actium: Experimental archaeology at Nicopolis. In *Nicopolis B: Proceedings of the Second International Nicopolis Symposium (11–15 September 2002)*, ed. Konstantinos L. Zachos, 333–341, 445–451. Preveza, Greece: Actia Nicopolis Foundation.

Newport Ship. 2010. Online at www.thenewportship.com. Accessed 3 February 2010.

Paley, Samuel M., and Donald H. Sanders. 2004. The citadel of Nimrud, Iraq: A virtual reality interactive model as a resource for world heritage preservation. In *Enter the past: The e-way into the four dimensions of cultural heritage, CAA2003, proceedings from the 31st Conference, Vienna, Austria, April 2003*, ezcd. Magistrat der Stadt Wien–Referat Kulturelles Erbe–Stadtarchæologie Wien, 541–543 and CD-ROM. British Archaeological Reports, International Series No. 1227. ArcheoPress: Oxford.

Pantelidis, Veronica S. 2009. Virtual reality and education: Information sources, a bibliography. Online at http://vr.coe.ecu.edu/vpbib.html. Accessed 2 February 2010.

Posluschny, A., K. Lambers, and I. Herzog, eds. 2008. *Layers of perception: Proceedings of the 35th International Conference on Computer Applications and Quantitative Methods in Archaeology (CAA), Berlin, Germany, April 2–6, 2007.* Vol. 10 plus CD-ROM (the relevant papers only appear on the CD-ROM). Bonn: Kolloquien zur Vor- und Frühgeschichte.

Redfern, Martin. 2004. The "Cutty Sark" faces collapse. Rev. 20 August 2004. Online at http://dofundodomar.blogspot.com/2004_08_01_dofundodomar_archive.html. Accessed 28 January 2010.

Refsland, Scot Thrane, Takeo Ojika, Alonzo C. Addison, and Robert Stone. 2000. Virtual heritage: Breathing new life into our ancient past. *IEEE Multimedia* 7 (2): 20–21.

RENCI 2010. Online at www.ecu.edu/renci/. Accessed 2 February 2010.

Richards, Nathan, Sami Seeb, Brian Diveley, and Michelle Liss. 2006. Virtual modeling and 3D photogrammetry for maritime heritage: Exercises in EOS PhotoModeler Pro 5.0. Research Report No. 18. Greenville, NC: Program in Maritime Studies, East Carolina University.

Sanders, Donald H. 1997. Archaeological virtual worlds for public education. *Computers in the Social Sciences Journal* 5 (3).

——. 1999. Virtual worlds for archaeological research and education. In *Archaeology in the age of the Internet—CAA97: Computer Applications and Quantitative Methods in Archaeology 25th Anniversary Conference, University of Birmingham, April 1997,* ed. L. Dingwall, S. Exon, V. Gaffney, S. Laflin, and M. van Leusen, 265. British Archaeological Reports No. S750. Oxford: Archaeopress.

——. 2001. Persuade or perish: Moving virtual heritage beyond pretty pictures of the past. In *Enhanced realities: Augmented and unplugged—Proceedings of the Seventh International Conference on Virtual Systems and Multimedia, 25–27 October 2001,* ed. Hal Thwaites and Lon Addison, 236–245. Los Alamitos, CA: IEEE Computer Society.

——. 2002. Virtual archaeology and museums: Where are the exhibits? In *Virtual archaeology: Proceedings of the VAST Euroconference, Arezzo, 24–25 November 2000,* ed. Franco Niccolucci, 187–194. British Archaeological Reports, International Series No. 1075. Oxford: ArcheoPress.

——. 2008. Why do virtual heritage? Case studies from the portfolio of a long-time practitioner. *Archaeology Magazine Online,* 13 March 2008. Online at www.archaeology.org/online/features/virtualheritage/. Accessed 14 November 2008.

Sanders, Donald H., and Eben Gay. 1996. VRML-Based public education: An example and a vision. *VRML Site Magazine.* Online at www.vrmlsite.com/dec96/spot2.html/. Accessed 28 January 2010.

Steffy, J. Richard. 1994. *Wooden ship building and the interpretation of shipwrecks.* College Station: Texas A&M University Press.

U.S. Navy. 2009. CSS *Alabama.* Department of the Navy, Navy History and Heritage Command, Underwater Archaeology Branch. Online at www.history.navy.mil/branches/org12-1.htm. Accessed 29 January 2010.

VENUS. 2008. Online at http://piccard.esil.univmed.fr/venus/newwebsite/. Accessed 2 February 2010.

VIZIN. 2010. The Institute for the Visualization of History Inc. Online at www.vizin.org. Accessed 2 February 2010.

Wachsmann, Shelley. *The Gurob Ship-Cart Model and Its Mediterranean Context.* College Station: Texas A&M University Press.

Wachsmann, Shelley, and Yaakov Kahanov. 1997. Shipwreck fall: The 1995 INA/CMS joint expedition to Tantura lagoon, Israel. *INA Quarterly* 24 (1): 3–18.

Wachsmann, Shelley, Yaakov Kahanov, and Jerome Hall. 1997. The Tantura B shipwreck: The 1996 INA/CMS joint expedition to Tantura lagoon. *INA Quarterly* 24 (4): 3–15.

Watts, Gordon P., and T. Kurt Knoerl. 2007. Entering the virtual world of underwater archaeology. In *Out of the blue: Public interpretation of maritime cultural resources*, ed. John H. Jameson Jr. and Della A. Scott-Ireton, 223–239. New York: Springer.

Wells, Audrey. 2008. Virtual reconstruction of a seventeeth-century Portuguese nau. MS thesis, Texas A&M University.

Witsen, Nicolaes. 1671. *Aeloude en Hedendaegse Scheepsbouw en Bestier*. Amsterdam.

WreckSight. 2009. Online at www.wrecksight.com. Accessed 4 February 2010.

CHAPTER 15

A DIGITAL LIBRARY PERSPECTIVE: THE SYNTHESIS AND STORAGE OF MARITIME ARCHAEOLOGICAL DATA TO ASSIST IN SHIP RECONSTRUCTION

CARLOS MONROY, FILIPE CASTRO, AND RICHARD FURUTA

INTRODUCTION

NAUTICAL archaeology encompasses a wide range of processes, techniques, and methodologies. Preservation is an area familiar to nautical archaeologists, mainly because artifacts, ship timbers, and fragments recovered from excavations have to be processed in order to ensure their conservation and dissemination. In a similar way, data and information pertaining to those artifacts have to be properly identified, structured, and stored to better serve the various stakeholders.

Writing about the information and data generated from archaeologically excavated shipwrecks and the need for the data's preservation and dissemination, Steffy (1994: 189) states:

> Piles of rotted timbers and broken artifacts constitute a wealth of information, yet much of that knowledge will remain unrecognized unless one develops a proper method of access to it. In the case of shipwrecks, though, access is the mastery of a discipline . . . which is essentially the means of access to the wealth of information stored in the remains of ships and boats and the orderly dissemination of the knowledge derived from them.

However, why is it important to properly contextualize these data? What principles should be followed? What are the benefits and dangers of "going digital"? How does current and future scholarship in nautical archaeology adapt to this change? In this chapter we will address these questions in an attempt to shed light on what has been done, what is being done, and what can be done in the future.

An ideal point of view would be one that encompasses equally both technology and archaeology. Our own perspective places more emphasis on the computer and information science side, but despite that bias, the ideas presented in this chapter spring from experience working with the Nautical Archaeology Digital Library (NADL), an NSF-funded and collaborative project with the Center for Maritime Archaeology and Conservation and the Center for the Study of Digital Libraries at Texas A&M University. This project is aimed at designing, implementing, and evaluating a set of informatics tools to catalog, store, and manage information relative to archaeological excavations and relate it to data in diverse formats, such as video, images, and text—namely, a body of shipbuilding treatises and related documents. In its first stage, this project focused on a particular case study: the excavation of a Portuguese Indiaman wrecked at the mouth of the Tagus River, near Lisbon, in Portugal, in September 1606 (Castro 2005). The Nautical Archaeology Digital Library built upon a number of projects ongoing at Texas A&M University's Center for the Study of Digital Libraries.

Despite the diverse disciplines involved in these projects—Hispanic and English literature, art history, and nautical archaeology—they share numerous things in common and form a whole greater than the sum of the parts. The work conducted by archaeologists and described in Doerr and Crofts (1999: 159) highlights the importance of associating the objects under study: "Archaeologists and paleontologists habitually deal with fragmented objects, which are then combined, with luck, into a single whole—a process that is highly unusual in other domains. Multiple fragments need to be identified and tracked during the entire process." Here we want to stress the importance of two levels of associations: (1) at the ship reconstruction level, the need for and importance of linking ship components; (2) at the scholarly activity level—with the goal of facilitating access to the objects under study and enhancing their dissemination to a wider audience—the interdisciplinary nature of nautical archaeology (in this case, with information and computer science). It was stimulating to see stated as an objective in the proposal for this handbook of maritime archaeology the phrase "the interdisciplinary nature of the field." It is becoming more common (although not exempt from challenges and controversies) to see the need for collaboration among scholars and disciplines; a good example is that of the digital humanities (Unsworth 2002).

TECHNOLOGY IN ARCHAEOLOGY

Although the principles and methods used in archaeological excavations have not changed much over the last few years (Ashmore and Sharer 2003; Renfrew and Bahn 2000; Thomas 1998), advances in computing, recording, and instrumentation technology have impacted both the way off-the-field work is carried out, and how the gathered data is stored, processed, and presented. Mapping tools and customizable databases, for instance, have transformed the work of archaeologists. Software such as HPASS (Green and Souter 2002), SITE SURVEYOR (Holt 2008), Photo-Modeler (Green, Matthews, and Turanli 2002), and Rhinoceros (Rhinoceros 2009) illustrate examples of applications used in nautical archaeology ranging from GPS and triangulation to CAD and 3D modeling.

In contrast to individual software and tools, the Petra Great Temple excavations (Egan, Bikai, and Zamora 2000; Joukowsky 1993) is a joint archaeological excavation in Jordan that illustrates the development of new technologies based on the archaeologists' needs. The Brown University SHAPE Laboratory (Hadingham 2000; SHAPE 2008) has developed various techniques and applied tools, such as free-form 3D models for geometric recovery, virtual environments, topography, and linguistics elements. The Theban Mapping Project (Reeves 1992; Reeves and Wilkinson 1996; Theban Mapping Project 2008) provides a comprehensive archaeological detailed map and database for every archaeological, geological, and ethnographic feature in Thebes, Egypt.

Within the scope of digital humanities, numerous scholars are embracing new technologies for the preservation, dissemination, and exploration of a wide range of collections. The Perseus Project (Crane 1988, 2002) is an example of a digital library in the context of cultural and historical heritage material. Originally focusing on ancient Greek culture, and currently including Roman and Renaissance collections, it provides a variety of visualization tools and navigation options for a collection of texts and images. The Digital Atheneum (Brown and Seales 2000, 2001) has developed new techniques for restoring, searching, and editing humanities collections. The Digital Imprint (Digital Imprint 1999) proposes a project to design standards for the electronic publication of archaeological site reports.

ARCHAEOLOGICAL DATA AND SHIP
RECONSTRUCTION

In nautical archaeology, ship reconstruction can take three forms: graphic, three-dimensional, and physical (Steffy 1994). Graphic reconstructions are primarily two-dimensional, and their weaknesses are sometimes addressed in three-dimensional models. A physical reconstruction, on the other hand, entails rebuilding the full-size vessel from the recovered and preserved timbers. This is the pinnacle of ship reconstruction, but it tends to be extremely expensive, complex, and time consuming. Regardless of the type of reconstruction, the final product tends to include reports composed of texts, photographs, and drawings.

In general, reconstructing an ancient and no-longer-existing object or environment is a daunting process, quite often subject to ambiguity. Archaeologists' decisions are based on limited and damaged physical evidence, similar existing artifacts, iconography, and textual references (Kensek, Swartz, and Cipolla 2004). One way to address the information used in the reconstruction of a physical object (temple, artifact, or ship) is to ensure that supporting evidence can be linked to the virtual object as a way to document the reconstruction process (Snyder 2004). In order to offer a meaningful interpretation of a reconstruction, Snyder (2008) also suggests the incorporation of expert commentary, primary sources, and graphic references.

Similarly, ship reconstruction can be based on inferences from partially recovered archaeological evidence and other written sources (Castro 2005; Van Duivenvoorde 2009). This is the case in the excavation of the Portuguese ship *Santo Antonio de Tanná*, whose length and breadth had to be inferred from surviving portions of the hull and parts of the frames, along with historical sources (Fraga 2007). These interpretations can be complemented with construction sequences described in textual sources such as shipbuilding treatises. A sample methodology for representing ambiguity in a nonintrusive way is proposed by Kensek and colleagues (2004). With special emphasis on ambiguity in 2D reconstructions, the authors link textual and visual information for documenting decisions made by archaeologists.

Studying the characteristics of the hull planking of *Batavia*, van Diuvenvoorde (2009) compares archaeological remains from other VOC Indiamen and yachts (VOC stands for Vereenige Oostindische Compagnie, or Dutch East India Company), along with shipbuilding charters dating to the early seventeenth century, and the late-seventeenth-century Dutch shipbuilding manuscripts of Witsen and van Ijk. Likewise, in studying the *Amsterdam*, an eighteenth-century Dutch Indiaman, Kist (1998: 44) mentions the positive outcome of employing historical records and archaeological evidence concurrently, asserting that "the differences between the model built from historical records and the real-life data from the archaeological situation were further investigated to arrive at a more detailed and comprehensive reconstruction." The author further highlights the benefits of using diverse sources for expanding the range of hypotheses pertaining to ship construction: "In some cases entirely new questions were raised about the way the ship was actually built, questions that would never have been asked working from one category of sources alone" (Kist 1998: 44).

Similarly, commenting on experimental archaeology and its application to the reconstruction of *Batavia*, Green (2006) indicates that written materials improve one's understanding of the construction of a particular vessel. While using dimensions and proportions described in contemporaneous shipbuilding treatises, Castro (2005) demonstrates a theoretical reconstruction of a Portuguese Indiaman based on very limited archaeological evidence, while Pevny (in this volume) discusses how textual evidence can be used as a guide to shipwreck reconstruction.

ENHANCING DIGITAL REPRESENTATIONS OF ARCHAEOLOGICAL DATA

A common characteristic of the previous examples is the need to connect parts of a rebuilt physical object with relevant sources and materials. Connecting relevant information serves two purposes. During the ship reconstruction phase, it enables scholars to associate a ship component under study with similar ship parts from other excavations or with descriptions in shipbuilding treatises or other written sources. In the postreconstruction period, they can support and document the decisions made, enhancing knowledge of the vessel's historical and technological contexts.

Speaking of virtual archaeological reconstructions, Forte (1997: 8) states that one of their goals is "to enhance and direct cognitive perceptions of antiquity." However, others (e.g., Kensek, Swartz, and Cipolla 2004: 175–176) warn of the risk associated with such reconstructions when supporting materials and evidence are not properly referenced:

> The risk is that virtual archaeological reconstructions can have lives of their own; they are seductive; they can seem viable. . . . Even careful scholars can be seduced by the realistic imagery, renderings, and animations. Although an archaeologist might know what the columns of a particular temple looked like (having found remains at the site), have a fairly good idea of the wall construction (from comparative buildings), but be a bit vague as to the roof of the building (some indications in text resources); still the rendering of this temple might look equally resolved, presenting the same degree of certainty for all aspects.

The use of textual and visual information in virtual ship reconstruction is characterized in the work of Hazlett (2007) and Wells (2008). Following textual descriptions in various shipbuilding treatises, Hazlett (2007) created a 3D model of a sixteenth-century Portuguese ship that constituted a database of all the timbers needed to build such a ship. The author captures the essence of his approach by calling it a "textual excavation." Although the reconstruction was primarily based on two written sources, it was complemented by additional texts, graphic materials, and archaeological evidence. By contrast, Wells (2008) created a 3D reconstruction of a Portuguese vessel based on interpreted archaeological evidence in the form of drawings. Well's iterative approach shows how new interpretations can affect the digital model.

In technical and specialized domains such as nautical archaeology, linking materials can be difficult given the media and language of the sources. One example is the case of photographs and technical illustrations that only partially show a section of a ship; given perspective, distance, and parallax errors, it is not always possible to reconcile such illustrations with other sources of data. Similarly, shipbuilding treatises written in different languages, words whose meaning changed over time, and technical concepts that are difficult to understand are also issues to contend with.

Given the collaborative nature of ship reconstruction, and in an effort to standardize data storage, it can be tempting to impose, from the technology side, rules about what and how information should be gathered and structured. Yet within archaeology and among individual scholars, diverse idiosyncratic practices are used. This observation also applies to large amounts of information from decades of research already archived. Thus, adopting a standardized model is challenging.

Despite these complexities and challenges, some degree of standardization and integration are possible. ETANA-DL demonstrates a conceptual model for cataloguing and storing information from numerous archaeological excavations, along with tools for browsing and visualizing that information (Shen et al. 2008). By contrast, Kansa (2005) proposes a model based on data mediation and data warehousing. A third example, Arachne, is a multidisciplinary initiative, encompassing numerous institutions, that provides an electronic repository (database) of the German Institute for Archaeology. According to the latest available statistics, their collection holds about 500,000 scanned images and 250,000 objects (Foertsch 2009).

The Digital Archive Network for Anthropology and World Heritage (DANA-WH 2009) is a distributed, interconnected repository of information pertaining to human heritage objects in various media, including two- and three-dimensional representations of artifacts. Likewise, OCHRE at the University of Chicago (OCHRE 2010) is a system based on an abstract representation that enables the integration from diverse sources, formats, and media.

These examples suggest that the adoption of a mechanism for describing and cataloguing archaeological artifacts is not only possible, but advisable. Also, since part of the post-excavation analysis entails comparing data and information from multiple sources, descriptions of the relationships among components are necessary. Nonetheless, proposing a comprehensive list of characteristics is not an easy undertaking because properties of the objects under study vary. In addition, the way in which ship components are related is unique. Even when there was a certain standardization (after the seventeenth century and in large-scale state shipyards), scantlings were always adjusted for each particular instance: scarfs, although classified in types, were hand-crafted and always different and dependent on the position of knots, waning edges, or wood grain patterns; and fastening holes were randomly positioned within very small areas, generally defined by rigid patterns (e.g., two staggered spikes per frame on each plank), thus generating unique combinations.

Nautical Archaeology Digital Library (NADL)

Texas A&M University's aforementioned Nautical Archaeology Digital Library has archaeologists embrace technology as part of their methodology in an effort to continue the pioneering work of J. Richard Steffy. Steffy's work in designing a relational database to store information pertaining to hundreds of shipwrecks deserves special consideration for several reasons. This was an attempt born from the archaeologists' needs rather than imposed from outside. Steffy realized the importance and difficulties associated with using a computational system in the conceptualization and description of archaeological data about ship components. Unlike presenting information as a list of ship timbers and fragments, as would be the case with a spreadsheet, his model intuitively represents properties and relationships among components.

Regardless of the required information about objects recovered both at the excavation site and at the different postprocessing stages, what is recorded has to follow a procedure to allow future reference to those objects, as well as thorough descriptions of their characteristics, conditions, and relationships. In this context, Steffy's approach for cataloguing wooden vessels suggests the following top-level categories: project details, principal data, hull components, auxiliary components, wood types, keel or keel plank, frames, planking, plank/frame, fastening systems, edge-joinery systems, and internal structures.

Although a complete explanation of every item in this model is beyond the scope of this chapter, a few examples help to illustrate how they are related and used. It also highlights some limitations. The first advantage this model provides is a method for categorizing elements. Categories can be used to narrow down retrieved elements during search operations. They can also be used for enhancing visualization by grouping items belonging to the same category.

Some items in the model indicate characteristics about ship components. For example, under the category "keel," the item "molded" indicates the height of the keel section. The item "sided" includes the keel section width, and the average floor timber or double frame siding at keel. In the case of the category "edge-joinery systems," information pertaining to single-layered mortise-and-tenon-joined hulls includes characteristics such as depth and width of the mortise, length and width of the tenon, distance from center to center between mortises, maximum diameter of the pegs (if present), and so on.

System Architecture

Growing out of the model pioneered by Steffy, the Nautical Archaeology Digital Library project has expanded and adopted a system architecture that enables it to undertake multisource data integration, as depicted in Figure 15.1. Documents (D_1, D_2, ... D_k), for example, are encoded in XML and segmented by page. Each document, which could be a treatise, thesis, dissertation, report, journal articles, and so on, is associated with a language, which then allows the use of the proper stemmer in the creation of a full text index. The full text index tool selected is Lucene (Apache Lucene Project 2009). Each word in the glossary is stemmed and searched in the full text index; the result is a set of documents that each contain that particular word. Identifying terms in the text of each document with entries in the glossary requires a parser and a tagger. The parser reads lines of text from the original XML transcriptions. An XSLT template removes existing tags, leaving only words. The tagger searches each (stemmed) word in the glossary. If a match is found, the word

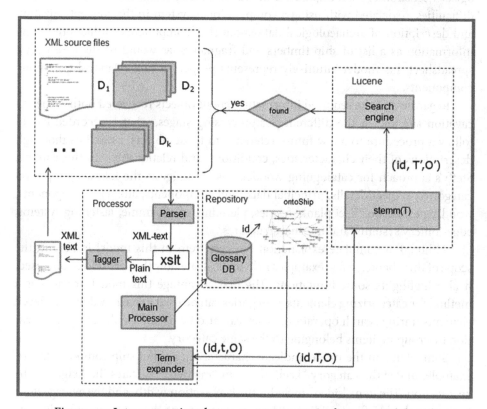

Figure 15.1 Interconnections between components in the proposed digital data management architecture. Reproduced with the kind permission of the Nautical Archaeology Digital Library project.

is enclosed in a tag with the corresponding identification key from the glossary. Words without match in the glossary are left unchanged. The new line is saved in the XML file. Matching words is carried out not only by searching for a word in a particular language. The term expander extends the query by using spellings and synonyms. Therefore, the original term *(id, T, O)* is transformed into *(id, T', O')*, where *id* is the term key, *T'* is the stemmed term, and *O'* are all the stemmed synonyms and spellings. In addition, tagging can be further enhanced by using the definitions from the ontology (called ontoShipDS), because it relates words and expresses relationships. These relationships allow the NADL user to summon a wide range of information in diverse formats, from tagged images to portions of texts on shipbuilding, to similar archaeological sites, outlining analogies and parallels, and contextualizing the object of the user's search (e.g., keel scarfs or floor timber/futtock fastening patterns).

A further component of the architecture is a glossary of nautical terms (called glosShip). This component is based on a relational database. In this model, a master table stores unique identifiers for each term. In an alternate table, all translations of that term along with its roles (synonyms and spellings) are stored. This includes definitions in each language. Similarly, there are two additional tables for taxonomy and categories.

From a computational perspective, the original entity-relation model (as proposed by Steffy) contained inconsistencies and redundancies. However, his design offers a unique depiction of information about the properties and relationships of ship components. This illustrates how an attempt to automate the storage of archaeologically generated data turned into what is primarily a mechanism for the preservation of knowledge about wooden vessels that had otherwise been almost impossible to achieve. But more importantly, his work provided the building blocks for the creation of an ontological representation and conceptualization of wooden ships.

The first step in the normalization of the original model required a thorough analysis of the database structure; concepts representing similar ideas were grouped. In addition, the original model influenced, and provided the foundation for the definition of, the six top-level categories: Component, Concept, Object, Property, Technique, and Ship. "Component" describes any physical object that is a structural part of the ship. "Concept" contains general information about a vessel, such as its type and dimensions. "Object" includes objects that do not play a structural role in the ship but are necessary for fastening, joining, and attaching components. "Property" describes the materials ship components are made of (for example, wood and metal). "Technique" lists the different techniques used in building a ship. Techniques, in turn, are divided into categories based on the components of the ship where they are employed (e.g., ceiling, chocking, nailing, and planking). "Ship," on the other hand, contains general information about (wooden) ships.

The structure of one category proposed in Steffy's original database, Hull Components, illustrates part of this transformation. Attributes such as single and double planking and common and transverse ceiling originally had their own entry in the table. Then two things surfaced. First, they belonged to two different categories: planking and ceiling. Therefore, they were converted from a noncategorized representation into a categorized one. Further discussions with domain experts suggested another conceptual ambiguity. If this table described components of a ship, the terms discussed here—ceiling and planking—were not really components, but rather techniques. This case was found in other tables, suggesting the creation of the Technique category. This new category was used to encompass any type of technique.

A second observation indicated that a number of properties (of ship components) in the original design were characterized further in specific separated individual tables. Each of these tables included its own list of properties. This was the case for Keel, Plank, and Frame. What emerged at this point was the need for the creation of a new category that summarized components in general. This finding, coupled with the contents of other tables, led to the creation of the category Components, which was then broken down into Hull Component, Auxiliary Component, and Internal Structure.

Another characteristic shared among objects in numerous tables was the material they were made of (for example, metal and wood). This characteristic led to the development of the Property category. "Wood" itself was then divided into various wood species used in the components of a ship. This makes it possible to represent the fact that any wooden component of a ship fits into a particular specie. All components that did not play a structural role on the ship were classified under the category Object. Similar to Property, this category enables objects to be associated with various structural components. For example, there are various techniques for fastening a frame to a plank, and each technique uses different objects, such as nails, treenails, and bolts. The original definition of the table titled "Plank/Frame Fastening Systems" is depicted in Figure 15.2. As the name suggests, this table contained information about the techniques used in fastening planks and frames. Of the contents in this table, only items 2 and 3 correspond to techniques. Item 4 is a property that applies only to metallic objects (e.g., nails). Items 5, 8, and 10 are properties that applied to certain objects described in 2. For example, "end" refers to the type of technique used in placing the nails. This technique, however, does not apply to treenails. Items 6, 7, and 9 describe measurements of certain objects. Item 6 refers only to shafts (item 5), item 7 only to nails (included in item 2), and item 9 to treenails (included in item 2). What this example illustrates is that a database can provide one with an initial understanding about a concept. However, it also shows the inconsistencies in describing properties, as well as the difficulties in finding relationships. For example, item 3 states that a wale can be fastened using a different method than the one used in fastening frames with planks.

Supporting Materials: Textual Representations of Ships

As stated earlier, two means of representing and describing ships are textual and visual. Textual representations are mainly contained (although not exclusively) in shipbuilding treatises, contracts, and descriptions. As they pertain to the

XI. **Plank/Frame Fastening Systems**
1. ID (vessel ID)
2. system (type of fastening system – [N] for nailed; [T] for treenailed; [N/T] for combinations; [L] for ligatured; [PT] for nails encased in plug treenails; [B] for bolted; [O] for other; [X] for unknown
3. wale (type of wale fastenings, if different than plank fasteners)
4. metal (type of metal)
5. shaft (square, round, or other)
6. thick (shaft thickness or diameter, in cm)
7. head (head diameter or maximum dimension, in cm)
8. end ([CL] if the end of the nail was simply bent over; [DCL] for double-clenched applications; [S] for straight nailing)
9. diam (treenail diameter, in cm)
10. wedge (if a treenail, was it wedged? yes or no)

Figure 15.2 Original definition of the table "Plank/Frame Fastening Systems" in Richard J. Steffy's model. Reproduced with the kind permission of the Nautical Archaeology Digital Library project.

representation of composite objects, these descriptions can complement visual abstractions of ships. A narrative accompanying an illustration often offers a more detailed description of what is graphically shown. Shipbuilding treatises are technical texts, both printed and manuscript. Although their contents vary, they describe (among other things), the properties and types of wood, methods, measurements, and construction sequences of a particular type of ship. Figure 15.3 offers partial depictions of various shipbuilding treatises. Superimposed rectangles correspond to labels used for indexing and retrieving those images in the collection.

Treatises offer valuable information about ship design, construction techniques, and the evolution of shipbuilding in general, always within a more general historical and cultural context. In a wider context, treatises provide numerous possibilities for linking textual descriptions with visual representations and archaeological evidence. Linked materials can help in testing hypotheses in the reconstruction of a damaged, incomplete, and (often) unknown composite physical object. They can also help in the disambiguation and understanding of terms, concepts, and construction techniques across numerous naval traditions and through time.

A digital library infrastructure for storing and presenting shipbuilding treatises is discussed in Monroy, Furuta, and Castro 2007. The NADL collection of treatises offers a diverse geographical, linguistic, and chronological background of written sources, at present representing 15 texts in Portuguese, French, Italian, Dutch, English, German, and Latin, spanning a period from the late sixteenth to the early eighteenth centuries. Unfortunately, not all of the documents have been transcribed; most are available only as digital images.

Making these sources searchable and allowing linkages between them is based on a tagging methodology. Images are manually tagged with labels that correspond to important words in the text depicted. Although this is a time-consuming process,

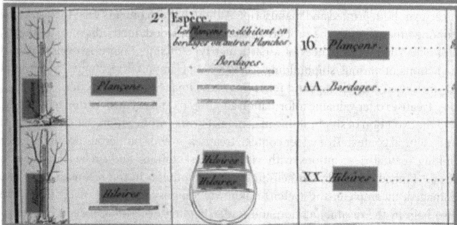

Figure 15.3 Partial depiction of tagged treatises: At the top, Bartolomeu's *Nautica Mediterranea* (1601) with the labels toggled on. In the middle, Bushnell's *The Complete Ship-wright* (1669). At the bottom, *Des bois propres au service des arsenaux* (1813). Reproduced with the kind permission of the Nautical Archaeology Digital Library project.

it is more accurate than applying optical character recognition. These labels are stored as text in a database, making them searchable. Figures 15.4 and 15.5 show tagged images of both treatises and photographs.

However, tagged texts are only the first step in enhancing the resources in the collection. Given the characteristics of the texts (written in diverse languages), a

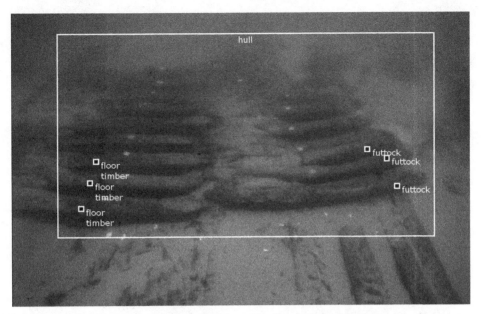

Figure 15.4 Partial depiction of a photograph of a section of the hull of the Pepper Wreck along with two types of labels: areas (hull) and points (futtocks and floor timbers). Photograph courtesy of Filipe Castro. Reproduced with the kind permission of the Nautical Archaeology Digital Library project.

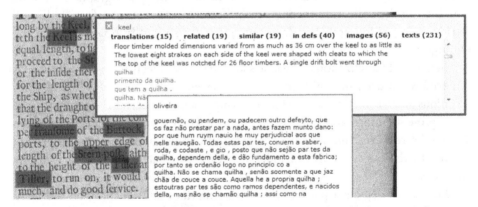

Figure 15.5 Partial detail of the Nautical Archaeology Digital Library interface, including the image of a treatise, labels, contextual information, and textual transcription. Reproduced with the kind permission of the Nautical Archaeology Digital Library project.

multilingual glossary of nautical terms was created. In this context, a glossary is useful for understanding definitions of words in a specialized domain and for allowing cross-language retrieval. The glossary allows terms to be categorized, which enables searching terms based on functional properties (structural, ornamental, joining, etc.) and spatial properties (location in the ship, such as stern, bow, and upper or lower decks).

Supporting Materials: Visual Representations of Ships

The components of a vessel can be also depicted graphically. Three of the most common types of visual representation are technical illustrations from the treatises, drawings, and photographs of timbers and ship fragments, whether in situ or following archaeological recovery. It is important to note that as an excavation progresses and as recovered timbers and ship remains undergo various conservation treatments, new photographs are generated, revealing patterns and details that were previously hidden. Each of these three sources offers different perspectives in the conceptualization of a vessel and can be used in various ways in the reconstruction of ships.

Visual representations can augment the understanding of a vessel and its components. For instance, text snippets in isolation can be difficult to contextualize. A visual environment provides extra clues for understanding a term or concept. Viewing a term in association with other ship components can enhance cognition on two levels: (1) the term itself, since related components give additional information, and (2) the ship as a whole, since the aggregation of components helps to conceptualize how a vessel was built and what techniques and materials were used.

Figure 15.4 shows an underwater photograph depicting the preserved section of a hull, including floor timbers and futtocks. The labels in the photograph have been previously inserted and can be used to index the photograph. Therefore, searching in the collection for the words "futtock," "floor timber," or "hull" will retrieve this photograph. Labels are also useful to identify objects within the photograph.

Better contextualization using labels for retrieving objects from the collection is achieved when used in conjunction with other elements. Because available transcriptions have been indexed using a full-text engine (Lucene), clicking on the labels presents information in a wider context. The expansion algorithm used in this model retrieves thumbnails of images containing labels matching the word entered in the query. It also includes text excerpts matching the query in any language.

Figure 15.5 depicts a partial view of the interface after clicking on the word "keel." In the background is the image of a treatise (*The Complete Ship-wright*, Bushnell 1669) along with labeled areas (dark semi-transparent rectangles). It also includes contextual information related to (1) *translations* of the word "keel" to other languages (in this case, 15 translations); (2) *related terms*, which are words in the definition of "keel" that have entries in the glossary (in this case, 19 words); (3) *similar terms*, which are words in the glossary that include the word "keel," for example, "bilge keel," "sister keel," and "drop keel" (19 instances); (4) *in definitions*, that is, words in the glossary whose definitions include the word "keel" (40 instances); (5) *images*, that is, illustrations or photographs that include the word "keel" (56 instances); and (6) lines in all texts where the word "keel" appears in any language (visible are English and Portuguese occurrences). In the foreground is a segment of a page after clicking on one of the returned texts (*Livro da fabrica das naus*, Oliveira c. 1580).

Defining an Ontology of Wooden Ships

The preceding sections covered textual and visual abstractions of ships. Regardless of the media employed, in the end the same reality is represented: a ship. In order to enhance the representation of ships, two approaches can be adopted. One is the use of metadata. Metadata is "data about data." It has a long history of use in library sciences because it can be used to describe books. For example, title, author, year of publication, and type of publication enable cataloging, classification, and searching. In the case of ships, metadata for describing a component of a ship (e.g., the keel) could be wood, length, width, and joints. This would allow users to search for keels based on the kind of wood, their dimensions, and what joining techniques might have been used.

A richer and more flexible approach is the use of an ontology. An ontology is the formalization and conceptualization of a domain. Using the example of the keel, a frame could be related to a keel, since they can be attached to each other. This kind of relationship is difficult to capture solely with metadata to be derived from the glossary.

The original conceptualization (expressed as a relational database) of ship components designed by Steffy was used as a starting point in the creation of a ship ontology. The first step was a preliminary analysis of the structure of the database. To facilitate this process, Protégé was used as an editing interface (Protégé 2009). Throughout various sessions, unknown concepts were clarified by nautical archaeology experts. This allowed the removal of redundancies and inconsistencies, while ensuring proper classification.

In order to define the scope of an ontology, it is important to formulate a list of questions (known as competency questions) that the ontology should answer (Gruninger and Fox 1995). Although it is impossible to list all potential questions, the following list provides a general idea of what the ontology should aim to answer: What kind of planking technique was used in a ship given the fastening objects found in an excavation? What were the frame dimensions of a ship based on a specific fastening technique? What planking pattern do holes and cuts in a timber suggest? What is the best joining method for a particular type of planking? Is it possible to see all assembling techniques for certain timbers? What can be learned from the wood used in building a vessel? What are the best types of woods for the various parts of a vessel? What do dimensions of a recovered piece suggest in terms of the size of another timber that was not found? In short, the ontology should be able to depict as many of the components of a wooden ship as possible; to describe their properties, how they are assembled, and what objects are used in their assembly; and to present instances of ships that document the techniques previously listed.

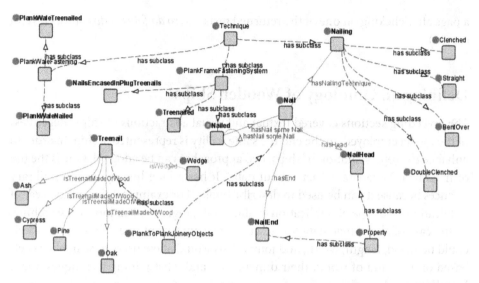

Figure 15.6 Graphic representation of the concepts and properties of Plank/Frame Fastening Systems defined in the ontology using Protégé. Reproduced with the kind permission of the Nautical Archaeology Digital Library project.

Unlike a database approach, an ontological representation enables a richer description of concepts. Figure 15.6 shows a graphical representation of a Plank/Frame Fastening System from ontoShipDS in Protégé. Various facts can be learned from this representation. For instance, the direction of the arrows indicates membership to classes. Thus, Plank/Frame Fastening System is a subclass of Technique. In turn, there are various Plank/Fastening Systems: Treenailed, Nailed, Combinations, NailsEncasedInPlugTreenails, Bolted, and Unknown. Also, it can be inferred that some fastening techniques use shafts and are made of metal.

Characteristics and properties of ship components and objects can also be described in an ontology. For example, a ship can be described in terms of certain properties such as general dimensions, which include length, breadth, length-to-beam ratio, depth in hold, and displacement. In ontoShipDS, these properties were categorized under Concepts. Although it can be argued that these categories could be considered properties (and conceptually they are), the adopted categorization suits the needs in this domain.

Figure 15.7 shows the photograph of a frame belonging to the Pepper Wreck (Castro 2005), with two additional pieces of information superimposed: a list of properties from the ontology, and a definition from the glossary (this is a mock-up). Properties from the ontology make explicit several additional facts about frames—for example, that there are various framing techniques, and that frames can be fastened, joined, or chocked, which in turn implies that there should be objects used in joining frames. In some cases rider frames (a frame that goes on top of the ceiling) can be also used along with frames. This list exemplifies the way the ontology and the glossary can augment objects in the collection.

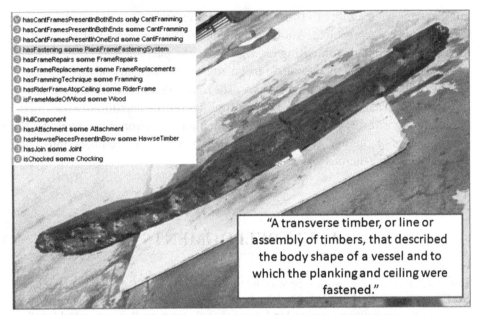

Figure 15.7 Photograph of a frame along with a list of properties defined in the ontology (top left), and a definition from the glossary (bottom right). Photograph by Filipe Castro. Reproduced with the kind permission of the Nautical Archaeology Digital Library project.

CONCLUSION

In this chapter we have outlined some ideas about the role of computational technology in assisting nautical archaeologists. Linking and associating supporting materials in more meaningful ways improves the contextualization of information. This in turn facilitates the understanding of the techniques used in ship construction. In addition, presenting related facts and data in more relevant ways enables the discovery of building patterns.

For nautical archaeologists, access to the contents of archived resources and the easy addition of new materials increase the availability of relevant information for documenting scholarly work. It can also reduce the time required to publish new archaeological findings. An important lesson learned throughout the work with NADL is how information technology infrastructure fosters multidisciplinary collaboration. Furthermore, the work of Richard Steffy highlights the impact of computing technology for ensuring long-term preservation of scholarly collections.

From the perspective of an integrated scholarly infrastructure, we are still in the early years of the use of information technology in nautical archaeology. Although the number of available tools has increased, and projects in digital media are more common, new questions have emerged.

It is clear that digital collections facilitate the dissemination of archaeological data. However, there is an ongoing debate about the associated issues with guaranteeing accessibility to those sources once existing formats change or software tools become obsolete. Another challenge is the conversion of archived information and data documenting excavations in the past decades.

It would be unfair not to also recognize here the benefits of this interdisciplinary collaboration to computer science. The materials and the scholarly practices in nautical archaeology offer unique opportunities for the creation of novel methodologies, algorithms, and interfaces. This fascinating environment resembles the long journeys of the age of exploration, when sailors would embark into often unknown and treacherous waters.

ACKNOWLEDGMENTS

This material is based on work supported by the National Science Foundation under Grant No. IIS-0534314. Special thanks to Dr. Wendy van Duivenvoorde for her invaluable perspective on nautical archaeology and to Mr. J. Richard Steffy for providing an invaluable collection of information on timbers recovered from underwater excavations.

REFERENCES

Apache Lucene Project. 2009. *Welcome to Lucene!* Rev. 25 February 2010. Online at http://lucene.apache.org/. Accessed 10 March 2010.

Ashmore, Wendy, and Robert Sharer. 2003. *Discovering our past: A brief introduction to archaeology.* New York: McGraw-Hill.

Brown, Michael, and William Seales. 2000. Beyond 2D images: Effective 3D imaging for library materials. *Proceedings of the 5th ACM (Association for Computing Machinery) Conference on Digital Libraries,* June 2000, San Antonio, TX, 27–36. New York: Association for Computing Machinery.

———. 2001. The digital Atheneum: New approaches for preserving, restoring and analyzing damaged manuscripts. *Proceedings of the First ACM/IEEE-CS Joint Conference on Digital Libraries,* June 2001, Roanoke, VA, 437–443. New York: Association for Computing Machinery.

Castro, Filipe. 2005. The Pepper Wreck: Nossa Senhora dos Mártires, Lisbon, Portugal. In *Beneath the Seven Seas,* ed. George Bass, 39–45. London: Thames & Hudson.

Crane, Gregory. 1988. The Perseus Project: An interactive curriculum on classical Greek civilization. *Educational Technology* 28 (11): 25–32.

———. 2002. Cultural heritage digital libraries: Needs and components. In *Proceedings of ECDL 2001,* ed. Maristella Agosti and Constantino Thanos. Lecture Notes in Computer Science No. 2458, 626–637. Berlin: Springer-Verlag.

Digital Archive Network for Anthropology and World Heritage. 2009. *The Digital Archive Network for Anthropology and World Heritage.* Rev. 10 January 2010. Online at http://www.dana-wh.net/home/. Accessed 30 August 2009.

Digital Imprint. 1999. *Society for American Archaeology Bulletin* 17 (5). Rev. 29 October 2009. Online at http://www.saa.org/Portals/0/SAA/publications/SAAbulletin/17-5/saa11.html. Accessed 15 January 2010.

Doerr, Martin, and Nicholas Crofts. 1999. Electronic Esperanto: The role of the object oriented CIDOC reference model. In *Proceedings of the International Cultural Heritage Informatics Meeting*, ed. David Bearman and Jennifer Trant, 157–173. Toronto: Archives & Museum Informatics.

Egan, Virginia, Patricia Bikai, and Kurt Zamora. 2000. Archaeology in Jordan. *American Journal of Archaeology* 104 (3): 561–588.

Foertsch, Reinhard. 2009. *ARACHNE—Datenbank und kulturelle Archive des Forschungsarchivs für Antike Plastik Koeln und des Deutschen Archaeologischen Instituts*. Rev. 1 January 2010. Online at http://arachne.uni-koeln.de/. Accessed 10 December 2009.

Forte, Maurizio. 1997. Introduction. In *Virtual archaeology: Re-creating ancient worlds*, ed. Maurizio Forte and Alberto Siliotti, 8–13. New York: Harry N. Abrams.

Fraga, Tiago. 2007. *Santo Antonio de Tanna*: Story and reconstruction. MA thesis, Texas A&M University.

Green, Jeremy. 2006. Nautical archaeology in Australia, the Indian Ocean and Asia. In *Maritime archaeology: Australian approaches*, ed. Mark Staniforth and Michael Nash, 97–110. New York: Springer.

Green, Jeremy, Sheila Matthews, and Tufan Turanli. 2002. Underwater archaeological surveying using Virtual Mapper: Different applications for different problems. *International Journal of Nautical Archaeology* 31 (2): 283–292.

Green, Jeremy, and Corioli Souter. 2002. Archaeological application of the HPASS (High Precision Acoustic Surveying System) to surveys of the HMS Pandora wreck-site and the Roman bridge at Maastricht. *International Journal of Nautical Archaeology* 31 (2): 273–282.

Gruninger, Michael, and Mark Fox. 1995. Methodology for the design and evaluation of ontologies. In *Proceedings of the Workshop on Basic Ontological Issues in Knowledge Sharing*, 1–10. August 1995. Montreal, Canada.

Hadingham, Evan. 2000. Secrets of a desert metropolis: The hidden wonders of Petra's ancient engineers. *Scientific American Discovering Archaeology* 2 (4): 70–74.

Hazlett, Alex. 2007. The nau of the Livro Náutico: Reconstructing a sixteenth-century Indiaman from texts. PhD diss., Texas A&M University.

Holt, Peter. 2008. *Site recorder database schema*. 3H Consulting Software. Plymouth, UK.

Joukowsky, Martha. 1993. Archaeological excavations and survey of the Southern Temple at Petra, Jordan. *Annual of the Department of Antiquities of Jordan* 38: 293–322.

Kansa, Eric. 2005. A community approach to data integration: Authorship and building meaningful links across diverse archaeological data sets. *Geosphere* 1 (2): 97–109.

Kensek, Karen, Lynn Swartz, and Nicholas Cipolla. 2004. Fantastic reconstruction or reconstructions of the fantastic? Tracking and presenting ambiguity, alternatives, and documentation in virtual worlds. *Automation in Construction* 13: 175–186.

Kist, Jennifer. 1998. Integrating archaeological and historical records in research. In *Maritime archaeology: A reader of substantive and theoretical contributions*, ed. Lawrence Babing and Hans van Tilburg, 39–46. New York: Plenum.

Krasniewicz, Louise. 2009. *CSA Newsletter: Digital publishing at UCLA's Institute of Archaeology*. Rev. Fall 1999. Online at http://csanet.org/newsletter/fall99/nlf9901.html/. Accessed 15 September 2009.

Monroy, Carlos, Richard Furuta, and Filipe Castro. 2007. Texts, illustrations, and physical objects: The case of ancient shipbuilding treatises. In *Proceedings of ECDL 2007*, ed.

László Kovács, Norbert Fuhr, and Carlo Meghini, 198–209. Lecture Notes in Computer Science No. 4675. Berlin: Springer.

OCHRE. 2010. *Welcome to OCHRE.* Rev. 30 March 2009. Online at http://ochre.lib.uchicago.edu/. Accessed 2 February 2010.

Protégé. 2009. *The Protégé Ontology Editor and Knowledge Acquisition System.* Rev. 1 January 2010. Online at http://protege.stanford.edu/. Accessed 20 May 2009.

Reeves, Nicholas. 1992. *After Tut'ankhamun: Research and excavation in the Royal Necropolis at Thebes.* London: Kegan Paul.

Reeves, Nicholas, and Richard Wilkinson. 1996. *The complete Valley of the Kings: Tombs and treasures of Egypt's greatest pharaohs.* London: Thames & Hudson.

Renfrew, Colin, and Paul Bahn. 2000. *Archaeology: Theories, methods and practice.* London: Thames & Hudson.

Rhinoceros. 2009. *Modeling Tools for Designers.* Rev. 1 January 2007. Online at http://www.rhino3d.com. Accessed 3 October 2009.

SHAPE. 2008. The SHAPE Lab @ Brown University. Rev. June 2004. Online at http://www.lems.brown.edu/vision/extra/SHAPE/. Accessed 15 December 2009.

Shen, Rao, Naga Vemuri, Weiguo Fan, and Edward Fox. 2008. Integration of complex archaeology digital libraries: An ETANA-DL experience. *Information Systems* 33: 699–723.

Snyder, Lisa. 2004. Real-time visual simulation models in an exhibition environment. In *Proceedings of IEEE Virtual Reality Workshop: Virtual Reality for Public Consumption,* ed. Yashushu Ikei, Martin Göbel, and Jim Chen, 267. Chicago, March 2004. New Jersey: Institute of Electrical and Electronics Engineers.

———. 2008. The devil in the details: Reconstructing Chicago's White City. Poster presented at the 2008 Chicago Colloquium on Digital Humanities and Computer Science. Chicago, November 2008.

Steffy, Richard. 1994. *Wooden ship building and the interpretation of shipwrecks.* College Station: Texas A&M University Press.

Theban Mapping Project. 2008. *Theban Mapping Project.* Rev. 1 January 2008. Online at http://www.thebanmappingproject.com/about/. Accessed 17 February 2010.

Thomas, David. 1998. *Archaeology.* Fort Worth: Harcourt Brace College Publishers.

Unsworth, John. 2002. What is humanities computing, and what is not? In *Jahrbuch für Computerphilologie,* ed. Georg Braungart, Karl Eibl, and Fotis Jannidis, 71–84. Paderborn: Mentis Verlag.

van Duivenvoorde, Wendy. 2009. More than just bits of hull: Expensive oak, laminate construction, and goat hair; New insights on *Batavia*'s archaeological hull remains. *Tijdschrift voor Zeegeschiedenis* 28 (2): 59–68, 72–73.

Wells, Audrey. 2008. Virtual reconstruction of a seventeenth century Portuguese nau. MS thesis, Texas A&M University.

PART III

SHIPS AND SHIPWRECKS

CHAPTER 16

....

EARLY SHIPBUILDING IN THE EASTERN MEDITERRANEAN

....

MARK E. POLZER

INTRODUCTION

....

WHEN did cultures in the eastern Mediterranean start building ships? The answer, quite simply, is that we don't know. Some researchers claim that stone implements and skeletal remains found on Crete and Sardinia and in southern Spain testify to seafaring in the Pleistocene by early hominids (Bednarik 1999; Facchini and Giusberti 1992; Johnstone 1988: 3; Martini 1992; Sondaar et al. 1995). While such assertions may one day be proven, they are not yet widely accepted, and methodological questions have been raised about the dating and interpretation of such evidence (Bower 1997, 2010; Cherry 1992). The earliest established evidence for sea trade and, by implication, the use of seagoing watercraft in the Mediterranean are Mesolithic stone tools found in Franchthi Cave in the Argolid (Jacobsen 1969: 343, 1973: 76–77, 82–85; Renfrew, Dixon, and Cann 1965: 225; see additional bibliographical information in Tzalas 1995: 459–462). Studies have shown that they were fashioned from obsidian gathered on the island of Melos in the Cyclades, which lies some 120 km across open sea from the mainland (Aspinall, Feather, and Renfrew 1972: 333; Cann and Renfrew 1964: 111; Renfrew et al. 1971: 242; see Johnstone 1973: 3–4 for a good summary). Those responsible for the obsidian were familiar with the sea and probably had been voyaging among the islands of the Aegean for a long time (Cann, Dixon, and Renfrew 1965: 225; Cherry 1990). What sort of vessels they employed is not known, but scholars have argued for both dugouts (Basch 1987: 77; Casson 1995: 31; Johnstone 1973: 6; Wachsmann 1998: 74) and reed craft (Johnstone 1973: 4–6; Tzalas 1995), based partly on available building materials and tools but also largely on later representations of descendant craft. The answer, perhaps, is both dugouts and reed craft, and others as well (Marangou 2003).

Indeed, the difficulty in studying the construction of early watercraft is precisely that most of the evidence is in the form of artistic representation—boat depictions decorating pottery, drawn on rocks, painted on walls, and sculpted in various media— that is often difficult to interpret and limited with respect to the details of construction. In order to understand how ancient shipwrights conceived and designed their hulls, and the constructional features—materials, scantlings, joinery, building techniques and procedures—that gave form and functionality to the vessels, we are best served by evidence from the ships themselves. Therefore, in the limited confines of this chapter, we will focus our discussion of early shipbuilding in the eastern Mediterranean on archaeological hull remains provided by shipwreck and terrestrial excavations. Egypt has proven to be the largest repository of early ancient watercraft; to date, archaeologists have found remains from more than 20 ancient boats spanning 2,500 years of Egyptian civilization. It is fitting, then, that we begin our discussion there.

EGYPT

Riverine Craft

Two Predynastic boat models from about 4000 BCE (Hayes 1964: 233; Brunton and Caton-Thompson 1928: 34, pl. 23.33) provide the earliest evidence for watercraft in ancient Egypt, although by then Egyptians probably had been building rafts capable of navigating the main channel of the Nile for at least three millennia (Hendrickx and Vermeersch 2000: 35). These early watercraft were simple bundles of reeds lashed together (Casson 1995: 11), but by the mid-fourth millennium BCE, Egyptians were constructing plank-built wooden boats (Ward 2004: 13). Beginning in dynastic times, boat representations by the thousands decorate the tombs and funerary monuments of Egypt's royalty and elite. In times of prosperity, these included both elaborate boat models and full-size boats interred with the deceased, either within or near the tomb and sacred enclosure (Ward 2000: 6–8). The earliest-known examples are 14 wooden boats discovered in 1991 buried in mud-brick, boat-shaped graves at the Early Dynastic enclosures at Abydos (O'Connor 2009: 185–194, with earlier accounts in O'Connor 1991, 1995; O'Connor and Adams 2001). Belonging to one of Egypt's First Dynasty kings, this fleet of boats represents the oldest planked watercraft in the world (Ward 2000: 39). The only boat so far examined has a narrow, shallow, crescent-shaped hull with rounded ends, flat bottom, and angled sides (Ward 2006: 125 fig. 7). Its hull is made from thick planks of local wood, probably tamarisk, cut in joggled shapes and held together with woven straps lashed through transverse rows of V- and L-shaped channels (O'Connor 1991: 12; Ward 2003: 20–21). While complete recordings of this and the other hulls must await full excavation, the reported features are broadly defining and demonstrate, through their survival in later funerary boats, a religious adherence to traditional forms and specific, even standardized, methods (Ward 2000: 140).

One such descendant craft, discovered in 1954, is the magnificent funerary boat of Khufu, Egypt's Fourth Dynasty ruler responsible for constructing the Great Pyramid at Giza (AbuBakr and Mustafa 1971; Jenkins 1980; Lipke 1984, 1985; Nour et al. 1960). The papyriform boat, like the pyramid, was a deliberate display of conspicuous wealth and power. It is an elegant and complex vessel constructed from almost 40 tons of imported Lebanese cedar and measuring over 43 m in length and 5.6 m in beam (Lipke 1984: 25, 97, 102). Like the Abydos boat, it has a flat bottom, formed by eight symmetrically placed planks, and angled sides that continue the planking symmetry (Lipke 1984: 104; Steffy 1994: 25). Builders first constructed the shell of the hull from thick planks with elaborately joggled edges (see Lipke 1984: 66 fig. 42). They inserted hardwood tenon coaks between plank edges to align them (Lipke 1984: 25, 64), and then tied the planks together at their ends and in other strategic areas of stress with ligatures (Lipke 1984: 66 fig. 42; Mark 2009: 138–145). Builders closed the seams by lacing ligatures—or woven straps (see Mark 2009: 138)—transversely from sheer to sheer over large, wooden battens and through rows of V-shaped channels cut into the interior side of the planks, but never penetrating their full thickness (Figure 16.1a). Edge mortises and lashing channels are the same standard size as those in the Abydos boat (Lipke 1984: 78).

Builders stabilized the hull by installing deck-level through-beams notched into the sheer strakes and trimmed flush with their outer surface (Figure 16.1b) (Lipke 1984: 107). They clamped the beams in place with notched longitudinal side stringers lashed around the beams to hold-downs (Figure 16.1c) (Lipke 1984: 21 fig. 11). These stringers provide much of the hull's longitudinal strength (Mark 2009: 147–148). A central carling, notched along its upper face to fit up under the beams and supported from below by stanchions resting on floor timbers, further buttresses the deck beams and distributes hull stresses (Figure 16.1d–f). Builders lashed together the entire assembly with ligatures (Lipke 1984: 119, 75 fig. 48, 123 fig. 73).

Another four funerary boats, discovered in 1894 buried outside the Twelfth Dynasty pyramid of Senwosret III at Dashur (Arnold 2002: 106–107; de Morgan et al. 1895: 81–83, pls. XXIX–XXXI; Ward 2000: 101–102) have been recorded and studied in detail (Creasman 2005; Haldane 1984; Ward 2000: 84–102). Like the Khufu boat, these vessels were built almost entirely of imported cedar (Ward 2000: 84–85), but include many timbers fashioned from the recycled planking of other, larger ships (Creasman 2005: 36, 130; Reisner 1913: 86; Ward 2000: 98–100; Ward and Zazzaro 2009: 41). This practice is also documented in early New Kingdom dockyard records (Glanville 1931–1932). However, at only about 10 m long and 2 m wide, the Dashur boats are much smaller and beamier than the Khufu and Abydos vessels (Ward 2000: 84 table 8). Their hulls have a crescent shape and full, rounded sections

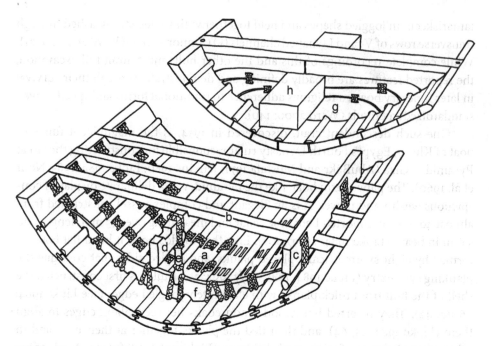

Figure 16.1 Sketch showing various features of Egyptian hull construction: (a) transverse
lashings; (b) deck-level beams; (c) side stringer and hold-down; (d) central carling;
(e) stanchions; (f) floor timber; (g) composite frame and beam assembly; (h) massive
longitudinal timber. Drawing by the author. After Landström 1970: 29 fig. 86 and Ward
2000: 125 fig. 70.

throughout (Creasman 2005: 31 fig. 15, 47 fig. 21, 89–90 figs. 39–40; Ward 2000: 86
fig. 37). They are built up from a thick central bottom strake consisting of planks
joined by superficial dovetail joints, and they have symmetrical sides, each with
three strakes and a gunwale. The gunwales replace the side stringers of Khufu's boat
as longitudinal stiffeners (Ward 2000: 102).

The hulls of these vessels differ from the Giza and Abydos examples mostly in
their edge joinery and lack of transverse lashing. Like their predecessors, the
Dashur builders used tenons between planks, but ones that are substantially longer
and more tightly fitted (Creasman 2005: 60–62, 102–103; Haldane 1984: 23–24;
Steffy 1994: 33; Ward 2000: 90). These are more than mere coaks; they not only
would have stiffened the hull longitudinally and prevented movement along seams,
but also would have contributed considerable transverse strength to the hull (Steffy
1994: 33). The Dashur builders deviated as well by employing superficial dovetail
fastenings, rather than ligatures, to connect all seams, although they located them
in similar positions. These joints acted in concert with compression forces to hold
the planks together (Ward 2000: 101–102). To accomplish this, builders united the
sides of the hulls with deck beams notched between sheer strakes and gunwales,
fixed with square treenails and rope girders, and supported from below with stanchions (Creasman 2005: 53–56; Haldane 1984: 16–19; Steffy 1994: 33–35; Ward 2000:
86 fig. 37, 87).

Cheryl Ward (Haldane 1984: 98–101; Haldane and Shelmerdine 1990: 535–539; Ward 2000: 93, 94–95 figs. 42–44) believes that the builders did in fact use ligatures to tie the planks and that the dovetail mortises were originally dilapidated lashing channels that nineteenth-century reconstructors modified and fitted with dovetail tenons (Haldane 1996: 240–241). However, the mortises would seem too narrow and shallow to have been lashing channels, and examples of dovetail joints found in boat timbers from Wadi Gawasis (see below) and their longtime use in Egyptian carpentry (Creasman 2005: 11 n. 33, 122–123 fig. 37; Lucas 1962: 513; Ward 2000: 93) suggest that they may indeed be original to the boats' construction.

Aside from recovered boat burials, excavations of ramps and causeways in the vicinity of the Middle Kingdom pyramid of Senwosret I at Lisht have unearthed more than 90 timbers of local tamarisk or acacia wood from dismantled boats reused as construction material (Haldane 1988, 1992: 108–112 for timber catalog, 1996: 236–239; Ward 2000: 108–117). A majority of these timbers comes from working vessels, so they provide evidence for hull construction in more mundane craft. Most of the planks have joggled edges, though the size and shape of the joggles vary (Ward 2000: 127 fig. 71). Fastening holes for tenons and ligatures are present in the planks, penetrating only their inner surface and edges, never their exterior face. The Lisht and Khufu builders used planks of a similar and substantial thickness, and both used ligatures to reinforce their assembly at points of stress. The Lisht boats also had large tenons, like those from Dashur, which provided much of their longitudinal and transverse rigidity. Additionally, the Lisht builders paired some mortise-and-tenon joints within the thickness of planks, thus increasing the strength of the edge joinery. In short, these vessels were sturdily built and probably were designed to transport heavy freight (Ward 2000: 110–111, 114).

This is further and perhaps most strikingly demonstrated by a frame assembly found among the timbers. The preserved portion of the frame consists of a curved floor timber and a pair of futtock-like timbers attached to the floor's upper face with mortise-and-tenon joints and lashings (Ward 2000: 120–121 figs. 65–67). The outer faces of the floor and upper timbers, where they touch the hull, have notches to accommodate planking seams fitted with battens, and three drilled holes indicate that the frame was treenailed to the hull (Ward 2000: 119, 120 fig. 65; note her reservations about the treenails on 126). Ward has reconstructed the Lisht frame as a vertical composite structure built up from floor timber to deck beam with successive elements (Figure 16.1g) (Ward 2000: 125 fig. 70). The frame components enclose a massive keelson-like timber (Figure 16.1h) that would have provided much of the hull's longitudinal strength and lowered the boat's center of gravity (Ward 2000: 121–123). Composite assemblies like this would have formed a series of stout bulkheads designed to bolster and stabilize a heavily built transport vessel and support heavy cargoes carried topside.

The remains of another utilitarian vessel, abandoned during Egypt's Late Period in the mid-fifth century BCE, was unearthed and damaged by workers trenching in Cairo's Mataria suburb in 1987. The hull has a rounded bottom similar to the Dashur boats, but is slightly shorter and beamier (Ward 2000: 129). Its sycamore fig planks are irregularly shaped, and some have joggled edges. The vessel has a keel plank, which reportedly protruded 1–2 cm below the outer surface of the hull (Ward 2000: 131). But what sets this boat apart from all other known Egyptian craft is that its builders used 2 cm diameter pegs to lock the large mortise-and-tenon joints in the planking assembly (Haldane 1996: 242; Ward 2000: 131). They did not peg every joint, and preservation and recording are insufficient to confirm whether they pegged tenons on both sides of a seam. Further complicating the picture is the fact that the pegs apparently protrude through planks, rather than being trimmed flush with their surfaces, and so might have been used to fix structural elements to the hull (Ward 2000: 133–134).

Collectively, these hulls show a remarkable consistency in Egyptian boat-building, while hinting at variability in design dictated by size and function (Table 16.1). Thus, builders of the small Dashur boats forwent the transverse lashings and frames that were so essential to the long and slender Khufu boat, and offset their absence by enlarging the mortise-and-tenon joints. Similarly, Lisht builders replaced beams and stanchions, like those in the Khufu and Dashur boats, with stout bulkheads in order to support much greater loads. The prudent use of short-length locally available woods and recycling of imported timber speaks to the adaptability of Egyptian shipwrights and their methods to economic and environmental conditions. The longevity of the basic characteristics of Egyptian hull construction—thick planks not penetrated below the water-line, joggled edges and coaks, battens and transverse lashings, stringers and gunwales, a reliance on compression, and integrated beams—testifies to the extraordinary success of this boatbuilding tradition. It is worth noting that significant departure from these practices does not show in the archaeological record until a late date, when Egypt was under heavy foreign influence (Ward 2000: 133).

Seagoing Vessels

Beyond the banks of the Nile, Egyptian seafarers engaged in active trade along the Levantine coast and in the Red Sea (Wachsmann 1998: 9–38, 327). The earliest-known depictions of obvious seagoing ships date to the Fifth Dynasty and decorate the funerary temple of Sahure at Abusir and the causeway of Unas at Saqqara (Borchardt 1913: pl. 12; Hassan 1955: 139 fig. 2; Wachsmann 1995: 11). The depicted hulls have crescent shapes, hogging trusses, and lashings or lacing running longitudinally below the sheer strakes and vertically at the extremities. Seagoing merchant galleys depicted in painted relief in Hatshepsut's New Kingdom mortuary temple at Deir el Bahri have similar constructional features, as well as through-beams protruding along the side of one of the ships (Säve-Söderbergh 1946: 14 fig. 1). Ships employed in Red Sea trade were built in the Nile shipyard at Gebtu (Koptos) and then disassembled for transport across the eastern desert to the coast via the Wadi Hammamat (Wachsmann 1998: 238–239; Ward 2000: 140). Recent studies and excavations at Wadi Gawasis (Bard and Fattovich 2007; Ward and Zazzaro 2009) and Ayn

Table 16.1 Hull construction features of ancient Eastern Mediterranean vessels

	Egyptian	Egyptian	Egyptian	Egyptian	Egyptian	Egyptian	Syro-Canaanite	Greek	Greek
Provenience									
Environmental design	riverine	riverine	riverine	riverine	seagoing	seagoing	seagoing	seagoing	seagoing
Purpose	funerary/ceremonial boat	funerary/ceremonial boat	working vessel/freighter	working vessel/freighter	trading vessel	trading vessel	trading vessel	trading vessel	trading vessel
Construction type	transverse lashing	unpegged mortise-and-tenon joints and compression	unpegged mortise-and-tenon joints and compression	mortise-and-tenon joints, some pegged	unpegged mortise-and-tenon joints and compression	tenon coaks and ligatures	pegged mortise-and-tenon joints	pegged lacing	pegged mortise-and-tenon joints (transitional)
Date	Early Dynastic–Old Kingdom	Middle Kingdom	Middle Kingdom	Persian Period	Middle Kingdom	Middle Kingdom	Late Bronze Age	Archaic	Late Archaic–Early Classical Period
Examples	Abydos boats (14), Khufu (2)	Dashur boats (4)	el-Lisht timbers	Mataria shipwreck	Wadi Gawasis and Ayn Sokhna timbers	Wadi Gawasis timbers	Uluburun, Cape Gelidonya shipwrecks	Giglio, Pabuç Burnu, Bon Porté, Cala Sant Vicenç, Place Jules Verne 9, Gela 1 shipwrecks	Place Jules Verne 7, César 1, Gela 2, Grand Ribaud F, Tektaş Burnu, Alonnesos, Porticello, Ma'agan Mikhael shipwrecks
Size and Shape									
Lengths (m)	20–43.6	9.25–10.2	–	11+	15	small vessel	11.5–16	9.5–25	10–25
L:B Ratio	7.8–10:1	4:3:1	–	2:1	–	–	3:1	4:1	3.3:1
Shape	long, slender with curved sheer	long, slender with curved sheer	–	–	–	–	beamy	slender; sharp, carriage return raking ends	beamy; raking-straight prow, curved stern; rockered keel

(*continued*)

355

Table 16.1 (continued)

Provenience	Egyptian	Egyptian	Egyptian	Egyptian	Egyptian	Egyptian	Syro-Canaanite	Greek	Greek
Section	lateral flat carriage return with rounded angled sides	rounded, carriage return beamy	rounded beamy	rounded	rounded	–	rounded	rounded	wine-glass shaped
Bottom	central strake(s)	–	central strake(s)	central strake/ keel-plank	central strake/keel-plank **Shell**	–	large, rudimentary, proto-keel	rectangular, almost square keel	rectangular keel
Planking	thick (10–15 cm), symmetrical planking	thick (7–13.5 cm), symmetrical planking	thick planks (8.5–18 cm)	thick planks (7–9 cm)	thick planks (up to 22 cm)	thin planks (2.5–4.2 cm)	thick planks (6–6.5 cm)	thin planks (2.5–4.5)	thin planks (2.5–5)
Plank Shape	joggled	narrow butt ends with wide middle	joggled	joggled and narrow butt ends with wide middle	–	straight	straight, long strakes	straight, long strakes	straight, long strakes
Plank Alignment	half-mortises in plank ends, ligatures	half-mortises, in plank ends, ligatures	half-mortises small tenons	small tenons	–	small tenons	–	dowels, temporary cleats/stays	temporary cleats/stays
Edge Joinery	transverse lashing with tenon coaks	dovetail joints with large tenons, compression forces	large tenons, compression forces	large mortise-and-tenon joints, some pegged	unpegged mortise-and-tenon joints, dovetail joints	tenon coaks	large, pegged mortise-and-tenon joints	longitudinal pegged lacing with edge coaks	pegged mortise-and-tenon joints
– coaks	tenons	long tenons	long tenons, some doubled	small mortise-and-tenon joints	long tenons	–	none	dowels, tenons	dowels at extremities and in repairs

356

– ligatures	at stress carriage return points	at stress points	none	at stress points	–	at stress points or for plank	–	for lacing	for lacing at extremities and for repairs
– lashing	transverse over battens	transverse over battens	transverse, over battens	transverse over battens	–	–	for frames	for frames	none
– seam stopping	possible use of wadding	possible use of wadding	–	caulking?	none	none	–	wadding	none
– lashing mortises	V- and L-shaped channels, from interior face, never penetrating through entire thickness of the plank	–	L-shaped channels, from interior face, never penetrating through entire thickness of the plank	L-shaped channels	–	–	L-shaped channels	–	–
– lacing/ lashing material	woven straps, halfa grass, papyrus?	woven straps, halfa grass, papyrus?	woven straps, halfa grass	–	–	–	copper straps and rope	monocots	flax, esparto grass, monocots
– coating	–	–	–	–	–	waterproofing along seams	–	pine tar/pitch on interior	pine tar/pitch on interior and exterior

Transverse Structure

Primary Support	deck-level beams	deck-level beams	integrated frame/deck-level beam bulkheads	deck-level beams	frames?	deck-level beams	rows of large, paired tenons	frames	frames

(continued)

357

Table 16.1 (*continued*)

Provenience	Egyptian	Egyptian	Egyptian	Egyptian	Egyptian	Syro-Canaanite	Greek	Greek
Frames	small floor timbers, used to distribute stresses and weight of deck/ upper works	none	massive composite frames integrated with deck-beams	–	small	–	made-frames alternating with top-timbers	made-frames alternating with top-timbers
Frame Attachment	lashed	–	treenailed, lashed	–	treenailed, lashed	–	lashed; top-timbers treenailed and lashed	double-clenched copper nails
Beams/Thwarts	transverse stiffening	transverse stiffening	transverse stiffening, integrated with frames	stiffening	–	–	transverse stiffening	transverse stiffening
Beam Attachment	notched and treenailed	dovetailed and treenailed	notched and treenailed	–	–	–	notched and treenailed into top-timbers	beams notched and treenailed into tops of frames
Longitudinal Structure								
Primary Support	side stringers	gunwales	gunwales and massive keelson-like timber, integrated with frames	–	–	proto-keel	keel, extended carriage return mast step	keel, extended mast step, wales
Secondary Support	central carling, used to distribute weight of deck/ upper works	–	–	–	–	–	–	–

Sokhna (Mathieu 2004; Pomey in press; el-Raziq et al. 2006) testify to hull construction methods and materials, and also to a well-organized industry for repairing, dismantling, storing, and reusing ships and their hull timbers. The recycling of ship timbers either for use in other hulls, as seen in the Dashur boats, or for use as construction material, as at Wadi Gawasis and el-Lisht, demonstrates a frugality that attests to economic concerns and the value of good timber in Egypt, especially imported conifers.

Hull planks, deck beams, and other timbers and fastenings found at these sites reflect the same building tradition seen in Egyptian riverine craft, but with adaptations for open-sea conditions. All hull planks are cedar, but with thicknesses of up to 22.5 cm, they are much heftier than those on riverine vessels (Ward and Zazzaro 2009: 31–32). Builders relied on this robustness to strengthen their hulls against the greater stresses encountered at sea. They further stiffened the shells of their ships by doubling up mortise-and-tenon edge joints in the thickness of planks, much as they did in heavy Nile freighters. However, builders of seagoing vessels also had to deal with the ravages of shipworms and other marine borers, and they may have provided for this with an additional, sacrificial thickness of at least 5 cm between joints and the outboard surface of hull planks (Ward and Zazzaro 2009: 41). In typical fashion, lashings through standard L-shaped channels reinforced stress points in the planking. Here, however, builders fortified these connections by using a combination of copper straps and ligatures, which they firmly compressed and locked within the channels with wooden wedges (Ward and Zazzaro 2009: 37, figs. 6 and 13). Deck beams seem stouter as well, thicker and wider than those of the Dashur boats, but otherwise of similar make (Ward and Zazzaro 2009: 31).

Ship timbers also include additional evidence for the use of dovetail joinery in Egyptian hull construction. Part of a keel plank has two dovetail mortises cut into its inboard face, and excavators found at least eight loose dovetail-tenon fragments made from local wood, probably acacia (Ward and Zazzaro 2009: 38 fig. 14). The keel-plank mortises are located in similar positions as those on the central strakes of the Dashur boats, and the tenons had all been chiseled or sawn into pieces and forcefully pried free of their mortises, indicating that they were fitted tightly (Ward and Zazzaro 2009: 37–38).

Particularly intriguing are five thin planks (2.5–4.2 cm) with small tenon coaks (Ward and Zazzaro 2009: 30 tables 1 and 2, 33–34, fig. 8, 36–37). Paired ligature holes, perhaps in rows running across plank widths, and what appears to be a tree-nail hole between them resemble frame fastenings found on Greek laced boats (see below), while the combination of edge tenons and lashed frames evokes some comparison to the construction of two seventh-century BCE boats, possibly Phoenician, at Mazarrón (see below).

Until recently, nautical archaeologists could only speculate as to how Egyptian shipwrights built their seagoing ships. The construction of riverine vessels designed to transport heavy cargoes, including huge granite blocks, giant stone obelisks, and other loads weighing many tons, offered clues as to how shipwrights dealt with great stresses in their hulls. But static loads, no matter how heavy, and the buffering forces of rough seas pose quite different challenges to planking joints, longitudinal stiffeners, and transverse framework. Ship timbers discovered along Egypt's Red Sea coast testify to the viability of Egyptian riverine construction, with some modification, for seagoing vessels. Several also provide tantalizing evidence for another constructional method that hints at a possible diffusion of technology between Egypt and the Aegean or Levant. We therefore turn our attention northward now, to the easternmost shores of the Mediterranean.

The Levant

In comparison to the vast corpus of evidence for Egyptian boats and ships, their construction, use, and sociocultural significance, knowledge of Near Eastern ships and seafaring is miniscule. The earliest-known mention of Syro-Canaanite ships is by Kamose (Seventeenth Dynasty) in his account of the capture of numerous Hyksos vessels laden with rich cargoes of trade goods (Wachsmann 1998: 39). Numerous other texts document cities along the eastern Mediterranean seaboard that were active in sea trade and provide information about the size of their fleets, inventories of ship's equipment, and even general indications of ship sizes (Hoftijzer and van Soldt 1998; Wachsmann 1998: 39–41, and additional bibliography therein).

The most detailed depiction of ships from this region is painted on the Theban tomb of Kenamun, an administrator under Amenhotep III of the Eighteenth Dynasty (Basch 1987: 63 figs. 111–112, 65 fig. 115; Daressy 1895; Davies and Faulkner 1947; Wachsmann 1998: 42–47). The scene includes a total of 11 ships with crescent-shaped hulls, tall vertical ends, and wickerwork and post screens running the full length of the sheer. A few strakes are delineated by seam lines, as are several possible butt joints. The only other construction features shown are a line of through-beam ends protruding from the side of the hulls below the sheer strake, and what appears to be a short run of lacing along the sheer at the bow of the ships. Typically, however, such evidence is not only limited, its interpretation is also problematic due to artistic factors. The lacing and through-beams, for example, may be Egyptianizing elements introduced by the artist, and not necessarily true features of the actual ships (Wachsmann 1998: 44; for additional examples of these features in Egyptian craft, see Glanville and Faulkner 1972: fig. 13; Landström 1970: figs. 64–72; Ward 2000: 36, 73 fig. 26).

Archaeological evidence for Levantine ships is provided by scanty hull remains from two Late Bronze Age shipwrecks excavated off the coast of Turkey. The older of these wrecks, dated to 1320 BCE ±15 years (Pulak 1998: 214; but revised in Manning et al. 2009: 184), was discovered off Uluburun, near Kaş, on Turkey's southwestern Anatolian coast. Eleven seasons of excavation recovered a combined 11 tons of copper and tin ingots; 175 cobalt blue, turquoise, and lavender glass ingots; jars of terebinth resin; African blackwood logs; elephant and hippopotamus ivory; tortoise shells and ostrich eggshells; Cypriot pottery; metal vessels; ritual faience drinking cups; luxurious carved ivory objects; seashell rings; beads of various designs and materials; gold and silver jewelry; a gold chalice; sets of pan-balance weights; an assortment of weapons, tools, and fishing equipment; and sundry spices and food-stuffs (Pulak 1998: 193–210). Shipboard items and its enormously rich and diverse cargo of raw materials and luxury goods indicate that the ship probably originated from one of the ports in the northern Carmel coast, possibly at Tel Abu Hawam (Pulak 2008: 299), and was almost certainly engaged in a trading venture of royal gift exchange (Pulak 1998: 220). A ship carrying such a cargo would rightly be expected to epitomize the best available methods and materials of construction for its day.

　Three small sections of preserved hull include parts of the ship's keel, garboards, and fragments of three port and seven starboard strakes (Pulak 1999: 234 fig. 2). Based on these remains and distribution of cargo, the cedar-built vessel is estimated to have been about 15–16 m long and 5 m in beam, and to have displaced approximately 34 tons (Lin 2003: 220, 224; Pulak 1999: 210, 212). The vessel's builders began with a rudimentary keel, or proto-keel, which they cut wider (sided 28 cm) than high (molded 22 cm) (Figure 16.2a). It extended about 2 cm beyond the outer hull, but protruded into the interior of the hull some 10 cm (Pulak 1999: 215–216, 234 fig. 2). Unlike most Egyptian boats, which relied on a central strake or bottom flat only slightly thicker than the garboards and planking, the Uluburun proto-keel was

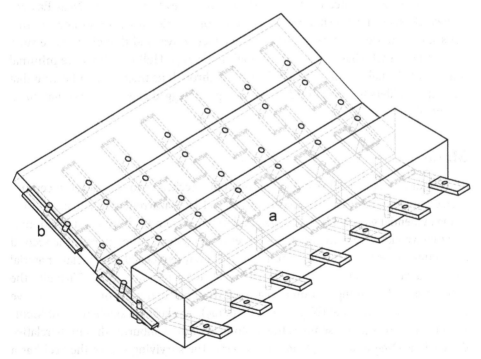

Figure 16.2 Isometric reconstruction of the Uluburun hull remains: (a) proto-keel; (b) pegged mortise-and-tenon joints. Drawing by W. van Duivenvoorde.

a more massive timber that acted as a spine and provided a good deal of longitudinal stiffening (Pulak 1999: 217). Hull planking was thick (6–6.5 cm) when compared
to later Mediterranean vessels, but not nearly as massive as that of Egyptian hulls
(Pulak 1999: 218). The preserved remains offer no evidence for framing, or any indication that builders used treenails, ligatures, or metal fastenings in assembling the
hull. However, nothing of the vessel's extremities survived, and the preserved portions of the hull may not be long or wide enough to include frames or bulkheads or
evidence for securing such structural elements to the planking (Pulak 1999: 215).

Builders joined the edges of their planks with large oak tenons (Pulak 1999: 237
fig. 5) and secured the seams by locking the tenons in their mortises with 2.2 cm
diameter oak pegs driven from inside the hull through the thicknesses of planks
and tenons (Figure 16.2b) (Bass 1989: 31 fig. 2; Pulak 1999: 212, 218–219, 232 table 1).
They cut deep mortises that extended well across the width of planks, and positioned them immediately adjacent to the nearest mortise cut from the opposite
edge (Pulak 1998: 211). In this manner the joints formed continuous lateral runs of
alternating paired tenons within the hull planking. The size and positioning of the
joints suggest that the builders intentionally designed them to act as internal
framing, perhaps in order to compensate for the lack of proper framing (Pulak
1999: 219–220). This construction must have proven sturdy, since the ship's crew
made no concessions for seams or planking scarfs—typically the weakest points in
a hull—when stowing heavy cargo within the hold directly against the hull (Pulak
1999: 218, 222–223).

Supporting evidence for this construction comes from another Near Eastern
shipwreck, that of a possible Syro-Canaanite or Cypriot vessel excavated off Turkey's southern Mediterranean coast at Cape Gelidonya, and thought to have sunk
around 1200 BCE (Bass 1967: 50–51; Pulak 1999: 214). Hull remains were minimal
but included a half-tenon with a hole pierced through its thickness, indicating that
the ship's builders had employed the same type of pegged edge joinery (Pulak 1999:
237 fig. 6).

Mazarrón

The remains of two small vessels abandoned or wrecked in the late seventh century
BCE on Spain's southeastern coast at Playa de la Isla, Mazarrón, may help fill in some
of the evidential gaps left by the sparse hull remains from Uluburun and Gelidonya.
The two wrecks were discovered in a Phoenician context, although only the second
and better-preserved wreck was found with securely associated Phoenician material
(Negueruela 2004: 230, 235; Negueruela et al. 1995: 190–191, 2004). Virtually the
entire keel and a joining section of planking from one extremity of the hull survive
from the Mazarrón 1 boat (Negueruela 1996: 165). The keel is a single piece of Mediterranean cypress that resembles the proto-keel of the Uluburun ship in its relative
dimensions (Negueruela 1996: 167, 2004: 237). The surviving end of the keel has a
short tongue that originally would have fit into a corresponding groove in the end
post (Negueruela 1996: 165, 167). The nine preserved hull strakes consist of pine

planks joined end-to-end with diagonal scarfs and edge-joined with olive tenons pegged in their mortises (Negueruela 1996: 165, 167; Ruiz 2008: 138). Plank edges are beveled so that they form a shallow V-shaped recess along the inboard seams of the strakes, somewhat reminiscent of the Khufu I planking (see Mark 2009: 151). Here, small ropes or twists of esparto grass lie within the recesses and are held in place with small ligatures laced over the seams in a continuous, one-pass diagonal pattern through holes predrilled along the sides of the planks (Negueruela 2004: 237; Negueruela et al. 2000: 1673). Preserved "frames" are small fig branches that have been trimmed of twigs or other protrusions, but otherwise left unshaped. They were tied lightly to the hull with ligatures presumably made from esparto as well (Negueruela 1996: 167; Negueruela et al. 2000: 1673, 2004: 467 fig. 13, 478).

Mazarrón 2 is larger and better preserved; in fact, almost the entire hull is intact. It measures 8.5 m long and 2.2 m at the beam, and has a sheer height of some 90 cm (Negueruela 2004: 235). The keel is a single timber scarfed to stem and sternpost with simple tongue-and-groove joints. From garboard to sheer the vessel's sides have nine strakes that are only 1.9–2.3 cm thick and are fastened together with small, pegged mortise-and-tenon joints (Negueruela 2004: 247). These planks, however, have no edge beveling or seam wadding. Light fig branches, 4–8 cm in diameter and running athwartship from sheer to sheer, are lashed to the hull interior every 40–50 cm (Cabrera et al. 1992: 39; Gómez-Gil Aizpurúa and Sierra Méndez 1996: 219; Negueruela 2004: 249). Also spanning the hull are seven benchlike thwarts that dovetail into the top of the seventh strake, except for two in the stern. The hull is coated inside and out with pitch (Negueruela 2004: 235–236).

Despite their importance, these two boats have yet to be recorded and studied in detail. As is clear from their small size and low freeboard, these vessels were not seagoing ships. Furthermore, questions as to their cultural designation remain. These vessels may have been small lighters associated with the mining and silver-founding activities at Punta de los Gavilanes (Mazarrón) and the surrounding areas (Aubet 2001: 339–340). In this light, the boats could be representative of indigenous watercraft, although some Phoenician influence might rightly be expected. Certainly, they have similarities with the Uluburun vessel that suggest a possible descendancy of their building method. Each of the vessels has a proto-keel, but in the Mazarrón boats, the proto-keel only projects outward from the hull, as the garboards are set flush with its inboard face. The vessels all rely on pegged mortise-and-tenon joinery to fasten strakes and secure seams. However, the Mazarrón hulls have much thinner planking and much smaller and more widely spaced joints, and adjacent joints are not paired as in the Uluburun ship. In all aspects, the Mazarrón construction is much less substantial. The use of seam wadding and the diminutive frames is curious. The latter seem more suited to cargo stowage for protecting the hull, and would have added little if any strength to the vessel's structure. In this regard they resemble the heavier branches of dunnage laid athwartship in the Uluburun hull (Pulak 1998: 197). What is certain is that builders assembled these hulls using pegged mortise-and-tenon joinery and not lacing, which they employed simply as tie-downs. For a shipbuilding tradition in which shell planking was laced together, we move now to the Aegean.

THE AEGEAN

No direct evidence for early seacraft in the Aegean exists until the Bronze Age (Wachsmann 1998: 69). Enigmatic, mostly ceramic vessels, known by archaeologists as "frying pans" because of their unusual shape, have been found at sites throughout the Aegean and on mainland Greece and Anatolia (Coleman 1985: 191–193). The flat surfaces of at least a dozen examples from Early Cycladic II tombs on Syros are decorated with incised illustrations of ships (Basch 1987: 80–81 figs. 159–167; Casson 1995: 30–31; Coleman 1985: 191–193, 199 ill. 5). The ships have one high extremity and a lower end that is angled upward slightly and has a short, horizontal projection. Some of the vessels are shown with vertical lines or a zigzag pattern along their hull, which may suggest laced or lashed construction (Basch 1987: 47, 86; Wachsmann 1998: 14). Similar ships would seem to be depicted by an Early Minoan I–II terracotta model found at Palaikastro in Crete (Basch 1987: 83 figs. 170–171; Evans 1964: 240 fig. 137; Wachsmann 1998: 71–73, 75 fig. 5.9), and three contemporary lead models from Naxos, though the latter have no stern projection (Casson 1995: 41–42; Renfrew 1967: 5; 1972: 318, 356–357, 358 fig. 17.7 and pl. 28, 3 and 4; Wachsmann 1995: 13, 1998: 69–70). Archaeologists have long debated what sort of early Aegean vessel is depicted, what function the horizontal projection served, and even which end of the craft is the bow and which the stern (e.g., Basch 1987: 84–85; Casson 1995: 41–42; Coleman 1985: 198–199; Johnstone 1973: 6–11; Johnstone 1982; Renfrew 1967: 5; 1972: 355–358; Roberts 1987; Wachsmann 1995: 12–14, 1998: 70–71). The latter question would seem to have been answered when excavations at Akrotiri, on the island of Thera, revealed a magnificent wall fresco that contains the most detailed portrayal yet found of Bronze Age Minoan ships (Marinatos 1974: 19–31, pl. 2; Wachsmann 1998: 86–99; for varying interpretations of the Thera ship scene and the vessels depicted, see also Raban 1984; Giesecke 1983; Wachsmann 1980). All of the boats portrayed in procession are fitted with a horizontal projection at their stern.

Unfortunately, no vestige of any early Aegean ship has yet surfaced in the archaeological record. To date, the earliest—in fact, only—pre-classical Aegean shipwreck to be excavated and studied by nautical archaeologists is that of a modest trading vessel, probably East Greek, that sank around 570–560 BCE at Pabuç Burnu, a small promontory on the southwestern Turkish coast just east of Bodrum (Greene 2003; Greene, Lawall, and Polzer 2008; Polzer 2004, 2009a). Six fragmentary planks are all that remain from its hull, but these preserve a surprising amount of evidence for the vessel's construction (Polzer 2009a, 2009b). Most prominently, the hull components were joined with ligatures laced along planking seams and lashed around frames. Interpretation of the preserved features is facilitated by evidence from beyond the physical confines of the Aegean, in areas of Greek colonization and trade, where archaeologists have excavated the remains of five Archaic Greek ships that have similar joinery and construction techniques. In chronological order, these include shipwrecks at Giglio (Italy, 600–580 BCE) (Bats 1996: 577; Bound 1985, 1991a, 1991b; Bound and Vallintine 1983; Cristofani 1996: 21–48; see Mark 2005: 40–42 for discussion of the vessel's origin), Bon Porté (France, circa 540–510 BCE) (Joncheray 1976; Kahanov and Pomey 2004; Liou 1974, 1975: 595–597; Pomey 1981, 1995, 1999a, 2001, 2002a, 2002b, 2003: 14; Pomey and Long 1992: 192), Cala Sant Vicenç (Majorca, 520–510 BCE) (Nieto and Santos 2009; Nieto et al. 2002, 2004, 2005), Place Jules-Verne (wreck 9, Marseille, circa 525–510 BCE) (Pomey 1995, 1999a, 2001, 2002b, 2003), and Gela (wreck 1, Sicily, 500–480 BCE) (Panvini 2001a). The construction features preserved in the hull remains from these wrecks are remarkably consistent in make, form, materials, and application, demonstrating in their totality a clearly definable shipbuilding tradition (as per Prins 1986: 23–24)— in this case, a Greek tradition (Table 16.1).

Construction evidence from five additional Greek shipwrecks, spanning the late sixth, fifth, and fourth centuries BCE, indicates that a major technological shift occurred in Greek shipbuilding that transformed Archaic laced construction into the so-called Graeco-Roman building tradition, exemplified in the well-preserved hull of the Kyrenia ship (Cyprus, 295–285 BCE) (Steffy 1985, 1994: 42–59). The evidence comes from the hull remains of the Place Jules-Verne 7 (Marseille, circa 525–510 BCE) (Pomey 1995, 1999a, 2001, 2002b, 2003), César 1 (Place Villeneuve-Bargemon, Marseille, 510–500 BCE) (Pomey 2001: 429–430), Grand Ribaud F (France, 510–490 BCE) (Long et al. 2001; Long, Gantès, and Drap 2002; Long and Sourisseau 2002; Pomey and Rival 2002), Gela 2 (450–425 BCE) (Panvini 2001b), and Ma'agan Mikhael (Israel, 410–390 BCE) (Kahanov and Linder 2004; Linder and Kahanov 2003) wrecks. Shipwrecks at Tektaş Burnu (Turkey, 440–425 BCE) (Carlson 2003; van Duivenvoorde forthcoming), Alonnesos (Greece, 420–400 BCE) (Hadjidaki 1996; Mantzouka 2004), and Porticello (Italy, 400–385 BCE) (Eiseman and Ridgway 1987; Lawall 1998) can also be included for the sake of completeness, although they have provided very little in the way of hull remains, due to poor preservation or incomplete excavation.

Ancient Greek shipwrights began building their hulls by first laying down the ship's spine, which they formed by joining keel to stem and sternpost using keyed box-scarfs, a particular hallmark of this building tradition (Pomey 1997a: 195). Small, rectangular (almost square) keels generally proportional to a vessel's length appear to have been the norm, as did rounded hulls.

Greek shipbuilders predominantly utilized pine in their hulls, as the wood was readily available, strong, durable, resistant to rot, and easily worked (Steffy 1994: 258–259). They connected planks end-to-end with diagonal, three-planed (Z), or curved (S) scarfs to form long, continuous strakes that generally ran from stem to sternpost. Like their Egyptian counterparts, they staggered scarfs so as not to locate joints in adjacent strakes next to one another. However, they used much thinner planks than Egyptian and Near Eastern builders. This probably was not predicated on the choice of joinery, as some have suggested (e.g., Mark 2005: 58–59, 62), but more likely was the product of how shipwrights conceived and approach the construction of their hulls. Within Greek shipbuilding itself, laced hulls could have planks as thick or thicker than mortise-and-tenon-joined planks. Hull dimensions and planking thicknesses indicate that the latter were related more to the size of a vessel than to the type of edge fastening employed (Polzer 2009b: 98–102).

The two essential elements of Greek laced joinery are ligatures and wooden coaks. Much as in Egyptian lashed joinery, coaks served the dual purpose of aligning planks during construction and, more importantly, reinforcing the seams to help prevent longitudinal slippage between strakes. Greek builders traditionally used cylindrical dowels (typically about 12 cm long and 1.0–1.5 cm in diameter) in laced hulls, which they centered within the thickness of planks and staggered across their sides (Figure 16.3a) (Bound 1985: 55; Joncheray 1976: 28; Pomey 1995: 471). However, the Pabuç Burnu (Polzer 2004: 111–113, 2009a: 31) and Cala Sant Vicenç (Nieto and Santos 2009: 27 fig. 22, 51) builders employed small hardwood tenons for coaks, while those responsible for the Gela 1 vessel inserted both dowels and tenons (Panvini 2001a: 21, 22 fig. 13, 25 fig. 20, 26 fig. 22). The Pabuç Burnu coaks represent the earliest archaeologically attested use of tenons in Greek shipbuilding.

The lacing system developed by the ancient Greeks was unique in its use of tetrahedral notches in conjunction with oblique ligature holes, seam wadding, and locking pegs (Polzer 2009a: 30; Pomey 1999b: 150). Builders first chiseled

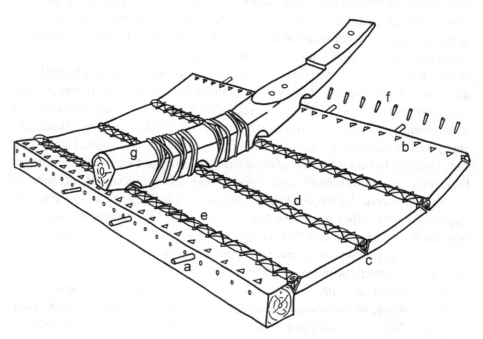

Figure 16.3 Hull construction features of typical Archaic Greek laced ships: (a) dowel coaks; (b) tetrahedral notches; (c) oblique ligature channels; (d) seam wadding; (e) double-helical lacing; (f) ligature pegs; (g) made-frame floor timber. Drawing by the author. After Pomey 1997b: 92.

small tetrahedral notches along each inboard side of a plank, close to the edge (Figure 16.3b). Using the notches as guides, they drilled a small, angled hole from the base of each notch through the thickness of the plank to the outside corner of the seam edge. The holes in one plank matched up with those in the adjacent plank to form a line of V-shaped lacing channels along the seam (Figure 16.3c). The notches also reduced the severity of the angles around which the lacing bent, which in turn reduced stress and wear on the ligatures (Polzer 2009b: 128–129). Additionally, they oriented the diagonal lacing turns across the inboard seams and kept the ligatures in proper alignment (Pomey 1995: 474, 1999b: 150), which helped distribute the resistance from the diagonal lacing evenly to the lateral and longitudinal loadings of the joint.

Shipwrights laid a strip of flax or other fibrous wadding along the inboard seam between the two lines of notches and laced a length of ligature through the holes and over the wadding, securing both wadding and seam (Figure 16.3d) (Pomey 1999b: 149, 150 n. 3; Nieto and Santos 2009: 54–55, fig. 47). Such wadding likely would have been ineffective at stopping a seam. Rather, it made it easier to maintain uniform tension on the ligatures when lacing multiple turns through a hole (Foerster Laures 1989: 266–267), and it provided a softer and more rounded surface over which to cinch the lacing taut. In this way, it acted much like a spring washer over which a nut is tightened.

Builders laced ligatures across the seams of their boats in a symmetrical double-helical pattern that produced at least one pass of the ligature between each hole and the three opposing holes in the adjacent plank (Figure 16.3e) (Nieto and Santos 2009: 27, fig. 22.6, 55–57, figs. 49 and 51). Ligature turns oriented perpendicularly to the seam joined the strakes and kept the seams from opening. The diagonal turns, on the other hand, helped to connect the strakes (as joints), but also to prevent them from moving longitudinally against one another (as stiffeners) (Polzer 2009b: 131–136).

Once builders had laced two strakes together, they drove tapered pegs into the lacing holes until they would go no farther, and then trimmed the pegs flush with the inner surface of the plank (Figure 16.3f). The primary function of the pegs was to lock the ligatures in their holes, which allowed the stretched parts of the lacing to be loaded to their breaking point (Coates 1985: 14). The pegs effectively isolated the ligature segments of each turn and created three independent "joints" between each pegged hole. This prevented the loosening of unloaded ligatures (due to flexing of the hull, wear, or breakage) from spreading to the loaded parts of the lacing and causing the lacing as a whole to slacken. In this way, the pegs enabled symmetrical helical lacing to resist shearing forces between planks, which otherwise it could not (Coates 1985: 17).

Greek builders strengthened their hulls transversely with internal framing comprised of preassembled "made-frames" (Figure 16.3g) alternating with top-timbers (Pomey 2003: 62 fig. 11.8). They fashioned the frames by connecting a single futtock to each end of the floor timbers using hook scarfs fixed with treenails. With wide, rounded inner surfaces and narrow outer surfaces notched over planking seams, the frames were ideally suited morphologically for lashing and for protecting seam joinery (Pomey 1997a: 195, 197 fig. 5). Between the frames and higher up the sides of the hull, shipwrights installed top-timbers with more rectangular sections. They both lashed and treenailed these to the planking, since ligatures alone are not particularly well suited for holding timbers in vertical positions (Polzer 2009a: 31; Pomey 1999b: 152).

The final step in completing the lower hull was paying the interior with a coating of pine tar, a common practice that continued throughout antiquity (Casson 1995: 211–212; Polzer 2009a: 31). The main function of the tar was to protect the interior of the hull and especially the exposed joinery elements—ligatures, wadding, and pegs—from seawater, condensation, and the elements, which could cause rot and jeopardize seam integrity.

Transition

Construction features evidenced in two shipwrecks from Marseille (Jules-Verne 7 and César 1) and those at Grand Ribaud, Gela (wreck 2), and Maʻagan Mikhael attest to a major shift in Greek shipbuilding in which pegged mortise-and-tenon joints and metal nails replaced pegged ligatures in hull joinery (Polzer 2009a: 33; Pomey 1997a). The builders of these vessels joined hull planks with mortise-and-tenon joints locked on both sides of the seam with wooden pegs driven perpendicularly through plank and tenon, and they attached frames with double-clenched copper nails driven from outside the hull (Table 16.1). Some pegged lacing is still present, but builders used it only to close and reinforce the end assemblies at stem and stern and to make repairs. In testament to their conservatism, builders continued to shape frames in the traditional manner even though it served no purpose, since they no longer lashed frames to the hull (Benini 2001: 101, 153 pls. XXXVI–XXXVII; Kahanov 2003: 88–95; Kahanov and Pomey 2004: 17; Long et al. 2001: 39–40; Pomey 2001: 430).

No full and convincing explanation for why this change occurred has yet been given, but it likely involved the growing transport of bulk cargoes in amphoras, the development of the Greek trireme, and a rapid buildup of state-supported naval fleets during the sixth and fifth centuries BCE (Mark 2005: 63–69). Mortises and pegged tenons were stiffer joints that were less vulnerable to wear and damage than pegged lacing and allowed for construction of stronger and more durable hulls (Polzer 2009a: 35–36).

The three Marseille wrecks, one (Jules-Verne 9) built in the traditional laced method and two (Jules-Verne 7 and César 1) constructed with the new joinery, are particularly serendipitous. They provide a close approximation of the date when the new joinery was adopted into Greek shipbuilding, and indicate that the change was sweeping, being incorporated into fishing boats and seagoing trading vessels alike (Pomey 1997a: 198, 2001: 431). A similar scenario is presented at Gela, where two ships of comparable size and carrying similar cargoes, but separated chronologically by half a century, were built using the two different types of hull joinery. The change seems to have been comprehensive: no Greek shipwreck earlier than

Jules-Verne 7 (last quarter of the sixth century BCE) has provided evidence for pegged mortise-and-tenon joinery, and none later than Gela 1 (first decades of the fifth century BCE) has yielded full laced construction.

Faulty seam joints, cracked planking, and the inability to apply the new joint to making repairs or to closing hull extremities testify to the newness of pegged mortise-and-tenon use in Greek shipbuilding and the novice proficiency of its practitioners (Polzer 2009a: 33; Pomey 1999b: 151, 1995: 478–479). Furthermore, the retention of made-frames, with their particular laced morphology, and the reversion to traditional laced-construction techniques in problematic areas of the hull confirm that these builders were working within the same tradition (Polzer 2009a: 34–35). The use of tenon coaks instead of traditional dowels in the Pabuç Burnu and Cala Sant Vicenç hulls may represent the first, critical step in this transitional process. Due to their shape, cylindrical dowels could not easily be pegged and therefore would not likely have evolved to take the place of lacing in edge joinery. The wider, flat tenon, on the other hand, was perfectly suited for pegging. This simple modification paved the way for pegged mortise-and-tenon joinery to evolve from and replace pegged lacing in Greek shipbuilding (Wachsmann 1998: 241). The gradual transition from dowel coak to tenon coak to pegged-tenon joint, along with supporting modifications to other construction features not attested in Near Eastern or Egyptian ships, strongly suggests a natural development of pegged mortise-and-tenon construction within the Greek tradition (Polzer 2009a: 34–36, 2009b: 159–174) rather than the wholesale importation of a foreign—most likely Phoenician—technology that many scholars suppose (Bass 2006: 14; Kahanov and Pomey 2004: 24–25; Mark 2005: 35, 67–68; Pomey 1997a: 201).

As the Archaic period of Greek history came to a close, so too did an Aegean tradition of building boats with ligatures whose roots probably stretched back to methods used by Stone Age obsidian traders, and perhaps even earlier ones. Greek shipwrights incorporated pegged mortise-and-tenon joinery into their construction at the beginning of classical antiquity and would adapt, modify, and perfect their techniques to take advantage of the strengths of the new joinery. All of the basic features resulting from these changes can be seen in the Kyrenia ship, by the end of the fourth century BCE.

CONCLUSION

All shipwrights in early antiquity constructed the hulls of their boats and ships by first building up a shell of planks, fastened together with some form of edge joinery, and then stiffening and reinforcing that shell with various forms of internal structure. The planking shell formed a watertight skin that enabled the boat to displace water and float, while bearing its own weight and that of crew, passengers, and all sorts of cargoes. The watertightness of such hulls was dependent primarily upon the strength of the planking joints and on the amount of relative movement between adjacent planks (Coates 1985: 11). The bending moment and tensile forces acting on a vessel's hull can cause hogging and open seams and are directly proportional to the hull's length and weight. The ancient seafaring cultures of the eastern Mediterranean each developed their own unique set of solutions to address these problems and create elegant, sturdy, and capable boats and ships well suited to their environments and intended purposes. Egyptian builders constructed vessels represented by Coates's (1985: 11–13) "boats with massive planks" model, wherein much of the hull's strength came from the thick, joggled planks themselves. Coaks and ligatures, transverse lashings and battens, side stringers and gunwales, and deck-level through-beams formed the compatible joinery and supporting structure necessary to ensure durability and watertightness (Coates 1985: 11). Near Eastern shipwrights built with thick planks as well, but relied more on massive internal mortise-and-tenon joints locked with wooden pegs to both close seams and fortify the hull. Their Aegean counterparts built vessels with smaller and more flexible planks joined with continuous, longitudinal lacing (Coates 1985: 15–18). Coaks, wadding, pegs, made-frames, and top-timbers all worked in concert to maintain seam integrity and strengthen the hull while still keeping it appropriately flexible. The ways in which these different builders conceived, designed, and constructed their watercraft—the materials they chose, the tools they used, and the techniques they developed—were all products of a unique coalescence of cultural, environmental, and economic circumstances. Nevertheless, it was the skill, experience, and ingenuity of the shipwrights themselves that, above all else, was the final and determining factor in the process.

REFERENCES

AbuBakr, `Abd al-Mun`im, and Ahmed Youssef Mustafa. 1971. The funerary boat of Khufu. In *Aufsätze zum siebzigsten Geburtstag von Herbert Ricke*, ed. `Abd al-Mun`im AbuBakr, 1–16. Wiesbaden: Steiner in Komm.

Arnold, Dieter. 2002. *The pyramid complex of Senwosret III at Dahshur: Architectural studies*. Publications of the Metropolitan Museum of Art Egyptian Expedition, no. 26. New York: Metropolitan Museum of Art.

Aspinall, Arnold, S. W. Feather, and Colin Renfrew. 1972. Neutron activation analysis of Aegean obsidians. *Nature* 237: 333–334.

Aubet, María Eugenia. 2001. *The Phoenicians and the West: Politics, colonies, and trade*. Trans. Mary Turton. 2nd ed. Cambridge: Cambridge University Press.

Bard, Kathryn A., and Rodolfo Fattovich, eds. 2007. *Harbor of the Pharaohs to the land of Punt: Archaeological investigations at Mersa/Wadi Gawasis, Egypt, 2001–2005*. Naples: Università degli Studi di Napoli "L'Orientale."

Basch, Lucien. 1987. *Le musée imaginaire de la marine antique*. Athens: Institut Hellénique pour la Préservation de la Tradition Nautique.

Bass, George F. 1967. *Cape Gelidonya: A Bronze Age shipwreck*. Transactions of the American Philosophical Society, no. 57, part 8. Philadelphia: American Philosophical Society.

———. 1989. The construction of a seagoing vessel of the Late Bronze Age. In *Tropis I. Proceedings of the 1st International Symposium on Ship Construction in Antiquity,*

Piraeus 1985, ed. Harry E. Tzalas, 25–35. Athens: Hellenic Institute for the Preservation of Nautical Tradition.

———. 2006. New techniques of archaeology and Greek shipwrecks of the sixth and fifth centuries BCE. *Proceedings of the American Philosophical Society* 150 (1): 1–14.

Bats, Michel. 1996. I Greci in Gallia e in Corsica. In *I Greci in Occidente*, ed. Giovanni Pugliese Carratelli, 577–584. Milan: Bompiani.

Bednarik, Robert G. 1999. Pleistocene seafaring in the Mediterranean. *Anthropologie* 37 (3): 275–282.

Benini, Alessandra. 2001. The second wreck at Gela: Notes on naval architecture. In *The Archaic Greek ship at Gela (and preliminary exploration of a second Greek shipwreck)*, ed. Rosalba Panvini, 97–106. Trans. Brian E. McConnell. Palermo: Salvatore Sciascia Editore.

Borchardt, Ludwig. 1913. *Das Grabdenkmal des Königs Sá hu-re' (Ausgrabungen der Deutschen Orient-Gesellschaft in Abusir 1902–1908, no. 7)*. Wissenschaftliche Veröffentlichungen der Deutschen Orient-Gesellschaft, no. 26. Leipzig.

Bound, Mensun. 1985. Early observations on the construction of the pre-classical wreck at Campese Bay, Island of Giglio: Clues to the vessel's nationality. In *Sewn plank boats: Archaeological and ethnographic papers based on those presented to a conference at Greenwich in November 1984*, eds. Seán McGrail and Eric Kentley, 49–66. Oxford: BAR.

———. 1991a. A wreck of likely Etruscan origin off the Mediterranean Island of Giglio (c. 600 B.C.). In *Recent advances in marine archaeology: Proceedings of the Second Indian Conference on Marine Archaeology of Indian Ocean Countries, January 1990*, ed. S. R. Rao, 43–50. Goa: Society for Marine Archaeology and National Institute of Oceanography.

———. 1991b. *The Giglio wreck: A wreck of the Archaic period (c. 600 BCE) off the Tuscan island of Giglio; An account of its discovery and excavation: A review of the main finds*. ENAΛIA Supplements, no. 1. Athens: Hellenic Institute of Marine Archaeology.

Bound, Mensun, and R. Vallintine. 1983. A wreck of possible Etruscan origin off Giglio Island. *International Journal of Nautical Archaeology* 12 (2): 113–122.

Bower, Bruce. 1997. Ancient roads to Europe. *Science News* 151 (1): 12.

———. 2010. Ancient hominids may have been seafarers: Hand axes excavated on Crete suggest hominids made sea crossings to go "out of Africa." *Science News* 177 (3): 14.

Brunton, Guy, and Gertrude Caton-Thompson. 1928. *The Badarian civilisation and predynastic remains near Badari, publications of the Egyptian Research Account and British School of Archaeology in Egypt*. London: British School of Archaeology in Egypt.

Cabrera, P., J. Pinedo, B. Roldán, J. S. Barba, and J. Perera. 1992. Campaña de cubrición del yacimiento subacuático de la Playa de la Isla (Mazarrón–Murcia). In *II Jornadas de arqueología suacuática en Asturias*, ed. J. A. Rodríguez Asensio, 37–43. Oviedo: Universidad de Oviedo.

Cann, J. R., J. E. Dixon, and Colin Renfrew. 1965. Obsidian in the Aegean. *Annual of the British School of Archaeology at Athens* 60: 225–247.

Cann, J. R., and C. Renfrew. 1964. The characterization of obsidian and its application to the Mediterranean region. *Proceedings of the Prehistoric Society* 30: 111–133.

Carlson, Deborah N. 2003. The classical Greek shipwreck at Tektaş Burnu, Turkey. *American Journal of Archaeology* 107: 581–600.

Casson, Lionel. [1971] 1995. *Ships and seamanship in the ancient world*. Reprint, Baltimore: Johns Hopkins University Press.

Cherry, John F. 1990. The first colonization of the Mediterranean islands: A review of recent research. *Journal of Mediterranean Archaeology* 3 (2): 145–221.

———. 1992. Palaeolithic Sardinians? Some questions of evidence and method. In *Sardinia in the Mediterranean: A footprint in the sea; Studies in Sardinian archaelogy presented to Miriam S. Balmuth*, ed. Miriam S. Balmuth, Robert H. Tykot, and Tamsey K. Andrews, 28–39. Sheffield: Sheffield Academic Press.

Childs, T. 2007. Copper. In *Harbor of the Pharaohs to the land of Punt: Archaeological investigations at Mersa/Wadi Gawasis, Egypt, 2001–2005*, ed. Kathryn A. Bard and Rodolfo Fattovich, 196. Naples: Università degli Studi di Napoli "L'Orientale."

Coates, John F. 1985. Some structural models for sewn boats. In *Sewn plank boats: Archaeological and ethnographic papers based on those presented to a conference at Greenwich in November 1984*, ed. Sean McGrail and Eric Kentley, 9–18. Oxford: BAR.

Coleman, John E. 1985. "Frying pans" of the Early Bronze Age Aegean. *American Journal of Archaeology* 89: 191–219.

Creasman, Paul P. 2005. The Cairo Dahshur boats. MA thesis, Texas A&M University.

Cristofani, Mauro. 1996. *Etruschi e altre genti nell'Italia preromana: Mobilità in età arcaica.* Archaeologica, no. 120. Rome: Giorgio Bretschneider.

Daressy, Georges. 1895. Une flottille phénicienne d'après une peinture égyptienne. *Revue Archéologique* 27: 286–292, pls. XIV–XV.

Davies, Norman de G., and R. O. Faulkner. 1947. A Syrian trading venture to Egypt. *Journal of Egyptian Archaeology* 33: 40–46, pl. VIII.

de Morgan, Jean-Jacques, M. Berthelot, Georges Albert Legrain, Gustave Jéquier, Victor Loret, and Daniel Fouquet. 1895. *Fouilles à Dâhchour.* Vol. 1, *Mars–juin 1894.* Vienna: A. Holzhausen.

Eiseman, Cynthia Jones, and Brunilde Sismondo Ridgway. 1987. *The Porticello shipwreck: A Mediterranean merchant vessel of 415–385 B.C.* Nautical Archaeology Series, no. 2. College Station: Texas A&M University Press.

el-Raziq, M. Abd, G. Castel, and P. Tallet. 2006. Ayn Soukhna et la mer Rouge. *Égypte, Afrique et Orient* 41: 3–6.

Evans, Arthur. 1964. *The Palace of Minos: A comparative account of the successive stages of the early Cretan civilization as illustrated by the discoveries at Knossos.* Vol. 2. New York: Biblo and Tannen.

Facchini, F., and F. Giusberti. 1992. *Homo sapiens sapiens* remains from the island of Crete. In *Continuity or replacement: Controversies in Homo sapiens evolution; Selected papers from the Symposium on Controversies in Homo sapiens Evolution, Zagreb, July 1988*, ed. Günter Bräuer and Fred H. Smith, 89–208. Rotterdam: A. A. Balkema.

Foerster Laures, Federico. 1989. Caulking in sewn boats? *International Journal of Nautical Archaeology* 18 (3): 266–267.

Giesecke, Heinz-Eberhard. 1983. The Akrotiri Ship fresco. *International Journal of Nautical Archaeology* 12 (2): 123–143.

Glanville, Stephen Ranulph Kingdon. 1931–1932. Records of a royal dockyard of the time of Thutmosis III: Papyrus British Museum 10056. *Zeitschrift für Ägyptische Sprache und Altertumskunde* 66, 68: 105–121, 7–41.

Glanville, Stephen Ranulph Kingdon, and Raymond Oliver Faulkner. 1972. *Catalogue of Egyptian antiquities in the British Museum.* Vol. 2, *Wooden model boats.* London: British Museum.

Gómez-Gil Aizpurúa, Carlos, and Juan Luis Sierra Méndez. 1996. Extracción y tratamientos del barco fenicio (barco I) de la Playa de la Isla (Puerto de Mazarrón, Mazarrón). *Cuadernos de Arqueología Marítima* 4: 217–228.

Greene, Elizabeth S. 2003. Endless summer: The 2002 excavation season at Pabuç Burnu, Turkey. *INA Quarterly* 30 (1): 3–11.

Greene, Elizabeth S., Mark L. Lawall, and Mark E. Polzer. 2008. Inconspicuous consumption: The sixth-century B.C.E. shipwreck at Pabuç Burnu, Turkey. *American Journal of Archaeology* 112 (4): 685–711.

Hadjidaki, Elpida. 1996. Underwater excavations of a late fifth century merchant ship at Alonnesos, Greece: The 1991–1993 seasons. *Bulletin de Correspondance Hellénique* 120 (2): 561–593.

Haldane, Cheryl Ward. 1984. The Dashur boats. MA thesis, Texas A&M University.

———. 1988. Boat timbers from El-Lisht: A new method of ancient Egyptian hull construction; Preliminary report. *Mariner's Mirror* 74: 141–152.

———. 1992. The Lisht timbers: A report on their significance. In *The pyramid complex of Senwosret I*, ed. Dieter Arnold, 102–112, pls. 15–32. New York: Metropolitan Museum of Art.

———. 1996. Ancient Egyptian hull construction. In *Tropis IV: Proceedings of the 4th International Symposium on Ship Construction in Antiquity, Center for the Acropolis Studies, Athens, 28–31 August 1991*, ed. Harry E. Tzalas, 235–244. Athens: Hellenic Institute for the Preservation of Nautical Tradition.

Haldane, Cheryl W., and Cynthia W. Shelmerdine. 1990. Herodotus 2.96.1–2 again. *Classical Quarterly* 40 (2): 535–539.

Hassan, Selim. 1955. The causeway of Wnis at Sakkara. *Zeitschrift für Ägyptische Sprache und Altertumskunde* 80 (2): 136–139.

Hayes, William Christopher. 1964. Most Ancient Egypt: Chapter 3. The Neolithic and Chalcolithic communities of northern Egypt. *Journal of Near Eastern Studies* 23 (4): 217–272.

Hendrickx, Stan, and Pierre Vermeersch. 2000. Prehistory: From the Palaeolithic to the Badarian culture (c. 700,000–4000 BCE). In *The Oxford History of Ancient Egypt*, ed. Ian Shaw, 17–43. Oxford: Oxford University Press.

Hoftijzer, J., and W. H. van Soldt. 1998. Texts from Ugarit pertaining to seafaring. In *Seagoing ships and seamanship in the Bronze Age Levant*, ed. Shelley Wachsmann, 333–344. College Station: Texas A&M University Press.

Jacobsen, Thomas W. 1969. Excavations at Porto Cheli and vicinity, preliminary report II: The Franchthi Cave, 1967–1968. *Hesperia* 38: 343–381.

———. 1973. Excavation in the Franchthi Cave, 1969–1971, part I. *Hesperia* 42 (1): 45–88, pls. 13–17.

Jenkins, N. 1980. *The boat beneath the pyramid: King Cheops' royal ship*. New York: Holt, Rinehart and Winston.

Johnstone, Paul. 1973. Stern first in the Stone Age? *International Journal of Nautical Archaeology* 2 (1): 3–11.

———. 1988. *The sea-craft of prehistory*. London: Routledge.

Johnstone, Paul F. 1982. Bronze Age Cycladic ships: An overview. In *Temple University Aegean Symposium: A symposium sponsored by the Department of Art History, Temple University, with the theme "Trade and travel in the Cyclades during the Bronze Age," Friday, March 5, 1982*, ed. Philip P. Betancourt, 1–8. Philadelphia: Department of Art History, Temple University.

Joncheray, J.-P. 1976. L'épave grecque, ou étrusque, de Bon Porté. *Cahiers d'Archéologie Subaquatique* 5: 5–36.

Kahanov, Yaacov. 2003. The hull. In *The Ma'agan Mikhael ship: The recovery of a 2400-year-old merchantman: Final report*. Vol. 1, ed. Elisha Linder and Yaacov Kahanov, 53–129. Haifa: Israel Exploration Society and University of Haifa.

Kahanov, Yaacov, and Eilisha Linder 2004. *The Ma'agan Mikhael ship: The recovery of a 2400-year-old merchantman: Final report*. Vol. 2. Haifa: Israel Exploration Society and University of Haifa.

Kahanov, Yaacov, and Patrice Pomey. 2004. The Greek sewn shipbuilding tradition and the Ma'agan Mikhael ship: A comparison with Mediterranean parallels from the sixth to the fourth centuries BCE. *Mariner's Mirror* 90 (1): 6–28.

Landström, Björn. 1970. *Ships of the pharaohs: 4000 years of Egyptian shipbuilding*. Garden City, NY: Doubleday.

Lawall, Mark L. 1998. Bolsals, Mendian amphoras, and the date of the Porticello shipwreck. *International Journal of Nautical Archaeology* 27 (1): 16–23.

Lin, Shih-Han Samuel. 2003. Lading of the Late Bronze Age ship at Uluburun. MA thesis, Texas A&M University.

Linder, Elisha, and Yaacov Kahanov. 2003. *The Ma'agan Mikhael ship: The recovery of a 2400-year-old merchantman: Final report*. Vol. 1. Haifa: Israel Exploration Society and University of Haifa.

Liou, B. 1974. Note provisoire sur deux gisements gréco-étrusques (Bon-Porté A et Pointe du Dattier). *Cahiers d'Archéologie Subaquatique* 3: 7–19.

———. 1975. Direction des recherches archéologiques sous-marines. *Gallia* 33: 571–605.

Lipke, Paul. 1984. *The royal ship of Cheops: A retrospective account of the discovery, restoration and reconstruction; Based on interviews with Hag Ahmed Youssef Moustafa*. BAR International Series, no. 225. Oxford: BAR.

———. 1985. Retrospective on the royal ship of Cheops. In *Sewn plank boats: Archaeological and ethnographic papers based on those presented to a conference at Greenwich in November 1984*, ed. Sean McGrail and Eric Kentley, 19–34. Oxford: BAR.

Long, Luc, Pierre Drap, Liucien-François Gantès, and Michel Rival. 2001. L'épave Grand Ribaud F: Rapport scientifique intermédiaire année 2001. Marseille: DRASSM.

Long, Luc, Liucien-François Gantès, and Pierre Drap. 2002. Premiers résultats archéologiques sur l'épave Grand Ribaud F (Giens, Var). Quelques éléments nouveaux sur le commerce étrusque en Gaule vers 500 avant J.-C. *Cahiers d'Archéologie Subaquatique* 14: 5–40.

Long, Luc, and Jean-Christophe Sourisseau. 2002. Épaves Grand Ribaud F (Giens). In *Les étrusques en mer: Épaves d'Antibes à Marseille*, ed. Luc Long, Patrice Pomey, and Jean-Christophe Sourisseau, 55–62. Aix-en-Provence: Musées de Marseille, Édisud.

Lucas, Alfred. 1962. *Ancient Egyptian materials and industries*. 4th ed., rev. and enl. by John Richard Harris. London: Edward Arnold.

Manning, Sturt W., Cemal Pulak, Bernd Kromer, Sahra Talamo, Christopher Bronk Ramsey, and Michael Dee. 2009. Absolute age of the Uluburun shipwreck: A key Late Bronze Age time-capsule for the east Mediterranean. In *Tree-rings, kings, and Old World archaeology and environment: Papers presented in honor of Peter Ian Kuniholm*, ed. Sturt W. Manning and Mary Jaye Bruce, 163–188. Oxford: Oxbow.

Mantzouka, Eleftheria. 2004. The transport amphoras from a fifth century shipwreck found off the island of Alonnesos, northern Sporades, Greece. MA thesis, East Carolina University.

Marangou, Christina. 2003. Neolithic watercraft in Greece: Circumstantial evidence and serious guesses. In *Boats, ships and shipyards: Proceedings of the Ninth International Symposium on Boat and Ship Archaeology, Venice 2000*, ed. Carlo Beltrame, 14–18. Oxford: Oxbow.

Marinatos, Spyridon. 1974. *Excavations at Thera VI: 1972 season*. Bibliotheke tes en Athenais Archaiologikes Hetaireias, no. 64. Athens: Archaiologiki Etaireia.

Mark, Samuel. 2005. *Homeric seafaring*. College Station: Texas A&M University Press.
———. 2009. The construction of the Khufu I vessel (c. 2566 BCE): A re-evaluation. *International Journal of Nautical Archaeology* 38 (1): 133–152.
Martini, F. 1992. Early human settlements in Sardinia: The Palaeolithic industries. In *Sardinia in the Mediterranean: A footprint in the sea; Studies in Sardinian archaelogy presented to Miriam S. Balmuth*, ed. Miriam S. Balmuth, Robert H. Tykot, and Tamsey K. Andrews, 40–48. Sheffield: Sheffield Academic Press.
Mathieu, Bernard. 2004. Les travaux de l'institut français d'archéologie orientale en 2003–2004. *Bulletin de l'Institut Français d'Archéologie Orientale* 104: 585–762.
Negueruela, Iván. 1996. Excavaciones arqueológicas subacuáticas realizadas por el Centro Nacional de Investigaciones Arqueológicas Submarinas en el yacimiento de la Playa de la Isla (Mazarrón): Memoria de la campaña de 1995. In *Memorias de arqueologia 10*, ed. Manuel Lechuga Galindo and María Belen Sánchez González, 162–180. Murcia: Región de Murcia, Consejeria de Educación y Cultura, Dirección General de Cultura.
———. 2004. Hacia la comprensión de la construcción naval fenicia según el barco "Mazarrón-2" de siglo VII a.C. In *La navegación fenicia: Tecnología naval y derroteros; Encuentros entre marinos, arqueólogos e historiadores*, ed. Victoria Peña, Carlos G. Wagner, and Alfredo Mederos, 227–278. Madrid: Centro de Estudios Fenicios y Punicos.
Negueruela, Iván, R. G. Gallero, M. San Claudio, A. M. Sanmartín, M. Presa, and C. Marín. 2004. Mazarrón-2: El barco fenicio del siglo VII a.C. Campaña de noviembre 1999/marzo 2000. In *El mundo púnico: Religión, antropología y cultura material; Actas II Congreso Internacional del Mundo Púnico, Cartagena, 6–9 de abril de 2000*, ed. Antonino González Blanco, Gonzalo Matilla Séiquer, and Alejandro Egea Vivancos, 453–484. Murcia: Universidad de Murcia, Instituto del Próximo Oriente Antiguo, Área de Historia Antigua.
Negueruela, Iván, J. Pinedo, M. Gómez, A. Miñano, I. Arellano, and J. S. Barba. 1995. Seventh-century BCE Phoenician vessel discovered at Playa de la Isla, Mazarron, Spain. *International Journal of Nautical Archaeology* 24 (3): 189–197.
———. 2000. Descubrimiento de dos barcos fenicios en Mazarrón (Murcia). In *Actas del IV Congreso Internacional de Estudios Fenicios y Púnicos: Cádiz, 2 al 6 de octubre de 1995*, ed. Maria Eugenia Aubet and M. Barthélemy, 1671–1679. Cádiz: Servicio de Publicaciones, Universidad de Cádiz.
Nieto, Xavier, and M. Santos. 2009. *El vaixell grec arcaic de Cala Sant Vicenç*. Monografies del CASC, no. 7. Barcelona: Museu d'Arqueologia de Catalunya.
Nieto, Xavier, Marta Santos, and Ferran Tarongí. 2004. Un barco griego del siglo VI a.C. en Cala Sant Vicenç (Pollença, Mallorca). In *La navegación fenicia: Tecnología naval y derroteros; Encuentros entre marinos, arqueólogos e historiadores*, ed. Victoria Peña, Carlos G. Wagner, and Alfredo Mederos, 197–225. Madrid: Centro de Estudios Fenicios y Punicos.
———. 2005. El barco griego de Cala Sant Vicenç (Pollença, Mallorca). In *Aequora, iam, mare . . . Mare, uomini e merci nel Mediterraneo antica: Atti del Convegno Internazionale, Genova, 9–10 Dicembre 2004*, ed. Bianc Maria Giannattasio, Cristina Canepa, Luisa Grasso, and Eliana Piccardi, 42–55. Madrid: All'Insegna del Giglio.
Nieto, Xavier, Ferrán Terongí, and Marta Santos. 2002. El pecio de Cala Sant Vicenç: El barco griego más antiguo de Baleares. *Revista de Arqueología* 258: 18–25.
Nour, Mohammad Zaki, Mohammad Salah Osman, Zaky Iskander, and Ahmad Youssof Moustafa. 1960. *The Cheops boats*. Part I. Cairo: Ministry of Culture and National Orientation, Antiquities Department of Egypt.

O'Connor, David. 1991. Boat graves and pyramid origins: New discoveries at Abydos, Egypt. *Expedition* 33 (3): 5–17.

———. 1995. The earliest royal boat graves. *Egyptian Archaeology* 6: 3–7.

———. 2009. *Abydos: Egypt's first pharaohs and the cult of Osiris*. New Aspects of Antiquity. London: Thames & Hudson.

O'Connor, David, and Matthew A. Adams. 2001. Moored in the desert. *Archaeology* 54 (3): 44–45.

Panvini, Rosalba. 2001a. *The Archaic Greek ship at Gela (and preliminary exploration of a second Greek shipwreck)*. Trans. Brian E. McConnell. Palermo: Salvatore Sciascia Editore.

———. 2001b. The second Greek wreck at Gela: Preliminary observations. In *The Archaic Greek ship at Gela (and preliminary exploration of a second Greek shipwreck)*, ed. Rosalba Panvini, 79–95. Trans. Brian E. McConnell. Palermo: Salvatore Sciascia Editore.

Polzer, Mark E. 2004. An Archaic laced hull in the Aegean: The 2003 excavation and study of the Pabuç Burnu ship remains. *INA Quarterly* 31 (3): 3–11.

———. 2009a. The VIth-century B.C. shipwreck at Pabuç Burnu, Turkey: Evidence for transition from lacing to mortise-and-tenon joinery in late Archaic Greek shipbuilding. In *Transferts technologiques en architecture navale méditerranéenne de l'antiquité aux temps modernes: Identité technique et identité culturelle: Actes de la Table Ronde d'Istanbul, 19–22 mai 2007, Institut Français d'Études Anatoliennes–Georges Dumézil*, ed. Patrice Pomey, 27–44. Paris: De Boccard.

———. 2009b. Hull remains from the Pabuç Burnu shipwreck and early transition in Archaic Greek shipbuilding. MA thesis, Texas A&M University.

Pomey, Patrice. 1981. L'épave de Bon Porté et les bateaux cousus de Méditerranée. *Mariner's Mirror* 67 (3): 225–243.

———. 1995. Les épaves grecques et romaines de la place Jules-Verne à Marseille. In *Comptes rendus des séances de l'année 1995 (avril–juin)*, 459–484. Paris: Académie des Inscriptions et Belles-Lettres.

———. 1997a. Un exemple d'évolution des techniques de construction navale antique: De l'assemblage par ligatures à l'assemblage par tenons et mortaises. In *Techniques et économie antiques et médiévales: Le temps de l'innovation; Colloque international (C.N.R.S.)*, ed. Dimitri Meeks and Dominique Garcia, 195–203. Aix-en-Provence: Editions Errance.

———. 1997b. *La navigation dans l'antiquitié*. Aix-en-Provence: Édisud.

———. 1999a. Les épaves grecques archaïques de la Place Jules-Verne. In *Parcours de villes: Marseille; 10 ans d'archéologie, 2600 ans d'histoire*, ed. Antoinette Hesnard, Manuel Moliner, Frédéric Conche, and Marc Bouiron, 35. Aix-en-Provence: Musées de Marseille and Éditions Édisud.

———. 1999b. Les épaves grecques du VIe siècle av. J.-C. de la place Jules-Verne à Marseille. In *Construction navale maritime et fluviale: Approches archéologique, historique et ethnologique; Actes du Septième Colloque international d'archéologie navale, Île Tatihou, 1994*, ed. Patrice Pomey and Éric Rieth, 147–154. Paris: CNRS Éditions.

———. 2001. Les épaves grecques archaïques du VIe siecle av. J.-C. de Marseille: Épaves Jules-Verne 7 et 9 et César 1. In *Tropis VI: Proceedings of the 6th International Symposium on Ship Construction in Antiquity, Lamia, 1996*, ed. Harry Tzalas, 425–437. Athens: Hellenic Institute for the Preservation of Nautical Tradition.

———. 2002a. Épave de Bon Porté 1. In *Les étrusques en mer: Épaves d'Antibes à Marseille*, ed. Luc Long, Patrice Pomey, and J.-Ch. Sourisseau, 113–116. Aix-en-Provence: Musées de Marseille, Édisud.

———. 2002b. Épaves Jules-Verne 9 et Jules-Verne 7. In *Les étrusques en mer: Épaves d'Antibes à Marseille*, ed. Luc Long, Patrice Pomey, and J.-Ch. Sourisseau, 121–123. Aix-en-Provence: Musées de Marseille, Édisud.

———. 2003. Reconstruction of Marseilles 6th century BCE Greek ships. In *Boats, ships and shipyards: Proceedings of the Ninth International Symposium on Boat and Ship Archaeology, Venice 2000*, ed. Carlo Beltrame, 57–65. Oxford: Oxbow.

———. In press. A Pharaonic sea-going ship of the Middle Kingdom (c. 2000 BCE) from Ayn Soukhna. In *Between continents: Proceedings of the Twelfth International Symposium on Boat and Ship Archaeology, Istanbul, 12–16 October 2009*, ed. Nergis Günsenin. Oxford: Oxbow.

Pomey, Patrice, and Luc Long. 1992. Le premiers échanges maritimes du midi de la Gaule du VIe au IIIe s. av. J.-C. à travers les épaves. In *Marseille grecque et la Gaule: Actes du Colloque international d'histoire et d'archéologie et du Ve Congrès archéologique de Gaule méridionale (Marseille, 18–23 novembre 1990)*. Études Massaliètes, no. 3, ed. Michel Bats, Guy Bertucchi, Gaëtan Conges, and Henri Tréziny, 189–198. Aix-en-Provence: Université de Provence.

Pomey, Patrice, and Michel Rival. 2002. Épave *Grand Ribaud F*. In *Les étrusques en mer: Épaves d'Antibes à Marseille*, ed. Luc Long, Patrice Pomey, and J.-Ch. Sourisseau, 117–119. Aix-en-Provence: Musées de Marseille, Édisud.

Prins, Adriaan Hendrik Johan. 1986. *A handbook of sewn boats: The ethnography and archaeology of Archaic plank-built craft*. Maritime Monographs and Reports, no. 59. Greenwich: Trustees of the National Maritime Museum.

Pulak, Cemal. 1998. The Uluburun shipwreck: An overview. *International Journal of Nautical Archaeology* 27 (3): 188–224.

———. 1999. The Late Bronze Age shipwreck at Uluburun: Aspects of hull construction. In *The Point Iria wreck: Interconnections in the Mediterranean ca. 1200 BCE; Proceedings of the International Conference, Island of Spetses, 19 September 1998*, ed. W. Phelps, Y. Lolos, and Y. Vichos, 209–238. Athens: Hellenic Institute of Marine Archaeology.

———. 2008. The Uluburun shipwreck and Late Bronze Age trade. In *Beyond Babylon: Art, trade, and diplomacy in the second millennium B.C.*, ed. Joan Aruz, Kim Benzel, and Jean M. Evans, 288–305, 306–310, 313–321, 324–333, 336–342, 345–348, 350–358, 366–378, 382–385. New York: Metropolitan Museum of Art; New Haven, CT: Yale University Press.

Raban, Avner. 1984. The Thera ships: Another interpretation. *American Journal of Archaeology* 88 (1): 11–19.

Reisner, George A. 1913. *Models of ships and boats*. Cairo: Institut Français d'Archéologie Orientale.

Renfrew, Colin. 1967. Cycladic metallurgy and the Aegean Bronze Age. *American Journal of Archaeology* 71: 1–20, pls. 1–10.

———. 1972. *The emergence of civilisation: The Cyclades and the Aegean in the third millennium B.C.* Studies in Prehistory. London: Methuen.

Renfrew, Colin, J. E. Dixon, and J. R. Cann. 1965. Obsidian in the Aegean. *Annual of the British School at Athens* 60: 123–248.

Renfrew, Colin, S. A. Durrani, H. A. Khan, and J. Taj. 1971. Obsidian source identification by fission track analysis. *Nature* 233: 242–245.

Roberts, Owain T. P. 1987. Wind-power and the boats from the Cyclades. *International Journal of Nautical Archaeology and Underwater Exploration* 16 (4): 309–311.

Ruiz, Rafael Azuar. 2008. *ARQUA: Museo Nacional de Arqueología Subacuática; Catálogo*. Madrid: Ministerio de Cultura, Dirección General deBellas Artes y Bienes Culturales, Subdirección General de Museos Estatales.

Säve-Söderbergh, Torgny. 1946. *The navy of the Eighteenth Egyptian Dynasty*. Uppsala Universitets Årsskrift, no. 6. Uppsala: Lundequistska Bokhandeln.

Sondaar, P. Y., R. Elburg, G. Klein Hofmeijer, F. Martini, M. Sanges, A. Spaan, and H. de Visser. 1995. The human colonization of Sardinia: A Late-Pleistocene human fossil from Corbeddu Cave. *Comptes Rendus de l'Académie des Sciences* 320: 145–150.

Steffy, J. Richard. 1985. The Kyrenia ship: An interim report on its hull construction. *American Journal of Archaeology* 89: 71–101.

——. 1994. *Wooden ship building and the interpretation of shipwrecks*. College Station: Texas A&M University Press.

Tzalas, Harry E. 1995. On the obsidian trail: With a papyrus craft in the Cyclades. In *Tropis III: Proceedings of the 3rd International Symposium on Ship Construction in Antiquity, 24–27 August 1989, Athens*, ed. Harry E. Tzalas, 441–469. Athens: Hellenic Institute for the Preservation of Nautical Tradition.

van Duivenvoorde, Wendy. In press. The fifth-century B.C. shipwreck at Tektaş Burnu, Turkey: Evidence for the ship's hull from nail concretions. In *Tropis IX: Proceedings of the 9th International Symposium on Ship Construction in Antiquity; Agia Napa, Cyprus, 25–30 August 2005*, ed. Harry E. Tzalas. Athens: Hellenic Institute for the Preservation of Nautical Tradition.

Wachsmann, Shelley. 1980. The Thera waterborne procession reconsidered. *International Journal of Nautical Archaeology* 9 (4): 287–295.

——. 1995. Paddled and oared ships before the Iron Age. In *The age of the galley: Mediterranean oared vessels since pre-classical times*, ed. Robert Gardiner, 10–35. London: Conway Maritime Press.

——. 1998. *Seagoing ships and seamanship in the Bronze Age Levant*. College Station: Texas A&M University Press.

Ward, Cheryl A. 2000. *Sacred and secular: Ancient Egyptian ships and boats*. Archaeological Institute of America Monographs New Series, no. 5. Philadelphia: University Museum, University of Pennsylvania.

——. 2003. Sewn planked boats from Early Dynastic Abydos, Egypt. In *Boats, ships and shipyards: Proceedings of the Ninth International Symposium on Boat and Ship Archaeology, Venice 2000*, ed. Carlo Beltrame, 19–23. Oxford: Oxbow.

——. 2004. Boatbuilding in ancient Egypt. In *The philosophy of shipbuilding*, ed. Frederick Hocker and Cheryl Ward, 13–24. College Station: Texas A&M University Press.

——. 2006. Boat-building and its social context in early Egypt: Interpretations from the First Dynasty boat-grave cemetery at Abydos. *Antiquity* 80: 118–129.

Ward, Cheryl, and Chiara Zazzaro. 2009. Evidence for Pharaonic seagoing ships at Mersa/Wadi Gawasis, Egypt. *International Journal of Nautical Archaeology* 39 (1): 27–43.

CHAPTER 17

THE SEAFARERS AND SHIPWRECKS OF ANCIENT GREECE AND ROME

DEBORAH N. CARLSON

INTRODUCTION

CLASSICAL archaeology, which comprises the study of the ancient Mediterranean's two greatest cultures—the Greeks and Romans—embraces several related disciplines, including art history, history, philology, and philosophy. The result is a symbiotic but delicately balanced and at times precarious relationship between the textual, visual, and material evidence. Some examples of a maritime nature: the classical scholar can draw on no substantive archaeological evidence for either piracy or grain cargoes, two issues of enduring historical consequence for the ancients, and there are almost no textual descriptions, much less discussion, of ancient ship construction technology; this knowledge has come exclusively from archaeological remains. Ancient warships, by contrast, lie somewhere in between, with virtually no direct physical evidence that predates the first millennium, but a considerable amount of information in illustrations, inscriptions, and literary sources. The reader is cautioned, therefore, that much of the relevant data regarding Greek and Roman seafaring lies outside the realm of archaeology and thus outside the focus of the present contribution. There are, however, a wide range of excellent publications, ranging from indices (Illsley 1996; Parker 1992) and sourcebooks (Meijer and Van Nijf 1992) to histories (Bass 1972, 1975; Blackman 1973; Du Plat Taylor 1965), syntheses (Casson 1995; Meijer 1986), and thematic studies (Hohlfelder 2008; Rauh 2003). Furthermore, because the maritime archaeology of the ancient Mediterranean involves dozens of countries with a seafaring past, the reader is encouraged not to overlook the many equally useful foreign-language titles, including those in French (Basch 1987; Pomey 1997; Pomey and Rieth 2005; Rival 1991), German (Bockius 2007; Göttlicher 2009; Höckmann 1985), Italian (Beltrame 2002; Gianfrotta and Pomey 1981), and Spanish (Nieto 1984).

Early History

It comes as no surprise that the search for evidence of ancient Greek and Roman seafaring and the development of underwater archaeology in the Mediterranean intensified dramatically with the creation of the Aqualung in the 1940s; reciprocally, an illustrated account of Jacques Cousteau's early dives on the ancient shipwreck(s) at Grand Congloué, near Marseille (Cousteau 1954), fueled a public thirst for SCUBA equipment that manufacturers could scarcely meet. But Cousteau and his French colleagues were not the first to be captivated by the promise of unearthing the physical remains of ancient Mediterranean voyages; by the early twentieth century important discoveries in Greece, North Africa, and Italy had demonstrated just how extraordinary and fragile a resource ancient shipwrecks are.

In 1900, a small group of Greek sponge fishermen, blown off course while on a return voyage to the eastern Mediterranean, sought refuge at Antikythera, a barren island that lies almost equidistant between Crete and the Greek mainland (Svoronos 1903). There, at depths of approximately 42–55 m (140–180 ft), the sponge divers happened upon a sunken cargo of ancient bronze and marble statuary (Bol 1972). Conscientiously, they notified the Greek Archaeological Service, and an expedition to the site was launched. Over the next nine months, helmet divers at Antikythera raised additional pieces of bronze and marble sculpture, about a dozen two-handled ceramic shipping containers called transport amphoras, some finer ceramic tablewares (jugs, plates, cups, pots), glass bowls, and wooden fragments of the ship's hull (Weinberg et al. 1965). Sadly, because so little was known about wood conservation at the time, these fragmentary elm planks were allowed to dry out, causing them to shrink and become distorted, but not before it was observed that they had been joined together at their edges by means of close-set mortises and tenons. The most intriguing find from Antikythera is a portion of a sophisticated calendrical device comprising more than two dozen bronze gears calibrated to predict eclipses according to the 19-year-long cycle observed by the classical Greek astronomer Meton (Price 1974). Recent research using computed tomography has shown that the month names on one dial are likely of Corinthian origin, while another dial corresponds to the four-year cycle of the Olympic games, as celebrated at one of four ancient Greek sanctuaries (Freeth et al. 2008). The Antikythera Mechanism, as it is commonly called, thus provides unparalleled evidence for the technical proficiency of the ancient craftsman, even if in its day the device functioned as little more than a conversation piece.

In 1907, it was again Greek sponge fishermen who discovered the remains of a large cargo vessel lost off the Tunisian coast at Mahdia in the second quarter of the first century BCE. This ship had been transporting various fine arts in bronze (statues, lamps, decorative appliqués, and pieces of furniture) as well as marble (kraters, freestanding sculptures, sculpted reliefs, inscribed blocks, column shafts, and Ionic capitals). When some of these finds appeared for sale in Tunisia, French archaeologist and then director of the Antiquities Service Alfred Merlin located the site and launched an excavation. Merlin himself did not dive on the wreck, but supervised the recovery effort from the surface and attempted to record the location of the finds on the seabed; if this document, now lost, had appeared in any of Merlin's numerous publications (Hellenkemper Salies 1994: 1107–1117), it would likely have been the earliest archaeological site plan of an ancient Mediterranean shipwreck. In the decades that followed Merlin's campaign, various individuals returned to the Mahdia wreck and recovered additional artifacts, including portions of the ship's hull, which show, among other things, that the vessel had two layers of mortise-and-tenon-joined planks, protected by an outer skin of lead sheathing. More than 80 years after Merlin's expedition, a comprehensive catalog of finds, including a hypothetical reconstruction of the original ship, was published in association with an exhibit at the Rheinisches Landesmuseum in Bonn, Germany (Hellenkemper Salies 1994).

Finally, just southeast of Rome, Italy, at Lake Nemi, two enormous ancient ships came to light in the 1920s as a result of an ambitious recovery project spearheaded by Benito Mussolini (Bonino 2003; Carlson 2002; Ucelli 1950). Though their existence had been known to explorers for almost five centuries, the two vessels—attributed to the Roman emperor Caligula (37–41 CE)—emerged from their 1,900-year-old grave after Mussolini ordered that the water be pumped out of the lake into a nearby valley via an ancient Roman conduit. This audacious effort revealed the remains of two impressive wooden hulls, each about 70 m (230 ft) long and 23 m (75 ft) in beam, lavishly appointed with marble columns, gilded copper roof tiles, relief sculpture, mosaic floors, and running water. Technical drawings of the massive vessels show that they had been assembled using a system of pegged mortise-and-tenon joinery similar to that used at Antikythera and Mahdia, but never before seen on such a magnificent scale. In order to build the broad flat bottoms that made the Nemi vessels more like floating palaces than seagoing ships, the ancient shipwright(s) utilized four smaller sister keels, two on either side of the central keel, and huge internal timbers scarfed together to form continuous frames that spanned the hold from port to starboard. The Lake Nemi ships thus provided maritime historians with precious insight into the scope of Imperial Roman shipbuilding technology. Little did they know how precious a glimpse it was, for both ships were completely destroyed when the museum they were housed in caught fire during the Second World War.

Despite their demise, the Nemi ships still rank as the largest vessels ever recovered from antiquity, but it is important to note that they were designed primarily to serve as Imperial houseboats and not as seagoing merchantmen. The largest-known ancient seagoing ship to date was discovered about 1.6 km (1 mile) off the Tyrrhenian coast of northern Italy at Albenga, in 1925. A recovery effort in 1950, using a salvage ship equipped with a bucket dredge, brought to the surface over 1,000 clay transport amphoras, most of which were badly damaged in the process. Between 1961 and 1971, Italian archaeologist Nino Lamboglia directed the excavation of the remaining cargo, which included thousands more amphoras stacked in at least four rows. Pieces of Campanian black glaze pottery found between the jars and a bed of volcanic pumice found beneath them suggest that the cargo was loaded near the Bay of Naples in the early first century BCE. The Albenga ship is believed to have been transporting about 11,000 amphoras, for a total capacity of some 450–500 tons (Lamboglia 1971).

While these early underwater exploits were revolutionary, they were, archaeologically speaking, "less expert than they might have been" (Rickman 2008: 7); at Antikythera, Mahdia, and Grand Congloué, archaeologists never dived on the site but, rather, remained topside, directing the excavation remotely and often establishing the relative provenience of artifacts by interviewing the divers who collected them. In the years that followed, as more Roman shipwrecks came to light in France and Italy, archaeologists gained a profound appreciation of the urgent need to protect underwater cultural heritage, even if in some cases it was too late. In 1957, French naval officer Philippe Tailliez directed the excavation of a partially looted first-century BCE shipwreck at Titan (Tailliez 1965), where exposure of the ship's double-planked hull revealed early evidence for the long-standing tradition of placing a coin inside the socket of the mast-step (Carlson 2007; Marsden 1965). The next year, Lamboglia initiated two brief exploratory campaigns on the late-second-century BCE shipwreck at Spargi, Sardinia, but by the early 1960s the wreck, which lay at a depth of only 18 m (60 ft), had been picked clean by looters, and very few artifacts were subsequently recovered (Beltrame 2000a; Lamboglia 1961; Pallarés 1986; Roghi 1965, 1966).

At Spargi, Lamboglia fixed a network of grid squares to the seabed to facilitate photographic documentation of the wreck before the excavation ever began, signaling an important shift in the philosophy of treating shipwrecks as submerged archaeological sites (Olschki 2008: 170–171). In 1960, at Cape Gelidonya, Turkey, archaeologist George Bass and journalist Peter Throckmorton pioneered many of the discipline's now-standard excavation techniques (Bass 1967, 1972, 1975). In 1976, Bass founded the Institute of Nautical Archaeology at Texas A&M University, a nonprofit organization responsible for some of the most historically and archaeologically significant shipwreck excavations in the Mediterranean. For chronological reasons, many of them (such as Uluburun, Yassıada, and Serçe Limanı) lie outside the reach of this chapter, but the very idea that a shipwreck could and should be excavated with the same precision, thoroughness, and diligence afforded a terrestrial site led to the recovery and reassembly, in the late 1960s, of the best-preserved ancient Greek vessel found to date, at Kyrenia, Cyprus (Katzev 2007; Steffy 1985).

CARGOES AND COMMODITIES

Raw Materials

The vast majority of goods shipped around and across the Mediterranean in Greco-Roman times were comestible items like wine, olive oil, *garum* (a fermented fish sauce especially popular with the Romans), spices, and grain, as well as other agricultural products, such as fruit, nuts, and even butchered meat. Apart from grain, which texts and depictions suggest was shipped either in sacks or loose in partitioned compartments within the hold, these commodities were typically transported in amphoras (Grace 1979; Peacock and Williams 1986). The longevity and ubiquity of the amphora as the standard commercial shipping container of classical antiquity make it a unique archaeological indicator of both the agrarian economy and maritime trade.

Because amphoras were produced, used, and reused by the Canaanites, Phoenicians, Greeks, and Romans in every corner of the Mediterranean and beyond over the course of nearly two millennia, they—like the ships that carried them—offer numerous opportunities for archaeological research. Some scholars analyze production through the excavation of kiln sites (Empereur and Picon 1986) and the examination of clay fabrics (Whitbread 1995); others focus on the physical properties of the jars themselves, including morphology (Lawall 1995, 2005), capacity (Matheson and Wallace 1982; Wallace 1986), prefiring stamps (Börker and Burow 1998; Finkielsztejn 2001), postproduction graffiti (Lawall 2000), and linings (Beck and Borromeo 1990) or contents (Hansson and Foley 2008; Rothschild-Boros 1981).

The study of shipwrecked cargoes and the study of amphoras, then, enjoy a symbiotic relationship. Most ancient Mediterranean ships excavated over the past half-century were laden with large consignments of one or two amphora types alongside smaller quantities or even lone examples (sometimes called singletons) of numerous other types (Figure 17.1); of course, this does not mean that a given ship visited all the destinations represented by the various amphora types it carried, for amphoras too were continually traveling and being repaired, restocked, and reused. The excavation of a sunken amphora carrier can tell us not only which types routinely circulated together, but also for how long such jars remained in service; in turn, the amphora cargo can inform us about where the ship had called and when it sank, as the amphoras themselves are often among the latest datable objects on board (e.g., Lawall 1998). Stamped amphoras, which were particularly prevalent in the Hellenistic period (323–31 BCE), have been instrumental in dating individual shipwrecks (e.g., Pulak et al. 1987: 43). For the economic historian, however, amphora stamps often generate more wide-ranging questions than they solve (Davies 2001: 27–29; Debidour 1998), challenging researchers to better harvest the qualitative potential of largely quantitative data.

Figure 17.1 The shipwreck of a first-century BCE amphora carrier at Madrague de Giens, France. Photograph by A. Chéné. Reproduced with the kind permission of Centre Camille Jullian, CNRS, Aix-en-Provence.

Noncomestible raw materials such as stone blocks, metal ingots, and timber also constituted a conspicuous and important part of ancient maritime commerce. For building stone, the classical Greeks were generally content to exploit local sources where possible, even if this meant coating limestone blocks with plaster to give the appearance of finely grained marble; smaller, portable objects like volcanic millstones were routinely transported by sea (Williams-Thorpe and Thorpe 1990, 1993). The Greeks were forced to rely on distant forests, however, to supply the vast quantities of wood needed for the construction of both buildings and ships (Meiggs 1982; Rackham 2001). While it is not uncommon to find ingots of iron, lead, tin, or copper among the remains of ancient shipwrecked cargoes, less durable organic commodities like timber and textiles almost never survive the millennia (if they ever sank at all). The practical importance of such archaeologically invisible materials, and the strategic importance of controlling the shipping lanes in which they were transported, are underscored by one anonymous fifth-century BCE Greek writer often referred to as the Old Oligarch: "If some city is rich in timber for ship-building, where will it dispose of it, if it does not have the consent of the ruler of the sea? What if a city is rich in iron or copper or flax? Where will it dispose of it, if it does not have the consent of the ruler of the sea? And yet, it is from these very materials that I get my ships, taking timber from one place, iron from another, copper from another, flax from another, and wax from another" (Marr and Rhodes 2008: 47). The maritime transport of timber derivatives like pine tar—used as a sealant and waterproofing agent, among other things—has been documented archaeologically at shipwreck sites on both sides of the Mediterranean (Beck and Borromeo 1990; Bound 1991: 23; Carlson 2003: 588–589; Eiseman and Ridgway 1987: 3).

It was primarily the Romans who cultivated an appetite for the import of exotic colored stones (including marbles, breccias, granites, and porphyries) from distant locations in Egypt, North Africa, and Asia Minor. Inscriptions on blocks either abandoned at the quarry or stockpiled for future use attest to the scope and organization of this Imperial system (Fant 1989, 2001; Waelkens, De Paepe, and Moens 1988), while dozens of sunken stone cargoes shed light on the size, nature, and date of the shipments that supplied the Roman marble trade. The archaeological evidence points to a steady increase in the frequency of shipments during the first three centuries CE and indicates that the majority were composed of architectural elements (generally blocks and monolithic column shafts cut into standardized lengths) weighing as much as 350–400 tons. That most marble carriers were transporting eastern stones westward, with many likely destined for Rome, is suggested by a concentration of wrecks off the Sicilian coasts (Purpura 2008). One of these, the Capo Granitola A shipwreck, was laden with at least 60 white marble blocks from Proconnesus Island in the Sea of Marmara, but small chips of other marble types found between these large blocks imply that the vessel had previously transported stones from other sources.

Finished Goods

The Romans' interest in exotic stones, set in motion during the last two centuries BCE, coincided with a growing desire for Greek art, from mosaics and paintings to metalwork and sculpture, whether bronze originals, stone copies, or even forgeries. The fervor appreciable in the personal correspondence of wealthy Roman collectors like Marcus Tullius Cicero spawned what many today regard as the world's first art market (Green 1993; Pollitt 1986). Maritime archaeological evidence for the ancient art trade first came to light in the early twentieth century with the shipwrecks at Antikythera and Mahdia, but since then dozens of other lost or jettisoned sculptures have surfaced, making the sea one of the most prolific sources of ancient bronze statuary (Mattusch 1997; Tzalas 2007); only very few examples, however, are clearly associated with shipwrecked assemblages (Eiseman and Ridgway 1987).

Other manufactured goods documented in Greco-Roman shipwrecks around the Mediterranean include buckets, lamps, and incense burners, dining couches and other furniture, terra-cotta tiles for roofing and construction, and glass. At present, the partially excavated Ouest Embiez 1 shipwreck in southern France provides precious archaeological evidence for the transport by sea, ca. 200 CE, of raw glass, or cullet, as well as finished goblets and flat panes (Bernard et al. 2007; Fontaine and Foy 2007). The nearly contemporaneous shipwreck at Grado, in northern Italy, carried more than 10,000 fragments of recyclable colored and clear glass (Silvestri

2008; Silvestri, Molin, and Salviulo 2008) inside a single wooden barrel, which is among the earliest intact examples of its kind.

Fineware pottery holds an especially conspicuous place in ancient maritime trade and a somewhat contested place in modern scholarship. Because virtually every ancient shipwreck has yielded some fineware ceramics (cups, bowls, plates, jugs, etc.), it has been argued that their importance as articles of trade has been overestimated as a direct result of their durability (Gill 1994). Unlike transport amphoras, which functioned above all else as inexpensive shipping containers for consumable substances, open shapes such as bowls, cups, and plates—whether decorated or not—can only have had an intrinsic value, and attempts to determine this value have generated some rather dynamic debate (Boardman 1988; Cook 1987; Johnston 1993; Vickers 1985). The study of postproduction mercantile marks, such as graffiti and dipinti, has advanced the discussion (Johnston 1979, 2006; Lang 1976), but we cannot presume that all such marks were commercial in nature; it has been suggested that Greek and Punic graffiti scratched onto various Attic black glaze pots loaded on board a ship that sank near El Sec, Majorca, in the middle of the fourth century BCE represent different notational systems applied to different pots by different people at different times (De Hoz 1989). Other marks likely denote the owner's abbreviated name, like the Greek EYΠ (EUP) incised onto the bottom of a fishplate from the captain's quarters of the Kyrenia wreck, where the only other fineware ceramics on board appear to have been in use by the four-man crew and *not* transported as cargo.

SEAGOING SHIPS

Construction Technology

The excavation of shipwrecks has enhanced modern knowledge of Greco-Roman ship construction probably more than any other aspect of ancient seafaring, for Classical authors are silent on the subject, and detailed depictions are extremely few. The standard and predominant method of Greek and Roman shipwrights, often referred to today as the shell-first technique, involved the assembly of a shell or skin of hull planks fastened to one another at their edges using pegged mortise-and-tenon joinery (Steffy 1994: 43–54). Because the planks were not bent around a preexisting skeleton of ribs, or frames, they had to be cut with saws and shaped with adzes to achieve the appropriate curvature, which predictably meant considerable wastage of timber.

The construction process began by attaching the stem and sternpost to the keel, which was notched—or rabbeted—along its upper, outside edge to receive the first hull plank, also called the garboard strake. Along the entire length of this rabbet, or notch, the shipwright carved a row of mortises, each about 5 cm wide and 3 cm deep, and then inserted a wooden tenon approximately 6 cm long into each mortise

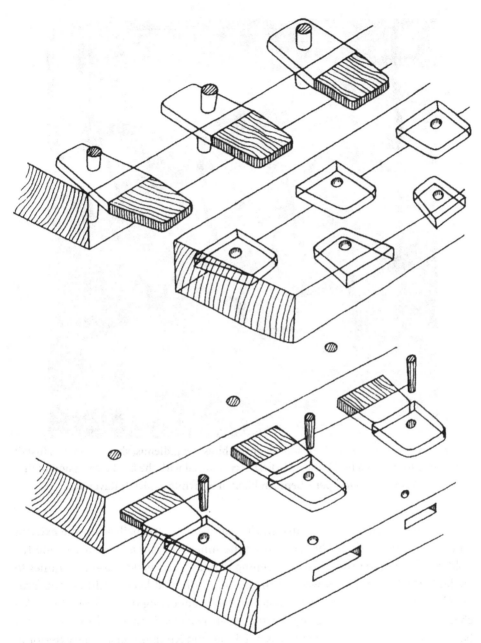

Figure 17.2 Schematic drawing of pegged mortise-and-tenon hull construction. Reproduced with the kind permission of Centre Camille Jullian, CNRS, Aix-en-Provence.

(Figure 17.2). Corresponding mortises were cut into the bottom edge of the garboard strake, which was then driven down snugly atop the tenons protruding from the keel. Small wooden pegs hammered through the tenons from the hull's exterior locked the plank(s) in place, and with the addition of subsequent rows of planks, a wooden shell was gradually realized. To provide the shell with some lateral rigidity, the shipwright installed frames (Figure 17.3), fastening them to the hull with copper

Figure 17.3 The funerary stele of shipwright Publius Longidienus, shown about to install a framing timber in a hull built shell-first. Reproduced with the kind permission of the Soprintendenza per I Beni Ambientali e Architettonici di Ravenna.

alloy (or, less often, iron) nails driven through wooden treenails from the exterior and double-clenched, or "hooked," over the inner face of each frame. Inside the hold, the mast-step was added, and ceiling planking was nailed atop the frames to facilitate the lading and stowage of the cargo. Additional lateral stiffness was provided by cross-beams framing the hatch(es) and supporting the deck planking. Archaeological evidence for the superstructure of ancient ships above the deck is scant because it very seldom survives (Gassend, Liou, and Ximenes 1984). The exterior of the hull might be coated with an antifouling substance such as orpiment and covered with a protective layer of lead or copper sheathing (Hocker 1995; Stieglitz 2004).

The predominance of pegged mortise-and-tenon joinery as the established method of the ancient Mediterranean shipwright brought about a technological uniformity in Greco-Roman shipbuilding that was characterized by significant change only at the beginning and end of the period under consideration here (450 BCE–400 CE). As discussed elsewhere in this volume (see Polzer), there is increasing evidence from shipwreck sites like Ma'agan Mikhael, Israel (Linder and Kahanov 2003), to suggest that the earlier and probably Greek technique of sewing or lacing hull planks together endured into the late fifth century BCE, coexisting with the pegged mortise-and-tenon technique, albeit on a much more limited scale. Likewise, a transition away from the canonical shell-first technique occurred in the fourth and fifth centuries CE, when shipwrights came to rely less on the integrity of the hull planking, as evidenced by the use of thinner planks joined by smaller, loose-fitting, and occasionally unpegged tenons (Boetto 2001; Van Doorninck 1976).

While the principal features of Greco-Roman ship construction—which included a primary shell of hull planks joined at the edges by means of pegged tenons set in mortises, and a secondary skeleton of floor timbers and alternating half-frames fastened to planks by nails driven through wooden dowels or treenails—remained largely unchanged for nearly a millennium, it would be misleading to suggest that ancient Mediterranean shipwrights embraced no innovation whatsoever. Many of these innovations occurred in conjunction with the construction of large vessels during the Roman era—like the Nemi ships, the dimensions of which necessitated that floor timbers be joined or scarfed together to form continuous frames that spanned the width of the entire hull. The 400-ton merchantman that sank at Madrague de Giens, France, between 75 and 60 BCE and was excavated by French archaeologists between 1972 and 1982 (Pomey 1982; Tchernia, Pomey, and Hesnard 1978), contains several construction features also utilized in other large vessels of the first century BCE, including double layers of hull planking and elaborate keel scarfs. The Madrague de Giens wreck, incidentally, provides some of the best direct evidence for the presence of ancient salvors, known in Latin as *urinatores* (Oleson 1976; Tchernia 1988).

During the first four centuries CE, some shipwrights began bolting selected frames to the keel, a decision that may (or may not) anticipate later construction techniques whereby frames were used to determine the profile of the upper hull (Pomey 2004: 31–32). Other variations were largely regional, as is the case with several Roman Imperial vessels belonging to what appears to be a distinct northwestern European shipbuilding tradition. A handful of well-studied wrecks from London (Marsden 1994: 33–104), Wales (Nayling and McGrail 2004), and Guernsey, in the Channel Islands (Rule and Monaghan 1993), supply the key features: a preference for oak, two or three thick keel planks in place of a conventional keel, a flat bottom, thick, heavy floor timbers, and hull planking that is not edge-joined but fastened to frames by means of thick iron nails, often driven through oak treenails. Though the origin and evolution of the type are debated, most scholars have embraced the designation Romano-Celtic (Ellmers 1996: 68–71; McGrail 2001: 196–206), citing several compelling parallels in Julius Caesar's account of the ships built by the Celtic Veneti of northwestern Gaul during their resistance in 56 BCE (*Bellum Gallicum* 3.13).

Rigging and Equipment

Hundreds of ship depictions in vase paintings, wall frescoes, and mosaic pavements make it abundantly clear that the square sail was the standard rig of both merchantmen and war galleys in the Greco-Roman Mediterranean (Casson 1995: 235–243). In both cases, the single, broad sail was hung on a mast stepped just forward of amidships, though in fighting ships this mast was easily removed so that it could be stowed quickly for tactical reasons. Beginning about 500 BCE we have pictorial evidence of a second, smaller, raking mast called an *artemon* set farther forward in the bow (Casson 1963, 1980); archaeological evidence for the presence of this fore-sail is limited chiefly to the socket where the *artemon* was stepped (Beltrame 1996).

While sails themselves do not survive underwater (though see Wild and Wild 2001), other elements of ancient rigging that are not uncommon finds on ship-wrecks include rope (Charlton 1996: 55–71; Sanders 2010), pulley blocks, deadeyes, and toggles (Polzer 2008), the latter likely serving to connect lines to the edge of the sail in order to keep it taut and prevent luffing. Arguably the most common relic of the ancient square sail is the brailing ring, usually of lead, but also of wood or animal horn (Whitewright 2007). Brailing rings were sewn onto the forward face of the sail at regular intervals to accommodate the brails—lines fastened to the foot of the sail that ran up the sail face, over the yard, and then down to the stern. Hauling in all of the brails furled an ancient square sail to the yard, while hauling in some of the brails shortened only part of the sail. In this way, an ancient square sail could be modified to achieve a sail of a different shape, such as a lateen (Casson 1971). A handful of sculpted reliefs on ancient tombstones indicate that Greco-Roman sailors also knew other fore-and-aft rigs, including the spritsail, at least as early as the second century BCE (Casson 1995: 243–244).

In the early 1980s, a group of archaeologists and researchers undertook an ambitious experiment to accurately replicate the 14 m long (46 ft long) merchant ship that sank off the coast of Kyrenia, Cyprus, in the early third century BCE. The construction of *Kyrenia II* (Figure 17.4) not only demonstrated the accuracy of the reconstructed lines drawings made of the original ship and the durability of hull planks joined by the mortise-and-tenon technique (Katzev and Katzev 1989); her sea trials, which included two 800 km voyages between Cyprus and Athens, also proved that an ordinary, beamy merchant vessel rigged with a single square sail could average speeds of 6–7 knots, routinely reach speeds of 10–12 knots, and sail 50–60° off the wind (Katzev 1989). *Kyrenia II*, in keeping with the evidence for all ancient Mediterranean seagoing ships, was maneuvered by two steering oars—one mounted on each stern quarter. In the hold of the original Kyrenia ship, excavators found a spare steering oar as well as a spare square sail, represented by a single assemblage of 176 lead brailing rings.

One of the most gripping and instructive accounts of an ancient sea voyage comes from the fifth book of the New Testament. The book of Acts (27–28) describes the journey of the Apostle Paul from Caesarea to Rome, ca. 60 CE (Fitzgerald 1990; Hirschfeld 1990). Traveling on an Alexandrian ship—in all probability a grain carrier—the group of nearly 300 passengers and crew encountered a nasty storm that drove their vessel from the southern coast of Crete across the Adriatic to Malta. As the ship was battered by the waves and the sea state grew increasingly dire, the crew jettisoned some of the cargo, then the ship's gear (27: 18–19). After two weeks on the open sea (27:27), sensing that land was near, the crew deployed a sounding lead to measure the depth of the water, which was 20 paces (about 30 m or 16 fathoms).

Figure 17.4 *Kyrenia II* under sail. Reproduced with the kind permission of
Patrice Pomey.

When the second reading came back at 15 paces (22 m or 12 fathoms), the crew
became fearful that the ship would run aground, so they cast four anchors from the
stern and hoped for daybreak. That the dropping of the anchors in this instance was
essentially an act of desperation is indicated by the fact that, almost immediately,
crew members readied the ship's boat under the guise of deploying the bow anchors,
while really intending to make their escape (27:30).

The story of Saint Paul's shipwreck provides one clear historical scenario to
explain the scatter across the seafloor of isolated artifacts such as amphoras, anchors,
and sounding weights. The study of anchors, like amphoras, has grown exponen-
tially with the advance of underwater archaeology and the controlled excavation of
shipwrecks. As a result, it is possible to discuss the key attributes and materials of
basic anchor types (Frost 1963; Kapitän 1984). One particularly diagnostic feature
of ancient wooden anchors is the stock, since this is often all that survives centuries
underwater: in the sixth century BCE stocks were typically of stone, while in the
fifth and fourth centuries BCE they were more often of wood with cores of lead,
poured into the stock while still molten. From the third century BCE until well into
the Roman Empire, solid lead stocks of various shapes and sizes, at first fixed and
later removable, were the norm (Haldane 1990: 21). Iron anchors, which are attested
in fifth-century BCE texts and fourth-century BCE shipwrecks, coexisted alongside
wooden anchors, making the discovery of both types in a single wreck especially
informative. But anchors are, by nature of their very function, often found at considerable distances from the vessels to which they belonged, making it difficult to

attribute them with certainty to a given shipwrecked assemblage; solitary finds may be almost impossible to date without analytical techniques that yield an absolute chronology. Of course no typology is all-inclusive; the anchor(s) in use on a small fishing skiff would have been very different from those on board a contemporaneous grain transport. Among the objects recovered from the large merchantman that sank at Madrague de Giens, France, was a small lead anchor stock presumably from a dinghy like the one mentioned in Saint Paul's shipwreck story.

Another piece of ancient ship's equipment that has survived in sufficient quantities to warrant the creation of a typology is the lead sounding weight (Oleson 2000). Ancient mariners relied on sounding weights not only to measure the depth of unfamiliar waters, but also to collect sediment samples from the sea bottom, which might indicate the presence of a river mouth or other geological landmark (Oleson 2008: 124). Sounding leads were the only navigational instrument available to the ancient sailor, who otherwise relied on topography (promontories, islands), monuments (temples, lighthouses), and clues from nature (breezes, currents, birds, fish, stars) to carry out his voyage. This reliance on land-based phenomena led many to conclude that ancient ships must have hugged the coast whenever possible, but the relatively recent discovery of numerous deepwater shipwrecks (Ballard 2008; McCann and Freed 1994; McCann and Oleson 2004; Wachsmann in this volume) implies that ancient ships often followed routes over the open sea. A recent assessment of ancient Greek literature suggests that on any given voyage sailors likely made use of both deep-sea and coastal routes, working out their itinerary gradually according to developing weather conditions (Morton 2001: 173–180).

Vessel Size

Superlatives make great headlines, whether it is the first, the fastest, or the farthest, and archaeological headlines are no exception, provided that it is either oldest or the biggest. Yet the question "How big were the biggest Greek and Roman ships?" begets no easy answer, in part because of conflicting evidence from numerous sources and periods. The very biggest ships survive only on paper, in the accounts of ancient authors like Pliny the Elder (23–79 CE), who described a ship commissioned by the emperor Caligula to transport the parts of a 500-ton Egyptian obelisk from Alexandria to Rome (*Natural History* 16.201, 36.70); the ship was ballasted with 800 tons of lentils, for a total deadweight of 1,300 tons. The *Isis*, a grain carrier following the same route when it was blown off course to Athens in the second century CE, became the focus of a parable by the satirist Lucian, who mentioned the ship's dimensions as 120 cubits (55 m) long and more than a quarter that in beam (apx. 15 m), and with a hold 29 cubits (14 m) deep (*Navigium* 5); resulting calculations of the vessel's burden range from 1,100 to 3,250 tons (Casson 1995: 186–188). And then there is the *Syracusia*, a three-masted, turreted, luxury grain carrier constructed by Hiero of Syracuse (306–215 BCE), supervised by the scientist Archimedes and bedecked with mosaic pavements, flower beds, a library, a bath, tanks for keeping live fish, and stables. The complete account of Hiero's superfreighter was penned by

Moschion, a Hellenistic paradoxographer, and transcribed in a quotation by Athenaeus (*Deipnosophistae* 5.206d–209b), ca. 200 CE. Modern estimates based on lading data supplied by Moschion put the *Syracusia*'s deadweight at anywhere between 1,700 and 4,200 tons (Casson 1995: 185–186).

Without port facilities to accommodate them (Pomey and Tchernia 1978), the mammoth vessels constructed by Hiero and Caligula were essentially unusable as anything other than eccentric imperial showpieces. The trend among scholars has typically been to trust in the veracity of the *Isis* figures and discount the credibility of the *Syracusia*, though two important articles argue exactly the opposite, suggesting that Lucian's ship is an allegorical illusion (Houston 1987) and that Moschion's account of Hiero's ship, while fabulous, is not fabricated (Turfa and Steinmayer 1999).

The challenge for archaeologists is in reconciling these written sources with existing shipwreck data, which indicate that the largest seagoing vessel found to date—the 500-ton merchantman uncovered at Albenga, Italy, in 1925—had just half the capacity of the most conservative estimates for *Isis*. Comparable vessels from the Roman Republican and Imperial periods, respectively, include the amphora carrier from Madrague de Giens, France (400 tons) (Figure 17.1), and the marble transport that sank at Isola delle Correnti, Italy (350 tons). The largest Greek ship identified thus far is the partially excavated late classical amphora wreck at Alonnesos, in the Sporades, with a probable capacity of 125 tons (Hadjidaki 1996). While it has been proposed that ships of 350–400 tons burden were not uncommon in classical Greece (Casson 1995: 172; Wallinga 1964), a faded customs inventory from an unknown Egyptian port suggests that the 40 or so Ionian and Phoenician ships that paid duty in 475 BCE were not capable of carrying more than about 30 tons of cargo each (Yardeni 1994). Thus, when it comes to the evidence for ship size, the historical sources focus on the exceptional, but the archaeological record reflects the mundane, leading us to the inescapable conclusion that vessels under 75 tons burden were the most common class in antiquity (Houston 1988; Parker 1992: 26), and largely responsible for making "the short hops and unpredictable experiences of *cabotage* . . . the basic modality for all movements of goods and peoples in the Mediterranean before the age of steam" (Horden and Purcell 2000: 365).

NAVAL FLEETS

In the years leading up to the Persian Wars—that fateful confrontation of the early fifth century BCE—Greek city-states across the Aegean were busy building fleets of warships and assembling crews of rowers to explore, colonize, and defend their rapidly expanding world. The majority of these vessels were pentecontors, or 50-oared ships, but modern knowledge of them, as of all ancient oared warships, is based almost completely on written accounts, inscriptions, vase paintings, and sculptural reliefs (Basch 1987). Unlike merchant ships, warships carried no heavy cargo to force them to the bottom; a damaged warship might either float away in pieces at the surface or be towed away by the victor for salvage, as galleys ranked among the most sophisticated and valuable instruments of war for their time.

The most famous ancient galley was undoubtedly the trireme, or *trieres*, the classical Greek ship of the line (Morrison 1995a). But with ramming as the primary tactical objective, a warship was only as effective as it was agile, and it was the Athenian oarsmen who held pride of place, secured in part by a stunning victory over the Persian fleet at Salamis in 480 BCE (Hale 2009; Strauss 2000). Naval inventories inscribed on marble blocks found in the Athenian port of Piraeus indicate that, in the last third of the fourth century BCE, each trireme was equipped with 170 oars (and 30 spares), and the oarsmen were classified according to one of three categories: thranites, zugites, or thalamites. Scholars have long debated exactly how the oarsmen aboard a trireme were arranged: did they sit on three superimposed benches, or were there three men on each bench (Coates 1995; Tilley 1990)? The discussion is fueled in part by iconography—of the hundreds of galleys depicted on Greek vases, not one shows more than two superimposed banks of rowers. But then, most of these depictions predate the trireme by a half-century or more, and nowhere are the paintings labeled to suggest what class of ship is depicted. Until archaeologists can provide more definitive physical evidence for ancient warships, one effective (but expensive) way to test current hypotheses is the construction of full-scale working models like the triple-banked *Olympias*, launched in 1987 by the Trireme Trust (Morrison, Coates, and Rankov 2000; Ravn et al. in this volume).

The legacy of the trireme continued into the fourth century BCE, with the construction of the "four" (Greek *tetreres*, Latin *quadrireme*) and the "five" (Greek *penteres*, Latin *quinquireme*). The competitive aggression of various Hellenistic monarchs fueled the development of polyremes with the creation of even larger classes, such as sixes, sevens, eights, tens, sixteens, twenties, and thirties. These numerical names, however, refer to the total number of rowers organized in two or three superimposed files, with perhaps as many as eight men pulling a single oar. One important change that took place aboard such larger warships was a tactical shift from ramming to boarding (Morrison 1995b); a second was the adoption of smaller, faster vessels like the liburnian (Höckmann 1997), which was favored among Illyrian pirates in the Adriatic, and the hemiolia (Casson 1958; Morrison 1980), which seems to have been especially popular among pirates in the eastern Mediterranean.

In 31 BCE, almost 450 years after the Battle of Salamis, another naval encounter once again ushered in long-lasting changes in the Mediterranean. Near the small town of Actium in northwestern Greece, a young Octavian routed the fleet of Mark Antony and Cleopatra, bringing a protracted civil war to a decisive end. The ships were different from those that had met at Salamis, of course, but the net result was the same: the smaller, lighter, and more agile liburnians under Octavian's command prevailed over Antony's larger, bulkier quinquiremes. After his victory, Octavian erected a commemorative stone monument that had as its centerpiece about 30 bronze rams taken from the captured ships (Murray and Petsas 1989; Sanders in this volume). In 1980, a similar ram was discovered in isolation off the coast of Athlit, Israel, with the bow timbers of the ship to which it was once affixed still inside (Casson and Steffy 1991). But the Athlit Ram, which weighs nearly one-half ton, proved to be smaller than any of the sockets on the Actium monument—a telling indication of how little we really know about the vessels that fought in some of history's most momentous naval battles.

River Craft

As the Roman Empire expanded northward, the great rivers of central Europe served as vital arteries from which the provinces and the legions were supplied and defended. Excavations at Mainz, Germany, formerly a Roman frontier town and administrative seat of Germania Superior, have revealed the remains of four long, low, undecked river boats of oak dating from the fourth century CE (Bockius 2006). The vessels, which are now displayed in Mainz's Museum für antike Schifffahrt, have been associated with textual descriptions of the *navis lusoria*—a small, light, fast ship that probably served as a patrol boat (Höckmann 1997). Farther north, in the ancient capital of Germania Inferior, today the small town of Zwammerdam in the Netherlands, Dutch archaeologists excavating a Roman fort on the Rhine in the 1970s uncovered three long, narrow flat-bottomed river barges (De Weerd 1978). While their enormous size (20–34 m in length) evokes Roman influence, elements of their construction, including the preference for oak, the use of large iron nails, and hard L-shaped chine strakes cut from a single piece of wood, seem decidedly indigenous (Hocker 2004: 68–72). Nearer the Mediterranean, much of the evidence for inland watercraft comes from the Adriatic, where at least half a dozen hulls indicate that boatbuilders in the Roman era were constructing flat-bottomed vessels by lacing planks together with ligatures (Beltrame 2000b; Bonino 1985). One of these, the 25 m long ship excavated at Comacchio on the River Po in northern Italy, was transporting a cargo of boxwood logs, lead ingots, and amphoras when it sank in the late first century BCE (Berti 1990).

CONCLUSION

No matter where, when, or to whom the development of underwater archaeology is attributed, the fact remains that the discipline was born in the Mediterranean and, in the course of just over one half-century, has significantly enhanced our understanding of Greco-Roman ships—their cargoes, construction, size, and

Figure 17.5 Numbered drawing of the vessel types depicted in the Althiburus Mosaic (from O. Höckmann, *Antike Seefahrt* fig. 52). Reproduced with the kind permission of Verlag C. H. Beck oHG.

operation—while simultaneously advancing related fields like amphora studies and dendrochronology (Kuniholm 2001; Kuniholm et al. 1992). While the quantity of raw archaeological data available for consideration is remarkable (Parker 1992), historically scholars have only sporadically utilized these data synthetically to draw conclusions about broader trends in maritime trade and economy (Horden and Purcell 2000: 368–372).

Part of the challenge of working with the existing corpus of ancient shipwreck material is that early underwater investigations were not always concerned with archaeological context or artifact conservation. In short, the quality of any archaeological data is only as reliable as the quality of the excavation that produced it. But resourceful scientists are constantly devising methods to extract new information from old objects, and to this end the intersections of shipwreck archaeology with fields such as palynology (Muller 2004) and dendromorphology (Liphschitz 2007) rank among some of the most exciting applications for future research. Thus, while the field continues to expand, with the discovery of additional ancient shipwrecks in some rather nontraditional contexts—including deep water and even on land, owing to the siltation of ancient harbors (Bruni and Abbado 2000; Lobell and Merola 2008)—we must be careful not to disregard those unpublished artifacts excavated decades ago that now line the shelves of museum storerooms.

Another enduring challenge for classical archaeologists is balancing the often delicate relationship between text, image, and artifact; a maritime illustration of one such relationship concerns the classification of various ship types. Ancient texts mention dozens of compounds of *navis*, the Latin word for ship. Terms like *navis longa* (long ship) and *navis tecta* (covered ship) describe a vessel's physical appearance, while *navis mercatoria* (ship of commerce) and *navis praedatoria* (ship of plunder) clearly pertain to function. Other examples, like *navis frumentaria* (grain ship), *navis lapidaria* (stone ship), and *navis vivaria* (ship for live fish), refer to the cargo a vessel carries. To this glossary of terms can be added a remarkable floor mosaic from a villa at Althiburus, Tunisia (Figure 17.5), decorated with labeled depictions of more than two dozen different vessels, many complete with details of their rigging or cargo (Duval 1949). It is thus against this rich backdrop of literary descriptions and artistic depictions that archaeologists endeavor to interpret and contextualize the remains of the vessels they excavate, and while we may never know for certain how the ancient Greeks and Romans classified these ships, attempting to solve such puzzles is half the fun.

REFERENCES

Ballard, Robert D. 2008. Searching for ancient shipwrecks in the deep sea. In *Archaeological oceanography*, ed. Robert D. Ballard, 131–147. Princeton, NJ: Princeton University Press.

Basch, Lucien. 1987. *Le musée imaginaire de la marine antique.* Athens: Hellenic Institute for the Preservation of Nautical Tradition.

Bass, George F. 1996. *Archaeology under water.* New York: Praeger.

———. 1967. Cape Gelidonya: A Bronze Age shipwreck. *Transactions of the American Philosophical Society* 57.8.

———. 1972. *A history of seafaring based on underwater archaeology.* New York: Walker.

———. 1975. *Archaeology beneath the sea.* New York: Walker.

———. 2005. *Beneath the Seven Seas: Adventures with the Institute of Nautical Archaeology.* London: Thames & Hudson.

Beck, Curt W., and Carl Borromeo. 1990. Ancient pine pitch: Technological perspectives from a Hellenistic shipwreck. In *Organic contents of ancient vessels: Materials analysis and archaeological investigation,* ed. William R. Biers and Patrick E. McGovern, 51–58. MASCA Research Papers in Science and Archaeology 7. Philadelphia: University Museum of Archaeology and Anthropology, University of Pennsylvania.

Beltrame, Carlo. 1996. Archaeological evidence of the foremast on ancient sailing ships. *International Journal of Nautical Archaeology* 25: 135–139.

———. 2000a. A review of the Roman wreck of Spargi (Sassari/Italy): Evidence of the commerce of luxurious furniture during late Republican Age. In *Schutz des Kulturerbes unter Wasser: Veränderungen europäischer Lebenskultur durch Fluß- und Seehandel: Beiträge zum Internationalen Kongreß für Unterwasserarchäologie (IKUWA '99), 18.–21. Februar 1999 in Sassnitz auf Rügen,* ed. Hildegard von Schmettow, 155–162. Lübstorf Archäologisches Landesmuseum für Mecklenburg-Vorpommern.

———. 2000b. Sutiles naves of the Roman age: New evidence and technological comparisons with pre-Roman sewn boats. In *Down the river to the sea: Proceedings of the Eighth International Symposium on Boat and Ship Archaeology,* ed. Jerzy Litwin, 91–96. Gdańsk: Polish Maritime Museum.

———. 2002. *Vita di bordo in Età Romana.* Rome: Istituto Poligrafico e Zecca dello Stato.

Bernard, Hélène, Marie-Pierre Jezegou, and Emmanuel Nantet. 2007. L'épave Ouest-Embiez 1, Var: Cargaison, mobilier, fonction commerciale du navire. *Revue Archéologique de Narbonnaise* 40: 199–233.

Berti, Fede. 1990. *Fortuna maris: La nave romana di Comacchio.* Bologna: Nuova Alfa.

Blackman, David J. 1973. *Marine archaeology.* London: Butterworths.

Boardman, John. 1988. Trade in Greek decorated pottery. *Oxford Journal of Archaeology* 9: 27–33.

Bockius, Ronald. 2006. *Die spätrömischen Schiffswracks aus Mainz: Schiffsarchäologisch-technikgeschichtliche Untersuchung spätantiker Schiffsfunde vom nördlichen Oberrhein.* Mainz: Verlag des Römisch-Germanischen Zentralmuseums.

———. 2007. *Schifffahrt und Schiffbau in der Antike.* Stuttgart: Theiss.

Boetto, Giulia. 2001. Les navires de Fiumicino. In *Ostia: Port et porte de la Rome antique,* ed. Jean-Paul Descoeudres, 121–130. Genève: Musée d'art et d'histoire.

Bol, Peter C. 1972. *Die Skulpturen des Schiffsfundes von Antikythera.* Berlin: Mann.

Bonino, Marco. 1985. Sewn boats in Italy: Sutiles naves and barche cucite. In *Sewn plank boats: Archaeological and ethnographic papers based on those presented at a conference at Greenwich in November 1984,* ed. Sean McGrail and Eric Kentley, 87–104. BAR International Series 276. Oxford: Tempus Reparatum.

———. 2003. *Un sogno ellenistico: Le navi di Nemi.* Rome: Felici.

Börker, Christoph, and Johannes Burow. 1988. *Die hellenistischen Amphorenstempel aus Pergamon.* New York: W. de Gruyter.

Bound, Mensun. 1991. *The Giglio wreck: A wreck of the Archaic period (c. 600 BCE) off the Tuscan island of Giglio.* Enalia Supplement 1. Athens: Hellenic Institute of Marine Archaeology.

Bruni, Stefano, and Marta Abbado. 2000. *Le navi antiche di Pisa: Ad un anno dall'inizio delle ricerche*. Firenze: Polistampa.

Carlson, Deborah. 2002. Caligula's floating palaces. *Archaeology* 55 (3): 26–31.

———. 2003. The Classical Greek shipwreck at Tektaş Burnu, Turkey. *American Journal of Archaeology* 107: 581–600.

———. 2007. Mast-step coins among the Romans. *International Journal of Nautical Archaeology* 36: 317–324.

Casson, Lionel. 1958. Hemiolia and triemiolia. *Journal of Hellenic Studies* 78: 14–18.

———. 1963. The earliest two-masted ship. *Archaeology* 16 (2): 108–111.

———. 1971. The origin of the lateen. *American Neptune* 31: 49–51.

———. 1980. Two-masted Greek ships. *International Journal of Nautical Archaeology* 9: 68–69.

———. 1995. *Ships and seamanship in the ancient world*. 2nd ed. Baltimore: John Hopkins University Press.

Casson, Lionel, and J. Richard Steffy. 1991. *The Athlit Ram*. College Station: Texas A&M University Press.

Charlton, William H., Jr. 1996. Rope and the art of knot-tying in the seafaring of the ancient Eastern Mediterranean. MA thesis, Texas A&M University.

Coates, John F. 1995. The naval architecture and oar systems of ancient galleys. In *The age of the galley: Mediterranean oared vessels since pre-Classical times*, ed. Robert Gardiner, 127–141. Annapolis: Naval Institute Press.

Cook, Robert M. 1987. Artful crafts: A commentary. *Journal of Hellenic Studies* 107: 169–171.

Cousteau, Jacques Y. 1954. Fish men discover a 2,200-year-old Greek ship. *National Geographic* 105 (January): 1–36.

Davies, John K. 2001. Hellenistic economies in the post-Finley era. In *Hellenistic economies*, ed. Zofia H. Archibald, John Davies, Vincent Gabrielsen, and G. J. Oliver, 11–62. New York: Routledge.

Debidour, Michel. 1998. Le timbrage des amphores: Une prerogative publique ou privée? *Ktema* 23: 275–286.

De Hoz, Javier. 1989. Les graffites mercantiles en occident et l'épave d'El Sec. In *Grecs et Ibères au IVe siècle avant Jésus-Christ: Commerce et iconographie*, ed. Pierre Rouillard and Marie-Christine Villaneuva-Puig, 117–130. Paris: de Boccard.

De Weerd, Martin D. 1978. Ships of the Roman period at Zwammerdam/Nigrum Pullum, Germania Inferior. In *Roman shipping and trade: Britain and the Rhine provinces*, ed. Joan du Plat Taylor and Henry Cleere, 15–21. CBA Research Report 24. London: Council for British Archaeology.

Du Plat Taylor, Joan. 1965. *Marine archaeology: Developments during sixty years in the Mediterranean*. New York: Crowell.

Duval, Paul-Marie. 1949. La forme des navires romains, d'après la mosaïque d'Althiburus. *Mélanges d'archéologie et d'histoire* 61: 119–149.

Eiseman, Cynthia J., and Brunilde S. Ridgway. 1987. *The Porticello shipwreck: A Mediterranean merchant vessel of 415–385 B.C.* College Station: Texas A&M University Press.

Ellmers, Detlev. 1996. Celtic plank boats and ships, 500 BCE–CE 1000. In *The earliest ships: The evolution of boats into ships*, ed. Robert Gardiner and Arne Emil Christensen, 52–71. Annapolis: Naval Institute Press.

Empereur, Jean-Yves, and Maurice Picon. 1986. A la recherche des fours d'amphores. In *Recherches sur les amphores grecques*, ed. Jean-Yves Empereur and Yvon Garlan,

103–126. Bulletin du Correspondance Hellénique Supplément 13. Athens: École
Française d'Athènes.

Fant, J. Clayton. 1989. *Cavum antrum phrygiae: The organization and operations of the
Roman imperial marble quarries in Phrygia*. BAR International Series 482. Oxford:
Tempus Reparatum.

———. 2001. Rome's marble yards. *Journal of Roman Archaeology* 14: 167–198.

Finkielsztejn, Gérald. 2001. *Chronologie détaillée et révisée des éponymes amphoriques
rhodiens, de 270 à 108 av. J.-C. environ*. BAR International Series 990. Oxford: Tempus
Reparatum.

Fitzgerald, Michael. 1990. The ship of Saint Paul: Comparative archaeology. *Biblical
Archaeologist* 53 (1): 31–39.

Fontaine, Souen Deva, and Danièle Foy. 2007. L'épave Ouest-Embiez 1, Var: Le commerce
maritime du verre brut et manufacturé en Méditerranée occidentale dans l'Antiquité.
Revue archéologique de Narbonnaise 40: 235–268.

Freeth, Tony, Alexander Jones, John M. Steele, and Yanis Bitsakis. 2008. Calendars with
Olympiad display and eclipse prediction on the Antikythera Mechanism. *Nature* 454:
614–617.

Frost, Honor. 1963. From rope to chain: On the development of anchors in the
Mediterranean. *Mariner's Mirror* 49: 1–20.

Gassend, Jean-Marie, Bernard Liou, and Serge Ximenes. 1984. L'épave 2 de l'anse des
Laurons (Martigues, Bouches-du-Rhône). *Archaeonautica* 4: 75–105.

Gianfrotta, Piero, and Patrice Pomey. 1981. *Archeologia subacquea: Storia, tecniche, scoperte
e relitti*. Milan: A. Mondadori.

Gill, David W. J. 1994. Positivism, pots and long-distance trade. In *Classical Greece: Ancient
histories and modern archaeologies*, ed. Ian Morris, 99–107. Cambridge: Cambridge
University Press.

Göttlicher, Arvid. 2009. *Fähren, Frachter, Fischerboote: Antike Kleinschiffe in Wort und Bild*.
BAR International Series 1922. Oxford: Archaeopress.

Grace, Virginia R. 1979. *Amphoras and the ancient wine trade*. Athenian Agora Picture
Book 6. Princeton, NJ: American School of Classical Studies at Athens.

Green, Peter. 1993. Late Hellenistic art, 150–30 BCE: The mass market in nostalgia. In
Alexander to Actium: The historical evolution of the Hellenistic age, 566–585. Berkeley
and Los Angeles: University of California Press.

Hadjidaki, Elpida. 1996. Underwater excavations of a late fifth century merchant ship at
Alonnesos, Greece: The 1991–1993 seasons. *Bulletin de Correspondance Hellénique* 120:
561–593.

Haldane, Douglas. 1990. Anchors of antiquity. *Biblical Archaeologist* 53: 19–24.

Hale, John R. 2009. *Lords of the sea: The epic story of the Athenian Navy and the birth of
democracy*. New York: Viking.

Hansson, Maria C., and Brendan P. Foley. 2008. Ancient DNA fragments inside classical
Greek amphoras reveal cargo of 2400-year-old shipwreck. *Journal of Archaeological
Science* 35 (5): 1169–1176.

Hellenkemper Salies, Gisela. 1994. *Das Wrack: Der antike Schiffsfund von Mahdia im
Rheinischen Landesmuseum Bonn, 8. September 1994–29. Januar 1995*. Köln: Rheinland
Verlag.

Hirschfeld, Nicolle. 1990. The ship of Saint Paul: Historical background. *Biblical
Archaeologist* 53 (1): 25–30.

Hocker, Frederick M. 1995. Lead hull sheathing in antiquity. In *TROPIS 3: Third
International Symposium on Ship Construction in Antiquity, Athens, 24–27*

August 1989, ed. Harry Tzalas, 197–206. Athens: Hellenic Institute for the Preservation of Nautical Tradition.

———. 2004. Bottom-based shipbuilding in northwestern Europe. In *The philosophy of shipbuilding: Conceptual approaches to the study of wooden ships*, ed. Frederick M. Hocker and Cheryl A. Ward, 65–93. College Station: Texas A&M University Press.

Höckmann, Olaf. 1985. *Antike Seefahrt*. Munich: C. H. Beck.

———. 1997. The liburnian: Some observations and insights. *International Journal of Nautical Archaeology* 26: 192–216.

Hohlfelder, Robert. 2008. *The maritime world of ancient Rome*. Memoirs of the American Academy in Rome, Supplement 6. Ann Arbor: University of Michigan Press.

Horden, Peregrine, and Nicholas Purcell. 2000. *The corrupting sea: A study of Mediterranean history*. Oxford: Blackwell.

Houston, George W. 1987. Lucian's *Navigium* and the dimensions of the *Isis*. *American Journal of Philology* 108: 444–450.

———. 1988. Ports in perspective: Some comparative materials on Roman merchant ships and ports. *American Journal of Archaeology* 92: 553–564.

Illsley, John S. 1996. *Indexed bibliography of underwater archaeology and related topics*. Oswestry: A. Nelson.

Johnston, Alan W. 1979. *Trademarks on Greek vases*. Warminster, England: Aris and Phillips.

———. 1993. Greek vases in the marketplace. In *Looking at Greek vases*, ed. Tom Rasmussen and Nigel Spivey, 203–231. New York: Cambridge University Press.

———. 2006. *Trademarks on Greek vases: Addenda*. Warminster, England: Aris and Phillips.

Kapitän, Gerhard. 1984. Ancient anchors—technology and classification. *International Journal of Nautical Archaeology* 13: 33–44.

Katzev, Michael L. 1989. Voyage of the *Kyrenia II*. *INA Newsletter* 16 (1): 4–10.

Katzev, Michael L., and Susan W. Katzev. 1989. *Kyrenia II*: Building a replica of an ancient Greek merchantman. In *TROPIS 1: First International Symposium on Ship Construction in Antiquity, Athens, 30 August–1 September 1985*, ed. Harry Tzalas, 163–176. Athens: Hellenic Institute for the Preservation of Nautical Tradition.

Katzev, Susan W. 2007. The ancient ship of Kyrenia, beneath Cyprus seas. In *Great moments in Greek archaeology*, ed. Pavos Valavanis, Vasileios Petrakos, and Angelos Delivorrias, 286–299. Los Angeles: J. Paul Getty Museum.

Kuniholm, Peter I. 2001. Dendrochronology and other applications of tree-ring studies in archaeology. In *The handbook of archaeological sciences*, ed. Don R. Brothwell and A. Mark Pollard, 35–46. London: John Wiley & Sons.

Kuniholm, Peter I., Carol B. Griggs, Shana L. Tarter, and Hope E. Kuniholm. 1992. A 513-year Buxus chronology for the Roman ship at Comacchio (Ferrara). *Bollettino di Archeologia* 16–18: 291–299.

Lamboglia, Nino. 1961. La nave romana di Spargi. In *Atti del II Congresso Internazionale di Archeologia Sottomarina, Albenga, 1958*, 141–166. Bordighera: Istituto Internazionale di Studi Liguri.

———. 1971. Il rilievo totale della nave romana di Albenga. In *Atti del III Congresso Internazionale di Archeologia Sottomarina, Barcelona, 1961*, 167–175. Bordighera: Istituto Internazionale di Studi Liguri.

Lang, Mabel. 1976. *The Athenian Agora XXI: Graffiti and dipinti*. Princeton, NJ: American School of Classical Studies at Athens.

Lawall, Mark L. 1995. Transport amphoras and trademarks: Imports to Athens and economic diversity in the fifth century B.C. PhD diss., University of Michigan.

———. 1998. Bolsals, Mendean amphoras and the date of the Porticello shipwreck. *International Journal of Nautical Archaeology* 27: 16–23.

———. 2000. Graffiti, wine selling, and the reuse of amphoras in the Athenian agora, ca. 430 to 400 B.C. *Hesperia* 69: 3–90.

———. 2005. Amphoras and Hellenistic economies: Addressing the (over)emphasis on stamped amphora handles. In *Making, moving, and managing: The new world of ancient economies, 323–31 BCE*, ed. Zofia H. Archibald, John K. Davies, and Vincent Gabrielsen, 188–232. Oxford: Oxbow.

Linder, Elisha, and Yaacov Kahanov. 2003. The hull. In *The Ma'agan Mikhael ship: The recovery of a 2400-year-old merchantman: Final report*, vol. 1, ed. Elisha Linder and Yaacov Kahanov, 53–129. Haifa: Israel Exploration Society and University of Haifa.

Liphschitz, Nili. 2007. *Timber in ancient Israel: Dendroarchaeology and dendrochronology.* Tel Aviv: Institute of Archaeology, Tel Aviv University.

Lobell, Jarrett A., and Marco Merola. 2008. Naples underground. *Archaeology* 61 (3): 22–28.

Marr, J. L., and Peter J. Rhodes. 2008. *The "Old Oligarch": The Constitution of the Athenians attributed to Xenophon.* Oxford: Oxbow.

Marsden, Peter. 1965. The luck coin in ships. *Mariner's Mirror* 51: 33–34.

———. 1994. *Ships of the port of London: First to eleventh centuries A.D.* London: English Heritage.

Matheson, Philippa M. W., and Malcolm B. Wallace. 1982. Some Rhodian amphora capacities. *Hesperia* 51: 293–320.

Mattusch, Carol C. 1997. Rescued from the sea: Shipwrecks and chance finds. In *The victorious youth*, 3–21. Los Angeles: J. Paul Getty Museum.

McCann, Anna M., and Joann Freed. 1994. *Deep water archaeology: A late Roman ship from Carthage and an ancient trade route near Skerki Bank off northwest Sicily.* JRA Supplementary Series 13. Ann Arbor: Journal of Roman Archaeology.

McCann, Anna M., and John P. Oleson. 2004. *Deep water shipwrecks off Skerki Bank: The 1997 survey.* JRA Supplementary Series 58. Portsmouth, RI: Journal of Roman Archaeology.

McGrail, Seán. 2001. *Boats of the world from the Stone Age to medieval times.* Oxford: Oxford University Press.

Meiggs, Russell. 1982. *Trees and timber in the ancient Mediterranean world.* Oxford: Clarendon.

Meijer, Fik. 1986. *A history of seafaring in the classical world.* New York: St. Martin's.

Meijer, Fik, and Onno Van Nijf. 1992. *Trade, transport, and society in the ancient world: A sourcebook.* New York: Routledge.

Morrison, John S. 1980. Hemiolia, trihemiolia. *International Journal of Nautical Archaeology* 9: 121–126.

———. 1995a. The trireme. In *The age of the galley: Mediterranean oared vessels since pre-classical times*, ed. Robert Gardiner, 49–65. Annapolis: Naval Institute Press.

———. 1995b. Hellenistic oared warships 399–31 BCE. In *The age of the galley: Mediterranean oared vessels since pre-classical times*, ed. Robert Gardiner, 66–77. Annapolis: Naval Institute Press.

Morrison, John S., John F. Coates, and N. Boris Rankov. 2000. *The Athenian trireme.* 2nd ed. Cambridge: Cambridge University Press.

Morton, Jamie. 2001. *The role of the physical environment in ancient Greek seafaring.* Leiden: Brill.

Muller, Serge D. 2004. Palynological study of antique shipwrecks from the western Mediterranean Sea, France. *Journal of Archaeological Science* 31: 343–349.

Murray, William M., and Photios M. Petsas. 1989. *Octavian's Campsite Memorial for the Actian War*. Transactions of the American Philosophical Society 79.4. Philadelphia: American Philosophical Society.

Nayling, Nigel, and Seán McGrail. 2004. *The Barland's Farm Romano-Celtic boat*. York: Council for British Archaeology.

Nieto, F. Javier. 1984. *Introdución a la arqueología subacuática*. Barcelona: CYMYS.

Oleson, John P. 1976. A possible physiological basis for the term *urinator*, "diver." *American Journal of Philology* 97: 22–29.

———. 2000. Ancient sounding-weights: A contribution to the history of Mediterranean navigation. *Journal of Roman Archaeology* 13: 293–310.

———. 2008. Testing the waters: The role of sounding-weights in ancient Mediterranean navigation. In *The maritime world of ancient Rome*, ed. Robert L. Hohlfelder, 119–176. Memoirs of the American Academy in Rome, Supplement 6. Ann Arbor: University of Michigan Press.

Olschki, Alessandro. 2008. Rimembranze archeologiche sottomarine. *Archaeologia Maritima Mediterranea* 5: 153–178.

Pallarés, Francisca. 1986. Il relitto della nave romana di Spargi: Campagne di scavo 1958–1980. *Archeologia Subacquea* 3: 89–102. Bollettino d'Arte Supplemento al 37–38.

Parker, Anthony J. 1992. *Ancient shipwrecks of the Mediterranean and the Roman provinces*. BAR International Series 580. Oxford: Tempus Reparatum.

Peacock, D. P. S., and D. Williams. 1986. *Amphorae and the Roman economy: An introductory guide*. New York: Longman.

Pollitt, Jerome J. 1986. *Art in the Hellenistic age*. New York: Cambridge University Press.

Polzer, Mark E. 2008. Rigging elements recovered from the Tantura B shipwreck, Israel. *International Journal of Nautical Archaeology* 37: 225–252.

Pomey, Patrice. 1982. Le navire romaine de la Madrague de Giens. *Comptes rendus de l'académie desinscriptions* (January–March): 133–154.

———. 1997. *La navigation dans l'antiquité*. Aix-en-Provence: Édisud.

———. 2004. Principles and methods of construction in ancient naval architecture. In *The philosophy of shipbuilding: Conceptual approaches to the study of wooden ships*, ed. Frederick M. Hocker and Cheryl A. Ward, 25–36. College Station: Texas A&M University Press.

Pomey, Patrice, and Eric Rieth. 2005. *L'archéologie navale*. Paris: Editions Errance.

Pomey, Patrice, and Andre Tchernia. 1978. Le tonnage maximum des navires de commerce romains. *Archaeonautica* 2: 233–252.

Price, Derek de Solla. 1974. Gears from the Greeks: The Antikythera Mechanism—a calendar computer from ca. 80 B.C. *Transactions of the American Philosophical Society* 64 (7): 1–70.

Pulak, Cemal, Rhys F. Townsend, Carolyn G. Koehler, and Malcolm B. Wallace. 1987. The Hellenistic shipwreck at Serçe Limanı, Turkey: Preliminary report. *American Journal of Archaeology* 91: 31–57.

Purpura, Valentina. 2008. I relitti con manufatti marmorei in Sicilia. *Archeologia Maritima Mediterranea* 5: 23–44.

Rackham, Oliver. 2001. *Trees, wood and timber in Greek history*. Oxford: Leopard's Press.

Rauh, Nicholas. 2003. Merchants, sailors, and pirates in the Roman world. Charleston, SC: Tempus.

Rickman, Geoffrey E. 2008. Ports, ships, and power in the Roman world. In *The maritime world of ancient Rome*, ed. Robert L. Hohlfelder, 5–22. Memoirs of the American Academy in Rome, Supplement 6. Ann Arbor: University of Michigan Press.

Rival, Michel. 1991. *La charpenterie navale romaine: Matériaux, méthodes, moyens*. Paris: Editions du CNRS.

Roghi, Gianni. 1965. Spargi. In *Marine archaeology: Developments during sixty years in the Mediterranean*, ed. by Joan du Plat Taylor, 103–118. New York: Crowell.

———. 1966. La vergogna di Spargi. *Mondo Sommerso* 8 (11): 1058–1060.

Rothschild-Boros, M. C. 1981. The determination of amphora contents. In *Archaeology and Italian society: Prehistoric, Roman and medieval studies*, ed. Graeme Barker and Richard Hodges, 79–89. BAR International Series 102. Oxford: Tempus Reparatum.

Rule, Margaret, and Jason Monaghan. 1993. *A Gallo-Roman trading vessel from Guernsey: The excavation and recovery of a third century shipwreck*. Guernsey Museum Monograph 5. Candie Gardens: Guernsey Museums & Galleries.

Sanders, Damien. 2010. Knowing the ropes: The need to record ropes and rigging on wreck-sites and some techniques for doing so. *International Journal of Nautical Archaeology* 39: 2–26.

Silvestri, Alberta. 2008. The coloured glass of Iulia Felix. *Journal of Archaeological Science* 35 (6): 1489–1501.

Silvestri, Alberta, G. Molin, and G. Salviulo. 2008. The colourless glass of Iulia Felix. *Journal of Archaeological Science* 35 (2): 331–341.

Steffy, J. Richard. 1985. The Kyrenia ship: An interim report on its hull construction. *American Journal of Archaeology* 38: 71–101.

———. 1994. *Wooden shipbuilding and the interpretation of shipwrecks*. College Station: Texas A&M University Press.

Stieglitz, Robert R. 2004. Copper sheathing and painting with orpiment at Elephantine Island (fifth century B.C.E.). *Bulletin of the American Schools of Oriental Research* 336 (November): 31–35.

Strauss, Barry. 2000. Democracy, Kimon, and the evolution of Athenian naval tactics in the fifth century B.C. In *Polis and politics: Studies in ancient Greek history*, ed. Pernille Flenstead-Jensen, Mogens H. Hansen, Thomas H. Nielsen, and Lene Rubinstein, 315–326. Copenhagen: Museum Tusculanum.

Svoronos, Ioannes N. 1903. *Die Funde von Antikythera*. Athens: Beck & Barth.

Tailliez, Philippe. 1965. Titan. In *Marine archaeology: Developments during sixty years in the Mediterranean*, ed. Joan du Plat Taylor, 76–93. New York: Crowell.

Tchernia, André. 1988. Les urinatores: Sur l'épave de la Madrague de Giens. *Cahiers d'Histoire* 33: 489–499.

Tchernia, André, Patrice Pomey, and Antoinette Hesnard. 1978. L'épave romaine de la Madrague de Giens (Var): Campagnes 1972–1975. *Gallia* Supplement 34. Paris.

Tilley, Alec F. 1990. Warships of the ancient Mediterranean. *American Neptune* 50: 192–200.

Turfa, Jean M., and Alwin G. Steinmayer Jr. 1999. The *Syracusia* as a giant cargo vessel. *International Journal of Nautical Archaeology* 28: 105–125.

Tzalas, Harry E. 2007. Bronze statues from the depths of the sea. In *Great moments in Greek archaeology*, ed. Pavos Valavanis, Vasileios Petrakos, and Angelos Delivorrias, 342–363. Los Angeles: J. Paul Getty Museum.

Ucelli, Guido. 1950. *Le navi di Nemi*. 2nd ed. Rome: La Libreria dello Stato.

Van Doorninck, Fred. 1976. The 4th century wreck at Yassi Ada: An interim report on the hull. *International Journal of Nautical Archaeology* 5: 115–131.

Vickers, Michael. 1985. Artful crafts: The influence of metalwork on Athenian painted pottery. *Journal of Hellenic Studies* 105: 108–128.

Waelkens, Marc, Paul De Paepe, and Luc Moens. 1988. Quarries and the marble trade in antiquity. In *Classical marble: Geochemistry, technology, trade*, ed. Norman Herz and Marc Waelkens, 11–28. Boston: Kluwer.

Wallace, Malcolm B. 1986. Progress in measuring amphora capacities. In *Recherches sur les amphores grecques*, ed. Jean-Yves Empereur and Yvon Garlan, 87–94. Bulletin du Correspondance Hellénique Supplément 13. Athens: École Françiase d'Athènes.

Wallinga, Herman T. 1964. Nautika (I): The unit of capacity for ancient ships. *Mnemosyne* 17: 1–40.

Weinberg, Gladys Davidson, Virginia R. Grace, G. Roger Edwards, Henry S. Robinson, Peter Throckmorton, and Elizabeth K. Ralph. 1964. The Antikythera shipwreck reconsidered. *Transactions of the American Philosophical Society* 55 (3): 3–48.

Whitbread, Ian K. 1995. *Greek transport amphorae: A petrological and archaeological study*. Athens: British School at Athens.

Whitewright, Julian. 2007. Roman rigging material from the Red Sea port of Myos Hormos. *International Journal of Nautical Archaeology* 36: 282–292.

Wild, Felicity C., and John P. Wild. 2001. Sails from the Roman port at Berenike, Egypt. *International Journal of Nautical Archaeology* 30: 211–220.

Williams-Thorpe, Olwen, and Richard S. Thorpe. 1990. Millstone provenancing used in tracing the route of a fourth-century B.C. Greek merchant ship. *Archaeometry* 32: 115–137.

———. 1993. Geochemistry and trade of eastern Mediterranean millstones from the Neolithic to Roman periods. *Journal of Archaeological Science* 20: 263–320.

Yardeni, Ada. 1994. Maritime trade and royal accountancy in an erased customs account from 475 B.C.E. on the Ahiqar Scroll from Elephantine. *Bulletin of the American Schools of Oriental Research* 293: 67–78.

CHAPTER 18

MEDITERRANEAN SHIP DESIGN IN THE MIDDLE AGES

ERIC RIETH

INTRODUCTION

THE term "design," which appears in the title of this essay, requires a short comment. A simple and plain definition of the word is given by the dictionary *Le Petit Robert*: "the act of conception . . . of thought, applying to an object" (*Petit Robert 1994*: 429). Among the further definitions of the verb "to design" provided by the same dictionary, one of them can be retained: "to create by reflection, the implementation of ideas" (*Petit Robert 1994*: 430). Taking into consideration these two definitions, the concept of "design" would seem to be associated (or even to merge) with an act of creation.

Consequently, within the framework of the history of naval architecture, which in this case is of primary interest, we will define the design of a ship in a much less restrictive way. On the one hand, the intellectual development process of an architectural concept, and on the other, the means, or instruments, to materialize this architectural concept. In other words, the term "design," seen from this perspective, encompasses the various ways of thinking about a ship according to its method and materials of construction, but also according to the economic conditions of the period, the social context, the status of the shipbuilder, and so on. These various manners of "thinking" do not necessarily suggest creativity, with all the share of originality and innovation that the word "creation" brings to mind. Moreover, the concept of design, as it is being presented here, can equally apply to the building of a ship-of-the-line as to a small fishing boat. There is always a process of design, more or less developed, behind every ship or boat.

It is quite certain that during the development of an architectural concept, all the characteristics that define a vessel (the hull, its system of propulsion, its steering mechanism, etc.) are taken into account. In a somewhat artificial way, in this discussion we will primarily limit ourselves to the study of one of these aspects: the development of the shape of the hull as seen from a geometrical point of view.

In the same light, "to think" and "to make," to design and to build, cannot be viewed as two separate, stand-alone processes; rather, they are closely dependent components of the same technical and cultural system. Medieval ships were not designed in isolation from the methods used to construct them. In fact, very often in the medieval period the man who worked out the architectural concept was also the one who directed its realization.

Before considering the methods of design, let us examine the main characteristics of medieval naval architecture.

A Mediterranean Architectural Tradition

It is in the specific geohistorical context of the medieval Mediterranean carvel "frame-first" architecture that we will examine the process of hull design. This architectural system is characterized by the privileged role granted to the frames, that is, the components of the transverse framing of the hull, both during the design phase and during construction. It is indeed starting from the frames, or, more accurately, from a section of the frames, that the volume of the hull is geometrically conceived. The frames play an active role in the development of a hull's shape, which is conceptualized through a "transverse" perspective of the hull (Basch 1972: 34–39). J. R. Steffy (1995: 419) elaborated on this process and professed that it should be viewed as an authentic "philosophy" of shipbuilding, thereby underlining the importance of the cognitive dimension related to this "transverse" perspective of a hull's shape. This architectural approach and logic is marked on two principal levels: the actual structure of the hull, on the one hand, and the processes of building it, on the other.

From both the structural and construction point of view, a basic distinction has to be made between the frames of the central part of the hull, corresponding to what is traditionally referred to as the "body," and the frames of the fore and aft parts of the hull, between the "body" and the stem- and sternpost. Beginning with the "body" of the hull, one observes that the molded, or predetermined, frames are generally larger (both in sided width and molded thickness) than in the case of "shell-first" construction, and have a relatively regular morphology. They are also distributed, starting with the master frame as the symmetry plane between the fore and aft parts of the hull, according to a more regular rhythm along the length of the vessel. In addition, the various components of the transverse framing, which vary typologically according to the time period under consideration (floor timbers, half-floors, futtocks, etc.), are from this point on jointed according to a number of methods. It is important to note that the floor timbers and half-floors are fixed to the keel in a quasi-systematic way. These transverse frames of the "body" of the hull act as a sort of "skeleton" and occupy a central position in the construction process. On the other hand, the joints between the frames of the ends and the keel are much less regular, as are the joints of their various components. It is not exceptional, for example, to note futtocks that are "floating," connected only to the hull planking.

On this structurally dominant transverse framing is laid the planking, with every plank (including the wales) being generally mechanically independent of one another. It is important, however, to underline that this carvel planking can be compared to a kind of wooden "shell" of the transverse framing, and that therefore it has a considerable mechanical function. Indeed, the carvel planking adds longitudinal stiffness to the frames and hull as a whole, bolstering the longitudinal structural components of the hull (e.g., the keelson, the stringers, or the ceiling planks). Moreover, this longitudinal stiffening is reinforced by means of caulking forced into the seams between the planks, which further compresses the edges of the planks.

From the point of view of the process or method of construction, frame-first architecture is characterized by the installation of a part of the predetermined frames on the keel, before any element of the planking. Consequently, the dominant structural role granted to the transverse framing is commensurate to the constructive sequence. This definition, obviously diagrammatic due to the limited space allowed for this general reflection, carries on to the much more elaborate construction architecture of the High Medieval Period, as exemplified by the Contarina 1 (Italy) (Bonino 1978) and Culip VI (Spain) (Rieth, Pujol, and Hamelink 1998) shipwrecks. But intermediate stages take place between this more matured level of development and the beginnings of the frame-first concept.

According to the current state of archaeological research, it is between the fifth and seventh centuries CE that great changes in the Mediterranean shipyards seem to have taken place. These changes followed two separate processes: one of "transition," and the other of "rupture" (Pomey and Rieth 2005: 175–183). It is the second of these processes, that of "rupture," that grants a primary role to the frames and transverse framing.

Archaeologically, this approach becomes evident through carvel planks, which, in general terms, no longer carry vestiges of assembly by pegged tenons and mortises. In the configuration that emerges, the planking, which is systematically associated with a caulking of the seams by means of a thread of oakum laid out in force, comes to cover the transverse framing that is already partly affixed to the keel. It is this transverse framing, now in a structurally active role, that plays the dominant part within the overall structure of the hull.

The study of this process of architectural rupture rested for a long time on the case of two wrecks from opposite parts of the Mediterranean. The first is that of the seventh-century CE wreck of Saint-Gervais II, located in the gulf of Fos-sur-Mer, close to Marseille (France) (Jézégou 1985a, 1985b), and the second that of Serçe Limanı (Turkey), dated from the first half of the ninth century CE (Steffy 1982, 1991, 2004). Since the excavation of these two wrecks, many other underwater excavations have brought additional examples to light. Such is the case, for example, with the wrecks of Dor 2001/1 (Israel) (Kahanov and Mor 2006; Mor and Kahanov 2006) and Tantura A (Israel) (Kahanov, Royal, and Hall 2004: 113–118), both dated to the turn of the sixth century CE. Other examples include the eighth-century CE wreck of Tantura F (Israel) (Barkai and Kahanov 2007), as well as the ninth-century CE wrecks of Tantura B (Israel) (Kahanov, Royal, and Hall 2004: 118–123) and Bozburun (Turkey) (Harpster 2002, 2005, 2006). This last wreck features the particular characteristic of a system of preassembled planking: small dowels inserted in the edges of the carvel planks were intended, it seems, to align and support the planks before they were attached to the preestablished frames. Despite this system of preassembly, the wreck of Bozburun, according to Matthew Harpster (2006: 98), corresponds to a "ship built in a frame-first manner." To these underwater sites one must add the extraordinary terrestrial "necropolis" of wrecks of the Theodosius harbor at Yenikapı, in Istanbul (Turkey). Without doubt, the 34 wrecks dated from the seventh to the eleventh centuries CE discovered thus far will lead to an in-depth reassessment of this history of naval architecture from the early Middle Ages in this oriental part of the Mediterranean.

It is important to note, in closing, that even though archaeological documentation has increased notably during the last decade, it still remains compartmentalized, both chronologically and geographically. The incomplete nature of this evidence raises the question of the representativeness of the archaeological sources, namely, wrecks, when attempting a historical analysis. Given this methodological problem, historical interpretations of the archaeological data must more often take the form of careful proposals rather than premature or hazardous assertions.

Having briefly defined the structural characteristics of frame-first architecture, let us approach the heart of our reflection: the design methods.

THE MASTER-MOLD METHOD

In a little-known work of great interest devoted to the dynasty of the Italian shipbuilders Camuffi, Mario Marzari (1991: 72) discusses the design method used in the arsenal of Venice during the fourteenth and fifteenth centuries and states that there were rules of "general use" constituting the common technical and cultural heritage of the shipbuilders. These rules were distinct from those of "particular use," which formed the specific technical and cultural heritage of each shipbuilder. Pierre Bouguer

(1746: xvi), one of the first French theorists of naval architecture (Ferreiro 2007), established a comparable distinction, stating that the knowledge of the shipbuilders of his
time, the middle of the eighteenth century, was based on "particular practices" that
always carried some "light modifications of the general maxims."

First of all, let us consider the great principles of these "general maxims" within
the chronological framework of the Middle Ages, more particularly between the
end of thirteenth century and the end of fifteenth, the period of technical maturity
of these "general maxims" and, moreover, a time when the written sources are more
precise. These principles rest on a fundamental fact: the architectural concept of the
hull as a whole does not rely on reduced scale representations such as lines plans.

The first stage of planning is a kind of "dimensional draft" of the hull, which
does not translate graphically; this is based on a number of technical criteria and
influenced by functional, economic, or administrative factors. The "draft," which
to the shipbuilder corresponds to a "mental finished representation" of the ship
under consideration, is based on the definition of a reduced number of longitudinal and transverse dimensions. These are fundamental dimensions established
according to simple proportional ratios and based on one or two structural reference dimensions (for example, the length of keel or the overall length between
stem- and sternposts—see Figure 18.1). The transverse dimensions, essential from
the point of view of frame-first design, relate the master frame (particularly the

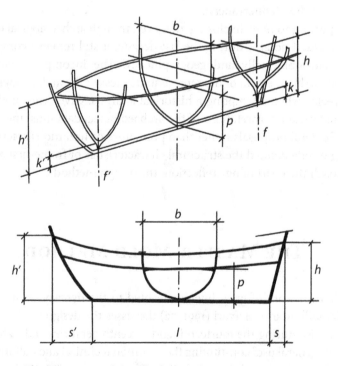

Figure 18.1 The "dimensional draft" of a merchant ship. After M. Marzari 1991.
Reproduced with the kind permission of M. Marzari.

length of the floor timber, the depth, and the maximum breath—see Figure 18.2) to two sections known as the tail frames, located at a certain distance fore and aft of the master frame. These are often the reference dimensions (though not always exclusively) that are mentioned in a contract between the dormant partners and the shipbuilder.

A second stage of planning involves establishing the values of the intermediate transverse dimensions that range between the master frame and the tail frames. The determination of these values, key to the design process, relies purely on graphic processes that rest on figures of practical geometry. The oldest examples, according to Venetian documents like the *Libro de Zorzi Trombetta da Modon* or the *Libro de Michele da Rodi*, appear to be the "half-moon," or *mezzo redondo*, and the "triangle," or *scagion*. These processes are carried out in full scale (1:1) and are based on the principle of progressive divisions (Figure 18.3). The progressive modifications of each

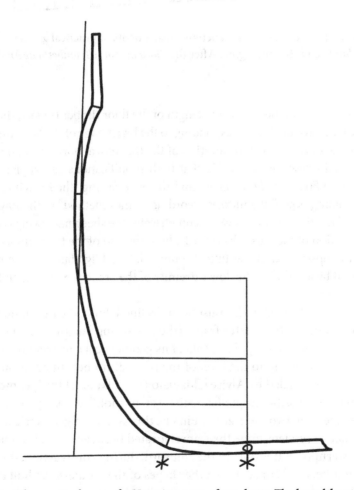

Figure 18.2 The master frame of a Venetian nave of 700 *botte*. The breadths at the floor timber, 3 feet above, 6 feet above, and at the *bocca* are indicated. After the *Libro de Zorzi Trombetta de Modon* fº 46.

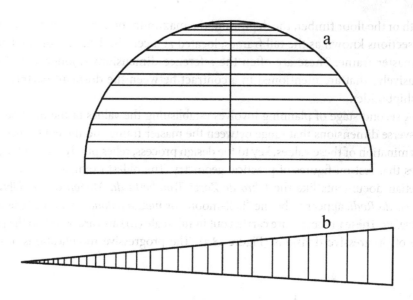

Figure 18.3 The two traditional Venetian "instruments of practical geometry": (a) the *mezo redondo* and (b) the *scagion*. After the *Libro de Zorzi Trombetta de Modon* f° 45.

frame relate mainly to the narrowing length of the floor timber (in fact, the length of a theoretical horizontal line corresponding to the lower edge of the floor timber), and to the increase of the rising (an elevation of the theoretical horizontal line above the keel). In certain cases, it is possible that both modifications can apply: the sheer-narrowing (the French *trébuchement*), and the bilge-fairing (the French *recalement*), a sort of "hauling down" the futtock according to the "method" of the English naval architectural treatises (Barker 1998). Geometrically, the sheer-narrowing is character-ized by a rotation of the arc of the futtock about the end of the floor timber, which in turn tilts the upper end of the futtock outward. The bilge-fairing is geometrically characterized by a sliding of the low extremity of the arc of the futtock on the end of the floor timber.

At this stage, three remarks must be underlined. First, the two basic modifica-tions of the values of the master frame (the narrowing length of the floor timber and the increase of its rising) do not affect its geometrical construction as a whole, which remains stable up to the level of the two tail frames. In addition, the geo-metrical processes called by Alvise Chiggiato (1987: lx; 1991) the "geometrical op-erators" make it possible to predetermine (or to mold) the shape of the frames located between the two tail frames. Finally, this system of geometrical operators proves unable to predetermine the frames located between the tail frames and the stem- and sternposts. It is only in the shipyard, during construction, downstream from the architectural concept, that the shapes of these outermost hull frames are determined.

The third stage of planning is one of transition between the definition of the architectural concept and its materialization in the shipyard. The aforementioned "instruments" in essence become a practical medium. Consequently, the contour of the master frame is traced on the ground, always in actual scale (1:1). Using this as a guide, three wooden "tools" are produced: a master mold accurately reproducing the contours of the master frame, a rising square (Figures 18.4 and 18.5), and a second square for the narrowing of the sheer line. Each of these wooden "tools" graphically represents, in full scale (1:1), the values of the various series of divisions obtained using the geometrical operators.

The combination of the horizontal (for the narrowing of the length of the floor timber), vertical (for the increase of the rising), and transverse (for the sheer-narrowing) planes of these mobile "tools," in the order presented, results in tracing the full contours of the body frames. In this stage of materialization of the architectural concept, the "instruments" of design become "tools" of construction, underlining the close association between the phases of design and construction. In a certain way, the operational chain between the "immaterial" design sequence and the "material" building sequence is uninterrupted.

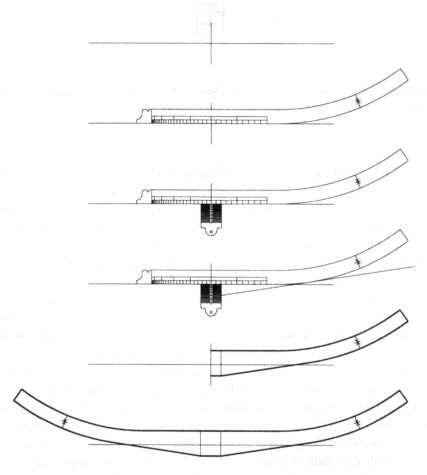

Figure 18.4 The floor-timber mold and the rising square as "tools" of construction. Drawing by M. Bondioli. Reproduced with the kind permission of M. Bondioli.

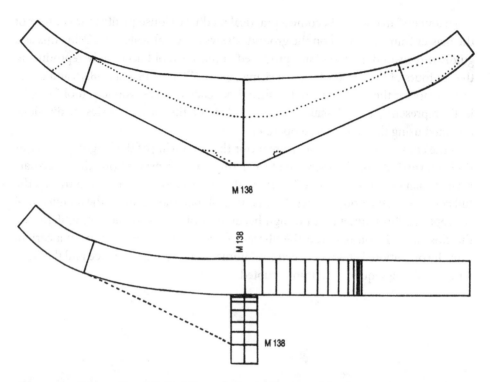

Figure 18.5 The medieval Culip VI wreck, Spain. Design of the floor timber M 138 using a floor-timber mold and a rising square. Floor-timber mold, rising square, and surmarks were reconstructed according to archaeological data. Drawing by E. Rieth.

As for the particular practices of shipbuilders, P. Bouguer's "light modifications of the general maxims," they correspond to specific choices made by a shipbuilder in matters relating to, for example, the ratios of proportions intended to establish the dimensional draft of the hull, the use of a determined geometrical operator, or the geometrical construction of the conceptual and structural contour of the master frame, which offers the "transverse" perspective of the hull. In this context, the practices of the medieval shipbuilders were probably more or less comparable to those of their eighteenth-century heirs that H. Duhamel du Monceau, founder of the first French state school of shipbuilding (1741), evokes in these terms: "Every shipbuilder is different in something in the figure [of the master frame] that he gives it, with the result that there are many methods to trace it, each shipbuilder by adopting one, that he believes preferable to all the others. . . .. these methods are different only by the way of tracing the arcs of circle or contour of the transverse plane of the ship at the place of its greater breath" (Duhamel du Monceau 1752: 186). These various ways of defining the contour of the master frame do not translate to different manners of designing hull shapes. All of these geometrical choices mark and personalize, in truth, the "general maxims" common to the shipbuilders. As for these "particular practices" of every shipbuilder, they result in two vessels of comparable size and function having different hull shapes. Particularly influential is the geometrical figure of the master frame, which controls the volume of the hull between the two tail frames.

HISTORY OF THE MASTER-MOLD METHOD

One of the oldest written references to the master-mold ship-design method permits us to trace the practice to the end of the thirteenth century, more precisely to 1273 CE. In a building contract (Fourquin 2001) for a *nave* being used to transport horses, and intended for the fleet of king Charles I of Anjou, the Latin word *sextis*, the Venetian equivalent of *sexto* or *sesto*, appears defined as a "particular mold which permits the whole series [of] frame[s] [to be] progressively different one from another, by means of marks inscribed on the surface" (Penzo 1999: 250). In the Venetian language, the design method of the master mold is called *di sexto* or *di sesto*. One of the oldest mentions, dated 17 February 1275, relates to principal dimensions (defining the "dimensional draft") of the *galea rubea of Provincia*, the "red galley of Provence," specifying that the galley was to have 96 molded frames. From the dimensional specifications of this great galley, or *capitane*, similar galleys were to be built for the fleet of Charles I of Anjou (Bellabarba 1996: 259).

It is then necessary to wait until the fifteenth century and the corpus of the Venetian "technical recipes" or practical "rule books" of naval architecture to have other attestations, always implicit, of this design method based on the various modifications of the master frame (Rieth 1996b: 139–141). Among these Venetian documents, the most famous is without doubt the so-called *Fabrica di Galere* manuscript, in reality *Libro di Marineria*, of which the text was partially published by the French historian Augustin Jal in 1840 (Alertz 2003; Bondioli 2003a, 2003b, 2003c).

With regard to these written sources, an important aspect must be underlined.In the *Fabrica di Galere*, as in the *Libro de Zorzi Trombetta da Modon*, *Ragioni antique spettanti all'arte del mare et fabriche de vasselli* and, of course, the manuscript of *Michele da Rodi*, the various modifications of the master frame that make it possible to predetermine the shape of the body frames are only named, not described. It is only at the end of the next century, in the year 1594 CE, that a Venetian manuscript, the *Visione* written by Baldissera Quinto Drachio (Rieth 1996b: 134–139), gives a description of this medieval design method by explaining the way in which the modifications of the master frame are defined according to the method of progressive divisions (the *partisone* of the Venetian documents). The two basic modifications, narrowing of the length and increasing the rising of the floor timber, are referred to respectively as *partisone del fondo* and *partisone della stella*, while the additional modifications of sheer-narrowing and bilge-fairing are in turn referred to as *partisone del ramo* and *partisone del scorer del sesto*.

Let us note that Drachio geometrically constructed the figure of the master frame according to the medieval method quoted in the *Libro de Z. Trombetta da Modon*: breadth considered on the level of the floor timber, 3 Venetian feet (1.04 m) above the floor, 6 Venetian feet (2.08 m) above the floor, as well as on the level of the greatest breadth, or *bocca*. In the sixteenth century, however, other means of tracing the contour of the master frame, using a combination of several tangent arcs of a circle, are attested to in Venetian and Iberian sources. These various types of geometrical constructions, more or less elaborate, correspond to the "particular practices" specific to every shipbuilder, always seen in relation to the "general maxims" shared by shipbuilders as a whole.

WERE OTHER DESIGN METHODS UTILIZED DURING THE MIDDLE AGES IN THE MEDITERRANEAN?

This question must be posed in spite of gaps in medieval documentation. Indeed, in the eighteenth century, at a time when according to the technocultural context the master-mold design method was still employed in private shipyards working for the trade and fishing industries, other design methods that relied on similar principles are attested. Two authors, the French P. Bouguer (1746: 37–40) and the Spanish G. Juan (1783: vol. 2, 15–18), mention, for example, two other methods elsewhere previously classified by the author as Method 1, "master mold and ribbands," in which the master mold is motionless and geometrically predetermined, and Method 2, "master mold, tail frames, and ribbands," in which only the master mold and the tail-frame molds, all motionless, are predetermined (Rieth 1996b: 97–108). To our knowledge, neither of these two design methods seems to be identified in medieval written sources.

An archaeological reference could be intercalated between the typical master-mold method and Method 2. It is the eleventh-century wreck of Serçe Limanı, Turkey, for which J. R. Steffy (1991: 1–9, 2004: 155–158) has advanced a hypothesis to reconstruct the geometrical process of the hull's design. This process calls upon the predetermination of a series of floor timbers ranging fore and aft of the duplicated full master frame (floor timber and futtocks)—the basic reference of the hull shape—and two other full frames acting more or less like tail frames. This process of geometrical design could correspond to a kind of "proto-master-frame method." In addition, a "proto-method" similar to that of the Serçe Limanı shipwreck would seem to be evident in the ninth-century wreck at Bozburun, Turkey (Harpster 2006). Importantly, Matthew Harpster relates this "proto-method" to a method of determining the tonnage described in a Byzantine document of the thirteenth century, the *Codex Palatinus Graecus* 367 of the Vatican Library (Harpster and Coureas 2008).

Although it may seem premature today to go beyond these two examples of Bozburun and Serçe Limanı, future research will perhaps allows us to reduce the realm of speculation. Meticulous research of the medieval written sources, and in particular private contracts of construction, could indeed uncover revealing indices of design methods different from those attested to in the usual Venetian sources. In fact, this reference to the Venetian sources raises the important question of whether the Venetian site of the Arsenal founded in 1104 CE should be considered a "closed" techno-cultural space. In other words, could the system of production controlled by the Senate, particularly in dealing with galley design, be extraordinary? Were the "instruments" of design used in the Arsenal—that is, within the framework of a state shipyard—the same ones employed in the private shipyards? Could there have been differences in the systems of production or the organization of production? Was the Arsenal a place of advanced naval technology, particularly when it came to the design of hulls, or was its perceived advantage more related to methods of effectively managing a shipyard? In addition, the discovery of new medieval wrecks could renew our "Venetian"-dominated perspective of hull design. Several examples, in addition to those of P. Bouguer and G. Juan, highlight the relative diversity of the methods derived from this same logic of design. In the context of traditional and vernacular shipyards in the eastern Mediterranean and the Black Sea, Kostas Damianidis (1993: 98–100) has thus far identified several similar design methods. One is a method observed along the Turkish littoral of the Black Sea that is based on the use of motionless molds of floor timbers on both sides of the master floor timber, ribbands to define the shape of the additional floor timbers, and, once the latter are established on the keel, a recourse to new ribbands to determine the shape of the futtocks.

In fact, a family of design methods, of which that of the master mold, the rising square, and the sheer-narrowing scale seem the most complete, could have been of use, synchronically and diachronically. These methods, while different, rest on the same principle of geometrical predetermination of the shape of the master frame (complete or partial) in relation to the "transverse" perception of the hull as a whole from both a conceptual and structural point of view. In the "advanced" method, all of the frames between the two tail frames would be predetermined by means of geometrical operators, and the function of the ribbands would be reduced to the definition, at the shipyards, of bow and stern frames. In the "primary" method, only the master frame (or even the master floor timber) would be predetermined, and the conceptual role of the ribbands, defining the hull longitudinally, would then be used to define, in the shipyard, the shape of the majority of the frames. These ribbands would act, according to the formula of Arne Emil Christensen, like "the shellbuilder's solution to skeleton problems" (Christensen 1973: 143). Between these two extreme solutions lie all the intermediate cases that have, and in the future will be, identified through both archaeological data and written sources.

In considering the present state of research concerning the predetermination of a hull's shape, it appears that a critical function is provided by the geometrical operators, which form the basis of the *partisone* of the Venetian documents. These

geometrical operators make it possible to define a series of gradually evolving modifications, without any calculation, using only an elementary figure of practical
geometry traced at actual scale on the ground of the shipyard or on a wooden
panel. In other words, this design method calls upon a purely practical geometrical
knowledge.

A PROGRESSIVE OR REGRESSIVE PHENOMENON?

Let us now consider the question of the existence of different levels of development
of the master-mold design method by examining, for example, postmedieval Iberian sources (Barker 2001; Castro 2007).

   Not until the beginning of the seventeenth century does the first definition of
the word *joba*, or "sheer-narrowing," appear in a Spanish treatise (Cano 1611: 108).
And not until 1613 is this important correction of the shape of the master frame
taken into account in a royal Spanish decree regulating the main dimensions of
merchant and war ships.

   In Portugal, it is in 1616 that sheer-narrowing, called *espalhamento*, is integrated
into the definition of an architectural concept in the treatise on carpentry by Manoel
Fernandes, *Livro de traças de carpintaria* (Rieth 1996a: 33–40). This more or less
contemporaneous appearance of the written term for sheer-narrowing in both
Spain and Portugal is not surprising, given that at the time Portugal was under the
domination of Spain.

   From a point of view of technical evolution and linear progress, it is certain that
this late use or, more precisely, late date of mention of sheer-narrowing in Iberian
documents could represent an innovation through which a correction of the breadth
increases the possibilities of controlling, prior to construction, the shape of the master frame. This aspect of innovation and progress does not elude G. Juan at the end
of the eighteenth century when, describing the differences between design with a
motionless master frame and ribbands, and the more elaborate master-frame
method, he notes that "other shipbuilders are more advanced, and put more precision in their practice" (Juan 1783: t. 2, 17).

   Is this model of progressive evolution, such as it appears through the
remark of G. Juan, applicable to the case of the medieval Mediterranean shipbuilders? In other words, is it possible that the master-frame method and the
rising-square method identified at the end of the thirteenth century could be
the result of a linear evolution that includes the wrecks of Bozburun (ninth
century) and Serçe Limanı (eleventh century)? Given the current state of
research, one cannot answer this question in more detail without perceiving
the concept of evolution as both progress and regression. Indeed, from the
point of view of technical evolution, one cannot put aside the phenomenon of
regressive evolution.

A remarkable contemporary illustration of this concept is provided by "traditional" shipbuilders of Newfoundland who in 1980 utilized a design method known as "whole-molding," the English equivalent to the master-mold and rising-square method, in a completely regressive fashion (Rieth 1996b: 192–193). The shipbuilders only predetermined the master frame and the two tail frames, whereas the "tools" of design (the master mold and the rising square) carried all the surmarks, allowing them, in theory, to predetermine the shape of all of the frames ranging between the two tail frames. According to the ethnologist David Taylor (1982), this technical regression should be explained through the inability of the shipbuilders to understand the significance of most of the surmarks present on the "tools." This manifested loss of knowledge of practical geometry would have occurred quickly, in the space of one or two generations of shipbuilders.

It is quite certain that one cannot, for lack of sources, transpose this contemporary example of regressive evolution to the Middle Ages. However, the possibility of a partial loss of knowledge must be kept in mind.

A third possibility must also be considered—the concurrent existence in the same cultural context of various levels of evolution. Thanks to the research undertaken in 1985 by the late John Patrick Sarsfield (1988, 1991), contemporary Brazil offers a perfect illustration of this phenomenon. In Valença, Bahia, shipbuilders worked according to the most elaborate master-mold and rising-square method (applying a particular means of correcting for the upper breadth), but in the state of Rio Grando do Norte, other Brazilian shipbuilders designed ships according to the most "primary" master-mold and ribbands method.

Therefore, if future research on medieval textual sources does not reveal a similar situation, it seems important to take into account the possibility of the concurrent existence of a number of development levels concerning design methods.

Knowledge of the Ancient Shipbuilders

The last aspect to be considered in this chapter pertains to the knowledge carried by the actual shipbuilders who designed their vessels according to the master-mold method. The medieval sources remain nearly silent on this subject. However, through the documents of the seventeenth and eighteenth centuries, and on the basis of a regressive historical approach, one can try to outline the extent of this medieval knowledge. A review of our current understanding is presented below, largely based on French sources.

During the second half of the seventeenth century, research on the theory of naval architecture was of central importance to the state, following the initiative of successive ministers Colbert and Seignelay under King Louis XIV and the development of what can be considered the first French Navy (Lemineur 1996: 34–74). It is during this same period that fundamental changes in design methods were first introduced in France, with the application of lines plans at the royal shipyards, that is, in a technical and sociocultural context called "erudite" and controlled by the state (Boudriot 1994: 7–58). Beginning with the eighteenth century, lines plans and the hydrostatic calculations become the "instruments of design" of the royal ship-yards. The master-mold method, the rising square, and the sheer-narrowing scale, which comprise the earlier medieval instruments of design, are still employed, but only in the context of private shipyards by shipbuilders who conformed, according to Duhamel du Monceau, to the method of the "ancient shipbuilders" (Rieth 1995).

It is thus in relation to the point of view of shipbuilders of the new generation, men for whom the lines plans and hydrostatic calculations were commonplace, that archaeologists can try to determine the knowledge of the "ancient shipbuilders." It is clear, however, that the design method of the "ancient shipbuilders" was perceived as inferior by the "new shipbuilders," whose technical and political objectives involved developing new instruments of design.

Let us recall first of all that the master-mold method, the rising square, and the sheer-narrowing scale, described as "extremely mechanic but rather ingenious" (Duhamel du Monceau 1752: 194), make it possible to predetermine only the frames ranging between the two tail frames (Duhamel du Monceau 1752: 194).

One of the primary characteristics of this earlier method is its nongraphic nature, which does not allow for information on the shape of the hull as a whole to be visualized on paper at a reduced scale. Duhamel du Monceau underlines one of the consequences of this characteristic for the shipbuilder with respect to his pro-ject: "One cannot know in advance the advantages and the drawbacks of the ship which one builds" (Duhamel du Monceau 1752: 195). Yet this absence of a full illus-tration of the shape of the hull prior to construction does not mean, for the ship-builder, an absence of architectural models of reference.

Obviously, the development of the architectural concept itself is supported by an "illustration," purely intellectual but effective, of the finished shape of the whole hull. Memory, without recourse to writing, drawings, or lines plans, appears to constitute one of the bases of the technical knowledge of the "ancient shipbuilders." The role of memory did not escape the intendant of the arsenal of Toulon. In a letter written to Colbert on 10 January 1670, he noted, "If I had only to take their feelings [those of the shipbuilders] . . . I could send all dimensions . . . considering the shipbuilders have all of them [the dimensions] in their memory, but they do not have any reasoning and cannot give rea-sons for which they grant one thing rather than another" (Lemineur 1996: 52).

This insight reveals another characteristic of technical knowledge based on memory: measurements, or, more exactly, rules of proportions, lead to the con-struction of the "dimensional draft" of the hull, as well as the master frame. This memory, often evoked in the documents of the modern period, is not a pure ab-straction. Quite to the contrary, it is nourished and composed of realities—that is, different types of ships or boats already built either by the shipbuilder himself, or by others. With evidence, this memory rests also and principally on the various master molds carefully preserved by the shipbuilder.

From this point of view, each new architectural project will tend to reproduce, with slight modifications, the tested architectural models of reference. In this context, any innovation that was not a clear improvement on an existing problem could lead to negative results. The result was a tendency toward conservatism. As Duhamel du Monceau observes (1752: 315), the majority of the "ancient" generation of shipbuilders "put all their application to copy the ships that they consider to be best."

In the design of a ship or a boat, a shipbuilder can rely on the tested model of another shipbuilder. Therefore, this particular knowledge relies on a certain collective dimension and, as a consequence, is also surrounded by a great deal of secrecy. P. Bouguer, a man of progress, underlines this concept by saying: "They [the "ancient shipbuilders"] observe a secrecy so important that their particular practices, though they are always only light modifications of the general maxims, constitute a sort of heritage . . . which is almost never transmitted but from father to son" (Bouguer 1746: xvi).

This knowledge, with its paradoxical contents clarified by P. Bouguer, remains acquired, memorized, and transmitted, either within the framework of a direct or indirect relationships, or in that of a corporation (another type of sociocultural closed space), according to the traditional methods of the artesian technical culture (Bocquet and Noël 1987: 229–241). As a cultural and also economical heritage, it must be protected. Seen through this perspective, the various master molds preserved by the shipbuilder represent a key to this heritage.

Thus, briefly outlined through the sources of the seventeenth and eighteenth centuries, this knowledge of the master-mold method, the rising square, and the sheer-narrowing scale that resided with the "ancient shipbuilders" could constitute a coherent interpretative screen of the knowledge of the medieval shipbuilders, which has been preserved to modern times by their heirs.

Concluding Thoughts

"Mediterranean Ship Design in the Middle Ages": perhaps it was quite ambitious to try to evoke this topic in only a few pages. Many aspects indeed remain unresolved, and many questions have not found answers. However, this only provides incentive to pursue this reflection further, supplement it, moderate it, and eventually correct it. In any case, it was essential to show that nautical archaeology cannot be summarized in a descriptive catalog of features—a corpus, however complete, of structural components, of types of assembly, and so on. A nautical archaeologist is not an engineer or a naval architect. He is defined primarily as a historian of the material sources represented by the remains of a ship or a boat. And through the restitution of the history of these remains, the process of archaeological study leads back to the origin, to some extent, to the history of the ship or the boat, to the point of its design.

Despite the gaps of our medieval sources, this chapter has attempted to restore the design methods used by the Mediterranean shipbuilders of the Middle Ages. And behind their nongraphic design methods, their knowledge of geometrical practice, their "instruments" and "tools" of which the master mold is the cultural symbol, they are always the men of the Middle Ages who appeared in filigree. In this manner, we do nothing but follow the proposal of J. R. Steffy, who, in his reference book *Wooden Shipbuilding and the Interpretation of Shipwrecks* (1994: 5), underlined that a "wooden ship has, in reality, far more than a lifeless structure. It began as a desire for profit, a hope for victory, or a dream of exploration or conquest in the minds of its originators.... The construction and operation of this vessel might have been influenced by hundreds or even thousands of people, some of whom, in some manner, left their marks on its remains." The key is always the people.

SELECTED PRIMARY SOURCES AND ASSOCIATED SECONDARY SOURCES

Anonymous, c. 1410. *Fabrica di galere.* Florence, National Library, Magliabecchiano, ms D 7, XIX.
  Anderson, R. C. 1945. Jal's memoire no. 5 and the manuscript *Fabrica di Galere. Mariner's Mirror* 31: 160–167
  Bellabarba, S. 1988. The square-rigged ship of the *Fabrica di Galere* manuscript. *Mariner's Mirror* 74: 113–130, 225–239.
  Jal, A., ed. 1840. *Archéologie navale*, vol. 2: 1–106. Paris.
Anonymous, fifteenth century. *Ragioni antique spettanti all'arte del mare et fabriche de vasselli.* Greenwich, National Maritime Museum, ms NVT 19.
  Bonfiglio, Dosio G., ed. 1987. *Ragioni antique spettanti all'arte del mare et fabriche de vasselli: Manoscritto nautico del sec. XV.* Venice: Comitato per la Publicazione delle Fonti Relative alla Storia di Venezia.
Drachio, B. Q. c. 1594. *Visione.* Venice, State Archives, Contarini, ms 19, arsenal, b.1.
  Lehmann, L. Th., ed. 1992. *Baldissera Quinto Drachio, la Visione del Dracchio.* Amsterdam.
Michele da Rodi. 1434–1435. *Libro.* Burndy Library.
  McGee, D. 2009. The shipbuilding text of Michael of Rhodes. In *Creating shapes in civil and naval architecture: A cross-disciplinary comparison*, ed. H. Nowacki and W. Lefèvre, 223–249. Leiden: Brill
  Long, P. O., D. McGee and A. M. Stahl, eds. 2009. The Book of Michael of Rhodes : A Fifteenth-century Maritime Manuscript. Cambridge, M. A. and London: MIT Press.
Z. Trombetta da Modon. c. 1445. *Libro.* London, British Library, Cotton, ms Titus A 26.
  Anderson, R. C. 1925. Italian naval architecture about 1445. *Mariner's Mirror* 11: 135–163.

REFERENCES

Alertz, U. 2003. The Venetian merchant galley and the system of *partisoni*—initial steps towards modern ship design. In *Boats, ships and shipyards: Proceedings of the Ninth International Symposium on Boat and Ship Archaeology, Venice 2000*, ed. Carlo Beltrame, 212–221. Oxford: Oxbow.

Alertz, U. 2009. Naval Architecture Digitalized Introducing Arithmetic and Geometry into Mediaeval Shipwrigthry. In Creating shapes in civil and naval architecture: A cross-disciplinary compraison, ed. H. Nowacki and W. Lefèvre, 251–277. Leiden: Brill.

Barkai, O., and Y. Kahanov. 2007. The Tantura F shipwreck, Israel. International Journal of Nautical Archaeology 36 (1): 21–31

Barker, R. 1998. English shipbuilding in the sixteenth century: Evidence of the processes of conception and construction. In Concevoir et construire les navires: De la trière au picoteuxTechnologies/Idéologies/Pratiques XIII(I); Technologies/Idéologies/Pratiques XIII(I), ed. Eric Rieth, 108–126. Ramonville Saint-Agne: Editions Erès.

———. 2001. Sources for Lusitanian shipbuilding. In Proceedings of the International Symposium Archaeology of Medieval and Modern Ships of Iberian-Atlantic Tradition, Lisbon 1998, ed. Francisco Alves, 213–228. Lisbon:Instituto Portugués de Arqueologia.

Basch, L. 1972. Ancient wrecks and the archaeology of ships. International Journal of Nautical Archaeology 1: 1–58.

Bellabarba, S. 1996. The origins of the ancient method of designing hulls: A hypothesis. Mariner's Mirror 82: 259–268.

Bocquet, A., and M. Nöel. 1987. Les hommes et le bois: Histoire et technologie du bois de la préhistoire à nos jours. Paris: Editions Hachette.

Bondioli, M. 2003a. The art of design and building Venetian galleys from the 15th to the 16th century. In Boats, ships and shipyards: Proceedings of the Ninth International Symposium on Boat and Ship Archaeology, Venice 2000, ed. Carlo Beltrame, 222–227. Oxford: Oxbow.

———. 2003b. Le galee: Storia degli studi. In Le navi della Serenissima: La "galea" di Lazise, ed. M. Capulli, 82–85. Venice: Marsilio.

———. 2003c. Introduzione allo studio della costruizone delle galee veneziane: Il contributo dei manoscritto. In Le navi della Serenissima: La "galea" di Lazise, ed. M. Capulli, 92–95. Venice: Marsilio.

Bonino, M. 1978. Lateen-rigged medieval ships: New evidence from wrecks in the Po Delta (Italy). International Journal of Nautical Archaeology 7 (1): 9–28.

Boudriot, J. 1994. Les vaisseaux de 50 et 64 canons: Historique 1650–1780. Paris: Editions Ancre.

Bouguer, P. 1746. Traité du navire, de sa construction, et de ses mouvements. Paris: Charles-Antoine Jombert.

Cano, T. [1611] 1964. Arte para fabricar y aparejar naos. Ed. M. E. Dorta. Reprint, Seville: La Laguna.

Castro, F. 2007. Rising and narrowing: 16th-century geometric algorithms used to design the bottom of ships in Portugal. International Journal of Nautical Archaeology 36 (1): 148–154.

Chiggiato, A. 1987. Le "ragioni antique" dell' architecturra navale. In Ragioni antique spettanti all'arte del mare et fabriche de vasselli, ed. D.G. Bonfiglio, 56–79. Venice: Comitato per la Publicazione delle Fonti Relative alla Storia di Venezia.

———. 1991. Contenuti delle architectura navali antiche. Ateneo Veneto 178: 141–211.

Christensen, A. E. 1973. Lucien Basch: Ancient wrecks and the archaeology of ships: A comment. International Journal of Nautical Archaeology 2 (1): 137–145.

Damianidis, K. 1993. Methods for controlling the form of vessels during shipbuilding in the eastern Mediterranean—18th and 19th centuries. In The evolution of wooden shipbuilding in the eastern Mediterranean during the 18th and 19th centuries, First International Workshop, ed. Kostas Damianidis, 97–105. Athens.

Duhamel du Monceau, H. L. [1752] 1994. *Elémens de l'architecture navale.* Paris: Charles-Antoine Jombert. Facsimile, Nice: Editions Oméga.

Ferreiro, L. D. 2007. *Ships and science: The birth of naval architecture in the scientific revolution, 1600–1800.* Cambrige, MA: MIT Press.

Fourquin, N. 2001. Un devis de construction navale de c. 1273. In *Pour une histoire du "fait maritime." Sources et champ de recherche,* ed. C. Villain-Gandossi and E. Rieth, 263–278. Paris: Editions du CTHS.

Harpster, M. 2002. A preliminary report on the 9th-century wreck CE hull found near Bozbrurun, Turkey. In *Tropis VII: 7th International Symposium on Ship Construction in Antiquity, Pylos 1999,* ed. H. Tzalas, 409–418. Athens: Hellenic Institute for the Preservation of Nautical Tradition.

———. 2005. Dowels as a means of edge-to-edge joinery in the 9th-century CE vessel from Bozburun, Turkey. *International Journal of Nautical Archaeology* 34 (1): 88–94.

———. 2006. Geometric rules in early medieval ships: Evidence from the Bozburun and Serçe Limanı vessels. In *Connected by the sea: Proceedings of the Tenth International Symposium on Boat and Ship Archaeology, Roskilde 2003,* ed. L. Blue, F. M. Hocker, and A. Englert, 95–98. Oxford: Oxbow.

Harpster, M., and N. Coureas. 2008. Codex Palatinus Graecus 367: A 13th-century method of determining vessel burden? *Mariner's Mirror* 34: 88–94.

Jézégou, M. P. 1985a. Eléments de construction sur couples observés sur une épave du haut Moyen Age découverte à Fos-sur-Mer (Bouches-du-Rhône). In *VI Congreso internacional de arqueologia submarina, Cartagena 1982,* 351–356. Madrid: Ministerio de Cultura.

———. 1985b. L'épave II de l'anse Saint-Gervais à Fos-sur-Mer (Bouches-du-Rhône): Un navire du haut Moyen Age construit sur squelette. In *Tropis I: 1st International Symposium on Ship Construction in Antiquity, Piraeus 1985,* ed. H. Tzalas, 139–146. Athens: Hellenic Institute for the Preservation of Nautical Tradition.

Juan, G. 1783. *Examen maritime théorique et pratique, ou traité de méchanique appliqué à la construction et à la manoeuvre des vaisseaux et autres bâtiment.* Trans. M. Levêque. Nantes: Malassis & Despilly.

Kahanov, Y., and H. Mor. 2006. The Dor 2001/1 wreck. Dor/Tantura Lagoon, Israel: Preliminary report. In *Connected by the sea: Proceedings of the Tenth International Symposium on Boat and Ship Archaeology, Roskilde 2003,* ed. L. Blue, F.M. Hocker, and A. Englert, 84–88. Oxford: Oxbow.

Kahanov, Y., J. Royal, and J. Hall. 2004. The Tantura wrecks and ancient Mediterranean shipbuilding. In *The philosophy of shipbuilding,* ed. F. M. Hocker and C. Ward, 113–127. College Station: Texas A&M University Press.

Lemineur, J.-Cl. 1996. *Les vaisseaux du roi Soleil.* Nice: Editions Oméga.

Marzari, M. 1991. *I Camuffo, uomini e barche: Cinque secoli di costruzioni navali.* Monfalcone: Edizioni della Laguna.

Mor, H., and Y. Kahanov. 2006. The Dor 2001/1 Shipwreck, Israel—a summary of the excavation. *International Journal of Nautical Archaeology* 35 (2): 274–289.

Penzo, G. 1999. *La gondola: Storia, progettazione e costruzione della piu straordinaria imbarcazione tradizionale di Venezia.* Venezia: Institituzione per la conservazione della gondola e la tutela del gondoliere.

Pomey, P., and E. Rieth. 2005. *L'archéologie navale.* Paris: Editions Errance.

Rieth, E. 1995. Duhamel du Monceau et la méthode des "anciens constructeurs." In *Etat, marine et société: Hommage à Jean Meyer,* ed. M. Acerra, J.-P. Poussou, M. Vergé-Franceschi, and A. Zysberg, 351–363. Paris: Presses de l'université de Paris-Sorbonne.

———. 1996a. A propos du terme espalhamento chez Manoel Fernandes (1616). *Neptunia* 203: 33–40.

———. 1996b. *Le maître-gabarit, la tablette et le trébuchet: Essai sur la conception non-graphique des carènes du Moyen-Age au XXe siècle*. Paris: Editions du CTHS.

Rieth, E., I. Pujol, and M. Hamelink. 1998. L'arquitectura naval. In *Excavacions arque-ològiques subaquàtiques a Cala Culip 2. Culip VI*, Monografies del CASC 1, ed. H. Palou, E. Rieth, M. Izaguirre, M. Jover, A. Nieto, M Pujol, X. Raurich, and C. Apestegui, 15–189. Girona: CASC Museu d'Arquelogia de Catalunya.

Robert, P. 1994. *Petit Robert: Dictionnaire de la langue française*. Paris: Editions Le Robert.

Sarsfield, J. P. 1988. Survival of pre-sixteenth century Mediterranean lofting techniques in Bahia, Bresil. In *Local boats: Proceedings of the Fourth International Symposium on Boat and Ship Archaeology, Porto 1985, British Archaeological Reports, International Series*, ed. O. L. Filgueiras, 63–86. Oxford: BAR.

———. 1991. Master frame and ribbands: A Brazilian case study with an overview of this widespread traditional carvel design and building. In *Carvel construction technique: Proceedings of the Fifth International Symposium on Boat and Ship Archaeology, Amsterdam 1988*, ed. R. Reinders and K. Paul, 137–145. Oxford: Oxbow.

Steffy, J. R. 1982. The reconstruction of the 11th century Serçe Limanı vessel: A preliminary report. *International Journal of Nautical Archaeology* 11 (1): 13–34.

———. 1991. The Mediterranean shell to skeleton transition: A northern European parallel? In *Carvel construction technique: Proceedings of the Fifth International Symposium on Boat and Ship Archaeology, Amsterdam 1988*, ed. R. Reinders and K. Paul, 1–9. Oxford: Oxbow.

———. 1994. *Wooden ship building and the interpretation of shipwrecks*. College Station: Texas A&M University Press.

———. 1995. Ancient scantlings: The projection and control of Mediterranean hull shapes. In *Tropis III: 3rd International Symposium on Ship Construction in Antiquity, Athens 1989*, ed. H. Tzalas, 417–428. Athens: Hellenic Institute for the Preservation of Nautical Tradition.

———. 2004. *Construction and analysis of the vessel*. In *Serçe Limanı: An eleventh-century shipwreck*. Vol. 1, *The ship and its anchorage, crew and passengers*, ed. G. F. Bass, S. Matthews, J. R. Steffy, and F. van Doorninck, 153–169. College Station: Texas A&M University Press.

Taylor, D. 1982. *Boat building in Winterton, Trinity Bay, Newfoundland*. Musée national de l'Homme, Centre canadien d'études sur la Culture traditionnelle, dossier 41. Ottawa: National Museum of Man.

CHAPTER 19

MEDIEVAL SHIPS AND SEAFARING

SUSAN ROSE

INTRODUCTION

To the Romans the Mediterranean was the *Mare Nostrum*, "our sea," and this familiar, almost cozy term perhaps reflects the way in which seafaring, whether by traders or by imperial fleets, was not seen as something extraordinary. In this the Romans followed the example of the Greeks, who for the most part lived in close contact with the sea, ships, and mariners. Europeans living in the confused and difficult times after the end of the late Antique period had more varied and complex relations with the maritime world. These relations changed gradually, particularly in the period between 1000 and 1500 CE. Many Europeans never saw the sea or had contact with any vessels other than river craft; others were skillful and careful ship builders and navigators gradually acquiring the skills and the confidence to make long voyages that by the end of the fifteenth century would span half the globe. Still others owed their living to the sea, whether as fishermen or traders, viewing the sea and ships in a practical and empirical way. Underlying these attitudes were the stern facts of geography and the natural world. Differences in the nature and conformation of the coastline and in climate, ocean currents, and prevailing winds all influenced humans' relationship with the sea. For these reasons, until around the mid-fifteenth century, seafaring in northern waters and the Western Approaches developed in a different way from that in the virtually landlocked Mediterranean and Black Seas. Each region will therefore be considered separately.

NORTHERN WATERS

The Vikings

In northern waters, especially once the Roman authorities had withdrawn, it would be easy to characterize seafaring as lawless and violent, an arena beyond the reach of any law where might was right. Long before the emergence of the Vikings as an identifiable group, robbery at sea was commonplace, widespread, and beyond the power of rulers to control (Haywood 1999: 41–81). It was probably hard to define exactly where legitimate trade shaded into robbery; this was an uncouth age when self-help was of more use than any appeal to rulers and their courts. Yet particularly in the world of the Norsemen, the sea and ships were a source of wonder, longing, and adventure. The poetry of the sagas is full of images of seafaring and the exhilaration of being on board a ship. A mariner's spirit "roams beyond the enclosure of the heart" and is drawn irresistibly to follow "the whale's path / over the sea's expanse" (Exeter Book, "The Seafarer," lines 58–60, quoted in Rose 2007: 1–2). At the same time, the Norsemen were skilled navigators and excellent boatbuilders. Their ability to voyage safely across the North Sea from Scandinavia to Shetland, Orkney, and the Faeroe Islands and then farther to Iceland, Greenland, and the enigmatic Vinland demonstrates this.

The archaeological evidence, provided by the well-known vessels excavated from burial mounds and others recovered from sites like Roskilde fjord, reveals the design and construction methods of Viking longships. There are clear differences in the details of hull design and rigging between those used as ceremonial or war craft, like the Oseberg or Gokstad ships, and those used for various trading purposes, like the vessel known as Skuldelev III (Crumlin-Pedersen 2002: 303–338; Ravn et al. in this volume). All, however, belong to the same tradition of shipbuilding, being clinker-built with a double-ended hull. The freeboard was lower on the warships intended to be rowed into battle than on vessels intended to carry cargo. These were normally sailed using one square sail on a mast stepped more or less amidships. There was a single steering oar at the stern. Written records complement this evidence. The Norse Sagas not only describe sea battles and raids but also give indications of the way the ships were sailed and navigated on long voyages (Marcus 2007: 35–99). The dismay caused by the state known as *hafvilla* is well described. The term meant that the ship's master and navigators had become completely disoriented and could no longer determine what course to follow. This occurred when the wind dropped or became fluky and uncertain, the sky was obscured by clouds so that no heavenly bodies could be seen, or a fog descended. Experienced seamen like the Vikings from at least the tenth century used the Pole Star and the Sun as direction-finding aids. They may have had some fairly crude way of estimating their northing or southing. They certainly were expert in the interpretation of small indications of their whereabouts, like the presence of seabirds and cloud patterns (Marcus 2007: 100–118). Other documents, such as the Anglo-Saxon Chronicle, make plain the fear inspired by the incursions of Vikings, so that coastal areas became dangerous and the sea a source of terror (Whitelock 1961: 85–86). Attempts made at defense included, in southern England, the organization of a small squadron of ships owned by the Crown (Rodger 1997: 7–17). This force had some success in encounters in bays and estuaries. More important was the acceptance of the idea by the beginning of the eleventh century that all seamen and ship owners had an obligation to contribute to the defense of the realm (Rodger 1997: 23–25).

Ship Types and the Maritime Community, 1100–1500 CE

The Bayeux Tapestry, made circa 1080 CE, after the cessation of Viking raids, depicts William the Conqueror's army embarked for the invasion of England on vessels much like some of those excavated at Skuldelev. The images of boatbuilders at work and their tools, also included, seem to belong to the same tradition (Thorpe 1973: figs. 37–46). It is probable that all along the shores of the North Sea and the Channel, Viking influence on ship design persisted for some time. The existence of a community of seafaring men with much in common, unaffected by the varying fortunes of realms and rulers, may lie behind the way in which many specialist terms relating to the building or equipping of ships can be found in a closely related format in many of the languages spoken in the same area. Sandahl (1982: 3–4) called such terms "Channel words." Examples are (in modern English spelling) "luff," "helm," and "bowline." Another indication of the cohesion of a specifically maritime community from the twelfth century are the many versions of the Laws of Oléron; this collection of "case law" relating to the duties of shipmasters and the rights of crewmen and other matters relating to the operation of ships can be found in almost all the languages of seafaring nations from this period (Ward 2009).

By the thirteenth century there is more visual and documentary evidence of changes in ships and seafaring. Images of ships are common on the seals of port towns, while illuminated manuscripts often include pictures of ships illustrating the lives of saints or incidents in chronicles (Flatman 2009) (Figure 19.1). Official documents include shipbuilding and repair accounts, orders assembling fleets and giving directions to their commanders, and the particulars of customs accounts, which often include details of merchant shipping such as tonnage and crew numbers (Friel 1983). Vessels may be described simply as *batella* (boat) or *navis* (ship) or by other apparently more specific terms, such as "hulk" or "cog." The excavation of the Bremen Cog and of the ships found in the Ijsselmeer has provided extensive and important information on the design and construction of fourteenth- and fifteenth-century workaday vessels (Gould 2000: 178–187; Hutchinson 1994: 15–21). However, it is still hard to relate the terms used in documents with precision either to images of ships or to those excavated. The image and inscription on the seal of New Shoreham has led to the conclusion that "hulks" were distinguished by their hull shape, in which the planking curved upward at both stem and stern, creating almost a banana-shaped profile.[1] On the other hand, the term "cog" can be found as early as the ninth century describing a Frisian vessel and as late as 1513–1516 CE in the customs accounts of Chichester (Burwash 1947: 193). It is used both of trading ships

Figure 19.1 The matrix of the seal of Rye, one of the leading Cinque Ports, dating from the fourteenth century. It shows the type of standardized ship image often found on the seals of port towns at this date. Reproduced with the kind permission of the author.

and warships. Clearly, it would be strange if developments in ship design did not take place during this span of time, making the term "cog" perhaps no more specific than *navis*. Looking at the iconographical record and excavated remains from the whole period, however, some common features do emerge. Cogs had hulls that were much beamier than Viking ships' had been. They were clinker-built, with a single mast supporting a yard with an oblong sail. The sail could be adapted to changing weather conditions either by reefing points or, later, by the use of bonnets, an extra strip of sail cloth attached at the foot of the sail. Gradually, from the late thirteenth to early fourteenth century the side rudder or steering oar was replaced with one hung on the sternpost. Temporary raised platforms, or castles, at the stern and the bow designed either to provide cabins for elite passengers or to be used in sea battles were also incorporated into the superstructure of some vessels. There could also be a top castle at the masthead for use as a lookout or from which missiles could be thrown (Gardiner 1994: 8–9). Ships like this could range in capacity from under 40 to over 300 tuns (that is, the standard Bordeaux wine barrels that were used to measure the capacity of a vessel). They were seaworthy, robust, and well suited to conditions in their home waters. Oared vessels, sometimes called galleys, also existed but were neither identical to the galleys of the Mediterranean nor as much favored by mariners as beamy "round" ships.[2]

Ships and Trade

Most seafarers of this period were involved in commercial trade. Some vessels might carry passengers; this could be a major part of their employment in a few places, like ports on the Kentish coast with regular crossings to France and Flanders, or for the shipmasters who carried pilgrims to the great shrine of St. James at Compostela. Their main business, however, was the transport of goods, whether coastwise from port to port, or across the Channel and the North Sea, through the Sound into and out of the Baltic, or southward to the ports on the north coast of Spain and on to Seville and Cartagena (Figure 19.2). Chaucer's description of the Shipman, one of the Canterbury Pilgrims, lists his ports of call—Gotland to the Cape of Finistere and then on to creeks in Brittany and Spain—and thus in fact gives a good idea of the range of English ships and mariners at the end of the fourteenth century (Coghill 1974: 28). The fleets of the Hanseatic towns regularly visited Iceland, Bergen, the League towns in the Baltic, and English ports (especially London and Lynn), and also sailed westward to Biscay for salt (Mackay and Ditchburn 1997: 211). Most voyages were fairly short, along well-used trading routes. Across the Channel to Normandy, Flanders, or

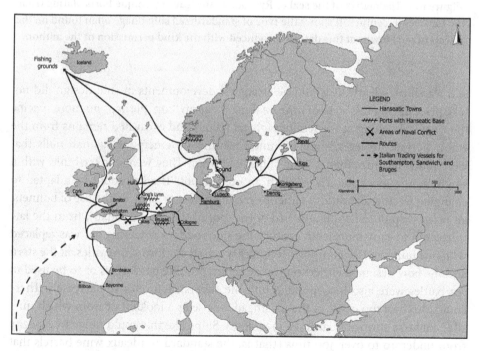

Figure 19.2 Map illustrating seafaring routes along the North Sea and the Baltic Sea.

Calais were the routes taken most frequently by English vessels (Rose 2007: 64–75). The longer and more demanding voyage from England or Flanders to Bordeaux for wine was normally made only by the larger ships, often traveling in convoy for fear of pirates, who, as in earlier times, infested most coasts.

Warfare at Sea

In this situation, more or less all ships, except the very smallest fishing boats or coastwise traders, carried arms of some kind. There was no real distinction between warships and commercial ships. Although, especially in England, any vessel in port might find itself arrested for service in a royal fleet, this commonly involved the logistical support of a royal expedition overseas, perhaps transporting soldiers and victuals north for Edward I's wars in Wales and Scotland or, later, across the Channel during the Hundred Years' War. Virtually every inlet capable of sheltering a ship could contribute to such fleets, while major ports like Sandwich, Southampton, Dartmouth, and Bristol were home to many vessels. A similar situation existed in Brittany and the coast of northern France. Sea battles were a rare occurrence that usually happened in sheltered coastal waters. This was the case at Sluys: in 1340 CE, Edward III managed to trap a French fleet in the shallow waters of the Scheldt estuary and won a crushing victory; he celebrated by issuing a gold noble featuring an image of himself on board his *Cog Thomas*. His fleet included a small group of "king's ships" whose role was, perhaps, to lead the arrested ships into battle and stiffen the resolve of their crews (Rose 2002: 63–65). The French Crown had initially attempted a different approach to acquiring a navy, setting up a galley-building yard at Rouen at the end of the thirteenth century, but this was not a great success; vessels from this yard were disregarded in favor of galleys hired from the Castilians and the Genoese (Rose 2002: 13–16). These vessels were well suited to mounting raids on the southern coast of England, a tactic that caused much destruction and also much fury in places like Winchelsea and Southampton (Rose 2002: 68–71). All seamen and merchants trading in these waters complained frequently and vociferously about losses to sea robbers, but often they, on other occasions, were guilty of the same crime.

Changes in the Fifteenth Century CE

Closer and more regular contact with shipping and seamen from Genoa, Venice, and the Florentine port of Pisa may have been one of the drivers behind the beginnings of change in both northern ships and seafaring in the fifteenth century. Pictorial evidence as well as evidence from ships' inventories and accounts makes clear that gradually over the course of the century changes were made in the rigging of some ships (Rose 1982: 191–194). Two-masted vessels with a mizzen mast, likely lateen-rigged, similar to that carved on a bench end in a church in King's Lynn, appeared in the first decades of the century but were replaced fairly quickly by the better-balanced three-masted rig, whose extra foremast probably carried a square sail like the main mast (Hutchinson 1994: 42–44). The source of these innovations may have been the Genoese carracks that regularly visited the south coast of England and Flanders on trading voyages (Figure 19.3). Some were also captured during Henry V's campaigns in 1415–1417 CE and incorporated into his fleet of royal ships. Royal interest in shipping was considerable at this time, with the Clerk of the King's Ships running a sophisticated shipbuilding and repair yard at Southampton (Rose 1982).[3] This interest was not maintained under Henry VI, but from the 1440s, some

Figure 19.3 A wooden carving illustrating a two-masted early-fifteenth-century sailing vessel that may be based on a Genoese carrack. It was originally on a bench end of the now demolished chapel of St. Nicholas at King's Lynn, Norfolk. Reproduced with the kind permission of the Victoria and Albert Museum, London.

of the most prominent noble families owned and built ships. This was especially the case with the Earl of Warwick, who in the 1460s and 1470s used them to advance his political aims with some tactical skill (Richmond 1998–1999: 1–19). The clinker-built hulls of the earlier period were now becoming obsolete as English shipwrights acquired the skills needed to build frame-first carvel hulls following the example of southern European shipwrights.[4] Cannon were also used at sea in small numbers, probably doing little more at first than adding to the noise and confusion of battles in which boarding an enemy vessel remained the major form of combat. Not until the final years of the century did Henry VII acquire ships carrying quite large numbers of guns of sufficient caliber to have at least the potential to be "ship-killing" weapons (Oppenheim 1896: 216–217, 261). Of the other rulers in northern Europe, the French Crown had ceased to have much interest in maritime matters. Its attention in the later years of the fifteenth century was focused on land warfare in Italy. In 1395–1400 CE, ships of members of the Hanseatic League conducted vigorous campaigns against the notorious *Vitalienbruder* pirates based in Frisia. Later in the century, the League also did its best to exclude English ships from the Icelandic trade and from trading directly with Baltic ports, largely through trade embargoes and the seizure of goods. There was little warlike activity in northern waters in the second half of the fifteenth century.

Long-Distance Voyages

This mention of the Icelandic trade, largely conducted by merchants from Bristol or Lynn who traded general goods for stockfish, indicates how English seamen were gradually becoming willing to sail farther afield, moving beyond the routes across the Channel or to Bordeaux. Some of the reasons behind this transition were political; the loss of Gascony to the French in 1453 CE ensured that the wine trade was no longer firmly in English hands. Seamen from Bristol or other western ports now looked more frequently to northern Spain and Portugal as alternative destinations. In 1457–1458 CE, Robert Sturmy of Bristol took three ships into the Mediterranean, probably with the intention of trying to break into the alum trade previously monopolized by the Genoese based in Chios. This voyage ended in disaster, but by the late 1470s other Englishmen were trading in the Mediterranean (Jenks 2006: 7–28). Improvements in ship design and seaworthiness, together with the spread of better navigational techniques, especially those developed by the Spanish and Portuguese, may have also increased the willingness of mariners to undertake longer voyages. Bristol records contain references that are not yet fully understood to voyages in the 1480s to somewhere called "the isle of Brasil," while in 1497 CE Cabot set out from this port on the voyage that took him to Newfoundland and North America. It is possible that, even though there is no trace in the records, adventurous traders from Bristol, or other West Country ports or perhaps French or Breton ports had made their way to the Newfoundland Banks and its fishery well before Cabot's journey (Rose 2007: 175). What is clear is that, although seamen in northern waters had been notable for their boldness in the centuries before 1000 CE, in the period around

1000 to 1500 CE most mariners in this region seemed to operate on a small scale, sticking to known routes and known technology. The sea was not seen or celebrated as a source of adventure or inspiration. For a more innovative and enterprising approach it is necessary to turn to seafaring and ships in southern Europe, in the Mediterranean and on the Atlantic coasts of Spain and Portugal.

THE MEDITERRANEAN REGION

Ship Types

In this region, seafaring clearly owed much to the mariners of Roman times; this tradition continued under the Byzantine Empire, which has been characterized as a thallasocracy (rule of the sea). It was also handed on to the Muslim rulers who, from the second half of the seventh century CE, after their capture of the Byzantine dockyard at Alexandria, commanded ships able to engage the Byzantine fleet (Unger 1980: 33–55, 96–102). Warships were predominantly oar-powered galleys that could be operated very effectively in these waters, despite their low freeboard and need for frequent halts in order to replenish the victuals and water needed by their crews. The design of these vessels, however, underwent considerable change over the period to 1500 CE (Figure 19.4). The bireme galleys of the later Roman period were replaced by the monoreme dromons of the Byzantines (Pryor and Jeffreys 2006). For longer voyages, these vessels probably used lateen sails as well as oars, rather than the square sails of antiquity. They were also equipped, for use in battle, with a "spur" at the bows projecting above the water (allowing boarders to pour across into an enemy ship or for its banks of oars to be broken up) rather than the underwater ram used to sink or capsize enemy ships in Roman times (Gardiner 1995: 101–116). Byzantine and later Muslim vessels could also be fitted with some kind of siphon mechanism in the bows for delivering Greek fire, the inflammable liquid that could cause devastating damage to an adversary (Rodgers 1967: 41–45).

Accounts exist from around 1270 CE for the building of galleys for Charles I of Anjou. These documents include dimensions and the technical terms used for the components of the hull and rigging. There was a foredeck, a poop deck raised above the sternpost, and a gangway running the length of the vessel between the banks of rowing benches. The average crew for galleys of this type was around 108 oarsmen and 36 marines, usually armed with crossbows. There would also be two sailing masters, four helmsmen, and a couple of ship's boys. A modern calculation has suggested that each crewman needed 22 kg of *biscotti* (the essential carbohydrate fuel for an oarsman) per month at sea. Nearly 70 liters of wine would also be provided per man for the same period. These requirements for a large crew and quantities of supplies limited the use of galleys (Gardiner 1995: 110–111).

Figure 19.4 Two three-masted Mediterranean "round ships" in the background with
a galley, mast raised, but no sail set. In the foreground off a rocky island are two
galleys prepared for battle. The one in the rear is a Muslim (probably Turkish) vessel,
while that in front is a galley of the Crusading Order of St. John of Jerusalem, which
was based on Rhodes during the fifteenth century. The disposition of the armed men
is clearly shown. From the Hours of Pierre de Bosredont. Reproduced with the kind
permission of the Pierpont Morgan Library, New York (G. 55, f. 140v).

Naval architecture manuals, or treatises, with directions for calculating the
form of the frames that made up the skeleton of a carvel-built hull, including basic
technical drawings, came into existence by the fifteenth century. These were produced by men with direct knowledge of the craft, even if the shipwrights themselves
were reluctant to share their secrets. They reflect the practices of the galley-building

yard of the Venetians, the Arsenale, easily the largest industrial enterprise in Europe. The best-known are those by Giorgio Trombetta (Anderson 1925) and Michael of Rhodes. By this date, in fact, Mediterranean galleys were successful and sophisticated vessels used to maintain regular trade routes running to a timetable. The trade network of the Venetians stretched from the port of Tana on the Sea of Azov to Sluys, the outport of Bruges in Flanders. The ships, of a standard design (described as "similar to each other as one swallow's nest to the next" by a fifteenth-century German pilgrim) (Gardiner 1994: 2004: 148), had two or even three masts carrying lateen sails used in favorable conditions, while the oarsmen rowing *alla sensile* (three men on the same bench each pulling a separate oar) powered the vessel in unfavorable winds or on the approach to a harbor. The alternative *a scallacio* system (three or more men to a bench all pulling on the same oar) was not used until the sixteenth century CE (Gardiner 1995: 123–126). The Genoese, Florentines, and Aragonese all had galley fleets designed in much the same way. The degree of state control over shipping and the organization and success of war fleets varied between these maritime powers. Control by the authorities was strongest in Venice, where not only were galleys built in a state-owned yard but there was also a state-owned rope walk, a state-owned bakery for the *biscotti*, and state-owned forests to produce timber for shipbuilding (Lane 1973: 363). Venetian galleys sailed on dates set by the authorities, with precise orders regarding the ports to be visited and the goods to be traded (Lane 1973: 339–342).

Merchants and shipmasters from these ports also operated round ships, or "coche" beamy sailing vessels whose design from the fourteenth century shared some features with the cogs of northern Europe. This was particularly the case with the adoption of the sternpost rudder, said to have been introduced into the Mediterranean by raiders from Bayonne circa 1304 CE (Gardiner 1994: 69–76). The most successful of these round ships were probably the carracks of the Genoese. They were used in bulk trades for goods like corn and alum, a fixative used in the cloth industry. They also carried cargoes of mixed goods, everything from dried fruits, wine, and olive oil to items like gold dust and grains of paradise, on voyages to Southampton, where the details of the cargoes are recorded in the local port books (Cobb 1961). They were also engaged in trade with both Muslim and Christian states throughout the Mediterranean. Venetian round ships were not as closely controlled as the galleys, although the authorities did become involved if there was any danger of war at sea.

Our knowledge of the shipping used at this period by the remnants of the Byzantine Empire and the Muslim rulers of the southern coasts of the Mediterranean is not so extensive (Figure 19.5). It has been pointed out that the prevailing seasonal winds, the sea currents, and the configuration of the coastline caused difficulties for mariners from the northern coast of Africa who wished to sail north (Pryor 1992: 12–24). It has also been suggested that aspects of the prevailing culture, especially in Egypt and Syria, were actively hostile to seafaring, seeing the sea as the abode of darkness (Hillenbrand 1999: 558–559). Evidence for this view is patchy. While Islamic rulers during the period of the Crusades were intimidated by Christian

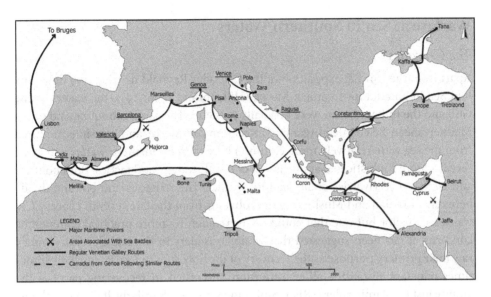

Figure 19.5 Map illustrating seafaring routes along the Mediterranean Sea and Black Sea.

fleets, such as the one that attacked Alexandria in 1174 CE, fairly extensive port facilities were built by a Seljuk sultan at Alanya on the southwest coast of Turkey in
the early thirteenth century (Hillenbrand 1999: 564–566). Saladin, moreover, pursued an active maritime policy against the Franks (Ehrenkreutz 1955: 100–116). The
Mamluk kingdom does not seem to have been much involved in maritime matters
after the final collapse of the Crusader states, but the rulers and inhabitants of the
Maghreb were competent mariners both as pirates and in more legitimate trade.

Castile was able to extend its maritime power into southern waters only after its
capture of Seville (1247–1248 CE) and finally Algeciras (1340–1344 CE) left the
Moors without ports on the Iberian coast (Rose 2002: 117–118). Piratical attacks by
both Christians and Moors on shipping in the western Mediterranean remained a
problem throughout the medieval period and beyond. In the Red Sea, in the Persian Gulf, and along the coast of East Africa as far south as Lamu and Zanzibar,
Arab trading ships remained as active as they had been for centuries. There is evidence from the first century BCE that seafarers in the region understood how to use
the seasonal pattern of the trade winds to reach India and return (see chapters by
Blue, and Gaur and Vora, in this volume). Until the arrival of Europeans in the
Indian Ocean, the ships used by local traders were constructed without the use of
iron. The hull planking was held together by a form of stitching using twisted cords
made of coir (the husk of coconuts). These open boats were navigated with skill
across the seas to India and the Malay Peninsula using charts, written sailing directions, and astronomical observations as early as the end of the tenth century
(Hourani 1995: 87–113). Certainly, this traffic across the Indian Ocean up the Persian Gulf and thence overland to Baghdad was one of the routes by which Chinese
goods reached the West.

Warfare at Sea in Southern Waters

The Crusades

Apart from the 1191 CE expedition of the Crusader Reynald de Chatillon down the Red Sea in an attempt to attack Mecca (Hillenbrand 1999: 293), the waters of the Gulf and the Indian Ocean were normally peaceful. The same cannot be said of the Mediterranean. Sea battles, organized attacks on commerce, and invasions mounted from the sea were relatively more common here than in northern waters and often reveal a more sophisticated appreciation of naval strategy and tactics. Both political and commercial rivalries could lead to conflict. The religious and cultural divide between Christian and Muslim regions, obvious from the late seventh century CE, was also a factor but one that could be overridden by more practical commercial concerns. It has been suggested that while Crusaders in the late eleventh century saw their primary purpose as the recovery of the holy sites in Jerusalem, their some-times reluctant Byzantine allies were more interested in recovering parts of the empire lost to Islamic rulers (Riley-Smith 1996: 22–26). Similarly, Italian merchants were happy to maintain a trading base at Alexandria despite papal injunctions against trading with Muslims.

The early success of the Crusading project owed a great deal to the fleets of both Byzantium and Italian maritime cities. Ships brought reinforcements and vital sup-plies to the Crusaders. The long trek overland from Burgundy or Germany to the Middle East, especially the dangerous and difficult march through Anatolia, was soon largely abandoned in favor of traveling by sea to ports in Syria from Italy or France. It is significant that the commanders of both the First and the Third Cru-sades clearly understood the urgent need to capture and hold cities on the coast—Antioch, Tripoli, Acre, and Jaffa. During the First Crusade, the successful siege of Antioch, which was a turning point in the whole expedition, owed much to the arrival of a Genoese fleet with supplies in November 1098. The fall of Acre to Richard I in 1191 was essential to any further military action in the Holy Land during the Third Crusade (Rose 2002: 35–42).

The Genoese-Venetian Wars

The sea traffic to Outremer, whether carrying military supplies, pilgrims, or trade goods, soon became of great importance to most Italian maritime cities. This in fact became the first arena in which the long-running conflict between Genoa and Venice took place. It is worth considering the nature of this rivalry and how it was fought out largely at sea. Both cities were largely dependent on maritime trade for their survival. Both wished to extend their influence in the eastern Mediterranean, the source of many of the luxuries that found a ready sale in western Europe. Both needed to establish bases in the region for their merchants and for access to ship-yard facilities for their fleets. The merchant elites and ruling classes of both cities also wished to be the dominant trading power in the region, particularly when it came to relations with the Empire in the East and its capital at Constantinople.

These basic factors caused poor relations between the two cities, which at times flared up into open warfare fought out largely by attacks on each other's commerce at sea and set-piece battles between their galley fleets (such as in the years 1257–1270, 1293–1299, 1350–1355, and 1378–1381 CE). Open warfare eventually came to an end not because either side had won a decisive victory or because the rivals had reached an acceptable compromise but because the advance of the Ottoman Empire altered the balance of power in the region. Genoa was forced to withdraw from the Aegean and the Black Sea, while Venice became in effect the leader of European opposition to the extension of Ottoman power (Dotson 2001, in Rose 2008: 427–439).

The way in which these wars were conducted forms a striking contrast with what has already been said about war at sea in northern waters, where it is hard to find any real strategic understanding of naval power. Northern rulers used ships in an almost casual way, with little continuity of purpose; there seems to have been the belief that at times of need suitable vessels would easily be found in the ports and pressed into royal service. There was no need for a continuous navy; ad hoc solutions to a crisis were sufficient.[5] Only in England during the reign of Henry V was there some indication of a different policy, expressed not only in the ships built for the Crown but in the mounting of regular sea-keeping patrols in the Channel until the Treaty of Troyes (1421 CE) made them redundant (Rose 1982: 47–52). In both Genoa and Venice, however, the continuing need for vessels able to fight at sea was well understood. Their solutions to the problem of how to organize and support such a fleet differed. Venice favored tight control by the state, while Genoa took a more "free enterprise" approach, but both were able to send strong, well-equipped fleets into battle.

John Dotson (1986, 2001), in a series of articles on the Genoese-Venetian wars, has emphasized the way in which the seasonal winds and trade routes of the Mediterranean allowed for a form of "control of the seas" by a well-led fleet. The galley fleet or the trading ships of the enemy could reliably be expected to be off certain narrows within a fairly short time span. For either city, attacks on its commerce were of much greater importance than the intermittent opportunistic piracy common in the English Channel—trading fleets were their lifeblood in a very real sense. Thus, for example the Venetians defeated Genoese galley fleets off Acre in 1258 CE, near Spetsai in 1263 CE, and at Trapani in 1266 CE, while the Genoese captured Venetian ships and the proceeds of a whole year's trade off Abydos (on the Gallipoli peninsula) in 1262 CE and a further four trading ships near Monemvasia. The most complex campaign in these years was probably that of 1264 CE, when the Genoese fooled the Venetians into thinking their fleet had sailed east to Pera when in fact it was lurking off Durazzo. On this occasion the Genoese successfully captured the entire Venetian galley fleet and the goods it was carrying. The only vessel to escape was a large round ship, the *Roccafortis* (Rose 2008: 408).

It is evident, however, from the way the Venetian-Genoese conflict waxed and waned that while each could do great damage to the other, each city lacked the ability to deliver a true knockout blow to its opponent. To do this, warfare at sea needed to be backed up by a campaign on land. The War of Chioggia (1378–1381 CE) brought Venice to the brink of disaster as the Genoese successfully recruited their Hungarian allies to attack by land. The Venetians in the fifteenth century suffered in a similar way at the hands of the Ottoman Empire. The Venetians could not hold on to the island of Negroponte once the Turkish land army was ashore, nor could they defend their crucial Peloponnesian bases, Modon and Coron, once the Turks had conquered the interior of the peninsula (Rose 2002: 109–116).

Roger of Lauria and the Aragonese

War between the Venetians and the Genoese was based on commercial rivalry. On the other hand, Peter III of Aragon used naval forces very effectively during the War of the Sicilian Vespers (1282–1302), a conflict with its roots in political and dynastic rivalries. He and Charles I of Anjou were in dispute over the Crown of the Regno, a kingdom which at this date (the late thirteenth century) included Naples, the south of Italy, and the island of Sicily. Some action at sea was probably inevitable given the fact that Peter also ruled Catalonia and its capital, Barcelona, while Charles was based in Provence, with the major port of Marseille. The naval aspects of the war have attracted much attention because the commander of Peter's fleet was Roger of Lauria, who has been hailed as an admiral fit to stand beside the most prominent figures of later ages (Pryor 1983, in Rose 2008: 295–316). His success may have been due to no more than the fact that he and perhaps his crews had more experience in galley warfare than their opponents and were personally brave and determined. For this relatively brief period, Aragon could well consider itself a naval power in a way that was not possible for many other medieval states. It is perhaps not surprising, with this heritage, that mariners from the western Mediterranean—the Catalans, Aragonese, and Genoese—were responsible for many of the advances in maritime skills in the fifteenth century discussed below.

Navigation and Seamanship

The mingling of seafarers from all the leading maritime powers of the Mediterranean in Iberian ports may have provided the stimulus for the great advances in the science of navigation during the fifteenth century. Even in Roman times a basic form of sailing directions existed. The *Periplus of Scylax of Caryanda* dates to the fourth century BCE and gives directions for voyages in the Mediterranean. The *Periplus of the Erythraean Sea* from 60 CE gives not only sailing directions but also useful tips for those trading in the Red Sea and across the Gulf to Persia (see Blue in this volume). The earliest surviving medieval sailing directions are the *Compasso da Navigare* (1250 CE), which included precise directions for entering major ports. A text like this may well have been used in conjunction with a chart, although the earliest surviving example is the *Carta Pisana* from 1274 CE. The *portolani* (as this and similar maps were called) depicted reasonably accurate coastal outlines; courses could be set using the rhumb lines leading from the maps' compass roses. Using

these and a magnetic compass, something which was now routinely in the possession of many shipmasters in this area, a suitable course could be laid off on the
chart. More general mapmaking also made great advances during the fourteenth
century CE; the best-known family of cartographers, based in Majorca, produced
major works like the Catalan Atlas of 1375 (Rose 2007: 51–56).

Other innovations included a system for estimating the course made good by a
vessel set out in the *Toleta de Marteloio* and the eventual extension to seafaring of a
method of determining the latitude of any point on the globe, originally devised in
classical times for use on land. This method entailed the measurement of the altitude of either the sun above the horizon at noon or the Pole Star at night using a
simplified astrolabe or other instrument. Calculations according to the rules and
tables to be found in books like the *Regimento do Astrolabio e do Quadrante* were
then necessary to establish a vessel's position in terms of latitude (Rose 2007: 56–59).
Longitude presented greater problems, which would not be solved until the eighteenth century. Navigation in this way was becoming not just a matter of hard-won
experience but a science based on astronomy and mathematics.[6] Mariners from the
western Mediterranean became more confident in their ability to voyage farther
afield, initiating settlement on the Canary Islands in the fourteenth century CE,
Madeira in 1420 CE, the Azores in 1427 CE, and the Cape Verde Islands in 1456 CE.
Some credit, at least for the steady accumulation of experience in more scientific
navigation and for the making of more accurate maps and charts, may be due,
according to some historians, to Henry the Navigator and his court, based at Sagres
(Parry 1974: 113–129; Phillips 1998: 213–219). The ultimate outcome, was, of course,
the discovery of the route around the Cape of Good Hope to India pioneered by the
Portuguese Bartolomeu Dias (1488 CE) and Vasco da Gama (1497–1499 CE) and
that across the Atlantic to the Caribbean first followed in 1492 CE by Christopher
Columbus, a Genoese supported by the rulers of Castile.

Conclusion

At the beginning of this discussion of medieval seafaring, emphasis was placed on
the way in which ships and seafarers in northern waters differed from those in the
south. The stormy waters of the North Atlantic, the fierce tides and shifting sandbanks of the Channel, and the North Sea made for a harsher maritime environment
than the more predictable seasonal changes in the winds and the weather of the
almost tideless Mediterranean. By the end of the fifteenth century CE, however,
these differences were much less pronounced. For use inshore, for fishing, or for the
transport of small local cargoes, all kinds of craft existed, exhibiting special adaptations for particular local circumstances: the need to beach on a stony shore, or to
launch into the surf; a rig adapted to long-reaching courses in steady winds, or one
suited to short tacks into a narrow harbor. On longer voyages, however, a degree of

consensus had been established as to the best and most practical design, which now became generally known as the caravel (Gardiner 1994: 91–98). Equally, shipmasters contemplating such a journey were expected to have at least some understanding of navigational instruments and their use at sea. The experienced but rough and ready mariner who as late as 1571 CE was described by William Bourne as laughing at charts and astronomical observations and saying he could do as well as "star shooters" by keeping an "account upon a boord" was gradually being edged out of seafaring (Rose 2004: 176). The new exponents of mathematical navigation were better educated and increasingly of a higher social rank. Columbus and Cabot were both prepared and able to negotiate with monarchs for support. Drake and his colleagues in Elizabeth's reign were familiar figures at court.

It is also the case that just as an earlier maritime community had spread knowledge of the Laws of Oléron widely along the sea lanes, mariners in both southern and northern Europe exchanged knowledge of techniques and courses. In 1477 CE Columbus probably made a voyage as far north as Iceland. Later in 1478 CE he traveled to Madeira and eventually married a close relation of one of the town's first settlers. He did not set out across the Atlantic without some good experience in long-distance voyages and the prevailing winds (Fernández-Armesto 2000: 14–17). Similarly, in another linking of the traditions of the North and the South, the Italian Cabot (Giovanni Caboto) set out from Bristol in a locally built vessel. We might also observe that the enthusiasm for new experiences found in Viking sagas seemed to be reborn in the plans of the most prominent seamen of the late fifteenth century CE. Columbus could even declare in 1498 CE that he believed he was on the brink of discovering "the Earthly Paradise where no man may go save by the grace of God" (Fernández-Armesto 2000: 104). Such fantasies were, of course, a long way from the experience of most workaday seamen plying short routes. They served, however, to ensure that ships and seafaring had a renewed prominence in European affairs at the end of the fifteenth century CE, with profound consequences for the future development of the world and its peoples.

NOTES

1. The inscription read as follows: *Hoc hulci signo vocor os sic nomine digno* (By the sign of a hulk I am called Mouth which is a worthy name). This becomes comprehensible when one learns that New Shoreham was earlier called Hulksmouth.

2. The English Crown ordered the building of so-called galleys for defensive purposes at the end of the thirteenth and in the mid-fourteenth centuries. Little or nothing is known about the way they were used. Balingers, a ship type combining both oars and sails, enjoyed some popularity as fast transports or raiders up to the first half of the fifteenth century (Unger 1980: 171–172; Tinniswood 1949 in Rose ed. 2008: 25–68).

3. Full details of Henry V's naval activities, including a transcription and translation of the account book of the Clerk of the King's Ships for 1422–1427, can be found in Rose 1982.

4. The Household Books and other documents relating to John Howard, Duke of Norfolk, in the second half of the fifteenth century contain mentions of ships called carvels, e.g., a listing from 1468 CE in which 8 out of 22 ships are described as carvels (Crawford 1992: xliv).

5. Sir John Fortescue, in his *Governance of England* (written in the 1470s), pointed out that it was too late to build a navy when the enemy were already at sea, but no English ruler took much notice of this until the sixteenth century (Lockwood 1997: 96–97).

6. The whole subject of navigation from classical times to the eighteenth century is discussed in E. G. R. Taylor's *The Haven-Finding Art: A History of Navigation from Odysseus to Captain Cook* (1956). Parts III and IV are most relevant for the medieval period.

REFERENCES

Anderson, R. C. 1925. Italian naval architecture about 1445. *Mariner's Mirror* 11: 135–163.

Burwash, Dorothy. 1947. *English merchant shipping 1460–1540*. Newton Abbot, England: David and Charles.

Cobb, Henry S. 1961. *The local port book of Southampton for 1439–40*. Southampton: Southampton University.

Coghill, Neville, ed. 1974. *The Canterbury Tales*. London: Folio Society.

Crawford, Anne. 1992. *The Household Books of John Howard, Duke of Norfolk, 1462–1471, 1481–1483*. Stroud: Alan Sutton.

Crumlin-Pedersen, Ole. 2002. *The Skuldelev Ships I: Topography, archaeology, history, conservation and display*. Roskilde: Viking Ship Museum.

Dotson, J. E. 1986. Naval strategy in the First Genoese-Venetian War 1257–1270. *American Neptune* 46: 84–90.

———. 2001. Foundations of Venetian naval strategy from Pietro II Orseolo to the Battle of Zonchio 100–1500. *Viator* 32: 113–125. Dotson 1986 and 2001 are reprinted in S. Rose, ed., *Medieval ships and warfare*, 403–439. Aldershot: Ashgate, 2008.

Ehrenkreutz, A. S. 1955. The place of Saladin in the naval history of the Mediterranean Sea in the Middle Ages. *Journal of the American Oriental Society* 75: 100–116. Reprinted in S. Rose, ed., *Medieval ships and warfare*, 235–251. Aldershot: Ashgate, 2008.

Fernández-Armesto, Felipe. 2000. *Columbus and the conquest of the impossible*. London: Phoenix Press.

Flatman, Joe. 2009. *Ships and shipping in medieval manuscripts*. London: British Library.

Friel, Ian. 1983. Documentary sources and the medieval ship: Some aspects of the evidence. *International Journal of Nautical Archaeology and Underwater Exploration* 12 (1): 41–62.

Gardiner, Robert, ed. 1994. *Cogs caravels and galleons: The sailing ship 1000–1650*. London: Conway Maritime Press.

———. 1995. *The age of the galley: Mediterranean oared vessels since pre-classical times*. London: Conway Maritime Press.

Gould, Richard A. 2000. *Archaeology and the social history of ships*. Cambridge: Cambridge University Press.

Haywood, John. 1999. *Dark Age naval power: A reassessment of Frankish and Anglo-Saxon seafaring activity*. 2nd ed. Hockwold-cum-Wilton: Anglo-Saxon Books.

Hillenbrand, Carole. 1999. *The Crusades: Islamic perspectives.* Edinburgh: Edinburgh University Press.

Hourani, George F. 1995. *Arab seafaring in the Indian Ocean in ancient and early medieval times.* Princeton, NJ: Princeton University Press.

Hutchinson, Gillian. 1994. *Medieval ships and shipping.* London: Leicester University Press.

Jenks, Stuart. 2006. *Robert Sturmy's commercial expedition to the Mediterranean (1457-8).* Bristol: Bristol Record Society.

Lane, Frederic C. 1973. *Venice: A maritime republic.* Baltimore: Johns Hopkins University Press.

Lockwood, Shelley, ed. 1997. *Sir John Fortescue: On the laws and governance of England.* Cambridge: Cambridge University Press.

Mackay, Angus, with David Ditchburn. 1997. *Atlas of medieval Europe.* London: Routledge.

Marcus, G. J. 2007. *The conquest of the North Atlantic.* 2nd ed. Woodbridge: Boydell Press.

Oppenheim, M. 1896. *Naval accounts and inventories of the reign of Henry VII 1485-8 and 1495-7.* London: Navy Records Society.

Parry, J. H. 1974. *The discovery of the sea.* London: Weidenfeld and Nicolson.

Phillips, J. R. S. 1998. *The medieval expansion of Europe.* Oxford: Clarendon Press.

Pryor, John H. 1983. The naval battles of Roger of Lauria. Reprinted in S. Rose, ed., *Medieval ships and warfare,* 295-332. Aldershot: Ashgate, 2008.

Pryor, John H. 1992. *Geography, technology, and war: Studies in the maritime history of the Mediterranean 649-1571.* Cambridge: Cambridge University Press.

Pryor, John H., and Elizabeth M. Jeffreys. 2006. *The age of the ΔPOMΩN: The Byzantine navy ca 500-1204.* Leiden: Brill.

Richmond, Colin F. 1998/1999. The Earl of Warwick's domination of the Channel and the naval dimension of the Wars of the Roses. *Southern History* 20/21:1-19.

Riley-Smith, Jonathan. 1996. *The Crusades: A short history.* London: Athlone Press.

Rodger, N. A. M. 1997. *The safeguard of the sea: A naval history of Britain.* Vol. 1, *660-1649.* London: HarperCollins.

Rodgers, William Ledyard. 1967. *Naval warfare under oars 4th to 16th centuries: A study of strategy tactics and ship design.* Annapolis: Naval Institute Press.

Rose, Susan. 1982. *The navy of the Lancastrian Kings: Accounts and inventories of William Soper, Keeper of the King's Ships 1422-27.* London: Navy Records Society.

———. 2002. *Medieval naval warfare 1000-1500.* London: Routledge.

———. 2004. Mathematics and the art of navigation: The advance of scientific seamanship in Elizabethan England. *Transactions of the Royal Historical Society,* 6th ser., 14: 174-184.

———. 2007. *The medieval sea.* London: Hambledon Continuum.

———, ed. 2008. *Medieval ships and warfare.* Aldershot: Ashgate.

Sandahl, Bertil. 1982. *Middle English sea terms.* Vol. 3, *Standing and running rigging.* Uppsala: Acta Universittatis Upsaliensis.

Taylor, E. G. R. 1956. *The haven-finding art: A history of navigation from Odysseus to Captain Cook.* London: Hollis and Carter.

Thorpe, Lewis. 1973. *The Bayeux Tapestry and the Norman Invasion.* London: Folio Society.

Tinniswood, J. T. 1949. English galleys 1272-1377. *Mariner's Mirror* 35: 276-315.

Unger, Richard W. 1980. *The ship in the medieval economy 600-1600.* London: Croom Helm; Montreal: McGill-Queen's University Press.

Ward, R. 2009. *The world of the medieval shipmaster: Law business and the sea, c. 1350-1450.* Woodbridge: Boydell.

Whitelock, Dorothy, with D. C. Douglas and S. I. Tucker. 1961. *The Anglo-Saxon chronicle.* London: Eyre and Spottiswoode.

CHAPTER 20

POSTMEDIEVAL SHIPS AND SEAFARING IN THE WEST

FRED HOCKER

INTRODUCTION

WHILE the conceptual underpinnings of the modern world, our ideas of what religion, economy, and politics are, were formed in the Middle Ages, the physical form and organization of the world today is a postmedieval creation, a result of accelerated growth in population and economy. Ships and seafaring were an essential part of that growth and expansion, connecting ever more remote parts of the world in a global economy and carrying European ambition into the farthest reaches of the world's oceans. In the last half-millennium, European seafarers and their American descendants established empires that harvested the raw materials and manufactures of six continents and concentrated the profits in a handful of great cities, from Amsterdam and London to Venice and Seville, to New York and Boston. At the same time, governments increasingly under the influence of economic forces challenged and defeated local rulers in distant oceans while exporting European wars to their overseas colonies. All of this required ships, harbors, and a sophisticated administrative infrastructure to manage them (Adams 2003). Even after the resurgence of indigenous economies in the Far East during the twentieth century and the expansion of their merchant fleets, the balance of naval power still reflects a postmedieval order, and European and American cities remain among the most influential financial and commercial centers in the world, a legacy of the maritime empires created in the sixteenth and seventeenth centuries.

Major Societal Trends

Demographics

The period after 1400 is characterized by growth and bureaucratization in most of Europe. The plagues and famines that had devastated the world for millennia tapered off in Europe after the early fifteenth century, and the population began to recover. It took decades or even centuries in some places for the population to return to pre–Black Death levels, but those who survived the horrors of the fourteenth century were wealthier due to the concentration of capital that resulted from mass mortality, and this capital surplus could be invested in economic ventures in larger quantities. While the smaller population may have reduced demand for staples and other bulk commodities, the increased wealth encouraged demand for luxury products, as did changed attitudes toward the balance between earthly and spiritual life. The growing population was increasingly urban in western Europe, which probably contributed to a rapid recovery of the market for foodstuffs. It also provided a concentration of potential labor for manufacturing everything from textiles to ships, and tended to concentrate information and expertise in the same location as capital.

Colonialism and Globalization

From the beginning of the fifteenth century, the maritime countries of western Europe began to consider extra-European expansion of their territory and influence (Scammell 1981). The borders between countries on the continent had largely been decided, and there was limited opportunity for expansion at the expense of neighbors. To the west and south, however, in the Atlantic Ocean and Africa, there was potentially rich land for the taking, not to mention the riches of the ocean itself, in the form of fish. The Azores, Canary, and Cape Verde Islands were quickly claimed and colonized, and the Iberian expansion continued down the coast of Africa. By the end of the century, the Spanish began to consider the possibility of breaking the traditional Italian monopoly on Far Eastern luxuries by finding a direct route to the Indies that would bypass the Mediterranean and the trans-Asian caravan routes. Most favored an eastward route around Africa, while others thought that sailing westward would lead directly to China, but the southern extent of Africa was unknown, and the existence of the Americas not even suspected, except perhaps by a few fishermen searching for cod in the northwestern Atlantic. Columbus reached the Americas in 1492, de Gama rounded the southern tip of Africa and entered the Indian Ocean in 1497, and the race to exploit the new routes and territories was on.

The new land to the west was initially unprofitable, but contact with well-organized indigenous societies revealed rich deposits of gold and silver, as well as agricultural products that could be sold in Europe. Exploiting these resources required co-option, subjugation, or extermination of the indigenous peoples, and the introduction of European diseases wiped out many of the original inhabitants, especially on the islands of the Caribbean. The rapid decline of the potential labor force for new plantations led to a demand for slaves, who were eventually imported in large numbers from Africa. High mortality continued, and the reproduction rate of the slave population was unable to keep up with demand, leading to the growth of a lucrative trade in human chattel.

Although the western route to the Indies was blocked, the eastern route paid immediate dividends. China, the most powerful and advanced civilization in the East, had embarked on its own program of exploration in the early fifteenth century, but withdrew from international ventures soon afterward, leaving a vacuum filled by merchants from Arabia, East Africa, and India. The Portuguese and the Spanish who followed them found an ocean divided among a large number of relatively small, regional powers with inferior military technology. Small European forces were able to defeat native ships in battle and intimidate local rulers, while exploiting existing rivalries to establish footholds in the important entrepôts of India, Indonesia, and Southeast Asia. They could then use these trading stations to collect the valuable commodities of the region, especially spices, and ship them back to Europe.

These overseas colonies and trading posts were an almost exclusively Iberian venture for nearly a century, but by the 1580s, Dutch and English entrepreneurs were eyeing the precious metals and agricultural profits of the New World and the spices of the East Indies with envy. They began to send their own colonists to establish settlements, mostly in North America, beyond the northern limits of the Spanish colonies. By the mid-seventeenth century, there were English, Dutch, French, and Swedish colonies in North America, and the Spanish had started to lose their grip on the Caribbean islands. By the late eighteenth century, the Swedes were gone, the French nearly so, and the English had emerged as the dominant colonial power in North America, leaving South America to the Spanish and Portuguese. In the Indian Ocean, Dutch merchants had begun to challenge the Iberian monopoly in the 1590s, and the consolidation of the Dutch effort into a single corporation, the Vereinigde Oostindische Compagnie (VOC, or United East India Company), in 1602 facilitated the concentration of Dutch resources and commercial expertise on the capture of the bulk of the lucrative spice trade, with a central administrative center at Batavia (modern Jakarta) (Gaastra 2003). The English arrived later, in an East India Company (EIC) of their own, and while it was never as commercially profitable as its Dutch counterpart, it did lead to far greater outright territorial acquisition, especially in India (Keay 1994). East India companies were formed in several other countries and trading centers established in secondary ports in the East, but none could compete effectively with the VOC and EIC. The VOC eventually closed during the Napoleonic period, and trade in the Far East opened up somewhat in the nineteenth century, but it continued to revolve around the centers established by the European powers well into the twentieth century, until the emergence of Japan, Korea, and China as international commercial giants after World War II.

The integration of the Far East and the Americas into a single global market, centered on Europe, had far-reaching implications not only for the world economy, but also for political developments. Wars between the European powers ceased to be purely European conflicts, as the trade income generated by overseas colonies was a strategic resource worth capturing or crippling. Privateers preyed on merchant shipping on the oceans, with perhaps the greatest single success coming in 1628, when a Dutch squadron captured that year's New World silver fleet on its way to Spain. Troops were sent to remote outposts to guard them against attack, or to attack enemy trading stations. The Seven Years' War (1756–1763), the first global war, began with battles between French and English forces in the North American wilderness.

Warfare

After thousands of years in which the technology of warfare had changed very little, with a traditional reliance on the horse, sword, spear, and bow, new weapons were introduced at the end of the Middle Ages. Gunpowder allowed armies to fight at greater distances and cause greater damage while at the same time reducing the effectiveness of fortifications and armor. It took over two centuries for this new technology to find its most useful applications, but by the end of the sixteenth century, guns were on their way to becoming the dominant weapon on land and at sea. Cannon could be deployed against castles or massed formations of men with devastating effect, and men armed with muskets and taught to maneuver and fire as a group could command a battlefield. Ships armed with cannon could be employed against shore installations or other ships.

Economic forces and goals had a greater role in warfare after the Middle Ages (McNeill 1982). While the Thirty Years' War (1618–1648), the bloodiest in history before 1914, started (but did not finish) over religious differences (Parker 1987), the Anglo-Dutch Wars (1652–1654, 1665–1667, and 1672–1674) that followed soon after were largely fought over commercial issues (Hainsworth and Churches 1998). Suppression or capture of enemy trade became an overt part of war aims and strategy, with naval vessels and privateers employed to blockade ports, capture enemy commerce, and starve the enemy of the income from foreign trade. The private companies trading in the East carried on their own wars and foreign policy, as if they were sovereign states. The VOC was empowered in its charter to raise troops, conclude alliances, and make war, and the EIC maintained its own army and navy in India well into the nineteenth century.

This new technology and its expanded scale were not cheap. Guns and gunpowder were not only expensive in themselves; the infrastructure needed to produce and use them effectively was also costly, and deploying forces on an expanded, global battlefield was not inexpensive. Ships built primarily as gun platforms had insufficient hold space to be used as profitable cargo carriers, and men armed with muskets had to be carefully trained and had to practice regularly, and so had to be fed and housed. Although maintaining a standing army and navy was not the only solution to the problem of military power, it eventually became the most effective solution adopted by large countries intent on achieving preeminence and defending themselves against similarly ambitious neighbors (Glete 2000). Medieval government machinery and taxation systems, focused on commandeered ships, annual campaigning seasons, and short-term service based on personal relationships, was inadequate to the task of fielding the new forces. The result was the growth of permanent bureaucracies to turn timber, iron ore, and farm boys into ships, guns, and soldiers.

Organization

The new global economy and the new warfare required a new approach to management. It required organization on a scale not seen since the Roman period. The construction of warships, the training of troops, the scheduling of cargoes, and the purchasing of provisions all required specialist skills in managing raw materials and people. The countries and companies that prospered were not necessarily those with the most resources, but those that could collect and utilize resources most efficiently (Glete 2002). Governments replaced or augmented their medieval households with professional administrative departments, to whom they devolved authority and from whom they expected reports and results. Commercial ventures changed from temporary associations of merchants to permanent corporations with separate legal identities.

The men who served in the new government departments were not exclusively from the established elites, but were often "new men," who had shown ability and produced results. In some cases, rulers took advantage of existing expertise by outsourcing government functions to private entrepreneurs (Hallenberg 2008). In others, they established university programs to train talented young men in the arts of administration. Even aristocrats entering government service had to demonstrate some degree of competence in order to advance. These men, in turn, reorganized the process of raising taxes, building ships, recruiting and feeding armies, and buying and selling commodities so that they could control both expectations and results. They created the committee structures that we still use today, with budgets, agendas, minutes, and progress reports, and insisted on a paper trail to record the process of management. Samuel Pepys, who made his career as the secretary of the Navy Board in England, was typical of such men (Ollard 1974).

Industrialization

The growth of modern military arms and commerce coincided with advances in the production of manufactures. Series production of armaments began in the early seventeenth century, if not before, with weapons produced to standard patterns in order to simplify training and the provision of ammunition. New materials came into common use, especially in ferrous metals. Wrought iron had been in use for millennia, but effective techniques for casting iron in large quantities first appeared in the sixteenth century, and by the end of the seventeenth century, cast iron had largely replaced bronze for cannon production (Caruana 1994). As these materials were introduced, the technology for working them advanced as well. Raw metal could be smelted and refined more consistently, and the machining technology for producing precision instruments and bearings that began to develop in the late eighteenth century made new types of machines possible. One of the central developments of the new metallurgy and machining technology was the introduction of mechanical power, independent of wind, water, or muscle, in the form of the steam engine (Hills 1993).

The improvements in transportation infrastructure were as significant as those in propulsion and vehicles. Starting in the late Middle Ages in Europe and the late eighteenth century in North America, canal projects began connecting the major river systems and rendering previously marginal waterways navigable, to create an inland transport network that could be linked with deepwater and coastal shipping in an integrated system (Ketner 1943; Shaw 1993). These inland systems tended to encourage the growth of major deepwater ports, as they connected oceanic routes with the hinterland.

SHIPBUILDING AND SEAFARING

Construction

There were two major developments in ship construction after 1400, both with far-reaching consequences. In the first, the importation of Mediterranean design and construction methods into northern Europe in the fifteenth century quickly replaced or marginalized shipbuilding traditions over a thousand years old. In the second, the introduction of new materials in the nineteenth century changed the fundamental concepts, scale, and organization of the shipbuilding process.

Since Roman times, most large vessels in northern Europe had been built in one of two major conceptual traditions. In Scandinavia, the British Isles, and the Slavic Baltic zone, the basic structure was a shell of overlapping, radially split planks riveted (Anglo-Scandinavian) or treenailed (Slavic) together and reinforced by relatively light frames and beams. This system, known as clinker construction, was one of the purest expressions of a shell concept seen in Europe, and through the careful balancing of material properties and dimensions, it was also one of the most elegant engineering solutions to the structural challenges of shipbuilding ever developed (Crumlin-Pedersen 2004). The ships produced were light, strong, flexible, and hydrodynamically superior, but they required materials of the highest quality, and hull forms may have been limited. In the Low Countries and northern Germany, hulls were built on a flat or flat-floored bottom of flush-laid planks, laid up and held together with temporary fastenings out to the turn of the bilge, before floor timbers were added. With the bottom completed, the sides were built up, often from overlapping planks fastened together with double-clenched nails. This bottom-based tradition tended to produce heavy, capacious hulls, as seen in cogs (Hocker 2004). Seagoing ships built in both traditions reached substantial size, over 300 tons deadweight capacity, by the early fifteenth century.

In the Mediterranean, frame-based design and construction methods had been developing since at least the late Roman period, and by the beginning of the fifteenth century they had reached a stage of sophisticated geometrical precision that was being committed to paper in the form of teaching manuals (Hocker and McManamon 2006; see also Rieth in this volume). Ships built in this tradition had been visiting northern ports since the thirteenth century if not before, exposing northern shipbuilders to hulls with flush-laid planks and a potentially wide range of hull forms. Mediterranean techniques began to be adopted along the Atlantic coast of Iberia and then France, and by the first third of the fifteenth century, builders in the Low Countries had begun to experiment with this new method, which they called carvel, probably after the Portuguese and Breton *caravelas* trading to Dutch and Baltic ports (van Beylen 1970; Hocker 2004). By the end of the century, carvels were under construction in the Baltic, and by the first quarter of the sixteenth century, clinker construction had been largely relegated to local and small craft, although a few large clinker hulks continued to be built in Scandinavia and England (Adams 2003).

The bottom-based builders of the Low Countries did not adopt the Mediterranean method completely, but chose certain elements of it that fit into the existing conceptual framework. They abandoned the lapstrake sides of the cog in favor of all-carvel planking, but continued to build big ships in a bottom-first sequence until at least the mid-seventeenth century (Witsen 1671; van Yk 1697). They realized many of the economic benefits of the new technique without having to develop the design methodology to make it work most effectively. This is probably one of the reasons that Dutch shipbuilders enjoyed a dominant position in the market for nearly a century, until the shipbuilders of other countries had mastered the new design techniques and could exploit them to produce a wider variety of hull forms to suit the needs of customers in a changing market.

The adoption of carvel construction in northern Europe coincided approximately with a sudden growth in the size of the largest ships in merchant use as well as the introduction of shipboard artillery. The largest ships more than doubled in size in the fifteenth century, from about 300 tons deadweight capacity to over 600 tons, and gunports for cannon were introduced at the end of the century, so it has often been suggested that carvel construction made these advances possible (for example, Greenhill 1976; Hutchinson 1994). The relationship between these developments is probably not that simple. The majority of the increase in ship size in the fifteenth century occurred before carvel construction had been widely adopted (Friel 1995; Hocker 1999), and the largest ships known in northern Europe before the eighteenth century, a trio of warships ordered by Henry V of England, were built before 1420 in a complex version of clinker construction (Friel 1993). These show that clinker construction could be adapted for immense ships, and their service history does not suggest that there was anything wrong with their construction.

Most of the largest fifteenth-century vessels known from both historical and archaeological sources are clinker-built. Carvel construction did not make large ships possible, but it probably did make them cheaper to build, an advantage not lost on
shipowners under economic pressure.

Carvel construction did not make cannon-armed warships possible either. It
has long been said that it is impractical or unsafe to cut gunports in a clinker hull
(for example, see Greenhill 1976 or Hildred 2009), but the clinker hulls of the fifteenth century were not Viking ships, made of thin planks and light, widely spaced
frames. They were heavily built ships, with scantlings not far different from those in
the carvel ships that eventually replaced them. They were still shell-based in design
and construction sequence, but framing had already begun to take a much larger
role in the structural strength than previously. Cutting a gunport into the side of
such a ship does not weaken it appreciably more than cutting a gunport in a similar
carvel ship, although making it watertight when closed is more complicated. Carvel
construction was probably advantageous for warships for the same reasons that it
was attractive to merchants: it was cheaper and offered more flexibility in hull form.

The adoption of Mediterranean design methods had social consequences as
well. Before the codification of a formal design method, the designer and builder of
a ship were necessarily the same person. Once a design could be written down or
drawn, the designer could deliver his idea to someone else for construction. This
had distinct advantages for governments wanting to build multiple ships to the
same design, and led to the separation of design and construction. Ship designers,
later called naval architects, were men of status and semi-academic standing, while
constructors were craftsmen. This elevation of the naval architect was already well
under way in Venice and the other Italian city-states in the fifteenth century (Hocker
and McManamon 2006) and, by the sixteenth, the process had reached northern
Europe (Baker 1586). By the seventeenth century, a naval architect might be
knighted, as Sir Anthony Deane was in England (Lavery 1981), and in the mid-
eighteenth century, schools of naval architecture began to be established (Ferreiro
2007). These completed the divorce of design and construction, since potential
naval architects were no longer educated as apprentices in the shipyard, but were
taught formal mathematics and design theory in a classroom. Constructors
remained responsible for design in merchant yards well into the nineteenth century,
but eventually the separation occurred here as well, largely due to the second great
development in construction.

Since at least the Mesolithic period, the primary raw material for watercraft had
been wood, whether it was the body of a dugout, the framework of a skin boat, or
the components of a plank-built vessel. Wood was plentiful, strong, tolerant of
water, grew in a wide variety of shapes, and could be worked with simple tools. It
grew in sufficient size to make very large vessels, up to about 80 m in hull length, if
properly shaped and fastened, and it was a renewable resource if properly managed.
Once governments started building warships on a regular basis, they quickly became
mindful of the strategic nature of timber and tried to manage the supply by re-
serving tracts of forest for government use, regulating the timber market, and even

practicing conscientious forestry, as the Venetians and Basques did as early as the sixteenth century (Lane 1934; Loewen 2007). Even so, the growing scale of shipbuilding put pressure on the resource, and shipbuilders were in competition for timber reserves with the metals industry, which had an even more voracious appetite for fuel. By the eighteenth century, if not earlier, shipyards were beginning to feel the effects of declining timber stocks in much of Europe (Batchvarov 2002).

One solution was to look abroad. Shipbuilding timber, primarily oak, had been exported from the Baltic since the fourteenth century (Dollinger 1970). There was an indigenous shipbuilding industry in the Baltic, with a major center at Danzig/Gdańsk, but the reserves of the Polish and Livonian forests far exceeded local needs, and a major trade in Baltic oak developed to feed the industries of northwestern Europe. This trade fell largely into the hands of Dutch merchants by the fifteenth century, and eventually most of the high-quality timber felled in Poland was marketed in Amsterdam (Unger 1978). The Baltic also produced high-quality mast timber of pine. The North American colonies were seen as a potential source of timber, since much of the eastern seaboard was covered with forest offering oak and pine of good quality and ready availability (Lott 1777). Still, European shipwrights were forced to economize in their use of wood, adapting construction methods to use smaller pieces of lower quality even as the demand for larger ships increased (Goodwin 1997; Sutherland 1711).

By the early nineteenth century, developments in metalworking made it possible to roll and form large structural shapes in iron, and it did not take long for shipbuilders to begin thinking of the possibilities that this material offered. Iron had already been used in the eighteenth century to replace some of the harder-to-find wooden components of a ship, such as knees, and to reinforce larger ships made up of small timbers (Goodwin 1997; Ollivier 1737), but eventually the idea of building a ship entirely of iron took hold. Some smaller vessels were built in the 1810s, but the growth of formal engineering knowledge and experience with the material suggested that iron ships could be built on a much larger scale than wooden ships. Iron offered much higher strength and stiffness for the volume it occupied, but required more formal mathematics and engineering in the design stage, effectively completing the divorce between designers and constructors (Scott Russell 1865).

Propulsion

Propulsion went through two similar major changes, more or less synchronized with the major changes in construction. One was a change in complexity, the other a change in nature. Until the eighteenth century, the only sources of propulsive energy for ships were wind and muscle power. The wind was harnessed by sails, human muscle by oars, paddles or towropes, and animal muscle by whims or towropes. One was cheap but unreliable, while the other was reliable but expensive. Both had limitations in larger ships. As ship size increases, the volume and weight increase at a faster rate than deck area available for oarsmen or sail handling. At the same time, the requirement for sail area rapidly reaches a point where a single sail is unmanageable, both because of material limit and human muscle limits.

More oars can be added by using multiple tiers of oars, as in an ancient *trieres*, or staggering the oarsmen on angled benches. If the geometry is carefully calculated, a rowing system can be built that effectively puts two or three oars in the space formerly occupied by one, as was done on *a scalaccio* Italian galleys in the late Middle Ages. An alternative is to use larger oars and assign several oarsmen to each oar, a development that appeared in the sixteenth century in Italy. This system has the advantage of requiring less skill on the part of the oarsmen, as only one man at each oar needs to be skilled; the rest follow the leader. In this case, fewer oarsmen have to be trained to a high level, and prisoners can be used for raw muscle power (Bondioli, Burlet, and Zysberg 1995).

Although galleys and oared craft continued to be used by navies in specialized circumstances, human-powered ships were largely obsolete by the beginning of the seventeenth century. The expansion of the European maritime world beyond home waters created a demand for large, efficient ships, and the principal trade routes could take advantage of reliable weather systems for long stretches. In this environment, what was needed was a more efficient sailing rig.

The limits of the single sail had been reached in the Mediterranean in ancient times, and larger ships there commonly carried two or three masts, in some cases with more than one sail on each mast. This idea took a longer time to reach northern Europe, but in the first or second decade of the fifteenth century, ships suddenly made the jump from a single mast to three—there is only limited evidence for an intermediate step with two masts (Brindley and Moore 1921). This change coincides with the sudden increase in ship size, suggesting that if a technological limit on ship size was reached in the Middle Ages, it was more likely related to propulsion than construction. By dividing the necessary sail area into several sails distributed over the length of the hull, not only could the total sail area be increased, but it could also be made more flexible, by allowing different combinations of sails to suit different conditions. The next stage was to divide the sail area on each mast into several sails, which seems to have happened soon after if not concurrently (Figure 20.1). By the end of the century, the basic configuration of what later came to be called the full-rigged ship had been established: three masts, with two or three large square sails on the fore- and mainmast and a combination of fore-and-aft and square sails on the mizzen (Anderson 1927). Sails could also be mounted on the bowsprit, and a fourth mast, the bonaventure, was sometimes seen on large ships in the sixteenth century, carrying a smaller lateen sail abaft the lateen mizzen. In the seventeenth century, a fifth mast, the spritsail topmast, was sometimes stepped on the end of the bowsprit. After about 1660, the square sails of the fore and main were supplemented by fore-and-aft sails bent onto the stays between the masts, further increasing flexibility. In the first half of the eighteenth century, the lateen mizzen was replaced by a simpler gaff sail, and the spritsail topmast disappeared (Harland 1984).

This basic rig was refined in the later eighteenth and nineteenth centuries by further subdivision of the sails and the introduction of more metal components, such as chain and wire in place of rope rigging (Biddlecomb 1848; Harland 1984; Lever 1808; Steel 1794), but it was essentially the full rig of the sixteenth century in

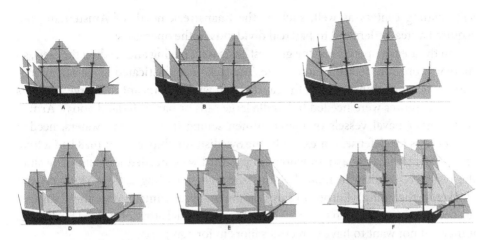

Figure 20.1 Evolution of the full-rigged ship 1540–1800 CE: (a) 1540 *Mary Rose* after Marsden 2009; (b) 1580 English galleon after Baker 1586; (c) 1628 *Vasa*; (d) 1670 English Third Rate after Deane (1670) with staysails added; (e) 1720 English 50-gun ship after original sailplan; (f) 1800 HMS *Leopard* after Winfield (1997). Drawing by Fred Hocker.

concept, and still carried the inherent limitations of wind power. The appearance of an alternative power source in the later eighteenth century, in the form of the reciprocating steam engine, encouraged inventors in North America and Europe to consider the possibilities of a steam-propelled vessel (see Crisman in this volume).

Manning

The growing economic role of the cost of materials and labor—especially the latter, after the fourteenth century—encouraged savings in construction and operation of ships. In both areas, there are two ways to look at cost: either as the absolute cost for the ship, or the cost per ton of capacity or displacement. Both are relevant, since a larger ship usually costs less per ton of capacity to build and operate, but costs more in absolute terms. Owners of limited capital might wish to build larger ships in order to realize the economies of scale that they offer, but not be able to amass the necessary absolute capital.

Construction costs could be reduced by using lighter or lower-quality materials, at the expense of durability, or through better organization of the process of acquiring materials and converting them into ships. The Dutch proved to be leaders in both areas from the sixteenth century onward, through better organization of the Baltic and German timber trades as well as the introduction of mechanical sawmills, usually wind-powered, and standardized construction methods (Unger 1978). Large, specialized workforces, as were found in some naval shipyards, were pioneered by the Venetians in the expansion of the Arsenale in the fifteenth century, in response to the final collapse of the Byzantine Empire and the growth of Ottoman sea power (Lane 1934). Such workforces were seen in major commercial shipbuilding centers as well, such as the Zaanstreek north of Amsterdam, but required a steady demand to pay real dividends to the operators.

In the area of operations, the greatest costs were paying and feeding the crew, so there was pressure to reduce crew size. The lack of sophisticated labor-saving machinery on most ships, beyond the capstan and windlass, meant that large amounts of muscle power were needed to handle large sails or oars (Harland 2003). Armed ships, either naval vessels or merchantmen sailing in dangerous waters, needed larger crews for defense. For example, the Swedish warship *Vasa* of 1628 had a total crew of approximately 450, of whom only a third were needed for sailing the ship; the rest were soldiers to man the guns and fight boarding actions (Pipping and Hocker forthcoming). European ships sailing in hotter climates or on long voyages needed to carry extra men to compensate for the normal attrition caused by disease, if they did not want to have to recruit sailors in foreign ports.

The manning ratios (men per ton of capacity) for merchant sailing ships were on a downward trend throughout the postmedieval period (Harland 1984), with a number of routes toward greater efficiency explored in different periods. Ships dependent on direct muscle power (galleys) were abandoned for merchant tasks early in the period, as the rising cost of labor made them uneconomical even for the high-value niche trades in which they had specialized. This trend was accelerated by the development of more efficient rigs that could sail closer to the wind, reducing the advantage of the galley. Muscle power made a brief return in local ferries in the nineteenth century, as horses were used to power paddle-wheel boats in markets insufficiently profitable for early steam vessels, but such vessels were extremely limited in range, and once efficient steam plants became common around midcentury, they disappeared (Crisman and Cohn 1998).

In sailing vessels, where the rig must be handled by hand, crew size is dictated in part by the energy needed to move the vessel: larger sails need more men to handle them. On the other hand, a larger vessel needs less propulsion energy per ton, since the main resistance to movement, skin friction on the submerged hull, increases at a slower rate than volume as ship size increases (Gillmer and Johnson 1982). The development of the multisail rig meant that individual sail size could be reduced while increasing overall sail power, so that fewer men were needed to handle a larger rig, as long as it was not necessary to set or strike all sails simultaneously. Rigs became more efficient and better able to handle heavier weather. The introduction of backstays, reef points, and footropes more or less simultaneously in the mid-seventeenth century (Anderson 1927) made ships much safer and were a decided advantage for oceanic sailors, who could not shelter from hard weather.

Steam-powered vessels, once they became purely mechanical and could dispense with a sailing crew, heightened the pressure on sail, accelerating the drive to reduce crews and maintain profitability as sailing ships were pushed into increasingly marginal trades in bulk goods and backwater routes. Further subdivision of the sail plan in the second half of the nineteenth century, by the introduction of split topsails and more masts, reduced crew requirements still more (Chapelle 1935; Harland 1984). The adoption of simpler and less labor-intensive fore-and-aft rigs on larger merchant ships in the later nineteenth century (Greenhill 1988) meant that very large ships could be operated with very small crews. By the early twentieth century, the largest sailing ships ever built, over 100 m long and with up to seven masts, were often sailing oceanic routes with crews of 20 men or fewer (Newby 1956). The reduction in the number of crew meant not only a reduction in operating cost, but also an increase in cargo capacity, as less space had to be devoted to accommodation and provisions. By the mid-nineteenth century, merchant crews (including officers) were no longer housed in the ends of the hold, as they had been for centuries, but were moved into deckhouses.

Naval vessels, because they needed men to fight the vessel and because their systems became ever more complex, saw crew size climb significantly with the introduction of heavy shipboard artillery at the beginning of the sixteenth century (Rodger 2004; Scammell 1987). A naval gun firing a ball weighing 5 kg or more weighed more than a ton and needed a gun crew of six to eight men to serve it. As the number of guns increased, the number of men did so as well, but the space for accommodation and provisions was still limited. Once ships started to depend on broadside gunnery, they could not carry enough men to man all of the guns simultaneously, so only one side of the ship could usually be reloaded and fought at one time. The space between the guns was used by the crew for eating and sleeping, and the introduction of hammocks in many navies in the mid-seventeenth century was an attempt to alleviate some of the crowding and maintain traffic flow through the ship; before this, men slept on the deck.

Ships

Merchantmen

The demographic and economic recovery of the fifteenth century, followed closely by the globalization of seafaring, had notable effects on the development of merchant ships and shipping. One of the most obvious effects, judging from historical records, is the wider range of ship sizes that came into use. It is also interesting to see how the new large ships were employed. Generally speaking, larger ships tend to be used on longer routes, where their economic advantages are most useful. Larger ships cost less per ton to operate, but until the container and RORO (roll on/roll off) revolution of the late twentieth century, they took longer to load and unload. Using a large ship on short-haul routes thus wastes some of its efficiency. The oceanic routes developed in the sixteenth century, while pioneered by small vessels, such as the Portuguese *caravela*, were eventually exploited by larger ships, which could carry the provisions needed for long journeys and still have abundant room for paying cargo. The largest seagoing ships in regular use in the early stages of globalization were Iberian vessels engaged in the East Indies trade, sailing the route from Europe, around the southern tip of Africa into the Indian and Pacific Oceans and back

(Boxer 1991). There were few places to provision on the way before European colonies were established in southern Africa, and mortality among the crews was relatively high, so large crews shared space with passengers, all of whose provisions for many months had to find space as well.

In local networks, there was relatively little change in the basic configuration of merchant vessels (Figure 20.2). In Scandinavia, clinker construction survived into the nineteenth century and even the twentieth in local craft, only abandoned finally when it proved impractical to adapt clinker hulls to diesel propulsion (Christensen 1992). The deck and hold layout of Dutch inland craft was well established in the early fifteenth century, as seen in the Almere cog of 1425 (Hocker and Vlierman 1997), and did not change substantially even with the introduction of iron and steam. There was some growth in size, but the increased local and regional demand seems to have been met more by increases in the number of ships, since existing harbor and canal facilities often established the maximum practical size for ships. It was more cost-effective in the short term to build more vessels than to rebuild the infrastructure.

Even larger deepwater ships needed adaptation to existing facilities. Remote ports had to be used and goods transshipped when vessels exceeded the capacity of harbors, a problem which had faced the Romans over 1,500 years earlier (see Oleson and Hohlfelder in this volume). Special floating drydocks were built in the eighteenth century to get large ships over the Pampus bar into the port of Amsterdam, a problem eventually solved by the construction of a canal leading directly to the

Figure 20.2 The so-called Ghost Wreck, a mid-seventeenth-century merchantman typical of the Dutch-built ships which dominated the trade in bulk goods between the Baltic and the North Sea, the busiest and most lucrative trade route in northern Europe, twice as profitable as the East Indies trade. Such ships were built for efficiency above all else, but carried enough decoration to suggest that their owners took some pride in their ships. Drawing by Niklas Eriksson. Reproduced with the kind permission of Deep Sea Productions.

North Sea in the later nineteenth century (Barnard 1872). One of the early uses of steam was in harbor tugs, which allowed the larger, less maneuverable sailing ships of the mid-nineteenth century to get into and out of established ports, helping to prolong the working life of sail (Gardiner 1994).

A clear trend in merchant shipping was specialization as the diversity of cargoes and routes grew. East Indiamen built for the long voyages around Africa were less economical and useful on intra-European routes and could not be easily adapted for other trades. Those not lost at sea were often broken up after relatively short working lives and the aggressive attack of tropical marine borers, instead of being passed on to more marginal trades. The nineteenth century saw the development of several fast-sailing types, after thousands of years in which virtually all merchant ships averaged less than 3 knots under sail. Chesapeake Bay shipbuilders adapted sloop and schooner designs used on Caribbean routes to produce a type of fast schooner, sometimes rigged as a brig, that came to be known as the Baltimore clipper (Figure 20.3) (Chapelle 1967; Footner 1998). Such vessels had very little cargo capacity, but their speed made them especially useful for smuggling high-value cargoes. Governments were forced to adopt similar designs for coastal patrols in order to suppress smuggling, and the type found

Figure 20.3 The Clydesdale Plantation vessel, a fast-sailing sloop built in the late eighteenth century CE and deliberately buried as cribbing to repair a rice plantation levee near Savannah, Georgia. It is a small version (14.5 m LOA) of the hull form tradition that produced the famous Baltimore clippers of the later eighteenth and early nineteenth centuries. Photograph by Tina Erwin. Reproduced with the kind permission of the Institute of Nautical Archaeology.

much use in privateering during the Napoleonic period. For a brief period in the 1840s and 1850s, there was sufficient demand for speed on long routes that American ship-builders, principally in New York and Boston, developed large, fast full-rigged ships with sharp sections and raking bows. These clipper ships famously carried prospectors to the gold fields of California via Cape Horn, setting sailing records that survive until today on some routes, but as soon as the demand disappeared, they were impractical (Cutler 1984). Modified clippers returned in the 1860s in the tea trade, where a pre-mium was paid for the first tea cargoes landed in England each year (Baker 1974).

Specialized ships were developed for the trade in human beings, both free and enslaved. In the eighteenth century, a booming trade in African slaves encouraged the development of ships with holds adapted to carry hundreds of people densely packed on shelves, with careful thought given to the optimum density of cargo—too many slaves and the mortality rate rose to an unacceptable level, too few and the maximum profit could not be achieved. In one respect, the horrors of the Middle Passage, as the trans-Atlantic part of the route from the Bight of Benin to the Carib-bean was called, are not the most terrifying aspect of the slave trade; it is the cool detachment with which English and American merchant shippers could discuss human beings as cargo in such brutally economic terms (Klein 1999). Great Britain outlawed the slave trade (although not slavery itself) within its dominions in 1807, and the United States outlawed the importation of slaves in the same year. Enforce-ment, primarily by the Royal Navy, forced slavers to become smugglers, and tended to concentrate the American end of the trade in the Caribbean, from which regional smugglers transported slaves to the North American mainland. Slave traders, who had formerly used medium-sized merchant vessels, had to shift to new vessel types, such as the Baltimore clipper, to smuggle their cargoes into American ports.

The initial settlement of the Americas in the sixteenth and seventeenth cen-turies had been accomplished with existing merchant ship types, their interiors adapted to carry passengers along with cargo. In the second half of the eighteenth century, the scale of trans-Atlantic traffic began to grow as the attractions of the New World appealed to many in war-torn Europe, and some shippers began to spe-cialize in passenger transport. By the nineteenth century, immigration had become a flood, and regularly scheduled trans-Atlantic service was established between many western European ports and North America, beginning in 1818. Major ship-ping lines developed around the Atlantic trade, operating large, full-hulled, full-rigged ships, called packets, which were still relatively fast, due mostly to their size (Chapelle 1967). While first-class passengers traveled well, the lessons learned in the slaving trade were put to use in the lower decks, packing the human cargo into tight, squalid conditions for the month-long crossing.

Until the nineteenth century, ships operating in international waters or off hos-tile coastlines were at risk of seizure or piracy. Privateering, using privately armed warships to capture enemy merchant vessels, was a potentially profitable enterprise in wartime, and entrepreneurs fitted out ships for this "trade" on a regular basis in the course of European wars. Privateers were not always discriminating in their choice of targets, and some nations practiced privateering in peacetime as a means of extorting revenue, in the form of tribute or transit fees, from foreign merchantmen and their home governments (see, for example, Lunsford 2005). To defend themselves, merchant vessels often carried armament of their own. East Indiamen, operating far from home, were sometimes armed almost as heavily as warships. This took up cargo space but was a necessary expense in dangerous waters. The alternative was to sail in government-backed convoys, protected by escorting warships.

Armed merchantmen largely disappeared after 1815 and the conclusion of the Napoleonic Wars, which saw extensive privateering. The long peace that followed in Europe and the agreements reached between the major and minor European powers meant an effective end to this type of sanctioned piracy, and a concerted effort was made to suppress unsanctioned piracy on the major sea lanes. Governments, especially those with inferior military forces, still resorted to commerce raiding during wartime (Hearn 1992), but it was discovered that convoying and naval patrol of the sea lanes were more effective against attack than the light armament with which merchantmen were equipped.

Warships

The adoption of gunpowder weapons on board ships at the end of the Middle Ages had far-reaching consequences, although it took over two centuries for effective tactics to be developed. Initially, small-caliber weapons, sometimes in large numbers, were mounted on the upper works of warships and used in much the same way as other projectile weapons against enemy personnel. Over the course of the fifteenth century, shipboard guns grew in size to resemble field artillery, mounted on wheeled carriages or bedded in heavy stocks that rested on the upper decks and fired over the railing (Caruana 1994). There were practical limits to the number of heavy guns that could be carried high above the water due to stability consequences, and at some point near the end of the century, the idea appeared of moving the heaviest guns to a lower deck, where they would fire through ports cut in the ship's side (Figure 20.4). The credit for the invention of gunports is traditionally assigned to a Breton shipwright around 1501 (see, for example, Hildred 2009 or Rodger 1997), but no one cites a primary source for this claim, and it is, in any case, impossible to prove. If the date is correct, there is evidence that it took a generation for gunports to be adopted by major navies: the recent study of *Mary Rose*, built in 1509 and rebuilt in the mid-1530s, suggests that not all of the lower tier of gunports were part of the original construction (Marsden 2009).

Once gunports became common, shipboard artillery fell into three main classes, based on basic configuration and size, although a much wider variety of names were used for individual types. One class was formed of light guns mounted on yokes and aimed with a tiller that was part of the gun. These swivel guns were mounted on the railings and used against personnel, as the earliest shipboard guns had been. Heavy guns, mounted on carriages, made up the other two classes: large-bore short guns (cannon) for short-range engagement and smaller-bore long guns (culverins) for longer range (Caruana 1994). The difference was initially

Figure 20.4 Contemporary drawing of a warship in a storm, showing the typical features of a sixteenth-century warship after the introduction of gunports. There is a single row of ports, low down in the hull, and the upper works have been lowered relative to the carracks of the early part of the century. These were the first ships that could use gunnery effectively, even if fully developed tactics were still nearly a century in the future.

due to the performance of early gunpowder, which burned slowly and inconsistently. Manufacturing improvements in the first half of the sixteenth century produced more powerful, consistent powder (Partington 1999), eliminating the need for the long, culverin class by the end of the century. Most naval carriage guns after 1700 were a hybrid of the old cannon and culverin groups and were classed by the size of the ball they fired. A demi-cannon thus became a "24-pounder." Because guns were expensive and had a potentially long service life, over a century in many cases, they were often carefully registered and accounted by a separate administrative department from the ships to which they were issued (Caruana 1994). If the registration number is still visible on a recovered gun, it is often possible to determine its service history.

The earliest guns had been forged of iron, welded together of staves formed around a mandrel and reinforced with hoops, or cast in bronze. Forged guns usually had separate breech chambers, while cast guns often had a solid breech and were loaded at the muzzle. Although guns were occasionally cast of iron from the beginning of the sixteenth century, cast iron did not become common until the mid-seventeenth century, and by 1700 most cannon were cast in iron, which was cheaper and lighter for equivalent strength, if properly cast. Smoothbore, cast iron muzzleloaders remained the most common type of ordnance until the mid-nineteenth century, when rifling and breechloading produced guns that were more accurate and fired faster.

The first ships to carry heavy guns were galleys, which mounted one or more guns at the bow. The guns were aimed by turning the ship toward the enemy. When similar guns were mounted on large sailing ships, the same methodology was used. The heaviest guns fired forward, over the bow, with lighter guns mounted along the sides. Even after the broadside guns began to grow in size, the heaviest guns were still at the bow, and the gunports were bowed, or angled toward the ends of the ship. The broadside guns were not used in a coordinated manner, but fired individually (Hildred 2011). Even *Vasa*, as late as 1628, has bowed ports.

Although they had been instrumental in proving the concept of heavy shipboard artillery, galleys disappeared quickly from most navies, except in niche applications, such as messenger craft in the Mediterranean, or inshore fleets in the Baltic archipelagos (Harris 1989). They simply could not carry enough firepower to justify their expense, and the design challenge in naval shipbuilding was to combine firepower and seaworthiness. This was relatively straightforward for ships carrying a single deck of heavy guns, but already by the mid-sixteenth century, the demand for firepower led to ships with two gundecks. This is a greater challenge, since the lower gundeck has to be uncomfortably close to the water and the upper gundeck dangerously high above the water. The loss of *Vasa* in 1628 demonstrated the difficulty of balancing all of the forces in such ships (Figure 20.5); insufficient initial stability allowed the ship to heel under a light breeze until the lower gunports were in the water, water rushed in to push the leeward side farther down, and the ship filled and sank (Cederlund 2006). The gunports were designed to seal when closed, and the ship would not have sunk that day if they had been closed, but then it would not have been possible to show off the ship's impressive armament. As most navies discovered, ships with multiple gundecks had to sail with the lower ports closed except in very calm weather, which tended to reduce the firepower advantage of the lower tier of guns.

After some experimentation, it was discovered that the most effective way to use the new armament was for crews to learn to load and fire their guns quickly, using gunnery as the primary weapon, and for ships to fight in groups, with organized tactics to concentrate the massed firepower of their broadsides. These tactics had been foreshadowed by Sweden and Denmark in the Northern Seven Years' War of 1563–1570 (Glete 2002), but were more fully developed by the English and the Dutch in their commercial wars of the mid-seventeenth century (Hainsworth and

Figure 20.5 The Swedish warship *Vasa*, built 1626–1628 CE, sunk 1628, raised 1961. *Vasa* is an example of Dutch shipbuilding practice in an early attempt at two complete gundecks, with a total planned armament of 72 bronze guns, most of them 24-pounders of a new, lightweight pattern. Reproduced with the kind permission of Statens maritima museer.

Churches 1998). To a certain degree, the development parallels the shift in infantry tactics on land toward carefully drilled formations of men with muskets maneuvered to focus their fire on specific objectives, rather than fighting as individuals. To exploit these tactics, many navies settled on a system that relied on larger ships built to similar designs for standardized armaments, called rates. First rates had three full gundecks, over 100 guns total, and were the largest ships in use, although relatively few were built. Second, third, fourth, and fifth rates followed, with fewer guns, down to a sixth rate with a single gundeck (Lavery 1983–1984). In addition to such ships, intended to fight in line-of-battle formation, navies built smaller ships, such as frigates and sloops, which could be used independently for patrolling sea lanes, interdicting commerce, or suppressing piracy (Auer 2008; Gardiner 1992). By the eighteenth century, major navies were building a few first rates as prestige ships, but the backbone of the line of battle was formed by two-deckers, with the 74-gun ship acknowledged by most navies as the best compromise of firepower, speed, and sea-worthiness (Boudriot 1986–1988; Lavery 1985).

Broadside gunnery in wooden sailing ships reached its apogee in the Napoleonic Wars (1793–1815), with the main naval combatants, England, France, and Spain, building large fleets and the nascent U.S. Navy scoring significant victories in single-ship combats and inland fleet actions. The winners and losers of the Napoleonic Wars became the leaders of the postwar navies, and they lapsed quickly into a conservatism rooted in their own glorious accomplishments, perpetuating antiquated designs and resisting the new technologies developed in the first half of the nineteenth century, but their resistance only delayed the introduction of iron and steam into naval use (Fuller in press). The last significant battle between wooden sailing ships using broadside gunnery was in 1864, between a Danish and an Austro-Prussian squadron at Helgoland, but the contemporary American Civil War saw the first successful use in anger of armored hulls, turret-mounted guns, submersibles, and electrically detonated mines (Perry 1965), marking the effective end of the naval technology developed in the sixteenth century.

Fishing Vessels

Although fishing in the postmedieval period was a widespread subsistence and commercial activity, and naval planners recognized fishing communities as a major source of seafaring expertise, fishing and its development do not often receive much attention from maritime archaeology. Fishermen from the British Isles and Iberia were some of the first European seafarers in the North Atlantic after the Vikings and were well established in North America by the first quarter of the sixteenth century (Proulx 2007). Fishing became a global industry, with specialized vessel types and a diversified economy, at an early stage.

The collapse of Baltic herring stocks in the late fourteenth century led to a large-scale movement of the herring fishery, one of the most profitable in Europe, out into the North Sea. Whereas the Baltic fishery had been dominated by Scandinavians, Dutch fishermen began to exploit the North Sea fishery early in the fifteenth century, using efficient vessels called busses. These vessels could sail offshore but, once on the fishing grounds, could be partly downrigged to make them more stable and easily handled by a small crew. By keeping their operating costs low and feeding an insatiable market for protein, especially in a period when the Church had decreed that fish were the only acceptable food on certain days of the week, herring fishermen fueled the growth of northern Dutch markets and contributed to the concentration of capital in Amsterdam and the other towns of Holland and Zeeland, which enabled them to expand their merchant fleets and operations (Unger 1978).

The fifteenth century also saw the beginnings of a long-distance cod fishery on the banks of the North Atlantic. What herring had been to medieval Europeans, cod became to the Renaissance and modern world. It was easier to preserve than herring and could be transported in bulk, and the fish were relatively easy to catch, with a much larger protein yield per fish. Dried cod became a staple of the European diet, even far from the sea, and the fish could be found throughout the North Atlantic. They were most numerous and easily caught on the shallow banks that lie near the European and North American coasts, and European fishermen ranged far out into the ocean in search of them. The Grand Banks off Newfoundland, with their extraordinary and apparently inexhaustible supply of fish, may have been reached in the fifteenth century, but were certainly being exploited in the sixteenth century by fishermen from the British Isles and Iberia (Kurlansky 1997). Once Canada and New England were settled, North American fishermen joined in the bounty. Because the fish could be preserved by salting on board, fishing vessels could stay on the banks for extended periods as they filled their holds. Specialized vessels were built to make the long passage and then ride hove to for weeks while fish were caught on individual hooks, deployed first from the sides of the vessel and later from smaller boats carried by a mother ship (Chapelle 1973). This methodology survived until the twentieth century, when engine power made it practical to drag (tow a net) for fish. Dragging was so efficient that it effectively wiped out the fishery by 2000.

While herring and cod were Atlantic fisheries with Atlantic markets, whaling became a global industry, with ships eventually employed on voyages years long, circling the world. Before the exploitation of petroleum and electricity on a large scale in the nineteenth century, the oil rendered from whale blubber provided the best-quality light and lubrication then available, but it was expensive. Whales had been hunted from the Atlantic coast of Europe, especially the Basque country, since perhaps the first millennium (Proulx 2007), although on a very small scale. With the discovery of the cod fishery and the abundant marine life of the North Atlantic, Basque whalers began to visit the rich hunting grounds of what they called *Terranova* in the early sixteenth century and to exploit the resource on a larger scale. Long-distance merchant ships built specifically for the trade carried whalemen, boats, and all of the equipment needed to shore stations established in Labrador. The whales were hunted from small boats and brought to shore to be cut up and tried (rendered) into oil, which was carried back to Europe on the merchant ships. The excavation of a largely complete ship and its associated boats and shore installation at Red Bay, Labrador, has provided a detailed picture of this phase of the whaling industry (Grenier, Bernier, and Stevens 2007).

In the seventeenth century, northern Europeans, especially the English and the Dutch, entered the whaling business in numbers and began to develop new methodologies. Shore whaling was still practiced, and the Dutch station on Spitzbergen has been excavated (Hacquebord and Vroom 1988), but offshore whaling from ships was introduced. The rendering installation was reduced in size until it could be carried on a ship, along with boats for catching the whales, so that the entire process of hunting and conversion to oil could take place at sea. As near-shore stocks of whales began to disappear in the eighteenth century, especially in the North Atlantic, offshore whaling grew in importance and voyages increased in duration. By the early nineteenth century, the Greenland right whale, the animal on which the industry had been born and nurtured, had been hunted to the edge of extinction, and whalemen had to look for new species and grounds to exploit. The sperm whale succeeded the right whale as focus of the industry, but such whales were pelagic and could not be found in numbers near shore. It was discovered that they were plentiful in the Pacific Ocean, so ships, primarily from New England, began to make extremely long voyages, around Cape Horn, in search of the potentially large profits from a successful voyage. The whale fishery probably reached its peak, in terms of ships and men employed, in the first half of the nineteenth century, but for ordinary sailors it was a dirty, smelly, low-paying business with much hardship. Whalemen were held in contempt by other mariners, the lowest of the low in a field that enjoyed little social status by the nineteenth century (Dolin 2007).

MARITIME ARCHAEOLOGICAL IMPLICATIONS

While Mediterranean maritime archaeology began and largely continues with ancient and early medieval ships, the history of maritime archaeology in northern Europe and North America is primarily the story of medieval and postmedieval shipwrecks. To a certain degree, this is a result of the physical visibility of such ships on the sea bottom—they are usually better preserved than older ships, relatively easy to find, and relatively easy to identify with the help of historical archives. They make good news stories, as they can often be tied to the popular history taught in schools.

At the same time, such ships have a cultural visibility that makes them appealing projects, which are readily supported by state agencies and commercial sponsors. In northern Europe especially, the growth of maritime archaeology was tied directly to popular cultural interest in perceived high points in national histories. In Denmark and Norway, the emphasis has been on ships of the Viking period, when stable central governments were first established and when these countries had their greatest foreign influence, either as imperial/colonizing powers or as pirates and raiders. In Germany, the post–World War II rejection of the imperialistic role chosen by Bismarck, Wilhelm II, and Hitler left Germans without a glorious, unified past that could be recalled with pride, but the discovery of the Bremen cog in 1962 offered a window on a positive, internationally influential past under the Hanse. In Sweden, the relocation of *Vasa* in 1956 coincided with postwar prosperity and renewed interest in the seventeenth century, called the Great Power Period in Sweden, when the country played a major role on the central European stage and effectively controlled the Baltic. In each of these cases, public and private funding were available for projects that were not necessarily primarily archaeological in nature, but iconic. In *Vasa*'s case it was also ironic, as the ship had never fought in a great battle but was an abject failure. Here, it was the association with a popular figure, King Gustav II Adolf, and the heroic efforts to salvage the ship in the 1950s, rather than the ship's own history, that mattered. This holds true even when there is no nation to remember—the recovery of the submersible CSS *Hunley* in Charleston, South Carolina,

SHIPS AND SHIPWRECKS

offers a socially acceptable way to recognize the heroes of a secessionist movement and to enshrine the idea of a Confederate nation, in a region of the United States where for some the Civil War never really ended (Horwitz 1998). As a result, the popular and academic concept of what a successful maritime archaeological project should be was established by the raising, conservation, and display of significant shipwrecks from the "great moments" of the past, and most of these great moments are relatively recent.

Postmedieval maritime archaeology tends to be focused much more on naval ships than classical or medieval maritime archaeology. These wrecks are readily visible on the sea bottom, since cannon are relatively easy to find and identify with remote sensing equipment, and they are also more visible as individual ships in the archives, since states tended to keep good records of naval procurement and losses. It is thus possible to link warships to specific events or people, which makes it easier to justify preservation to the public. There is a merchant ship archaeology, but it lived for many years in the shadow of naval ships. The exceptions here are Germany, largely due to antimilitary academic and popular attitudes after World War II, and the Netherlands, due to the discovery of hundreds of merchant shipwrecks in the reclaimed land of the former Zuiderzee.

The development of postmedieval maritime archaeology has also been bound up more tightly with the development of avocational diving and treasure hunting than other periods. The gold and silver cargoes transported across the Atlantic by Spain after 1500 attracted treasure hunters already in the seventeenth century (Earle 2007), and even though most such ventures fail, the lure of sunken treasure is hard for even hard-nosed businesspeople to resist. Well-preserved shipwrecks in the colder waters of northern Europe and the American Great Lakes are a natural attraction for SCUBA divers, and these areas have seen the greatest avocational involvement in the documentation and study of historic ships.

Current submerged heritage management programs in northern Europe and the Americas are largely shaped by postmedieval sites. This is once again the result of their visibility, both archaeologically and culturally. They may resonate more directly with the general public and elected representatives than the ships of vanished civilizations, and they offer plenty of substance, in both physical remains and historical source material, to attract scholars and amateurs. Because of their potential commercial value, they are also often under the greatest threat.

REFERENCES

Adams, J. 2003. *Ships, innovation and change: Aspects of carvel shipbuilding in northern Europe 1450–1850*. Stockholm Studies in Archaeology 24/Stockholm Marine Archaeology Reports 3. Stockholm: Göteborgs Universitet Acta Univ.
Anderson, R. C. 1927. *The rigging of ships in the days of the spritsail topmast 1600–1720*. Salem: Marine Research Society Salem.

Auer, J. 2008. Fregat and snau: Small cruisers in the Danish navy 1650–1750. PhD diss., University of Southern Denmark.

Baker, M. 1586. *Fragments of ancient English shipwrightry*. Pepys Library, Magdalene College, Cambridge.

Baker, W. F. 1974. *Running her easting down: A documentary of the development and history of the British tea clippers, culminating with the building of the* Cutty Sark. Caldwell, UK: Caxton.

Barnard, J. G. 1872. *Report on the North Sea Canal of Holland and on the improvement of navigation from Rotterdam to the sea*. Washington, DC: U.S. Army.

Batchvarov, K. 2002. The framing of seventeenth-century men-of-war in England and other northern European countries. MA thesis, Texas A&M University.

Biddlecombe, G. 1848. *The art of rigging: Containing an explanation of terms and phrases and the progressive method of rigging expressly adapted for sailing ships*. London: Norie and Wilson.

Bondioli, M., R. Burlet, and A. Zysberg. 1995. Oar mechanics and oar power in medieval and later galleys. In *The age of the galley: Mediterranean oared vessels since pre-classical times*, ed. R. Gardiner, 172–205. London: Conway Maritime Press.

Boudriot, J. 1986–1988. *The seventy-four gun ship: A practical treatise on the art of naval architecture*. 4 vols. Rotherfield: Jean Boudriot.

Boxer, C. R. 1991. *The Portuguese seaborne empire 1415–1825*. 2nd ed. Manchester: Carcanet.

Brindley, H. H., and A. Moore. 1921. Square-rigged vessels with two masts. *Mariner's Mirror* 7: 194–217.

Caruana, A. 1994. *The history of English sea ordnance I: The age of evolution 1523–1715*. Rotherfield: Jean Boudriot.

Cederlund, C. O. 2006. *Vasa I: The archaeology of a Swedish warship of 1628*. Stockholm: Statens maritima museer.

Chapelle, H. I. 1935. *The history of American sailing ships*. New York: W. W. Norton.

———. 1967. *The search for speed under sail 1700–1855*. New York: Bonanza.

———. 1973. *The American fishing schooners 1825–1935*. New York: Model Shipways.

Christensen, A. E. 1992. *Gamle norske trebåter: Bevaring og vedlikehold*. Norske Båter VI. Oslo: Grøndahl Dryer.

Crisman, K. J., and A. B. Cohn. 1998. *When horses walked on water: Horse-powered ferries in nineteenth-century America*. Washington, DC: Smithsonian Books.

Crumlin-Pedersen, O. 2004. Nordic clinker construction. In *The philosophy of shipbuilding: Conceptual approaches to the study of wooden ships*, ed. F. Hocker and C. Ward, 37–64. College Station: Texas A&M University Press.

Cutler, C. C. 1984. *Greyhounds of the sea: The story of the American clipper ship*. 3rd ed. Annapolis, MD: HarperCollins.

Dolin, E. J. 2007. *Leviathan: The history of whaling in America*. New York: Tantor Media.

Dollinger, P. 1970. *The hanse*. London: Alfred Kroener.

Earle, P. 2007. *Treasure hunt: Shipwreck, diving and the quest for treasure in the age of heroes*. London: Thomas Dunne Books.

Ferreiro, L. 2007. *Ships and science: The birth of naval architecture in the scientific revolution 1600–1800*. Cambridge: MIT Press.

Footner, G. M. 1998. *Tidewater triumph: The development and worldwide success of the Chesapeake Bay pilot schooner*. Mystic, CT: Mystic Seaport Museum.

Friel, I. 1993. Henry V's *Grace Dieu* and the wreck in the R. Hamble near Bursledon, Hampshire. *International Journal of Nautical Archaeology* 22 (1): 3–19.

———. 1995. *The good ship: Ships, shipbuilding, and technology in England 1200–1520*. Baltimore: British Museum Press.

Fuller, H. J. In press. *Technology and the mid-Victorian Royal Navy: Ironclads and naval innovation*. New York: Routledge.

Gaastra, F. S. 2003. *The Dutch East India Company: Expansion and decline*. Leiden: Walburg Pers.

Gardiner, R. 1992. *The first frigates: Nine- and twelve-pounder armed frigates 1748–1815*. London: Conway Maritime Press.

———, ed. 1994. *The golden age of shipping: The classic merchant ship, 1900–1960*. London: Conway Maritime Press.

———, ed. 1995. *The age of the galley: Mediterranean oared vessels since pre-classical times*. London: Conway Maritime Press.

Gillmer, T. C., and B. Johnson. 1982. *Introduction to naval architecture*. Annapolis, MD: Naval Institute Press.

Glete, Jan. 2000. *Warfare at sea, 1500–1650: Maritime conflicts and the transformation of Europe*. London: Routledge.

———. 2002. *War and the state in early modern Europe: Spain, the Dutch Republic and Sweden as fiscal-military states, 1500–1660*. London: Routledge.

Goodwin, P. 1997. *The construction and fitting of the English man-of-war 1650–1850*. London: Conway Maritime Press.

Greenhill, B. 1976. *Archaeology of the boat*. London: A and C Black.

———. 1988. *Merchant schooners*. Annapolis, MD: Naval Institute Press.

Grenier, R., M.-A. Bernier, and W. Stevens, eds. 2007. *The underwater archaeology of Red Bay: Basque shipbuilding and whaling in the 16th century*. Ottawa: Parks Canada.

Hacquebord, L., and W. Vroom, eds. 1988. *Walvisvaart in de gouden eeuw: Opgravingen op Spitsbergen*. Amsterdam: De Bataafsche Leeuw.

Hainsworth, D. R., and C. Churches. 1998. *The Anglo-Dutch naval wars 1652–1674*. Stroud: Alan Sutton.

Hallenberg, M. 2008. *Statsmakt till salu*. Stockholm: Nordic Academic Press.

Harland, J. 1984. *Seamanship in the age of sail: An account of the shiphandling of the sailing man-of-war 1600–1860, based on contemporary sources*. Annapolis, MD: U.S. Naval Institute Press.

———. 2003. *Capstans and windlasses: An illustrated history of their use at sea*. Piermont, NY: Pier Books.

Harris, D. G. 1989. *F. H. Chapman. The first naval architect and his work*. London: Naval Institute Press.

Hearn, C. G. 1992. *Gray raiders of the sea: How eight Confederate warships destroyed the Union's high seas commerce*. Camden: Louisiana State University Press.

Hildred, A. 2009. The fighting ship. In *Mary Rose your noblest shippe: Anatomy of a Tudor warship*, ed. P. Marsden, 297–344. The archaeology of the *Mary Rose* 2. Portsmouth, UK: Mary Rose Trust.

———, ed. 2011. *Weapons of warre: The armaments of the* Mary Rose. The archaeology of the *Mary Rose* 3. Portsmouth, UK: Mary Rose Trust.

Hills, R. L. 1993. *Power from steam: A history of the stationary steam engine*. Cambridge: Cambridge University Press.

Hocker, F. 1999. Technical and organisational development in European shipyards 1400–1600. In *Maritime topography and the medieval town*, ed. J. Bill and B. L. Clausen, 21–32. Copenhagen: National Museum.

———. 2004. A bottom-based concept of shipbuilding in northwestern Europe. In *The philosophy of shipbuilding: Conceptual approaches to the study of wooden ships*, ed. F. Hocker and C. Ward, 65–93. College Station: Texas A&M University Press.

Hocker, F., and J. McManamon. 2006. Medieval shipbuilding in the Mediterranean and written culture at Venice. *Mediterranean Historical Review* 21 (1): 1–37.

Hocker, F., and K. Vlierman. 1997. *A small cog, wrecked on the Zuiderzee in the early 15th century*. Lelystad, the Netherlands: NISA.

Horwitz, T. 1998. *Confederates in the attic: Dispatches from the unfinished Civil War*. New York: Vintage.

Hutchinson, G. 1994. *Medieval ships and shipping*. London: Cassell.

Keay, J. 1994. *The honourable company: A history of the English East India Company*. New York: HarperCollins.

Ketner, F. 1943. *Amsterdam en de binnenvaart door Holland in de 15e eeuw*. Bijdragen voor Vaderlandsche Geschiedenis en Oudheidkunde, 8th ser., vol. 4. Leiden: E. J. Brill.

Klein, H. S. 1999. *The Atlantic slave trade*. Cambridge: Cambridge University Press.

Kurlansky, M. 1997. *Cod: A biography of the fish that changed the world*. New York: Penguin.

Lane, F. 1934. *Venetian ships and shipbuilders of the Renaissance*. Baltimore: Ayer.

Lavery, B. 1981. Introduction to A. Deane, *Deane's doctrine of naval architecture*, annotated ed. London: Conway Maritime Press.

———. 1983–1984. *The ship of the line*. 2 vols. London: Conway Maritime Press.

———. 1985. *The 74-gun ship* Bellona. London: Conway Maritime Press.

———. 1987. *The arming and fitting of English ships of war 1600–1815*. London: U.S. Naval Institute Press.

Lever, D. 1808. *The young sea officer's sheet anchor, or the key to the leading of rigging and to practical seamanship*. Leeds: John Richardson.

Loewen, B. 2007. The Basque shipbuilding trades: Design, forestry and carpentry. In *The underwater archaeology of Red Bay: Basque shipbuilding and whaling in the 16th century*, ed. R. Grenier, M.-A. Bernier, and W. Stevens III, 253–298. Ottawa: Parks Canada.

Lott, Y. 1777. *An account of proposals made for the benefit of His Majesty's naval service*. London: W. Owen, J. Wilkie, and F. Noble.

Lunsford, V. W. 2005. *Piracy and privateering in the golden age Netherlands*. New York: Palgrave Macmillan.

Marsden, P., ed. 2009. Mary Rose *your noblest shippe: Anatomy of a Tudor warship*. The archaeology of the *Mary Rose* 2. Portsmouth, UK: Mary Rose Trust.

McNeill, W. H. 1982. *The pursuit of power: Technology, armed force, and society since A.D. 1000*. Chicago: ACLS Humanities.

Newby, E. 1956. *The last grain race*. London: Lonely Planet.

Ollard, R. 1974. *Pepys: A biography*. London: Allison and Busby.

Ollivier, B. 1737. Remarques sur la marine des Anglais et des Hollandais. Annotated translation published by D. Roberts as *18th century shipbuilding: Remarks on the navies of the English and the Dutch*. London: Jean Boudriout, 1992.

Parker, G., ed. 1987. *The Thirty Years' War*. Rev. ed. New York: Routledge.

Partington, J. R. 1999. *A history of Greek fire and gunpowder*. Baltimore: Johns Hopkins University Press.

Perry, M. F. 1965. *Infernal machines: The story of Confederate submarine and mine warfare*. Baton Rouge: Louisiana State University Press.

Pipping, O., and F. Hocker. Forthcoming. Vasa II: *The wind is fair; Seamanship in the early 17th century*. Stockholm: Statens maritima museer.

Proulx, J.-P. 2007. Basque whaling in Labrador: An historical overview. In *The underwater archaeology of Red Bay: Basque shipbuilding and whaling in the 16th century*, ed. R. Grenier, M.-A. Bernier, and W. Stevens, I-25–96. Ottawa: Parks Canada.

Rodger, N. A. M. 1997. *The safeguard of the sea: A naval history of Britain 660–1649*.
    London: W. W. Norton.

Scammell, G. V. 1981. *The world encompassed: The first European maritime nations c.*
    800–1650. London: Routledge.

———. 1987. The sinews of war: Manning and provisioning English fighting ships c.
    1550–1650. *Mariner's Mirror* 73: 351–376.

Scott Russell, J. 1865. *The modern system of naval architecture*. London: Day and Son
    Lithographers.

Shaw, R. L. 1993. *Canals for a nation: The canal era in the United States 1790–1860*. Lexington:
    University Press of Kentucky.

Steel, D. 1794. *The elements and practice of rigging and seamanship*. London: David Steel.

Sutherland, W. 1711. *The ship-builders assistant: or, Some essays towards compleating the*
    art of marine architecture. London: R. Mount, A. Bell, and R. Smith.

Unger, R. 1978. *Dutch shipbuilding before 1800*. Assen: Van Gorcum.

Van Beylen, J. 1970. *Schepen van de Nederlanden van de late middeleeuwen tot het*
    einde van de 17e eeuw. Amsterdam: P. N. van Kampen.

Van Yk, C. 1697. *De nederlandsche scheepsbouwkonst open gestelt*. Amsterdam:
    Ian ten Hoom.

Witsen, N. 1671. *Aeloude en hedendaegsche scheeps-bouw en Bestier*. Amsterdam: Casparus
    Commelijn.

CHAPTER 21

SOUTHERN AFRICAN SHIPWRECK ARCHAEOLOGY

BRUNO E. J. S. WERZ

INTRODUCTION

THE southern African region includes three independent states that border the sea. These are Namibia, to the west; South Africa, in the south-central part; and Mozambique, to the east (Figure 21.1). During the last 500 years, thousands of ships came to an untimely end in the waters and on the shores of this region. Their physical remains represent an important part of the world's maritime cultural heritage. Although the research potential of southern African historic shipwrecks is substantial, very few scientific investigations into this heritage have been undertaken to date.

The first part of this contribution briefly sketches the physical geographic setting of the region's shores and the adjacent coastal waters. Following this, some aspects relating to southern African shipwreck archaeology are discussed, including the nature and potential of wrecks for scientific historical-archaeological investigations. The final section describes some aspects of specific studies in maritime archaeology that have been undertaken in the region so far. These examples focus on shipwrecks that date to the earlier period of navigation in these parts: the sixteenth to eighteenth centuries CE. Threats to the underwater cultural heritage, attempts to protect this heritage, education and training in maritime archaeology, and other aspects of shipwreck resource management will not be discussed here, as these have been reported upon extensively elsewhere (Bell-Cross 1980; Brown 1987; Deacon 1988; Gribble 2002; Hamilton 1994; Van Meurs 1985; Oberholzer 1987; Rudner 1981; Smith 1988; Werz 1990b, 1993c, 1994a, 1994b, 1999a, 1999b, 2003a, 2007, 2009c).

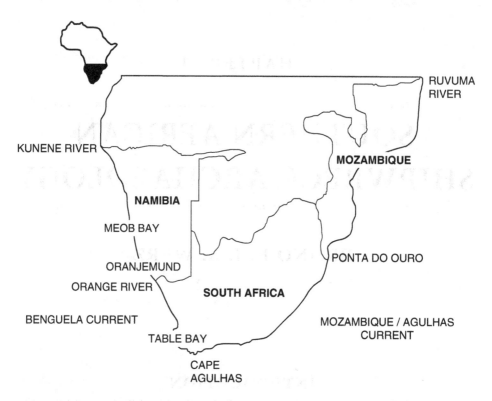

Figure 21.1 Plan of the southern African region. Illustration by the author.

THE AREA OF INTEREST

The northwestern extreme of the southern African region is indicated by the mouth of the Kunene River, at approximately 17° 15′ S–11° 45′ E, the border between Angola and Namibia. The northeastern demarcation is indicated by the mouth of the Ruvuma River, separating Tanzania from Mozambique, at 10° 28′ S–40° 30′ E. Cape Agulhas, on the southern coast of South Africa, at 34° 50′ S–20° 00′ E, is the southernmost tip of the region. This cape is also the geographical division between the Atlantic Ocean, to the west, and the Indian Ocean, to the east. The combined coastline of the region is roughly 7,000 km long. Of this total distance, approximately 1,500 km falls within the borders of Namibia, from the Kunene River to the Orange or Gariep River mouth to the south. The coastline of South Africa stretches over approximately 3,000 km, from the mouth of the Orange River to Ponta do Ouro, on the border with Mozambique. The coastal region of the latter state runs from Ponta do Ouro to the Ruvuma River and has a length of about 2,500 km (Hydrographer South African Navy 1979a, 1982; Werz 1999b, 2007).

The Namibian coast consists mostly of sand and gravel beaches, with rocky headlands and cliffs in places. In many instances, salt pans and high shifting sand dunes back the shore. The coastal area is bounded by the Namib Desert to the east and has few natural places of refuge. Walvisbaai, situated almost in the center, and Lüderitz, farther south, are the only two ports along the entire coast. The coastline of South Africa is also quite rugged and consists of rocks and cliffs, interspersed with sandy beaches. Some coral reefs are found near the northeast coast. Few natural harbors of refuge exist in the area. The most important of these are Saldanha Bay, False Bay, Mossel Bay, and Algoa Bay. Deep waters surround the coastal regions of both Namibia and South Africa, and this factor together with the long fetch and the strong prevailing winds often cause violent sea conditions. Because of this combination of natural factors, both states have a high-energy coastline. The greater part of the coast of Mozambique is characterized by sandy beaches, backed by a belt of tropical forest. Coral reefs can be found along the coast, which has several natural harbors of refuge, including Inhambane, Beira, and Mozambique Island.

To the west, the Atlantic Ocean bounds the western coasts of Namibia and South Africa. The continental shelf, from the low-water mark to the 200 m isobath, is generally quite narrow in these parts. A notable exception is the shelf region off Cape Agulhas. The Indian Ocean borders South Africa to the south and east, as well as the coast of Mozambique. In the latter area, the continental shelf extends quite a distance offshore. The predominant current off Namibia and the western coast of South Africa is the Benguela Current, which flows in a northerly direction, parallel to the coast. Most of its cold water is brought to the surface by upwelling, a result of the prevailing winds from the southerly direction, which cause the surface layer of water to be transported away from the coast. The warm to temperate Mozambique-Agulhas Current flows in a south-southwesterly direction past Mozambique and the South African eastern and southern coasts. The Benguela and Agulhas Currents converge off South Africa's southern coast, which often causes unpredictable conditions at sea (Hydrographer South African Navy 1975, 1979a, 1979b, 1982; Werz 1999b, 2007).

THE NATURE AND POTENTIAL OF SHIPWRECKS

Namibia, South Africa, and Mozambique are, historically speaking, not maritime nations. This assertion is supported by the fact that no archival records or archaeological evidence exists of local vessels being produced here before the mid-seventeenth century CE, at least not in Namibia and South Africa. There is thus not much of a seafaring tradition, and local interest in aspects of maritime history is limited. One result of this disinterest is that an encompassing inventory of historic shipwrecks in southern African waters is not available.

The unavoidable incompleteness of historical records that are dispersed in different archives throughout the region and overseas is also a restricting factor in this regard. The majority of shipwrecks have thus not been located, positively identified, or recorded in great detail, especially those of the earlier periods. Some lists of wrecks exist, but most of these are not comprehensive. In many cases they only contain information on the name and nationality of vessels that foundered, the year of sinking, and the approximate location where an incident occurred. Unfortunately, some of the information provided is not correct. Other inventories, compiled by interested private individuals or salvage operators, are not accessible for obvious reasons.

A list of shipwrecks off the coast of Namibia, which was compiled by dedicated amateur historians over the years, indicates that a minimum of 350 vessels met their end here. This list has been deposited at the Namibia Scientific Society in Windhoek and is available for public scrutiny. Some data contained therein have also been reported upon in internal communications of the Namibia Scientific Society and the Namibia Underwater Federation (Gunter von Schumann, Namibia Scientific Society and Namibia Underwater Federation, pers. comm.). Available but limited data for selected shipwrecks in Mozambique can be found on some Internet sites. In this context, information made available by Arqueonautas Worldwide, a shipwreck exploration company based in Portugal, must be mentioned. This company cooperates with Patrimonio Internacional, an organization that is partly owned by the Mozambican government (Arqueonautas Worldwide 2001, 2006). These Web sites do not provide information on the number of Mozambican shipwrecks as a whole; rather, they focus on salvage excavation projects that both companies are involved in.

The most complete records to date concern the shipwreck potential in South African waters. Since the early 1990s, the South African Heritage Resources Agency (previously known as the National Monuments Council) has managed a database that combines information from several older wreck lists, some of which have been published (Kennedy 1955; Rawe and Crabtree 1978; South African Shipping News 1982, 1983, 1984; the unpublished *List of South African Shipwrecks* in the National Library of South Africa). In 2002, the database contained over 2,200 entries of which some 1,914 are historical shipwrecks that are protected by law. The general consensus is, however, that the total number of vessels may well be more, even passing the 3,000 figure (Gribble 2002). Further archival work is thus required. This may be illustrated by an example of the shipwreck potential in a smaller area.

Since 1989, a research program has been undertaken that focuses on the Table Bay area near Cape Town. Known under the acronym MAP (Maritime Archaeological Project of Table Bay), several studies have been undertaken on a variety of aspects of the region's cultural heritage sites (Werz 1990a, 1992b, 1993a, 1993b, 1993c, 1999b, 2004, 2009c, in press). One of these studies concerns the shipwreck potential in the bay. A first study, based on the aforementioned lists, indicated the presence of 358 wrecks (Werz 1999b). Later research revealed that some of the entries in the lists were not correct and that some vessels had not sunk in the area, thus reducing the number of losses. In contrast, some previously unknown data were collected that in turn increased the potential slightly. Currently, references exist for 360 shipwrecks in Table Bay, but further research may increase this number (Werz 2003b, 2004, 2009c).

Except for the last 150 years or so, very few references to locally constructed vessels exist. Due to the fact that Namibian and South African coastal waters are dangerous for navigation and border on inhospitable shores, prehistoric indigenous people were not tempted to develop seagoing craft. Life was focused on the interior, even more so as sufficient living space and food resources could be obtained here for the sparse population. Although some small bands of people lived off the sea, their activities were limited to collecting crustaceans and shellfish from the inter-tidal zone or fishing from the beach (Avery 1975; Van Andel 1989; Werz 1999b). Archaeological evidence of these shorebound activities is abundant in southern Africa, in the form of coastal hunter-gatherer campsites, shell middens, and fish traps (Figure 21.2). In this context, it is noteworthy that the oldest artifacts ever found underwater in the world are Acheulean hand axes that were probably used by beachcombing hominids. These stone tools were excavated some distance offshore

Figure 21.2 Indigenous people of the Cape of Good Hope as seen by seventeenth-century CE callers. In the background, Table Mountain and Table Bay. Herbert (1634).

in Table Bay at a depth between 7 and 8 m. Based on typology, they have been dated to between 300,000 and 1.4 million years ago (Werz 1999b, 2004, 2009c; Werz and Flemming 2001). Nevertheless, the archaeological record has not revealed a trace of evidence for the use of oceangoing rafts or crafts in prehistoric times.

A dearth of precolonial coastal navigation is also supported by the lack of anthropological and ethnographic evidence (Van Warmelo 1977). Exceptions are a few rock paintings some distance from the sea in the Western Cape Province of South Africa that depict seagoing craft of a European origin (Figure 21.3). The images were probably produced by local artists that had observed passing ships and are not evidence for an indigenous tradition of navigation (Johnson 1960; Johnson and Maggs 1979; Yates, Manhire, and Parkington 1993). A possible exception that should not be overlooked, however, concerns Mozambique. Because the coastal waters of this country are more hospitable than those elsewhere in the region, being situated along the warm Indian Ocean and having a less savage coastline, it is possible that Mozambique's indigenous prehistoric people did take to the sea on occasion. This was certainly the case once the dhow was introduced by Arab traders during the sixteenth or seventeenth century (Landström 1972). This vessel type enabled trading and fishing activities and is still very much in use by locals. Based on the above, it can be concluded that the shipwreck potential in southern African waters is dominated by vessels that were developed and constructed elsewhere.

There is scanty documentary evidence for foreign landfalls prior to the sixteenth century CE. The oldest mention in this regard is from the Greek historian Herodotus. He refers to a Phoenician expedition consisting of some ships that supposedly sailed around Africa as early as 600 BCE. During this voyage, which took about three years, the Phoenicians made some stopovers. It has been alleged that during one of these stops they abandoned one of their vessels. During the nineteenth century, rumors

Figure 21.3 Rock painting of a sailing ship from Noordbron/Heidedal, Western Cape Province, South Africa, suggesting a Dutch East Indiaman of the seventeenth or eighteenth century (dimensions approximately 36 by 27 cm). After Johnson 1960: 113.

emerged that parts of an old wreck had been located near Cape Town that could be attributed to this Phoenician ship. Some investigations followed over the years, but none of these were conclusive. A renewed effort to locate the supposed site of the wreck was undertaken in the late 1980s. This work revealed some ancient wood fragments. Radiocarbon analysis, however, indicated that their age was beyond the dating range, whereas a study of the wood anatomy indicated a locally occurring species (O'Sullivan 1990; Werz 1997).

Much stronger indications relate to sporadic contacts between Arabic and Indian traders and Africans of the Mozambican region. Archaeological evidence for this is provided by Persian ceramics and glass beads that were found in Chibuene. Occupation at this place dates back to the eighth to ninth century CE, which may be associated with early overseas contacts in the region (Werz 1997).

Hundreds of years after the Arabs and Indians first gained access to the region from the east, the Portuguese started to explore the western coast of the African continent. In search of the riches of the East, such as spices and exquisite textiles, they sent out expeditions to explore the sea route to Asia. During the second half of the fifteenth century CE, the West African coast was reconnoitered during a number of consecutive journeys. In 1488, Bartolomeu Diaz rounded the southernmost tip of Africa. Ship and crew managed to reach present-day Mossel Bay on the southern coast of South Africa before Diaz was forced to return by his crew. On the return voyage, he observed a promontory and erected a *padrao*, or memorial cross, there. The landmark was initially called the Cape of Storms, but this name was later changed into Cabo de Boa Esperanza, or Cape of Good Hope. Ten years later, explorer Vasco da Gama finally reached the coast of India at Calicut (De Kock 1981; Raven-Hart 1967; Werz 2010).

Within a few decades, the Portuguese managed to establish an extensive trading network and their ships plied the sailing routes that led them past present-day Namibia and South Africa. Although they needed places where fresh provisions and drinking water could be obtained, the greater part of the Namibian coast was too hostile for this purpose. The South African coast seemed a more feasible option, and occasionally landfalls were made here. An example is the visit of Francisco d'Almeida to Table Bay. After having departed Cochin in India, on 19 November 1509, d'Almeida and his men entered the bay. Once ashore, they started bartering with indigenous people, but complained that these people took what they fancied. An altercation ensued. Bent on revenge, the commander decided on a punitive expedition that failed miserably. More than 50 Portuguese were killed, including d'Almeida, who was fatally wounded by a spear through his throat (Raven-Hart 1967). This was not a unique event, and several early contacts between those from overseas and indigenous people seem to have ended in bloodshed. This may be one of the reasons why no permanent Portuguese foothold was established on the South African coast, unlike other areas along Africa's West Coast, such as São Jorge da Mina (Elmina) on the Gold Coast, and in Mozambique (Boxer 1991).

Several Portuguese ships met their demise in southern African waters and provide evidence for the earlier periods of European maritime activity in the region.

References exist to at least 10 Portuguese shipwrecks, dating to the period 1550–1699, that sank along the coast of South Africa (Werz 1999b). Some of these wrecks were discovered and excavated by profit-motivated salvage divers who produced very few publications from these activities (Allen and Allen 1978b; Sachs and Smith 1981). In addition, only limited scientific research has been undertaken on their history and material culture (Auret and Maggs 1982; Axelson 1985; Bell-Cross 1981; Maggs 1984; Smith 1986; Stuckenberg 1986). Portuguese wrecks have also been recorded along the Namibian coast, and one of these, the Oranjemund shipwreck, was recently excavated by archaeologists (Werz 2008b, 2009a, 2009b, 2010). The Oranjemund shipwreck probably dates to the 1530s, making it the oldest wreck of European origin ever discovered in sub-Saharan Africa. Other Portuguese ships are known to have foundered off Mozambique. These were located by private companies and also subjected to invasive investigations, but very little published information has been made available to date (Arqueonautas Worldwide 2001).

During the late sixteenth century, the Dutch followed in the wake of the Portuguese. At the time, the Dutch Republic was engaged in the Eighty Years' War (1568–1648 CE) with Spain and its ally Portugal. Several smaller companies emerged in the Netherlands that undertook trading missions to the East and threatened to undermine the Portuguese dominance in Asia. This strategic factor was soon recognized by the national government of the Netherlands. As a result of this, but also because internal competition between the individual companies harmed the national economy, the government decided to step in. This intervention resulted in the establishment of the Verenigde Oostindische Compagnie (VOC), or United Dutch East India Company, in 1602.

During the nearly two centuries in which the VOC was active, from 1602 to 1799, it focused on trade with Asia and occasionally fought the Portuguese, and later the French and English, for commercial control. The VOC became the largest commercial company the world had ever known, overshadowing the English East India Company (EIC) as well as its French and Scandinavian counterparts. An indication of this size is that during the period of its existence, the organization used some 1,772 ships. Of these vessels, approximately 1,581 were purpose-built and constructed at the company's dockyards. All told, the ships undertook at least 4,789 outbound and 3,401 return voyages. These figures amount to an impressive minimum total of 8,190 transoceanic trips, or an average of about four and a half voyages per vessel (Werz 1999c).

During the long sea voyages, ships often called at Table Bay near the southern tip of Africa. At this point, roughly halfway between Europe and Asia, fresh provisions and drinking water were obtained. Also, crew members who were too sick to continue the journey often found temporary relief. This use was especially the case from 1652 onward, when the company founded a permanent refreshment station on the shores of Table Bay. This station, which developed into the city of Cape Town, remained in VOC hands until the end of the eighteenth century, when the company ceased to exist. The refreshment station was established as a result of a shipping disaster. Although some other VOC ships had sunk in Table Bay in previous years, the wrecking of the *Haarlem* in 1647 finally tipped the scale. This ship foundered near the eastern coastline of the bay and became a total loss. The officers and crew managed to reach safety, but had to spend about a year in a makeshift camp before being rescued by a returning fleet. During their stay, the people from the *Haarlem* reconnoitered the area and came in contact with indigenous people. Unlike in previous encounters with Portuguese callers, in this case the locals and the Dutch established friendly relations. When they returned to the Netherlands, the people from the *Haarlem* reported favorably on their stay and made practical suggestions for the establishment of a permanent base in the region (Werz 1999b, 2004, 2009c, in press).

Since 1988, research into this aspect of the early recorded history of the Cape of Good Hope has been undertaken on an ad hoc basis, including literature and archival research based on relevant historic documents and cartographic evidence. An analysis of these sources resulted in the demarcation of a specific area that may well contain the original location of the survivor camp and the wreck of the *Haarlem*. Photogrammetric surveys of this area were carried out in 1994 using terrestrial and aerial photographs. This research was followed by metal detector and magnetometer searches, as well as limited test excavations. Work undertaken to date has not revealed convincing archaeological evidence for the presence of the camp or the wreck. Nevertheless, additional fieldwork is planned, as the site has significant symbolic meaning. The contacts that were made between the people from the *Haarlem* and the local population lie at the roots of the multiracial and multicultural South African nation of today (Werz 1999b, in press).

Besides the *Haarlem*, the VOC lost several other vessels in the southern African region. From 1602 to 1796, the company had to write off some 104 outward-bound and 140 returning ships, totaling about 244 vessels. Archival information has indicated that of this total, approximately 28 outward-bound and 24 homeward-bound ships, or 21% of VOC shipwrecks worldwide, foundered along the South African coast. A substantial number of accidents took place in Table Bay, as this anchorage was not always a safe harbor (Werz 1999b, 1999c, 2004, 2009c). Several VOC shipwrecks have been discovered over the years, and nearly all of them were exploited for private gain. Such activities pertain to the remains of the *Huis te Crayensteyn* (1698), *Merestein* (1702), *Bennebroek* (1713), *Vis* (1740), *Reigersdaal* (1747), and *Middelburg* (1781). Few artifacts from these sites ended up in museums, and hardly any reliable information was recorded, although aspects of their salvage have been discussed in a limited number of academic publications (Klose 2000; Lightley 1976; Marsden 1976) or reported elsewhere (Meltzer 1984; Turner 1988). This rather negative balance is partly compensated by extensive research involving the *Oosterland* (1697) and the *Waddinxveen* (1697). These ships were discovered during the late 1980s by amateur divers who reported their find immediately. Long-term cooperation between the discoverers, the University of Cape Town, and the South African authorities followed. This cooperation resulted in the first scientific maritime archaeological project in southern African waters. Due to its significance, the project will be discussed in more detail below (Werz 1992b, 1993a, 1999b, 2004, 2009c).

Remains of Dutch East Indiamen have also been found elsewhere in the region. At least one such wreck, the *Bredenhof* (1753), was reported in Mozambique (Werz 1999b). There are strong indications that another VOC ship, the *Vlissingen* (1747), went down off Meob Bay on the Namibian coast. Even though the wreck of this ship has not been found to date, the *Vlissingen* will be discussed in more detail later, because it resulted in a unique research design and was the first exercise in maritime archaeology undertaken in Namibia (Werz 2006, 2007, 2008a).

Although the Dutch played an important role in the region for nearly two centuries, other nations also plied the sea routes that led past southern Africa. The Portuguese continued unabated with their trading activities and created a foothold in Mozambique in the sixteenth century. English, Danish, and French East India Company ships regularly passed the Cape during the seventeenth and eighteenth centuries, as did a variety of other merchantmen, slavers, whalers, and warships from different nations. Some examples of ships that wrecked during this period include the English East Indiaman *Dodington* (1755) (Allen and Allen 1978a) and *Nicobar*, a Danish Asiatic Company vessel that sank off South Africa's south coast in 1783 with a cargo of plate money (Herbert and Tingström 1999).

During the nineteenth century, the southern African region saw major political and socioeconomic changes. The British took the Cape by force and later extended their influence throughout South Africa. Namibia became a colony of Germany, whereas parts of Mozambique had already been colonized by Portugal centuries before. Shipping traffic increased and other nations from the Americas and Australasia became involved as a result of global economic expansion. Technology also developed, and a number of new vessel types were introduced. These changes are to some extent reflected in the remains of the ships that went down in the waters of the region. Some South African projects that dealt with nineteenth-century shipwrecks involved the EIC ship *Arniston* (1815) near Waenhuiskrans, the *Brunswick* (1805) and the Dutch warship *Bato* (1806) in False Bay near Cape Town, as well as the Royal Netherlands Navy ship *Amsterdam* (1817) in Algoa Bay. Two other vessels were excavated on beaches at Blaauwbergstrand, near Cape Town, and at Plettenberg Bay but have not yet been identified. There are, however, strong indications that they too originate from the nineteenth century. All of these wrecks were partly investigated by historians and archaeologists, but they have been described only in unpublished reports that are lodged at the South African Heritage Resources Agency. Parts of the English troopship *Birkenhead* (1852) were salvaged by divers, and the recovered artifacts from this ship have been dispersed. Nevertheless, a representative collection is under the control of the South African government, and all artifacts were registered by a Cape Town museum (Kayle 1990).

A large-scale survey of wrecks was undertaken during 1991 and 1992 on the direct order of the South African National Cabinet. The purpose of this project, also known as Operation Sea Eagle, was to locate and identify the maritime archaeological heritage around Robben Island in Table Bay. Work included archival and library research, magnetometer surveys, and underwater searches by navy divers and the author. The results of this project were to assist in the formulation of a management policy for the island, which subsequently became a UNESCO World Heritage site. On the basis of relevant records it could be established at the time that at least 22 ships foundered in the 1-nautical-mile security zone surrounding the island. This potential has increased since, as a result of recent accidents. The vessels that met their demise here originated from eight different nations and consist of 14 different types. Their time range covers more than 300 years, from 1694 to 1998, and about 50% date to the nineteenth century.

During fieldwork, the coast and seabed around the island were surveyed in detail. This work took some six months in total, during which 15 shipwreck sites were located and successfully identified. Although it was concluded that surface and underwater conditions resulted in the fragmentation of most wrecks, it has been formally acknowledged that they represent an important part of the maritime heritage of not only southern Africa, but the world as a whole (Martin and Werz 1999; Werz 1993b, 1994b, 1999b, 2001, 2003a; Werz and Martin 1994).

Shipwreck Archaeology in Southern Africa: Some Case Studies

From the above it is apparent that although the southern African potential of historic wrecks is quite substantial and diverse, very few scientific investigations of this heritage have been undertaken to date. This state can be attributed to such factors as the limited number of qualified maritime archaeologists in the region, which is partly a result of an underdevelopment of teaching in the field; a lack of specialist research institutions; and a lack of financial support (Werz 1994a, 1999a, 1999b, 2003a, 2007). Even though these circumstances have had a direct impact on both research infrastructure and research output, some projects have been realized successfully since 1990. Three of these, which have some common characteristics, will be discussed in more detail here.

The specific projects that were selected contributed to the introduction of acceptable standards for shipwreck research in southern Africa. Their outcomes therefore have direct value to legislators and heritage resource management practitioners in the region. The projects described below were also undertaken under the auspices of, or with close cooperation from, national governments. Full-scale excavation of the Oranjemund shipwreck was ordered and financed by the Namibian government. Research related to the Dutch East India Company ship the *Vlissingen* was supported by the Dutch government and the Namibian National Monuments Council, whereas the excavations of the wrecks of the VOC vessels *Oosterland* and *Waddinxveen* were the result of cooperation between the discoverers of both wrecks, the University of Cape Town, and the South African authorities. A third aspect that needs to be mentioned is that the three projects were undertaken under the guidance of a qualified maritime archaeologist with international experience. This person was assisted by terrestrial archaeologists, other professionals, and interested amateurs. An internationally acceptable standard for applied fieldwork procedures and research could thus be achieved, whereas excavation results and analysis of research data have been reported in the scientific literature.

The material culture that was recovered during two of the projects, the *Vlissingen* and the Oranjemund wreck, has been kept together under the supervision of the Namibian National Museum. This was unfortunately not the case with the *Oosterland* and the *Waddinxveen*. The lesser part of the artifact collection from both sites was sold by the people who discovered the wrecks to recoup fieldwork expenses they incurred. These sales were completed in consultation with the South African authorities and in accordance with national legislation that was in force at the time. This legislation was revised during the 1990s to prevent future dispersal of shipwreck artifacts. Nevertheless, a representative collection that includes the greater part of the excavated material from both wrecks has been kept by the South African government, while the remainder that ended up in private hands was first fully documented, analyzed, and conserved (Werz 1992b, 1993a, 1993c, 1999b, 2003a, 2004, 2009c).

The Oranjemund Shipwreck

On 1 April 2008, archaeological material was uncovered by chance in a high-security diamond-mining area close to Oranjemund, Namibia. Initial analysis indicated that the finds dated to the sixteenth century and that they were associated with a shipwreck. Soon after the discovery, the Namibian government took charge of the project and commissioned a full-scale investigation of the wreck. During September and October 2008, all material was excavated and removed under supervision of the author, who had been appointed principal investigator of the project (Werz 2008b, 2009a, 2009b, 2010).

The site was situated on the seabed and made accessible by temporary reclamation. The distance from the shoreline was approximately 30 m and the depth between 7 and 8 m below mean sea level. The wreck site covered a surface area of approximately 18 by 16 m and contained remnants of the original ship including several partial ground futtocks, from about midships toward the stern. No remains of the keel were found. Three distinct areas in the eastern section of the site contained structural remains. These were situated immediately adjacent to a natural obstruction, a rocky seabed outcrop, against which the vessel probably foundered.

The areas to the north, west, and south of the structural remains revealed a number of ferrous concretions. These were cemented to the bedrock and contained an array of pewter tableware, navigational and barber/surgeon equipment, personal possessions, and other artifacts. To the north of the rocky outcrop and to the north and northeast of the structural remains was an area that revealed a concentration of roughly and irregularly cast metal ingots, probably tin and lead. A number of these ingots had been deposited in deep erosion pockets; the remainder covering the surface. Partly on top of the structural remains and immediately south thereof was a substantial concentration of round copper ingots. The depositional pattern of cultural material indicated that the keel was deposited on the seabed in a NNE–SSW direction.

During excavation, marine deposits were identified underneath sections of the hull structure. These deposits indicated that the wreck had been exposed to a high-energy marine environment. The wreck was not buried immediately, but remained vulnerable to the destructive forces of the swell and currents until relatively recently. Evidence of this was provided by fragments of rubber found in deposits underneath the structural remains. Biological deterioration caused by marine borers (*Teredo navalis*) and possibly gribble (*Limnoria*) was also observed.

As part of the documentation process, video footage, aerial photographs, differential global positioning system (DGPS) readings, Total Station Theodolite readings, and laser-scan surveys of the excavation area were undertaken. The data thus acquired do not only serve as a survey record but will be invaluable for a detailed interpretation of the site at a later date. The application of the various survey techniques was essential, as time was extremely limited.

It was concluded that the ship originally was a merchant vessel of Portuguese origin that foundered shortly after 1525 CE. The vessel was on the outward-bound voyage to Asia when it probably struck a submerged rock close to shore. Provisional identification pertaining to the vessel's type and nationality, as well as relative accurate dating, was obtained from the material culture and especially the numerous coins, which provided for a *terminus post quem* of post-1525. Further historical research indicated that the wreck is probably that of the *Bom Jesus*, which was lost in 1533 CE.

The Oranjemund shipwreck is a find of international significance and worldwide interest. The next phase of the project will focus on the conservation and further documentation of the excavated material. Parallel to this task, future interdisciplinary research will be undertaken to investigate aspects of the history of the ship and the origin of its contents. The end goal is to have the shipwreck preserved and displayed in a special museum, together with all the material that was excavated from the site. Additionally, extensive ongoing research, publication, and education on various levels will be undertaken. It is hoped that this primary example of world heritage will serve an important educational role and enhance the current status of southern African shipwreck archaeology.

The *Vlissingen* (1747)

During September 2001, members of the Namibia Underwater Federation and the Namibian National Monuments Council undertook an archaeological survey in the Meob Bay area, Namibia, under the supervision of the author. The project was sponsored in part by the Dutch Ministry of Foreign Affairs. The aim was to collect further information to assist in the formulation of a plan to locate a suspected historic shipwreck. To this effect, terrestrial archaeological test excavations and field walks, as well as aerial and underwater observations, were undertaken (Werz 2006, 2007, 2008a).

Already in 1993, numerous identical copper coins identified as VOC *doits* had been washed ashore at Meob Bay. The coins were all minted in 1746 CE in the province of Zeeland in the then Dutch Republic for use in the overseas territories. It was therefore surmised that their likely source of origin was the wreck of an outward-bound VOC ship. Circumstantial evidence supported this view. During the eighteenth century, the whole of the Namibian coastline was virtually *terra incognita*. No historic records exist of a settlement in the Meob region predating the nineteenth century. The southernmost Portuguese strongholds on Africa's west coast only went as far south as Angola, whereas the Dutch East India Company station at the Cape of Good Hope was situated much farther south. Ships only passed near the coast on occasion, as nothing much was to be gained in the region and the shores are very inhospitable.

The logical conclusion therefore was that an outward-bound Dutch East Indiaman, carrying a cargo of specie, had met its demise here. This consignment consisted of identical *doits* that were never put into circulation, which was confirmed by their appearance. The coins were all found in a band that was several kilometers long, but only a few hundred meters wide. This band ran parallel to the shoreline and bordered on the high-water mark, indicating that the source of the coins was situated offshore. Most *doits* were exposed and lying on the surface, while some were covered by only a few millimeters of beach sand. These circumstances implied that they had been deposited on the beach in relatively recent times.

The 2001 excavations were undertaken in five sections spread over a distance of approximately 3,290 m along the shore. In each section, two grids were established. The smaller grids, each measuring 10 by 30 m, were situated as close to the high-water mark as possible. The larger grids, ranging from 30 by 50 m up to 30 by 150 m, were positioned farther inland. A total of 222 coins were excavated from the grids. Their dispersal pattern revealed that these finds are concentrated near the high-water mark, with densities decreasing farther inland, supporting the viewpoint that their source was situated offshore. Substantial parts of wreckage must thus still be underwater, as proven by the regular washing up of coins that continues to this day. Parts of the ship, including heavier items such as cannon, anchors, and ballast, may well be covered by sandbanks. Extensive field walks and aerial surveys did not reveal any such material on land, with the possible exception of a copper cauldron. Underwater searches were hampered by bad visibility and exceptionally strong swells and currents. As a result, no trace of any cultural material was observed by divers.

Further archival research has given a strong indication of the identity of the supposed wreck. Using the year that was provided by the *doits* as a *terminus post quem*, initial searches in the Dutch National Archives in The Hague focused on outward-bound ships that left the Netherlands between 1746 and 1758. This last year was chosen randomly as a *terminus ante quem*, as it seemed improbable that a substantial quantity of identical coins that had never been put in circulation would have been kept in store for long. Although some ships were reported to have been lost between 1746 and 1758, the approximate places of their demise were recorded in all cases except for one. None of these coincided with the Meob Bay area, or in fact with any position along the Namibian coast. It thus became clear that there was only one likely candidate: the *Vlissingen* (Figure 21.4). This ship was reported as having been lost sometime after departure, without an indication of its last position. Further archival research therefore concentrated on this vessel.

Documentary evidence provided an indication of events that led up to the disaster that claimed the ship. In all probability, the accident was caused by a combination of different factors, including the age of the vessel; the fact that hull damage was reported shortly after departure; references to the poor state of health of a number of people on board, which probably resulted in a high death rate; and adverse weather conditions. Archival research provided further information on the *Vlissingen* and those aboard, including details of previous voyages, cargoes transported, as well as personal details of officers and crew.

The project achieved its objectives successfully. Many data were collected that will prove vital for a second-phase fieldwork campaign. If future work on the *Vlissingen* can be undertaken, it should be done in close cooperation between the Namibian and Dutch governments, specialists, and dedicated members of the public. Only in this way can proper management of the project, an acceptable

Figure 21.4 Woodcut depicting a standard Dutch East Indiaman of the first half of the eighteenth century. The general appearance of the *Vlissingen*, as well as the *Oosterland* and *Waddinxveen*, would have been similar. After Werz 2006: 22.

research output, and increased public education be assured. The fact that the wreck has not been tampered with increases its value as an exponent of southern African maritime heritage.

The *Oosterland* and the *Waddinxveen* (1697)

The wrecks of the VOC ships *Oosterland* and *Waddinxveen* were found in Table Bay, South Africa, by sport divers during the late 1980s. The finds were reported, and permits for their excavation and study were issued by the South African authorities. The project was guided by the author, who is the founding contributor of maritime archaeology in southern Africa, in close cooperation with the discoverers of both wrecks, the University of Cape Town, the South African Cultural History Museum, and the South African National Monuments Council. This undertaking was the first scientific maritime archaeological project in southern Africa and has contributed to several positive developments. These include specialized academic teaching and public education, improved shipwreck regulation and legislation, and increased understanding of underwater cultural heritage (Martin and Werz 1999; Werz 1989, 1990a, 1992a, 1992b, 1993a, 1993c, 1994a, 1999a, 1999b, 2003a, 2004, 2009c; Werz and Klose 1994; Werz, Lee-Thorp, and Miller 1991; Werz and Martin 1994).

From the outset, the simultaneous study of both wrecks was developed on a broad base, including intra- and interdisciplinary approaches. An example of the intradisciplinary research approach is the extensive archival work that was undertaken in Dutch and South African archive repositories. Historical data, studied in conjunction with the material culture from the wrecks, allowed for their positive identification. Other historical information enabled for the re-creation of events pertaining to both vessels, such as their sinking. Detailed information on previous journeys, trade goods that were loaded on board, and items that were salvaged soon after the disaster have been recorded. Also, personal information of officers and crew, including their names, rank, place of origin, and other data, has been secured.

Historical research revealed that both ships were on their return voyage to the Netherlands when disaster struck. The *Oosterland*, a ship of 160 ft (48.8 m) and constructed in the period 1684–1685, had already completed three successful journeys to the Dutch East Indies. Returning from the port of Galle in Ceylon (Sri Lanka) on the first leg of the fourth homeward-bound voyage, it entered Table Bay on 6 or 7 May 1697 in the company of four other vessels. About two weeks later, a returning VOC fleet from Batavia (Jakarta) consisting of 12 ships entered the roads. Among them was the *Waddinxveen*, a 145 ft (44.2 m) ship that was on its second homeward-bound voyage. A few days later, weather conditions deteriorated dramatically and resulted in a violent storm. Pushed by the strong winds, the *Oosterland* and the *Waddinxveen* broke their anchor cables and were driven to shallow waters close to shore. Both foundered in close proximity of each other, between 13.00 and 15.00 hrs on Friday, 24 May 1697. The disaster claimed 140 lives in all.

Interdisciplinary approaches came into play during fieldwork and artifact analyses. As part of the predisturbance phase, side-scan sonar surveys and a study of the morphology of the near-shore zone and adjacent beach were undertaken. This survey allowed for a better understanding of relevant site formation processes. An important aspect during the disturbance phase was the development of an appropriate survey system. These techniques resulted in a level of accuracy similar to most terrestrial excavations. A number of artifacts and samples were retrieved and subjected to different material analyses. Some of the information obtained in this way could be combined with historical data, thus enhancing the research output. Interdisciplinary research was undertaken with the assistance of oceanographers, hydrographers, geologists, surveyors, material scientists, botanists, and computer specialists. One of the practical results of this cooperation was the development of a geographic information system (GIS) for shipwreck projects, representing a first for Africa.

Fieldwork extended over several years, although natural conditions often made underwater work difficult. Nevertheless, the project proved that maritime archaeological excavation on an acceptable level can be undertaken off the coasts of southern Africa. Evidence of this was provided by the valuable contextual and provenance information recorded for all collected artifacts, even though both wreck sites were heavily fragmented and scattered over a substantial area. Fieldwork, in combination with post-excavation analyses, has refuted the unfounded claim of many local treasure hunters that shipwrecks in southern African waters have lost their scientific value due to the breakup and dispersal of cultural material.

This project has thus set a benchmark for regional maritime archaeological excavations. Experiences gained from the excavation and study of the *Oosterland* and the *Waddinxveen* have benefited other projects, such as the *Vlissingen* and the Oranjemund shipwreck. It can therefore be concluded that the *Oosterland* and *Waddinxveen* project has played a most important role in the development of maritime and specifically shipwreck archaeology in the southern African region.

CONCLUSION

To date, the southern African region has not revealed convincing archaeological, ethnographic, or historic evidence for the existence of local seagoing craft in precolonial times. The known potential of shipwrecks therefore consists of vessels that originated from elsewhere. Reliable recorded maritime activity in the region dates back to the late fifteenth century CE, when Portuguese vessels started to visit these shores. The oldest archaeological evidence of this is provided by the Oranjemund shipwreck, probably the *Bom Jesus*, dating to 1533 CE. From the mid-seventeenth century until the end of the eighteenth century, the Dutch East India Company played a central role in the region's maritime traffic. As a result of this, a substantial number of vessels were lost. Several VOC shipwrecks that were located have been exploited for commercial gain in past years. Nevertheless, two others, the *Ooster-land* and the *Waddinxveen*, were the subject of the first scientific maritime archaeo-logical project in the region. These excavations were followed in 2001 by another project, the first of its kind for Namibia, involving the VOC ship *Vlissingen*.

Some databases provide an indication of the shipwreck potential in southern African waters. Although these sources are not complete and do not always provide reliable information, they do reflect the quantity and diversity of this underwater cultural heritage. From the records it is clear that the greatest number of shipping incidents occurred during the nineteenth century, which can be explained by an explosive growth of maritime traffic, stimulated by global political-economic ex-pansionism. Technical developments during this period, resulting in the develop-ment of new vessel types, also contributed to an increased diversity of ships represented in the archaeological record. From the above it will be clear that a cru-cial aspect of the southern African shipwreck potential is that it can provide com-parative material for sixteenth- through nineteenth-century shipwreck studies elsewhere in the world.

REFERENCES

Allen, Geoffrey, and David Allen. 1978a. *Clive's lost treasure*. London: Robin Garton.
——. 1978b. *The guns of Sacramento*. London: Robin Garton.
Arqueonautas Worldwide. 2001. *Arqueonautas worldwide*. Rev. 10 July 2001. Online at www.arq.de. Accessed 12 January 2010.
——. 2006. Arqueonautas Worldwide Publications. Online at www.arq-publications.com. Accessed 12 January 2010.
Auret, C., and Tim Maggs. 1982. The great ship *Sao Bento*: Remains from a mid-sixteenth century Portuguese wreck on the Pondoland coast. *Annals of the Natal Museum* 25: 1–39.
Avery, Graham. 1975. Discussion on the age and use of tidal fishtraps (visvywers). *South African Archaeological Bulletin* 30: 105–113.
Axelson, Eric. 1985. Recent identifications of Portuguese wrecks on the South African coast, especially of the *Sao Gonçalo* (1630), and the *Sacramento* and *Atalaia* (1647). In *Estudos de História e Cartografia Antiga Memórias* 25, 43–61. Lisboa: Instituto de Investigação Científica Tropical.
Bell-Cross, Graham. 1980. Research policy on shipwrecks. *Southern African Museums Association Bulletin* 14: 1–2.
——. 1981. Problems associated with the location and identification of early shipwrecks. *Southern African Museums Association Bulletin* 15: 326–340.
Boxer, Charles R. 1991. *The Portuguese seaborne empire 1415–1825*. Manchester: Carcanet.
Brown, A. G. K. 1987. Maritime archaeology in South Africa: Dead on arrival? *Bulletin of the Australian Institute for Maritime Archaeology* 11: 1–4.
De Kock, W. J. 1981. Explorers and circumnavigators of the Cape. In *500 years: A history of South Africa*, ed. C. F. J. Muller, 1–17. Pretoria: Academica.

Deacon, Hillary J. 1988. Practice and policy in maritime archaeology. *South African Archaeological Bulletin* 43: 123–125.

Gribble, John. 2002. Past, present and future of maritime archaeology in South Africa. In *International handbook of underwater archaeology*, ed. Carol V. Ruppé and Janet F. Barstad, 553–567. New York: Kluwer Academic/Plenum.

Hamilton, C. I. 1994. South Africa. In *Ubi sumus? The state of naval and maritime history*, ed. John B. Hattendorf, 313–324. Newport, RI: Naval War College Press.

Herbert, Jimmy, and Bertel Tingström. 1999. *Nicobar: The biggest plate money find in the world*. Stockholm: Royal Coin Cabinet.

Herbert, Thomas. 1634. *A relation of some yeares travaile, begunne Anno 1626. Into Africa and the greater Asia . . .* London: William Stansby and Jacob Bloome.

Hydrographer South African Navy. 1975. *South African sailing directions*. Vol. 1, *General information*. Kenwyn, SA: Directorate of Hydrography.

———. 1979a. *South African sailing directions*. Vol. 2, *The coasts of South West Africa and the Republic of South Africa from the Kunene River to Cape Hangklip*. Kenwyn, SA: Directorate of Hydrography.

———. 1979b. *South African sailing directions*. Vol. 3, *The coasts of the Republic of South Africa from Table Bay to Great Kei River*. Retreat, SA: Hydrographic Office Maritime Headquarters.

———. 1982. *South African sailing directions*. Vol. 4, *The coasts of the Republic of South Africa and Transkei from East London to the Mocambique border*. Tokai, SA: Hydrographic Office Maritime Headquarters.

Johnson, Townley R. 1960. Rock paintings of ships. *South African Archaeological Bulletin* 15: 111–113.

Johnson, Townley R., and Tim M. Maggs. 1979. *Major rock paintings of southern Africa*. Cape Town: David Phillip.

Kayle, Allan. 1990. *Salvage of the Birkenhead*. Johannesburg: Southern Book Publishers.

Kennedy, R. F. 1955. *Shipwrecks on and off the coasts of Southern Africa: A catalogue and index*. Johannesburg: Johannesburg Public Library.

Klose, Jane. 2000. Oriental ceramics retrieved from three Dutch East India Company ships wrecked off the coast of southern Africa: The *Oosterland* (1697), *Bennebroek* (1713) and *Brederode* (1785). *Transactions of the Oriental Ceramic Society* 64: 63–81.

Landström, Björn. 1972. *Het schip: De geschiedenis van het schip van primitief vlot tot atoom-onderzeeboot*. Hoofddorp, the Netherlands: Septuaginta.

Lightley, Robert A. 1976. An 18th century Dutch East Indiaman, found at Cape Town, 1971. *International Journal of Nautical Archaeology and Underwater Exploration* 5 (2): 305–316.

Maggs, Tim. 1984. The great galleon *São João*: Remains from a mid-sixteenth century wreck on the Natal south coast. *Annals of the Natal Museum* 26: 173–186.

Marsden, Peter. 1976. The *Meresteyn*, wrecked in 1702, near Cape Town, South Africa. *International Journal of Nautical Archaeology and Underwater Exploration* 5 (2): 201–219.

Martin, Colin G. C., and Bruno E. J. S Werz. 1999. Geographical Information Systems applied to maritime archaeology, with specific reference to the Table Bay project. *Southern African Field Archaeology* 8: 86–100.

Meltzer, Lalou. 1984. The treasure from the shipwreck, Reijgersdaal (1747). *Bulletin of the South African Cultural History Museum* 5: 5–19.

National Library of South Africa. *List of South African shipwrecks*. Unpublished ms. Cape Town: National Library of South Africa.

Oberholzer, Hannes. 1987. *Beleid vir die bewaring van die materiële kultuurerfenis*. Bloem-
    fontein: Nasionale Museum.
O'Sullivan, Bernard. 1990. A report on drilling and trenching on the Woltemade Flats,
    Cape Town, in 1988 and 1989. *South African Journal of Science* 86: 487–488.
Raven-Hart, Richard. 1967. *Before van Riebeeck: Callers at South Africa from 1488 to 1652*.
    Cape Town: C. Struik.
Rawe, Jim, and Anne Crabtree. 1978. *Shipwrecks of the southern Cape: A guide to the wrecks
    and their references for the coastline and islands between Lamberts Bay and Cape
    Agulhas*. Cape Town: Atlantic Underwater Club.
Rudner, Jalmar. 1981. The legal protection of historical shipwrecks in South Africa. *South-
    ern African Museums Association Bulletin* 14: 317–319.
Sachs, Peter, and C. Smith. 1981. Shipwrecks and salvage on the Eastern Cape coast.
    Southern African Museums Association Bulletin 14: 320–325.
Smith, Andrew B. 1986. Excavations at Plettenberg Bay, South Africa, of the camp-site of
    the survivors of the wreck of the *São Gonçalo*, 1630. *International Journal of Nautical
    Archaeology and Underwater Exploration* 15 (1): 53–59.
———. 1988. When is marine salvage "archaeology"? *South African Archaeological Bulletin*
    43: 122–123.
South African Shipping News. 1982. Marine casualties southern African waters 1552 to 1913.
    South African Shipping News and Fishing Industry Review 37 (6): 18–50.
———. 1983. Marine casualties southern African waters 1914 to 1945. *South African Shipping
    News and Fishing Industry Review* 38 (6): 3–15.
———. 1984. Marine casualties southern African waters 1946 to 1984. *South African
    Shipping News and Fishing Industry Review* 39 (6): 3–29.
Stuckenberg, Brian. 1986. Recent studies of historic Portuguese shipwrecks in South Africa.
    Academia de Marinha: 5–16.
Turner, Malcolm. 1988. *Shipwrecks and salvage in South Africa, 1505 to the present*. Cape
    Town: C. Struik.
Van Andel, Tjeerd H. 1989. Late Pleistocene sea levels and the human exploitation of the
    shore and shelf of southern Africa. *Journal of Field Archaeology* 16: 133–155.
Van Meurs, L. H. 1985. *Legal aspects of marine archaeological research*. Cape Town: Institute
    of Marine Law, University of Cape Town.
Van Warmelo, N. J. 1977. *Anthropology of southern Africa in periodicals to 1950: An analysis
    and index*. Johannesburg: Witwatersrand University Press.
Werz, Bruno E. J. S. 1989. Saving a fragment of the underwater heritage: A multi-faceted
    approach. *Cabo: Yearbook of the Historical Society of Cape Town* 4 (4): 13–17.
———. 1990a. A maritime archaeological project in Table Bay. *South African Archaeological
    Bulletin* 45: 121.
———. 1990b. A preliminary step to protect South Africa's undersea heritage. *International
    Journal of Nautical Archaeology and Underwater Exploration* 19 (4): 335–337.
———. 1992a. Tafelbaai gee sy geheime prys. 'n Histories-argeologiese ondersoek van die
    VOC-skip *Oosterland*. *Huguenot Society of South Africa Bulletin* 29: 54–60.
———. 1992b. The excavation of the *Oosterland* in Table Bay: The first systematic exercise in
    maritime archaeology in southern Africa. *South African Journal of Science* 88: 85–89.
———. 1993a. Maritime Archaeological Project Table Bay: Aspects of the first field season.
    South African Archaeological Society Goodwin Series 7: 33–39.
———. 1993b. Shipwrecks of Robben Island, South Africa: An exercise in cultural resource
    management in the underwater environment. *International Journal of Nautical
    Archaeology* 22 (3): 245–256.

———. 1993c. South African shipwrecks and salvage: The need for improved management. *International Journal of Nautical Archaeology* 22 (3): 237–244.

———. 1994a. Maritime archaeology, shipwreck salvage and the role of museums: Some comments. *Southern African Museums Association Bulletin* 20: 8–10.

———. 1994b. Searching for shipwrecks off Robben Island: An exercise in cultural resource management. *Southern African Field Archaeology* 3: 26–32.

———. 1997. Maritime archaeology. In *The archaeology of sub-Saharan Africa: An encyclopedia*, ed. John O. Vogel, 558–560. New York: Garland.

———. 1999a. Between the devil and the deep blue sea: The development and future of maritime archaeology in South Africa. In *Maritime archaeology: Challenges for the new millennium symposium*. Cape Town: World Archaeological Congress 4, 1–12. Available at www.wac.uct.ac.za/symposia/s032.asp/.

———. 1999b. *Diving up the human past: Perspectives of maritime archaeology, with specific reference to developments in South Africa until 1996*. British Archaeological Reports International Series 749. Oxford: BAR.

———. 1999c. Ships of wood and men of steel: Trans-oceanic voyages to the Cape of Good Hope during the seventeenth century. *The early immigration experience in global perspective symposium*. Cape Town: World Archaeological Congress 4, 1–8. Available at www.wac.uct.ac.za/symposia/s032.asp/.

———. 2001. A graveyard of ships: Maritime archaeological research and management of shipwrecks near Robben Island, South Africa. In *Conference proceedings of the 1998 International Congress on Islands in Archaeology, Starnberg, Germany: Archäologie unter Wasser* 3, ed. Wolfgang Schmid, Hubert Beer, and Birgit Sommer, 247–254. München: Bayerische Gesellschaft für Unterwasserarchäologie.

———. 2003a. Cape of Storms or Cape of Good Hope? The development of maritime archaeological research in South Africa and prospects for the future. In *Maritime heritage*, ed. Carlo A. Brebbia and T. Gambin, 75–85. Southampton, UK: Wit Press.

———. 2003b. *Strategic Environmental Assessment (SEA) for the Port of Cape Town and Environmental Impact Assessment (EIA) for the expansion of the Container Terminal Stacking Area: Specialist study in maritime archaeology*. Cape Town: National Ports Authority.

———. 2004. *"Een bedroefd, en beclaaglijck ongeval": De wrakken van de VOC-schepen* Oosterland *en* Waddinxveen *(1697) in de Tafelbaai*. Zutphen, the Netherlands: De Walburg Pers.

———. 2006. The "Vlissingen": A Dutch East India Company ship that perished along the Namibian shore in 1747. In *Namibia and the Netherlands: 350 years of relations*, ed. Huub Hendrix, 20–30. Windhoek, Namibia: Embassy of the Kingdom of the Netherlands.

———. 2007. A suggested blueprint for the development of maritime archaeological research in Namibia. *Journal of Namibian Studies* 2: 103–121.

———. 2008a. Not lost without a trace: The DEIC ship *Vlissingen*, assumed to have foundered near Meob Bay in 1747. *Journal of Namibian Studies* 4: 47–74.

———. 2008b. *The Oranjemund shipwreck project: Phase 2 excavation report*. Unpublished report.

———. 2009a. Ship in the desert: The Namibian treasure wreck. *Salon: Journal of the Society of Antiquaries of London*: 1–8.

———. 2009b. The Oranjemund shipwreck, Namibia: The excavation of sub-Saharan Africa's oldest discovered wreck. *Journal of Namibian Studies* 6: 81–106.

———. 2009c. *The shipwrecks of the* Oosterland *and* Waddinxveen: *1697, Table Bay*. Johannesburg: Zulu Planet.

————. 2010. Sub-Saharan Africa's oldest shipwreck: Historical-archaeological research of an Early Modern Era Portuguese merchantman on the Namibian coast. *Mariner's Mirror* 96 (4): 430–442.

————. In press. *Overture to the South African "Rainbow Nation": 17th century accounts of the wrecking of the* Haarlem *and the establishment of the Cape.* Johannesburg: Zulu Planet.

Werz, Bruno E. J. S., and Nicholas C. Flemming. 2001. Discovery in Table Bay of the oldest handaxes yet found underwater demonstrates preservation of hominid artifacts on the continental shelf. *South African Journal of Science* 97: 183–185.

Werz, Bruno E. J. S., and Jane E. Klose. 1994. Ceramic analysis from the VOC-ship *Oosterland* (1697). *South African Journal of Science* 90: 522–526.

Werz, Bruno E. J. S., Julia A. Lee-Thorp, and Duncan E. Miller. 1991. Amber finds from Table Bay. *International Journal of Nautical Archaeology* 20 (3): 247–249.

Werz, Bruno E. J. S., and Colin G. C. Martin. 1994. Hydrographic surveys in aid of maritime archaeological research: The example of the Table Bay Project. *Hydrographic Journal* 72: 3–15.

Yates, Royden, Anthony Manhire, and John Parkington. 1993. Colonial era paintings in the rock art of the south-western Cape: Some preliminary observations. *South African Archaeological Society Goodwin Series* 7: 59–70.

....

CHAPTER 22

THE RED SEA

....

LUCY BLUE

INTRODUCTION
....

THE Red Sea, so called due to the red hue of the desert landscape that straddles its shores, lies between 30°N and 12°30′N and is one of the youngest seas on the planet (Figure 22.1). Extending over 1,900 km, this long, narrow body of water is the product of a triple rift system: the Arabian Plate and two parts of the Africa Plate (the Nubian and the Somalian). To the south it is linked through the narrow straits of the Bab al Mandab to the Gulf of Aden and the Arabian Sea and hence to the Indian Ocean. In the north, since the construction of the Suez Canal in the nineteenth century, and much earlier by an indirect canalized link to the River Nile, the Red Sea connects with the Mediterranean Sea (Head 1987; Tomber 2008: 65–66; Cooper 2009). Thus, despite its arid and inhospitable desert coastline, it has been an important highway for maritime trade and shipping along and across its length since antiquity.

ENVIRONMENTAL CONTEXT
....

The Red Sea has a negligible tidal range (max. of 90 cm) but is dominated by fierce and persistent north-northwesterly winds, particularly in its northern reaches. In the south, the Indian Ocean monsoon weather patterns dictate the wind regime, causing the wind to blow from the north in the winter and the south in the summer. The prevailing winds have greatly influenced the way that ancient seafarers navigated these treacherous waters, contributing to the traditional view that the Red Sea

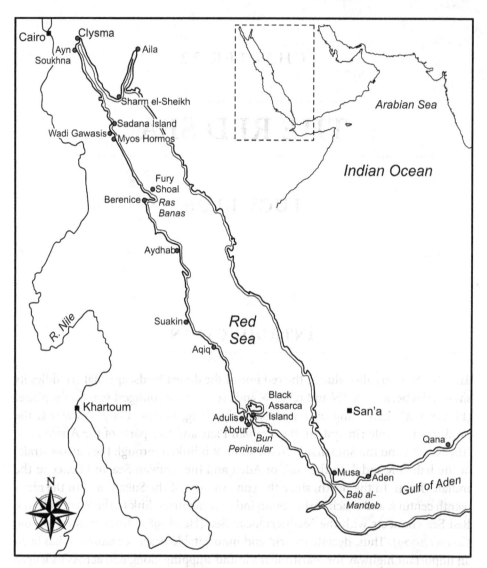

Figure 22.1 Map of the Red Sea indicating the location of sites referred to in the text. Reproduced with the kind permission of the Quseir al-Qadim Southampton University project.

served as a barrier to maritime communications (Davies and Morgan 1995; Facey 2004; Whitewright 2007). Despite the tough weather regime and what was, in fact, frequent maritime traffic, remarkably few shipwrecks have been discovered to provide us with an insight into the nature of seafaring and trading activities.

The limited number of shipwrecks identified in the Red Sea to date is both a product of the environmental context and limited systematic research. Preservation is a critical issue in this region, as the coral coastline, warm seas, and deep waters are not conducive to the preservation of shipwreck and organic materials, at least in locations and depths accessible to divers. Until recently, relatively little research had been conducted in this region, either underwater or on land, contributing to the scarce shipwreck archive available for academic research. Thus, this chapter will address the limited shipwreck evidence and also draw on a range of diverse evidence, from coastal settlements, silted port sites, and maritime artifacts, to ancient texts, iconographic images, and ethnographic indicators of past activities, in order to provide some insight into the maritime archaeological record of the Red Sea.

Prehistory

Some of the earliest evidence for human activity in a coastal environment anywhere in the world can be found along the southern shores of the Red Sea. Recent discoveries confirm that in the Middle Stone Age, some 125,000 years ago, early modern humans (*Homo sapiens*) settled a coastal strip on the Buri Peninsula, in what is now modern Eritrea (Bruggemann et al. 2004; Walter et al. 2000). Palaeolithic flake and blade tools discovered at the site of Abdur were found in association with discarded shallow marine molluscs and crustaceans, which included edible oysters that may have been harvested and processed at the site. Not only does this discovery have implications for early human exploitation of the marine resource; it also, when viewed in the context of other Palaeolithic discoveries on both sides of the Red Sea and in light of subsequent lower sea levels, serves as evidence for some of the earliest coastal migrations out of Africa (Bailey and Flemming 2008; Bailey et al. 2007; Stringer 2000).

Direct evidence for prehistoric maritime activities in the Red Sea region is extremely scarce. Material culture of a similar nature recovered from sites on both sides of the southern Red Sea gives an indication of the extent of maritime contact, communication, and trade along the waterway. However, the nature of maritime activities is rather restricted to evidence largely derived from the Nile Valley, from wall paintings, reliefs, and inscriptions that describe, among other things, trips to the mythical land of "Punt." "Punt" was located somewhere yet to be determined, in the southern region of the Red Sea or beyond (Kitchen 2009). Trade was conducted primarily to import frankincense and other exotic commodities to the pharaohs. Evidence for such voyages date from the Old Kingdom onward, and one of the primary sources of data relating to the nature of the vessels undertaking these voyages comes from the temple of Hatshepsut at Deir el-Bahri (circa 1473–1458 BCE), where a wonderful relief displays a naval expedition to Punt, illustrates the route, the trade goods, and most importantly the ships that conducted this trade (Bard and Fattovich 2007: 17–23; Casson 1971: fig. 18). Until recently the only physical evidence available for ships and boats of this era were confined to the Nile Valley (Vinson 1994; Ward 2000). However, recent finds excavated in caves at the site of Wadi Gawasis (Bard and Fattovich 2007), on the Egyptian Red Sea coast some 23 km south of Safaga, add to our knowledge of this trade. Limestone anchors first identified in the

1970s (Sayed 1977), plus over 40 ship planks, structural elements, and rigging components, are among the wealth of archaeological finds dating to the Middle and
New Kingdom. A number of steering blades up to 2 m long were also discovered
(Ward and Zazzaro 2007). The primary ship construction technique noted is that of
double, unpegged mortise-and-tenon joints. Some ligature holes have also been
identified on the planks, often in association with copper strips; this method of
fastening appears to be unique to the region.

A second site that promises further insight into the construction of Twelfth
and Thirteenth Dynasty ships is the site of Ayn Soukhna on the coast of the Gulf of
Suez in the Sinai, where charred remains of stored ship timbers were recently
located (El-Raziq, Castel, and Tallet 2006). The timbers belong to ships constructed
of planks secured by double rows of unpegged mortise-and-tenon joints with intermittent stitching. Excavations at both of these sites are ongoing, and further publications will no doubt reveal more insight into the construction of early Red Sea
vessels.

Based on the limited evidence available, it would appear that the construction of the Wadi Gawasis ship timbers share some similarities with finds from
the Nile Valley region. As in the Khufu, Dashur, and Lisht vessels from the Nile
Valley, which are all of a similar date, none of the fastenings used in their construction penetrate the thickness of the hull. Both Khufu and Lisht have ligature
fastenings, although, rather than copper, "rope" in the case of Khufu and "plaited
strips of twisted grass fibers" for Lisht are the materials employed (Ward 2000:
115–119). Similarly, mortise-and-tenon fastenings are present in all four vessels.
Thus, the traditions of the Red Sea and Nile Valley, while not identical, have parallels and would appear to differ from the limited remains we have of vessels
from the subsequent Roman era, when the influence of Mediterranean shipbuilding tradition exerts a greater influence.

ROMAN RED SEA PORTS AND TRADE

From at least the middle of the second millennium BCE and no doubt earlier,
vessels were plying the waters of the Red Sea to "Punt" and beyond to bring back
myrrh and frankincense, along with other exotic artifacts of trade and tribute
(Bard and Fattovich 2007; Casson 1989: 11, n. 2). Subsequent voyages were undertaken by Phoenician, Arab, and Indian seafarers. However, it was not until descriptions given by the classical geographers, most importantly the *Periplus Maris
Erythraei* (Casson 1989), written by an anonymous Greek author in the mid-first
century CE and describing voyages within the Red Sea and beyond, that detailed
evidence for these seafaring activities was forthcoming (Sidebotham 1986). Thus,
under Ptolemaic rule, and later when Egypt became part of the Roman Empire,
merchants plied the route to Arabia and India in ever-increasing numbers. Key to

this expansion of trade and maritime activity was the role of harbors in facilitating an interface between land and sea and as a conduit for the transfer and storage of goods.

> Of all the designated harbours of the Erythraean Sea and the ports of trade on it, first comes Egypt's ports of Myos Hormos and, beyond it, after a sail of 1800 stades to the right, Berenicê. The ports of both are bays of the Red Sea on the edge of Egypt. (*Periplus Maris Erythraei* 1)

It would be no exaggeration to suggest that the sister ports of Myos Hormos and Berenice were Rome's gateway to the East. Founded by Ptolemy II Philadelphus sometime in the mid-third century BCE, the ports would later become central points in a communications axis that stretched from the Mediterranean to the coasts of India. Strabo (*Geog.* 2.5.12) indicated that over 120 ships sailed annually for southern Arabia and India from the port of Myos Hormos. Both ports have been identified and partially excavated and provide valuable insight into the nature of maritime trade (Casson 1989; Peacock and Blue 2006; Sidebotham 1986; Sidebotham and Wendrich 2007; Tomber 2008; Whitcomb and Johnson 1979, 1982a, 1982b).

The Roman town of Myos Hormos (Islamic Quseir al-Qadim) was located on a peninsula, with the sea on one side and a lagoon, now silted, on the other. Excavations revealed part of a late-first-century BCE to early-third-century CE Roman waterfront in the lagoon to the west of the main settlement (Blue 2007). The harbor extended from the edge of a narrow strip of late Pleistocene coral bedrock out into the lagoon to form a wharf or jetty constructed of amphorae (Figure 22.2). Amphorae, packed with earth, broken amphorae shards, and lithics, were arranged in rows and then sealed by a surface of trampled earth. The structure formed an artificial extension to the foreshore that facilitated and extended access across the waterlogged sediments at the margins of the lagoon. The amphorae within it date the feature to the late first century BCE or early first century CE. This feature is unique along the Red Sea coast but finds parallels in the Mediterranean Sea (Bernal et al. 2005). Another wharflike feature was noted to the north of the "jetty" in the form of a stone seawall that was later replaced by stone blocks arranged in a series of headers and stretchers consolidated with mortar (Blue 2007). During the course of the first century CE the harbor is believed to have been subject to siltation. By the beginning of the third century CE, the site was abandoned, perhaps partially because the harbor silted up completely.

In the narrow entrance to the mersa or bay at Quseir al-Qadim a few amphorae dating to the first century CE have been identified at a water depth of over 40 m. It is believed that these amphorae were jettisoned from a vessel as she struggled to enter the harbor, as the remains are not substantial enough to indicate a shipwreck (Underwood, pers. comm.).

Berenice appears to have suffered a similar fate to its sister port of Myos Hormos. The anchorage slowly infilled with sediment over time. The site was settled in the Ptolemaic period, was occupied until the sixth century CE, and

Figure 22.2 Myos Hormos: View of the Roman harbor amphorae foundation of the jetty "hard" in the silted lagoon. Reproduced with the kind permission of the Quseir al-Qadim Southampton University project.

was extensively excavated by a Dutch and American team (Sidebotham and Wendrich, 1995, 1996, 1999, 2000). It is located on a headland with a silted lagoon to the south, which is believed to have been the ancient harbor. A series of large walls, up to 1.2 m wide and mostly constructed from coral blocks, were identified around the edges of the settlement and were interpreted as seawalls or quays for boats to moor against. Although the anchorage was first utilized in the Ptolemaic period, the identified quays largely date to the first century CE, with one example toward the east of the site dating to the fifth century CE (Harrell 2007). Today the site and its former harbor are cut off from each other by a sandbar, the formation of which is likely to have led to the demise of the port in the sixth century CE.

An important question that remains to be answered relates to the exact nature of the ships that sailed the Red Sea during the Roman period. Roman merchantmen are known to have operated here often alongside vessels from the Indian Ocean. How these boats differed in their construction has yet to be determined; however, maritime artifacts have been uncovered from excavations at both Myos Hormos and Berenice, largely in secondary contexts, that provide some clues. These include fragments of wooden planking, all of which display mortise-and-tenon fastenings characteristic of ship construction techniques of the Roman Mediterranean, together with a number that have in situ pegs (treenails) that would have secured the tenons. This type of edge fastening is typical of the shell-first tradition of shipbuilding that was common in the Mediterranean until the late Antique period (Pomey 2004; Steffy 1994: 23–78; Carlson in this volume). Little is known about the construction of indigenous ships of the Indian Ocean during this period, but they are generally described, by Mediterranean observers, as being of the sewn construction technique (Procopius *Bel. Pers* I.xix.23–26; *Periplus Maria Erythraei* 36; Hourani 1995: 92). However, the remains of planking from Myos Hormos and comparable reused planks from Berenice (Vermeeren 1999: 316) may indicate that at least some of the shipping engaged in the trade between the Red Sea and the wider Indian Ocean was constructed according to the Mediterranean shipbuilding tradition of the time. Further evidence to support the Mediterranean nature of the vessels comes in the form of rigging components and other maritime finds found at the two sites. At Myos Hormos, these components include approximately 169 brail rings (made from both horn and wood), a deadeye, and various sheaves from rigging blocks (Figure 22.3). Several fragments of sailcloth were also discovered at both sites, some still with brail rings attached (Whitewright 2007; Wild and Wild 2001). The general form of the deadeye, sheaves, brail rings, and sailcloth is consistent with vessels operating in the Mediterranean basin during this period, and together they comprise most of the components required to rig a square-sailed vessel (Whitewright 2007). Finally, a graffito of a Mediterranean-style ship found at Berenice reinforces this emerging concept that Mediterranean-style ships prevailed in the Red Sea (Sidebotham 1996: 315–317; Figure 22.4). However, many of the rigging components and plank timbers found were made from Indian teak (*Tectona grandis*) or Indian or East African blackwood (*Dalbergia* sp.), and the sailcloth was made of Indian cotton woven in an Indian weave. This raises the possibility that the rigging and hull elements from Myos Hormos and Berenice are perhaps representative of sailing vessels of Indian Ocean origin, albeit rigged in a Mediterranean style. Thus, the finds from these two critical ports have provided significant insight into the nature of ships of trade and of the ports they frequented that participated in Indo-Roman trade.

Additional ports along the Red Sea coast were critical to both Indo-Roman and late Antique trade both within the Red Sea and beyond (Casson 1989; Peacock and Blue 2007b). From north to south the most important ports of trade also included Clysma, Aila, Ptolemais Theron, Adulis, Muza, and Qana. Ptolemais Theron is believed to have been located close to the modern village of Aqiq in southern Sudan (Casson 1989: 51; Seeger et al. 2006), and according to Strabo (*Geog.* 16.4.7) the port was founded as a base to support hunting elephants ordered by Ptolemy II Philadelphus (286–246 BCE). Muza has been associated with modern Mocha in Yemen. Aden (Eudaimon Arabia) is a major port even today, and is one of the very few to remain viable from the time of the *Periplus Maris Erythraei*, even though the precise

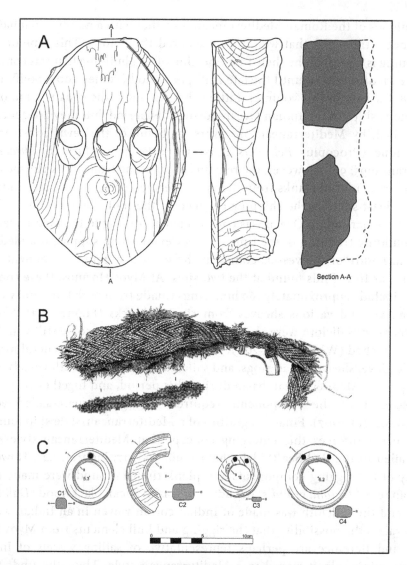

Figure 22.3 Maritime artifacts from the Roman Red Sea port of Myos Hormos: (a) Deadeye from the standing rigging of a sailing ship rigged with a Mediterranean square-sail, mid- to late second century CE, made from *Dalbergia* sp. (b) Sail fragment or Indian cotton with attached wooden brail ring, late first or early second century CE. (c) Examples of wooden brail rings with one (C1) or two (C3 and C4) attachment holes. C2 dates between the mid-second and mid-third centuries CE and is made from *Dalbergia* sp. C3 dates between the late first and early second centuries CE and is made from a wood of Indian origin, *Wrightia* sp. Reproduced with the kind permission of J. Whitewright.

location of the Roman port has yet to be discovered. The *Periplus Maris Erythraei* (26: 8.22–32) describes it as the meeting place for ships coming from India and Egypt, as neither would attempt to undertake the complete journey. The natural harbor, still utilized today, is sheltered and capacious; at about 10 km wide and 5 km deep, it is more substantial than any of the ports hitherto considered. The site of

Figure 22.4 Berenice ship graffito after Sidebotham 1996 and Sidebotham and
Wendrich 1995: 315–317. Reproduced with their kind permission.

Qana (Kane) is well known and has been the subject of a long-term excavation
(Sedov 2007). The site lies on a peninsula overlooked by the citadel of Husn al-
Ghurab. There are sandy bays to the north and south that would have been excellent
for beaching boats, although no harbor installations have yet been found (Peacock
and Blue 2007b).

A recent survey at the port of Adulis sheds light on the location of both its ports
of trade. The site is located on the shore of the Gulf of Zula, coastal Eritrea, and
operated as a port from at least the time of the *Periplus Maris Erythraei* until the
period of Aksumite trade between the fourth and seventh centuries CE (Peacock
and Blue 2007a). Adulis is connected to the great city of Aksum on the Ethiopian
plateau by a tortuous mountain route. It was a source of luxuries such as ivory, shell,
and horn, and afforded a good harbor on the route to India. Recent discoveries have
confirmed the location of the two ports that at different times served the city of
Adulis. One is the harbor of Gabaza, which is located on the mainland to the south
of Adulis. The Red Sea winds are less ferocious here, and ships would moor in the
lee of Diodorus Island just offshore. The second is the harbor on the offshore island
of Orienê, modern Dese. Oreinê had a magnificent lagoonal harbor and an adjacent
settlement in the central valley of the island (Peacock and Blue 2007a).

SHIPWRECKS

Fury Shoals

Lying around a coral outcrop known as the Fury Shoals, to the north of Ras Banas, Egypt, is a Roman shipwreck referred to as the Fury Shoals wreck. The vessel lies in 7–10 m of water and is believed to have sunk after she hit the coral reef. As a result of the exposed and shallow nature of the vessel, much of her cargo has been washed away or removed by divers. The site, which holds no visible signs of hull remains, consists of Dressel 2–4 type amphorae that date the wreck to the first century CE.

Black Assarca Island

A wreck dating to between the late fourth and early seventh century CE was partially excavated in 1997 off the island of Black Assarca, a barren rock outcrop located off the Buri Peninsula, Eritrea. The wreck sits on a sandy seabed in 4–6 m of water and is approximately 9 m long. Among other artifacts, the cargo consists predominantly of amphorae of a type the excavators referred to as "Assarca Types I–III." These amphorae appear to have strong parallels with those produced in Aqaba during this period, known as Aqaba or Aila amphorae (Tomber 2008: 92). Only a few amphorae remained intact, but many contained traces of pitch. No hull remains were identified, but the vessel was only excavated to 1 m below the sandy seabed. The site is believed to be linked with late Roman and Byzantine trade in the Red Sea and particularly with Adulis and the Kingdom of Aksum, which was, until the rise of Islam, the predominant power in the region (Pedersen 2000).

Sadana Island

Between 1994 and 1998, INA-Egypt conducted the excavation of an Ottoman period shipwreck near Sadana Island, Safaga, to the north of Quseir on the Egyptian Red Sea coast. The vessel dated to the second half of the eighteenth century and because of its location is referred to as the Sadana Island wreck. The ship lies in 28–40 m of water and is more than 50 m long and at least 15 m wide; it may have carried up to 900 tons of cargo. Over 3,500 artifacts were recovered, about one-third of which were pieces of Chinese porcelain intended for the Middle Eastern market. The vessel also carried earthenware vessels, including *kullal* (small clay water vessels), glass bottles, and copper artifacts associated with the galley. Recovered organic materials included a substantial cargo of coffee, as well as frankincense and coconuts, and a number of tree branches (Haldane 1996; Khalil and Mustafa 2002; Ward 2001). The vessel was characterized by massive hull timbers of oak and pine joined by iron fastenings. The floors were widely spaced, and two layers of planking were recorded toward the stern of the vessel. Three levels of huge knees were identified, indicating a three-decked vessel. Despite the large amount of Chinese porcelain, which suggests strong links with the Kangxi period Qing dynasty, the excavators believe the ship was a Muslim vessel, possibly Egyptian in origin (Haldane 1996; Khalil and Mustafa 2002; Ward 2001). A ship of a slightly earlier date with a similar cargo was excavated in the region of Sharm el-Sheikh, although on this shipwreck very few porcelain shards remained among the many *kullal* water vessels (Raban 1971).

Islamic Ships, Shipwrecks, and Seafaring of the Red Sea and Indian Ocean

The Red Sea was as important to medieval shipping as it was to Indo-Roman trade; trade goods and, importantly, pilgrims en route to the holy city of Mecca were conveyed through ports such as Al-Quseir, Aydhab, Suakin, and Jeddah (Tibbetts 1971, 1961). However, our knowledge of ships of the Islamic era is limited, since shipwrecks of this period in the Red Sea continue to be as elusive as those of earlier periods. Fortunately, excavation of the medieval necropolis of Quseir al-Qadim has proved to be a fruitful source for Islamic ship-finds (Blue 2006, although subsequent reinterpretation of the timber species has altered the original findings, as indicated below). Planks recovered in reused contexts, such as covering a cist-type grave that dates to between the late twelfth and early fifteenth centuries CE, appear formerly to have been sewn ship timbers (McGrail and Kentley 1985). These timbers were regularly shaped planks (700–980 mm in length; 100–160 mm in breadth; 30–35 mm average thickness; Figure 22.5). The wood is in very poor condition, and six of the seven planks are of an unidentified hardwood, probably non-native to Egypt. The preliminary identification of some of these timbers as teak wood (Blue 2006) is now known to be incorrect (see Whitewright, Blue, and Thomas forthcoming). The planks were originally fastened together with fibers sewn through holes along the edges. A few of the holes still contained fibers of coconut coir and were secured with wooden pegs, with traces of bitumen still visible on at least one side of the planks. A number of the holes located along the plank edges were fed by a channel or groove recessed into the wood on one side of the timber. The recess extended at a right angle from the hole to the plank edge. Some of these recessed channels had coconut coir in situ. The fact that both the bitumen and the recesses for the coir stitches are uniformly located on the same side of the planks would indicate that this side of the planks had originally been on the outside of the hull. The practice of cutting recessed channels from the stitch hole to the edge of the plank on the outside of the hull has been identified as a feature of sewn boat construction and is seen as a means of protecting the coir stitch. As Severin (1985: 283) observed in the construction of the Omani Boom Sohar, "A groove was cut between

Figure 22.5 Islamic sewn boat timbers reused on a tomb from Quseir al-Qadim.
Reproduced with the kind permission of the Quseir al-Qadim Southampton
University project.

the pairs of holes, on the outside of the hull, so that the cord was recessed and protected from chafe."

A second tomb was recorded at the Islamic necropolis of Quseir al-Qadim. In
contrast to the first, this tomb was covered in short, stocky, and irregularly shaped
reused timbers that had once been fastened by iron nails. These may also have been
ship planking and date to a similar period. What is different is their iron fastenings,
which, if the interpretation as ship timbers proves correct, could have interesting
implications for our understanding of the construction of vessels in this period (see
below; Whitewright, Blue, and Thomas forthcoming). Evidence for further timber
and rigging elements from the twelfth- to fifteenth-century Islamic settlement of the
site is extremely limited. However, during previous excavations at the site (Whitcomb
and Johnson 1979, 1982a, 1982b), one of the many fragments of paper recovered was
noted to depict an image of a ship. Dating to the Mamluk period, thirteenth through

fourteenth century, the vessel appears to be "single masted, perhaps with a yardarm to hold a lateen sail," and "seems to have a substantial deck-house amidships" (Nicolle 1989: 181, fig. 28). The image, however, is extremely crude and damaged, thus limiting detailed interpretation.

The distinguishing feature of Arab craft of the Indian Ocean and the Red Sea from antiquity until the late twentieth century is generally agreed to be "the use of fiber, rather than nails, to sew the planks of hulls together" (Said 1991: 107). The earliest-known sewn boats come from Ras al-Jinz in Oman and date to the third millennium BCE (Cleuziou and Tosi 2000). The first historical reference to "small sewn boats" is in the first-century CE *Periplus Maris Erythraei* (Casson 1989: 141, 15.5.30). However, most of the evidence for what has become known as the traditional Arab construction technique is restricted to later references by travelers, historians, and geographers, and to a few sketchy iconographic depictions (Hourani 1995).

In the sixth century CE in the Persian Gulf, it appears that "all the boats which are found in India and on this sea . . . are bound together with a kind of cording" (Procopius *Bel. Pers.* I.19.23). Abu-Zaid Hassan of Siraf, writing in the tenth century CE, describes how the people of Oman traveled to the Maldives and Laccadives and, having felled and prepared the timbers, stripped the bark of coconut trees to produce yarn, "wherewith they sew the planks together." In the twelfth century CE, Ibn-Jubayr describes the sewn vessels built at 'Aydhab in more detail: "for they are stitched with cords of coir, which is the husk of the coconut; this they thrash until it becomes stringy, then they twist from it cords with which they stitch the ship" (Hourani 1995: 92; McGrail 2001: 72). The painting that accompanies the 1237 CE manuscript of Al Hariri's *Maqamat* from Iraq is a most convincing image of a sewn vessel. It shows a double-ended vessel with sewn planking (Hourani 1995: 92, plate 7). Marco Polo visited the Persian Gulf twice at the end of the thirteenth century CE and describes the ships as "bad" and states how "many get lost for they have no iron fastenings, being only stitched together with cord made from the husk of Indian nut" (Johnstone and Muir 1964). Vasco da Gama noted Arab vessels along the coast of Mozambique in the fifteenth century CE built without nails, their planks being held together by cords, as did Lancaster a century later (Johnstone and Muir 1964). Even today, there are a number of examples of stitched vessels in use around the shores of the Red Sea and Indian Ocean, including the *sambuk* of the Dhofari coast of Oman, and the *masula* of India (McGrail and Kentley 1985).

The implication, therefore, is that iron nails were not adopted in the construction of boats and ships in the region until the arrival of the Portuguese and that even then the practice of attaching planks by means of stitching was not comprehensively abandoned (Hornell 1942; Johnstone and Muir 1964; Moreland 1939). However, if the timbers from the second tomb at Quseir al-Qadim are in fact ship timbers, this would indicate the use of iron nails well before the arrival of the Europeans, at least in this part of the Red Sea (Whitewright, Blue, and Thomas forthcoming).

THE MARITIME ETHNOGRAPHIC RECORD

Recourse to ethnographic data has provided insight into the dying traditions of boat and ship construction along the shores of the Red Sea and beyond, supplementing the limited iconographic dataset and thin archaeological record. Besides the few remaining examples of traditional sewn vessels, which are now limited to a small number of boats in Yemen, and a handful of tied/lashed log rafts, the only other example of traditional boatbuilding practice that survives in the Red Sea and the northern reaches of the Indian Ocean is the log boat or dugout referred to as a *huri*. *Huri* are known to have operated in the Indian Ocean and Red Sea region for at least two millennia (*Periplus Maris Erythraei* 15), so they have great historical depth. Boxhall (1989: 295) states, "The small *huri* a canoe . . . is to be found on almost every coast of the Indian Ocean." The word *huri* is believed to to have come from the Sanskrit word *hoda*, which was later known in Hindu as *hōṛī* (Glidden 1942). Limited interest has been shown in these vessels in the past (Hornell 1920: 148, 1942; LeBaron Bowen 1952: 198; Moore 1920: 138; Prados 1997), but recently the University of Southampton has undertaken a comprehensive survey of the vessels along the shores of the Red Sea and the Indian Ocean in order to arrive at a better appreciation of their distribution, constructional variety, and shape through time.

Traditions are changing and many of these windows into the past are rapidly disappearing. Studies of an ethnographic nature help to provide specific detail of how similar vessels could have been constructed in the Red Sea during antiquity, providing a record of a dying tradition, as many boats are being replaced by reinforced fiberglass. At the same time, these studies allow us to ask bigger questions about the criteria that determine construction techniques and how these change depending on the effects of, among other things, environment, culture, and history. This approach has both "width," in that there are many different types still in existence that operate in environmentally similar conditions, and "depth," in that there is a good historical record (Adams 2003; Blue 2003; McGrail et al. 2003).

CONCLUSION

This short section has attempted to summarize what is known to date about the maritime archaeological record of the Red Sea. Unfortunately, the current archive does not constitute a reliable shipwreck database, there are few iconographic representations of boats, and the documentary evidence is restricted to comments from ancient travelers and sailors' guides such as the *Periplus Maris Erythraei* (Casson 1989). Regardless, we have to work with the material available to explore the nature of maritime activities, cultures, trade, and boats and ships of the region and try to determine how these have changed over time. There is much more to be discovered and learned about this crucial sea that provides a corridor from the Indian Ocean via river and canal to the Mediterranean Sea, thus stimulating maritime activities that have played a critical role for millennia.

REFERENCES

Adams, J. A. 2003. *Ships, innovation and social change—Aspects of carvel shipbuilding in northern Europe 1450–1850*. Stockholm Studies in Archaeology 24. Stockholm Marine Archaeology Reports 3. Stockholm: Stockholm Universitet.

Bailey, G. N., and N. Flemming. 2008. Archaeology of the continental shelf: Marine resources, submerged landscapes and underwater archaeology. *Quaternary Science Reviews* 27 (23–24): 2153–2165.

Bailey, G. N., N. Flemming, G. C. P. King, K. Lambeck, G. Momber, L. Moran, A. Al-Sharekh, and C. Vita-Finzi. 2007. Coastlines, submerged landscapes and human evolution: The Red Sea Basin and the Farasan Islands. *Journal of Island and Coastal Archaeology* 2 (2): 127–160.

Bard, K. A., and R. Fattovich, eds. 2007. *Harbor of the pharaohs to the land of Punt: Archaeological investigations at Mersa/Wadi Gawasis Egypt, 2001–2005*. Naples: Università Degli Studi di Napoli "L'Orientale."

Bernal, D., A. M. Saez, R. Montero, J. J. Diaz, A. Saez, D. Moreno, and Y. T. Toboso. 2005. Instalaciones fluvio-maritimas de drenaje con anforas Romanas: A propositio del embarcadero flavio del cano de sancti pertir (San Fernando, Cadiz). *Revista de Prehistoria y Aqueologia de la Universidad de Sevilla* 14: 179–230.

Blue, L. 2003. Maritime ethnography: The reality of analogy. In *Boats, ships and shipyards: Proceedings of the 9th International Symposium on Boat and Ship Archaeology, Venice 2000*, ed. C. Beltrame, 334–338. Oxford: Oxbow.

———. 2006. Sewn boat timbers from the medieval Islamic port of Quseir al-Qadim on the Red Sea coast of Egypt. In *Connected by the sea: 10th International Symposium of Boat and Ship Archaeology, Roskilde, Denmark*, ed. L. Blue, F. Hocker, and A. Englert, 277–283. Oxford: Oxbow.

———. 2007. Locating the harbour: Myos Hormos/Quseir al-Qadim; A Roman and Islamic port on the Red Sea coast of Egypt. *International Journal of Nautical Archaeology* 36 (2): 265–281.

Boxhall, P. 1989. Arabian seafarers in the Indian Ocean. *Asian Affairs* 20: 287–295.

Bruggemann, J. H., R. T. Buffler, M. M. Guillaume, R. C. Walter, R. von Cosel, B. N. Ghebretensae, and S. M. Berhe. 2004. Stratigraphy, palaeoenvironments and model for the deposition of the Abdur Reef Limestone: Context for an important archaeological site from the last interglacial on the Red Sea coast of Eritrea. *Paleogeography, Palaeoclimatology, Palaeoecology* 20: 179–206.

Casson, L. 1971. *Ships and seafaring in the ancient world*. Princeton, NJ: Princeton University Press.

———. 1989. *The Periplus Maris Erythraei*. Princeton, NJ: Princeton University Press.

Cleuziou, S., and M. Tosi. 2000. Ra's al-Jinz and the prehistoric coastal cultures of the Ja'alan. *Journal of Oman Studies* 11: 19–73.

Cooper, J. 2009. Egypt's Nile–Red Sea canals: Chronology, location, seasonality and function. In *Connected hinterlands: Proceedings of Red Sea Project IV held at the University of Southampton, September 2008*, ed. L. Blue, J. Cooper, R. Thomas, and J. Whitewright, 195–209. Society for Arabian Studies Monographs. BAR S2052. Oxford Archeopress.

Davies, S., and E. Morgan. 1995. *Red Sea pilot*. London: Imray Laurie Norie and Wilson.

El-Raziq, M. A., G. Castel, and P. Tallet. 2006. Ayn Soukhna and la mer Rouge. *Egypte, Afrique and Orient* 41: 3–6.

Facey, W. 2004. The Red Sea: The wind regime and location of ports. In *Trade and travel in the Red Sea region: Proceedings of the Red Sea Project I; Society for Arabian Studies Monographs No. 2*, ed. P. Lunde and A. Porter, 7–17. BAR International Series 1269. Oxford: BAR.

Glidden, H. W. 1942. A comparative study of Arabic nautical vocabulary from Al-'Aqabah, Transjordan. *Journal of American Oriental Society* 62 (1): 68–71.

Haldane, C. 1996. Sadana Island shipwreck, Egypt: Preliminary report. *International Journal of Nautical Archaeology* 25 (2): 83–94.

Harrell, J. A. 2007. Geology. In *Berenike 1999/2000: Report on the excavation*, ed. S. E. Sidebotham and W. Wendrich, 166–168. Los Angeles: Cotsen Institute of Archaeology, University of California.

Head, S. M. 1987. Introduction. In *Key environments: The Red Sea*, ed. A. J. Edwards and S. M. Head, 1–21. Oxford: Pergamon.

Hornell, J. 1920. The origins and ethnological significance of Indian boat designs. *Memoirs of the Asiatic Society of Bengal* 7: 134–256.

———. 1942. A tentative classification of Arab sea-craft. *Mariner's Mirror* 28: 11–40.

Hourani, G. F. 1995. *Arab seafaring in the Indian Ocean*. Princeton, NJ: Princeton University Press.

Johnstone, T. M., and J. Muir. 1964. Some nautical terms in the Kuwaiti dialect of Arabic. *Bulletin of the School of Oriental and African Studies* 27: 299–332.

Khalil, E., and M. Mustafa. 2002. Underwater archaeology in Egypt. In *International handbook of underwater archaeology*, ed. C. V. Ruppé and J. F. Barstad, 519–534. New York: Plenum Series in Underwater Archaeology.

Kitchen, K. 2009. Ancient polities and interrelations along the Red Sea and its west and east hinterlands. In *Connected hinterlands: Proceedings of Red Sea Project IV held at the University of Southampton, September 2008*, ed. L. Blue, J. Cooper, R. Thomas, and J. Whitewright, 3–8. Society for Arabian Studies Monographs, BAR S2052. Oxford Archeopress.

LeBaron Bowen, R. 1952. Primitive watercraft of Arabia. *American Neptune* 12: 186–221.

McGrail, S. 2001. *Boats of the world*. Oxford: Oxford University Press.

McGrail, S., L. Blue, E. Kentley, and C. Palmer, eds. 2003. *Boats of South Asia*. London: Routledge.

McGrail, S., and E. Kentley, eds. 1985. *Sewn plank boats—archaeological and ethnographic papers based on those presented to a conference at Greenwich in November 1984*. National Maritime Museum, Greenwich, Archaeological Series No. 10. BAR International Series 276. Oxford: BAR.

Moore, A. 1920. Craft of the Red Sea and the Gulf of Aden. *Mariner's Mirror* 6 (1): 73–76; 6 (2): 98–105.

Moreland, W. H. 1939. The ships of the Arabian Sea about A.D. 1500. *Journal of the Royal Asiatic Society of London* 1: 63–74.

Nicolle, D. 1989. Shipping in Islamic art. *American Neptune* 49 (3): 168–197.

Peacock, D., and L. Blue, eds. 2006. *Myos Hormos—Quseir al-Qadim: Roman and Islamic ports on the Red Sea*. Vol. 1, *Survey and Excavations 1999-2003*. Oxford: Oxbow.

———, eds. 2007a. *The ancient Red Sea port of Adulis, Eritrea*. Oxford: Oxbow.

———. 2007b. Appendix: The topography of Periplus ports; A comparison. In *The ancient Red Sea port of Adulis, Eritrea*, ed. D. Peacock and L. Blue, 135–140. Oxford: Oxbow.

Peacock, D., and D. Williams, eds. 2007. *Food for the gods: New light on the ancient incense trade*. Oxford: Oxbow.

Pedersen, R. K. 2000. Under the Erythaean Sea: An ancient shipwreck in Eritrea. *INA Quarterly* 27 (2/3): 3–12.

Pomey, P. 2004. Principles and methods of construction in ancient naval architecture. In *The philosophy of shipbuilding: Conceptual approaches to the study of wooden ships*, ed. F. Hocker and C. Ward, 25–36. College Station: Texas A&M University Press.

Prados, E. 1997. Indian Ocean littoral maritime evolution: The case of the Yemeni *Huri* and *Sambuq*. *Mariner's Mirror* 83 (2): 185–198.

Raban, A. 1971. The shipwreck off Sharm el-Sheikh. *Archaeology* 24 (2): 146–155.

Said, F. 1991. *Oman: A seafaring nation*. 2nd ed. Oman: Ministry of National Heritage and Culture, Sultanate of Oman.

Sayed, A. M. 1977. Discovery of the 12th Dynasty port of Wadi Gawasis on the Red Sea shore. *Revue d'Égyptologie* 29: 140–178.

Sedov, A. 2007. The port of Qana' and the incense trade. In *Food for the gods: New light on the ancient incense trade*, ed. D. Peacock and D. Williams, 71–111. Oxford: Oxbow.

Seeger, J. A., S. E. Sidebotham, J. A. Harrell, and M. Pons. 2006. A brief archaeological survey of the Aqiq region (Red Sea coast) Sudan. *Sahara* 17: 7–18.

Severin, T. 1985. Construction of the Omani Boom *Sohar*. In *Sewn plank boats—archaeological and ethnographic papers based on those presented to a conference at Greenwich in November 1984*, ed. S. McGrail and E. Kentley, 279–288. National Maritime Museum, Greenwich, Archaeological Series No. 10, BAR International Series 276. Oxford: BAR.

Sidebotham, S. E. 1986. *Roman economic policy in the Erythra Thalassa 30 BCE–CE 217*. Leiden: E. J. Brill.

———. 1996. The Ship Graffito. In *Berenike 1995: Preliminary report of the 1995 excavation at Berenike and the survey of the Eastern Desert*, ed. S. E. Sidebotham and W. Z. Wendrich, 315–317. Leiden: Research School of Asian, African and Amerindian Studies (CNWS).

Sidebotham, S. E., and W. Z. Wendrich, eds. 1995. *Berenike '94: Report of the excavations at Berenike (Egyptian Red Sea coast) and the survey of the Egyptian Eastern Desert*. Leiden: Research School of Asian, African and Amerindian Studies (CNWS).

———, eds. 1996. *Berenike '95: Report of the excavations at Berenike (Egyptian Red Sea coast) and the survey of the Egyptian Eastern Desert*. Leiden: Research School of Asian, African and Amerindian Studies (CNWS).

———, eds. 1999. *Berenike '97: Report of the excavations at Berenike (Egyptian Red Sea coast) and the survey of the Egyptian Eastern Desert including excavations at Shenshef*. Leiden: Research School of Asian, African and Amerindian Studies (CNWS).

———, eds. 2000. *Berenike '98: Report of the excavations at Berenike (Egyptian Red Sea coast) and the survey of the Egyptian Eastern Desert, including excavations at Kalalat*. Leiden: Research School of Asian, African and Amerindian Studies (CNWS).

———, eds. 2007. *Berenike 1999/2000: Report on the excavation*. Los Angeles: Costen Institute of Archaeology, University of California.

Steffy, J. R. 1994. *Wooden ship building and the interpretation of shipwrecks*. College Station: Texas A&M University Press.

Stringer, C. 2000. Coasting out of Africa. *Nature* 405 (May): 24–27.

Tibbetts, G. R. 1961. Arab navigation in the Red Sea. *Geographical Journal* 127: 322–334.

———. 1971. *Arab navigation in the Indian Ocean before the coming of the Portuguese*. London: Royal Asiatic Society of Great Britain and Ireland.

Tomber, R. 2008. *Indo-Roman trade: From pots to pepper*. London: Duckworth Debates in Archaeology.

Vermeeren, C. E. 1999. Wood and charcoal. In *Berenike 1997: Report of the 1997 excavations at Berenike and the survey of the Egyptian Eastern Desert including excavations at Shenshef*, ed. S. E. Sidebotham and W. Z. Wendrich, 307–324. Leiden: Research School CNWS.

Vinson, S. M. 1994. *Egyptian boats and ships*. Buckingham: Shire.

Walter, R. C., et al. 2000. Early human occupation of the Red Sea coast of Eritrea during the last interglacial. *Nature* 405 (May): 65–69.

Ward, C. 2000. *Sacred and secular: Ancient Egyptian ships and boats*. Boston: Archaeological Institute of America.

———. 2001. The Sadana Island shipwreck: A mid-eighteenth century CE merchantman off the Red Sea coast of Egypt. *World Archaeology* 32: 371–385.

Ward, C., and C. Zazzaro. 2007. Finds: Ship evidence. In *Harbor of the pharaohs to the land of Punt: Archaeological investigations at Mersa/Wadi Gawasis Egypt, 2001–2005*, ed. K. A. Bard and R. Fattovich, 135–163. Naples: Università Degli Studi di Napoli "L'Orientale."

Whitcomb, D. S., and J. H. Johnson. 1979. *Quseir al-Qadim 1978: Preliminary report*. Cairo: American Research Centre in Egypt.

———. 1982a. *Quseir al-Qadim 1980: Preliminary report*. American Research Centre in Egypt, Vol. 7. Cairo: Malibu.

———. 1982b. Season of excavation at Quseir al-Qadim. *American Research Centre in Egypt, Newsletter* 120: 24–30.

Whitewright, J. 2007. How fast is fast? Technology, trade and speed under sail in the Roman Red Sea. In *Natural resources and cultural connections of the Red Sea: Proceedings of the Red Sea Project III*, ed. J. P. Starkey and T. Wilkinson, 77–78. Society for Arabian Studies Monographs No. 5, BAR International Series 1661. Oxford: BAR.

Whitewright, J., L. Blue, and R. Thomas. Forthcoming. Ships and ships fittings. In *Myos Hormos—Quseir al-Qadim: Roman and Islamic ports on the Red Sea. Vol. 2, The finds from the 1999–2003 excavations*, ed. D. Peacock and L. Blue. Oxford: Archeopress.

Wild, F. C., and J. P. Wild. 2001. Sails from the Roman port of Berenice. *International Journal of Nautical Archaeology* 30: 211–220.

CHAPTER 23

MARITIME ARCHAEOLOGICAL STUDIES IN INDIA

ANIRUDDH S. GAUR AND KAMLESH H. VORA

INTRODUCTION

IN ancient Indian literature the ocean was referred to as *Ratnakara*, "the bestower of wealth," and a famous Indian myth, *Samudramanthan* (The Churning of the Ocean), echoes this concept of scanning the seabed for pearls, gems, and medicinal seaweeds. Conversely, the destruction by the sea of coastal towns such as Dwarka on India's west coast and Poompuhar on the east have been frequently referred to in ancient literature. Legends are woven around these phenomena observed and passed on from generation to generation.

An ancient Sanskrit text, the *Arthasastra* of Kautilya, provides information regarding a government official called the *navadhyaksha*, the "superintendant of shipping," who was in charge of oceangoing ships and strictly enforced rules for the management of ports. He was empowered to destroy pirates and punish those who did not follow the rules or pay proper taxes (Shamasastry 1915: 105). Further, the anonymous author of the *Periplus of the Erythrean Sea*, dating back to about 60 CE, mentions a chain of ports along the Indian coast (Schoff 1912). The ancient texts, including Indian (such as Sanskrit, Pali, and Tamil Sangam) and foreign sources (Ptolemy's *Geography*, Arian's *Indica*, etc.), have also made ample reference to the existence of harbors and ports along the Indian coast during the historical and medieval periods.

India played a major role in the Indian Ocean trade and the development of shipbuilding technology between 2500 BCE and 1700 BCE (S. R. Rao 1988). The Arabian Sea basin of the Indian Ocean, with its unique winds and currents, shaped the sailing and navigation techniques of the region. The trade network of the third millennium BCE that flourished between the Harappan region, the Persian Gulf, and Mesopotamia was oceanic by its nature and included the Oman Peninsula and Bahrain.

The study of maritime history of India commenced in the first decade of the twentieth century and was largely based on literary data, particularly *Vedas*, *Ramayana*, *Mahabharata*, *Puranas*, and other contemporary Sanskrit, Pali, and Prakrit literature (Mookerji 1912). In the middle of the last century, the large-scale excavations of several Harappan sites in India and Bronze Age sites in the Persian Gulf countries revealed evidence of active maritime interaction between these two geographical regions (see Blue in this volume). There are numerous literary references, as well as sculptural and archaeological evidence, indicating active maritime traditions during the historical period all along the Indian coast. However, it was not until the last quarter of the previous century (in 1981) that a center for marine archaeology was established at the National Institute of Oceanography, Goa, and underwater exploration of the Indian coast began in earnest. In the beginning of the twenty-first century an underwater archaeology wing was established in the Archaeological Survey of India, Government of India.

Submerged Sites and Ports along the Indian Coast

Maritime archaeological investigations have been undertaken at various places along the Indian coast (Figure 23.1) during the last two decades. Several of the known sites are primarily indicated by a concentration of stone anchors (Table 23.1). Brief descriptions of a few important sites are offered below.

Dwarka

The ancient city of Dwarka, situated on the extreme west coast of the Indian territory, occupies an important place in the cultural and religious history of India. The fabulous architecture of the Dwarka temple has attracted tourist from all over the world. It is generally believed that Lord Krishna founded the town by reclaiming land from the sea (Gupt 1944). During its glorious past, Dwarka was a city of beautiful gardens, deep moats, several ponds, and palaces, but it is traditionally believed

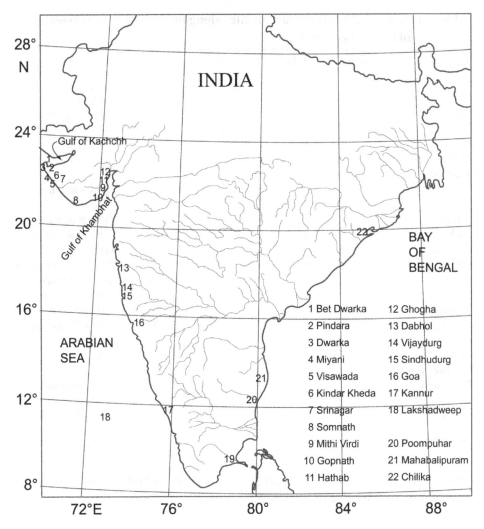

Figure 23.1 Important marine archaeological sites along the Indian coast.
Illustration by the author.

to have become submerged just after the death of Lord Krishna. Due to its historical importance and association with the Indian epic *Mahabharata*, Dwarka continues to attract archaeologists and historians for the antiquity of the site and the historicity of the *Mahabharata*.

Dwarka was the first site in India to be explored by maritime archaeologists, and investigations continued for almost two decades. Extensive diving operations have been undertaken in depths ranging from the intertidal zone to water 25 m deep, 1 km off Dwarka. The nearshore underwater topography consists of beach rock formations, covered with dense vegetation. Thick sand deposits in the small channels are occasionally noticed. Topography beyond 10 m water depth is sandy with rock boulders and sparse vegetation. A number of artifacts were discovered

Table 23.1 Stone anchors from various sites along the Indian coast (current as
of November 2008)

Site	Composite anchors	Indo-Arabia type anchors	Ring stone anchors	Total	References
Dwarka	35	63	25	123	Gaur et al. 2008
Bet Dwarka	25	17	—	42	Gaur et al. 2005
Miyani	2	6	4	12	Gaur et al. 2007b
Visawada	10	2	2	14	Gaur et al. 2007b
Kindar Kheda	1	—	—	1	Gaur et al. 2004
Srinagar	1	—	—	1	
Ghumli	—	—	1	1	Gaur and Tripati 2006
Somnath	35	2	6	43	Gaur et al. 2008
Mithi Virdi	—	4	—	4	Gaur et al. 2005d
Gopnath	—	1	—	1	Gaur and Bhatt 2008
Hathab	—	4	—	4	Gaur and Bhatt 2008
Ghogha	1	18	—	19	Gaur and Bhatt 2008
Dabhol	—	4	—	4	Gaur et al. 2007
Vijaydurg	1	23	—	24	Sila et al. 1998
Sindhudurg	3	5	—	8	Sila and Gaur 1997
Goa	—	4	1	5	Sila et al. 2003
Kerala	—	1	—	1	Sila et al. 2005
Lakshadweep	—	1	—	1	
Tamilnadu	1	4	—	5	Athiyaman and Jaykumar 2004
Orissa	5	—	—	5	Sila and Patnaik 2008

during offshore explorations in water 3–16 m deep. Broadly, these artifacts can be
divided into the following two categories.

Stone Structures

Several stone structures of various shapes and sizes were noticed off Dwarka. A few
semicircular structures joined with a hard mortar are partially intact (Figure 23.2).
Structures with two or three courses have been noticed in at least 10 locations. The
semicircular structures were constructed by using L-shaped blocks with provision
for dowels to join two stone blocks. Besides semicircular structures, a large number
of rectangular structures have been noticed in this area. They are scattered over a
vast area and do not follow any regular plan. However, at a few places, two or three
courses of blocks appear to be the remains of fallen structures. These blocks are
found close to the semicircular structures, which indicate that these might have
been parts of a larger structure of jetty.

   Earlier (S. R. Rao 1990), the underwater structures, particularly the semicircular ones, were described as the remains of bastions of a fort wall similar to that at
Harappan and dating to the historical and medieval periods. However, the absence
of any other artifacts, like pottery, suggests that this may not be a habitation site

Figure 23.2 Structural remains off Dwarka. Photograph by the author.

(Gaur, Sundaresh, and Sila 2004a). In view of this fact, the remains noticed off Dwarka might be parts of a jetty. The circular and semicircular structures are presumably the bases of pillars and the rectangular dressed blocks portions of the superstructure of a jetty that extended from shore to 300 m offshore. Sankalia (1966: 10) has mentioned that "Sayajirao Gaekwad of Baroda had built a dock along the Gomati creek and a landing place on the opposite side, with huge stone pillars to facilitate tying the ship." It is quite likely that the remains lying on the shore and offshore regions are remains of the same dock. The presence of stone anchors lying along these structures also supports this hypothesis.

Stone Anchors

The discovery of 123 stone anchors of different shapes and sizes was another important feature of the Dwarka investigations. The anchors were noted between the intertidal zone and water 16 m deep, with the greatest concentration in water 6 to 8 m deep. Broadly, these anchors have been divided into three groups: composite, Indo-Arabia, and ring stone anchors. Composite anchors are often chiseled out of a thin limestone block and are triangular (Figure 23.3). They often include an upper circular hole known as a rope hole and two rectangular lower holes referred to as fluke holes. These anchors range from 16 to 496 kg and were probably used by local fishermen for short voyages. Indo-Arabia anchors were cut from a long block of hard stone and are characterized by a tapering upper end pierced with a circular hole and a wider lower end containing two rectangular holes on either face of the

Figure 23.3 Composite stone anchor off Dwarka. Photograph by the author.

block. These anchors are larger than the composite anchors, ranging from 82 to 668 kg, and were used by large vessels used for extended voyages, such as the Arabian dhow. Similar anchors have been reported from several port sites in India and Sri Lanka and on the Arabian and East African coasts. Twenty-four ring stone anchors of various sizes were also located at Dwarka, ranging from 20 to 245 kg in weight. Similar ring stone anchors have been reported from Oman waters (Vosmer 1999).

Bet Dwarka

The island of Bet Dwarka is situated about 30 km north of Dwarka at the entrance of the Gulf of Kachchh. It is famous for its temple dedicated to the Lord Krishna. The island is a narrow, crooked strip of sand and rock about 13 km long. The area is referred to as the Gulf of Barake in the Greek sea guide *Periplus Maris Erythraei* (Schoff 1912), although Ptolemy mentioned Barake as an island in the Gulf of Kanthi, which has been identified as the Gulf of Kachchh (McCrindle 1885).

In the seventeenth century BCE, the late Harappan people established their settlement on the northwest part of the island and took advantage of the rich fish and shellfish resources available around the island, as evidenced by a large fishhook and several shell artifacts recovered from the site (Gaur and Sundaresh 2003; 2004; Gaur, Sundaresh, and Vardhan 2005). The scanty habitation deposit suggests that the site was abandoned after a couple of centuries. The southeastern coast of the

island was again inhabited during the eighth century BCE and the population expanded dramatically, reaching its zenith during the historical and medieval periods.
Bet Dwarka continued to be an important center of maritime activity until the
emergence of the Okha port in the Okhamandal area in the mid-twentieth century.

Archaeological Finds

Underwater explorations were carried out near the present Bet Dwarka passenger
jetty during two seasons in 2001 and 2002. A large number of artifacts, including
amphorae shards, lead anchors, lead ingot, a hand mill of stone, and 42 stone
anchors, were located in water depths between 5 and 8 m.

The large quantity of amphorae shards that were discovered include examples
with morphology very similar to Roman amphora types of the fourth through fifth
century CE. These ceramic wares were mainly used for exporting wine and olive oil
originating in the Roman Empire. As olive oil was in less demand in India and the
shards exhibit a resin coating, it is most probable that the majority of the Indian
finds represent wine amphorae (Gaur, Sundaresh, and Sila 2006).

The Bet Dwarka expeditions also uncovered 42 composite and Indo-Arabia
anchors stone lying close to the present jetty in 6 to 8 m of water. The majority of the
composite anchors were cut from locally available limestone blocks. Their circular
upper hole is often broken, whereas the lower two rectangular holes tend to be preserved. The anchors are very similar to those reported from Dwarka and other
places in Saurashtra. The Indo-Arabia anchors are predominantly made of a hard
rock such as basalt, although some examples are made of limestone. The stone
anchors have been dated to the historical and medieval periods. In addition to the
stone anchors, the expeditions also uncovered two 70 kg lead anchors in the vicinity
of the amphorae. They are circular in shape, with an axial hole, and are very similar
to ring stone anchors recovered from Dwarka and other places in Saurashtra.

Pindara

The ancient temple site of Pindara is on the northern Saurashtra coast in the Gulf of
Kachchh about 36 km west of Khambhalia and 24 km from Kalyanpur. To the west
of Pindara is a vast marshy land known as Okha Rann. Pindara is a well-sheltered
area free from open sea waves, with mud flats extending 2 km inland of the high
water line and shallow waters extending well offshore. The average tidal range in the
region is 1 to 4 m.

During low tide in Pindara, a huge temple complex (10 by 10 m) is exposed
about 300 m from the high-water line (Gaur, Sundaresh, and Sila 2007a). A floor
area of dressed limestone blocks (Figure 23.4) is well preserved, although the superstructure has been destroyed and the stone blocks have been washed or taken away.
The temple was dedicated to the Lord Shiva, as a *yoni* is present in the sanctum
(*garbhagriha*). In the iconography of Shaivism, the *yoni* with the phallic linga, Shiva's symbol. The two symbols together represent the eternal process of creation and

Figure 23.4 Remains of a tenth-century CE temple exposed during low tide off Pindara.
Photograph by the author.

regeneration. The architectural feature of the submerged complex corresponds more or less with the existing temple on the shore of Pindara. The size of the submerged temple must have been contemporary to other surviving temples in the Pindara group of temples that date to the seventh through tenth centuries CE. The archaeological evidence indicates that the shoreline has changed significantly during the last 1,000 years on the Saurashtra coast.

The Gulf of Khambhat

The Gulf of Khambhat is famous for the high tidal range (up to 11 m) it experiences during full and new moon phases, making it the highest in India. In the ancient Sanskrit literature there is a reference (Panikkar and Srinivasan 1971) to a 10 m (510 *angulas*) rise in sea level during a full moon. This reference corresponds well with present-day conditions. The author of *Periplus of the Erythrenean Sea* also described the tidal range in the gulf and the challenges it posed to navigation. Similar difficulties extend to modern times; pilot services are provided by the contemporary port authorities in order to aid with navigation (Schoff 1912). The location of Harappan sites such as Lothal, Budhel, Padri, and Hanuman-no-Timbo indicate that people of the oldest civilization on the subcontinent were attracted to this

Figure 23.5 A Far Eastern–type stone anchor exposed during low tide off Hathab.
Photograph by the author.

extraordinary natural phenomenon, which they used very effectively for overseas trade and commerce.

The important medieval port at Ghogha is situated in the middle of the western bank of the Gulf of Khambhat. Ghogha was a famous boatbuilding center during the Mughal period (sixteenth and seventeenth centuries CE) (Habib 1982). Being located at a strategic point on the western end of the gulf, Ghogha was attacked and captured several times by local rulers such as Gohel Rajputs and Mohammedans. With the emergence of Bhavnagar in the early nineteenth century, Ghogha lost its importance as major port in the Gulf of Khambhat.

A large number of stone anchors have been discovered near Ghogha. The majority of anchors belong to Indo-Arabia types that have been dated to between the eighth and fourteenth centuries along the Saurashtra coast (Gaur, Sundaresh, and Sila 2004b). Interestingly, for the first time associated Islamic glazed ware was collected in the vicinity of the anchors.

Four stone anchors have also been observed at Hathab, a historical period site that is mentioned in *Periplus of the Erythrenean Sea* (Schoff 1912). Three anchors fall in the Indo-Arabia anchor category while one example is very different and reported for the first time in Indian waters (Figure 23.5). It is made of laterite stone with a shallow and wide groove on all four faces of the block. It is very similar to examples reported from Chinese, Japanese, and Korean waters dated to the twelfth to fourteenth centuries (Yang 1990; Qin Zhang 1989). This is the first direct underwater archaeological evidence of Indo-Chinese trade during the medieval period.

Besides the aforementioned anchors, there are also two unfinished Indo-Arabia anchors from Hathab and one from Ghogha, suggesting that raw material for stone anchors was obtained locally and that some manufacturing may have occurred in the area.

The Maharashtra Coast

Maharashtra has a coastline running over 720 km along the Arabian Sea, extending from Dahanu and Bordi in the north to Goa in the south. Bays, creeks, and rivers offer a number of safe harbors and anchorages along the coast, and the unknown Greek writer of the *Periplus of the Erythrean Sea* mentions a chain of port towns (Sopara, Kaliyana, Chaul, Dabhol, Vijaydurg, and Vengurla). Investigations at a few sites, namely Dabhol, Vijaydurg, and Sindhudurg, yielded material culture.

Dabhol

Dabhol is situated at the confluence of the river Vashishthi and the Arabian Sea. This port was referred to as Palaepatmae by the author of the *Periplus of Erythrean Sea* (Schoff 1912) and was of great importance in the fourteenth through sixteenth centuries as the principal port of the South Konkan region, carrying on trade with ports in the Mediterranean, the Red Sea, and the Persian Gulf (Brown 1902).

During the coastal survey, a temple dedicated to an iron anchor was noted near the present-day jetty of Dabhol. It is locally known as Loyaleshwar. The Marathi word *loyali* refers to a type of anchor used even today by the fishermen across the Maharashtra and Gujarat coasts. The temple has been renovated, and marble and granite flooring and wall tiles have been added. However, tradition suggests that the temple is at least 200 years old. An iron anchor with a long, square-section shank and ring at the upper end is situated in the sanctum (*garbhagriha*) and is being worshipped as a god. The style of anchor appears to be of the British admiralty type. The lower two prongs are buried, but the entire shaft is exposed and painted in red.

In the course of the survey, four stone anchors were found near the jetty. One of the anchors had wooden fluke remains in the holes, which were removed. These are typical Indo-Arabia stone anchors (Gaur, Sundaresh, Sila, and Vora 2007). One of the anchors has quarry marks, leaving no doubt as to the technique of obtaining raw material, which is similar to that of ancient India. The chisel marks are visible, and the width of one mark is about 5 cm, with a similar distance between two marks. The raw material of two anchors appears to be Deccan Traps basalt, and the remaining two anchors are of sedimentary rock. One anchor is unfinished, as one of the holes was only partially chiseled.

The location of the modern town is on a sheltered harbor, which the geophysical exploration indicated was also the case during antiquity. The river Vashishthi is navigable up to Chiplun, which was historically a marketplace (Nairne 1896). The development of the current harbor caused the loss of the remains of an old jetty and other structures related to maritime activities, but traces are still noticeable in certain locations and are indicative of construction patterns. Blocks of basalt (Deccan Traps) were frequently used in the construction of jetties and are similarly employed today, although the quality of the masonry has improved. Historic jetties were constructed perpendicular to the shore unlike modern jetties, which are oriented parallel to the coast.

Vijaydurg

The ancient port of Vijaydurg is situated on the southern bank of the river Vaghotan in Sindhudurg district. It has been referred as Byzanteion by Ptolemy (McCrindle 1885) and as Byzantine in the *Periplus of Erythrenean Sea* (Schoff 1912). In the seventeenth century CE, Vijaydurg became an important naval base of the Maratha Kingdom on the western coast of India. The historical record indicates frequent naval battles between Europeans and Maratha kings, resulting in several shipwrecks in Vijaydurg waters (Apte 1973).

A tidal dockyard, built by the Maratha admiral Kanhoji Angre in the seventeenth century CE, is located 3 km upstream on the Vaghotan River. Later, the dockyard was renovated by Anand Rao Dhulap, who also increased the landing capacity. The dimensions of the tidal dock are 110 by 75 m, and it had the capacity to hold ships of 500 tons. The entrance of the dock is 7 m wide at the base and 12 m at the top (Sila and Gaur 1997a). The southern and eastern sides are cut out of natural rock, while the third side is a dry masonry construction.

During the archaeological investigation, eight stone anchors of Indo-Arabia type were noticed in the Vijaydurg Fort. These anchors had been reused as niche lintels in the second parapet wall of the fort. There are also 15 Indo-Arabia anchor and one composite anchor lying around the dockyard. Perhaps these were used as mooring bits when the dock was in use (Sila et al. 1998).

Sindhudurg Fort

The fort of Sindhudurg is situated about 1 km off Malvan on a low-lying rocky island. The fort was built by the Maratha King Shivaji in the mid-seventeenth century CE. A survey around the fort yielded eight stone anchors, including three of the composite type and five of the Indo-Arabia type (Sila and Gaur 1997b). They were made of laterite stone that is locally available.

Tamilnadu Coast

Tamilnadu, with its 800-km-long coastline, is dotted with several ancient ports, which played a dominant role in internal and external trade. The earliest form of Tamil literature, known as Sangam literature and dating to the early centuries of the Christian era, contains glimpses of the seaborne commerce carried on between the ports of Tamilnadu and countries of Southeast Asia and Ceylon (Raman 1988). The author of *Periplus of Erythrenean Sea* also mentions a chain of ports on the

Tamilnadu coast (Schoff 1912). Marine archaeological investigations have been
undertaken at Poompuhar and Mahabalipuram.

Poompuhar

The ancient town of Poompuhar is situated at the point where the river Kaveri joins
the Bay of Bengal. Sangam period texts such as *Silappatikaram* and *Pattinappalai*,
and later ones, including *Manimekhalai* and *Ahananaru*, vividly describe Poompuhar as the capital port city of the Early Cholas. A coastal survey in 1962 revealed the
vestiges of ancient habitations, including terra-cotta ring wells, pottery, bricks, and
beads. These features and artifacts have been dated to the early centuries of the
Christian era. A wharf at Kilaiyur and a water reservoir at Vanagiri are other important archaeological finds near Poompuhar (Soundar Rajan 1994).

The terrestrial excavations in and around Poompuhar brought to light a square
copper coin with a tiger emblem that was the royal crest of the Early Cholas. Other
finds included beads of semi-precious stones and amphora pieces. The most significant discovery was an I-shaped brick structure, which was exposed in the ancient
channel of the Kaveri River, now completely silted, at Kilaiyur. This brick structure,
with a drain for the flow of water and a platform supported by wooden posts for
handling cargo, served as a wharf built in the channel of the river (S. R. Rao 1987).

Three ring-wells were noticed near Vanagiri village during low tide. One of
them was exposed to a depth of 45 cm and was formed of three courses of bricks,
each 15 cm high and 6 cm thick at the rim. The diameter of the ring was 75 cm. Two
other ring-wells were also measured and were found to have nearly the same diameter and thickness of rim.

A brick structure exposed in the intertidal zone was excavated to obtain a cross
section. The structure extended to 120 cm below the surface and was constructed of
11 courses of brick resting on natural soil. The structure measures 4 m in length and
1.2 m in width and is aligned parallel to the shore. On the basis of brick size (36 by
18 by 6 cm) the structure is assigned to the third century BCE (S. R. Rao et al.
1995–1996: 12). Another brick structure was located during low tide. This L-shaped
structure measures 3.25 m in length by 1.2 m in width and is exposed during May
and June when beach sediments are removed by the waves and currents. The
remains of these brick structures in the intertidal region indicate that ancient city of
Poompuhar has been partially destroyed by the sea.

An offshore survey opposite the mouth of the Kaveri River identified a disturbed structure buried in the sediments. Excavation was carried out in the vicinity
to ascertain the size and shape of the structure and uncovered some dressed blocks.
There is no trace of any mortar on the blocks, as they are heavily eroded. The pottery
collected from the area includes black-and-red ware, red ware, and an amphora
shard (Gaur, Sundaresh, and Sila 2005). The shapes are not recognizable, as a result
of having been tumbled by the sea.

A few dressed sandstone blocks were located north of the Kaveri River mouth.
The area is covered with fine black sand. A potential archaeological site was suggested

by a geophysical survey to the north of Poompuhar, opposite to Kadaikkadu. Extensive excavations in this area using an airlift revealed several stone blocks. Among the pottery uncovered was the rim of a bowl or jar of gray ware originating from 1 m below the seabed. The ceramic evidence suggests that the habitation belongs to the early Christian era (Gaur 1997).

Dredging in the shallow portion of the site revealed three courses of sandstone blocks extending in a north–south direction, but it is difficult to determine the layout of the original buildings because the structures are disturbed. The occurrence of black-and-red ware of the megalithic period suggests that this area was inhabited during Sangam Period. Similar types of structures and pottery reported from the northern side of Poompuhar indicate that ancient Poompuhar extended 2 km along the coast.

The survey also identified two stone structures in 23 m of water off Poompuhar. According to side-scan sonar data, Structure I is oval in shape and measures approximately 24 by 20 m (T. C. S. Rao 1991). The middle of the structure, which is about 1 m deep, projects approximately 2 m above the seabed. An open space filled with rubble was located on the northern side of the structure. Chiseling and hammering exposed a very porous laterite stone, while airlift excavations by the side of the structure suggest a substantial coarse sand deposition at least 2 m thick. Structure II consists of two smaller structures lying about 40 m northwest of Structure I. These structures are oriented in an east–west direction and are 10 to 12 m apart. They are heavily disturbed and scattered. The local fishermen of region call these structures *koil*, meaning a temple. It is possible that the structures are natural (not man-made).

The explorations at Poompuhar and Tranquebar clearly demonstrate that the sea has gradually encroached on the land during the last 2,000 years. It is worth mentioning here that in 1973 the Kannagi statue was installed at the shore of Poompuhar about 200 m away from the high-water line, and by 1994 it had to be moved 150 m landward because the structure was being destroyed by the sea. Similarly, other monuments at Poompuhar were also destroyed due to coastal erosion.

A mid-seventeenth-century map of Tranquebar on display in the Dansborg Museum shows a complete plan of the town along with the then-shoreline. A careful study of the map suggests that the town was well protected by a seaward fort wall and that the Siva temple was landward of the fort wall. It is estimated that during the seventeenth century, the shoreline was at least 50 m away from the fort wall and the temple was located around 250 to 300 m from the shoreline (Sundaresh, Gaur, and Nair 1997). This observation unequivocally suggests that the shoreline has transgressed about 300 m in the last 300 years, infringing at an average rate of 1 m per year.

Mahabalipuram

Mahabalipuram, famous as a center of ancient art and architecture, is situated about 55 km south of Chennai (formerly known as Madras). There is a popular tradition among the locals detailing the submergence of the ancient city of Mahabalipuram that was recorded by European travelers in the eighteenth and nineteenth centuries (Ramaswami 1980). Marine archaeological survey at Mahabalipuram was undertaken about 500 m east of the Shore Temple. The investigation revealed the presence of fallen and scattered walls and structures. The remains of some of these structures can be seen running parallel to the shore for several meters at depths ranging between 5 m and 10 m. The large number of dressed and rectangular blocks suggests that they were part of a large building complex. At several places divers noticed steps leading to high platforms (Sundaresh et al. 2004). It is difficult to determine a site plan, however, as the structures have been badly damaged and are covered with thick biological growth.

The presence of archaeological structures off Mahabalipuram raises many interesting questions, such as when they were constructed and how and why they happened to be there. In the absence of datable material culture evidence, the underwater structures can be dated only based on the local traditions and available literature. Ancient Tamil texts do not directly mention Mahabalipuram, but the poem *Perumpanarrupadai* (dedicated to Tondaiman Ilamtriraiyan, a king of Kanchipuram) describes a port called Nirppeyarvu, which could be identified with either Kanchipuram or Mamallapuram (Ramaswami 1980: 12). It has been inferred that the Pallava King Mamalla first set his workers to construct the town in the seventh century CE, thereafter known as Mamallapuram. The name Mahabalipuram, therefore, is of a very late origin.

The study of sea-level and shoreline change may shed light on the date of submergence for these structures. The sea level fluctuated several times between 2 m and 6 m during the Holocene on both coasts of India (Banerjee 2000; Merh 1987). Another study revealed that a major and important factor affecting the Mahabalipuram coast is erosion (Mahapatra and Hariprasad 1999), and a third study suggests that the rate of erosion around Mahabalipuram is 55 cm/yr (Ramaiyan, Prasad, and Suresh 1997). If the same rate prevailed during the last 1,500 years, then the shoreline at that time might have been approximately 800 m eastward, and all the structures noticed underwater would have been on land. However, the rate of erosion may not be constant over a long period, and the Bay of Bengal is also prone to severe cyclones that can damage or submerge a large part of land in a very short time.

Study of Shipwrecks along
the Indian Coast

India has over 7,000 km of coastline and around 5,000 years of maritime history, which creates the potential for a large number of shipwrecks on her coast. However, no proper records of shipwrecks are preserved, except some literary references, prior to the arrival of Europeans in the Indian Ocean. Archival records preserved throughout India suggest a large number of shipwrecks dating between the early sixteenth century and the nineteenth century CE. A few shipwrecks have been explored in Goa, Lakshadweep, and Poompuhar waters. A few important shipwrecks are discussed here.

Goa

Archival records of the Portuguese period provide information on shipwrecks along the Goa coast. Marine archaeological exploration of Goa revealed two shipwrecks, one at Sunchi Reef and another near St. George's Reef.

Sunchi Reef extends in a north–south direction across the entrance to the bay and separates the bay from the Arabian Sea. Investigations around the middle of the reef revealed cargo material from a shipwreck, including granite blocks (Sila et al. 2004). The orientation of these blocks is random, and they lie in gaps in the bedrock. Four iron cannon were another important find from this wreck. They rest on high-tabled rock and are covered with a thick layer of encrustation of marine growth. The brass barrel of a handgun, trapped below the dressed granite blocks, was also found. The barrel has two notches; the front side is intact, and the rear one, which is meant for fixing the barrel to the wooden part of the gun, is broken. Elephant tusk (ivory) and hippopotamus teeth, recovered from beneath the granite blocks and partially buried in the sediment, were among other important finds from this wreck. Further investigation also brought to light a large number of potsherds and glass bottles. On the basis of the pottery characteristics and a single thermoluminescence date, the wreck has been dated to the mid seventeenth century CE.

St. George's Reef lies near Grande Island and is exposed during low tide. Investigations there yielded a large number of terra-cotta artifacts, such as chimney bricks, roof, ridge, and floor tiles, a hollow column drum, a Corinthian-type column capital, and a drainage pipe, as well as timber from the ship (Sila, Gaur, and Sundaresh 2003). All terra-cotta artifacts were intended for house construction. Excavation was carried out up to 1 m below the seabed, and several broken roof tiles and floor tiles were noted. Floor tiles are square and have deep grooves at regular intervals; some are stamped with the words "Basel Mission Company 1865." Finally, several bricks made of white clay intended for chimneys or other industrial purposes were also located at the wreck site. The St. George wreck appears to represent a late-nineteenth- to early-twentieth-century wooden-hulled vessel carrying house building materials originating from the Basel Mission Company manufacturing center in the South Kanara region.

Lakshadweep Islands

Islands have played an important role in ancient maritime trade and commerce. The Lakshadweep Islands lie on the sea route between western Asia and northern Africa to one side and southern Asia and Sri Lanka to the other. The oldest reference to Lakshadweep Island, albeit indirect, is found in the first-century CE text *Periplus of the Erythrean Sea*. Describing the trade of the Malabar Coast, the unknown author mentions "tortoiseshell from the islands off Limurike," the latter being the name given to Malabar or part of it in ancient times (Schoff 1912: 45).

There are no archival records of shipwrecks on the islands prior to the seventeenth century CE. There are, however, a few indirect references to naval battles from inscriptions. One, from Vaylur in Tamilnadu, mentions that Rajasimha (680–720 CE) conquered the islands (Sastri 1925–1926: 152). Another, from the temple of Rajarajeswar at Tanjavur, mentions that the Chola King Raja Rajendra (1018–1019 CE) conquered many islands (Mannadiah 1977: 39). These naval wars reflect the strategic importance of the Lakshadweep Islands.

Shipwreck in Bangaram Island

Archaeological Survey of India, in association with the Indian Navy, surveyed a shipwreck dated to the late eighteenth century off Bangaram Island in 9–40 m of water (Tripathi 2004). A large number of bricks, shards of thick brown-glazed storage jars, pieces of wood, corroded and cemented parts of the ship, utensils of copper, shards of porcelain, pottery with embossed designs, and green-glazed shards, in addition to four cannon, an iron anchor, two complete brown-glazed pots, and a bronze bell with the inscription "Prince Royal 1792" were important finds from the wreck (Tripathi 2004). Archival records indicate that a number of ships were named *Prince Royal* and more commonly *Princess Royal*. Fifteen vessels, named *Princess Royal* are listed in the Lloyd's register. These were constructed between 1763 and 1791, and nine of them were sheathed. The list of lost ships of British East India Company also mentions a ship by name, *Prince Royal*. If the year inscribed on bell corresponds to the construction of ship, then none of the above-listed ships could be identified with the excavated wreck. The excavator (Tripathi 2004) believes that ship was lost in 1795–1796 during her return voyage from China.

Steamship Wrecks

In 1994, the National Institute of Oceanography conducted a marine archaeological survey off Minicoy Island of the Lakshadweep Archipelago and located three steamship wrecks. One of the wrecks lies about 200 m from the shore at a water depth that changes significantly from 4–15 m depending on the seabed topography. The ship sank parallel to the shore and tilted toward the deeper waters. It is approximately 100 m long and 20 m broad (Gaur et al. 1998). The hull frames are well preserved and scattered to both starboard and port. The wreck rests on a slope, hence the starboard frames are more disturbed than the port ones. The engine consists of three vertical cylinders with a heavy flywheel and survives to a height of about 3 m, excluding the flywheel. The cylinder blocks are formed of several iron pieces bolted together with machined wrought iron bolts fastened with wrought iron nuts. The width of the flywheel is 1.4 m, and the diameter is 4.5 m. It is attached to the shaft, which is well preserved. The length of the shaft, as far as the propeller, is 27 m, with four square bearings at 5 m intervals. One of the most interesting features is the anchor chain, which is connected to the anchor lying in deeper water indicating initial anchorage before the wreck of ship. The visible length of chain is over 100 m, with links about 30 cm long and in good condition. A completely preserved propeller with all four blades was observed. The length of each blade is about 80 cm with a maximum breadth of about 35 cm and appears to be made of a brass alloy.

A second wreck was located about 200 m north of the first wreck, lying perpendicular to the shore in 4–15 m of water. It is estimated to be over 100 m long. The boilers and engine parts are well preserved. The ship is tilted toward starboard and is similar to first wreck in shape, size, and type. The aft portion of the ship has fallen into deeper water, and the hull is heavily corroded in most places. The propeller shaft is broken in two. A smaller part is attached to the engine, but the longer portion, together with the propeller, was broken and slipped down the slope. Two huge boilers were noted; they are cylindrical, watertight boxes about 5 m in height and 2 m in diameter.

These wrecks were probably cargo ships. Although identification of the ships is not possible at present, further exploration may be useful in obtaining some clue regarding their origin. At present, they face a potential threat in that commercial companies may obtain licenses to salvage them.

Poompuhar

An eighteenth-century shipwreck was discovered during offshore investigations in Poompuhar. Earlier, Vora (1987) reported the presence of some anomalies on the seafloor at water depths of 17 to 18 m. The echogram indicates a height above the seabed between 2.5 and 3 m for these objects, and they appear to be buried in coarse grained sediment. The results of a side-scan sonar survey carried out at the site location indicated two anomalies separated by 5 or 6 m of sand. It seems likely that these are two sections of a single shipwreck, the larger of which appears to be the wreck's fore part. The wreck is tilted to one side, and heavy barnacle encrustation and sediment deposits make it very difficult to determine the vessel's orientation. A heavily encrusted cannon, two gunpowder boxes, and several unidentified objects were also recorded. Between the two parts of the wreck, two circular structures were observed; these appear to be the hatches of cargo holds. Airlift operations inside these holds were difficult due to thick encrustation.

The ship had a wood hull; a large number of wooden planks were exposed during the excavation. A large assortment of small and large copper-alloy nails were recovered. A rudder gudgeon of copper alloy was another important find from this wreck, as were several lead ingots observed in the smaller of the two sections (Gaur et al. 1997). Due to barnacle growth, the ingots were cemented together, but a few ingots were retrieved with careful chiseling. Based on their shape, size, and imprints, the ingots could be classified into three broad groups. The first category is composed of boat-shaped ingots averaging 68.6 kg in weight, with "W:BLACKETT" inscribed on the obverse and the year 1791 or 1792 stamped on the reverse. The ingots of the second category are similar in shape to the first category but are slightly smaller, averaging 63 kg. These ingots are impressed with the symbol "D" with a crown above on the obverse, and stamps with various symbols, such as a heart and a smaller "D" with a crown, on the reverse. The ingots of the last category are rectangular and average 65.5 kg in weight, and no inscriptions other than a few characters are apparent on both faces.

Determining the identification, exact date, and origin of the wreck is not possible in the absence of additional data. However, on the basis of the dates inscribed on the ingots, it can be suggested that the ship was wrecked after 1792. Archival records do not include any indication of a shipwreck in this area. From the survey, the wreck appears to be of a moderately sized vessel, approximately 50 m long. It should be noted that the cannon and gunpowder boxes adjacent to the wreck do not rule out the possibility that this was a cargo vessel, as these carried armament.

Conclusion

Marine archaeological research during the last two and half decades has revealed a number of sites of interest along the Indian coast, including ancient ports, jetties, and shipwrecks. The extensive explorations of the Saurashtra coast revealed several ancient ports and jetties. Interestingly, archaeological discoveries suggest that natural phenomena like tidal variations were used very effectively by past residents of the Gulf of Kachchh and the Gulf of Khambhat. Due to changes in the coastline, a number of sites originally on the coast are now lying far into the hinterland, suggesting topographical changes. Similarly, a few sites, such as Pindara and Bet Dwarka, that were originally on land are now submerged in the intertidal zone.

Discovery of a large copper fishhook from a Bronze Age (late Harappan) context suggests that Bet Dwarka Island attracted early settlers because of the availability of marine resources such as fish and shellfish. The discovery of amphorae shards and lead anchors from Bet Dwarka also suggest that the island was a focal point of international trade and commerce during the early centuries of the Christian era. Similarly, Dwarka, Somnath, Miyani, and Visawada were important port towns during the historical and medieval periods. Ghogha in the Gulf of Khambhat was an important Indo-Arabia trading point on the Saurashtra coast. One of the most important aspects of the existence of several ancient ports on the Saurashtra coast must have been the availability of natural resources such as semiprecious stones and wood for boatbuilding, in addition to rich agricultural products (wheat, barley, and cotton). During the Bronze Age and the historical period, marine shells were another major attraction for the coastal settlements along the Gujarat coast. The great tidal variations on the Saurashtra coast were also responsible for the active participation of hinterland sites in maritime activities, particularly in the development of ports along tidal creeks.

Coastal explorations of the Maharashtra coast yielded stone anchors at Dabhol, Vijaydurg, and Sindhudurg, which indicate that these were active port towns during the medieval period. Interestingly, Dabhol has a temple dedicated to an anchor. Stone anchors of different sizes continue to be found in Goa, Kerala, and Lakshadweep, and on the Tamilnadu coast in the context with the historical and the medieval periods. In the absence of the remains of port installations, stone anchors are an indicator of anchorage points close to the port and also the size of vessels calling at the port. Although, if there are only one or two anchors, they may have accidentally fallen from a ship.

Though archival records suggest that a large number of shipwrecks should exist in Indian waters, relatively few have been found. The possible reason for this paucity of archaeologically recorded shipwrecks is the high sedimentation rate along the coast, combined with the tropical waters: these conditions lead to the quick burial of most wrecks and the rapid deterioration of portions that remain above the seabed. However, a few shipwrecks have been explored, and detailed work is in progress. Although two of the three shipwrecks found around Goa do not have any wood remains, heavy metal artifacts like cannon, granite blocks, and pottery have been recovered from these wrecks. Shipwrecks in Lakshadweep and Poompuhar are well preserved, and a detailed study is awaited. Although maritime archaeology based on literary data has been taught in various universities across the country since the middle of the twentieth century, during the last two decades the importance of the study of maritime archaeology has grown significantly, resulting in the establishment of underwater archaeology centers in Archaeological Survey of India, Tamil University, Thanjavur, and the National Institute of Oceanography, Goa, which was established in 1981. A few institutions and universities regularly send students to the National Institute of Oceanography, Goa, for small projects dealing with ancient ports, boatbuilding, and other traditional maritime activities. These are encouraging indications of the future of the marine archaeological studies in India. However, a huge effort is needed, given the subcontinent's long coastline and deep-rooted maritime history.

ACKNOWLEDGMENTS

We are thankful to the director, National Institute of Oceanography, for permission to publish this article. Thanks are also due to my colleagues of the Marine Archaeology Center for various assistance. This is NIO contribution number 4544.

REFERENCES

Apte, B. K. 1973. *A history of the Maratha navy and merchantships.* Bombay: State Board for
Literature and Culture.

Athiyaman, N., and P. Jayakumar. 2004. Ancient anchors off Tamil Nadu coast and ship
tonnage analysis. *Current Science* 86 (9): 1261–1267.

Banerjee, P. K. 2000. Holocene and late Pleistocene relative sea level fluctuations along the
east coast of India. *Marine Geology* 167: 243–260.

Brown, L. H. S. 1902. *From Calcutta to Bombay coasting: The handbook to the ports on the
coast of India between Calcutta and Bombay.* London: J. D. Potter.

Gaur, A. S. 1997. Ceramic industries of Poompuhar in an integrated approach to marine
archaeology. In *An integrated approach to marine archaeology,* ed. S. R. Rao, 127–132.
Goa: Society for Marine Archaeology.

Gaur, A. S., and B. K. Bhatt. 2008. Marine archaeological explorations on western coast of
the Gulf of Khambhat. *Man and Environment* 33 (2): 99–104.

Gaur, A. S., and T. Sila. 2006. Marine archaeological explorations on the southwestern
coast of Saurashtra, India. *Journal of Indian Ocean Archaeology* 3: 81–89.

Gaur, A. S., and Sundaresh. 2003. Onshore excavation at Bet Dwarka Island, in the Gulf of
Kachchh, Gujarat. *Man and Environment* 28 (1): 57–66.

———. 2004. A Late Bronze Age copper fish-hook from Bet Dwarka, Gujarat: An evidence
on the advance fishing technology. *Current Science* 86 (4): 512–514.

Gaur, A. S., Sundaresh, P. Gudigar, and T. Sila. 1997. An 18th century shipwreck off
Poompuhar Tamil Nadu coast (India). *International Journal of Nautical Archaeology*
26 (2): 118–126.

Gaur, A. S., Sundaresh, and B. Kumar. 2005. The biggest stone anchors from Mithi Virdi.
Journal of Indian Ocean Archaeology 2: 110–114.

Gaur, A. S., Sundaresh, and A. D. Odedra. 2004. New light on the maritime archaeology of
Porbandar, Saurashtra coast, Gujarat. *Man and Environment* 29 (1): 103–107.

Gaur, A. S., Sundaresh, and T. Sila. 2004a. Dwarka: An ancient harbour. *Current Science* 86
(9): 1256–1260.

———. 2004b. Grapnel anchors from Saurashtra: Remnants of Indo-Arabia trade route in
Indian Ocean. *Mariner's Mirror* 90 (2): 134–151.

———. 2005. Underwater explorations of a Sangam period port town at Poompuhar, east
coast of India. In *Revealing India's past: Recent trends in art and archaeology,* ed. R. K.
Sharma and Devendra Handa, 33–43. New Delhi: Aryan Books International.

———. 2006. Evidence for Indo-Roman trade from Bet Dwarka waters, west coast of India.
International Journal of Nautical Archaeology 35 (1): 117–127.

———. 2007a. Submerged temple complex off Pindara, on the northwestern coast of
Saurashtra. *Man and Environment* 32 (2): 37–40.

———. 2007b. Remains of the ancient ports and anchorage points at Miyani and Visawada,
on the west coast of India: Study based on underwater investigations. *Mariner's Mirror*
93 (4): 428–440.

Gaur, A. S., Sundaresh, T. Sila, and K. H. Vora. 2007. New evidence on the maritime
activity at Dabhol on the Maharashtra coast. *Puratattva* 37: 186–192.

Gaur, A. S., Sundaresh, and P. Vardhan. 2005. Ancient shell industry at Bet Dwarka.
Current Science 89 (6): 941–946.

Gaur, A. S., Sundaresh, and K. H. Vora. 2005. *Archaeology of Bet Dwarka Island: An
excavation report.* New Delhi: Aryan Books International.

————. 2008. *Underwater archaeology of Dwarka and Somnath (1997–2002)*. New Delhi: Aryan Books International.

Gaur, A. S., K. H. Vora, Sundaresh, T. Sila, and P. Gudigar. 1998. Exploration of steam engine wrecks off Minicoy Island, Lakshadweep, India. *International Journal of Nautical Archaeology* 27 (3): 225–236.

Gupt, M. L., trans. 1944. *Shri Vishnu Purana (5.23, 13–15)*. Gorakhpur: Geeta Press.

Habib, I. 1982. *An atlas of the Mughal Empire*. Delhi: Oxford University Press.

Mahapatra, G. P., and M. Hariprasad. 1999. Shoreline changes and their impact on the archaeological structures at Mahabalipuram. *Gondwana Geological Magazine* 4: 225–233.

Mannadiah, M. S. 1977. *Gazetteer of India: Union territory of Lakshadweep*. Coimbatore: Information Department of Union Territory of Lakshadweep.

McCrindle, J. W. 1885. *Ancient India as described by Ptolemy*. New Delhi: Today & Tomorrow.

Merh, S. S. 1987. Quaternary sea level changes: The present status vis-à-vis record along coast of India. *Indian Journal of Earth Science* 14 (3–4): 235–251.

Mookerji, R. K. 1912. *Indian shipping: A history of the sea-borne trade and maritime activities of the Indians from the earliest times*. Bombay: Longmans.

Nairne, A. K. [1896] 1988. *History of the Konkan*. Delhi: Asian Educational Services.

Panikkar, N. K., and T. M. Srinivasan. 1971. The concept of tide in ancient India. *Indian Journal of History of Science* 6 (1): 36–50.

Qin Zhang, Y. 1989. A 12th–13th century stone anchor of Southern Sang recently discovered on the coast of the South China Sea. *Bulletin of the Australian Institute of Maritime Archaeology* 13 (2): 27–32.

Ramaiyan, M., E. Krishna Prasad, and P. K. Suresh. 1997. Shoreline oscillation of Tamilnadu coast. In *Proceedings of the Second Indian National Conference on Harbour and Ocean Engineering* (INCHOE-97), 1177–1182. Thiruvanantpuram: Indian National Conference on Harbour and Ocean Engineering.

Raman, K. V. 1988. Port towns of Tamilnadu: Some field data and the prospects of marine archaeology. In *Marine archaeology of Indian Ocean countries*, ed. S. R. Rao, 114–118. Goa: National Institute of Oceanography.

Ramaswami, N. S. 1980. *Mamallapuram, an annotated bibliography*. Madras: New Era.

Rao, S. R. 1987. *Progress and prospects of marine archaeology in India*. Goa: National Institute of Oceanography.

————. 1988. The future of marine archaeology in Indian Ocean countries. In *Marine archaeology in Indian Ocean countries*, ed. S. R. Rao, 21–25. Goa: National Institute of Oceanography.

————. 1990. Excavations of legendary city of Dvaraka in the Arabian Sea. *Journal of Marine Archaeology* 1: 59–98.

Rao, S. R., T. C. S. Rao, A. S. Gaur, T. Sila, Sundaresh, and P. Gudigar. 1995–1996. Underwater explorations off Poompuhar, 1993. *Journal of Marine Archaeology* 5–6: 7–22.

Rao, T. C. S. 1991. Marine geophysical surveys off Kaverippattinam for archaeological investigations. *Journal of Marine Archaeology* 2: 21–31.

Sankalia, H. D. 1966. Dwarka in literature and archaeology. In *Excavations at Dwarka*, ed. Z. A. Ansari and M. S. Mate, 1–17. Poona: Deccan College.

Sastri, H. K. [1925–1926] 1983. The Vayalur Inscription of Rajasimha II. *Epigraphia Indica* 18: 145–152.

Schoff, W. H. [1912] 1974. *The periplus of the Erythraean Sea: Travel and trade in the Indian Ocean by a merchant of the first century*. New Delhi: Munshiram Manoharlal.

Shamasastry, R., trans. 1915. *Kautilya's Arthashastra*. Book 2. Bangalore: Government Press.

Sila, Tripati, and A. S. Gaur. 1997a. Onshore and nearshore explorations along the Maharashtra Coast: With a view to locating ancient ports and submerged sites. *Man and Environment* 22 (2): 73–84.

——. 1997b. Stone anchors from Sindhudurg Fort on the west coast of India. *International Journal of Nautical Archaeology* 26 (1): 51–57.

Sila, Tripati, A. S. Gaur, and Sundaresh. 2003. Anchors from Goa waters, central west coast of India: Remains of Goa's overseas trade contacts with Arabian countries and Portugal. *Bulletin of Australian Institute of Maritime Archaeology* 27: 97–106.

Sila, Tripati, A. S. Gaur, Sundaresh, P. Gudigar, and S. N. Bandodker. 1998. Historical stone anchors from Vijaydurg, Maharashtra, west coast of India. *Bulletin of Western Australian Museum* 22 (1 and 2): 1–8.

Sila, Tripati, A. S. Gaur, Sundaresh, and K. H. Vora. 2004. Shipwreck archaeology of Goa: Evidence of maritime contacts with other countries. *Current Science* 86 (9): 1238–1260.

Sila, Tripati, A. Manikfan, and M. Mohamed. 2005. An Indo-Arabia type of stone anchor from Kannur, Kerala, west coast of India. *International Journal of Nautical Archaeology* 34 (1): 131–137.

Sila, Tripati, and A. P. Patnaik. 2008. Stone anchors along the coast of Chilika Lake: New light on the maritime activities of Orissa, India. *Current Science* 94 (3): 386–390.

Sila, Tripati, Sundaresh, A. S. Gaur, P. Gudigar, and S. N. Bandodkar. 2003. Exploration of Basel Mission Company shipwreck remains at St. George's Reef off Goa, west coast of India: Impact of the Basel Mission Co. on society and culture. *International Journal of Nautical Archaeology* 32 (1): 111–120.

Soundar Rajan, K. V. 1994. *Kaveripattinam excavations 1963–73: A port city on the Tamil Nadu coast*. Memoir of Archaeological Survey of India No. 90. New Delhi: Archaeological Survey of India.

Sundaresh, A. S. Gaur, and R. R. Nair. 1997. Our threatened archaeological heritage: A case study from Tamil Nadu coast. *Current Science* 73 (7): 593–598.

Sundaresh, A. S. Gaur, T. Sila, and K. H. Vora. 2004. Underwater investigations off Mahabalipuram, Tamil Nadu, India. *Current Science* 86 (9): 1231–1237.

Tripathi, A. 2004. Princes royal: Excavation of ancient shipwreck in the Arabian Sea. *Current Science* 86 (9): 1246–1250.

Vora, K. H. 1987. A note on the geophysical explorations for marine archaeology of Tamilnadu coast. *International Journal of Nautical Archaeology* 16 (1): 159–164.

Vosmer, T. 1999. Maritime archaeology, ethnography and history in the Indian Ocean: An emerging partnership. In *Archaeology of seafaring: The Indian Ocean in the ancient period*, ed. H. P. Ray, 291–312. New Delhi: Pragati.

Yang, Q. Z. 1990. South Song stone anchors in China, Korea and Japan. *International Journal of Nautical Archaeology* 19 (2): 113–121.

CHAPTER 24

A SURVEY OF EAST ASIAN SHIPBUILDING TRADITIONS DURING THE ERA OF CHINESE MARITIME EXPANSION

RANDALL J. SASAKI

INTRODUCTION

FOR millennia, the peoples of East Asia have used vessels for travel on their lakes, rivers, and seas. Despite a growing interest in Asian history and archaeology, Western scholars are only gradually beginning to understand the rich and complex maritime culture of this region. It must be understood that the term "East Asia" includes vast areas of ocean and landmass encompassing complex and independent shipbuilding traditions that, while in no way uniform, were interrelated. In this short summary, I introduce East Asian shipbuilding technology, as well as maritime history, based on archaeological remains of vessels. For the purposes of this chapter, East Asia is roughly defined as corresponding to the area of modern-day China, Korea, and Japan, although the reader must be aware that political boundaries and the very concept of a nation differed in the past (Figure 24.1). The main focus of this survey is on the Song dynasty (960–1279 CE), the Yuan dynasty (1271–1368 CE) and onto the middle of Ming dynasty (1368–1644 CE) of China, roughly from the mid-tenth century to the mid-fourteenth century, corresponding to the period when

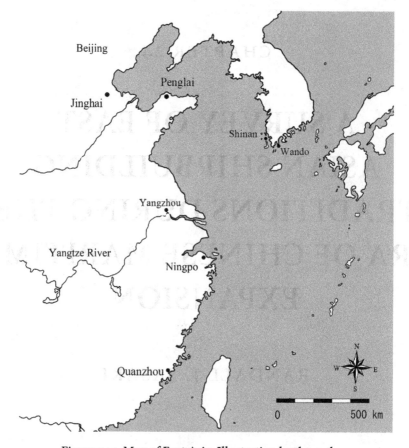

Figure 24.1 Map of East Asia. Illustration by the author.

China was effectively the world's maritime superpower. Perhaps this time period may be called the era of China's maritime expansion. Although it appeared to dominate the maritime scene of East Asia, China was heavily influenced by the outside world and interactions within Asia, creating a rich and diverse maritime tradition (Table 24.1 and Figure 24.2). As this is only a preliminary overview of East Asian shipbuilding technology, those who are interested in a more detailed study should refer to Van Tilburg 2007, Herron 1998 and other sources listed in the references.

BEFORE THE CHINESE MARITIME EXPANSION

The Early Periods (Until 617 CE)

There are many Chinese texts that mention patrons of boatbuilding, including Fu Hsi, who lived around 2852 BCE, mentioned in *Yi Jing*, "The Book of Changes," and Emperor Yü, who lived around 2000 BCE near Ningbo, mentioned in *Shi Yi Ji*

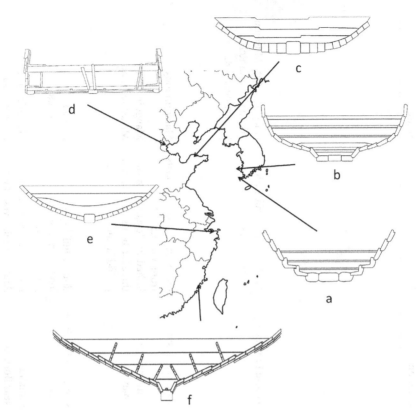

Figure 24.2 Schematic models of cross sections of typical vessels from East Asia from the Song and Yuan dynasties (not to scale): (a) Shibidongpado Boat; (b) Anjwado Ship; (c) Penglai No. 1 Ship; (d) Jinghai Boat; (e) Ningbo Ship; and (f) Quanzhou Ship. Illustration by the author.

(Worcester 1971: 7–8). The Chinese character for "boat/ship" appears on the earliest evidence of writings in the Shang dynasty (1600–1046 BCE), attesting to a long and thriving boatbuilding tradition in China (Worcester 1971). Cave paintings and several clay models of vessels have been discovered dating to as early as 7,000 years ago, but it is difficult, if not impossible, to identify how the vessels were constructed; their slender shape with U-shaped cross section may represent a log boat (Wang 2000: 13–16). As suggested by Nishimura (1925), rafts were most likely in use since antiquity, but archaeological evidence is rare. However, this type of vessel probably played a significant role in the history of the development of Asian watercraft. Scholars, such as Hornell (1934), Needham (1971), and Worcester (1971), rely on ethnographic and historical records to indicate the widespread use of rafts in the past.

The archaeological remains of boats provide a clearer picture of the development of the earliest forms of naval architecture in China, and from these it is known that the Chinese extensively built log boats. More than 40 log boats have been excavated from almost all coastal provinces, from Lianing in the north to Hainan in the

Table 24.1 Timeline of Chinese dynasties and vessels mentioned in the text

Dynasty	Date	Name	Brief Description	Location	Source
Xia dynasty	2100–1600 BCE	log boats discovered throughout East Asia			Xi 1999
Shang dynasty	1600–1046				
Western Zhou dynasty	1046–771				
Eastern Zhou dynasty	770–256				
Spring and Autumn Period	722–476				
Warring States Period	475–221				
Qin dynasty	221–206				
Western Han dynasty	206 BCE – CE 9	Wujin Boat	flat-bottomed craft with chine strakes	Jiangsu Province	Chagzhou City Museum Wujin Cultural Relics Department 1982
Xin dynasty	9–23				
Eastern Han dynasty	25–220				
Three Kingdoms	220–265				
Jin dynasty	265–420	Pontian Boat (CE 260–430)	one of the earliest log boats from Southeast Asia	Malay Peninsula	Manguin 1993
		Butuan Boat 1 (CE 260–550) Itachigawa, Morokuwa, Oiwazato log boats	lashed-lug (cleat) log boat three log boats from Kofun period Japan	Mindanao Japan	Manguin 1993 Miyashita 2006
Southern and Northern dynasties	420–589				
Sui dynasty	581–618	Pingdu Boat Shanghai Boat	double-hull log boat log boat base with extended planks	Shandong Province Shanghai	Xi 1999 Wang 1983
Tang dynasty	618–907	Sambirejo (CE 610–775) Belitung Shipwreck	lashed-lug (cleat) log boat Arab or Indian vessel with Chinese cargo	Sumatra Near Borneo	Manguin 1993 Flecker 2000

Ship	Dynasty/Period	Date	Location	Description	Reference
Intan Shipwreck	Five Dynasties and Ten Kingdoms	907–960	Southeast Asia	local Southeast Asian vessel with Chinese cargo	Flecker 2001
Grand Canal Boats	Northern Song dynasty	960–1127	Anhui Province	eight flat-bottomed river craft	Kan et al. 2001
Rugao Ship			Jiangsu Province	possible first example of bulkhead use	Nanjin Museum 1974
Anapuchi Pond Boat			Korea	flat-bottomed craft with chine strakes	Kim 1994
Jinghai Boat (Yuanmengkou Ship)			Near Tianjing	local flat-bottomed watercraft	Tianjing City Cultural Relics Administration 1983
Jiading Ship (Fengbinyang Bay Ship)			Near Shanghai	local watercraft with bulkhead	Ni 1979
Ningbo Ship			Zhejiang Province	estuary/oceangoing vessel	Lin et al. 1991
Quanzhou Shipwreck	Liao dynasty	916–1125	Fujian Province	large seagoing vessel	Green et al. 1998
Shibidongpado Shipwreck	Jin dynasty	1125–1234	Korea	small watercraft with double chine strakes	Yuan 2006
Wando Shipwreck	Southern Song dynasty	1127–1279	Korea	small watercraft with chine strakes	Green and Kim 1989
Huaguang No. 1 Ship			Paracel Islands	large six-layered planked cargo vessel	Zhao 2009
Taean Treasure Ship			Korea	possible large Korean cargo vessel	The National Research Institute of Maritime Cultural Heritage of Korea 2009

(continued)

Table 24.1 (continued)

Dynasty	Date	Name	Brief Description	Location	Source
Yuan dynasty	1271–1368	Butuan Boat 2 (CE 1270–1410)	lashed-lug (cleat) log boat	Mindanao	Manguin 1993
		Shinan Shipwreck	large cargo vessel from China on way to Japan	Korea	Cultural Property Maintenance Office 1984
		Takashima Underwater Site	warships from China and Korea crushed by a typhoon	Japan	Sasaki 2008
		Penglai No. 1	Chinese patrol vessel	Shandong Province	Cultural Relics Bureau of Penglai City 2006; Yuan 2006
		Talido Ship	traditional Korean watercraft	Korea	
Ming dynasty	1368–1644	Penglai No. 2	Chinese patrol vessel	Shandong Province	Cultural Relics Bureau of Penglai City 2006
		Penglai No. 3	hybrid Chinese and Korean vessel	Shandong Province	Cultural Relics Bureau of Penglai City 2006
		Penglai No. 4	Korean ship found in China	Shandong Province	Cultural Relics Bureau of Penglai City 2006
		Pattaya Shipwreck	Southeast Asian hybrid vessel	Thailand	Green and Intakosai 1983
		Phu Quoc Shipwreck	Southeast Asian hybrid vessel	Vietnam	Flecker 2007
		Jindo Log Boat	possible Chinese log boat—extended lengthwise	Korea	Mokpo Conservation Institute 1993
		Anjwa Ship	large traditional Korean watercraft	Korea	National Maritime Museum of Korea 2006
Qing dynasty	1644–1911				

south, as well as from inland provinces, implying that log boats were ubiquitous in China (Wang 2000; Xi 1999). The earliest log boat dates to the Neolithic period, but the majority of them date from the millennia between the Spring and Autumn Period (1122–256 BCE) to the Han dynasty (206 BCE–220 CE). The number of archaeologically documented log craft gradually declines during the Tang dynasty (618–907 CE).

Various shapes and construction techniques can be seen on these vessels, and lengths vary between 7 and 14 m. The importance of log boats to East Asia as a whole becomes evident when we realize that over 200 log boats have been excavated in Japan alone, and the use of such vessels persisted until recently (Miyashita 2006). Although the significance and accuracy of textual sources is debatable, some documents add support to the importance of the log boat in maritime China; the fabled emperor Huang Ti, believed to have lived around 2697 BCE, is himself said to have built a boat by hollowing out logs (Worcester 1971: 11–12).

When China began to develop a more advanced material culture, its civilization began to spread. In the north, particularly in Japan, a sudden influx of imported goods appeared in the late Jōmon or early Yayoi periods, around 300 BCE or perhaps earlier (Mizoguchi 2002: 116–196; Seth 2006: 31). The Japanese learned metallurgy, rice cultivation, and other advanced cultural traits, including writing and bureaucratic administrative systems, from China and Korea (Totman 2005: 38). Ships from Japan and Korea were built with log boats as their base. Shipwrights added planks to increase freeboard, creating an efficient, seaworthy craft, or split the log in two to insert flat bottom planks, creating a vessel with a wider beam (Adachi 1998: 33).

A maritime-oriented population known as the Yueh, who made the famous bronze Dong-son drums, lived in southern China and northern Vietnam and were involved with the Chinese in commercial and political activities beginning in the first century CE (Nguyễn 1993: 21–35; Taylor 1983: 4). In addition, Chinese monks traveling to India, while mostly preferring the land route, also traveled by sea (Ishizawa and Ikuta 1998: 77, 87–95). Different seafaring traditions existed in the region, such as the sewn plank boats recorded in Hainan Island and elsewhere (Manguin 1985). Perhaps the Chinese learned many aspects of shipbuilding from the people of Southeast Asia. At this early stage, however, the process through which shipbuilding technology was transferred from one culture to another is difficult to assess.

Several clay models of vessels have been discovered from the Han dynasty, some equipped with oars and superstructures (Xi 1999: 76–78). These models appear to be of planked vessels, but their internal structures and method of hull assembly cannot be determined. On the other hand, the actual remains of some preserved vessels provide an excellent idea of how East Asian vessels were made in this period. One interesting vessel from the Sui dynasty (581–618 CE) was excavated in Pingdu, Shandong Province, in 1976. This was a double-hulled log boat, connected with beams and decks between the two hulls. This unique discovery provides an example of how shipwrights utilized their resources skillfully. The length of the vessel was over 23 m, with the hollowed-out hulls connected together using complex scarfs to extend their overall dimensions (Xi 1999: 20–21). Another vessel, dated to about 2,000 years ago, was excavated in Wujin, Jiangsu Province. Although most of the hull had been lost, there were sufficient remains to illustrate a transitional form from log boat to planked vessel. This boat had a flat bottom plank with two curved log-boat-like planks as chine strakes. The components were connected using pegged mortises and tenons (Chagzhou City Museum Wujin Cultural Relics Department 1982). Another vessel with a transitional form, discovered near Shanghai, had a hollowed log as the base with planks about 5 cm thick attached above, and multiple beams supporting the hull (Wang 1983: 51). The vessel is dated to the Sui dynasty and carries a keel-like feature; triangular and 40 cm high, it narrows from 90 cm wide at the top to 40 cm wide near its bottom (Xi 1999: 26–27). A shallow hollowed-out section, only about 10 cm on either side of its centerline, was removed to create the appearance of a log canoe. Possible "stem" and "stern" sections, both upturned, were attached to the log base using hooked scarfs.

The Tang Dynasty (618–907 CE)

Beginning in the sixth century CE, Arab and Persian merchants began to sail directly to China. By 618 CE, they were already creating a trading settlement in what will later become Canton, and a large population of Arabs and Persians lived in Yangzhou on the Yangtze River (Reischauer 1946: 142–144). The Yangtze estuary became the center of communication where a great shipbuilding tradition flourished (So 2000). The activities of Arab merchants were extensive, even reaching Korea (Seth 2006: 85). Koreans were also active in trade, acting as intermediaries between China and Japan (Mori 1972). The Chinese were initially less active in the business of international commerce (Lo 1969: 60–61). Nonetheless, the fame of the Tang dynasty stems from the expansion of an extensive trade network. This brought goods from India and Southeast Asia to China, and from China to the rest of Asia. The people who lived in extreme northern Asia were also incorporated into the trade system: for example, furs were exported from Sakhalin and Manchu to China and Japan (Anno 1999: 12). The trade was based on a tribute system wherein officials from a country brought goods to the Tang court and the government resold the items to private individuals; foreign merchants had to accept Chinese overlordship and culture to engage in any commercial activity (Kamei 1986: 4–21).

One of the most significant archaeological finds that reveals the maritime culture of the Tang dynasty is the Belitung shipwreck, dated to between 618 and 628 CE and found between Borneo and Sumatra (Flecker 2000). The ship was laden with a Chinese cargo, but the vessel is believed to be the product of Arab or Indian shipwrights. This hypothesis is based on the shipwreck having the characteristic laced construction techniques found in the Indian Ocean and on the species of wood used to build it (Flecker 2000: 211–216; Hourani 1995). The Belitung vessel had a distinctive U-shaped keel with a curved rise at the prow where it was fitted to the sternpost (Flecker 2000: 201).

Another vessel discovered in Southeast Asia, the Intan shipwreck from the tenth century CE, was also carrying a ceramic cargo from southern China, as well as various goods from Southeast Asia and the Middle East (Burningham 2003: 266). Although the hull was not well preserved, it was possible to identify that the planks were joined by edge-joined dowels, the characteristic construction technique of the region (Flecker 2001: 126–140). Such a local craft carrying this varied cargo implies that a large maritime network existed connecting the people of the Indian Ocean to Pacific Asia.

Archaeological evidence of Chinese vessels has yet to be discovered in Southeast Asia, but several vessels have been excavated in the continental area of China. In 1999, a total of eight vessels were discovered near Huaibei, Anhui Province, along the ancient Grand Canal, which was used during the Sui and Tang dynasties (Kan, Gong, and Xi 2001: 35). Ship No. 1 was 9.6 m long and 1.8 m in beam, a slim and fast vessel used to maneuver in the canal. The planks were connected using iron nails, suggesting a distinctive Chinese way of plank joinery compared to lacing found in ships built in the Indian Ocean and the edge-joined dowel common in Southeast Asia. It was a flat-bottomed vessel, with four bottom planks 6–7 cm thick, but no chine strakes survive. The vessel had transverse beams as well as floor timbers, but no attached bulkheads. Evidence suggests that *chunam*, which is white putty made by mixing tung oil, straw, and sometimes ash, may have been used for waterproofing the seams (Kan, Gong, and Xi 2001). Along with this vessel, another late Sui or early Tang boat discovered in Rugao, Jiangsu Province, is considered one of the most important vessels excavated in China from this period. What makes this example unique is that it is possibly the earliest excavated Chinese ship that utilized bulkheads for structural support. With a reconstructed length of 18 m and beam of 2.58 m, the vessel was built using iron nails to connect the planks, and *chunam* was used for waterproofing (Nanjin Museum 1974).

Despite the extent of Arab and Southeast Asian commercial activities in the area, it is difficult to assess their influence on the Chinese shipbuilding tradition. The vessels discovered from Sui and Tang periods are not from the coast but from inland waterways, where the local tradition of the log boat appears to have matured to a fully planked vessel. A number of typical "Chinese" features can be seen on the ships from this period, including the use of iron nails to connect planks and the use of *chunam*. One thing to note is that the use of bulkheads may be relatively new at this stage.

THE ERA OF MARITIME EXPANSION: THE SONG AND YUAN DYNASTIES (960–1368 CE)

Despite the glorious history of the Tang dynasty, the government was weakened by internal struggle and the empire collapsed; after a period of chaos, the new Northern Song dynasty was established (960–1127 CE) (Lo 1969: 64). Initially, the

Northern Song dynasty held the country in unity, but invading Khitans and Jurch-
ens from the north soon took over control of the northern half of China. In response,
the Song moved their capital to the south and created the Southern Song dynasty
(1127–1279 CE). It was no longer possible to maintain the lucrative overland trade
with western Asia (the traditional Silk Road); in order to defend and finance the
country, the court encouraged overseas trade, and maritime commerce became a
dependable source of income (Shiba 1983: 105–106). To protect against pirates, in
1132 CE a professional navy was established, and prizes were offered for new naval
innovations. It was by this route that major nautical inventions appeared, including
the marine compass (Levathes 1997: 43; Van Tilburg 1994: 2).

   A stronger commercial and cultural link between Northeast Asia and China
developed during this time period. Korea, under the Goryeo dynasty (918–1392
CE), established by descendants from a powerful merchant family, developed strong
maritime connections with other Asian nations using their ships (Choi 2006: 68).
One indication of the geographical range of the maritime sphere of East Asia is the
fact that the Goryeo dynasty was visited by Arab traders beginning in 1024 CE (Seth
2006: 84–85). Japan was also involved in international trade. Hakata, located on
Kyūshū Island, became a major international city where merchants from the Southern Song visited frequently, creating what may be called a "China Town" (Batten
2006). For the people of southern China, the trade with Japan was profitable because
Japan based the value of coin on the value of its metal, while China minted coin to
collect taxes and its value was artificially fixed by the government (Schottenhammer
2001: 130–140). This difference in "exchange rate" led to a mass exodus of Chinese
coins to Japan, with as much as 10,000 tons of coins per year exported to Japan
(Tanaka 1986: 42). The Yuan dynasty Shinan shipwreck exhibits the mechanism of
trade that took place during this period. This vessel, which originated in China and
was en route to Japan when it shipwrecked in Korea, had seven million brass and
copper coins on board; the earliest coin dated from 14 CE (Kamei 1986: 183–186).
These ancient coins had no value in China but were highly valuable in Japan. Mori
(1972) notes that if no written documents were available, archaeologists would conclude that Japan was invaded by southern China, as, concurrently, imported Chinese porcelain virtually replaced the local ceramic industry in some areas. Coins
and merchandise were also exported to Southeast Asia and beyond; Chinese coins
have been found in Java and as far away as Ceylon (Shiba 1983: 106).

   The Southern Song's status as a maritime empire was destroyed by more powerful invaders from the north: the Mongols. Initially, the Mongols lacked an organized naval force and were thus kept at bay along the Yangtze River (Rossabi 1988:
82). To defeat the naval empire of the Southern Song, it was necessary to curb the
profits from trade; the solution for the Mongols was to conquer the Southern Song's
trading partners, Korea and Japan (Saeki 2003: 72). Korea suffered from Mongol
invasions beginning in 1231 CE and was finally conquered in 1273 CE (Nahm 1988:
90–91). In the following year, Khubilai Khan sent 900 vessels built in Korea to attack
the international trading city of Hakata in western Japan, but retreated after only a
few days of fighting (Ota 1997: 5–34). Soon after this failed invasion of Japan, the

Mongols succeeded in conquering the Southern Song dynasty and established the Yuan dynasty, becoming the sole rulers of China (Rossabi 1988: 208). Again in 1281 CE, Khubilai amassed more than 3,000 vessels from China and 900 ships from Korea to conquer Japan. When the fleet approached the island of Takashima in western Japan, the winds and waves of a strong typhoon crushed the invader's vessels to pieces; the Japanese believed that the wind was brought by the gods, so the word *kamikaze*, or "divine wind," was born (Saeki 2003: 140–149). The remains of the invading fleets, which contained vessels built in Korea, along the Yangtze River, and in Fujian Province, were discovered on the island of Takashima in recent years (Delgado 2009; Sasaki 2008). Khubilai's intractable desire led to a series of invasions in Southeast Asia, all of which eventually failed (Saeki 2003: 191–192).

Despite the Mongol conquests, trade flourished in East Asia. Fortunately, much evidence of ships and seafaring traditions survives to this day. While it is not possible to list all the available evidence or discuss all the ships that have been discovered, the better-known examples, those that show characteristic traits of the area and time in which they were constructed, are described below. The descriptions start with vessels built in China, followed by Korea and Japan. Unique construction features of vessels and maritime practices will be illustrated for each area. Although the detailed relationships between the maritime traditions are less clear at this time, there was a steady interaction of people and technology across the region.

The Study of Ships from China

Many historical accounts have been written over the centuries in China, dealing with politics, poetry, science, and everyday life. Nonetheless, G. R. G. Worcester, an expert in traditional Chinese river craft of the Yangtze River, once wrote, "China holds scholarship in high honor, but apparently they did not concern themselves with naval history or nautical lore" (Worcester 1971: 335). Other scholars, including Joseph Needham, noted that comprehensive nautical treatises were rarely written in China (Needham, Ling, and Gwei-Djen 1971: 380). Many documents, including one entitled *Tai Bai Yin Jie*, describes the types and sizes of vessels used, but no details can be learned about the internal structure of the hulls (Wang and Zhang 2004). The encyclopedia of medieval China, *Tian Gong Kai Wu*, has a section for shipbuilding, and it states, "When building a vessel, the bottom of a ship serves as a foundation, and is laid down first" (Yabuuchi 1955). An extensive study of written documents such as this may reveal some details about China's nautical tradition; however, these historical accounts will not be discussed here. A grasp of the study of Chinese literature and an understanding of Chinese characters are necessary to be able to conduct a meaningful discussion.

Foreigners also wrote accounts about the ships they encountered in China. Italian merchant Marco Polo, for example, visited China during Khubilai's reign. He described Chinese vessels, shipbuilding practices, and naval organization in remarkable detail. Polo wrote, "Vessels have some thirteen compartments or severances in the interior, made with planking strongly framed." He also describes the use of lime paste mixed with tree oil and hemp to waterproof the seams, as well as the use of multiple layers of planking; it is said that with each repair, Chinese ship-wrights added one extra layer of planks, and they added up to six layers of planks (Yule 1993: 250–251). To add credibility to Polo's account, Chinese researchers recently announced the discovery of the Huaguang No. 1 ship, a relatively large vessel with five or six layers of planks (Zhao 2009). Ibn Battuta, an Arab traveler who visited China around 1347 CE, described a shipbuilding practice he observed, albeit briefly. According to his account, the bottom was laid down first, and then the two "walls" (side planking?) were installed. After this, another "wall" series (bulk-heads?) was put across the hull (Mackintosh-Smith 2002: 223–224).

The study of iconography should also bring to light more detail on Chinese shipbuilding traditions, but anything other than a brief discussion is beyond the scope of this chapter. The study conducted by Needham (1971) is an excellent refer-ence, and Wang (2000) has compiled a large collection of Chinese iconography that requires further analysis. The study of iconography entails a thorough investigation of its source; many drawings were copied, and they were not designed to impress people with accuracy. Despite this general trend, several pieces are well worth noting for their accurate depictions of ships. One example is *Qing Ming Shang He Tu*, or "The Spring Festival along the River." This painted scroll drawn in the North-ern Song period is considered one of the masterpieces of Chinese art, portraying details of city life and multiple riverboats, even including the nailing patterns on planks (Ihara 2003). The artist depicts flat-bottomed vessels with planks fastened with an ample supply of nails, equipped with superstructures, decks, rudders, wind-lasses, and other shipboard items that may be comparable to archaeological data. Another work of art is the *Moko Shurai Ekotoba* scroll, or the "Mongol Invasion Scroll," most likely created in 1293 CE (Conlan 2001: 5). This scroll depicts scenes from the Mongol invasions of Japan, illustrating multiple vessels of various sizes. Some vessels are large and wide, and others may have multiple decks, while a number appear to be narrow boats made for speed.

It is known that during the Sung dynasty, such cities as Quanzhou in Fujian Province became an international center of trade (Li 1986: 282–283). Jung-Pang Lo, a Chinese maritime historian, mentions an account from the early Song period about a state official in the north who ordered vessels to be built in Quanzhou spe-cifically for overseas travel; the shipwrights that received the orders replied that the flat-bottomed types specified were not suited for open seas and that deeper-hulled vessels should be used instead (Lo 1969: 79). This account demonstrates that dif-ferent shipbuilding traditions existed in China and, perhaps, that different areas specialized in their own construction methods. These differences in hull character-istics are mostly visible through the archaeological evidence. More than 50 vessels have been excavated and reported on in China; the small representative sample dis-cussed here begins in the north of the region and proceeds southward.

A vessel dating to the early Song dynasty and discovered in Jinghai, Tianjin, is an excellent example of the local traditional craft that existed in northern China. It is a flat-bottomed and box-shaped boat built without the use of bulkheads. Instead, the hull derived its major strength from a series of crossbeams of unfashioned wood (Tianjing City Cultural Relics Administration 1983: 58, 67). Small frames and stanchions were also made with curved branches. The transition from the bottom to the straight sides of the hull was marked by a thick and slightly rounded strake; otherwise, there is no distinction between the bottom planks (Tianjing City Cultural Relics Administration 1983: fig. 5). The watercraft was most likely used as a barge for transporting goods locally, and it shows remarkable similarity to the Korean vessels described below.

The Jiaodong peninsula of Shandong province extends out to the Yellow Sea, making it suitable for seafarers, both Chinese and foreign, who wished to replenish their supplies or wait for the wind to change. The importance of Penglai City, a waterfront castle located on Jiaodong peninsula, is evident throughout Chinese dynasties. The city developed into a systematic water and land fortification during the Song dynasty and was well fortified during the Ming dynasty (Cultural Relics Bureau of Penglai City 2006: 217). The excavation of the waterfront fort yielded a total of four ancient vessels. Penglai Ships Nos. 1 and 2 were dated to the Ming dynasty and exhibited characteristics of the Chinese shipbuilding tradition, including bulkhead construction, the use of a keel, and planks joined by iron nails set diagonally. Penglai Ship No. 3 appears to be a possible hybrid vessel showing both Korean and Chinese shipbuilding characteristics, while Penglai Ship No. 4 appears to be a Korean vessel (Cultural Relics Bureau of Penglai City 2006: 217). Penglai Ships Nos. 3 and 4 will therefore be discussed below with Korean vessels.

Penglai Ships Nos. 1 and 2 were most likely used as military vessels along the near shore and rivers. The remaining length of the vessels is close to 30 m, while the maximum beams are about 6m (Xi 1999: 209–211). Both vessels have relatively flat midship profiles, but the angles of dead rise become sharper toward the prow. A keel that protrudes slightly on the inside of the hull, or perhaps what may be called a keel plank, is present in both cases, and elaborate hooked scarfs join the gradually rising stem and stern keel pieces, supported by an additional timber above the keels (Dun et al. 1994: 20–21). All planks were nailed together using square iron nails placed diagonally from inside the hull, as well as nails placed within the seams going through the width of one plank and connecting to the plank below it. The shipwrights used iron nails as long as 50 cm, and the planks were almost square, approximately 20 cm by 20 cm, becoming narrower toward the turn of the bilge. The vessels also employed mortise-and-tenon construction for bulkhead connections, along with iron nails (Dun et al. 1994: 25). The joinery between the bulkhead and the planks for Penglai Ship No. 1 must be illustrated in detail (Figure 24.3). It uses L-shaped iron brackets; the shorter side of the "L" is fitted inside the seams of the planks, while the longer side is nailed to the surface of the bulkheads (Xi 1999: fig. 7/11).

An early Song dynasty vessel discovered near Jiading in Shanghai exhibits a partially flat-bottomed, partially angled hull. Perhaps it is a transitional form between the flat-bottomed boat and the rounded-hull vessel characteristic of the Yangtze estuary (Ni 1979). Only a small section about 6.23 m long was discovered;

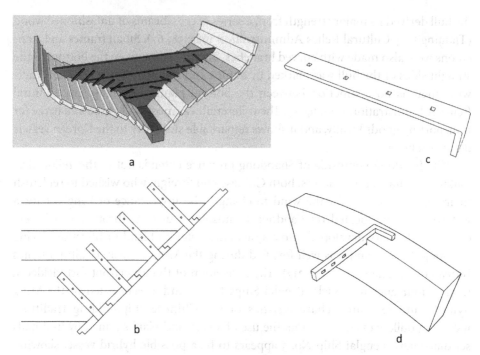

Figure 24.3 Simplified models of selected joining methods for plank-bulkhead connection: (a) model of the Shinan Ship showing the stiffeners; (b) configuration of L-shaped brackets found on the Quanzhou Ship; (c) L-shaped bracket; and (d) method for attaching L-shaped brackets as seen on the Penglai No. 1 Ship. Illustration by the author.

however, it revealed that the scarfs' positions were random (Ni 1979: fig. 2). This fact is significant because vessels dating later than the Jiading ship typically carried their scarfs at the bulkhead stations. The random positioning of the scarfs may imply that the bulkheads were inserted as an afterthought and that bulkhead structures were not considered an integral part of a ship's structure at the time. Considering the possible early date of this vessel, the concept of the bulkhead may not have been fully developed.

Another vessel was discovered at a Song dynasty shipyard in Ningbo. This vessel had a rounded to V-shaped hull with a keel, seven bulkheads, wales, and two tabernacle steps to hold masts. Although the 9.3 m long hull did not survive after the excavation, detailed recordings provide insights into the shipbuilding practices of the time (Lin, Genqi, and Green 1991). As seen with Penglai Ships Nos. 1 and 2, the keel plank (26 cm sided and 18 cm molded) protrudes inside the hull. The lowest bulkhead of the ship is actually a curved piece of wood functioning as a frame, and the bulkhead planks were laid on top of this base. The Ningbo ship had planks that varied in width from 21 to 42 cm, but the thicknesses were uniform, between 6 and 8 cm (Lin, Genqi, and Green 1991: 306–308). Thus, the shape of the planks differed from the ones seen in the ships from Penglai. Iron nails were used as the primary means of fastening the hull (Lin, Genqi, and Green 1991: 302).

The most famous excavated and fully reported shipwreck from East Asian waters may be the Quanzhou shipwreck, made in Fujian Province or south of the Yangtze River during the late Song dynasty. The vessel, more than 20 m long and constructed with transverse bulkheads, carried a cargo of spices, wood, and exotic materials from Southeast Asia. The Quanzhou ship has a keel wider than it is tall, at 27 cm molded and 42 cm sided (Green, Burningham, and Museum of Overseas Communication History 1998: 282). The garboard is larger than the other planks and was firmly attached to the keel. The planks are joined using iron nails driven diagonally from outside. The multilayering of planks provides additional longitudinal stiffening (Green, Burningham, and Museum of Overseas Communication History 1998: 286). The use of L-shaped iron brackets (similar to one found on Penglai No. 1) to connect the planks and bulkheads is an important feature of the Quanzhou ship (Figure 24.4). These brackets are set from the outside of the plank going through the thickness and nailed to the surface of the bulkhead (Green, Burningham, and Museum of Overseas Communication History 1998: 289–291). The Quanzhou ship was literally covered with *chunam*, and it is said that "no nail was left behind" without the putty; every seam and nail hole, including internal structures, was sealed with an ample amount of *chunam* (Li 1986: 279).

The Shinan ship, a large cargo vessel mentioned above, also had a large and wide keel, 50 cm molded and 71 cm sided. The garboards, thicker than other planks, were strongly attached to the keel. One difference from the Quanzhou ship is that

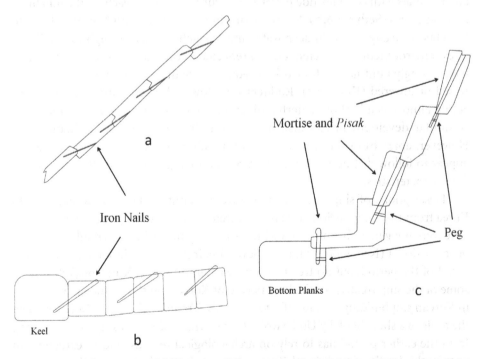

Figure 24.4 Schematic models showing differences in plank joinery: (a) Quanzhou Ship; (b) Penglai No. 1 and No. 2 Ships; and (c) the Wando Boat. Illustration by the author.

the lowest bulkhead timber of the Shinan ship is thicker than the other bulkhead timbers, acting as a frame (Cultural Property Maintenance Office 1984: 127–129). The keel, the garboards, and the lowest bulkhead timber formed the foundation of the vessel. While the Quanzhou ship utilized multiple layers of planking, the Shinan ship had only one layer but was built with thick plank sheathing (Cultural Property Maintenance Office 1984). The planks and bulkheads were firmly assembled with stiffeners, a wooden form of an "iron bracket," as seen in the Quanzhou ship. The bulkhead is cut following the shape of the hull, indicating that the planks might have been assembled first. The positions of the plank scarfs are symmetrical between the starboard and port sides, but notably they are not dependent on the bulkhead positions, as they are not aligned under the bulkheads (Cultural Property Maintenance Office 1984: fig. 8/1).

The Study of Ships from Korea and Japan

It is natural to assume that Korea, a peninsula similarly to Italy, would develop a strong maritime tradition. The southern and western coasts of Korea face Japan and China, respectively, and were important loci of trade. Korea often acted as a middleman in trade between Japan and China and developed a rich maritime tradition (Choi 2006: 67–73).

When approaching Korea from the sea, mariners faced numerous small islands and mudflats with complex tide patterns and currents before reaching the inhabited mainland area (Seth 2006: 7). In this environment, a vessel must have the ability to both take a steady course in deep water and navigate craftily through the shallows. These environmental characteristics are reflected in traditional Korean craft, which have strongly built flat-bottomed hulls equipped with large rudders that could be raised or lowered (Kim 1994). Rudders were lowered when sailing in open seas, acting almost as a keel or centerboard, and raised when navigating the mudflats. A similar development can also be seen on Chinese vessels (Needham 1971). However, apart from the functionality of a rudder, Korean and Chinese vessels appear to follow distinctive styles, the two developing independently and sharing few characteristics.

Descriptions of ships written in a travel account of the 1124 CE embassy to Korea from the Chinese Song dynasty are well known, and it appears that the Chinese were not generally impressed with the crudely made, boxlike, double-transom boats of Korea (Needham 1971: 603). Several paintings provide some account of a vessel of the period, but no treatises were written this early. Kim (1994) illustrates some of the ship treatises of the later period of Korea, and those who are interested in Korean shipbuilding should refer to his study. Traditional ships of Korea are also the topic of a short book by Underwood (1976). The evidence of ships and seafaring from the earlier period has to rely on archaeological records, and researchers can now study details of traditional Korean watercraft, thanks to more than a dozen shipwrecks excavated and reported in recent years (Kim 2006).

A sophisticated shipbuilding tradition can be seen in a log boat dating to the thirteenth and fourteenth centuries CE excavated in Jindo, Korea. The vessel, 16.85 m long and 2.34 m wide, used two logs to extend the length of the vessel. An interesting feature is the locking mechanism found at the junction connecting the two hollowed-out logs. Bracing timbers were laid on top of the seam, and complex carvings were made to fit the locking mechanism in place (Mokpo Conservation Institute 1993). Similar mechanisms were present on several log boats found in Japan, including those found at Itachigawa, Morokuwa, and Oiwazato (Miyashita 2006: 40–47). While the tradition of log boats continued in the region, Koreans also began to develop more robust vessels. The first archaeological example of such a vessel was found at Anapuchi Pond, dating to the seventh to ninth centuries CE. The vessel, less than 6 m long and with upturned ends, has a large rectangular bottom timber carved from a single log. The bottom piece is connected to L-shaped chine strakes on either side. The timber has two cleats with a hole where transverse timbers were placed and secured (Kim 1994: 41–44). These cleats are similar to those found on Bronze Age vessels in England, including the Ferriby boats (Wright 1985; McGrail 1985). A similar boat was found at Takashima, Japan (Takashima Board of Education 2001). Only the bottom timber survived, but the upturned end and a cleat with a hole was preserved. Perhaps this vessel was used during the Mongol invasion of Japan in the thirteenth century; however, considering the proximity of the island to Korea and the heavily disturbed nature of the site, along with slightly earlier dates obtained from carbon-14 dating, the vessel may have wrecked on an earlier visit to Japan. Otherwise, it may serve as evidence that a similar construction technology was widespread in the area.

Several vessels have been excavated in Korea that date between the eleventh and fourteenth centuries CE. The traditional Korean flat-bottomed vessels relied on heavy, robust hull timbers and numerous transverse beams. Ethnographic, historical, and archaeological records point to a tradition of shipbuilding based on using wooden fasteners and no iron nails (Kim 1994: 8–37). The vessels were made of flat bottom planks joined by *jangsak*, a long tenon or internal framing piece that goes through several planks. The robust side planking was connected with a *pisak*, a large tenon put through the mortise cut completely through the upper planks and into the middle of the plank below, and pegged only through the bottom end (Figure 24.4). The lateral strength of the vessels was derived from through-beams; frames and bulkheads were not used on traditional Korean vessels. Both stern and bow ended abruptly with transoms. Choi (2006) and Kim (2004) provide a synthesis on traditional boats.

The Sibidongpado vessel, dated to the eleventh century or the early twelfth, was found carrying celadon ware (protected with dunnage) and other personal items on board, offering archaeologists a chance to study the seafaring life of the Goryeo dynasty period. The Sibidongpado vessel had two overlapping L-shaped chine strakes, which is unique and perhaps the only excavated example of such a construction in the world (Yuan 2006: fig. 10). The Wando boat, less than 10 m long, was discovered in southern Korea and dates to the eleventh century (Green and

Kim 1989: 39). The vessel features heavy bottom planks and one L-shaped chine strake, giving it a boxlike appearance in cross section (Kim 1994: fig. 26). The Wando boat had five bottom planks, each 18–20 cm thick and 30–32 cm wide (Green and Kim 1989: 39). Two rectangular recesses are present near midships, where taberna- cles for the mast were placed (Kim 1994: fig. 26). These two vessels seem to be the only vessels that featured the L-shaped chine strake, and all later vessels had the first side planks directly attached to the bottom planks.

The Talido Boat from the fourteenth century had three bottom strakes; the vessel was 10.5 m in length and only 2.7 m in beam, suggesting a fast boat that had navigated the coast of Korea (Yuan 2006). The Anjwa boat from the fourteenth century also had three bottom strakes. The estimated length of the vessel is 17 m, and the hull shows extensive use of beams to support the lateral stress. Several tiles were found, indicating that the ship had a galley. An evidence of caulking as well as a use of markings for constructing the hull was observed (National Maritime Museum of Korea 2006). One interesting vessel is the Taean ship, known as the "treasure boat of the Goryeo dynasty." A large number of unique and precious cel- adon wares, and numerous wooden and bamboo tags, were found with the cargo, illustrating shipping practices at the time. The planks, 30–40 cm wide and 12–15 cm thick, were unusually thin compared to the typical 20 cm or thicker planks found on Wando and other vessels. The Taean ship also used *pisak* for connecting planks; these were positioned through the planks diagonally, and driven though the upper edges of planks (National Research Institute of Maritime Cultural Heritage of Korea 2009).

The discussion of Korean ships cannot end without a mention of the Penglai shipwrecks from northern China. Although only a small section of the hull sur- vived, Penglai Ship No. 4 is certainly a vessel that originated in Korea, based on the mast tabernacle slots, the shape of the bottom planks, and the joinery method using *jangsak* (Yuan 2006: 505–506). Penglai Ship No. 3 is a unique vessel that exhibits the characteristics of both Korean and Chinese traditions. The vessel has Chinese-like bulkheads and mast step, but the hull was composed of three bottom planks joined with *jangsak*. The planking were joined using both iron nails and *pisak* (Yuan 2006: 498–505). It can be suggested that the vessel was built in Korea and later reinforced or rebuilt in China, but it is difficult to provide a definitive interpretation.

The shipbuilding tradition of Japan is not well known, unfortunately. Ships prior to this period of Chinese maritime expansion have been excavated from sev- eral land sites; Miyashita (2006) describes the development of Japanese ships from a log-boat-based tradition to semi-built vessels. No hull remains, except for those from the underwater Takashima site, have been excavated in the country, and researchers must rely on iconography and written documents for the studying the Japanese maritime tradition. Very little evidence exists prior to the sixteenth cen- tury, but it suggests that some of the ships were based on log boats with added sides, while other vessels may have developed into *tanaita-tsukuri*. These boats featured a flat-bottomed base with side planks directly attached; heavy beams were used to support the hull laterally, perhaps somewhat similar to traditional Korean vessels

(Adachi 1998: 31). The *Moko Shurai Ekotoba* scroll mentioned above is one good source of iconography that depicts small Japanese boats among the much larger Mongol invading vessels.

The Decline of Shipping during the Ming Dynasty (1368–1644 CE) and the First European Influences

The empire that Khubilai held together began to crumble after his death. Continuous warfare during the Song and Yuan dynasties led to a decline in the land's productivity; because of this decline, coupled with succession troubles and famine, the Yuan dynasty was soon overthrown, and the powerful Ming dynasty was born (1368–1644 CE). Perhaps paradoxically, the voyages of the Ming admiral Cheng He, with his "treasure ships," in the early fifteenth century are often quoted as the height of East Asia's maritime legacy (Stewart 2008: 117–135; Levathes 1997). It is argued, however, that the main concern of the Ming court in regard to those missions was to re-create the tribute system that flourished during the Tang dynasty, not to reestablish the once profitable private shipping framework that existed during the Song dynasty (Cheng 1991; Levathes 1997; Lo 1958: 154–158). Although envoys were sent to India and the Middle East, shipping in China was in decline during and before this time (Cheng 1991: 28). By the middle Ming period, the ruling class suddenly stopped its support of overseas expansion (Stewart 2008: 117–135; van Tilburg 1994: 28). The completion of the Grand Canal in 1411 CE also led to the decline of the sea route and the construction of large draft vessels (Lo 1958: 159). In the past, grain from southern China was brought to northern China by sea using large grain transport vessels; now, small and shallow-draft vessels could transport grain via canals and rivers. The reopening of overland trade through central Asia further weakened maritime commerce.

Without competition, Japanese maritime power grew. While Korea had suffered the most damage from the Mongol invasions, the Chinese also suffered from weaker mercantile activities as a result. Before the invasions, Japan relied on Korean and Chinese vessels to travel overseas; afterward, however, they began to sail to China using their own ships (Kamei 1986: 32). This imbalance of maritime power led to the strengthening of the *wakō*, so-called Japanese pirates who in fact mainly consisted of the marginal populations that lived along the coastal regions of Japan, Korea, and China (Anno 1999: 7). Beginning in the early fourteenth century CE, these pirates began to burn and pillage villages along the Korean and Chinese coasts, disrupting maritime activities in the area (Tanaka 1986: 125–169). By the end of the sixteenth century, the great shipbuilding tradition that dominated the region was lost in China.

Many Chinese traders and shipwrights migrated to Southeast Asia, where the Chinese shipbuilding tradition continued. Large Chinese communities developed during the Ming dynasty in Southeast Asia, including Malacca, Palembang, and Aceh (Cheng 1991: 14–16). This led to the development of new trade routes, and the resultant mix of people and cultures created a new Southeast Asia. Traditional vessels in the region were built using lacing as well as edge-joined dowels. Such vessels discovered at Pontian, Butuan, and Sambirejo suggest that lacing was gradually replaced with the use of dowels (Manguin 1993: 260). When the Chinese moved into Southeast Asia, the so-called hybrid ships of Southeast Asia developed. A growing number of archaeological examples, including the Pattaya and PhuQuoc wrecks, provide a basic idea of how these vessels were constructed using Chinese shipbuilding technology but incorporating the local Southeast Asian tradition. A few typical characteristics, including the V-shaped hull with a keel, multiple planking, and the use of bulkheads, can be attributed to Chinese-influenced techniques, while the use of dowels to connect the planks is a notable local shipbuilding trait (Flecker 2007). Chinese shipwrights played a major role in designing the vessels, but it is argued that local shipbuilders from Southeast Asia constructed them (Flecker 2007: 81–82). There are numerous varieties and differences between Southeast Asian vessels and Chinese vessels, as well as differences within those groups themselves.

During the late Ming dynasty, European powers began to show some influence over the East Asian maritime sphere. In 1543 CE, muskets were introduced to Japan; at that time the country was torn by civil wars. The rapid spread of the technology led to the unification of Japan, and by 1592 it had become strong enough to invade Korea (Swope 2005: 11). The Japanese used the muskets effectively on land, quickly taking most of the country (Seth 2006: 140). Japanese Samurai with muskets were no match, however, when the Ming forces came to aid the Koreans with massive cannon developed by the Portuguese (some carrying interesting names, such as the "Crouching Tiger Cannon") (Swope 2005: 27). In addition, Japanese supply lines through the open water were cut by the efficient use of Korean naval forces (Swope 2005: 22). The Ming court aided the Koreans by sending 200 or more vessels built in Fujian Province, all armed with a variety of firearms (Swope 2005: 34). Perhaps the most famous story from the invasion of Korea is the invention of the Turtle Boat, developed by Korean admiral Yi Sun-Shin; the wooden vessel was protected against the Japanese muskets with iron plates, had spikes to repel the enemy from boarding, and was equipped with large cannon on all sides (Kim 1994: 207–242).

Despite regional conflict in the northeast, shipping continued uninterrupted throughout Asia. Ships from Thailand came to Okinawa and Korea (Robinson 2000: 113), and it is recorded that vessels from Palembang sailed to the port of Obama in western central Japan (Amino 1992: 89). Tsukumoto (1992) refers to "the Asian Inner Sea," the areas connecting Japan, Okinawa, and Southeast Asia, with China at the center. The Red Seal Ships of Japan are worthy of note; these vessels sailed to China and Southeast Asia from Japan during the sixteenth century and into the seventeenth (Adachi 1998: 38–46). The vessels exhibited Chinese, Japanese, and Western construction features. Although the internal structure and construction techniques are not known, the rigging and shipboard equipment can be studied from existing iconography. A European-style rudder was attached to the sternpost, and the rigging shows a peculiar mix of Chinese and European sails. The main propulsion consisted of Chinese batten lug sails; European sails, including spritsail, topsails, and often lateen-rigged mizzen masts, were added to provide extra maneuverability as well as speed when following the direct wind. The Japanese built Western-style ships with the help of shipwrecked sailors and shipwrights who visited Japan (Ishii 1995: 61–72). However, Western influence was curbed as, due to zealous missionary activities in Japan, the shogun began a series of efforts to control the spread of Christianity, culminating in the ban on overseas trade by the Japanese, and a ban on all trade with European countries except the Dutch; the latter were confined to the small artificial island of Deshima in Nagasaki harbor (Totman 2005: 221–227).

Shipping in China did not cease, but the economy refocused on internal development and the use of sustainable resources. Lo (1958: 165) states that in China, self-cultivation and nonexpansion became the norm, and antimilitary and antiexpansion thinking prevailed, enforced by state officials. Some of the vessels made during the eighteenth century in China and Southeast Asia that visited Japan can be seen on the *Tōsen no zu*, an excellent scroll painting stored at Matsuura Historical Museum in Nagasaki, Japan (Ōba 1974). The use of seagoing vessels may have declined compared to the Song period, but vessels with flat or rounded bottoms were well adapted for inland use. Domingo de Navarrete, a Spanish Dominican missionary who visited China at this time, mentioned that "there are more vessels in China than in all the rest of the world" (Needham, Ling, and Gwei-Djen 1971: 423). Watercraft played an important role in the daily life of Chinese people and still do. However, by the time the scientific study of shipbuilding reached China and detailed recordings of ships began to be made, most of the great ships of China had been replaced by the flat-bottomed coastal and river vessels that became the iconic image of Chinese junks.

CONCLUSION

Archaeological evidence collected from shipwrecks, combined with textual and iconographic data, allow scholars to study the seafaring history, seafaring practices, and shipbuilding technologies of East Asia. The vessels of East Asia appear to have developed from a log boat tradition and evolved into planked vessels by the Sui dynasty. Perhaps seafaring populations from the Indian Ocean and Southeast Asia contributed to this technological advancement. China experienced a great maritime expansion during the Song and Yuan dynasties, influencing maritime practice in Southeast Asia and northern East Asia, as seen in some hybrid vessels. While shipbuilding traditions across the region influenced each other, distinctive regional traditions are also visible. Maritime trade and shipping in China began to decline during the Ming dynasty; by the time European nations appeared on Chinese shores, the glorious maritime tradition that once existed had been lost. Recent studies of this lost tradition are bringing new interpretations to the maritime culture of the world. Many aspects of these maritime traditions require further research, including the study of harbors, navigation, naval tactics, and shipboard life. Although this account is limited in its scope, I hope it will act as a gateway into appreciating the depth of East Asian maritime culture and the research that has been undertaken so far.

REFERENCES

Adachi, Hiroyuki 安達祐之. 1998. *Nihon no Fune—Wasen Hen* 日本の船—和船編 *(Ships of Japan—Wasen)*. Tokyo: Fune no Kagakukan 船の科学館.

Amino, Yoshihiko 網野喜彦, ed. 1992. *Higashi-Shinakai to Seikai Bunka* 東シナ海と西海文化 *(The East China Sea and the culture of southern seas)*. Tokyo: Syōgakukan 小学館.

Anno Masayuki 安野眞幸. 1999. Higashi Asia no nakanochyūsei Nihon 東アジアの中の中世日本 (Medieval Japan within the East Asian context). *Hirosaki Daigaku Kyōiku Gakubu Kiyō* 弘前大学教育学部紀要 82: 1–17.

Batten, Bruce. 2006. *Gateway to Japan: Hakata in war and peace 500–1300*. Honolulu: University of Hawaii Press.

Burningham, Nick. 2003. Reviews: The archaeological excavation of the 10th century Intan shipwreck. *International Journal of Nautical Archaeology* 32 (2): 266.

Changzhou City Museum, Wujin Cultural Relics Department 武进县文化馆常州市博物馆. 1982. Jiangsu Wujin Xian Chutu Han Dai Mu Chuan 江苏武进县出土汉代木船 (The Han dynasty wooden ship from Jiangsu province, Wujin district). *Kao-gu* 考古 2: 373–376.

Cheng, Pin-Tsun. 1991. The First Chinese diaspora in Southeast Asia in the fifteenth century. In *Emporia, commodities, and entrepreneurs in Asian maritime trade, c. 1400–1750*, ed. Roderich Ptak and Dietmar Rothermund, 13–28. Stuttgart: Franz Steirer Verlag.

Choi, Wan Gee. 2006. *The traditional ships of Korea*. Trans. Jean Young Lee. Seoul: Ewha Womans University Press.

Conlan, Thomas. 2001. *In little need of divine intervention*. Ithaca, NY: East Asia Program, Cornell University.

Cultural Property Maintenance Office 文化財管理局. 1984. *Shinan Haejeo Yumul Jaryo Pyeon II* 新安海底遺物資料編 *(Shinan Underwater Site Artifacts Report)*. Seoul: Ministry of Culture and Publicity 文化広報部.

Cultural Relics Bureau of Penglai City 蓬莱市文物局. 2006. *Penglai Gu Chuan* 蓬莱古船 *(Ancient ships from Penglai)*. Penglai: Cultural Relics Publishing House 文物出版社出版发行.

Delgado, James. 2009. *Khubilai Khan's lost fleet: In search of a legendary Armada*. Berkeley and Los Angeles: University of California Press.

Dun, He 顿贺, MaoCheng Wang 王茂盛, XiaoChunYuan 袁晓春, and Shi Heng Luo 罗世恒. 1994. Penglai Gu Chuan de Jie Gou ji Jian Zao 蓬莱古船的结构及建造 (The Penglai Ship structure and construction). *Wuhan Shipbuilding* 武汉造船 1: 18–28.

Flecker, Michael. 2000. A 9th-century Arab or Indian shipwreck in Indonesian waters. *International Journal of Nautical Archaeology* 29 (2): 199–217.

———. 2001. *The archaeological excavation of the 10th century Intan shipwreck.* BAR International Series 1047. Oxford: BAR.

———. 2007. The South-China-Sea tradition: The hybrid hulls of South-East Asia. *International Journal of Nautical Archaeology* 36 (1): 75–90.

Green, Jeremy, Nick Burningham, and Museum of Overseas Communication History. 1998. The ship from Quanzhou, Fujian province, People's Republic of China. *International Journal of Nautical Archaeology* 27 (4): 277–301.

Green, Jeremy, and Vidya Intakosai. 1983. The Pattaya wreck site excavation: An interim report. *International Journal of Nautical Archaeology* 12 (1): 3–13.

Green, Jeremy, and Zae Geun Kim. 1989. The Shinan and Wando sites, Korea: Further information. *International Journal of Nautical Archaeology* 18 (1): 33–41.

Herron, Richard. 1998. The development of Asian watercraft: From the prehistoric era to the advent of European colonization. PhD diss., Texas A&M University.

Hornell, James. 1934. The origin of the junks and sampan. *Mariner's Mirror* 30: 331–337.

Hourani, George. 1995. *Arab seafaring in the Indian Ocean in ancient and early medieval times.* Princeton, NJ: Princeton University Press.

Ihara, Hiroshi 伊原弘. 2003. *SeimeiJogazu o Yomu* 清明上河図を読む *(Read the Qing Ming Shan He Tu).* Tokyo: Bensei Shuppan 勉誠出版.

Ishizawa, Yoshiaki 石澤良昭, and Shigeru Ikuta 生田滋. 1998. *TōnanAjia no dentō to hatten* 東南アジアの伝統と発展 *(The tradition and development of Southeast Asia).* Tokyo: Chūō Kōronsha 中央公論者.

Kamei, Meitoku 亀井明徳. 1986. *Nihonbōekitōjishi no Kenkyū* 日本貿易陶磁史の研究 *(A study of Japanese imported ceramics).* Tokyo: Dōhōsha 同朋舎.

Kan, Xuhang 阚绪杭, Changqi Gong 龚昌奇, and LongfeiXi 席龙飞. 2001. Sui Tang Yunhe Liuzi Tang Chuanji qi Tuodo de Yanjiu 隋唐运河柳孜唐船及其拖舵的研究 (Study of ancient ships and rudders in the Tang dynasty). *Journal of Haerbin Institute of Technology (Social Science Edition)* 哈尔滨工业大学学报 *(社会科学版)* 3 (4): 35–38.

Kim, Seong-beom. 2006. Current situation and perspective of underwater archaeology in Korea and Shinan underwater relics. In *International symposium in celebration of the 30thanniversary of the Shinan wreck excavation: Shinan underwater relics and 14th century Asian marine trades,* 407–421. Mokpo: National Maritime Museum of Korea.

Kim, ZaeGeun 金在瑾. 1994. *HangugeuBae* 韓国의船 *(Korean ship).* Seoul: Seoul University Press.

Levathes, Louise. 1997. *When China ruled the sea.* New York: Oxford University Press.

Li, Guo-Qing. 1986. Archaeological evidence for the use of Chu-nam on the 13th century Quanzhou Ship, Fujian province, China. *International Journal of Nautical Archaeology* 18 (4): 277–283.

Lin, S., D. Genqi, and J. Green. 1991. Waterfront excavations at Dongmenkou, Ningbo, Zhe Jiang province, PRC. *International Journal of Nautical Archaeology* 20 (4): 299–311.

Lo, Jung-Pang. 1958. The decline of the early Ming navy. *Oriental Extremus* 5: 149–168.

———. 1969. Maritime commerce and its relation to the Sung navy. *Journal of the Economic and Social History of the Orient* 12 (1): 57–101.

Mackintosh-Smith, Tim. 2002. *The travels of Ibn Battutah.* Oxford: Picador.

Manguin, Pierre-Yves. 1985. Sewn-plank craft of South-East Asia: A preliminary survey. In *Sewn plank boats: BAR International Series 276*, ed. Sean McGrail and Eric Kentley, 19–343. London: Oxford University Press.

———. 1993. Trading ships of the South China Sea. *Journal of the Economic and Social History of the Orient* 36 (3): 253–280.

McGrail, Sean. 1985. The Brigg "Raft"—Problems in reconstruction and in the assessment of performance. In *Sewn plank boats: BAR International Series 276*, ed. Sean McGrail and Eric Kentley, 165–194. London: Oxford University Press.

Miyashita, Hiroaki. 2006. Ancient ships of Japan. MA thesis, Texas A&M University.

Mizoguchi, Koji. 2002. *An archaeological history of Japan: 30,000 B.C. to A.D. 700*. Philadelphia: University of Pennsylvania Press.

Mokpo Conservation Institute 목포해양유물보존처리소. 1993. *Jindo Pyokpari Tongnamu Pae: Palgul Chosa Pogoso* 진도벽파리통나무배 :발굴조사보고서 *(Report on the excavation of the Jindo Logboat)*. Mokpo, Korea: Mokpo Conservation Institute for Maritime Archaeological Finds.

Mori, Katsumi. 1972. The beginning of overseas advance of Japanese merchant ships. *Acta Asiatica* 23: 1–24.

Nahm, Andrew. 1988. *Korea: Tradition and transformation*. Elizabeth, NJ: Hollym.

Nanjing Museum 南京博物院. 1974. Rugao Faxian de Tang Dai Mu Chuan如皋发现的唐代木船 (Discovery of a Tang dynasty wooden ship at Rugao). *Wen Wu* 文物 5: 84–94.

National Maritime Museum of Korea. 2006. *The excavation of Anjwaship, Sinan*. Mokpo: National Maritime Museum of Korea.

National Research Institute of Maritime Cultural Heritage of Korea. 2009. *Taean treasure ship*. Seoul: National Research Institute of Maritime Cultural Heritage of Korea.

Needham, Joseph, Wang Ling, and Lu Gwei-Djen. 1971. *Science and civilization in China*. Vol. 4, *Physics and technology; Part III, Civil engineering and nautics*. Cambridge: Cambridge University Press.

Nguyễn, Khắc Viện. 1993. *Vietnam: A long history*. Hanoi: Gioi.

Ni, Wenjun 倪文俊. 1979. Jiading Fenbing Song Chuan Fajue Jianbao嘉定封浜宋船发掘简报 (Excavation report on the Song dynasty vessel from Jiading Fenbing). *Wen Wu* 文物 12: 32–36.

Nishimura, Shinji. 1925. *Ancient rafts of Japan*. Tokyo: Society of Naval Architects.

Ōba, Osamu. 1974. Scroll paintings of Chinese junks which sailed to Nagasaki in the 18th century and their equipment. *Mariner's Mirror* 60: 351–362.

Ōta, Koki太田弘毅. 1997. *Mōko Shūrai: Sono Gunjishiteki Kenkyū* 蒙古襲来：その軍事史的研究 *(Mongol invasion: The study of its military history)*. Tokyo: Kinseisha錦正社.

Reischauer, Edwin. 1946. Notes on T'ang dynasty sea routes. *Harvard Journal of Asiatic Studies* 5 (2): 142–164.

Robinson, Kenneth. 2000. Centering the king of Chosen: Aspects of Korean maritime diplomacy, 1392–1592. *Journal of Asian Studies* 59 (1): 109–125.

Rossabi, Morris. 1988. *Khubilai Khan—his life and times*. Berkeley and Los Angeles: University of California Press.

Saeki, Kōji 佐伯弘次. 2003. *Mongol Shūrai no Shyōgeki* モンゴル襲来の衝撃 *(The impact of the Mongol invasion)*. Nihon no Chūsei (Medieval Japan) 日本の中世 9 . Tokyo: Chūō Kōron Shinsha 中央公論新社.

Sasaki, Randall. 2008. The origin of the Lost Fleet of the Mongol Empire. MA thesis, Texas A&M University.

Schottenhammer, Angela. 2001. The role of metals and the impact of the introduction of Huizi paper notes in Quanzhou on the development of maritime trade in the Song period. In *The emporium of the world: Maritime Quanzhou, 1000–1400*, ed. Angela Schottenhammer, 95–176. Leiden: Brill Academic.

Seth, Michael. 2006. *A concise history of Korea: From the Neolithic period through the nineteenth century*. Lanham, MD: Rowman & Littlefield.

Shiba, Yoshinobu. 1983. Sung foreign trade: Its scope and organization. In *China among equals*, ed. Morris Rossabi, 89–115. Berkeley and Los Angeles: University of California Press.

So, Billy. 2000. *Prosperity, region, and institutions in maritime China: The South Fukien pattern, 946–1368*. Cambridge, MA: Harvard University Press.

Stewart, Gordon. 2008. *When China was the world*. Philadelphia: Da Capo.

Swope, Kenneth M. 2005. Crouching tigers, secret weapons: Military technology employed during the Sino-Japanese-Korean War, 1592–1598. *Journal of Military History* 69 (1): 11–41.

Takashima Board of Education 長崎県鷹島町教育委員会. 2001. *Takashima Kaitei Isek V—Takashima-chō Bunkazai Chōsa Hōkokushyo Dai 4 Shū* 鷹島海底遺跡V—鷹島町文化財調査報告書 第4集 (*Takashima Underwater Site V—Takashima Cultural Relics Report 4*). Nagasaki: Takashima Board of Education 長崎県鷹島町教育員会.

Tanaka, Takeo 田中健太. 1986. *Kamakura Bakufu to Mōko Shūrai* 鎌倉幕府と蒙古襲来 (*The Kamakura Bakufu and the Mongol invasion*). Tokyo: Gyōsei ぎょうせい.

Taylor, Keith. 1983. *The birth of Vietnam*. Berkeley and Los Angeles: University of California Press.

Tianjin City Cultural Relics Administration 天津市文物管理处. 1983. Tianjin Jinghai Yuan Menkou Song Chuan de Fajue 天津静海元蒙口宋船的发掘 (The excavation of a Song vessel at Jinghai near Tianjin). *Wen Wu* 文物 7: 54–58, 67.

Totman, Conrad. 2005. *A history of Japan*. 2nd ed. Malden, MA: Blackwell.

Tsukamoto, Manabu 塚本学. 1992. Naikai o meguruchiiki 内海を巡る地域 (Regions in the Inner Sea). In *Ajiya no naka no Nihonshi IV* アジアの中の日本史 IV (*Japanese history in Asia, Vol. 4*), ed. AranoYasunori 荒野 泰典 et al., 29–53. Tokyo: Tokyo Daigaku Shuppankai 東京大学出版会.

Underwood, Horace. [1934] 1976. *Korean boats and ships*. Reprinted in *Transactions of the Korean branch of the Royal Asiatic Society*, vol. 23, part 1. Seoul: Yonsei University Press.

Van Tilburg, Hans. 1994. The maritime history and nautical archaeology of China in Southeast Asia: Song to early Ming dynasty (960–1435 CE). MA thesis, East Carolina University.

———. 2007. *Chinese junks on the Pacific: Views from a different deck; New perspectives on maritime history and nautical archaeology*. Gainesville: University Press of Florida.

Wang, Guanzhuo 王冠倬. 2000. *Zhongguo Gu Chuan Tu Pu* 中国古船图谱 (*Catalog of ancient Chinese ships*). Beijing: San lianshudian 三联书店.

Wang, Long 王龙, and Wancai Zhang 张文才. 2004. *Tai Bai Yin Jing: Quan Jie* 太白阴经:全解 (*Tai Bai Yin Jing, with commentary*). Changsha: Yue Lu Shu She 丘麓书社.

Wang, Zhengshu 王正书. 1983. Chuan Yang He Gu Chuan Fajue Jianbao 川杨河古船发掘简报 (Excavation report on the ancient vessel from Chuan Yang He). *Wen Wu* 文物 7: 50–53, 93–97.

Worcester, G. R. G. 1971. *The junks and sampans of the Yangtze*. Annapolis, MD: Naval Institute Press.

Wright, Edward. 1985. The North Ferriby Boats—A revised basis for reconstruction. In *Sewn plank boats: BAR International Series 276*, ed. Sean McGrail and Eric Kentley, 105–144. London: Oxford University Press.

Xi, Longfei 席龙飞. 1999. *Zhong Guo Zao Chuan Shi* 中国造船史 *(The history of Chinese shipbuilding)*. Shanxi: Hubei Jiayu Chuban She 湖北教育出版社.

Yabuuchi, Kiyoshi 薮内清. 1955. *Ten Kō Kai Butsu no Kenkyū* 天工開物の研究 *(A study of Tian Gong Kai Wu)*. Tokyo: Kōsei Shuppan 恒星出版.

Yuan, Xiao Chun 袁晓春. 2006. Chongguo Penglai Shucheng Guchuanbo Fajueyu Chengguo 中国蓬莱水城古船发掘与成果 (The result of the excavation of the ancient ship at Penglai Water Castle, China). In *International Symposium in Celebration of the 30th Anniversary of the Shinan Wreck Excavation: Shinan underwater relics and 14th century Asian marine trades*, 493–512. Mokpo: National Maritime Museum of Korea.

Yule, Henry. [1871] 1993. *The travels of Marco Polo*. Reprinted in *The Book of Ser Marco Polo the Venetian concerning the kingdoms and marvels of the East*. London: John Murray; New York: Dover.

Zhao, Jiabin 赵嘉斌. 2009. Current developments in underwater archaeology in China. Presented at the 19th Indo-Pacific Prehistory Association Congress, 5 December 2009, Hanoi, Vietnam.

CHAPTER 25

AUSTRALIAN MARITIME ARCHAEOLOGY

MARK STANIFORTH

INTRODUCTION

EVERYTHING has a history and even a "prehistory," so a brief history, and prehistory, of maritime activity around the coastline of the world's largest island is perhaps appropriate here (Broeze 1998). The first point that needs to be made is that Australia is and, as far as human history and prehistory is concerned, always has been an island, completely surrounded by the sea. It has no terrestrial boundaries with any other nation and no land bridges to anywhere nor, as far as we know, has it had any in the last 200,000 years or so. Australia is quintessentially a maritime nation where sea travel and transportation has been vitally important and, to a certain extent, even in the age of the airplane, it still is. Certainly until the twentieth century everyone, or their ancestors, and literally every "thing" or artifact that was not made there arrived by sea.

MARITIME ARCHAEOLOGICAL POTENTIAL

In terms of the chronology so loved by archaeologists the earliest, "ancient" sea voyages that we can infer must have taken place in order for the first human beings to get to Australia, not hundreds or even a few thousand years ago, but at least 50,000 years ago. Indigenous people have been in Australia for a very, very long time, and they arrived there by voyaging in some form of watercraft, making them among the earliest "maritime" people that we know of. Unfortunately, it is unlikely, though not entirely impossible, that we will ever find physical, archaeological evidence of the earliest watercraft; but interesting experimental maritime archaeology can still be attempted (Bednarik 1998, 2002). Nevertheless, as a result of rising sea levels since the Last Glacial Maximum (LGM), some of the earliest terrestrial archaeological sites associated with Australia's indigenous peoples have been inundated and now lie beneath the sea (Allen and O'Connell 2003; Bowdler 1995; Flemming 1982; Nutley 2000, 2006: 84–88, 2007). Consequently, part of the maritime archaeological potential in Australian waters goes back at least 50,000 years, and over the past 20 years, Charles Dortch (1991, 1998, 2002) of the Western Australian Museum has started to demonstrate some of that potential.

Despite being an island, Australia was never completely isolated, and the indigenous peoples were never cut off from the rest of the world. People, and animals like the dingo, arrived while others probably left, and maritime trade and interaction with peoples to the north of Australia, in what is now Indonesia, Papua New Guinea, and the islands of Melanesia, though not consistent or extensive, at least occurred (MacKnight 1976). There are those who argue for other maritime contacts with Australia, sometimes from much farther away than the islands to the north of Australia, including China, but there is currently no archaeological evidence for any such visits (Connah 1988: 7).

Such was the situation when the first Europeans—the Portuguese and, soon after them, the Spanish—arrived in the Indian and Pacific Oceans in the years around and shortly after 1500 CE. There is currently no archaeological, or historical, evidence for European presence in Australia or its surrounding waters until about a century later: we know that the Dutch deliberately, and accidentally, came into contact with Australia after 1600 CE. Soon afterward the Dutch, the British, and others started to suffer shipwrecks around Australia; the first that we know of was the English East India Company ship *Trial*, lost in 1622 (Green 1977a). Over the last four centuries thousands of vessels have been lost in the waters around Australia. These shipwrecks, together with jetties, submerged aircraft, and material associated with maritime industries, such as whaling and shipbuilding, comprise the maritime archaeological potential that exists in Australia and its surrounding waters (Green 1990; Henderson 1987; McCarthy 2004; Nash 2007a; Nutley 2006: 88–96; Staniforth and Hyde 2001; Staniforth and Nash 2006).

WESTERN AUSTRALIAN BEGINNINGS

The finding of two seventeenth-century Dutch East India Company (VOC) ships during the early 1960s (*Batavia*, lost in 1629, and *Vergulde Draeck*, sunk in 1656) prompted the Western Australian Government to enact legislation designed to protect shipwrecks with the Museum Act Amendment Act of 1964. While this provided

the legislative basis for the protection of historic shipwrecks such as the VOC shipwrecks, there were still no trained, experienced, or qualified maritime archaeologists working in Australia in the late 1960s. This changed in 1971 when the Western
Australian (WA) Museum employed Jeremy Green, who had worked on shipwrecks in the UK with Colin Martin and in the Mediterranean with people like
George F. Bass and Michael Katsev (McCarthy 2006: 2). Green brought others to
Western Australia from overseas, like Myra Stanbury and Patrick Baker, who would
become long-serving staff members of the Maritime Archaeology Department.
Also in the 1970s, other key staff like Graeme Henderson and Michael McCarthy
joined the department and, at the same time, the Materials Conservation Department was gearing up to conserve the artifacts generated by large-scale underwater
archaeological excavations (Pearson 1974, 1977; MacLeod 1989).

Beginning in the 1970s, the WA Museum has conducted a number of terrestrial
and underwater excavations of VOC shipwrecks such as *Batavia* (1629), *Vergulde
Draeck* (1656), and *Zeewijk* (1727) under the Dutch Shipwrecks Program (Figure 25.1)
(Gibbs 2002; Green 1975, 1977b, 1978b, 1989, 1991; Ingelman-Sundberg 1976, 1977;
Orme and Randall 1987; Pasveer, Black, and van Huystee 1998; Stanbury 1998).
Excavations of later period sites like the ex-slaver *James Matthews* (1841), the

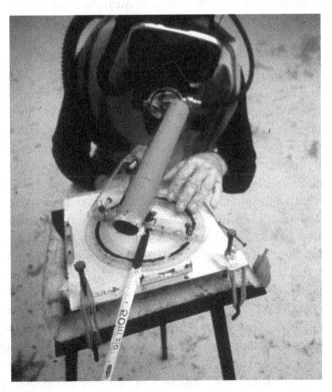

Figure 25.1 Maritime archaeologist using an underwater theodolite on the site of the
Dutch East India Company ship *Zeewijk*. Photograph by Patrick Baker. Reproduced
with the kind permission of the Western Australian Museum.

merchant vessel *Eglinton* (1852), and SS *Xantho* were conducted under the Colonial Shipwrecks Program (Baker and Henderson 1979; Henderson 1975a, 1975b, 1976, 1978, 2008; Henderson and Stanbury 1983; McCarthy 1986, 1988, 2000; Stanbury 2003). Maritime Archaeology Department staff have also produced a variety of publications for the general public (Cairns and Henderson 1995; Henderson 1980b; Henderson and Henderson 1988; Kenderdine 1994). Much of the excavated material is held by the Maritime Archaeology Department, and some is on display in the Western Australian Museum's Shipwreck Galleries in Fremantle (Green, Gainsford, and Stanbury 2004; Hosty 2006: 155–157).

UNDERWATER CULTURAL HERITAGE MANAGEMENT

The enactment of the Australian federal government's Historic Shipwrecks Act in 1976 fundamentally changed the management of historic shipwrecks, and consequently the nature of maritime archaeology, in Australia (McCarthy 2006: 3). From being an activity that throughout most of the 1970s was almost exclusively carried out in the state of Western Australia, all of the Australian states had to at least consider their options for the protection and management of historic shipwrecks. This change took some considerable time to work through, given that Australia is a federation of states, each with its own government system and bureaucracy. Some states, like Western Australia and Queensland, moved relatively quickly to request that the federal government apply the Historic Shipwrecks Act to the waters off their state (Jeffery 2006: 125). Western Australia already had existing legislation in the form of the Maritime Archaeology Act of 1973, which applied to the sites not covered by the federal legislation, and others, like South Australia and Victoria, subsequently enacted their own parallel legislation. Primarily after the introduction of a tertiary course in maritime archaeology in Western Australia in 1980 (see below), a number of states appointed qualified maritime archaeology graduates to positions within their government agencies and museums responsible for historic shipwrecks. A few states lagged behind: Victoria and Tasmania took six years to request that the Historic Shipwrecks Act apply to waters around their coast, and New South Wales (NSW) managed to hold out until 1988 before appointing the first qualified maritime archaeology graduate to a position in the NSW Department of Planning (Anderson, Philippou, and Harvey 2006; Green 1995; Hosty and Stuart 1994; Jeffery 2006; McCarthy 1998, 2006; Staniforth 2000). Nevertheless, the 1980s were a golden decade in terms of job growth for maritime archaeology graduates, at least in the field of underwater cultural heritage management.

Also during the 1980s the federal government delegated part of the responsibility for the administration of the Historic Shipwrecks Act to a state government agency or museum in each state. Annually the federal government provides a small amount of funding to supplement the funding each state provides (Anderson, Philippou, and Harvey 2006: 140–141). Whether the state agency called the delegated authority a museum, as it proved to be in Western Australia, Queensland, and the Northern Territory, or a government heritage agency, as it was in Victoria, NSW, South Australia, and Tasmania (the only state to select a National Park Service as a delegated authority), appears to have been a historical accident or a case of who put their hand up first. Nevertheless, the inherent conflict of interest between museums as excavators, or consumers, of historic shipwrecks and their role as protectors of historic shipwrecks, enforcers of the Historic Shipwrecks Act, and issuers of permits to disturb and excavate shipwreck sites has been obvious, and challenged, over the years (Staniforth 1993, 2007a). By 1988, all Australian states had some sort of program in underwater cultural heritage management, and most had grown as much as they were going to. Twenty years later, unfortunately, there has been little or no job growth in the sector, and many of the positions are still held by the same persons who held them in 1988, although that is beginning to change as people leave or retire. Succession planning is acknowledged to be a significant issue, but financial constraints have effectively prevented action in most cases.

The delegated authority in each state plays an important role in the administration and enforcement of legislation, but this management role is rarely the highest priority for any archaeologist working for government (Cooper et al. 1995). Nevertheless, Australian underwater cultural heritage managers have developed some effective enforcement programs, including the appointment and training of historic shipwreck inspectors, and have made a small number of successful prosecutions for infringements of historic shipwrecks legislation and regulations (Cassidy 1991; Gurney 1994; Jeffery 1987, 1999; Nutley 1998, 2000). Of greater importance have been the public education programs established and operated in most states (Anderson, Philippou, and Harvey 2006; McCarthy 2003; Nash 2003a; Nutley 1987). One of the most publicly visible features of these education programs has been what Mike McCarthy (1981) first termed the "underwater display case," which subsequently developed into historic shipwreck or maritime heritage trails in most Australian states (Philippou and Staniforth 2003; Smith 2003; Strachan 1995).

One of the most significant achievements of underwater cultural heritage management in Australia has been the development of a National Historic Shipwrecks Database (National Historic Shipwrecks Database Web site). Importantly, this database is backed up by detailed historical, archival, and individual site investigation documentation and regional surveys, all of which are held in agency files; these documents sometimes appear as publications for the general public (see, for example, Anderson 1997; Anderson and Cahir 2003; Clark and Jung 2001; Coroneos 1997; Coroneos and McKinnon 1997; Foster 1987–1990, 1996; Jordan 1995; Nash 2001, 2007b; Nutley 1996). Unfortunately, while these kinds of publications are available for most Australian states, in particular Western Australia, South Australia, and Victoria, but they are conspicuously absent for other states, most notably Queensland.

THE TEACHING OF MARITIME ARCHAEOLOGY

The need for tertiary-level teaching in maritime archaeology was first acknowledged in the mid-1970s, when the Western Australian Museum canvassed several options for university teaching in maritime archaeology, including a three-year bachelor's degree course and a graduate diploma (Penrose 1978). The introduction of the Historic Shipwrecks Act in 1976 highlighted the need for more people trained in underwater archaeological techniques than existed in Australia at the time. So in 1980, a 12-month Graduate Diploma in Maritime Archaeology (GDMA) was introduced by the WA Institute of Technology (later renamed Curtin University); it was taught in association with the Department of Maritime Archaeology at the WA Museum. The GDMA was offered on five occasions between 1980 and 1995 (in 1980–1981, 1981–1982, 1986, 1990, and 1995–1996). It had an intake of approximately 10 to 12 students, and the principal emphasis was on practical knowledge and the application of underwater archaeology field techniques (Henderson 1987: 167–168; Hundley 1983; Penrose 1983).

A significant number of the maritime archaeologists and underwater cultural heritage managers who are currently working in Australia were trained through the GDMA program, and Jeremy Green (1995: 39) has argued that the GDMA "helped to promote a sense of cohesiveness in maritime archaeology in Australia." Nevertheless, the 1995–1996 course was the last time that the GDMA was offered in Western Australia, and in 2000 it was decided that Curtin University would no longer offer the GDMA option. In 2008 a new Master of Applied Maritime Archaeology degree was introduced, this time by the University of Western Australia (UWA) but also taught in association with the Department of Maritime Archaeology at the WA Museum.

James Cook University (JCU) in Townsville, Queensland, commenced the teaching of maritime archaeology at the undergraduate level in 1993, and later, in 2002, at the graduate level. Unfortunately, teaching in maritime archaeology at JCU has dwindled in recent years as faculty such as Associate Professor Peter Veth and Dr. Martin Gibbs have left for positions elsewhere. Nevertheless, JCU has produced at least four PhD graduates over the past decade or so, including Dr. Mike McCarthy, who works in the Department of Maritime Archaeology at the WA Maritime Museum; Dr. Nigel Erskine, who is now at the Australian National Maritime Museum in Sydney; Dr. Brad Duncan, who works for NSW Heritage Office, and Dr. Bill Jeffery, who in recent years has been working primarily in Micronesia (McCarthy 2000; Erskine 2004; Duncan 2006; Jeffery 2008).

In 1996 Flinders University in Adelaide, South Australia, introduced traditional "on-campus" teaching of maritime archaeology at the undergraduate level, with a third-year course called Maritime Archaeology (ARCH 3005). In addition to lecture-based classes, the Maritime Archaeology Program runs a regular annual Maritime Archaeology Field School, usually in association with one or more partner government agencies (Figure 25.2). In 2002, the Graduate Program in Maritime Archaeology was established (Flinders University Web site). It has now drawn students from more than 10 countries, including Australia, Canada, Holland, Italy, Japan, New Zealand, the Netherlands, South Africa, United Kingdom, and the United States (Staniforth 2008a, 2008b). The Maritime Archaeology Program publishes high-quality honor's and master's theses in the Flinders University Maritime Archaeology Monographs Series (Nash 2006b; Nutley 2007). In addition, since 1999, the author (who completed his own PhD at Flinders University) has been involved in supervising PhD candidates, including Dr. Nathan Richards, who now teaches maritime archaeology as a tenure-track assistant professor in the Maritime Studies Program at East Carolina University in the United States (Richards 2002, 2008; Staniforth 1999, 2003). Currently, in 2010, there are four PhD students at Flinders University, all on scholarships, who are conducting research in the field of maritime archaeology.

Figure 25.2 Diver taking notes during the Maritime Archaeology Program Field School survey at Streaky Bay in February 2009. Photograph by Mark Staniforth. Reproduced with the kind permission of the Maritime Archaeology Program, Flinders University.

MARITIME ARCHAEOLOGY RESEARCH

The sheer volume of site investigation, survey, and excavation cannot be covered in a chapter of this length. Instead I consider four case studies that can provide some insights into the types and extent of maritime archaeological research that has been conducted over more than three decades in Australia. The four case studies are HMS *Sirius*, HMS *Pandora*, *Sydney Cove*, and the Archaeology of Whaling project.

HMS *Sirius* (1790 CE)

HMS *Sirius* was built at Rotherhithe on the River Thames in 1781 as the Baltic trader *Berwick* and was purchased on the stocks by the Admiralty in November 1781 for use as an armed naval storeship. In 1785 she was laid up "in ordinary," but the following year she received an extensive overhaul and was commissioned in the Royal Navy as a 511-ton, sixth-rate 20-gun frigate. She was the flagship, and largest, Royal Navy vessel to accompany the First Fleet to Australia in 1788. In 1790 HMS *Sirius* (under the command of Captain John Hunter), together with HMS *Supply*, made a voyage to Norfolk Island carrying convicts and Royal Marines. They intended to establish a colony there and hopefully start growing food for themselves and the Port Jackson colony. For HMS *Sirius*, the voyage ended in disaster on 13 March 1790 when the ship was driven backward onto the reef near the new settlement of Kingston (Nash 2006a: 56–58; Stanbury 2007: 25–26). The wreck of HMS *Sirius* was a very significant event in Australian history generally and in the history of Norfolk Island specifically. The connections to the events of the First Fleet and British convict settlement of Australia make the site of great significance to Australians. Although the approximate position of the site had always been known, until the 1980s there had been no accurate survey work done to evaluate or record the extent of the archaeological material. Furthermore, very little work had been done to catalog the artifacts believed to be from HMS *Sirius* held in the Norfolk Island museums or by island residents.

With funding from the Australian Bicentennial Authority (ABA), sponsorship from private companies, and support from a number of museums and government agencies, three seasons of fieldwork were conducted in 1985, 1987, and 1988. These archaeological expeditions were led by maritime archaeologist Graeme Henderson of the WA Museum and included a team of about 12 experienced professional maritime archaeologists and avocational volunteers (Henderson and Stanbury 1988; Stanbury 1991, 1994, 2007). A fourth expedition, funded by the Australian Federal Government's Historic Shipwrecks Program, took place in 2002 (Erskine 2002).

The site is located in very shallow water of 2 to 3 m depth that is regularly subjected to heavy wave action. Experience gained on shallow-water, "surf-zone" sites in Western Australia, such as *Batavia*, had shown that valuable information could still be obtained from such sites. The survey and recording work was carried out using SCUBA equipment and conducted from an inflatable dive boat anchored on the seaward side of the surf zone. Apart from a substantial ballast pile consisting of cast-iron ballast pigs (or ingots) known as kentledge, most of the artifacts were located in gullies and holes in the limestone reef flat. The four expeditions and a program of artifact conservation and cataloging carried out over the last 20 years and largely funded with grants from the federal government's Historic Shipwrecks Program provided accurate survey data, as well as raising and conserving hundreds of small artifacts. The archaeological assemblage contains a wide variety of material, from a copper coin to large anchors, but most consists of material primarily associated with the structure of the ship, its fastenings and fittings, and a smaller amount of equipment and personal belongings relating to the crew and passengers.

Many specialist reports have been written, and articles have been published in respected international journals such as the *International Journal of Nautical Archaeology* as well as a popular paperback book called *Sirius—Past and Present* (Henderson 1993; Henderson and Stanbury 1988; Kimpton 1992; Stanbury 1991, 1994). A commemorative plaque has been placed on the site, while artifacts from *Sirius* are now on display in the Norfolk Island Museum (Pier Store), and some loan material has been on display at the Australian National Maritime Museum (ANMM) in Sydney (Figure 25.3). In addition, some material from HMS *Sirius* was incorporated into a major exhibition that toured Australia during 1988 and 1989 titled *Shipwreck— Discoveries from our Earliest Shipwrecks 1622–1797* (Hosty 2006: 160–161).

Figure 25.3 Diver at the interpretive plaque on the *Sirius* wreck, Norfolk Island, in 1991. Reproduced with the kind permission of the Australian Bicentennial Authority.

HMS *Pandora* (1791 CE)

As a consequence of the famous and well-documented mutiny aboard HMS *Bounty* on 26 April 1789, the Royal Navy dispatched the 24-gun frigate HMS *Pandora* (under the command of Captain Edward Edwards) to the South Pacific in 1790 (HMS *Pandora* Web site). HMS *Pandora* was a Porcupine Class, sixth-rate frigate built in 1779 that was equipped not only with enough stores and material for the long "South Sea" voyage but also with sufficient spares to refit HMS *Bounty* should they manage to recapture that vessel. The task was to capture the 25 mutineers and bring them back to the United Kingdom for trial, and the mission was partly successful: 14 of the *Bounty* mutineers were captured in Tahiti, where it was also reported that two others had been killed. The remaining nine mutineers under Fletcher Christian had evaded capture by sailing to remote Pitcairn Island, where they burned HMS *Bounty* and would remain undetected until 1808. After unsuccessfully searching for four months, Captain Edwards decided to sail back to the United Kingdom through the northern end of the Great Barrier Reef. Unfortunately, HMS *Pandora* ran onto a reef-top during the night of 29 August 1791 and sank into deeper water the next day (Gesner 1991, 1997, 2007; Nash 2006a: 58–62).

Despite a number of expeditions to search for the wreck in the 1960s and 1970s, it was not until November 1977 that the site of HMS *Pandora* was relocated with the assistance of an airborne magnetometer carried aboard an RAAF (Royal Australian Air Force) maritime reconnaissance aircraft. The wreck was reported to the Australian Federal Government and initially inspected in April 1979 by a team led by maritime archaeologist Graeme Henderson, and including Pat Baker, from the WA Museum (Henderson 1980a). The site is in an extremely remote location, some 50 nautical miles offshore, which during the 1970s would have fallen outside the claimed offshore jurisdiction of some, perhaps many, countries. Nevertheless, Australia had recently passed the Historic Shipwrecks Act of 1976, which claimed a 200-nautical-mile jurisdiction, so HMS *Pandora* was declared a historic shipwreck in November 1979. The Queensland Museum was made responsible for managing historic shipwrecks, including HMS *Pandora*, in Queensland, and in 1981 the museum appointed Ron Coleman as curator of maritime archaeology. Also in 1981, HMS *Pandora* was given protected zone status, under which a permit is required for anyone entering a zone that extends for a radius of 500 m from the wreck. The site is still a protected zone, which probably makes it one of the longest periods (now 30 years) of direct, and effective, government control over access to a historic shipwreck anywhere in the world.

Between 1983 and 1989, the Queensland Museum undertook several expeditions to survey and partially excavate the site (Figure 25.4). Initial funding came from the Australian Federal government, and with support from maritime archaeologists in a variety of interstate organizations, as well as volunteers, some test excavations were completed and a permanent grid structure was established on site. It was found that a substantial section of the lower ship's timbers had survived on the starboard side, including relatively intact areas of the lower hull as well as the collapsed remains of

Figure 25.4 Diver on the anchor during the excavation of HMS *Pandora* wreck, Queensland. Reproduced with the kind permission of the Queensland Museum.

upper works and cabins with their contents (Coleman 1988a, 1988b; Gesner 1988, 1990, 1991; Henderson 1986: 129–142; MacKay and Coleman 1992).

The remains of HMS *Pandora* lie in approximately 30 to 34 m of water, which, together with the remote location more than 600 km from the nearest major port (Cairns), makes any archaeological investigation both person-intensive and expensive. By about 1990 the problems of the short dive times allowable with SCUBA and the need to hire "live-aboard" vessels for large teams had led to the conclusion that without large-scale funding the excavations should probably cease. Expeditions in 1993 and 1995 concentrated on sediment and core sampling with only limited excavation but also, importantly in light of subsequent developments, trialed the use of a surface-supplied breathing apparatus (SSBA), which increased dive times and improved communications (Gesner 1993; Guthrie et al. 1994; Ward, Larcome, and Veth 1999a, 1999b).

The situation changed in the mid-1990s, when the Queensland state government offered the Queensland Museum $1 million for the project, subject to matching funds being raised from the private sector. The nonprofit Pandora Foundation was established in Townsville in 1996 and raised a further $2.5 million from local businesses and donations, placing the *Pandora* project back on track to continue excavations. The Queensland government subsequently announced that it would provide more than $17.5 million for a major museum development (the Museum of Tropical Queensland) in Townsville, which would house and exhibit the *Pandora* material in one of the new museum's major galleries (Hosty 2006: 158).

A series of five expeditions between 1995 and 1999 raised several thousand artifacts, including ship's equipment, human skeletal remains, and crew items, and collected artifacts from the Pacific islands as well (Gesner 2000, 2007). Over the years, a number of research reports, catalogs, and commentaries based on the material culture assemblages from HMS *Pandora* have been completed (Campbell and Gesner 2000; Pigott 1995; Randell 1999; Steptoe and Wood 2002; Staniforth 2006: 28–31). The collected artifacts or so-called "artificial curiosities" are of considerable interest for what they tell us about the cultural interactions between the "West" and the "Other". British exploration vessels and their crews would collect the material culture of the indigenous inhabitants of Australasia and the Pacific. The recovered artifacts from HMS *Pandora* are of particular importance, as they represent collecting by all social strata among the Pandora officers and crew, rather than just the "official" or elite collections that made their way into collections of the British Museum, the Museum of Natural History, and the like (Campbell 1997; Fallowfield 2001; Illidge 2002; Staniforth 2006: 37–39). After the 1999 expedition the project focused on the opening of the new Museum of Tropical Queensland in April 2000. Despite plans to continue excavation work, no further expeditions have taken place to date (Nash 2006a: 62). There is considerable maritime archaeological potential remaining on the HMS *Pandora* site, particularly in the bow area, which has not been excavated to date. In addition, the existing archaeological assemblages provide excellent comparative collections for other investigations of late-eighteenth-century Royal Navy vessels in other parts of the world (Elkin 2006; Redknap 1997).

Sydney Cove (1797 CE)

The *Sydney Cove* was wrecked on 9 February 1797 during a voyage from Calcutta (Kolkata) in India to the newly established penal colony at Port Jackson (Sydney). The vessel had been consigned by Campbell and Clark, a small trading enterprise which was involved in trading European, Indian, and Chinese goods, primarily around the coasts of the Indian subcontinent, and for which trading to Australia would be a new venture (Staniforth 2003: 65–99). The *Sydney Cove* was carrying a speculative, mixed cargo, including rice, sugar, tobacco, salted meats, tar, vinegar, soap, candles, leatherware, Indian textiles, livestock, and Chinese tea and porcelain, as well as 7,000 gallons (31,500 liters) of rum (Nash 2002, 2006a, 2007b).

The site of *Sydney Cove* was located by sport divers in January 1977 in only 4 to 6 m of water, approximately 400 m off Preservation Island in Bass Strait. Despite the recent enactment of the Commonwealth Historic Shipwrecks Act (1976), the Tasmanian government chose to declare the underwater site itself, and the associated land sites that included salvaged cargo and the survivors' camp, a Historic Site on 29 March 1977 under the Tasmanian National Parks and Wildlife Act of 1970. Survey work and test excavations were undertaken in the late 1970s, and further work was carried out in the 1980s to install permanent survey controls around the wreckage. Some artifacts, including the partially intact rudder and two cannon, were raised during this early work (Atherton and Lester 1982; Clark and Nash 1988; Clark and Smith 1986; Lester 1982, 1984; Nash 1991; Strachan 1986a, 1986b).

A program of archaeological excavation on the underwater site was carried out between 1991 and 1994 under the direction of Mike Nash of the Tasmanian Parks and Wildlife Service, with funding from the Federal Historic Shipwrecks Program and conservation assistance from the Queen Victoria Museum in Launceston. Support also came in the form of personnel and equipment from federal and interstate government agencies, backed up by numerous volunteers. Diving operations were conducted using surface-supplied air from an 11 m charter vessel (*Strait Lady*), and SCUBA tanks were used only for photographic and video recording. A total of 216 m² of the site were excavated using water dredges, and underwater recording was carried out with a rigid grid frame system (Figure 25.5). Among the artifact assemblages were more than 200 kg of mostly broken polychrome overglaze and blue underglaze Chinese export porcelain, which was commonly imported into the Australian colonies before 1830. Porcelain, in addition to its functional utility, tells us about some of the meanings that were attached to ceramics in the early colony (Staniforth 2003: 86–99; Staniforth and Nash 1998). The meanings of artifacts, as I have argued previously, are not fixed but are "attached" to things by people through culturally derived behaviors and attitudes as symbols of status and wealth (Staniforth 2003: 143–158).

Figure 25.5 Divers excavating under a grid frame on the *Sydney Cove* site, Tasmania, in 1993. Photograph by Mike Nash. Reproduced with the kind permission of the Tasmanian Parks and Wildlife Service.

The *Sydney Cove* excavation also revealed interesting features about the construction of *Sydney Cove*, such as the use of traditional Indian methods of protecting the hull, including the use of waterproof resins and a thin layer of sacrificial planking, over which a layer of woolen felt and copper sheathing was laid, following the latest imported technology (Nash 2006a: 60). The final expedition in March 1994 reburied the entire hull remains using more than 500 polypropylene sandbags, and periodic monitoring has demonstrated this to be a cheap but effective means of stabilizing the site after excavation (Nash 2006a, 2007a).

To commemorate the bicentenary of the loss of *Sydney Cove*, an exhibition was developed that opened at the Queen Victoria Museum in Launceston in February 1997. This exhibition traveled around Australia for two years, funded by the Federal *Visions* exhibition touring program, before returning to Launceston, where the archaeological assemblage is now held. In 2002 and 2004 two further terrestrial expeditions were conducted to locate and excavate part of the survivors' camp, which included at least one dwelling, at the south end of Preservation Island (Nash 2006b).

The Archaeology of Whaling Project

Whaling was probably the most important extractive maritime industry operating in Australasia during the late eighteenth and first half of the nineteenth centuries. Since the 1980s, cultural heritage managers and archaeologists working for government and museums had become increasingly interested in whaling primarily from a site management perspective: either shore-based whaling, largely by terrestrial, or historical archaeologists, or whaling shipwrecks, primarily by maritime archaeologists. Much of this work either took the form of individual site investigations or larger-scale regional surveys (Atkinson 1987; Bell 1991; Evans 1993a, 1993b; Jones and Staniforth 1996; Kostaglou 1995a, 1995b; Kostaglou and McCarthy 1991; McIlroy 1986; Nash 1990; Randall 1987; Townrow 1997). In addition, some academic archaeologists were considering whaling sites (Gibbs 1995). One interesting result of this work was that, despite their potentially vulnerable location on the coastal fringe, archaeological evidence of dozens of shore-based whaling stations have survived to the present day. This is particularly important given the level of secrecy that surrounded shore-based whaling at the time, which means that very little (and, in some cases, no) written evidence exists about the whaling stations.

In 1997, Susan Lawrence of La Trobe University and I decided to establish the Archaeology of Whaling in Southern Australia and New Zealand (AWSANZ) project in an attempt to draw together some of the various researchers who were interested in whaling. The first activity that the AWSANZ project undertook was to host a symposium and publish the submitted papers, which provided a baseline from which further work could be conducted (Lawrence and Staniforth 1998). One of the strengths of an Australasia-wide comparative study of whaling is that the different whaling stations and vessels all operated within what constituted a single industry, with few of the state and national boundaries and differing jurisdictions that exist today (Gibbs 2006: 78). This has also led to more global comparative study with room for further international comparisons, such as with the British and American whaling activity in the Pacific as well as with shore-based whaling activities in other countries (Jateff 2007; Staniforth 2007b; Van Tilburg in this volume).

Since 1997, a number of primarily academically based research projects and excavations have been conducted, sometimes as an extension of, or in collaboration with, cultural heritage management work (Lawrence 2001a, 2001b, 2007; Nash 2003; Paterson 2006; Staniforth, Briggs, and Lewczak 2001). This research has revealed elements of the living and working conditions experienced at the whaling stations and shows that status was expressed in terms of the possession of certain types of glass and tablewares (Gibbs 1996; Lawrence 2001a).

AIMA AND THE AVOCATIONALS

One of the great strengths of Australian maritime archaeology over the years has been the Australasian (formerly Australian) Institute for Maritime Archaeology (AIMA), which was formed in Adelaide in 1981 (AIMA Web site). The AIMA membership includes not only trained, professional maritime archaeologists (which would be a very small and exclusive club indeed) but many other interested people. AIMA also provides a national umbrella body for the avocational (amateur) organizations that exist in some, but not all, Australian states, including the Maritime Archaeology Association of Western Australia (MAAWA), the Society for Underwater Historical Research (SUHR), and the Maritime Archaeology Association of Victoria (MAAV) (Souter 2006).

Regular annual conferences have been run by AIMA for more than 25 years, usually in September. These conferences had their origin, even before the formation of AIMA, in the grandiosely named Southern Hemisphere Conferences on Maritime Archaeology, both held in Adelaide, in 1977 and 1981 (Green 1978a; Jeffery and Amess 1983). The annual AIMA conferences not only bring together most Australian maritime archaeologists and underwater cultural heritage managers each year to talk about their work, exchange ideas, and hold various meetings, but have also provided the opportunity for many others to come to Australia from all over the world. For a country that is not on the way to anywhere in particular, it would be very easy to become, and remain, a parochial backwater, but the AIMA conferences have provided one way to help prevent that from happening. For more than a decade now the annual AIMA conference has usually been held jointly with the annual conference of one or more of the other related organizations in Australia (and New Zealand), including the Australasian Society for Historical Archaeology (ASHA), the Australian Association for Maritime History (AAMH), and the Australian Archaeological Association (AAA).

Another important contribution made by AIMA has been the regular publication of the *Bulletin of the Australasian Institute for Maritime Archaeology*, initially twice a year but in recent years only once a year, as well as a quarterly newsletter that is available on the AIMA Web site. In the late 1990s AIMA purchased a license to run the internationally recognized Nautical Archaeology Society (NAS) training program, which was then tailored to suit the Australian situation (Moran and Staniforth 1998). AIMA/NAS training has proved of enormous benefit to AIMA, providing a flow of new membership, fulfilling important public education and awareness needs, and being used by universities to train students (Souter 2006: 169–171). Finally, AIMA plays an important role in helping to maintain ethical standards in Australian maritime archaeology. Although not a professional body in the sense of requiring professional qualifications in order to be a member, as required, for example, by the Australian Association of Consulting Archaeologists (AACA Web site) and the International Council on Monuments and Sites (ICOMOS Web site), AIMA does have a Code of Ethics and regularly enters into ongoing debates about what constitutes ethical practice in maritime archaeology (Coroneos 2006).

AUSTRALIA AND THE REST OF THE WORLD

Australian maritime archaeologists often individually, but sometimes with institutional support and backing, have taken leading roles in a variety of regional Asia-Pacific and international activities. For more than two decades, for example, Jeremy Green of the WA Museum has taken a leading role in teaching maritime archaeology in Thailand, China, and Sri Lanka through programs organized by SEAMEO-SPAFA (Southeast Asian Ministers of Education Organization—Regional Centre for Archaeology and Fine Arts) as well as conducting research on VOC ships in Malaysia and Asian-built vessels throughout the region (Atkinson et al. 1989; Green 1983a, 1983b, 1983c, 1986, 2006; Green and Harper 1982, 1983; Green, Harper, and Intakosi 1987; Green et al. 1995; Green, Burningham, and Museum of Overseas Communication History 1998; Green, Devendra, and Parthesius 1998).

Graeme Henderson was the first head of the International Committee on the Underwater Cultural Heritage (ICUCH Web site) and took a leading role in the drafting of both the 1996 ICOMOS Charter on the Protection of Underwater Cultural Heritage (ICOMOS Web site) and the 2001 UNESCO Convention on the Protection of the Underwater Cultural Heritage (UNESCO Web site). David Nutley has been the secretary and is now vice president of ICUCH. I have served for two terms on the Advisory Council on Underwater Archaeology (2000–2008) (ACUA Web site), including three years as deputy chair (2001–2003) and three years as chair (2004–2007), as well as three years on the board of the Society for Historical Archaeology (SHA) in my capacity as ACUA chair.

CONCLUSION

In recent decades Australia has developed legislation for the protection of the historic shipwreck component of its underwater cultural heritage, established more or less effective cultural heritage management programs in each of the states, and conducted a number of significant excavations of historic shipwrecks. Some excellent museum exhibitions, a very strong publications record, a genuine commitment to public education in most Australian states, and some good tertiary education programs have also been important successes over the years. Australian maritime archaeology has a long history of "holistic" approaches to the integration of related underwater and terrestrial archaeological sites, going back to the 1970s *Zeewijk* excavations, and extending to recent times with the AWSANZ project.

If these are some of the strengths of Australian maritime archaeology, one of its weaknesses has been the relative lack of funding to date for what one might term "pure" or academic research; the Australian Federal government did commission a national research plan for historic shipwrecks in the mid-1990s (Edmonds et al. 1995), but then ignored it. Another, and to some extent related, weakness, which was true of the twentieth century but is becoming much less so in the twenty-first century, is the number of PhD graduates in Australian maritime archaeology. This number has climbed dramatically in the last decade and looks likely to increase still further over the next decade.

REFERENCES

AACA—Australian Association for Consulting Archaeologists. Online. Available at www.aacai.com.au. Accessed 4 December 2008.

AIMA—Australasian Institute for Maritime Archaeology. Online at www.aima.iinet.net.au. Accessed 4 December 2008.

Allen, J., and J. F. O'Connell. 2003. The long and the short of it: Archaeological approaches to determining when humans first colonised Australia and New Guinea. *Australian Archaeology* 57: 5–18.

Anderson, R. 1997. *Wrecks on the reef.* Melbourne: Heritage Council.

Anderson, R., and A. Cahir. 2003. *Surf coast wrecks: Historic shipwrecks between Point Lonsdale and Cape Otway 1853–1940.* Melbourne: Heritage Victoria.

Anderson, R., C. Philippou, and P. Harvey. 2006. Innovative approaches in underwater cultural heritage management. In *Maritime archaeology: Australian approaches,* ed. M. Staniforth and M. Nash, 137–150. New York: Springer/Kluwer/Plenum.

Atherton, K., and S. Lester, 1982. Sydney Cove (1797) site work 1974–1980: An overview. *Bulletin of the Australian Institute for Maritime Archaeology* 6: 1–18.

Atkinson, K. 1987. The significance of the Rowley Shoals wreck to the study of whaling in the South Seas. *Bulletin of the Australian Institute for Maritime Archaeology* 11 (2): 1–7.

Atkinson, K., J. N. Green, R. Harper, and V. Intakosi. 1989. Joint Thai-Australian underwater archaeological project 1987–1988. *International Journal of Nautical Archaeology* 18 (4): 299–315.

Baker, P., and G. Henderson. 1979. James Matthews excavation: A second interim report. *International Journal of Nautical Archaeology* 8: 225–244.

Bednarik, R. G. 1998. An experiment in Pleistocene seafaring. *International Journal of Nautical Archaeology* 29 (2): 139–149.

———. 2002. The first mariners project. *Bulletin of the Australian Institute for Maritime Archaeology* 26: 57–64.

Bell, P. 1991. Research and management issues arising from sites associated with the South Australian bay whaling and sealing industries. *Bulletin of the Australian Institute for Maritime Archaeology* 15 (2): 45–58.

Bowdler, S. 1995. Offshore islands and maritime exploration in Australian prehistory. *Antiquity* 239: 945–958.

Broeze, F. J. A. 1998. *Island nation: A history of Australian and the sea.* St. Leonards, NSW: Allen and Unwin.

Cairns, L., and G. Henderson. 1995. *Unfinished voyages—shipwrecks of Western Australia 1881–1900.* Nedlands: University of Western Australia Press.

Campbell, J. 1997. Eighteenth century wooden clubs from HMS *Pandora. Bulletin of the Australian Institute for Maritime Archaeology* 21: 1–8.

Campbell, J., and P. Gesner. 2000. Illustrated catalogue of artefacts from the HMS *Pandora* wrecksite excavations 1977–1995. *Memoirs of the Queensland Museum—Cultural Heritage Series* 2 (1): 53–159.

Cassidy, W. 1991. Historic shipwrecks and blanket declaration. *Bulletin of the Australian Institute for Maritime Archaeology* 15 (2): 4–6.

Clark, P., and S. Jung. 2001. Beyond the wrecked ship: The Northern Territory's shipwreck database. *Bulletin of the Australian Institute for Maritime Archaeology* 25: 43–52.

Clark, P., and M. Nash. 1988. Sydney Cove *Historic Shipwreck (1797).* Occasional Paper 19. Hobart: Tasmanian Parks and Wildlife Service.

Clark, P., and T. Smith. 1986. Recent site work on the *Sydney Cove* (1797). *Bulletin of the Australian Institute for Maritime Archaeology* 10 (2): 44–49.

Coleman, R. 1988a. The currency of cultural change and 18th century Pacific exploration. *Bulletin of the Australian Institute for Maritime Archaeology* 12 (1): 41–50.

———. 1988b. A "Taylor's" common pump from HMS *Pandora. International Journal of Nautical Archaeology* 17 (3): 201–204.

Cooper, M. A., A. Firth, J. Carman, and D. Wheatley. 1995. *Managing archaeology.* London: Routledge.

Coroneos, C. 1997. *Shipwrecks of Encounter Bay and Backstairs Passage.* Australian Institute for Maritime Archaeology Special Publications No. 8.

———. 2006. The ethics and values of maritime archaeology. In *Maritime archaeology: Australian approaches,* ed. M. Staniforth and M. Nash, 111–122. New York: Springer/Kluwer/Plenum.

Coroneos, C., and R. McKinnon. 1997. *Shipwrecks of Investigator Strait and the Lower Yorke Peninsula.* Australian Institute for Maritime Archaeology Special Publication No. 9.

Dortch, C. 1991. Rottnest and Garden Island prehistory and the archaeological potential of the adjacent continental shelf, Western Australia. *Australian Archaeology* 33: 38–43.

———. 1998. The erosion factor in sea floor investigations of prehistoric occupation deposits. *Australian Archaeology* 47: 37–42.

———. 2002. Preliminary underwater survey for rock engravings and other sea floor sites in the Dampier Archipelago, Pilbara Region, Western Australia. *Australian Archaeology* 54: 8–17.

Duncan, B. 2006. *The maritime archaeology and maritime cultural landscapes of Queenscliffe: A nineteenth century Australian coastal community*. PhD thesis. School of Anthropology, Archaeology and Sociology, James Cook University, Townsville.

Edmonds, L., S. Kenderdine, G. Nayton, and M. Staniforth. 1995. *Historic Shipwrecks National Research Plan*. Unpublished report. Canberra: Department of Communications and the Arts.

Elkin, D. 2006. HMS Swift: Scientific research and management of underwater cultural heritage in Argentina. In *Underwater cultural heritage at risk: Managing natural and human impacts*, ed. R. Grenier, D. Nutley, and I. Cochran, 76–78. Paris: UNESCO.

Erskine, N. 2002. *HMS Sirius Expedition Report*. Unpublished report for the Australian federal government, Norfolk Island.

———. 2004. *Bringing back the Bounty: An archaeological study of the mutineer settlement at Pitcairn Island 1790–1856*. PhD thesis, School of Anthropology, Archaeology and Sociology, James Cook University, Townsville.

Evans, Kathryn. 1993a. Shore based whaling in Tasmania archaeological research project. Vol. 1, A social and economic history. Hobart: Report for the Tasmanian Parks and Wildlife Service.

———. 1993b. Shore based whaling in Tasmania archaeological research project. Vol. 2, Site histories. Hobart: Report for the Tasmanian Parks and Wildlife Service.

Fallowfield, T. 2001. Polynesian fishing implements from the wreck of HMS *Pandora*: A technological and contextual study. *Bulletin of the Australian Institute for Maritime Archaeology* 25: 5–28.

Flemming, N. 1982. *Sirius Expedition—Cootamundra Shoals Survey 1982: Expedition reports*. 4 vols.

Flinders University—Maritime Archaeology Program. Online. Available at https://ehlt.flinders.edu.au/archaeology/postgrad_programs/coursework/maritime/. Accessed 4 December 2008.

Foster, L. 1987–1990. *Port Phillip shipwrecks: An historical survey*. 4 vols. Occasional Report Series. Melbourne: Victoria Archaeological Survey.

———. 1996. *The Wild Coast wrecks*. Melbourne: Heritage Victoria.

Gesner, P. 1988. The *Pandora* project: Reviewing genesis and rationale. *Bulletin of the Australian Institute for Maritime Archaeology* 12 (1): 27–36.

———. 1990. Situation report: HMS *Pandora*. *Bulletin of the Australian Institute for Maritime Archaeology* 14 (2): 41–46.

———. 1991. Pandora: An archaeological perspective. Brisbane: Queensland Museum.

———. 1993. Managing *Pandora*'s box—the 1993 *Pandora* expedition. *Bulletin of the Australian Institute for Maritime Archaeology* 17 (2): 7–10.

———. 1997. Pandora. In *The British Museum encyclopedia of maritime and underwater archaeology*, ed. J. Delgado, 305–307. London: British Museum Press.

———. 2000. HMS *Pandora* project—a report on Stage 1: Five seasons of excavations. *Memoirs of the Queensland Museum—Cultural Heritage Series* 2 (1): 1–52.

———. 2007. HMS *Pandora* 1791: Pursuit of the Bounty. In *Shipwreck archaeology in Australia*, ed. M. Nash, 39–50. Nedlands: University of Western Australia Press.

Gibbs, M. 1995. The historical archaeology of shore-based whaling in Western Australia 1836–1879. PhD thesis, Archaeology, University of Western Australia.

———. 2002. Maritime archaeology and behaviour during crisis: The wreck of the VOC ship Batavia (1629). In *Natural Disasters, catastrophism and cultural change*, ed. J. Grattan and R. Torrence, 66–86. New York: Routledge.

———. 2006. Maritime archaeology at the land-sea interface. In *Maritime archaeology: Australian approaches*, ed. M. Staniforth and M. Nash, 69–81. New York: Springer/Kluwer/Plenum.

Green, J. N. 1975. The VOC ship *Batavia* wrecked in 1629 on the Houtman Abrolhos, Western Australia. *International Journal of Nautical Archaeology* 4 (1): 43–64.

———. 1977a. *Australia's oldest wreck: The loss of the* Trial, *1622*. BAR Supplementary Series No. 27. Oxford: British Archaeological Reports.

———, ed. 1977b. *The loss of the Verenigde Oostindische Compagnie jacht* Vergulde Draeck, *Western Australia, 1656*. 2 vols. BAR Supplementary Series No. 36. Oxford: British Archaeological Reports.

———, ed. 1978a. *Papers from the First Southern Hemisphere Conference on Maritime Archaeology*. Melbourne: Oceans Society of Australia.

———. 1978b. The Western Australian Museum Maritime Archaeology Department and the Dutch Wreck Programme. In *Papers from the First Southern Hemisphere Conference on Maritime Archaeology*, ed. J. N. Green, 62–68. Melbourne: Oceans Society of Australia.

———. 1983a. The Koh Si Chang excavation report 1983. *Bulletin of the Australian Institute for Maritime Archaeology* 7 (2): 9–37.

———. 1983b. The Song dynasty shipwreck at Quanzhou Fujian province, People's Republic of China. *International Journal of Nautical Archaeology* 12 (3): 253–261.

———. 1983c. The Shinan excavation, Korea: An interim report on the hull structure. *International Journal of Nautical Archaeology* 12 (4): 293–302.

———. 1986. The survey of the VOC fluit *Risdam* (1727), Malaysia. *International Journal of Nautical Archaeology* 15 (2): 93–104.

———. 1989. *The AVOC retourschip* Batavia, *wrecked Western Australia, 1629: Excavation report and artefact catalogue*. BAR International Series No. 489. Oxford: British Archaeological Reports.

———. 1990. *Maritime archaeology: A technical handbook*. New York: Academic Press.

———. 1991. The planking-first construction of the VOC ship *Batavia*. In *Fifth International Symposium on Boat and Ship Archaeology*, ed. R. Reinders and K. Paul. Monograph No. 12. Oxford: Oxbow.

———. 1995. Management of maritime archaeology under Australian legislation. *Bulletin of the Australian Institute for Maritime Archaeology* 19 (2): 33–44.

———. 2006. Nautical archaeology in Australia, the Indian Ocean and Asia. In *Maritime archaeology: Australian approaches*, ed. M. Staniforth and M. Nash, 97–109. New York: Springer/Kluwer/Plenum.

Green, J. N., N. Burningham, and Museum of Overseas Communication History. 1998. The ship from Guanzhou, Fujian province, People's Republic of China. *International Journal of Nautical Archaeology* 27 (4): 277–301.

Green, J. N., S. Devendra, and R. Parthesius, eds. 1998. *Galle Harbour project 1996–1997*. Special Publication No. 4. Fremantle: Australian National Centre of Excellence for Maritime Archaeology.

Green, J. N., M. Gainsford, and M. Stanbury. 2004. *Department of Maritime Archaeology, Western Australian Maritime Museum: A compendium of projects, programmes and publications 1971–2003*. Special Publication No. 9. Fremantle: Australian National Centre of Excellence.

Green, J. N., and R. Harper. 1982. The excavation of the Ko Kradet wreck site, Thailand. *International Journal of Nautical Archaeology* 11 (2): 164–171.

———. 1983. *The excavation of the Pattaya wrecksite and survey of three other sites, Thailand, 1982.* Special Publication No. 1. Fremantle: Australian Institute for Maritime Archaeology.

Green, J. N., R. Harper, and V. Intakosi. 1987. *The maritime archaeology of shipwrecks and ceramics in Southeast Asia.* Special Publication No. 4. Fremantle: Australian Institute for Maritime Archaeology.

Green, J. N., T. Vosmer, P. Clarke, R. Santiago, and M. Alvares. 1995. Interim report on the joint Australian-Philippines Butuan boat project, October 1992. *International Journal of Nautical Archaeology* 24 (3): 177–181.

Gurney, K. 1994. Recent changes to historic shipwrecks legislation in Victoria: Something borrowed and something new. *Bulletin of the Australian Institute for Maritime Archaeology* 18 (1): 47–50.

Guthrie, J., L. Blackhall, D. Moriarty, and P. Gesner. 1994. Wrecks and marine microbiology: A case study from the *Pandora*. *Bulletin of the Australian Institute for Maritime Archaeology* 18 (2): 19–24.

Henderson, G. 1975a. *James Matthews* excavation summer 1974–1975. *Australian Archaeology* 3: 40–45.

———. 1975b. Post settlement sites: *James Matthews* excavation. *International Journal of Nautical Archaeology* 4 (2): 371.

———. 1976. *James Matthews* excavation: Summer 1974, interim report. *International Journal of Nautical Archaeology* 5 (2): 245–251.

———. 1978. Developing a colonial wrecks programme in western Australia. In *Papers from the First Southern Hemisphere Conference on Maritime Archaeology*, ed. J. N. Green, 69–72. Melbourne: Oceans Society of Australia.

———. 1980a. Finds from the wreck of HMS *Pandora*. *International Journal of Nautical Archaeology* 9 (3): 237–243.

———. 1980b. *Unfinished voyages—shipwrecks of western Australia 1622–1850.* Nedlands: University of Western Australia Press.

———. 1986. *Maritime archaeology in Australia.* Nedlands: University of Western Australia Press.

———. 1993. The wreck of the *Sirius*. *Australian Geographic* 29: 100–117.

———. 2008. The wreck of the ex-slaver *James Matthews*. *International Journal of Historical Archaeology* 12: 39–52.

Henderson, G., and K. J. Henderson, 1988. *Unfinished voyages—shipwrecks of western Australia 1851–1880.* Nedlands: University of Western Australia Press.

Henderson, G., and M. Stanbury. 1983. The excavation of a collection of cordage from a shipwreck site. *International Journal of Nautical Archaeology* 12 (1): 15–26.

———. 1988. *The* Sirius *past and present.* Sydney: Collins.

HMS *Pandora*—Queensland Museum. Online. Available at www.qm.qld.gov.au/features/pandora/pandora.asp. Accessed 4 December 2008.

Hosty, K. 2006. Maritime museums and maritime archaeological exhibitions. In *Maritime archaeology: Australian approaches*, ed. M. Staniforth and M. Nash, 151–162. New York: Springer/Kluwer/Plenum.

Hosty, K., and I. Stuart. 1994. Maritime archaeology over the last twenty years. *Australian Archaeology* 39: 9–19.

Hundley, P. 1983. Educational programs in maritime archaeology. In *Proceedings of the Second Southern Hemisphere Conference on Maritime Archaeology*, ed. W. F. Jeffery and

J. Amess, 69–77. Adelaide: South Australian Department of Environment and
    Planning and the Commonwealth Department of Home Affairs and Environment.
ICOMOS—Charter on the Protection of Underwater Cultural Heritage. 1996.
    Online at www.international.icomos.org/charters/underwater_e.htm/. Accessed
    4 December 2008.
ICUCH—International Committee on Underwater Cultural Heritage. Online at www.
    icuch.org/artman/publish/index.shtml/. Accessed 4 December 2008.
Illidge, P. 2002. The Tahitian mourner's costume: A description of use, composition and
    relevant artefacts from HMS *Pandora*. *Bulletin of the Australian Institute for Maritime
    Archaeology* 26: 65–74.
Ingelman-Sundberg, C. 1976. The VOC ship *Zeewijk* 1727: Report on the 1976 survey of the
    site. *Australian Archaeology* 5: 18–33.
———. 1977. The VOC ship *Zeewijk* lost off the western Australian coast in 1727.
    International Journal of Nautical Archaeology 6 (3): 225–231.
Jateff, E. 2007. *Hain't bin found yet: The search for archaeological evidence of shore whaling at
    Diamond City*. Monograph Series No. 14. Adelaide: Flinders University Maritime
    Archaeology.
Jeffery, W. F. 1987. A cultural resource management programme for shipwrecks in South
    Australia. *Bulletin of the Australian Institute for Maritime Archaeology* 11 (1): 39–56.
———. 1999. Australia. In *Legal protection of the underwater cultural heritage: Federal,
    regional and international perspectives*, ed. S. Dromgoole, 1–17. The Hague: Kluwer Law
    International.
———. 2006. Historic shipwrecks legislation. In *Maritime archaeology: Australian approaches*,
    ed. M. Staniforth and M. Nash, 123–135. New York: Springer/Kluwer/Plenum.
———. 2008. *War graves, munition dumps and pleasure grounds: A post-colonial perspective
    of Chuuk Lagoon's submerged World War II sites*. PhD thesis, School of Anthropology,
    Archaeology and Sociology, James Cook University, Townsville.
Jeffery, W. F., and J. Amess, eds. 1983. *Papers from the Second Southern Hemisphere
    Conference on Maritime Archaeology*. Adelaide: SA Department of Environment
    and Planning.
Jones, M. D., and M. Staniforth. 1996. *Fowlers Bay whaling site archaeological program*.
    Adelaide: Report for the SA Museum and ANZSES.
Jordan, D. 1995. *East coast wrecks: A thematic historical survey*. Melbourne: Heritage
    Victoria.
Kenderdine, S. 1994. *Shipwrecks 1656–1924: A guide to historic wrecksites of Perth*.
    Fremantle: Western Australian Maritime Museum.
Kimpton, G. 1992. Construction of replica anchor stocks and a carronade carriage for
    display of artefacts from HMS *Sirius* (1791). *Bulletin of the Australian Institute for
    Maritime Archaeology* 16 (2): 31–38.
Kostaglou, P. 1995a. *Shore based whaling in Tasmania archaeological research project*. Vol. 1,
    Industry overview and recommendations. Hobart: Report for the Tasmanian Parks and
    Wildlife Service.
———. 1995b. *Shore based whaling in Tasmania archaeological research project*. Vol. 2,
    Results of fieldwork. Hobart: Report for the Tasmanian Parks and Wildlife Service.
Kostaglou, P., and J. McCarthy. 1991. *Whaling and sealing sites in South Australia*. Special
    Publication No. 6. Australian Institute for Maritime Archaeology.
Lawrence, S. 2001a. Foodways on two colonial whaling stations: Archaeological and
    historical evidence for diet in nineteenth century Tasmania. *Journal of the Royal
    Australian Historical Society* 87 (2): 209–229.

———. 2001b. Whaling in the South Seas: Archaeological evidence of Australia's first industry. *Mains'l Haul, Journal of Pacific Maritime History* 37 (3–4): 4–11.

———. 2006. *Whalers and free men: Life on Tasmania's colonial whaling stations.* Melbourne: Australian Scholarly Publishing.

Lawrence, S., and M. Staniforth, eds. 1998. *The archaeology of whaling in Southern Australia and New Zealand.* Special Publication No. 10. Gundaroo: Australasian Society for Historical Archaeology and Australian Institute for Maritime Archaeology.

Lester, S. 1982. The rudder of the *Sydney Cove* (1797) reassembly, construction and assessment of importance. *Bulletin of the Australian Institute for Maritime Archaeology* 6: 19–31.

———. 1984. The importance of a shipwreck: The *Sydney Cove* (1797). *Papers and Proceedings of the Tasmanian Historical Research Association* 31 (3): 1–12.

MacKay, J., and R. Coleman, 1992. *The 24-gun frigate* Pandora *1779.* London: Conway Maritime Press.

MacKnight, C. 1976. *Voyage to Marege: Macassan trepangers in northern Australia.* Carlton: Melbourne University Press.

MacLeod, I. D. 1989. The application of corrosion science to the management of maritime archaeological sites. *Bulletin of the Australian Institute for Maritime Archaeology* 13 (2): 7–16.

Maritime Archaeology Department, WA Museum. Online at www.museum.wa.gov.au/collections/maritime/march/march.asp/. Accessed 4 December 2008.

McCarthy, M. 1981. The underwater display case. *Bulletin of the Australian Institute for Maritime Archaeology* 5: 42–52.

———. 1986. The excavation and raising of the SS *Xantho* engine. *International Journal of Nautical Archaeology* 15 (2): 173–176.

———. 1988. SS *Xantho*: The pre-disturbance, assessment, excavation and management of an iron steam shipwreck off the coast of Western Australia. *International Journal of Nautical Archaeology* 17 (4): 339–348.

———. 1998. Australian maritime archaeology: Changes, their antecedents and the path ahead. *Australian Archaeology* 47: 33–38.

———. 2000. *Iron and steamship archaeology: Success and failure on the SS* Xantho. New York: Springer/Kluwer/Plenum.

———. 2003. The holistic approach to the maritime heritage: Western Australia case study. *Bulletin of the Australian Institute for Maritime Archaeology* 27: 25–34.

———. 2004. Historic aircraft wrecks as archaeological sites. *Bulletin of the Australian Institute for Maritime Archaeology* 28: 81–90.

———. 2006. Maritime archaeology in Australasia: Reviews and overviews. In *Maritime archaeology: Australian approaches*, ed. M. Staniforth and M. Nash, 1–11. New York: Springer/Kluwer/Plenum.

McIlroy, J. 1986. Bathers Bay Whaling Station, Fremantle, Western Australia. *Australasian Historical Archaeology* 4: 43–50.

Moran, V., and M. Staniforth. 1998. The AIMA/NAS Part 1 Training Program. *Bulletin of the Australian Institute for Maritime Archaeology* 22: 137–138.

Nash, M. 1990. Survey of the historic ship *Litherland. Bulletin of the Australian Institute for Maritime Archaeology* 14 (1): 13–20.

———. 1991. Recent work on the *Sydney Cove* historic shipwreck. *Bulletin of the Australian Institute for Maritime Archaeology* 15 (1): 37–47.

———. 2001. *Cargo for the colony: The wreck of the merchant ship* Sydney Cove. Woden: Navarine.

———. 2002. The *Sydney Cove* shipwreck project. *International Journal of Nautical Archaeology* 31 (1): 39–59.

———. 2003a. The Tasmanian Maritime Heritage Program. *Bulletin of the Australian Institute for Maritime Archaeology* 27: 43–58.

———. 2003b. *The bay whalers: Tasmania's shore based whaling industry*. Canberra: Navarine.

———. 2006a. Individual shipwreck site case studies. In *Maritime archaeology: Australian approaches*, ed. M. Staniforth and M. Nash, 55–67. New York: Springer/Kluwer/Plenum.

———. 2006b. *Investigation of a survivors camp from the Sydney Cove shipwreck*. Monograph Series No. 2. Adelaide: Flinders University Maritime Archaeology.

———, ed. 2007a. *Shipwreck archaeology in Australia*. Nedlands: University of Western Australia Press.

———. 2007b. *Sydney Cove* 1797: Cargo for the colony. In *Shipwreck archaeology in Australia*, ed. M. Nash, 51–63. Nedlands: University of Western Australia Press.

National Historic Shipwrecks Database. Online. Available at www.environment.gov.au/cgi-bin/heritage/nsd/nsd_list.pl/. Accessed 4 December 2008.

Nutley, D. 1987. Maritime Heritage Protection: Education as the long arm of the law. *Bulletin of the Australian Institute for Maritime Archaeology* 11 (1): 29–33.

———. 1996. Shipwrecks, sharks and shattered timbers—the shipwreck atlas of New South Wales. *Bulletin of the Australian Institute for Maritime Archaeology* 20 (2): 9–10.

———. 1998. Ten years of shipwreck access and management in New South Wales. *Bulletin of the Australian Institute for Maritime Archaeology* 22: 115–118.

———. 2000. Developing a methodology for identifying, assessing and managing inundated archaeological sites in Australia. *Bulletin of the Australian Institute for Maritime Archaeology* 24: 35–36.

———. 2003. Benefits of a formal understanding between the NSW Marine Parks Authority and the NSW Heritage Office. *Bulletin of the Australian Institute for Maritime Archaeology* 27: 71–76.

———. 2006. Underwater archaeology. In *Maritime archaeology: Australian approaches*, ed. M. Staniforth and M. Nash, 83–96. New York: Springer/Kluwer/Plenum.

———. 2007. *Surviving inundation: An examination of environmental factors influencing the survival of inundated indigenous sites in Australia within defined hydrodynamic and geological settings*. Monograph Series No. 10. Adelaide: Flinders University Maritime Archaeology.

Orme, Z., and N. Randall. 1987. A survey of the historical limestone structures on West Wallabi Island, Houtman Abrolhos. *Bulletin of the Australian Institute for Maritime Archaeology* 11 (2): 25–31.

Pasveer, J., A. Black, and M. van Huystee. 1998. Victims of the *Batavia* mutiny: Physical, anthropological and forensic studies of the Beacon Island skeletons. *Bulletin of the Australian Institute for Maritime Archaeology* 22: 45–50.

Paterson, A. 2006. *Understanding the Sleaford Bay tryworks: An interpretive approach to the industrial archaeology of shore based whaling*. Monograph Series No. 3. Adelaide: Flinders University Maritime Archaeology.

Pearson, C. 1974. The Western Australian Museum Conservation Laboratory for maritime archaeological material. *International Journal of Nautical Archaeology* 3 (2): 295–305.

———. 1977. On site conservation requirements for the marine archaeological excavations. *International Journal of Nautical Archaeology* 6 (1): 37–46.

Penrose, J. D. 1978. Education in maritime archaeology. In *Papers from the First Southern Hemisphere Conference on Maritime Archaeology*, ed. J. N. Green, 104–109. Melbourne: Oceans Society of Australia.

———. 1983. Education in maritime archaeology—an Australian perspective. In *Proceedings of the Second Southern Hemisphere Conference on Maritime Archaeology*, ed. W. F. Jeffery and J. Amess, 65–68. Adelaide: South Australian Department of Environment and Planning and the Commonwealth Department of Home Affairs and Environment.

Philippou, C., and M. Staniforth. 2003. Maritime Heritage Trails in Australia: An overview and critique of the interpretive programs. In *Submerged cultural resource management*, ed. J. D. Spirek and D. A. Scott-Ireton, 135–141. New York: Springer/Kluwer/Plenum.

Pigott, L. 1995. The surgeon's equipment from the wreck of HMS *Pandora*. *Bulletin of the Australian Institute for Maritime Archaeology* 19 (1): 23–28.

Randall, N. 1987. Western Australia's shore-based whaling heritage. *Bulletin of the Australian Institute for Maritime Archaeology* 11 (2): 33–36.

Randell, S. 1999. The effects of material type on concretion formation: A case study from the HMS *Pandora*. *Bulletin of the Australian Institute for Maritime Archaeology* 23: 51–55.

Redknap, M., ed. 1997. *Artefacts from wrecks: Dated assemblages from the late Middle Ages to the Industrial Revolution*. Oxford: Oxbow.

Richards, N. 2002. *Deep structures: An examination of deliberate watercraft abandonment in Australia*. PhD thesis. Department of Archaeology, Flinders University, Adelaide.

———. 2008. *Ships' graveyards: Abandoned watercraft and the archaeological site formation process*. Gainesville: University Press of Florida.

Smith, T. 2003. Shipwreck trails: Public ownership of a unique resource? In *Submerged cultural resource management*, ed. J. D. Spirek and D. A. Scott-Ireton, 121–133. New York: Springer/Kluwer/Plenum.

Souter, C. 2006. Cultural tourism and diver education. In *Maritime archaeology: Australian approaches*, ed. M. Staniforth and M. Nash, 163–176. New York: Springer/Kluwer/Plenum.

Stanbury, M. 1991. Scientific instruments from the wreck of HMS *Sirius* (1790). *International Journal of Nautical Archaeology* 20 (3): 195–221.

———. 1993. Maritime history, archaeology and museums. *Bermuda Journal of Archaeology and Maritime History* 5: 215–228.

———. 1994. *HMS* Sirius *1790: An illustrated catalogue of artefacts recovered from the wrecksite at Norfolk Island*. Australian Institute for Maritime Archaeology Special Publication No. 7.

———. 1998. Land archaeology in the Houtman Abrolhos. In *The ANCODS Colloquium*, ed. J. N. Green, M. Stanbury, and F. Gastra, 101–107. Australian National Centre of Excellence for Maritime Archaeology Special Publication No. 3.

———. 1999. *Dependent colonies: The importation of material culture and the establishment of a consumer society in Australia before 1850*. PhD diss., Department of Archaeology, Flinders University, Adelaide.

———. 2000. A future for maritime archaeology? *Australian Archaeology* 50: 90–93.

———. 2003. *The barque* Eglinton: *Wrecked western Australia 1852*. Australian Institute for Maritime Archaeology Special Publication No. 13.

———. 2007. HMS *Sirius*: Relic of the first fleet. In *Shipwreck archaeology in Australia*, ed. M. Nash, 25–38. Nedlands: University of Western Australia Press.

Staniforth, M. 1993. Maritime history, archaeology and museums. *Bermuda Journal of Archaeology and Maritime History* 5: 215–228.

———. 1999. *Dependent colonies: The importation of material culture and the establishment of a consumer society in Australia before 1850.* Doctoral thesis, Flinders University, Adelaide.

———. 2000. A future for Australian maritime archaeology? *Australian Archaeology* 50: 90–93.

———. 2003. *Material culture and consumer society.* New York: Springer/Kluwer/ Plenum.

———. 2006. Artefact studies. In *Maritime archaeology: Australian approaches,* ed. M. Staniforth and M. Nash, 27–40. New York: Springer/Kluwer/Plenum.

———. 2007a. Australian approaches to defining and quantifying underwater cultural heritage—learning from our mistakes. In *Managing the marine cultural heritage: Defining, accessing and managing the resource,* ed. J. Stachell and P. Palma, 25–30. Research Report 153. York: Council for British Archaeology.

———. 2007b. *The history and archaeology of the Gaultois shore-based whaling station in Newfoundland, Canada.* Monograph Series No. 6. Adelaide: Flinders University Maritime Archaeology.

———. 2008a. Strategies for teaching maritime archaeology in the 21st century. *Journal of Maritime Archaeology* 3: 93–102.

———. 2008b. Collaboration is the key: Developing field and work skills in collaboration with government, museum and commercial underwater cultural heritage organizations. In *Proceedings of the 13th Annual Meeting of the European Association of Archaeologists* (Zadar, Croatia, 18–23 September 2007), ed. R. Radic, Rossi A. Gaspari, and A. Pydyn, 111–120. Profil, Zagreb: Hrvatsko arheolosko drustvo.

Staniforth, M., S. Briggs, and C. Lewczak. 2001. Unearthing the invisible people: European women and children and aboriginal people at South-Australian shore-based whaling stations. *Mains'l Haul, Journal of Pacific Maritime History* 36 (3): 12–19.

Staniforth, M., and M. Hyde, eds. 2001. *Maritime archaeology in Australia: A reader.* Blackwood, SA: Southern Archaeology.

Staniforth, M., and M. Nash. 1998. *Chinese export porcelain from the wreck of the Sydney Cove (1797).* Special Publication No. 12. Gundaroo, NSW: Australasian Society for Historical Archaeology and Australian Institute for Maritime Archaeology.

———, eds. 2006. *Maritime archaeology: Australian approaches.* New York: Springer/ Kluwer/Plenum.

Steptoe, D. P., and W. B. Wood. 2002. The human remains from HMS *Pandora. Internet Archaeology* 11. http://intarch.ac.uk/journal/issue11/steptoe_index.html/.

Strachan, S. 1986a. *The history and archaeology of the Sydney Cove Shipwreck (1797): A resource for future site work.* Canberra: Research School of Pacific Studies, Australian National University.

———. 1986b. A research design for European influenced shipbuilding in India and Southeast Asia: The *Sydney Cove* (1797). *Bulletin of the Australian Institute for Maritime Archaeology* 10 (2): 37–44.

———. 1995. Interpreting maritime heritage: Australian historic shipwreck trails. *Historic Environment* 11 (4): 26–36.

Townrow, K. 1997. *An archaeological survey of sealing and whaling sites in Victoria.* Melbourne: Heritage Victoria.

UNESCO Convention on the Protection of the Underwater Cultural Heritage. 2001.
    Online at http://portal.unesco.org/en/ev.php-URL_ID=13520&URL_DO=DO_
    TOPIC&URL_SECTION=201.html/. Accessed 4 December 2008.
Ward, I., P. Larcome, and P. Veth. 1999a. Sedimentary processes and the *Pandora* wreck,
    Great Barrier Reef, Australia. *Journal of Field Archaeology* 26 (1): 41–53.
———. 1999b. A new process-based model for wreck site formation. *Journal of
    Archaeological Science* 26: 561–570.

CHAPTER 26

HISTORIC PERIOD SHIPS OF THE PACIFIC OCEAN

HANS K. VAN TILBURG

INTRODUCTION

THE Pacific Ocean, stretching some 9,300 nautical miles (17,223 km) from Panama to Mindanao, encompasses over 179 million km² (69 million square miles) of surface area. This is larger than the area of all land masses on the planet combined; it is the largest and deepest ocean in the world, fringed by at least 11 separate seas. In some ways the Pacific Ocean has been a barrier, the distance and time required for successful crossings imposing a strict reckoning on unskilled seafarers. But for those who understood the winds and the currents, in many ways the Pacific has also been a highway, an expansive and mobile blue bridge allowing communication between all the habitable locations within this sea of islands.

The ship is the single central object for all migration and communication within this oceanic world. In an area as large as the Pacific, there are naturally a multitude of different vessel designs, reflecting the many different seafaring cultures and locations and historical periods. But what gives ships their significance? What makes Pacific shipwrecks representative of historic periods? It must be more than an accident of geography, for the list of known Pacific shipwrecks is simply too long for such an open approach. There must be some specific criteria. For example, candidates might be defined by construction sufficient to navigate open ocean passages, the longest of seagoing legs. Additionally, selected ships should capture elements of historical periods that shaped the Pacific maritime past in major ways, including vessels of exploration and migration, early trade, pelagic whalers, Gold Rush ships, lumber schooners, iron-hulled square-rigged ships, early naval vessels, and wreck sites associated with particularly significant Pacific events. There is, of course, no unbroken record of submerged archaeological sites depicting continuous maritime activity—maritime archaeology in the Pacific is too new a field compared with that of the Mediterranean or Atlantic—but a selected summary of archaeological site work, rather than a comprehensive survey, might serve to illuminate specific chapters of our seafaring past within the Pacific region.

PACIFIC DOUBLE-HULLED VOYAGING CANOES

Long before Western discoveries, virtually all of the inhabitable islands of the Pacific had been contacted by Pacific Island voyagers in what is coming to be recognized today as the single greatest marine migration ever to take place. Over hundreds of years, double-hull voyaging canoes, guided by specialists trained in noninstrumental navigation, moved eastward into the Pacific, bearing the men and women and all necessary supplies to support permanent remote settlement. Oceanic voyaging canoes of advanced design demonstrated a proven technical ability as Austronesian sailors learned to successfully cross thousands of miles of open ocean sometime between 1,400 and 900 BCE. Some of this ability was apparent to eighteenth- and nineteenth-century Western explorers, such as Captain James Cook, for not all canoe construction or traditional voyaging came to a halt with the advent of Western ships in the Pacific region (Neich 2006: 200). The idea of long-distance non-instrument navigation, of intentional voyaging and colonization, later proved difficult for twentieth-century scholars, who have only recently begun to understand the true outlines of this achievement.

Works such as A. C. Haddon and James Hornell's *Canoes of Oceania* (1936), Ben Finney's *Voyage of Rediscovery* (1994), and K. R. Howe's *Vaka Moana: Voyages of the Ancestors* (2006) go a long way in presenting the technical aspects of the voyaging canoe evolution to the general public. The pre–iron age lashed double-hulled canoe design was clearly the preeminent Pacific vessel of exploration and migration, a cultural platform of immense importance. The double-hull voyaging canoe had no need for ballast in order to maintain stability, and therefore was almost incapable of sinking. As an ironic consequence, unfortunately very little archaeological signature has been left for the maritime archaeologist, a fact that made Dr. Yoshi Sinoto's terrestrial wet site excavations in the early 1970s all the more important.

Sinoto, chairman of the anthropology department of Hawai'i's Bernice P. Bishop Museum, accomplished some of the only archaeological work on voyaging canoes to date. The construction of the hotel Bali Hai on the island of Huahine in French Polynesia initiated the survey of a canoe construction site containing shell, bone, wooden artifacts, and stone tools. The wet site location had been inundated by a tsunami and covered with a thick layer of sand and silt, but the long planks of the voyaging canoes, along with splashboards from the bows, steering paddle, and outrigger boom, remained (Sinoto 1983: 11). These traces of canoes, together with contemporary eighteenth- and nineteenth-century observations, contributed to the current Pacific-wide revival of canoe construction and non-instrument navigation. The replica Hawaiian voyaging canoes *Hokule'a* and *Hawai'iloa* are two well-known examples of this revival (Figure 26.1). Still, it is an odd situation that, for such an influential nautical accomplishment, there is so little actual physical record. In the Pacific, where archaeology must contribute to the story of human migration, the maritime field is faced with an unsinkable ironless target. Even if they had sunk, voyaging canoes, an advanced technology, lacked the solid iron features found in galleons and other Western vessels, leaving no signal for the magnetometer.

Spanish Manila Galleons

Survey tools can locate European galleons, though, and these sixteenth-century ships were the first Western vessels to venture into the Pacific. As with the voyaging canoes, archaeologists are again faced with an absence of survey data, but for completely different reasons. Soon after the remnants of Magellan's small fleet completed their remarkable first circumnavigation in 1522 CE, the challenge for the

Figure 26.1 Drawing of the Hawaiian double-hulled voyaging canoe *Hokule'a*, a performance-accurate replica with oceanic spritsail rig. Reproduced with the kind permission of Ben Finney.

Spanish was to find a way back to Mexico from their newly established trade entrepôt in the Philippines, thus avoiding transgressing Portuguese waters in Southeast Asia. In 1565, Adrés de Urdaneta found the westerlies of the North Pacific, and merchantmen began their annual transpacific trek to and from Acapulco and Manila, forging the way for 250 years of Western global maritime network. The extraction of wealth from East Asia depended on ships capable of crossing the Pacific. These large, slow galleons, many of which were built in the Philippines by Southeast Asian laborers under the direction of Spanish shipwrights, were the first Western-style vessels truly capable of safely making the crossing.

Despite the long-standing search, discovery, and excavation of some of these sites, almost nothing is known of Manila galleon construction. Just as they were the richly laden prey of the historic period, galleon shipwrecks have been the targets of treasure hunters for many decades, and sites have been heavily impacted by commercial efforts focusing more on recovery and less on archaeological survey. Some 40 Manila galleons went missing in the Pacific, most lost in the Philippines and the Mariana Islands. Wrecks on Guam include the *San Pablo* in 1568, the *Nuestra Senora de Pilar* in 1690, and the *Nuestra Senora del Buen Viaje* in 1754. Researchers are investigating the possible galleon site known as the "Beeswax wreck" near Nehalem, Oregon (Stenger 2005). In general, much is known about the cargo, but the small number of case studies adds little information about these types of ships themselves.

The 2,000-ton vice-flagship *Nuestra Senora de la Concepcion*, reportedly the largest vessel afloat at the time of its loss, was driven ashore during a storm at Aguingan Point, Saipan, on 20 September 1638. Some of the cargo and most of the cannon were retrieved by Spanish authorities in 1674. Some of the remaining treasure of the *Concepcion* was recovered by William M. Mathers, of Pacific Sea Resources, in 1987 and 1988. These excavations yielded more than 1,300 pieces of gold jewelry in the form of chains, crucifixes, beads, buckles, filigree buttons, rings, and brooches set with precious stones. Mathers completed an artifact recovery report in 1990. The artifact collection went to a Japanese company planning to display the finds in a hotel. The hotel was never built, and the company returned the collection to the government of the Northern Mariana Islands (Mathers, Parker, and Copus 1990).

The wreck site of the galleon *San Agustin*, the oldest known shipwreck in California, has been the subject of more than four decades of search (von der Porten 2001: 57). In exception to the above, the *San Agustin* project is directed more toward retrieving archaeological information and locating the ship's hull remains. This Spanish vessel of exploration, commanded by Juan Rodrigues Cermeño, was driven ashore by a storm in November 1595, while anchored for reprovisioning in Drakes Bay on the southern shore of Point Reyes. Soon after the crew abandoned the vessel and continued southward to Acapulco in a small launch, members of the Coast Miwok tribe began opportunistic salvage, and today artifacts and porcelain shards are scattered along the bay's coastline (Russell 2009: 58). Archaeological work in the 1940s and 1950s focused on these artifacts from coastal midden sites.

The wreck of the ship itself has not yet been located, but an archaeological survey of the vessel could address several important questions about the Manila galleon trade, the possible incorporation of Asian ship construction methods, and early cultural contacts in California. The National Park Service (NPS) and the National Oceanic and Atmospheric Administration (NOAA) together began a systematic remote-sensing survey of the area in 1982, but fieldwork was postponed for years due to litigation of a commercial salvage claim. In 1997 and 1998 the survey resumed, covering 4 square miles with magnetometer and side-scan sonar, resulting in approximately 60 high-priority targets. Shark-proof enclosures used for ground-truthing anomalies were also tested. The work continued in 2007 in partnership with NPS and NOAA's Office of Coast Survey, collecting multibeam bathymetry, and extended into 2008 with the joint NPS/NOAA/University of California at Berkeley Tamál-Húye/Drakes Bay Submerged Cultural Resources Project (Russell 2007: 32).

PACIFIC WHALING VESSELS

Manila galleons were a consistent and long-lived element of global trade, yet two or three ships in a vast ocean in no way rendered the Pacific a "Spanish Lake." Western presence was rare indeed. Only in later centuries did the gradual trickle of explorers and Western mariners entering the region eventually become a rushing stream. Whalers represent the bulk of that sudden onslaught of vessel activity. Whaling ships and the whaling industry played a large role in maritime activities in the Pacific throughout most of the nineteenth century.

In many cases whalers were not only hunters but also explorers in new archipelagos and (for better or worse) cultural ambassadors of sorts for the West, the often inadvertent agents of drastic change in remote Pacific island settings. The first Western whaling vessels rounded Cape Horn in 1788 CE, and the industry progressively exploited whale populations as it moved slowly northward over time, from the onshore grounds off South America, to the equatorial line, to a broad swath of the North Pacific known as the Japan Grounds, and finally to the farthest accessible Arctic reaches of the Bering Strait and Chukchi Sea. Many ships were purpose-built for the hunt and outfitted for extended cruises of three to five years (Figure 26.2). By the mid-nineteenth century the American whaling fleet from Nantucket and New Bedford had grown to hundreds of vessels, for whale oil was the source of lighting and lubrication in growing cities, and whale bone or baleen was shaped into a myriad of common products. Until petroleum products became commercially viable, whaling was a global industry of great economic and even international importance. Following the American Civil War, whaling activities in the Pacific declined, though the last sailing voyages in pursuit of the bowhead whale in the Arctic Sea continued into the early twentieth century. The wooden ships were

Figure 26.2 Whalers outfitting at New Bedford, many bound for multiyear voyages to the Pacific. Reproduced with the kind permission of NOAA National Marine Fisheries Service.

replaced by steam catcher boats and mechanized floating factories, though few whales remained.

There is an emerging focus on the archaeology of historic whaling in the Pacific region. In 1997, a maritime archaeology conference at La Trobe University initiated the Archaeology of Whaling in Southern Australia and New Zealand (AWSANZ) project (Lawrence and Staniforth 1998: 7). In 2008, NOAA's Maritime Heritage Program sponsored a whaling heritage symposium, inviting archaeologists, historians, cultural practitioners, and marine biologists to explore the connections between maritime archaeology, whaling history, the marine environment, indigenous whaling cultures, and marine mammal populations. For NOAA, the whaling shipwreck represents a window on a critical marine industry that impacted our relationship with marine resources and the ocean itself. It is seafaring history combined with environmental history and natural resources. A number of recently discovered shipwreck sites are adding to our combined knowledge of this period.

The low, hazardous coral atolls of the Northwestern Hawaiian Islands, lying between Honolulu and the Japan Grounds, an area discovered to be rich with sperm whales in 1820, led to the loss of at least 10 whaling ships. As part of the evolving management plan for the Papahānaumokuākea Marine National Monument,

NOAA's Maritime Heritage Program has been conducting site surveys and assessments (O'Regan, Van Tilburg, and Gleason 2008: 15). Five of these 10 whalers have been located. The *Gledstanes*, a 428-ton ship built in Lieth, Scotland, in 1827, ran aground in heavy surf at Kure Atoll on 9 June 1837. Under difficult conditions, three boats were launched, and captain and crew made landfall on nearby Ocean Island. A 38-foot vessel named *Deliverance* was constructed from the wreckage; whale spades were fashioned into axes for this work, and lances became augers and chisels. In 2008, NOAA divers discovered the wreck site on the exposed shallow reef crest of the atoll and conducted noninvasive site survey. Only the heaviest elements, such as anchors, cannon, trypot portion, and iron ballast bars, appear at the site, but these artifacts describe some of the outfitting of an early-nineteenth-century whaler, as well as the atoll site formation process (Van Tilburg 2009: 22).

The *Parker*, a 406-ton New Bedford whaler, ran onto the northern reef of Kure Atoll on 24 September 1842. The position of the wreckage inside the shallow atoll corresponds to historical reports of a fierce storm at the time, bringing a large portion of the vessel into the lagoon. The vessel broke apart quickly, her crew unable to salvage provisions for what would turn out to be eight months of harsh privation on Ocean Island. The wreck site, discovered in 2002, consists of deck equipment and head gear from the bow section: anchors, windlass, hawse pipes, chain, fastenings, and rigging (National Marine Sanctuaries 2006a). No wooden remains were apparent. Kure Atoll lies in the vicinity of the Japan Grounds, a broad swath of ocean stretching far to the east of the Japanese islands (Van Tilburg 2003: 31).

The oldest shipwrecks in the Hawaiian Islands found so far, the *Pearl* and *Hermes*, were two British South Seas whaling vessels. While sailing in consort from Honolulu toward the Japan Grounds in search of sperm whale oil, they struck Pearl and Hermes Atoll on the night of 24 April 1822. The 258-ton *Hermes* struck first, the larger 327-ton *Pearl* going onto the reef just to the east. The carpenters of the two ships built a rescue schooner (again) named *Deliverance*, and even though a passing vessel eventually took on board most of the crew, a group sailed the *Deliverance* successfully back to the main Hawaiian Islands and used the funds from her auction to establish the first Western shipyard in the islands. The artifacts of these wreck sites (ballast iron, rudder hardware, anchors, fastenings, etc.) describe the wrecking process and the material culture of the London-based South Seas fishery (Figure 26.3). The musket balls and cannon balls and large cannon reflect the diversity of threats inherent in Pacific voyaging in the early part of the century (O'Regan, Van Tilburg, and Gleason 2008: 16; National Marine Sanctuaries 2006b).

The fifth whaling wreck site, discovered by NOAA divers in 2008 at French Frigate Shoals, has only recently been identified as the Two Brothers, Captain Pollard's second ill-fated vessel following the earlier loss of the whaler Essex in 1820. Additionally, the *Jacob A. Howland*, a New Bedford whaler lost at Johnston Atoll in 1889, has been discovered recently (Lobel 2003: 8). And the burned remains of a whaler, possibly the Hawaiian-registered vessel *Harvest*, along with three other ships, have been tentatively located on Pohnpei in the Caroline Islands of Micronesia (Carrell 1991: 286).[1] Four whaling vessels were burned and sunk at that location

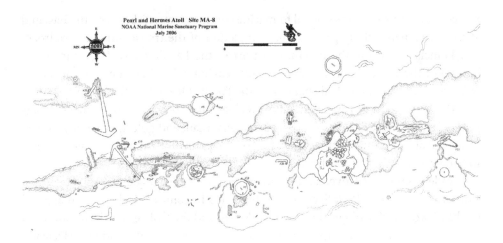

Figure 26.3 Wreck-site plan of the British whaler *Pearl*, lost in 1822, Pearl and Hermes Atoll, Northwestern Hawaiian Islands. Reproduced with the kind permission of NOAA Office of National Marine Sanctuaries.

in 1865 by CSS *Shenandoah*, the infamous Confederate raider that captured 37 prizes in the Pacific (Whittle 2005: 215).

These multiple site discoveries (many only in the preliminary stages), along with several whalers investigated in Australia, highlight the potential for international collaboration in whaling heritage research, and begin to make possible the comparison of artifacts and features and individual wreck site processes. Interest in whaling ships is also spreading into the western Arctic and the Chukchi Sea. According to Alaska's shipwreck database, over 140 whaling vessels were lost in that region (Tornfelt and Burwell 1992). The New Bedford whaling fleet suffered large losses in the 1870s as groups of ships were trapped and crushed by shifting pack ice, the ships pushing farther north in response to the declining profit margin of whale oil (Bockstoce 1986: 143). These are included in an emerging NOAA research project titled "Lost Fleets of the Western Arctic." Historically, whaling in the Pacific was clearly a multicultural and multinational phenomenon.

WEST COAST GOLD RUSH STEAMERS

The nineteenth century was the boom period for many different maritime trades in the wide Pacific besides whaling. Beginning in 1848 maritime activity increased all along the Pacific coast of North and South America, responding to the discovery of gold in California. Ultimately, the Panama Route (featuring the railroad connection at the isthmus), serviced by fast Pacific side-wheel steam vessels running between Panama and San Francisco, made the hazardous sailing voyage around Cape Horn unnecessary. This link was critical to marine communications between the East and West coasts, particularly prior to the completion of the transcontinental railroad. San Francisco became the preeminent port of the Pacific Coast (Delgado 1990). Several of these West Coast steamers sank, leaving behind evidence of the social, economic, and technological changes on the Pacific Ocean frontier.

The 211 ft (64.3 m) wooden side-wheel steamer *Tennessee*, built in 1848, was placed in Pacific service. She carried passengers, mail, and gold specie between San Francisco and Panama for three years before going aground in the fog at the entrance to San Francisco Bay on 6 March 1853. The ship broke apart in the surf of what was later called Tennessee Cove, her machinery occasionally being exposed by seasonal storms. The National Park Service field team, led by James P. Delgado and assisted by the Miwok Archaeological Preserve of Marin and the College of Marin, surveyed the scattered machinery of the steamship's engines between 1980 and 1982 (Delgado 2002: 230).

The 1,290-ton wooden side-wheel steamer *Winfield Scott*, built in 1850, began her Pacific service in 1852 on the San Francisco-Panama Route. On 2 December 1853, the ship missed the foggy Santa Barbara Channel and ran onto the rocks off Anacapa Island, California. Today the *Winfield Scott* wreck site reveals steam engine components and scattered iron wreckage partially buried in the sand, along with portions of the two paddle wheels. Local divers originally discovered the wreck sometime after World War II, and artifacts were removed. The National Park Service conducted an initial survey in 1981. As the wreck is located in both the Channel Islands National Park and the NOAA Channel Islands National Marine Sanctuary, both NPS and NOAA maritime archaeologists continue to document and monitor the wreck, a popular dive destination in Southern California (Marx 2001: 10). Permanent datums have been established, and a number of artifacts such as copper drifts are currently stored in situ pending funds for recovery and conservation. NOAA and NPS now work in collaboration with Coastal Maritime Archaeological Resources (CMAR) and the California State Lands Commission in monitoring the site.

The loss of *Brother Jonathan*, a 220 ft (67 m) wooden side-wheel steamer built in 1851, is popularly known as California's greatest maritime disaster. Constructed for the Panama Route, the ship was sold in 1856 and placed on the San Francisco to Vancouver run, carrying passengers for the Fraser Canyon Gold Rush in British Columbia and earning a reputation for fast passages. Departing Crescent City, California, where she had been sheltering from a heavy gale, the steamer ran onto a submerged rock on 30 July 1865, tearing a large hole in her hull. In the rough seas, only 11 crewmen, 5 women, and 3 children managed to reach Crescent City in a small surf boat; 205 people perished at sea. Also on board were boxes of gold specie ($80,000) and the U.S. Army payroll ($200,000), cargo that touched off salvage efforts in the deep, cold, and dark waters off the state's northwestern coast. These efforts were unsuccessful, until in 1993 Deep Sea Research, led by Donald Knight, finally discovered traces of the shipwreck at a depth of 84 m (275 ft). Ultimately, thousands of artifacts were brought to the surface, including 1,207 coins (mainly

$20 Double Eagles), which were auctioned off for more than $5 million in 1999, the first legal sale of gold coins from a U.S. shipwreck (Powers 2006: 313).

Not unlike other high-profile commercial projects, the recovery effort touched off a legal battle that began even before the wreck was located (California State Lands Commission v. Deep Sea Research Inc.). The state claimed rights to historic shipwrecks in its waters under established state and federal laws, notably the Abandoned Shipwreck Act of 1987, which removes historic wrecks from Admiralty awards. The district court, however, found that the state "had not established by a preponderance of the evidence that the ship is abandoned, embedded in the seafloor, or eligible for listing in the National Register as is required" (Cornell University 2008). The wreck was later determined eligible. Review of the case reached the U.S. Supreme Court, which declined to resolve whether the *Brother Jonathan* was abandoned. The definition of "abandonment" regarding historic wrecks remains controversial. No published archaeological research has been completed for the wreck. The popular book *Treasure Ship: The Legend and Legacy of the S.S.* Brother Jonathan, by Dennis Powers (2006), documents the recovery project for a general audience.[2]

Pacific Lumber Schooners

Compared to the high-profile stories of gold-laden ships, the historical importance of regular working vessels is often overlooked. Multimasted sailing schooners, though, played a large role in the economic development of the region, for these tall ships of distinctive American design were often the unsung maritime workhorses of the late nineteenth century. Strongly built and inexpensive to operate (the combination of fore-and-aft rigs and steam donkey engines needed less crew), many of these wooden schooners had originally been designed for the West Coast lumber trade following the Gold Rush boom in California. This was simply treasure of a different sort, for during the Gold Rush, fortunes were made in many different ways. Later the lumber schooners could be found fulfilling a variety of Pacific roles, such as carrying salmon or cod or even ice in the Alaskan fisheries, or copra, the dried meat or nut of the coconut, in the South Seas, or sugar or coal. At least 130 four-masted lumber schooners were built on the Pacific coast between 1887 and 1904, many in places like Coos Bay, Oregon, or Puget Sound, Washington—areas that were the source of their own scantlings as well as their cargo (MacGregor 1997: 154). More than 50 major shipbuilders had operations on the West Coast. These large wooden schooners were crucial to American shipping between the Civil War period and World War I.

The four-masted 600-ton schooner *Churchill* was built in North Bend, Oregon, and launched in April 1900, by shipwright Asa Meade Simpson (Figure 26.4). *Churchill* was carrying a cargo of copra from Nukualofa, Tonga, to Seattle, Washington, when she ran aground on a reef at French Frigates Shoal in the Northwestern Hawaiian Islands on 27 September 1917. All of her 12-man crew was rescued by a local motorized fishing sampan, but on returning to Honolulu the men filed affidavits charging Captain Charles Granzow with the intentional destruction of the ship; these charges were later dropped (District Court Case No. 1309: 1918). In 2007, the NOAA maritime heritage team began a noninvasive survey of the site, which was initially discovered by divers with the NOAA Coral Reef Ecosystem Division in October 2005 (Pacific Islands Fisheries Science Center 2008). Diagnostic artifacts included parts of the windlass, three large iron anchors, ship's pumps, chains, fastenings, and numerous blocks and rigging components, but no donkey engine or boiler (National Marine Sanctuaries 2007). All the anchors, rigging, pumps, and deck equipment appeared consistent with the 178 ft (54 m), 600-ton schooner *Churchill*. Historical documents mentioned several salvage efforts being initiated from Honolulu (*Pacific Commercial Advertiser*, 2 November 1917: 10). Survey work in 2008 completed the site map. Members of NOAA maritime heritage staff are currently working with volunteers to analyze the evidence and confirm a positive identification of the site.

The Underwater Archaeology Society of British Columbia (UASBC), one of the most active avocational groups in the maritime field, has also conducted some limited reconnaissance work on Pacific schooners (UASBC 2007). The 1,729-ton five-masted schooner *K. V. Kruse* was launched in 1919 and served in the Australian trade. On 26 January 1941, the large schooner, converted into a barge, broke her

Figure 26.4 Historical photo of the Pacific schooner *Churchill*, launched at Coos Bay, Oregon, in 1900. Photograph provided by Steve Priske.

tow in Hecate Strait, British Columbia. Located the following day and secured, the *K. V. Kruse* was then torn from her moorings by a fierce gale and finally went onto a reef 125 miles (200 km) away in Alaska's Cordova Bay (*Daily Colonist*, 13 February 1941: 1). The UASBC has also initiated a preliminary survey of the wreck of the 731-ton four-masted schooner *Alumna*, launched by Asa Meade Simpson in 1901 (James 2007).

By an odd stroke of fate, three Pacific lumber schooners, all built by the Hall Brothers Shipyard in the Puget Sound between 1883 and 1888, ended up wrecked near each other in the Channel Islands off Southern California. The beached remains of *J. M. Colman*, *Dora Bluhm*, and *Comet*, three-masted, single-decked lumber schooners, became the focus of Matthew Russell's 1996 master's thesis at East Carolina University, and the project was conducted with assistance from the Channel Islands National Park and the National Park Service's Submerged Resources Center. This case study demonstrated the usefulness of a systematic approach to beached shipwreck sites, even if those shipwrecks comprised only scattered and disarticulated remains (Russell 2005: xii).[3]

IRON SQUARE-RIGGED SHIPS

The large lumber schooners had found a regional Pacific niche, but the great iron square-rigged ships took the search for efficient carrying capacity under sail to its furthest expression. The iron (and later steel) hulled "downeasters," the last age-of-sail commercial carriers at a time when steam propulsion was revolutionizing marine transportation, were familiar Pacific long-haul vessels, large enough to compete economically in the coal, grain, lumber, guano, salmon, jute, and copra trades during the late nineteenth century (Greenhill 1993: 90). A few of these wind-driven ships of the industrial age remain afloat as museum vessels (*Star of India*, *Falls of Clyde*, *Balclutha*), the remains of many more rest on the bottom of the ocean. The design of ferrous ships evolved over time as shipwrights gained experience in iron construction.

The three-masted ship *Ivanhoe* was built in 1868 on the river Clyde by shipbuilder John C. Reid and Company in Glasgow, Scotland. She began life as an English emigrant ship carrying passengers to Australia, and later shifted to the long-haul bulk cargo trades. The vessel was a tramp coal carrier when she dragged anchors and went on the rocks at Port Allen, Kaua'i, on 25 December 1915. The shipwreck site, a shallow high-energy environment on the rocks of a lee shore, was surveyed in September 2007 by students in the East Carolina University Program in Maritime Studies, with assistance from NOAA archaeologists, over a three-week period. The survey was part of a multiyear ferrous shipbuilding project, better defining traditions in Anglo-American iron and steel ship construction (Richards 2009).

The four-masted bark *Goldenhorn* was a fairly typical medium clipper. She was built in Scotland in 1883 by the firm Russell and Company and was carrying a cargo of bituminous coal from New South Wales, Australia, to San Pedro, California, when she was lost on the southwest side of Anacapa Island, California, on the night of 12 September 1892. The area was marked by strong currents and dense fog (Channel Islands National Marine Sanctuary 2008). The crew successfully abandoned ship into two boats and rowed to Santa Barbara across the channel. Some salvage occurred thereafter.

National Park Service divers initiated survey at the *Goldenhorn* wreck site in 1985, and further work in 1993 and 1994 provided more detailed assessment. The wreck is now monitored by NPS and NOAA divers. The features lie in relatively shallow water, where wave action has flattened the hull over time, breaking it apart along the turn of the bilges among the rocky shoals. Brass and other yellow metal fittings are noticeably absent from the site, though approximately half of the hull is still visible, as well as a great deal of wire rigging and other structural components. Fortunately for the interpretation of the *Goldenhorn* site, the accounting records of the ship's construction and outfitting have survived, giving a complete inventory for vessels of this type (Channel Islands National Marine Sanctuary 2008).

The three-masted 258 ft (78.6 m) British ship *Dunnottar Castle* was built in Glasgow, Scotland, in 1874. While bound for Wilmington, California, from Sydney, Australia, with a cargo of coal, the ship grounded hard in the coral reef at Kure Atoll on 15 July 1886 and was held fast. Though efforts were made to jettison the cargo and repair the damaged hull, the stricken vessel could not be refloated, and the crew abandoned ship for the nearby deserted island. Subsequently, the chief officer and six seamen took one of the boats and made a 52-day passage to Kaua`i. While they were gone, the majority of the 28-man crew were rescued from the island by the ship *Birnam Wood* and transported to Valparaiso, Chile.

Dunnottar Castle was broken apart and flattened in place over time by strong ocean swells. In 2006, Kure Atoll refuge staff (State of Hawai`i Division of Forestry and Wildlife) discovered the wreckage by accident while transiting across the lagoon. The initial dive by NOAA archaeologists revealed the broken but extensive remains of the late-nineteenth-century sailing ship. Many of the wooden components, loose materials, and organic fabrics have been swept away, but the heavier elements remain. Large sections of iron hull plate, iron frames, rigging, masts, auxiliary steam boiler, keelson, anchors, windlasses, winches, capstans, davits, rudder and steering gear, cargo hatches, bowsprit, hawse pipes, chain locker, ballast stone, deadeyes, chains, stringers, bitts, ladders, and so on, are solidly encrusted in place on the sea bottom. Large blocks of coal are also lodged in place. The wreck of the *Dunnottar Castle* is a near complete assemblage of the major elements of a late-nineteenth-century commercial carrier, a heritage resource now protected by the Papahānaumokuākea Marine National Monument, from the days when our maritime commerce was driven by steel masts and canvas, wind power, and human hands (National Marine Sanctuaries 2006c).[4]

THE OLD STEAM NAVY IN THE PACIFIC

Where merchantmen and whalers go, navies soon follow; and for American ships and sailors, this led the U.S. Navy in stages across the Pacific, protecting the interests of U.S. citizens abroad and surveying hazardous archipelagos. American military expansion in the region progressed slowly and unevenly over time, though, for prior to the completion of the Panama Canal, communication between oceans was difficult, and national interest was definitely centered on the East Coast. The Pacific fleet in the nineteenth century generally consisted of a small collection of the ships that could be spared from the Atlantic and the Gulf of Mexico. Various Pacific duties, such as coastal patrol, protection of Pacific mail steamers, showing the flag, and so forth, often fell to individual vessels far from home.

The American side-wheel steamer USS *Saginaw* was the first vessel built at California's Mare Island naval shipyard in 1859 and the first warship built on the West Coast. The ship, a brig-rigged steamer, captures a critical period of American naval involvement in the Pacific, the transitional phase between steam and sail. *Saginaw*'s service spanned the Pacific and took her to distant ports in China and Japan, and along the West Coast from Central America to Alaska. During the Civil War, *Saginaw* cruised between San Francisco and Panama, protecting the Pacific steam liners from Confederate raiders like CSS *Shenandoah*. Her final cruise involved supporting an attempt to develop a coal depot at Midway Island, which had been claimed by the United States in 1867. The *Saginaw* was transporting a team of Boston hardhat divers from Midway back to San Francisco when she wrecked at Kure Atoll on 29 October 1870. Survivors spent two months on Ocean Island (today called Green Island) while five volunteers made a perilous 1,500 mile (2,400 km) open-boat voyage to the main Hawaiian Islands. Four of these five died in the rough nighttime landing on Kaua'i. The fifth, coxswain William Halford, made his way to Honolulu with news of his stranded shipmates (Read 1912: 109).

The wreck site was discovered by NOAA divers in 2003, and further noninvasive survey took place in 2006 (National Marine Sanctuaries 2006d). Topography and surf zone conditions prohibited trilateration and measurements of many areas, but the team located and photographed the major elements of the ship, including bow and stern Parrott rifled pivot guns, 24-pounder broadside howitzers, one of two steam oscillating engine cylinders, port and starboard paddle-wheel shafts, anchors, brass steam machinery, boiler tubes, boiler face, rigging components, fasteners, rudder hardware, davits, sounding lead, and other material. Some of the brass and iron artifacts have become solidly embedded in the calcareous algae of the substrate, and very little wood remains. Site distribution reflects the historical record of the bow breaking off at the initial impact point, and midships machinery falling into the reef just south of the bow, with the stern itself being pushed farther south by current and swell and lighter components eventually falling into the back reef zone.

PACIFIC MEMORIALS AND WAR GRAVES

From the decades prior to the American Civil War and the old steam navy to the events of World War II and beyond, the military presence has had an increasingly profound effect in the Pacific. Though shipwrecks of World War II are featured in another chapter (Neyland in this volume), there are several that are of central importance to the Pacific and to Hawai`i in particular. Indeed, as a whole, the Pacific has been heavily impacted by the amphibious and naval aviation campaigns during World War II, and any cursory examination of areas like Chuuk (Truk) Lagoon or Guadalcanal or Bikini Atoll or the Aleutian Archipelago reveals numerous submerged naval resources (Carrell 1991; Jeffrey 2007; Van Tilburg 2002). There is no other single episode in modern history that has had more influence in shaping the modern Pacific than the events associated with World War II. The legacy of that period is reflected in numerous shipwrecks and submerged aircraft throughout the region. Several deserve specific mention here.

The battleship USS *Arizona* BB-39 was launched from the New York Navy Yard in 1915. In 1921 she became part of the Pacific fleet. She was moored at quay F-7 on the east side of Ford Island when Pearl Harbor was attacked by the Imperial Japanese Navy on the morning of 7 December 1941. One of the aerial bombs that struck the ship penetrated the forward ammunition magazine; the resulting massive explosion immediately sank the vessel. Most of the ship's 1,177 casualties occurred in that single moment (Lenihan 1989: 34). Much has been written about the loss of USS *Arizona* and about the reverence felt for this site, as well as the place it occupies in the American national narrative. In addition to the ship's status as a war grave and memorial, the wreck is an archaeological site as well, one that continues to contribute data about the nature of submerged World War II cultural resources (Figure 26.5).

In 1983 the NPS Submerged Resources Center initiated survey of the site, since published as *Submerged Cultural Resource Study: USS* Arizona *Memorial and Pearl Harbor National Historic Landmark* (Lenihan 1989). Subsequent field projects took place in 1998, 1999, 2000, and 2001; at various times the Submerged Resources Center partnered with academic, commercial, and military groups (National Park Service Submerged Resources Center 2003). Follow-up studies on biofouling and metals corrosion, as well as a site monitoring program, continue today. Multiple lines of inquiry revolve around questions of structural integrity, the specific processes of deterioration, the amount and location of fuel oil remaining in the ship, and the possibilities for long-term site preservation. NPS rangers at Pearl Harbor, archaeologists from the NPS Submerged Resources Center, and metallurgists from the University of Nebraska at Lincoln, as well as the National Institute of Standards and Technology, are working together in this investigation (Johnson, Weins, and Makinson 2000; Makinson et al. 2002; Russell 2002). Study of the wreck site has created the first detailed database on the environmental interactions between the harbor and the large steel battleship. Beyond archaeological or management

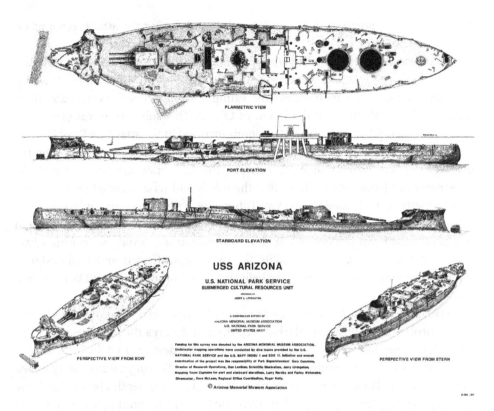

Figure 26.5 Drawings of the battleship USS *Arizona*, sunk at Pearl Harbor on 7 December 1941. Reproduced with the kind permission of Jerry L. Livingston, National Park Service.

perspectives, though, the shipwreck is still considered sacred ground, a war grave of central importance to national memory.

The target ship USS *Utah* AG-16 (formerly battleship BB-31) was also at Pearl Harbor on 7 December 1941, and it was sunk during the attack. USS *Utah* was built before World War I and was much modified in the intervening years. Sources indicate that at least two torpedoes hit forward on *Utah*'s port side. The ship soon began to fill and take on an increasing list to port; it capsized completely at 8:12 a.m., trapping sailors inside (Lenihan 1989: 46). The site of USS *Utah*, still emergent on the west side of Ford Island, was surveyed by the NPS Submerged Resources Center in 1986–1987 as part of the work on USS *Arizona* and Pearl Harbor. Measured sketches and trilateration produced accurate site maps. The NPS team found the exposed portions of the starboard side heavily rusted. The hull overall is virtually complete and undistorted, lying with the port side partially buried in the fine silt. Torpedo impact areas are therefore not visible. Severed salvage cables dominate the ship's side from midships aft. Access holes cut in an attempt to free personnel are visible in several places. Some of the armament, not used during the attack, remains on board (Lenihan 1989: 107).[5]

In 2002 researchers with the Hawai'i Undersea Research Laboratory (HURL), part of NOAA's National Undersea Research Center and the University of Hawai'i, discovered a small two-man submarine sitting upright in over 365 m (1,200 ft) of water off the south shore of the island of O'ahu. This submarine was one of the Japanese Imperial Navy's five secret weapons involved in the attack on Pearl Harbor, which heralded America's entrance into World War II in the Pacific. Following the discovery, letters were exchanged between the U.S. State Department and the government of Japan, establishing that the wreck and its associated artifacts were now property of the United States (Van Tilburg 2007: 189). Properly understood, the submarine is not only an archaeological site, but also a significant historic site and war grave, worthy of respect and in situ preservation. According to historian Paul Kemp, "the Ko-Hyoteki were possibly the most sophisticated and well-designed midget submarines used by any of the belligerents in the Second World War" (Kemp 1999: 70).

Five of the small submarines, code-named Ko-Hyoteki or "Target A," took part in the surprise attack on Pearl Harbor, deployed in the area the previous night by a larger fleet of mother subs. The following morning the destroyer USS Ward reported what appeared to be a conning tower and periscope following a barge being towed into the harbor. Ward opened fire with its deck guns and depth charges, and one shot appeared to strike the target directly at the base of the conning tower, but there was no explosion. The sub descended into the area of the exploding depth charges, leaving behind an oily slick. The first enemy planes arrived at Pearl Harbor over an hour later.

The search for the Ko-Hyoteki sunk by USS Ward began in 1988 with the joint National Park Service and U.S. Navy project known as Operation Seamark, a collaboration that soon grew to support numerous naval maritime archaeology projects over half the globe (Lenihan 2002: 192). Over the next decade, numerous side-scan sonar surveys near Pearl Harbor were conducted by the Park Service, the navy, and several private companies. These consistently revealed aircraft, landing craft, barges, and ships, but no Japanese sub. Finally, in March 2002 HURL discovered the site outside the original 1988 survey area. The sub appeared upright and intact, in relatively good condition, with a slight list to port. Both torpedoes were still in their tubes, and no extensive exterior damage was visible except for a shell hole at the base of the conning tower's starboard side, corresponding to USS Ward's report. Silt, corrosion, and "rusticles," similar to the microbial structures seen on the Titanic, were evident on the outside of the hull (NOAA Ocean Explorer 2008). The sub rested on hard substrate at its midsection, the bow extending unsupported over a scour area. A programmatic agreement for preservation management of the site has been drafted between NOAA, NPS, the Naval History & Heritage Command, State Historic Preservation Division, and the Advisory Council on Historic Preservation, proposing joint-agency collaboration in the Pacific (Van Tilburg 2007: 188).

CONCLUSION

This selection of ships of the Pacific Ocean cannot be a comprehensive survey; rather, it is only a summary of certain representative sites that fall into critical historical periods. Each of the historical vessel types discussed, from voyaging canoes to galleons to whalers, from steamers to lumber schooners to battleships, all had their particular heyday in the Pacific, and all then vanished from the scene. Each left a trace, reflecting the wide range of human seafaring activity.

Over the past two decades, maritime programs and institutions involved in maritime archaeology have been slowly increasing in the Pacific. The field has benefited greatly from the work of the National Park Service Submerged Resources Center, many projects having been completed on the West Coast, at Pearl Harbor, in Micronesia, and elsewhere. NOAA, through its Office of National Marine Sanctuaries and its Office of Ocean Exploration and Research, now highlights shipwreck resources throughout the Hawaiian archipelago and American Samoa, and beyond (Van Tilburg 2008). Collaborative efforts between federal agencies, states, and outside partners play a large role in this as well. Furthermore, in French Polynesia the Groupe de Recherche en Archéologie Navale (GRAN), a nonprofit organization created in 1980, has been compiling an inventory of the archipelago (Vecella 2006: 77). And for the past 22 years, the University of Hawai`i's Marine Option Program, supported by the Maritime Archaeology and History of the Hawaiian Islands Foundation (MAHHI), and NOAA's Office of National Marine Sanctuaries, has offered an annual symposium on the maritime history and underwater archaeology of Hawai`i and the Pacific (MAHHI 2008).

The Pacific is so large and the potential archaeological resources there so varied that it is immediately important to address the question of directions in research. Because there are limited resources to dedicate to such a vast area, projects need to be chosen with care. Besides the periods and vessel types mentioned here, what are other major historical themes to which maritime archaeology can make a contribution in the Pacific? What are the gaps in knowledge that can be addressed by this field? Certainly, there is the potential to broaden the focus beyond shipwrecks alone and address indigenous Pacific island resources, such as submerged remnant fishponds and fish traps. And there is the challenge of understanding the significance of shipwreck sites from island or non-Western perspectives, including current uses that can go beyond the established Western preservation model (Jeffery 2007).

Maritime archaeology has a long way to travel in the Pacific and a wide number of directions from which to choose. There are a host of challenges facing this field: the logistical obstacles involved in remote site work and the safety considerations associated with high-energy shallow-water environments are two that spring instantly to mind. But the resource's great potential continues to be the driving motivation for survey. This field of study is a relative latecomer to the Pacific, yet this ocean basin is the largest on the planet. Even though tourists in Waikiki might perceive the ocean surface as flat and featureless, albeit a pleasing blue color, there is, as always, much more beneath the surface.

NOTES

1. Fieldwork at these sites was conducted by Suzanne Finney, a University of Hawai'i PhD candidate.

2. For further information on Pacific Gold Rush steamers, see Delgado 1995 and the NPS survey of the *Tennessee* in San Francisco.

3. For further information on Pacific lumber schooners, see Delgado 1986 and the NPS survey of the *Neptune* in San Francisco.

4. For further information on Pacific iron-hulled shipwrecks, see Gibbs 1983 and the *Peter Iredale*, Oregon.

5. For further information on Pearl Harbor World War II surveys, see Van Tilburg and Conlin 2007.

REFERENCES

Bockstoce, John R. 1986. *Whales, ice, and men: The history of whaling in the western Arctic.* Seattle: University of Washington Press.

Carrell, Toni, ed. 1991. *Micronesia: Submerged cultural resources assessment.* Santa Fe: National Park Service.

Channel Island National Marine Sanctuary. 2008. *Goldenhorn.* Online at http://channelislands.noaa.gov/shipwreck/dbase/cinms/goldenhorn1.html/. Accessed 22 November 2008.

Cornell University. 1998. California v. Deep Sea Research Inc. Online at http://supct.law.cornell.edu/supct/html/96-1400.ZO.html/. Accessed 25 November 2008.

Daily Colonist (Victoria, B.C.). 13 February 1941.

Delgado, James P. 1986. Documentation and identification of the two-masted schooner *Neptune. Historical Archaeology* 20 (1): 95–108.

———. 1990. *To California by sea: A maritime history of the California Gold Rush.* Columbia: University of South Carolina Press.

———. 1995. The wreck of the *Tennessee. Journal of the West* 33 (4): 14–21.

———. 2002. Maritime and underwater archaeology on the Pacific Coast. In *International handbook of underwater archaeology,* ed. Carol V. Ruppé and Janet F. Barstad, 221–246. New York: Kluwer Academic/Plenum.

District Court of the Territory of Hawaii Case No. 1309, U.S. v. Charles Granzow, 12 July 1918.

Finney, Ben. 1994. *Voyage of rediscovery: A cultural odyssey through Polynesia.* Berkeley and Los Angeles: University of California Press.

Finney, Suzanne S. 1999. What sank where: A survey of ships and shipwrecks in the harbors of Pohnpei, based on historical sources and information concerning possible diagnostic elements to aid an archaeological survey of Madolenihmw Harbors. University of Hawai`i Marine Option Program report.

Gibbs, James A. 1983. *Shipwrecks of the Pacific coast*. Portland, OR: Binford & Mort.

Greenhill, Basil. 1993. The iron and steel sailing ship. In *Sail's last century: The merchant sailing ship 1830–1930*. London: Conway Maritime Press.

Haddon, A. C., and James Hornell. 1936. *Canoes of Oceania*. Honolulu: Bishop Museum Press.

Howe, K. R. 2006. *Vaka Moana, voyages of the ancestors: The discovery and settlement of the Pacific*. Honolulu: University of Hawai`i Press.

James, Rick. 2008. Communication with author, 17 September.

Jeffery, William. 2007. War graves, munition dumps and pleasure grounds: A post-colonial perspective of Chuuk Lagoon's submerged World War II sites. PhD diss., James Cook University.

Johnson, D. L., W. N. Weins, and J. D. Makinson. 2000. Metallographic studies of the U.S.S. *Arizona*. *Microstructural Science* 27: 85–91.

Kemp, Paul. 1999. *Midget submarines of the Second World War*. London: Chatham.

Lawrence, Susan, and Mark Staniforth, eds. 1998. *The archaeology of whaling in southern Australia and New Zealand*. Gundaroo, NSW: Australasian Society for Historical Archaeology and the Australian Institute for Maritime Archaeology.

Lenihan, Daniel J., ed. 1989. *Submerged cultural resources study: USS* Arizona *Memorial and Pearl Harbor National Historic Landmark*. Santa Fe, NM: National Park Service.

———. 2002. *Submerged: Adventures of America's most elite underwater archaeology team*. New York: Newmarket Press.

Lobel, Philip. 2003. *Marine life of Johnston Atoll, central Pacific Ocean*. Oregon: Natural World Press.

MacGregor, David R. 1997. *The schooner: Its design and development from 1600 to the present*. London: Chatham.

MAHHI. 2008. 1989–2009 Symposia Abstracts. Online at www.mahhi.org/previous_abstracts.html/. Accessed 2 June 2009.

Makinson, John D., Donald L. Johnson, Matthew A. Russell, David L. Conlin, and Larry E. Murphy. 2002. In situ corrosion studies on the battleship USS *Arizona*. *Materials Performance* 41 (10): 56–60.

Marx, Deborah. 2001. Archaeological investigation of the Gold Rush steamship *Winfield Scott*. *Stem to Stern* 16: 10.

Mathers, William, Henry S. Parker, and Kathleen A. Copus, eds. 1990. *The recovery of the Manila galleon* Nuestra Senora de la Concepcion. Sutton, VT: Pacific Sea Resources.

National Marine Sanctuaries. 2006a. *Parker*. Online at http://sanctuaries.noaa.gov/maritime/expeditions/parker.html/. Accessed 18 November 2008.

———. 2006b. *Pearl*. Online at http://sanctuaries.noaa.gov/maritime/expeditions/pearl.html/. Accessed 18 November 2008.

———. 2006c. *Dunnottar Castle*. Online at http://sanctuaries.noaa.gov/maritime/. Accessed 18 November 2008.

———. 2006d. *Saginaw*. Online at http://sanctuaries.noaa.gov/maritime/expeditions/saginaw.html/. Accessed 18 November 2008.

———. 2007. Site of the possible four-masted schooner *Churchill*. Online at http://sanctuaries.noaa.gov/maritime/expeditions/pmnm/churchill.html/. Accessed 22 November 2008.

———. 2008. Whaling Heritage Symposium. Online at http://sanctuaries.noaa.gov/maritime/whaling/welcome.html/. Accessed 18 November 2008.

National Park Service. 2003. Submerged Resources Center. Online at http://home.nps.gov/
    applications/submerged/. Accessed 12 October 2008.

Neich, Roger. 2006. Voyaging after the exploration period. In *Vaka Moana, voyages of
    the ancestors: The discovery and settlement of the Pacific*, ed. K. R. Howe, 198–245.
    Honolulu: University of Hawai'i Press.

NOAA Ocean Explorer. 2008. RMS *Titanic* Expedition 2003. Online at
    http://oceanexplorer.noaa.gov/explorations/03titanic/rusticles/rusticles.html/.
    Accessed 2 June 2009.

O'Regan, Deirdre, Hans Van Tilburg, and Kelly Gleason. 2008. Whaling shipwrecks in the
    northwestern Hawaiian Islands. *Sea History* 125: 14–19.

Pacific Commercial Advertiser (Honolulu). 2 November 1917.

Pacific Islands Fisheries Science Center. 2008. Coral Reef Ecosystem Division. Online at
    www.pifsc.noaa.gov/cred/. Accessed 4 November 2008.

Powers, Dennis. 2006. *Treasure ship: The legend and legacy of the S.S.* Brother Jonathan.
    New York: Citadel Press.

Read, George H. 1912. *The last cruise of the* Saginaw. Boston: Houghton Mifflin.

Richards, Nathan. 2009. Communication with author. 2 June.

Russell, Matthew A. 2002. USS *Arizona:* Preserving an American icon. *Immersed*
    7 (3): 38–45.

———. 2005. *Beached shipwreck archaeology: Case studies from Channel Islands National
    Park*. Santa Fe: Submerged Resources Center.

———. 2007. The Tamál-Húye archaeological project: Cross-cultural encounters in
    sixteenth century northern California. *Society for California Archaeology Newsletter*
    41 (2): 32–34.

———. 2009. Encounter at Tamál-Húye: The archaeology of cross-cultural interactions in
    sixteenth-century northern California. *Proceedings of the Society for California
    Archaeology: Papers Presented at the 2007 Annual Meeting of the Society for California
    Archaeology* 21: 58–62.

Sinoto, Yosihiko. 1983. The Huahine excavation: Discovery of an ancient Polynesian canoe.
    Archaeology 36: 10–15.

Stenger, Alison. 2005. Physical evidence of shipwrecks on the Oregon coast in prehistory.
    Oregon Archaeological Society Newsletter 54 (8).

Tornfelt, Evert E., and Michael Burwell. 1992. *Shipwrecks of the Alaskan shelf and shore*.
    Alaska: U.S. Department of the Interior Minerals Management Service.

Underwater Archaeology Society of British Columbia. 2007. Underwater Archaeology
    Society of British Columbia. Online at www.uasbc.com/index.cfm/. Accessed 22
    November 2008.

Van Tilburg, Hans. 2002. U.S. Navy shipwrecks in Hawaiian waters: An inventory of
    submerged naval properties. Naval Historical Center report.

———. 2003. Kure and Midway Atoll Maritime Heritage Survey. NOAA Office of National
    Marine Sanctuaries report.

———. 2007. The Japanese midget sub at Pearl Harbor. In *Out of the blue: Public
    interpretation of maritime cultural resources*, ed. John H. Jameson and Della
    A. Scott-Ireton, 182–195. New York: Springer Press.

———. 2008. American Samoa Maritime Heritage Inventory. NOAA Office of National
    Marine Sanctuaries report.

———. 2009. British whalers in the Pacific: The discovery of the *Gledstanes*. *Sea History* 127:
    22–26.

Van Tilburg, Hans, and David Conlin. 2007. Pearl Harbor: West Loch site reconnaissance, August 2007. NOAA Office of National Marine Sanctuaries/NPS Submerged Resources Center Technical Report No. 25.

Vecella, Robert. 2006. The GRAN Underwater Inventory of French Polynesia. In *Finishing the interrupted voyage: Papers of the UNESCO Asia-Pacific Workshop on the 2001 Convention on the Protection of the Underwater Cultural Heritage*, ed. Lyndel V. Prott. Leicester: Institute of Art and Law.

Von der Porten, E. P. 2001. Manila galleon porcelains on the American West Coast. *Taoci: Revue annuelle de la Société française d'Étude de la Céramique orientale* 2: 57–61.

Whittle, William C., Jr. 2005. *The voyage of the CSS* Shenandoah: *A memorable cruise.* Tuscaloosa: University of Alabama Press.

CHAPTER 27

....

THE ARCHAEOLOGY OF STEAMSHIPS

....

KEVIN CRISMAN

INTRODUCTION

....

THE symbol and substance of the dawning nineteenth century arrived at Albany, New York, in August 1807, accompanied by a raucous fanfare resembling "the pounding of a dozen forge hammers" (*Missouri Republican*, 25 June 1835). Residents of the upper Hudson River beheld a fantastic vision: a large boat proceeding upriver at 4 miles an hour, belching smoke and sparks from its metal chimney and lashing at the water with a pair of whirling paddle wheels. It was Robert Fulton's *North River Steamboat*, completing its first 120 mile (190 km) passage from New York City in only 32 hours (Marestier 1957: 5). Whether they knew it or not, the citizens of Albany were witnessing a revolution in transportation. Henceforth, the combination of a steam-generating boiler, a piston and crank, and paddles or propellers would dramatically broaden the possibilities for travel across the water, alter human perceptions of time and distance, and reengineer cultures and landscapes. The century of the steamboat had officially begun.

Steam propulsion was a radical departure from the old and familiar. From the very beginning of human seafaring endeavors, all watercraft were limited to three modes of propulsion: muscle, currents, and wind. These had worked for millennia, but with obvious limitations. Muscle power—paddling, rowing, or poling—is hard to maintain over long distances and can move only limited amounts of cargo. Currents are generally monodirectional, making it difficult to return to the start point without a lot of effort. And wind, the longtime favorite for moving vessels over great distances, has the drawback of being erratic in its strength, duration, and direction.

Steam overcame all of these limitations, although it would create new and unforeseen challenges for its users.

Fulton's *Steamboat* was underpowered and unreliable, and made a clatter "sufficient to frighten the very sturgeon from the river," but it proved more than a passing novelty (*Missouri Republican*, 25 June 1835). Over the following years and decades, many of the technical and logistical difficulties of steam propulsion were overcome. The numbers of boats grew slowly at first, but production vastly increased as the century progressed. By midcentury, steam would overtake sail in many important routes and trades, and by the end of the century there were no oceans, or rivers and lakes of consequence where steam did not play a role in the transportation of people and goods.

The nineteenth century is a relatively well-documented era compared to previous centuries, and the story of maritime steam has been preserved in histories, technical journals, traveler's accounts, plans and sketches, and, after the 1840s, photographs. Not everything was recorded, however, for much of the development took place on an informal trial-and-error basis that left scant traces for us to follow. The gaps are sometimes surprising. We know, for example, that steamboats began navigating the Mississippi River and its tributaries in 1811, but our first good set of plans for one of them, the *Buckeye State*, comes from 1850, four decades and many hundreds of boats later (Kane 2004: 85). How were the earlier boats designed and built, and what were their operational parameters? In what ways was life and work aboard steamboats different from earlier types of ships? Clearly, there is a vital role for archaeology in our modern-day rediscovery of the age of steam, just as there has been for the ships and seafarers of earlier eras.

PRELUDE TO SUCCESS

Fulton's 1807 *Steamboat* has rightfully been credited as the world's first commercially successful steamboat, but it was not the first steamboat. Rather, Fulton's creation marked the end of a long period of inspiration and dogged development. The idea of propelling boats by paddle wheels extended back to the classical and medieval eras, when various mechanisms using human or animal power were proposed (Crisman and Cohn 1998: 3–10). Steam's expansive power was also recognized in earlier millennia, and its potential for driving machinery was investigated. Entertaining steam toys were built and tested, but it was only in the second half of the seventeenth century that Europe's industrialization and new dedication to scientific inquiry led to machines with practical applications.

Though crude, these early inventions pointed the way to the future. Around 1690 Denis Papin developed the steam piston as well as the safety valve to relieve excess steam pressure; in 1699 Thomas Savery patented a steam-powered pump that could be used to lift water out of mines; and in 1712 Thomas Newcomen patented an engine that condensed steam to create a vacuum, which in turn drew a piston back and forth in a cylinder. Steam-propelled boats were discussed at this time, and in 1736 Jonathan Hulls patented his idea for a Newcomen-engine-powered stern-wheeler, but the great size, irregular motion, and low horsepower of the first engines thwarted efforts in this direction (Flexner 1978: 13–16; Morgan 1977: 102–103).

By the second half of the eighteenth century, inventors in France, England, and the United States were competing to produce a functioning steamboat. In France, several experimental boats were built for testing on the rivers, and one of them, the work of the Marquis de Jouffroy d'Abbans, is believed to be the first ever to paddle ahead under steam. This was in June 1783. Unfortunately, after 15 minutes the boat's seams were shaken open and it had to be run ashore. Jouffroy could raise no funds to build another, and so was unable to build on this success (Flexner 1978: 41–47).

In Great Britain, steam technology was given a boost by the work of James Watt, who added an external condenser to the Newcomen design to greatly improve its efficiency; he and financier Matthew Boulton then went into business in the late 1770s manufacturing low-pressure steam engines for pumping out mines. Crucial improvements followed. In 1781, Watt patented a crank arrangement for converting a piston's reciprocal action into rotary motion, and in 1783 he patented a double-acting engine that pulled from both sides of the piston (Flexner 1978: 38–39). With these improvements the elements necessary to build a working steamer were in place. Several boats would be built in the following years. One of them, a small catamaran with center-mounted paddles and a tiny, 4 in (10 cm) diameter cylinder, ran on Dalswinton Loch in Scotland for several days in 1788. William Symington designed the machinery for two canal towboats, each named *Charlotte Dundas*, which underwent trials in 1801 and 1803 (Osborne 1995: 63–78). These boats all worked, but western Europe's well-developed transportation system gave investors little incentive to back an expensive and still-unreliable form of propulsion.

Things were different on the other side of the Atlantic. Late-eighteenth-century North America was sparsely populated and had little industry, but its immense size and crude transportation network provided a greater incentive to develop steam. In the 1780s and 1790s several American inventors embarked on the quest to build a steamboat that could work on the continent's waterways. Most notable among them was the talented but erratic John Fitch. A native of Connecticut who settled in Philadelphia, Fitch operated in something of a scholarly vacuum and ended up reinventing many of the steamboat's basic elements. For propulsion he employed an odd arrangement of vertical dipping paddles that resembled mechanical duck feet. His first boat had a successful debut on the Delaware River in August 1787; his third boat ran a scheduled passenger service on the river in 1790, paddling 3,200 to 4,800 km (2,000 to 3,000 miles) with few mechanical problems. There was one hitch, however: the public did not patronize the boat, perhaps because of its novelty, or perhaps due to Fitch's reputation for eccentricity. It was permanently laid up at the end of the year, and Fitch was unable to put any other boats into service (Fitch 1976; Johnston 1983: 14–19; Morrison 1958: 5–11).

Despite Fitch's failure, interest in steam ran strong in America. Other inventors at this time included James Rumsey, whose hydraulic jet design proved impractical; John Stevens, who between 1802 and 1804 built two screw-propeller boats that crossed the Hudson River between New Jersey and New York; Samuel Morey, who experimented with paddle-wheel configurations and ran a small steamer in the waters around New York City; Oliver Evans, who pioneered the use of high-pressure steam to drive a piston; and Robert R. Livingston, a wealthy New York businessman who sought to develop steam on the Hudson River (Marestier 1957: 4–5; Morrison 1958: 11–19). Again, none of these men quite managed the leap from invention to widespread commercial application.

It was Pennsylvanian Robert Fulton who finally succeeded. A highly talented, driven man like Fitch, Fulton was equipped with better social skills and an ability to absorb the best ideas of others and combine them in his own projects. He traveled to Europe as a young man, in 1787, to develop his techniques as a portrait painter, but instead involved himself in engineering and mechanical projects: canals, mills, submarines, underwater mines, and steamboats. In 1802, he became acquainted with steamboat enthusiast Robert R. Livingston (then U.S. minister to France), and the two entered into a partnership. In 1806, Fulton returned to America, where he and Livingston dedicated themselves to building a boat for the Hudson (Morgan 1977).

The new vessel, built in the New York City yard of Charles Browne, measured 142 ft long by 14 ft beam (43.28 m by 4.26 m), giving it the high length-to-beam ratio (L/B ratio) of 10:1. The design incorporated Fulton's ideas on the best form for a steamboat and featured flat floors, a hard chine, near-vertical sides, and a flat sheer; contemporary observers described the hull as bargelike (Marestier 1957: 7–8, 17; Ridgely-Nevitt 1981: 21–23). It was outfitted with an imported Boulton and Watt low-pressure engine that turned a pair of side wheels (originally exposed, the wheels were later housed to reduce spray and protect them from collisions). Fulton, not ready to trust in the reliability of the machinery, also provided the vessel with two masts and sails. Initially known as just *The Steamboat*, it was subsequently registered as *The North River Steamboat of Clermont* in honor of Livingston's New York estate; later generations would know the boat as the *Clermont* (Morgan 1977: 138).

EARLY STEAMBOATS: *VERMONT*, *PHOENIX*, AND *LADY SHERBROOKE*

The first season of navigation by Fulton and Livingston's *Steamboat* in 1807 ended with scant profit, but a wealth of practical experience. The hull was found to be too lightly constructed and was rebuilt both larger and stronger, with passenger accommodations that set the high standard for which nineteenth-century American steamers were famed. As word of the boat's comfort, speed, safety, and reliability spread, business picked up considerably, and by 1809 the partners were building their second boat, *The Car of Neptune* (Morgan 1977: 148–149, 153–155, 166).

The Steamboat's passage to Albany and back in 1807 secured for Fulton and Livingston a statewide monopoly on steamboat use in New York waters, a concession intended to encourage the development of commercial steam. They acquired a similar monopoly from Louisiana in 1811, effectively gaining control of Mississippi River steamer traffic as well. This initially worked to the advantage of their operations—six boats were serving on the Hudson in 1814, as well as several steam ferryboats—but also involved the partners and their heirs in constant litigation to protect their monopoly rights against interlopers. Other steam promoters also acquired state monopolies, hampering the movement of boats and generating a mountain of legal proceedings. The issue was only settled in 1824 with the landmark *Gibbons vs. Ogden* case, in which the U.S. Supreme Court ruled that interstate commerce could be regulated only by Congress, not by individual states (Sutcliffe 2004: 219–220). Government-granted monopolies on steam navigation were thereby eliminated.

By all accounts, the steamboats that followed *The Steamboat* improved rapidly in their design, construction, and machinery, although the nature of the changes is not always clear from the records. There were certain features common to boats in service at this time. A single low-pressure condensing cylinder was standard, and both boilers and machinery were mounted low in the hold. They were flush-decked, with small deck houses or no deck structures at all, and were usually steered by a wheel located on an open platform amidships. "Guards," the extensions of the main deck beyond the sides of the hull, supported and protected the housed-over paddle wheels. Many early boats had masts and sails to assist the underpowered engines or to allow navigation in the event of breakdown.

The boats built in the years between 1807 and 1813 followed the general barge-like design of *The Steamboat*, with its flat bottom, flat sheer, angled bilges, and high length-to-beam ratio. These characteristics led to excessive hogging and sagging that shortened a vessel's lifespan (Fulton's *Paragon* of 1811 suffered from a "wavy" deck due to longitudinal weakness). In 1813, the steamer *Fulton* was built for use on the semi-open waters of Long Island Sound: it featured heavier construction, a modest deadrise to the floors, a rounded rather than angled turn of the bilge, and a pronounced curve to the sheer. This model was found to work well and last longer, and it would become typical of eastern river, lake, and coastal steamboats built after *Fulton* (Marestier 1957: 7, 22).

Four wrecks from the first 10 years of commercial steam have been located and studied. The earliest, *Vermont*, was built on Lake Champlain in 1808 by the brothers John and James Winans and was the first commercial steamer to follow *The Steamboat*; the Winans brothers circumvented the Fulton-Livingston monopoly by registering their vessel in Vermont. *Vermont* was fitted with a 20-horsepower engine, side-lever bell crank machinery, a large flywheel to even out the motion of the crank, and side wheels that had no coverings. Evidence suggests there were two masts as well. The vessel was steered by a tiller at the stern, an arrangement that did not allow the pilot a good forward view (hence the elevated amidships wheel on later boats). *Vermont* entered service in June 1809 and made regular biweekly runs up and down the length of the lake, although the War of 1812 interrupted Canadian traffic for two and a half years. In the spring of 1815, shortly after *Vermont* resumed passages to Canada, the crank shaft separated and punched a hole through the hull, sending the boat to the bottom of Quebec's Richelieu River (Blow 1966; Ross 1997: 23–26).

Vermont's lower hull was salvaged in 1953 by a group planning to display it in a museum of lake history, but the museum was never built, and the hull deteriorated in a barn. While the structure is no longer intact, photographs and a set of basic plans give us some idea of the design and assembly (Barranco 1963; Fowler 1974: 33–34; Ross 1997: 202). *Vermont* measured about 125 ft in length and 20 ft in beam (35.57 m by 6.09 m), with an L/B ratio of 6.25:1. The hull was lightly timbered and had flat floors like Fulton's *North River Steamboat*, but photos show that the bottom and sides met at the bilges with a curve or bevel rather than a hard angle. The evidence indicates that *Vermont*'s design had much in common with Fulton's earliest steamers, although the lake boat's L/B ratio was less extreme.

The hulls of two steamboats intended to compete with *Vermont* have also been archaeologically studied. These were *Ticonderoga* and *Phoenix*, built by a consortium of Albany financiers who attempted to break the Fulton-Livingston monopoly on the Hudson River in 1811. Shut down by a court ruling the next year, the Albany group then gained the right to operate on the New York waters of Lake Champlain. Incorporated as the Lake Champlain Steamboat Company, they began building their first boat in the winter of 1813–1814. Unfortunately, the War of 1812 was raging on the lake at this time, and the company's partly finished steamer hull was purchased by the U.S. Navy and finished as the 17-gun schooner *Ticonderoga* (Crisman 1983).

The steamboat company's next vessel was launched in the spring of 1815 and christened *Phoenix*. Measuring 147 ft in length by 27 ft in beam (44.8 m by 8.23 m), and rated at 336 tons, it was equipped with a 45-horsepower engine capable of propelling the vessel at 8 mph (12.8 kmh). *Phoenix* was finely appointed with men's and women's cabins, a barbershop, and a smoking room, all located below deck. The steamboat ran for five seasons, and in 1817 it carried President James Monroe across the lake during his "Era of Good Feeling" tour of the U.S.-Canadian border. *Phoenix* met a tragic end, catching fire and burning to the waterline during a nighttime passage in September 1819. Six lives were lost (Davison 1981: 7–8, 10–11; Ross 1997: 29–35).

Both *Ticonderoga* and *Phoenix* have undergone archaeological study; the former was raised from the lake in 1958 and displayed outside a museum in Whitehall, New York (Figure 27.1), and the latter was found beneath 18.3–33.5 m (60–110 ft) of water in the northern lake. Only the lower portions of the two hulls survived decay and fire, but it is evident from the substantial timber dimensions, slight rise to the floors, and curved rather than angled bilges that the Lake Champlain Steamboat Company was building its first vessels in the heavier style of the steamboat *Fulton*. *Ticonderoga*, with its length of approximately 120 ft and beam of 24 ft (36.6 m by 7.3 m), had

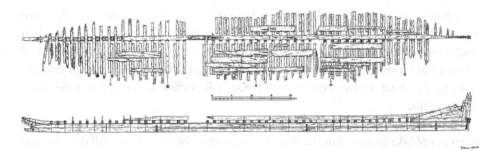

Figure 27.1 Plan and profile of the 17-gun Schooner *Ticonderoga*. Laid down in late 1813 by the Lake Champlain Steamboat Company, the hull was converted on the stocks into a U.S. Navy warship. A large add-on keel improved the sailing abilities and stability of the narrow, shallow steamboat design. The hull was cut into short lengths during its salvage in 1958. Drawing by Kevin Crisman.

an L/B ratio of 5:1, while *Phoenix* had an L/B ratio of 5.4:1, both considerably less than Fulton's early boats and *Vermont* (Marestier 1957: 8).

The two wrecks revealed interesting features. *Ticonderoga*'s steamboat hull form was not well suited for conversion into a sailing warship. The navy's shipwrights found the original 10 in (25.4 cm) molded keel too weak and shallow for their purposes and added a substantial 14 in (35.5 cm) molded false keel to stiffen the vessel longitudinally and improve stability and lateral resistance under sail. Even with this deeper bite in the water, the relatively narrow hull was probably top-heavy when its cannon were mounted on deck. It may be significant that while *Ticonderoga* had 20 gunports, it never mounted more than 17 cannon (Crisman 1983: 8–9, 62–63).

Despite *Phoenix*'s fiery demise, the surviving lower hull has yielded clues to the steamer's layout and appearance (Figure 27.2). The propulsion machinery was salvaged shortly after the sinking, but the placement of the engine and side wheels slightly abaft the midship frame could be determined by two sister keelsons and two pairs of shorter bed timbers that were mortised to fit the upright posts and braces of the crank mechanism's frame. A mass of bricks and mortar aft of the engine showed the likely location of the boilers, while a notch in the keelson tells us that *Phoenix* stepped a single mast halfway between the midship frame and bow (Davison 1981: 48–65). Ceramic fragments and other fire-scorched artifacts recovered from between the frames provided clues to the boat's interior and passenger amenities. The distribution of shell-edged pearlware dishes, transfer print and hand-decorated tea wares, stoneware storage jars, and glass bottles suggest that there was a storage locker for provisions in the forward part of the hold, that food preparation took place on the port side of the boiler space, and that there was a dishware storage cupboard on the starboard side of the boilers (Hadden 1995).

Fulton and Livingston's success on the Hudson inspired Canadian businessman and brewer John Molson to form a steamboat company to serve the busy St. Lawrence River freight and passenger trade between Quebec and Montreal. His first boat, *Accommodation*, was launched in August 1809, followed by *Swiftsure* in 1812

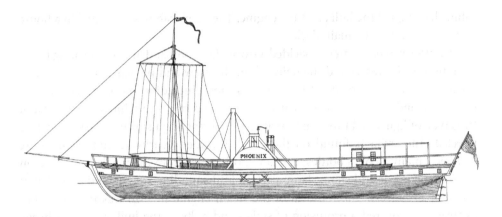

Figure 27.2 Conjectural reconstruction of the Lake Champlain steamboat *Phoenix*.
Launched as the second steamboat on Lake Champlain in 1815, *Phoenix* was typical of
early American steamships, with its engine and boiler in the hold, lack of superstructure,
and auxiliary sailing rig. This profile was reconstructed from evidence found on the
wreck, contemporary descriptions of the vessel, and similar steamships shown in Jean
Baptiste Marestier's *Memoir on Steamboats*. Drawing by Kevin Crisman.

and *Malsham* in 1814. In 1817, ten years after *The Steamboat*'s first passage, Molson
launched his fourth steamer, *Lady Sherbrooke*. Powered by an imported Boulton
and Watt engine, the latter vessel measured 147 ft in length by 34.8 ft in breadth
(44.8 m by 10.6 m), identical in length to *Phoenix* but substantially beamier (L/B
ratio 4.2:1). *Lady Sherbrooke*'s career got off to a rough start when a flood in January
1818 left the vessel high and dry for nearly a year. Thereafter, for eight seasons, the
steamboat made regular trips between Quebec and Montreal, suffering occasional
mishaps and on one passage transporting 800 Irish immigrants up to Montreal. By
1826, the hull was starting to show its age, and at the end of the season it was stripped
of machinery and abandoned in a side channel of the river below Montreal (Bélisle
1994: 10–11, 82–83).

The listing, partially buried hull of *Lady Sherbrooke* was located in 1983 and
underwent systematic excavation from 1984 to 1990. An estimated 60% of the hull
survived, and the buried portions of the port side proved to be in excellent condition (Lépine, Stewart, and Bélisle 1991). Preserved elements included the keel, endposts, and rudder; most of the portside frames and planking to the level of the main
deck; parts of the port guard structure; and many of the heavy longitudinal timbers
that supported and braced the engine and port-side shafts and paddle wheel. The
hull was flat-floored, with a hard curve at the bilges; timber dimensions and fastenings were substantial throughout and included extensive diagonal bracing under
the clamps. Molson's steamboat was very solidly built, perhaps in anticipation of
collisions with river ice or other boats (Bélisle and Lépine 1986, 1988). The engine
and paddle wheels were located slightly forward of amidships, the crew's quarters
and galley were forward of the engine, and the boilers, cargo hold, and women's

cabin all occupied the hull abaft the engine. The men's cabin was located in a house on the after end of the main deck.

Lady Sherbrooke's interior yielded a trove of features and artifacts relating to the operation of the vessel and the daily life of the crew and passengers. In the stern, excavators found remnants of the women's cabin, including stairs, paneled doors, partitions, and bunks, some of which still retained traces of white or yellow paint (this type of lightweight internal carpentry does not often survive in early steamer wrecks). The artifacts found on the wreck included pearlware and earthenware ceramics, many alcohol bottles, beef and pork bones from the meals consumed on board, pipe bowls and stems, lamp parts, a lead sounding weight, and a myriad of other small objects. The removal of the steam engine in 1826 was thorough, but excavators recovered a profusion of spikes and bolts in the hull, as well as heavy chisels that may have been used to separate machinery from its bed timbers. Altogether, *Lady Sherbrooke* provides our best archaeological example of a vessel built during the first decade of steam propulsion in North America.

PADDLES AND PROPELLERS ON NORTH AMERICAN WATERS

The commercial success of the Fulton-Livingston enterprise and other early steamboat companies spurred participation by forward-thinking mariners and investors, and the numbers of boats grew year by year. By the beginning of the 1820s steamboats were working on most major rivers in eastern North America, as well as the Mississippi and its tributaries. The end of the War of 1812 opened the Great Lakes to paddleboats: *Frontenac* and *Ontario* began service on Lake Ontario in 1817, and the next years saw the aptly named *Walk-in-the-Water* steaming up Lake Erie (Simmons 1988: 192–193; Smith 2005: 16–22). The end of the war also made it safe for steamboats to venture along the coasts or even farther out to sea. The first steam engine–equipped vessel to brave the Atlantic, the *Savannah*, crossed from Savannah, Georgia, to Liverpool in 1819. *Savannah* was essentially a sailing ship with an auxiliary engine, and because it was not possible to carry enough fuel for the entire trip, most of the voyage was made under sail alone (Marestier 1957: 20–22; Ridgely-Nevitt 1981: 58–65). The first vessel to ply the open seas as a full-fledged steamboat was the *Robert Fulton*, which began service between New York, Charleston, and New Orleans in 1820. This vessel, along with *Savannah*, started a process that would culminate in regular steam passenger service between North America and Europe by 1840 (Ridgely-Nevitt 1981: 52–57, 99).

It was readily apparent to steamboat designers and builders that one type of hull and machinery would not fit all conditions, and vessels increasingly diversified to meet varying navigational and commercial needs. Bearing in mind that exceptions will inevitably spoil every generalization, we can discern certain trends in the steamboats navigating eastern rivers, the Great Lakes, and coastal regions in the second quarter of the nineteenth century. These bodies of water offered deep or moderately deep water, so steamers were built with substantial, durable construction and sleek, rounded hull forms that provided good sea-keeping abilities (particularly the lake and coastal boats). Because steamboats did not have the same issues with windage as sailing ships, designers built up from the main deck, adding larger and more elaborate superstructures that provided airy, bright accommodations for passengers. Most of these boats continued to use low-pressure condensing engines, which provided adequate power and had a relatively good safety record. Beginning in the 1820s eastern river, lake, and coastal steamers adopted the "walking beam"—a tilting lever mounted on an "A" frame that extended above the superstructure—to transfer the piston's motion to the crank that turned the paddle shaft (Ridgely-Nevitt 1981: 68–69). Walking beams would be characteristic of American paddle steamers into the twentieth century. After 1840, propellers began to be used, starting with lake boats. As engines and propulsion systems became more powerful and reliable, sailing rigs were gradually eliminated.

A substantial number of steamer wrecks from the mid- and later nineteenth century have been located and examined by archaeologists in recent decades, particularly on the Great Lakes and Lake Champlain. One of the more significant finds was the propeller steamship *Indiana*, sunk off Whitefish Point, Michigan, in the cold, clear waters of Lake Superior. This vessel, built in Vermillion, Ohio, in 1848, operated for nearly 10 years as a general-purpose "package freighter" carrying passengers and cargoes around Lakes Erie, Huron, and Michigan. In 1858, *Indiana* began hauling iron ore from Lake Superior to Cleveland, Ohio, but in June of that year, while down-bound on Superior, the boat developed a sudden, catastrophic leak around its sternpost and foundered in about 36.5 m (120 ft) of water (Robinson 1999: 26–72, 98).

Indiana was discovered by wreck hunters in 1972 and identified by the "PROP INDIANA" stamped into the wooden handle of a handcart. The deckhouse was missing, and the steamboat's impact with the lake bottom had broken the stem and caused the bow to splay open, but the wreck was otherwise in a remarkably complete condition. Of great interest to technological historians was the propulsion system, particularly the early propeller. Between 1979 and 1984 the vertical "beehive" boiler, single-piston engine and frame, and propeller were salvaged for documentation and display by the Smithsonian Institution. Study of the wreck was resumed from 1991 to 1993, when construction details were recorded and lines were taken from the hull (Johnston and Robinson 1993; Robinson 1999: 72–81, 92–123).

Indiana appears to have been typical of the early propeller steamers of the Great Lakes. It had two decks, a round stern and plain stem, and one mast, and measured 146.5 ft in length and 23 ft in beam (44.7 m by 7.01 m), giving it an L/B ratio of 6.37:1. The relatively high L/B ratio reflects a trend toward longer, leaner steamboats as the century progressed and builders began adding truss or arch systems to increase longitudinal strength (Morrison 1958: 51). *Indiana* was fitted with a simple, lightweight "hog chain truss" to support the ends, particularly the machinery-and-boiler-laden stern (Robinson 1999: 199–211). In general *Indiana*'s construction was solid, with substantial frames and planking, sister keelsons, and dagger knees reinforcing all of the deck beams.

The archaeological study of *Indiana*'s hull and machinery revealed that the vessel was sunk by its own propeller. The 9 ft 7¾ in (2.94 m) diameter propeller assembly consisted of a cast iron hub with four rolled iron blades, each of which was secured by two rows of bolts. When the wreck was first discovered, the propeller was broken off its shaft and lying near the stern, and one of the four blades was sheared off the hub and missing. The lost blade was found in 1992, lodged in the base of the sternpost in a manner to suggest that it struck with terrific force. In addition, the post had deep impact gouges above the propeller shaft, the inner post was badly split, and the outer shaft bearing was cracked. All of this suggested that, perhaps as a result of metal fatigue, the blade broke off the spinning propeller, struck the stern, and opened up the plank and timber seams, causing the rapid flooding that sank the *Indiana* (Robinson 1999: 235–244).

WESTERN RIVER STEAMBOATS AND THE *HEROINE*

The area drained by the Mississippi River encompasses most of the continental United States between the Appalachian and Rocky Mountains, and its potential for settlement and economic exploitation was recognized long before the U.S. government acquired the river's western basin with the Louisiana Purchase of 1803. There was one immense hurdle to development, however, and that was the region's inaccessibility. The Mississippi provided a pathway out of the continent, but its powerful currents could not be stemmed by sailing craft. Upriver traffic was limited to small boats that were towed by laborers walking along the shore. American steam inventors and promoters saw navigation of the western rivers as the ultimate prize for their efforts. Indeed, during an early trial run of *The Steamboat* in the summer of 1807, Fulton wrote to Livingston: "Whatever may be the fate of steamboats for the Hudson, everything is completely proved for the Mississippi, and the object is immense" (Hunter 1969: 8).

In 1811, a venture headed by Fulton and Livingston built the first boat for the West at Pittsburgh, Pennsylvania. Called *New Orleans*, the boat measured 116 ft in length by 20 ft in beam (35.35 m by 6.09 m) and was propelled by a low-pressure engine and a pair of side wheels. This vessel successfully descended the length of the Ohio and Mississippi rivers, but its relatively deep draft and low power limited it to service between New Orleans and Natchez, Mississippi. *New Orleans* was also the first steamer to be sunk by that nemesis of river boats, the submerged log or "snag" (Kane 2004: 45, 57).

New Orleans illustrated many of the problems that steamboats would encounter on the western rivers. In order to work effectively in swift-moving, very shallow waters, it was necessary to build hulls with minimal draft and equip them with very powerful engines. Determining the optimal characteristics for the western steamboat required about a quarter century. It was found that the best design was similar to *The Steamboat* of 1807: a long, narrow, flat-bottomed hull that was very lightly constructed throughout. Because shallow hulls provided scant stowage, working, or living space below deck, builders compensated with a design that accommodated boilers, fuel, machinery, and some cargo on the main deck. Crew and passenger quarters were also located on the main or upper decks. All of this was housed over with a light wooden superstructure. The result was a distinctive boat that resembled a warehouse on a barge, topped by a pair of tall, iron chimneys and an enclosed pilothouse (Hunter 1969: 61–120).

The low-pressure condensing-type steam engine's inability to generate sufficient power on western rivers was overcome by switching to the high-pressure direct-acting steam engine first championed by Oliver Evans. Not only were high-pressure engines more powerful; they were also lighter, more compact, and far easier to manufacture and maintain, and they were more responsive in situations when a kick of extra power was needed. With these advantages, it is not surprising that by the 1820s nearly all boats navigating the western rivers employed high-pressure engines (Hunter 1969: 121–180). There was one drawback, however, and it was a big one: high-pressure steam exceeded the limits of contemporary engineering and manufacturing knowledge, and western steamboats exploded often and violently. Throughout the nineteenth century these boats were widely regarded as floating bombs (Brockmann 2002).

As the problems of western river navigation were overcome, steam took off. By 1821, there were 72 boats in service; by 1832, there were an estimated 220 in motion around the Mississippi basin, prompting French engineer Michel Chevalier (1961: 209, 216) to write: "The circulation of steamboats is as necessary to the west as blood is to the human system." The evolution of engines and hulls on the rapidly expanding western frontier was, for the most part, undertaken by anonymous shipwrights and mechanics working on a "let's try it and see what happens" basis. It is therefore not surprising that our knowledge of the early boats tends to be spotty and anecdotal (Hunter 1969: 175–180).

A wreck sunk in southeastern Oklahoma's Red River has provided archaeologists with what is thus far the earliest archaeologically documented example of a western river steamer (Lees and Arnold 2000). Excavated between 2001 and 2008, the vessel was preserved up to the level of the main deck at the bow, amidships, and stern, and still retained parts of both paddle wheels, a pair of large iron flywheels, the piston-supporting cylinder timbers, and the complete rudder and tiller assembly (Figure 27.3). Inside the hull, excavators found barrels of pork and flour, a modest collection of tools, hardware, and personal belongings, machinery elements, water and steam pipes, boiler mounts and sheet-metal casing, fire grates, and numerous firebox bricks (Crisman 2007).

Figure 27.3 The wreck of the steamboat *Heroine* in the Red River. The shallow, fast-moving, hazard-filled western rivers of North America proved challenging to steamboat builders and operators (as well as to maritime archaeologists studying steamboat wrecks). *Heroine* was snagged and sunk by a submerged log, then entombed under 30 feet (9 m) of sand for 150 years until a shift in the river exposed the wreck once more. Photograph by Carrie Sowden.

The centerline-mounted cylinder timbers and two flywheels indicated that the wreck was a single-piston boat, and therefore likely predated the 1840s, when twin-piston boats became the standard on western rivers (Hunter 1969: 144–146). The wreck's location on the upper Red River was not accessible to larger steamboats until after 1838, when Henry Shreve cleared a path through a 240 km (150 mile) logjam in northwestern Louisiana known as the "Great Raft." These parameters helped researchers to identify the vessel as *Heroine*, a steamer snagged while delivering supplies to the U.S. Army's Fort Towson in May 1838.

Heroine was a very average 150-ton steamboat of its era. Built on the Ohio River at New Albany, Indiana, in 1832, for most of its career the vessel was owned and operated by a captain from Louisville, Kentucky. Like most western steamers before the middle of the century, *Heroine* operated as a "transient boat", a type defined by Louis Hunter (1969: 317) as "free lances roving from trade to trade wherever business beckoned, without any fixed field of operations and without schedule or regularity." The steamer mostly navigated the Ohio and Mississippi rivers between Louisville, St. Louis, and New Orleans, but made occasional side trips up lesser rivers. Cargoes included agricultural commodities such as salt pork, tobacco, whiskey, produce, livestock, barrel staves, and assorted manufactured goods; in the winter, cotton bales were delivered to New Orleans.

Advertised in the newspapers as an "upper cabin" steamer, *Heroine* carried first-class passengers exclusively on the upper (or "boiler") deck, where they enjoyed separate men's and women's cabins, a bar, three meals a day, and river vistas from the galleries and roof. Deck passengers paid one-third of an upper cabin fare, but camped on the main deck amid machinery and cargo, and prepared their own meals on a communal stove. Contemporary newspapers tell us of noteworthy events in *Heroine's* life, such as the boiler explosion that killed the captain's nephew in 1835, and indicate that in 1836 the steamer carried volunteers to fight in the Texas Revolution. *Heroine* appears to have been sold to a new owner in late 1837 and put to work on the lower Red River; it was one of the first boats to pass through the newly opened "Great Raft" shortly before being snagged in the spring of 1838 (Crisman 2005).

Heroine's hull was sufficiently preserved to permit reconstruction of its lines and internal assembly (Figure 27.4). The boat measured 136.66 ft in length by 20.33 ft in molded beam (41.65 m by 6.19 m), giving the hull an L/B ratio of 6.73:1; the guards added 6 ft (1.82 m) of breadth to each side of the main deck. For its size the hull was remarkably shallow, with a depth of hold of only 6 ft (1.82 m); the Roman numeral "V" was carved into the stem, indicating the approximate draft when fully laden. The bow featured a sharply raked stem and moderately fine entrance; amidships the vessel had a full, somewhat boxy shape, with slight rise to the floors, rounded-knuckle bilges, and slightly out-flaring sides; the stern had a tapering run surmounted by a low, finely molded transom. A broad-bladed "barn door" rudder hung off the sternpost on two pintles.

Heroine was fashioned principally from white oak with pine deck planking, and the hull was iron-fastened throughout. Construction was very light by the standards of contemporary wooden vessels built for the Great Lakes, eastern rivers, or high

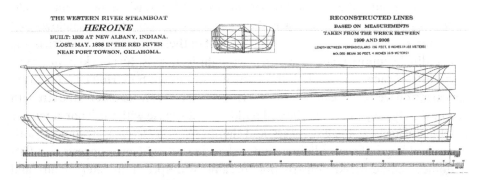

Figure 27.4 Reconstructed lines of the Steamboat *Heroine*. Built in 1832, *Heroine* entered service 21 years after the first steamboat navigated the Ohio and Mississippi Rivers. Its long, narrow hull, curving bow, and boxy section amidships show the development of the classic western steamboat form, although the vessel lacks the hog chain truss support system that would be typical of western steamboats built after 1840. Lines by Kevin Crisman.

seas. The keel was little more than a plank 4 in (10.16 cm) thick, only twice the thickness of the bottom and side planking. Frames were widely spaced and of modest
dimensions; they consisted of a floor, two first futtocks cut to fit the turn of the bilge,
and two top timbers. The keelson was molded 9 in (22.8 cm) and, together with a
pair of bilge stringers and two pairs of clamps, was notched down over the frames
and bolted in place to provide much of the hull's longitudinal stiffness. Deck beams
were also of modest dimensions and were not reinforced with knees of any type.
Judging from everything seen in *Heroine*'s construction—the high L/B ratio, lightweight frames and planking, minimal fastenings, and lack of knees—it is no wonder
that most western steamboats generally wore out after five years of service (Hunter
1969: 100–101).

One place in the hull was notable for its heavier construction: the bow. The 12
forwardmost square frames in *Heroine*'s hull had doubled floor timbers, and there
were substantial cant frames and breast hooks as well, all to better withstand
groundings and collisions. There was also a watertight "snag chamber bulkhead" to
prevent flooding of the entire vessel if a log punctured the bow. These precautions
did not avert disaster in May, 1838, for the snag that sank *Heroine* tore open the port
bilge well aft of this location.

Cast iron machinery elements recovered from the wreck included paddle- and
flywheel flanges, flywheel rims, paddle and main shafts, pillow blocks, a cam and
cam yokes, and a cylinder bed plate (Figure 27.5). When *Heroine* was built, large-
scale steelmaking techniques were undeveloped, so most of the machinery was
made of cast iron. The problems inherent in using this brittle material were evident
in the many breaks and repairs in the flanges, while numerous wedges and shims
on the pillow blocks showed just how challenging it must have been for the engineer to keep the machinery aligned on the flexible wooden deck of a steamboat
(Grieco 2005).

Heroine provides us with a look at the evolution of the steamboat on western
rivers 20 years after Fulton and Livingston's *New Orleans*, when most (but not all)
of the key features were in place. Two elements typical of later shallow-draft
steamboats were absent from *Heroine*. The first of these was a hog chain truss, the
longitudinal support system that used wrought iron rods, turnbuckles, and support posts—braces—to hold up the ends of a steamboat hull. Hog chains started
appearing on western steamboats in the late 1830s and early 1840s, and the strength
and flexibility they imparted allowed builders to dispense with the labor-intensive
notching of keelson, bilge stringers, and clamps seen on *Heroine*. Steamboat yards
began building hulls even lighter, and archaeological evidence suggests that flat-
bottomed, chine-based construction became widespread in later small- and
medium-sized river steamers (Kane 2004: 100–104).

The second significant change in western boats that became commonplace after
1840 was the employment of two cylinders to turn the side wheels independently.
This arrangement eliminated the cumbersome flywheels and provided greater
power and maneuverability (Hedrick 1998: 67–70). The support provided by hog
chains facilitated yet another change in western steamboat propulsion in the second

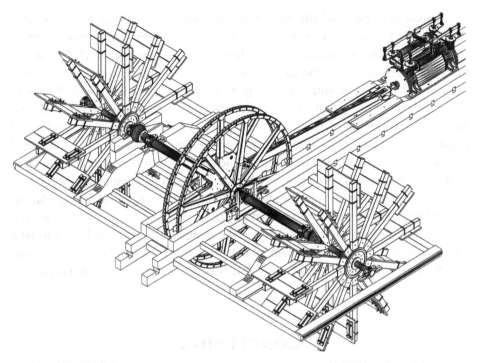

Figure 27.5 Isometric view of *Heroine's* propulsion machinery. A single-piston boat, *Heroine* required a pair of iron-rimmed flywheels mounted amidships to even out the motion of the crank (or "pitman"). Steamboats of this era relied on cast iron machinery (nothing stronger was available), but the brittle material fared very poorly in the hard service of the western rivers. *Heroine's* machinery had numerous breaks and repairs. CAD drawing by Glenn Grieco.

half of the century: the gradual shift from side wheels to a sternwheel. Heavy pistons and a paddle wheel were installed on cantilevered cylinder timbers that extended beyond the transom, an arrangement that better protected the wheel from damage, permitted quick adjustment of the paddle depth, and allowed steamboats to work in very shallow rivers (Bates 1968: 23–31).

The wrecks of more than a score of western river steamboats dating to the 1850s or later have been found and subjected to some level of archaeological study (Kane 2004: 33–43). Two boats among them that snagged in the Missouri River with full cargoes—the side-wheeler *Arabia* (lost in 1856) and the stern-wheeler *Bertrand* (lost in 1865)—have been fully excavated and their contents conserved and displayed in purpose-built museums. Both vessels were up-bound, laden with supplies to support the growing populations of the trans-Mississippi west: hardware, foodstuffs, clothing, luxury items, and personal belongings (Corbin 2000; Hawley 2005; Petsche 1974). The collections from the two wrecks reveal the variety and quantity of a typical steamboat cargo and illustrate how these vessels transplanted the material culture of an industrial society into the frontier hinterlands of nineteenth century North America.

Arabia, *Bertrand*, and the other post-1850 wrecks show that while the river steamer type matured in its general characteristics, a surprising level of variation continued in steamers' construction techniques (Kane 2004: 97–114). One wreck that has undergone excavation and intensive recording, the stern-wheeled Missouri River boat *Montana*, illustrates how large and complex some of these craft were in the later stages of the steamboat era. Built in 1878–1879 in Pittsburgh, Pennsylvania, *Montana* had a length of 252 ft, a beam of 48.66 ft (76.8 m by 14.8 m), and a hull registered at 959 tons. Despite its immense size, *Montana* was a "mountain steamer," with a raftlike form and lightweight, flexible construction that provided the minimal draft necessary to navigate the shallow and hazardous Missouri River. By 1879, the extension of railroads was leading to a decline in steamboat use throughout the United States, but *Montana* managed to stay in service for five years. In the end, the light assembly contributed to its demise. The steamer hit a railroad bridge in 1884 and sank in shallow water, and then, unable to support the weight of water on one side, the hull tore open along the centerline (Corbin and Rodgers 2008: 14–20, 117).

CONCLUSION

The nineteenth century witnessed astounding advances in science, engineering, and industry. All three would combine to produce a transportation revolution that radically shrank human concepts of space and time (Hindle and Lubar 1986: 109–124; Meyer 1948). An essential first step in that revolution was the use of boilers and pistons to transform heat into steam and thereby turn a wheel. Maritime steam would effect changes around the world, but in North America its effects were particularly noticeable. Over the first half of the century steamboats were probably the most important technological contributor to the profound transformations that took place in the continent's environment and social landscape. Maritime archaeology has allowed us to see for ourselves the processes of invention, engineering, and construction that made the steamboat a reality. It has also allowed us to more clearly see what steam propulsion meant to the people who lived and worked within its smoky, steamy realm.

REFERENCES

Barranco, A. Peter. 1963. Dimensions of Str. *Vermont* raised from the Richelieu River in 1953. Notes and plans on file with K. Crisman, Texas A&M University, College Station.
Bates, Alan L. 1968. *The western rivers steamboat cyclopoedium*. Leonia, NJ: Hustle Press.
Bélisle, Jean. 1994. *À propos d'un bateau a vapeur*. Ville LaSalle, Québec: Éditions Hurtubise.

Bélisle, Jean, and André Lépine. 1986. *Le Projet Molson I: Rapport préliminaire de la quatrième campagne de fouilles (1986) sur le site de l'épave Molson I, un bâtiment à vapeur du début du XIXe siècle.* Quebec: Comité d'Histoire et d'Archéologie Subaquatique du Québec.

———. 1988. *Rapport préliminaire de la quatrième campagne de fouilles (1987) sur la site de l'épave du* Lady Sherbrooke *c. 1817–1827, un bâtiment à vapeur de la Molson Line.* Quebec: Comité d'Histoire et d'Archéologie Subaquatique du Québec.

Blow, David J. 1966. *Vermont I*: Lake Champlain's first steamboat. *Vermont History* 34 (April): 115–122.

Brockmann, R. John. 2002. *Exploding steamboats, Senate debates, and technical reports: The convergence of technology, politics, and rhetoric in the Steamboat Bill of 1838.* Amityville, NY: Baywood.

Chevalier, Michel. 1961. *Society, manners, and politics in the United States.* Ithaca, NY: Cornell University Press.

Corbin, Annalies. 2000. *The material culture of steamboat passengers: Archaeological evidence from the Missouri River.* New York: Kluwer Academic/Plenum.

Corbin, Annalies, and Bradley A. Rodgers. 2008. *The steamboat* Montana *and the opening of the West.* Gainesville: University Press of Florida.

Crisman, Kevin. 1983. *The history and construction of the United States schooner* Ticonderoga. Alexandria, VA: Eyrie.

———. 2005. The *Heroine* of the Red River. *INA Quarterly* 32 (2): 3–10.

———. 2007. Easy as one-two-three: Completing the steamboat *Heroine* excavation, 2005–2006. *INA Quarterly* 34 (2): 3–12.

Crisman, Kevin J., and Arthur B. Cohn. 1998. *When horses walked on water: Horse-powered ferries in nineteenth-century America.* Washington, DC: Smithsonian Institution Press.

Davison, Rebecca, ed. 1981. *The* Phoenix *project.* Burlington, VT: Champlain Maritime Society.

Fitch, John. 1976. *The autobiography of John Fitch.* Philadelphia: American Philosophical Society.

Flexner, James T. 1978. *Steamboats come true.* Boston: Little, Brown.

Fowler, Barney. 1974. *Adirondack album.* Schenectady, NY: Outdoor Associates.

Grieco, Glenn. 2005. Modeling an early western steamboat engine. *INA Quarterly* 32 (4): 7–11.

Hadden, Lester James. 1995. Ceramics from the American steamboat *Phoenix* (1815–1819) and their role in understanding shipboard life. MA thesis, Texas A&M University.

Hawley, Greg. 2005. *Treasure in a cornfield: The discovery and excavation of the steamboat* Arabia. Kansas City, MO: Paddle Wheel.

Hedrick, David Layne. 1998. The investigation of the Caney Creek shipwreck, Archaeological Site 41MG32. MA thesis, Texas A&M University.

Hindle, Brooke, and Steven Lubar. 1986. *Engines of change: The American Industrial Revolution, 1790–1860.* Washington, DC: Smithsonian Institution Press.

Hunter, Louis C. 1969. *Steamboats on the western rivers: An economic and technological history.* New York: Octagon Books.

Johnston, Paul F. 1983. *Steam and the sea.* Salem, MA: Peabody Museum of Salem.

Johnston, Paul Forsythe, and David Stewart Robinson. 1993. The wreck of the 1848 propeller *Indiana*: Interim report. *International Journal of Nautical Archaeology* 22 (3): 219–235.

Kane, Adam I. 2004. *The western river steamboat.* College Station: Texas A&M University Press.

Lees, William B., and J. Barto Arnold. 2000. Preliminary assessment of a wreck in the Red River, Choctaw County, Oklahoma, USA. *International Journal of Nautical Archaeology* 29 (1): 120–125.

Lépine, André, David Stewart, and Jean Bélisle. 1991. *Lady Sherbrooke*: Une fenêtre sur les débuts de la navigation à vapeur sur le Saint-Laurent. *La Plongée* 18 (4).

Lytle, William M., and Forrest R. Holdcamper. 1975. *Merchant steam vessels of the United States, 1790–1868*. Staten Island, NY: Steamship Historical Society of America.

Marestier, Jean Baptiste. 1957. *Memoir on steamboats of the United States of America*. Mystic, CT: Marine Historical Association.

Meyer, Balthazar Henry. 1948. *History of transportation in the United States before 1860*. Carnegie Institute of Washington Publication No. 215C.

Missouri Republican. 1835. St. Louis, 25 June.

Morgan, John S. 1977. *Robert Fulton*. New York: Mason Charter.

Morrison, John H. 1958. *History of American steam navigation*. New York: Stephen Daye Press.

Osborne, Brian D. 1995. *The ingenious Mr. Bell*. Argyll, Scotland: Argyll.

Petsche, Jerome. 1974. *The steamboat* Bertrand: *History, excavation, and architecture*. Washington, DC: National Park Service.

Ridgely-Nevitt, Cedric. 1981. *American steamships on the Atlantic*. Newark: University of Delaware Press.

Robinson, David S. 1999. *Indiana:* The history and archaeology of an early Great Lakes propeller. MA thesis, Texas A&M University.

Ross, Ogden. [1930] 1997. *The steamboats of Lake Champlain 1809 to 1930*. Quechee, VT: Vermont Heritage Press Reprint Series.

Simmons, Joe J., III. 1988. Steamboats on inland waters: Prime movers of Manifest Destiny. In *Ships and shipwrecks of the Americas: A history based on underwater archaeology*, ed. George F. Bass, 189–206. London: Thames and Hudson.

Smith, Maurice D. 2005. *Steamboats on the lakes: Two centuries of steamboat travel through Ontario's waterways*. Toronto: James Lorimer & Company.

Sutcliffe, Andrea. 2004. *Steam: The untold story of America's first great invention*. New York: Palgrave Macmillan.

CHAPTER 28

CARIBBEAN MARITIME ARCHAEOLOGY

MARGARET LESHIKAR-DENTON

INTRODUCTION

MARITIME environments, such as oceans, seas, bays, lakes, rivers, marshes, and cenotes, and the landscapes bordering them, hold maritime archaeological sites (Bass 1972, 1988, 2005; Delgado 1997; Grenier, Nutley, and Cochran 2006; Leshikar-Denton and Luna Erreguerena 2008; Ruppé and Barstad 2002). They can be at the interface of land and sea, or in the deepest oceans. There are prehistoric and historical heritage sites that, through archaeology, reveal aspects of human culture from ancient to recent times. Lost ships, boats, canoes, local watercraft, and aircraft, as well as salvage and survivors' campsites, fishing-related areas, navigational aids, anchorages, careening places, ports, harbors, coastal settlements, towns, wharves, shipbuilding sites, coastal forts and defenses, and lighthouses all represent clues to the past. Among them are catastrophic sites, eroded sites, inundated terrestrial sites, and places where cultural material was accidentally lost or purposely deposited into the water.

TREASURE AND HERITAGE VALUE

Archaeological sites in the Caribbean reflect the presence of the earliest indigenous and migrating inhabitants, European explorers and colonizers, multicultural settlers, enslaved and indentured laborers, passing merchants, and the cultures of today (Leshikar-Denton 1997c, 1998, 2001a, 2001b, 2002, 2004; Leshikar-Denton and Luna Erreguerena 2008; Smith 1988b; UNESCO 2004). While appreciation of this finite cultural heritage exists, a dominant problem, especially for shipwrecks, is the perceived commercial value of real and imagined treasure cargoes. The quest for treasure endangers all underwater cultural heritage (UCH) sites in the Caribbean. The actions of commercial salvors are a persistent menace to heritage professionals and the UCH they seek to study, manage, and protect.

REGIONAL AND INTERNATIONAL DEVELOPMENTS

The Caribbean Sea both links and separates Caribbean countries (Figure 28.1). Each of these countries has a unique history, but all share a common maritime heritage with their neighbors. In spite of cultural, linguistic, and legislative differences, island nations are working toward common goals to address their underwater and maritime cultural heritage, especially for the benefit of Caribbean culture, education,

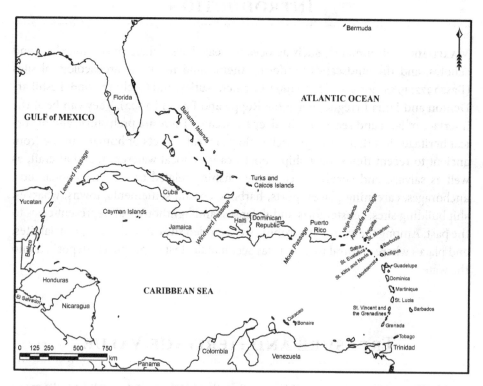

Figure 28.1 Map of the Caribbean. Drawing by Piotr Bajawoski. Reproduced with the kind permission of the Center for Maritime Archaeology and Conservation, Texas A&M University.

and tourism, but also for the world community (Leshikar-Denton 1998, 2001a, 2001b, 2002, 2004; Leshikar-Denton and Luna Erreguerena 2008; UNESCO 2004). In 1997, the Forum of Ministers of Culture of Latin America and the Caribbean established a technical commission on underwater and maritime cultural heritage (UCH) known as the Latin American and Caribbean Group (GRULAC). GRULAC met in Santo Domingo in 1998 and 1999 and agreed to support the ICOMOS International Charter on the Protection and Management of Underwater Cultural Heritage (ICOMOS 1996), then wrote the Santo Domingo Declaration, a statement of their united views regarding UCH, in preparation for a series of expert meetings held by UNESCO in Paris between 1998 and 2001. At the Paris meetings, 88 countries adopted the UNESCO Convention on the Protection of the Underwater Cultural Heritage (UNESCO 2001), which established an international legal framework. The 2001 Convention came into force on 2 January 2009. At this writing, GRULAC countries represent 14 of the 36 ratifications on record (Argentina, Barbados, Cuba, Ecuador, Grenada, Haiti, Honduras, Mexico, Panama, Paraguay, Saint Kitts and Nevis, Saint Lucia, Saint Vincent and the Grenadines, and Trinidad and Tobago), reflecting the importance of UCH to the collective region, in a world setting.

CASE STUDIES OF CARIBBEAN HERITAGE LEGISLATION, MANAGEMENT, AND RESEARCH

The foundations of Caribbean maritime archaeology are built on recurring themes, including heritage legislation, management, research, meaning to descendant communities, and the future (Leshikar-Denton and Luna Erreguerena 2008). Creativity in protection and management of UCH and cooperation in sharing knowledge, technical skills, and professional expertise are key concepts in the region. Help can come from beyond the Caribbean, but sustainability must come from within it.

In the Caribbean today, most island countries are participating in regional meetings and initiatives to address their UCH and working to create a larger base of knowledge and awareness of the region's rich underwater and maritime history. Significant discoveries and scientific archaeological projects under way in certain countries over the past three decades have laid a foundation, while other countries are just beginning the process. It has not been possible to include every Caribbean island country, but the experiences of many are described in the following sections. Although not the target of this article, nearby countries sharing Caribbean coastlines and/or a common history have faced comparable problems and achieved progress. Bermuda, often grouped with the Caribbean islands, has experienced discord with treasure hunters; the Bermuda Maritime Museum, founded in 1974, has made great strides by inviting cooperative research projects with overseas institutions (Harris 1997, 2008; Smith and Harris 2002). In 2001, Bermuda passed the Historic

Wrecks Act, which emulates many aspects of the 2001 UNESCO Convention Annex. Mexico, treated elsewhere in this book, has a strong history with UCH protection and management and has ratified the 2001 UNESCO Convention (Leshikar-Denton and Luna Erreguerena 2008; Luna Erreguerena 1997, 1998, 2002). Panama, although the first country in the world to ratify the 2001 UNESCO Convention, faces conflicting issues concerning UCH; researchers from the Institute of Nautical Archaeology (INA) and Ships of Discovery searched for vessels lost there by Columbus (Smith 1988a), while the Playa Damas shipwreck has been impacted by treasure hunters (Castro and Fitzgerald 2006). The U.S. state of Florida is also a location of conflicting interests. Treasure salvors are permitted to excavate and commercially gain from shipwrecks, while simultaneously research is being conducted by professional university and state archaeologists, and interpretive maritime trails and shipwreck preserves have been established for the public benefit (Bratten 1998; Cozzi 1998; Jameson and Scott-Ireton 2007; Scott-Ireton 1998, 2003; Smith 1991, 1994, 2002; Smith et al. 1995; Smith et al. 1999). Case studies of Caribbean island heritage legislation, management, and research follow.

British Overseas Territories

Anguilla

In the mid-1990s, the Anguilla government established the Historic Wrecks Advisory Committee (HWAC) to review proposals from groups requesting permission to commercially work the 1772 inbound Spanish merchantmen *El Buen Consejo*, and *Jesús, María y José* (Conrich 1997). These ships were part of a *flota* of 16 vessels sailing from Spain to Veracruz when they were lost on the reefs of Anguilla with nearly 1,000 people aboard, including 52 Franciscans who wrote about the loss of the 70-gun warship *El Buen Consejo* and the 40-gun merchant vessel *Jesús, María y José*, providing a phenomenal written record.

Meanwhile, ICOMOS International Committee on Underwater Cultural Heritage (ICUCH) members sent information on protecting UCH to the government (Leshikar-Denton 2002). HWAC member Bob Conrich reached out to archaeology professionals; as a result, archaeologists from East Carolina University (ECU) and the Maritime Archaeological and Historical Society (MAHS), under the direction of Bradley Rodgers, documented the Spanish wrecks (Conrich 1997). The team produced a site map of *El Buen Consejo* and an analysis for the government, who declared the site an Underwater Archaeological Preserve (Azevedo 2009). But the government is still entertaining commercial proposals, so the fate of the ships remains unclear.

In 2010, UCH legislation remains to be addressed (Bob Conrich, pers. comm.). The good news, however, is that a comprehensive UCH survey initiated by Lilli Azevedo and a team of graduate students from the University of Southampton, England, is under way (Azevedo 2009, pers. comm.). The 2009 Anguilla Shipwreck Survey identified seven historic wrecks, including two nineteenth-century sailing vessels with windlasses, a cluster of nine cannon (Figure 28.2), a site with four anchors, a nineteenth-century site with copper fastenings, a twentieth-century barge, and several isolated anchors and cannon. Meanwhile, the Anguilla Archaeo-logical and Historical Society and Azevedo promoted the island's maritime heritage through a series of field trips, public lectures, radio interviews, and community activities to educate the public and raise awareness. A land-based Heritage Trail, set to open in April 2010, will promote the island's heritage and encourage Anguillians to think about managing the past in the present (Anguillian 2010).

The Cayman Islands

The Cayman Islands enacted the Abandoned Wreck Law in 1966. The law vests in the Crown all shipwrecks that have been lying on the seabed for at least 50 years, providing blanket protection, but falls short of recognizing them as cultural prop-erty (Leshikar-Denton 1997b, 2002; Leshikar-Denton and Luna Erreguerena 2008; Leshikar-Denton and Scott-Ireton 2008). It allows for permitting prospectors, who receive at least half of the wreck's value. If government keeps salvaged artifacts, it must pay the prospector a percentage of their appraised value, effectively giving up rights to more than 50% of a shipwreck and paying the salvor to buy it back. A

Figure 28.2 Project Director Lillian Azevedo (right) and team member Molly Crossthwaite (left) document a cluster of nine cannon on a site in Anguilla. Photograph by Carl Grout. Reproduced with the kind permission of the 2009 Anguilla Shipwreck Survey.

marine archaeology committee established by the Ministry of Culture in the 1990s assessed the law as inadequate, but new legislation is still forthcoming; a new law should take into account standards set in the 1996 ICOMOS Charter and the 2001 UNESCO Convention. Meanwhile, Cayman has denied all applications from treasure hunters, and prosecutions for violations resulting in imprisonment and fines are on record. Other local legislation affecting the marine environment, material culture, and heritage sites includes the Marine Conservation Law, first enacted in 1978; a 1979 law that established the Cayman Islands National Museum (CINM); and a 1987 law creating the National Trust for the Cayman Islands.

The Cayman Islands has benefited from a chronology of steps taken to creatively manage its UCH, but has yet to establish a competent management authority. Thirty years ago, Roger Smith and a team from INA, at the invitation of the government, surveyed the waters of Little Cayman, Cayman Brac, and Grand Cayman and documented 77 sites, primarily shipwrecks (Leshikar-Denton 1996, 1997a; Smith 1981, 2000). During the 1979–1980 project, they test-excavated the Turtle wreck, believed to be an English turtle-fishing sloop that was burned in 1670 by Spanish privateer Manuel Rivero Pardal, and the Duck Pond Careenage, used for overhauling vessels for at least three centuries. Documentary research indicated that vessels such as the Dutch West Indiaman *Dolphijn*, lost in 1629, and the pirate ship *Morning Star*, run aground in 1722, had come to grief in Cayman's waters. Smith (2000) wrote *The Maritime Heritage of the Cayman Islands* based on this work.

Between 1990 and 1993, Margaret Leshikar-Denton, affiliated with Texas A&M University (TAMU), INA, and the CINM, investigated the 1794 Wreck of the Ten Sail—the British HMS *Convert* and 9 ships of her 58-ship merchant convoy that were lost together on the East End reefs of Grand Cayman during the French Revolutionary Wars (Figure 28.3) (Leshikar 1992, 1993; Leshikar-Denton 1997c, 2005, in press; Leshikar-Denton and Pedley 1994). HMS *Convert*, the captured French *l'Inconstante*, was leading the fleet from Jamaica to Europe when the frigate wrecked with her original ordnance of 12-pounder cannon; this factor contributed to later identification of the site. The archival research and archaeological survey led to an exhibition at the CINM that was visited by Britain's Queen Elizabeth II; a National Archive publication; a postal service stamp issue; a Currency Board commemorative coin; and a Visual Arts Society art competition. A book is also in progress (Leshikar-Denton in press). The government also dedicated a land-based park at East End to the Wreck of the Ten Sail, providing a view of the reefs where the convoy struck.

Between 1990 and 2006, Leshikar-Denton served as archaeologist for the CINM, where she and teams of archaeologists and avocational volunteers, assisted at times by Department of Environment staff and boats, enlarged the islands' shipwreck inventory to over 140 sites, spanning five centuries and 15 nationalities, and highlighting rare sites in need of special protection, such as HMS *Jamaica* (1715) and *San Miguel* (1730). They also test-excavated an early-eighteenth-century turtle-fishing encampment on the north coast of Grand Cayman and a historic step-well used for centuries on the western harbor-front. Surveys for prehistoric sites by University College London in 1992 and 1995 (Drewett 1992, 1996) and the Florida

Figure 28.3 An encrusted eighteenth-century anchor believed to be associated
with the Wreck of the Ten Sail lies exposed on the seabed of the Cayman Islands.
Photograph by Mike Guderian. Reproduced with the kind permission of the Wreck
of the Ten Sail Project.

Museum of Natural History in 1993 (Stokes and Keegan 1993) on all three islands
came up with negative results. Ball State University field school teams documented
the *Geneva Kathleen*, a three-masted lumber schooner wrecked in 1930 (National
Shipwreck Inventory n.d.).

In 2003 a Maritime Heritage Trail (MHT) Partnership, facilitated by Leshikar-
Denton and Della Scott-Ireton, launched the interactive land-based Cayman Islands
Maritime Heritage Trail, consisting of 36 sites located throughout the three islands.
This trail includes a range of themes: early explorers, maritime place-names, historical anchorages, shipwrecks, wrecking practices, lighthouses, seaside forts, shipbuilding, turtle-fishing, and hurricanes (Leshikar-Denton and Scott-Ireton 2007,
2008; Maritime Heritage Trail Partners 2003). In 2003, Bert Ho and Florida State

University students assisted in documenting the Norwegian-flagged *Glamis* (lost in 1913), providing groundwork for a future shipwreck preserve (Ho 2004; Leshikar-Denton and Ho 2004). Leshikar-Denton advocates a creative layered approach to protecting, managing, and interpreting Cayman's UCH through traditional legislative means and by using creativity to interpret maritime sites on land, create shipwreck preserves at robust sites, and conduct specialized archaeological investigation on sensitive early sites; she is advocating for development of a sustainable maritime archaeology program.

Turks and Caicos Islands

The Turks and Caicos Islands Historic Wrecks Ordinance (1974) is modeled on the United Kingdom's Protection of Wrecks Act (1973) (Leshikar-Denton 2002: 285). But whereas wrecks must be designated for protection in the British law, the Turks and Caicos law provides blanket protection for shipwrecks that have been on the seabed for at least 50 years. If persons unlawfully possess part of a wreck, or use explosives, a pressure hose, or a vacuum hose on a historic wreck, they can be fined or imprisoned, but the government can release artifacts to a permittee. The Turks and Caicos National Museum (TCNM), a publicly funded nonprofit trust, sanctioned by but independent of the government, helped the government develop permit applications designed to exclude all but professional scientific work. This process has not stopped the government from considering recent proposals from salvors.

The Turks and Caicos Islands have granted permits to treasure salvors in the past and have allowed historical shipwrecks to be salvaged in the seas surrounding the islands (Keith 1997c, 2006). In 1980, Caribbean Ventures discovered a sixteenth-century shipwreck that they incorrectly announced was Columbus's *Pinta*. The government called on Colin Martin at the Scottish Institute of Maritime Studies to verify its age. Soon INA was contacted and the treasure hunters were prohibited from continuing, and from 1982 to 1985 Donald Keith's team excavated the Molasses Reef wreck (Keith 1987, 1988, 1997b, 1997c, 2001, 2006). They transported the artifacts to TAMU, where they began conservation treatments on the collection. In 1988, Keith founded a nonprofit organization, Ships of Discovery, which carried the conservation treatments of the Molasses Reef wreck artifacts, including surviving timbers, to their conclusion. This work laid the foundations for heritage management in the Turks and Caicos Islands.

The Molasses Reef wreck is the only Caribbean shipwreck that has been completely excavated by scientific archaeological methods (Keith 1987, 1988, 1997b, 1997c, 2001, 2006; Keith and Simmons 1985). It dates from the 1520s, making it the earliest shipwreck discovered in the Western Hemisphere. Fragments of late-fifteenth- to early-sixteenth-century Spanish ceramics and an array of armaments, including swivel guns, cannon, shoulder arms, crossbows, swords, shot, and grenades, were discovered on the site (Figure 28.4). Although only 2% of the hull survived below the ballast pile, these remains suggest that the Molasses Reef wreck was of the poorly understood caravel ship type. In order to fill in missing pieces of information, researchers conducted test-excavations on two similar sixteenth-century shipwrecks, also located in the Caribbean. Treasure hunters had worked on the Highborn Cay wreck in the Bahamas, resulting in the loss of most of its artifacts, but the salvors were uninterested in the hull; the team of archaeologists exposed and studied a well-preserved section, including the main mast step carved out of the keelson (Keith 1988: 58–60, 1997a; Smith 1993: 200–203). In collaboration with Mexico's National Institute of Anthropology and History (INAH), the Bahía Mujeres wreck, located off the northeastern coast of the Yucatán Peninsula, was also investigated (Delgado 1997: 48; Keith 1988: 56–59; Luna Erreguerena 1997: 51, 1998: 37–38; Smith 1993: 203–204). The vanguard research on these wrecks has illuminated how early vessels of this period were built, armed, and provisioned.

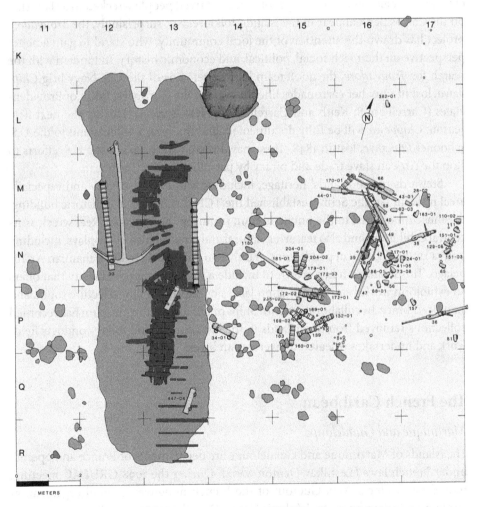

Figure 28.4 Molasses Reef wreck plan showing the distribution of ordnance across the site, outline of the ballast mound, hull remains beneath the ballast, and grooves in the seabed corresponding to frame locations. Illustration by Donald Keith. Reproduced with the kind permission of Ships of Discovery.

Ships of Discovery is conducting cooperative field projects with the TCNM and received significant grants from the National Oceanographic and Atmospheric Administration's Ocean Exploration Program in 2006 and 2008 toward the search for the slave ship *Trouvadore*, which was a Spanish vessel lost off East Caicos in 1841 (Keith and Carrell 2007, 2009; Keith and Sadler 2005; NOAA 2008; Sadler 2008; Slave Ship Trouvadore 2008). One hundred ninety-three African people headed for slavery in Cuba made up *Trouvadore*'s cargo; their fortunes changed as a result of the wreck. The islands' population suddenly expanded with first-generation Africans. Slavery was illegal in the British territory, so most of these people were indentured into the salt industry of the Turks and Caicos and gained their full freedom soon thereafter. The archaeology team test-excavated a site off East Caicos that Keith and Toni Carrell hypothesize is *Trouvadore*, in part because of documentary evidence, but also because vestiges of a story of freed people wrecked in a slave ship on the Caicos Bank appear in the islands' folklore. Not surprisingly, the *Trouvadore* project has drawn the attention of the local community, who stand to gain a better perspective on their rich social, political, and economic history. In tandem with the search for *Trouvadore*, the 2008 team located remains of the U.S. Navy brig *Chippewa*, lost in 1816; her carronades line the reefs of the Northwest Point of Providenciales (Carrell 2008; Keith and Carrell 2009; NOAA 2008). During the next field season, *Chippewa* will be fully documented, and the search will expand to the U.S. schooner *Onkahye*, lost in 1848. These naval vessels were part of the U.S. efforts to stop the African slave trade and piracy by patrolling in the Caribbean.

Stewards of the islands' heritage, including Ships of Discovery and especially local resident Grethe Seime, established the TCNM. Located in a historic building, the museum opened to the public in 1991, featuring the Molasses Reef wreck as its central exhibition, and also featuring natural and cultural history displays, including a circa 1100 CE Lucayan paddle, one of only two discovered in the Bahamian Archipelago. This institution has grown to include a museum support facility that offers an exhibition workshop, conservation labs, a curatorial facility, a lecture room, and an office/library. In collaboration with Ships of Discovery, the museum has recorded collections removed from the islands in the last century, and today conducts fieldwork and undertakes research in overseas archives.

The French Caribbean

Martinique and Guadeloupe

The islands of Martinique and Guadeloupe are departments of France and operate under French laws (Leshikar-Denton 2002). During the 1998 GRULAC meeting, retired naval officer Max Guérout of the French nongovernmental organization Groupe de Recherche en Archéologie Navale (Naval Archaeology Research Group) (GRAN) reported that GRAN had worked on a project to inventory the shipwrecks of Martinique. Although the GRAN fieldwork, under the leadership of Guillaume François (1991–1997), was discontinued due to a lack of funds, a Web site (www.archeonavale.org/martinique) presents the work that has been accomplished (Henry Petitjean Roget and Gérard Richard, pers. comm.). It features archival and archaeological work undertaken, resulting in a list of 90 ship losses between the seventeenth and twentieth centuries. The list includes 73 archaeological sites, 19 of which can be identified by the ship's name; among them are *Notre Dame De Bonne Espérance*, lost in 1687; HMS *Raisonable*, wrecked in 1762; and *Le Cygne*, a casualty in 1808. Petitjean Roget and Richard also highlighted that Jean Pierre Moreau, a specialist in naval archaeology, has done extensive archival research in France, Spain, and England; he published a work entitled *Guide des trésors archéologiques sous-marins des Petites Antilles* (Guide to Archaeological Treasures of the Lesser Antilles) featuring ships lost between the sixteenth and eighteenth centuries (Moreau 1988).

The Netherlands Antilles

The Netherlands Antilles is composed of Saint Maarten, Saint Eustatius, and Saba, located east of Puerto Rico, and Curaçao and Bonaire, located near the coast of Venezuela. The 1992 Convention on the Protection of the Archaeological Heritage of Europe, or Treaty of Malta, applies to European archaeological heritage and extends to the Netherlands Antilles; thus, the Dutch islands are amending local legislation to comply with the European Treaty (Leshikar-Denton 2002; Leshikar-Denton and Luna Erreguerena 2008: 25–53; Nagelkerken and Ayubi 1997).

From 1982 to 1988, in collaboration with the College of William and Mary, the Archaeological and Anthropological Institute of the Netherlands Antilles (AAINA) carried out fieldwork in the historical anchorage at Orange Bay, Saint Eustatius (Nagelkerken 1985; Nagelkerken and Ayubi 1997). They delineated the location and size of the anchorage by the dispersion of Dutch, French, and English ceramics, glass, bricks, tiles, and beads lost by seventeenth- and eighteenth-century European seafarers.

In Bonaire, Wil Nagelkerken and Raymond Hays, under the auspices of AAINA and with volunteers from the Maritime Archaeological and Historical Society (MAHS), surveyed the historical anchorage of Kralendijk, adjacent to Fort Orange, to identify the site's maritime historical landscape, based on the distribution, classification, and source of artifacts exposed on the seabed (Nagelkerken and Hayes 2002, 2008). They recovered 600 artifacts from Holland (65%), England (22%), France (13%), and Germany (1%), and determined that peak use of the anchorage had occurred from 1775 to 1850. They also identified the Dutch warship *Sirene*, lost in 1831, within the anchorage.

In Curaçao, AAINA investigated the Dutch frigate *Alphen*, which exploded and sank in Santa Anna Bay in 1778; excavations followed from 1994 to 1998 (Haviser 1997; Leshikar-Denton 2002; Nagelkerken 1989). *Alphen* is the only underwater site on the Curaçao monuments list. AAINA also conducted a survey in response to dredging during repair of a quay wall of the Handelskade (commercial wharf) at the entrance to Santa Anna Bay in 1993, resulting in a limited surface collection of seventeenth- to nineteenth-century materials (Nagelkerken 1998).

The British steamship SS *Mediator* collided with another ship in the entrance to Willemstad harbor in 1884; it sank rapidly with over 750 tons of "fine goods" (Nagelkerken et al. 2008). Archaeologists discovered the remains in 1986 and made plans to preserve the site in situ. It was cleared of overburden and mapped, and measures are in place to protect it from damage caused by ship traffic. The *Mediator* is being readied for local and tourist diving in combination with displays at the Curaçao Maritime Museum, with maritime archaeology education coordinated by MAHS, cultural resource management provided by the STIMANA Foundation, and promotional activities assigned to the UNIEK CURAÇAO Foundation.

Archaeologists under the auspices of the Saint Maarten National Heritage Foundation, the Ministry of Culture, the Department of Planning and Environment, and Maritime Archaeology and Research mapped HMS *Proselyte*, a captured Dutch frigate that wrecked in 1801 in Saint Maarten (Bequette 1996). They carried out the work from 1994 to 1995, with a view toward developing a management plan to protect the site from ongoing looting, and recommended placing the recovered artifacts in the Saint Maarten Museum in Philipsburg.

The Commonwealth of Puerto Rico

Puerto Rico, an unincorporated territory affiliated with the United States, established the Consejo para la Conservación y Estudio de Sitios y Recursos Arqueológicos Subacuáticos (Council for the Conservation and Study of Underwater Archaeological Sites and Resources) in 1987 under Law No. 10, and created the Office of Underwater Archaeology to register sites, investigate illegal salvage, issue permits, and evaluate the impact of coastal development on cultural resources (Fontánez-Aldea 1997; Hall 1997b; Leshikar-Denton 2002). The Consejo is compiling an inventory of underwater sites, currently numbering over 200 shipwrecks, and has recorded at least 12 of them. Richard Fontánez, formerly with the Consejo, pointed out that between 1992 to 1995 Consejo archaeologists investigated the Spanish steamship *Alicante*, wrecked in 1881; documented an eighteenth-century English warship wrecked on the Laurel Reefs of La Parguera, Lajas; verified sites described by Miguel "Pili" Pagan at Mona Island, on the coast of Sardinera Beach; and documented the Cerro Gordo sites in Vega Alta, a shipyard of the seventeenth to nineteenth centuries (Richard Fontánez, pers. comm.). Under the direction of Jerome Hall, and in cooperation with Richard Wills, they recorded a PT boat in Desecheo Island, and two aircraft—a B-29 in Aguadilla and a PBY Catalina flying boat in La Parguera—for the U.S. Navy. They also inspected Buoy 4 in San Juan to confirm and investigate the vessels *Manuela* and *Cristobal Colon*, lost during the Spanish-American War.

Other sites recorded in Puerto Rico include the seventeenth-century Rincón Astrolabe wreck (Garcia Ortiz 2005); the *Antonio López*, an 1898 casualty of the

Spanish-American War, which today is a National Landmark and listed on the National Register of Historic Places (Fontánez, pers. comm.); three historical anchorages in the waters of Mona Island where 30 anchors of various time periods and nationalities were recorded by Frank Cantelas, Wayne Luzardi, Roger and K.C. Smith, Jerome Hall, and Fontánez; and an inventory of the Cayo Ratones in Cabo Rojo, where a semi-submerged indigenous archaeological site was investigated by Fontánez, Gustavo García, and Consejo personnel Juan Vera and Amilcar García.

Surprisingly with such professional work under way, in 2007 the Puerto Rican government considered a new regressive bill in favor of commercial exploitation. Thanks to the prompt and unified intervention of local archaeologists and international colleagues and institutions, it was vetoed (Juan Vera, pers. comm.). In 2009, two senators again proposed the excavation of submerged archaeological sites in order to alleviate the island's financial crisis (Gustavo García, pers. comm.). Fortunately, the reaction of the public and the government has not been favorable to the proposal.

In 2008, the Puerto Rican Instituto de Investigaciones Costaneras (IIC), the Centre for Maritime Archaeology and Conservation (CMAC) at TAMU, and INA conducted surveys on the northern coast of Puerto Rico between Loíza and San Juan Bay (Castro 2008: 70). Noting a rich prehistory, and Spanish colonization from 1509 under Juan Ponce de León, the long-term project goals are to study the island's full history through its submerged cultural heritage and to create public awareness about this significant and varied maritime heritage. The 2008 team, including Fontánez, Filipe Castro, and Gustavo García, among others, located important sites in an area where pre-Columbian settlements existed and at least 66 ships have wrecked (Castro 2008).

Independent Countries in the Greater Antilles

Bahamas

The Bahamas Abandoned Wrecks Act (1965) is a law that values historic shipwrecks for their monetary potential rather than as cultural heritage resources; it is inadequate to protect the islands' UCH (Patman 2004: 112–113). Treasure hunters working with and without authorization have compromised many sites. Although the Antiquities, Monuments and Museums Act (1998) has been implemented, it does not specifically address UCH. The Antiquities, Monuments and Museums Corporation (AMMC) has served only as an advisory agency on salvage issues (Grace Turner, pers. comm.). According to Michael Pateman (2004: 113), a position paper has been put before government recommending that the Abandoned Wrecks Act be repealed; that shipwrecks be considered archaeological resources rather than treasure troves; that significant sites be reserved as marine parks; and that only reputable research institutions be allowed to conduct research. So far one Bahamian, Grace Turner, has completed academic training in underwater archaeology; she received her MA in 2004 from TAMU.

Professional archaeology in the Bahamas includes a 1986 INA test-excavation of the sixteenth-century Highborn Cay wreck, mentioned above (Keith 1988: 58–60,

1997a; Smith 1993: 200–203). In the early 1990s the sixteenth-century St. Johns Bahamas wreck was discovered on the Little Bahama Bank, and the government granted an excavation permit to salvors (Smith 1993: 204–205; Malcom 1997: 351–352).

A 500-year-old Lucayan burial canoe was discovered lying on a submerged ledge at a depth of 18 m in Stargate blue hole, a submerged cenote of Andros Island, in May 1995 (Chris Amer, pers. comm.; SCIAA 2009). The Bahamian government invited assistance from the University of South Carolina's Institute of Archaeology and Anthropology (SCIAA). Chris Amer and Jonathan Leader spearheaded an investigation to archaeologically record, recover, and conserve the canoe. The 2 m long craft, made from Madeira wood, is the oldest artifact of its type ever recovered in the Caribbean region. It is undergoing conservation treatments in the Pompey Museum, Nassau, under the direction of Director General of Heritage Gail Saunders at the National Archives of the Bahamas. Discovery of the canoe and Lucayan skeletal remains in blue holes brought about the realization that Lucayans developed cultural use of both dry and submerged caves within the archipelago (Grace Turner, pers. comm.).

Cuba

In Cuba, activities directed at underwater cultural heritage are controlled by the Ministry of Culture under Laws No. 1 and No. 2 of 4 August 1977: Ley de Protección al Patrimonio Cultural (Law for the Protection of Cultural Heritage) and Ley de los Monumentos Nacionales y Locales (Law of National and Local Monuments) (Echeverría Cotelo 2004; Fernández González and Escobar Guio 1998; Leshikar-Denton 2002: 290). Cuba has created decrees and regulations to implement both laws, signed other international treaties that relate to UCH, and charged specialized Cuban agencies with responsibilities. Site inventories are being developed and assessed, excavations and conservation of remains have been undertaken, and artifacts have been exhibited at the Museum of San Salvador de La Punta of the Office of the Historian of Havana (Echeverría Cotelo 2004: 52–55, 118–121). Preservation of cultural heritage is a priority in Cuba, with laws, institutions, and museums established for preservation of cultural heritage, including that from underwater sites. Various media suggest, however, that Cuba is engaging in cooperative ventures with foreign treasure-hunting groups (Arnaut 1998; Billings 2002). While there has been a lack of clarity regarding scientific underwater and maritime archaeological research in the country, important colonial shipwrecks, such as the Cayo Ines de Soto site, thought to contain a ship lost in 1555–1556, are present (Roger Smith, pers. comm.). Cuba ratified the 2001 UNESCO Convention on 26 May 2008, so this is an excellent opportunity for the country to adjust its relationships with salvors and to abide by and promote the fundamental principles of that international document.

Dominican Republic

In 1979, the Dominican Republic created the Comisión de Rescate Arqueológico Submarino (Commission of Underwater Archaeological Rescue) (CRAS), an agency under the auspices of the Dominican Navy and charged with salvaging, conserving, and exhibiting UCH by locating sites, granting permits, supervising exploration activities, and developing a laboratory to catalog and conserve artifacts (Report 1998). Not to be confused with scientific archaeological projects that do not include salvage, CRAS excavated a number of historic shipwrecks: *Nuestra Señora de la Pura y Limpia Concepción* (lost in 1641 on Silver Bank); *Nuestra Señora de Guadalupe* and *Conde de Tolosa* (lost in 1724 in Samaná Bay); the French warship *Scipión* (lost in 1782 in Samaná Bay); and the French vessels *Diómedes* and *Imperial* (lost in 1806). Objects from these historic sites are on exhibition at the Museo de las Reales Atarazanas (Royal Shipyards Museum), the Museo de Arqueología Submarina del Faro a Colón (Columbus Lighthouse Underwater Archaeology Museum), and the Museo de las Casas Reales (Royal Houses Museum), while several books discuss the findings (Borrell 1983a, 1983b; Borell et al. 1997; Santiago 1990).

The Dominican Republic has published a compendium of the country's cultural heritage legislation (Brea-Franco and Victoriano 1998). In June 1998, the country hosted and headed GRULAC's first meeting of the Technical Commission on Underwater Cultural Heritage. They knew of 400 shipwrecks in the waters of Hispaniola, and though cooperative agreements with commercial salvage interests had been reached in the past two decades, the country began to work exclusively with universities and maintain all recovered artifacts within the country.

Scientific projects undertaken in the Dominican Republic include INA's 1980s surveys for vessels lost during the first two Columbus voyages: the *nau Santa María*, and the caravels *Mariagalante, Gallega, San Juan*, and *Cardera* (Smith 1988a). Indiana University and PanAmerican Consultants also searched for Columbus's ships in the 1990s (James and Beeker 1994); in addition, they conducted fieldwork at a prehistoric plaza and a cenote containing Taino artifacts at Manantial de la Aleta in East National Park (Foster and Beeker 1997). Jerome Hall and his team from the Pan-American Institute of Maritime Archaeology excavated the Monte Christi shipwreck, lost around 1652–1656 (Hall 1991, 1992, 1993, 1994, 1997a). The ship, thought to be an English-built merchantman carrying a Dutch cargo of clay pipes, wrecked while interloping into the Spanish colony.

By the Decree of 26 June 1999, the Dominican Republic created the National Office for the Protection of the Underwater Cultural Heritage, which replaced all previous authorities responsible for this patrimony. This decree, mindful of UNESCO and ICOMOS initiatives, was an important development for UCH in the Dominican Republic and the whole Caribbean region. But recent news suggests changes of attitudes in successive political situations, with renewed threats to UCH (Pineda 2009).

Haiti

During the 1998 GRULAC meeting in Santo Domingo, Harold Gaspar reported knowledge of more than 200 shipwrecks in Haitian waters and related that the country had issued a decree on 26 September 1995 creating a National Office of

Marine Archaeology. Its mission was to establish a policy on marine archaeology, maintain an inventory of sites, manage prospecting activities, promote scientific investigations, encourage international cooperation, and create marine archaeological reserves and parks to increase museum and tourism activities. In 1998 the agency had not been instituted, and Gaspar expressed concern that without a good legal framework, UCH is threatened (Gaspar 1998; Leshikar-Denton 2002). A positive development is that on 9 November 2009, Haiti ratified the 2001 UNESCO Convention.

In 1998, Haiti signed an agreement with the French NGO GRAN to document slave routes in Haiti and the Dominican Republic, in association with a UNESCO initiative; the subject of slave ships was included in the project design, with Max Guérout as principal investigator (Report 1998). The UNESCO slave routes project is ongoing (Khakifa and Chan-Mow 2006).

Jamaica

Jamaica began heritage management initiatives as early as the nineteenth century (Gray 1997, 2008; Leshikar-Denton 2002; Leshikar-Denton and Luna Erreguerena 2008). The Institute of Jamaica (IJ) was established in 1879, the Jamaica National Trust Commission Act in 1958, and the Jamaica National Heritage Trust Act in 1985. Professional archaeology in the country extends back to the 1980s. So it was unexpected when Jamaica issued a permit directed at UCH to a U.S.-based commercial firm in 1999 and renewed the permit in 2002, while also hosting a UNESCO meeting in support of the 2001 UNESCO Convention. Jamaica National Heritage Trust (JNHT) archaeologists, upholding professional standards in their permit requirements, continuously blocked progress for the permittee. In 2007, Jamaica changed course again, in favor of heritage preservation, but a lack of clarity on the issue remains. The stated mission of JNHT Technical Director of Archaeology Dorrick Gray is to encourage Jamaica to ratify the UNESCO Convention; develop specific national legislation; issue permits only for professional research; initiate an inventory of UCH; increase training; seek assistance from divers, fishermen, and the public to identify sites; and educate stakeholders about proper action to take when historical sites are found.

One of the most significant heritage sites in the Caribbean is the remains of the bustling English colonial city of Port Royal, Jamaica, which was founded in 1655, and most of which subsided into Kingston Harbour during a catastrophic earthquake in 1692. Studies of the site fit within an emerging body of "disaster archaeology literature" (Gould 2007; Grattan and Torrence 2002). Nonscientific excavations of the sunken city began when the IJ sponsored underwater work by Edwin Link and the National Geographic Society in the late 1950s, resulting in a pre-1692 map of Port Royal, and by Robert Marx from 1966 to 1968, whose team excavated caches of artifacts. By 1969 Philip Mayes began terrestrial archaeological excavations, involving young Jamaicans, and the creation of the Jamaican Archaeological Research Centre in the Old Naval Hospital at Port Royal.

Scientific underwater archaeology and conservation of artifacts from Port Royal commenced in the 1980s, when TAMU and INA, under the direction of Donny Hamilton and in association with the JNHT, began a program at the site (Clifford 1991; Hamilton 1991, 1997, 2004, 2006, 2008; Leshikar-Denton and Luna Erreguerena 2008; Smith 2008). Hamilton led field schools at Port Royal from 1981 to 1990, excavating eight buildings and a ship that crashed through one of them during the disaster (Figure 28.5); Gray began his training in underwater archaeology with Hamilton's team. Conservation of recovered artifacts was completed at TAMU, while Jamaica has established museums at Port Royal to interpret and display part of the collection. Many reports, theses, and dissertations have resulted from this work, providing a window into all aspects of life in seventeenth-century Port Royal. But Hamilton cautions that this rich body of archaeological data, much of which remains to be excavated, poses long-term post-excavation difficulties related to conservation, curation, display, and publication (Hamilton 2004: 49).

In the 1980s and 1990s, INA archaeologists searched for the remains of Columbus's caravels *Capitana* and *Santiago de Palos*, both of which ran aground during the explorer's fourth voyage, in 1503, in St. Ann's Bay (Geddes 1992; Neville, Neyland, and Parrent 1992; Smith 1988a). The Columbus sites eluded them, but the group located six eighteenth-century merchantmen. Greg Cook directed a team of INA/JNHT archaeologists in the study of one of these ships, a British sloop called the Reader's Point wreck. The vessel was likely scuttled during the American Revolutionary War after a career as a merchant-trader (Cook 1997).

In the 1980s, INA also helped the Jamaican government conduct surveys on the Pedro Banks for early shipwreck sites constantly threatened by treasure hunters (Gray 2008; Leshikar-Denton 2002; Leshikar-Denton and Luna Erreguerena 2008). Limited scientific work has been conducted in the area because of distance from the mainland, difficult logistics, and lack of funding. In 1983, the IJ sponsored work by Leshikar-Denton, who recorded the building of a traditional Jamaican dugout canoe using hand tools (Leshikar 1985, 1988). Meanwhile, scientific archaeological projects have also focused on colonial sites, sites of enslaved populations, and prehistoric Taino sites, many of which have maritime aspects (Armstrong and Hauser 2009).

Independent Countries in the Lesser Antilles

Barbados

The 20th country to ratify the 2001 UNESCO Convention was Barbados. The country's action on 2 October 2008 triggered the three-month process whereby the Convention came into force on 2 January 2009.

The Barbados Museum and Historical Society (BMHS) is respected for its contributions to preserving the cultural heritage of Barbados (Leshikar-Denton 2002). Exhibits at the museum show a keen interest in the island's rich prehistoric and historical archaeological legacy. However, only recently has Barbados begun to

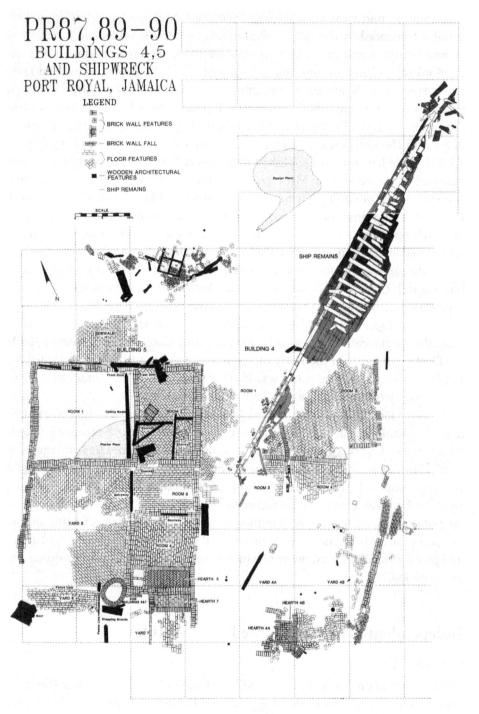

Figure 28.5 Port Royal, Jamaica, Building 4/5 excavation plan, showing remains of a ship that crashed into Building 4. Reproduced with the kind permission of the Port Royal Project, Center for Maritime Archaeology and Conservation, Texas A&M University.

address UCH. Since the 1990s, Barbados has received applications from organizations seeking to salvage shipwrecks in the island's waters; wisely, no such permits have been issued (Cummins, pers. comm.). Barbados has conducted an examination to delimit its Exclusive Economic Zone in accordance with the 1982 United Nations Convention on the Law of the Sea. Related to this action, the government has considered that a professional underwater archaeological survey should be conducted in order to evaluate the extent and nature of cultural remains existing in Barbados's waters.

Over the past decade, Barbados has been working toward development of a proposed law, the 2006 Preservation of Antiquities and Relics Bill, which includes underwater heritage (UNESCO 2008). During the 2008 Saint Lucia UNESCO meeting, Barbados representative Angelique Brathwaite of the Coastal Zone Management Unit (CZMU) updated the forum with information that major activities directed at UCH will not be undertaken in Barbados until passage of the 2006 bill. She noted that the 1998 Coastal Zone Management Act includes a measure of protection for UCH, especially shipwrecks, although specific regulations still need to be adopted. She highlighted that the BMHS under Director Alissandra Cummins is the principal contact for issues related to heritage matters and that the CZMU will work in association with the BMHS on UCH issues. Brathwaite noted that over 200 wrecks are reported to lie in the waters of Barbados.

Dominica

During the 2008 Saint Lucia UNESCO meeting, Terry Raymond of the Dominica National Commission for UNESCO and John Grimmer of the nonprofit organization Society for Heritage, Architectural Preservation and Enhancement (SHAPE) explained that in Dominica the focus has been on terrestrial heritage rather than UCH (UNESCO 2008). SHAPE has undertaken most of the island's work in heritage preservation. There is a problem with looting in Dominica, but there is also a ban on artifacts being taken out of the country. When Hurricane Dean uncovered a wreck, the local watersports association stepped in to help protect the site; by such action, dive operators empower themselves to protect their own industry. Raymond and Grimmer maintain that Dominica should initiate a shipwreck inventory and ratify the 2001 UNESCO Convention.

Nagelkerken, Knepper, and Hays (2004) have reported that they conducted a harbor survey of Roseau, Dominica. Meanwhile, the Gli Gli Carib Canoe Project has been undertaken by local heritage advocates: a traditional Carib canoe was constructed and sailed throughout the Eastern Caribbean to draw attention to and promote discourse around the history of Carib peoples and their culture throughout the region (Gli Gli 1997).

Grenada

According to heritage conservation officer Michael Jessamy, the framework for protection of UCH in Grenada is the National Trust Act of 1967, a law inadequate

regarding UCH (UNESCO 2008). He believes that the new Regional Heritage
Association (RHA) will provide a means for Eastern Caribbean States to collaborate
on heritage issues. He reported that a list of at least 174 wrecks in the waters of Grenada is being developed, and he expressed concern about pending development
plans at Port Louis, with no UCH assessments having been made. There is also a
shortage of capacities at museums to handle artifacts from shipwreck sites. On the
positive side, Grenada has a project in place with France to develop protected
underwater areas. In early 2009, a historic shipwreck was reported to Jessamy by a
local dive operation; discussions are under way to address how the dive operation
might assist government in ways to protect and manage the site (Jessamy, pers.
comm.). Grenada ratified the 2001 UNESCO Convention on 15 January 2009.

Saint Kitts and Nevis

McClean Hobson, director of Maritime Affairs for Saint Kitts and Nevis, attended
the 2008 Saint Lucia UNESCO meeting. He explained to the forum that the National
Conservation and Environmental Management Act (1987) and the Merchant Shipping Act (2002) afford some protection for UCH, with the 1987 Act enforced by the
Physical Planning and Environment Unit (UNESCO 2008). Terrestrial sites have
received more attention, but a pilot project undertaken in 2003 suggests the presence of more than 200 wrecks in the Basseterre Bay area. Hobson stated that taking
artifacts from them is prohibited.

Public opinion has been heading in the right direction. A recent article pointed
out that the islands' historical wrecks are threatened without adequate legal protection (SKNVibes.com 2008). In light of looting of UCH in neighboring Caribbean
islands, it called for a coordinated effort to reduce the risk to UCH, to identify and
record all of the wrecks in the islands' waters, and to ratify the 2001 Convention,
noting among benefits that it provides for states to take common action against
illegal recovery and trafficking of cultural property and to help each other by seizing
such UCH in their territories. It also includes practical guidelines on how to conduct research and to create a common approach to protecting UCH. Saint Kitts and
Nevis ratified the 2001 UNESCO Convention on 3 December 2009.

Saint Lucia

The Saint Lucia Archaeological and Historical Society, under the leadership of Eric
Branford, has a history of conducting professional research on Saint Lucia's terrestrial archaeological heritage. In 2003, Branford began efforts to bring professional
maritime archaeologists to Saint Lucia for a meeting about the 2001 UNESCO Convention. In 2003, Toni Carrell, Dorrick Gray, and Leshikar-Denton facilitated the
first regional meeting, hosted by the Saint Lucia National Commission for UNESCO.
A second meeting, organized jointly by the UNESCO Kingston Cluster Office for
the Caribbean and the Saint Lucia National Commission for UNESCO, was held in
2008 (UNESCO 2008). On 1 February 2007, Saint Lucia became the first Caribbean
country to ratify the 2001 UNESCO Convention and turned its attention toward

assisting and informing other Caribbean countries about its benefits. Soon afterward, Barbados, Cuba, Grenada, Haiti, Saint Kitts and Nevis, Saint Vincent and the Grenadines, and Trinidad and Tobago ratified the convention. Meanwhile, Branford helped formalize the RHA. Saint Lucia is a leader in promoting ethical protection and management of UCH, especially in the Eastern Caribbean subregion.

Saint Vincent and the Grenadines

Peter Pursglove, legal consultant in international law and treaties for the Ministry of Legal Affairs, reports that many ships wrecked in Saint Vincent and the Grenadines (SVG), but there is limited information available on UCH (UNESCO 2008). There is no inventory or database, and there are no specific national laws directed at UCH. He noted, however, that major pieces of legislation that attempt to protect local heritage include the Saint Vincent and the Grenadines National Trust Act, the Preservation of Historical Building and Antiques Act, the Marine Parks Act No. 9, the National Parks Act, the Fisheries Act, the Wild Life Act, and the Forest Resources Act. No public education has been undertaken, and there are no practical measures in place to excavate wrecks or to address trafficking or pillaging. SVG has developed awareness about protection, while noting that there are challenges. Pursglove maintained that presently there are inadequate financial resources to ensure adequate control, and that legislation can only be developed and enforced with adequate financing. However, SVG are capacity-building in diverse areas, including youth, and working to increase heritage preservation awareness among different segments of the population.

In 1997–1998, in cooperation with the Saint Vincent government and the Organization of American States, Florida State University and the Institute of Maritime History collaborated in the Kingstown Harbour Project to investigate an eighteenth-century shipwreck (FSU 2009). Remote sensing, surface mapping, artifact recovery, and limited excavations were undertaken.

On 8 November 2010, Saint Vincent and the Grenadines ratified the 2001 UNESCO Convention, becoming the most recent Caribbean country to sign on to this international treaty.

Trinidad and Tobago

According to Vel Lewis, director of the Trinidad National Museum and Art Gallery, French ships lost in a 1677 battle with the Dutch were discovered in the early 1990s during harbor dredging on the island of Tobago (Leshikar-Denton 2002; Lewis 1998). Soon thereafter, Trinidad and Tobago introduced the United Kingdom–based Protection of Wrecks Act (1994). Under the law, sites are the property of the state and can be designated as restricted areas; it is mandatory for finders to report wrecks; licenses may be issued; and there are penalties for illegal activity. In 1997 the government appointed a technical advisory committee to advise on site designation and license approvals and to consider conservation and disposition of artifacts. The intention was to compile an inventory of sites with the help of the local military museum, review the 1994 legislation, and develop a set of guidelines to approve requests from international bodies who expressed interest in working in the country. It is encouraging that on 27 July 2010, Trinidad and Tobago ratified the 2001 UNESCO Convention.

THE FUTURE

Despite limited resources, many Caribbean countries are addressing protection and management of their UCH in creative ways, while others are just getting started. The road is long and rugged, but the responsibility to protect and manage the region's UCH is compelling. Where shall we focus our energies? Perhaps it is best to build on the foundations that have been laid.

The 2001 UNESCO Convention and the 1996 ICOMOS Charter are the international documents in our tool kit to provide guidance. In the following order, Saint Lucia, Cuba, Barbados, Grenada, Haiti, Saint Kitts and Nevis, Trinidad and Tobago, and Saint Vincent and the Grenadines have ratified the 2001 Convention. Now all other Caribbean countries should follow their lead. Specific national legislation should be developed in tandem with the concepts provided in these international documents; in particular, commercial exploitation of UCH should be completely disallowed.

A number of policies point the way forward. Countries should identify key persons, train them, and place them in existing or newly developed competent authorities to guide in professional identification, protection, management, research, conservation, and interpretation of UCH. While gladly accepting cooperation from overseas institutions and individuals, sustainable regional and local programs and networks must be created. Look to the examples of INA, Ships of Discovery, TAMU, ECU, and the University of Southampton in Jamaica, the Cayman Islands, the Turks and Caicos Islands, and Anguilla to see how individual projects and passionate people can lead to national capacity building. Preserve sites in situ as a first option, but empower museums to interpret results of specialized archaeological excavation and research on significant sites where recovery and conservation are appropriate. Develop site inventories to know what UCH exists and to make informed decisions about how to protect and manage sites. Be aware that UCH treated in a sustainable way can provide benefits to education, culture, and tourism.

Unique responsibilities accompany archaeological excavation. They must be undertaken selectively and in such a way that scientific objectives, adequate funding, professional staff, and provisions for documentation, conservation, curation, reporting, and public interpretation are part of the overall plan. Multidisciplinary and multi-institutional collaborations need to be encouraged; regional and international cooperation benefit all peoples. Of primary importance is communication among governments, professionals, and the public in order to gain the most from the Caribbean's UCH. To succeed we must be creative, persevere, and, most of all, cooperate.

REFERENCES

Abandoned Wreck Law 5. 1966. Revised 1997. Cayman Islands: Cayman Islands Government.

Anguillian. 2010. Heritage Trail moves forward with help from local businessman Rayme Lake. *The Anguillian*. Rec. 5 February 2010. Online at www.anguillian.com/article/articleview/7910/1/140/. Accessed 5 February 2010.

Armstrong, Douglas V., and Mark W. Hauser. 2009. A sea of diversity: Historical archaeology in the Caribbean. In *International handbook of historical archaeology*, ed. Teresita Majewski and David Gaimster, 583–612. New York: Springer.

Arnaut, Gordon. 1998. Sunken loot worth millions suddenly in reach. *New York Times*, 27 November. Online at www.cubanet.org/CNews/y98/nov98/27e5.htm. Accessed 4 March 2010.

Azevedo, Lillian. 2009. The Anguilla Archaeological and Historical Society's 2009 Shipwreck Survey. *Maritime Archaeological and Historical Society (MAHS) News* 20 (2): 7–10.

Bass, George F., ed. 1972. *A history of seafaring based on underwater archaeology*. London: Thames and Hudson.

———, ed. 1988. *Ships and shipwrecks of the Americas*. London: Thames and Hudson.

———, ed. 2005. *Beneath the Seven Seas*. London: Thames and Hudson.

Bequette, Kathryn E. 1996. The HMS *Proselyte* project: Survey of an eighteenth-century British frigate in Great Bay, Saint Maarten. In *Underwater archaeology*, ed. S. R. James Jr. and C. Stanley, 73–75. Cincinnati: Society for Historical Archaeology.

Billings, Malcolm. 2002. Hunting for Cuba's hidden treasure. *BBC News*, 23 November. Online at http://news.bbc.co.uk/2/hi/programmes/from_our_own_correspondent/2503019.stm/. Accessed 4 March 2010.

Borrell, B., and J. Pedro. 1983a. *Arqueología submarina en La República Dominicana*. Santo Domingo: Comisión de Rescate Arqueológico Submarino.

———. 1983b. *Historia y rescate del galeon* Nuestra Senora de la Concepción. Santo Domingo: Comisión de Rescate Arqueológico Submarino.

Borrell, B., J. Pedro, Eugenio Pérez Montás, and Cruz Apestegui. 1997. *La Aventura del Guadalupe*. Barcelona and Madrid: Lunwerg.

Bratten, John R. 1998. Recent artifact finds from the Emanuel Point ship. In *Underwater archaeology*, ed. L. E. Babits, C. Fach, and R. Harris, 38–44. Atlanta: Society for Historical Archaeology.

Brea-Franco, Luis O., A. Ramón, and M. Victoriano. 1998. *Hacia un programa de desarrollo cultural para la República Dominicana, informes sobre el diagnóstico participativo del sector cultural*, Vol. 1: *Compendio de legislación cultural*. Santo Domingo: Consejo Presidencial de Cultura.

Carrell, Toni L. 2008. Uncovering Chippewa. *Times of the Island* 3: 97–102. Online at www.timespub.tc/2008/09/uncovering-chippewa/#commenting/. Accessed 5 February 2010.

Castro, Filipe. 2008. Puerto Rico. *SHA Newsletter* 41 (3): 70.

Castro, Filipe, and Carlos Fitzgerald. 2006. The Playa Damas shipwreck: An early sixteenth-century shipwreck in Panama. In *Underwater cultural heritage at risk: Managing natural and human impacts*, ed. Robert Grenier, David Nutley, and Ian Cochran, 38–40. Paris: ICOMOS.

Cayman Islands Maritime Heritage Trail Partners. 2003. *The Cayman Islands Maritime Heritage Trail, Grand Cayman and Sister Islands* (poster/brochures). Cayman Islands: Maritime Heritage Trail Partners.

Clifford, Sheila A. 1991. A preliminary report on a possible 17th-century shipwreck at Port Royal, Jamaica. In *Underwater archaeology: Proceedings from the Society for Historical Archaeology Conference*, ed. J. D. Broadwater, 80–83. Richmond: Society for Historical Archaeology.

Conrich, Bob. 1997. Neocolonialism in Anguilla. In *Underwater archaeology*, ed. D. C. Lakey, 44–49. Corpus Christi, TX: Society for Historical Archaeology.

Cook, Gregory D. 1997. Reader's Point wreck. In *Encyclopaedia of underwater and maritime archaeology*, ed. J. P. Delgado, 334. London: British Museum Press.

Cozzi, J. 1998. Hull remains of the Emanuel Point ship. In *Underwater archaeology*, ed. L. E. Babits, C. Fach, and R. Harris, 31–37. Atlanta: Society for Historical Archaeology.

Delgado, James P., ed. 1997. *Encyclopaedia of underwater and maritime archaeology*. London: British Museum Press.

Drewett, Peter L. 1992. *The Cayman Islands: Their potential in prehistoric research*. Institute of Archaeology Report. London: University College London.

———. 1996. *An archaeological survey of Cayman Brac and Little Cayman together with a test excavation in Great Cave, Cayman Brac, 1995*. Institute of Archaeology Report. London: University College London.

Echeverría Cotelo, Jorge. 2004. Cuba: The protection of underwater cultural heritage. In *Patrimonio cultural subacuático/Underwater cultural heritage*, ed. V. Marín, 52–55, 118–121. Havana: UNESCO.

Fernández González, Eddy, and Francisco Escobar Guio. 1998. CUBA. Presentations at the first meeting of the Technical Commission on Underwater Cultural Heritage, 15 June 1998. Santo Domingo: Forum of Ministers of Culture and Officials Responsible for Cultural Policy of Latin America and the Caribbean.

Fontánez-Aldea, Richard. 1997. Puerto Rico. In *Encyclopaedia of underwater and maritime archaeology*, ed. J. P. Delgado, 330. London: British Museum Press.

Foster, John W., and Charles D. Beeker. 1997. The conquest of a sinkhole: Initial archaeological investigations at El Manantial de la Aleta, East National Park, Dominican Republic. In *Underwater archaeology*, ed. D. C. Lakey, 27–32. Corpus Christi, TX: Society for Historical Archaeology.

FSU (Florida State University) Anthropology Web site. 2009. The Kingston Harbour Project. Online at www.anthro.fsu.edu/research/uw/research/ships/. Accessed 14 February 2009.

Garcia Ortiz, Gustavo Adolfo. 2005. *The Rincón Astrolabe shipwreck*. MA thesis, Texas A&M University.

Gaspar, Harold. 1998. Haiti. Presentation at the first meeting of the Technical Commission on Underwater Cultural Heritage, 15 June 1998. Santo Domingo: Forum of Ministers of Culture and Officials Responsible for Cultural Policy of Latin America and the Caribbean.

Geddes, Donald G., III. 1992. Archival research: The search for the Columbus caravels at St. Ann's Bay, Jamaica. In *Underwater archaeology: Proceedings from the Society for*

Historical Archaeology Conference, ed. D. H. Keith and T. L. Carrell, 148–151. Kingston, Jamaica: Society for Historical Archaeology.

Gli Gli, the Carib Canoe Project. 1997. Online at www.avirtualdominica.com/gligli/index. html/. Accessed 16 February 2009.

Gould, Richard J. 2007. *Disaster archaeology*. Salt Lake City: University of Utah Press.

Grattan, John, and Robin Torrence, eds. 2002. *Natural disasters, catastrophism and cultural change*. London: Routledge.

Gray, Dorrick E. 1997. Managing underwater archaeological resources: The Jamaican experience. Unpublished paper presented at the 30th Annual Society for Historical Archaeology Conference, 8–12 January, Corpus Christi, TX.

———. 2008. The Jamaican version: Public archaeology and the protection of underwater cultural heritage. In *Underwater and maritime archaeology in Latin America and the Caribbean*, ed. Margaret E. Leshikar-Denton and Pilar Luna Erreguerena, 245–257. Walnut Creek, CA: Left Coast Press.

Grenier, Robert, David Nutley, and Ian Cochran, eds. 2006. *Underwater cultural heritage at risk: Managing natural and human impacts*. Paris: ICOMOS.

Hall, Jerome L. 1991. The 17th-century merchant vessel at Monte Cristi Bay, Dominican Republic. In *Underwater archaeology: Proceedings from the Society for Historical Archaeology Conference*, ed. J. D. Broadwater, 84–87. Richmond: Society for Historical Archaeology.

———. 1992. A brief history of underwater salvage in the Dominican Republic. In *Underwater archaeology: Proceedings from the Society for Historical Archaeology Conference*, ed. D. H. Keith and T. L. Carrell, 35–40. Kingston, Jamaica: Society for Historical Archaeology.

———. 1993. The 17th-century merchant shipwreck in Monte Cristi Bay, Dominican Republic: The second excavation season interim report. In *Underwater archaeology: Proceedings from the Society for Historical Archaeology Conference*, ed. S. O. Smith, 95–101. Kansas City, MO: Society for Historical Archaeology.

———. 1994. Spanish coins, Dutch clay pipes, and an English ship: The 1993 Monte Cristi shipwreck project interim report. In *Underwater archaeology: Proceedings from the Society for Historical Archaeology Conference*, ed. R. P. Woodward and C. D. Moore, 32–39.Vancouver, BCE: Society for Historical Archaeology.

———. 1997a. Monte Cristi wreck. In *Encyclopaedia of underwater and maritime archaeology*, ed. J. P. Delgado, 283–284. London: British Museum Press.

———. 1997b. Puerto Rico: Island of enchantment? Paper presented at the Annual Society for Historical Archaeology Conference, 8–12 January, Corpus Christi, TX.

Hamilton, Donny L. 1991. A decade of excavations at Port Royal, Jamaica. In *Underwater archaeology: Proceedings from the Society for Historical Archaeology Conference*, ed. J. D. Broadwater, 90–94. Richmond: Society for Historical Archaeology.

———. 1997. Port Royal. In *Encyclopaedia of underwater and maritime archaeology*, ed. J. P. Delgado, 316–318. London: British Museum Press.

———. 2004. Port Royal: A buried treasure. In *Patrimonio cultural subacuatico/Underwater cultural heritage*, ed. V. Marín, 34–35, 102–103. Havana: UNESCO.

———. 2006. Port Royal, Jamaica: Archaeological past and development potential. In *Underwater cultural heritage at risk: Managing natural and human impacts*, ed. Robert Grenier, David Nutley, and Ian Cochran, 49–51. Paris: ICOMOS.

———. 2008. Port Royal, Jamaica: Archaeological past, present, and future. In *Underwater and maritime archaeology in Latin America and the Caribbean*, ed. Margaret E.

Leshikar-Denton and Pilar Luna Erreguerena, 259–269. Walnut Creek, CA: Left Coast Press.

Harris, Edward C. 1997. Underwater cultural resource management in Bermuda since World War II: The decline of Bermuda's underwater cultural resources. Unpublished paper presented at the 30th Annual Society for Historical Archaeology Conference, 8–12 January, Corpus Christi, TX.

———. 2008. Bermuda's shipwreck heritage. In *Underwater and maritime archaeology in Latin America and the Caribbean*, ed. Margaret E. Leshikar-Denton and Pilar Luna Erreguerena, 201–207. Walnut Creek, CA: Left Coast Press.

Haviser, J. B. 1997. Curaçao. In *Encyclopaedia of underwater and maritime archaeology*, ed. J. P. Delgado, 121. London: British Museum Press.

Historic Wrecks Ordinance, 1974. Turks and Caicos Government.

Ho, Bert. 2004. An archaeological study of *Glamis*: The role of a 19th-century iron barque. MA thesis, Florida State University.

ICOMOS International Charter on the Protection and Management of Underwater Cultural Heritage. 1996. Paris: ICOMOS. Online at www.international.icomos.org/charters/underwater_e.htm/. Accessed 31 January 2009.

James, Stephen R., and Charles Beeker. 1994. The fifteenth-century shipwrecks of La Isabela: Current investigations. In *Underwater archaeology: Proceedings from the Society for Historical Archaeology Conference*, ed. R. P. Woodward and C. D. Moore, 3–7. Vancouver, BCE: Society for Historical Archaeology.

Jameson, John H., and Della A. Scott-Ireton. 2007. *Out of the blue: Public interpretation of maritime cultural resources*. New York: Springer.

Keith, Donald H. 1987. The Molasses Reef wreck. PhD diss., Texas A&M University.

———. 1988. Shipwrecks of the explorers. In *Ships and shipwrecks of the Americas*, ed. G. F. Bass, 45–68. London: Thames and Hudson.

———. 1997a. Highborn Cay wreck. In *Encyclopaedia of underwater and maritime archaeology*, ed. J. P. Delgado, 192–193. London: British Museum Press.

———. 1997b. Molasses Reef wreck. In *Encyclopaedia of underwater and maritime archaeology*, ed. J. P. Delgado, 279–281. London: British Museum Press.

———. 1997c. Problems and progress in underwater archaeology in the Turks and Caicos Islands. In *Underwater archaeology*, ed. D. C. Lakey, 38–43. Corpus Christi, TX: Society for Historical Archaeology.

———. 2001. The Molasses Reef wreck and the Turks and Caicos National Museum: More than just another site. In *Memorias del Congreso Científico de Arqueología Subacuática ICOMOS*, coords. P. Luna Erreguerena and R. M. Roffiel, 200–212. Mexico City: Instituto Nacional de Antropología e Historia.

———. 2006. The Molasses Reef wreck. In *Underwater cultural heritage at risk: Managing natural and human impacts*, ed. R. Grenier, D. Nutley, and I. Cochran, 82–84. Paris: ICOMOS.

Keith, Donald H., and Toni L. Carrell. 2007. The search for *Trouvadore*, 2006 season. Report to the Department of Environment and Coastal Resources, Turks and Caicos Islands. Unpublished report on file, Ships of Discovery, Corpus Christi, TX.

———. 2009. The search for the slave ship *Trouvadore* and the US Navy anti-slavery patrol in the TCI: Three ships, one story. Symposium Abstract for Conference on Historical and Underwater Archaeology. Presenters Keith, Carrell, James W. Hunter III, Jason Burns, Michael Krivor, Veronica Veerkamp. Toronto: Society for Historical Archaeology.

Keith, Donald H., and Nigel Sadler. 2005. The search for the slave ship *Trouvadore*, 2004 season. Report to the Department of Environment and Coastal Resources, Turks and Caicos Islands. Unpublished report on file, Ships of Discovery, Corpus Christi, TX.

Keith, Donald H., and Joe Simmons. 1985. Analysis of hull remains, ballast and artifact distribution of a 16th-century shipwreck, Molasses Reef, British West Indies. *Journal of Field Archaeology* 12 (4): 411–424.

Khalifa, Aisha Bilkhair, and Jocelyn Chan-Mow. 2006. First meeting of the Renewed International Scientific Committee of *The Slave Route Project*, Final Report. Paris: UNESCO. Online at www.unesco.org/culture/en/slaveroute/pdf/Report_7th_Session_ISC_(February_2006).pdf/. Accessed 4 March 2010.

Leshikar, Margaret E. 1985. Construction of a dugout canoe in the parish of St. Ann, Jamaica. In *Proceedings of the Sixteenth Conference on Underwater Archaeology*, ed. P. F. Johnston, 48–51. Society for Historical Archaeology Special Publication Series No. 4. Pleasant Hill, CA: Society for Historical Archaeology.

———. 1988. The earliest watercraft: From rafts to Viking ships. In *Ships and shipwrecks of the Americas*, ed. G. F. Bass, 13–32. London: Thames and Hudson.

———. 1992. Investigation of the Wreck of the Ten Sail, Cayman Islands, British West Indies. In *Underwater archaeology: Proceedings from the Society for Historical Archaeology Conference*, ed. D. H. Keith and T. L. Carrell, 30–34. Kingston, Jamaica: Society for Historical Archaeology.

———. 1993. The 1794 Wreck of the Ten Sail, Cayman Islands, British West Indies: A historical study and archaeological survey. PhD diss., Texas A&M University.

Leshikar-Denton, Margaret E. 1996. Underwater cultural resource management in Mexico and the Caribbean. In *Underwater archaeology*, ed. S. R. James Jr. and C. Stanley, 57–60. Cincinnati: Society for Historical Archaeology.

———. 1997a. Problems and progress in underwater cultural resource management in the Caribbean, Bermuda and Mexico. In *30th Annual Conference on Historical and Underwater Archaeology: Abstracts*, 36. Corpus Christi, TX: Society for Historical Archaeology.

———. 1997b. Underwater cultural resource management: A new concept in the Cayman Islands. In *Underwater archaeology*, ed. D. C. Lakey, 33–37. Corpus Christi, TX: Society for Historical Archaeology.

———. 1997c. Caribbean, Cayman Islands, Wreck of the Ten Sail. In *Encyclopaedia of underwater and maritime archaeology*, ed. J. P. Delgado, 86–89, 91–92, 416. London: British Museum Press.

———. 1998. Maritime archaeology in the Caribbean. In *Indian Ocean Week 1997 Proceedings*, ed. G. Henderson, 62–72. Perth: Western Australian Museum.

———. 2001a. Caribbean underwater cultural heritage at Y2K. In *Memorias del Congreso Científico de Arqueología Subacuática ICOMOS*, coords. P. Luna Erreguerena and R. M. Roffiel, 70–73 and addendum. Mexico City: Instituto Nacional de Antropologia e Historia.

———. 2001b. Caribbean underwater cultural heritage in the Year 2001. *Foundation Magazine* (Cayman National Cultural Foundation) 1: 1.

———. 2002. Problems and progress in the Caribbean. In *International handbook of underwater archaeology*, ed. C. Ruppé and J. Barstad, 279–298. New York: Kluwer Academic/Plenum.

———. 2004. The situation in the Caribbean. In *Patrimonio cultural subacuático/ Underwater cultural heritage*, ed. V. Marín, 10–15, 80–85. Havana: UNESCO.

———. 2005. Tracing the Wreck of the Ten Sail, Grand Cayman, Cayman Islands. In
    Beneath the Seven Seas, ed. G. Bass, 206–209. London: Thames and Hudson.

———. In press. *The Wreck of the Ten Sail*. Gainesville: University Press of Florida.

Leshikar-Denton, Margaret E., and Bert Ho (with contributions by D. Scott-Ireton, A.
    Evans, and W. Anderson). 2004. *The probable Glamis site: Archaeological mapping and
    potential for a shipwreck preserve, Grand Cayman, Cayman Islands*. Cayman Islands
    National Museum Shipwreck Preserve Series 1. Cayman Islands: CINM.

Leshikar-Denton, Margaret E., and Pilar Luna Erreguerena. 2008. *Underwater and
    maritime archaeology in Latin America and the Caribbean*. World Archaeological
    Congress, One World Archaeology Series. Walnut Creek, CA: Left Coast Press.

Leshikar-Denton, Margaret E., and Philip E. Pedley, eds. 1994. The Wreck of the Ten Sails,
    vol. 2 of *Our Islands' Past*. Grand Cayman: Cayman Islands National Archive and
    Cayman Free Press.

Leshikar-Denton, Margaret E., and Della A. Scott-Ireton. 2007. A maritime heritage trail
    and shipwreck preserves for the Cayman Islands. In *Out of the blue: Public interpreta-
    tion of maritime cultural resources*, ed. John H. Jameson and Della A. Scott-Ireton,
    64–84. New York: Springer.

———. 2008. The Cayman Islands' experience: Yesterday, today, and tomorrow. In *Under-
    water and maritime archaeology in Latin America and the Caribbean*, ed. Margaret E.
    Leshikar-Denton and Pilar Luna Erreguerena, 221–244. Walnut Creek, CA: Left Coast
    Press.

Lewis, Vel. 1998. Trinidad and Tobago. Presentation at the First Meeting of the Technical
    Commission on Underwater Cultural Heritage, 15 June. Santo Domingo: Forum of
    Ministers of Culture and Officials Responsible for Cultural Policy of Latin America
    and the Caribbean.

Luna Erreguerena, Pilar. 1997. Stepping stones of Mexican underwater archaeology. In
    Underwater archaeology, ed. D. C. Lakey, 50–53. Corpus Christi, TX: Society for
    Historical Archaeology.

———. 1998. Aspects of Mexican underwater archaeology. In *Indian Ocean Week 1997
    Proceedings*, ed. G. Henderson, 36–41. Perth: Western Australian Museum.

———. 2002. Mexico: A country with a rich underwater legacy. In *International handbook
    of underwater archaeology*, ed. C. Ruppé and J. Barstad, 269–278. New York: Kluwer
    Academic/Plenum.

Malcom, Corey. 1997. St. John's Bahamas wreck. In *Encyclopaedia of underwater and
    maritime archaeology*, ed. J. P. Delgado, 351–352. London: British Museum Press.

Moreau, Jean Pierre. 1988. *Guide des trésors archéologiques sous-marins des Petites Antilles
    d'après les archives anglaises, espagnoles françaises des XVI°, XVII°, XVIII° siècles*.
    Clamart: Jean Pierre Moreau.

Nagelkerken, Wil. 1985. Preliminary report on the determination of the location of the
    historical anchorage at Orange Bay, St. Eustatius, Netherlands Antilles. In *Proceedings
    of the Sixteenth Conference on Underwater Archaeology*, ed. P. F. Johnston, 60–76.
    Society for Historical Archaeology Special Publication Series No. 4. Pleasant Hill, CA:
    Society for Historical Archaeology.

———. 1989. Survey of the Dutch frigate *Alphen*, which exploded and sank in 1778 in the
    harbour of Curaçao. In *Proceedings of the Thirteenth International Congress for
    Caribbean Archaeology*, ed. E. Ayubi and J. Haviser, 771–792. Willemstad, Curaçao:
    Archaeological-Anthropological Institute of the Netherlands Antilles.

———. 1998. Nineteenth-century Dutch Pearlware recovered in the harbor of Curaçao,
    Netherlands Antilles. In *Underwater Archaeology*, ed. L. E. Babits, C. Fach, and R.
    Harris, 104–110. Atlanta: Society for Historical Archaeology.

Nagelkerken, Wil, and Edwin Ayubi. 1997. Underwater cultural resource management in the Netherlands Antilles. Paper presented at the 30th Annual Society for Historical Archaeology Conference, 8–12 January, Corpus Christi, TX.

Nagelkerken, Wil, and Raymond Hayes. 2002. *The historical anchorage of Kralendijk, Bonaire, Netherlands Antilles, including the Wreckage of the Dutch Brigantine Sirene (1831).* STIMANA Marine Archaeological Series 2. Curaçao: STIMANA.

———. 2008. The historical anchorage of Kralendijk, Bonaire, Netherlands Antilles. In *Underwater and maritime archaeology in Latin America and the Caribbean,* ed. Margaret E. Leshikar-Denton and Pilar Luna Erreguerena, 293–301. Walnut Creek, CA: Left Coast Press.

Nagelkerken, Wil, Dennis Knepper, and Raymond Hayes. 2004. Preliminary report from a survey of the historical anchorage in the harbour of Roseau, Dominica. Foundation for Marine Archaeology of the Netherlands Antilles (STIMANA).

Nagelkerken, Wil, Theo van der Giessen, Raymond Hayes, and Dennis Knepper. 2008. Development of maritime archaeological tourism using the wreck of the English SS *Mediator* in Curaçao. In *Underwater and maritime archaeology in Latin America and the Caribbean,* ed. Margaret E. Leshikar-Denton and Pilar Luna Erreguerena, 283–292. Walnut Creek, CA: Left Coast Press.

National Shipwreck Inventory. n.d. Unpublished files, Cayman Islands Government.

Neville, John C., Robert S. Neyland, and James M. Parrent. 1992. The search for Columbus's last ships: The 1991 field season. In *Underwater archaeology: Proceedings from the Society for Historical Archaeology Conference,* ed. D. H. Keith and T. L. Carrell, 148–151. Kingston, Jamaica: Society for Historical Archaeology.

NOAA Ocean Explorer. 2008. Search for the slave ship *Trouvadore* 2008 and the US Navy ships *Chippewa* and *Onkahey.* Online at http://oceanexplorer.noaa.gov/explorations/08trouvadore/welcome.html/. Accessed 5 February 2010.

Pateman, Michael. 2004. The evolution of the protection of underwater cultural heritage in the Bahamas. In *Patrimonio cultural subacuático/Underwater cultural heritage,* ed. V. Marín, 46–47, 112–113. Havana: UNESCO.

Pineda, Jorge. 2009. Sunken treasure hunt yields fabulous baubles of Dominican coast. *Domincan Today,* 24 November 2009. Online. Available at www.dominicantoday.com/dr/local/2009/11/24/33981/Sunken-treasure-hunt-yields-fabulous-baubles-off-Domini-can-coast/. Accessed 4 March 2010.

Protection of Wrecks Act. 1973. United Kingdom Government.

Protection of Wrecks Act. 1994. Trinidad and Tobago Government.

Report on the Status of the Convention for Safeguarding Underwater Cultural Heritage. 1998. Tenth Meeting of the Forum of Ministers of Culture and Officials Responsible for Cultural Policy of Latin America and the Caribbean, 4–5 December, Bridgetown, Barbados.

Ruppé, C., and J. Barstad, eds. 2002. *International handbook of underwater archaeology.* New York: Kluwer Academic/Plenum.

Sadler, Nigel. 2008. The sinking of the slave ship *Trouvadore*: Linking the past to the present. In *Underwater and maritime archaeology in Latin America and the Caribbean,* ed. Margaret E. Leshikar-Denton and Pilar Luna Erreguerena, 209–220. Walnut Creek, CA: Left Coast Press.

Santiago, Pedro J. 1990. *Estudios sobre comercio maritimo, naufragios y rescates submarinos en la Republica Dominicana.* Santo Domingo: Comisión de Rescate Arqueológico Submarino and Museo de las Casas Reales.

Santo Domingo Declaration. 1998. Forum of ministers of culture and officials responsible for cultural policy of Latin America and the Caribbean: First meeting of the technical commission on underwater cultural heritage, 16 June.

SCIAA (South Carolina Institute of Archaeology and Anthropology). 2009. Special
    projects, Bahamas. Online at www.cas.sc.edu/sciaa/. Accessed 14 February 2009.
Scott-Ireton, Della A. 1998. An examination of the Luna colonization fleet. In *Underwater
    archaeology*, ed. L. E. Babits, C. Fach, and R. Harris, 25–30. Atlanta: Society for
    Historical Archaeology.
———. 2003. Florida's underwater archaeological preserves. In *Submerged cultural resource
    management: Preserving and interpreting our sunken maritime heritage*, ed. J. D. Spirek
    and D. A. Scott-Ireton, 95–105. New York: Kluwer Academic/Plenum.
SKNVibes.com. 2008. A call for ratification of culture convention. 1 April. Basseterre, St.
    Kitts and Nevis: SKNVibes.com.
Slave Ship Trouvadore. 2008. Online at www.slaveshiptrouvadore.com. Accessed 5
    February 2010.
Smith, C. Wayne. 2008. Preservation of waterlogged archaeological glass using polymers.
    In *Underwater and maritime archaeology in Latin America and the Caribbean*, ed.
    Margaret E. Leshikar-Denton and Pilar Luna Erreguerena, 271–282. Walnut Creek,
    CA: Left Coast Press.
Smith, Clifford E., Jr., and Edward C. Harris. 2002. Underwater cultural heritage in
    Bermuda. In *International handbook of underwater archaeology*, ed. C. Ruppé and J.
    Barstad, 299–312. New York: Kluwer Academic/Plenum.
Smith, Roger C. 1981. The maritime heritage of the Cayman Islands: Contributions in
    nautical archaeology. MA thesis, Texas A&M University.
———. 1988a. The voyages of Columbus: The search for his ships. In *Ships and shipwrecks of
    the Americas*, ed. G. F. Bass, 33–44. London: Thames and Hudson.
———. 1988b. Treasure ships of the Spanish Main: The Iberian-American maritime
    empires. In *Ships and shipwrecks of the Americas*, ed. G. F. Bass, 85–106. London:
    Thames and Hudson.
———. 1991. Florida's underwater archaeological preserves. In *Underwater archaeology:
    Proceedings from the Society for Historical Archaeology Conference*, ed. J. D. Broadwa-
    ter, 43–46. Richmond, VA: Society for Historical Archaeology.
———. 1993. *Vanguard of empire*. Oxford: Oxford University Press.
———. 1994. The ship at Emanuel Point: An examination of Florida's earliest shipwreck. In
    *Underwater archaeology: Proceedings from the Society for Historical Archaeology
    Conference*, ed. R. P. Woodward and C. D. Moore, 14–18. Vancouver: Society for
    Historical Archaeology.
———. 2000. *The maritime heritage of the Cayman Islands*. Gainesville: University Press of
    Florida.
———. 2002. Florida frontiers: From ice age to New Age. In *International handbook of
    underwater archaeology*, ed. C. Ruppé and J. Barstad, 143–167. New York: Kluwer
    Academic/Plenum.
Smith, Roger C., John R. Bratten, Joe Cozzi, and Keith Plaskett. 1999. *The Emanuel Point
    ship: Archaeological investigations, 1997–1998*. Report of Investigations No. 68.
    Pensacola: Archaeology Institute, University of West Florida.
Smith, Roger C., James Spirek, John Bratten, and Della Scott-Ireton. 1995. *The Emanuel Point
    ship: Archaeological investigations, 1992–1995*. Tallahassee: Bureau of Archaeological
    Research, Division of Historical Resources, Florida Department of State.
Stokes, Ann V., and William F. Keegan. 1993. *A settlement survey for prehistoric archaeological
    sites on Grand Cayman*. Department of Anthropology Miscellaneous Project Report
    52. Gainesville: Florida Museum of Natural History.
UNESCO. 2004. *Patrimonio cultural subacuático (Underwater cultural heritage): América
    Latina y el Caribe*. Havana: UNESCO.

————. 2008. Final report on the 27–28 March 2008 Regional Seminar on the Protection of the Underwater Cultural Heritage. Saint Lucia: Saint Lucia National Commission for UNESCO.

UNESCO Convention on the Protection of the Underwater Cultural Heritage. 2001. Paris: UNESCO. Online at http://portal.unesco.org/en/ev.php-URL_ID=13520&URL_DO=DO_TOPIC&URL_SECTION=201.html/. Accessed 31 January 2009.

UNESCO/ICUCH/Ministry of Culture of Colombia Heritage Direction (w/d) Memoirs. 2004. Regional workshop seminar of Latin American and the Caribbean community about UNESCO's Convention on the Protection of the Underwater Cultural Heritage. Bogota: UNESCO.

CHAPTER 29

MARITIME ARCHAEOLOGY OF THE NORTHERN GULF OF MEXICO: ARCHAEOLOGY FROM THE AGE OF EXPLORATION TO THE TWILIGHT OF SAIL

AMY BORGENS

INTRODUCTION

THE Gulf of Mexico was charted in the early sixteenth century CE as part of an expansive exploration of the New World launched by the Spanish Crown. Its discovery instigated a competition for territorial acquisition in the Gulf as Spain, France, and England, and later the United States vied for dominance in the region. By the mid-1800s, centuries of boundary disputes, insurgencies, and revolutions culminated in a reenvisioned Gulf of Mexico, wherein European occupation had been supplanted by emerging independent powers.

The subtropical waters of the Gulf are bounded by the United States, Mexico, and Cuba. Florida has the largest expanse of Gulf coastline in the United States, followed by Louisiana, Texas, Alabama, and Mississippi. The Mexican portion of the Gulf Coast extends from the state of Tamaulipas to the northern tip of Quintana Roo, a distance of approximately 2,240 km (1,392 miles) (see Luna Erreguerena in this volume). Important historic ports in the Gulf include Pensacola, Mobile, New Orleans, and Galveston in the United States; Veracruz, Mexico; and Havana, Cuba (Figure 29.1). It is estimated that there are over 4,000 shipwrecks in the Gulf of Mexico; 75% to 80% of these wrecks are believed to lie within 6.2 miles of the coastline (Garrison et al. 1989: 85, 118; Pearson et al. 2003: 3-2, 4-2, 7-4).

The ability to conduct archaeological work in the region is hindered by many of the same environmental attributes that led to the original wreck events. The coastal topography was (and is) often shallow, necessitating the use of vessels that were smaller and better adapted to shallow bays and rivers. Even for such craft, bay and riverine entry could be very difficult. Weather patterns in the Gulf include two periods that produce damaging storms: the hurricane season, from late June through November, and the strong northers that develop between October and April. These same hazards persist today and can make long-term archaeological documentation of wreck sites difficult.

High-visibility dive environments in some areas of the Gulf facilitate discovery and recordation of wreck sites. Such conditions also enable historic sites to be more easily scavenged by collectors and salvagers. Government involvement and intervention has led to the protection of some archaeological sites. Florida, for example, has a large number of shipwrecks in high-visibility environments. The state has

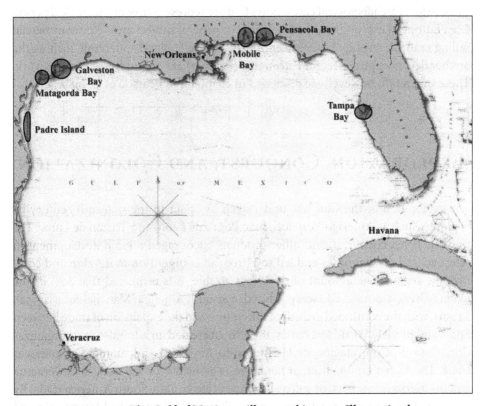

Figure 29.1 The Gulf of Mexico as illustrated in 1808. Illustration by the author modified from Dessiou 1808.

actively pursued public outreach initiatives, including the creation of state preserves for historic wrecks and the production of materials to educate recreational divers about shipwreck sites (Smith, Finegold, and Stephens 1990; Scott-Ireton 2003; see Cohn and Dennis in this volume). Unfortunately, government actions to protect these wrecks often postdate the recovery of their respective artifact assemblages.

Outside these high-visibility areas, much of the Gulf of Mexico is considered a "blackwater" environment in which shipwrecks are located accidentally, often by commercial fishermen, or through remote-sensing surveys. A large portion of marine archaeological survey and testing in the Gulf of Mexico is done within these low-visibility conditions ahead of oil and gas industry growth, public works, and urban development. Many government-mandated projects do not receive the capital and scholarly research of academic studies; however, they attest to the variety of wrecks in Gulf waters. Refinements in remote-sensing data collection techniques, coupled with increased regulatory oversight, and oil and gas expansion have spurred an increase in detection of historic wrecks within the Gulf (see Gearhart in this volume).

The following discourse summarizes the area's specific shipwreck sites so that the breadth of work and variety of wreck types for the region can be illustrated. Historical periods are emphasized to demonstrate the quantity, or lack thereof, of archaeological discoveries related to notable historic events. Each section is dedicated to brief archaeological case studies that are representative of a historical period (e.g., European exploration, the Civil War) or general subject area (e.g., commercial sailing craft, steamships). Seventeenth-century Gulf inland watercraft such as the birchbark canoe, pirogue, and *bateau plat* (flatboat) are not addressed in this work. These watercraft, however, are discussed in chapter 4 of Pearson et al. 1989.

EXPLORATION, CONQUEST, AND COLONIZATION

The exploration of the Gulf was undertaken by Spain in the sixteenth century by explorers such as Amerigo Vespucci, Juan Ponce de León, and Tristán de Luna.[1] The trade in silver, cochineal, and other products encouraged a rapid development in select coastal communities and led to European competition to develop and colonize the region. The amount of trade was sizable. It is estimated that 80% of the world's silver (1550–1800 CE) was produced in Spanish America (Marichal 2006: 25–52). In 1503, with the continued growth of the empire and the expansion of trade between Spain and its New World territories, the Crown created an administrative organization, Casa de Contratación de las Indies, to formalize and monitor its overseas trade. The *Nueva España* fleet, or *flota*, was responsible for the trade with Veracruz and the *Tierra Firme* fleet, or *galeones*, concentrated on the South America trade. By the mid-sixteenth century, the two fleets collectively disembarked from Spain and met at the Cape Verde Islands before separating and heading for their respective localities. For the return trip, the fleets rendezvoused at Havana before proceeding for Spain through the Straits of Florida. The fleet system reached its peak between 1590 and 1600; the last fleet set sail in 1789 (Parry 1990: 56–59; Peterson 1975: 52–96). The trade routes utilized by Spanish fleets invariably made them susceptible to inherent seaborne hazards, such as hurricanes, and the man-made threats of privateering and warfare.

An early shipwreck discovered in the northern Gulf of Mexico was from a *Nueva España* fleet. Its discovery and salvage prompted the creation and enactment of state legislation to protect historic wreck sites. *Espíritu Santo* was one of four ships that disembarked from Veracruz in April 1554, carrying 400 individuals and freighted with silver, gold, cochineal, and other products destined for Spain. During the voyage from Veracruz to Havana in late April, a storm blew the vessels due west toward the coast. Three of the four vessels—the *San Esteban*, *Santa María de Yciar*, and *Espíritu Santo*—broke apart on the shore at Costa de Madalena, present-day Padre Island, Texas. More than 300 passengers and crew would eventually perish. A salvage expedition was launched by Spain in July 1554, though only 70% of the 51,330 pounds of precious metal were recovered in the effort (Davis 1977: 15–17, 24, 34).

In late 1967, Platoro Inc., a treasure-hunting enterprise from Gary, Indiana, began to salvage one of the wrecks. A court order halted work in December, since the locations of the wrecks were in Texas tidal waters and, as such, were considered the property of the state. Due to the manner of recovery, and the loss of invaluable information regarding artifact provenience and the wreck itself, a state antiquities code was passed that established the Texas Antiquities Committee (TAC, now merged with the Texas Historical Commission [THC]). The TAC launched field efforts in 1972 and 1973 and documented the *Espíritu Santo* and *San Esteban*. Additional surveys in 1974 and 1975 located two magnetic anomalies associated with the wreck sites. Ground-truthing of the anomalies located more artifacts and identified a site that is believed to be a small Spanish salvage vessel. The site of the third wreck, *Santa María de Yciar*, was presumed to have been largely destroyed by dredging of the Mansfield Cut in the 1940s. A variety of materials were recovered from *Espíritu Santo* and *San Esteban*, including navigational tools, chain mail, ceramics, stoneware, woodworking tools, silver *reales*, and bombards (Arnold and Weddle 1978; Smith 1988: 89).

The oldest identified shipwreck in Florida was part of a Spanish expedition to colonize the Florida coast. It was discovered in 1992 during a state survey for historic wreck sites in Pensacola Bay. Two multiyear investigations of the site, known as the Emanuel Point shipwreck, were conducted under a partnership between the Florida Bureau of Archaeological Research (BAR), the University of West Florida (UWF), and the Historic Pensacola Preservation Board. The Emanuel Point shipwreck, believed to be one of the larger vessels in the fleet of Tristán de Luna, was located in 4 m (13 ft) of water in Pensacola Bay near Emanuel Point. Luna led an expedition of 11 vessels in 1559 to establish a colony at the port of Ochuse (modern Pensacola). The expedition arrived in August only to be struck by a hurricane the following month. All but four of the ships were destroyed, and the loss of life and damage to supplies doomed the colony. The site was abandoned in 1561 and would not be revisited until a presidio was established at the location in 1698 (Smith 2001: 295; Smith 2009: 79; Worth 2009: 83–84).

The well-preserved hull, estimated to measure 28–29 m (92–95 ft) in length, was buried under a mound of ballast stones, indicating that the vessel's original cargo was likely salvaged. Over 5,000 artifacts were recovered from within the bilge and on the periphery of the site, including wooden tools, galley ware, faunal remains, ceramics, over 3,000 g of liquid mercury, and an armor breastplate (Smith 2001: 295–300; Smith et al. 1998, 1999). A second vessel from the fleet was discovered in 2006 during remote-sensing surveys conducted by archaeologists from UWF. Diver investigations of the site in 2007, known as the Emanuel Point II shipwreck, defined the extent of the wreck and confirmed the vessel's nationality (Clark 2007; Cook 2009: 93–100). The wreck has been the focus of concurrent UWF field schools whose activities are chronicled on the project's "field journal," which is hosted online by the Museum of Underwater Archaeology.

The Spanish Crown was not alone in its efforts to colonize and explore the Gulf of Mexico. During the late seventeenth and early eighteenth centuries, France founded the port of New Orleans and established settlements at Biloxi Bay and Mobile Bay. An ill-fated attempt to colonize the Texas coast was led by French explorer Robert Cavelier, Sieur de La Salle, in 1865. The expedition was originally composed of four vessels and over 300 crew and settlers. In February 1686, the last remaining vessel, the *barque longue La Belle*, foundered during a storm on the southern shore of Matagorda Bay. A 1978 survey conducted by the TAC attempted to locate the vessel but was unsuccessful. A second survey by the THC in 1995 finally discovered the wreck at a depth of 3.7 m (12 ft) (Figure 29.2). Concerns regarding detailed data recovery of the site in low-visibility conditions influenced the decision to create a cofferdam around the wreck of *La Belle* so that the site could be drained and approached as a terrestrial excavation (Bruseth and Turner 2005: 37–41, 48).

At the time of its discovery, *La Belle* was considered one of the most important archaeological finds in North America and was one of the largest conservation projects ever undertaken in the United States (Locke 1999: 70). During the course of the 1996–1997 excavation, nearly a million artifacts were recovered (including 750,000 glass beads), some of which were contained in the 85 barrels and 10 chests of goods stored within the hull. Artifacts from *La Belle* include three bronze cannon, an iron swivel gun, flintlock muskets, rigging, navigational tools, woodworking tools, galley ware, and trade goods such as glass beads, brass pins, and iconographic rings. The remaining hull, measuring 15.9 by 4 m (52.3 by 13 ft) and representing 40% of the vessel, was disassembled on site and transported to the Conservation Research Laboratory at Texas A&M University (TAMU) for treatment. Detailed cleaning of the timbers revealed Roman numerals carved into the keel and many of the major frames (see Pevny in this volume). This numerical system divided the hull into four quadrants, with the main mast as the central point. This feature indicated that *La Belle* was created as a "ship kit" wherein the constituent pieces could be carried as cargo and later assembled (Bruseth and Turner 2005).

Figure 29.2 The hull of *La Belle*, following excavation and removal of the artifact assemblage. Reproduced with the kind permission of the Texas Historical Commission.

The earliest historic shipwreck site off the Louisiana coast was found by Texas shrimper Curtis Blume in 1979. *El Nuevo Constante* was one of two Spanish fleet vessels blown aground during a hurricane in 1766. *El Nuevo Constante* was initially part of the *Nueva España* fleet of 1765, though delays in preparing for the journey prevented the ship from joining the convey. Instead *El Nuevo Constante* departed later in the company of two other merchant ships (Pearson and Hoffman 1995: 23–24). Following the discovery, the state of Louisiana, through the Department of Culture, Recreation, and Tourism, entered into an agreement with Curtis Blume and his associates to excavate the site. Archaeological investigations of the wreck commenced in 1980 and concluded in February 1981. Divers recorded the remaining 38.9 by 7.9 m (127.5 by 26 ft) of hull. Hundreds of artifacts were recovered from the site, including three 9-pounder cannon, copper ingots, silver and gold bullion, lead sheathing, ceramics, and glassware (Pearson 1981; Pearson and Hoffman 1995).

REDEFINING THE GULF COAST TERRITORIES

The late eighteenth and early nineteenth centuries in the northern Gulf of Mexico were characterized by two emerging nationalistic trends: the movements within New Spain to secede from European control, and aggressive actions by the new U.S. power to expand its borders.[2] Louisiana, with its pivotal port, New Orleans, was acquired in 1804 by the United States as part of the Louisiana Purchase. Spanish Florida was ceded to Great Britain in 1763, though the territory fell under Spanish control again with the Treaty of Paris in 1783. With ratification of the Adams-Onís Treaty in 1821, the United States ultimately gained control of West Florida (which included present-day Mississippi, Alabama, and a portion of Louisiana) and east Florida.

As the United States gained Spanish lands east of the Mississippi River, the new nation also unofficially aided insurgencies in New Spain by supplying arms and assisting the privateer navies employed by the revolutionaries. After Mexican independence in 1821, however, the United States pursued its own interests by encouraging and financially assisting the Texas Revolution (1835–1836), and later by instigating the Mexican-American War (1846–1848). The annexation of the Republic of Texas in 1845 and the acquisition of California, Nevada, Utah, and portions of New Mexico, Colorado, Arizona, and Wyoming in 1848 (as part of the Treaty of Guadalupe Hidalgo) completed the United States' expansion to its current continental boundaries. Less than two decades later, Gulf U.S. territories would align themselves with the Confederate States of America.

Early Naval Activities and Privateering in the Gulf of Mexico

During the late eighteenth and early nineteenth centuries there was an increase in privateering in the region. The French privateers were being driven from the Caribbean by the British Navy at a time when insurgent groups in New Spain were in need of an improvised fleet. The cooperation between these groups was discovered to be beneficial to both parties: French privateers acquired letters of marque to harass Spanish shipping, and the revolutionaries in turn gained the cooperation of the armed French privateer squadrons. With the United States engaged in war with Britain (1812–1815), the federal government likewise issued letters of marque for American vessels wishing to engage British shipping. Over 180 privateers were operating out of the eastern Caribbean, Cuba, and New Orleans during the early nineteenth century (Faye 1940: 433). Spanish and British naval fleets patrolled the Gulf, in addition to the small Spanish and U.S. coastal squadrons trying to control the rampant privateering. In this hostile climate, merchant vessels were sometimes defensively armed to protect against such hazards.

Gulf regional navies, mirroring the use of small watercraft for coastal maritime commerce, were often composed of small versatile vessels. The Spanish, United States, and Mexican coastal fleets included vessels such as *galeras* (galleys), sloops, gunboats, large launches, pilot boats, and schooners. Privateers in the Gulf utilized multiple vessel types: armed corvettes, ships, gunboats, schooners, oared feluccas and small launches, and merchant cargo carriers. Many privateer vessels were constructed or selected to be fast and easily maneuverable in shallow water. Though this period is accentuated by naval, privateer, and related merchant losses, the wrecks of few armed vessels have been discovered.

Two shipwrecks at Deadman's Island, Florida, attest to the location's use for careening and repairing vessels during the British occupation. The Deadman's Island shipwreck was discovered in 1988 and documented by UWF students in conjunction with BAR; the Town Point wreck was discovered in 1993 and investigated by archaeologists from Southern Oceans Archaeological Research Inc. The size and condition of the vessels, recovered artifacts, and historic research identified candidates for the shipwrecks, though there is no conclusive evidence to pair the wreck with its historical counterpart. The wrecks at Deadman's Island are likely the remains of the sloops-of-war HMS *Florida* (a patrol schooner) and the 14-gun HMS *Stork*. The vessels were abandoned at the island in 1778 and 1779, as both were too unfit to repair (Scott-Ireton 2009; Smith 1999: 93–97).

The wreck of another armed sailing craft was discovered at the historical entrance into Matagorda Bay by the National Underwater Marine Agency (NUMA) in 1998. An English carronade manufactured by the Low Moor Foundry and post-dating 1795 was recovered from the site and is the property of the state of Texas (Dodsworth 1971: 127–128; Wilbanks, Hal, and McKee 2000). This deeply buried wreck site has not been reassessed since its initial discovery and could be related to known privateer wrecks or to the Mexican military sloop *General Bustamante*, wrecked in 1830 and lost in the area (Elozúa 1830; Borgens 2004: 46–47).

A deepwater wreck off the coast of Louisiana could be an early-nineteenth-century privateer. In the summer of 2007, an investigation of a shipwreck off the Louisiana coast was conducted by researchers from TAMU and Minerals Management Service (MMS; now the Bureau of Ocean Energy Management, Regulation, and Enforcement [BOEMRE]). The wreck study included documentation of the site and recovery of visible artifacts. Due to the depth of the shipwreck, 1,220 m (4,000 ft), a remotely operated vehicle (ROV) was utilized for the artifact recovery. The site, termed the Mardi Gras shipwreck, is characterized by a northwest–southeast linear artifact distribution measuring 14.8 by 4.4 m (48.5 by 14.3 ft). The major features visible above the sediment were a single stove, a 9-pounder cannon, a box of mixed arms, and examples of ferrous shot (Figure 29.3). Approximately 10% of the site was investigated during the study. The investigation of the shipwreck is considered the deepest underwater archaeological excavation conducted in the Gulf of Mexico. Over 2,000 artifacts were recovered from the site, including a

Figure 29.3 Detail of the Mardi Gras shipwreck. The weapons box and hull timbers were exposed during excavation. Photomosaic created from ROV images provided courtesy of Texas A&M University.

cannon, two Mexican-minted silver *reales* (one dated 1808), British-manufactured navigational tools, buttons, creamware, French spoons, and earthenware that is possibly French and German in origin (Ford et al. 2008; Randall 2008). The wooden-hulled sailing vessel is tentatively identified as a schooner. Given its assorted armament, this vessel could qualify as either a small privateer vessel or a defensively armed merchantman. In 2009 MMS announced that the wreck may be the U.S. privateer *Rapid*, which sank off the coast of Louisiana in 1813 while eluding a British naval vessel (Ford, Borgens, and Hitchcock 2010: 95).

The Texas Revolution

The struggle for Texas's independence had a naval component consisting of two separate fleets. The early Texas Navy of four armed schooners (*Liberty*, *Independence*, *Brutus*, and *Invincible*) was created in 1836 and was all but lost by 1837 (Powers 2006). A new navy was formed in 1839 and included the steam warship *Zavala*; the sloop-of-war *Austin*; brigs-of-war *Branch T. Archer* and *Wharton*; schooners-of-war

San Jacinto, *San Bernard*, and *San Antonio*; and the auxiliary vessels *Potomac* and *Louisville* (*Striped Pig*). By 1845 most of the fleet was unserviceable and two vessels had been lost (Jordan 2006).

Two vessels from these naval fleets have been the focus of remote-sensing investigations and testing; one additional vessel was discovered accidentally during maintenance dredging. The 25.5 m (83.7 ft) schooner *Invincible* ran aground at Galveston in August 1837 during an engagement with two Mexican naval vessels. Surveys conducted by NUMA in 1986 and 1988 for the *Invincible* discovered two historic wreck sites, but did not conclusively identify the remains of the vessels (Oertling 1992). The 25 m (82 ft) schooner *Brutus* sank at her anchorage in Galveston Harbor during a hurricane in 1837. Dredging of the Galveston Ship Channel in 1884 recovered two of the vessel's cannon and timbers, though at the time the wreck's identity was unknown. The cannon were subsequently purchased and displayed at a local residence before becoming inadvertently buried during the grade-raising project that elevated the city of Galveston after the hurricane of 1900 (Ryan 1982: 1). One of the cannon was recovered in 1974 during a commercial construction project and is now on display at the Texas Seaport Museum at Galveston (*Galveston Daily News* 1986: 16A). The shipwreck itself has not been relocated and is presumed to have been destroyed by dredging activity.

The steamship *Zavala* was purchased as the 61.3 m (201 ft) double-walking-beam side-wheel steamer *Charleston* and outfitted with four medium 12-pounder cannon and one long 9-pounder. Though *Zavala* is recognized as the earliest steam warship in the Gulf of Mexico, the naval career of *Zavala* was far from illustrious. The vessel was seldom used and was eventually abandoned at a Galveston wharf. Cartographic research and magnetometer investigations by NUMA and the TAC in 1986 located the derelict vessel buried in an empty Galveston lot. Testing of the site identified ship timbers and a riveted iron boiler more than 4.6 m (15 ft) in length. The steamship wreck has not been the subject of further archaeological investigations (Arnold, Cussler, and Gronquist 1990; Baldwin 1995).

Several merchant vessels carrying supplies and volunteers for the Texas cause wrecked along the Texas coast (Powers 2006: 207–213). The remnants of such a small sailing craft was discovered at Pass Cavallo, Texas, by NUMA in 1998 during the survey for La Salle's vessel *l'Aimable*, which wrecked in 1685 (Wilbanks, Hal, and McKee 2000; Weddle 2009). A second investigation of the site in 1998 by the THC and members of the Southwest Underwater Archaeology Society recovered a variety of artifacts, including bayonets, saber fragments, English and Spanish muskets, and ferrous and lead shot. Probing of the site did not identify extant hull remains. The vessel is possibly the remains of the 20.7 m (68 ft) New Orleans merchant schooner/gunrunner *Hannah Elizabeth*, which grounded at the pass before being overtaken by a Mexican naval vessel and boarded. *Hannah Elizabeth* was recaptured by a Texas vessel but broke apart while being salvaged. This wreck is the only Gulf underwater site to have military artifacts similar to those recovered from Texas Revolution era military sites (Borgens 2004).

The U.S. Civil War

Following secession of most of the Confederate states, Abraham Lincoln issued a proclamation declaring a blockade of all Confederate ports. Maritime commerce conducted from these areas during this time was vital to southern supply lines and the economic stability of the Confederacy. The West Gulf Blockading Squadron, commanded by Admiral David G. Farragut, was tasked with blockading Gulf ports from Pensacola to the Rio Grande (Soley 1898: 123). Major naval conflicts occurred at New Orleans, Galveston, Sabine Pass (Texas), and Mobile Bay as Union and Confederate forces fought over control of these pivotal locations. Vessels utilized in Gulf engagements included traditional sailing vessels as well as screw-steamers, side-wheel steam warships, converted ferry-gunboats, and newly introduced vessel types such as ironclads and monitors.

In April 1862 a Union naval force of 17 vessels commanded by Admiral Farragut advanced toward the port of New Orleans. After heavily bombarding Fort Jackson and Fort St. Philip for five days, on 24 April Farragut engaged a Confederate fleet of 27 vessels, comprising ironclads, steamers, launches, and towboats converted to gunboats. Though most of the Union fleet endured, only six Confederate vessels were still afloat following the battle (some were later scuttled). Following capitulation of the Confederate squadron, New Orleans surrendered on 25 April 1862. A remote-sensing investigation and testing at Fort St. Philip was conducted by Goodwin and Associates Inc. in 1991. The magnetometer data, in combination with coring samples of the anomalies, led to the identification of two Civil War wrecks: the ironclad CSS *Louisiana* and the tugboat-converted-to-gunboat *Defiance*. Both vessels are deeply buried under sediment and have not been the subject of subsequent investigations (Irion, Beard, and Heinrich 1994).

Months after the Union success at New Orleans, an attack was commenced on Galveston, a vital conduit for the exportation of southern cotton. Galveston was occupied by Union forces, without contest, in October 1862, but was recaptured by Confederate forces on 1 January 1863. Following the loss, a Union fleet remained offshore and subjected the city to occasional bombardment (Cotham 1998: 142). As a means of circumventing another naval loss at Galveston, a Union attack was commenced at Sabine Pass on 8 September 1863. A small detachment of fewer than 50 men at Fort Griffin successfully sank three Union vessels, thereby forcing the retreat of the remaining gunboats, 22 troop transports, and a combined military force of more than 6,000 men (Cotham 2004: 125–147).

Several vessels associated with Civil War naval activities in Texas have been investigated. USS *Westfield*, flagship of the West Gulf Blockading Squadron, was destroyed by its captain during the Battle of Galveston on 1 January 1863. It was rediscovered in 2005 by archaeologists from PBS&J (now Atkins) during a remote-sensing survey conducted for the U.S. Army Corps of Engineers in Galveston Bay (Gearhart et al. 2005). Though the location of the shipwreck was depicted on historical charts, contemporaneous salvage and modern bay maintenance was thought to have destroyed the wreck. The gunboat USS *Westfield* was a 64.9 m (213 ft) former

Staten Island ferry sold to the navy by Cornelius Vanderbilt in 1861 and converted to an armed gunboat. Reconnaissance dives of the site in 2006 did not locate any remaining hull but identified machinery, shot, protective boiler plating, and a 9 in Dahlgren cannon. Large artifacts and sediment from the dispersed debris field were recovered in late 2009. Over 7,800 artifacts have been examined by archaeologists from PBS&J, including shells, shot, shell fuses, Union belt buckles, hull plating, and ship fasteners (Gearhart et al. 2010; Borgens 2010). The "sister ship" to *Westfield*, USS *Clifton*, was investigated in 1994 by Espey, Huston and Associates Inc. (EH&A, now PBS&J) in an effort to assess the condition of the wreck. The site, buried under marsh grass at Sabine Pass, was determined to have been impacted by jetty construction and salvage in the past (Hoyt, Schmidt, and Gearhart 1994).

USS *Hatteras* was part of the fleet of five warships engaged in the bombardment of Galveston following the Union loss of the port. The Confederate commerce raider CSS *Alabama* approached Galveston on 11 January 1863, anticipating the presence of Union transport vessels. USS *Hatteras* was sent to investigate and, after a brief engagement lasting less than twenty minutes, was sunk. The wreck of the 64 m (210 ft), 1,126-ton sidewheel steamer *Hatteras* was initially detected as a source of net hangs for local fisherman. A salvage group discovered the wreck site in the mid-1970s and attempted to acquire rights to the vessel. They were successfully challenged in 1978 by the U.S. Navy, which retains ownership of wrecked U.S. military vessels (see Neyland in this volume). *Hatteras* has been the focus of continued investigation over the years by BOEMRE working jointly with the THC, Naval History and Heritage Command, and, in the past, the Institute of Nautical Archaeology (INA) at TAMU (Arnold and Anuskiewicz 1995: 82–87). Monitoring of the site continued in 2004, with an MMS-sponsored study conducted by PBS&J as part of a larger National Register assessment of wreck sites. The wreck is buried, with only the tops of the paddle-wheel hubs and a portion of the shaft visible (Enright et al. 2006: 37–40).

Denbigh was a 55.5 m (182 ft) iron-hulled British sidewheel steamship that served as one of the most successful blockade-runners of the Civil War. The vessel was abandoned and burned after grounding off Bolivar Peninsula, Texas, in May 1865. The site of the wreck, a charted wreck obstruction, was identified as *Denbigh* through a series of investigations by INA beginning in 1997. *Denbigh* lies in 1.8 m (6 ft) of water and is evident at low tide. Ship features visible in the water column include the paddle wheels, machinery, boilers, and valve chest. The engine and portions of the hull were documented during excavations conducted in 2000 and 2001. Artifacts recovered during the course of work include portions of machinery, ceramic shards, a doll's leg, and coal (Arnold 2003; Arnold, Oertling, and Hall 2001).

Faced with embarrassing and unexpected naval losses in Texas, the Union redirected its efforts to Mobile Bay, Alabama. Mobile was the last significant Gulf port under Confederate control. The Confederate defenses at Mobile consisted of the batteries at Fort Morgan and Fort Gaines, four warships, and strategically placed torpedoes (mines) and obstructions. On 5 August 1864 a Union fleet entered Mobile Bay and, in the early morning hours, commenced firing on Fort Morgan. The Battle of Mobile Bay ended when the Confederates surrendered on the ironclad

CSS *Tennessee*. Fort Gaines and Fort Morgan succumbed on 8 and 23 August, respectively, and the city of Mobile capitulated the next year, on 26 April 1865, as part of the Confederate surrender of its forces east of the Mississippi. Naval losses accrued in the battle were the steamer CSS *Gaines*, the monitor USS *Tecumseh* (by torpedo), and the tug USS *Philippi* (Wakefield 1987).

Remote-sensing and diver investigations of the battle site since the 1960s have identified the locations of all three Union vessels (Watts 1998). Four vessels sunk by Confederate troops as defensive obstructions—ironclad *Phoenix*, steamboats *Cremonia* and *Carondelet*, and an unknown flat—were also discovered during remote-sensing surveys conducted by EH&A in the mid-1980s. The wreck of the tug *Thomas Sparks* (1866) was also discovered at this time. These vessels are in variable states of preservation; some wrecks were sparse and somewhat disarticulated sites, but two vessels (USS *Tecumseh* and *Phoenix*) were well preserved (Irion 1985; Irion and Bond 1984; Watts et al. 1998).

The 68.6 m (225 ft) ironclad monitor USS *Tecumseh* lies intact and upside down in 10.7 m (35 ft) of water. It has been the subject of a series of investigations, beginning with a project launched by the Smithsonian Institution in 1965. Preliminary reports from diver investigations indicated that the turret was intact but disconnected from the deck; identified a mooring ring and the counterbalance for the rudder; and uncovered part of a propeller blade. Artifacts recovered at the time included shards of dinnerware, a section of deck plating, and an anchor. The Smithsonian Institution, in cooperation with Expeditions Unlimited Inc. (EUI), planned to have the vessel exhumed and restored. Divers from EUI investigated the wreck and discovered extensive teredo damage to the deck and turret chambers. The interior of the hull was also examined and determined to be in good condition. The project failed after the death of the key investor and has not resumed since 1975. Researchers from East Carolina University reassessed *Tecumseh* in 1993 and discovered that the site was buried under sediment, with only an 2.4 by 1.8 m (8 by 6 ft) section exposed (Watts et al. 1998: 43–56).

The 82.6 m (271 ft) *Phoenix* was one of only two side-wheel ironclads designed for the Confederate Navy. The vessel was never commissioned, having been damaged during its initial launch. The ironclad was not part of the original bay defenses but was sunk to fill a channel through the defensive line as the Union Navy approached Mobile. On 24 August 1864, Union troops blew *Phoenix* up to clear entry. The wreck of *Phoenix* was rediscovered by archaeologists from EH&A in 1984 and was the focus of diver investigations conducted by researchers from Florida State University (FSU) over a five-day period in 1993. Scouring of the interior hull on the starboard side exposed a depth of over 3 m (10 ft). The hull was discovered to be mostly intact, with portions of deck planking observed at both the bow and the stern. Exterior hull features were buried under sediment (Ball 1998: 80–91; Gearhart 1986).

Two western Florida wrecks from this period have been the subject of archaeological investigations. The 25 m (82.5 ft), wooden-hulled USS *Narcissus* sank in January 1866 off Egmont Key (near Tampa Bay) as the armed steam tug was returning to New York to be decommissioned. The vessel grounded on a shoal and exploded, killing all 25 aboard. The wreck was discovered in 1983 by two Florida dive masters. An attempt to obtain salvage rights failed in 1987, as the wreck was located within the Pinellas County Aquatic Reserve. Major features of the site include the steam machinery and portions of the boiler, propeller shaft, and large propeller. The site has been investigated by such groups as the Florida Division of Historical Resources (FDHR), TAMU, and the Florida Aquarium, and is the focus of a UWF master's thesis study (Powell 1999: 17; Tumbleson Morris 2009). The remains of the blockade runner *Kate Dale* were recently positively identified in the Hillsborough River in Tampa Bay, though the identity of the known wreck site has been the source of speculation since the 1960s. The 24.4 m (80 ft) sloop was burned to the waterline by Union troops in October 1863. The wreck is the focus of a project conducted by the Florida Aquarium (Morelli 2008).

COMMERCIAL SAILING VESSELS IN THE GULF OF MEXICO

New Orleans was the preeminent northern Gulf port in the eighteenth and nineteenth centuries. By 1810, six years after its acquisition by the United States, it was the largest city south of Baltimore and the fifth most populous city in the nation. Maritime activity at New Orleans was a diverse combination of upriver trade and international commerce. During this time, approximately half of the vessels arriving at New Orleans originated from U.S. ports. Close to a quarter of the vessels disembarked from Spanish colonies, while slightly fewer emanated from Britain and France and their respective colonies (Clark 1970: 275, 313–314). The largest quantity of U.S. vessels that registered or enrolled at New Orleans between 1804 and 1870 were constructed in northeastern states (38% to 52%); only 17% to 31% of vessels for the same period were produced by Gulf shipyards (Works Progress Administration 1941–1942). Schooners were the predominant vessel used to conduct trade in the Gulf of Mexico. Gulf-built schooners of the early nineteenth century were, on average, about 27% smaller than those produced in the North (Borgens 2008: 57–58). Archaeological examples of the early Gulf sailing craft are rare.

One exception is the Mica shipwreck site, which lies at a depth of 808 m (2,650 ft) and is located approximately 64.4 km (40 miles) southeast of the Mississippi River mouth. The wreck was discovered in 2001 by ExxonMobil during a routine postinstallation inspection of an oil and gas pipeline. The wreck, believed to be an early-nineteenth-century two-masted schooner, measures 20.4 m (67 ft) from stempost to sternpost. The overall length of the vessel was deduced as 22 m (72 ft). During inspection it was discovered that the pipeline had been laid atop the exposed vessel, in essence bisecting the wreck perpendicular to the keel and "flattening" the midship portion of the wreck site. Archaeologists and researchers from MMS and

TAMU supervised the ROV investigation of the site. Recovered artifacts include a lead hawser pipe, copper alloy fasteners, and portions of copper sheathing (Atauz et al. 2006; Jones 2004).

The Viosca Knoll wreck site is an unidentified, coppered, wooden-hulled sailing craft also dating to the early nineteenth century. The wreck was discovered in 2003 during a deep-tow survey for a proposed pipeline in the Viosca Knoll lease block area, offshore in the Gulf of Mexico. It was investigated as a separate site assessment in 2006 by archaeologists from C&C Technologies and MMS using a ROV. The wreck lies at a depth of 613.8 m (2,010 ft) and measures approximately 42.7 by 11 m (140 by 36 ft). The port side is visible 0.6–1.8 m (2–6 ft) above the seafloor, exposing the turn of the bilge; the stempost projects at least 3.4 m (11 ft) above the sediment. A 6.4 m (21 ft) section of standing rigging, tentatively identified as the mainstay, lies on the seafloor adjacent to and outside the wreck. Hatch openings, deck beams, lodging knees, and hanging knees were visible on or within the hull. A portion of the stern section was discovered to have been damaged by a possible cable drag. Artifacts associated with the wreck but displaced from the vessel were a patent stove, an earthenware crock, and a possible lantern. The shape of the hull and remnant rigging indicate that the wreck is likely a brig or brigantine (Church and Warren 2008: 17–23).

A well-preserved example of a late-nineteenth-/early-twentieth-century flat-bottomed schooner is the site known as the 303 Hang wreck. This wreck is located a mile offshore of Freeport, Texas, and was discovered in 1990 when it was impacted by the burial of a new gas pipeline. Archaeologists from Panamerican Consultants Inc. spent 10 days documenting the vessel, whose lower hull was complete and measured approximately 30.5 m (100 ft) long, with a beam of 7.2 m (23.5 ft). The level of vertical preservation extended from the keel to the lower portions of the rear starboard chain plate. A pipeline lies diagonally across the stern of the vessel and is covered by a sandbag cap. Historical research did not identify a wreck candidate for the two-masted schooner, which was burdened with a cargo of anthracite coal (James, Hudson, and Hudson 1991).

A common vessel type along the Gulf Coast at this time was the centerboard schooner. An early example of this type of craft is located along a muddy slough in the Blackwater River in Pensacola Bay. The early- to mid-nineteenth-century vessel, known as the Bethune Blackwater Schooner, is extremely well preserved. The vessel is 90% complete, with the exception of the masts, cabin house, and part of the bow, the latter of which was burned to create space for the construction of a dock. The vessel is an estimated 29.3 m (96 ft) long, with a 7.9 m (25.9 ft) beam and 2 m (6.7 ft) draft. The pump, handspike windlass, and rigging fittings were diagnostic for identifying the rig and time period for the vessel. The Florida Division of Historical Resources was informed about the vessel in 1988, and a preliminary assessment of the site was conducted in February and April 1988. Documentation of exterior hull features was conducted by volunteer workers and students in July 1989. The vessel is located within an area that was integral to the production and exportation of bricks and lumber and was likely used to carry these products to Gulf and Atlantic ports (Baumer 1990).

The only example of a well-preserved Gulf-built scow schooner, *Lake Austin*, was discovered near Port Aransas, Texas, in 1966 and excavated from the beach using large machinery (Figure 29.4). The scow schooner was typically 9.8–15.2 m (32–50 ft) in length and was a common vessel type of the western Gulf. It was first used by early Texas colonists (Chapelle 1951: 332–336). The *Lake Austin* wreck, identified by its registration number, was a 21 m (69 ft), 53-ton scow centerboard schooner built in Matagorda Bay in 1881 that grounded during a norther in 1903. The vessel was carrying a cargo of lumber when it was lost (*Daily Advocate* 1903; Johnson n.d.). *Lake Austin* had a single deck with a cargo hold that was evenly bisected by a bulkhead that ran the length of the vessel. There were two cabins at the stern and two small storage rooms in the bow, each separated from the hold by a bulkhead. The vessel was intended to be restored and displayed as a tourist attraction. However, months after its discovery, after public interest waned, it was burned as a perceived traffic hazard (Hoyt 2006: 7–8; Johnson n.d.; Ramage 1963: 10).

Other examples of historic centerboard vessels used in the Gulf include the Mississippi-built, 7.97-ton schooner *Governor Stone*, built in 1877, which has been

Figure 29.4 *Lake Austin* in 1966. Photograph by M. Johnson. Reproduced with the kind permission of the Texas Historical Commission.

fully restored (albeit in a slightly altered form) and resides in Pascagoula, Florida (McClure 2003, 2004), and the Ballast Cove wreck. This latter vessel was the subject of a four-year investigation conducted by FSU. The site is located near Dog Island, off the coast of Florida. The vessel is only partially preserved on the starboard side to just below the turn of the bilge. The keel length is 19.7 m (64.6 ft), and the center-board is offset on the starboard side of the keel. It has been identified as a mid- to late-nineteenth-century schooner-rigged sailing vessel. Over 1,400 artifacts were recovered from the site, including door hardware, fasteners, rigging hardware, ceramics, and pipe fragments (Horrell 2005: 127–183).

Toward the end of the nineteenth century, the use of steamers supplanted the use of many sailing vessels for commercial shipping. As steam transportation began to eclipse that of sail, large, multimasted vessels were often still effective for transporting large bulk cargoes such as railroad iron, coal, and lumber. As the usefulness of these vessels declined, however, many were converted to barges or schooner barges, though barges and schooner barges were also purpose-built at this time. Conversion usually involved removal of the bowsprit, upper masts, and deckhouse (Morris 1984: 1, 11). Near the mouth of the Blackwater River in Pensacola Bay is the graveyard of at least 15 abandoned wooden-hulled vessels. A survey of the wrecks conducted in 1991 iden-tified four early-twentieth-century schooner barges, three of which were believed to be the 45.7 m (150 ft) *Palafox*, 42 m (138 ft) *Dinty Moore*, and 54.9 m (180 ft) *Geo. T. Lock*. The fourth vessel has not been conclusively identified. *Palafox* and *Geo. T. Lock* were built as three- and four-masted schooners in 1917 but later converted to schooner barges. *Dinty Moore* was purpose-built as a schooner barge in 1921. All three vessels were built in Gulf ports. These watercraft were abandoned in the Blackwater River in the 1930s, salvaged, and later burned to the waterline. In 2003 and 2004, students from UWF documented the lower hulls, which are relatively complete and well-preserved (Franklin, Morris, and Smith 1991; Holland 2006; Sjordal 2007).

THE STEAM AGE

Territorial changes in the Gulf and the growing economic opportunities of the early nineteenth century heightened immigration into the region. Foreseeing new oppor-tunities for commerce and expansion, entrepreneur Charles P. Morgan transferred much of his New England–based business to the Gulf of Mexico in mid-1838, after introducing two of his steamers on Gulf service in 1837 (Baughman 1968: 19–25). Morgan's steamship service, the Harris and Morgan Steamship Line, facilitated travel between major Gulf ports and accelerated localized growth and market diver-sification, particularly at Galveston. Soon other companies opened competitive routes or offered freight and passenger service to other portions of the Gulf.

Steam travel at this early time was not without complications, both mechanical and weather-related, and Morgan and other steamer services lost many vessels in the

Gulf. The luxurious 50.6 m (166 ft), 365-ton Morgan side-wheel steamer *New York* was broken apart off Galveston in 1846 during a storm (Figure 29.5). Seventeen passengers and crew perished, and between 30,000 to 40,000 dollars in specie and banknotes were lost with the ship (*Daily Picayune* 1846). Gentlemen of Fortune LLC (GOF), a salvage group based in Louisiana, relocated the wreck in 1990. The discovery of the ship's bell in 2005 led to the vessel's identification, and an admiralty claim was successfully filed on the site in 2006. The wreck site was the focus of investigations by MMS in 1997 and 1998 and is the subject of a MMS-sponsored study to assess hurricane impacts on selected shipwreck sites in the Gulf of Mexico (Gearhart et al. 2010). The vessel is broken forward of the engine and is preserved to the turn of the bilge. The crosshead engine is collapsed but retains its major component parts. Artifacts recovered by GOF and later documented by PBS&J included the ship's bell, tools, dinnerware, a pocket watch, sheathing, door hardware, buttons, and assorted bottles (Irion and Ball 2001: 48–56; D. Jones, Borgens, and Ball 2009). GOF also recovered a large collection of gold and silver coins from the site (Bower 2008).

Remnants of the SS *Perseverance* (1852), another early wooden-hulled Morgan steamer, were discovered during a remote-sensing survey conducted by the THC in 2006. The 57 m (187 ft) steamer burned to the waterline at Indianola, Texas, in 1856 (Baughman 1968: 105; Hoyt 2007; Works Progress Administration 1941–1942, vol. 5: 207). Less than three decades later, the Morgan steamer SS *Josephine* foundered during a storm in February 1881. The wreck of the iron-hulled *Josephine* lies in 11.6 m (38 ft) of water off the coast of Mississippi. Much of the lower hull of the vessel is buried and intact. In 1997 and 1998 divers from MMS conducted remote sensing of the site and investigated major exposed features of the wreck, including the paddle wheels, the base of the smokestack, and the collapsed walking-beam engine. Side-scan imagery from 1997, collected when the wreck was more exposed, showed two objects that are believed to be twin boilers lying forward of the paddle wheel. The

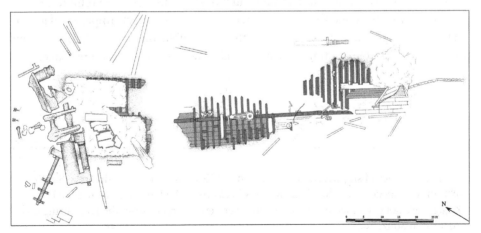

Figure 29.5 Detail of the SS *New York* site plan. Exposed portion of the SS *New York* recorded by PBS&J in 2007. Illustration by the author. Reproduced with the kind permission of Minerals Management Service.

engine cylinder was not located during the course of investigations and is believed to be either missing or buried within the hull (Irion and Ball 2001: 53–56). Other prominent steamer losses in the Gulf that have been the focus of archaeological investigations include Morgan's 71.3 m (234 ft) steamer SS *Mary*, which ran aground at Aransas Pass, Texas, in 1876; *City of Waco*, an 42.7 m (140 ft) Mallory line propeller steamer that inexplicably caught fire and sank in 1875 off Galveston Bay; and the twin-screw Florida coastal steamer SS *Tarpon* (built 1887), which foundered off Panama City in 1937 (Hall 2005: 1–3; Horlings and Galloway 2001; Hoyt 1990).

CONCLUSION

The archaeology of the Gulf of Mexico is characterized by a large and diverse collection of international and regional vessels, from the small coastal schooner to large warships and passenger steamers. Some of the oldest shipwreck sites in North America are located within Gulf waters. Hundreds of shipwrecks have been identified within the region through remote-sensing surveys, archaeological investigations, and the activities of commercial fishing and oil development. Much of the archaeology in the Gulf of Mexico occurs in blackwater environments, and projects in this area are often short-term investigations that involve a combination of remote-sensing surveys, diver reconnaissance, and limited site documentation. Shipwreck sites that are located in high-visibility environments like the western coast of Florida or in shallow, accessible locations have in many cases been afforded more attention and a higher level of study. Although there is a preponderance of material for early shipwreck sites and those from the Civil War, indigenous coastal craft and wooden-hulled sailing vessels from the early colonial period are relatively unknown. The variable preservation of wreck sites in salt water and limitations in mandated remote-sensing requirements can make these early vessels difficult to detect. Improved data-collection techniques and an increased emphasis on public outreach initiatives can aid in discovering and protecting the Gulf's invaluable maritime cultural resources.

NOTES

1. A number of shipwrecks along the Florida Keys are from Spanish *flotas* (Smith 1988; Smith, Finegold, and Stephens 1990). Wrecks from the Florida Keys and the Dry Tortugas are not discussed in this study. An overview of wrecks from the Dry Tortugas is provided in Souza 1998.

2. Underwater archaeological sites related to the Mexican-American War have not been recorded in the northern Gulf of Mexico, though three coastal terrestrial sites that were vital to the supply and movement of troops (Brazos Santiago Depot, Fort Polk, and

Indianola) have been investigated (Banks 1983; Gearhart 1987; Hoyt 2007; Hoyt, Gearhart, and Myers 1991). Two predreadnought vessels from the Spanish-American War are located in the Gulf, though neither loss is associated with U.S. naval engagements. The gunboat USS *Castine* and the Indiana-class battleship USS *Massachusetts* are both historically significant vessels that sank (one deliberately) off the Gulf Coast in the 1920s. Both vessels, located off Louisiana and Florida, respectively, have been the subject of archaeological investigations (Delgado 1998: 266; Enright et al. 2006; Jones 2007; Smith et al. 1999: 15). Twentieth-century naval shipwrecks are not addressed in this manuscript, though a substantial number of wrecks have been documented (Arnold et al. 1998; Church et al. 2007; Enright et al. 2006; Hoskins, Borgens, and Enright 2007; Warren et al. 2004).

REFERENCES

Arnold, J. Barto. 2003. The *Denbigh* project 2002: Excavation of a Civil War blockade runner. *Bulletin of the Texas Archeological Society* 74: 131–140.

Arnold, J. Barto, and R. J. Anuskiewicz. 1995. USS *Hatteras*: Site monitoring and mapping. In *Underwater archaeology: Proceedings from the Society for Historical Archaeology Conference*, ed. Paul F. Johnston, 82–87. Rockville, MD: Society for Historical Archaeology.

Arnold, J. Barto, Clive Cussler, and Wayne Gronquist. 1990. The survey for the *Zavala*, a steam warship of the Republic of Texas. Paper presented at Society for Historical Archaeology Conference on Historical and Underwater Archaeology, January 1990, Tucson, AZ.

Arnold, J. Barto, Jennifer Goloboy, Andrew W. Hall, and Rebecca A. Hall. 1998. *Texas' liberty ships: From working-class heroes to artificial reefs.* Austin: Texas Parks and Wildlife Department.

Arnold, J. Barto, Thomas J. Oertling, and Andrew W. Hall. 2001. The *Denbigh* project: Excavation of a Civil War blockade-runner. *International Journal of Nautical Archaeology* 30 (2): 231–249.

Arnold, J. Barto, and Robert Weddle. 1978. *The nautical archaeology of Padre Island: The Spanish shipwrecks of 1554.* New York: Academic Press.

Atauz, A. D., W. Bryant, T. Jones, and B. Phaneuf. 2006. *Mica shipwreck project: Deepwater archaeological investigation of a 19th-century shipwreck in the Gulf of Mexico.* New Orleans: U.S. Department of the Interior, Minerals Management Service, Gulf of Mexico OCS Region.

Baldwin, Elizabeth R. 1995. T. S. S. Zavala: The Texas Navy's steamship-of-war. The INA Quarterly 22 (3): 10–15.

Ball, David A. 1998. *Phoenix* and the Confederate obstructions of Upper Mobile Bay, Alabama (1MB28). MA thesis, Florida State University.

Banks, Cynthia R. 1983. Brazos Santiago Depot and Fort Polk, Cameron County, Texas: Contexts of the site and analysis of the ceramics from 1967 and 1980 investigations. MA thesis, University of Texas.

Baughman, James P. 1968. *Charles Morgan and the development of southern transportation.* Nashville: Vanderbilt University Press.

Baumer, David R. 1990. *Bethune Blackwater Schooner.* Florida Archaeological Reports 21. Tallahassee: Bureau of Archaeological Research, Division of Historical Resources, Florida Department of State.

Borgens, Amy A. 2004. Analysis of the Pass Cavallo shipwreck assemblage, Matagorda Bay,
    Texas. MA thesis, Texas A&M University.
———. 2008. Historical context. In *Archaeological excavation of the Mardi Gras shipwreck
    (16GM01), Gulf of Mexico Continental Slope*, ed. Ben Ford, Amy Borgens, William
    Bryant, Dawn Marshall, Peter Hitchcock, Cesar Arias, and Donny Hamilton, 39–74.
    New Orleans: U.S. Department of the Interior, Minerals Management Service, Gulf of
    Mexico OCS Region.
———;. 2010. USS *Westfield*: The loss and rediscovery of a Civil War ferry-gunboat in
    Galveston Bay. *Current Archeology in Texas* 12 (2): 1–8.
Bower, Q. David. The treasure ship S. S. New York: her story 1837–1846. Wolfeboro, NH:
    Stacks.
Bruseth, James E., and Toni S. Turner. 2005. *From a watery grave: The discovery and excava-
    tion of La Salle's shipwreck* La Belle. College Station: Texas A&M University Press.
Chapelle, Howard L. 1951. *American small sailing craft: Their design, development, and
    construction*. New York: W. W. Norton.
Church, R., D. Warren, R. Cullimore, L. Johnston, W. Schroeder, W. Patterson, T. Shirely,
    M. Kilgour, N. Morris, and J. Moore. 2007. *Archaeological and biological analysis of the
    World War II shipwrecks in the Gulf of Mexico: Artificial reef effect in deep water*. New
    Orleans: U.S. Department of the Interior, Minerals Management Service, Gulf of
    Mexico OCS Region.
Church, R. A., and Daniel J. Warren. 2008. *Viosca Knoll wreck: Discovery and investigation of
    an early nineteenth-century wooden sailing vessel in 2,000 feet of water*. New Orleans: U.S.
    Department of the Interior, Minerals Management Service, Gulf of Mexico OCS Region.
Clark, John G. 1970. *New Orleans 1718–1812: An economic history*. Baton Rouge: Louisiana
    State University Press.
Clark, Megan. 2007. *UWF archaeologists discover second oldest shipwreck in the U.S*. Rev. 19
    October 2007. Online at http://uwf.edu/uwfMain/press/topstoryarch.
    cfm?emailID=17683/. Accessed 28 November 2008.
Cotham, Edward T., Jr. 1998. *Battle on the bay: The Civil War struggle for Galveston*. Austin:
    University of Texas Press.
———. 2004. *Sabine Pass: The Confederacy's Thermopylae*. Austin: University of Texas Press.
Cook, Gregory D. 2009. Luna's ships: Current excavation on Emanuel Point II and
    preliminary comparisons with the first Emanuel Point shipwreck. *Florida Anthropolo-
    gist* 62 (3–4): 93–99.
Daily Advocate (Victoria). 1903. *Lake Austin* lost. 9 December.
Daily Picayune (New Orleans). 1846. Wreck of the *New York*. 10 September.
Davis, John L. 1977. *Treasure, people, ships, and dreams*. Austin: Texas Antiquities Commit-
    tee and the Institute of Texan Cultures of the University of Texas at San Antonio.
Delgado, James P. 1998. *Encyclopedia of underwater and maritime archaeology*. New Haven,
    CT: Yale University Press.
Dessiou, J. Foss. 1808. A general chart of the West Indies and Gulf of Mexico. Map
    reproduction, collection of author.
Dodsworth, C. 1971. The Low Moor Ironworks, Bradford. *Industrial Archaeology* 8
    (2): 122–164.
Elozúa, Antonio. 1830. Letter to Mier y Terán, 21 June 1830. In *The Béxar Archives at the
    University of Texas Archives*, ed. Chester V. Keilman and Carmela Leal. Austin:
    University of Texas at Austin Library, 1967–1971. Microfilm.
Enright, Jeffrey M., Robert L. Gearhart, Doug Jones, and Jenna Enright. 2006. *Study to
    conduct National Register of Historic Places evaluations of submerged sites on the Gulf of*

Mexico Outer Continental Shelf. New Orleans: U.S. Department of the Interior,
    Minerals Management Service, Gulf of Mexico OCS Region.
Faye, Stanley. 1940. Privateers of Guadalupe and their establishment in Barataria. *Louisiana
    Historical Quarterly* 23 (1): 428–444.
Ford, Ben, Amy Borgens, William Bryant, Dawn Marshall, Peter Hitchcock, Cesar Arias,
    and Donny Hamilton. 2008. *Archaeological excavation of the Mardi Gras shipwreck
    (16GM01), Gulf of Mexico Continental Slope*. New Orleans: U.S. Department of the
    Interior, Minerals Management Service, Gulf of Mexico OCS Region.
Ford, Ben, Amy Borgens, and Peter Hitchcock. 2010. The "Mardi Gras" shipwreck: Results
    of a deep-water excavation, Gulf of Mexico, USA. *International Journal of Nautical
    Archaeology* 39 (1): 76–98.
Franklin, Marianne, John William Morris III, and Roger C. Smith. 1991. *Submerged
    historical resources of Pensacola Bay, Florida: The Pensacola Shipwreck Survey Phase
    One*. Florida Archaeological Reports 25. Tallahassee: Bureau of Archaeological
    Research, Division of Historical Resources.
Galveston Daily News. 1986. GHF notes: Cannon ready. 11 May.
Garrison, Ervan G., Charles P. Giammona, Frank J. Kelly, Anthony R. Tripp, and
    Gary A. Wolff. 1989. *Historic shipwrecks and magnetic anomalies of the northern
    Gulf of Mexico: Reevaluation of Archaeological Resources Management Zone 1*,
    Vol. 3, Appendices. New Orleans: U.S. Department of the Interior, Minerals
    Management Service, Gulf of Mexico OCS Region.
Gearhart, Robert L. 1986. The *Phoenix*: Mobile's unknown ironclad. Paper presented at
    Seventeenth Annual Conference on Underwater Archaeology, Sacramento, CA.
———. 1987. *A baseline assessment of the cultural resources within the proposed Playa
    del Rio development including an archaeological survey of Phases IA and I-B*. Austin:
    Espey, Huston & Associates.
Gearhart, Robert L., Amy Borgens, Sara Hoskins, and Doug Jones. 2010. Investigation and
    recovery of Site 41GV151 (USS *Westfield*), Texas City Channel Improvement Project,
    Galveston County, Galveston Bay Texas. Draft report submitted to the U.S. Army
    Corps of Engineers, Galveston District. Austin: PBS&J.
Gearhart, Robert L., Doug S. Jones, Jeffrey M. Enright, Jenna Enright, and Ty Summerville.
    2005. *Close-order remote-sensing survey of five anomalies and the proposed channel
    modifications for historic properties investigations, Texas City Channel Improvements,
    Galveston Bay, Texas*. Austin: PBS&J.
Gearhart, Robert L., Doug Jones, Amy Borgens, Sara Laurence, Todd DeMunda, and Julie
    Shipp. 2010. Impacts of recent hurricane activity on historical shipwrecks in the Gulf
    of Mexico Outer Continental Shelf. New Orleans: U.S. Department of the Interior,
    Bureau of Ocean Energy Management, Regulation and Enforcement, Gulf of Mexico
    OCS Region.
Hall, Andy. 2005. *City of Waco* located in Galveston Bay. *Current Archeology in Texas* 7 (1):
    1–3.
Holland, Lora K. 2006. Maritime technology in transition: Historical and archaeological
    investigations of the schooner barge *Geo. T. Lock* (8SR1491). MA thesis, University of
    West Florida.
Horlings, Rachel, and Marc Galloway. 2001. *The wreck of the SS Tarpon*. Tallahassee:
    Florida Bureau of Archaeological Research and Florida State University's Program in
    Underwater Archaeology.
Horrell, Christopher E. 2005. Plying the waters of time: Maritime archaeology and history
    on the Florida Gulf Coast. PhD diss., Florida State University.

Hoskins, Sara, Amy Borgens, and Jenna Enright. 2007. *Eligibility testing of the unknown shipwreck (41OR90) adjacent Highway 10 at the Neches River Bridge, Orange County, Texas.* Austin: PBS&J.

Hoyt, Steven D. 1990. *National Register assessment of the SS* Mary, *Port Aransas, Nueces County, Texas.* Austin: Espey, Huston & Associates.

———. 2006. Shipwreck investigation priorities of the Marine Archeology Program: A guide for future investigations. Manuscript on file at the Texas Historical Commission.

———;. 2007. Indianola investigations: Phase 2. *Current Archeology in Texas* 9 (November): 8–9.

Hoyt, Steven D., Robert L. Gearhart, and Teresa L. Myers. 1991. *Submerged historic resources investigations, Brownsville Channel and Brazos Santiago Depot (41CF4), Cameron County, Texas.* Austin: Espey Huston & Associates.

Hoyt, Steven D., James S. Schmidt, and Robert L. Gearhart. 1994. *Magnetometer survey of Sabine Pass Channel and assessment of the* Clifton, *41JF65, Jefferson County, Texas and Cameron Parish, Louisiana.* Austin: Espey, Huston, & Associates.

Irion, Jack B. 1985. *Archaeological testing of the Confederate obstructions, 1MB28, Mobile Harbor, Alabama.* Austin: Espey, Huston, and Associates.

Irion, Jack B., and David A. Ball. 2001. The *New York* and *Josephine*: Two steamships of the Charles Morgan Line. *International Journal of Nautical Archaeology* 30 (1): 48–56.

Irion, Jack B., David V. Beard, and Paul V. Heinrich. 1994. *Remote sensing investigations of Civil War era shipwrecks in the vicinity of Fort St. Philip, Plaquemines Parish, Louisiana.* New Orleans: Goodwin and Associates.

Irion, Jack B., and Clell Bond. 1984. *Identification and evaluation of submerged anomalies, Mobile Harbor, Alabama.* Austin: Espey Huston & Associates.

James, Stephen R., Jack C. Hudson, and Kay G. Hudson. 1991. *The 303 Hang: Archaeological investigations of a two masted schooner wrecked offshore Freeport, Brazoria County, Texas.* Tuscaloosa, AL: Panamerican Consultants.

Johnson, Malcom L. n.d. *Lake Austin*, a coastal trading schooner. Unpublished report on file at the Texas Historical Commission, Austin.

Jones, Douglas S. 2007. Too much top for its bottom: The historical and archaeological identification of the USS *Castine* and the significance of U.S. gunboats in the early steel navy. MA thesis, East Carolina University.

Jones, Douglas, Amy Borgens, and Dave Ball. 2009. Wrecks in the washing machine: Documenting the *New York* and evaluating the effects of recent hurricane activity on Gulf of Mexico shipwrecks. In *ACUA Underwater Archaeology Proceedings*, ed. Erika Laanela and Johnathon Moore, 71–81. Columbus, OH: PAST Foundation.

Jones, Toby N. 2004. The *Mica* shipwreck: Deepwater nautical archaeology in the Gulf of Mexico. MA thesis, Texas A&M University.

Jordan, Jonathon W. 2006. *Lone Star navy: Texas, the fight for the Gulf of Mexico, and the shaping of the American West.* Washington, DC: Potomac Books.

Locke, Robert. 1999. Reviving a sunken dream: A spectacular shipwreck tells the tale of a doomed French venture into Texas. *Discovering Archaeology* 1 (5): 70–81.

Marichal, Carlos. 2006. The Spanish-American silver peso: Export commodity and global money of the Ancient Regime, 1550–1800. In *From silver to cocaine: Latin American commodity chains and the building of the world economy, 1500–1800*, ed. Steven Topik, Carlos Marichal, and Zephyr Frank, 25–52. Durham, NC: Duke University Press.

McClure, Kathryn S. 2003. *Governor Stone*: A nineteenth-century Gulf Coast schooner. MA thesis, Florida State University.

———. 2004. *Governor Stone*: Analysis of an 1877 two-masted schooner from the Gulf of Mexico. *International Journal of Nautical Archaeology* 33 (2): 297–314.

Morelli, Keith. 2008. Long-lost ship may surrender Civil War secrets. Media General News Service. Rev. 23 May 2008. Online at www.newsadvance.com/lna/news/state_regional/article/long_lost_ship_may_surrender_civil_war_secrets/5146/. Accessed 11 November 2008.

Morris, Paul. 1984. *Schooners and schooner barges*. Orleans, MA: Lower Cape.

Oertling, Thomas J. 1992. Survey for the Texas Navy warship *Invincible*. Galveston: National Underwater and Marine Agency.

Parry, John H. 1990. *The Spanish seaborne empire*. Berkeley and Los Angeles: University of California Press.

Pearson, Charles E. 1981. El Nuevo Constante: *Investigation of an eighteenth century Spanish shipwreck off the Louisiana Coast*. Baton Rouge: Louisiana Archaeological Survey and Antiquities Commission, Department of Culture, Recreation, and Tourism.

Pearson, Charles E., George J. Castillo, Donald Davis, Thomas E. Redard, and Allen R. Saltus. 1989. *A history of waterborne commerce and transportation within the U.S. Army Corps of Engineers New Orleans District and an inventory of known underwater cultural resources*. Baton Rouge: Coastal Environments.

Pearson, Charles E., and Paul E. Hoffman. 1995. *The last voyage of* El Nuevo Constante: *The wreck and recovery of an eighteenth-century Spanish ship off the Louisiana coast*. Baton Rouge: Louisiana State University Press.

Pearson, Charles E., Stephen R. James Jr., Michael C. Krivor, S. Dean El Darragi, and Lori Cunningham. 2003. *Refining and revisiting the Gulf of Mexico Outer Continental Shelf Region High Probability Model for Historic Shipwrecks*. New Orleans: U.S. Department of the Interior, Minerals Management Service, Gulf of Mexico OCS Region.

Peterson, Mandel. 1975. *The funnel of gold*. Boston: Little, Brown.

Powell, Christine, ed. 1999. In the field. *INA Quarterly* 26 (2): 16–17.

Powers, John. 2006. *The first Texas navy*. Austin: Woodmont Books.

Ramage, Margaret. 1963. Wrecked schooner's cargo built Port Aransas home. *Corpus Christi Caller-Times*. 19 June.

Randall, Keith. 2008. Unusual artifacts found in Mardi Gras shipwreck. Rev. 31 October 2008. Online at http://dmc-news.tamu.edu/templates/?a=6898&z=15/. Accessed 23 November 2008.

Ryan, Pandora. 1982. Sole surviving link to early Texas navy on display. *Galveston Daily News*. 17 March.

Scott-Ireton, Della A. 2003. Florida's underwater archaeological preserves. In *Submerged cultural resources management: Preserving and interpreting our sunken maritime heritage*, ed. James D. Spirek and Della A. Scott-Ireton, 95–106. New York: Plenum.

———. 2009. Shared heritage: British shipwrecks in Florida. In *Shared heritage: Joint responsibilities in the management of British warship wrecks overseas; International Seminar, 8 July 2008, University of Wolverhampton*, ed. Steven Gallagher, 45–57. London: English Heritage.

Sjordal, Paul. 2007. *The history and archaeology of ship abandonment at Shields Point*. MA thesis. University of West Florida.

Smith, Roger C. 1988. Treasure ships of the Spanish Main: The Iberian-American maritime empires. In *Ships and shipwrecks of the Americas: A history based on underwater archaeology*, ed. George E. Bass, 85–106. New York: Thames and Hudson.

———. 1999. Pensacola's colonial maritime resources. In *Archaeology of colonial Pensacola*, ed. Judith A. Bense, 91–120. Gainesville: University of Florida Press.

———. 2001. The Emanuel Point ship: A 16th-century vessel of Spanish colonization. In *Pré-Actas do Simpósio Internacional Arqueologia dos Navios Medievais e Modernos de Tradição Ibero-Atlântica*, ed. F. J. S. Alves, 58–60. Lisbon: Centro Nacional de Arqueologia Náutica e Subaquática.

———. 2009. Luna's fleet and the discovery of the first Emanuel Point shipwreck. *Florida Anthropologist* 62 (3–4): 79–81.

Smith, Roger C., John R. Bratten, J. Cozzi, and K. Plaskett. 1998. The Emanuel Point ship: Archaeological investigation 1997–1998. Tallahassee: Bureau of Archaeological Research, Division of Historical Resources, Florida Department of State.

Smith, Roger C., Robert Finegold, and Eric Stephens. 1990. Establishing an underwater archaeological preserve in the Florida Keys: A case study. *APT Bulletin* 22 (3): 11–18.

Smith, Roger C., James D. Spirek, John R. Bratten, and Della Scott-Ireton. 1999. The Emanuel Point ship: Archaeological investigations 1992–1995. Tallahassee: Bureau of Archaeological Research, Division of Historical Resources, Florida Department of State.

Soley, J. R. 1898. *The navy in the Civil War: The blockade and the cruisers*. London: Sampson, Low, Marston & Company.

Souza, Donna J. 1998. *The persistence of sail in the age of steam: Underwater archaeological evidence from the Dry Tortugas*. New York: Plenum.

Tumbleson Morris, Nicole. 2009. Letter to author. 23 February.

Wakefield, John F., ed. 1987. *Battle of Mobile Bay 1864*. Incidents in the American Civil War. Revised 2000. Florence, SC: Honors Press.

Warren, Daniel, Robert Church, Roy Cullimore, and Lori Johnston. 2004. *ROV investigations of the DKM U-166 shipwreck site to document the archaeological and biological aspects of the wreck site*. Lafayette, LA: C&C Technologies.

Watts, Gordon P., Tim Hastings, Stan Dunlap, and Stan Duncan. 1998. Mobile Bay shipwreck survey: Investigation and assessment of Civil War shipwrecks off Fort Morgan Point, Mobile, Alabama. Greenville: East Carolina University.

Weddle, Robert S. 2009. *The wrecking of La Salle's ship* Aimable *and the trial of Claude Aigron*. Austin: University of Texas Press.

Worth, John E. 2009. Documenting Tristán de Luna's fleet, and the storm that destroyed it. *Florida Anthropologist* 62 (3–4): 83–92.

Wilbanks, Ralph L., Wes Hal, and Gary E. McKee. 2000. Search for *L'Aimable*. Scottsdale, AZ: National Underwater and Marine Agency.

Works Progress Administration. 1941–1942. *Ship registers and enrollments of New Orleans*. 6 vols. Baton Rouge: Louisiana State University.

CHAPTER 30

SHIPWRECK ARCHAEOLOGY IN SOUTH AMERICA

DOLORES ELKIN

INTRODUCTION

THIS chapter, as stated in the title, focuses on the archaeological study of shipwrecks, which, admittedly, is just one component of what the concepts of "maritime," "nautical," and "underwater" archaeology usually encompass. On the one hand, some selection criteria had to apply in order to provide a minimal degree of insight into each of the case studies presented. On the other, although ships are cultural products that have a great potential to teach us about technology, trade, and many other aspects of the society to which they relate (Adams 2001), South American archaeologists are only beginning to address them, whereas other types of prehistoric and historic sites have been thoroughly studied and published for many decades in most of the region.

It is probably worth clarifying, too, that this chapter deals with shipwreck archaeology itself; various matters related to the management, public presentation, or purely historical approach to shipwrecks are intentionally left out. Watercrafts or parts of vessels that have only been studied out of their original archaeological context will also be excluded.

THE REGION

South America is a huge geographical region, with hundreds of thousands of kilometers of coastline in the form of oceans, archipelagic waters (particularly in southern Chile), rivers, lakes, and other waterways, stretching from tropical to subantarctic environments.

Since prehistoric times, native peoples ventured into the water using rafts, boats, and other devices, some of which have been occasionally recorded in rock art. Later in time, particularly in the era of the European discovery and exploration of the Americas, an increase in nautical activity began to take place involving ships of diverse natures. By the nineteenth and early twentieth centuries, specifically until the opening of the Panama Canal in 1914, commercial vessels from all over the world sailed around South America.

For such a vast area and such a rich potential in terms of nautical heritage, it is quite surprising that the specialty of underwater archaeology was not born in South America until the mid-1990s, considerably later than in other parts of the world presented in this book. Surrounded by a considerable number of treasure hunters, souvenir collectors, and other threats (Leshikar-Denton and Erreguerena 2008), a handful of archaeologists and undergraduate students gradually began conducting research in Brazil, Argentina, Chile, and Uruguay, and they were eventually followed by scholars in other counties. The following sections, arranged in alphabetical order by country, outline the current state of archaeological research of shipwrecks in the region.

Argentina

In the mid-1990s Argentina witnessed the birth of two underwater archaeology research groups: one based at the National Institute of Anthropology (INAPL) in Buenos Aires and directed by the author (Elkin 2002a), and the other at the National University of Rosario (Santa Fe Province) and directed by historian Mónica Valentini, often working in collaboration with architect Javier García Cano of the Albenga Foundation (Valentini 2003).

Both teams conduct various activities pertaining to maritime cultural heritage, including research, management, education, and public outreach (Elkin 2003; Valentini 2003). Archaeologically, the INAPL Underwater Archaeology Program (PROAS) has focused on shipwrecks, while the Rosario team has dealt with a greater variety of sites. In addition, the link between the INAPL program and the National Research Council (CONICET) has developed some form of "specialization" in archaeological research.

Shipwreck Studies Conducted by the Underwater Archaeology Program (PROAS) of the National Institute of Anthropology

Under the auspices of PROAS, four archaeological research projects focused on shipwrecks are being conducted in three different locations in Patagonia, in southern Argentina. The PROAS program, in conjunction with the Naval Hydrographic Service and other entities, is also developing a shipwreck database that until now has focused on the Río de la Plata, and to a lesser degree on the South Atlantic Ocean. However, even for the Río de la Plata shipwreck database, the work so far has concentrated on historical, hydrographic, and geomorphological data, addressing archaeology only through the interpretation and modeling of the nautical aquatic landscape of the river (Guagliardo 2007). Therefore, this work will not be described in the present chapter.

HMS Swift *(Puerto Deseado, Santa Cruz)*

HMS *Swift* was a 14-gun sloop-of-war sent in 1769 CE to the British base of Port Egmont, in the Malvinas/Falkland archipelago, under the command of Captain George Farmer. In early March 1770, while conducting an exploratory trip in the region, *Swift* had to seek shelter in the continental estuary of Port Desire (Puerto Deseado) after several days of bad weather. Close to the entrance of the estuary *Swift* ran aground, but the crew managed to free the vessel. Subsequently pushed by the wind farther up the estuary, the ship grounded again on another rock. After several hours of unfruitful maneuvers, *Swift* sank (ADM 5304; Gower 1803).

Due to the critical situation faced by the survivors, six volunteers and the ship's master were sent back to Port Egmont to get help. After successfully completing an amazing journey of 370 nautical miles in a six-oared cutter, all 88 survivors of the *Swift* shipwreck were rescued about a month after the accident (ADM 5304; Gower 1803).

Over two centuries later, an Australian Army officer named Patrick Gower—a descendant of the ship's lieutenant, Erasmus Gower—traveled to Puerto Deseado carrying a diary published in 1803 that included an account of the wreck and its general location. The local community did not know about the loss of *Swift*, but the seed was sown, and a few years later a group of local divers decided to look for the wreck. Using Gower's diary, maritime charts, topographic information, and their own personal knowledge of the area, they soon found the remains of *Swift*. It was February 1982. In the first stages of activities conducted at the site in the 1980s and early 1990s, about 100 artifacts were recovered and taken to a local museum that was specially built to host the *Swift*'s finds.

In 1998, at the request of the provincial authorities, the underwater archaeology team of the National Institute of Anthropology initiated an ongoing systematic archaeological investigation of the site under the direction of the author. The Brozoski Museum in Puerto Deseado has remained in charge of the conservation, curation, display, and management of the collection.

The ship lies on its port side at a maximum depth of 18 m, and it is estimated that about 60% of the original wooden hull structure is preserved (Murray, Elkin, and Vainstub 2002–2003). Except for the ship structure rising above the seabed, the remaining hull components, including most of the main deck, as well as the artifacts and ecofacts associated with the vessel, have been covered by fine-grained silt. This anaerobic environment has allowed for remarkably good preservation conditions.

The archaeological assemblage excavated during the last eight years has been recovered mainly from the officers' quarters in the stern of the ship. It includes a great variety of artifacts made of ceramic, metal, glass, wood, stone, and bone, as well as several additional organic remains usually associated with clothing, food, rigging, and stowage materials (Elkin 2002a, 2003, 2008; Elkin et al. 2000, 2001, 2007; Murray, Elkin, and Vainstub 2002–2003). Recently a complete human skeleton was found within the excavation zone at the stern, inside the great cabin.

Aside from the historical contextualization of *Swift* within the geopolitical arena of the time (Dellino 2007), the main research themes conducted within the *Swift* project include contemporary technologies, the relationship between material culture and status, ship construction, diet, site formation processes, and, triggered by the finding of human remains, health and other bioanthropological topics.

The analyses of the material culture associated with the officers and the ordinary seamen of *Swift* are based on the hypothesis that differences in material quality reflect differential social status within the crew. The higher-quality items, which should be associated with the officers, are also expected to reflect the technological progress that characterized the European region in the eighteenth century.

The methodology that allows addressing this topic consists of the study of materials already recovered from the officers' quarters, as well as from areas in the lower deck amidships (excavated since 2008), an area that is expected to be associated with ordinary seamen. In both cases, standard typological-technical analyses are complemented with chemical characterization of selected items in order to assess indicators such as manufacture techniques and composition of the artifacts. For this latter purpose, the team includes the interdisciplinary participation of specialists in chemistry capable of conducting elemental and compositional analyses of organic and inorganic materials.

The results achieved to date show that the officers of *Swift* indeed owned or used some objects of relatively high quality (such as tableware made of porcelain and refined earthenware; see Elkin et al. 2007), although some other items were quite coarsely made (De Rosa et al. 2007; Ciarlo, pers. comm. 2008). As for the lower classes within the ship's crew, the artifact sample obtained to date is not sufficient to allow us to draw significant conclusions, but excavations in areas likely associated with ordinary seamen are planned for future field seasons.

Another line of investigation is the modifications that were made to the vessel after its original construction, since significant alterations have already been identified in both the rigging and the deck layout (Murray, Elkin, and Vainstub 2002–2003). Our hypothesis is that these changes were made with the purpose of adapting the vessel to transoceanic sailing and other aspects of its service. In the areas of the ship recently opened for excavation, modifications probably intended to increase the internal space of the ship were found, especially the space occupied by ordinary seamen, since the original design of the ship (NMM 3606A) assigned a reduced space for them. On the other hand, certain design aspects related to seaworthiness, specifically the hull shape, do not seem to have been modified, since it is believed that they would have been sufficient for the vessel's new purpose (Murray, Elkin, and Vainstub 2002–2003; Murray, pers. comm. 2009).

The question of what was consumed on board *Swift* has guided one of the main lines of research since the beginning of the project (Elkin 1997). Many items are listed as supplied by the Victualling Board for vessels of the period and on a number of instances references are made specifically to supplies carried by *Swift*. However, archaeology can provide an independent and objective tool to find out what was actually carried on board (Elkin 2008).

The galley of the ship has not been fully excavated, and the food items that have been recovered have come mostly from the officers' quarters. To a lesser degree, some were found inside glass and ceramic containers located on the surface of the sediment in different sectors of the ship. To date, various condiments and other botanical remains have been identified (Museo Argentino de Ciencias Naturales 1983; Rodríguez 2002; Picca, pers. comm. 2006). These include white mustard (*Brassica aff alba*) and two species of pepper (*Piper nigrum* and *Pimenta officinalis*), none of which are mentioned as supplied by the navy in the several documents we have consulted. Nutmeg (*Myristica fragrans*), raisins (*Vitis vinifera*), and squash (*Cucurbita* sp.) were also found. An interesting food category consists of penguin eggs, identified by their eggshells as king penguin (*Aptenodytes patagonicus*) (Frere, pers. comm. 2000). This provides evidence in terms of the use of local resources to complement the provisions supplied by the Admiralty's Victualling Board (Elkin 2008).

In regard to drink on board, chemical analyses were performed on the content of different types of bottles that were found with their cork stoppers in place. One cylindrical "wine" bottle contained a variety of sweet, sherry-type white wine (Dirección Nacional de Química 1982). The contents of the square "gin" bottles were unfortunately found to be highly contaminated with seawater, but a gas liquid chromatography analysis revealed that some ethanol still remained in the samples (UDV Laboratory 2001).

The monitoring and study of natural site formation processes constitute another component of the investigation of the *Swift* wreck site. Marine organisms, such as the kelp *Macrocystis pyrifera* and tunicates of different species, have colonized many of the exposed timbers. This biofouling causes mechanical and chemical effects on the ship's structure and exposed artifacts (Bastida et al. 2004, 2008; Grosso 2008).

Another issue addressed is the action of marine wood borers, which has already been confirmed for this site even in hardwood materials (Bastida et al. 2004; Grosso 2008). Evidence of postdepositional attack by wood borers has also been confirmed, although whether or not it continues at present is not yet known. The hull components, as well as various wooden artifacts and experimental wooden panels, are being thoroughly studied and/or monitored in relation to this problem (Bastida et al. 2004, 2008; Grosso 2008). The potential action of wood-boring molluscs on the site is also a relevant conservation issue, given that wood is the main component of the site.

The last main strand of research within the *Swift* project originated in the 2005–2006 field season, when a complete human skeleton was found in the captain's cabin and subsequently excavated after consultation and agreement with UK authorities. Several historical documents indicate that three people perished when the ship sank: the cook, Richard Griffiths (age 30), and two private marines—Robert Rusker (age 21) and John Ballard (age 23) (ADM 33-688, ADM 5304; Gower 1803). The present research hypothesis is that these skeletal remains correspond to one of the two private marines (Barrientos et al. 2007). The first studies were conducted by means of visual and radiological techniques. Sex and age indicators revealed that the skeletal remains indeed belonged to a male approximately 25 years of age (range 17–34). This osteological conclusion would be consistent with the sex and age of either of the marines who died in the accident, but the strongest evidence supporting our hypothesis is the identification of traces of a red woolen jacket, which would have been part of a private marine's uniform (Maier et al. 2010). Additionally, it can be stated that the remains represent an individual who stood 1.67 m tall, was probably right-handed, and enjoyed generally good bone and dental health, other than a class II malocclusion (retrognathism), a few cavities, and abundant tartar. A current goal is to identify the person at the individual level. Mitochondrial DNA has already been successfully extracted from *Swift*'s skeleton (Moraga, pers. comm. 2008), and attempts are made to extract nuclear DNA as well. The remaining task would then consist of conducting genealogical research in the UK in the hope of finding descendants of either Rusker or Ballard, extracting DNA samples from them, and comparing their DNA with that obtained from the human remains found on *Swift*.

The last type of study that will be conducted on the archaeological bones from the *Swift*, regardless of the person's identity, is carbon and nitrogen stable isotope analysis, which may shed light on the individual's diet. The results will be confronted with the historical records referring to the standard diet aboard *Swift* and comparable vessels of the time (ADM 111/65).

Hoorn *(Puerto Deseado, Santa Cruz)*

The *jacht Hoorn* was one of the two ships of the Dutch expedition led by Jacob Le Maire and Willem C. Schouten during the early seventeenth century in search of a new passage to the Spice Islands. After crossing the Atlantic Ocean, she entered into the Deseado estuary (currently Santa Cruz Province, Argentina) and was lost by accidental fire in December 1615 while being careened on the pebble shore.

In 2003, a project was started with the purpose of locating and studying the remains of the vessel, under the direction of Damián Vainstub and Cristian Murray, from PROAS-Argentina and Martijn Manders, from the National Service for Archaeological Heritage (ROB) of Holland. The initial methodological approach was twofold (Murray et al. 2007). On the one hand, it involved the compilation and analysis of historical documents related to the *Hoorn*'s voyage and its context. This comprised materials such as the journals written by the leaders of the expedition (Le Maire 1622; Schouten 1618), as well as maps and iconographic sources. On the other hand, the approach included a careful interpretation of the coastal geomorphology with the purpose of identifying potential sectors where a vessel like the *Hoorn* could have been intentionally beached and careened. One of these areas yielded some ceramic shards scattered among the pebbles (Figure 30.1), which were subsequently assigned to the chronological and geographical context under study and which in turn helped to delimitate the search and work area.

A terrestrial archaeological survey was initiated along the wide intertidal coastline with the aid of metal detectors. Several test pits were excavated in areas with the highest surface artifact density. One of these sectors included a cluster of seemingly allochthonous (non-native) rocks, something later confirmed by petrographic studies (Murray et al. 2007; Vainstub and Murray 2006). This originated the hypothesis of possible ballast.

Other archaeological surface or subsurface finds included melted metallic fragments that seemed to be associated with the fire on board. While the aforementioned archaeological evidence led to the belief that the primary deposit resulting from the

Figure 30.1 In situ Rhineland (probably Westerwald) blue and gray stoneware shard from the *Hoorn* (Santa Cruz, Argentina). Photo by R. Bastida, PROAS—Instituto Nacional de Antropología.

burning of the *Hoorn* had been located, no evidence of the ship's structure was found on land. As a result, the search was extended to the underwater environment.

The first season of underwater work in search of further remains from the *Hoorn* began with a SCUBA-diving reconnaissance survey of the subtidal area, mainly focusing on topography, sedimentary characteristics, visibility, and currents (Murray et al. 2007; Vainstub and Murray 2006). A second field season surveyed a larger area of seabed adjacent to the coast by means of geophysical remote-sensing technology (side-scan sonar and magnetometer), combined with selected SCUBA-diving immersions to review anomalies (Murray et al. 2007: 353).

The main results of the three-year-long *Hoorn* project can be summarized as follows: The location of the wreck site has been identified, with a primary deposit of archaeological materials related to the fire and destruction of the ship. These materials include melted metallic fragments made of pewter and brass alloys, silver, and lead, some of which contain seeds and carbon fragments, as well as copper nails. All of these artifacts were found in association with a group of allochthonous rocks that are interpreted to be part of the vessel's ballast (Marconetto et al. 2005; Vainstub and Murray 2006). Additionally, and scattered along the line of high tide, about 170 ceramic shards were found, showing evidence of rolling and weathering. Many of them bear inscriptions and seals and have been assigned to Raeren, Frechen, and Westerwald stonewares (Elkin and Murray 2006).

The complementary underwater survey identified ferrous concretions in the subtidal zone adjacent to the land concentration located in the intertidal zone. The bathymetric characteristics of the area possibly acted as a natural "trap," preventing further dispersal of artifacts. X-ray studies conducted on the concretions revealed the impressions of corroded iron artifacts such as nails, fittings, and bolts (Ciarlo 2006; Murray et al. 2007). No wood or hull remains were found either on land or underwater. The explanation may lie in a combination of factors, including the effects of a very dynamic intertidal zone environment on site formation processes, and the salvage of wood both by the original crew of the Dutch expedition, as well as by aboriginal or nonaboriginal people in later times. The project achieved its main goal of locating and surveying the wreck site of the *Hoorn*, the earliest identified shipwreck site in Argentina to date (Elkin and Murray 2006; Murray et al. 2007; Vainstub and Murray 2006).

BG2 (Puerto Madryn, Chubut)

In 2004, a project began in the province of Chubut, with the initial goals of assessing, conducting nonintrusive surveys, and providing educational, public outreach, management, and tourism guidelines for historic and modern shipwrecks. The specific area selected for the work was the UNESCO World Heritage site of the Valdés Peninsula, as well as the adjacent coastal city of Puerto Madryn. Around 30 shipwrecks are located there, 6 of which were selected for preliminary surveys on the basis of their historical, archaeological, and/or touristic significance (Elkin and Murray 2006). Due to the criteria followed in this chapter, only

site BG-2 will be presented, as it has been subject to the most thorough archaeological study.

BG2 is an unidentified wooden wreck site named after the former name of the
bay in which it is located, Bahía Galenses, in the southern coastal segment of Puerto
Madryn city. Lying in the intertidal zone of the beach, it consists of a 28 m long
section of a hull that was becoming increasingly exposed to the elements. A preliminary nonintrusive survey suggested that the original vessel may have been built in
the eighteenth or nineteenth century.

With the goal of conducting a more specific assessment of the cultural and
chronological affiliation of this wreck, two archaeological field seasons were carried out in 2006. The work consisted of completing a site plan of the exposed structure, digging several test pits around the perimeter in order to better understand
the nature and position of the structure, excavating three cross-section trenches in
the middle and end sectors of the site (considered potentially diagnostic), surveying diagnostic features of the structure, and taking samples of the wooden
structure, metal fittings, and any other material that could contribute to its understanding (Murray et al. 2008). The archaeological research revealed that the structure is part of a wooden sailing ship, probably a merchant or fishing vessel of
300–500 tons burden, which could have sunk due to a fire in what appears to be the
mid-nineteenth century. Botanical taxonomic analysis indicated that European
and American wood was used in the construction of the vessel. Interestingly, the
archaeological evidence seems to coincide with historical documentation that indicates the presence of a shipwreck in the area by the time the first Welsh settlers
arrived (British Admiralty 1883; Ap Iwan 1889 in Coronato 1997), as well as with the
reported salvage of wood from such a wreck by the Welsh (Coronato 1997; Jones
1993, 2000), as some of the buried timbers show evidence of nonrecent cutting with
an axe or a similar sharp edge tool. Further botanical and chemical analyses will be
conducted for BG-2, and it is hoped that they will provide a better understanding
of this wreck site.

Shipwrecks in Monte León National Park (Santa Cruz)

Monte León is a recently created national park in the Santa Cruz Province of Argentina that includes 40 km of ocean coastline. The National Parks Administration
requested that the PROAS team conduct a baseline assessment of the maritime heritage of the park's coastline as part of the park's general management plan. It is
worth noting that one of the ships of Magellan-Elcano's voyage around the world
(1519–1522 CE), the *nau Santiago*, wrecked against the rocky Patagonian shore
(Pigafetta 2003 [circa 1526]), potentially within what is now the Monte León
National Park.

Research began with a thorough compilation and analysis of primary and secondary historical sources referring to the Magellan-Elcano expedition and the loss
of the *Santiago*, as well as of other seafaring activity in the area, in order to assess
the presence of possible archaeological resources. Additionally, information was

gathered from various sources regarding previous activities directed at shipwrecks, including the development of private and public artifact collections. After this initial stage, two field seasons were conducted within the national park, and the selected methodology consisted of coastal and intertidal surveys along parallel transects, conducted as much as possible during low-tide periods. The hypothesis of the location of the remains of the *Santiago* indicated that the intertidal zone, which averages around 500 m wide, was the area with greatest archaeological potential. Materials previously extracted from the area by local people were also recorded. As of yet, only interim manuscript reports of the study are available (Elkin 2007), although a paper for publication is currently being prepared.

The main results of the work can be summarized as follows. Although no evidence of the *Santiago* was found—and, for diverse reasons, it is unlikely that such evidence will ever be found—several scattered shipwreck remains were located, documented, and sampled for further laboratory studies. The initial interpretation of the material indicated that they consist of a minimum of two wooden shipwrecks dating probably from the second half of the nineteenth century, both between 300–500 tons burden. At least one of them was built with European woods. The combination of this preliminary conclusions and the analysis of documentary sources led the research team to propose the hypotheses that the vessel remains surveyed in Monte León could correspond to the North American bark *Mary E. Parker* (1874 CE) and the Norwegian bark *Cuba* (1878 CE). Further studies, botanical and other, are expected to shed more light on the Monte León wreck sites.

Shipwreck Studies by the National University of Rosario

The School of Anthropology of the National University of Rosario has mostly dealt with submerged sites other than shipwrecks. However, the director of the group, Mónica Valentini, has published or copublished on at least three projects involving shipwrecks (Valentini 2003: 40–41). These projects include an unsuccessful search for a German submarine in Patagonia (see Valentini et al. 2001 for a description of the methodology and techniques applied); a ship sunk in the Río de la Plata that may have played a role in one of the battles during the war against Brazil in the first quarter of the nineteenth century; and a wreck near the beach resort of Reta, on the ocean coast of the province of Buenos Aires. The projects were collaborative efforts with the Albenga Foundation and on occasion with other institutions.

Survey and excavation of the Reta shipwreck conducted in 2002 revealed a nearly 30 m long wooden structure located on the beach above the intertidal zone. Metallographic and chemical studies were subsequently made on samples of plates and tacks from the metal sheathing, and they revealed that the first consisted of a copper-zinc alloy (60% and 40%, respectively), which was patented by Muntz in 1832 and shortly thereafter became of general use (Lorusso et al. 2003). The authors have concluded that the ship very probably dates to the late nineteenth century (Valentini 2003: 40).

At the beginning of 2009, together with archaeologist Marcelo Weissel from the Heritage Area of the Buenos Aires City Government and architect Javier García Cano from the School of Architecture of the University of Buenos Aires, Valentini became one of the three codirectors responsible for the study of a wooden ship-wreck unexpectedly uncovered during construction works in the city. So far the characteristics of the hull and of artifacts such as cannons, pottery, and coins indicate that the ship was an eighteenth-century merchant vessel (Comisión para la Preservación del Patrimonio Histórico Cultural 2009).

BRAZIL

Brazil was the first country in South America to begin conducting activities related to underwater cultural heritage, under the direction of archaeologist-diver Gilson Rambelli. Together with historians and other specialists from related disciplines, Rambelli has also been responsible for training students and supervising their work conducted in different underwater sites, some of them prehistoric.

The main challenge that Rambelli and his coworkers in Brazil had to face was the recurrent presence of treasure hunters, who were often supported by governmental agencies and the national legislation (Rambelli 2002, 2006). This situation might explain why, aside from his unpublished master's and PhD theses (Rambelli 1998, 2003), Rambelli's work has mostly focused on creating awareness about the rich Brazilian underwater cultural heritage. It is worth remarking, however, that at this time a number of shipwrecks are being periodically recorded and monitored for an archaeological chart of submerged sites (Rambelli 2006), while a book on the shipwreck of the nineteenth-century steamer *Conde d'Aquila* is expected to be published in the near future (Rambelli, pers. comm. 2008).

The Recife Shipwreck (Lamarão I)

Recife is an important port located on the northeastern coast of Brazil (state of Pernambuco), off which a large number of ships have been reported lost since the sixteenth century. In 2000, shrimp fishermen accidentally located an unidentified wooden shipwreck lying in the external portion of the harbor at a depth of 12 m. Since that time, the site has been archaeologically studied by Carlos Rios, currently a PhD student in archaeology at the Federal University of Pernambuco, with the goal of assessing the cultural and chronological context of the vessel. Rios has undertaken bibliographic research about wrecks and types of vessels recorded for the area, completed a survey and plan of the site, recovered surface artifacts, and excavated two sections of the site. Bathymetric recording and sediment sampling were also conducted in order to address issues such as site formation processes (Rios 2008).

Ship construction features and artifact interpretation led to the conclusion that the wreck corresponds to a merchant sailing vessel dating to between 1750 and 1850 CE; fire was likely the main cause of the sinking. The hull, which was covered with copper sheating, measured 54 m long and 15 m wide, with an estimated draft of around 5 m (Rios 2008). Four anchors were found close to the shipwreck, but on the basis of indicators such as position and typology, Rios (2008) believes that they did not belong to the shipwreck under study, whose anchors may have been salvaged.

As for the artifact collection, the ceramics consist mostly of utilitarian wares, with the exception of a type of faience transfer-print, while the glass is mostly blown. In both cases they can be dated to the eighteenth and nineteenth centuries. A few animal bone fragments, some of which could be identified as pork, were also found. Rios (2008) argues that this material and some other discovered artifacts may be intrusive. As it was not possible to establish the identity of the vessel, this shipwreck is called Lamarão I on the basis of its location within the Recife harbor area.

CHILE

Chile has recently been developing several initiatives oriented toward the preservation, public outreach, and investigation of the country's underwater cultural heritage. Local archaeologist and diver Diego Carabias Amor, a graduate of Universidad de Chile and later employed by the national heritage agency (Comisión Nacional de Monumentos), has played a leading role in this process, beginning as an undergraduate student around a decade ago. Spanish archaeologist Pedro Pujante Izquierdo, based in Chile at the Universidad Internacional SEK, has also contributed toward these common goals. In the following sections three case studies of archaeological shipwreck investigations conducted in Chile will be presented.

Submerged Valparaíso Project (Fifth Region—Valparaíso)

The bay of Valparaíso, particularly by the mid-nineteenth century, was one of the most important ports along the seafaring routes of the South Pacific, and historical documents indicate that approximately 500 vessels have been lost in this area since the end of the sixteenth century. A project oriented at archaeologically assessing the underwater cultural heritage of the Valparaiso bay was developed by the Centro de Ciencias y Ecología Aplicada (CEA) of the Universidad del Mar in Chile, in collaboration with the Groupe de Recherche en Archéologie Navale of France (Carabias and Chapanoff 2006; Carabias et al. 2006; Chapanoff and Carabias 2004).

The first of two phases of the Valparaíso Project were geared toward the location of submerged sites within 10 predetermined search areas by means of a geophysical remote sensing survey (magnetometer and side-scan sonar). The second phase involved underwater visual assessment of magnetic anomalies and side-scan sonar targets, followed by nonintrusive basic recording. In total, around 30 selected sites up to 45 m in depth were examined (Carabias and Chapanoff 2006: 216–220).

Preliminary results arising from the processing of 4 of the 10 search units within the bay show that the majority of sites can be dated to the nineteenth and twentieth centuries. Carabias and Chapanoff (2006: 220–221) believe the lack of earlier shipwrecks can be explained by a combination of factors, including the high degree of sedimentation and the significant anthropic modification of the coastline, which has been periodically advancing and which may well be covering old anchorings. Despite the preliminary nature of the results, the distribution and characteristics of the located wreck sites is already revealing patterns in the occupation and use of the maritime space of the bay.

It is worth noting also that this project was the first one of its kind in South America in using first geophysical and then direct diving recording of the shipwreck remains.

HMS *Wager* (Eleventh Region—Aysen)

HMS *Wager* was a British frigate that was part of Lord Anson's expedition to the South Seas, a fleet of eight vessels sent by the British Admiralty to the South Pacific in the context of territorial disputes and smuggling after the end of the War of Spanish Succession. The frigate, which carried a complement of 160 men and 28 guns, sank off the Pacific archipelagic coast of southern Chile in May 1741. The wrecking of HMS *Wager* led to considerable interaction between the ship's survivors and local indigenous groups that had a maritime-oriented economy and lifestyle.

Since 2006, archaeological research supported by the Universidad del Mar and other institutions has been conducted with the general goal of locating, surveying, and interpreting the archaeological remains of the HMS *Wager*. A second component of the archaeological investigations has been to study the indigenous groups and their intercultural contact with the European survivors.

The expected general location of the HMS *Wager* site was established on the basis of documentary sources, such as those written by the survivors or religious missionaries who came in contact with indigenous people inhabiting the area following the event. The field survey combined systematic and selective sampling methods, taking into account changes to the central and southern coastlines in western Patagonia and their implications for differential archaeological preservation, mostly of the prehistoric record. The underwater surveys were conducted in the subtidal zone, based on the materials found on land and information gathered through documentary sources (Carabias 2007).

A total of 14 archaeological sites—mostly prehistoric shell middens—were found during the fieldwork (Carabias 2007, 2008a, 2008b). In terms of locating the HMS *Wager* wreck site, the expedition came across the promising remains of a wooden hull measuring approximately 5.5 m by 4.5 m, as well as additional scattered pieces of timber, all of which were located at the bottom of a shallow stream in the northwest sector of Wager Island. This cluster was originally found by a group of British explorers who reported the find, and was subsequently defined by Carabias as site Wager 10 (Carabias 2007).

The main structural assemblage is a hull section formed by at least four frames, joined to eight outer planks by a series of treenails (Figure 30.2). Samples were taken from wooden elements such as frames, planking, and treenails, and an additional sample was obtained from a botanical fiber used as caulking material. At the time of writing, these samples were still undergoing analysis in different specialized laboratories in Chile. The interpretation of the structure is that it is part of a robust war or trade vessel, and the construction method and material coincide with those of a vessel like HMS *Wager*, a frigate originally built for trading purposes in the East Indies (Carabias 2007). The fact that the site location is consistent with several documentary sources that refer to the loss of HMS *Wager* on the northern coast of the island provides further support for considering that the site does indeed correspond to Anson's vessel.

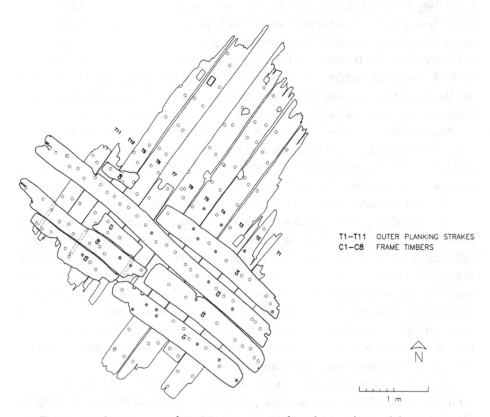

T1–T11   OUTER PLANKING STRAKES
C1–C8   FRAME TIMBERS

N

1 m

Figure 30.2 Structure 01 of site Wager 10, part of Lord Anson's vessel, lost in 1741 (Aysen, Chile). Drawing by C. Murray for Wager Research Project. Reproduced with the kind permission of D. Carabias.

The Mejillones Shipwreck (Second Region—Antofagasta)

The Universidad Internacional SEK conducted an archaeological shipwreck study in Bahia Mejillones under the direction of Pedro Pujante Izquierdo (Pujante 2001, 2007, n.d.). The team surveyed and excavated the remains of an unidentified wooden vessel that had been looted in previous years. After conducting archival historical research in Spain, it was concluded that the remains correspond to the Spanish merchant vessel *San Martín*, lost in 1759 CE in Mejillones (Antofagasta, Chile) during a voyage from El Callao (Perú) to Spain. Interestingly, the study revealed that the frame construction system of the vessel seems to represent a transitional phase between a system that was common in the first four decades of the eighteenth century, one that required large pieces of wood per frame, and the "English" system that was later adopted, in which each frame was made of a series of adjacent futtocks.

COLOMBIA

Shipwreck archaeology—and actually maritime or nautical archaeology in general—in Colombia is still in a very embryonic stage. Well-trained, young, and enthusiastic diving archaeologists, mostly related to a private nongovernmental organization called Fundación Terra Firme, have begun to develop various initiatives involving education, public outreach, and awareness about the underwater cultural heritage of the country (Del Cairo and García Chávez 2006).

A project currently under way consists of an archaeological and historical map of Cartagena Bay (García Chávez 2006: 188). Actual archaeological work has not yet been conducted or reported (García Chávez, pers. comm. 2008) but hopefully will take place in the near future.

URUGUAY

Until very recently Uruguay's legislation allowed the activities of treasure hunting and other forms of commercial exploitation of historic shipwrecks. Archaeologists and students from the country's National Heritage Commission have devoted more than a decade (see Martínez 1995 for the first steps) to combating treasure hunting, creating awareness, and training their nationals in the protection and investigation of the underwater cultural heritage. The legislation in Uruguay has now changed, and submerged cultural heritage that remains in its waters will be protected from commercial exploitation. It is likely, however, that some time will have to pass until either the National Heritage Commission or the Universidad de la República (the latter now training students, conducting environmental impact studies, and initiating some research projects) is able to progress sufficiently along the line of archaeological investigations.

An initiative worth mentioning is the Submerged Cultural Resources Inventory. A first field season was conducted in 2005 under the joint direction of archaeologists from the University of Southampton (Jon Adams and Jorge M. Herrera Tovar) and from Uruguay (Valerio Buffa and Alejo Cordero, the latter from the Heritage Commission), with the collaboration of the Argentinean PROAS team. Forty kilometers of ocean coastline were surveyed with remote sensing equipment, and two sites were located.

The rich nautical heritage of Río de la Plata has been addressed by Uruguayan archaeologist Antonio Lezama from Universidad de la República, but mostly from a historical perspective (Lezama 2008). In a way, this is similar to the aforementioned work on the same river undertaken by Argentinean archaeologist Juan Pablo Guagliardo (2007), although the latter has also taken into account geomorphological data that plays an important role in the development of an archaeological landscape model. In any case, the actual material remains of the hundreds of vessels lost in this river since the sixteenth century have rarely been subjected to archaeological recording and interpretation.

Occasionally, researchers from the Archaeology Department of Uruguay's National Heritage Commission have conducted archaeological surveys of historic shipwreck remains that either were not attractive to commercial salvagers or were left behind after the looting had taken place. This was the case, for example, of wooden hull remains located in the intertidal zone near Cabo Polonio. The timbers are visible along some 30 m and reveal the existence of two decks (Buffa and Cordero, pers. comm, in Elkin 2002b). Another shipwreck surveyed by the same team is located in a beach called Santa Rosa, some 40 km east of the city of Montevideo, and will be briefly described below.

The Santa Rosa Shipwreck (Department of Canelones)

The Santa Rosa shipwreck site consists of portions of a wooden ship structure semi-buried along the homonymous beach. The archaeological research involved the identification of structural elements, naval design and construction indicators, wood types present, and site formation processes. The study was focused on the most representative section of the vessel (Figure 30.3), an articulated structure that covers an area of 72 m² and includes frames, inner and outer planking, and knees (both iron hanging knees and wooden lodging knees). Some of the fittings consist of iron bolts, but the majority were treenails (Buffa and Cordero 2001). The structure was interpreted as part of the upperworks of a two- or three-deck vessel. The angle of the cant frames indicated that this section of the structure was located close to either the bow or the stern of the ship.

Botanical analyses of various wood samples obtained from the structural components have identified a soft wood: Gimnosperma of the family *Pinaceae*, subfamily

Figure 30.3 The shipwreck of Santa Rosa (Canelones, Uruguay). Reproduced with the kind permission of the Comisión Nacional de Patrimonio Cultural, Uruguay.

Abietoideae, genus *Picea*. It is highly probable that this corresponds to an autochthonous North American spruce species: either the white, red, or black spruce (Inda and Del Puerto 2001, in Buffa and Cordero 2001).

The study has concluded that the remains correspond to those of a large vessel—over 1,200 tons—built in North America around the middle of the nineteenth century, as indicated by certain construction features, such as the metal knees (Buffa and Cordero 2001).

CONCLUSION

The overview presented above reveals quite a varied degree of research undertaken by different South American countries. Moreover, vast geographical areas seem to be lacking underwater archaeological studies altogether, whether specifically nautical, or related to the use of the ocean and inland waterways in general. The potential, therefore, remains enormous.

Nonetheless, one can only expect the growth of the discipline in this region given the number of undergraduate and graduate archaeology students that are currently in the stage of acquiring the necessary skills and experience to take up the challenge.

This is particularly the case for Perú (Ausejo, pers. comm. 2010), Colombia (García Chávez, pers. comm. 2008), Uruguay (Vienni, pers. comm. 2008), and Brazil (Rios, pers. comm. 2008). Countries like Ecuador and Paraguay apparently lack such local development, but the fact that they are both among the first states to have ratified the UNESCO Convention for the Protection of Underwater Cultural Heritage justifies an optimistic perspective. Bolivia has already been sending delegates to regional meetings regarding the UNESCO convention, and apparently local archaeologists-divers are beginning to conduct studies on submerged sites.

The field of conservation of waterlogged materials, an essential partner in fore-shore and underwater archaeology, is less mature than the archaeology front in South America, and capacity building is widely acknowledged as an urgent need. Argentina and Chile are the only countries that seem to have local conservators working with underwater cultural heritage, but they are only a handful of people. Progress in this field is additionally constrained by access to costly equipment such as freeze-dryers, commonly used in countries with better-developed maritime archaeology practice.

Among some positive actions, hands-on training of South American conservators in overseas venues with expertise in the specialty has already started. As an example, an Argentinean conservator from the National Institute of Anthropology undertook a four-week-long internship in 2008 at the Mary Rose Trust in England with sponsorship from that institution and from UNESCO-ICUCH.

Hopefully all these new initiatives will yield fruitful results in the very near future, and the mutual collaboration between countries that has characterized the region since the first steps will continue to take place.

REFERENCES

Adams, J. 2001. Ships and boats as archaeological source material. *World Archaeology* 32 (3): 292–310.
ADM 111/65. 1769. *Victualling board and committees.* Public Record Office, London.
ADM 33-688. 1770. *Swift* complement. Public Record Office, London.
ADM 5304. 1770. *Court martial to the HMS* Swift. Public Record Office, London.
Ap Iwan, L. 1889. Chronicle of a voyage to Valdes Peninsula in 1886. *Y Celt Y Bala*, 15 March.
Barrientos, G., M. Béguelin, V. Bernal, M. Del Papa, S. García Guraieb, G. Ghidini, P. González, and D. Elkin. 2007. *Estudio bioarqueológico del esqueleto recuperado en la corbeta británica del siglo XVIII HMS* Swift *(Puerto Deseado, Santa Cruz).* Octavas Jornadas Nacionales de Antropología Biológica. Salta, 1–5 October. Ms. on file, Instituto Nacional de Antropología, Buenos Aires.
Bastida, R., D. Elkin, M. Grosso, M. Trassens, and J. P. Martin. 2004. The British sloop of war HMS *Swift* (1770): A case study of the effects of biodeterioration on the underwater cultural heritage of Patagonia. *Corrosion Reviews. Special Issue: Biodeterioration of Cultural Heritage* 22 (5–6): 417–440. London: Freund.

Bastida, R., M. Grosso, and D. Elkin. 2008. The role of benthic communities and
    environmental agents in the formation of underwater archaeological sites. In
    Underwater and maritime archaeology in Latin America and the Caribbean, ed.
    M. Leshikar-Denton and P. Luna Erreguerena, 173–185. Walnut Creek, CA:
    Left Coast Press.
British Admiralty. 1883. *Chart of New Gulf* (1876). Capt. H. Fairfax, HMS *Volage*.
Buffa, V., and A. Cordero. 2001. *Arqueología marítima en el fortín de Santa Rosa: El
    potencial de los hallazgos costeros*. Paper presented at the XIV Congreso Nacional
    de Arqueología Argentina (Simposio Arqueología Subacuática, Investigaciones en
    Arqueología Subacuática-Teoría, Metodos y Técnicas). Universidad Nacional
    de Rosario, September. Ms. on file, Instituto Nacional de Antropología, Buenos Aires.
Carabias, A. D. 2007. *Proyecto Wager: Enfoques integradores en arqueología marítima;
    Prospección arqueológica combinada costera y subacuática Islas Wager—Byron,
    Archipiélago guayaneco, región de Aisén—Trabajo de terreno no. 1: 15 de noviembre
    al 03 de diciembre de 2006. Informe de avance*. April. Ms. on file, Arka Consultores,
    Santiago de Chile.
———. 2008a. *Enfoques metodológicos integradores en arqueología marítima: Contribuciones
    a la comprensión del Paisaje Cultural Marítimo de la Patagonia Occidental en el Siglo
    XVIII a partir del estudio de la fragata Wager*. V Congreso de Arqueología, Colombia.
    Bogotá, November.
———. 2008b. *The HMS Wager Research Project: An integrative approach to culture contact
    studies in 18th-century western Patagonia, southern Chile*. Paper presented at IKUWA 3
    Conference, London, July.
Carabias, D., and M. Chapanoff. 2006. Proyecto Valparaíso Sumergido: Resultados
    preliminares de un plan de evaluación del patrimonio cultural subacuático de la bahía
    de Valparaíso, Chile. In *Historias sumergidas: Hacia la protección del patrimonio
    cultural subacuático en Latinoamérica*, ed. C. Del Cairo Hurtado and M. C. García
    Chávez, 213–227. Bogotá: Universidad Externado de Colombia.
Carabias, D., M. Chapanoff, and R. Ortiz. 2006. Arqueología marítima, sensoramiento
    remoto y SIG en espacios portuarios: Resultados de un plan de evaluación del
    patrimonio cultural subacuático en la Bahía de Valparaíso. Trabajo presentado en el
    Simposio de Arqueología Histórica, XVII Congreso Nacional de Arqueología Chilena,
    9–14 October 2006, Valdivia.
Chapanoff, M., and D. Carabias. 2004. La arqueología subacuática y el estudio de los
    recursos culturales sumergidos: Resultados preliminares de la investigación
    "Valparaíso sumergido: Evaluación del patrimonio cultural subacuático de la
    Bahía de Valparaíso." In *Actas de las III Jornadas de Historia Naval y Marítima*,
    ed. Museo Naval y Maritimo, 81–85. Valparaíso: Museo Naval y Marítimo.
Ciarlo, N. 2006. Metodología de estudio de artefactos ferrosos corroídos en un medio
    subacuático. Un caso de estudio: Las concreciones del sitio Hoorn. *La Zaranda de
    Ideas—Revista de Jóvenes Investigadores en Arqueología* 2: 87–106.
Comisión para la Preservación del Patrimonio Histórico Cultural. 2009. Novedades en la
    obra de restauración de la embarcación española en Puerto Madero. *Boletín digital de
    la Comisión para la Preservación del Patrimonio Histórico Cultural*. Buenos Aires:
    Secretaría de Cultura, Gobierno de la Ciudad de Buenos Aires. Online at www.
    buenosaires.gov.ar/areas/cultura/cpphc/boletines_online_anteriores/noticias_abril09.
    php/. Accessed April 2009.
Coronato, F. 1997. The first Welsh footstep in Patagonia: The primitive location of Port
    Madryn. *Welsh History Review* 18 (4): 639–666.

Del Cairo, C., and M. C. García Chávez, eds. 2006. *Historias sumergidas—hacia la protección del patrimonio cultural subacuático en Latinoamérica.* Bogotá: Universidad Externado de Colombia.

Dellino-Musgrave, V. 2007. *Maritime archaeology and social relations: British actions in the Southern Hemisphere.* New York: Springer Series in Underwater Archaeology.

De Rosa, H., D. Elkin, N. C. Ciarlo, and F. Saporiti. 2007. Characterization of a coin from the shipwreck of HMS *Swift* (1770). *Technical Briefs in Historical Archaeology* 2: 32–36.

Dirección Nacional de Química. 1982. *Informe sobre muestras de materiales hallados en la ría Deseado.* Unpublished report. Ms. on file, Instituto Nacional de Antropología, Buenos Aires.

Elkin, D. 1997. Proyecto Arqueológico HMS *Swift.* Ms. on file, Instituto Nacional de Antropología, Buenos Aires.

———. 2002a. Water: A new field in Argentinian archaeology. In *International handbook of underwater archaeology*, ed. C. V. Ruppé and J. F. Barstad, 313–332. New York: Kluwer Academic/Plenum.

———. 2002b. News from South America—maritime archaeology in the Atlantic coast of Uruguay: "Cabo Polonio" and "Castillo Grande." *AIMA Newsletter* 21 (3): 10–11.

———. 2003. Arqueología marítima y patrimonio cultural subacuático en Argentina: El trabajo actual desarrollado por el Instituto Nacional de Antropología y Pensamiento Latinoamericano. *Protección del Patrimonio Cultural Subacuático en América Latina y el Caribe 26–33.* La Habana: UNESCO—Oficina Regional de Cultura para América Latina y el Caribe.

———. 2007. *Estudio arqueológico marítimo en el Parque Nacional Monte León: Informe final.* Interim report presented to Administración de Parques Nacionales. Ms. on file, Instituto Nacional de Antropología, Buenos Aires.

———. 2008. Maritime archaeology in Argentina at the Instituto Nacional de Antropología. In *Underwater and maritime archaeology in Latin America and the Caribbean*, ed. M. Leshikar-Denton and P. Luna Erreguerena, 155–171. Walnut Creek, CA: Left Coast Press.

Elkin, D., A. Argüeso, R. Bastida, V. Dellino-Musgrave, M. Grosso, C. Murray, and D. Vainstub. 2007. Archeological research on HMS *Swift*: A British sloop-of-war lost off Patagonia, southern Argentina, in 1770. *International Journal of Nautical Archaeology* 36 (1): 32–58.

Elkin, D., and C. Murray. 2006. Arqueología subacuática en Chubut y Santa Cruz. In *Arqueología de la Costa Patagónica—perspectivas para la conservación*, ed. I. Cruz, M. S. Caracotche, M. X. Senatore, and B. Ladrón de Guevara, 109–124. Río Gallegos: Universidad Nacional de la Patagonia Austral.

Elkin, D., D. Vainstub, A. Argueso, and V. Dellino. 2001. Proyecto Arqueológico H.M.S. *Swift* (Santa Cruz, Argentina). In *Memorias del Congreso Científico de Arqueología Subacuática—ICOMOS*, Colección Científica, Serie Arqueología, ed. P. Luna Erreguerena and R. Roffiel, 143–162. Mexico City: Instituto Nacional de Antropología e Historia.

Elkin, D., D. Vainstub, A. Argueso, and C. Murray. 2000. H.M.S. *Swift*: Arqueología submarina en Puerto Deseado. *Desde el país de los gigantes: Perspectivas arqueológicas en Patagonia*, vol. 2, 659–671. Río Gallegos: Universidad Nacional de la Patagonia Austral.

García Chávez, C. 2006. Caminos recorridos, fronteras por superar: Arqueología subacuática en Colombia. In *Historias sumergidas—hacia la protección del patrimonio cultural subacuático en Latinoamérica*, ed. C. Del Cairo and M. C. García Chávez, 177–191. Bogotá: Universidad Externado de Colombia.

Gower, E. 1803. *An account of the loss of His Majesty's sloop "Swift," in Port Desire on the coast of Patagonia, on the 13th of March, 1770.* London: Winchester and Son.

Grosso, M. 2008. *Arqueología de naufragios: Estudio de procesos de formación naturales en el sitio HMS* Swift *(Puerto Deseado, Santa Cruz).* Tesis de Licenciatura en Ciencias Antropológicas—Orientación Arqueología, Facultad de Filosofía y Letras, Universidad de Buenos Aires (2006). Publicación electrónica *CD 2* Tesis de Licenciatura del Departamento de Ciencias Antropológicas, Facultad de Filosofía y Letras de la Universidad de Buenos Aires.

Guagliardo, J. P. 2007. El infierno de los marinos: Distribuciones de naufragios en el Río de la Plata (Siglos XVI–XX). *Cuadernos del Instituto Nacional de Antropología y Pensamiento Latinoamericano* 21 (2006/2007): 51–65.

Inda, H., and L. Del Puerto. 2001. *Identificación de las muestras de material leñoso WYT1, informe de laboratorio: Laboratorio de Estudios del Cuaternario del Uruguay* (LEQ), UNCIEP, Facultad de Ciencias, UDELAR. Ms. on file, Montevideo.

Jones, L. [1898] 1993. *La colonia galesa.* Rawson, Argentina: El Regional.

———. [1926] 2000. *Historia de los comienzos de la colonia en la Patagonia.* Trelew, Argentina: Fundación Ameghino.

Le Maire, J. 1622. *Spieghel der Australische Navigatie Door den Wijt vermaerden ende cloeck moedighen Zee-Heldt, Jacob le Maire.* Amsterdam: Michiel Colijn. In *De ontdekkingsreis van Jacob Le Maire en Willem Cornelisz Schouten in de jaren 1615–1617*, ed. W. A. Engelbrecht and P. J. van Herwerden (1945), vol. 1 (49), 1–101. The Hague: Linschoten Vereeniging Collection, Martinus Nijhoff.

Leshikar-Denton, M., and P. Luna Erreguerena, eds. 2008. *Underwater and maritime archaeology in Latin America and the Caribbean.* One World Archaeology Series. Walnut Creek, CA: Left Coast Press.

Lezama, A. 2008. Navigation in the Río de la Plata. In *Underwater and maritime archaeology in Latin America and the Caribbean*, ed. M. Leshikar-Denton and P. Luna Erreguerena, 187–200. Walnut Creek, CA: Left Coast Press.

Lorusso H., Svoboda, H. G., and H. M. De Rosa. 2003. Caracterización microestructural de componentes metálicos hallados en el pecio de Reta. *Jornadas SAM/CONAMET* 2003: 1103–1106.

Maier, M. S., B. A. Gómez, S. D. Parera, D. Elkin, H. De Rosa, N. C. Ciarlo, and H. Svoboda. 2010. Characterization of cultural remains associated to a human skeleton found at the site HMS *Swift* (1770). *Journal of Molecular Structure* 978: 191–194.

Marconetto, B., P. Picca, H. De Rosa, and C. Murray. 2005. El naufragio del *Hoorn* (1615), materiales de un sitio intermareal (Santa Cruz–Argentina). In *Arqueología de Fuego-Patagonia.* Actas de las VI Jornadas de Arqueología de la Patagonia, Punta Arenas, November, 343–349. Punta Arenas: Ed. CEQUA.

Martínez, E. 1995. Problemática de la arqueologia subacuatica en el Uruguay. In *Actas del VIII Congreso Nacional de Arqueología Uruguaya*, ed. M. Consens, J. M. Lopez Mazz, and C. Curbelo, 389–391. Montevideo: Imprenta y Editorial Surcos.

Murray, C., D. Elkin, and D. Vainstub. 2002–2003. The Sloop-of-War HMS *Swift*: An archaeological approach. In *The age of sail: The international annual of the historic sailing ship*, ed. Nicholas Tracy, 101–115. London: Conway Maritime Press.

Murray, C., M. Grosso, D. Elkin, F. Coronato, H. De Rosa, María A. Castro, R. Bastida, and N. Ciarlo. 2009. Un sitio costero vulnerable: El naufragio de *Bahía Galenses* (Puerto Madryn, Chubut, Argentina). In *Arqueología de la Patagonia: Una mirada desde el último confín*, ed. M. Salemme, F. Santiago, M. Álvarez, E. Piana, M. Vázquez, and E. Mansur, Tomo 2: 1093–1108. Ushuaia, Argentina: Editorial Utopías.

Murray, C., D. Vainstub, M. Manders, and R. Bastida. 2007. El naufragio del *Hoorn*—1615— prospecciones costeras y subacuaticas en la ria Deseado (Santa Cruz–Argentina). In *Arqueología de Fuego-Patagonia: Actas de las VI Jornadas de Arqueología de la Patagonia, Punta Arenas, November 2005*, 351–355. Punta Arenas: Ed. CEQUA.

Museo Argentino de Ciencias Naturales. 1983. *Informe sobre muestras de materiales hallados en la ría Deseado*. Unpublished report. Ms. on file, Instituto Nacional de Antropología, Buenos Aires.

NMM Draughts, Box 52 no. 3606A ("sheer and profile" *Swift & Vulture*). London: National Maritime Museum.

NMM Draughts, Box 52 no. 3642 ("Decks" *Swift*). London: National Maritime Museum.

Pigafetta, A. [ca. 1526] 2003. Primer viaje en torno al globo: Noticias del Nuevo Mundo, con los dibujos de los países descubiertos, escritas por Antonio Pigafetta, gentilhombre vicentino y caballero de Rodas. In *La primera vuelta al mundo*, ed. J. S. de El Cano et al., 185–325. Madrid: Miraguano Ediciones/Ediciones Polifemo.

Pujante Izquierdo, P. 2001. La investigación del patrimonio cultural sumergido en Chile: El programa de arqueología subacuática de la Universidad Internacional SEK. In *Revista de la Escuela de Antropología* 6: 155–169. Rosario: Universidad Nacional de Rosario, Facultad de Humanidades y Artes, Escuela de Antropología.

———. 2007. Primeros resultados de una intervención subacuática en Chile: El proyecto Bahía Mejillones. Buenos Aires: *NAYA*. Noticias de Antropología y Arqueología (CD-Rom).

———. N.d. CD naya primeros resultados de una intervención subacuática en Chile: El proyecto Bahía Mejillones. Online at www.naya.org.ar/articulos/submar05.htm/. Accessed April 2007.

Rambelli, G. 1998. *Arqueología subaquática e sua aplicação à arqueología brasileira: O exemplo de baixo vale do Ribeira de Iguape*. Tesis de Maestría en Arqueología. Ms. on file, Facultad de Filosofía, Letras e Ciencias Humanas, Universidad de São Paulo.

———. 2002. *Arqueología até debaixo d'água*. São Paulo: Maranta.

———. 2003. *Arqueología subaquática do baixo vale do Ribeira*. Tesis de Maestría en Arqueología. Ms. on file, Facultad de Filosofía, Letras e Ciencias Humanas, Universidad de São Paulo.

———. 2006. Los desafíos de la arqueología subacuática en Brasil. In *Historias sumergidas: Hacia la protección del patrimonio cultural subacuático en Latinoamérica*, ed. C. Del Cairo Hurtado and M. C. García Chávez, 88–100. Bogotá: Universidad Externado de Colombia.

Rios, C. 2008. Identificação arqueológica de um naufrágio na área do Lamarão externo do porto do Recife, PE, Brasil. *Revista CLIO*. Recife: Universidad Federal de Pernambuco.

Schouten, W. C. 1618. *Journal ofte Beschryvinghe van de wonderlicke reyse ghedaen door Willem Cornelisz: Schouten van Hoorn, inde Jaren 1615, 1616 en 1617*. Amsterdam: Willem Jansz Blaeu. In *De ontdekkingsreis van Jacob Le Maire en Willem Cornelisz Schouten in de jaren 1615–1617*, ed. W. A. Engelbrechtand and P. J. van Herwerden, vol. 1, no. 49, 149–220. The Hague: Linschoten Vereeniging Collection, Martinus Nijhoff.

UDV Laboratory. 2001. *Report on the content of bottles from the HMS* Swift *archaeological site*. Unpublished report. Ms. on file, Instituto Nacional de Antropología, Buenos Aires.

Vainstub, D., and C. Murray. 2006. Proyecto Hoorn: Un naufragio holandés en la Patago- nia. In *Problemáticas de la arqueologia contemporanea: Actas del XV Congreso Nacional de Arqueología Argentina, Río Cuarto, Septiembre 2004*, 1: 397–404. Río Cuarto: Universidad Nacional de Río Cuarto.

Valentini, M. 2003. Reflexiones bajo el agua: El papel de la arqueología subacuática en la protección del patrimonio cultural sumergido en la Argentina. *Protección del Patrimonio Cultural Subacuático en América Latina y el Caribe*, 36–43. La Habana: UNESCO—Oficina regional de Cultura para América Latina y el Caribe.

Valentini, M., J. García Cano, M. Jasinski, and F. Soreide. 2001. Técnicas no intrusivas de prospección y registro subacuático: Experiencias y potencial en Argentina. *Actas del XIII Congreso Nacional de Arqueología Argentina*, 203–212. Córdoba.

CHAPTER 31

UNDERWATER ARCHAEOLOGY OF THE WORLD WARS

ROBERT S. NEYLAND

INTRODUCTION

SHIPWRECKS from the World Wars are incredibly numerous and, with the exception of *Titanic*, likely the most prominent underwater archaeological sites of the twentieth century—a century that witnessed two world wars and an undeclared Cold War. Ship losses rose dramatically in both World War I and World War II, resulting in a cumulative loss of more ships than in any previous conflict in history and very likely all the preceding naval wars combined. Naval aviation had its beginnings a few years prior to World War I, provided valuable service during that war, and came into its prime during World War II, expanding sea combat to the air, and adding an entirely new category of submerged wrecks to the archaeological record. World War II produced far more destruction at sea than occurred during World War I or the conflicts of the Cold War.

World War ship and aircraft wrecks are exceedingly complex sites consisting of ships and aircraft from many different nations representing a diversity of types and sizes, ranging from craft as large as aircraft carriers to vessels as small as two-manned Japanese mini-submarines. Aerial battles and ship bombardment contributed not only to the sinking of ships but also to the loss of thousands of aircraft. Besides the larger warships, the range of wrecks includes landing craft, military transports, and merchant vessels. Shipwrecks of the world wars litter the world's waters—principally the Atlantic and Pacific oceans and the Mediterranean and Caribbean seas, but elsewhere as well. Even lakes situated far from the oceans, such as Lake Michigan, which hosted naval aviation training, hold the remains of military aircraft (Cooper 1994: 134–139; Neyland and Grant 1999: 46–51). Sunken surface ships, submarines, and aircraft represent a uniquely global maritime landscape of twentieth-century naval warfare.

World War I and II wreck sites have many different meanings to different groups of people. They are the physical reminders of conflicts that touched all of the world's nations and transformed the modern world. Ship casualties equate to human losses; war graves that today stand as memorials to the events of the world wars and to those who lost their lives in battle or in support of the war effort. For our past, current, and future generations, these wrecks are the grave sites of comrades and brothers, fathers and grandfathers. Even as memories fade, these wrecks will remain in memoriam.

The wrecks are not only reminders of the fallen but also have a current role as important marine habitats. Like flowers blooming on the battlefield, these ships in their sinking have become thriving underwater resources filled with sea life and providing recreation and a food source for humans. There is a dark side as well, for many of the wrecks represent potential environmental disasters from releases of oil and other toxic substances.

WORLD WAR SHIP SINKINGS

Numbers of ships lost during combat rose dramatically throughout the twentieth century, but predominantly during World War II. Ship loss numbers speak for themselves: naval warships lost by all nations during this conflict exceeded 1,450. As recorded, the U.S. Navy lost 167 ships, the Royal Navy 359, Germany 244, Italy 119, and Japan 402. Recorded aerial attacks account for 561 losses, submarine action 330, surface attacks 262, mine warfare 800, and accidents 82. Other countries also lost warships, but in relatively fewer numbers: the USSR 70, France 41, the Netherlands 15, Norway 10, Greece 9, Poland 6, and neutrals and others a combined 14 (Brown 1995: 228). The above are only naval surface ship losses; they do not include World War II merchant vessel or submarine losses. Submarine losses for Germany alone amount to 784, for the Japanese Navy 124, and for the U.S. Navy 52 (Naval History Division 1963: 8, 159–174; Joint Army-Navy Assessment Committee 1947: 1–28).

By comparison to its midcentury counterpart, the great number of losses during World War I appears measured. The U.S. Navy lost only one warship, USS *San Diego*, the wreck site of which is discussed below. World War I cost the Royal Navy, among the preeminent naval powers at the time, 254 warships, including 13 battleships (His Majesty's Stationary Office 1919: 7–8). It is important to note, however, the great number and importance of merchant marine losses, which for Britain in World War I total 2,479 vessels and a loss of 14,287 lives. In addition, Britain reported fishing vessel losses of 675 craft and 434 lives (His Majesty's Stationary Office 1919: 162–163). Human losses were also grave in U-boats during both conflicts, with over 5,400 officers and sailors lost during World War I and 27,491 men during World War II (Kemp 1997: 7–8).

During World War II, the war in Europe alone resulted in staggering losses of shipping and lives. Brigadier Peter Young (1966) calculates that at the height of German U-boat successes, during the four-month period between July and October 1942, the Allies lost 396 ships (over 2 million tons). Although these losses were sharply reduced as anti-U-boat operations increased, by the time of the German surrender, U-boats had sunk 2,828 Allied and neutral ships. German U-boat construction totaled 1,162 built, of which 785 were eventually destroyed.

The numbers are so staggering that different sources provide far different figures. For example in the Pacific, Brown (1990: 229) lists 402 Japanese warships lost, while the Joint Army-Navy Assessment Committee report (February 1947: vi) gives Japan's losses as 686 naval vessels and 2,346 merchant vessels, with a combined tonnage of 10,583,755 tons. The same report credits the U.S. Navy as the sole Allied force responsible for sinking 611 Japanese naval vessels and 2,117 merchant craft, primarily through submarine and aircraft attacks (February 1947: vii).

SHIP-SINKING WEAPONS

These unprecedented losses are attributed to changes in warfare that resulted from the technological development of weapons capable of sinking ships rather than merely damaging or capturing them. In the second half of the nineteenth century, naval warfare began to change dramatically with innovations in steam power, iron hull design, exploding shells, revolving turrets, and mine and torpedo warfare. These advances made it far easier to destroy and sink ships than ever before. Innovations in technology were closely linked with advancing industrial capacity in metallurgy and the application of mass production methods to ships and weapons. World War I saw the continued development and production of submarines, mines, and aerial bombardment. Advances in offensive weapons were countered by defensive innovations resulting in warships increasing their speed and defensive firepower, as well as adding heavier armor and thicker bulkheads (Brown 1990: 6, 14). Increasing ship size also equated to increased survivability, since larger ships with their greater hull capacity could stay afloat longer with a flood of incoming water than smaller ships could. Larger vessels, however, also came under greater concentrated attacks.

Although the Allies would eventually counter developments such as the German acoustic homing torpedo and the Japanese Type 93 Long Lance torpedo with their own acoustic anti-submarine torpedo and radar, both Axis weapons took a heavy toll on shipping during World War II (Brown 1990: 16). Aerial bombardment became increasingly deadly to watercraft during the war with the design of heavy-armor-piercing bombs and guided weapons such as the rocket-propelled glider bomb and the ballistic guided bomb. Underwater concussion alone, even from near misses, could sink a vessel. Improved fire control from computers and radar also made naval artillery more deadly. Mines, which had been used successfully in warfare since the American Civil War, became even greater hazards with magnetic, acoustic, and pistol-detonated varieties, some of which incorporated intricate devices to prevent defusing (Brown 1990: 17). Finally, increased aerial attacks resulted in better ship defenses using anti-aircraft gunnery. The Royal Navy and U.S. Navy developed and used radar proximity-fused ammunition, which took its toll on Axis aircraft (Brown 1990: 18). It was these repeated innovations in technology that made twentieth-century naval warfare unprecedented in destruction of ships, aircraft, and personnel. These advances in ship-sinking weapons have equated to more shipwrecks for future generations to consider as potential archaeological sites, war graves, and environmental hazards.

ARCHAEOLOGICAL RESEARCH ON WORLD WAR SHIPWRECKS AND SUNKEN AIRCRAFT

World War archaeological research has primarily focused on identifying the locations of wrecks and causes of sinking rather than the broader cultural, economic, and technological research questions asked by archaeologists working with earlier time periods. Underwater explorers have sought to put pins on the map demarcating the locations of notable naval shipwrecks such as *Bismarck*, USS *Yorktown*, Japanese mini-submarines, the Japanese aircraft carriers *Kaga* and *Akagi*, and U.S. Navy submarines or German U-boats (Archibald 1999; Dunmore and Marshall 2002; Means 2001; Tully and Parshall 2005). For the most part, these are expeditions of exploration asking the fundamental research question, "Where is it?"; and frequently they become the focus of a television documentary. Sometimes the expedition attempts to ask a leading question, such as what caused the ship to sink or, in the case of the *Lusitania*, whether it was carrying munitions (Greenhill 2008). There is also an increasingly common type of search and discovery project, generally on a smaller scale but no less successful in outcome, characterized by endeavors funded by private entrepreneurs, avocational archaeologists, or historians who have a passion for the story and adventure. The relatively low cost and availability of remote-sensing technology and increased efficiency of these searches is frequently resulting in new discoveries of shipwrecks from the world wars (Barnette 2009). A contributing factor to the ease of these discoveries is that many of these wrecks are relatively large, metallic vessels and thus relatively easier than ancient shipwrecks to image with remote-sensing tools.

Keith Muckelroy (1978) considered the study of shipwrecks from our recent past unnecessary due to the existence of extensive written documentation. World War I wrecks were only 64 years old at most, World War II no more than 39 years past, and we were in the midst of the Cold War (Muckelroy 1978: 10). What Muckelroy did not consider was the value of archaeological identification and documentation for discovery, preservation as memorials and grave sites, and long-term management. Although the world wars are far better known than historical events from earlier periods of human history, professional archaeologists have applied archaeological principles and formulated research questions on the ship and aircraft wrecks of these conflicts. Like other research in historical archaeology, such questioning can confirm, complement, or contradict the historical records. One example of this research is reassessing the location of reported losses and providing more accurate positions when possible. There are of course other questions worth answering; for example, a study of World War II aircraft in Australian waters by Julie Ford (2006) recommended comparing Australian-built aircraft to foreign-built aircraft obtained through lend-lease programs. Ford (2006: 40–41) also suggested analyzing the differences in training aircraft versus operational craft. Very intelligently, Silvano Jung (2005) not only used archaeological documentation to not only record Catalina PBY flying boats lost during the Japanese attack on Darwin Harbor, but also compared and contrasted the wreck sites to interpret the attack, destruction, and sinking of the flying boats. Michael McCarthy (1998: 61) suggested that a specialized set of archaeological questions should apply to submarines focusing on human adaptation to prolonged working and living in confined spaces. These vessels, he argues, form a separate class of sunken shipwreck representing a specific cultural community.

Practicing archaeologists engage in searching for and locating World War shipwrecks as part of their professional responsibilities. Archaeological surveys occur most frequently to evaluate sites under their respective nation's historic preservation laws. Archaeologists assess and document the state of preservation of wrecks creating detailed site plans to use in management strategies. This is done in preparation for the site being established as a memorial (e.g., USS *Arizona* located in Pearl Harbor), for listing on a government register of historic sites (e.g., the National Register of Historic Places in the United States), or for evaluating environmental or human impacts. An example of the latter, the wrecks at Bikini Atoll, sunk during atomic bomb testing of Operation Crossroads, were documented by National Park Service archaeologists prior to their transfer to the Republic of the Marshall Islands for use as a marine park (Delgado, Lenihan, and Murphy 1991). Such reports usually have a specific format, including a large historical overview section, and chapters discussing project background, site description, and significance. Although there is some archaeological analysis, it usually relates primarily to how the site compares to the extensive historic record. In the case of nominations to the National Register of Historic Places, World War II sites only recently met the notional 50-year test of time to be considered eligible for listing. Sites are also archaeologically documented, as in the recent case of U-boats off the North Carolina coast, in order to determine their state of preservation, rate of corrosion, and deterioration (NOAA 2008). This information can be used as a benchmark against which to measure future human and environmental impacts to the wrecks and estimate their longevity. Aviation archaeology is peopled with a large number of enthusiasts searching for aircraft wrecks both within the United States and abroad. The aircraft wreck sites are in general much more fragile and ephemeral than shipwrecks and present somewhat different challenges for preservation and research (Wessex Archaeology 2008: 31–35; see Fix in this volume).

U.S. NAVY WORLD WAR ARCHAEOLOGY

The Naval History and Heritage Command (NHHC; formerly Naval Historical Center), through its Underwater Archaeology Branch, analyzes World War wrecks as part of its responsibilities of managing U.S. Navy ship and aircraft wrecks, as well as assisting foreign navies with their wrecks located in U.S. waters. The U.S. Navy's wrecks are distributed in virtually every major body of water, those from World War II being by far the most numerous and widespread of all the navy's shipwrecks. They represent many of the basic questions formulated in World War archaeology: Where did the ship or aircraft sink? Does the wreck site confirm the reported cause of sinking, or, if the cause of sinking is unknown, can a cause be determined from the wreck? What is the state of preservation? In most cases, new information concerning these wrecks is presented to the NHHC by people who are intentionally searching for the wrecks or who inadvertently find them.

U-1105

Surprisingly, one of the first sites for which the Underwater Archaeology Branch devised a management strategy was that of a former German U-boat, *U-1105*. The U-boat had surrendered and was turned over to the navy after World War II as a war prize. It was then brought to the United States, where it underwent a period of study focusing on its protective rubber coating, an innovation applied to its hull in an attempt to inhibit sonar detection. After the research was complete, the U-boat was used in explosives testing in Maryland's Chesapeake Bay. It was eventually sunk there and forgotten until the wreck was discovered by sport divers in 1985. In 1994 it became Maryland's first historic shipwreck preserve, and it is currently available for divers to visit from April to December (Shomette 1994). *U-1105* retains its structural integrity and is relatively well preserved when compared to U-boat wrecks that have been impacted by divers seeking souvenirs, such as the U-boats located off the coast of North Carolina (Kozak 2008).

World War I Cruiser USS *San Diego*

Another example of an assessment and documentation conducted for management and historic preservation purposes was that undertaken by navy divers on the World War I cruiser USS *San Diego*, which is located in 33.5 m (110 ft) of water off Fire Island National Seashore, New York. *San Diego*, originally USS *California*, was one of three armored cruisers authorized by Congress in 1899. These vessels were slightly over 503 ft (153 m) in overall length and 69 ft (21 m) beam. Vessels such as *San Diego* were designed after the Spanish-American War for cruising the Caribbean and western Pacific Ocean. They possessed longer steaming range and heavier ordnance and armor than their predecessors. On the morning of 19 July 1918, while en route to Portsmouth, New Hampshire, *San Diego* suffered an external explosion amidships on the port side. The port engine room immediately flooded and was disabled. The captain attempted to turn the ship north to ground her in shallow water (Figure 31.1). The flooding spread through damaged compartments until the starboard engine became disabled and the ship, listing to port, was adrift. The order was given to abandon ship. Only 25 minutes after the explosion, *San Diego* rolled over and sank. Only 6 men out of the 1,255 crew members were lost. The captain initially reported they had been struck by a torpedo from a German U-boat, but the Navy Court of Inquiry determined that the ship has been sunk by a mine previously laid by U-156. *San Diego* was the only capital warship lost by the U.S. Navy in World War I. The wreck today lies inverted on the sea bottom, with the mine-damaged area clearly visible on the port side, abreast the number 4 smokestack. The explosion resulted in a 1.5 m (5 ft) diameter hole 3.5 m (12 ft) below the waterline. In addition to this hole, hull plates were crushed for 7.5 m (20 ft) between the lower edge of the armor plate and the bilge keel in the vicinity of the hole. Forward of this area, plate butts and seams were bent, and numerous rivets and shims were sprung or missing (Gentile 1989: 67–69). Site formation processes have resulted in continued deterioration of *San Diego*; during the last 90 years, the wreck has been buffeted by storms and hurricanes. Visitors have reported increasing deterioration and hull collapse, perhaps hastened by diver penetrations into the interior and artifact recovery over the years. In the 1960s and 1970s, the vessel's bronze propellers were recovered, one of which was lost while under way to shore and never relocated (Gentile 1989: 82). Dr. James K. Orzech, who led a navy diving investigation of the wreck site, stated in his letter to the sport diver community, "Ironically, as a shipwreck, it [*San Diego*] has outlived most other warships from that era" (NHHC/UAB Records, letter dated 18 November 1995). In 1995, U.S. Navy Mobile Diving and Salvage (MDSU) Unit 2 conducted a site assessment of the shipwreck at the request of the NHHC (then Naval Historical Center). MDSU's objectives were provided by NHHC archaeologists to cause minimal impact to the wreck and consisted of assessing the historical integrity of the wreck site, verifying that ordnance was present, documenting the deterioration of the wreck, meeting with local divers, and providing video and photographic coverage of the survey. A single 6 in naval gun projectile was recovered, taken into custody by Navy Explosives Ordnance Demolition technicians, and intentionally exploded as a test to confirm that ordnance still posed a danger. A rudimentary site map was prepared showing the areas of damage and penetration by divers. The most important outcome was the site's listing on the National Register of Historic Places following its nomination by Dr. Orzech. The wreck site was determined to be dangerous for penetration due to collapsing interior structures, separating hull plates, and significant amounts of ordnance (Mobile Diving Salvage Unit 2, 1995). This wreck, like others of its ilk, is a significant marine habitat for a variety of species, and is known particularly for its community of lobsters.

Operation Neptune

On D-Day, 6 June 1944, Allied forces consisting of American, British, Canadian, Free French, Polish, Norwegian, and other nationalities mounted an invasion of northern Europe. In a 24-hour period, over 5,000 ships transported 175,000 Allied troops and 50,000 vehicles across 50 to 90 nautical miles (93 to 167 km). The transport and naval operation continued throughout the month of June as the front was secured and reinforced.

The Western Naval Task Force was organized into three assault forces: Force O, designated for Omaha beaches and including 775 vessels; Force U, designated for Utah beaches and including approximately 865 vessels; and follow-up force B.

Figure 31.1 USS *San Diego* site plan. USS *San Diego* (Armored Cruiser No. 6) sank on 19 July 1918 after striking a floating mine laid by *U-156*. Painting by Francis Muller, 1920. Reproduced with the kind permission of the Navy Art Collection, Naval History and Heritage Command, Washington, D.C.

During D-Day, shore batteries and sea mines brought about most of the U.S. naval casualties and losses. Of the two, mines took the greatest toll on Operation Neptune's ships. Official records report that by 19 June, the navy had lost at least 162 vessels (Report of Lost and Non-Operational Ships and Craft, serial 00147, 1944). Of these, about 60 ships and craft went down in the mine-swept channels off Utah and the Banc du Cardonnet. By May 1944, the Banc du Cardonnet was one of four mined barriers in Seine Bay (Department of the Navy 2008: 12–20). During the first 18 days of the D-Day invasion, a total of 221 mines (magnetic, acoustic, and remote ignition) were detonated or cut in the Utah area. While Allied intelligence indicated extremely heavy enemy defenses, Allied ships were unprepared for new German pressure-acoustic and pressure-magnetic mines. These mines were laid in the Cardonnet shoals and became Force U's greatest hazard, as Allied ships were not equipped to sweep for them (Figure 31.2).

An intentional effort to locate and document World War II wrecks by the U.S. Navy's underwater archaeologists took place from 2000 to 2002. At this time, the NHHC mounted a survey expedition to locate and identify U.S. Navy losses incurred

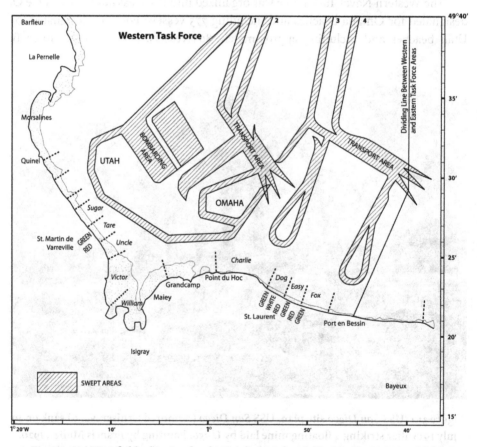

Figure 31.2 Minefields showing banks. Reproduced with the kind permission of the Underwater Archaeology Branch, Naval History and Heritage Command, Washington, D.C.

during the 1944 Operation Neptune, which aimed at landing Allied forces on the coast of Normandy, France. The archaeological survey area covered approximately 80 km² off Omaha and Utah beaches, Pointe du Hoc, the heavily mined Banc du Cardonnet, and the Pointe-et-Raz-de-la-Percée. The archaeological survey relied on remote-sensing data collection through the use of marine magnetometer, side-scan sonar, multibeam echo sounder, and a remotely operated vehicle (ROV) equipped with video and still photography. Not surprisingly, the combined survey areas yielded over 1,400 magnetic and over 300 acoustic targets (Neyland 2009: 38).

Omaha Beach

Surviving wrecks discovered at Omaha Beach included the large oceangoing tug USS *Partridge* and troop transport *Susan B. Anthony*. The survey also confirmed the presence of four duplex-drive Sherman tanks and extensive remains of the Mulberry artificial harbor installed at St.-Laurent-sur-Mer. USS *Partridge*, torpedoed by a German E-boat, suffered additional explosions in both boilers and the magazine. Its wreckage, buried under the seafloor, spread over 7,500 m², with only 2.8 m (9 ft) of hull rising into the water column. *Susan B. Anthony*, a passenger steamer launched in 1930 and acquired for a troop transport by the navy in 1942, struck a mine directly under its number 4 cargo hold on 7 June. The forward masts, booms, and bow guns were still clearly visible on the wreck. There was also substantial impact to the number 1 cargo hold, indicating that perhaps the ship struck more than one mine. Nearby, the Mulberry artificial harbor survey recorded a long line of caissons running parallel to shore for 0.88 nautical miles (1.65 km), and another set 300 m (984 ft) long and perpendicular to shore (Figure 31.3). The caissons were constructed of concrete in England and then towed across the channel. Several caissons were well preserved, while others survived only as rubble. The Mulberry survey also noted the remnants of a Whale, or floating roadway, that formed part of the artificial harbor, and the steel or concrete supporting pontoons, called Beetles, which floated the Whales. Despite the presence of fishing gear, including traps and buoys, and the constant threat of entanglement that prevented a search of the entire area, eight block ships and nine caissons were recorded. Several craft could not be located at the positions reported in action reports or hydrographic records, including Landing Ship Tank *LST-496*. In addition, a scattering of artifacts not associated with an identified shipwreck were found that might represent lost cargo from a landing craft or other vessel.

Utah Beach

The Utah Beach survey grid revealed the remnants of SS *Charles Morgan*, USS *Tide*, USS *Rich*, *LCT-524*, a landing craft, two barges, and the Gooseberry 1 harbor installation. *Tide*, an Auk Class minesweeper, had just finished sweeping for mines and was hauling its gear aboard when an explosion from a mine broke the ship's back, tearing away bulkheads and leaving a gaping hole in its hull. *Rich*, a Buckley Class

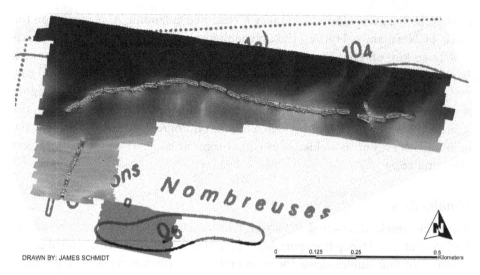

Figure 31.3 Remains of artificial harbor "Mulberry" consisting of concrete caissons
located at Omaha Beach. At bottom right, the wreck of an unidentified ship lies
across the eastern caissons. Reproduced with the kind permission of the Underwater
Archaeology Branch, Naval History and Heritage Command, Washington, D.C.

destroyer, was also sunk by mines. Both shipwrecks were heavily salvaged after the
war, to the extent that today *Tide* and *Rich* are represented only by debris fields.

Tide provides an excellent example of how many D-Day ships met their fate.
On 5 June 1944, USS *Tide* (AM-125) departed from Tor Bay in convoy with Minesweeper Squadron A, assigned to the Utah area. During the night of D-Day, *Tide*
moved in close to shore, guarding the Carantan estuary to prevent the egress of
German E-boats based up the river. Two days later, early in the morning on 7 June,
Tide, USS *Threat* (AM-124), and USS *Swift* (AM-122) proceeded close inshore
between St. Marcouf and Barfleur to clear lanes for the fire-support ships (USS
Swift Log Book 1944). At 09:35, after recovering its mine-sweeping gear, *Tide*
drifted over the Cardonnet Banks and struck a mine. The mine exploded under
the vessel on the starboard side with such force that it lifted the ship out of the
water (Crane 1944). LCDR George Crane's inspection revealed that all bulkheads
aft of the forward crew compartment were open and water had flooded the after
engine room. At 09:45 *Tide* began sinking by both the bow and stern. USS *Pheasant*
came along to port side to evacuate the crew as the ship listed to starboard. USS
Threat came along to starboard and fastened to *Tide* as that ship lurched to starboard. At 09:50 the executive officer, LCDR Crane, ordered, "All hands prepare to
abandon ship," and *Threat, Swift, Pheasant*, a patrol craft, and a USCG Higgins
boat from USS *Bayfield* assisted in evacuating the wounded (Historical Material
vol. 2 1945). At 10:10, *Swift* attempted to tow *Tide* to the beach, but as the towline
strained, *Tide* broke in two and sank in about 14 m (45 ft) of water (USS *Swift* [AM
122] Log Book 1944).

The remote-sensing survey on *Tide* confirmed cracked hull plates from the explosion and noted such identifiable features as a large winch and ring gear and a hawser tube. A scallop dredge and abandoned fishing traps provided an indication of possible recent human impacts to the wreck site from fishing. In addition, faint net drag marks in the sea bottom indicated that fishing activities continue to impact *Tide*. More intact wrecks than *Tide* and *Rich* were a Landing Barge Vehicle (LBV) and Landing Barge Emergency Repair (LBE). *Charles Morgan*, a Liberty Ship, was struck by a single 500-pound bomb dropped by an aircraft. More damaging than the bomb, however, was the postwar salvage, which reduced the hull to less than a meter of structure rising above the sea bottom. Archival data differed from the actual location of SS *Charles Morgan* found during the archaeological survey. In addition, despite extensive obstruction from fishing gear, the harbor installation in the Baie du Vey was surveyed, and the remains of 10 American vessels sunk as caissons were recorded (Department of the Navy 2008: 108–115).

Banc du Cardonnet

The Banc du Cardonnet survey grid contained the remains of *LST-523*, *LCT-777*, *LCT-244*, *LCT-305*, *LCI-232*, *PC-1261*, a Sherman tank, a possible U.S. Army DUKW (General Motors used a model naming terminology in which the *D* indicates a vehicle designed in 1942, the *U* represented "utility (amphibious)," the *K* indicated all-wheel drive, and the *W* indicated two powered rear axles), two other motorized vehicles, a barge, USS *Meredith*, *LST-523*, HMS *Minster*, and 10 other unidentified wrecks. *Meredith's* lower hull is embedded in the sea bottom, but a portion of the vessel's stern rises about 2.9 m (9.5 ft) off the seafloor and clearly exhibits impacts from postwar salvage. *Meredith* was part of a salvage contract awarded to the Belgian firm Van Loo sometime in 1960 (Information Request, No Series 1969). Resting upside down, *LST-523* is relatively more complete but exhibits substantial impacts both amidships and in the bow area. A blue polypropylene line circles around part of the ship's structure, an indication that sport divers frequently visit the site.

Discrepancies in the archival record were also evident at Banc du Cardonnet. *LST-244*, for example, was identified as lost at Banc du Cardonnet, but the archaeological survey did not locate the wreck, and later archival data indicates that it was returned to the United Kingdom and possibly scrapped there (Department of the Navy 2008: 60). Similarly, *LCT-777* is a charted wreck site off Utah, and the wreck of an LCT was found at the charted location. Oral histories and a photograph showing *LCT-777* upside down on the shore, however, indicate that the charted wreck might be a different LCT (Department of the Navy 2008: 64–65).

Pointe du Hoc and Pointe et Raz de la Percee

The Pointe du Hoc survey discovered only one unidentified wreck site, probably *LCA-860* or *LCA-914*, both reportedly sunk while making their way to Pointe du

Hoc. The Pointe-et-Raz-de-la-Percée survey grid contained one wreck site as well, identified on nautical charts as an LST. The remaining hull structure and machinery are not indicative of an LST; rather, they are more consistent with that of a large Landing Craft Infantry (LCI) (Department of the Navy 2008: 125–126).

Site Formation Processes on D-Day Wrecks

The NHHC archaeological surveys identified the remains of several navy ships and small craft lost during the Normandy invasion. There was more damage to many of the wreck sites, particularly the larger ships, than could be attributed to the detonation of mines or bombs. Damage to the wreck sites was also a result of intentional Allied efforts to salvage and sink vessels and the voracious demand for scrap iron after the war. Allied attempts to keep the channels and sea lanes open often resulted in removing obstructions with the most expedient methods available. In circumstances where damaged ships or wrecks could not be salvaged or removed, United States and British ships would destroy nonoperational craft in place. USS *Arikara* (AT-98) and USS *Swivel* (ARS-36) reported sinking nonoperational vessels with demolition charges, making firing runs, or a combination of the two. In the case of sunken vessels such as the torpedoed *LST-314*, a British ship dropped depth charges to level the sunken wreckage (USS *Arikara* Log Book 1944; USS *Swivel* Log Book 1944; USS *Pope* Log Book 1944).

Some of the heaviest damage to the wrecks occurred from postwar salvage operations. The French metal industry had a huge demand for scrap metals for nearly 15 years following the war. Local diver and salvor Jacques Lemonchois remembered that demolition sites were everywhere on the Normandy coast. Lemonchois related that for those shipwrecks whose hulls rose above the seabed, salvage companies such as his used a blowtorch and explosives to cut the structure just above the mud line. According to Lemonchois, it took five years to reduce *Susan B. Anthony* to only 10 m (33 ft) of hull above the seafloor (personal interview, July 2001). Société Métallurgique de Normandie (1957: 5) reported that between 1953 and 1957, approximately 25,000 tons of metal were delivered to its Aciérie *Martin* scrapyard. The best-preserved wrecks were the previously unrecorded small craft and landing barges, who were probably too small to be targeted by salvage crews.

Despite the 65 years under the sea and the actions of human wrecking and salvage, the Normandy wrecks represent the full spectrum of Operation Neptune ships, including Liberty ships, troop transports, destroyers, minesweepers, landing ships and craft for tanks and infantry, Sherman tanks, a submarine chaser, and a variety of barges and other wreckage. They memorialize the events in which sailors and soldiers lost their lives either in battle or in support of the war effort. Today, these act as artificial reefs supporting a variety of sea life and the local fishing and diving communities. The caissons, in particular, provide a healthy fishing ground, evidenced by the number of commercial nets and recreational fishing boats that frequent the harbor area.

World War Wrecks as Environmental Hazards

Shipwrecks of the World Wars pose environmental concerns. Although USS *Arizona* is listed as a National Landmark and a well-visited National Memorial rises above the wreck, it also contains thousands of barrels of bunker oil, and there are concerns that there will one day be an oil spill in environmentally sensitive Pearl Harbor, Hawai'i. Visitors to the memorial are greeted by small droplets of oil rising to the surface from *Arizona's* hull. For some this is a moving experience, as if the ship still bleeds after all these years. For others, such as the commanders at the naval base Pearl Harbor, the oil droplets that hint at a potential spill are a matter of concern. The National Park Service, in coordination with the U.S. Navy, has completed many years of hull testing and corrosion sampling trying to determine the nature of the threat. Their studies suggest that the integrity of the hull is sufficiently strong and that there is no imminent threat of a catastrophic spill (Wilson 2007: 14–18; Foecke et al. 2009). *Arizona*, however, is just one of hundreds of ships lost during the World Wars that contain bunkers of oil, asbestos, or other hazardous or radioactive materials. The navy anticipates that there are over 800 United States government oil-containing wrecks in the Pacific (Mair 2007: 569). Likewise, NOAA is generating a national database, called RUST, which lists shipwrecks that are potential environmental and public safety hazards (Zelo, Overfield, and Helton 2009). Elsewhere in the world, the Norwegian government, concerned about mercury in *U-864* and potential health and environmental hazards, awarded a salvage contract to Mammoet Salvage BV to raise the submarine. In this latter case, archaeology is of less concern than public safety (Ocean News and Technology 2009). The same may be the case for the several nuclear submarines lost during the Cold War, such as USS *Thresher* and *Scorpion*, which raise concerns of radioactive hazards. Many of our naval and commercial shipwrecks from the twentieth and twenty-first centuries will present health and environmental hazards for the public and the marine archaeologist.

The largest recovery of oil from a World War II U.S. Navy shipwreck is that from USS *Mississinewa*. *Mississinewa* (AO-59), a ship fleet oiler, was the only vessel successfully sunk by a Japanese suicide *kaiten*, which was essentially a manned torpedo (Figures 31.4 and 31.5). Similar to a mini-submarine, the *kaiten* was not designed to bring its single pilot home; rather, like a kamikaze pilot, *kaiten* pilots intended to meet death in order to deliver a demoralizing blow to their enemy. *Mississinewa* was anchored in Ulithi Atoll, Palau, on 20 November 1944 with her cargo tanks filled to capacity with 404,000 gallons (1,529.3 m³) of aviation fuel, 9,000 barrels (1,430.89 m³) of diesel oil, and 90,000 barrels (14,308.86 m³) of fuel oil. At 05:47, shortly after reveille, a heavy explosion rocked the oiler; fumes in an aviation gas cargo tank ignited, causing a massive second explosion and fires. The ship was engulfed in its bunker fuel oil and aviation fuel. The fire reached the after magazine, causing it to explode. Thereafter, the ship was abandoned and sank with a loss of 63 men as well as the Japanese *kaiten* pilot. Of the five *kaiten* sent against U.S. ships, only this one succeeded at meeting its objective. The explosion and fire from the

Figure 31.4 Japanese *kaiten* (Type 2 or Type 4) human torpedo, on display in East Willard Park, Washington Navy Yard, Washington, DC, October 1974. Total length of this *kaiten* is 54.5 feet and 4.5 feet diameter; it was built in 1945 after the sinking of USS *Mississinewa*. Reproduced with the kind permission of the Photographic Archives, Naval History and Heritage Command, Washington, D.C.

Mississinewa were so large, however, that the Japanese Naval Command overoptimistically reported that three aircraft carriers had been hit and accordingly expanded the *kaiten* program (Mair 2007: 469–471).

On 6 April 2001, a search for *Mississinewa* was successfully undertaken by Bent Prop, a group of divers with an avocational interest in archaeology and Pacific Ocean WWII history. Bent Prop divers eventually located the wreck and notified the government of Palau, which in turn expressed its willingness to treat the wreck as a memorial for the sailors who perished in the explosion and fire (Mair 2007: 576–577). A short time after this discovery, a severe typhoon struck the atoll, creating exceptionally high waves and impacting the wreck site. *Mississinewa* began to leak oil at an estimated 360 gallons an hour. The potential for environmental damage to the lagoon was enormous. Not only would marine and avian life be impacted; the residents of the islands who depended on subsistence fishing would also lose their sustenance and livelihood (Mair 2007: 557).

In 2001, the U.S. Navy's Supervisor of Diving and Salvage Command conducted a survey of the wreck in response to concerns voiced by the local government about

Figure 31.5 USS *Mississinewa* (AO-59) sinking in Ulithi anchorage after she was hit by a Japanese suicide *kaiten*, 20 November 1944. Reproduced with the kind permission of the Photographic Archives, Naval History and Heritage Command, Washington, D.C.

oil being released from the site. The U.S. Navy and members of Bent Prop plugged the leaks during this initial survey. The Yap State government petitioned the U.S. government to remove the oil from the wreck because of the continual leakage, the large volume of remaining oil, and the sensitive marine and lagoon ecology. The U.S. Navy agreed to remove as much oil as possible due to the leaks having begun again, stronger than before, and the imminent environmental damage (Mair 2007: 569–570). The navy estimated that at least 2,062,116 gallons (7,805.96 m³) of Navy Special Fuel Oil (NSFO) remained in the intact cargo tanks. The U.S. Navy salvage team arrived in February 2003, and divers used "hot taps" to drill into the oil tanks and remove all accessible oil. In all, the U.S. Navy removed 1.8 million gallons (6,813.74 m³) of oil, preventing an environmental disaster and preserving the

Mississinewa for the future (Mair 2007: 570). The governor of Yap State nominated the USS *Mississinewa* to the National Register of Historic Places in order to memorialize its historic significance and recognize it as a war grave (Mair 2007: 577). Oil leakage from *Mississinewa* resulted in the Pacific Regional Environment Programme (SPREP) developing a regional Pacific strategy for marine pollution from WWII wrecks and the development of an inventory, including 3,854 vessels for the Pacific alone. When this inventory is combined with the Atlantic, Mediterranean, and Indian Ocean (AMIO) database of 3,953 WWII wrecks, the total count is over 7,807 vessels worldwide, of which 861 are tankers and oilers (Monfils 2009: 3–4).

Munitions are another hazard that can pose a public safety risk. Such is the case with the Liberty Ship SS *Richard Montgomery*, which sank in 1944 with its cargo of 7,000 tons of munitions near a heavily populated area in the Thames estuary. It is apparent that while some of the munitions on the wreck are capable of detonation, the likelihood of a major explosion is remote. It would likely be more dangerous to attempt to salvage the munitions than to leave the wreck in place but prevent collision from passing ships with Montgomery's mast and derrick, disturbance in general, and regularly monitor the site. Most experts agree that the best way to minimize the risk is to leave the wreck alone. As the wreck breaks up, however, individual munitions will become free and will represent smaller but multiple hazards within the area (Maritime and Coastguard Agency 2000: 6–17).

War Graves and Private Searches

A number of private individuals and organizations have dedicated themselves to locating World War shipwrecks and aircraft. There is a special fascination for locating lost submarines of the World Wars, as well as those from earlier periods. Surprisingly, there are no accurate numbers for submarines still unaccounted for. NHHC's current research indicates that there are still at least 15 "missing" U.S. Navy submarines from WWII. Other nations, such as the United Kingdom, are also missing an uncertain number of submarines, while Germany has perhaps as many as 26 U-boats unaccounted for (Bauer 1991; Friedman 1995; Evans and Kimber 1986; Malcolmson 2010; Sharpe 1998). A recent discovery involved USS *Grunion*, reported missing while on patrol off the island of Kiska in the Aleutian Islands. In July 1942, *Grunion* sank two Japanese sub chasers and damaged a third near Kiska, one of two islands in the Aleutians that had been captured by the Japanese during the early months of World War II. *Grunion*'s last message was on 30 July 1942, when it reported by radio the receipt of a navy message ordering its return to the naval base at Dutch Harbor, Alaska. When it did not return to base, it entered the records as "overdue and presumed lost." USS *Grunion* was located not by the navy, nor by archaeologists, but by a search team led by the son of LTCDR Mannert Abele, captain of the *Grunion*. The ship was found in 300 m (1,000 ft) of water off Kiska Island following a lengthy search with the help of Civil Air Patrol Lt. Col. Robert J. Miller, who flew his Cessna 182 over the wreck site, employing the Archer hyperspectral system. Following up on a likely anomaly, an ROV was deployed to confirm and document the find. The cause of *Grunion*'s loss is still undetermined, and various theories remain, including that it was sunk by Japanese naval vessels on patrol in the area, suffered an internal explosion, or even struck an underwater reef (Associated Press 2007).

Other recent discoveries of navy submarines by private groups include USS *Lagarto*, discovered in 67 m (220 ft) of water in the Gulf of Thailand, and USS *Wahoo*, discovered in 65 m (213 ft) of water in the La Perouse Strait between the Russian island of Sakhalin and the Japanese island of Hokkaido. In both cases, all hands were lost, and members of descendants' families were involved with the discoveries and identification of the wrecks (ABC News Technology and Science 2007; Rush 2005; Naval History and Heritage Command 2006).

The involvement of descendants in surveying for lost shipwrecks is a personal and sensitive experience for all of those involved. In most archaeology, the archaeologists have become detached from the tragedy of human loss by the passage of time. This is not the case for ship losses from World War II and Cold War conflicts such as the Korean and Vietnam wars. For these wars the immediate family members are still living. The discovery and investigation process is thus influenced and—as shown by the above examples—motivated by a need to bring grief resolution for the families of those missing in action. For the survivors and families of those lost, the wrecks are first and foremost war graves. It is their sensitivity as war memorials that can help build consensus about protecting these shipwrecks.

CONCLUSION

Marine archaeologists interested in the World Wars will have no scarcity of archaeological sites to dive on, research, and analyze for centuries to come, provided that iron hulls have longevity similar to that of wooden hulls. Preservation studies conducted on USS *Arizona* by the National Park Service suggest that such wrecks can remain intact for some time if not disturbed by human actions or located in harsh marine environments with strong currents or storms that act to break the wrecks apart. There is still much to be learned concerning the corrosion processes at work on these shipwrecks, and this research will have value for future generations, given the environmental concerns posed by wrecks with oil and munitions on board. The sheer numbers of World War ship and aircraft losses could keep all of today's marine archaeologists and those coming out of graduate schools busy for the rest of their careers should they devote themselves exclusively to documenting these wrecks. However, it is unlikely that most will regard such relatively recent shipwrecks as offering more compelling archaeological research questions than those from our ancient, less-well-documented past.

The archaeological work that has been done to date on World War sites has chiefly involved locating the wrecks and establishing management strategies for historic/heritage preservation as well provide protection for grave sites. These efforts have an international scope, including not only ships of the United States but those of other nations as well (Sciboz 2000). These wrecks are recognized by current generations as informal memorials to both the fallen and those who served. As generations pass, the wrecks of the World Wars will continue to be remembered and honored in the same fashion that American Civil War battlefields are honored over 150 years later.

Environmental concerns and archaeology will have to be mediated with World War sites, since twentieth-century warfare has produced more long-term health and environmental hazards than previous conflicts. This may present challenges for the archaeologist and historic/heritage preservationist, especially in cases where environmental and human safety concerns override the benefits of archaeological research. In these cases, researchers will have to answer questions regarding the extent of environmental risk, rate of hull corrosion, and deterioration of munitions in addition to, or perhaps instead of, preparing historical analyses. Underwater archaeology will have to continue to incorporate multidisciplinary scientific approaches, including such specialties as material analysis, corrosion engineering, and environmental science.

World War wrecks continue to be found with amazing frequency. In fact, four previously unknown wrecks were reported to the NHHC while this work was being drafted: the SS *City of Rayville*, the first U.S. merchant casualty of WWII; the German *U-40*, lost during World War I; the U.S. Navy submarine USS *Flier*; and a Navy Hellcat aircraft discovered in a California lake (Associated Press Miami Herald 2009; McIntosh 2009; NHHC UAB USS *Flier* and aircraft files). Shipwreck finds from the World Wars will undoubtedly continue until all the larger ships and notable aircraft have been found, for such is the fascination with discovery and the history of the lost ships and aircraft of those conflicts.

REFERENCES

ABC News Technology and Science. 2007. A WWII submarine finally comes home: Divers find the USS *Wahoo*, most storied of U.S. subs. Online at http://a.abcnews.com/ Technology/Story?id=2670734&page=2/. Accessed 9 December 2009.

Archbold, Rick, and Robert D. Ballard. 1999. *Return to Midway: The quest to find the* Yorktown *and the other lost ships from the pivotal battle of the Pacific War*. New York: Random House.

Associated Press, Fox News. 2007. Wreckage of World War II submarine found off Aleutian Islands. Rev. 24 August 2007. Online at www.foxnews.com/story/0,2933,294356,00. html/. Accessed 9 December 2009.

Associated Press, Miami Herald. 2009. News, World, US WWII shipwreck found off Australia's coast. 1 April.

Barnette, Michael C. 2009. Looking for a needle in a sea of haystacks. Online at http:// uwex.us/remotesensing.html/. Accessed 9 December.

Bauer, K. Jack, and Stephen S. Roberts. 1991. *Register of ships of the U.S. Navy, 1775–1990: Major combatants.* Westport, CT: Greenwood Press.

Brown, David. 1990. *Warship losses of World War Two.* Annapolis: Naval Institute Press.

Cooper, David J. 1994. In the drink: Naval aviation resources and archaeology. In *Underwater Archaeology Proceedings from the Society for Historical Archaeology Conference,* ed. Robyn P. Woodward and Charles D. Moore, 134–139. Vancouver: Society for Historical Archaeology.

Crane, LTCDR George (USNR). 1944. Narrative by Lieutenant Commander George Crane, USNR. USS *Tide,* Normandy Invasion. Film No. 278. Recorded 8-31-44. Washington, DC: Operational Archives Branch, Naval History and Heritage Command, Washington Navy Yard.

Delgado, James P., Daniel J. Lenihan, and Larry E. Murphy. 1991. *The archaeology of the atomic bomb: A submerged cultural resources assessment of the sunken fleet of Operation Crossroads at Bikini and Kwajalein Atoll Lagoons.* Southwest Cultural Resources Center Professional Papers No. 37. Sante Fe: National Park Service.

Department of the Navy. 2002. Archaeological remote sensing of Operation Neptune: The D-Day landings at Omaha and Utah Beaches, Normandy, France. Field Season 2001. Washington, DC: Naval Historical Center, Underwater Archaeology Branch.

———. 2008. Archaeological remote sensing of the D-Day landings: Utah and Omaha Beaches, Normandy, France. Washington, DC: Naval Historical Center, Underwater Archaeology Branch.

Dunmore, Spencer, and Ken Marschall. 2002. *Lost subs: From Hunley to the Kursk; the greatest submarines ever lost—and found.* New York: HarperCollins.

Evans, A. S. 1986. *Beneath the waves: A history of HM Submarine losses.* London: William Kimber.

Foecke, Tim; Li Ma, Matthew A. Russell, David Conlin, and Larry E. Murphy. 2009. Investigating archaeological site formation processes on the battleship USS *Arizona* using finite element analysis. *Journal of Archaeological Science* (in press).

Ford, Julie. 2006. *WWII aviation archaeology in Victoria.* Flinders University Maritime Archaeology Monographs Series No. 1. Adelaide: Flinders University, Department of Archaeology.

Friedman, Norman. 1995. *U.S. submarines through 1945: An illustrated design history.* Annapolis: United States Naval Institute

Gentile, Gary. 1989. USS *San Diego.* Philadelphia: Gary Gentile.

Greenhill, Sam. 2008. Secret of the *Lusitania*: Arms find challenges Allied claims it was solely a passenger ship. MailOnline, 20 December. Online at www.dailymail.co.uk.

His Majesty's Stationary Office, London. 1977. *British vessels lost at sea 1914–18: Reprints of 1919 navy losses and merchant shipping (losses).* Cambridge: Patrick Stephens.

Historical Material (Vol. 2). 1945. Collection of personal experiences accounts of naval personnel. Serial 00200, 13 February. World War II Action and Operational Reports. Box 58 (TF 125, 5–6-44 to TF 129). Records Relating to Naval Activity During World War II. Records of the Office of the Chief of Naval Operations. Record Group 38. NARA.

Information Request. 1969. USS *Meredith.* No Series. 22 May. Washington, DC: Ship's History Branch, Naval History and Heritage Command, Washington Navy Yard.

Joint Army-Navy Assessment Committee. 1947. Japanese naval and merchant shipping losses during World War II by all causes. Washington, DC: U.S. Government Printing Office.

Jung, Silvano. 2005. Archaeological investigation of the World War Two Catalina flying boat wreck sites in East Arm, Darwin Harbour: An appraisal of results. In *Darwin*

archaeology: Aboriginal, Asian and European heritage of Australia's top end, ed. Patricia
  Bourke, Sally Brockwell, and Clayton Fredericksen, 85–95. Darwin, NT: Charles
  Darwin University Press.

Kemp, Paul. 1997. *U-boats destroyed: German submarine losses in the World Wars*.
  Annapolis: Naval Institute Press.

King, Fleet Admiral E. J. 1946. *U.S. Navy at war 1941–1945*. Washington, DC: United States
  Navy Department.

Kozak, Catherine. 2008. NOAA goes diving for U-boats in North Carolina. *Virginia-Pilot*,
  21 July.

Mair, Michael. 2007. *Oil, fire and fate: The sinking of the USS* Mississinewa *(AO-59) in
  WWII by Japan's secret weapon*. Santa Ana, CA: Seven Locks Press.

Malcolmson, George A. 2010. Personal e-mail communication from Archivist Royal Navy
  Submarine Museum, Gosport, 22 January. Copy in Naval History and Heritage
  Command, Underwater Archaeology Branch, British Submarine File. Washington
  Navy Yard.

Maritime and Coastguard Agency. 2000. Report on the wreck of the SS *Richard
  Montgomery*. November. Online at www.mcga.gov.uk/c4mca/2000_survey_report_
  montgomery.pdf/. Accessed 9 December 2009.

McCarthy, Michael. 1998. The submarine as a class of archaeological site. *Bulletin of
  Australian Institute for Maritime Archaeology* 22: 61–70.

McIntosh, Lindsey. 2009. Great War U-boat found in North Sea 100 years on the bottom.
  Times (London), 27 March.

Means, David, and Rob White. 2001. Hood *and* Bismarck: *The deep sea discovery of an epic
  battle*. London: Channel 4 Books.

Mobile Diving and Salvage Unit Two. 1995. USS *San Diego* (ACR-6) surveyed by USN
  divers: Report to Naval Historical Center. Naval History and Heritage Command,
  Underwater Archaeology Branch Records, Washington Navy Yard.

Monfils, Rean. 2009. The global risk of marine pollution from WWII shipwrecks:
  Examples from the seven seas. Online at www.seaaustralia.com/documents/.
  Accessed 9 December.

Muckleroy, Keith. 1978. *Maritime archaeology*. Cambridge: Cambridge University Press.

Navy History Division. 1963. *United States submarine losses: World War II*. Washington,
  DC: Office of the Chief of Naval Operations.

Naval History and Heritage Command. 2006. Underwater Archaeology Branch records.
  Washington Navy Yard.

Neyland, Robert S. 2009. The underwater navy at Normandy. *Naval History* 23 (3): 37–40.

Neyland, Robert S., and David Grant. 1999. Navy aircraft as artifacts. In *Underwater
  archaeology*, ed. Adriane A. Neidinger and Matthew A. Russell, 46–51. Tucson: Society
  for Historical Archaeology.

NOAA, National Marine Sanctuaries. 2008. Battle of the Atlantic expedition. Rev. 15 July.
  Online at http://sanctuaries.noaa.gov/missions/battleoftheatlantic/u701.html/.
  Accessed 9 December 2009.

Ocean News and Technology. 2009. Mammoet awarded U-864 salvage in Norway. *Ocean
  News and Technology* 15 (1): 12.

Peterson (USCG), Lt. Craig R. 2007. A proposed annex to the wreck removal convention
  treaty to address environmental hazards of sunken World War II naval vessels.
  University College, University of Denver, Capstone Project for Master of
  Environmental Policy and Management. Rev. 15 May 2007. Online at www.seaaustralia.
  com/documents/NAVY%20WRECKS-Petersen.pdf/. Accessed 9 December 2009.

Report of Lost and Non-Operational Ships and Craft. 1944. General Records of the
    Department of the Navy, 1798–1947. Record Group 80, serial 00147. NARA.
Rush, David. 2005. Veterans Day ceremony highlights newly found USS *Lagarto*. Rev. 15
    November 2005. Online at www.navy.mil/search/display.asp?story_id=21011/.
    Accessed 9 December 2009.
Sciboz, Bertrand. 2000. *Épaves: Des costes de France*. Edilarge: Ouest-France.
Sharpe, Peter. 1998. *U boat fact file detailed service histories of the submarines operated*.
    Leicester, UK: Midland.
Shomette, Donald. 1994. The U-1105 survey: A report on the 1993 archaeological survey of
    18ST636, a Second World War German submarine in the Potomac River, Maryland.
    Naval History and Heritage Command, Underwater Archaeology Branch Records,
    Washington, DC.
Société Metallurgique de Normandie. 1957. Vol. 5. Archives Société Mellurgique de
    Normandie. Colombelles-Caen, France.
Tully, Anthony, and Jonathan Parshall. 2005. *Shattered sword: The untold story of the Battle
    of Midway*. Dulles: Potomac Books.
USS *Arikara* (ATF 98) Log Book. 1944. No series, 5 January to 30 June. Logs of U.S. naval
    ships and stations, 1801–1946. Records of Bureau of Naval Personnel. Record Group
    24. NARA.
USS *Pinto* (ATF 90) Log Book. 1944. Logs of U.S. naval ships and stations, 1801–1946. No
    series, 1 January to 30 June 30. Records of Bureau of Naval Personnel. Record Group
    24. NARA.
USS *Swift* (AM 122) Log Book. 1944–1945. No series, 1 January 1944 to 30 June 1945. Logs of
    U.S. naval ships and stations, 1801–1946. Records of the Bureau of Naval Personnel.
    Record Group 24. NARA.
USS *Swivel* (ARS 36) Log Book. 1943–1945. No series, 6 October 1943 to June 1945. Logs of
    U.S. naval ships and stations, 1801–1946. Records of Bureau of Naval Personnel.
    Record Group 24. NARA.
Wessex Archaeology. 2008. Aircraft crash sites at sea: A Scoping Study archaeological
    desk-based assessment: Final report. Prepared for English Heritage, Wiltshire.
Wilson, Brent M., Donald L. Johnson, Hans Van Tilburg, Matthew A. Russell, Larry
    E. Murphy, James D. Carr, Robert J. De Angelis, and David L. Conlin. 2007. Corrosion
    studies on the USS *Arizona* with application to a Japanese midget submarine. *JOM
    Journal of the Minerals, Metals and Materials Society* 59 (10): 14–18.
Zelo, Ian, Mike Overfield, and Doug Helton. 2009. NOAA's Abandoned Vessel Program
    and Resources and Under Sea Threats project—partnerships and progress for
    abandoned vessel management. Online at http://response.restoration.noaa.gov/book_
    shelf/1056_05-A-324-IOSC%20-%20AVP_RUST%20Zelo2.pdf/. Accessed
    9 December 2009.

PART IV

MARITIME CULTURE AND LIFE ASHORE

CHAPTER 32

THE MARITIME CULTURAL LANDSCAPE

CHRISTER WESTERDAHL

INTRODUCTION

THE first application of the specific concept of a maritime cultural landscape dates to the middle of the 1970s. From the beginning, it referred to a "fossil" or "relic" archaeological landscape, a landscape of survivals, but that could as well subsume landscapes of today. From its very inception it referred to a cross-disciplinary mode of research and the obliteration of the archaeological border between sea and land, while recognizing the overriding importance of the position of this border in the past so as to analyze and interpret remains and their meanings. The geographical background for the concept was originally Scandinavia, whose coasts have experienced maximum land upheaval since the Ice Age, and thus a strong chronological motive is apparent from the beginning.

When I was invited to write this text, I realized that I had to sin against one of the principles of the handbook: not to stress one's own personal part in the subject treated. I did, however, have a key role in the development of the concept and its contents. I hope, therefore, that I am excused for giving rather much to the history of the concept. The main issues in its development and its applications will also be pursued to some extent.

It is extremely gratifying after so many years to realize that while the *Encyclopedia of Maritime and Underwater Archaeology* (Delgado 1997) did not mention the maritime cultural landscape, the present work not only gives a whole chapter (this one) to the rise and scope of the general concept but a number of other chapters also deal with particular aspects of it, such as harbors, shipyards, and coastal archaeology (see, respectively, Oleson; Hohlfelder, Moser, and Ford). The shipwreck sites that took up virtually all the material of the earlier volume have at last been reduced to a more reasonable role in the subject matter of maritime archaeology. In most cases, they can be meaningfully analyzed as an integral part of the maritime cultural landscape. It cannot be denied that maritime archaeology has so far gathered most of its material from such sites, a fact willingly and thankfully admitted. Ship technology is still seminal in the discipline, not the least as an independent dating instrument.

Cultural Landscape

The term "cultural landscape" (or, in German, *Kulturlandschaft*) as applied to the past was the creation of German cultural geographers such as August Maitzen, Wilhelm Müller-Wille, and others. It had a more profound influence in Sweden than in the rest of the North and was partly absorbed into archaeological thinking. It was originally used to summarize the material remains and structures of inland agrarian economies, irrespective of period. Thus, agriculture was at the basis of this definition. On the other hand, a coherent cultural landscape of hunting, fishing, and gathering at sea or in lakes, forests, and mountains had early been observed by the Swedish ethnologist Åke Campbell (1936).

Insofar as a *maritime culture* existed parallel to the agrarian mainstream, as was exposed by the prominent maritime ethnologist Olof Hasslöf, a fisherman's son of Bohuslän, West Sweden, the potential of a cultural landscape based on maritime activities could be inferred. What was obviously needed was tangible material proof with a scientific concern, and preferably an extensive amount of material evidence. Many small pioneering surveys had already been completed by dedicated skin divers; and while the value of oral tradition was known and place-names had had a certain role in Scandinavian studies, the main emphasis among the pioneers was underwater material culture. On the other hand, the official ancient monuments survey, not only in Sweden but in many other northern European countries as well, primarily recorded remains on land and marked them as sites on topographical or economic maps. Cartography and differing scales prevented the same happening to sea charts, except for wrecks dangerous to shipping. There was no consistent coordination between these efforts of underwater amateurs (as they then were) and the professional terrestrial archaeologists. *The conceptual border was thus drawn tightly at the shore between water and land.* This theme will recur in the hermeneutic aspects of the cognitive landscape of early historical and prehistoric times (discussed below). Apart from this instinctive barrier, uniting underwater and terrestrial aspects in a maritime cultural landscape might still be problematic to some, since humans live on land, not underwater. But any interpretation of past cultures should indeed depend on contemporary remains found in both spheres.

BACKGROUND: SURVEYING

Any holistic view of maritime culture must supersede this border between water and land, be it conceptual, administrative, material, or instinctive. My first extensive interviews of maritime people (fishers, both full- and part-time; pilots; lighthouse attendants; divers, professional and amateur; or generally coastal people—coastal of origin though perhaps not living there now) took place at Lake Vänern, Sweden, in the 1960s. Sites of shipwrecks were but one of several objectives (Westerdahl 2003a, 2003b). Later, the chance offered to me in 1975 by the National Maritime Museum of Stockholm to survey the oral statements and traditions of a limited harbor area in connection with steelworks in Luleå, Norrbotten, northern Sweden, produced a promising number of wreck sites. My innovation in this survey was, however, to focus on other material that was connected to, but not identified with, the ship-wreck sites. The occurrence of historic shipwrecks must have relied on a logistic network of the past, which could be recorded in the same process. The widening of my survey objectives was actively supported by the museum and garnered private sponsorship for continued work along the coast. During the seven years between 1975 and 1982, the survey in Norrbotten was extended to the northern outskirts of Stockholm, a stretch of approximately 1,250 km, not counting the undulating coast-line, nor archipelagos and islands. Even though it was extensive, the survey was never thought of as exhaustive in scope. It had to be complemented all the time by excursions to fill in gaps, and in fact these excursions continue to the present day.

Still, the survey was mainly restricted to the shore and to underwater remains (Figure 32.1). A growing realization that the extensive submerged material was indeed of concern to the heritage authorities led to the inclusion of (more) mari-time remains in subsequent official surveys of ancient monuments. This process was also in line with a successively broadened application of the concept of (pro-tected) ancient monument (Swedish *fornminne*).

HISTORY OF THE CONCEPT

Det maritima kulturlandskapet first appears as a caption in Swedish (Westerdahl 1978). There the term was defined as "the network of sea routes and harbors, indi-cated both above and under water." The development of ship technology during the period circa 1500–1800 had admittedly transformed this network. But other pro-cesses were even more important in a longer time perspective. The world's most pronounced land upheaval or rebound since the last ice age (286 m at Skuleberget, Ångermanland) had a particular role. The land rise could be keenly observed even during the life of an individual. Recent remains at the shore were lifted to dry land in considerably less than 100 years, partly due to rapid sedimentation and

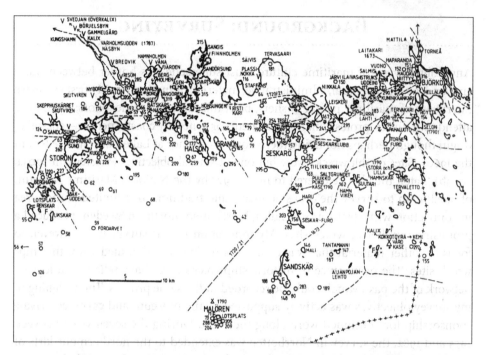

Figure 32.1 Map number 1 (of 35) of the Swedish Norrland survey 1975–1982, with relevant place-names and numbered wreck and foundering sites. F = fishing harbor, V = shipyard, anchor signs = harbors. The border with Finland is to the right. After Westerdahl 1987.

stabilizing vegetation. Thus, the maritime cultural landscape was chronologically multilayered. But certain periods of the past could also be sketched along ancient shorelines, especially when it was discovered that upheaval was not entirely linear in time. Transgressions had stabilized the shoreline for longer periods of time at certain intervals, usually at 20 m intervals, corresponding to changes in the iso-static/eustatic balance. Thus, the relevant maritime landscapes and the ancient coastal configurations could be traced back to the first humans who exploited marine resources. Yet it took some time for this fact to be acknowledged by archae-ological surveys, even though it was apparent in local studies that maritime settle-ment finds tended to cluster at certain height curves, as recent as the last 1,000 years. Clearly, these clusters should indicate harbors or landing places in the vicinity. This occurrence emphasized the need for an observant study of the topographical landscape. Since then, height curves have been at the basis of any study.

Among the remains listed were—apart from shipwrecks—harbors and ports, including emergency harbors, anchorages, sea inns or taverns (with stage function), ballast sites, shipyards (or boatbuilding sites), maritime settlements, and piers or other such constructions, as well as landing places (Westerdahl 1978, 1980). Most of the material remains were likely to be indicated by place-names, but toponyms were not yet considered as an independent source to "the maritime mind" (see below). Although the place-names were extremely important even in this early text, their indicative use was restricted to the functions that were immediately related to shipping and, to some lesser extent, to fishing. Maritime cultures were thus not understood in their entire scope. The history of sailing ships and their routes, networks, and crews still determined the course of the survey.

However, it was stressed in the first paper on the subject that "a holistic study and interpretation of maritime remains in their own cultural landscape presuppose *crossdisciplinary* insights," which meant that the surveyor had to personally obtain such insights (Westerdahl 1978). Sources should include interviews, archaeological surveys, archival material, place-names, historical sources, cartographic material,

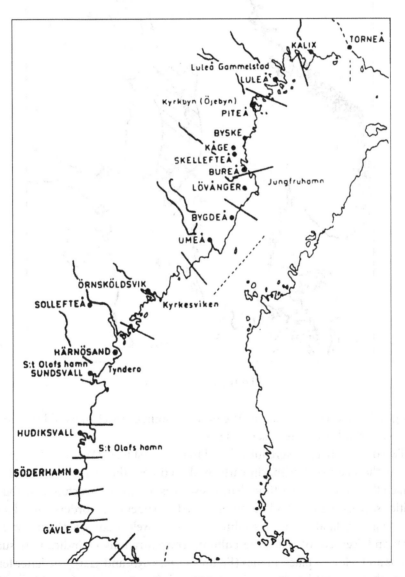

Figure 32.2 Maritime cultural areas. This is a very preliminary attempt, but it shows the survey area of northeastern Sweden, 1975–1982. After Westerdahl 1980.

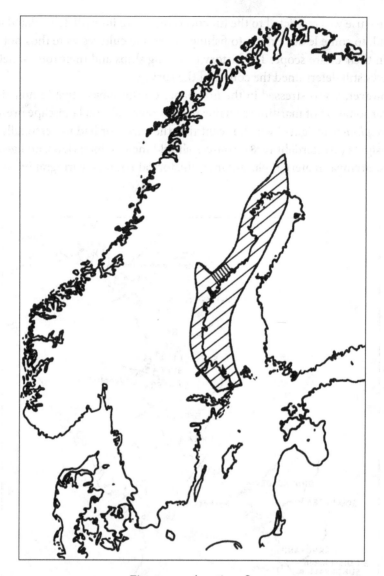

Figure 32.2 (*continued*)

iconographic sources, and so on. The need for source criticism would require considerable versatility on the observer's part.

Two other concepts were introduced in these first texts (Westerdahl 1978, 1980, 1986) on the analysis of primarily early modern times: "the maritime cultural areas," of which the borders of maritime elements such as settlement structures, boatbuilding traditions, place-names, and so on appeared to supersede borders introduced or emanating from land conditions, administrative as well as cultural (Figure 32.2a and 32.2b); and "centers of maritime culture," concentrations of indications such as remains and relevant place-names (Figures 32.3a, 32.3b, and 32.4). The latter term in fact sought to establish a connection between different aspects of maritime culture, emphasizing a kind of hierarchical buildup of functions, always based on fishing.

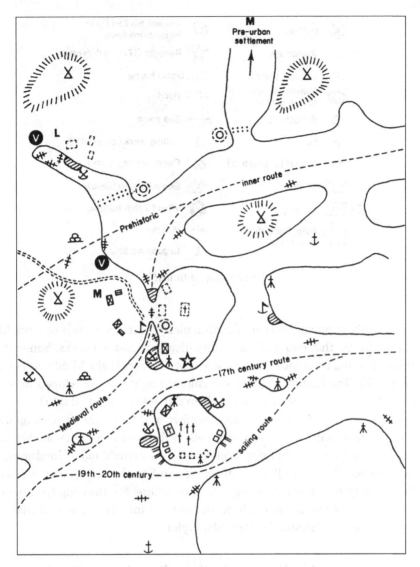

Figure 32.3 A center of maritime culture. A fictitious area along the Swedish Baltic coast with possible elements as it appears today. The sketch was originally produced by my friend Annika Sander, Museum of Skellefteå, based on several prototype drawings by me. The harbor function is paramount. Ruins of chapel and churchyard fences, a sea inn, a repair shipyard, possibly a customhouse, landing places, and so on are indicated. Land rise and changing ship technologies give a chronological displacement sequence for trade and shipping c. 1000–1700 CE, from the shallow bays and channels inland outward to the outer and deeper routes between islands. But fishing and other local sustenance is still carried out starting from the shallow inner parts, only with seasonal settlement in the archipelagoes. These sites provide the first pilots and transport service in the form of stage traffic by boat. After Westerdahl 1980.

Figure 32.3 (*continued*)

It worked partly as an application of central place theory in a study of a maritime cultural landscape that emphasized communications and networks. Some of the indications pointed to an inception of these central places in the Middle Ages (circa 1050–1550 CE). The centers of maritime culture might have developed into port cities, but the overwhelming majority of them did not (Westerdahl 1982).

I used these general ideas in a large number of lectures and articles, applying them in turn to specific subjects or elements of the landscape (such as shipyards, countryside sites [Westerdahl 1987]; stone mazes [Westerdahl 1996b]; and seamarks [Westerdahl 2006b]) as well as to provinces and to the larger region (mostly Nordic) from 1976 onward. Although its implications for studying the cognitive landscape were not realized at the time, the seminal importance of oral traditions and place-names was stressed in Westerdahl 1980.

Acceptance and Application in Scandinavia

International support for the conceptual contents of the term appeared gradually. For example, in 1978 Ole Crumlin-Pedersen had applied partly the same perspective, although without using the specific term "maritime cultural landscape," for Roskilde Fjord in Denmark (Crumlin-Pedersen 1978). A recurring idea was that the land should be seen from the sea (cf. Cooney 2004), often in connection with the ships and their performance: "Perhaps some of the answers to questions concerning the origins of our towns not at all to be found within the town limits, but on board a vessel closing in with the coast" (Crumlin-Pedersen 1978: 75). The answers could be in the heads of the sailors as well as in the construction, draft, and propulsion of the vessel. The significance of the ancient seaman's appreciation and experience for the topographical location of landing sites along a shallow coastline is still stressed by Ilves (2004).

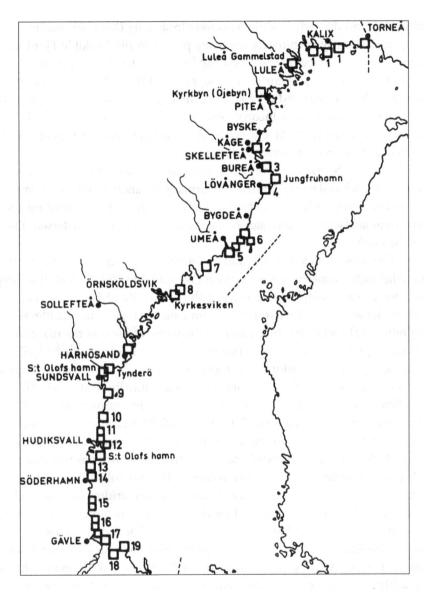

Figure 32.4 Centers of maritime culture along the survey coast. A preliminary
view. After Westerdahl 1980.

Another impressive illustration of the concept, what could be called the maritime archaeology of land, was the atlas of the island Funen in Denmark (Crumlin-
Pedersen, Porsmore, and Thrane 1996). While no oral survey material is presented
in this study, it is a demonstration of the potential of an already existing cross-
disciplinary survey of material, including place-names (see the extensive summary
and the introduction on the landscape by Crumlin-Pedersen). The function of late
prehistoric harbors in the cultural landscape, especially on the island of Gotland,
had already been explored by Cederlund (1980, on the basis of Lundström 1971,
1976). On this island, a substantial number of small harbors dating to the late Iron

(Viking) Age and the early Middle Ages were located by Dan Carlsson (1994). The landing sites from approximately the same period in the Roskilde Fjord area of Zealand, Denmark, were discussed on the basis of extensive excavations by Jens Ulriksen (1997). Iron Age preurban developments of the Baltic have been mapped by Johan Callmer (1994) and others. These smaller sites gradually disappeared as they concentrated or became incorporated in medieval towns, which tended to be situated on the coast in inlets and fjords, at estuaries, or along rivers due to their dependence on waterborne traffic (Bill 1999).

The Swedish Norrland survey concerned an area with strong land uplift. In western Denmark and parts of northern Germany the ancient shorelines have sunk considerably, in some places 17 m below present sea level. The potential for a Stone Age cultural landscape underwater is staggering (Fischer 1995; Pedersen, Fischer, and Aaby 1997).

The first major article published in an international language on the maritime cultural landscape concept was in German (Westerdahl 1986). By that time, preparations for a cross-disciplinary project at the University of Umeå, Sweden, were already under way, with a focus on three main aspects: (1) patterns of settlement and living milieu, (2) social structures, and (3) the world of ideas of the maritime cultural landscape. The initiative came from the leading ethnologist Phebe Fjellström; archaeology, geography, history, and toponomy followed suit. Despite lively and productive discussions and the support of local museums, little came out of it except an excellent pilot project and the realization that such an approach necessarily must incorporate a cognitive perspective (Holstein 1988). This tacit "endorsement" of the scientific significance of nonmaterial traditions and place-names changed the attitude of other disciplines toward maritime archaeology in a positive way.

The archipelagoes of western and southern Finland hold a huge potential for the study of past maritime culture. In Zilliacus 1990 the maritime cultural landscape was synthesized in articles by way of partly the same source materials, especially place-names, that I used. One of the authors, the archaeologist Tapani Tuovinen, published his dissertation in 2002 with quantitative methods (sighting vistas) to assess the perspectives of coastal cairns from different periods. In nearby Estonia, the maritime landscape was addressed in a special issue of *Estonian Journal of Archaeology* (2004). Despite these projects, the term "maritime cultural landscape" for a long time remained largely unknown outside the Nordic area. However, its scope was already coming into focus.

Publication of a Handbook and Its Material

In 1987 and 1989, I published the results of the Norrland coastal survey of the years 1975–1982 as *Norrlandsleden I–II* (The Norrland Sailing Route I–II); the title was true to the original definition of the maritime cultural landscape as mainly a network of routes and harbors (Westerdahl 1987–1989). The first volume of this publication, which contains a fairly extensive English summary, purports to be a handbook comprising a systematic maritime archaeological survey or inventory, mainly covering the Scando-Baltic area. The second volume contains a catalog and registers of the area, with the site descriptions partly adapted to an English audience. The explicit intention was later to distill an outline of the maritime cultural landscape of the Middle Ages (circa 1050–1550 CE) from the collected multiperiod material. Several other significant historical periods could be outlined: for example, the periods of advanced sails, 1550–1750 CE and 1750–1850 CE (just before the Industrial Revolution along the Norrland coast) and the period of rapid change in route and harbor structures, circa 1850–1950 CE. But all such chronology is based on local or regional contexts.

By 1980, the following counts of site types and elements of the maritime cultural landscape had been registered (with additions/alterations up into 1990 within parentheses; Westerdahl 1998: 100; cf. Westerdahl 1980: 315):

Oral tales not associated directly with wrecks: 307 (400)
Identified shipwrecks: 745 (1,000)
Founderings: 729 (900)
Unknown foundering sites: 9 (2; the decrease is due to the discovery of
    place-names etc. which had disappeared on maps)
Net fastenings: 376 (400)
Unconfirmed indications on sonar: 23 (50)
Loose finds (indicating wrecks): 95 (100)
Undetermined positions/localities in general: 59 (62). These localities are
    often explained by faulty descriptions of the localities involved.
Harbors, havens, anchorages, seasonal fishing harbors: 538 (600)
Sites where ballast was unloaded: 56 (100)
Place-names of relevance to maritime culture: 131 (200)
Shipyards: 234 (300)
Route blockages: 6 (7)
Canals: 1 (2)

These categories were the basis for a further analysis of the landscape. In part II the marked elements of each of the 35 original maps were subdivided into:

Principal sailing routes/destinations (main towns/ports)
Older sailing routes
Older sailing marks and beacons
Early lighthouses
Pilot stations
Harbors (all categories, including landing sites and clear-ways)
Ballast sites
Fishing harbors
Shipyards
Place-names of maritime interest
Number of foundering/wreck sites (all details given individually to each
    site in the catalog).

The whole range of remains of shipping and fishing in Sweden has since been summarized by Norman 1995, with the emphasis on ancient monuments included in an official ancient monuments survey. Later, sites that may denote power centers, Crown or Church ownership, fortifications, medieval church sites, maritime chapels (Westerdahl 2006c), import finds, and market sites pinpointed by the historical material were given further systematic attention as central places. The medieval time horizon based on the Norrland survey has never been published, though summaries do exist (Westerdahl 1991).

It is apparent that harbors and havens are of seminal importance, citing the first idea of a network of sea routes leading to these points. Despite the universal significance of the haven-finding art in maritime cultures (Taylor 1956), there are only a few studies published on the typology of harbors, particularly for prehistory (topographical features in Bjerck 1985, Blue 1997, urban locations in Bill 1999). I have discussed rest or emergency harbors in Norrland and somewhat farther south in the Baltic, quoting sailing directories of recent times (seventeenth to eighteenth centuries; e.g., Westerdahl 1997b).

Included in the handbook part of my publications are, however, some elements that so far have not been mentioned. A special feature of the Norwegian coastal landscape is the approximately 800 ancient boathouses, from the Roman Iron Age into the Middle Ages. The boathouses are found all over the North Atlantic but are particularly dense in Norse coastal settlements (Stylegar and Grimm 2005). The study of them initiated an analysis of their general maritime context, military aspects, social organization, and administrative units (Myhre 1985, 1995; Grimm 2001, 2006).

Additional features of military significance are underwater fortifications and pile and stone blockages, sometimes with sunken ships. The dating of these features in Denmark appears to go back to the pre-Roman Iron Age, beyond the year 0. Blockages of this kind are so far not found in Norway or Finland, but they are quite common, although likely later, in present-day Sweden (Crumlin-Pedersen 1986; Westerdahl 1989; Rieck 1991; Nørgård Jørgensen 1996, 2002).

GOING INTERNATIONAL

The concept of the maritime cultural landscape was first published in English (Westerdahl 1992a) during my first time as a senior lecturer of maritime archaeology at the University of Copenhagen. The old definition stressing the network of sea routes and harbors had been replaced with a more explicit connection to maritime culture. Thus, the maritime cultural landscape was derived from a culture that was conceptually different from inland (agricultural) culture. This does not, however, mean that either of the two cultural concepts was isolated. On the contrary, a considerable number of communities and individuals partook in both (Ohnuki-Tierney 1972; cf. Meløe 1990). Very few, if any, maritime cultures of the past were entirely dependent on marine resources. Marine resources are necessary for hunters and gatherers and important as a reserve for coastal agrarian communities (Fitzhugh 1975; Yesner 1980; Erlandson 2001; Westerdahl 2009).

The same person or family group was engaged economically both on the sea and on land. But what is important here is that the *cognitive* expressions differed from each other. An example is the cultural landscape of the ice in the Bothnian Sea, where the outward expressions changed from year to year. The ice disappears entirely, although some features of the landscape reappear constantly, such as the major open channels (Russian *polynya*). However, human utilization of the ice, with its necessary terms and adaptations, remains basically the same. This is accordingly a cultural landscape, although it is not, in contrast to what has so far been studied in archaeology, studded with material remains or relic cultural layers.

In Westerdahl 1992a, the Swedish term *sjöbruk*, literally "use of the sea," introduced by Olof Hasslöf in the 1950s, was used. Translations to other languages were supposed to convey the same feeling of "a juxtaposition to agriculture" that is apparent in the Swedish (Scandinavian) term for "agriculture," *jordbruk* or *åkerbruk*. It should be possible to construct new terms of the same denotation with a foundation in each language. The same problems arise with translations of the phrase "maritime cultural landscape" if it is to bear the same connotations as the original application. This cognitive landscape "denotes the mapping and imprinting of the functional aspects of the surroundings in the human mind. Man in landscape, landscape in man" (Löfgren 1981; Westerdahl 1992a: 5). It should definitely have been pointed out more emphatically that it is not only the functional aspects that are imprinted in the human mind, but also the concomitant transcendent and ritualized features. However, a link to function, whether economic or social, always appears to exist in other cognitive representations that are not directly techno-practical.

Maritime culture would then be defined as "human utilization (economy) of maritime space by boat: settlement, fishing, hunting, shipping, and, in historical times, its attendant subcultures, such as pilotage, and lighthouse and seamark maintenance" (Westerdahl 1992a: 5). It should include any hermeneutic kind of human relationship to the sea. In general, it is possible to talk of *aquatic adaptations* (Erlandson 2001). Island and coastal settlements are included almost by definition. Rivers and lakes would be considered as well, but not only as part of the transport landscape (e.g., Vedru 2004; Westerdahl 2003a, 2003b). A natural (or necessary) way of discovering aspects of the landscape, environmental as well as the cognitive, would be by way of local traditions. This material would reasonably be collected in interviews or various kinds of participant observation. It is important to remember that the holistic study of settlement must include the use of resources other than strictly marine ones.

However, I feel that the value of the approach of maritime culture for *prehistoric* archaeology had been pointed out enough in Westerdahl 1992a. Neither was the vast potential of landscape studies in the scope of maritime archaeology observed to its full potential. The first to do so was in fact the maritime archaeologist Marek Jasinski at the University of Trondheim, Norway, who pointed out that maritime (as opposed to "marine" or "underwater") archaeology had been given a new direction by the concept "maritime cultural landscape" (Jasinski 1993a, 1993b). A rigorous scrutiny of the elements of the maritime cultural landscape produced a number of aspects, essentially subheadings of the larger landscape (Westerdahl 1997a, 2000). The original definitions are still valid, but further comments are given here:

1. The *economic landscape*, or the landscape of sustenance, of fishing (ruins of seasonal settlements, fish traps, net sinkers, etc.), hunting (traps, sheds), and gathering (traces in the natural landscape), but also including elements of coastal agriculture (settlements, fields with terraces, fences, traces of grazing on islands). The landscape of fishing in eastern Sweden, and its ramifications, has been analyzed by Norman (1993). The ambition is to include the archaeological structure of the agrarian landscape at the coast in the marine-focused economic landscape (Mägi 2004).

2. The *landscape of transport and communications* (communicative landscape): routes, seamarks, pilotage, harbors, roads, portages. Not to be overlooked is the exceedingly important factor of navigation, including transit lines and the assignment of place-names that order the landscape, its points and its borders.

3. The *power landscape*, that of mansions of great chieftains, as administrative and central places. This landscape could well include the landscape of defense, a *territorial landscape*, or landscape of allegiance (but is there not a landscape of resistance to internal power as well?), which would include the social landscape of class structures, settlement patterns, boathouses, blockages, other fortifications.

4. The *outer resource landscape*, more specifically for supplying material and resources for shipbuilding, including sails (production of wool, etc.) and cordage (lime bast, etc.).

5. The *inner resource landscape*, emphasizing the necessary surplus for ship expeditions and trade.

6. The *cognitive landscape*, the mental map as expressed in oral traditions and place-names, including the ritual and symbolic landscape. This aspect, particularly place-names, may carry connotations of all the others. It is the only aspect that is not necessarily shared with terrestrial cultures.

7. The *recreative (leisure) landscape*. A recent restructuring of the landscape for leisure cottages, marinas, and so on.

It would be rather logical also to include an eighth landscape, the *urban landscape*, but the survey situation normally subsumed it under transport and communication. It is also an exceedingly difficult subject, likely to be individualized in research for each site (but see Bill and Clausen 1999).

These aspects, in combination and in conjunction with natural topography, thus create the cultural landscape in the human mind, now or then. However, it seems reasonable that a particular historical situation, such as war, mobilized one or two cognitive aspects, such as the territorial (or allegiance) factor. The aspects mingle effortlessly to form facets of the same feature. For example, coastal portages are not just an element of transport; they might be the objects of power and control, and they might also mark borders of cognitive (transport) zones (Tveit and Elvestad 2006; Westerdahl 2006a). The landscape of shipbuilding easily fits into the economic, social, and power aspects.

So far, however, the landscape may appear far more static and permanent than it actually was. Unfortunately, the temporal dynamic in the landscape might be lost in this process of analyzing and integrating aspects: the seasonal and thereby cyclical variations are extremely important to humans, and humans may enhance and even create variable landscape features, not the least cognitive ones.

Despite the growing realization that place-names not only indicated maritime activities but could also be a seminal source of the cognitive landscape, the categories listed in the *International Journal of Nautical Archaeology* article (Westerdahl 1992a) were still very much related to shipping, and to a lesser degree fishing and farming in the maritime landscape:

Names of sailing routes, including harbor, wreck, and foundering indicators, such as names of individual ships, names of ship types, names of origin, and names of a person or profession/title.

Names of harbors: The main cargo is often named at loading places and anchorages (iron, wood, etc).

Names of beacons (often only with a faint, indirect relationship to the sailing routes): These concern sites of warning fires (Westerdahl 2002a).

Names of sailing marks: These are used at a dangerous spot, later sometimes marked by a modern seamark or a lighthouse (Westerdahl 2006b).

Names of warning (danger names): The earliest one known to me may in fact be Scandinavia, originally denoting the dangerous sand banks of Falsterbo, Skåne, southern Sweden (Svennung 1953).

Names denoting the sailing route itself or navigation in it (e.g., crossing of transit lines): The latter points to the determination of reference points on land or where there is a divergence of routes.

Names at ferry routes or fords: They could denote the call for boats or signal systems (smoke) as well as the functions of ferrying or fording themselves.

Authority names: The symbolical connotations of this toponym group are obvious. Later this name group to some extent triggered the term "cognitive landscape."

Migrant names: Showing maritime cultural, particularly commercial, contacts. On the aspect of special jurisdiction, mainly referring to maritime localities, especially islands, see Westerdahl 2003c.

Another subtitle in Westerdahl 1992a concerns the way place-names convey the landscape's *aspects of defense* (further in Westerdahl 2002a). Finally, the *inland names* indicating transportation are particularly interesting to the phenomenon of portages (Westerdahl 2006a). Basically, the same categories are still of current interest today, but the range is much greater. A professional linguist's view is found in Holmberg 1991.

It must be emphasized that it is never as simple as recording place-names on maps, old or new or in archives. Some of the most interesting place-names may not be found except in oral tradition. This may not necessarily mean that they only denote very small localities. A systematic field survey of any local area is absolutely necessary.

Stemming from the study of the cultural landscape of the sea, although also including land roads and rivers, is the concept of *traditional zones of transport geography*, or *transport zones* for short. This concept has been treated in several articles (Westerdahl 1992a, 1994, 1995, 1996a, 1997a, 1999, 2000). Transport zones consist of route corridors in elongated and easily recognizable sociocultural space, but not identical with any single route or only following coasts (Figure 32.5). The maritime

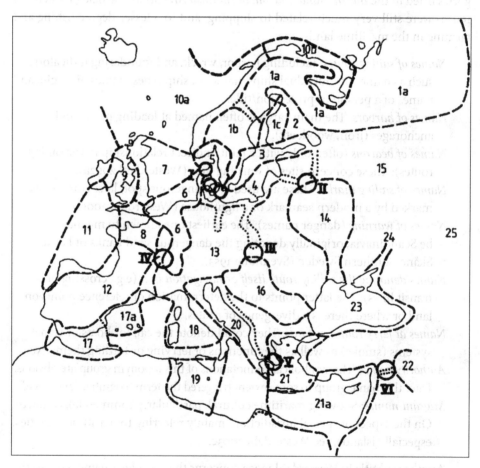

Figure 32.5 Transport zones of Europe and the Levant. The *durées* assumed to mark the European Middle Ages, with borders and transit points (circles) drawn at dangerous points (e.g., the Skaw and Falsterbo in Scandinavia, Cape Maleas in Greece) and several portages (dotted lines). The inner seas of Braudel (1986/1949) are marked in the Mediterranean, many of them valid for classical antiquity as well. After Westerdahl 1995.

cultural landscapes along these zones show close connections, by way of similar-ities in ships and the shipping system, place-name types, coastal settlement char-acter, sizes and patterns, and sometimes a common trading language or vocabulary. The zones are influenced by and have an influence on cultural borders and border zones. Some of the boundaries of these zones appear to be based on natural conditions, such as topography (dangerous spits of land), prevailing wind directions, and currents as well as conditions of maritime culture and transport (type of goods, adapted boatbuilding, type of propulsion, etc.). Thus, the concept of transport zones also purports to contribute to explaining differences in ship and boat types. Vessel adaptations are expected to be dual: both to nature and to culture.

The transitions between two zones could mean the change of boat or vessel type, or a different means of transport (e.g., portage), sometimes with seasonal implications, such as the difference between summer (open waters) and winter (frozen land and waters). Transit points or areas were found at the sites for transshipment, such as at the neck of an isthmus or in the estuaries of important and navigable rivers. There may be several such transit points at rapids along waterways. Land roads are a part of this purview (Westerdahl 2008).

Originally these zones were understood as quite small, meaning likewise small cognitive worlds for communities—on one side of a border the known world, on the other a somewhat vaguer outside (cf. Braudel 1986/1949). Limitations of trans-portation techniques were decisive. The sizes of zones appear to have varied with time. Some express continuous *durées*, whereas others are discontinuous. Transport zones may later encompass the whole world as trade routes, but the old borders of smaller zones are still to be found; they show up occasionally in certain cultural elements or in traditional coastal shipping. Archaeologically, remains of the old pattern can be demonstrated. The phenomenon of *transport enclaves* or *niches*, meaning concentrated all-year settlements of maritime people serving as trans-porters, skippers, and crews and assisting sea transport in various ways, including harbor functions, change of vessel, portage, and pilotage, can sometimes be related directly to the intensive use of such a zone.

Apart from seasonal variations, we find among the transport zones, extending to land corridors, mainly the following zone types (Westerdahl 2000: 15):

1. Trans-isthmian zones (cross-ridge/cross-watershed) land zones (Sherratt 1996a; Westerdahl 1996a; Sherratt 2006; Larsson 2006)
2. Ferry corridors or routes of regular transportation across waters (often not just a short ferry tour)
3. Zones based on river valleys or other far-reaching water courses
4. Estuary lagoon zones, protected by extensive sand spits or barriers (perhaps 25% of the coasts of the globe could be said to belong to this category!)
5. Lake zones (Westerdahl 1999, 2003a and b)
6. Zones of the open sea

The World

Impressive attention was given the maritime cultural landscape at a conference dedicated entirely to the subject at Kiel, Germany: Maritime Kulturlandschaften am Beispiel des Ostseeraumes (Maritime Cultural Landscapes Exemplified by the Baltic Area), held in September 1996. The organizing body was the Arbeitskreis fur genetische Siedlungsforschung in Mitteleuropa, the working circle for settlement history in Middle Europe, harking back to the prestigious German creation of a historical cultural geography of the last century.

The archaeologist Michael Müller-Wille was an important initiator and referred in particular to research in southern Scandinavia (Müller-Wille 1997). My contribution contained the principal thoughts on the contents of maritime cultural landscapes (Westerdahl 1997a). The contributions with geographical, historical, archaeological, and ethnological implications ranged from Iron Age to medieval settlements on the Baltic coast, and from the urban port milieu to the leisure landscapes of today. To continue the urban aspect, the port of Bristol was treated as a maritime cultural landscape by Parker (1999).

From an international perspective, the northern Irish survey work *Strangford Lough: An Archaeological Survey of the Maritime Cultural Landscape* in 2003 was a landmark (or seamark?) (McErlean, McConkey, and Forsythe 2003). Within the same area, the Irish Sea, is the study of South Argyll (Ragan 2001). A similar project concerns Achill Island in western Ireland.

What is even more striking, perhaps, is the worldwide extension of studies with the same focus such as those published in *Seascapes*, the title of a 2003 thematic issue of *World Archaeology*. The maritime cultural landscape concept was most extensively discussed by Brad Duncan in his dissertation, where, among other important comments, he points out the difficulty of drawing a border between land and sea in human life (Duncan 2006: 1–37). Island landscapes are at the root of the maritime sphere. Paul Rainbird's *Island Archaeology* is an important addition to ideas on maritime culture. An innovative study of sailor's gravestones of the United States is that of David Stewart (2007). Important holistic studies concern the past maritime cultural landscape of the Lake Ontario area (Ford 2009). Work on reconstructed coastal landscapes also concern Native American Newfoundland (Bell and Renouf 2003). Among particular elements of the landscape, historical shipyards have been the objects of scrutiny (Jason Moser [2007] and Ben Ford [2007] in the United States, Christian Lemee [1997] in Denmark).

In the Indian Ocean, the works of Himanshu Prabha Ray have shown the same versatility in finding a maritime landscape of human significance (Prabha Ray 2003, 2007). Other studies on important maritime sites concern East Africa (Breen and Lane 2004; McConkey and McErlean 2007; Pollard 2008). The long-term conception of the landscape in Braudelian terms (Braudel 1986/1949) has been explored eminently and critically by Horden and Purcell (2000) for the Mediterranean and Johan Rönnby (2006) for the central Baltic. The *longue durée* appeared already in the theory of traditional transport zones. It appears that the Mediterranean is finally getting the same attention from the current point of view, and not only for the classical period (Knapp 1997; Morton 2001). Critical discussions on mari-time landscape perception and archaeology, however few, include Firth (1994) and Parker (2001).

Special sessions dedicated to the maritime cultural landscape have nowadays become commonplace at conferences and congresses of maritime archaeology. Maybe it would be a good idea to integrate in general archaeology as well as to specialize.

COGNITIVE AND RITUAL LANDSCAPE

What about the cognitive factor? Partly under impulses derived from postproces-sual archaeology, I finally launched a theory in 2004 on the cognitive cultural land-scape in prehistory (Westerdahl 2005, 2007).

The ritual landscape among sailors and fishermen in early modern times (Solheim 1939, 1940 on fishing taboos; Henningsen 1961 on sailors' baptism) was explored preliminarily in Westerdahl 2002b, but received more attention in Wester-dahl 2004, finally spilling over into the Middle Ages and possibly prehistory. The basic feature appears to be the contrast between the sea and the land, leading to ritual behavior. This behavior is normally called superstition in modern times, but it seems originally to have been a consistent system of belief. Nature is experienced as fickle, and ritual produces human magic to avert danger. It was once widely believed, at least in northern Europe, that catching danger in a ritual web of language and vocabulary would render it innocuous.

This contrast of elements is in my opinion firmly anchored in fishing, in the combination of land and sea pursuits that is so characteristic of maritime culture. This environmental dichotomy is reasonably reflected by cognition in the maritime landscape. Basic patterns for naming and remembering are supplied during naviga-tion for the everyday economy in this landscape, particularly by way of contours of land, skerries, and transit lines between these features. Barber (2004: 445) points to the Maori word *tohu* for alignment landmarks, what Nordic people would call *me(d)*. These techniques may appear elementary to an experienced surveyor in the age of GIS and GPS (e.g., Dean et al. 1992: 110, fig. 45, repeated in Bowens 2008: 90, fig. 11.8), but the implications for the cognitive landscape of past maritime culture are important (e.g., Hovda 1941a, 1941b, 1948, 1961). By way of coordinated place-names, a visual landscape analysis (terrestrial in Gansum, Jerpåsen, and Keller 1997; Keller 1993) can be applied at sea following the coast and its landmarks.

In the current sphere of meanings, I am finally drawing together ethnoarchae-ology, place-names, and some major prehistoric shore-aligned monumental cate-gories of the Nordic area—Stone Age and Bronze Age rock carvings (Figure 32.6a and 32.6b), Bronze Age and Iron Age coastal cairns, and medieval stone mazes. I am trying to interpret their location as a part of the maritime cultural landscape. The

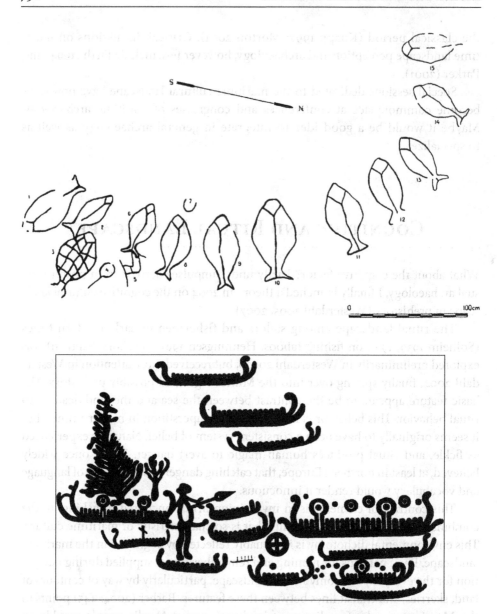

Figure 32.6 Fish and ships. Rock carvings from the late Neolithic and the Bronze
Age of the North. The location of rock carvings at the seashore is the relevant
perspective in this text, but it cannot be denied that ships are among the most
common among the motifs. Fish, in this case halibuts, are in fact rather rare.
After Gjessing 1936:pl. LXX.

ritual quality of the shore in connection with Nordic rock carvings have been
emphasized by Sognnes (1994) and Helskog (1999). Another area where the cognitive dualism of sea and land can be detected in various ways is the Inuit (and
historic Thule) culture of Greenland and northern Canada (Zeilich-Jensen 1974;
McGhee 1977).

I suspect strongly that this cognitive idea is globally widespread, although expressions may vary and may reflect highly complicated issues. The multifarious issues concerning the interpretation of landscape use and preferences include rock resources on islands as well as the location of holy places at any water's edge (e.g., Bradley 2000: 18–32, 81–96, 132–146).

In my current hypothesis on the North, other major monument groups such as ship settings (multiperiod) and phenomena such as ship burials (Iron Age) and wetland offerings (multiperiod) indicate various aspects of what I have called *hydro-liminality*. The social and cognitive meanings of monuments, other phenomena, and figurative representations have varied incessantly, and are indeed multivocal or polysemous in the same time span, but I still believe that the basic structure of a "cosmological" contrast, dualism, dichotomy, or opposition appears to be there.

My view is that the structural translation of the sea/land relationship affected various other essential dichotomies of the maritime mind, such as life/death and male/female. The sea could be either one, but was mostly death and mostly female. It was also a strongly corporeal opposition, affecting the senses: certain colors (black is the color of land, white that of the sea) and sounds (more difficult to establish in recorded traditions) were thought of as opposed. In the Nordic context, the living incarnations of land are male and the great "royal" (horned) land animals—elks, moose, or stags, and probably reindeer (caribou); those of the sea are female—boats and the great sea animals, especially whales and seals.

These incarnations, made symbols and metaphors, can represent and replace each other on both sides of the waterline as *liminal agents*. It is assumed that the application of a liminal agent in the opposite element meant that an act was taboo and therefore produced the strongest possible magic power. The transfer from one world to another was not factual but was expressed by words, names, and various applications in the liminal area, that is, the shore or onboard the boat. I am convinced that the current dichotomy dates originally from the Mesolithic, to judge from recorded economies of settlements and the location and the motives of rock carvings. But even though the symbols and their meanings may vary, the basic dual relationship remains. Of course, I should have referred here to Claude Lévi-Strauss and classical structuralism (Tilley 1990), but in fact the idea stems directly from a study of maritime cultures.

Considerably more work will be required in this hypothetical field, not the least for each of the main categories of remains, such as rock carvings, burial cairns, stone mazes, and so on. Perhaps the experience of maritime archaeology might even be seen to contribute to concepts and theories of its older sister? Important points, for example on the liminal foreshore, were pointed out by Cooney (2004), and the notion of the sea as the place of no return is discussed in the same journal by Lindenlauf (2004). There are important contributions already offered on the relationship of megaliths and other monuments to the sea, on the liminal qualities of Atlantic cliff forts, and on Orkney and northern Scotland (Cunliffe 2001: 9–10; Scarre 2002a, 2002b; Phillips 2004). In particular, I want to mention McNiven's maritime spiritscapes of indigenous Australians (McNiven 2004). Lars Larsson tries to interpret burials at the Mesolithic shore of South Scandinavia as an effort to stop the inexorable changes in water level (Larsson 2004). The huge isostatic/eustatic changes in the North must have profoundly influenced human thoughts on the transcendent (Westerdahl 2000: 11).

Some other ideas already to some extent published concern the application of the cognitive landscape to place-names, seamarks (Westerdahl 2006c), and topographical features such as overland portages (land spits, isthmi; Sherratt 1996a, 2006; Westerdahl 2006a). The latter were characterized as monuments in the landscape—landscape portals, transit points in transport zones, meeting places, nodes of power and control of transportation, catalysts of the adaptation of transport vessel types and techniques, and finally as watersheds in the cognitive worlds of mobile humans.

EXIT AUCTOR

The term "maritime cultural landscape" emerged in Scandinavia in its particular context of land rise (and to some extent the opposite)—a comparatively young cultural area, dating only from the end of the last ice age. However, it appears that its conceptual contents can be used universally, even though some may prefer to vary its name ("culture landscape," "seascape," "waterscape," "island archaeology," etc.). The concept has simply to be adjusted to any specific context. The potential of maritime cultural landscapes even back into Palaeolithic times is huge (Erlandson 2001). The study of maritime culture and its landscape ought to mean the exploration of all kinds of human relationships to the sea, or very plausibly to any large body of water. The scope will always be the leaps from physically major to minor features, even tiny ones. Apart from the obvious, almost any kind of unexpected material could be used as a source. Classifications of elements or aspects such as those made above are not an end in themselves. There are many matters still unexplored in the maritime cultural landscape. I am painfully aware that this text may not have done justice to all of the positive efforts that have already been made from a global perspective.

There are indeed many efforts currently made across the globe to make the "maritime cultural landscape" concept even more meaningful and enrich our appreciation of the maritime heritage. The references made here are certainly by no means exhaustive for the present history of the term, let alone for its contents.

REFERENCES

Barber, Ian. 2004. Sea, land and fish: Spatial relationships and the archaeology of South Island Maori fishing. *World Archaeology* 35 (3): 434–448.

Bell, Trevor, and M. A. P. Renouf. 2003. Prehistoric cultures, reconstructed coasts: Maritime Archaic Indian distribution in Newfoundland. *World Archaeology* 35 (3): 350–370.

Bill, Jan. 1999. Port topography in medieval Denmark. In *Maritime topography and the medieval town*, ed. J. Bill and B. Clausen, 231–261. Copenhagen: PNM Studies in Archaeology and History.

Bill, Jan, and B. Clausen, eds. 1999. *Maritime topography and the medieval town*. Copenhagen: PNM Studies in Archaeology and History.

Bjerck, Hein Bjartmann, 1989. *Forskningsstyrt kulturminneforvaltning på Vega, Nordland*. En studie av steinaldermenneskenes boplassmønstre og arkeologiske letemetoder. Gunneria 61. Trondheim, Universitetet i Trondheim. Vitenskapsmuseet. 2nd edition 1995.

Blue, Lucy. 1997. Cyprus and Cilicia: The typology and palaeogeography of second millennium harbours. In *Res maritimae: Cyprus and the eastern Mediterranean from prehistory to late antiquity*, ed. S. Swiny, R. Hohlfelder, and H. Wylde Swiny, 31–41. Atlanta: Scholars Press.

Bowens, Amanda, ed. 2008. *Underwater archaeology: The NAS guide to principles and practice*. 2nd ed. Portsmouth: Nautical Archaeology Society/ Blackwell.

Bradley, Richard. 2000. *An archaeology of natural places*. New York: Routledge.

Braudel, Fernand. 1986 (1949). *The Mediterranean and the Mediterranean world in the age of Philip II*. Vols. 1–2. Glasgow: Collins.

Breen, Colin, and Paul J. Lane. 2004. Archaeological approaches to East Africa's changing seascapes. *World Archaeology* 35 (3): 434–448.

Callmer, Johan. 1994. Urbanization in Scandinavia and the Baltic Region c CE 700–1100: Trading places, centres and early urban sites. In *Developments around the Baltic Sea in the Viking Age*, ed. B. Ambrosiani and H. Clarke, 50–70. Stockholm: Birka Studies 3 and the Twelfth Viking Congress.

Campbell, Åke. 1936. *Kulturlandskapet: En etnologisk beskrivning med särskild hänsyn till äldre svenska landskapstyper* (The cultural landscape: An ethnological description with particular respect to older Swedish landscape types). Verdandis småskrifter 387. Stockholm.

Carlsson, Dan. 1991. Harbours and trading places on Gotland CE 600–1000. In *Aspects of maritime Scandinavia*, ed. O. Crumlin-Pedersen, 145–158. Roskilde: Viking Ship Museum.

Cederlund, Carl Olof. 1980. Marknadshamn, gårdshamn, fiskehamn eller övernattningshamn (Market harbour, farmstead harbour, fishing or overnight?). In *Människan, kulturlandskapet och framtiden*, 176–184. Stockholm: Kungliga Vitterhets Historie och Antikvitetsakademien.

Cooney, Gabriel. 2004a. Introduction: Seeing land from the sea. *World Archaeology* 35 (3): 323–328.

———, ed. 2004b. Seascapes. *World Archaeology* 35 (3).

Crumlin-Pedersen, Ole. 1978. Søvejen til Roskilde (The sea route to Roskilde). *Historisk Årbog for Roskilde Amt*, 3–79. Roskilde: Viking Ship Museum.

———. 1986. Ship finds and ship blockages CE 800–1200. In *Archaeological formation processes: The representativity of remains from Danish prehistory*, ed. K. Kristiansen, 215–228. Copenhagen: Nationalmuseum.

———. 1988. Schiffe und Seefahrtswege im Ostseeraum während des 9.–12. Jahrhunderts (Ships and sea routes in the Baltic Sea area). *Bericht der Römisch-Germanischen-Kommission* 69, 530–563. Mainz: Zabern.

———. 1996. Studiet af det maritime kulturlandskab (The study of the maritime cultural landscape). In *Atlas over Fyns kyst i jernalder, vikingetid og middelalder*, ed.

O. Crumlin-Pedersen, E. Porsmose, and H. Thrane, 10–20. Odense, Denmark: Odense universitetsforlag.

Crumlin-Pedersen, O., E. Porsmore, and H. Thrane, eds. 1996. *Atlas over Fyns kyst i jernalder, vikingetid og middelalder* (Atlas of the coast of Funen in the Iron Age, the Viking Age and the Middle Ages). Odense, Denmark: Odense universitetsforlag. Extensive summary in English, pp. 283–299.

Cunliffe, Barry. 2001. *Facing the ocean: The Atlantic and its peoples 8000 BCE–CE 1500.* Oxford: Oxford University Press.

Dean, Martin, B. Ferrari, I. Oxley, M. Redknap, and K. Watson, eds. 1992. *Archaeology underwater: The NAS guide to principles and practice.* Dorchester: Nautical Archaeology Society/Archetype.

Delgado, James, ed. 1997. *Encyclopedia of underwater and maritime archaeology.* London: British Museum.

Duncan, Brad G. 2006. The maritime archaeology and maritime cultural landscape of Queenscliffe: A nineteenth century Australian community. PhD diss., School of Anthropology, Archaeology and Sociology, James Cook University.

Erlandson, Jon M. 2001. The archaeology of aquatic adaptations: Paradigms for a new millennium. *Journal of Archaeological Research* 9 (4): 287–350.

Estonian Journal of Archaeology. 2004. *Estonian Journal of Archaeology* 8 (2). Special issue on maritime landscapes.

Firth, Anthony. 1994. Three facets of maritime archaeology: Society, landscape and critique. Unpublished paper, Southampton University.

Fischer, Anders, ed. 1995. *Man and sea in the Mesolithic: Coastal settlement above and below present sea level.* Oxbow Monograph 53. Oxford: Oxbow.

Fitzhugh, William. 1975. A comparative approach to northern maritime adaptations. In *Prehistoric maritime adaptations of the circumpolar zone*, ed. W. Fitzhugh, 339–386. Mouton: World Anthropology.

Ford, Ben. 2007. Down by the water's edge: Modeling shipyard locations in Maryland, USA. *International Journal of Nautical Archaeology* 36 (1): 125–137.

———. 2009. Lake Ontario maritime cultural landscape. PhD diss., Texas A&M University.

Gansum, Terje, Gro B. Jerpåsen, and Christian Keller. 1997. *Arkeologisk landskapsanalyse med visuelle metoder* (Archaeological analysis of landscape by way of visual methods). AmS-Varia 298. Stavanger, Norway: Arkeologisk museum i Stavanger.

Gjessing, Gutorm. 1936. *Nordenfjelske ristninger og malinger av den arktiske gruppe.* Oslo: Instituttet for sammenlignende kulturforskning.

Grimm, Oliver. 2001. Norwegian boathouses from the late Roman and migration periods: An analysis of their military function. In *Military aspects of the aristocracy in Barbaricum in the Roman and early migration periods*, ed. B. Storgaard, 55–66. Copenhagen: National Museum.

———. 2006. Grossbootshaus-Zentrum und Herrschaft (Great boathouses and dominion): Zentralplatzforschung in der nordeuropäischen Archäologie (1–15 Jahrhundert) mit Beiträgen von Boris Rankov und Frans-Arne Stylegar, Ergänzungsbände zum Reallexikon der Germanischen Altertumskunde Bd 52. Berlin: Walter de Gruyter.

Helskog, Knut. 1999. The shore connection: Cognitive landscape and communication with rock carvings in northernmost Europe. *Norwegian Archaeological Review* 32 (2): 73–92.

Henningsen, Henning. 1961. Crossing the Equator: Sailor's baptism and other initiation rites. Copenhagen: Munksgaard.

Holmberg, Bente. 1991. Maritime place names. In *Aspects of maritime Scandinavia CE 200–1200*, ed. O. Crumlin-Pedersen, 233–240. Roskilde: Viking Ship Museum; Oxford: Blackwell.

Holstein, Lars, ed. 1988. *Det maritima kulturlandskapet: Artiklar och studier från Bottenviksprojektet.* Umeå, Sweden: University of Umeå.

Horden, Peregrine, and Nicholas Purcell. 2000. *The corrupting sea: A study of Mediterranean history.* Hoboken, NJ: Wiley-Blackwell.

Hovda, Per. 1941a. Okse, galt, hund og andre dyrenevne i skjernamn (Ox, boar, dog and other animal names on skerries). *Bergens museums årsbok: Historisk- antikvarisk rekke nr 7.* Bergen: Museum of Bergen.

———. 1941b. Kjerring, i stadnamn frå sjøen (*Kjerring*, referring to [old] women, in place-names at sea). *Maal og Minne 1941*, 37–47.

———. 1948. Stadnamn og sjøfiske (Place-names and sea fishing). *Namn och Bygd*, 51–66.

———. 1961. *Norske fiskeméd: Landsoversyn og to gamle médbøker* (Norwegian transit lines [or, rather, crossing points for such transit lines] in fishing: A national survey and two old notebooks with transit lines). *Skrifter fra Norsk Stadnamnarkiv 2.* PhD diss., Oslo/ Bergen.

Ilves, Kristin. 2004. The seaman´s perspective in landscape archaeology. *Estonian Journal of Archaeology* 8 (2): 163–180.

Jasinski, Marek. 1993a. Maritimt kulturlandskap: Arkeologisk perspektiv (Maritime cultural landscape: An archaeological perspective). *Viking 1993*, 129–140.

———. 1993b. The maritime cultural landscape: An archaeological perspective. *Archeologia Polski* 38 (1): 7–21.

Keller, Christian. 1993. Visuelle landskapsanalyser i arkeologien (Visual landscape analyses in archaeology). *Årbok 1991/1992. Universitetets Oldsaksamling.* Oslo: University Museum.

Knapp, A. Bernard. 1997. Mediterranean maritime landscapes: Transport, trade and society on Late Bronze Age Cyprus. In *Res maritimae: Cyprus and the eastern Mediterranean from prehistory to late antiquity*, ed. S. Swiny R. Hohlfelder, and H. Wylde Swiny, 153–162. Atlanta: Scholars Press.

Larsson, Gunilla. 2006. An ethnoarchaeological approach to the problem of portages. In *The significance of portages: Proceedings of the First International Conference of the Significance of Portages 29th September–2nd October 2004*, British Archaeological Reports (BAR) International Series 1499, ed. C. Westerdahl, 151–168. Oxford: BAR.

Larsson, Lars. 2004. Land, water and symbolic aspects of the Mesolithic in southern Scandinavia. *Before Farming* 2003/4 (3): 1–13.

Lemee, Christian. 1997. A ship-cemetery on the B&W site in Copenhagen. In *Down the river to the sea: Eighth International Symposium on Boat and Ship Archaeology*, ed. J. Litwin, 235–240. Gdańsk: Polish Maritime Museum.

Lindenlauf, Astrid. 2004. The sea as a place of no return in ancient Greece. *World Archaeology* 35 (3): 416–433.

Löfgren, Orvar. 1981. Människan i landskapet—landskapet i människan (Man in landscape—landscape in man). In *Tradition och miljö*, ed. L. Honko and O. Löfgren, 235–261. Lund, Sweden: Liber.

Lundström, Per. 1971. Lagunhamnarnas tid (The time of the lagoon harbours). *Sjøfartshistorisk årbok.* Bergen: Maritime Museum of Bergen.

———. 1976. Förhistoriska och medeltida hamnar: En undersökningsmodell (Prehistoric and medieval harbors: A model for investigation). In *Rapport maritimhistoriskt symposium*, ed. C.-O. Cederlund and U. Wessling. Luleå, Sweden: Luleå kommun.

Mägi, Marika. 2004. "Ships are their main strength": Harbour sites, arable lands and chieftains on Saaremaa. *Estonian Journal of Archaeology* 8 (2): 163–180.

McConkey, Rosemary, and Thomas McErlean. 2007. Mombasa Island: A maritime perspective. *International Journal of Historical Archaeology* 11 (2): 99–121.

McErlean, Thomas, Rosemary McConkey, and Wes Forsythe. 2003. *Strangford Lough: An archaeological survey of the maritime cultural landscape*, ed. B. Scott. Belfast: Blackstaff Press.

McGhee, Robert. 1977. Ivory for the sea woman: The symbolic attributes of a prehistoric technology. *Canadian Journal of Archaeology* 1: 141–149.

McNiven, Ian J. 2004. Saltwater people: Spiritscapes, maritime rituals and the archaeology of Australian indigenous seascapes. *World Archaeology* 35 (3): 329–349.

Meløe, Jacob. 1990. The two landscapes of northern Norway. *Acta Borealia* 1: 68–80.

Modeer, Ivar. 1936. *Färdvägar och sjömärken vid Nordens kuster: Namntolkningar.* (Routes and seamarks at the coasts of the North: Interpretations of place-names). Uppsala: Arbeten utgivna av Vilhelm Ekmans universitetsfond.

Morton, Jamie. 2001. *The role of the physical environment in ancient Greek seafaring.* Leiden: Brill.

Moser, Jason D. 2007. *Lower Eastern Shore shipyard survey: Archaeological and historical investigations.* Crownsville: Maryland Historical Trust.

Müller-Wille, Michael. 1997. Maritime archäologie: Fallbeispiele aus dem südlichen Skandinavien (Maritime archaeology: Case studies from southern Scandinavia). *Siedlungsforschung Archäologie-Geschichte-Geographie Band* 15: 9–31.

Myhre, Bjørn. 1985. Boathouses as indicators of political organisation. *Norwegian Archaeological Review* 18: 36–60.

———. 1997. Boathouses and naval organization. In *Military aspects of Scandinavian society in a European perspective CE 1–1300*, ed. A. Nørgård Jørgensen and B. L. Clausen, PNM Studies in Archaeology and History Vol. 2, 169–183. Copenhagen: National Museum.

Nørgård Jørgensen, Anne. 1996. Sea defence in Denmark CE 200–1300. In *Military aspects of Scandinavian society*, ed. A. Nørgård Jørgensen and B. Clausen, PNM Studies in Archaeology and History Vol. 2, 200–209. Copenhagen: National Museum.

———. 2002. Naval bases in southern Scandinavia from the 7th to the 12th century. In *Maritime warfare in northern Europe: Technology, organisation, logistics and administration 500 BCE–1500 CE*, ed. A. Nørgaard Jørgensen, J. Pind, and L. Jørgensen. Publications from the National Museum. PNM Studies of Archaeology and History Vol. 5, 125–158. Copenhagen: National Museum.

Norman, Peter. 1993. *Medeltida utskärsfiske: En studie av fornlämningar i kustmiljö* (Medieval open sea fishing). Nordiska museet Handlingar 116. Stockholm: Nordiska museet.

———. 1995. *Sjöfart och fiske: De kustbundna näringarnas lämningar* (Shipping and fishing: Remains of coastal economies). Fornlämningar i Sverige 3. Stockholm: Riksantikvarieämbetet.

Ohnuki-Tierney, Emiko. 1972. Spatial concepts of the Ainu of the northwest coast of southern Sakhalin. *American Anthropologist* 74: 426–457.

Parker, Anthony J. 1999. A maritime cultural landscape: The port of Bristol in the Middle Ages. *International Journal of Nautical Archaeology* 28 (4): 323–342.

———. 2001. Maritime landscapes. *Landscapes* 1: 22–41.

Pedersen, Lisbeth. 1995. 7000 years of fishing: Stationary fishing structures in the Mesolithic and afterwards. In *Man and sea in the Mesolithic*, ed. A. Fischer, 75–86. Oxford: Oxbow.

Pedersen, Lisbeth, Anders Fischer, and B. Aaby, eds. 1997. *The Danish Storebælt since the ice age—man, sea and forest.* Copenhagen: Storebælt.

Phillips, Tim. 2004. Seascapes and landscapes in Orkney and northern Scotland. *World Archaeology* 35 (3): 371–384.

Pollard, Edward. 2008. Inter-tidal causeways and platforms of the 13th to 16th century city-state of Kilwa Kisiwani, Tanzania. *International Journal of Nautical Archaeology* 37 (1): 98–114.

Prabha Ray, Himanshu. 2003. *The archaeology of seafaring in ancient South Asia.* Cambridge: World Arch.

———. 2007. Crossing the seas: Connecting maritime spaces in colonial India. In *Cross currents and community networks*, ed. H. Prabha Ray and Edward A. Alpers, 50–78. New Delhi: Oxford University Press.

Ragan, Elizabeth Anne. 2001. *Coastal archaeology and complex societies: The maritime cultural landscape of south Argyll (Scotland).* Philadelphia: University of Pennsylvania.

Rainbird, Paul. 2007. *The archaeology of islands.* Topics in Contemporary Archaeology. Cambridge: Cambridge University Press.

Rieck, Flemming. 1991. Aspects of coastal defence in Denmark. In *Aspects of Maritime Scandinavia CE 200–1200*, ed. O. Crumlin-Pedersen, 83–96. Roskilde: Viking Ship Museum.

Rönnby, Johan. 2007. Maritime durées: Long-term structures in a coastal landscape. *Journal of Maritime Archaeology* 2: 65–82.

Scarre, C. 2002a. A pattern of islands: The Neolithic monuments of north-west Brittany. *European Journal of Archaeology* 5: 24–41.

———. 2002b. Coast and cosmos: The Neolithic monuments of northern Brittany. In *Monuments and landscapes of Atlantic Europe: Perception and society during the Neolithic and the Early Bronze Age*, ed. C. Scarre, 84–102. London: Routledge.

Sherratt, Andrew. 1996. Why Wessex? The Avon route and river transports in later British prehistory. *Oxford Journal of Archaeology* 15 (2): 211–236.

———. 2006. Portages: A simple but powerful idea in understanding human history. In *The significance of portages: Proceedings of the First International Conference of the Significance of Portages 29th September–2nd October 2004*, British Archaeological Reports (BAR) International Series 1499, ed. C. Westerdahl, 1–13. Oxford: BAR.

Sognnes, Kalle. 1994. Ritual landscapes: Toward a reinterpretation of Stone Age rock art in Trøndelag, Norway. *Norwegian Archaeological Review* 27 (1): 29–50.

Solheim, Svale. 1939. Ålmenne fordomar ved fiske (General prejudice in fishing). *Ord og sed* 5 (83): 5–72.

———. 1940. Nemningsfordommer ved fiske (Naming prejudice in fishing). PhD diss., Det Norske Videnskaps Akademi, Oslo.

Stewart, David. 2007. Gravestones and monuments in the maritime cultural landscape. *International Journal of Nautical Archaeology* 36 (1): 112–124.

Stylegar, Frans Arne, and Oliver Grimm. 2005. Boathouses in northern Europe and the North Atlantic. *International Journal of Nautical Archaeology* 34 (2): 253–268.

Svennung, Josef. 1953. *Scadinavia und Scandia: Lateinisch-nordische Namenstudien.* Uppsala Universitets Årsskrift 1953: 4. Uppsala: University of Uppsala.

Taylor, Elizabeth G. R. 1956. *The haven-finding art.* London: Hollis and Carter.

Tilley, Christopher. 1990. Claude Lévi-Strauss: Structuralism and beyond. In *Reading material culture*, ed. C. Tilley, 3–81. Oxford: Basil Blackwell.

Tuovinen, Tapani. 2002. *The burial cairns and the landscape in the archipelago of Åboland, SW Finland, in the Bronze Age and the Iron Age.* Acta Universitatis Ouluensis Humaniora B 46. Oulu, Finland: University of Oulu.

Tveit, Turid, and Endre Elvestad. 2006. Portages of power—a preliminary report from Rogasland, Norway. In *The significance of portages: Proceedings of the First International Conference of the Significance of Portages 29th September–2nd October 2004,* British Archaeological Reports (BAR) International Series 1499, ed. C. Westerdahl, 77–83. Oxford: BAR.

Ulriksen, Jens. 1997. *Anløbspladser: Besejling og bebyggelse i Danmark mellem 200 og 1100 e. Kr; En studie af söfartens pladser på baggrund af undersögelser i Roskilde fjord* (Landing places: Shipping and settlement in Denmark between CE 200 and 1100; A study of the sites of shipping on the basis of excavations in Roskilde fiord). Roskilde: Viking Ship Museum.

Vedru, Gurly. 2005. People on river landscapes. *Estonian Journal of Archaeology* 8 (2): 181–197.

Westerdahl, Christer. 1978. Marinarkeologisk inventering med utgångspunkt från ett norrländskt exempel (Maritime archaeological survey with the basis in an example from Norrland). MA thesis, Stockholm University.

———. 1980. On oral traditions and place names: An introduction to the first stage in the establishment of a register of ancient monuments for the maritime cultural heritage. *International Journal of Nautical Archaeology* 9 (4): 311–329.

———. 1982. Maritima kulturcentra i östra Sverige: En preliminär katalog med kartor (Centers of maritime culture in eastern Sweden: A preliminary catalog with comments). *Medd/MAS* 4 (5): 24–37.

———. 1986. Die maritime Kulturlandschaft: Schiffe, Schiffahrtswege, Häfen; Überlegungen zu einem Forschungsansatz (The maritime cultural landscape: Ships, sea routes and harbours; Discussion of a research strategy). *Deutsches Schifffahrtsarchiv* 9: 7–58.

———. 1987. Varvsplatser utanför städerna, och deras omvärld, i fält och i källor: Inventering på svenska sidan av Bottenhavet och Bottenviken (Shipyards outside the cities, and their environment, in the field and in sources: Survey on the Swedish side of the Bothian Sea). In *Bottnisk Kontakt III,* ed. G. Björklund, 73–87. Jakobstad, Finland: Jakobstads Museum.

———. 1987–1989. *Norrlandsleden I–II: Beskrivning av och källor till det maritima kulturlandskapet* (The Norrland route: A description, and the sources for the maritime cultural landscape). *Arkiv för norrländsk hembygdsforskning XXIII–XXIV.* Härnösand, Sweden: Länsmuseet Murberget. Extensive summaries in English, part I: 313–327; part II: passim.

———. 1991. Norrlandsleden: The maritime cultural landscape of the Norrland sailing route. *Aspects of Maritime Scandinavia CE 200–1200,* ed. O. Crumlin-Pedersen, 105–120. Roskilde: Viking Ship Museum.

———. 1992a. The maritime cultural landscape. *International Journal of Nautical Archaeology* 21 (1): 5–14.

———. 1992b. The use of maritime space in the Baltic. In *Pre-printed papers,* Vol. 2. *Maritime studies: Ports and ships; Medieval Europe, York 1992,* 61–79. York: University of York.

———. 1994. Maritime cultures and ship types: Brief comments on the significance of maritime archaeology. *International Journal of Nautical Archaeology* 23 (4): 265–270.

———. 1995. Traditional transport zones in relation to ship types. In *Shipshape: Essays for Ole Crumlin-Pedersen*, ed. O. Olsen, F. Rieck, J. Skamby Madsen, 213–230. Roskilde: Viking Ship Museum.

———. 1996a. Amphibian transport systems in northern Europe: A survey of a medieval way of life. *Fennoscandia archaeologica* 13: 28–41.

———. 1996b. Stone maze symbols and navigation: A hypothesis on the origin of coastal stone mazes in the north. *International Journal of Nautical Archaeology* 24 (4): 267–277.

———. 1997a. Maritime Kulturlandschaften am Beispiel des Ostseeraumes: Einführung in die Tagungsthematik. *Siedlungsforschung* 15: 33–52.

———. 1997b. En bortglömd värld i utskären: Natthamnar i Bottniska viken; Om Nyströms seglingsbeskrivning längs norrlandskusten 1788 (A forgotten world in the outskerries: On the sailing description of the Norrland coast by Nyström 1788). In *Bottnisk Kontakt VIII*, ed. B. Wännström, 115–121. Piteå, Sweden: Piteå Museum.

———. 1998. The Norrland Survey and its aftermath. In *The marine archaeology of the Baltic Sea area*, ed. M. Lindström, 100–104. Stockholm: University College, Huddinge.

———. 1999. Inland water boats and shipping in Sweden: The great lakes; The application of a theory on transport zones and maritime enclaves. In *Construction navale maritime et fluviale: Approches archéologiques, historique et ethnologique; Proceedings (Actes) 7th ISBSA. Archaeonautica 14 1998*, ed. Patrice Pomey and Éric Rieth, 135–143. Paris: CNRS.

———. 2000. From land to sea, from sea to land: On transport zones, borders and human space. In *Down the river to the sea*, ed. J. Litwin, 11–20. Gdańsk: Polish Maritime Museum.

———. 2002a. The cognitive landscape of maritime warfare and defence. In *Maritime warfare*. PNM Studies of Archaeology and History, vol. 5, ed. A. Nörgaard Jörgensen and B. Clausen, 155–176. Copenhagen: National Museum.

———. 2002b. The ritual landscape at sea. In *Maritime Archäologie heute / Maritime archaeology today*, ed. K. Krueger and C. O. Cederlund, 51–72. Rostock: Koch.

———. 2003a. Maritime culture in an inland lake? In *Maritime heritage*, ed. C. Brebbia and T. Gambin, 17–26. Southampton: WIT.

———. 2003b. *Vänern-landskap, människa, skepp: Om en maritim inlandskultur vid Vänern; En studie kring människor, båtar, vattentransport och segelsjöfart från förhistorien till tiden före sekelskiftet 1900* (Vänern-landscape, man, ship: On a maritime inland culture at [Lake] Vänern; A study of people, boats, water transport and sailing from prehistory to the turn of the century 1900). Skärhamn, Sweden: Båtdokgruppen.

———. 2003c. Holy, profane and political: Territoriality—extraterritoriality; A problem with borders; Some notes and reflections. In *Accurata descriptio: Studier i kartografi, numismatik, orientalistik och biblioteksväsen tillägnade Ulla Ehrensvärd*, ed. G. Bäärnhielm, 467–495. Stockholm: Kungliga Biblioteket (The Royal Library).

———. 2004. Lindesnes och sjömäns dopseder (Lindesnes and the rituals of sailor's baptism). *Agders Historielag. Årsskrift* 80: 105–136.

———.2005. Seal on land, elk at sea: Notes on and applications of the ritual landscape at the seaboard. *International Journal of Nautical Archaeology* 34 (1): 2–23.

———. 2006a. On the significance of portages: A survey of a new research theme. In *The significance of portages: Proceedings of the First International Conference of the Significance of Portages 29th September–2nd October 2004*, ed. C. Westerdahl, 15–51. British Archaeological Reports (BAR) International Series 1499. Oxford: BAR.

————. 2006b. Äldre sjömärken: Ett nordeuropeiskt perspektiv (Ancient seamarks : A northern European perspective). *Norsk Sjøfartsmuseum. Årbok 2006*, 101–177. Oslo: Norsk Sjøfartsmuseum.

————. 2006c. Skärgårdskapell i Norden: En kortfattad översikt med några reflexioner (Archipelago chapels of the North: A brief survey with some reflections). *Hikuin* 33: 155–186.

————. 2007. Maritime cosmology and archaeology. *Deutsches Schifffahrtsarchiv* 2: 7–54.

————. 2008. The relationship between land roads and sea routes in the past—some reflections. *Deutsches Schifffahrtsarchiv* 29: 59–114.

————. 2009. Fish and ships: Towards a theory of maritime culture. *Deutsches Schifffahrtsarchiv* 30: 191–236.

————. In press a. Shipyards and boatbuilding sites as social history: An aspect of the maritime cultural landscape of the North. *Deutsches Schifffahrtsarchiv* 2010. Bremerhaven: German Maritime Museum.

————. In press b. Ancient sea marks: A social history in a northern European perspective. *Deutsches Schifffahrtsarchiv* 2010. Bremerhaven: German Maritime Museum.

Yesner, David R. 1980. Maritime hunter-gatherers: Ecology and prehistory. *Current Anthropology* 21 (6): 727–750.

Zeilich-Jensen, Leif. 1974. *Den centraleskimåiska världsbilden: Huvuddragen av eskimåisk religion mot bakgrunden av termerna för orientering* (Central Eskimo conception of the world: Principal traits of Eskimo religion against the background of the terms for orientation). PhD diss., Acta Universitatis Stockholmiensis.

Zilliacus, Kurt, ed. 1990. *Finska skären: Studier i åboländsk kulturhistoria utgivna av Konstsamfundet* (Finnish skerries: Studies in the cultural history of the archipelago of Åboland). Helsinki: Konstsamfundet.

CHAPTER 33

COASTAL ARCHAEOLOGY

BEN FORD

INTRODUCTION

MARLOW in Joseph Conrad's *Heart of Darkness* understood the "delightful mystery" of blank spaces on maps; even those partly filled offer the opportunity to find a niche and make a contribution. For Marlow these spaces were Africa, South America, Australia, and the Arctic, but for archaeology many of the blanks occur along our coasts, the strips of land and water between the well-defined domains of underwater and terrestrial archaeologies (Erlandson and Fitzpatrick 2006: 23; Gawronski 2003: 133; Loveluck and Tys 2006: 161; Stilgoe 1994: ix). Just as Marlow's equatorial Africa was partly filled with rivers, lakes, and place-names, the coast is not archaeologically blank. Several seminal studies in littoral archaeology serve as landmarks, but the shore has been far less mapped and measured than other areas. How else could recent shoreline surveys of such diverse places as Kilwa Kisiwani, Tanzania; Kingston, Canada; and the north Kent Coast of England, all areas with strong traditions in coastal archaeology, well-known archaeological potential, large coastal populations, and active diving, fishing, and shellfish-gathering communities, yield such substantial and significant results (Moore 2008; Paddenberg and Hession 2008; Pollard 2008)?

Clearly, coastal archaeology is a growth field for maritime archaeology in terms of the data that can be gathered, but "the living edge" between land and water is also a fruitful realm for the development of archaeological theory (Walker 1990: 271). The coast is a difficult environment for archaeologists in terms of preservation, access, and methods. Similarly, past peoples recognized the coast as a natural boundary, perhaps the most obvious boundary on the landscape, and, as a result, imbued it with spiritual and cultural associations. Often these associations focused on the sea's dangerous or cleansing nature (Cooney 2004: 326; Flatman

2011; Lindenlauf 2004; O'Sullivan and Breen 2007: 125). The liminal nature of the coast was also important to many cultures; borders are often the domain of the Trickster (e.g., Hermes, Loki, Satan, Coyote and Raven, Krishna, Eshu, Elegba, or Anansi) and are special places demarcating the line between safety and danger or known and unknown (Hyde 2008). However, people in the past did venture across this boundary; if they had not, there would be no maritime cultures and consequently no maritime archaeology.

Thus, the coast was as much a bridge between terrestrial and maritime lives as a perceptual, physical, or cultural border. As such, the coast links terrestrial and underwater archaeology into a unified maritime archaeology. Ships and their cargoes were produced on land, as were most sailors; yet seaborne trade, transportation, recreation, and warfare formed the foundation of many ancient cultures. Neither terrestrial nor underwater archaeology alone wholly tell the stories of these maritime cultures, but combined, connected by coastal archaeology, these archaeologies allow for a fully developed maritime archaeology. What follows in this chapter is a summary of the nature and development of coastal archaeology as well as a discussion of how coastal archaeology interdigitates with maritime archaeology and a synthesis of the major theoretical trends in littoral archaeology. Figure 33.1 depicts the geographic distribution of the examples cited.

DEFINITION OF COASTS: CULTURAL AND ENVIRONMENTAL PROCESSES

The coast is generally defined as the area where marine processes such as erosion, deposition, and storm surge influence terrestrial processes and vice versa (coastal process zone). This zone can range from hundreds to thousands of meters in width depending on the slope and substrate of the coastal margin; if climatic impacts are added to the equation, then the coastal margin can be expanded to several hundred kilometers. These impacts certainly affect cultures not normally classified as maritime, but the activity zone where human undertakings are influenced by the coast is of more immediate concern to coastal archaeology. The coastal activity zone can often be as limited as 5–10 km on either side of the waterline, but it can extend much farther inland when considering cultures that forage both along the coast and in the uplands as part of their seasonal round (Fulford, Champion, and Long 1997: 22; Westley and Dix 2006: 13). The definition of coast should consequently be left open and defined for each culture and region depending on the pertinent research questions.

Adding to the difficulty of defining "coast" and by extension "coastal archaeology" is the fact that the coast is a moving target (see chapters by Delgado and Firth in this volume). The 500,000-year-old hominin site at Boxgrove, West Sussex, UK, formed on a coastal mudflat but is now 46 m above the sea and 11 km inland.

Number	Reference
19	Staniforth and McGonigle 2007
20	Bell and Renouf 2003
21	Fitzhugh and Phaneuf 2008
22	O'Sullivan 2001, 2004; O'Sullivan and Breen 2007
23	McErlean et al. 2003
24	Hale 2003
25	Noble 2006
26	Oxley 2000
27	Bell and Neumann 1997; Goldberg and Macphail 2006; Parker 1999
28	Crawford 1927
29	Goldberg and Macphail 2006
30	Loveluck and Tys 2006
31	Milne 1985; Milne et al. 1998; Paddenberg and Hession 2008
32	Pieters et al. 2006
33	Gawronski 2003
34	Fischer 2007
35	Lemee 1997
36	Westerdahl 2003
37	Rönnby 2007; Welinder 1997

Number	Reference
1	Vainstub and Murray 2008
2	Russell 2005; Torben et al. 2001
3	Fedje et al. 2000
4	Rissolo and Glover 2008
5	Leshikar-Denton 1993
6	Murphy 1990
7	Reitz 2004
8	Faught 2004
9	Jordan-Greene 2007
10	Sorek and Harris 2003
11	Claasen 1982
12	Ford 2007; Moser 2007
13	Emory 2000
14	Bernstein 2006
15	Moore 2005, 2008
16	Knoerl 1994
17	Vrana and Vander Stoep 2003
18	Ringer 2003

Number	Reference
38	Westerdahl 1992, 2006
39	Král 1997
40	Reinders
41	Boyce et al. 2003; Raban 1989
42	Kennett and Kennett 2006
43	Peacock and Blue 2007
44	McConkey and McErlean 2007; Quinn et al. 2006
45	Pollard 2008
46	Parkington 2006
47	Gaur et al. 2004, 2005
48	Parida 1999
49	Shimin et al. 1991
50	McNiven 2003
51	Richards and Staniforth 2006
52	Duncan 2006
53	Ash 2005
54	Bullers 2005
55	Flores 2009; Lauer and Aswani 2009
56	Belcher 2009

Figure 33.1 Sites and locations mentioned in the text. Illustration by the author.

Scandinavian coastal sites can be found as much as 100 km inland due to glacio-isostatic rebound over the last 13,000 years (Goldberg and Macphail 2006: 151–152). Similarly, wharves and coastal harbor structures of less antiquity are often found buried far from the modern shoreline as a result of land filling and the seaward press of harbor facilities (Heintzelman 1986; Stone et al. 2008). The majority of the recent archaeological record, however, is submerged. We are currently experiencing one of the highest sea levels of the past 120,000 years, surpassed only by the previous interglacial period, when sea levels were approximately 6 m higher than they are today. Thus, with the exception of high latitudes and regions subjected to tectonic uplift, the littoral sites from approximately 120,000 to 5,000 years ago are submerged (Ehlers and Gibbard 2004; Erlandson 2001: 300; Erlandson and Rick 2008: 4; Faught 2004; Fedje and Josenhans 2000; Flemming 2004; Murphy 1990).

The relative inaccessibility of many sites along the world's ancient coastlines has led to what Jon Erlandson (2001: 291) has termed the "coastal paradox," wherein the dearth of evidence for early coastal adaptations is compared to the complexity and sedentism of groups that did adopt a coastal lifeway after 5,000 years ago. While current work on submerged prehistoric sites is striving to address this paradox (see Firth in this volume), changes in sea level are still a confounding factor in coastal archaeology, and extreme care is necessary in interpreting the environmental setting of coastal sites. Simply put, sites that are on the shoreline today may have been inland sites with little maritime contact when they were occupied, and, conversely, sites that are now far removed from the littoral may have been coastal when they were inhabited (Bell and Renouf 2003; Fulford, Champion, and Long 1997: 112; Goldberg and Macphail 2006: 155).

Changes in sea level also cause changes in the nature of the coast; due to variations in topography and bottom material, rising and falling waterlines are not parallel, and significantly different coastal environments can be created at different levels of the coast. For example, shell-fish-productive rocky points formed in several South African locations circa 3,000 years ago as sea levels changed. The creation of these environments led to shifts in habitation and subsistence patterns among the local population to take advantage of the new resources (Parkington 2006: 76). In addition to natural changes in the littoral environment, anthropogenic alterations must also be kept in mind. Activities such as quarrying, farming, and filling can drastically change the quality of the shore, creating new embayments while obliterating old ones (Pilon 2008).

Acknowledging that many coastal sites are now submerged leads to the principal concern of coastal archaeology—erosion. Many submerged prehistoric sites were doubtlessly destroyed by erosion as sea levels rose, while sites currently in littoral areas are threatened by coastal erosion (Erlandson 2001: 291; Waters 1997: chap. 6). Sea-level rise is listed as a threat to World Heritage Archaeological Sites, and the United Kingdom National Trust predicts that 500 archaeological sites and historic structures will be lost to erosion over the next century (Colette 2007: 52; 2005). An understanding of the formation processes and geoarchaeology of coasts is consequently important to interpreting the archaeology of this environment, but that is beyond the scope of this chapter. Goldberg and Macphail (2006), Waters (1997), and Feibel (2001) provide good introductory discussions of coastal processes as related to archaeology. In addition to erosion caused by wave action, coastal sites are susceptible to ice damage, the ravages of storms, and increased coastal development. Approximately 60% of the world population lives within 100 km of the coast, and much of the current development is in areas with long histories of human activity (Cooney 2004: 327; Erlandson and Rick 2008: 1). Thus, coastal sites are threatened by natural factors, human-influenced natural factors (e.g., climate change), and cultural factors. These threats certainly contribute urgency to coastal archaeology but are not grounds to abandon all hope. Significant discoveries have been made in submerged coastal sites.

History and Development of Coastal Archaeology

There is a protracted tradition of studying the coast, and coasts have long been understood as an important cultural resource, although intensive study of the littoral is a relatively recent development in maritime archaeology. For example, submerged forests were noted along the British coast as early as 1170, with more systematic recording beginning in the eighteenth century (Goldberg and Macphail 2006: 163). Similarly, many of the significant early discoveries in nautical archaeology, such as the Ferriby boats, *Amsterdam*, and *Grace Dieu*, were made along shorelines (Anderson 1934; Clarke et al. 1993; Friel 1993; Gawronski 1990; Wright 1994). There were also early forays into coastal archaeology that utilized methods remarkably similar to those employed today. For example, O. G. S. Crawford's 1927 exploration of Lyonesse off the Cornish coast made use of intertidal survey methods, oral history, archival research, and aerial photography to investigate a submerged prehistoric landscape. While Crawford believed that the land surface had sunk rather than the sea level risen, his observations on the effects of erosion on coastal sites match those of English Heritage seven decades later (Adams 2006; Crawford 1927; Fulford, Champion, and Long 1997: 40). Nicholas Flemming's (1971) work on submerged terrestrial sites in the Mediterranean also predates much of the modern emphasis on integrated maritime archaeology and coastal studies.

Despite these early examples of a holistic approach to coastal sites, much of the archaeological work in the littoral has been divided along the waterline (Cooney 2004: 323; Erlandson 2006: 299). In addition to being divided along methodological and environmental boundaries, terrestrial and underwater archaeologists have also traditionally given themselves over to studying specific site types along the coast. Underwater archaeologists have tended to focus on ports and beached shipwrecks, while terrestrial archaeologists have given the majority of their attention to shell middens, with a secondary interest, primarily European, in the coastal location of barrows and tombs. While these foci are somewhat limiting in geographic scope, often ignoring "off-site" cultural resources, they have proven to be productive approaches, providing a wealth of data about specific locations and the foundation for many of the methods and theoretical perspectives applied to coastal archaeology.

Ports have long been a focus of maritime archaeology, and they remain an important aspect (see Oleson and Hohlfelder in this volume), but the emphasis on them seems to have fluoresced during the 1980s (Boyce et al. 2003; Flemming 1971; Milne 1985; Parida 1999; Parker 1999; Pasquinucci and Weski 2004; Raban 1989, 1985, 1986, 1988; Rudolph 1980). During this period, even texts with titles that implied a broader scope were dominated by port studies. For example, *Archaeology of Coastal Changes*, edited by Avner Raban (1988), included 13 chapters, 9 of which focused on ports. While they may have been overemphasized in the archaeological literature, it must be said that ports provided a natural starting point for coastal archaeology, a gateway between the elements, and, given their importance to the formation of cities and the distribution of goods, a focus on them was not inappropriate (Naylor 2004; Walker 1990: 279). Port archaeology has also expanded in recent years and benefited from multidisciplinary approaches allowing for well-developed and methodologically deep studies, such as that conducted at Adulis on the Red Sea (Peacock and Blue 2007).

Paralleling the level of effort and interdisciplinary approaches often dedicated to ports by underwater and nautical archaeologists, shell middens have been a tremendously productive subject of study for terrestrial archaeologists; middens have been investigated on every continent except Antarctica (Milner, Craig, and Bailey 2007; Parkington 2006: 120; Stein 1992). Recent work on shell middens utilizing rigorous methods, including isotope analysis, has led to new insights on human impacts on the marine food web (Erlandson and Rick 2008; Reitz 2004). Shell midden work has also provided intriguing data on cultural change and colonization. Cheryl Claasen's (1982) analysis of shell middens in coastal North Carolina, for instance, found that the seasonal use of shellfish increased with the rise of horticulture, as compared to foragers, who collected shellfish year-round, and agriculturalists, who relied only lightly on shellfish. She also noted that in late prehistoric shell middens there was a shift from early spring exploitation to summer exploitation, possibly indicating a change in the local seasonal round to take advantage of trading opportunities provided by European visits to the North Carolina coast during the summer months.

Just as port studies have limitations in that they focus on only the major nodes of coastal commerce, shell middens illuminate only limited facets of coastal subsistence. Shell tends to preserve well, and, as a result, middens can lead to a biased sample of what was likely an often opportunistic subsistence regime based on a wide range of marine resources, including fish and shellfish, but also taking advantage of such windfalls as red tides and beached whales (Parkington 2006: 14; Westley and Dix 2006: 11). It is only when fish traps, habitation sites, isolated landings and wharves, coastal monuments, beached vessels, and the myriad other sites and features that form the coastal archaeological record are taken into account along with middens and ports that a complete picture of human utilization of the coast can begin to form.

Tentative steps were taken in the direction of an integrated coastal maritime archaeology during the 1980s, but the field burgeoned during the following decade. Seán McGrail's (1983, 1985) articles on landing places and coastal structures laid the foundation for later work by showing the value of informal littoral facilities that bridged the waterline and by formulating a typology of basic coastal sites. Building on this and other early work, many of the large-scale coastal surveys conducted during the 1990s that took into account resources above and below the mean high-water mark give the sense that the surveyors are attempting something new, exciting, and potentially very productive (Aberg and Lewis 2000; Bell and Neumann 1997; O'Sullivan 1995, 2001). By the time of the 2003 Land and Sea: Integrative Archaeologies conference held at the University of Southampton, England, there was a strong association between the terrestrial and underwater archaeologies of the coast (Adams 2006).

All of these examples are from Britain and Ireland, which has largely led the English-speaking archaeological community in the development of coastal archaeology through an active concern for the management of coastal sites. The British model for coastal archaeology generally relies on systematic pedestrian surveys of the foreshore at low tide combined with aerial photography and intensive recording of identified sites to record the full range of sites within the coastal landscape. As a result of this inclusive approach, reports on the coastal archaeology of Britain and Ireland often span multiple periods and include multiple types of sites, both the romantic and the mundane (Aberg and Lewis 2000; Fulford, Champion, and Long 1997; McErlean, McConkey, and Forsythe 2003). A recent survey of the Kent shoreline, for example, recorded sites ranging from a submerged forest to a torpedo station and from fish traps to a medieval saltern, as well as jetties, quays, and hulks (Paddenberg and Hession 2008). An intertidal archaeological survey on the Shannon estuary, Ireland, investigated Neolithic occupation sites and forests preserved in submerged landscapes, while also accounting for fishtraps abandoned in the nineteenth century (O'Sullivan 2001). Based on the wide range of well-recorded features along their coasts, British and Irish scholars have become thankfully unafraid of interpreting the coastal archaeological record and have been among the leaders in applying archaeological theory to the littoral. As will be discussed below, much of this work deals with agency among maritime peoples and attempts to move beyond how the coast was used to address how it was perceived and constructed by its inhabitants and how it, in turn, constructed their perceptions (O'Sullivan 2004; O'Sullivan and Breen 2007).

Scholars in Britain and Ireland, however, have not been alone in their development of an integrated coastal maritime archaeology. Coastal archaeology in the British Isles was and is heavily influenced by developments in northern Europe, particularly the maritime cultural landscape approach (see Westerdahl in this volume). Northern European scholars have been perhaps even more aggressive in their theorization of the coast and have provided the explicit underpinnings of much of the current research in littoral archaeology (Fischer 2007; Król 1997; Lemee 1997; Pieters, Verhaeghe, and Gevaert 2006; Rönnby 2007; Westerdahl 1992).

Interesting shoreline projects are also taking place in Australia (see Staniforth in this volume; Ash 2005; Bullers 2005; Duncan 2006; Lawrence and Staniforth 1998; Richards and Staniforth 2006), India (Gaur, Sundaresh, and Sila 2004; Gaur, Sundaresh, and Vardhan 2005: 941–946; Gaur and Vora in this volume), Pakistan (Belcher 2009), Israel (Breman 2003), China (Shimin, Genqi, and Green 1991), the Mediterranean (Reinders 2001), Argentina (Elkin in this volume; Vainstub and Murray 2006), Mexico (Rissolo and Glover 2008), Oceania (Flores 2009; Jones 2009; Lauer and Aswani 2009), and elsewhere. A particularly strong integrated shoreline survey has been undertaken on Mombosa Island, Kenya. Building on the well-established tradition of coastal, or "Swahili," archaeology throughout eastern Africa, this survey has integrated historical documents, oral history, surface archaeology, and marine remote sensing into an excellent synthesis of the maritime heritage of the island (McConkey and McErlean 2007; Pollard 2008: 98; Quinn et al. 2006).

A wide range of integrated coastal archaeological investigations have also been undertaken in the United States, primarily as graduate theses and federal management projects (Emory 2000; Ford 2007, 2009; Jordan-Greene 2007; Knoerl 1994;

Leshikar-Denton 1993; Moser 2007; Russell 2005; Spirek and Harris 2003; Vrana and Stoep 2003). Archaeologists working along the Canadian coasts and shores have similarly embraced an integrated approach (Fitzhugh and Phaneuf 2008; Moore 2008, 2005; O'Sullivan 1995; Ringer 2003; Staniforth and McGonigle 2007). The majority of these studies differ from the British and northern European models in that they do not adopt the broad landscape approach; rather, they focus on specific sites. Both approaches strive to dissolve the boundary between terrestrial and underwater archaeology in an effort to create a seamless archaeology of the coast, but the Canadians have largely opted to investigate specific sites with both exposed and submerged components instead of treating the coast as a geographic unit to be investigated en masse. For example, James Ringer's (2003) investigations at Canso, Nova Scotia, focused on the submerged portion of a previously excavated fishing station and united the terrestrial and submerged findings to address questions of site function, seasonality, ethnic association, and the economic development of the fisheries.

COASTAL ARCHAEOLOGY AS A FACET OF MARITIME ARCHAEOLOGY

The majority of the projects discussed above were tremendously productive, yielding more sites, features, and data than archaeologists had initially hoped for and further reinforcing the fact that the coast has been the location of intensive occupation throughout human history (Walker 1990: 275). Furthermore, coastal data sets tend to include sites of multiple periods, allowing for analyses that address cultural change and continuity better than is generally possible with relatively finite shipwreck investigations. Thus, the coast is a storehouse of data that bears on such important issues as migration (Westley and Dix 2006), subsistence (Torben, Erlandson, and Vellanoweth 2001), and early industry (McErlean et al. 2007). For instance, Rick Torben and his colleagues' (2001) analysis of the faunal assemblage and artifact collection from Daisy Cave, California, showed that early Americans relied heavily on fish that were procured with a varied and complex toolkit that included boat fishing. These findings challenged the previous assumption that fish were a low-productivity food and showed the power of coastal archaeology to fundamentally change archaeological perceptions of past lifeways. An increased appreciation of the data stored in the coast not only helps address archaeological questions but also aids in the management of unidentified or underrecorded sites. As coastal erosion and development increasingly become a concern, "coastal survey provides a more reliable and better-quantified basis for future strategic planning on the coast, and for more targeted scientific research" (Paddenberg and Hession 2008: 150) where the submerged landscape is not "mis-represented as a sterile plain of beguiling blue . . . [with] historic shipwrecks . . . scattered like decoys to allure the attention of our legislators away from the wider vision of submerged national archaeological resources" (Tomalin 2000: 96).

The archaeology of the coast is clearly important in its own right, but it has the added power of being an integrative force in maritime archaeology. It capitalizes on the "weakness of the artificial seam" that separates terrestrial and underwater archaeologies and permits for a more holistic maritime archaeology (Tomalin 2000: 85). Whether the linkage between terrestrial and underwater archaeologies is methodological or theoretical, coastal archaeology serves to harmonize them (Adams 2006: 2; O'Sullivan and Breen 2007: 62; Oxley 2000: 31; Van der Noort and O'Sullivan 2006: 147; Westerdahl 2006). Many historic peoples who lived in proximity to a coast moved freely from terrestrial pursuits, such as agriculture, to maritime occupations, including fishing and commerce (Lance 1987; O'Sullivan and Breen 2007: 62; Westerdahl 2003). These farmers, fishermen, and sailors no doubt recognized the different environments, threats, and opportunities associated with both land-based and maritime pursuits but seem to have transitioned easily from one occupation to the other as the need arose. The coast formed a figurative (and, in the case of quays and wharves, a literal) bridge between multiple aspects of their working lives. In a broader sense, the littoral also formed a bridge between terrestrial transportation, production, and consumption systems, and the water-based production and transportation systems that were so important in the efficient movement of cargo from one point to another. With increasing regularity beginning with the Age of Discovery, goods seldom reached their point of consumption without being transported by ship or boat. As a result, the coast connects well-established subfields of historical/postmedieval archaeology, linking shipwreck studies with the investigations of settlements and industrial sites.

Beyond playing a functional role in maritime life, the coast figured prominently in the spiritual lives of many coastal peoples. Boundaries are important in many belief systems, and the coast is among the most naturally demarcated boundaries, making it a fruitful realm for spiritual development (see Westerdahl in this volume). As described by Edward Pollard (2008), the Digo culture of Tanzania provides a good example of a religious use of the coast. The Digo host annual ceremonies consisting of prayers and sacrifices of animal blood, sweets, and rice that begin at sacred land sites (*kaya*) and progress to corresponding sites offshore (*mzimu*). *Kaya* and *mzimu* are situated close to each other and to the coastline and are represented on the landscape by anomalies such as large trees, caves, upwellings of cold spring water, and portions of lagoon bottoms that are perpetually disturbed. Thus, each sacred site is unique and easily identified by members of the culture but also serves to link the two halves of the physical landscape together into a single spiritual landscape. From an archaeological perspective, Ian McNiven (2003) has noted culturally distinct, but potentially functionally similar, sites among Australian Aboriginal people.

THEORY AND METHOD IN COASTAL ARCHAEOLOGY

Theory

Much of the early theoretical development of coastal archaeology was driven by questions of environmental possibilism and economic or subsistence-derived explanations of littoral use (Van der Noort and O'Sullivan 2006: 25, 146). While the environment remains a primary research focus in coastal archaeology, which is appropriate given that coasts are among the most dynamic ecosystems on the planet, archaeological interpretations of the role that nature plays in human littoral occupations have become far more nuanced. There is also a growing literature on topics such as social identity, perception of the coast, and the role of coastal change in state formation.

Social Identity

Attributing agency to littoral inhabitants is a recurring theme in much recent coastal archaeology. These studies promote the social identity and actions of past peoples to the forefront. While these studies still address economic practices and environmental changes, which are contingent on and drivers of social relations, more weight is given to the actions of individuals and groups (Van der Noort and O'Sullivan 2006: 113). Much of this research is designed to investigate how people conceived of the coast, what distinctions they made between water and land, what special knowledge they maintained, how the natural rhythms of the coast structured their lives, how they valued and interacted with littoral environments, and how they interacted with other coastal peoples and inland peoples. The underlying argument is that the coast is different from the uplands and has different spaces, resources, and rhythms that arguably provide power to those who have the knowledge and skills to utilize them (Rönnby 2007; Van der Noort and O'Sullivan 2006: 36, 43, 82; Vickers 1993). The knowledge necessary to inhabit the coast, and the distinction of the coast from the uplands, lead to unique types of perception that make coastal communities a distinct subculture or potentially an identifiable culture.

A particularly clear example of this difference of perception is the case of sounds or inlets. Sounds are safe havens for seafarers, locations to be aware of and run to in case of a storm or to anchor in for the night. However, from the perspective of landsmen, sounds and their associated streams are an obstacle requiring a ferry, ford, or bridge. The opposite is true of portages. For a seafarer, the portage is an interruption of their easy passage requiring additional effort to move the cargo, if not the entire vessel, over the contrary ground, whereas for a terrestrial traveler the portage permits uninterrupted travel between two potentially confounding bodies of water (Westerdahl 2006: 77–78). In addition to shaping their worldviews around the coastal environment, shore dwellers also modify their surroundings to influence how their communities and the surrounding landscape are perceived. For example, the causeways on the coast surrounding Kilwa Kisiwani, Tanzania, had various functional purposes, including navigation aids, water access, and breakwaters, but they were also ceremonial sites and often associated with mosques. The mosques and associated causeways increased each other's visibility and advertised the Islamic allegiances of the port. These structures conveyed to the predominantly Muslim traders plying the coast that Kilwa Kisiwani was a safe and wealthy port and, therefore, a worthwhile place to do business (Pollard 2008).

The use of coastal structures to advertise local allegiances illustrates another aspect of coastal social archaeology, the interconnectedness of coastal peoples (Noble 2006). Travel by water was generally faster and far easier over long distances than travel on land: it is possible to move four to five times faster by small boat or canoe than on foot, and for much of the premodern era, a journey had to be only long enough to outweigh the cost of loading the cargo aboard a vessel to make water transport more efficient than the comparable overland route (Hugill 2005: 108; O'Sullivan and Breen 2007: 56). This ease of association among coastal peoples bordering the same body of water, combined with the similar knowledge bases, arguably similar perceptions of their environment, and the often-marginalized nature of coastal peoples in relation to inland peoples in terrestrial cultures, often led coastal peoples to develop a greater identification with geographically more distant coastal communities than with more proximal land communities (Loveluck and Tys 2006; Naylor 2004; Verhaeghe 2006: 215–219 for a counterexample). The relatively frictionless nature of water travel led to a greater emphasis on social distance than geographic distance. This general maritime group identity often manifests itself archaeologically in the relative abundance of trade commodities in coastal zones (Loveluck and Tys 2006; Naylor 2004).

Continuity and Dynamism

The social identity of coastal peoples was not static, of course; rather, it was constantly being constructed and modified, like all other living cultures. Yet Fernand Braudel's theory of the *longue durée* and his concern with continuity of social structures permeates much of the theoretical discussion of coastal archaeology. Many of these studies argue, either explicitly or implicitly, that the sea engenders certain social structures and that these structures are held in common among peoples living on particular coasts for an extended period of time (Aberg and Lewis 2000; Bernstein 2006; Julig 2007; O'Sullivan 2004; Rönnby 2007; Van der Noort and O'Sullivan 2006); however, it is also possible that coastal culture transcends geographic regions, establishing continuity not only through time but also through space (McErlean, McConkey, and Forsythe 2003: xix). This argument is very powerful because it allows for the consideration of a coastal culture that, while not monolithic, is distinct and warrants close study by coastal archaeologists. When applied well, the *longue durée* can be a very fruitful means of studying the coast. Aidan O'Sullivan (2004), for example, effectively argues that fish weirs are evidence of multigenerational continuity of traditions among coastal Irish and British peoples, despite major upheavals, such as the Anglo-Norman invasion. Indeed, he suggests that abandoned medieval fishtraps might have served hundreds of years later as a mnemonic for local fishing communities as to where the best fishing grounds might be located, giving archaeological sites in the maritime environment a cultural role that is often suggested by archaeologists to apply to reused barrows or other landward monuments. Similarly, David Bernstein (2006) posits that pre-Contact Native American peoples in coastal southern New England retained relatively constant subsistence, settlement, and technological patterns for millennia, while inland groups cycled through various patterns in response to environmental fluctuations. A somewhat different interpretation of similar evidence is provided by Lynn Ceci (1990).

Cultural continuity is clearly a viable theoretical perspective for coastal archaeology but it is largely based on assumptions of stability in the coastal environment. There is a substantial body of research, however, that proves the dynamism of the littoral (Erlandson and Fitzpatrick 2006; Welinder 1997; Westley and Dix 2006). Not only is the coastal environment not uniform from one geographic area to the next; it is also subject to seasonal and long-term variations. Geographic and seasonal variations can be adapted to by an individual culture and do not necessarily interrupt the continuity of that culture's coastal adaptations. However, long-term variations may lead to disruptions of the *longue durée*. Following the last glacial maximum, the changes in sea level due to the addition of meltwater and isostatic rebound would have been noticeable within individual lifetimes in some regions and would have been pronounced enough to be preserved in the cultural memory of other groups (Welinder 1997; Westley and Dix 2006). In addition to the rise or fall of the waterline, the associated changes in the flora and fauna as well as the climate of a landscape would have had a pronounced effect on local inhabitants. In these situations the continuity of coastal culture was almost certainly disrupted. For these cultures, the *longue durée* may not apply, or perhaps a more nuanced interpretation that takes into account cultural momentum in the face of environment change and addresses the adaptation of the old culture to the new environment while keeping identifiable aspects of old culture is appropriate.

Rise and Transition of the State

Coastal archaeology also has the potential to interact with established realms of archaeological theorization, such as the causes for the rise of the state. Douglas and James Kennett (2006) argue that sea-level change and the associated climate change were part of the multivariate process that led to early state formation in southern Mesopotamia. To oversimplify their model, the Kennetts argue that rising sea levels allowed for more irrigation and increased carrying capacity of lands in southern Mesopotamia; however, as sea-level rise slowed, the demands on the environment outstripped the ability of the population to support itself, resulting in the aggregation of groups and competition between groups. Thus, the human response to local sea-level change, in association with other more widely argued factors such as circumscription, population increase, warfare, trade, and irrigation, led to the formation of the early state.

The role of the coast also figures prominently in discussions of the transition from maritime-oriented states to inland, territory-oriented states during the post-medieval and modern periods (Hugill 2005; Mackinder 1942). Beginning circa 1400, maritime-oriented states were able to dominate large areas through naval power and commerce. Although wide-ranging, this power was relatively weak because ultimate control over the land was only within the range of the naval guns and the ability to blockade ports. However, prior to circa 1800, the vast majority of peoples were not far removed from the sea, even if neither we nor they would classify them as maritime or coastal peoples. With the advent of the nineteenth century, and new technology such as the telegraph and locomotive, as well as improved bureaucratic management, it became possible for populations and states to expand much farther inland. These territory-based states, relying on strong control of massive expanses of land, quickly overshadowed the maritime states during the nineteenth and twentieth centuries, resulting in a burgeoning emphasis on inland communities. This shift may, in part, be responsible for the relative neglect of coasts among twentieth-century archaeologists and may explain why more maritime-oriented cultures, such as the English and Irish, have been on the forefront of coastal archaeology.

Coastal Archaeology and the Environment

Perhaps the most commonly explored aspect of coastal archaeology is the relationship between coastal archaeology and the littoral environment. The coastal environment is among the most fragile and dynamic environments on earth, making it difficult to separate archaeology in this region from questions of the environment and environmental change (Head 2000; Walker 1990). Similarly, coastal archaeologists are often politically involved in environmental protection because of the very real threat that environmental change poses to the resources that they study (Van der Noort and O'Sullivan 2006: 31). Most of the archaeological focus on the coastal environment, consequently, can be divided into two categories: a concern with change in the coastal environment either through human or natural forces, and an interest in adapting to or managing changes in the coastal environment and their impacts on archaeological sites.

Humans affect every environment that they inhabit, and the coast, with its tendency to aggregate both land- and water-based impacts, is widely, intensively, and regularly impacted by humans, both intentionally and unintentionally (Bourne 2006; Halpern et al. 2008). Some of these alterations, such as land-making, sediment collection around groins and piers, and stone quarrying, take place directly on the coast, but other impacts, including increased sedimentation from plowed fields and increased runoff from urban canyons, are generated well inland. While the intensity of these human effects increased dramatically with the Industrial Revolution, there is ample evidence of human coastal alterations from antiquity (Inman 1978; Steffen et al. 2004; Walker 1990; Wood 2000). Further complicating the study of coastal change, many of the human impacts on the landscape are at the level of soils and nutrients (Goldberg and Macphail 2006: chap. 9) and, as demonstrated by sea-level rise following the last glacial maximum, the natural environment is also capable of drastic fluctuations without substantial human input.

The difficulty in parsing cultural and natural changes to the environment has led to an ecological approach among coastal archaeologists and many other scientists. In this approach, humans are considered within their environment, rather than above or external to it, and the complicated relationships between human and environmental actions and reactions are studied. The difficulty is that there is very little good ecological data prior to the twentieth century, and most ecological studies span little more than a few decades. Consequently, most data sets were established well after humans had begun to drastically affect the environment, and much of the data lacks a deep time dimension. Several archaeologists and historians have stepped into this void. Much of the archaeological data is drawn from shell midden sites and analyzes changes in animal size and species representation as a result of human predation; however, the results of human changes to the physical environment are also considered (Erlandson and Fitzpatrick 2006: 18; Head 2000; McErlean 2007: 92; Reitz 2004; Rick and Erlandson 2008). There is also a growing literature of historical ecology that draws on archival research (Starkey, Holm, and Barnard 2008) and serves as a bridge between the archaeological data and the growing corpus of research on coastal, marine, and global environmental change (Halpern et al. 2008; Pauly et al. 1998; Steffen et al. 2004).

In light of these physical and biological changes to the coast, many archaeologists are concerned about the preservation of our coastal heritage. In addition to erosion, human development is the primary threat to coastal archaeological sites, and an unknown number of sites are irretrievably lost each year (Erlandson and Fitzpatrick 2006: 20; Fulford, Champion, and Long 1997: 47). Unlike eroded sediments that are redeposited down current or diminished species that may eventually repopulate a degraded environment, lost archaeological sites cannot be regenerated. While both natural and cultural resource preservation are faced with the maxim that the coast will continue to change, the effects of this change are felt more grievously by coastal heritage. It is impractical to preserve and protect all coastal sites, but it is important to record all coastal sites. In this way, we will have a database of what has been lost and what types of sites once populated the landscape. This database will be useful not only as a research tool to study past coastal peoples, but also as a means to manage the remaining coastal sites and make judgments about what types of resources are worth protecting (O'Sullivan and Breen 2007: 243; Paddenberg and Hession 2008: 151).

Method

Lastly, a few words on the methods used to record these resources are appropriate. There are existing texts on recording intact and disarticulated hulls along the coasts as well as basic coastal archaeological survey (Fulford, Champion, and Long 1997; Milne, McKewan, and Goodburn 1998; Russell 2005), and coastal archaeologists are also encouraged to draw on the considerable amount of research conducted on the natural environment of coastlines and estuaries in preparation for any littoral survey (Hale 2000: 51). Similarly, the works cited in this chapter provide a sampling of the wide range of techniques utilized and challenges overcome in conducting coastal archaeology.

Coastal surveys should be conducted at low tide to take advantage of the greatest amount of exposed shoreline. These surveys can be cautiously completed on foot, and the greater the tidal variation, the more of the shore that can be accessed and surveyed conveniently. The major coastal survey of Strangford Lough benefited from a large tidal swing, exposing as much as one-third of the lough at low tide (McErlean, McConkey, and Forsythe 2003: 1). The lack of tidal variation is one of the primary differences between conducting a coastal survey along an ocean and a shoreline survey along a large lake or small sea. However, even in a lacustrine environment or along coasts that have minimal tidal variation, both SCUBA diver surveys, mirroring walking surveys on exposed land, and remote-sensing surveys can be effectively employed (see chapters by Gearheart and Quinn in this volume). The combination of a sub-bottom profiler/ground-penetrating radar assessment and sediment cores taken on- and offshore would also benefit coastal surveys by permitting the reconstruction of past shorelines and their associated environments. Regardless of the tidal variation within a survey area, archaeologists should bear in mind the height and timing of the tides, as they will influence the safety of the surveyors and their ability to locate and potentially excavate sites (Fulford, Champion, and Long 1997: 83–84). Conceptually, the coast should be viewed from the water at both low and high tide. Many of the coastal inhabitants would have known and accessed coastal sites from this direction rather from inland. Many questions of settlement location and importance can be answered simply by viewing a site from the water.

Finally, the archaeologist should weigh the integrity of the site against its long-term preservation. Many valuable coastal sites have been identified in low-energy environments, such as the human and cattle footprints preserved at Goldcliff along the Severn River, England, and these are naturally rewarding areas to search for coastal archaeological sites (Goldberg and Macphail 2006). However, it has also been shown that vessels run aground or sunk in shallow, energetic waters may be preserved beneath the seabed by a scour-related settling and covering process that leaves the lower hull and artifacts buried beneath the level of initial wrecking (McNinch, Wells, and Trembanis 2006). While this process does not apply to most inundated terrestrial sites (for a counterexample, see Patel 2009), there is still a need to investigate moderate and high-energy environments. Sites have been located in these areas, and these are the sites at the greatest risk. A coastal site that retains some integrity, has the potential to answer relevant research questions, and is threatened by erosion, development, or another force should be preferentially excavated before a nonthreatened site.

CONCLUSION

Through proper management, careful excavation, continued survey, and judicious preservation, the coastal archaeological record is a tremendous storehouse of data on maritime culture. As has been argued here, this data has the ability to answer a variety of questions about past maritime peoples, ranging from cognitive studies to questions of subsistence. What is more, coastal archaeology has the potential to form a tangible and theoretical bridge between underwater and terrestrial archaeology, making it fundamental to the study of the maritime past.

ACKNOWLEDGMENTS

Dr. Aidan O'Sullivan and Jessi Halligan offered several useful suggestions on an earlier draft of this chapter that have resulted in a substantially stronger final product. My fellow editors are also to be commended for their hard work and attention to detail that made this chapter readable.

REFERENCES

Aberg, Alan, and Carenza Lewis, eds. 2000. *The rising tide: Archaeology and coastal landscapes*. Oxford: Oxbow.

Adams, Jonathan. 2006. Editorial article: From the water margins to the centre ground? *Journal of Maritime Archaeology* 1: 1–8.

Anderson, R. C. 1934. The Bursledon Ship. *Mariner's Mirror* 20: 158–170.

Ash, Aidan. 2005. *A nice place for a harbour or is it? Investigating a maritime cultural landscape: Port Willunga, South Australia*. Maritime Archaeology Monograph and Report Series No. 4. Adelaide, South Australia: Flinders University.

Belcher, William R. 2009. Understanding ancient fishing and butchery strategies of the Indus Valley civilization. *SAA Archaeological Record* 9 (5): 10–14.

Bell, Martin, and Heike Neumann. 1997. Prehistoric intertidal archaeology and environments in the Severn Estuary, Wales. *World Archaeology* 29 (1): 95–113.

Bell, Trevor, and M. A. P. Renouf. 2003. Prehistoric cultures, reconstructed coasts: Maritime Archaic Indian site distribution in Newfoundland. *World Archaeology* 35 (3): 350–370.

Bernstein, David J. 2006. Long-term continuity in the archaeological record from the coast of New York and southern New England, USA. *Journal of Island and Coastal Archaeology* 1 (2): 271–284.

Bourne, Joel K., Jr. 2006. Loving our coasts to death. *National Geographic* 210 (1): 60–87.

Boyce, J. I., E. G. Reinhardt, A. Raban, and M. R. Pozza. 2003. The utility of marine magnetic surveying for mapping buried hydraulic concrete harbour structures: King Herod's harbour, Caesarea Maritima, Israel. Marine Archaeology Paper 03-01. Toronto: Marine Magnetics Corporation.

Breman, Joseph. 2003. Marine archaeology goes underwater with GIS. *Journal of GIS in Archaeology* 1: 25–32.

Bullers, Rick. 2005. *Convict probation and the evolution of jetties at Cascades, the coal mines, Impression Bay and Saltwater River, Tasman Peninsula, Tasmania: An historical perspective.* Maritime Archaeology Monograph and Reports Series No. 7. Adelaide, South Australia: Flinders University.

Ceci, Lynn. 1990. Radiocarbon dating "village" sites in coastal New York: Settlement pattern change in the middle to Lake Woodland. *Man in the Northeast* 39: 1–28.

Claassen, Cheryl Patricia. 1982. Shellfishing patterns: An analytical study of prehistoric shell from North Carolina coastal middens. PhD diss., Harvard University.

Clarke, Richard, Martin Dean, Gillian Hutchinson, Sean McGrail, and Jan Squirrell. 1993. Recent work on the R. Hamble wreck near Bursledon, Hampshire. *International Journal of Nautical Archaeology* 22 (1): 21–44.

Colette, Augustin. 2007. *Case studies on climate change and world heritage.* Paris: UNESCO World Heritage Centre.

Cooney, Gabriel. 2004. Introduction: Seeing land from the sea. *World Archaeology* 35 (3): 323–328.

Crawford, O. G. S. 1927. Lyonesse. *Antiquity* 1: 5–15.

Duncan, Brad. 2006. Maritime infrastructure heritage project stage one: Melbourne region. Melbourne, Australia: Heritage Victoria.

Ehlers, J., and P. L. Gibbard, eds. 2004. *Quaternary glaciations—extent and chronology.* 3 vols. New York: Elsevier.

Emory, Scott A. 2000. The Vineyard Shipbuilding Company: From wood shavings to hot sparks. MA thesis, East Carolina University.

Erlandson, Jon M. 2001. The archaeology of aquatic adaptations: Paradigms for a new millennium. *Journal of Archaeological Research* 9 (4): 287–350.

———. 2006. Book review essay: Beneath the seven seas; Shipwrecks, seafaring, and archaeology. *Journal of Island and Coastal Archaeology* 1 (2): 299–303.

Erlandson, Jon M., and Scott M. Fitzpatrick. 2006. Oceans, islands, and coasts: Current perspectives on the role of the sea in human prehistory. *Journal of Island and Coastal Archaeology* 1 (1): 5–32.

Erlandson, Jon M., and Torben C. Rick. 2008. Archaeology, marine ecology, and human impacts on the marine environment. In *Human impacts on ancient marine ecosystems: A global perspective*, ed. T. C. Rick and J. M. Erlandson, 1–19. Berkeley: University of California Press.

Faught, Michael K. 2004. The underwater archaeology of paleolandscapes, Apalachee Bay, Florida. *American Antiquity* 69 (2): 275–289.

Fedje, Daryl W., and Heiner Josenhans. 2000. Drowned forests and archaeology on the continental shelf of British Columbia, Canada. *Geology* 28 (2): 99–102.

Feibel, Craig S. 2001. Archaeological sediments in lake margin environments. In *Sediments in archaeological context*, ed. J. K. Stein and W. R. Farrand, 127–148. Salt Lake City: University of Utah Press.

Fischer, Anders. 2007. Coastal fishing in Stone Age Denmark—evidence from below and above the present sea level and from human bones. In *Shell middens in Atlantic Europe*, ed. N. Milner, O. E. Craig, and G. N. Bailey, 54–69. Hampshire, UK: Oxbow.

Fitzhugh, William, and Erik Phaneuf. 2008. The Gateways Project 2007: Land and underwater excavations at Hare Harbor, Mecatina. Washington, DC: Arctic Studies Center, Smithsonian Institution.

Flatman, Joe. 2011. Places of special meaning: Westerdahl's Comet, "agency," and the concept of the "maritime cultural landscape." In *The Archaeology of maritime landscapes*, ed. B. Ford. New York: Springer.

Flemming, Nicholas C. 1971. *Cities in the sea*. Garden City, NY: Doubleday.

——, ed. 2004. *Submarine prehistoric archaeology of the North Sea*. York, UK: English Heritage/Council for British Archaeology.

Flores, Carola. 2009. Shell middens in a Pacific Island Village, Baraulu, Roviana Lagoon, Western Salomon Islands. *SAA Archaeological Record* 9 (5): 19–21.

Ford, Ben. 2007. Down by the water's edge: Modeling shipyard locations in Maryland, USA. *International Journal of Nautical Archaeology* 36 (1): 125–137.

——. 2009. Lake Ontario maritime cultural landscape. PhD diss., Texas A&M University.

Friel, Ian. 1993. Henry V's *Grace Dieu* and the wreck in the R. Hamble near Bursledon, Hampshire. *International Journal of Nautical Archaeology* 22 (1): 3–19.

Fulford, Michael, Timothy Champion, and Antony Long, eds. 1997. *England's coastal heritage: A survey for English Heritage and the RCHME*. Archaeological Report No. 15. London: English Heritage.

Gaur, A. S., Sundaresh, and Tripati Sila. 2004. Dwarka: An ancient harbour. *Current Science* 86 (9): 1256–1260.

Gaur, A. S., Sundaresh, and P. Vardhan. 2005. Ancient shell industry at Bet Dwarka. *Current Science* 89 (6): 941–946.

Gawronski, Jerzy. 1990. The Amsterdam Project. *International Journal of Nautical Archaeology* 19 (2): 53–61.

——. 2003. The Hogendijk Shipyard in Zaandam and the VOC Shipyard Oostenburg in Amsterdam: Examples of recent archaeological slipway research in the Netherlands. In *Boats, ships and shipyards: Proceedings of the Ninth International Symposium on Boat and Ship Archaeology, Venice 2000*, ed. C. Beltrame, 132–143. Oxford: Oxbow.

Goldberg, Paul, and Richard Macphail. 2006. *Practical and theoretical geoarchaeology*. Malden, MA: Blackwell.

Hale, Alex. 2000. The archaeological potential of the Scottish intertidal zone: Some examples and an assessment. In *The rising tide: Archaeology and coastal landscapes*, ed. A. Aberg and C. Lewis, 51–60. Oxford: Oxbow.

Halpern, Benjamin, et al. 2008. A global map of human impact on marine ecosystems. *Science* 319: 948–952.

Head, Lesley. 2000. *Cultural landscapes and environmental change*. London: Arnold.

Heintzelman, Andrea. 1986. Colonial wharf construction: Uncovering the untold past. *Log of Mystic Seaport* 37 (4): 124–135.

Hugill, Peter J. 2005. Trading states, territorial states and technology. In *Global geostrategy: Halford Mackinder and the defence of the West*, ed. B. W. Blouet, 107–124. London: Frank Cass.

Hyde, Lewis. 2008. *Trickster makes this world*. Edinburgh: Canongate Books.

Inman, Douglas. 1978. The impact of coastal structures on shorelines. Paper presented at Proceedings of the Symposium on Technical, Environmental, Socioeconomic and Regulatory Aspects of Coastal Zone Management, 14–16 March, San Francisco, CA

Jones, Sharyn. 2009. Sailing at once in several seas, digging and I-Witnessing in Lau. *SAA Archaeological Record* 9 (5): 15–18.

Jordan-Greene, Krista. 2007. A maritime landscape of Deadman's Island. MA thesis, University of West Florida.

Julig, Patrick. 2007. A brief report on a Killatney Pukaskwa Pit (BlHi-10). *Ontario Archaeological Society Arch Notes* 12 (3): 9–10.

Kennett, Douglas J., and James P. Kennett. 2006. Early state formation in Southern Mesopotamia: Sea levels, shorelines, and climate change. *Journal of Island and Coastal Archaeology* 1 (1): 67–99.

Knoerl, Thomas Kurt. 1994. Beneath Niagara: A methodological approach to an inundated eighteenth-century site. MA thesis, East Carolina University.

Król, D., ed. 1997. *The built environment of coastal areas during the Stone Age*. Gdańsk, Poland: Archaeological Museum in Gdańsk.

Lance, Joyce Weese Barr. 1987. *Follow the North Shore*. Gouverneur, NY: MRS.

Lauer, Matthew, and Shankar Aswani. 2009. Indigenous ecological knowledge as situated practices: Understanding fishers' knowledge in the Western Solomon Islands. *American Anthropologist* 111 (3): 317–329.

Lawrence, S., and Mark Staniforth, eds. 1998. *The archaeology of whaling in Southern Australia and New Zealand*. Gundaroo, New South Wales: Australian Society for Historical Archaeology and Australian Institute for Maritime Archaeology.

Lemee, Christian. 1997. A ship-cemetery on the B&W site in Copenhagen. In *Down the river to the sea: Eighth International Symposium on Boat and Ship Archaeology*, ed. J. Litwin, 235–240. Gdańsk: Polish Maritime Museum.

Leshikar-Denton, Margaret. 1993. The 1794 wreck of the *Ten Sail*, Cayman Islands, British West Indies: A historical study and archaeological survey. PhD diss., Texas A&M University.

Lindenlauf, Astrid. 2004. The sea as a place of no return in ancient Greece. *World Archaeology* 35 (3): 416–433.

Loveluck, Chris, and Dries Tys. 2006. Coastal societies, exchange and identity along the Channel and southern North Sea shores of Europe, CE 600–1000. *Journal of Maritime Archaeology* 1: 140–169.

Mackinder, Halford J. 1942. *Democratic ideals and reality*. New York: Henry Holt.

McConkey, Rosemary, and Thomas McErlean. 2007. Mombasa Island: A maritime perspective. *International Journal of Historical Archaeology* 11 (2): 99–121.

McErlean, Thomas. 2007. Archaeology of the Strangford Lough kelp industry in the eighteenth- and early-nineteenth centuries. *Historical Archaeology* 41 (3): 76–93.

McErlean, Thomas, Caroline Earwood, Dermot Moore, and Eileen Murphy. 2007. The sequence of early Christian period horizontal tide mills at Nendrum Monastery: An interim statement. *Historical Archaeology* 41 (3): 63–75.

McErlean, Thomas, Rosemary McConkey, and Wes Forsythe. 2003. *Strangford Lough: An archaeological survey of the maritime cultural landscape*. Northern Ireland Archaeological Monographs No. 6. Belfast, Northern Ireland: Blackstaff.

McGrail, Sean. 1983. The interpretation of archaeological evidence for maritime structures. In *Sea studies*, ed. P. Annis, 33–46. Greenwich, UK: National Maritime Museum.

———. 1985. Early landing places. In *Conference on Waterfront Archaeology No. 2*, ed. A. E. Herteig, 12–18. Bergen, Norway: Historisk Museum Bergen.

McNinch, Jesse E., John T. Wells, and Arthur C. Trembanis. 2006. Predicting the fate of artefacts in energetic, shallow marine environments: An approach to site management. *International Journal of Nautical Archaeology* 35 (2): 290–309.

McNiven, Ian J. 2003. Saltwater people: Spiritscapes, maritime rituals and the archaeology of Australian indigenous seascapes. *World Archaeology* 35 (3): 329–349.

Milne, Gustav. 1985. *The port of Roman London*. London: B.T. Batsford.

Milne, Gustav, Colin McKewan, and Damian Goodburn. 1998. *Nautical archaeology on the foreshore: Hulk recording on the Medway*. Swindon, UK: Royal Commission on the Historical Monuments of England.

Milner, Nicky, Oliver E. Craig, and Geoffrey N. Bailey, eds. 2007. *Shell middens in Atlantic Europe*. Hampshire, UK: Oxbow.

Moore, Jonathan, ed. 2005. *Rideau Canal National Historic Site of Canada: Submerged Cultural Resource Inventory*. Ottawa: Underwater Archaeology Service, Ontario Service Centre, Parks Canada Agency.

———. 2008. Fort Henry Historic Site of Canada: Submerged Cultural Resource Inventory; 2004, 2006, and 2007 Surveys. Ottawa: Underwater Archaeology Service, Ontario Service Centre, Parks Canada Agency.

Moser, Jason D. 2007. Lower Eastern Shore shipyard survey: Archaeological and historical investigations. Crownsville, MD: Maryland Historical Trust.

Murphy, Larry. 1990. *8SL17: Natural site-formation processes of a multiple-component underwater site in Florida*. Southwest Cultural Resources Center Professional Papers No. 39. Santa Fe: National Park Service.

National Trust. 2005. *Shifting shores: Living with a changing coastline*. London: National Trust for Places of Historic Interest and Natural Beauty.

Naylor, John. 2004. Access to international trade in middle Saxon England: A case of urban over-emphasis? In *Close encounters: Sea- and riverborne trade, ports and hinterlands, ship construction and navigation in antiquity, the Middle Ages and in modern time*, ed. M. Pasquinucci and T. Weski, 139–148. Oxford: Archaeopress.

Noble, Gordon. 2006. Harnessing the waves: Monuments and ceremonial complexes in Orkney and beyond. *Journal of Maritime Archaeology* 1: 100–117.

O'Sullivan, Aidan. 1995. Intertidal archaeological surveys in the estuarine wetlands of North Munster. *International Journal of Nautical Archaeology* 24 (1): 71–73.

———. 2001. *Foragers, farmers and fishers in a coastal landscape: An intertidal archaeological survey of the Shannon estuary*. Dublin: Royal Irish Academy.

———. 2004. Place, memory and identity among estuarine communities: Interpreting the archaeology of early medieval fish weirs. *World Archaeology* 35 (3): 449–468.

O'Sullivan, Aidan, and Colin Breen. 2007. *Maritime Ireland: An archaeology of coastal communities*. Stroud, UK: Tempus.

Oxley, Ian. 2000. Maritime Fife: An integrated study of the maritime archaeological and historical resources of Fife. In *The rising tide: Archaeology and coastal landscapes*, ed. A. Aberg and C. Lewis, 29–38. Oxford: Oxbow.

Paddenberg, Dietlind, and Brian Hession. 2008. Underwater archaeology on foot: A systematic rapid foreshore survey on the North Kent coast, England. *International Journal of Nautical Archaeology* 37 (1): 142–152.

Parida, A. N. 1999. Ancient ports on the eastern coast of India. In *Maritime heritage of India*, ed. K. S. Behera. New Delhi: Aryan Books International.

Parker, A. J. 1999. A maritime cultural landscape: The port of Bristol in the Middle Ages. *International Journal of Nautical Archaeology* 28 (4): 323–342.

Parkington, John. 2006. *Shorelines, strandlopers and shell middens*. Cape Town: Creda Communications.

Pasquinucci, Marinella, and Timm Weski, eds. 2004. *Close encounters: Sea- and riverborne trade, ports and hinterlands, ship construction and navigation in antiquity, the Middle Ages and in modern time*. BAR International Series 1283. Oxford: Archaeopress.

Patel, Samir S. 2009. Swept away: Rediscovering the ruins of a great medieval center beneath the North Sea. *Archaeology* 62 (1): 43–45.

Pauly, Daniel, Villy Christensen, Johanne Dalsgaard, Rainer Froese, and Francisco Torres Jr. 1998. Fishing down marine food webs. *Science* 279 (5352): 860–863.

Peacock, David, and Lucy Blue, eds. 2007. *The ancient Red Sea port of Adulis, Eritrea.* Oxford: Oxbow.

Pieters, Marnix, Frans Verhaeghe, and Glenn Gevaert, eds. 2006. *Fishery, trade and piracy.* Brussels: Flemish Heritage Institute.

Pilon, Jean-Luc. 2008. Getting over the falls: The archaeological heritage of Rockcliffe Park. *Ontario Archaeological Society Arch Notes* 13 (1): 7–16.

Pollard, Edward. 2008. Inter-tidal causeways and platforms of the 13th- to 16th-century city-state of Kilwa Kisiwani, Tanzania. *International Journal of Nautical Archaeology* 37 (1): 98–114.

Quinn, Rory, Wes Forsythe, Colin Breen, Donald Boland, Paul J. Lane, and Athman Lali Omar. 2006. Process-based models for port evolution and wreck site formation at Mombasa, Kenya. *Journal of Archaeological Science* 34: 1449–1460.

Raban, Avner, ed. 1985. *Harbour archaeology: Proceedings of the First International Workshop on Ancient Mediterranean Harbours, Cesarea Maritima.* BAR International 257. Oxford: BAR.

——, ed. 1986. *Cities on the sea—past and present: 1st International Symposium on Harbours, Port Cities and Coastal Topography.* Haifa: University of Haifa.

——, ed. 1988. *Archaeology of coastal changes.* BAR International Series 404. Oxford: BAR.

——. 1989. *The harbours of Cesarea Maritima.* BAR International Series 491. Oxford: BAR.

Reinders, Reinder. 2001. The coastal landscape between Thermopylai and Demetrias from a maritime point of view. In *Tropis VI*, ed. H. Tzalas, 457–492. Athens: Hellenic Institute for the Preservation of Nautical Tradition.

Reitz, Elizabeth J. 2004. "Fishing down the food web": A case study from St. Augustine, Florida, USA. *American Antiquity* 69 (1): 63–83.

Richards, Nathan, and Mark Staniforth. 2006. The Abandoned Ships' Project: An overview of the archaeology of deliberate watercraft discard in Australia. *Historical Archaeology* 40 (4): 84–103.

Rick, Torben C., and Jon M. Erlandson, eds. 2008. *Human impacts on ancient marine ecosystems: A global perspective.* Berkeley: University of California Press.

Ringer, R. James. 2003. Underwater archaeology at Canso: Investigating the underwater component of a 17th- to 19th-century Nova Scotia fishing community. In *Mer et monde: Questions d'archeologie maritime*, ed. C. Roy, 188–211. Quebec City: Association des archeologues du Quebec.

Rissolo, Dominique, and Jeffrey B. Glover. 2008. Maya maritime trade and interaction along the Yucatan Coast: The view from Vista Alegre. Paper presented at 107th American Anthropological Association Annual Meeting, 19–23 November, San Francisco, CA.

Rönnby, Johan. 2007. Maritime durées: Long-term structure in a coastal landscape. *Journal of Maritime Archaeology* 2: 65–82.

Rudolph, Wolfgang. 1980. *Harbor and town: A maritime cultural history.* Altenburg, Germany: T. Lux Feininger.

Russell, Matthew A. 2005. *Beached shipwreck archaeology: Case studies from Channel Islands National Park.* Submerged Resources Center Professional Reports No. 18. Santa Fe: Submerged Resources Center, Intermountain Region, National Park Service.

Shimin, Lin, Du Genqi, and Jeremy Green. 1991. Waterfront excavations at Dongmenkou, Ningbo, Zhe Jiang Province, PRC. *International Journal of Nautical Archaeology* 20 (4): 200–311.

Spirek, James, and Lynn Harris. 2003. Maritime heritage on display: Underwater examples
    from South Carolina. In *Submerged cultural resource management*, ed. J. A. Spirek and
    D. A. Scott-Ireton, 165–176. New York: Plenum.

Staniforth, Mark, and Martin McGonigle. 2007. *The Gaultois and Balaena shore-based
    whaling stations in Newfoundland, Canada*. Flinders University Maritime Archaeology
    Monograph Series No. 6. South Australia: Shannon Research Press.

Starkey, David, Poul Holm, and Michaela Barnard, eds. 2008. *Oceans past: Management
    insights from the history of marine animal populations*. Sterling, VA: Earthscan.

Steffen, W., A. Sanderson, P. D. Tyson, J. Jager, P. A. Matson, and B. Moore III. 2004. *Global
    change and the face of the earth system: A planet under pressure*. Heidelberg, Germany:
    Springer.

Stein, Julie K., ed. 1992. *Deciphering a shell midden*. New York: Academic Press.

Stilgoe, John R. 1994. *Alongshore*. New Haven, CT: Yale University Press.

Stone, Linda, Diane Dallal, Meta Janowitz, and George L. Miller. 2008. A view of colonial
    New York from the South Ferry Terminal excavations in New York City. *NYSAA
    Newsletter* 3 (1): 3–6.

Tomalin, David. 2000. Stress at the seams: Assessing the terrestrial and submerged
    archaeological landscape on the shore of the *Magnus Portus*. In *The rising tide:
    Archaeology and coastal landscapes*, ed. A. Aberg and C. Lewis, 85–98. Oxford: Oxbow.

Torben, Rick, Jon M. Erlandson, and René Vellanoweth. 2001. Paleocoastal marine fishing
    on the Pacific coast of the Americas: Perspectives from Daisy Cave, California.
    American Antiquity 66 (4): 595–613.

Vainstub, D., and C. Murray. 2006. Proyecto Hoorn: Un naufragio holandés en la
    Patagonia. In *Actas del XV Congreso Nacional de Arqueología Argentina, Río Cuarto,
    Septiembre 2004*, 397–404. Río Cuarto: Universidad Nacional de Río Cuarto.

Van der Noort, Robert, and Aidan O'Sullivan. 2006. *Rethinking wetland archaeology*.
    London: Gerald Duckworth.

Verhaeghe, Frans. 2006. Living on the edge of the land: A few preliminary conclusions. In
    *Fishery, trade and piracy: Fishermen and fishermen's settlements in and around the
    North Sea area in the Middle Ages and later*, ed. M. Pieters, F. Verhaeghe, and
    G. Gevaert, 215–219. Brussels: Flemish Heritage Institute.

Vickers, Daniel. 1993. Beyond Jack Tar. *William and Mary Quarterly* 50 (2): 418–424.

Vrana, Kenneth J., and Gail A. Vander Stoep. 2003. The maritime cultural landscape of the
    Thunder Bay National Marine Sanctuary and Underwater Preserve. In *Submerged
    cultural resource management*, ed. J. D. Spirek and D. A. Scott-Ireton, 17–28. New York:
    Plenum.

Walker, H. Jesse. 1990. The coastal zone. In *The Earth as transformed by human action:
    Global and regional changes in the biosphere over the past 300 years*, ed. B. L. I. Turner,
    W. C. Clark, R. W. Kates, J. F. Richards, J. T. Mathews, and W. B. Meyers, 271–294. New
    York: Cambridge University Press.

Waters, Michael R. 1997. *Principles of geoarchaeology*. Tucson: University of Arizona Press.

Welinder, Stig. 1997. The Stone Age landscape of coastal southeast Sweden at the Neolithic
    transition. In *The built environment of coastal areas during the Stone Age*, ed. D. Król,
    87–97. Gdańsk: Archaeological Museum in Gdańsk.

Westerdahl, Christer. 1992. The maritime cultural landscape. *International Journal of
    Nautical Archaeology* 21 (1): 5–14.

———. 2003. Maritime culture in an inland lake? In *Maritime heritage*, ed. C. A. Brebbia
    and T. Gambin, 17–26. Southampton, UK: WIT Press.

————. 2006. The relationship between land roads and sea routes in the past—some reflections. *Deutsches Schifffahrtsarchiv* 29: 59–114.

Westley, Kieran, and Justin Dix. 2006. Coastal environments and their role in prehistoric migrations. *Journal of Maritime Archaeology* 1: 9–28.

Wood, J. David. 2000. *Making Ontario: Agricultural colonization and landscape re-creation before the railway.* Kingston, ON: McGill-Queen's University Press.

Wright, Edward V. 1994. The North Ferriby Boats—a final report. In *Crossroads in ancient shipbuilding: Proceedings of the Sixteenth International Symposium on Boat and Ship Archaeology, Roskilde 1991,* ed. C. Westerdahl, 29–34. Oxford: Oxbow.

....

CHAPTER 34

SUBMERGED PREHISTORY IN THE NORTH SEA

....

ANTONY FIRTH

INTRODUCTION

....

THE prehistory of the North Sea changed on Friday, 8 February 2008, at least for me. Peter Murphy, English Heritage, forwarded me an e-mail from Hans Peeters, his colleague in the Dutch cultural heritage agency. The e-mail related the discovery of 28 Paleolithic hand axes at a wharf in the Netherlands, found in gravel that had been dredged up off Great Yarmouth, on the east coast of England. Attached to the e-mail was a photograph of one of the hand axes. I forwarded it around my colleagues with a note: "We've not been making it up all these years, after all ..."

The reason the e-mail had been copied to me is that Wessex Archaeology runs a program that encourages people working for marine aggregate companies to report anything they find that might be of archaeological interest. The initiative is based on a protocol established by English Heritage and the British Marine Aggregate Producers Association (BMAPA), to which most of the companies dredging sand and gravel are affiliated. Although the wharf where the hand axes were found was owned by a Dutch company not directly involved in the protocol, the gravel was being dredged by Hanson Aggregates Marine Ltd. (HAML), a member of BMAPA, from a stretch of seabed known as Area 240, which refers to the license granted by the Crown Estate that enables HAML to dredge aggregate there.

HAML regularly reports dredged-up artifacts to us through the protocol, so we were able to alert them to this new discovery quickly. They immediately recognized the significance of the hand axes and moved their dredgers away from the part of Area 240 where they had been active. Meanwhile, in the Netherlands, Dutch archaeologists were collaborating with the finder, Mr. Meulmeester, who had been visiting the wharf to look for fossilized animal bones and mammoth teeth among the heaps of gravel.

As well as the good relations between professionals and amateurs that enabled Mr. Meulmeester to bring his finds to the attention of the Dutch authorities, it is worth pointing out the collaboration across the North Sea in the field of prehistory, the positive relationship between archaeologists and the aggregate industry, and the recognition within the aggregate industry of the archaeological significance of the discovery. Such relationships are central to understanding why the investigation of prehistory in the North Sea is currently so dynamic. While the prehistory of the North Sea has been generating interest—at least episodically—for over a century (see Coles 1998; Gaffney 2009), interest has grown significantly over the last decade or so. There are a range of investigations and initiatives under way involving various teams for which the North Sea Prehistory Research and Management Framework (NSPRMF) now provides a focal point (Murphy 2007; Peeters, Murphy, and Flemming 2009). These investigations are generating results that are not merely encouraging, but—as with the Area 240 hand axes—potentially paradigm-shifting. The relevant literature is expanding rapidly, and the following account is necessarily selective and UK-based; moreover, the pace of change is such that my account is bound to be outdated by the time it reaches print.

The hand axes were dredged about 13 km from the East Anglian coast, from a water depth of about 25–27 m. The place where they were found was being targeted for a particular grade of gravel to meet the specific requirements of the Dutch wharf. Each pass of the aggregate dredger removes a strip about 1.2 m wide and 20–50 cm deep, and the track followed by the draghead is monitored electronically for contractual purposes, which enables the dredge tracks to be mapped. Altogether there were 75 hand axes, flakes, and cores (Figure 34.1), with the remains of woolly mammoth, woolly rhino, bison, reindeer, and horse found at the same time (Glimmerveen, pers. comm. 2008). One of the striking things about the first photographs of the hand axes was that they seemed so "fresh," implying that they might have been found in a primary context—that is to say, more or less where they were left by the people who created and used them. Closer examination indicated that the finds had come from a number of different depositional contexts, falling roughly into three groups: some exposed on the seafloor; some from an eroding surface, possibly the seafloor; and some seeming to originate from a primary context, including many hand axes forming a homogenous typological group (Peeters, pers. comm. 2008). Hand axes are not readily ascribed to chronological groups, but a Middle Paleolithic date (from about 300,000 to 30,000 years ago) was tentatively suggested.

In summary, the Area 240 hand axes demonstrate the presence of artifacts at or close to the surface of the seabed, apparently associated with faunal remains, in an exposed location in the North Sea, having experienced at least one and possibly several major glacial periods and now subject to the direct impact of modern industry. In itself, this situation vindicated the precautionary approach that had been developed by archaeologists and the aggregate industry to the possible effects of

Figure 34.1 Part of the hand axe assemblage from Area 240 (Wessex Archaeology).

dredging on the marine historic environment since the mid-1990s. But the likelihood that at least some of these ancient artifacts from the floor of the North Sea were in primary context offered a decisive shift in implication.

A 700,000-YEAR STORY

An earlier pivotal moment in understanding the prehistory of the North Sea was the 2005 publication of results from investigations at Pakefield on the coast of East Anglia (Parfitt et al. 2005). Flint artifacts excavated from coastal exposures presented unequivocal evidence of human presence dating back to 700,000 years ago, being the earliest evidence for humans north of the Alps. As well as extending British prehistory backward by 200,000 years, the investigations established that fine-grained deposits containing archaeological material had survived numerous major glacial events and subsequent marine inundations. Geophysical investigations and coring off Pakefield in 2006 confirmed that deposits from the same sequence extended below the sea (Wessex Archaeology 2008a). Not only had prehistory gained a much longer timescale, but archaeologically significant deposits spanning the entire period were present beneath the North Sea despite the massive processes that had occurred over hundreds of millennia.

The most recent increase in sea levels approached current levels at the start of the Neolithic around 6,000 years ago, which means that the North Sea was a predominantly maritime environment by that time, although some small islands may still have been present (Gaffney, Fitch, and Smith 2009: 145–146). Leaving aside evidence of prehistoric seafaring from various points around the North Sea, the archaeological potential of the North Sea presents the possibility of discoveries on former land from about 700,000 to 6,000 years ago. However, current evidence suggests that human inhabitation was intermittent, with several periods of long absence. While the extreme conditions of maximum glaciation may have been one factor encouraging people to disappear from Britain, it is not the only explanation. On the one hand, there is evidence for inhabitation during very cold periods (Wenban-Smith 2002: 10), while on the other hand some periods of very favorable conditions provide no evidence of humans (Stringer 2006). Evidence from under the North Sea could play a big role in changing current understandings of the presence and absence of humans in the region.

Conventionally, the prehistory of the North Sea falls into two main periods:

- The Paleolithic, from circa 700,000 years ago through several glacial/ interglacial cycles including the Last (Devensian) Glacial Maximum (LGM). The term "Paleolithic" has also been used to include the period from about 13,500 to 11,300 years ago when Britain was reinhabited by people after the LGM, encompassing an initial period of improving climate (the Late Glacial/ Windermere Interstadial [Bølling-Allerød period]) and an abrupt but short period of climatic worsening (the Loch Lomond [Younger Dryas] Stadial).
- The Mesolithic period, from about 11,300 to 6,000 years ago, which accompanies the start of the Holocene as climate improved after the Loch Lomond Stadial, with Preboreal, Boreal, and Atlantic phases reflected in changing vegetation.

In studying submerged prehistory, however, it has proved more useful to use the Last Glacial Maximum about 18,000 years ago as the key division—marked by extensive glaciation, very low sea level, and apparent human absence in Britain—rather than the traditional Paleolithic-Mesolithic split.

A Basic Model for Submerged Prehistoric Contexts in the North Sea

Marine aggregates are playing a central role in the investigation of submerged prehistory because there is a prima facie relationship between the aggregate that industry seeks to exploit—especially in the southern North Sea and English Channel—and the areas most likely to contain important archaeological material. Specifically, the marine aggregate industry often targets sands and gravels sorted and deposited by rivers that extended across the continental shelf when the sea level was lower.

Repeatedly, sea level has fallen very significantly in the North Sea at times when Britain and the Continent were inhabited by our predecessors. Major periods of glaciation have been accompanied by sea-level reductions of up to 130 m. These major glacial periods and the interglacials between them are commonly referred to in terms of Marine Isotope Stages (MIS—formerly Oxygen Isotope Stages, or OIS), because they correlate with curves for global temperature derived from the investigations of deep ocean sediment cores. The stages count backward from the present interglacial, MIS 1. Glacial periods are represented as "even" numbers and interglacials as "odd" numbers, though some of the glacials/interglacials named by earlier researchers have since been shown to span multiple MIS.

As well as causing large areas of seabed to be exposed as land, lower sea-level causes river systems to cut down to achieve a steeper profile that, along with glacial and periglacial processes, resulted in massive processes of erosion and deposition (Antoine et al. 2003). The energetic environment transported sediment downstream, moving and sorting gravel and sand and washing out the finer sediments. In the warmer periods (interglacials) following glaciations, rivers regraded themselves to shallower inclines so that sands and gravels stagnated in the river basins or were reworked by braiding channels. The subsequent return to glacial conditions resulted in renewed down-cutting and remobilization of the sands and gravels, repeating the process. The surviving sand and gravel features now form a major source of aggregate for construction. We are currently in an interglacial (warm) period and sea level is high, so while deposits in the upper catchments of rivers can be excavated on land, gravel and sand in the lower catchments of the same rivers can only be obtained by marine dredging (Bellamy 1998; Wenban-Smith 2002: 1–2).

The submerged river gravels are considered to be of high potential for prehistoric archaeology for several reasons. First, the sedimentary processes affecting pieces of natural flint (the major component of gravel) also apply to flint artifacts made by humans, so such artifacts have been eroded and deposited in river valleys in among the gravels and sand. There is a long history of aggregate workers discovering Paleolithic hand axes in gravel quarries on land, and the river gravels have been a primary source for antiquarians and early archaeologists. Hence, both the principle underlying the formation of these deposits, and long experience on land, indicates that now-submerged river gravels have high potential for the presence of "derived" artifacts—meaning artifacts used and deposited upstream that have been eroded and redeposited downstream, outside their original context. Second, the rivers may have provided accessible routes to people (Lang and Keen 2005), as well as landforms—such as gravel bars and islands—favorable to inhabitation. Third, rivers, estuaries, and coastal zones offered rich resources not only of flint for tools but of various forms of wildlife and plants. Fourth, as the rivers slowed to shallower gradients and fine-grained material was deposited, soils would have developed and organic growth occurred—not only offering resources but also providing sediment cover within which artifactual and paleo-environmental data can be preserved. These reasons point to the potential presence not only of derived material, eroded and reworked from elsewhere, but also of artifactual material in primary or little-disturbed contexts.

As well as the direct relationship between submerged prehistory and marine aggregate dredging that arises from the coincidence of interest in river gravels, river valley deposits are a focus of scientific investigation and study by the aggregate industry itself (Bellamy 1998). Aggregate companies invest in surveys to establish the extent and character of aggregate deposits that they can use, but also to avoid the fine-grained sediments deposited in proximity to river gravels because they contaminate the aggregate and are a commercial hazard. Hence, the marine aggregate industry and archaeologists have a mutual interest in understanding the location and formation of river gravels and associated deposits.

Returning to sea-level change, the interplay of climatic, geological, and marine processes is very complex and not very well understood at scales relevant to archaeologists. The interplay is especially complex in parts of Scotland, Ireland, and Scandinavia, as rebounding of the earth's crust following the release of the weight of ice has caused sea level to fall as well as rise relative to land (Ballantyne 2004; Kelley et al. 2006; Wickham-Jones and Dawson 2006). This effect is very marked on the western coast of Scotland, where prehistoric sites can be found on raised beaches today, while contemporary sites from farther north are expected to be submerged. In contrast, in the southern North Sea it is possible to advance a general climate-driven model for submerged prehistory comparable to Bridgland's model of terrace formation (Bridgland 1994, 1996; Wymer 1999: 25–29), though it must be recognized that the South is also subject to complexity caused by uplift and tectonic factors and that river systems are not the only source of archaeologically significant surfaces and deposits. Bellamy (1995) offers a six-phase model that addresses multiple cycles, but the basic cycle has four phases (Table 34.1; Figure 34.2). A key characteristic of submerged prehistory in the North Sea is that this general sequence has occurred not once, but repeatedly. Within each phase there are opportunities for people to inhabit and exploit the changing landscape, though the overall sequence at any location is likely to be complex because erosion, deposition, and stability will reflect shorter-term cycles of environmental change.

It is the gentler sequences associated with vegetation in the early interglacial phase that are usually of greatest interest to archaeologists. Showing themselves as fine-grained deposits and peaty layers, there may be very good survival of a range of paleo-environmental indicators and material capable of scientific dating. It may also be possible for artifactual material to survive in these contexts, either buried on the hard surfaces of earlier, harsher times, or occurring within or on top of the deposits associated with the improving environment. The promise of direct, artifactual evidence—comprising not only inorganic material such as worked flint but also organic components preserved by waterlogging—in immediate association with rich, scientifically datable, paleo-environmental remains places a premium on the identification of sites where these circumstances might occur.

Table 34.1 Four-phase model of prehistoric contexts

Phase	Principal Changes in Environment	Implications for Inhabitation	Processes Affecting Site Formation
Onset of glacial periods	As climate cools, conditions become harsher; vegetation becomes tundralike; sea-level falls; and rivers cut downward to the steeper gradients necessary to meet lower sea levels.	New areas of land become available as sea level falls.	Erosion is the dominant process, but it is accompanied by the accumulation (aggradation) of gravel features on the exposed continental shelf as material moves downstream.
Glacial periods	The climate and associated conditions are maintained for thousands of years, with marked variations over a range of timescales, even including seasonal changes in meltwash and deposition.	At the height of glaciation, the main focus of inhabitation seems to have been farther south and east in continental refuges, but people may have exploited the glacial front in periods of climatic amelioration or in summer months.	Fully glacial periods characterized by highly dynamic erosion and deposition.
Early interglacials	As glacial gives way to interglacial and the climate ameliorates, vegetation and fauna become more temperate.	The improving climate creates vast, productive environments capable of extensive use.	Postglacial amelioration characterized by gentler depositional environments and the development of vegetated surfaces.
Later interglacials	Sea level rises; river gradients become less steep and deposition occurs. Rising sea level causes the tidal limit of rivers to be pushed upstream. Fresh water valleys become saline estuaries and then fully marine. Areas that were once land are inundated.	Inhabitable land lost to the rising sea. Major changes to estuaries and landforms.	Coastal and marine processes apply. Marine deposition in estuaries and low-energy environments. Erosion and reworking by tides and storms in exposed or constricted environments.

After Bellamy 1995.

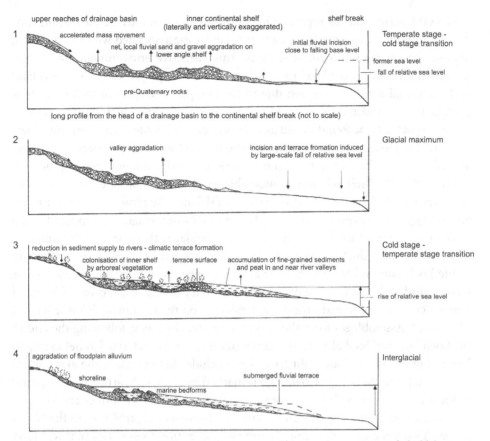

Figure 34.2 Bellamy's model (1995) of processes affecting the continental shelf during glacial cycles. Reproduced with the kind permission of the Geological Society.

DOGGERLAND

Only a few years ago it was only the most recent episode of sea-level rise and environmental improvement—that is, the onset of the Holocene following the Devensian glaciation—that was considered to be of real archaeological consequence in the North Sea. In other words, attention has focused on the North Sea as a lost land of the Mesolithic, envisaged as "Doggerland" by Coles (1998). Processes associated with the Devensian glaciation were considered likely to have heavily reworked evidence from earlier periods, so that although the presence of pre-Devensian artifacts could not be ruled out, their archaeological value would have diminished greatly (although not entirely; see Hosfield 2007).

The period after the Last Glacial Maximum saw a general process of sea-level rise and climatic amelioration—interrupted by the 1,000-year "blip" of deterioration in the Loch Lomond Stadial—enabling populations of modern humans to rein-habit Britain from the Continent beginning around 13,500 years ago. Broadly, the post-LGM period can be regarded as a progression from low sea level and tun-dralike conditions, to a verdant, temperate landscape associated with fine-grained, organic, and peaty sediment sequences. This attractive environment was subse-quently inundated as sea level rose, although the changing relation between land and sea varied across the region due to the complex interplay of factors such as postglacial rebound and tectonics. Human artifacts associated with this progression can be expected to be found in situ as well as in derived contexts, and exhibit differ-ences in assemblages across the period. The reason for these differences in artifact assemblages may be a combination of functional, environmental, geographic, and cultural factors. Their relation to assemblages on the other side of the English Channel and the North Sea is also a source of debate. The reinhabitation of Britain around 13,500 years ago is marked by Creswellian assemblages that appear to be a distinct variation of the late Magdalenian assemblages that characterize much of western Europe at the time (Barton et al. 2003). The Final Paleolithic in Britain, up to the Loch Lomond Stadial about 12,800 years ago, includes assemblages such as those found at the densely used site at Hengistbury on the south coast of England that are comparable to Federmesser assemblages on the Continent (Conneller and Ellis 2007). Assemblages from the very start of the Holocene, following the end of the Loch Lomond Stadial around 11,500 years ago, are characterized as belonging to Long Blade/Bruised Blade industries. To conclude this overview, the start of the early Mesolithic about 11,300 years ago is marked by changes in artifacts in response to the increasingly wooded environment and changing fauna (Cooper 2006).

In encapsulating the potential of post-LGM submerged prehistory in the North Sea as "Doggerland," Coles (1998) stimulated attention to material that was long known but nebulous. Her article underlined the possible role of the North Sea as a place inhabited in its own right rather than merely as a "land bridge" for those just passing through, and considered the influence of such a land on processes of cul-tural change from Mesolithic to Neolithic. New discoveries, technological advances, administrative changes, industrial pressures, and the injection of major funding (see below) have added momentum to the exploration of "Doggerland," and there is a growing and highly relevant literature for students of North Sea prehistory (Coles 1998; Gaffney, Thomson, and S. Fitch 2007; Gaffney, Fitch, and Smith 2009; Hazell 2008; Waddington 2007; Waddington and Pedersen 2007; Ward, Larcombe, and Lillie 2006; Ward and Larcombe 2008).

"Doggerland" takes its name from the Dogger Bank, a shallow area of the North Sea toward Denmark at about the same latitude as Yorkshire in northeast England. However, as a concept concerned with inhabitation and cultural change, Dogger-land has a much wider extent, encompassing all of the area that would have been available to late Upper Paleolithic and Mesolithic people between the Continent and Britain, including the English Channel and most of the North Sea (Coles 1998: figs. 9, 10). Key discoveries have come largely from the southern North Sea, but relevant material has also been found to the east of Shetland, hundreds of kilome-ters to the north (Long, Wickham-Jones, and Ruckley 1986). Given such extents, it is unsurprising that the different provinces of Doggerland will have had different histories—certainly in terms of the physical processes they experienced. Areas of North Doggerland, from the Dogger Bank northward, will have been more directly affected by Devensian ice, whereas South Doggerland, from the English Channel through to the broad band of the southern North Sea between East Anglia and the Dutch and German coasts, would have remained ice-free. In the course of Doggerland's history, from the LGM 18,000 years ago to the sea approaching its current level about 6,000 years ago, other physical factors such as drainage, topography, sedimentation, flora, and fauna would have varied in time and space. Doggerland requires differentiation in physical terms, therefore, and—for fear of imposing today's nationalistic prejudices—such differentiation needs also to anticipate cultural diversity within the land we are imagining.

Undoubtedly, detailing the histories of Doggerland will continue to be a highly important and productive avenue for many years to come. However, it is also clear now that there is evidence underwater on which the story of the vast span of human history prior to the LGM in the North Sea can be based.

Before Doggerland

Recent discoveries such as the Area 240 hand axes suggest that not all pre-Devensian artifacts from the North Sea have been repeatedly redeposited. It appears that there are instances where fine-grained material and/or artifacts in near-primary contexts have survived subsequent glacial periods. It is possible, therefore, to encounter stratigraphic sequences which provide relative dates for deposits attributable to the four phases outlined above but which float in absolute terms because they cannot be assumed to be post-Devensian in date. Although introducing additional complications, we stand to gain considerable insights into very early periods of prehistory by accessing paleoenvironmentally rich, waterlogged, fine-grained, in situ sequences, containing organic artifacts as well as worked flint. There is every chance that prehistory in the North Sea could fundamentally change the basis for understanding the earliest inhabitants of this part of the globe.

The pre-LGM story comprises the Lower Paleolithic, the Middle Paleolithic, and the early Upper Paleolithic. The Lower Paleolithic (which began around 700,000 years ago) encompasses the earliest forms of human activity during a series of interglacial and glacial stages (MIS 17; MIS 16; MIS 15–13 [Cromerian]; MIS 11 [Hoxnian]; MIS 9), but also major glacial stages for which there is currently no evidence of human presence (MIS 12 [Anglian]; MIS 10). The Lower Paleolithic includes our earliest predecessors (whose species is as yet unknown) and *Homo heidelbergensis*, whose remains were found at the 500,000-year-old site at Boxgrove, in Sussex. Direct evidence for human activity generally consists of tools made from flint and other suitable stone, with rare but highly significant discoveries of human remains. Tool assemblages have been characterized as Mode 1, comprising tools made from flakes, and Mode 2, which are assemblages that include hand axes. Mode 1 equates to "Clactonian" and Mode 2 to "Achuelian," but the two different types of assemblages both are present throughout the Lower Paleolithic and later and are not considered to represent different periods or distinctive peoples (Wymer 1999: 6–12).

The addition of Levallois (also known as prepared core, Mode 3, or Mousterian) toolmaking techniques to the existing technologies marks the start of the Middle Paleolithic around 300,000 years ago, at the turn from MIS 9 (Purfleet Interglacial) to MIS 8 (glacial) (Schreve et al. 2007). The Middle Paleolithic reflects the emergence of Neanderthal populations, though for long periods they seem to have been confined to Continental Europe. Sites in Britain are known from both MIS 8 (glacial) and MIS 7 (Averley Interglacial), but there appears to be a long period of human absence from 175,000 to 60,000 years ago, encompassing not only glacial stage MIS 6 but also favorable conditions in interglacial stage MIS 5 (Stringer 2006: 103–112).

Neanderthals returned to Britain around 60,000 years ago, toward the end of glacial stage MIS 4, within the Devensian period, creating hand-axe-rich assemblages that include characteristic *bout coupé* hand axes. From around 30,000 years ago there is also evidence for early modern humans (Cro-Magnon) with distinctive industries (Leaf Point, Aurignacian, and Gravettian; see Jacobi 2007), marking the start of the Upper Paleolithic. While there is evidence that Neanderthals in Britain overlapped with modern humans, Neanderthals appear to have become extinct as the climate worsened; Britain was inhabited to about 25,000 years ago, but further climatic deterioration leading up to the LGM seems to have driven people out of the region and into more temperate refuges on the Continent until their post-LGM return (Stringer 2006: 132–133).

THE NORTH SEA

Cultural affinities with Continental Europe, temporal patterns in human presence and absence, and the changing availability of lands that are now submerged all point to the North Sea and English Channel as having a direct relevance to pre-LGM prehistory as well as to the story of Mesolithic Doggerland. The North Sea not only has a long human history; it is also very extensive geographically. It is only semi-enclosed: to the north it simply opens out between Scotland and Norway; in the east it connects to the Baltic; and it links to the Atlantic in the west through the English Channel. Its articulation with these other basins, and the areas that surround them, is an important characteristic of the North Sea. These water-based links are yet more profound when considering the major rivers that flow into the North Sea. As indicated above, such rivers played a major role not only in the formation of prehistoric deposits that are now submerged, but also in the patterning of human activity. These physical links are important because it is reasonable to assume that at various times in prehistory the North Sea has been less of a distinct region than a major meeting point, with a catchment that encompasses much of northern and western Europe.

In addition to being very well connected, the North Sea is quite shallow and has very gentle relief. With the exception of various deeps (which may themselves have been formed relatively recently), the southern North Sea is typically less than 50–70 m deep. During major glacial episodes, when sea level may have been over 100 m lower than today, the entire area of the North Sea would have been land, with properly marine conditions hundreds of miles distant in the Western Approaches of the English Channel and in the Norwegian Trench. Even during intermediate periods, at the onset of glacial conditions or during the return to temperate interglacials, sea levels lower than 30–40 m, which would have occurred over tens of thousands of years, would have made much of the southern North Sea available for inhabitation.

Early prehistoric archaeology is transnational in outlook; the relative sparseness of sites—especially sites with primary contexts—means that researchers draw data and inferences from across northwestern Europe and beyond. Many of the research questions relate to very large areas—the processes by which our predecessors came to be in northwest Europe; their relation to human evolution; how technologies are related; how the environment changed—are all problems with large geographical scope. An understanding of the prehistory of areas and catchments adjacent to the North Sea is essential, and not only because discoveries underwater are as yet so very rare. As a frame of reference, the whole of northwestern Europe—both wet and dry—is more appropriate than simply what currently lies underwater. Equally, knowing what happened in lands that are now beneath the North Sea is clearly crucial for archaeologists more familiar with the terrestrial record. Many research questions turn on the articulation between Britain and the Continent, and the North Sea may well be the arena in which major events were played out. For all we currently know, early prehistoric sites found on present-day land may be but pale reflections and distant echoes of the main action, at places that are now submerged.

Geography was undoubtedly a factor in whatever actions took place in the lands beneath the North Sea. As noted above, the relief is generally slight, but the environmental processes taking place were at times immense. The seabed should not be regarded as a passive stage, revealed in today's contours as if by pulling the plug out of the basin. As researchers are already demonstrating, the North Sea in prehistory is better understood as a sequence of places—located in time and space, having specific environmental characteristics (topography; flora; fauna), and inhabited by people for whom the locality had meaning (Barton et al. 1995; Mithen 2004; Pannett 2007). In some cases fragments of these places may be extensive, abutting each other at roughly the same time, but in other cases there is time-depth, where chronologically distinct places lie stratified one upon another.

Given the slight relief, relatively minor variations in topography may have been significant. It is reasonable to assume that watercourses and their catchments had a strong structuring effect, but the structuring effect may have been different from period to period. With such low-lying landscapes, it seems likely that the "break in slope" more or less coinciding with today's coastline may also have been important, especially where there were high erosion-resistant cliffs. Even allowing for erosion over tens and hundreds of thousands of years, early prehistoric material associated with today's coastal cliffs should be considered in the light of contemporary topographies that may have encompassed extensive plains that are now beneath the sea.

In addition to local and perhaps regional geographic influences, there are some gross factors that undoubtedly have an effect on how North Sea prehistory is to be interpreted. One of the most significant questions concerns the breaching of the English Channel. At the time of the earliest inhabitation of the North Sea, there was an intact upland (the Weald-Artois ridge) encompassing southeastern England and the near Continent, resulting from the upward folding of geological strata over 15 million years ago and revealed in section on both sides of the Straits of Dover, most obviously in the white chalk cliffs of Dover and Cape Blanc Nez. To the north of this upland, the North Sea formed a basin into which flowed many of the rivers draining England, northern and eastern France, the Low Countries, and Germany; these rivers included the Thames, Scheldt, Meuse, Humber, Rhine, Ems, Weser, and Elbe. To the south of the upland was the basin of the English Channel, into which flowed the rivers of central and northern France (Authie, Somme, Bresle, Seine) and southern England (Ouse, Adur, Arun, Solent, Hampshire Avon).

While this upland was intact, the North Sea basin—during interglacial periods—would have drained to the north, between Scotland and Norway, but during glacial periods this route was blocked by ice, and a large lake formed. This lake overtopped the Weald-Artois upland, causing massive erosion that cut a gorge between Dover and Calais and a major paleo-valley down through the English Channel to the Atlantic. At times of higher sea level, as today, the top of this valley forms the Straits of Dover.

The form and timing of the overtopping and creation of the Straits of Dover and Channel paleo-valley has been disputed, but recent work indicates that the first, catastrophic breach occurred during the Anglian glaciation (MIS 12) (Gupta et al. 2007; Toucanne, Zaragosi, Bourillet, Cremer et al. 2009a; Toucanne, Zaragosi, Bourillet, Gibbard et al. 2009b). Prior to the Anglian glaciations, the rivers in the North Sea catchment, such as the Thames and Rhine, drained northward, whereas in the later glaciations the North Sea rivers ran through the Straits of Dover to add to the catchment of the English Channel river flowing southwest. Augmented by these previously north-flowing rivers, the English Channel river would at times have been colossal, draining the ice sheets from the whole of northwestern Europe. Its presumed force may have rendered it impassable, contributing to the scarcity or absence of humans in Britain in the later part of the Middle Paleolithic (Stringer 2006: 107–108). The relationship between the English Channel and the North Sea is a further caution against considering the North Sea in isolation.

Humans were not the only things that ebbed and flowed through the North Sea region: large and small animals, birds, fish, marine mammals, invertebrates, and different forms of plant life moved too as conditions changed. These changes are subjects of study in their own right, but they also provide proxies for understanding the environments in which people lived, and they count among the resources upon which people may have drawn (Mol et al. 2008).

The characteristics of watercourses such as rivers, lakes, and sea, both as barriers and as resource-rich conduits, warrant particular attention. They are likely to have been the most affected by sea-level rise as the climate ameliorated in each interglacial. As has been pointed out with respect to more or less every factor in this chapter, the pace, consequences, and causality of the relationship between sea-level rise and human inhabitation is not usually known, but it should be borne in mind that trends discernable in the relatively long term are likely to have been accompanied by episodic changes in tides, storminess, erosion, and flooding.

Motives and Mechanisms

Given the enormous complexity of prehistory in the North Sea and, at present, the very small number of known archaeological sites, why has there been such a rapid growth in interest? Undoubtedly there are some big, beguiling prizes; each discovery is likely to make a significant and widely relevant contribution to knowledge, both in archaeology and in other disciplines relating to quaternary science and climate change. Recent technological developments are also having a big effect, especially with respect to data quality, position-fixing, processing, and presentation. But the biggest factor bringing attention—and especially resources—to bear on North Sea prehistory has been the motivation to better manage the archaeological resource that is thought to be present, especially in the context of perceived pressure from industrial activities.

Concern about the impacts of marine development on prehistoric archaeology has been central to the emergence of archaeology within the Environmental Impact Assessment (EIA) process in the United Kingdom. In particular, state archaeologists in local government raised concerns in the mid- to late 1990s about the effects of marine aggregate dredging on prehistoric material off the Isle of Wight and Sussex in the English Channel. The aggregate industry responded positively, both at the company level and through the industry's trade body, the British Marine Aggregate Producers Association (BMAPA), to the specific issues and to more general concerns (Russell and Firth 2007).

The next steps were led by aggregate companies on individual site-specific EIA studies and by BMAPA through strategic studies (e.g., Wenban-Smith 2002). BMAPA also initiated the development of guidance, published with English Heritage in April 2003, that gave full weight to the consideration of prehistoric material (BMAPA and English Heritage 2003). BMAPA went on to initiate a Protocol for Reporting Finds of Archaeological Interest, which has applied to all BMAPA companies since August 2005 (BMAPA and English Heritage 2005). It was this protocol that enabled swift communication and action in regard to the artifacts discovered by Mr. Meulemeester.

Consideration of early prehistory also featured in regional studies such as the Bristol Channel Marine Aggregates: Resources and Constraints project (Posford Haskoning and ABP Research and Consultancy 2000) and in the East Channel Regional Environmental Assessment (REA) (Posford Haskoning 2002). Although sponsored by industry rather than by government, the East Channel REA anticipated the introduction of the Strategic Environmental Assessment (SEA Directive), which requires public authorities to consider the impacts of their plans on, among other things, the archaeological heritage. The aggregate industry's REA program— now encompassing the South Coast, Thames, East Anglia, and Humber—has been the principal driver for the recent acquisition and archaeological interpretation of high-quality regional-scale geophysical and geotechnical data.

While marine aggregate dredging has played a central role in addressing prehistoric archaeology, it is interwoven with other important strands. Systematic fieldwork in coastal wetlands and especially intertidal areas in the Severn (Rippon 2001), Scilly (Ratcliffe and Straker 1996) Solent (Allen and Gardiner 2000), Essex (Wilkinson and Murphy 1995), and Humber (Van de Noort and Ellis 1995) in the 1980s and 1990s demonstrated the presence of prehistoric material at and below today's sea level, stretching back to the Mesolithic and including organic remains and paleo-environmental data that enabled interdisciplinary collaboration with sea-level scientists (Long and Roberts 1997). Development-led investigations of deep alluvial sequences beneath reclaimed coastal land established that significant material could be investigated well below sea level, especially by integrating archaeological investigations with the geotechnical investigations that developers were carrying out for engineering purposes (Bates and Barham 1995; Barham et al. 1995; Firth 2000; Sidell et al. 2000). The project's scope—investigating relevant deposits in intertidal areas and in deep sequences beneath reclaimed land—was extended to fully submerged sites by studies at Bouldnor Cliff, which had been surveyed by archaeologists in the 1980s but gained far greater significance through the discovery by divers of Mesolithic flint tools at about 11.5 m below Ordnance Datum in 1999 (Momber 2000). Studies by Wessex Archaeology for the EIA for an unsuccessful port proposal—Dibden Terminal—in Southampton Water enabled the close integration of different forms of desk-based, geophysical, geotechnical, and diver-based investigations to address not only the post-LGM sequence but also the underlying gravel terraces of the paleo-Solent, which have an important history of Paleolithic research (Wessex Archaeology 2000).

While there were many strands of relevant investigation on the UK side of the North Sea pointing to its potential for prehistoric archaeology, proof had to be sought from the Continental side—especially Denmark and the Netherlands— in the form of investigations of the sort showcased in *Man and Sea in the Mesolithic* (Fischer 1995). The sense that the potential on the UK side was as yet unrealized in the mid-1990s is underlined, perhaps, by the fact that in *Man and Sea in the Mesolithic* the only papers focusing on Britain were concerned with

Scotland's Atlantic coast. As noted above, Coles's 1998 review of older investigations in light of more recent sea-level studies provided a welcome rallying point and the new term "Doggerland," against which investigations of North Sea prehistory could be framed.

Additional awareness was generated by the inclusion of thematic reports on prehistory as part of the UK Department of Trade and Industry's SEA program, accompanying plans for future oil and gas exploitation (e.g., Flemming 2002). In turn, this led to a transnational conference on submerged prehistory in London in May 2003, subsequently published as *Submarine Prehistoric Archaeology of the North Sea* (Flemming 2004). A key objective of the conference had been to encourage cross-border collaboration, which has come to fruition through the development of the North Sea Prehistory Research and Management Framework (NSPRMF) (Peeters, Murphy, and Flemming 2009).

From 2002, the preparation of Environmental Impact Assessments and subsequent surveys prior to and during construction of offshore wind farms (COWRIE 2007) has introduced another strand into the investigation of North Sea prehistory. Large volumes of high-quality geophysical data have been examined by archaeologists, and archaeological assessment, analysis, and scientific dating of samples from cores is becoming accepted practice. Importantly, offshore wind farms generally require foundations that are piled deeply down to tertiary bedrock, so investigations are required to address extensive sequences many meters in length, well beyond the range normally considered for ports, cables, or aggregates.

It is marine aggregate dredging, however, that has continued to provide the most important underpinning to North Sea prehistory, especially following the introduction of the Aggregate Levy Sustainability Fund (ALSF). The Aggregate Levy is a tax on primary aggregate production that, by making aggregate more expensive, is intended to encourage more careful use. Part of the revenue from the tax is directed back into applied research through the ALSF, which has been used to fund a wide range of different types of project intended to improve overall sustainability. Since 2002, when the ALSF was introduced, very substantial sums have been directed to research relating to seabed prehistory, encouraging a surge of research interest in prehistory offshore, including the North Sea (Bates, Bates, and Dix 2009; Gaffney, Thomson, and Fitch 2007; Gaffney, Fitch, and Smith 2009; Gupta et al. 2004; Newell and Garner 2007; Plets et al. 2007; Wessex Archaeology 2008b; Westley, Dix, and Quinn 2004). The ALSF is currently funding a series of Regional Environmental Characterization (REC) surveys, focusing on the REA areas referred to above, which are resulting in extensive geophysical and geotechnical datasets that are being interpreted archaeologically to shed further light on submerged prehistory in the English Channel and North Sea (Newell and Measures 2008).

In the preceding paragraphs it has been implicit that the principal means of managing prehistoric archaeology on the seabed has been through investigations and research that are closely tied to development pressures, rather than through designation of sites using heritage legislation. This seems likely to continue in the United Kingdom at least, although in Scottish waters the limitations in the framework for statutory protection for early prehistoric sites are now being overcome by the Marine (Scotland) Act 2010.

SOME QUESTIONS

Notwithstanding advances in the use of acoustic survey methods, the prospect of being able to "eyeball" the bed of the North Sea over any more than a few square meters at a time is likely to remain beyond our capabilities. Even the apparently simple demand of being able to know—within a few square meters—where prehistoric archaeological material might be present is a very significant objective. The attempt to reach such a simple end entails layer upon layer of complexity, the pursuit of which invites a series of investigative questions:

- How can prehistoric material be observed by archaeologists on and within the seabed?
- How has prehistoric material been affected by human activities over the last two millennia?
- How has archaeological material been eroded, reworked, and redeposited by glacial, periglacial, terrestrial, coastal, and marine processes through successive climatic cycles?
- How did particular locations come to be chosen for activities that resulted in archaeological traces being left behind?
- How did people inhabit the lands of the North Sea at different times and in different places?

The questions might also be regarded—in reverse—as a series of filters: people have to have been present in the region; material has to have been left as a result of human activity; the material will have been affected by natural postdepositional processes; the material may then have been affected by human activities at sea; and the material—having been subject to these processes—has to be visible to available methods. Favorable circumstances are needed at each level for archaeological material to come to the attention of archaeologists; but equally, the rarity of discoveries to date need not imply that these filters have conspired against the survival of significant material, only that our capabilities and understanding are still very limited.

As many of the authors cited above demonstrate, each of these questions is a research area in its own right, warranting specialized consideration that could usefully exhaust at least a decade of dedicated research. Moreover, each of these research areas is not only a concern of archaeologists; other scientists too—geologists, geophysicists, engineers, climate scientists, and so on—are actively investigating these areas for their own purposes. The insights they generate are valuable, but the research agendas of other sciences will not necessarily lead in the overall direction that archaeologists might want to take.

Despite the apparent convenience of dealing with each research question discretely, especially where there is another science within which to embed, it is better not to treat these questions as separable; the primary and fundamentally archaeological question of human habitation in the area of the North Sea has to be held in mind at every stage, and the pursuit of each question should test and inform pursuit of the others.

Returning to the artifacts from Area 240, Wessex Archaeology has embarked on a series of investigations funded by the ALSF. We hope to refine methods that will enable us to observe the source of the artifacts on the seabed and to relate it to its surroundings through a combination of techniques, making best use of existing geophysical and geotechnical data from industry and carrying out intensive sub-bottom surveys, which are themselves nested within regional surveys currently under way. We hope to confirm the presence and location of artifactual material by adopting benthic sampling techniques used by marine ecologists and geologists. If a sufficiently localized site is found, this work will be supplemented by coring of the sedimentary sequence or by diver-based observations, followed by a program of analysis and scientific dating. These investigations should help clarify how prehistoric material can best be observed on the seabed by archaeologists.

While the primary focus of the planned investigations is methodological, we expect to recover a suite of data that will enable us to address some of the other questions set out above. We already know that the Area 240 artifacts have been impacted by aggregate dredging; this was how they came to be discovered. Evidence from the artifacts themselves and from geophysical investigations should indicate whether they have, until now, remained relatively undisturbed by earlier marine activities, such as previous aggregate dredging or decades of trawling. Aside from the relatively few documented instances of prehistoric archaeological material being recovered by dredgers or in trawls, there is little evidence upon which to base estimates of human impacts on prehistoric resources in the North Sea—what proportion might have already been destroyed, and what proportion might yet survive. It is clear that human pressures will continue and even grow, though increasing awareness, capability, and provision in marine management should mean that future impacts can be properly assessed and mitigated.

The Area 240 artifacts are already shedding light on the climate-driven processes that tend to overwrite the human patterning of original deposition in the North Sea. As indicated above, at least some of the artifacts appear to be little disturbed, despite having been through at least one major glacial cycle. It is hoped that geophysical and geotechnical data obtained at local and regional scales will help reveal the sequence of processes that the site has undergone, not only informing investigation of this particular site but providing clues as to the processes and possible survival of artifactual material at other North Sea locations.

If it can be established that at least some of the artifacts reflect some form of original patterning rather than being aggregated by postdepositional processes, then it should be possible to draw some inferences about why that particular place was favored, and perhaps what kinds of activities took place there. The apparent juxtaposition with faunal remains may be significant, especially if some kind of relationship can be found between them, such as cut-marks on bones or other signs of processing or use. The apparent presence of fine-grained deposits is tantalizing too, because of the potential survival of paleo-environmental indicators such as the microscopic remains of plants and insects, pollen, and plankton. If relationships between all these elements can be confirmed, then it should be possible to provide a reasonably detailed picture of the artifact site as a place of human activity, perhaps at different times and in different environmental conditions.

Success in characterizing a place where prehistoric people were active will bring us a step closer toward conclusions about how the North Sea was inhabited in the past. Comparisons with other places and evidence—whether through scientific dating, sedimentary architecture, or comparable artifacts—will enable researchers to build Mr. Meulemeester's discovery into overarching narratives of early prehistoric inhabitation of northwestern Europe. Where the discovery will fit in this narrative and what it means overall will take some time to unfold, and in due course, even more extraordinary discoveries will be made.

POSTSCRIPT

Since this chapter was drafted, Wessex Archaeology has carried out detailed investigations in Area 240 and the wider region and has recovered further artifactual material (Tizzard, Baggaley, and Firth in press). Further work to understand the dates and environmental contexts of these deposits is currently under way.

ACKNOWLEDGMENTS

I would like to acknowledge Jan Meeulemester and the staff of Hanson Aggregates Marine Limited, the British Marine Aggregate Producers Association, English Heritage, and the Netherlands cultural heritage agency for their respective roles in bringing the artifacts from Area 240 to everyone's attention. Investigations in the area where the artifacts were found have been funded through the Aggregate Levy Sustainability Fund (ALSF) administered by English Heritage and the Marine Environment Protection Fund. I would also like to thank Louise Tizzard, Julie Gardiner, and Ingrid Ward for comments on early versions of this chapter, and the editors for their constructive criticism and patience.

REFERENCES

Allen, M. J., and J. Gardiner. 2000. *Our changing coast: A survey of the intertidal archaeology of Langstone Harbour, Hampshire.* CBA Research Report 124. York: Council for British Archaeology.

Antoine, P., J.-P. Coutard, P. Gibbard, B. Hallegouet, J.-P. Lautridou, and J.-C. Ozouf. 2003. The Pleistocene rivers of the English Channel. *Journal of Quaternary Science* 18 (3–4): 227–243.

Ballantyne, C. K. 2004. After the Ice: Paraglacial and post-glacial evolution of the physical environment of Scotland, 20,000 to 5000 BP. In *Mesolithic Scotland and its neighbours: The early Holocene prehistory of Scotland, its British and Irish context, and some northern European perspectives,* ed. A. Saville, 27–43. Edinburgh: Society of Antiquaries of Scotland.

Barham, A. J., M. R. Bates, C. A. Pine, and V. D. Williamson. 1995. Holocene development of the Lower Medway Valley and prehistoric occupation of the floodplain area. In *The Quaternary of the lower reaches of the Thames,* ed. D. R. Bridgland, P. Allen, and B. A. Haggart, 339–350. Durham: Quaternary Research Association.

Barton, R. N. E., P. J. Berridge, M. J. C. Walker, and R. E. Bevins. 1995. Persistent places in the Mesolithic landscape: An example from the Black Mountain uplands of South Wales. *Proceedings of the Prehistoric Society* 61: 81–116.

Barton, R. N. E., R. M. Jacobi, D. Stapert, and M. J. Street. 2003. The late-glacial reoccupation of the British Isles and the Creswellian. *Journal of Quaternary Science* 18 (7): 631–643.

Bates, M., and A. J. Barham. 1995. Holocene alluvial stratigraphic architecture and archaeology in the Lower Thames area. In *The Quaternary of the lower reaches of the Thames,* ed. D. R. Bridgland, P. Allen, and B. A. Haggart, 85–98. Durham: Quaternary Research Association.

Bates, R., M. Bates, and J. Dix. 2009. Contiguous palaeo-landscape reconstruction: Transition zone mapping for marine-terrestrial archaeological continuity. Online at http://ads.ahds.ac.uk/catalogue/archive/cplr_eh_2009/downloads.cfm/. Accessed 21 March 2010.

Bellamy, A. G. 1995. Extension of the British landmass: Evidence from shelf sediment bodies in the English Channel. In *Island Britain: A Quaternary perspective,* ed. R. C. Preece, 47–62. Geological Society Special Publication No. 96. London: Geological Society.

———. 1998. The UK marine sand and gravel dredging industry: An application of Quaternary geology. In *Advances in aggregates and armourstone evaluation,* ed. J.-P. Latham, 33–45. Engineering Geology Special Publication No. 13. London: Geological Society.

BMAPA (British Marine Aggregate Producers Association) and English Heritage. 2003. *Marine aggregate dredging and the historic environment: Guidance note.* London: British Marine Aggregate Producers Association and English Heritage.

———. 2005. *Protocol for reporting finds of archaeological interest.* London: British Marine Aggregate Producers Association and English Heritage.

Bridgland, D. R. 1994. *Quaternary of the Thames.* Geological Conservation Review. London: Chapman and Hall.

———. 1996. Quaternary river terrace deposits as a framework for the Lower Palaeolithic record. In *The English Palaeolithic reviewed: Papers from a day conference held at the*

Society of Antiquaries of London, 28 October 1994, ed. C. Gamble and A. J. Lawson, 23–39. Salisbury: Trust for Wessex Archaeology.

Coles, B. J. 1998. Doggerland: A speculative survey. *Proceedings of the Prehistoric Society* 64: 45–81.

Conneller, C., and C. Ellis. 2007. A final Upper Palaeolithic site at La Sagesse Convent, Romsey, Hampshire. *Proceedings of the Prehistoric Society* 73: 191–227.

Cooper, L. P. 2006. Launde, a Terminal Palaeolithic camp-site in the English Midlands and its North European context. *Proceedings of the Prehistoric Society* 72: 53–93.

COWRIE. 2007. *Historic environment guidance for the renewable energy sector*. Newbury: COWRIE.

Firth, A. 2000. Development-led archaeology in coastal environments: Investigations at Queenborough, Motney Hill and Gravesend in Kent, UK. In *Coastal and estuarine environments: Sedimentology, geomorphology and geoarchaeology*, ed. K. Pye and J. R. L. Allen, 403–417. Geological Society Special Publication No. 175. London: Geological Society.

———. 2006. Marine aggregates and prehistory. In *Underwater cultural heritage at risk: Managing natural and human impacts*, ed. R. Grenier, D. Nutley, and I. Cochran, 8–10. Paris: ICOMOS.

Fischer, A., ed. 1995. *Man and sea in the Mesolithic: Coastal settlement above and below present sea level*. Oxbow Monograph 53. Oxford: Oxbow.

Flemming, N. C. 2002. The scope of strategic environmental assessment of North Sea areas SEA3 and SEA2 in regard to prehistoric archaeological remains. Rev. 2002. Online at www.offshore-sea.org.uk/consultations/SEA_3/TR_SEA3_Archaeology.pdf/. Accessed 21 March 2010.

———, ed. 2004. *Submarine prehistoric archaeology of the North Sea: Research priorities and collaboration with industry*. CBA Research Report 141. York: Council for British Archaeology.

Gaffney, V., S. Fitch, and D. Smith. 2009. *Europe's lost world: The rediscovery of Doggerland*. CBA Research Report 160. York: Council for British Archaeology.

Gaffney, V., K. Thomson, and S. Fitch. 2007. *Mapping Doggerland: The Mesolithic landscapes of the southern North Sea*. Oxford: Archaeopress.

Gupta, S., J. Collier, A. Palmer-Felgate, J. Dickinson, K. Bushe, and S. Humber. 2004. Submerged Palaeo-Arun River: Reconstruction of prehistoric landscapes and evaluation of archaeological research potential. Unpublished report for English Heritage (ALSF 3277/3543). Online at http://ads.ahds.ac.uk/catalogue/archive/palaeoarun_eh_2007/downloads.cfm/. Accessed 21 March 2010.

Gupta, S., J. S. Collier, A. Palmer-Felgate, and G. Potter. 2007. Catastrophic flooding origin of shelf valley systems in the English Channel. *Nature* 448: 342–346.

Hazell, Z. J. 2008. Offshore and intertidal peat deposits, England: A resource assessment and development of a database. *Environmental Archaeology* 13 (2): 101–110.

Hosfield, R. 2007. Terrestrial implications for the maritime geoarchaeological resource: A view from the Lower Palaeolithic. *Journal of Maritime Archaeology* 2 (1): 4–23.

Jacobi, R. 2007. A collection of early Upper Palaeolithic artefacts from Beedings, near Pulborough, West Sussex, and the context of similar finds from the British Isles. *Proceedings of the Prehistoric Society* 73: 229–325.

Kelley, J. T., J. A. G. Cooper, D. W. T. Jackson, D. F. Belknap, and R. J. Quinn. 2006. Sea-level change and inner shelf stratigraphy off Northern Ireland. *Marine Geology* 232: 1–15.

Lang, A. T. O., and D. H. Keen. 2005. Hominid colonisation and the Lower and Middle Palaeolithic of the West Midlands. *Proceedings of the Prehistoric Society* 71: 63–83.

Long, A. J., and D. H. Roberts. 1997. Sea-level change. In *England's coastal heritage: A survey for English Heritage and the RCHME*, ed. M. Fulford, T. Champion, and A. Long, 25–49. Archaeological Report 15. London: English Heritage.

Long, D., C. R. Wickham-Jones, and N. A. Ruckley. 1986. A flint artefact from the northern North Sea. In *Studies in the Upper Palaeolithic of Britain and North West Europe*, ed. D. A. Roe, 55–62. BAR International Series 296. Oxford: British Archaeological Reports.

Mithen, S. 2004. The "Mesolithic experience" in Scotland. In *Mesolithic Scotland and its neighbours: The early Holocene prehistory of Scotland, its British and Irish context, and some northern European perspectives*, ed. A. Saville, 246–260. Edinburgh: Society of Antiquaries of Scotland.

Mol, D., J. De Vos, R. Bakkar, B. Van Geel, J. Glimmerveen, H. Van Der Plicht, and K. Post. 2008. *Kleine Encyclopedie van het leven in het Pleistoceen: Mammoeten, Neushoorns en andere Dieren van de Noordzeebodem* (Little encyclopedia of living in the Pleistocene: Mammoths, rhinoceroses and other animals of the North Sea floor). Diemen, the Netherlands: Veen Magazines.

Momber, G. 2000. Drowned and deserted: A submerged prehistoric landscape in the Solent, England. *International Journal of Nautical Archaeology* 29 (1): 86–99.

Murphy, P. 2007. The submerged prehistoric landscapes of the southern North Sea: Work in progress. *Landscapes* 8 (1): 1–22.

Newell, R. C., and D. J. Garner. 2007. *Marine aggregate extraction: Helping to determine good practice*. Lowestoft, UK: Marine ALSF c/o Cefas.

Newell, R. C., and J. Measures. 2008. *Marine Aggregate Levy Sustainability Fund (MALSF) Science Review 2008*. Lowestoft, UK: ALSF-MEPF.

Pannett, A. 2007. A Post-processual flight of fancy? Microlith production and enculturation of landscape in the Mesolithic of Caithness. In *Mesolithic studies in the North Sea Basin and beyond: Proceedings of a conference held at Newcastle in 2003*, ed. C. Waddington and K. Pedersen, 151–158. Oxford: Oxbow.

Parfitt, S. A., et al. 2005. The earliest record of human activity in northern Europe. *Nature* 438: 1008–1012.

Peeters, H., P. Murphy, and N. Flemming. 2009. *North Sea Prehistory Research and Management Framework (NSPRMF) 2009*. Amersfoort, the Netherlands: Rijksdienst voor het Cultureel Erfgoed.

Plets, R., J. Dix, A. Batsos, and A. Best. 2007. Characterization of buried inundated peat on seismic (Chirp) data, inferred from core information. *Archaeological Prospection* 14: 261–272.

Posford Haskoning. 2002. East Channel: Regional environmental assessment. Unpublished report for East Channel Association.

Posford Haskoning and ABP Research and Consultancy. 2000. Bristol Channel marine aggregates: Resources and constraints. Unpublished report for the Welsh Assembly, Department for Environment, Transport and the Regions (DETR), and the Crown Estate.

Ratcliffe, J., and V. Straker. 1996. *The early environment of Scilly: Palaeoenvironmental assessment of cliff-face and intertidal deposits, 1989–1993*. Truro, UK: Cornwall Archaeological Unit.

Rippon, S., ed. 2001. *Estuarine archaeology: The Severn and beyond*. Archaeology in the Severn Estuary 11. Bristol: Severn Estuary Levels Research Committee (SELRC).

Russel, M., and A. Firth. 2007. *Working alongside the marine historic environment: An aggregate dredging industry perspective*. Rotterdam: CEDA Dredging Days.

Schreve, D., P. Harding, M. J. White, D. R. Bridgland, P. Allen, F. Clayton, D. H. Keen, and K. E. H. Penkman. 2007. A Levallois knapping site at West Thurrock, Lower Thames, UK: Its Quaternary context, environment and age. *Proceedings of the Prehistoric Society* 72: 21–52.

Sidell, J., K. Wilkinson, R. Scaife, and N. Cameron. 2000. *The Holocene evolution of the London Thames: Archaeological excavations (1991–1998) for the London Underground Limited Jubilee Line Extension Project*. MOLAS Monograph 5. London: Museum of London Archaeology Service.

Stringer, C. 2006. *Homo britannicus: The incredible story of human life in Britain*. London: Penguin.

Tizzard, L., P. A. Baggaley, and A. J. Firth. In press. Seabed prehistory: Investigating palaeo-landsurfaces associated with a Palaeolithic tool find, North Sea. In *Underwater archaeology and the submerged prehistory of Europe*, ed. J. Benjamin, C. Bonsall, C. Pickard, and A. Fischer. Oxford: Oxbow.

Toucanne, S., S. Zaragosi, J. F. Bourillet, M. Cremer, et al. 2009a. Timing of massive "Fleuve Manche" discharges over the last 350 kyr: Insights into the European ice-sheet oscillations and the European drainage network from MIS 10 to 2. *Quaternary Science Reviews* 2009: 1–19.

Toucanne, S., S. Zaragosi, J. F. Bourillet, P. L. Gibbard, et al. 2009b. A 1.2 Ma record of glaciation and fluvial discharge from the western European Atlantic margin. *Quaternary Science Reviews* 28: 2974–2981.

Van de Noort, R., and S. Ellis, eds. 1995. *Wetland heritage of Holderness: An archaeological survey*. Hull, UK: School of Geography and Earth Resources.

Waddington, C., ed. 2007. *Mesolithic settlement in the North Sea basin: A case study from Howick, North-East England*. Oxford: Oxbow.

Waddington, C., and K. Pedersen, eds. 2007. *Mesolithic studies in the North Sea Basin and beyond: Proceedings of a conference held at Newcastle in 2003*. Oxford: Oxbow.

Ward, I., and P. Larcombe. 2008. Determining the preservation rating of submerged archaeology in the post-glacial southern North Sea: A first-order geomorphological approach. *Environmental Archaeology* 13 (1): 59–83.

Ward, I., P. Larcombe, and M. Lillie. 2006. The dating of Doggerland: Post-glacial geochronology of the southern North Sea. *Environmental Archaeology* 11 (2): 207–218.

Wenban-Smith, F. 2002. *Palaeolithic and Mesolithic archaeology on the seabed: Marine aggregate dredging and the historic environment*. Salisbury: Wessex Archaeology.

Wessex Archaeology. 2000. Dibden Terminal Technical Statement: Archaeology Impact Assessment. TS/A1. Unpublished report.

———. 2008a. Seabed prehistory: Gauging the effects of marine aggregate dredging—final report. Vol. 7. Happisburgh and Pakefield exposures. Online at . www.scribd.com/doc/2989835/Vol-VII-HappisburghPakefield/. Accessed 21 March 2010.

———. 2008b. Seabed prehistory: Gauging the effects of marine aggregate dredging—final report. Vol. 8. Results and conclusions. Online at www.scribd.com/doc/2989799/Vol-VIII-Results/. Accessed 21 March 2010.

Westley, K., J. Dix, and R. Quinn. 2004. A re-assessment of the archaeological potential of continental shelves. Online at http://ads.ahds.ac.uk/catalogue/archive/continent-shelves_eh_2008/downloads.cfm/. Accessed 21 March 2010.

Wickham-Jones, C. R., and S. Dawson. 2006. The scope of Strategic Environmental Assessment of North Sea Area SEA7 with regard to prehistoric and early historic archaeological remains. Online at www.offshore-sea.org.uk/consultations/SEA_7/SEA7_PreArchaeology_CWJ.pdf/. Accessed 21 March 2010.

Wilkinson, T. J., and P. L. Murphy. 1995. *The archaeology of the Essex Coast*. Vol. 1, *The Hullbridge survey*. East Anglian Archaeology No. 71. Chelmsford: Essex County Council.

Wymer, J. 1999. *The Lower Palaeolithic occupation of Britain*. Salisbury: Wessex Archaeology.

CHAPTER 35

ANCIENT HARBORS IN THE MEDITERRANEAN

JOHN P. OLESON AND ROBERT L. HOHLFELDER

INTRODUCTION

By at least the Early Bronze Age it had become clear to the inhabitants of the Mediterranean region that travel and the transport of merchandise by sea offered several significant advantages over conveyance by land: ships and rafts could carry very heavy weights; under the right conditions the wind provided powerful, sustained propulsion; and the "pathless ways of the sea" required neither maintenance nor permission for passage. Nevertheless, potential seafarers first had to construct ships, which soon became the largest and most complex machines in the ancient world, and they had to master the many arts of navigation. Small boats can be launched from land, and beached upon arrival at their destination, as long as the beaches are not exposed to high waves. Throughout history, estuaries, river mouths, and protected coves facilitated these maneuvers, which were simplified by the absence of large tidal changes in the Mediterranean and the restriction of most major storms to the winter season.

At some point, however, most likely in the late third or early second millennium BCE, the obvious advantages of larger ships for long-distance trade triggered a search for ways to accommodate and protect a ship between voyages and during the loading or off-loading of cargo. We know nothing about the earliest stages of harbor design, and less than we would like about harbor design and construction during the Bronze Age, a period of intense maritime trade in the eastern Mediterranean. The archaeological and literary evidence is richer for Phoenician and Greek harbors of the eighth through fifth centuries BCE, and overwhelming for harbors of the Hellenistic through Roman Imperial periods. The evolution of harbor design was driven by the changing characteristics of the ships that used the facilities, the economic needs of the individuals and groups that constructed them, and changes in available tools and techniques. The symbiotic feedback between the economy and technology is particularly marked in the history of harbor construction.

Hundreds of harbor sites of varying sizes and designs can be documented around the Mediterranean during the 500 years of most intense trade in that area (200 BCE to 300 CE), and undoubtedly many smaller harbors have escaped detection (Flemming 1971: 27–33). The catalog published by Lehmann-Hartleben in the early twentieth century (1923: 240–287) includes 303 harbors, and most of these he identified only from ancient literary references. Subsequent archaeological research has added many more to the list. The majority of these sites were in use in earlier periods as well, to one degree or another. In consequence, this survey has to be very selective in its focus. We have chosen to present an outline of the development of harbor technology in the ancient Mediterranean, along with case studies of some particularly important or illuminating sites, accompanied by discussion of the special problems that confront the archaeologist investigating an ancient harbor site. The scope of the topic explains why so few useful general studies of ancient harbors have appeared since Lehman-Hartleben's magisterial survey: Blackman 1982, 2008b; Casson 1995: 361–370; de Souza 2000; Flemming 1971; Frost 1972, 1974, 1995; Lehmann-Hartleben 1926; Reddé 1986; Reddé and Golvin 2005; Rickman 1988, 2008; Rougé 1966: 107–171, 1974; Shaw 1972. A gazetteer of individual ancient harbors with the important bibliography can be found in Blackman 2008b: 664–665, and a collection of ancient sources regarding Greek and Roman harbors in Humphrey, Oleson, and Sherwood 1998: 471–481.

THE DEVELOPMENT OF ANCIENT HARBORS

Harbors of the Bronze Age

Relief sculpture and paintings (particularly in Egypt), some royal archives, and a few shipwrecks provide us with ample evidence for the intensity of trade by sea in the eastern Mediterranean during the Bronze Age (Wachsmann 1998), but the remains of the contemporary harbors are elusive (Blackman 1982: 90–93; Blue 1997; Casson 1995: 361–363; Frost 1972, 1974, 1995; Raban 1985, 1991; Shaw 1972: 88–90). Along high-energy coastlines, the typical harbor sites could be open bays, nearly enclosed bays, bays framing headlands, anchorages in the lee of a promontory, and offshore islands or reefs (Shaw 2006: 51–59). On low-energy, low-lying coasts, harbor sites might include river valleys, lakes associated with rivers, deltas, and lagoons (Flemming 1971). Unfortunately, the rise in relative sea level in the eastern

Mediterranean since the Bronze Age has obscured or destroyed many of the early harbor sites (Blue 1997; Marriner, Morange, and Saghled-Beyhoun 2008; Raban 1985). The earliest harbor remains so far documented may be those of the late third millennium at Lothal in India, outside the Mediterranean world, where a basin was excavated close to the city walls and lined with walls of baked clay and bitumen. Channels possibly intended for ships connected the basin with the Sabamati River and the Indian Ocean (Blackman 1982: 90–92; Shaw 1972: 89; cf. Leshnik 1968). Similar facilities were constructed slightly later within the walls of Ur, on the Euphrates, and by at least 1800 BCE along the Nile, at Thebes (Blackman 1982: 92; Kemp and O'Connor 1974). Large, slow-moving rivers provide a relatively safe refuge for ships, and the alluvial soil along their banks can easily be excavated to provide docking space away from the current (Kemp and O'Connor 1974). This is probably the type of installation shown on many Egyptian tomb reliefs. In the tomb of Kenamun at Thebes (c. 1375 BCE), a relief depicts personnel using stepped ramps to unload goods from Syro-Canaanite merchant ships moored bow-first to a platform or pavement (Wachsmann 1998: 42–60). Reliefs from the mortuary temple of Queen Hatshepsut at Deir el Bahri show Egyptian cargo ships loading goods at Punt (Somalia?). The ships are moored bow to the beach, and goods are being carried through shallow water and up gangplanks (Wachsmann 1998: 18–29).

Since no other rivers the size of the Nile open into the eastern Mediterranean, the use of beach harbors was probably the typical practice in this region during the Bronze Age. This is one possible explanation for the absence of verifiable archaeological remains of harbors from this period. Frost (1972, 1973, 1974) suggests that along the Levant, offshore islands and reefs, such as those at Tyre, Sidon, and Aradus, were shaped by quarrying to serve as protection for large trading ships (Blackman 1982: 92; Marriner, Morange, and Carayon 2008; Raban 1995). The situation at Alexandria, Egypt, was similar (Goddio 1998; Goddio and Bernand 2004). The semi-protected south-facing beach at Tyre traditionally was given the name "Egyptian harbor," presumably because it received ships from that region during the season that beach landings were feasible (Poidebard and Lauffray 1951). At Dor, south of Ptolemais (Haifa), several low islands just offshore provided partial protection and attracted ships from at least the Middle Bronze Age. Raban (1985, 1987) has proposed that a substantial wall and pavement just below present sea level, along the south edge of the tel (occupation mound) at Dor, are remains of a Bronze Age quay (Figure 35.1). An Egyptian papyrus document records a visit to this harbor by the priest Wenamun sometime around 1100 BCE (Casson 1991: 47–53). He went on to Byblos, where the harbor consisted of a small natural bay (Wachsmann 1998: 40–41). The frescoes found at Akrotiri, which seem to date to the seventeenth century BCE, show several coastline settlements, but no artificial ports (Wachsmann 1998: 86–91). The ships are simply beached. Cuttings in the bedrock along the coastline of Crete have been associated with Bronze Age maritime activity, although it is impossible to verify the chronology of the installations (Raban 1991; Shaw 2006). Remains of a basin excavated in the coastline, apparently designed for ships, have been identified near the Mycenaean palace of Pylos (Zangger

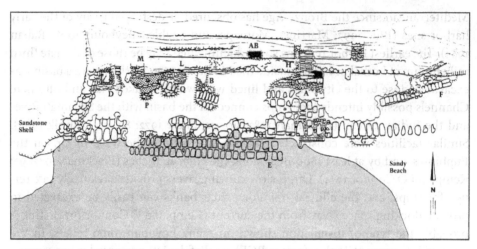

Figure 35.1 Plan of the quay at the south edge of Tel Dor from Raban 1987: 121.
Reproduced with the kind permission of the American Schools of Oriental Research.

1997: 613–625). In summary, during the Bronze Age, harbors generally were passive
in character, consisting of naturally sheltered beaches and bays, or at their most
elaborate of basins excavated in riverbanks and shorelines.

Phoenician, Greek, and Etruscan Harbors

Although these same designs, and some of the same harbors, continued in use into
the Iron Age, new sites were made available to shipping from the ninth or eighth
centuries BCE by means of walls built into the sea as breakwaters (Blackman
1982: 182–193; Casson 1995: 363–370; Shaw 1972: 90–94). The Phoenicians, the greatest
maritime traders in this period, seem to have pioneered this technique, and the
earliest structures appear at sites they occupied: Tabbat el-Hammam in Syria
(Braidwood 1940), Tyre in Lebanon, and Athlit in Israel (Raban 1985; Haggi 2010).
These breakwaters were constructed of blocks of the local *kurkar* bedrock on gravel
foundations, the blocks laid with their short ends facing out to increase their resistance to erosion. At first the breakwaters were used to augment the protection offered by offshore islands and reefs, but in the long run such structures allowed for
the construction of completely artificial harbors at otherwise inhospitable locations.
Although disruption of the shoreline currents with breakwaters could cause problems with siltation, it was probably easier to deal with the silt behind a wall than
with that deposited in a shallow basin excavated behind the shoreline. At Sidon and
Dor, there are surviving examples of rock-cut channels that funneled wave water
into the basin behind the breakwater, fostering a current that helped keep the
anchorage clear (Poidebard and Lauffray 1951). The Carthaginians, Phoenician colonists, carried all of these techniques with them to the western Mediterranean. Offshore islets augmented with breakwater walls can be seen at Apollonia (Laronde
1996) and Leptis Magna (Bartoccini 1958), while artificial basins were excavated in

the soil of the coastline at Carthage (Appian, *Punic Wars* 8.14.96; Cintas 1973; Hurst 1994; Hurst and Stager 1978) and Motya (Isserling 1974), and in the bedrock at Mahdia. In the Carthaginian context these in-shore basins were termed *cothons*.

While the low, unbroken coastlines and sandy beaches of the Levant and North Africa fostered use of the designs described above, the broken, karstic landscape of the Aegean offered innumerable naturally protected bays. As a result, artificial harbor structures become common in this region only in the seventh and sixth centuries BCE, as competition for trade and resources became intense. The earliest such structure that can be dated is the long rubble-mound breakwater at Samos, attributed by Herodotus to Polykrates, who ruled around 530 BCE (*Histories* 3.60). Only a commercially successful tyrant could afford such expenditure. A similar structure at the rich sanctuary of Delos may be as early as the seventh century BCE (Duchêne and Fraisse 2001; Paris 1916). Piraeus, the port city of Athens (Garland 1987), is a good example of the typical Greek harbor (*limen*) of the classical period, in which several natural bays were enhanced by the provision of breakwaters (*chomata*) built out from shore. These provided a safe anchorage (*hormos*), which might be provided with quays if the traffic warranted it. A commercial harbor (*emporion*) required porticoes, offices, and warehouses, while a naval base (*neorion*) was supplied with shipsheds (*neosoikoi*) for the military ships, and arsenals (*skeuothekai* or *hoplothekai*) for their gear (Casson 1995: 362–363). One development of the intensely competitive classical period was the *limen kleistos*, a harbor basin enclosed within the city walls, with a mouth narrow enough to be closed off with a chain that could keep out enemy vessels (Lehmann-Hartleben 1923: 65–74). Knidos provides a well-preserved example (Lehmann-Hartleben 1923: 126–127) (Figure 35.2). Some of these "closed harbors," such as Zea at the Piraeus and the circular harbor at Carthage, were specifically military ports, devoted to the expensive triremes and other oared war vessels that had to be stored out of the water in ship sheds (Blackman 2008: 657–660; Morrison, Coates, and Rankov 2000). The separation of military from commercial harbors reflects both the growing disparity in the design of warships and merchant ships after the eighth century BCE and the increasing sophistication of maritime technology in general.

Despite this general increase in sophistication, beach harbors remained common. The ideal harbor of the Phaeacians, described by Homer (*Odyssey* 6.262–269), consisted of beaches on either side of a projecting headland, with a channel connecting the two. The unique location of Corinth, next to the narrow isthmus that connected the Peloponnesos with the mainland of Greece, ensured its prosperity from the Bronze Age through the Byzantine period. The city controlled the land trade that used the isthmus and also attracted sea traders who did not wish to make the long and risky voyage around the southern tip of the Peloponnesos to the west (Strabo, *Geography* 8.6.20). Goods could be bought and sold at both Kenchreai, the Aegean harbor (Scranton, Shaw, and Ibrahim 1978), and Lechaion, the harbor on the west-facing Gulf of Corinth (Paris 1915; Rothaus 1995). The fact that the Lechaion harbor was a *cothon* raises interesting questions concerning the influence of Phoenician or Carthaginian harbor technology on Corinthian

Figure 35.2 View of northern harbor of Knidos, with towers. Reproduced with the
kind permission of L. Vann.

engineers. In the sixth century BCE, possibly under Periander, a paved roadway 8
km long, the *diolkos* ("haul across"), was built across the isthmus, allowing teams of
oxen to haul ships or their cargoes across on dollies (MacDonald 1986; Raepsaet
2008: 592–594).

The Etruscans, a major Mediterranean sea power until around 400 BCE, for the
most part accommodated their ships in river mouths and lagoons, or beached them.
The Arno, Ombrone, Marta, and Tiber rivers are all associated with important
Etruscan cities, and they formed routes to the interior of the peninsula. At one of
the mouths of the Po River, the trading centers of Adria and Spina were built on
artificial islands, like an ancient Venice (Kracht 1995). Ships bound for Pisa (Bruni
2003; Camilli 2004) or Rusellae (Naumann 1963) could anchor in large natural
lagoons adjacent to the habitation area. Rubble-mound breakwaters gave partial
protection to anchorages at Pyrgi (Oleson 1977) and Graviscae, while at Populonia
a breakwater constructed of large stone blocks provided extra protection to a deep
natural bay (McCann 1977) (Figure 35.3). These harbors handled the export of vast
amounts of grain, iron blooms, and minerals to the Greek world, paid for with olive
oil, wine, fine ceramics and other manufactured goods, and silver.

Hellenistic Harbor Engineering

The marked increase in prosperity and sea trade during the Hellenistic period, the
concentration of wealth and power among the monarchs of large kingdoms, and the

Figure 35.3 Breakwater of the Etruscan port at Populonia. Reproduced with the kind permission of J. P. Oleson.

growing size of warships and merchant vessels resulted in the construction of increasingly large and elaborate harbors. Alexandria, the outlet for all the wealth of Egypt, was particularly splendid (Strabo, *Geography* 16.1.6–10; Goddio 1998) (Figure 35.4). A causeway 1,250 m long connected the offshore island of *Pharos* with the mainland, forming two large basins that were further protected by exterior and interior breakwaters and enhanced with quay walls and dry docks (Athenaeus, *Deipnosophistae* 5.204c–d). A canal connected the western basin with Lake Mareotis and the Nile. Ptolemy II (283–246 BCE) hired Sostratos of Knidos to build a lighthouse 100 m tall on *Pharos* to guide mariners to the harbor, which otherwise was difficult to find on such a low-lying coast (Brodersen 1992; Giardina 2010). Pliny (*Natural History* 36.83) reports that Sostratos also built the first harborside colonnades, at Knidos, an indication of a new focus on the harbor as a hallmark of urban sophistication. The harbor of the maritime power Rhodes was equally elaborate, incorporating several basins, as well as a colossal bronze statue of the god Helios, designed by Chares of Lindos around 280 BCE (Pliny 34.41; Brodersen 1992). The growing self-consciousness of harbor engineering in the mid-third century BCE is symbolized by the composition of the *Limenopoïka* (*Handbook of Harbor Construction*) by Philon of Byzantium, of which we unfortunately know only the title (Blackman 2008: 643). It remained difficult for engineers to predict the behavior of sediments behind breakwater or jetty walls. King Attalos Philadelphos (159–138 BCE) attempted to improve the river harbor of Ephesus by building jetties at the mouth of

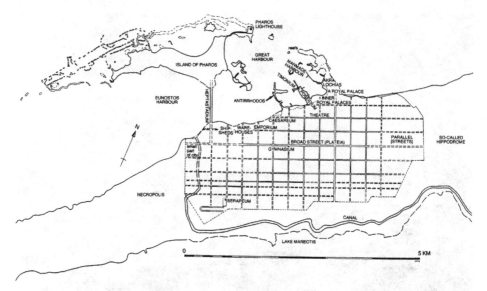

Figure 35.4 Plan of Alexandria. Reproduced with the kind permission of J. MacKenzie.

the Cayster River, but he only managed to clog the harbor basin with sediment (Strabo, *Geography* 14.1.24).

Roman Harbor Engineering

No further real progress in harbor engineering was made, however, until the development of hydraulic concrete by the Romans around 200 BCE (Blake 1947: 308–318; Blackman 1982: 196–197; Gazda 2001; Lechtman and Hobbs 1987; Lugli 1957; Oleson 1988; Oleson et al. 2004, 2006). Since portions of the valuable section in Vitruvius's *De architectura* that deals with harbor construction (5.12) probably were derived from Hellenistic handbooks, it is worthwhile quoting them. While Vitruvius summarizes these early practices, he also makes clear the unique character of the Roman contribution to harbor engineering.

> Harbors that have an advantageous natural location, with projecting headlands or promontories that shape naturally curved or angled recesses, seem to be the most useful. Colonnades or shipyards are to be constructed around the circumference, or entrances from the colonnades to the markets. Towers are to be built on either side [of the entrance to the harbor], from which chains can be drawn across by means of winches. If, however, we have no natural harbor situation suitable for protecting ships from storms, we must proceed as follows. If there is an anchorage on one side and no river mouth interferes, then a mole composed of concrete structures or rubble mounds is to be built on either side and the harbor enclosure constructed in this manner.
>
> Those concrete structures that are to be in the water must be made in the following fashion. Earth [*pulvis*, i.e., volcanic ash] is to be brought from that region which runs from Cumae to the promontory of Minerva and mixed in the mortar used in these structures, in the proportions of two parts earth to one of

lime. Next, in the designated spot, formwork enclosed by stout posts and tie beams is to be let down into the water and fixed firmly in position. Then the area within it at the bottom, below the water, is to be leveled and cleared out, [working] from a platform of small crossbeams. The building is to be carried on there with a mixture of aggregate and mortar, as described above, until the space left for the structure within the form has been filled. (*De architectura* 5.12.1–3)

Standard mortars and plasters of varying quality, composed of hydrated lime, beach or river sand, and water, had been used in the circum-Mediterranean world since the sixth or seventh millennium BCE (Gourdin and Kingery 1975; Kingery, Vandiver, and Prickett 1988). Hydraulic mortar differs in that a pozzolanic additive either supplements or is substituted for the relatively pure silica sand. For the Roman engineers working underwater, this pozzolanic additive was a sandlike volcanic ash, *pulvis puteolanus* ("powder from Puteoli"), surviving in Italian as *pozzolana*, a term now anglicized and applied to a variety of materials—such as sintered ash—that have the same effect on modern cement (Vitruvius, *On Architecture* 6.8.9; Blake 1947: 324–352; Lugli 1957: 363–442; Massaza 1988). Pozzolanic materials allow the mortar to set under water, out of contact with atmospheric CO_2. Roman engineers quickly realized the special suitability of this material for the construction of hydraulic installations, bridge footings, and harbor structures. The mastery of hydraulic concrete, combined with other engineering innovations, enabled Roman engineers to construct harbors anywhere political, economic, or military considerations dictated, not simply where advantageous physical features existed.

It is likely that this great technological advance first occurred in the region around the port city of Puteoli (modern Pozzuoli) at the north end of the Bay of Naples (Brandon, Hohlfelder, and Oleson 2008; Jaschke 2010; Lechtman and Hobbs 1987: 89; Oleson et al. 2004; Piromallo 2004), and the breakwater there may be the earliest harbor structure built with this material. Strabo (*Geography* 5.4.6) describes the advantages of the local pozzolana:

> Puteoli has become a great trade centre, since it has man-made harbors—thanks to the natural quality of the sand. Measured out in proper proportion to the lime, the sand forms a strong bond and cures solidly. In consequence, by mixing the sand-ash [*ammokonía*] with the lime, they can run breakwaters out into the sea and turn open beaches into protected bays, so that the largest merchant ships can moor there safely.

Both Pliny the Elder (*Natural History* 16.202, 35.166) and Seneca (*Questions about Nature* 3.20.3) echo Vitruvius's praise of *pulvis puteolanus*. Vitruvius (2.6.1) also provides our only detailed description of the wooden formwork into which Roman concrete was poured (Brandon 1996, 1999; Oleson 1988; Schläger 1971). As Vitruvius makes clear, only the use of hydraulic mortar allows the concrete to be placed in forms filled with seawater.

Concrete piers or breakwaters could be placed on a sandy seabed but more frequently were laid on top of submerged rubble foundations of the type built by Policrates in the sixth century BCE. Pliny the Younger (*Letters* 6.31.15–17) provides a unique eyewitness account of this type of breakwater under construction at Centumcellae (Civitavecchia) in the early second century CE.

The breakwater on the left has already been reinforced with construction of the greatest stability, while that on the right is in the process of being built. At the harbor entrance a freestanding mole rises from the sea to serve as a breakwater against seas brought in by the on-shore wind and to provide safe entrance to ships on either side. The technique by which the mole is built has got to be seen. A wide barge brings enormous stones right up to it and throws them in one on top of another. Their weight keeps them in position, and little by little a sort of rampart is constructed. A kind of stony hump can already be seen rising above the water which breaks the waves that beat upon it and tosses the spray high in the air with a great roar; the sea all around is white with foam. Masses of concrete will be laid on top of the stones, and as time passes it will come to resemble an island.

Making use of the new concrete technology, by the mid-second century BCE Roman harbor engineers began to construct large and successful harbor installations at sites along the shelving Italian coastline that otherwise would have remained unprotected. The harbor of Cosa is the earliest well-studied example (Ciampoltrini and Rendini 2004; McCann et al. 1987), and hundreds of others followed the spread of Roman power throughout the Mediterranean and into the Atlantic (Blackman 1982, 2008b). There is growing evidence that all the harbors employing hydraulic concrete made use of pozzolana imported from the region around Puteoli, attesting to an enormous trade in this specialized construction material (Oleson et al. 2004, 2006).

Not surprisingly, Roman harbors have attracted the most attention from modern archaeologists, since relatively few harbors of the pre-Roman period made use of extensive man-made structures. In contrast, during the period of most intensive maritime commerce in the ancient Mediterranean—from 200 BCE to 300 CE (Parker 1992: 1–33)—the evolution of ancient nautical technology, the growth of the political and economic imperatives for maritime commerce, and the evolving engineering skills for building new harbors or renovating existing ones all peaked. The demands of the Roman economy required more, often bigger, and varied maritime installations, thus enhancing the potential survivability of archaeological targets of interest. Sometimes such archaeological features that have fortuitously survived were components of the major nodes in the transportation and commercial network that nurtured the empire.

Given the immensity of the evidence for Roman imperial harbors, only two examples will be presented in detail here, as case studies: Sebastos and Aperlae. Sebastos, later called Portus Augusti, the artificial harbor built for King Herod's port city of Caesarea Maritima or Caesarea in Palaestine (Israel), is in some ways both the prototype and the archetype of the great emporia of the imperial world. Great harbors like this one were linked by a series of sea-lanes that enabled commercial goods, people, and ideas to move throughout the Mediterranean in a manner not seen again until the nineteenth century. Nevertheless, through the Roman imperial period modest, sometimes almost invisible anchorages or roadsteads, such as Aperlae in southern Turkey, continued to function, handling the bulk of the local trade and regional cabotage that constituted a significant portion of the ancient maritime commerce. Coasting between seaside settlements, small boats tramped along the Mediterranean littoral trading wherever they could buy or sell to their advantage. Periodically these modest vessels entered the large emporia to exchange regional for international products. The system in play was much like the one so familiar to air travelers today—a central international airport fed by smaller, local airfields. Maritime commerce moving to and from regional markets to the great harbors most likely represented the bulk of seaborne trade in antiquity, even though little evidence for such traffic appears in the extant ancient texts. The shipwrecks found at Skerki Bank seem to have been engaged in this sort of trade (McCann and Oleson 2004: 203–210).

Both Sebastos and Aperlae have been investigated in some detail in the recent past and can serve as case studies for what harbor archaeology can accomplish at inundated sites, employing a range of excavation and survey techniques at Sebastos, and a simple, nondestructive survey at Aperlae.

The Harbor of Sebastos: Taming Poseidon through Technology

The great international emporia such as Portus/Ostia, Massalia, Carthage, Alexandria, and Caesarea were the focal points of the maritime trading network that enabled the Romans to declare proudly but accurately that the Mediterranean was *mare nostrum*. Moreover, their very size made it more likely that some of their ancient features have survived. Sebastos had the distinction of being the first completely artificial harbor constructed at the outset of the imperial era, and its successful completion marked a real breakthrough in the technology of harbor construction (Brandon 2008; Branton and Oleson 1992; Hohlfelder 1996, 1997, 2000, 2003; Hohlfelder, Brandon, and Oleson 2007; Holum and Hohlfelder 1988; Oleson et al. 1994; Raban 1989, 2009) (Figure 35.5). Lacking local builders with sufficient experience in constructing maritime installations, Herod sought and received help from Rome (Hohlfelder 2000). Roman master builders in the Italian tradition, challenged in new ways by the topography, geology, and siltation regime of the Levant, expanded existing technology and experimented with new building protocols to construct the installations his port city required (Brandon 2008; Hohlfelder, Brandon, and Oleson 2007, 2008).

The key to the construction of a large artificial harbor basin on an exposed coastline was hydraulic concrete. The soft local building stone, a calcareous sandstone known as *kurkar*, was used for the rubble foundation pad and for infill walls, but the core of the two long breakwaters (500 m and 200 m long, c. 60 m wide) was composed of enormous blocks of concrete. Because of the exposed shoreline, many of these were cast in single-use barge forms, which were floated out to the intended site and filled with mortar and aggregate until they sank in position (Brandon 1996, 1998, 2008).

Through his close connections with Augustus and Marcus Agrippa, Herod was also able to obtain thousands of tons of raw material and access to the freighters to transport the material to the building site. Recent fieldwork at Sebastos has

Figure 35.5 Reconstruction of Sebastos. Reproduced with the
kind permission of C. Brandon.

indicated that approximately 52,000 tons of pozzolana had to be imported from the
Bay of Naples some 2,000 km to the west (Hohlfelder, Brandon, and Oleson
2007: 414). The bulk transport of pozzolana on this scale had not been known or
even suspected based on the surviving literary sources. Enormous amounts of lime,
rubble, and timber also had to be imported (Vortruba 2007).

Josephus (*Jewish War* 1.408–414, *Jewish Antiquities* 15.331–341) provides long
descriptions of the harbor, the manner of construction, and its splendid final appearance (Oleson in Raban 1989: 51–53). Once complete, the breakwaters were paved
and furnished with colonnades and vaulted warehouses. As at Alexandria, a tall
lighthouse, named Drusion after one of Augustus's heirs, guided mariners along the
low-lying coast to the north-facing entrance channel. Large concrete blocks, rising
well above sea level and carrying ornamental columns, were cast in position just
outside the harbor entrance, framing ships entering the harbor. These *pilae* probably helped to break waves that might otherwise have made entry difficult, and they
may also have helped prevent the deposition of silt in the entrance channel. Local
expertise was tapped for a further desilting mechanism. As in the Phoenician harbor at Sidon, channels cut in the bedrock at the base of the southern breakwater
allowed wave action to pile water up in the harbor basin, thus creating a gentle current out through the entrance. Another feature that may have been of local inspiration was the provision of low subsidiary breakwaters (*prokumatia*) at sea level
outside and parallel to the main southern breakwater, to add protection and reduce
spray from waves. There was also a small inner basin and quay.

The Roman master builders who supervised the building of Sebastos brought with them the accumulated experience of Roman harbor construction plus the creativity to expand this knowledge to meet the formidable natural challenges posed by the site selected by the king for his new port city. Their resourcefulness, creativity, and human energy combined to execute the king's grandiose vision and in the process produced a great technological leap forward in harbor engineering. After the construction of King Herod's harbor, nothing was beyond the reach of future harbor builders. The engineers of Portus itself, with its dual harbors built by Claudius and Trajan to serve the imperial capital of Rome, owed much to the engineering advances attributable to the builders of Sebastos.

Aperlae: A Secondary Harbor of the Lycian Coast

The southern coast of the Anatolian Peninsula is characterized by high, rugged mountains that plunge into the sea, creating many inlets, bays, and small islands, all blocked from easy access to the interior by almost impenetrable mountain ridges. In antiquity, any seaside communities that developed along this littoral had to be dependent on the sea for communication, commerce, and survival. Aperlae, only casually mentioned in ancient literature, was one such settlement. It was established sometime in the third century BCE and was not abandoned until late in the seventh century CE (Hohlfelder 2005a, 2005b). The fair-weather harbor of Aperlae was simple, but it provided access to an important sea-lane that ran along the southern Anatolian coast. Because of its modest size, limited docking facilities, and location at the head of an exposed, narrow, shallow inlet, deepwater freighters never came to call. Rather, it was a node of a regional network of maritime connectivity that both began and ended at Andriake, the harbor of the Lycian metropolis of Myra (Hohlfelder and Vann 2000a). This international emporium functioned as the gateway for many Lycian maritime communities similar to Aperlae.

An archaeological survey of the harbor and submerged portion of this site was carried out by divers using snorkels (Hohlfelder and Vann 1998; Vann and Hohlfelder 1999). Since no excavation or use of SCUBA equipment was permitted, the archaeological results are preliminary, but they allow a reconstruction of the town's maritime life. The Aperlites clearly were able to adapt to the challenges posed by the location of their town at the head of shallow Asar Bay, completely exposed to the southwest. The residents managed to survive and prosper not by building extensive harbor installations, but rather by accepting and embracing the natural patterns of wind and sea. This was the secret to the survival of hundreds of similar small maritime settlements around the Mediterranean.

In its Hellenistic era, when the Lycian coastline often changed political hands, the city probably had few if any permanent harbor installations along its then unprotected seafront. At this time the residents of Aperlae seem to have made do with the natural shoreline, perhaps augmented by some wooden piers. As conditions in Asia Minor stabilized and improved under the Romans, permanent ashlar seawalls appeared along the waterfront both to define and stabilize its perimeter.

A small jetty (approximately 22 m long) was also built out perpendicular to the waterfront quay to provide some limited shelter from the prevailing west-southwest winds that beat down the bay every afternoon. The jetty could have accommodated no more than three small coastal traders. No effort was ever made to build a break-water closer to the mouth of the bay, to provide an all-weather, protected basin for coasters bound for and arriving from Andriake. Since the inhabitants of Roman Aperlae appear to have had capital and the technical resources sufficient for such a project, it seems likely that they did not feel the outlay was justified. Aperlae thrived on the export of purple cloth dyed on site (Hohlfelder and Vann 2000a; Leadbetter 2003). Small coastal traders equipped with sail and oars could have worked their way out of Asar Bay, and in the early morning, when the diurnal land breezes were favorable, such a departure would have been easy. The approximately 20-nautical-mile trip to Andriake would have been safe from the prevailing offshore winds that came from the west or northwest. The return voyage would have been more diffi-cult, but not impossible for a captain who knew how to best use the local winds.

The decision of the people of Aperlae not to invest in harbor facilities beyond their immediate needs provides an important model. Not every coastal town could accommodate large deepwater freighters, nor did they need to do so. Small coastal communities, particularly ones like Aperlae that had a millennial existence, found ways of dealing with the winds and the sea. The mariners who came and went from this and other seaside settlements throughout the Mediterranean were by nature resourceful. To survive and prosper, they had to deal with the realities of nature. While the study of the great emporia like Portus, Sebastos, Piraeus, Carthage, and Massalia (Euzennat 1980; Hesnard, Maurel, and Bernardi 2001) is more immedi-ately compelling, Aperlae reminds us that small matters as well, for it is in the typ-ical rather than the exceptional that the fullness of the ancient maritime experience can best be found (Horden and Purcell 2000: 123).

THE SPECIAL CHALLENGES OF
HARBOR EXCAVATION

The techniques of survey and excavation depend on the geomorphology of an ancient harbor site. Those that now have been raised above ancient sea level by local tectonic activity can be treated as any land excavation (Hadjidaki 1988). Others that have been covered by siltation may start out as a normal land project but usually end up as what some have called an amphibious or mud excavation owing to the high water tables that are common to such sites. Most often, pumps are put to use to remove water from the zone of archaeological activity and cofferdams installed to stabilize trench walls. Fieldwork conducted at Caesarea on what was called the Inner Harbor area provides an excellent example of this type of maritime archae-ology (Raban 1989: 131–142, 2009: 199–206; Yule and Barham 1999), as does the work on the inner lagoon at Cosa, a small Italian port town sustained by a large maritime industrial complex (McCann et al. 1987: 98–128). Yenikapı (in Istanbul) also has challenged archaeologists with similar issues (Covington 2009; Rose and Aydingün 2007; Delgado in this volume).

Fieldwork on submerged harbor sites involves both challenges and opportunities, many of which are now summarized in a handy format by Bowens (2009; see also Raban 1989: 239–267). The logistics are usually somewhat easier than with archaeological projects in deeper coastal waters or in deep submergence archaeology (see Wachsmann in this volume). For example, a shore-based total station can be used to locate points on exposed ruins to provide their exact location on a pre-disturbance site survey map and also to facilitate their later use as base points for subsequent measurements underwater. Buoys floated over a baseline established underwater can be sighted from a total station as well to provide an exact location for a particular artifact discovered during survey or excavation.

The proximity to shore of drowned sites usually means that archaeologists are working in relatively shallow water (usually 10 m or less, and rarely over 15 m), where many of the physiological concerns of working in deeper water (e.g., decompression diving and nitrogen narcosis) are not an issue. SCUBA diving on such sites requires only compressed air rather than more exotic mixed gases, but, as always, proper diving protocols must be observed, since embolisms and hypothermia can occur at any depth. All these factors can reduce budgetary needs and frequently extend the portion of time that can be spent on site. A single tank of air usually can provide a diver with more than an hour of bottom time, with no physiological restrictions beyond fatigue or cold to prevent the use of a second or even third tank of air to continue the work. Surface-supplied air can also be used for teams engaged in excavation rather than survey. Safety boats or diving platforms with support personnel are usually necessary in shallow-water archaeological projects just as for those in deeper water, but they can be less costly to rent or operate. Further, the shallow depth of water covering the site itself and its closeness to the shore are also factors that enhance the safety and general ease of operations.

But while there are decided physiological advantages to harbor excavation, nature often offsets these positive factors with difficulties not often encountered during shipwreck excavation in deeper waters. Storms and currents play havoc with archaeological remains along shorelines. Sand moves about with unpredictable frequency and in random ways. Often ruins visible one day can disappear overnight, as bottom sands set in motion by storm seas or currents cover a site or in-fill a trench being dug near an underwater feature such as a quay wall. This process of natural in-filling often takes far less time than the original excavation did.

Artifacts also can move about in storms, when the sea exposes artifacts and transports them to some other point within the harbor basin. This "artifact drift" can also occur overnight, meaning that any area being excavated might have received some intrusive finds. This reality of harbor excavation makes it very risky to assume the integrity of any excavation area, even one that might first appear to represent a sealed locus or a closed deposit (Holum and Hohlfelder 1988: 91). Thus, stratigraphic archaeology, the gold standard of terrestrial archaeology, should be followed whenever possible as the preferred technique for excavating beneath the sea in submerged sites, but the data uncovered will always be less secure. For example, artifacts found in association with underwater features may not be synchronous. Even potsherds found beneath a Roman concrete *pila* can postdate the placement of this structure, since storms and current often scour the fill from beneath such blocks and deposit artifacts transported from elsewhere.

Adverse surface conditions often diminish underwater visibility around shallow water sites, impeding even simple tasks such as sketching or photographing an artifact or determining the dimensions of a feature with a tape measure. Likewise, storms often prohibit the use of underwater excavating or survey equipment. When the sea is running high, an excavating tool, like a dredge or an airlift, or a survey instrument, like an air probe, can bounce erratically and with such force that its careful use becomes impossible. Under rough conditions, excavation with this type of equipment can easily result in the loss or even the accidental destruction of fragile artifacts. Turbulence and currents caused by surface conditions can produce underwater seasickness in a diver, which is decidedly unpleasant at best and in extreme cases potentially fatal even in shallow water. A project director must always be aware of the weather and its impact on the well-being and safety of all personnel and on their ability to conduct underwater operations that meet the meticulous disciplinary standards of archaeology. When the sea is rough, safety and scientific requirements dictate that work must stop. Work sites in deeper water, as on shipwreck projects such as the Uluburun wreck in the 1980s and 1990s or currently at the Kizilburun wreck, normally are less disturbed by moderate seas.

But the most important challenge presented by the archaeology of drowned sites is their broad chronological range. Harbors often were in operation for centuries, even millennia (e.g., Piraeus, Caesarea, Aperlae). A shipwreck, by contrast, embodies the frozen moment in time when the vessel foundered. In submerged harbor archaeology, there is often an overwhelming volume of artifacts without secure provenance, plus features that may have been constructed or repaired at different points in a site's chronological continuum. In this regard the drowned harbor is much like a terrestrial site. A wealth of evidence confounds the investigator. The random nature of the discovery pattern and the difficulty of definitively associating any of these finds with the structural remains of the harbor itself produce issues never faced by the deepwater shipwreck archaeologist. Yet in these problems of physical scale and temporal range, there are opportunities afforded by a site with a long and varied existence to provide new insights into our historical record or to expand or question conventional wisdom. The underwater explorations of Aperlae and Caesarea serve as examples of how such archaeological challenges have expanded our knowledge of maritime life in classical antiquity.

Nondestructive survey methods of site exploration have also been brought to bear on harbor sites that are now both underwater and on land. Poidebard pioneered the use of aerial photography for the documentation of the harbors of Tyre and Sidon in the 1930s (Poidebard 1939; Poidebard and Lauffray 1951), and Schmiedt made use of military aerial photographs in his examination of Italian harbor sites (Schmiedt 1972, 1975). More recently, Google Earth has begun to put satellite imagery at the disposal of archaeologists. C. Brandon employed multibeam sonar, a survey tool usually associated with deepwater surveys of the ocean floor, in a pioneering search of the harbor area of Caesarea to construct the best map of the extant remains produced during more than 40 years of archaeological investigation (Brandon 2008). Ground-penetrating radar was recently combined with geological sampling in a survey of Phoenician sites in Portugal directed by S. Wachsmann to offer some insights into the life and times of these Iron Age trading outposts west of the Pillars of Hercules (Wachsmann et al. 2009). An international team of scholars has recently completed a massive nondestructive survey of the area of ancient Portus (Keay et al. 2005). Using a wide range of geophysical, topographic, and cartographic surveys combined with field walking and aerial photography, Keay and his colleagues have vastly expanded our knowledge of the environs of Rome's imperial harbors near the mouth of the Tiber River and added a significant body of new data concerning Rome's imperial trade and maritime infrastructure.

As the new century opens, maritime archaeologists are far better prepared to meet the special requirements of working in inundated harbors or habitations. Excavating and survey techniques developed and modified during the last decades of the twentieth century will continue to be used and refined, as new methodologies are developed as well. Building on the past ensures the promise of future work, as scholars continue to search for the secrets of ancient harbors.

CONCLUSION

The evolution of harbors in the ancient world can be linked to both changing social needs and the development of the technology available for their construction. Simple shelving beaches, offshore islands, roadsteads on either side of a promontory, protected embayments, inlets, and riverine estuaries met the needs of the earlier ancient mariners. Such natural anchorages never fell completely from use. Throughout the course of ancient Mediterranean history, they were employed where necessary and appropriate for meeting the maritime needs of some coastal communities. Even today at the small coastal towns that neighbor the ruins of ancient Aperlae, one can see small coasters anchoring as close to shore as possible to facilitate off-loading sacks of charcoal or cases of soft drinks. The crew slips over the side into the shallow water and wades ashore carrying their boat's cargo on their shoulders. The simplicity of this resourceful solution to the absence of permanent harbor installations reminds us of its obvious timelessness. This scene would have been repeated in ancient coastal settlements throughout the Mediterranean.

These ad hoc solutions to problems faced by small communities sustained by regional coastal trade, however, did not suffice for the larger hub or gateway port cities, such as Sebastos, that were the emporia for international trade. When a greater requirement for maritime transport led to the building of larger ships to meet this demand and to advances in technology to permit more sophisticated building in the sea, the modification of natural harbors (like Alexandria or the ones in the Bay of Naples) or the construction of new ones on a grand scale (like Sebastos, Portus, Leptis Magna, and the harbors of Constantinople) could occur. The ruins of these larger installations require more sophisticated archaeological investigations.

The exploration techniques and the research questions that drive archaeological investigations have evolved as well over the past five decades from snorkel surveys to the use of SCUBA gear and now to the employment of the latest computer software and state-of-the-art underwater survey tools. Hundreds of potential targets await serious archaeological investigation, and new ones are surely waiting to be discovered. At this writing, our understanding of ancient harbors and the role they played in defining the relationship of the classical civilizations to the sea remains very incomplete. New research questions and technology will drive our search for answers. There are still many issues that require investigation: for example, siltation regimes in harbor basins, the character and stability of sub-bottom strata, the determination of cultural sequences through examination of cores of harbor sediments, the role of local and imported materials in harbor construction, the origins and mechanism of the spread of harbor-engineering skills, the character of river harbors and their role in integrating sea and land transport networks, and the character of subsidiary harbor structures such as ship sheds and water-supply systems. The investigation of ancient harbors will continue to enrich our appreciation of the maritime world of antiquity and the role the sea played in the life and times of the ancient Mediterranean civilizations.

REFERENCES

Only a sample of the enormous bibliography concerning ancient harbors can be presented here. Some survey articles are presented here even though they are not cited in the text. Delgado 1998 includes entries on a number of harbor sites. Longer bibliographies of ancient harbors can be found in Blackman 1982, 2008.

Ahrweiler, H. 1974. L'escale dans le monde byzantine. *Revue du Societé Jean Bodin* 32: 161–178.

Bartoccini, R. 1958. *Il porto romano di Leptis Magna.* Bollettino del Centro di Studi per la Storia dell'Architettura, suppl. 13. Rome: Centro di Studi per la Storia dell'Architettura.

Blackman, D. J., ed. 1973a. *Marine archaeology.* Colston Papers 23. London: Butterworths.

———. 1973b. Evidence of sea level change in ancient harbours and coastal installations. In *Marine archaeology,* ed. D. J. Blackman, 115–139. London: Butterworths.

———. 1982. Ancient harbours in the Mediterranean. *International Journal of Nautical Archaeology* 11 (2): 79–104; 11 (3): 185–211.

———. 1988. Bollards and men. *Mediterranean Historical Review* 3: 7–20.

———. 1995. Naval installations. In *The age of the galley*, ed. R. Gardiner, 224–233. London: Conway Maritime Press.

———. 1996. Further evidence for the use of concrete in ancient harbor construction. In *Caesarea Maritima: A retrospective after two millennia*, ed. A. Raban and K. G. Holum, 41–49. Leiden: Brill.

———. 2005. Archaeological evidence for sea level changes. *Zeitschrift für Geomorphologie*, n.s. Suppl. 137: 61–70.

———. 2008a. Roman shipsheds. In *The maritime world of ancient Rome*, ed. R. Holhlfelder, 23–36. Ann Arbor: University of Michigan Press.

———. 2008b. Sea transport, part 2: Harbors. In *The Oxford handbook of engineering and technology in the classical world*, ed. J. P. Oleson, 638–670. New York: Oxford University Press.

Blake, M. E. 1947. *Ancient Roman construction in Italy from the prehistoric period to Augustus*. Washington, DC: Carnegie Institution.

Blue, L. K. 1997. Cyprus and Cilicia: The typology and palaeography of second millennium harbors. In *Res maritimae: Cyprus and the eastern Mediterranean from prehistory to late antiquity*, ed. S. Swiney, R. Hohlfelder, and H. Swiney, 31–43. Atlanta: Scholars Press.

Bowens, A., ed. 2009. *Underwater archaeology: The NAS guide to principles and practice*. Oxford: NAS and Blackwell.

Braidwood, R. 1940. Report on two sondages on the coast of Syria. *Syria* 21: 183–226.

Brandon, C. J. 1996. Cements, concrete, and settling barges at Sebastos: Comparisons with other Roman harbor examples and the descriptions of Vitruvius. In *Caesarea maritima: A retrospective after two millennia*, ed. A. Raban and K. G. Holum, 25–40. Leiden: Brill.

———. 1999. Pozzolana, lime, and single-mission barges (Area K). In *Caesarea papers 2*, Journal of Roman Archaeology Suppl. 35m, ed. K. Holum, A. Raban, and J. Patrich, 169–178. Portsmouth, RI: JRA.

———. 2008. Roman structures in the sea: Sebastos, the Herodian harbor of Caesarea. In *The maritime world of ancient Rome*, ed. R. Holhlfelder, 245–254. Ann Arbor: University of Michigan Press.

Brandon, C., R. L. Hohlfelder, and J. P. Oleson. 2008. The concrete construction of the Roman harbours of Baiae and Portus Iulius, Italy: The ROMACONS 2006 field season. *International Journal of Nautical Archaeology* 37: 374–392.

Brandon, C., R. L. Hohlfelder, J. P. Oleson, and C. Stern. 2005. The Roman Maritime Concrete Study (ROMACONS): The harbour of Chersonisos in Crete and its Italian connection. *Méditerranée* 1 (2): 25–29.

Branton, G., and J. P. Oleson. 1992. The technology of King Herod's harbour. In *Caesarea papers: Straton's Tower, Herod's Harbour, and Roman and Byzantine Caesarea*, Journal of Roman Archaeology, Suppl. 5, ed. R. L. Vann, 49–67. Ann Arbor: JRA.

Brodersen, K. 1992. *Reiseführer zu den Sieben Weltwundern: Philon von Byzanz und andere antike Texte*. Frankfurt: Insel Verlag.

Bruni, S. 2003. *Il porto urbano di Pisa antica: La fase etrusca, il contesto e il relitto ellenistico*. Milan: Silvana.

Camilli, A. 2004. Le strutture "portuali" dello scavo di Pisa-San Rossore. In *Le strutture dei porti e degli approdi antichi: Atti del II Seminario ANSER, Roma—Ostia Antica, 16–17 April 2004*, ed. A. Gallina Zevi and R. Turchetti, 67–86. Soveria Mannelli: Rubbettino.

Casson, L. 1991. *The ancient mariners*. 2nd ed. Princeton, NJ: Princeton University Press.

———. 1995. *Ships and seamanship in the ancient world.* Rev. ed. Princeton, NJ: Princeton University Press.

Ciampoltrini, G., and P. Rendini. 2004. Il sistema portuale dell'*ager Cosanus* e delle isole del Giglio e di Giannutri. In *Le strutture dei porti e degli approdi antichi: Atti del II Seminario ANSER, Roma—Ostia Antica, 16–17 April 2004,* ed. A. Gallina Zevi and R. Turchetti, 127–150. Soveria Mannelli: Rubbettino.

Cintas, P. 1973. *Le port de Carthage.* Manuel d'archéologie punique, vol. 2. Paris: A. and J. Picard.

Covington, R. 2009. Discovering Yenikapı. *Saudi Aramco World* 60 (1): 8–17.

Cunliffe, B. 2001. *Facing the ocean: The Atlantic and its peoples, 8000 BCE–CE 1500.* Oxford: Oxford University Press.

Delgado, J. P. 1998. *Encyclopedia of underwater and maritime archaeology.* New Haven, CT: Yale University Press.

De Souza, P. 2000. Western Mediterranean ports in the Roman Empire, first century B.C. to sixth century A.D. *Journal of Mediterranean Studies* 10: 229–254.

Duchêne, H., and P. Fraisse 2001. *Le paysage portuaire de la Délos antique: Recherches sur les installations maritimes, commerciales et urbaines du littoral délien.* Exploration archéologique de Délos, 39. Athens: École française d'Athènes.

Euzennat, M. 1980. Ancient Marseille in the light of recent excavations. *American Journal of Archaeology* 84: 133–140.

Felici, E. 1993. Osservazioni sul Porto Neroniano di Anzio e sulla tecnica romana delle costruzioni portuali in calcestruzzo. In *Archeologia subacquea* 1, ed. P. A. Gianfrotta, P. Pelagatti, E. Felici, and P. G. Monti, 71–104. Rome: Istituto Poligrafico e Zecca dello Stato.

———. 2002. Scoperte epigraphiche e topographiche sulla costruzione del porto neroniano di *Antium.* In *Archeologia subacquea* 3, ed. P. A. Gianfrotta, P. Pelagatti, E. Felici, and P. G. Monti, 107–122. Rome: Istituto Poligrafico e Zecca dello Stato.

Flemming, N. C. 1971. *Cities in the sea.* Garden City, NY: Doubleday.

Frost, H. 1971. Recent observations on the submerged harbourworks at Tyre. *Bulletin du Musée de Beyrouth* 24: 103–111.

———. 1972. Ancient harbours and anchorages in the eastern Mediterranean. In *Underwater archaeology: A nascent discipline,* 95–114. Paris: UNESCO.

———. 1973. The offshore island harbour at Sidon and other Phoenician sites in the light of new dating evidence. *International Journal of Nautical Archaeology* 2: 75–94.

———. 1974. Mediterranean harbours: Bronze and Iron Ages; Les grandes escales, I. *Recueils de la Société Jean Bodin* 37: 35–41.

———. 1995. Harbours and proto-harbours, early Levantine engineering. In *Cyprus and the sea,* ed. V. Karageorghis and Michaelides, 1–21. Nicosia: University of Cyprus–Cyprus Ports Authority.

Gallina Zevi, A., and R. Turchetti. 2004. *Le strutture dei porti e degli approdi antichi: Atti del II Seminario ANSER, Roma—Ostia Antica, 16–17 April 2004.* Soveria Mannelli: Rubbettino.

Garland, R. 1987. *The Piraeus.* London: Duckworth.

Gazda, E. K. 2001. Cosa's contribution to the study of Roman hydraulic concrete: An historiographic commentary. In *Classical studies in honor of Cleo Rickman Fitch,* ed. N. W. Goldman, 145–177. New York: Peter Lang.

———. 2008. Cosa's hydraulic concrete: Towards a revised chronology. In *The maritime world of ancient Rome,* ed. R. Hohlfelder, 265–290. Ann Arbor: University of Michigan Press.

Gianfrotta, P. A. 1996. Harbor structures of the Augustan age in Italy. In *Caesarea maritima: A retrospective after two millennia*, ed. A. Raban and K. G. Holum, 65–76. Leiden: Brill.

Gianfrotta, P. A., P. Pelagatti, E. Felici, and P. G. Monti. 1993. *Archeologia subacquea 1.* Rome: Istituto Poligrafico e Zecca dello Stato.

———. 2002. *Archeologia subacquea.* Vol. 3. Rome: Istituto Poligrafico e Zecca dello Stato.

Giardina, B. 2010. *Navigare necesse est: Lighthouses from antiquity to the Middle Ages: History, architecture, iconography and archaeological remains.* BAR International Series, S2096. Oxford: Archaeopress.

Goddio, F. 1998. *Alexandria: The submerged royal quarters.* London: Periplus.

Goddio, F., and A. Bernand. 2004. *Sunken Egypt: Alexandria.* London: Periplus.

Gotti, E., J. P. Oleson, L. Bottalico, C. Brandon, R. Cucitore, and R. L. Hohlfelder. 2008. A comparison of the chemical and engineering characteristics of ancient Roman hydraulic concrete with a modern reproduction of Vitruvian hydraulic concrete. *Archaeometry* 50 (4): 576–590.

Gourdin, W. H., and W. D. Kingery. 1975. The beginnings of pyrotechnology: Neolithic and Egyptian lime plaster. *Journal of Field Archaeology* 2: 133–150.

Hadjidaki, E. 1988. Preliminary report of excavation at the harbor of Phalasarna in West Crete. *American Journal of Archaeology* 92: 463–479.

Haggi, A. 2010. Report on underwater excavation at the Phoenician Harbour, Atlit, Israel. *International Journal of Nautical Archaeology* 39: 278–285.

Hesnard, A., C. Maurel, and P. Bernardi. 2001. La topographie du port de Marseille, de la fondation de la cité à la fin du Moyen Âge. In *Marseille: Trames et passages urbains de Gyptis au Roi René; Actes du colloque international d'archéologie, Marseille 3–5 Nov. 1999*, ed. A. Guilcher, J. Guyon, and M. Pagni, 159–202. Aix-en-Provence: Edisud.

Hohlfelder, R. L. 1985. The building of the Roman harbour at Kenchreai: Old technology in a new era. In *Harbour archaeology*, ed. A. Raban, 165–172. British Archaeological Reports International Series No. 257. Oxford: BAR.

———. 1996. Caesarea's master harbor builders: Lessons learned, lessons applied? In *Caesarea maritima: A retrospective after two millennia*, ed. A. Raban and K. G. Holum, 77–101. Leiden: Brill.

———. 1997. Building harbours in the early Byzantine era: The persistence of Roman technology. *Byzantinische Forschungen* 24: 367–380.

———. 2000. Beyond coincidence? Marcus Agrippa and King Herod's harbor. *Journal of Near Eastern Studies* 59: 241–253.

———. 2003. Images of homage, images of power: King Herod and his harbour, Sebastos. *Antichthon* 37: 13–31.

———. 2005a. Swimming over time: Glimpses of the maritime life of Aperlae. In *Terra marique: Studies in art history and marine archaeology in honor of Anna Marguerite McCann*, ed. J. Pollini, 187–210. Oxford: Oxbow.

———. 2005b. Aperlae in Lycia: Ancient maritime life beyond the great harbors. *Classical Ireland* 12: 13–30.

———. 2008. *The maritime world of ancient Rome.* Ann Arbor: University of Michigan Press.

Hohlfelder, R. L., C. Brandon, and J. P. Oleson. 2007. Constructing the harbour of Caesarea Palaestina: New evidence from the ROMACONS field campaign of October 2005. *International Journal of Nautical Archaeology* 36: 409–415.

————. 2008. The Roman Maritime Concrete Study: A brief summary of fieldwork from 2002 to 2005. In *The maritime world of ancient Rome*, ed. R. Hohlfelder, 297–304. Ann Arbor: University of Michigan Press.

Hohlfelder, R. L., and R. L. Vann. 1998. Uncovering the secrets of Aperlae, a coastal settlement of ancient Lycia. *Near Eastern Archaeology* 61: 26–37.

————. 2000a. Cabotage at Aperlae, Lycia. *International Journal of Nautical Archaeology* 29: 126–135.

————. 2000b. Built on snails and faith. *Discovering Archaeology* 2: 78–87.

Holum, K., and R. L. Hohlfelder. 1988. *King Herod's dream: Caesarea on the sea.* New York: W. W. Norton.

Horden, P., and N. Purcell. 2000. *The corrupting sea: A study of Mediterranean history.* Oxford: Oxford University Press.

Houston, G. W. 1988. Ports in perspective: Some comparative materials on Roman merchant ships and ports. *American Journal of Archaeology* 92: 553–564.

Humphrey, J. W., J. P. Oleson, and A. N. Sherwood. 1998. *Greek and Roman technology: A sourcebook.* London: Routledge.

Hurst, H. R. 1994. *Excavations of Carthage: The British mission.* Vol. 2.1, *The Circular Harbour, North Side.* London: British Academy.

Hurst, H., and L. E. Stager. 1978. A metropolitan landscape: The late Punic port of Carthage. *World Archaeology* 9 (3): 334–346.

Isserling, B. S. J. 1974. The cothon at Motya: Phoenician harbor works. *Isis* 27: 188–194.

Jaschke, K. 2010. *Die Wirtschaft- und Socialgeschichte des antiken Puteoli.* Pharos 26. Rahden, Germany: Verlag Marie Leidorf.

Keay, S., M. Millett, L. Paroli, and K. Strutt. 2005. *Portus: An archaeological survey of the port of Imperial Rome.* Rome: British School of Archaeology.

Kemp, B., and D. O'Connor. 1974. An ancient Nile harbour: University Museum excavations at the "Birket Habu." *International Journal of Nautical Archaeology* 3: 101–136.

Kingery, W. D., P. B. Vandiver, and M. Prickett. 1988. The beginnings of pyrotechnology, part II: Production and use of lime and gypsum plaster in the pre-pottery Neolithic Near East. *Journal of Field Archaeology* 15: 219–244.

Kracht, P. 1995. Adria und Spina: Zwei bedeutende antike Handelszentren. *Münstersch Beiträge zur antiken Handlegeschichte* 14: 51–60.

Laronde, A. 1988. Le port de Lepcis Magna. *Comptes Rendus de l'Académie des Inscriptions et Belles-Lettres:* 337–353.

————. 1996. Apollonia de Cyrénaïque, archéologie et histoire. *Journal des Savants* 1996 (1): 3–49.

Leadbetter, B. 2003. Diocletian and the Purple Mile of Aperlae. *Epigraphica Anatolica* 36: 127–136.

Lehmann-Hartleben, K. 1923. *Die antiken Hafenlagen des Mittelmeeres: Beiträge zur Geschichte des Städtebaus im Altertum.* Klio, Beiheft 14. Leipzig: Dieterich.

————. 1926. Limen. *Paulys Real-Encyclopädie des classischen Altertumswissenschaft* 13.1: 547–569.

Leshnik, L. S. 1968. The Harappan "port" at Lothal: Another view. *American Anthropologist* 70: 911–922.

Lugli, G. 1957. *La tecnica edilizia romana, con particolare riguardo a Roma e Lazio.* 2 vols. Rome: Giovanni Bardi.

MacDonald, B. R. 1986. The Diolkos. *Journal of Hellenic Studies* 106: 191–195.

Marriner, N., C. Morange, and N. Carayon. 2008. Ancient Tyre and its harbours: 5000 years of human-environment interactions. *Journal of Archaeological Science* 35: 1281–1310.

Marriner, N., C. Morange, and M. Saghled-Beyhoun. 2008. Geoarchaeology of Beirut's ancient harbour, Phoenicia. *Journal of Archaeological Science* 35: 2495–2516.

Massaza, F. 1998. Pozzolana and Pozzolanic cements. In *Lea's chemistry of cement and concrete*, 4th ed., ed. P. C. Hewlett, 471–636. New York: Arnold.

McCann, A. M. 1977. Underwater excavations at the Etruscan port of Populonia. *Journal of Field Archaeology* 4: 275–296.

———. 2008. Response to "Cosa's hydraulic concrete: Towards a revised chronology." In *The maritime world of ancient Rome*, ed. R. Hohlfelder, 291–296. Ann Arbor: University of Michigan Press.

McCann, A. M., J. Bourgeois, E. K. Gazda, and J. P. Oleson. 1987. *The Roman port and fishery of Cosa.* Princeton, NJ: Princeton University Press.

McCann, A. M., and J. P. Oleson. 2004. *Deep-water shipwrecks off Skerki Bank: The 1997 survey.* Journal of Roman Archaeology, Suppl. 58. Portsmouth, RI: JRA.

McKenzie, J. 2007. *The architecture of Alexandria and Egypt 300 BCE–CE 700.* New Haven, CT: Yale University Press.

Meiggs, R. 1973. *Roman Ostia.* 2nd ed. Oxford: Oxford University Press.

Milne, G. 1985. *The port of Roman London.* London: Batsford.

Morrison, J. S., J. F. Coates, and N. B. Rankov. 2000. *The Athenian trireme: The history and reconstruction of an ancient Greek warship.* 2nd ed. Cambridge: Cambridge University Press.

Müller-Wiener, W. 1994. *Die Häfen von Byzantion-Konstantinupolis-Istanbul.* Istanbul: German Archaeological Institute.

Naumann, R. 1963. Die Hafen von Rusellae. *Rassegna Monetaria* 70: 39–43.

Oleson, J. P. 1977. Underwater survey and excavation in the port of Pyrgi (Santa Severa), 1974. *Journal of Field Archaeology* 4: 297–308.

———. 1988. The technology of Roman harbours. *International Journal of Nautical Archaeology* 17: 147–158.

Oleson, J. P., C. Brandon, S. M. Cramer, R. Cucitore, E. Gotti, and R. L. Hohlfelder. 2004. The ROMACONS Project: A contribution to the historical and engineering analysis of hydraulic concrete in Roman maritime structures. *International Journal of Nautical Archaeology* 33 (2): 199–229.

———. 2006. Reproduction of a Roman maritime structure with Vitruvian hydraulic concrete. *Journal of Roman Archaeology* 19: 29–52.

Oleson, J. P., M. A. Fitzgerald, A. N. Sherwood, and S. E. Sidebotham. 1994. *The harbours of Caesarea Maritima.* Vol. 2, *The finds and the ship.* BAR International Series, S594. Oxford: Tempus Reparatum.

Paris, J. 1915. Contributions à l'étude des ports antiques du monde Grec: I, Lechaeum. *Bulletin de Correspondance Hellénique* 39: 5–16.

———. 1916. Contributions à l'étude des ports antiques du monde Grec: II, Les etablissements maritimes de Delos. *Bulletin de Correspondance Hellénique* 40: 5–71.

Parker, A. J. 1992. *Ancient shipwrecks of the Mediterranean and the Roman provinces.* BAR International Series, S580. Oxford: Tempus Reparatum.

Piromallo, M. 2004. Puteoli, porto di Roma. In *Le strutture dei porti e degli approdi antichi: Atti del II Seminario ANSER, Roma—Ostia Antica, 16–17 April 2004*, ed. A. Gallina Zevi and R. Turchetti, 267–278. Soveria Mannelli: Rubbettino.

Poidebard, A. 1939. *Un grand port disparu: Tyr; Recherches aériennes et sous-marines, 1934–36.* Paris: Paul Geuthner.

Poidebard, A., and J. Lauffray. 1951. *Sidon: Aménagements antiques du port de Saida; Étude aérienne, au sol, et sous-marine, 1946–50.* Beirut: Ministère des Travaux Publics.

Pollini, J. 2005. *Terra marique: Studies in art history and marine archaeology in honor of Anna Marguerite McCann*. Oxford: Oxbow.

Raban, A. 1985. The ancient harbours of Israel in biblical times (from the Neolithic period to the end of the Iron Age). In *Harbour archaeology: Proceedings of the First International Workshop on Ancient Mediterranean Harbours, Caesarea Maritima, 24–28 June 1983*, ed. A. Raban, 11–44. BAR International Series, S257. Oxford: British Archaeological Reports.

———. 1987. The harbour of the sea peoples at Dor. *Biblical Archaeologist* 50: 118–126.

———. 1989. *The harbours of Caesarea Maritima*. Vol. 1, *The site and the excavation*, ed. J. P. Oleson. BAR International Series, S491. Oxford: BAR.

———. 1991. Minoan and Canaanite harbours. In *Thalassa: L'Egee prehistorique et la mer*, ed. R. Laffineur and L. Basch, 129–145. Aegaeum 7. Liège: Université de Liège.

———. 1995. The heritage of ancient harbour engineering in Cyprus and the Levant. In *Cyprus and the sea*, ed. V. Karageorghis and Michaelides, 139–188. Nicosia: University of Cyprus–Cyprus Ports Authority.

———. 2009. *The harbour of Sebastos (Caesarea Maritima) in its Roman Mediterranean context*, ed. M. Artzy, B. Goodman, and Z. Gal. BAR International Series, S1930. Oxford: Archaeopress.

Raban, A., and K. G. Holum 1996. *Caesarea maritima: A retrospective after two millennia*. Leiden: Brill.

Raepsaet, G. 2008. Riding, harnesses, and vehicles. In *Oxford handbook of engineering and technology in the classical world*, ed. J. P. Oleson, 580–605. New York: Oxford University Press.

Reddé, M. 1986. *Mare nostrum*. Bibliothèque des Écoles françaises d'Athènes et de Rome 260. Rome: École française de Rome.

Reddé, M., and J.-C. Golvin. 2005. *Voyages sur la Méditerranée romaine*. Errance: Actes Sud.

Rickman, G. E. 1988. The archaeology and history of Roman ports. *International Journal of Nautical Archaeology* 17: 257–267.

———. 2005. Portus Romae? In *Terra marique: Studies in art history and marine archaeology in honor of Anna Marguerite McCann*, ed. J. Pollini, 232–237. Oxford: Oxbow.

———. 2008. Ports, ships, and power in the Roman world. In *The maritime world of ancient Rome*, ed. R. Hohlfelder, 5–22. Ann Arbor: University of Michigan Press.

Rose, M., and S. Aydingün. 2007. Under Istanbul. *Archaeology* 60 (4): 34–40.

Rothaus, R. 1995. Lechaion, western port of Corinth: A preliminary archaeology and history. *Oxford Journal of Archaeology* 14: 293–306.

Rougé, J. 1966. *Recherches sur l'organization du commerce maritime en méditerranée sous l'empire romain*. Paris: SEVPEN.

———. 1974. Les escales romaines avant les grandes conquêtes. *Revue de la Société Jean Bodin* 32: 95–116.

Schläger, H. 1971. Die Texte Vitruvs im Lichte der Untersuchungen am Hafen von Side. *Bonner Jahrbücher* 171: 150–161.

Schlimme, L. 1984. Hafen. *Reallexikon für Antike und Christentum* 13: 297–305.

Schmiedt, G. 1972. *Il livello antico del mar Tirreno*. Florence: Olschki.

———. 1975. *Antichi porti d'Italia: Gli scali Fenicio-Punici: I porti della Magna-Grecia*. Florence: Istituto Geografico Militare.

Scranton, R. L., J. W. Shaw, and L. Ibrahim. 1978. *Kenchreai: Eastern port of Corinth*. Vol. 1, *Topography and architecture*. Leiden: Brill.

Shaw, J. W. 1972. Greek and Roman harbour-works. In *A history of seafaring based on underwater archaeology*, ed. G. Bass, 87–112. New York: Walker and Company.

———. 2006. *Kommos: A Minoan harbor town and classical sanctuary in southern Crete.* Princeton, NJ: American School of Classical Studies at Athens.

Taylor, J. du Plat, ed. 1965. *Marine archaeology: Developments during sixty years in the Mediterranean.* London: Hutchinson.

Testaguzza, O. 1970. *Portus.* Rome: Julia.

Uggeri, G. 1968. La terminologia portuale romana e la documentazione dell' "Itinerarium Antonini." *Studi Italiani di Filologia Classica* 40: 225–254.

Vann, R. L., and R. L. Hohlfelder. 1999. Survey of the ancient harbors in Turkey: 1997 season at Aperlae in Lycia. *Alzrastrimia Sonuclari Toplantisi* 16: 443–460.

Vortruba, G. 2007. Imported building materials of Sebastos Harbour, Israel. *International Journal of Nautical Archaeology* 36: 225–235.

Wachsmann, S. 1998. *Seagoing ships and seamanship in the Bronze Age Levant.* College Station: Texas A&M University Press.

Wachsmann, S., R. K. Dunn, J. R. Hale, R. L. Hohlfelder, L. B. Conyers, E. G. Ernenwein, P. Sheets, M. L. P. Blot, F. Castro, and D. Davis. 2009. The paleo-environmental contexts of three possible Phoenician anchorages in Portugal. *International Journal of Nautical Archaeology* 38: 221–280.

Yule, B., and A. J. Barham. 1999. Caesarea's inner harbour: The potential of the harbour sediments. In *Caesarea maritima: A retrospective after two millennia*, ed. A. Raban and K. G. Holum, 262–284. Leiden: Brill.

Zangger, E. 1997. The Pylos Regional Archaeological Project, part II: Landscape evolution and site preservation. *Hesperia* 66: 549–641.

CHAPTER 36

....

SHIPYARD ARCHAEOLOGY

....

JASON D. MOSER

INTRODUCTION

....

As our understanding of the limits of archaeological data based solely on ship-wrecks has grown, we have broadened our archaeological horizons to include all material culture of the maritime world. This concept advancing the broader inter-pretation of maritime sites was introduced as the maritime cultural landscape, which includes all of the material remains at the shoreline, under or above water (Westerdahl in this volume). The interface between the land and the water, is one of the most dynamic environmental zones in which humans regularly work. This zone also contains some of the densest collections of maritime archaeological sites in the world. These sites include shipwrecks and a diversity of maritime structures, in-cluding wharves, piers, quays, and shipyards, that were necessary for maintenance, commerce, and communication (Ford in this volume).

Arguably one of the most fascinating site types within the maritime cultural landscape is the shipyard. Shipyards are interesting because they are intimately linked with both the ships that they built and the cultures that built them. They provide a tangible link between event-based site occurrences (e.g., shipwrecks) and the larger contemporaneous context (e.g., culture) in which these seagoing vessels were constructed. Like the vessels they built, shipyards were part of a system that influenced the globalization of exploration, commerce, communication, migration, and the dispersal of cultures throughout the world. Because of their role in ship design and construction, shipyards directly reflected the predominant socioeco-nomic forces in which watercraft were intended to operate. Between the fifteenth and nineteenth centuries the primacy of European shipbuilding was one of three key developments that "led to an imbalance, or 'asymmetry' between different parts of the globe" (Braudel 1992: 385).

Despite their importance, shipyards are perhaps one of the least often investigated types of industrial archaeological sites (Gawronski 2003b: 133; Pitt and Goodburn 2003: 191; Wilson 2003: 2). Maritime sites in general, and shipyards specifically, have not seen "the academic exploration their offspring, e.g. ships, receive" (Emory 2000: 32). There are a variety of cultural, academic, and practical reasons for this underrepresentation of shipyard excavations.

Many shipyards are located along urban waterfronts that are still in use and, therefore, largely inaccessible to systematic investigations due to urban land-use patterns (Gums and Shorter 2000). In rural areas, shipyards are infrequently investigated because of the ephemeral nature of these sites, which are often confused with other maritime sites (Ford 2001; Thompson 1993). When promising rural sites have been identified, archaeologists have had difficulty in excavating and interpreting such large, dynamic industrial sites. Despite these difficulties, a growing number of maritime and historical archaeologists have begun investigating these sites.

A Brief Archaeological Survey of Shipyards in Antiquity

The primary focus of this chapter is postmedieval shipyards, but it is worth mentioning that a few earlier shipyards have been archaeologically identified and studied. A number of slipways in the Mediterranean have been identified; however, these were designed to store warships out of the water. The best-known examples are the Zea slipways and ship sheds in Piraeus, Greece (Blackman 2003). Excavations of these slipways have revealed extensive infrastructure designed to support the Athenian navy (Baika 2003). Most other slipways investigated throughout the Mediterranean appear to represent similar storage facilities rather than shipbuilding locations; however, evidence of several shipbuilding yards have been identified at Thurii, Italy; Carthage; and Marseille (Blackman 2003: 86). Also, at Tel Dor, Israel, three sloping slipways were identified cut into the rock along the shoreline. Originally, they were probably 30 m in length and ranged between 3.8 and 4.5 m in width (Raban and Linder 1978: 243). Sockets for wooden supports were also identified at the Tel Dor slipways.

The identification of medieval and pre-medieval shipyards represents a difficult task. Only the largest military shipyards were likely to have preserved extensive archaeological evidence of their functions. Overall, the lack of permanent shipyards probably reflected the general lack of capital that was available to the artisan classes (Friel 1995). This scarcity of capital and the fluctuation of shipbuilding work at particular locations may have forced medieval shipwrights to migrate and probably discouraged the development of permanent shipyards.

LITERATURE REVIEW

Monographs, articles, and technical reports about Anglo-European shipbuilding and shipyards can generally be categorized as primarily historical or archaeological. The historical shipbuilding literature is quite extensive; however, most studies focus on military ship production at large British dockyards (Coad 1983; Dodds and Moore 1984; Goodwin 1987; Lavery 1989; Morriss 1983; Rodger 1986; Winklareth 2000). Other historical studies have focused on broader social, geographic, and economic aspects of shipbuilding. These works often include shipyards and ship-building as a small part of a larger work. In addition to these major historical works, there are a considerable number of monographs focusing on local shipbuilding communities (Briggs 1970; Grant 2000; Peckham 2002; Peterson 1989; Rowe 1929; Story 1991; Welch 1993; Wood 1997). In general, these works are particularistic and focus primarily on one family of shipwrights, one shipyard, or the history of a town strongly tied to shipbuilding.

One historical work by Richard Barker (1998) is useful to archaeologists because it discusses the practice of early European and Mediterranean shipbuilding traditions. This valuable article uses contemporaneous sources to describe medieval and post-medieval ship launching. Barker synthesizes previous research and provides his own interpretations of primary sources, which indicate that the conveyance of watercraft from land into the water was a difficult process. This article focuses on the details of substructures and cradles necessary for supporting a vessel during the launch process, how these structures differed across regions, and how they changed through time.

The Good Ship by Ian Friel (1995) includes a discussion of English shipbuilding and shipyards between 1200 and 1520. One of Friel's (1995: 49–52) most important revelations was that many shipyards purchased most of their timber supplies from nonlocal sources. Such a system suggests that timber availability did not tie early shipbuilders to specific building locations, nor did the availability of supplies diminish shipbuilding at rural locations. Rather, the concentration of shipbuilders in urban areas was probably stimulated by merchants who provided both the capital and the markets for new vessels (Friel 1995: 53).

Another useful synthetic historical study includes John Bradford Hunter's (1999) dissertation documenting Boston's transition from a peripheral to a core shipbuilding center. Hunter documents the expansion of the shipbuilding industry during the early nineteenth century and convincingly connects the rise of such cen-ters to the local availability of inexpensive timber and low-cost labor. William H. Thiesen's (2000) dissertation is also a useful source. In this study, Thiesen docu-ments the influence of technology in American shipyards on both shipyards and ship design. While historical in focus, this study is useful to those trying to understand the transformation of ship production from a craft-based tradition to industrial-based production. Thiesen's study is particularly useful to archaeologists for his descriptions of variability of the physical structures associated with ship-yards, and how such structures changed diachronically.

The second category of writing about shipyards uses archaeological investigations for source material. These works consist of archaeological reports, theses, and dissertations that are not readily available, as well as more widely available sources (Eddins 2000; Gawronsky 2003a; Gawronsky 2003b; Pitt and Goodburn 2003; Loewen and Cloutier 2003; Morby 2000; Moser and Cox 1999; Moser 2007; Pastron and Delgado 1991; Peterson 2002; Seidel 1993; Stammers 1999; Thompson 1993). Despite the usefulness of many of these works, they are frequently compromised by a limited research design, and/or the size and scope of the investigations that were conducted. A review of a few of these archaeological investigations summarizes the direction of research and documents the major successes and failings of these investigations.

T. W. Courtney (1974, 1975) was one of the first archaeologists to report excavations at a shipyard. In 1972, Courtney began excavations at the Royal Dockyard at Woolwich (1512–1869) in advance of efforts to redevelop the property. Because of the large area of the Woolwich Dockyard, Courtney (1974: 4) focused his research on specific activity areas. These investigations focused on portions of a building slip, a mast house, the surgeons' quarters, the central yard, the clock house, sawpits, pitch houses, roadways, a steaming kiln, a smithy, a double dock, and a steam and hammer house. These investigations were useful for identifying particular structures at Woolwich and for understanding the context of specific features, their associations with particular dockyard operations, and how they may have changed through time.

In 1994, Jonathan Adams (1994) and the University of Southampton reported on archaeological investigations at Bucklers Hard, a shipyard located on the Beaulieu River, England. Adams identified portions of four slipways, including several that were disturbed by later waterfront development. Such disturbances are often a part of shipyard archaeology and illustrate the difficulty of excavating in such environments. The archaeological work at Bucklers Hard mapped extant timber features, and completed topographic and bathymetric surveys to identify slipway features. Only limited areas of the shipyard were excavated stratigraphically (Adams 1994: 26). Consequently, the project provided reliable information about the horizontal extents of the slipways, but only limited chronological sequences of the slipway construction.

A report by Cynthia Peterson (2002) on excavations at the Dubuque Boat and Boiler Works on the Mississippi River in Dubuque County, Iowa, stands out for its synthesis of previous United States shipyard investigations. Peterson summarizes her database research of the Historic American Building Survey (HABS)/Historic American Engineering Record (HAER), National Historic Landmarks (NHL), and the National Register of Historic Places (NRHP). These searches identified elements of 14 shipyards recorded within the HABS/HEAR and NHL databases and elements of 13 shipyards listed on the NRHP. Peterson also contacted maritime researchers and State Historic Preservation Offices (SHPO) in 34 states and documented 70 shipyards, boatyards, marine railways, and related shipyard components that had been assigned official archaeological site numbers. Unfortunately, few of these sites have ever been investigated beyond a simple archaeological reconnaissance or identification survey.

Another synthetic study of shipyard sites used models based on geographic information systems (GIS) to examine the location of Chesapeake Bay shipyards (Ford 2001;

2006). Ford predicted the location of shipyards by using secondary historical sources to identify potential environmental and cultural variables that were associated with shipyards. Ford developed a model that used proximity to historic urban centers, the degree of protection offered, the channel width, the suitability of soils for construction, the suitability of the soil for tobacco cultivation, and the presence of timber appropriate for shipbuilding as the major determinants of shipyard locations (Ford 2001: 10).

Damian Goodburn (1999), in an examination of the postmedieval London waterfront, noted that elements of watercraft infrequently recovered from ship-wrecks are often preserved in anaerobic freshwater environments associated with some shipyards. His studies have also correlated tool marks on wood recovered from shipyards with the types of tools and the practices of shipwrights from partic-ular periods. He found that axes and pit saws were used to transform timber into stems, frames, knees, and beams, while adzes were mainly used for "secondary shaping, final trimming and smoothing" (Goodburn 1999: 174). The study of these timbers and refuse can also determine the type and the availability or scarcity of wood species used in shipbuilding (Goodburn 1999: 178–179).

Jerzy Gawronski (2003a, 2003b) investigated the Oostenburg shipyard in Amster-dam and the Hogendijk shipyard in Zaandam, Netherlands. Both of these investigations serve as models for theoretical and methodological approaches to investigating shipyard sites. At the seventeenth-century Vereenigde Oost-Indische Compagnie (VOC) ship-yard at Oostenburg, Gawronski (2003b: 15) focused on the layout and construction of the slipways. The scale of effort in constructing the VOC shipyard, the longevity of its ship-building operations, and the efficiency of its design and layout indicated engineering foresight and innovation in the organization of industrial production at this shipyard.

Archaeological excavations at the Hogendijk shipyard located on the river Zaan, approximately 20 km northwest of Amsterdam, suggest a marked difference in shipyard organization and design from the VOC Oostenburg facilities (Gawron-ski 2003a: 132). The excavations at Hogendijk identified four slipways constructed from recycled ship timbers that operated between 1575 and 1650 (Gawronski 2003a: 132). While the number and approximate sizes of the Hogendijk shipyard slipways were similar to those at Oostenburg, the quality of the construction and the financial cost of the construction investment in launching infrastructure were considerably lower and less permanent than those at Oostenburg. The methods used to construct the Hogendijk shipyard slipways appear to have been more hap-hazard, shorter-term, or economically restricted than those used at Oostenburg.

SHIPYARD DESIGN

Shipyards were commonly located in sheltered coves, harbors, and rivers with water that was sufficiently deep to launch large vessels at high tide (Stammers 1999: 256; Thiessen 2000: 31–32). Besides shipbuilding, shipyards performed routine maintenance and repaired vessels, and broke up older vessels to salvage timber and other materials. Although it is less frequently investigated, ship repair was the "bread and butter" of many shipyards (Stammers 1999: 254). No matter what their functions, shipyards were constrained by the physical attributes of the yard space. The number of vessels under construction or repair was limited by the amount of space available to build or repair the vessel and to store timber.

Space at urban shipyards may have been particularly limited due to the constraints of the high economic value of waterfront space. To build a sloop in the eighteenth century required approximately 225 loads (320 m^3 or 11,250 ft^3) of timber, while large eighteenth-century warships required over 3,700 loads (5,250 m^3 or 185,000 ft^3) (Dodds and Moore 1984). Michael Stammers (1999) found that English shipyards ranged from as small as 423 m^2 in size to as large as 24,280 m^2. Those shipyards with inadequate space were forced to stack and rearrange timber to keep it accessible. Despite potential disadvantages of smaller spaces, urban shipyards possessed greater access to specialized laborers, investment capital, market information, and customers (Hunter 1999: 138).

There are few early historical accounts specifically describing the practical aspects of constructing slipways and of launching a vessel. Every shipyard required at least one set of slipways or shipways for each vessel that was under construction. Larger shipyards also used dry-docks for the same purpose. Slipways and dry-docks were two of the largest and most durable features present at a shipyard. They were at the center of construction activities, and at least two were required to maintain continuous shipbuilding production. Multiple slipways also assisted in the seasoning of timber on the stocks (Stammers 1999: 259). Peckham (2002: 37) suggests that shipyards that constructed multiple vessels simultaneously usually built them in different stages. Once one vessel was launched and was being fitted and rigged, another vessel was reaching completion, often while a third vessel was just beginning on the stocks.

Ship repair and ship breaking were two other activities that were often completed at shipyards but could also be completed at nonshipbuilding sites. Repair and ship-breaking activities are difficult to archaeologically distinguish, since both activities produce similar artifact patterns. Documentary evidence for these activities indicates that ship repair was a substantial component of shipyard business. In ship breaking, timber and fittings were salvaged from old vessels and sold for scrap and firewood, while reusable timbers were sold for the construction of new vessels. Investigations at a mid-nineteenth-century ship-breaking yard in San Francisco, California, suggest that this yard was organized to salvage the hulks abandoned along the waterfront following the California Gold Rush (Pastron and Delgado 1991). Evidence of reused elements of ships has been identified in shipwrecks and at shipyards around the world. Although ship breaking may have required skilled labor, it does not seem to have required the same infrastructure that was required to build vessels (Pastron and Delgado 1991).

SHIP LAUNCHING

The earliest boatbuilding sites probably constructed small watercraft directly on the shoreline above the high tide line. Late Viking Age (circa 950–1100 CE) vessels were launched and drawn from the water on a wooden slipway called a *hlunnr* (Jesch 2001: 170). By the thirteenth century, historical evidence suggests that trenches or launching channels were excavated from the site of the ship construction to the shoreline to facilitate launching (Barker 1998; Friel 1995: 55). Later, by the fifteenth century, royal vessels were regularly built and repaired in more formal repair locations called tidal docks (Friel 1995: 56–57). The development of this method of launch and repair corresponded with increasing vessel sizes and ultimately may have spurred the development of the first English dry-dock in 1495. Alternatively, more formal methods of launching and repair may have corresponded with the acceptance of frame-first construction techniques.

Dry-Docks

The dry-dock was "used for repairing and sometimes for building ships, which can be emptied of water and refilled as required" (Trinder 1992: 216). They were the culmination of 200 years of technological refinement and an improvement over careening or hauling vessels up a slipway for repair (Barker 1998). Careening was an uneconomical and sometimes dangerous technique for repairing vessels (Goelet 1986: 1), but "was commonly applied to smaller vessels hauled into shallow water at high tide and laid on one side leaving the other accessible for cleaning or repair when the tide receded" (Goelet 1986: 8). Careening could also be completed on a grid of timber framing placed in the water near shore, sometimes also referred to as a gridiron, but they are not well documented in the archaeological record. The remains of a probable mid-eighteenth-century careening frame were identified at the Stephen Steward shipyard near Annapolis, Maryland (Thompson 1993). Often, careening required a precision similar to that which was required to launch a new vessel. As a result of the potential for damaging a vessel while making such repairs (see, e.g., Goelet 1986: 14), dry-docks were often preferred for completing major repairs. Dry-docks were also preferred for building first-rate naval vessels that were too large to be built on ordinary slips (Falconer 1780; Dodds and Moore 1984: 30).

Over time, dry-dock designs were refined to improve efficiency and reduce the maintenance and labor costs necessary to operate them. By the seventeenth century, military dry-docks were common, but private dry-docks were available only in the major ports. By 1660, 16 privately owned dry-docks were in operation in London (Barker 1991). Edmund Dummer (1651–1713), the Surveyor of Naval Works, was responsible for the introduction of the stone dry-dock at the Plymouth dockyard (Coad 1983: 50). Prior to this, dry docks were made from earth, timber, and brick (Pitt and Goodburn 2003: 200). In the United States, the earliest known dry-dock was constructed in Boston by a private group of Charlestown residents circa 1677 (Seasholes 2003: 387). The archaeological remains of a timber wall on the northeast side of this dry-dock were identified by excavations in 1986–1987 (Seasholes 2003: 389). American naval dry-docks were not constructed until after the War of 1812, as the government began construction of a conventional navy. Stone and timber dry-docks were completed at the Charlestown Navy Yard in Boston and the Gosport Naval Shipyard in Norfolk in 1833. By the mid-nineteenth century, large floating dry-docks had begun to replace terrestrial dry-docks (Clark 1827).

Traditional Slipways

Prior to the mid-nineteenth-century proliferation of commercial dry-docks, most large European merchant vessels were probably constructed on slipways. "Slipway" is a generic term referring to the place that a ship is constructed and launched. Falconer (1780: 270) defines a slip as a "place lying with a gradual descent on the banks of a river convenient for shipbuilding." The strength and complexity of the slipway was generally determined by the type of soils that were present on a site, the types of vessels that were constructed, and the slipway's intended life cycle.

To build slipways, shipbuilders either utilized natural slopes or modified the existing shoreline. If an angle was too shallow, the vessel could become stuck fast on the launching ways. Such an event twice prevented the USS *Constitution* from being launched; a month-long reconstruction of the slipway with a steeper slope was required before the frigate could be successfully launched (Marquardt 2005). Conversely, a slope that was too steep could cause loss of control during the launch and damage to the vessel. One notable example of such an occurrence was the overly severe launching slope that caused the 60-gun frigate *L'Original* to break her back and sink at her launch in Quebec (Marcil 1995: 101). Slipways' slopes varied greatly, but the angle was generally greater than 3° and less than 11° (Thiessen 2000: 31–32).

Most slipways can be divided into multiple components, including the substructure, groundways, launching ways, and cradle (Figure 36.1). In addition to the major components, there were various supporting, shoring, and scaffolding elements. The substructure was often constructed by driving "a sufficient number of rows of piles into the ground at proper locations to support keel blocking, ways and staging, spacing them as close as necessary to attain the desired end" (Desmond 1998: 66). They provided the structural support for the subsequent components of the slipway and also supported the vessel during its construction. Slipways that were constructed on stable subsoil required the construction of only a limited substructure to support the weight of the vessel. In some instances this may have been achieved through cutting down the shoreline along the bank. Excavations at the Woolwich Dockyard indicate that the earliest slipways (circa 1680–1750) were constructed of transverse oak beams, bolted to the bedrock and in-filled with rubbish (Courtney 1974: 24).

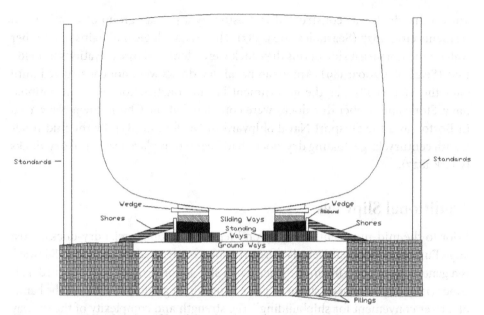

Figure 36.1 Generalized profile of the slipway substructure and vessel. Illustration by the
author after Carmichael 1919: 153.

Excavations at the Oostenburg shipyard have demonstrated the extent of the
preparations that went into creating a suitable substructure on which to build a
vessel. The archaeological remains of the 1660s slipway consisted of a slipway constructed of wooden flooring covering an area measuring approximately 12 m by 50
m (Gawronski 2003b: 18). The slipway substructure consisted of piles that were tenoned into the notched underside of unfinished pine beams, which were fixed horizontally to the pilings. The central axis of the substructure was reinforced with
additional support and heavier timbers, most likely to support the keel blocks.

Excavations at the eighteenth-century Stephen Steward Shipyard near Annapolis, Maryland, recorded a large feature complex consisting of a 15 m by 7 m scatter of
brick and oyster shell with three in situ timbers on the eastern side (Thompson
1993: 48). There was also space for two additional timbers on the west side of the
brick bed, suggesting that timbers were removed. Two other shipbuilding elements
that were associated with this feature included five scaffolding poles and a large
timber dogshore. This feature complex was part of a side-launch slipway (Thompson 1993). The history of side launching is not well documented; however, photographs of shipyards employing side-launching techniques suggest that it was utilized
in locations where the channel was narrow or the water depth was relatively shallow.
Unlike the other examples discussed in this chapter, the slipway substructure at the
Steward Shipyard was constructed from brick and shell. It is unclear whether additional timber elements were present below the brick and oyster (Thompson 1993).

Excavations at the Hogendijk Shipyard (circa 1550–1650) identified four slipways with no substructure. Slipway B, the most complete, possessed a partially

intact plank floor, 8 m by 18 m, that was originally 30 m long (Gawronski 2003a: 136). Three distinct episodes of construction and/or reconstruction were identified at Slipway B. The slipways had no evidence of substructure, even though they were constructed on unstable subsoil (Gawronski 2003a: 137). As a result, the slipways settled into the subsoil and had to be replaced every 25 years.

The second component of a slipway is the groundway, which consisted of large permanent timbers often fixed and/or fastened to the pilings of the substructure. Groundways formed the platform supporting the blocks and, later, the launching ways (Desmond 1998: 205). Archaeological evidence of groundways suggests a great degree of variability in their construction. Excavations of a slipway at the royal ship-yard at Saint Charles, Quebec, identified a timber grid sloping toward the water (Loewen and Cloutier 2003: 32). Blaise Ollivier described such a structure as a "gril-lage" or "bed," and Diderot and d'Alembert called it a "ladder" (Loewen and Clout-ier 2003: 32). Dendrochronologies of timbers from this slipway indicate that the grillage dated to circa 1663 and was repaired in the 1690s, with a wharf and flooring added in 1739 (Loewen 2009). The excavation of portions of the grillage seemed to indicate a hybrid system in which the timber grid served as both the substructure and the groundways. The use of pilings or other substructure was probably unnec-essary due to the stability of the clay subsoil at the site.

In addition to the permanent elements of the slipway, there were numerous temporary timbers that were installed anew for each launch. The shoring, standards, and scaffolding were erected as the vessel was assembled on the keel blocks. The keel blocks elevated the keel of the vessel several feet off the slipway or dry-dock to allow workers access to the bottom of the vessel. Shoring usually consisted of heavy tim-bers that kept the vessel in place while it was under construction, and smaller tim-bers that prevented it from tipping while on the keel blocks. Evidence from Dutch shipyards suggests that the bottom-first construction method may have used shorter keel blocks, while the frame-first construction method may have required higher keel blocks that allowed shipwrights to fasten the garboard and adjacent planks (Barker 1998: 68).

Barker (1998) reprises Chapman's description of the construction and launch of a small eighteenth-century vessel, in which the vessel was supported at points at the turn of the bilges during the launch. These bilgeways consisted of inclined planking located on the floor of the slipway directly below the vessel being launched. The scaffolding was often used to allow shipwrights and caulkers access to the sides of the vessels as it was being planked.

After the hull's construction was completed, the vessel was raised and the keel blocks were removed, then the vessel was lowered into place. Vertical supports were secured between the vessel and the bilgeways. The transfer of the entire weight of the vessel to these bilgeways required that they be securely fastened to the slipway and strongly anchored to pilings and posts along the slipway.

The third component of slipways, the launching or sliding ways, consisted of a large timber or plank, or several pieces that were bolted together and installed on the slipway parallel to the orientation of the slipway to carry a vessel from the building slip into the water (Desmond 1998; Stalkart 1787: 212). These timbers could be temporary, or they could be fixed in place, but they do not often survive archaeologically.

The launching ways served as a smooth platform on which the fourth and final component, the cradle, rested. The upper portion of the cradle conformed to the shape of the ship's bottom, to which it was securely attached (Falconer 1780). The lower surface of the cradle consisted of two runners that sat directly upon the launching ways. The runners of the cradle sat on opposite sides of the ship's bottom at the turn of the bilge (Stalkart 1787). As a result, this type of launching way is sometimes called "bulgeways" or "bilgeways." The hull of the vessel rested on the cradle, which rested on the launching ways and which carried the weight of the vessel and the cradle as it slid down the launching ways. To further smooth a ship's launch, the launching ways were often coated with soap or tallow for lubrication (Falconer 1780).

Barker (1998) has documented the relatively recent development of the shipyard cradle and its intricacies. In general, the cradle was a wooden framework that was custom fitted to each ship under construction. It was a temporary structure designed to hold the vessel upright during its launching. The cradle, bilgeways, poppets, and standing ways had to be very stable and strong to support the force of gravity as the weight of the vessel pushed downward, the transverse forces that pushed the bilgeways apart, and the forces of buoyancy that lifted the vessel during the final moments of the launch. Floating momentarily placed dynamic stresses on the hull as part of the vessel was supported by the buoyancy of the water, while the remainder of the hull was still on the slipways.

When it was ready for launch, the final restraints were removed, and both the cradle and the vessel traversed down the slope of the slipways into the water. If the launch was successful, most of the cradle ended up in the water at the base of the slipway as a tangled mass of wood. From historical documents it appears that there were differences between methods of launching and cradle construction that were often based on regional traditions. Some launching techniques may not have required cradles. Peckham (2002: 26) described the side launch of the *Emerald* in Essex, Connecticut, during the early twentieth century. He stated that the completed *Emerald* was lowered onto its starboard side and that she slid down the ways on one bilge. This method of launch was considerably less expensive than building a cradle.

Marine Railways

The development of the marine railway in the early nineteenth century dramatically changed the nature of shipbuilding and ship repair. The development of the marine railway allowed smaller shipyards to compete with many of the larger shipyards without having to build expensive dry-docks. The first marine railway was called the Patent Slipway. The Patent Slipway was invented by Thomas Morton in 1818 to haul vessels out of the water in order to make repairs to the hulls (Morton 1819). A new Patent Slipway cost between £450 to £1,900 depending on the size of the slipway that was constructed and the size of the vessels it could handle (George 1873). A dry-dock was 10 times as expensive to construct and was also more costly to operate.

First developed in Great Britain, the Patent Slipway consisted of two components: a set of inclined parallel iron rails, and a carriage (Figure 36.2). The rails formed the groundways and the bilgeways of the slipway, and they extended well below the water and beyond the high-water mark. The rails were inclined and generally oriented perpendicular to the direction of the shoreline, although they could also be angled. The carriage consisted of a well-constructed cradle with wheels that traversed the iron rails of the slipway. The carriage was pulled up the slipway by a system of chains or cables that were powered by winches. Initially these systems were driven by horses, but later they were powered by steam engines (George 1873). The advantage of the marine railway was the ease of launching a vessel or drawing a vessel out of the water for repair. Also, unlike the slipway cradle, the marine railway carriage was reusable.

A similar innovation in the United States resulted in the development of a technique for pulling a vessel out of the water called an "Inclined Plane." There are conflicting accounts of when the first marine railways were built in the United States, but the earliest documented example was constructed for the U.S. Navy at the Washington Naval Yard. The railway was first proposed and designed by Commodore John Rodgers in 1821 and completed in 1823 (Adams and Christian 1975; Morrison 1909; Rumm 1978). The first civilian marine railway may have been built in 1824, in Salem, Massachusetts, by the Salem Marine Railway Company (Rumm 1978; Theisen 2000). Three years later the *Franklin Journal and American Mechanics' Magazine* produced an in-depth description of the Rail-way Dock, built by

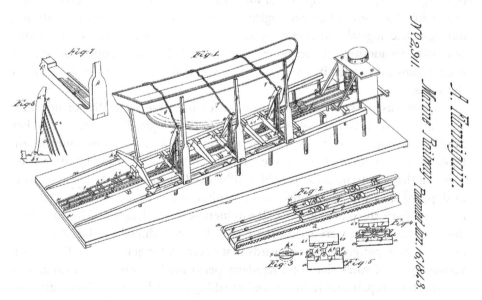

Figure 36.2 Illustration of an 1843 marine railway design (U.S. Patent No. 2911).

Mr. John Thomas in New York City (Sullivan 1827). The New York marine railway
was described as 300 ft (90 m) long, and it was initially powered by horses (Morrison 1909).

Investigations of the merits of dry-docks and marine railways by several committees of the Franklin Institute reported that the marine railway was more practical than a dry-dock and more economical than the custom of "heaving down"
(Sullivan 1827: 84–85). It was reportedly "convenient, expeditious and economical,
for the smaller class of ships of war" (Sullivan 1827: 84–85). In addition, dry-docks
were believed to be too humid, dark, and confining for proper repair work. Finally,
the committee also observed that marine railways were better adapted to the coastlines of the mid-Atlantic and southeastern United States.

Shipyard Typologies

The work at Oostenburg and Hogendijk indicates the usefulness of comparative
approaches in shipyard archaeology. One such approach uses a typology to organize
and classify site-level data into manageable and meaningful categories. Scott Emory
(2000: 36) was the first to develop such a typology by organizing late-nineteenth-
century shipyard sites into a ranked hierarchy based on his study at the Vinyard
Shipbuilding Company in Milford, Delaware. This typology used vessel size and
type as a means of providing a basic system of classification and comparison of
shipyards (Emory 2000: 36). Such a stratified typology also emphasized the resources that were available to the military in state-level societies. Although Emory's
typology is unique, it is impractical for comparing many older wooden shipyard
sites. Often the scattered archaeological remains and the limited area investigated
during archaeological studies of shipyards do not lend themselves to ready comparison with one another. Furthermore, without detailed historical documentation, it
is often difficult to identify the types of vessels that were constructed at specific
shipyards.

A more useful typology must account for the wide variability in shipyards
and the limited areas of the site that are often archaeologically investigated. When
available, it should also incorporate information about the local environment, the
types of vessels constructed, and the intensity and duration of shipbuilding operations at that location. These variables influenced the ultimate design and layout
of shipyard sites and likely influenced the initial site selection. The types of work
that were performed at shipyards also influenced their design and layout. Expedient shipyards that were used briefly and then abandoned produced different
archaeological patterns than shipyards that operated for generations. Finally, the
various types of work that were regularly performed at shipyards, such as new
construction, repair and refitting, and breaking and salvage, produced different
patterns.

The overall form of a shipyard, like all other archaeological sites, was dictated by its function, the general constraints of the site location (e.g., topography, water depth, and land availability), and the specific function of individual components at the site. The refinements and modifications of these components were achieved through efficiencies in the organization of capital, labor, supplies, and process. Therefore, the archaeological comparison of the physical structures at specific shipyards provides a basis for creating a typology that in turn will enable a more rigorous interpretation of these sites. A typology can assist in drawing broader comparisons between shipyards and the development of models that describe patterns and processes that created the degree of variability exhibited by shipyards.

Based on this, I suggest a new typology that classifies data about the shipyard infrastructure derived from archaeological and historical investigations. Fortunately, a physical structure that was present at all shipbuilding sites and was one of the most visible and durable aspect of shipbuilding was the slipway, dry-dock, or marine railway. The investment in these pieces of fixed infrastructure can serve as a proxy measurement of the shipyard size, function, and production intensity. The differences between slipways can be measured and compared both quantitatively and qualitatively. If sufficient information is available from excavations, comparisons could be measured precisely of individual slipways. Such comparisons could be based on the size and quality of slipway, or energy or construction costs. Despite the considerably variability in scale, these real differences between sites could be measured and compared. Other information, such as the presence or absence of a blacksmith's shop, storage sheds, saw houses, saw pits, utility buildings, worker housing, slave quarters, and other structures and features often associated with shipyards, further refine this typology.

The advantages of this typology include the fact that it is based on measurable aspects of material culture, such as the number of launching ways, their permanency, the method of launching (e.g., slipway, dry-dock, marine railway), culturally sensitive traditions of ship launching (e.g., side, bow, or stern launching), and the complexity of the slipway that was required to support the construction and launch of watercraft. This typology incorporates both historical and archaeological data as long as it is sufficiently detailed. Such a typology has the advantage of comparisons between different regions and continents and can be applied to different time periods. This proposed typology ranks shipyards into five broad categories or tiers.

Tier I

Tier I shipyards were the largest shipyards in operation. Tier I shipyards were exclusively state-owned and -operated shipyards. They represent the mobilization of power and resources of the state and are found only with the creation of large navies. These shipyard sites exhibit extensive horizontal and vertical integration of their labor forces and construction processes. The Royal British shipyards, the large Ming shipyard excavated at Nanjing, and the Venetian Arsenal Nuovoare are perhaps some of the best-known examples of Tier 1 shipyards (Church 2007). In addition to assembling and repairing warships, they also provided a variety of other services, including rope making, anchor- and sailmaking, and victualling, in support of the construction and maintenance of the fleet. The centralization of these industries into one location permitted a higher level of control over the rate of production and quality. The dockyards of many postmedieval European and Mediterranean naval powers operated Tier I shipyards.

By the end of the eighteenth century and the beginning of the nineteenth, Great Britain was the dominant naval force in the world. The size and scale of the Royal Naval Dockyards reflected the importance of the navy for the maintenance of Great Britain's colonies. These dockyards possessed multiple dry-docks, wet-docks, and slipways as well as a large, diversified permanent workforce, and they are the best-understood Tier I shipyards due to the extensive documentation of their development. As Coad (1983: 15) states, prior to the mid-eighteenth century, "the Royal dockyards could lay claim to being the industrial centers of England, if not in terms of absolute numbers, certainly in the variety of crafts and trades to be found in them or closely associated with them." The dockyards were used as fleet bases; they had sheltered moorings, ordnance yards, gunpowder stores, victualling yards, and, eventually, naval hospitals in addition to the structures necessary to build and launch a ship of the line (Coad 1983: 19). However, it was the presence of multiple slipways and dry-docks at such yards that distinguished Tier I sites from any other.

Tier II

Tier II sites were equally well organized and possessed a large labor force. The VOC shipyard at Oostenburg, Amsterdam, is an example of a Tier II site. These sites differ from Tier I sites because, although they could also be owned or supported by the government, they were typically smaller than Tier I sites. Investigations at the VOC shipyard in Amsterdam documented three slipways and demonstrated the scale of effort in constructing the shipyard, the longevity of its shipbuilding operations, and the efficiency of its design and layout, all of which indicated a large degree of engineering foresight and innovation in the organization of industrial production. Excavations have identified a portion of the harbor, two launching slips, and a number of structures associated with the shoreline. The number of pilings and the scale of construction denoted a large shipbuilding and repair facility that was well capitalized.

Tier III

Tier III shipyards were well organized, had a substantial labor force, and could build or repair multiple vessels simultaneously. The Stephen Steward shipyard is an eighteenth-century colonial and Revolutionary War period shipyard located on the West River approximately 10 miles (16 km) south of Annapolis, Maryland. This site is a well-documented and -preserved and extensively excavated shipyard. Selected portions of the site have been the focus of multiple archaeological investigations

(Gibb and Moser 1999; Moser and Cox 1999; Seidel 1993; Thompson 1993). Historical documents indicate that at least two ships were built "on the stocks" simultaneously (Green 1989: 118). The size and scope of this shipyard and the site infrastructure are considerably smaller than those of Tier I and II shipyard sites; however, the Steward shipyard site is larger and more sophisticated than many other American shipyards of this period.

Tier IV

Relatively few Tier IV shipyards have been identified. They were small shipyards with some investment in permant infrastructure, but were usually organized to build or repair only one vessel at a time. The Wicomico Creek Shipyard discovered during a shoreline survey in Somerset County, Maryland, is an example of a Tier IV shipyard due to the presence of a single slipway (Moser 2007). The shipyard was initially identified by the presence of a large wooden slipway adjacent to a modern pier. The slipway is subrectangular in plan, and its overall dimensions are approximately 35 ft by 100 ft (10.7 m by 30.5 m). The slipway is divided into two distinct areas designated as the upper and lower slipway. The upper slipway, located along the shoreline, is composed of five large transverse timbers set into shallow trenches, with only the upper half of the timbers visible. These timbers may represent groundways and a construction area. The lower slipway is composed of over 5,000 closely abutting individual pine pilings that form a continuous wood floor over an area of approximately 63 ft by 35 ft (19.2 m by 10.7 m). The pilings were driven into the creek bed, forming a slope. The creek channel deepens rapidly beyond the end of the slipway, from 4 ft to 8.5 ft (1.2 m to 2.6 m) at a distance of approximately 50 ft (15 m) beyond the last pilings. Dendrochronology analysis indicates that the large timbers of the upper slipway were felled circa 1800 (Moser 2007). This information, in conjunction with historical research, indicates that the tract was part a shipyard operated and later owned by shipwright Daniel Whitney. Whitney is known to have constructed several large vessels in the area, including the 292-ton *Commodore Rodgers*, and he may have been involved in the construction of the 325-ton *Shepherdess* (Moser 2007). The remainder of the shipyard has not been completely investigated.

Tier V

Tier V shipyards were small, expediently organized shipyards with little permanent infrastructure and were likely used for constructing or repairing few vessels. The archaeological remains of these shipyards are often ephemeral and easily mistaken for other waterfront activities. One example of such a shipyard was operated north of Annapolis, Maryland, by Benjamin Salyer. Salyer was a colonial shipwright who became entangled in legal and financial difficulties. A series of county court cases, newspaper advertisements, and the account book of a local merchant identify a sailing vessel Salyer was contracted to construct and describe the schedule of payment for this work. The vessel was described as measuring 48 ft (14.6 m) along the keel, 20 ft (6.1 m) in beam, 10 ft (3 m) at the hold, and 4 ft (1.2 m) between the decks, and her upper works were supposed to be completed as "galley built" (MSA Anne Arundel County Judgments, Liber ISB 2, folio 35). The vessel was most likely constructed on a 5-acre (2-hectare) tract located on the north side of the Magothy River (MSA, Unpatented Surveys, No. 446) owned and operated by a partnership of merchants who employed Salyer.

The shipyard was never completely described; however, court cases against Salyer contained an inventory of items at the shipyard and debts he owed (MSA, Anne Arundel County Judgment Records, Liber ISB 2, folio 297). Salyer owed money for 270 ft (80 m) of pine plank, 2,000 ft (610 m) of 2 in (5 cm) plank, and a debt of £6.14.2½ incurred for the use of a slave named Sambo for 60 days' worth of work. Other items at the shipyard included two beds, tools, one anvil and one pair of bellows, bar iron, a great hammer, a little hammer, a 5-pound maul, a scriving chisel, carpenters' tools, and a crowbar (MHS, Thomas Williamson's Account Book). Like most Tier V shipyards, Salyer's shipyard has not been identified archaeologically. It is likely that most similar shipyards will also be identified through historical research and then perhaps identified archaeologically. Shipyards such as Benjamin Salyer's rarely possessed the permanent infrastructure necessary to readily identify such sites archaeologically or cartographically.

Conclusion

A review of the historical and archaeological literature indicates that relatively few shipyards have been investigated archaeologically. Furthermore, many of these archaeological investigations have focused on relatively small areas of the overall shipyard. The few shipyards that have been archaeologically investigated and the diversity of data collected at these sites have created difficulties in contextualizing the results of many of these excavations. Specific historical data has played a critical role in understanding the operations of shipyards; however, much of the historical literature has resulted in overly generalized statements about shipbuilding. Even when accurate, many of these generalizations are often only applicable to a particular region or time period.

At present, the best method for reliably comparing shipyard sites involves the thorough documentation of fixed shipyard infrastructure, which serves as a proxy measurement of the intensity and longevity of shipbuilding or repair. The most visible elements of shipyard infrastructure were those associated with the construction and launch of vessels. The slipways, dry-docks, and marine railways were the most important infrastructure elements at these shipyards. Data about the details of these structures indicate a great deal about the capital and energy required to build and operate these shipyards, as well as the potential aspirations of the owners.

Through the use of comparative analysis it is then possible to describe the wide degree of cultural variability between shipyards through time. The typology presented in this article is not intended to be a definitive method for comparing these types of maritime sites. Instead, it suggests a conceptual framework for understanding the distinctions and similarities between similar types of sites.

In fact, there are problems inherent in the use of infrastructure as a proxy measurement for capitalization of shipyards. Among the most difficult of these is associated with the analysis of site infrastructure at sites occupied for many generations or centuries. Since these shipyards continued to operate, the infrastructure was continually upgraded, reused, and abandoned. Slipways that were too small may have been abandoned, only to be modified and put into use again at later dates. Such longer operations make the infrastructure more difficult to classify. This factor is somewhat offset by the fact that shipyards that were in operation for longer periods of time often left greater quantities of historical data in the records and archives.

The review of the current state of shipyard archaeology and the typology presented in this chapter suggest future directions for collecting and organizing the data in a way that may prove more fruitful for large-scale comparative analysis. As a whole, shipyard archaeology is a relatively new and exciting topic. Our understanding of the role of shipyards is growing more sophisticated. These unique locations at the interface between the land and the sea directly linked local communities around the globe. Such contacts exposed shipbuilders to wide variety of shipbuilding techniques, technology, ideas, and culture (Wilson 2003). Shipyard archaeology is an opportunity to interpret shipbuilding within a larger context of the maritime landscape. Its pursuit opens the door to developing more complex and accurate models of industry, commerce, technology, and economics of different periods and regions. The development and refinement of such models will provide a richer understanding of the maritime landscape (Wilson 2003: 2).

ACKNOWLEDGMENTS

I would like to thank everyone who has so generously assisted with my dissertation research and this article by contributing their time and expertise. In particular, I wish to thank Stephen R. Bilicki and Dr. Susan Langley, without whom this chapter would not have been possible. I want to thank all the volunteers who assisted in the fieldwork, including Jennifer Gardner, Sherri Marsh, Dr. Mark Staniforth, Paul Touart, Michael Worthington, Dr. James G. Gibb, Dionisios K. Kavadias, Pete Lesher, and Troy Nowak. I would also like to thank Dr. Rochelle Marrinan, Dr. Glen Doran, Dr. Christer Westerdahl, Dr. Brad Loewen, and Richard Barker for intellectual contributions to this project. Finally, I am deeply grateful for the efforts and support of the editors of this volume, whose hard work and unflagging efforts made this chapter possible.

REFERENCES

Adams, George R., and Ralph Christian. 1975. Washington Navy Yard: National Register of Historic Places Inventory Form. Nashville: American Association for State and Local History.

Adams, Jonathan. 1994. *Buckler's Hard: The Beaulieu River Project, Report No. 1.* Southampton: University of Southampton.

Amer, Christopher F., and Carlton A. Naylor. 1996. Prichard's Shipyard (38CH1049): Investigations at South Carolina's largest colonial shipyard. In *Mount Pleasant archaeological heritage*, ed. Amy Thompson McCandles, 36–49. Mount Pleasant, SC: Town of Mount Pleasant.

Anonymous. 1827. Observations on the Floating Dock, Invented by Commodore Barron: As Described in the Franklin Journal for January, 1827, and Recommended by a Select Committee, to the Merchants of Philadelphia. *Franklin Journal and American Mechanics Magazine* 3: 87–91.

Baika, Kalliopi. 2003. Operating on shipsheds and slipways: Evidence of underwater configuration of slipways from Neosoikos of "Trypiti." In *Boats, ships and shipyards: Proceedings of the Ninth International Symposium on Boat and Ship Archaeology*, ed. Carlo Beltrame, 103–108. Oxford: Oxbow.

Barker, Richard. 1991. Careening: Art and anecdote. *Mare Liberum* 2 (1991): 177–207.

———. 1998. Cradles of navigation: Launching ships in the age of discoveries. *Limites Do Mare Da Terra* (1998): 67–87.

Blackman, David. 2003. Progress in the study of ancient shipsheds: A review. In *Boats, ships and shipyards: Proceedings of the Ninth International Symposium on Boat and Ship Archaeology*, ed. Carlo Beltrame, 81–91. Oxford: Oxbow.

Braudel, Fernand. 1992. *Civilization and capitalism, 15th–18th century: The structure of everyday life.* Berkeley and Los Angeles: University of California Press.

Briggs, L. Vernon. [1889] 1970. *History of shipbuilding on North River, Plymouth County, Massachusetts, with genealogies of the shipbuilders, and accounts of the industries upon its tributaries, 1640 to 1872.* New York: Coburn Brothers.

Carmichael, Andrew W. 1919. *Practical ship production.* New York: McGraw-Hill.

Church, Sally K. 2007. Book review of the Ming Dynasty Baochuanchang Shipyard in Nanjing. *International Journal of Nautical Archaeology* 37 (1): 198–200.

Clark, Edward. 1827. Report of the Committee of Inventions, of the Franklin Institute, on the Plan of a Floating Dry Dock, Invented by Edward Clark, Civil Engineer. *Journal of the Franklin Institute* 3: 424–427.

Coad, Jonathan G. 1983. *Historic architecture of the Royal Navy.* London: Victor Gollancz.

Courtney, Terry W. 1974. Excavations at the Royal Dockyard, Woolwich, 1972–1973, part one: The building slips. *Journal for the Society of Post-Medieval Archaeology* 8: 1–28.

———. 1975. Excavations at the Royal Dockyard, Woolwich, 1972–1973, part two: The central area. *Journal for the Society of Post-Medieval Archaeology* 9: 42–102.

Desmond, Charles. [1919] 1998. *Wooden ship-building.* Vestal, NY: Vestal Press.

Dodds, James, and James Moore. 1984. *Building the wooden fighting ship.* New York: Facts on File Publications.

Eddins, John T. 2000. *Archaeological investigations for the branch relocation of Naval Sea Systems Command, Washington Navy Yard, Washington D.C.* Washington, DC: Louis Berger Group.

Emory, Scott. 2000. The Vinyard Shipbuilding Company: From wood shavings to hot sparks. MA thesis, East Carolina University.

Falconer, William. 1780. *An universal dictionary of the marine*. London: T. Caddel.

Ford, Ben. 2001. Shipbuilding in Maryland, 1631–1850. MA thesis, The College of William and Mary.

———. 2006. Down by the water's edge: Modeling shipyard locations in Maryland, USA. *International Journal of Nautical Archaeology* 36 (1): 125–137.

Friel, Ian. 1995. *The good ship: Ships, shipbuilding and technology in England 1200–1520*. Baltimore: Johns Hopkins University Press.

Gawronski, Jerzy. 2003a. The Hogendijk Shipyard in Zaandam and the VOC Shipyard Oostenburg in Amsterdam: Examples of recent archaeological slipway research in the Netherlands. In *Boats, ships and shipyards: Proceedings of the Ninth International Symposium on Boat and Ship Archaeology*, ed. Carlo Beltrame, 132–143. Oxford: Oxbow.

———. 2003b. Slipways of the VOC Shipyard Oostenburg in Amsterdam: A maritime site where tradition and innovation meet. In *Mer et monde: Questions d'archeologie maritime*, ed. Christian Roy, Jean Belisle, Marc-Andre Bernier, and Brad Loewen, 10–22. Quebec: Association des Archeologues du Quebec.

George, J. Rees C. E. 1873. Description of the patent slip at Evans Bay, Wellington, and on the mode of erecting or constructing the same. *Proceedings of the Royal Society of New Zealand 1868–1961*, no. 6: 14–25.

Goelet, Michael Peter. 1986. The careening and bottom maintenance of wooden sailing vessels. MA thesis, Texas A&M University.

Goodburn, Damian. 1999. Echoes of axes, adzes and pitsaws. In *Old and new worlds*, ed. G. Egan and R. Michael, 171–179. Oxford: Oxbow.

Goodwin, Peter. 1987. *The construction and fitting of the English man of war, 1650–1850*. Annapolis: Naval Institute Press.

Grant, Ellsworth S. 2000. *"Thar she goes!": Shipbuilding on the Connecticut River*. Essex, CT: Greenwich Publishing Group.

Green, Karen Mauer. 1989. *The Maryland Gazette 1721–1761: Genealogical and historical abstracts*. Galveston: Foundation Press.

Gums, Bonnie L., and George W. Shorter Jr. 2000. Mobile's waterfront: The development of a port city. In *Archaeology of southern urban landscapes*, ed. Amy L. Young, 30–51. Tuscaloosa: University of Alabama Press.

Huffington, Paul, and J. Nelson Clifford. 1939. Evolution of shipbuilding in southeastern Massachusetts. *Economic Geography* 15 (4): 362–378.

Hunter, John Bradford. 1999. Boston and its maritime world, 1790–1850: Trade circuits, proto-industrialization and the historical geography of shipbuilding in New England. PhD diss., Pennsylvania State University.

Jesch, Judith. 2001. *Ships and men in the late Viking Age: The vocabulary of runic inscriptions and Skaldic verse*. Woodbridge, UK: Boydell Press.

Lavery, Brian. 1989. *Nelson's navy: The ships, men and organization 1793–1815*. London: Conway Maritime Press.

Loewen, Brad. 2009. Personal communication re: Translation of the article Le Chantier Naval Royal. E-mail to Jason D. Moser.

Loewen, Brad, and Celine Cloutier. 2003. Le Chantier Naval Royal à Québec et le savoir maritime au XVIIIe siècle. In *Mer et monde: Questions d'archeologie maritime*, ed. Christian Roy, Jean Belisle, Marc-Andre Bernier, and Brad Loewen, 23–42. Quebec: Association des archeologues du Quebec.

Marcil, Eileen Reid. 1995. *The Charley-Man: A history of wooden shipbuilding at Quebec 1763–1893*. Ontario: Quarry Press.

Marquardt, Karl Heinz. 2005. *The 44-gun frigate USS* Constitution: *"Old Ironsides."* London: Conway Maritime Press.

Maryland State Archives (MSA). MSA C91-21, Anne Arundel County Judgment Records, Liber ISB 2, folios 35 and 297, 1754.

———. MSA S1212454, Land Office, Unpatented Surveys, Certificate No. 454, 1751.

Maryland Historical Society (MHS). MS 913. Thomas Williamson Account Book, 1746–1749. Account Book on file at Maryland Historical Society, Baltimore, Maryland.

Morby, Sarah J. 2000. Pritchard's Shipyard: A landscape analysis of South Carolina's largest colonial and antebellum shipyard. MA thesis, University of South Carolina.

Morrison, John Harrison. 1909. *History of New York ship yards.* New York: W. F. Sametz and Company.

Morriss, Roger. 1983. *The Royal Dockyards during the Revolutionary and Napoleonic Wars.* Leicester: Leicester University Press.

Morton, Thomas. 1819. Mr. Morton's Method for Dragging Ships Out of the Water on Dry Land. In *The Repertory of Patent Inventions of Arts, Manufactures, and Agriculture. The Philosophical Transactions and Scientific Journals of All Nations Intelligence Relating to the Useful Arts, Proceedings of Learned Societies and Notices of All Patents Granted for Inventions,* Vol. 35, 2nd ser.: 272–276.

Moser, Jason D. 2007. *Lower Eastern Shore shipyard survey: Archaeological and historical investigations.* Report prepared on behalf of the Chesapeake Bay Maritime Museum.

Moser, Jason D., and C. Jane Cox. 1999. *Stephen Steward's Shipyard (18AN817): Geophysical, archaeological, and historical investigations.* Annapolis, MD: Lost Towns Project.

Pastron, Allen G., and James P. Delgado. 1991. Archaeological investigations of a mid-19th century ship-breaking yard, San Francisco, California. *Historical Archaeology* 25 (3): 61–77.

Peckham, Courtney Ellis. 2002. *Essex shipbuilding: Images of America.* Charleston: Arcadia.

Peterson, Cynthia L. 2002. *Phase III data recovery at Site 13DB571, a.k.a. the former Dubuque Boat and Boiler Works, at the proposed location of the Mississippi River Discovery Center, Section 30, T89N-R3E, City of Dubuque, Dubuque County, Iowa.* Iowa City: University of Iowa, Office of the State Archaeologist.

Peterson, William N. 1989. *"Mystic Built" ships and shipyards of the Mystic River, Connecticut, 1784–1919.* Mystic: Mystic Seaport Museum. Mystic: Mystic Seaport Museum.

Pitt, Ken, and Damian M. Goodburn. 2003. 18th- and 19th-century shipyards at the south-east entrance to the West India Docks, London. *International Journal of Nautical Archaeology* 32 (2): 191–209.

Raban, Avner, and Elisha Linder. 1978. Dor: A Hellenistic shipyard. *International Journal of Nautical Archaeology* 7 (3): 243.

Rodger, N. A. M. 1986. *The wooden world: An anatomy of the Georgian navy.* New York: W. W. Norton.

Rowe, William Hutchinson. 1929. *Shipbuilding days in Casco Bay 1727–1890: Being footnotes to the maritime history of Maine.* Yarmouth: Southworth Press.

Rumm, John C. 1978. *From inclined plane to railway dry dock: The marine railway—its origins and development through the mid-19th century.* Columbus: Ohio State University Press.

Seasholes, Nancy S. 2003. *Gaining ground: A history of landmaking in Boston.* Cambridge: MIT Press.

Seidel, John L. 1993. *Preliminary report: 1993 Archaeological Society of Maryland field session at Steward's Shipyard (18AN817).* Crownsville: Maryland Historical Trust.

Stalkart, Marmaduke. 1787. *Naval Architecture, or the Rudiments and Rules of Ship-Building in a series of Drafts and Plans, with Observations Tending to the further Improvement of that Important Art.* 2nd ed. London: Letter Press.

Stammers, Michael. 1999. Slipways and steamchests: The archaeology of 18th and 19th century wooden merchant shipyards in the United Kingdom. *International Journal of Nautical Archaeology* 28 (3): 253–264.

Story, Dana A. 1991. *Growing up in a shipyard: Reminiscences of a shipbuilding life in Essex, Massachusetts.* Mystic: Mystic Seaport Museum.

Sullivan, John L. 1827. A Description of the American Marine Rail-Way, as Constructed at New York. *Franklin Journal, and American Mechanics' Magazine,* 3: 73–85.

Thiesen, William Harold. 2000. From practical to theoretical shipbuilding: The rationalization of an American craft, 1820–1920. PhD diss., University of Delaware.

Thompson, Bruce F. 1993. *Preliminary report of archaeological investigations at the Stephen Steward Shipyard Site 18AN817.* Crownsville: Maryland Historical Trust.

Trinder, Barrie. 1992. Dry dock. In *The Blackwell encyclopedia of industrial archaeology,* ed. Barrie Trinder, 216. Oxford: Blackwell.

United States Patent Office. 1843. Andrew Flannigan's Marine Railway, Patent No. 2911. Online at http://patft.uspto.gov/netahtml/PTO/srchnum.htm/. Accessed 31 March 2010.

Welch, Richard Floyd. 1993. *An island's trade: Nineteenth century wooden shipbuilding on Long Island* (New York). Stony Brook: State University of New York at Stony Brook.

Wilson, Garth. 2003. The culture of shipbuilding in Canada. *Mer et monde: Question d'archeologie maritime,* ed. Christian Roy, Jean Belisle, Marc-Andre Bernier, and Brad Loewen, 1–9. Quebec: Association des archeologues du Quebec.

Winklareth, Robert J. 2000. *Naval shipbuilders of the world from the age of sail to the present day.* London: Chatham.

Wood, James L. 1997. Shipbuilding: Scotland's past in action. Edinburgh: NMS.

CHAPTER 37

SHIP ABANDONMENT

NATHAN RICHARDS

INTRODUCTION

GROWING out of a foundation in maritime and insurance law, "ship abandonment" is a term that relates to "shipownership," or more specifically the transfer of vessel possession. Indeed, the doctrine of "ship abandonment" is at the core of marine insurance classification, and the phrase references the process via which a ship-owner hands a vessel over to their underwriter upon the loss of their watercraft. In practice, it also has a specific connotation that refers to giving up control of a vessel upon its *total loss* (whether actual or constructive) (see Holman 1953: 45, 53–54; Lloyd's of London 1973: 423, 1981: 488, 500–501, 1991: 370, 380; Stevens 1947: 6, 64). While these definitions are predominantly concerned with wrecked watercraft, to the archaeologist the word "abandonment" relates to a variety of behaviors that include the accidental and catastrophic but also concern the deliberate and well rehearsed (and therefore fall outside of marine insurance concerns). In other words, all watercraft, irrespective of their fate, come to be abandoned in some way by the people who used them, whether they are people scurrying to leave a sinking ship, or merchants seeking to dispose of their unwanted craft. To put it differently, the events and processes that are represented in ship abandonment activities are important cultural site formation processes, ones that are often characterized as the transformation of an object from a systemic (use) context into an archaeological context (Schiffer 1972, 1996).

This exploration of the theme of ship abandonment is divided into two sections. First, extending from the discussion above, it examines classification of abandonment behaviors and activities in order to show how understanding abandonment and discard events and processes can alter the way we extract meaning from abandoned vessels for the purposes of illuminating the thoughts and activities of past peoples. Second, it looks at the long history of ship abandonment studies by maritime historians and archaeologists. These studies, both particularistic and comparative, involve sites ranging from vessel fragments and isolated ship-finds to large clusters of watercraft (ships' graveyards). Together, they paint a picture of the diverse contexts within which ship abandonment occurs and illustrate the significance of the resource and the potential for future study.

CLASSIFICATION OF ABANDONMENT BEHAVIOR AND ACTIVITY

In maritime archaeology, the phrase "ship abandonment" is most often used in relation to the act of "ship discard," or the purposeful act of discarding vessels, most often culminating in the creation of ships' graveyards or marine boneyards. As such, it stands in distinction to "Shipwreck," which implies catastrophic loss. The *Oxford English Dictionary* defines a shipwreck as "what is cast up from a wreck; the remains of a wrecked vessel; wreckage," and the "destruction or loss of a ship by its being sunk or broken up by the violence of the sea, or by its striking or stranding upon a rock or shoal" (Simpson and Weiner 1989: 280). At the heart of these definitions it is clear that catastrophic events are what turn ships to shipwrecks. From such categorization, it also follows that discarded vessels, those ships deliberately thrown away or disposed of by their owners, do not fit the traditional definition of "shipwreck." These semantic differentiations are pivotal for understanding the nature of abandonment processes, discard activities, and, most importantly, the role of *behavior* in the creation of certain types of archaeological sites. From a behavioral perspective, it is clear that catastrophes and deliberately determined acts will induce different responses in human beings. Where the traces of a shipwreck represent the powerlessness of humans within a hostile natural world, the remains of discarded vessels represent the power that humans have within the landscapes of their own construction, the *cultural environment*.

Some researchers have commented on this shipwreck/abandonment dichotomy as it applies to ship abandonment. Donald Shomette, for instance, considers abandoned vessels an "important variation of the shipwreck category" (Shomette 1995a: 6–7; see also Babits and Corbin-Kjorness 1995: 38–39). Shomette's view focuses more attention on the role of human agency as a historical force and a significant influence on altering both the landscape and the archaeological record. Shomette distinguishes between "abandonments at sea," which emerge from catastrophic events, and "old or useless wrecks," which are often disposed of due to their obsolescence and condition, allowing for the behavioral aspects of the archaeological remains of watercraft to be better understood.

Growing from Shomette's explicitly behavioral definition is the work of Richards in *Ships' Graveyards: Abandoned Watercraft and the Archaeological Site Formation Process* (2008), which maintains that abandoned vessels are not a variation of shipwreck, but a discrete component of the maritime archaeological record. For Richards, this distinction is important in understanding that the processes interacting with a ship on its journey from its life of use to its integration as a component of the archaeological record are not just many and diverse, but also have major ramifications for how we can read the archaeological record and how archaeological resources can be used in research. Moreover, these distinctions are significant because they demonstrate the relationship between abandonment activities and cultural processes.

In this way, the dichotomous relationship between wrecked ships and discarded ships is also important because both categories of maritime archaeological site exist at the extremes of a behavioral spectrum concerned with the nature of human decision-making processes (agency). Within this continuum, there are essentially three major classifications of abandonment behavior. According to Richards, each type (mentioned below) illustrates a range of cultural behaviors associated with the loss and discard of watercraft.

Catastrophic abandonment takes place when the desertion of a ship becomes a prerequisite in the preservation of life. The passenger steamer RMS *Titanic* (1912) was abandoned when it hit an iceberg, as were the English naval frigate HMS *Pandora* (1791), when it struck the Great Barrier Reef, and the English flagship of the Virginia Company, *Sea Venture* (1609), when it collided with the islands of Bermuda (Ballard and Archbold 1995; Gesner 1991: xi, 13, 14, 2000: 1; Harris and Adams 1997: 365–366). This also commonly occurs when a crew abandons a vessel because of perception of an *impending* disaster. When the vessel does not sink, the vessel becomes derelict (see Lloyd's of London 1973: 425, 1981: 493). In these situations ships invariably become shipwrecks, and "abandonment" becomes synonymous with "escape." The decision occurs without consideration of the value of the vessel undergoing abandonment, and the end product is a bona fide *shipwreck*.

Consequential abandonment occurs when there is a need to ruin a ship in order to protect lives, cargo, and other structures from damage or destruction. One variation of this is seen in the example of the fire on the merchantman *General Knox* in August 1894 while it was lying alongside a New York wharf. Because the vessel was a threat to everything nearby, it was scuttled in order to extinguish the flames (Matthews 1987a: 135). Also included in this category are cases of the nonaccidental wrecking of vessels after mishaps at sea where the deliberate destruction of the ship is needed in order to create better circumstances for the preservation of life and cargo. One occurrence was the wrecking of the "Country" trade merchantman *Sydney Cove* near Preservation Island, Tasmania, in 1797. In this case, the threat of losing cargo due to a leaking hull and bad weather impelled the captain to deliberately run the vessel aground on the closest shoreline (Nash 1996: 22).

Despite catastrophic circumstances leading to the destruction of these ships, it is clear that the act of abandonment in all cases occurred because inaction would create a more substantial tragedy (often defined in terms of more significant loss to goods instead of human lives). Within this definition, the loss of the watercraft is always a consequence of actual or imminent catastrophe, but decisions occur with some thought concerning value and the potential losses and gains that would culminate with the act of abandonment. In this light, the phrase "consequential abandonment" becomes synonymous with the phrase "deliberate wrecking."

With both *catastrophic* and *consequential* abandonment, some degree of human decision making plays a role in the way events pan out. When deliberately running a vessel aground in order to save crew and cargo, for instance, a captain will have some time to make choices regarding the location for the ship's abandonment. Indeed, research regarding wreck patterning strongly suggests that even in the worst catastrophic circumstance, the intended route from point of departure to anticipated port of destination already reflects a large degree of decision making concerning potential risks to ship, lives, and merchandise (see Duncan 2000; Murphy 1983; Souza 1998). It is important to remember, however, that the decisions are not being made *at the leisure* of individuals, but are instead *being forced* upon them, and their options are normally limited. Hence, both types of abandonment are examples of *premature loss*.

Whether deliberately or catastrophically wrecked, the occurrence of loss through an element of surprise is the reason that definitions of abandonment within marine insurance exist. If a vessel is lost unintentionally, for reasons not attributable to the owner or operator, the ship will remain covered by insurance. Any captain or owner not seeking to reduce their loss, or not choosing to abandon their ship under such circumstances, will be legally negligent.

This is not the case with *deliberate abandonment*, which occurs when the act of abandonment involves premeditation in every sense. In these cases abandonment under marine insurance definitions do not apply, as the act of disposal is a planned one, without urgency, and without genuine threat to life or cargo. Here the act of destruction or discard is in every way intentional. Deliberately abandoned vessels are significantly different from catastrophically or deliberately wrecked watercraft because their final resting place, the intactness of their hull, and the inclusion of any material within their hull are totally determined by human intentions, decision-making processes, and actions. The only exemption to this occurs where a vessel befalls catastrophe en route to its location of discard, or where there are accidents during preparations for its disposal. For example, the barkentine *City of Adelaide* was wrecked on Magnetic Island, Queensland (Australia), before the proposed time for disposal, and one bay from its intended destination (Parsons and Plunkett 1995: 3). While this might suggest that such circumstances fall under a definition of *catastrophic abandonment*, it is worth considering that with *deliberate abandonment*, the location of discard is not the most crucial factor in the process. Arguably, despite a catastrophic aspect to the loss of vessels such as *City of Adelaide*, it is normally the facilitation of the loss of the vessel that drives its owner, irrespective of the location and circumstances of abandonment. Of more importance are the decision to abandon and the implementation of the processes that prepare the ship for its integration into the archaeological record. Exceptions occur only when people repair and refloat an abandoned vessel for further use, where it remains until it is somehow lost to human use a second time.

While the term "abandonment" may imply a relinquishing of function, it does not imply a loss of cultural value. Although the abandonment of vessels occurs because they are unwanted, sometimes the act of discard occurs with the intention of creating a new function for the vessel following its deposition. Subsequently, all abandoned watercraft (whatever the category) often retain cultural, economic, and technological value. This is best understood if we look at what maritime archaeology has discovered via the study of deliberately abandoned watercraft.

CASE STUDIES IN MARITIME ARCHAEOLOGY

Over a number of decades, maritime researchers have learned much about the past from the study of deliberately abandoned ships. The watercraft representative of this theme have proven to be as diverse and dispersed as their shipwrecked counterparts. So, too, these unwanted vessels correspond to other categories of archaeological sites—from examples many thousands of years old, to the continuing, present-day use of the sea as a dumping ground and ships as reusable objects.

Archaeological studies of abandoned watercraft exist within three major site types: isolated ship-finds, discarded and recycled disarticulated vessel components, and accumulations of watercraft known popularly as "ships' graveyards," "marine boneyards," and "rotten rows." Running throughout these site types are a number of concurrent themes representing many extinct or rare behavioral traits, as well as ones that continue to thrive.

Ritualistic Discard

One such theme is the concept of sacrificial and ritualistic discard (or "symbolic reuse") best seen in the votive offering of vessels (an offering of personal property to fulfill a religious vow), and the reutilization of ship hulls as graves. Since at least the seventeenth century, there have been reports of the reuse of ships as tombs in Scandinavia. Poetic works dating to many hundreds of years earlier also describe this activity, and researchers believe that many hundreds of such sites exist (Bruce-Mitford 1974: 81–82; Müller-Wille 1974: 187). Five sites that have been extensively recorded and published—the Snape Boat, the Sutton Hoo vessels, the Oseberg Ship, the Tune Ship, and the Gokstad Ship, dating to between the seventh and tenth centuries—best exemplify this site type (Christensen 1972: 166, 168; 1987: 6, 20–22, 27, 1997a, 1997b; Evans 1987a: 114, 1987b: 116, 1997a, 1997b). Vessels such as the Hjortspring Boat (circa 350 BCE) and other possible sites found in Danish bogs are believed to represent votive offerings (Christensen 1972: 162, 167, 1987: 86, 114;

Delgado 1997: 193). Many Egyptian boat-graves appearing in the Archaic period (First and Second dynasties), as illustrated by the royal monuments at Abydos, in the necropolis of the nobles at Helwan, and in the Fourth Dynasty at Giza, have been interpreted similarly. These sites include a number of well-known studies, like the Cheops Ships (circa 2600 BCE) and Dahshur Boats (circa 1850 BCE), as well as other archaeological work indicating that other pyramids had pits that once held ceremonial watercraft (El-Baz 1988; Jenkins 1980: 158; Miller 1988).

Structural Adaptation

In comparison to studies of the symbolic reuse of watercraft, studies of vessels reflecting functional and structural adaptation are much more common. In particular, the use of intact, articulated hulls as buildings, or foundations, is a subject well represented in archaeological literature. There are three variations on this theme of abandoned vessel as structure, relating to the types of post-abandonment functions that watercraft often serve. These include reclamation schemes, foundations, and buildings. What binds all three is their dependence to a large degree on the articulation of the extant hull (see also Delgado in this volume).

The reclamation of ground adjacent to waterways for creating more secure foundations for built structures is a common use for abandoned watercraft. Notable examples of this are located at Portus Augusti (Ostia, Italy), the B&W Engine Factory Site (Christianshavn, Denmark), and a number of sites in the ancient port of London, including the New Guys' House Boat (second century CE) and the County Hall Ship (190–225 CE) (Lemee 1997; Lemee, Schiellerup, and Gothche 1996; Marsden 1994: 11, 97, 104).

Related to reclamation, discarded watercraft may also provide solid foundations for buildings. Probably the most famous case of the use of an articulated hull for this purpose is the Ronson Ship. The Ronson Ship was used in the reclamation of land along New York's East River sometime during the mid-eighteenth century, when it was stripped, deliberately sunk, spiked through its hull with a set of piles, and filled with sand and rocks for use as a caisson or "crib hulk." By the conclusion of reclamation, the vessel was under meters of debris, and two street blocks from the waterfront (Reiss 1987: 90, 1997: 349–350; Steffy 1996: 125–128).

The reuse of ship hulls as above-ground structures also has a long history and is well represented in historical and archaeological literature. There are many examples of watercraft being converted into terrestrial structures, such as the various hulks of Port Stanley (Falkland Islands); an unidentified nineteenth-century vessel at the Royal Navy Dockyard, Bermuda (believed to be either *Dotterel*, *La Tourterelle*, or *Antelope*); the unfortunate *Arkansas*, *Niantic*, and *Apollo* (abandoned at the San Francisco waterfront during the California Gold Rush); and two wooden ships abandoned in New Zealand, *Edwin Fox* and *Inconstant*. These watercraft served a variety of functions, from victualling stores and slave dwellings to warehouses, barns, taverns, hotels, restaurants, offices, jails, churches, landing stages, and wharves (Aldsworth 1989: 109–110, 128–129; Delgado 1979; Edwin Fox Restoration

Society Inc. 1987; O'Keefe 1999). Such activities also continue in the present day, albeit less frequently. For example, ships and boats can still be found in a variety of reuse functions, such as old herring boats from Lindisfarne, England, halved and boarded up for use as fishing sheds, or transformed into breakwaters, artificial reefs, piers, hotels, bathhouses, bridges, fish depots, chapels, restaurants, mills, work-shops, or circus big tops (Figure 37.1) (Fisher 1979: 468–469; Richards 2008: 132–134, 137–143).

Salvage and Recycling

The act of abandoning and dismantling watercraft for the salvage and utilization of their component parts is another common activity that demonstrates the many ways in which unwanted vessels may retain value. Demolition, an act involving the systematic separation of vessel components, is a different form of abandonment because here the versatility of a ship's component parts has become more important than the hull structure. Nevertheless, recycling has connection to human decision-making processes concerned with the assessment of the suitability of watercraft components for other applications. The transformation of an object as large as a vessel from its initial use to another function is evidence of certain behavioral traits, from the ability to take risks in new markets through to the ability to think inge-niously in times of economic stress and find new uses for unutilized watercraft.

Figure 37.1 A view of the Tangalooma Ships' Graveyard, Moreton Island,
Queensland, showing reuse of vessels as breakwater and small boat harbor.
Reproduced with the kind permission of the author.

In addition to their potential use as fuel, another reason for dismantling and breaking down wooden vessels is their value and suitability for the manufacture of other structures. The recycling of ship's timbers allows for some economic reimbursement to the shipowner and may reduce costs for the construction of new ships.

There are two site types representative of the reuse of disarticulated watercraft timbers: actual ship-breaking industry sites, and sites where humans reused the salvaged timbers. There are few locations currently known that represent ship-breaking industries and activities in antiquity. Such places are difficult to identify due to the problems in distinguishing between the archaeological signatures of ship breaking and shipbuilding. Indeed, the high likelihood that shipbuilding and ship-breaking activities coexisted at the same site poses a major challenge to maritime archaeological research.

The remains of nine late Roman Rhine boats (circa fourth century CE) found in an ancient Roman harbor at Mainz, Germany, in 1967, are probably the best-known sites believed to represent ship-breaking activities (Hockmann 1993). One other example is work undertaken by Christoffersen (1991: 57) on the island of Funen (Fyn), Denmark, where he identified a ship-breaking or shipbuilding yard from the Scandinavian Iron Age (circa 1500 CE).

Similarly, ships' timbers found reused as decking at a site on the Thames foreshore in London in 1995 were interpreted as evidence of a ship-breaker's yard (Milne in Hammond 1995: 4). These timbers, reassembled as a grid, created a platform on which ships needing repair would lie. The site dates from at least 1838, when the vessel *Temeraire* was broken up in the vicinity (Hammond 1995: 4). Individual ship breaking and timber reuse has also been noted in a number of sites. These include the third-century BCE Kyrenia Ship (deck built from previously used timbers), the Sea of Galilee/Kinneret Boat (also partially constructed from used timbers, and interpreted as a working vessel subsequently used for spare parts), and numerous medieval Viking boats (Crumlin-Pedersen 1986: 142, 1994: 67–68; Steffy 1985: 94, 1990: 43–47; Wachsmann 1987: 81–82).

The recycling of timber salvaged from watercraft is a very different process from the structural reuse of entire vessels. Salvagers choose timbers from unwanted vessels for their shape. This is the case even when vessel components, such as large sections of planking, are relatively complete. With the odd exception, the selection strategy in the reuse of ships' timbers has been to choose "flat planking of fairly constant width" (as noted by Hutchinson 1998: 110). In certain cases, researchers have been able to make identifications of vessel types from the discovery of nonplanking components in archaeological deposits, observations of treenail hole spacing, and the dimensions of planks and fastenings. In this context, an uncharacteristic modification to usually complete ship components is an indication of reuse. Heal and Hutchinson (1986: 213) used this reasoning to show the intentional structural reduction and reuse of an incomplete log boat found at Tamworth, Shropshire. The holes and tool marks on this boat indicate that it is another clear example of modification for subsequent utilization. Damian Goodburn (1990: 332–333) has also used such a rationale to determine that the fragments of a vessel obtained after its destruction by a mechanical excavator were from a wrecked vessel, not from a structure using reused components from an abandoned watercraft.

The existence of recycled ships' timbers in shipwrecks, abandoned vessels, or waterside structures can tell us about a range of behaviors associated with the tendency to retain, destroy, or improve aging ships. They may even inform us about the changing costs of ship production over time.

Evidence of the reuse of dismantled ship timbers also comes from Lisht, Egypt. These timbers were found around the early Twelfth Dynasty Middle Kingdom pyramid of Senwosret I (1959–1914 BCE) and are believed to be from watercraft associated with monumental structures in the area (Ward-Haldane 1988: 142; Haldane 1992: 102–103). Other evidence of the reuse of ships' timbers in the context of subsequent building activity comes much later (between the tenth and seventeenth centuries CE) in western and northern Europe. Archaeologists have found these types of sites at medieval period waterfronts from Dublin, Ireland, to Bergen, Norway. In particular, a number of British studies have extensively documented ship timber reutilization at a number of locations around London, York, Bristol, Hartlepool, Newport, and Newcastle (Hutchinson 1998: 56, 65, 69, 105–106, 108–110; Marsden 1994: 141, 152–159, 1996: 9, 22, 30, 41–54, 113–127, 136–144, 160–172, 175, 179, 181, 217–221).

These studies are important for what they tell us about the condition of the vessels before salvage (reused timbers were often old or had been repaired) and illustrate the process of watercraft abandonment in the past. They give some insight into the nature of trade and technology in antiquity and inform us about the changing nature of the use of particular ships. Such comparisons are useful in our assessment of similar behaviors evident in the reuse of watercraft or parts of watercraft in more modern times, such as at the Falkland Islands (Stammers and Kearon 1992: 109).

In the era of iron and steel vessels, the use of salvaged materials from abandoned ships takes on a new characteristic due to the dominant role that ferrous-hulled vessels and their salvage play in relation to watercraft abandonment. Wooden ship scantlings can be reused only if they are sound and physically suitable to a new structure or object. Iron and steel, however, can be melted down and re-formed. Here the shape, condition, and size of the material salvaged from the dismantled vessel becomes unimportant due to the transformable features of the ferrous materials. Large groups of unwanted ships become refined veins of iron and steel, ready for mining (Figure 37.2).

Ships' Graveyards

The term "ship's graveyard" is often used by researchers for all collections of ships, such as the region popularly known as the "Graveyard of the Atlantic," and Yassiada (Bright 1993; Throckmorton 1970: vii). These sites, however, contain a high concentration of wrecked vessels rather than deliberately discarded watercraft, and are

Figure 37.2 The remains of *Sunbeam* (1857–1910), in the Garden Island ships'
graveyard (Port Adelaide, South Australia), show the scars of salvage activities
associated with scrapping from the Great Depression of the 1930s and World War II.
Reproduced with the kind permission of the author.

more appropriately called "ship traps." True ships' graveyards represent the gamut of
watercraft abandonment behaviors.

These graveyards are accumulations of watercraft retired and deliberately
abandoned by their owners following a decision that the vessels are ineffective or
inadequate for their intended purpose. The following criteria serve as a basis for
the determination of whether a region or location is indeed a ships' graveyard: one
discarded vessel lies in close proximity to other abandoned watercraft, watercraft
are discarded due to decisions regarding their suitability for use, and the location of
abandonment is determined by the consensus of a group of people. Ships end up
in ships' graveyards because their owners see more benefit in their discard and
destruction than in their use and care.

Such sites are the culmination of many of the behaviors linked with carrying
out the sacrifice, adaptation, and reuse outlined above. Woven into the fabric of the
everyday occurrence of vessel abandonment in the modern world are the same
behaviors and ideals that constituted the discard of watercraft in ages gone by. Even
watercraft deliberately abandoned in the present day provide a record of the
circumstances of their working lives and operating environments. They are also
representations of the continuation of traditions inextricably linked with the
economic and technological transitions of human societies, and are documents of
such changes themselves.

There are two types of ships' graveyards. In the first, vessels are deliberately abandoned in the context of war. This often involves the strategic use of watercraft as barriers against the enemy penetration of navigable waterways or strategic shorelines. The second type is a more general accumulation due to the dumping of unwanted vessels. This distinction is important for two reasons. The dumping of vessels within conflict-related graveyards often occurs at one given time, or at least over a very short period. The vessels are often disposed of due to imminent enemy capture, the perception that the vessel might be used against its owner, or as a defensive measure intended to slow the advance of an adversary. Due to the relatively short period for planning and implementation in this scenario, these sites may have rich artifact assemblages. These graveyards are widespread geographically and, in many cases, incorporate large numbers of watercraft.

In the second type of ships' graveyard, vessels are disposed of over an extended period. These dumping areas, often described with much flowery prose as the places where ships "are retired," accumulate a large number of diverse types of vessels (Figure 37.3). Historians and sailors alike have tended to see these locations as miserable places, not worthy of more than passing comment, or as eyesores, nuisances, or hazards to navigation, a veritable hell for "once glorious ships" (see, e.g., Matthews 1987b: 52; Moore 1970: 3). Nevertheless, researchers may find many examples of ships' graveyards in the historical record, and in some cases, documents have prompted maritime archaeologists to examine these conflict- and obsolescence-laden sites.

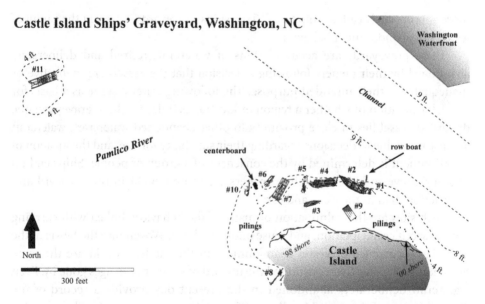

Figure 37.3 Plan view of the Castle Island ships' graveyard (Washington, North Carolina), a collection of at least 11 watercraft representing the diverse local trades and environments of the Tar-Pamlico river system. Reproduced with the kind permission of the Program in Maritime Studies, East Carolina University.

Discard, Strategy, and Conflict

The history of conflict-inspired abandonment is at least as old as the European Nydam boat finds (350–400 CE) and is represented by many case studies, from the late Saxon Clapton Logboat (Great Britain) and the sixteenth-century Mukran wreck (Germany) to the large post-thirteenth-century CE assemblages of vessels in Kalmar Harbor (Sweden) and eleventh-century CE block-ships at Skuldelev, Jydedybet, and Skane (Denmark) (Bill 1997: 388–389; Christensen 1972: 162, 164; Crumlin-Pedersen 1972: 69–70; 1991a: 42, 45; Einarsson 1997: 219–220; Marsden et al. 1989: 89, 95, 99, 109–110; Rieck 1991: 90–91, 1996; Springmann 1998: 120–123). Abandonment in the context of conflict tends to follow a number of themes related to the strategic use of watercraft. By far the most common strategies of abandonment during conflict entail the scuttling of one's own vessel or fleet, the demolition of incomplete vessels, or the destruction of a vessel by its captor. Evading vessel capture and avoiding the transfer of useful goods to an enemy appears to have been the most common reason for its occurrence. In Europe, such activities date from at least the seventeenth century, when the English destroyed their ships during the Second Anglo-Dutch War (1662–1667 CE). Later on, in 1690, the English and Dutch committed similar acts against their own fleets, something repeated by the French in 1704 during the English attack on Toulon (Warner 1968: 50–58). In North America, similar events occurred in connection with the French and Indian War/Seven Years' War (1756–1763 CE), in the prelude to and during the American War of Independence (1776–1783 CE), during the War of 1812 (1812–1815 CE), and during the American Civil War (1861–1865 CE). Conflict-abandonded ships are represented in investigations of the Wiawaka and James River bateaux (shallow-draft river vessels) sites, the French frigates *Machault*, *Marquis de Malauze*, and *Bienfaisant*, and the British sloop *Boscawen* (all lost in the French and Indian War); the privateer *Defence*; and the remains of HMS *Betsy* and the Cornwallis Cave wreck at Yorktown (American Revolutionary War) (Broadwater 1997; Crisman 1997; Johnston 1997; Shomette 1997: 98–99; Switzer 1998; Zacharchuk and Waddell 1984; Zarzynski 1997).

Naval scuttling strategies have persisted into the twentieth century, and there were many instances of the deliberate destruction of vessels during the World Wars. For example, the largest conflict-related destruction of naval vessels in history occurred on 21 June 1919, when the German Navy destroyed 74 of its own vessels at Scapa Flow (Orkney Islands, Great Britain) to prevent British capture (Van Der Vat 1998).

In other situations, navies may abandon their vessels in a manner that transforms them into devastating weapons. Many terms apply to the strategic abandonment of vessels used in this way during wartime. These terms fall within two categories: vessels modified for aggression (fire-ships), and vessels modified for defense (block-ships) (Blackburn 1978: 142; Kemp 1988: 112).

Despite a relationship between these strategies of naval engagement and catastrophic abandonment, many of these ships provide clues regarding the behaviors that brought about their abandonment. For instance, the Skuldelev vessels are important because evidence has shown that at least one vessel (Skuldelev 5) was of advanced age, had been regularly patched, had been built or repaired with recycled materials, and at the time of deposition was probably bordering on unseaworthy (Crumlin-Pedersen 1991b: 75). This illustrates the persistent economic angle to discard events of all varieties.

Likewise, the manner in which the British Navy scuttled HMS *Betsy* in 1781 during the Battle of Yorktown illustrates the methods used to ensure its destruction. Archaeological investigation of the vessel showed that *Betsy* was sunk with the use of a "scuttle-hole," where the inner starboard planking had been cut carefully with hammer and chisel to facilitate the vessel's sinking (Broadwater 1988: 806, 810).

Another variation on the theme of conflict-inspired abandonment relates to the aftermath of war. The changing economic conditions that emerge after conflict often have a marked effect on the tendency to abandon watercraft. As Daniel Lenihan has commented, "It is typical for societies to discard the tools of war when the conflict has ended. War weary nations focus on rebuilding . . . actively forgetting the carnage recently experienced" (Lenihan 1998: 294). While a tendency to abandon may be attributable to economic transitions in a burgeoning postwar world, it is also often due to the decreased need for warships and to costs associated with retarding their eventual deterioration (see, e.g., the work on *Ticonderoga* and *Eagle*: Cassavoy and Crisman 1996: 177, 179, 185–186; Crisman 1995: 4–8).

In other circumstances, a victorious military force may compel defeated groups to discard their fleets. Here discard activities are colored by undeniable political meaning. It is noteworthy, for instance, that Allied forces scuttled or scrapped most of Japan's remaining naval fleet in the aftermath of the World War II, despite the technological advancement of many ships, such as the Japanese battleship *Nagato* (1920–1946) (Delgado 1996: 18).

The phenomenon of sinking target ships is another example of conflict-inspired deliberate abandonment. This activity occurs largely outside wartime, where nations test the effectiveness of weapons on naval targets. While target ships are normally isolated occurrences, sometimes military weapons testing has created extensive ship discard sites. The ships associated with the Operation Crossroads atomic tests in the Kwajalein and Bikini Atolls in the Republic of the Marshall Islands in 1946 are the best example of this. These tests emerged from American fears that the advent of atomic warfare at Hiroshima had made the world's navies fortresses of redundant scrap. The tests constituted the destruction of ex-U.S. Navy combat vessels struck off the active list and German and Japanese war-prizes (Lenihan 1998). Reminders to the world of the power of the United States, these test were the first shots in the atomic-era games of the Cold War, sparking other nations in their own quests to strive for nuclear capability. The fact that five submarines used in this operation were not redundant at the time of their use in the tests further illuminates these activities' arm-flexing intentions (Delgado 1996: 21–22).

Discard, Trade, and Technology

When we refer to the dumping of unwanted vessels within the context of mercantile obsolescence and economic redundancy, there are two kinds of sites. First, there are isolated abandonment sites. These are watercraft dumped in solitary locations along the coasts and waterways of most maritime nations. There are many examples in historical and archaeological literature of such vessels (see, e.g., Claesson 1996: 16–17; Fenwick 1997: 175–176; Merriman 1997: 1, 10; Rusho 1962: 37, 39).

The nature of shipping and ship owning suggests that the number of vessels abandoned over time simply because they are of no further use has to be immense. The frequency of this behavior in relation to the use of the sea and other waterways as a dumping ground is nowhere better illustrated by the number and scale of watercraft disposal sites littered in and around the shorelines of almost every maritime nation.

For instance, archaeologists discovered eighteenth-century bateaux in 1974 and 1984 at the Musée de la Civilisation (Quebec City), further illustrating the tendency of humans to use vessels in waterside construction (they had been used as temporary dams) (La Roche 1987: 108–110). Another, more recent Canadian ships' graveyard is located at the southern end of the Great Cataraqui River in the inner harbor of the city of Kingston, Ontario. The collection includes many vastly different vessels, from unnamed barges discarded in the 1860s to the screw-steamer *C. D. 110*, abandoned in 1965. Many such vessels underwent conversion for post-abandonment uses as breakwaters and pier extensions, drastically altering the shape of the coastline (Moore 1995a, 1995b).

In the United Kingdom, abandoned-ship surveys at places such as Whitewall Creek (River Medway), Kidwelly (Dyfed), and on the River Tamar, and Shropshire Union Canal have added substantially to archaeological methodology (Emery 1997: 4; Milne, McKewan, and Goodburn 1998; Watson 1993: 7; Wood 1996: 6–7). One standout project is the Maritime Fife Project. Initial findings concerning one of the study areas dating to the World War I have indicated that "there is some evidence to suggest that craft may have been stockpiled in anticipation of periods of more favorable trading conditions that never came" (Dobson 1997: 3). The existence of ship stockpiles illustrates the underlying reasons that guide abandonment behavior, and shows how curatorial and reuse behaviors can exist concurrently at abandoned watercraft sites.

Other investigations of ships' graveyards expose the environmental factors that may direct the location of ships' graveyards. Environmental damage, caused by cultural activities in the landscape, is something that Somasiri Devendra (1993: 22) cites as a catalyst for the discard of watercraft in Sri Lanka. Here alterations in the landscape were noticeable in changes along rivers and at river mouths, which had been brought about by deforestation connected with plantations. This resulted in alteration to the rivers' water levels, the erosion of riverbanks, and the transformation of streams into mere trickles of water. Environmental ruin resulted, as well as the destruction of the networks used by waterborne transport. The other inevitable effect was the eventual abandonment and concealment by encroaching silt of large river craft that could no longer travel the waterways.

Ships' graveyards also tell us about the way humans structure their use of bodies of water. Geographical factors played a role in the abandonment of watercraft at Port Stanley in the Falkland Islands. In this case, vessel abandonment occurred due to the island's strategic position close to notoriously dangerous Cape Horn, and its importance as a location for ship repair or abandonment (Dean 1997a: 148–150; Dean and Miller 1979: 35; Smith 1985: 3; Southby-Tailyour 1985: 9; Throckmorton 1976: 35, 1987a: 211). The sites at Port Stanley, extensively documented by historians and archaeologists alike, are additionally important because of what they tell us about the techniques people used in abandoning and reusing the ships (see, e.g., Bound 1990, 1993; Cumming and Carter 1990; Lellman 1933; Stammers 1997; Stammers and Baker 1994; Stammers and Kearon 1991; Throckmorton 1987b: 98–100). In particular, Stammers and Kearon (1992: 109) have suggested that local quarried stone was dumped into the hold of the abandoned nineteenth-century merchantman *Jhelum* to prevent it from floating off.

Port Stanley is also significant because it has a history of structures such as storage hulks and jetties constructed from unwanted vessels. In certain instances, jetties were constructed by connecting several vessels and driving piles through them for stability and support. These ships were used for storage purposes almost to the present day. Other vessels, such as *Fennia*, were salvaged, and components were then used in dockside structures, such as in jetties joining two other ships, *Actaeon* and *Charles Cooper*. Alternatively, some, vessels became makeshift coal bunkers (Dean 1997b: 18; Lawson 1986: 18; Smith 1985: 25; Southby-Tailyour 1985: 10; Throckmorton 1976: 39).

In the case of his Mallows Bay investigation (Maryland), Shomette makes a number of observations with repercussions for how we perceive the logistics of abandonment and the cultural site formation processes at discard sites. This includes observations about the time taken to burn wooden vessels and the tendency to fill abandoned watercraft with sand, gravel, stone, or dredge spoil to ensure its sinking (Hopkins 1995; Langley 1995; Shomette 1994, 1995b, 1996: 201–338). Shomette also uses the ships' graveyard to discuss the lucrative (but risky) nature of the scrap metal industry, identify a relationship between scrap metal prices and wartime economies, chart the growth of subsistence salvage during economic depression, and chronicle pre–World War II fluctuations in metal prices due to Japanese demand for scrap (Shomette 1994: 83, 95, 1996: 256, 259, 262–263, 271, 275). Ships at the Mallow's Bay site also indicate the persistence of many of the placement assurance strategies already listed: piles had been driven through their hulls to stop them from floating into navigation channels (Shomette 1996: 283).

Australian researchers have been researching ship abandonment sites for many decades (for a review of the literature see Richards 2005). While mirroring many of the studies above, the Australian research has also included regional or national interpretations of the temporal and spatial distribution of ship abandonment sites as a microcosm of technological, economic, and social change in adjacent communities

(Figure 37.4) (see Doyle 2000; Richards 2003, 2008; Richards and Staniforth 2006). In addition, other examinations of regional ship abandonment have looked at the way that discarded watercraft represent themes such as geographical isolation and larger geopolitical occurences (see Richards 2003, 2004).

All of these studies reinforce the fact that shipowners do not simply abandon unwanted vessels when worn out. The actual reasons for abandonment vary from a combination of processes associated with general economic and technological change, to more specific, regional developments such as changes to port infrastructure and the development of alternative modes of transportation, as well as vessel age and condition. The effects of changing networks of transportation themselves seem to change with circumstance, and there is some divergence of opinion regarding the growth of alternative transportation, the redirection of resources into alternative transport infrastructure, and its effects on economic growth, which directly relates to discard trends (Hunter 1993: 179, 181, 218, 484–488, 504, 585–606; Paine 2000: 113).

CONCLUSION

Reflecting carefully planned decision-making processes, abandoned ships represent the abandonment of one function for the adoption of another. These changes may require a transformation of structures or functions, or may constitute a symbolic reuse. The decision to create, retain, and destroy a vessel may also depend on whether the vessel matches criteria emerging from the consequences of economic

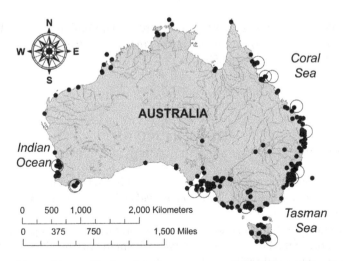

Figure 37.4 Map of Australia showing the current understanding of the distribution of abandoned watercraft and the location of designated Commonwealth ship disposal areas. Reproduced with the kind permission of the author.

and technological change. These transitions reflect the changing needs and desires of maritime people and are related to technological, economic, and social issues.

The studies mentioned briefly above illustrate that people abandon watercraft for many reasons. What connects these motives are the deliberate acts that bring about the transformation of usable ships into archaeological sites. The site formation processes and the archaeological signatures left in the wake of these planned acts of destruction are important clues in the extraction of intention and agency from the archaeological record. Additionally, the identification of discard and reuse mechanisms in the material record and the archaeological signatures that accompany them has the potential to illuminate many aspects of the past. The physical clues from ship abandonment sites and the behaviors that can be inferred from them have been found on similar sites from many periods around the world, and they illuminate a global maritime culture, as well as a myriad of regional variations. This reinforces our understanding that ships are not simply the tools of commerce, industry, and warfare; they are also objects replete with the qualities of particular cultures, as well as the "maritimity" of culture. Moreover, a ship's creation, retention, and destruction tell us much about the changing circumstances of social, technological, and economic change through time and illuminate the changing role and importance of aquatic transportation across human history. Understanding how and why owners abandon ships is not a simple matter of augmenting history. As the final phase in the life of tried and tested technologies, we may find clues to the catalysts and consequences of other changes within human societies.

NOTE

Portions of this material appeared earlier in Richards 2008, *Ships' Graveyards: Abandoned Watercraft and the Archaeological Site Formation Process*, and have been reprinted with permission of the University Press of Florida.

REFERENCES

Aldsworth, F. G. 1989. Excavations at the former Royal Naval Dockyard, Bermuda: A nineteenth century slave hulk. *Bermuda Journal of Archaeology and Maritime History* 1: 109–130.

Babits, L. E., and A. Corbin-Kjorness. 1995. Final report on an archaeological survey of the western shore of the Pungo River from Wades Point to Woodstock Point. Unpublished ms., East Carolina University.

Ballard, R. D., and R. Archbold. 1995. *The discovery of the* Titanic: *Exploring the greatest of all lost ships*. Toronto: Madison.

Bill, J. 1997. Skuldelev Ships. In *Encyclopedia of underwater and maritime archaeology*, ed. J. P. Delgado, 388–389. London: British Museum Press.

Blackburn, G. J. 1978. *The illustrated encyclopedia of ships, boats, vessels and other water-borne craft*. London: John Murray.

Bound, M. 1990. The hulk *Jhelum*: A derivative expression of late British Indiaman ship-building. *International Journal of Nautical Archaeology* 19 (1): 43–47.

———. 1993. Iron beam end fastenings: Fell's Patent No. 8186; A puzzle resolved. *Mariner's Mirror* 79: 338–342.

Bright, L. 1993. Beached shipwreck dynamics. In *Underwater archaeology proceedings from the Society for Historical Archaeology Conference, Kansas City, MO*.

Broadwater, J. D. 1988. Yorktown shipwreck. *National Geographic* 173 (6): 802–823.

———. 1997. Yorktown shipwrecks. In *Encyclopedia of underwater and maritime archaeology*, ed. J. P. Delgado, 471–472. London: British Museum Press.

Bruce-Mitford, R. 1974. *Aspects of Anglo-Saxon archaeology*. London: Victor Gollancz.

Cassavoy, K. A., and K. J. Crisman. 1996. The War of 1812: Battle for the Great Lakes. In *Ships and shipwrecks of the Americas: A history based on underwater archaeology*, ed. G. F. Bass, 169–188. London: Thames and Hudson.

Christensen, A. E. 1972. Scandinavian ships from earliest times to the Vikings. In *A history of seafaring based on underwater archaeology*, ed. G. F. Bass, 159–180. New York: Thames and Hudson.

———. 1987. *Guide to the Viking Ship Museum*. Oslo: Universitetets Oldsaksamling.

———. 1997a. Gokstad Ship. In *Encyclopedia of underwater and maritime archaeology*, ed. J. P. Delgado, 172–174. London: British Museum Press.

———. 1997b. Oseberg Ship. In *Encyclopedia of underwater and maritime archaeology*, ed. J. P. Delgado, 302–303. London: British Museum Press.

Christoffersen, J. 1991. Iron Age finds in Funen (Fyn)—some archaeological problems of defining maritime sites. In *Aspects of maritime Scandinavia CE200–1200*, ed. O. Crumlin-Pederson, 55–66. Roskilde: Viking Ship Museum.

Claesson, S. 1996. *Annabella*: The excavation of a nineteenth-century coasting schooner in Cape Neddick, Maine. *INA Quarterly* 23 (2): 16–21.

Crisman, K. J. 1995. "Coffins of the Brave": A return to Lake Champlain's War of 1812 ship graveyard. *INA Quarterly* 22 (1): 4–8.

———. 1997. Boscawen. In *Encyclopedia of underwater and maritime archaeology*, ed. J. P. Delgado, 69–70. London: British Museum Press.

Crumlin-Pedersen, O. 1972. Wrecks in the North Sea and the Baltic. In *Underwater archaeology: A nascent discipline, UNESCO*, 65–75. Paris: United Nations Educational, Scientific and Cultural Organization.

———. 1986. Aspects of wood technology in medieval shipbuilding. In *Sailing into the past*, ed. O. Crumlin-Pederson and M. Vinner, 138–149. Roskilde: Viking Ship Museum.

———. 1991a. Maritime aspects of the archaeology of Roman and migration-period Denmark. In *Aspects of maritime Scandinavia CE 200–1200*, ed. O. Crumlin-Pederson, 41–53. Roskilde: Viking Ship Museum.

———. 1991b. Ship types and sizes CE 800–1400. In *Aspects of maritime Scandinavia CE 200–1200*, ed. O. Crumlin-Pederson, 69–82. Roskilde: Viking Ship Museum.

———. 1994. Medieval ships in Danish waters. In *Crossroads in ancient shipbuilding*, ed. Christer Westerdahl, 65–72. Oxford: Oxbow.

Cumming, E. M., and D. J. Carter. 1990. The *Earl of Abergavenny* (1805), an outward bound English East Indiaman. *International Journal of Nautical Archaeology* 19 (1): 31–33.

Dean, M., and S. Miller. 1979. The story of the *St Mary*. *Falkland Islands Journal* 1979: 35–41.

Dean, N. 1997a. Falklands wrecks and hulks. In *Encyclopedia of underwater and maritime archaeology*, ed. J. P. Delgado, 148–150. London: British Museum Press.

———. 1997b. Actaeon. In *Encyclopedia of underwater and maritime archaeology*, ed. J. P. Delgado, 18. London: British Museum Press.

Delgado, J. P. 1979. No longer a buoyant ship: Unearthing the Gold Rush storeship *Niantic*. *California History* 63 (4): 316–325.

———. 1996. *Ghost fleet: The sunken ships of Bikini Atoll*. Honolulu: University of Hawai'i Press.

———. 1997. Hjortspring Boat. In *Encyclopedia of underwater and maritime archaeology*, ed. J. P. Delgado, 193. London: British Museum Press.

Devendra, S. 1993. Remains of riverine craft: Material for ecological and community studies. *Bulletin of the Australian Institute for Maritime Archaeology* 17 (2): 17–24.

Dobson, N. 1997. Maritime Fife completes Phase 2. *Nautical Archaeology: Society Newsletter for the World of Underwater, Foreshore, Ship and Boat Archaeology* (Spring): 1–3.

Doyle, C. 2000. An examination of associations between significant historic events and the loss and discard of vessels in the Townsville Catchment, 1865–1981. Master's thesis, James Cook University.

Duncan, B. 2000. Signposts in the sea: An investigation of the shipwreck patterning and cultural seascapes of the Gippsland Region, Victoria. Honors thesis, James Cook University.

Edwin Fox Restoration Society. 1987. *The Story of the* Edwin Fox. 2nd ed. Picton, New Zealand: Toneden Promotions.

Einarsson, L. 1997. Kalmar Harbour wrecks. In *Encyclopedia of underwater and maritime archaeology*, ed. J. P. Delgado, 219–220. London: British Museum Press.

El-Baz, F. 1988. Finding a pharaoh's funeral bark. *National Geographic* 173 (4): 513–533.

Emery, M. 1997. Successful search for sunken boats. *Nautical Archaeology: Society Newsletter for the World of Underwater, Foreshore, Ship and Boat Archaeology* (Spring): 4.

Evans, A. C. 1987a. The coming of the Anglo-Saxons. In *History from beneath the sea: Shipwrecks and archaeology*, ed. P. Throckmorton, 112–115. Melbourne: RD Press.

———. 1987b. A kingly burial. In *History from beneath the sea: Shipwrecks and archaeology*, ed. P. Throckmorton, 116–122. Melbourne: RD Press.

———. 1997a. Snape Boat. In *Encyclopedia of underwater and maritime archaeology*, ed. J. P. Delgado, 392. London: British Museum Press.

———. 1997b. Sutton Hoo. In *Encyclopedia of underwater and maritime archaeology*, ed. J. P. Delgado, 411–413. London: British Museum Press.

Fenwick, V. H. 1997. Graveney Boat. In *Encyclopedia of underwater and maritime archaeology*, ed. J. P. Delgado, 175–176. London: British Museum Press.

Fisher, A. C., Jr. 1979. Two Englands. *National Geographic* 156 (4): 442–481.

Gesner, P. 1991. *Pandora: An archaeological perspective*. Brisbane: Queensland Museum.

———. 2000. HMS Pandora Project—a report on Stage 1: Five seasons of excavation. *Memoirs of the Queensland Museum: Cultural Heritage Series* 2, 1: 1–52.

Goodburn, D. 1990. Fragments of an early carvel-built vessel from Camber, East Sussex, England. *International Journal of Nautical Archaeology* 19 (4): 327–334.

Haldane, C. 1992. The Lisht Timbers: A preliminary report. In *The pyramid complex of Senwosret I at Lisht: Metropolitan Museum of Art Egyptian Expedition XXV; The southern cemeteries at Lisht III*, ed. D. Arnold, 102–112 and plates. New York: Metropolitan Museum of Art.

Hammond, N. 1995. Graveyard of wooden ships found on Thames foreshore. *Nautical Archaeology: Society Newsletter for the World of Underwater, Foreshore, Ship and Boat Archaeology* (Autumn): 4.

Harris, E. C., and J. R. Adams, 1997. Sea venture. In *Encyclopedia of underwater and maritime archaeology*, ed. J. P. Delgado, 365–366. London: British Museum Press.

Heal, S. V. E., and G. Hutchinson. 1986. Three recently found logboats. *International Journal of Nautical Archaeology* 15 (3): 205–213.

Hockmann, O. 1993. Late Roman Rhine vessels from Mainz, Germany. *International Journal of Nautical Archaeology* 22 (2): 125–135.

Holman, M. R. 1953. *A handy book for shipowners and masters.* 15th ed. London: Commercial Printing and Stationery Company.

Hopkins, F. 1995. The final anchorage: The WW1 Emergency Fleet wrecks at Mallow's Bay. *Underwater archaeology proceedings from the Society for Historical Archaeology Conference* (1995): 72–76.

Hunter, L. C. 1993. *Steamboats of the western rivers: An economic and technological history.* New York: Dover.

Hutchinson, G. 1998. *Medieval ships and shipping.* Leicester: Leicester University Press.

Jenkins, N. 1980. *Boat beneath the pyramids.* New York: Thames and Hudson.

Johnston, P. F. 1997. Cornwallis Cave wreck. In *Encyclopedia of underwater and maritime archaeology*, ed. J. P. Delgado, 110–111. London: British Museum Press.

Kemp, P. K., ed. 1988. *The Oxford companion to ships and the sea.* Oxford: Oxford University Press.

La Roche, D. 1987. The small boat finds at the "Musée de la Civilisation" in Quebec City. In *Underwater archaeology proceedings from the Society for Historical Archaeology Conference*, ed. A. Albright, 108–113. Savannah: Society for Historical Archaeology.

Langley, S. B. M. 1997. Mallows Bay. In *Encyclopedia of underwater and maritime archaeology*, ed. J. P. Delgado, 257–258. London: British Museum Press.

Lawson, E. 1986. Egeria: The nineteenth century Canadian built sailing ship at Port Stanley. *Falkland Islands Journal* (1986): 15–19.

Lellman, K. V. 1933. The hulks at Stanley Harbour. *Sea Breezes* 16: 270–271.

Lemee, C. 1997. A ship cemetery on the B&W site in Christianshavn. *Maritime Archaeology Newsletter from Roskilde Denmark* 9 (December): 29–34.

Lemee, C., P. Schiellerup, and M. Gothche. 1996. Ships and shipyards in Copenhagen. *Maritime Archaeology Newsletter from Roskilde* 7 (December): 16–20.

Lenihan, D. J. 1998. From Pearl to Bikini: The underwater archaeology of World War II in the Pacific. In *Excavating ships of war*, ed. M. Bound, 294–302. Oswestry, UK: Anthony Nelson.

Lloyd's of London. 1973. *Lloyd's Calendar: 1973.* London: Lloyd's of London.

———. 1981. *Lloyd's Calendar: 1981.* London: Lloyd's of London.

———. 1991. *Lloyd's Calendar: 1991.* London: Lloyd's of London.

Marsden, P. 1994. *Ships of the Port of London: First to eleventh centuries.* London: English Heritage.

———. 1996. *Ships of the Port of London: Twelfth to seventeenth centuries.* London: English Heritage.

Marsden, P., et al. 1989. A Late Saxon logboat from Clapton, London Borough of Hackney. *International Journal of Nautical Archaeology* 18 (2): 89–111.

Matthews, F. C. 1987a. *American merchant ships 1850–1900: Series 2.* New York: Dover.

———. 1987b. *American merchant ships 1850–1900: Series 1.* New York: Dover.

Merriman, A. M. 1997. *The Cypress Landing shipwreck of Chocowinity Bay: A North Carolina sail flat; An archaeological and historical study*. East Carolina University Research Report No. 9. Greenville: Program in Maritime History and Nautical Archaeology.

Miller, P. 1988. Riddle of the Pyramid Boats. *National Geographic* 173 (4): 534–550.

Milne, G., C. McKewan, and D. Goodburn. 1998. *Nautical archaeology on the foreshore: Hulk recording on the Medway*. London: Royal Commission on the Historical Monuments of England.

Moore, A. 1970. *Last days of mast and sail: An essay in nautical comparative anatomy*. Oxford: Clarendon Press.

Moore, J. 1995a. Kingston Inner Harbour survey: A preliminary archaeological survey of submerged and partially submerged vessels (BbGc-29 to BbGc-42) in the Inner Harbour, Kingston, Ontario; Report for the Marine Museum of the Great Lakes at Kingston.

———. 1995b. The boneyard below the bridge. *Freshwater: A Journal of the Marine Museum of the Great Lakes of Kingston* 11 (1–4): 3–28.

Müller-Wille, M. 1974. Boat-graves in northern Europe. *International Journal of Nautical Archaeology* 3 (2): 187–204.

Murphy, L. E. 1983. Shipwrecks as a data base for human behavioral studies. In *Shipwreck anthropology*, ed. R. A. Gould, 65–90. Albuquerque: University of New Mexico Press.

Nash, M. 1996. *Cargo for the colony: The wreck of the merchant ship* Sydney Cove. Sydney: Braxus Press.

O'Keefe, M. 1999. The shipwreck under the city: The *Inconstant*, Wellington, New Zealand. *Bulletin of the Australian Institute for Maritime Archaeology* 23: 121–125.

Paine, L. 2000. *Down east: A maritime history of Maine*. Gardiner: Tilbury House.

Parsons, R. H., and G. Plunkett. 1995. *Scuttled and abandoned ships in Australian waters*. Adelaide: Self-published.

Reiss, W. 1987. The ship beneath Manhattan. In *History from beneath the sea: Shipwrecks and archaeology*, ed. P. Throckmorton, 185–187. Melbourne: RD Press.

———. 1997. Ronson Ship. In *Encyclopedia of underwater and maritime archaeology*, ed. J. P. Delgado, 349–350. London: British Museum Press.

Richards, N. T. 2003. The role of isolation in cultural site formation: A case study from Strahan, Tasmania. *Bulletin of the Australasian Institute for Maritime Archaeology* 27: 77–84.

———. 2004. The role of geo-politics in cultural site formation: A case study from the Northern Territory. *Bulletin of the Australasian Institute for Maritime Archaeology* 28: 97–106.

———. 2005. The archaeological examination of watercraft abandonment in Australia: A retrospective. *Bulletin of the Australasian Institute for Maritime Archaeology* 29: 61–76.

———. 2008. *Ships' graveyards: Abandoned watercraft and the archaeological site formation process*. Gainesville: University Press of Florida.

Richards, N. T., and M. Staniforth. 2006. The Abandoned Ships Project. *Historical Archaeology* 40 (4): 84–103.

Rieck, F. 1991. Aspects of coastal defence in Denmark. In *Aspects of maritime Scandinavia CE200–1200*, ed. O. Crumlin-Pederson, 83–96. Roskilde: Viking Ship Museum.

———. 1996. Nydam: A wealth of finds in a dangerous environment. *Maritime Archaeology Newsletter from Roskilde Denmark* 7 (December): 5–6.

Rusho, W. J. 1962. Charles Spencer and his wonderful steamboat. *Arizona Highways* 37 (8): 34–39.

Schiffer, M. B. 1972. Archaeological context and systemic context. *American Antiquity* 37: 156–165.

———. 1996. *Formation processes of the archaeological record*. Salt Lake City: University of Utah Press.

Shomette, D. G. 1994. The shipwrecks of Mallows Bay: An historic overview; Report prepared for the Maryland Historical Trust by the St. Clements Island–Potomac River Museum, Colton Point, Maryland. Centreville, MD.

———. 1995a. *Tidewater time capsule: History beneath the Patuxent*. Centreville, MD: Tidewater.

———. 1995b. From maritime antiquarianism to underwater archaeology along the Potomac corridor, 1825–1994. In *Underwater archaeology proceedings from the Society for Historical Archaeology Conference; Washington, D.C., 1995*, ed. P. F. Johnston, 64–71. Tucson: Society for Historical Archaeology.

———. 1996. *Ghost Fleet of Mallows Bay: And other tales of the Lost Chesapeake*. Centreville, MD: Tidewater.

———. 1997. Chesapeake flotilla. In *Encyclopedia of underwater and maritime archaeology*, ed. J. P. Delgado, 98–99. London: British Museum Press.

Simpson, J. A., and E. S. C. Weiner, eds. 1989. *The Oxford English dictionary*. Vol. 25, *Ser–Soosy*. 2nd ed. Oxford: Oxford University Press.

Smith, J. 1985. *Condemned at Stanley: Notes and sketches on the hulks and wrecks at Port Stanley, Falkland Islands*. Chippenham, UK: Picton Print.

Southby-Tailyour, E. 1985. *Falkland Island shores*. London: Conway Maritime Press.

Souza, D. J. 1998. *The persistence of sail in the age of steam: Underwater archaeological evidence from the Dry Tortugas*. New York: Plenum Press.

Springmann, M. 1998. The Mukran wreck, sunk off of the Isle of Rugen, Germany, in 1565: A preliminary report. *International Journal of Nautical Archaeology* 27 (2): 113–125.

Stammers, M. K. 1997. Jhelum. In *Encyclopedia of underwater and maritime archaeology*, ed. J. P. Delgado, 218. London: British Museum Press.

Stammers, M. K., and J. Baker. 1994. Fell's Patent Knees—some evidence of their use. *International Journal of Nautical Archaeology* 80: 474–476.

Stammers, M. K., and J. Kearon. 1991. The *Jhelum*—an East Indiaman? *International Journal of Nautical Archaeology* 20 (4): 351–353.

———. 1992. *The Jhelum: A Victorian merchant ship*. Stroud, UK: Sutton.

Steffy, J. R. 1985. The Kyrenia Ship: An interim report on its hull construction. *American Journal of Archaeology* 89 (1): 71–101.

———. 1990. The boat: A preliminary study of its construction. In *The excavation of an ancient boat in the Sea of Galilee (Lake Kinneret)*, ed. S. Waschmann, 29–47. Jerusalem: Israel Antiquities Authority.

———. 1996. The thirteen colonies: English settlers and seafarers. In *Ships and shipwrecks of the Americas: A history based on underwater archaeology*, ed. G. F. Bass, 107–128. London: Thames and Hudson.

Stevens, E. F. 1947. *Dictionary of shipping terms and phrases*. London: Sir Isaac Pitman and Sons.

Switzer, D. C. 1998. The *Defence*. In *Excavating ships of war*, ed. M. Bound, 182–193. Oswestry, UK: Anthony Nelson.

Throckmorton, P. 1970. *Shipwrecks and archaeology: The unharvested sea*. London: Victor Gollancz.

———. 1976. The American heritage in the Falklands. *Sea History* 4: 36–71.

———. 1987a. Bones on a beach. In *History from beneath the sea: Shipwrecks and archae-ology*, ed. P. Throckmorton, 210–214. Melbourne: RD Press.

———. 1987b. The shipwright's art. In *History from beneath the sea: Shipwrecks and archaeology*, ed. P. Throckmorton, 92–100. Melbourne: RD Press.

Van Der Vat, D. 1998. *The Grand Scuttle: The sinking of the German fleet at Scapa Flow in 1919*. Edinburgh: Birlinn.

Wachsmann, S. 1987. The Galilee Boat. In *History from beneath the sea: Shipwrecks and archaeology*, ed. P. Throckmorton, 81–83. RD Press: Melbourne.

Ward-Haldane, C. 1988. Boat timbers from El-Lisht: A new method of ancient Egyptian hull construction; Preliminary report. *Mariner's Mirror* 74: 141–152.

Warner, O. 1968. *The navy*. Harmondsworth, UK: Penguin.

Watson, K. 1993. Wreck rescue: Nautical archaeology in the River Medway. *Nautical Archaeology: Society Newsletter for the World of Underwater, Foreshore, Ship and Boat Archaeology* (August): 7–8.

Wood, A. 1996. Hulk survey, Kidwelly, Dyfed. *Nautical Archaeology: Society Newsletter for the World of Underwater, Foreshore, Ship and Boat Archaeology* (Spring): 6–7.

Zacharchuk, W., and P. J. A. Waddell. 1984. *The excavation of the Machault: An 18th-century French frigate*. Quebec: Environment Canada.

Zarzynski, J. 1997. Wiawaka bateaux cluster. In *Encyclopedia of underwater and maritime archaeology*, ed. James P. Delgado, 463–464. London: British Museum Press.

CHAPTER 38

....

MARITIME COMMUNITIES AND TRADITIONS

....

JESSE RANSLEY

INTRODUCTION

....

IT is first worth clarifying the meaning of "maritime communities and traditions" in this volume. In its truest sense, the phrase covers everything we address as maritime archaeologists, from ships, shipboard society, ports, communications, and trade to coastal communities' relationships with the water and conceptions of maritime space. However, when maritime communities, and in particular "maritime traditions," are discussed within archaeological discourse, the terms most often imply either small, contemporary, indigenous communities or folklore traditions from European or North American contexts. It is a discussion not of big concepts, of maritime traditions in the sense of global trade, colonization, or naval technology, but of small-scale "tradition" and local maritime "practices."

Moreover, rather than a cohesive academic field, it is a collection of research areas and sources on which we draw. Three main strands within this broad subject can be identified: oral histories and folklore traditions, studies of contemporary "traditional" boats, and ethnography that has a maritime locus of study. Probably as a result of this breadth, there is little well-developed critical dialogue about these research areas as sources on maritime communities and traditions, particularly in the context of their larger relationship with maritime archaeology. Common to all three sources is a focus on the present or recent past of particular communities. For both traditional boat studies and oral histories there is also a particular sense of "rescue" evoked through recording disappearing traditions, although they draw on disparate material and linguistic aspects of maritime communities. Ethnographies represent a different approach, and they do not, for the most part, set out to examine the maritime traditions of the communities they study. They are used by maritime archaeologists less frequently and most effectively when they are geographically proximate, so that in effect they represent ethnohistorical background to archaeological studies (e.g., Barber 2003). This chapter will look in detail at these three sources of information on maritime communities and traditions, and the next section will address the history and context of each research field, discuss their aims and methods, and offer key examples.

Once this brief review is complete, consideration will be given to why a chapter discussing maritime communities and traditions is included in a handbook of maritime archaeology, exploring what maritime archaeologists use these sources for. In discussing their research, many maritime archaeologists refer to their sailing or seafaring experiences or their understanding of local maritime traditions and "folklore" in informal ways. These are often useful expressions of experiential understandings of seamanship or living in maritime environments. However, the relationship between maritime traditions and maritime archaeology is less clear than we might at first assume. It is somewhat fractured, and complicated by the problem of how we draw on spatially and temporally disparate societies to illuminate maritime archaeological narratives and interpretation. There are, of course, examples of both the strengths and the limitations of using these varied research studies in maritime archaeological interpretation. However, the broader opportunity they offer archaeologists of exploring the multiplicity of other ways of living in and understanding the maritime world should not be undervalued. In particular, they emphasize the fact that our social practices, ontology, and values are not the same as those of other contemporary communities, and are therefore not necessarily applicable to past communities. Considering these different studies allows us to examine the assumptions on which we build our interpretations.

The final section will briefly touch on new directions in studies of maritime communities and traditions, including uses of maritime traditions in current cultural discourse. It will focus particularly on the notion of *maritime heritage*, and the sociopolitical and economic ways the concept of *maritime traditions* is employed in contemporary societies.

SOURCES AND SUBJECTS

Sources

Tappan Adney's extraordinary work at the turn of the last century on the construction of bark canoes and skin boats, including meticulous records, drawings, illustrations, essays, and 110 boat models, illustrates the long-held scholarly interest in maritime communities and traditions (Adney and Chapelle 2007; Jennings 2004). It also highlights a historical focus on the loss of maritime traditions in indigenous communities experiencing social and economic changes, which we see in both oral history projects and traditional boat studies. There are many contemporary connections in the objectives of these two research areas, and some studies link them together, including the exceptional work of the Traditional Boats of Ireland project (MacCárthaigh 2008). However, there are clear differences in their development, their methods, and the contexts within which studies are undertaken. This is amplified further when ethnographic studies of maritime communities are considered. We will therefore review each source individually and look at typical examples and methods, as well as the strengths and weaknesses of each as sources on maritime traditions.

Before that, it is worth noting briefly the variety of other historical and visual sources of information on maritime communities. For example, works by colonial administrators and European adventurers, while they require the reader to be mindful of cultural and historical contexts, are significant sources on maritime traditions. Though colored by colonial perspectives, Wilson's (1909) meticulous work on the vessels in Bombay harbor, Villiers's (1969) personal account of Arab seafaring in the 1930s, and Moore's (1970) work on rigging practices in the last days of commercial sail are uniquely valuable sources. Archaeologists are used to drawing on historical documents, firsthand accounts, and the archives of individuals such as Adney and Wilson. However, beyond these perhaps familiar examples, there are numerous others that, although we do not have the space to address them in detail, ought to be highlighted, including visual sources such as early ethnographic film of expanded logboat building in Finland (Vilkuna and Nikkilä 1936), a vast array of boat and ship models and plans, and large collections of maritime art and photography (e.g., the UK National Maritime Museum's extensive collection: www.nmm.ac.uk/collections/index.cfm/).

Traditional Boat Studies

There is a large corpus of literature on traditional boats, but though this field has a long-established scholarly history and breadth of research, it is not easily named. The phrase "boat ethnography" is often used (e.g., McGrail 1984), and it is interesting if rather problematic, since these studies do not employ ethnographic methodologies. Others suggest the phrase "ethnographic boat recording" or simply "boat recording" (Blue, pers. comm.). In this discussion the phrase "traditional boat studies" will be used, though it is still imperfect. Whatever they are termed, these studies are the source most often associated with maritime archaeology. This is to be expected, since researchers in this field are often archaeologists themselves (e.g., Insoll 1993), particularly maritime archaeologists, as well as naval architects, maritime historians, mariners, and boat enthusiasts. In addition, their research publications are found in the *International Journal of Nautical Archaeology* and *Mariner's Mirror*, among other journals, as well as in more popular magazines, such as *Classic Boat*, *Wooden Boat*, and *Maritime Life and Traditions*. As these last three titles suggest, these studies focus on the material aspects of maritime communities, specifically their boats and boat-related activities. Moreover, since it is only in the last 20 years that maritime archaeology as a whole has become more theoretically engaged and expanded its objects of study beyond boats and shipwrecks to include prehistoric maritime communities and more social, even reflexive, archaeological readings (McGrail 1987: 1; Ransley 2005), there has been a long-term affinity in the technological focus of the two fields. Both traditional boat studies and maritime archaeology have been critiqued in the past for their tendency to privilege boats and ships, their construction and performance and physical remains, over their social context (Ransley 2007: 224). Given the great number of studies and this connection to maritime archaeology, as well as a lack of critical discussion of the field, it is worth looking at this source in some detail.

Most characteristically, these studies involve surveys of particular types of traditional boats (such as Kentley's [1985] study of southern Indian sewn boats and Chittick's [1980] research in Somalia), or the traditional boats of a particular region (e.g., Heath's [2004] work on Arctic kayaks or McKee's [1983] study of the traditional working boats of Britain). More occasionally, they combine studies of vernacular craft and their associated, declining, artisanal industries (MacPolin 1992; Wilkins 2001). This is a robust area of research and publication, and in recent years the depth and diversity of these studies has expanded. Some are the product of lifelong obsessions (Heath 2004; H. C. Petersen 1986). Others result from the technological fascination of maritime archaeologists (McGrail et al. 2003). Many tell us as much about the researcher as about the boats (Lundberg 2003). All of them have in common technical descriptions and records of the boats, with plans and photographs, alongside notes on distribution, construction methods, and propulsion. The methodological process of recording these boats in the field is comparable to archaeological survey (Figure 38.1). In fact, the Traditional Boats of Ireland project has produced guidelines on surveying heritage boats for the many enthusiasts wishing to contribute to the project via their Web site (MacCárthaigh, Becker, and Kearon 2007).

Yet although the current context of these studies is often documenting the remaining examples of artisanal watercraft and associated fishing traditions in parts of the world where their production and use is rapidly declining (McGrail et al. 2003; MacCárthaigh 2008; Muscat 1999; H. C. Petersen 1986), the methods and objectives have been shaped by the history of the field. Colored by the classificatory expeditions of early anthropology, these studies are, for the most part, *solely* a practice of recording and classifying. Boats are conceived in the context of a technological progression, as objects made for functional reasons and through causal relationships with use, economics, materials, and environment—so much so that Vermoden has identified the twin dichotomies of "a dehumanised technology and a dematerialised society" within the field (Vermoden 2006: 227). Though this issue is pivotal to how we utilize these studies and it may be easy to critique their sometimes reductive methods and approaches, it should also be recognized that they begin

Figure 38.1 Recording *kattumaram* in southern Kerala, India, in 2006 for the Traditional Boats in Context project, supported by the Society for South Asian Studies. Reproduced with the kind permission of the University of Southampton.

from historically situated perspectives and are shaped by a particular, culturally specific paradigm.

Hornell's *Water Transport* (1946) is often seen as the archetype for studies of traditional boats. The book is a scholarly, remarkably comprehensive catalog of traditional watercraft from around the globe but is also focused on the vessels' construction, propulsion, and categorization. It is, in effect, a classificatory survey, not so very different from the books on "native craft" produced by the colonial administrators of South Asian ports (Wilson 1909), to Paris's nineteenth-century works (1841–1843), or even to Bowrey's earlier historical descriptions of indigenous craft (Hill 1958). All pursue the practice of recording and classifying from an apparently objective, external position without sociocultural context. Their purpose is creating a reference collection, and their objective is recording in and of itself: "I shall endeavour to marshal in due order the major part of knowledge within our ken concerning the origins of the many devices upon which men, living in varying stages of culture, launch themselves afloat upon river, lake and sea" (Hornell 1946:xv). The work is intertwined with eighteenth- and nineteenth-century scientific positivism and the colonial imperative, "the patrimony of scientific mastery and imperial might" (McClintock 1995: 26). It reflects the notion of the masculist gaze quantifying, objectifying, and constituting the subject (McClintock 1995: 25–28; see also Rose 1993; Thomas 2004: 199). It is colored by their respective colonial contexts, producing work and knowledge that is firmly situated, both historically and philosophically (Haraway 1988). Within this cultural framework there are, naturally, no attempts to qualify, analyze, or understand the motivations, assumed purpose, or supposed applications of the work. Equally and unsurprisingly, these studies are not concerned with the multivalent relations between people, boats, and water that produce the watery worlds of these communities. They are driven by a different impetus and framed by a particular theoretical paradigm: a *modern*, Western understanding of the world. Accordingly, within this paradigm, boats are addressed as technology rather than as material culture, without recognition of human-object intersubjectivity (Marshall and Gosden 1999), or the role they play in producing place, identity, and the social world in maritime communities.

This approach and conception of boats continued after Hornell (1946) and through the twentieth century, with the systematic, regional, or typological field studies of Greenhill (1966), McKee (1983), and McGrail (2001) and, most recently, Rajamanickam (2004) and Pohl (2007), among others. Yet whatever the critiques and explanations of the socially disembedded perspective of these studies, they have in common a distinct, learned fascination with the variety, construction, distribution, propulsion, uses, and building techniques of indigenous boats. This has provided us with a remarkable reference collection on watercraft around the world. The different accounts also reflect personal interests in fishing, crewing, migration, boat rituals, and mythologies, as well as individual approaches and sometimes idiosyncratic writing styles, providing an unexpectedly dynamic body of literature. For example, Horridge's work on the *prahu* of Indonesia is particularly engaging: "Prahu-chasing, like bird-watching, is a sport that grows on you, so beware . . . to spot a new one and especially to find the last surviving example of an old traditional type . . . to seek them being built is like searching out the rookeries of some rare sea-bird" (1985:xvi).

This continuity of research aims and approach is reflected in field methodologies. Remarkably, in the most part, these studies are still based on short field surveys not so dissimilar to Hornell's, with little ethnographic sensibility in the conception, objectives, or methodologies used. However, more recent studies have expanded their scope, addressing boats in greater detail: from technical recording, photography, boat plans, and lines, to recording *how* the boatbuilder constructs the vessel (including their materials and tools), the boat's equipment and its use (including types of fishing, whether it works inshore or offshore, etc.), its propulsion and handling, weather and sea states, launching and landing (Figure 38.2), and the number and organization of crew, among other details (McGrail et al. 2003; E. Petersen 2000). The University of Southampton's Traditional Boats in Context project, for example, examines variations in the construction and use of *kattumaram* (coastal fishing vessels) in southern India but focuses on questions of innovation and choice by exploring the social, economic, and environmental context of the boats (Blue et al. forthcoming). It documents details of their use, the building process, and local perceptions of the boats by interviewing fishermen and boatbuilders (Figure 38.3), as well recording the boats' distribution, propulsion, and construction. At the same time, Vermoden's (2006: 227) interest in challenging "the dichotomy between techniques and rituals" in his study of Indonesian boats, by

Figure 38.2 The *kattumaram* from Figure 38.1 in use, as a lone fisherman paddles out across the surf, timing his effort around the rhythm of the breakers. Reproduced with the kind permission of the University of Southampton.

connecting local beliefs and systems of meaning with boatbuilding, remains rare. Unfortunately, his particular focus on the sequence of decisions and material and social engagement involved in boat making still remains an alternative perspective within the field. However, in general, this new depth of detail provides greater technical context (even if it is conceived, for the most part, within a social-constructivist framework). In fact, this quality and specificity of detail is seen as crucial to the "rescue" aim of more recent studies, now that they are focused on recording too-often rare indigenous boats.

Oral Histories and Folklore Traditions

Within the disparate but interconnected corpus of maritime oral histories and folklore tradition studies, there is often a parallel sense of recording the disappearing maritime traditions of fast-changing communities. However, there is a linguistic rather than a material focus to both oral histories and folklore traditions. In this sense "histories" is the key term. Again, there is a blurring of terminology within this field. Here the term "oral *histories*" refers to individual narratives of the past, to personal life histories, while "oral" or "folklore *traditions*" refers to communal stories of the past (although the term "folklore" is somewhat problematic in postcolonial contexts; see Agrawal 1995; Damm 2005, 2006; Lane 2006; Silitoe 1998).

By their very nature, oral histories are tied to the recent past through the living memory of individuals and are personal perspectives. Often connected to local oral history projects, they are also mediated through the intentions and skill (or otherwise)

Figure 38.3 Discussing different variations of *kattumaram* with the visiting *meistri*
(boatbuilder), during a break from building a new *kattumaram* in the coastal
village of Ambalathu Mula, Kerala. Reproduced with the kind permission
of the University of Southampton.

of the researcher collating them. It is perhaps easier to discern the potential influence
of the researcher, and their subjective perspective, in studies that draw on linguistic
evidence rather than more tangible material evidence (like boat technology); and
there is certainly an extensive disciplinary debate on methodological and analytical
issues of collating personal oral histories (e.g., Perks and Thomson 1998). *Deep Sea
Voices*, a collection of recollections and photographs of a small group of women from
the fishing communities of northeast England, is a good example of this approach
(Lazenby and Lazenby 1999). Drawing on a project of the National Fishing Heritage
Centre, Grimsby, it sets out as its explicit aim to present the voices of women from
these "unique race-apart communities" and to explore their lives and attitudes within
what has been "portrayed, pilloried and parodied as an overtly masculine domain"
(Lazenby and Lazenby 1999: 8). It carefully avoids analysis or synthesis of the oral
histories, selected in an attempt to let "the tremendous depth, integrity, humility and
good humour of its contributors' speak" (Lazenby and Lazenby 1999: 8), and it does so
successfully. Yet the explicit agenda of the researchers is also clear in the subjects covered and structure of the book. On the other hand, Thompson's *Living the Fishing*
(1983), which addresses parallel British fishing communities, is a useful example
because it draws on a *mix* of sociology, anthropology, and history, through oral

histories, photographs, and personal and community archives. It addresses changes in these communities from the late nineteenth century into the late twentieth. Oral histories are the key source, yet it blends the ethnohistorical background with case studies of fishing communities in East Anglia, northwestern England, and Scotland; it offers a broader analysis of community, identity, and family in changing socioeconomic circumstances.

Maritime oral traditions and folklore collections include a wide range of studies with less-well-defined parameters. They range from the oral traditions and stories of particular communities, such as dreaming stories of Australian Aboriginal peoples (Wunungmurra and Wunungmurra 2003), to Scandinavian maritime epics and regional maritime folklore collections (Bois 1996; Greenhill 1985). They also include more general works such as Beck's *Folklore and the Sea* (1973), as well as discussions of maritime language (Colcord 1977) and the many collections of European and North American maritime songs (Creighton 1979; Smith 1888). Oral traditions document a community's unwritten past and have all the nuance, bias, and metaphors of written histories, along with a particular linguistic fluidity. The broader discourse on communal oral traditions reflects their importance alongside this apparent ambiguity. Scholars have, for example, discussed the knowledge systems they reflect and produce (Agrawal 1995; Greenstein 1995; Silitoe 1998) and how they are analyzed (Marshall 2006; Pálsson 1992; particularly Sørenson 1992), particularly in relation to archaeology (Gazin-Schwartz and Holtorf 1999; Helm 2004; Pikirayi 2004).

Much of the discussion reflects on how oral traditions are created and transformed through time, and how they carry meanings and messages, as well as the cultural purposes they serve (teaching, producing, and maintaining social identities) and the insights they offer into people's lives, beliefs, values, and understandings of their world and into social organization and practices (e.g., White, Miescher, and Cohen 2001). At heart, this discourse is about reading oral traditions and folklore texts in "contextually informed ways" (Marshall 2006: 74). It cannot be assumed that a *tradition*, be it either social practice or meaning, can be extracted from them directly. This is especially true of written and published collections, where the process of transferring oral traditions to the page is crucial (i.e., fieldwork collating first-person narrations or research into literary and historical texts) and the perspective of the researcher needs to be considered. Some texts respond to postcolonial discourse (e.g., Spivak 1999) and the epistemologically reflexive arguments of scholars such as Haraway (1988) to self-consciously present alternative voices. Others, such as Smith's work (1888), are historical sources in themselves or appeal to an intangible contemporary sense of collective maritime heritage (Lunn and Day 2004). So, though oral traditions about the maritime past offer access to what maritime communities value and choose to remember, this is rarely easily translatable.

Ethnographies of Maritime Communities

In contrast to the previous source, ethnographic studies of maritime communities are rooted in a distinct anthropological academic and fieldwork tradition.

Ethnographic fieldwork, in the classic Malinowskian tradition (1967), involves participant observation, a methodology of cultural immersion by the ethnographer. As Ingold (2008: 21) explains, "The objective of ethnography is to describe the lives of people other than ourselves, with an accuracy and sensitivity honed by detailed observation and prolonged first-hand experience." Anthropology draws on ethnography to pursue critical understanding of human life and society, to explore the ways in which people know and produce the world. Originally bound to the colonial project, early schools of anthropology were built on the notion that it would be a science of society, recording the multiplicity and *evolution* of social systems (Degerando 1800; Morgan 1887; White 1949) and deciphering universal cultural laws. In the period since, the field has moved through conceptual and epistemic shifts, acknowledging that the "butterfly approach" proposed by Lévi-Strauss (Ingold 2008: 23), the classification of all the discrete, self-contained societies of the world, does not reflect the overlapping, fluid, and changing nature of social life. Hence, there is a considerable body of reflexive discourse on ethnographic field methodologies and ethics (Brewer 2000; Bromley and Carter 2002; Gupta and Ferguson 1997), as well as the subjectivity and complexities of ethnographic texts (Clifford and Marcus 1986) and the nature of anthropological knowledge (Fabian 1983; Hastrup and Hervik 1994; Marcus and Fischer 1986). In more recent decades, there has, for example, been a shift to foregrounding the voices of individuals from the community being studied alongside that of the ethnographer (Coffey 1999). There is not space to engage fully with this extensive discourse here, but we should note that this holistic approach to studying maritime communities is far from the "dehumanised technology" of traditional boat studies. In fact, in much ethnography there has until very recently been a characteristic disinterest in the role material culture or technology plays in producing society, in favor of human relationships (Dolwick 2008). Moreover, these studies reflect the people and subjects the ethnographer encounters and chooses to purse (Marcus 1995). They are unlikely to focus on all elements of maritime communities and may well not examine, for example, the practicalities and technologies of seafaring.

Among the pertinent examples, Busby's (2000) brilliant ethnography of a southern Indian fishing village draws on the everyday lives of both men and women, on boats, fishing, fish-selling, and families, to address the ontologies of this maritime community. She uses her ethnography to consider their understandings of the performative nature of gender in particular. In contrast, Chou's (2002) ethnography is focused on identity and exchange among Indonesian sea nomads. There are also studies that focus on people's relationships with their environment and the pressures for change in coastal communities, such as Ruohomaki's (1997) fascinating study of southern Thai maritime villages. Meanwhile, Tilley's (2002) work on traditional canoes in Micronesia returns to material culture—the boats—to examine their social meanings and metaphors. Through this, he aims to address how objects contribute to making social identities and the mutually transformative coproduction of human-object (in this case human-boat) relations (2002: 27). These four "maritime" examples alone provide markedly diverse conceptual foci and ethnographic objects of study. Though they have a common depth and culturally holistic approach, they draw out very different subjects for analysis.

There is also a significant group of ethnographies that look specifically at fisheries. The world fisheries crisis of the 1970s and the 1982 United Nations Convention on the Law of the Sea shaped interest in sea management and indigenous fisheries among anthropologists interested in development studies and the politics of indigenous rights (e.g., Cordell 1989; Scott and Mulrennan 1999). Johannes and MacFarlane's (1991) work on traditional fishing in the Torres Strait Islands, for example, is published by the Fisheries Division of the Australian Commonwealth Scientific and Industrial Research Organisation. Plus, many anthropologists working among marine specialist aboriginal communities, or "saltwater peoples," of Australia are interested in "customary marine tenure" and the demands of many "saltwater peoples" for legal recognition of their Native Title rights to their seas (McNiven 2003: 332). These examples reflect more recent diversification of ethnographic objects of study and, in some cases, anthropological engagement with contemporary political contexts.

Strengths and Weaknesses

Both the merits and the limitations of traditional boat studies are bound to their focus on boats as technology. Disembedding boats from their sociocultural context is a significant limitation to the interpretive value of the studies. However, their value as a technological reference collection, which is a clear demonstration to any maritime archaeological researcher of the variety and technological diversity of boats and boat-related activities, should not be underestimated. Yet it needs to be recognized that traditional boat studies subscribe to an evolutionary narrative of boat technology, viewing archaeological finds simply as examples with which to fill gaps as construction techniques are traced through time and space (e.g., Hornell's [1946:xv] discussion of "stages of culture"; Lundberg 2003). This evolutionary narrative alone is the framework through which boats are addressed in relation to each other. The relationships identified are technical, typological, abstracted, and temporally separated. So the tangle of interactions between different boats, people and all the animate and inanimate things of the world—from wind and water to fish and nets—is beyond their scope. Despite expansion in these studies, there remains a lack of ethnographic detail about the social meaning and understandings behind specific maritime traditions. The focus on contemporary communities allows a depth of analysis of boats and their uses, but these studies still lack the voices of the people within those communities. The technological focus, categories, and even terminology are supplied by the researcher and are unlikely to reflect the concerns of the communities themselves. Yet if the particular perspective of these studies is acknowledged, they can offer a wealth of details and insights into different ways of constructing and using boats.

Similarly, the case specificity of oral history studies is both an asset and a drawback. On the one hand, they record the voices of tradition; on the other, they are by their very nature partial and subjective. If traditional boat studies are shaped by researchers' categories and concerns, the data here is shaped by the individuals they talk to and what those individuals wish to talk about (as much as the questions the researchers ask). Both provide unique but incomplete views. Moreover, these studies provoke very relevant questions about how we use people's words and whether we can deconstruct and analyze their personal stories. Oral and folklore traditions have a parallel significance, in that they are the stories maritime communities collectively choose to tell and with which their collective identity, concerns, and perspectives are entwined. Yet these traditions also raise a number of questions: what these stories are used for; the different contexts in which they are passed on, changed, or edited; and how they are collated and why. Both oral histories and folklore traditions have a particular value as primary sources, but as a direct result they are ambiguous material to analyze for information on maritime traditions and practices.

Ethnography has a valuable sociocultural depth, which allows us to consider the particular aspects of maritime culture in which we are interested within the larger web of social interactions, connections, and relations of these communities. As texts, ethnographies can be invaluable in situating the various voices within their historically particular context (including that of the ethnographer). However, they also reflect the research interests and encounters of the ethnographer, the "chains, paths, threads, conjunctions, or juxtapositions" which they followed (Marcus 1995: 105). So, as sources on maritime communities and traditions, they may not explore the particular details of technology, economy, or environment sought, though they can provide a more holistic depth of cultural information.

The imperative with each of these sources is critical reading—understanding the nature of the source, its partial perspective and particular focus. Above all, we need to recognize these sources' epistemic and historical background and situate them— these *knowledges*—in the context within which they were produced. Moreover, overall, these sources leave us with particular elements of maritime communities and traditions that are more comprehensively addressed, such as boat construction and technology, fishing and marine subsistence activities, seamanship (including propulsion, navigation, etc.), and others that are largely unexplored, such as ritual practices and the social organization of communities and families, as well as constructions of gender and understandings of maritime space, place, and identity.

USES AND ISSUES

Uses in Maritime Archaeology

At this point, we ought to ask why maritime archaeologists engage with these sources, and to consider the relationship between studies of maritime communities and traditions and maritime archaeology. Maritime archaeologists have drawn on this material in various ways. The use of historical documents is perhaps the most common. Alford (1992) uses references to logboats in historical records from North and South Carolina in the eighteenth and nineteenth centuries to suggest a migration of construction methodology with the refugee French Huguenots. This kind of technological focus on vessels and their historical connection (often in historical maritime archaeology, and especially in North American contexts) is the most common and least problematic use. There are also examples of archaeological studies drawing on early historical sources, particularly classical travel narratives and early navigation texts, such as the *Periplus Maris Erythraei* (Casson 1989; Huntingford 1980; see Blue, and Gaur and Vora, in this volume), though these are treated as primary historical sources with appropriate critical reading.

There are also particular, technical analogies drawn from traditional boats and applied to excavated boat remains (Prins 1986; see also Sorokin 2003). McGrail (1996: 232) even frames traditional boat studies with the additional, specific objective of recording contemporary, traditional craft for the benefit of archaeological interpretation, "to be of maximum use to archaeologists." Related work by Prins (1986) makes an explicit attempt to address traditional boat studies as a kind of ethnoarchaeology, a sources of evidence on which archaeology can draw (McGrail 1980: 41). In a different vein, Westerdahl has drawn on a variety of sources on maritime traditions, including folklore and ethnohistorical material, in his discussion of maritime ritual landscapes in Nordic Europe (2005), while McNiven (2003) uses Australian ethnographic work on "saltwater peoples" (Petersen and Rigsby 1998; Sharp 2002) in his analysis of the archaeology of Australian indigenous seascapes (see also Barber 2003). Yet beyond these examples, and despite McGrail's (1996) appeals, there are in fact quite limited examples of sources on maritime communities and traditions being used in maritime archaeological studies. So why is there such a fractured, undertheorized dialogue between these related areas of study?

Maritime Traditions: Past and Present Maritime Communities

One of the primary issues behind this fractured relationship is the complexities of drawing on contemporary sources in maritime archaeological studies, specifically the challenge of using this material in the interpretations of the (often distant) maritime archaeological past. McGrail (1987: 3) himself acknowledges that "ethnographic analogues must be treated with great caution. . . . the fact that hide boats (Hornell 1946) and reed rafts (Delaney 1976) were recently used in the west of Ireland does not prove that they were in use there millennia or even centuries ago." Yet the evolutionary narrative of boats and "origin stories" (Lundberg 2003) that characterizes all traditional boat studies, and particularly McGrail's work, conflates the present and past in just this way. More than this, however, and as we have already seen, these studies produce, to use Haraway's (1988) term, "situated knowledges." Marshall (2006: 73) warns that "our failure to appreciate the historical, particularly the colonial, context of most ethnography and ethnoarchaeology has severely compromised all interpretations archaeologists have drawn from it." Given the problem of spatial and temporal dislocation, and given that the sources on which we draw are situated knowledges, the use of analogy—either technological or social—is very problematic. Once we make analogous connections between disparate communities, we are in danger of making uniformitarian assumptions and of essentializing these societies in our analysis. It could be argued, for example, that the dehumanized technology and essentialized maritime traditions presented in traditional boat studies authorizes maritime archaeologists to make simplistic technological analogies across spatial and temporal distances, which further dislocates technology from social drivers and context in maritime archaeological interpretations.

This is as true for archaeological engagements with oral histories, folklore traditions, and traditional boat studies as it is for ethnoarchaeological engagements, though the disciplinary debate in ethnoarchaeology is well developed and worth considering in some detail (Barrett and Fewster 1998; Fewster 2001; Hamilakis 2001; Lucas 2001; Wobst 1978; Wylie 1985). For though at heart ethnoarchaeology addresses the role artifacts—material *things*—play in producing the world, there is a social reductionism inherent in using analogies to draw archaeological interpretation from ethnographic sources. A typical functionalist study, for example, may address ceramic manufacture, supply of materials, waste, and distribution among "less developed" contemporary communities to provide models for the interpretation of archaeological contexts (e.g., Allchin 1994). The individuals studied and the nuances of their social relationships become generalized exemplars that stand for the whole society. At its most conservative, ethnoarchaeology looks for "ethnofacts"—about metalworking, systems of pastoralism, or South Asian sewn boats, for example—and constitutes these observed "facts" as objective, transposable, cultural truths to be used to interpret prehistoric pastoralist movement or the function of specific objects found in metalworking sites of Bronze Age Britain (Prins 1986). Thus, the potential myriad of meanings, messages, and reasons for undertaking similar actions in different ways in different contexts, and the basic capriciousness of human choice, are lost as particular, multivalent social actions are fixed into archetypal models. As Smith (2001: 128) has suggested, "When ethnographic inquiry starts from social constructionist assumptions, the question of human agency is immensely complicated."

There is considerable debate about the problematics of this approach in postprocessual ethnoarchaeological discourse, and there are numerous studies that move beyond this narrow understanding of ethnoarchaeology. Among them are those that use contemporary examples to illuminate archaeological interpretations, to address archaeological epistemology reflexively, or to broaden potential readings of archaeological material (e.g., Tilley 1996; Whittle 1997), rather than to provide a model to construct an idea of the past around. In fact, Marshall (2006: 73) suggests that the interpretive limits of the approaches adopted by ethnoarchaeology are becoming increasing apparent, since whether they pursue the symbolic/structuralist approach of Hodder (1982) or processual/functionalist methods (David and Kramer 2001), "ethnoarchaeology remains a fundamentally ahistoric endeavour."

What underpins the use of analogy is the difficult and complex notion of uniformitarianism—the idea that the primary processes that shape our social world are common to all societies (in the past as well as the present). For in making analogies, whether functionalist or symbolic, these studies often make the implicit assumption that underlying all cultures is a systemic uniformity (a governing social structure or organization), a system of social action that can be deciphered, broken down into smaller component pieces of "natural" behavior (Lucas 2001: 182), and transferred across time and space (e.g., Bhattacharya and Bhattacharya 2002). The correlate assumption within much of this work is that those contemporary societies being studied are "a latter-day survival of a stage passed elsewhere in the world" (Gosden 1999: 9), an echo of the social-evolutionary concepts of early anthropology (Morgan 1887; White 1949). Thomas (2004: 241) identifies three contexts involved in the use of cultural analogies: namely, "the context within which archaeologists work; the temporal other of the past; and the ethnographic or spatial other." Beneath these various assumptions about the comparability of societies, it is the relations between these three contexts, and the process of creating an "other" that is embedded within them, that is so problematic. There is a danger in projecting modern, Western understandings of the world onto the ethnographic other and conflating this with the past; something reflected in MacEachern's (1994: 245) astute description of ethnoarchaeology as "the intersection of living people and archaeological constructions."

Though it may be starkest in functionalist ethnoarchaeology, and in the technical analogies advocated by McGrail and Prins, there are potentially parallel problems in socially reductive engagements with maritime oral and folklore tradition. Damm (2005: 78–79), among others, is critical of extracting details from oral traditions, a practice sometimes referred to as the "pick and mix approach" (Marshall 2006: 73). It is a critique that goes back to the early work of Lévi-Strauss (1969), among other anthropologists, on myth and folklore and is bound to early uniformitarian assumptions in anthropology. Yet it is also true of Westerdahl's (2005) work on maritime "ritual landscapes" in Nordic Europe, which conflates time and space, using folklore and ethnohistorical examples that are both particular and decontextualized to produce essentialist and problematically broad interpretations about coastal Nordic cosmology and cognitive landscapes. As Marshall (2006: 73) argues, "If we are to incorporate insights from oral traditions we must develop methodologies that allow such traditions to speak with their own voices rather than being merged into ours."

McNiven's (2003) work on the archaeology of Australian indigenous seascapes and the ontologies of coastal "saltwater peoples" draws on a breadth of ethnographic work as well as oral traditions. The notion of seascapes—the seamlessness of land and water in the cognitive and experiential landscapes of these coastal communities—which he discusses has the potential to alter the way many archaeologists imagine maritime communities in the past. Yet McNiven exhibits a tendency to gather elements of somewhat scattered examples to weave into his archaeological story. This is in contrast to Philips's (2000) work on Maori oral tradition and archaeology, which Marshall (2006: 74) discusses, where "each form of data is allowed to tell its own story" and the different forms are only brought together into a synthesized narrative at the end. It is worth adding a word of caution about McNiven's (2003: 244–245) concluding assertions that ritual "orchestration of seascapes . . . are fundamental to specialized maritime hunter-gatherers in a broad range of cultural contexts, both past and present." He universalizes his interpretation of this one example, in which he posits ritual sites (including shell middens and intertidal archaeological sites) as a fundamental part of local seascape ontologies (a universalism that may be all too seductive to archaeologists investigating prehistoric shell middens in northwestern Europe). It would certainly be socially reductive to interpret similar archaeological structures by mapping the "ritual orchestration of seascapes" as a defining feature onto the communities that produced them.

A need for rigorous respect of case specificity is clear. Above all, it should be remembered that for the most part archaeological questions do not, and should not, shape our sources on maritime communities and traditions. However, the material can be used to ask questions of archaeology. This distinction is crucial, not least because the idea of studying one culture with the express intention of using it as a mechanism for understanding the past is ethically problematic, as well as methodologically flawed.[1] Yet though there is much to critique about the philosophical assumptions at the heart of ethnoarchaeological analogy, there is a danger in becoming so culturally particularist as to render any discussion circular and paralyze archaeological engagements with any of these sources. However, there is room to maneuver between these opposing positions, and within the question of the nature and process of analogy. Exploring potential alternative ways of fishing, boatbuilding and engaging with the maritime world in order to open up our perspective is different from extracting "ethnofacts" in the present to transfer to the past. Successfully managing this involves being explicit about what we are using these sources for and how, and allowing such traditions to tell their own stories. This means endeavoring to undertake studies with an open mind, rather than shaping them through our preestablished conceptual framework; it means not looking for what we expect and then either interpreting material to fit that or drawing on decontextualized sources selectively to support our interpretive narrative.

Barber (2003), for example, successfully combines ethnohistorical and ethnographic literature to expand environmentally determinist, archaeological interpretations of Maori fishing practices in South Island, New Zealand, which emphasized extractive opportunism and foraging theory. Part of the success of his approach is rooted in the fairly limited spatial and temporal dislocation of the two types of evidence (there is continuity of Maori occupation of the area over most of the last millennia), but Barber (2003: 435) still recognizes the limits to this approach in his discussion and is cautious in what he asks of the material and what interpretations he draws from it. Vermonden considers works by Marshall Carucci (1995) and Barlow and Lipset (1997) that address emic understandings of boats and look beyond the boat as a functional object. He regards this approach positively, though

he is evidently concerned with the dangers of cultural particularism and an emphasis on local specificities that give the impression that local societies operate as
isolated units (Vermonden 2006: 228). Thomas (2004: 239) has identified both the
value of a more general archaeological awareness and the increasing use of ethnographic examples within the work of postprocessual archaeologists (e.g., Tilley
1996; Whittle 1997). There is a significant difference between deciphering "ethnofacts" about sewn-boat construction and use in contemporary southern Asia and
applying them to Bronze Age Britain (Prins 1986) and drawing on alternative understandings of seascapes, or how maritime communities produce identities, to illuminate our own assumptions and open up archaeological readings of the past.

What Makes a Community Maritime?

By way of one final word of caution regarding the apparently simple question of
what the term "maritime" means, it is telling that even within this short chapter the
term has been stretched to include inland boats and waterways, as well as riverine
and estuarine communities. It may appear to be a simple question of geography and
economy, but the term is more conceptually slippery. McGrail (pers. comm.), for
example, suggests that we might do well to define the geographical limits of "maritime culture" by drawing on Homer's idea of a nonmaritime culture. In *The Odyssey*
Homer describes a nonmaritime people as

> a people who know nothing of the sea, and never use salt with their food, so that
> crimson-painted ships and the long oars that serve those ships as wings are quite
> beyond their experience. He gave me this infallible sign (which I now reveal to
> you)—when I met some other traveller who referred to the oar I was carrying on
> my shoulder as a "winnowing-fan." (2003: 307)

Yet even when our examples fit geographically, what do we mean by a "maritime community"? Most coastal communities exploit both marine and terrestrial
resources. They are not isolated coastal communities facing only toward the sea.
Even the classic historical and archaeological examples of maritime communities,
such as the communities of the Scottish Islands or Viking society, were also farming
communities. Do the groups that live on the sea, such as Indonesian sea nomads,
represent a truer maritime community (Chou 2002)? Or perhaps the seafaring
communities of the Arabian Sea had a truly maritime culture (Villiers 1969)? Could
it even refer to shipboard society, to communities produced within the maritime
sphere? And what of the other terms and categories used: "saltwater peoples,"
"estuarine" or "coastal communities"? Are the differences in the experiences and
lives lived on inshore islands (in contrast to offshore islands), in coastal/inshore
seascapes (in contrast to estuarine worlds), or on the sea rather than the ocean of
relevance here? Even when examining practices and technology rather than social
worlds, case specificity is of utmost importance. We need to consider the terms we
are using and whether we are dividing communities into categories current in our
discipline (and in our conceptual framework), rather than categories current in the

realities of the people involved. It may be that the very idea of a "maritime community," and the scholarly discussion over what defines one, would have little meaning for those living in watery worlds in the past. We might do well to consider that the term itself, imposed as it is by scholars on past peoples, may limit or bias our interpretations, the questions we ask, and the stories we tell about these communities, before we even begin.

NEW RESEARCH DIRECTIONS

Having begun this chapter with the assertion that maritime archaeology addresses maritime communities and traditions in terms of small-scale, local maritime practices, this section will highlight research in which maritime archaeologists, anthropologists, and historians are exploring a broader conception of maritime tradition. Pálsson's (1994) work on embodied knowledge, experience, and learning in Icelandic fishing is a particularly good example. The study connects social relationships within the community, including master-apprentice relationships, to personal enskillment through actively engaging with the environment in order to acquire understanding of fishing and seafaring. This pivotal work has influenced a number of subsequent studies to look at the experiential nature of seafaring skill and the way it shapes people's identities and social status. Among them, King's (2007) work on corporeal interdependency and the performance of masculinity on Australian shark-fishing boats is illuminating. McNiven's (2003) and Barber's (2003) work has already been mentioned, and there is a growing group of studies now focusing in more detail on identity and landscape, on how people and place are made in particular watery communities (Cobb 2007; Ransley 2009; Sturt 2006). Moreover, there has been a significant shift in the approach of many maritime archaeologists who engage in maritime ethnography research, and traditional boat scholars have begun to debate the problematics of analogy (Blue 2003).

More recently still, a growing number of scholars have begun to look at the cultural currency of the idea of "maritime tradition" for contemporary communities, and the different ways we construct and use the notion of a "maritime community" (and it is this research, rather than questions of geography or economy, which is likely to finally answer the question of what makes a community maritime). This area of maritime heritage research draws on contemporary perceptions and cultural uses of the maritime past. It examines the identity politics involved in national, regional, and local agendas and even the notion of "maritimity" as a cultural concept. For example, how and why is the notion of a "maritime nation" or "our maritime past" deployed (Lunn and Day 2004)? What is behind this continuing cultural discourse, the popularity in the United Kingdom of the *Mary Rose*, and of historic dockyards and Nelson's story, or of the *Vasa* in Sweden (Day and Lunn 2003; Leffler 2004)? What are the contemporary cultural meanings of smaller local maritime heritage projects (Lindgren 1999)? What is the impetus behind the oral history projects of the National Fishing Heritage Centre (Lazenby and Lazenby 1999) or the Traditional Boats of Ireland project (MacCárthaigh 2008)?

Nadel-Klein's (2003) research among communities in western Scotland, where the decline of fishing has led to doubts over their economic and cultural survival, explores the local sense of maritime identity and tradition alongside the growing tourist industry to examine the various ways a "maritime heritage" is constructed (2003). Stefanou's (2008) work on Greek maritime heritage and national identity looks at constructions of maritime tradition and a maritime past in local, regional, and national contexts, and considers the different means through which a national maritime narrative is produced, from the many private maritime museums to community reenactments of past maritime events. Andrews's (2007) research on the complex maritime "heritage-scape" of Bermuda includes the personal discourses of salvage divers and the conflicting notions of maritime tradition and heritage deployed in local identity politics.

These studies of maritime traditions and communities speak to maritime archaeology in a different way: they center on what is being done with the knowledge and materials produced by the discipline and address maritime archaeology as a source for the production of maritime tradition rather than maritime traditions as a source for archaeological interpretation. They explore the uses to which maritime archaeological knowledge is put in the contemporary world and the cultural and even the socioeconomic politics behind many of the archaeological projects we are involved in, which color our work, our approaches, and even our objects of study. These interesting and potentially fruitful areas of research offer a very different contextualization of maritime archaeological sites, subjects, and research.

NOTE

1. Gosden has even argued that "ethnoarchaeology is immoral, in that we have no justification for using the present of one society simply to interpret the past of another" (1999: 9). However, if this position is taken to its logical conclusion—that we cannot morally draw any understandings or theoretical constructs from contemporary or near-contemporary societies to color archaeological interpretation—then it handicaps most, if not all, archaeological discourse.

REFERENCES

Adney, Edwin Tappan, and Howard I. Chapelle. [1964] 2007. *The bark canoes and skin boats of North America.* New York: Skyhorse.

Agrawal, Arun. 1995. Dismantling the divide between indigenous and scientific knowledge. *Development and Change* 26 (3): 413–439.

Alford, Michael B. 1992. Origins of Carolina split-dugout canoes. *International Journal of Nautical Archaeology* 21 (3): 191–203.

Allchin, Bridget, ed. 1994. *Living traditions: Studies in the ethnoarchaeology of South Asia.* Oxford: Oxbow.

Andrews, Charlotte. 2007. Tricky listening: Museological inclusion of archaeologically alternative views to Bermuda's underwater cultural heritage. *Museological Review* 12: 13–32.

Barber, Ian. 2003. Sea, land and fish: Spatial relationships and the archaeology of South Island Maori fishing. *World Archaeology* 35 (3): 434–448.

Barlow, Kathleen, and David Lipset. 1997. Dialogics of material culture: Male and female in Murik outrigger canoes. *American Ethnologist* 24 (1): 4–36.

Barratt, John C., and Kathyrn J. Fewster. 1998. Stonehenge: Is the medium the message? *Antiquity* 72: 847–852.

Beck, Horace Palmer. 1973. *Folklore and the sea.* Middletown, CT: Wesleyan University Press.

Bhattacharya, D. K., and Deepra Bhattacharya. 2002. Agro-pastoralism in contemporary ethnography: Its relevance in explanation of archaeological material in India. In *Archaeology and interactive disciplines*, ed. S. Setter and Radi Korisettar, 155–168. Manohar: ICHR.

Blue, Lucy. 2003. Maritime ethnography: The reality of analogy. In *Boats, ships and shipyards: Proceedings of the 9th International Symposium on Boat and Ship Archaeology, Venice 2000*, ed. Carlo Beltrame, 334–338. Oxford: Oxbow.

Blue, L., J. Whitewright, J. Ransley, and C. Palmer. Forthcoming. Traditional craft in context—the *kattumarram* of South Asia. *International Journal of Nautical Archaeology*.

Bois, G. J. C. 1996. *Jersey maritime folklore.* Jersey, UK: Jersey Maritime Museum.

Brewer, John D. 2000. *Ethnography.* Buckingham: Open University Press.

Bromley, David G., and Louis F. Carter, eds. 2002. *Toward reflexive ethnography: Participating, observing, narrating.* London: JAI.

Busby, Cecilia. 2000. *The performance of gender: An anthropology of everyday life in a South Indian fishing village.* London: Athlone Press.

Casson, Lionel. 1989. *The Periplus Maris Erythraei: Text with introduction, translation and commentary.* Princeton, NJ: Princeton University Press.

Chittick, Neville. 1980. Sewn boats in the western Indian Ocean, and a survival in Somalia. *International Journal of Nautical Archaeology* 9 (4): 297–309.

Chou, Cynthia. 2002. *Indonesian sea nomads: Money, magic, and fear of the Orang Suku Laut.* New York: Routledge.

Clifford, James, and George E. Marcus, eds. 1986. *Writing culture: The poetics and politics of ethnography.* Berkeley and Los Angeles: University of California Press.

Cobb, Hannah. 2007. *Media for movement and making the world: An examination of the Mesolithic experience of the world and the Mesolithic to Neolithic transition in the northern Irish Sea basin.* PhD diss., University of Manchester.

Coffey, Amanda. 1999. *The ethnographic self: Fieldwork and the representation of identity.* London: Sage.

Colcord, Joanna Carver. [1945] 1977. *Sea language comes ashore.* New York: Arno Press.

Cordell, John. 1989. *A sea of small boats.* Cambridge, UK: Cultural Survival.

Creighton, Helen. 1979. *Maritime folksongs.* St. Johns, Newfoundland: Breakwater Books.

Damm, Charlotte. 2005. Archaeology, ethno-history and oral traditions: Approaches to the indigenous past. *Norwegian Archaeological Review* 38 (2): 73–87.

———. 2006. Towards a glocal archaeology? *Norwegian Archaeological Review* 39 (1): 75–79.

David, Nicolas, and Carol Kramer. 2001. *Ethnoarchaeology in action*. Cambridge: Cambridge University Press.

Day, Ann, and Ken Lunn. 2003. British maritime heritage: Carried along by the currents? *International Journal of Heritage Studies* 9: 289–305.

Degerando, Joseph-Marie. [1800] 1969. *The observation of savage peoples*. Berkeley and Los Angeles: University of California Press.

Delaney, James. 1976. Fieldwork in south Roscommon. In *Folk and farm*, ed. C. Ó. Danochair, 15–29. Dublin: Royal Society of Antiquaries of Ireland.

Dolwick, Jim. 2008. In search of the social: Steamboats, square wheels, reindeer and other things. *Journal of Maritime Archaeology* 3 (1): 15–41.

Fabian, Johannes. 1983. *Time and the other: How anthropology makes its object*. New York: Columbia University Press.

Fewster, Kathryn. 2001. The responsibilities of ethnoarchaeologists. In *The responsibilities of archaeologists—archaeology and ethics*, ed. Mark Pluciennik, 65–73. BAR International Series 981. Oxford: Archaeopress.

Gazin-Schwartz, Amy, and Cornelius J. Holtorf, eds. 1999. *Archaeology and folklore*. Routledge: London.

Gosden, Chris. 1999. *Anthropology and archaeology: A changing relationship*. New York: Routledge.

Greenhill, Basil. 1966. *The boats of East Pakistan*. Reprinted from *Mariner's Mirror* 1957, vol. 43. London: Society of Nautical Research.

Greenhill, Pauline. 1985. *Lots of stories: Maritime narratives from the Creighton collection*. Ottawa: National Museums of Canada.

Greenstein, Ran. 1995. Rethinking the colonial process: The role of indigenous capacities in comparative historical inquiry. *South African Historical Journal* 32: 114–137.

Gupta, Akhil, and James Ferguson, eds. 1997. *Anthropological locations: Boundaries and grounds of a field science*. Berkeley and Los Angeles: University of California Press.

Hamilakis, Yannis. 2001. Archaeology and the burden of responsibility. In *The responsibilities of archaeologists: Archaeology and ethics*, ed. Mark Pluciennik, 91–96. BAR International Series No. 981. Oxford: Archeopress.

Haraway, Donna. 1988. Situated knowledges: The science question in feminism and the privilege of partial perspective. *Feminist Studies* 14 (3): 575–599.

Hastrup, Kirsten, and Peter Hervik, eds. 1994. *Social experience and anthropological knowledge*. New York: Routledge.

Heath, John D. 2004. *Eastern Arctic kayaks: History, design, technique*. Fairbanks: University of Alaska Press.

Helm, Richard. 2004. Re-evaluating traditional histories on the coast of Kenya: An archaeological perspective. In *African historical archaeologies*, ed. Andrew Reid and Paul Lane, 59–89. London: Kluwer Academic/Plenum.

Hill, A. H. 1958. Some early accounts of the Oriental boat. *Mariner's Mirror* 44: 1–217.

Hodder. Ian. 1982. *Symbols in action*. Cambridge: Cambridge University Press.

Homer. 2003. *The Odyssey*. Translated by Emile Victor Rieu and D. Christopher H. Rieu. London: Penguin.

Hornell, James. 1946. *Water transport: Origins and early evolution*. Cambridge: Cambridge University Press.

Horridge, Adrian G. 1985. *The prahu: Traditional sailing boat of Indonesia*. Singapore: Oxford University Press.

Huntingford, George Wynn Brereton. 1980. *The periplus of the Erythraean Sea*. London: Hakluyt Society.

Ingold, Tim. 2008. Anthropology is *not* ethnography. *British Academy Review* 11: 21–23.

Insoll, Timothy. 1993. A note on a sewn canoe in use at Gao, the Republic of Mali. *International Journal of Nautical Archaeology* 22 (4): 345–350.

Jennings, John. 2004. *Bark canoes: The art and obsession of Tappan Adney*. Buffalo, NY: Firefly.

Johannes, Robert Earle, and J. W. MacFarlane. 1991. *Traditional fishing in the Torres Strait Islands*. Hobart: CSIRO Division of Fisheries.

Kentley, Eric 1985. Some aspects of the masula surf boat. In *Sewn plank boats*, ed. Seán McGrail and Eric Kentley, 303–317. BAR International Series 276. Oxford: Archaeopress.

King, Tanya J. 2007. Bad habits and prosthetic performances: Negotiation of individuality and embodiment of social status in Australian shark fishing. *Journal of Anthropological Research* 63: 537–560.

Lane, Paul. 2006. Oral histories and indigenous archaeology: An Africanist perspective. *Norwegian Archaeological Review* 39 (1): 70–73.

Lazenby, Craig, and Jenny Lazenby, eds. 1999. *Deep sea voices*. Stroud, UK: Tempus.

Leffler, Phyllis. 2004. Peopling the portholes: National identity and maritime museums in the U.S. and U.K. *Public Historian* 26 (4): 23–48.

Lévi-Strauss, Claude. 1969. *The raw and the cooked*. New York: Harper & Row.

Lindgren, James M. 1999. "Let us idealize old types of manhood": The New Bedford Whaling Museum, 1903–1941. *New England Quarterly* 72 (2): 163–206.

Lucas, Gavin. 2001. *Critical approaches to fieldwork: Contemporary and historical archaeological practice*. London: Routledge.

Lundberg, Anita. 2003. Time travels in whaling boats. *Journal of Social Archaeology* 3 (3): 312–333.

Lunn, Ken, and Ann Day. 2004. Britain as island: National identity and the sea. In *History, nationhood and the question of Britain*, ed. Helen Brocklehurst and Robert B. Phillips, 124–136. London: Palgrave Macmillan.

MacCárthaigh, Críostóir, ed. 2008. *Traditional boats of Ireland: History, folklore and construction*. Cork: Collins Press.

MacCárthaigh, Críostóir, Colin Becker, and John Kearon. 2007. Heritage Council guidelines, Traditional Boats of Ireland Project. Rev. 12 December 2007. Online at www.tradboats.ie/heritage-council-guidelines.php/. Accessed 13 March 2010.

MacEachern, Scott. 1994. "Symbolic reservoirs" and cultural relations between ethnic groups: West African examples. *African Archaeological Review* 12: 203–222.

MacPolin, Dónal Mac. 1992. *The Drontheim: Forgotten sailing boat of the north Irish coast*. Dublin: PlayPrint.

Malinowski, Bronislaw. 1967. *A diary in the strict sense of the term*. London: Routledge.

Marcus, George E. 1995. Ethnography in/of the world system: The emergence of multi-sited ethnography. *Annual Review of Anthropology* 24: 95–117.

Marcus, George E., and Michael M. J. Fischer. 1986. *Anthropology as cultural critique*. Chicago: University of Chicago Press.

Marshall, Yvonne. 2006. Situating voices. *Norwegian Archaeological Review* 39 (1): 73–74.

Marshall, Yvonne, and Chris Gosden. 1999. The cultural biography of objects. *World Archaeology* 31 (2): 169–178.

Marshall Carucci, L. 1995. Symbolic imagery of Enewetak sailing canoes. In *Seafaring in the contemporary Pacific islands*, ed. Richard Feinberg, 16–33. DeKalb: Northern Illinois University Press.

McClintock, Anne. 1995. *Imperial leather: Race, gender and sexuality in the colonial contest.* Routledge: London.

McGrail, Seán. 1980. Ships, shipwrights and seaman: Sources of evidence. In *The Viking World*, ed. James Graham-Campbell, 38–63. London: Weidenfeld & Nicolson.

———. 1984. Boat ethnography and maritime archaeology. *International Journal of Nautical Archaeology* 13 (2): 149–150.

———. 1987. *Ancient boats in north-west Europe.* London: Longman.

———. 1996. The study of boats with stitched planking. In *Tradition and archaeology: Early maritime contacts in the Indian Ocean—proceedings of the International Seminar Techno-Archaeological Perspectives of Seafaring in the Indian Ocean 4th Century BCE–25th Century CE*, ed. Himanshu Prabha, P. Ray, and Jean-Francois Salles, 225–238. New Delhi: Manohar.

———. 1997. *Studies in maritime archaeology.* BAR British Series 256. Oxford: Archaeopress.

———. 2001. *Boats of the world: From the Stone Age to medieval times.* Oxford: Oxford University Press.

McGrail, Seán, Lucy Blue, Eric Kentley, and Colin Palmer. 2003. *Boats of South Asia.* London: Routledge Curzon.

McKee, Eric. 1983. *Working boats of Britain.* London: Conway Maritime Press and National Maritime Museum.

McNiven, Ian J. 2003. Saltwater people: Spiritscapes, maritime rituals and the archaeology of Australian indigenous seascapes. *World Archaeology* 35 (3): 329–349.

Moore, Alan. 1970. *Last days of mast and sail: An essay in nautical comparative anatomy.* London: David and Charles Reprints.

Morgan, Lewis H. 1887. *Ancient society.* Chicago: C. H. Kerr.

Muscat, Joseph. 1999. *The Dgħajsa and other traditional Maltese boats.* Malta: Fondazzjoni Patrmonju Malti.

Nadel-Klein, Jane. 2003. *Fishing for heritage.* Oxford: Berg.

Pálsson, Gísli, ed. 1992. *From saga to society: Comparative approaches in early Iceland.* Enfield Lock, Middlesex, UK: Hisarlik Press.

———. 1994. Enskilment at sea. *MAN* 29 (4): 901–927.

Paris, Edmond. [1841–1843]. *Essai sur la construction navale des peuples extra-européens.* Paris: Arthus Bertrand.

Perks, Robert, and Alaistair Thomson, eds. 1998. *The oral history reader.* London: Routledge.

Petersen, Erik. 2000. *Jukung-boats from the Barito Basin, Borneo.* Roskilde: Viking Ship Museum.

Petersen, H. C. 1986. *Skinboats of Greenland.* Roskilde: Viking Ship Museum.

Petersen, Nicolas, and Bruce Rigsby, eds. 1998. *Customary marine tenure in Australia.* Sydney: University of Sydney Oceania.

Philips, Caroline. 2000. *Wiahou journeys: The archaeology of 400 years of Maori settlement.* Auckland: Auckland University Press.

Pikirayi, Innocent. 2004. Less implicit historical archaeologies: Oral traditions and later Karanga settlements in south-central Zimbabwe. In *African historical archaeologies*, ed. Andrew Reid and Paul Lane, 243–267. London: Kluwer Academic/Plenum.

Pohl, Henrik. 2007. From the *kattumaram* to the *fibre-teppa*—changes in boatbuilding
    traditions on India's East Coast. *International Journal of Nautical Studies* 36 (2):
    382–408.

Prins, Adrian Henrik Johan. 1986. *A handbook of sewn boats: The ethnography and
    archaeology of Archaic plank-built craft*. Maritime Monographs and Reports No. 59.
    London: National Maritime Museum.

Rajamanickam, G. Victor. 2004. *Traditional Indian ship building—memories, history,
    technology*. New Delhi: New Academic.

Ransley, Jesse. 2005. Boats are for boys: Queering maritime archaeology. *World Archaeology*
    37 (4): 621–629.

———. 2007. Rigorous reasoning, reflexive research and the space for "alternative
    archaeologies"? Questions for maritime archaeological heritage management.
    International Journal of Nautical Archaeology 36 (2): 221–237.

———. 2009. *The backwater boats of Kerala: Identity, place and the world of Munruthuruthu*.
    PhD diss., University of Southampton.

Rose, Gillian. 1993. *Feminism and geography: The limits of geographical knowledge*. Oxford:
    Oxford University Press.

Ruohomaki, Olli-Pekka. 1997. *Livelihoods and environment in southern Thai maritime
    villages*. PhD diss., University of London.

Scott, Colin, and Monica Mulrennan 1999. Land and sea tenure at Erub, Torres
    Strait: Property, sovereignty and the adjudication of cultural continuity. *Oceania*
    70: 146–176.

Sharp, Nonie. 2002. *Saltwater people: The waves of memory*. Crows Nest: Allen & Unwin.

Silitoe, Paul. 1998. The development of indigenous knowledge: A new applied anthropology.
    Current Anthropology 39 (2): 223–252.

Smith, Laura Alexandrine. 1888. *The music of the waters: A collection of the sailors' shanties,
    or working songs of the sea, of all maritime nations: Boatmen's, fishermen's, and rowing
    songs, and water legends*. London: Kegan Paul, Trench & Co.

Smith, Michael P. 2001. Beyond the postmodern city: Rethinking ethnography in
    transnational times. In *Transnational urbanism: Locating globalization*, ed.
    M. P. Smith, 123–144. Malden: Blackwell.

Sørenson, Peben M. 1992. Some methodological considerations in connection with the
    study of the sagas. In *From saga to society: Comparative approaches in early Iceland*, ed.
    Gísli Pálsson, 27–41. Enfield Lock, Middlesex, UK: Hisarlik Press.

Sorokin, Petr. 2003. Investigation of traditional boatbuilding for the reconstruction of
    medieval Russian boats. In *Boats, ships and shipyards: Proceedings of the Ninth
    International Symposium on Boat and Ship Archaeology, Venice 2000*, ed. Carlo
    Beltrame, 190–194. Oxford: Oxbow.

Spivak, Gayatri Chakravorty. 1999. *A critique of postcolonial reason: Toward a history of the
    vanishing present*. Cambridge, MA: Harvard University Press.

Stefanou, Eleni. 2008. Maritime heritage and the shaping of national identity: The case of
    the Historical Archive-Museum of Hydra, Greece. In *SOMA 2005: Proceedings of the
    IX Symposium on Mediterranean Archaeology, Chieti (Italy), 24–26 February 2005*, ed.
    Olivia Menozzi, M. L. Di Marzio, and D. Fossataro, 463–470. BAR International Series
    No. 1739. Oxford: Archaeopress.

Sturt, Fraser. 2006. Local knowledge is required: A rhythmanalytical approach to the late
    Mesolithic and early Neolithic of the East Anglian fenland, UK. *Journal of Maritime
    Archaeology* 1: 119–139.

Thomas, Julian. 2004. *Archaeology and modernity*. London: Routledge.

Thompson, Paul, Tony Wailey, and Trevor Lummis. 1983. *Living the fishing*. London: Routledge and Kegan Paul.

Tilley, Christopher. 1996. *An ethnography of the Neolithic: Early prehistoric societies of southern Scandinavia*. Cambridge: Cambridge University Press.

———. 2002. Metaphor, materiality and interpretation. In *The material culture reader*, ed. Victor Buchli, 23–55. Oxford: Berg.

Vermoden, Daniel. 2006. Western European design boat building in Buton (Sulawesi, Indonesia): A "sequence of operations" approach. In *Connected by the sea: Proceedings of the Tenth International Symposium on Boat and Ship Archaeology, Roskilde 2003*, ed. Lucy Blue, Fred Hocker, and Anton Englert, 227–234. Oxford: Oxbow.

Vilkuna, Kustaa, and Eino Nikkilä. 1936. *The birth of an Aspen logboat (Haaparuuhen synty)*. Photography and editing: Eino Mäkinen. Production: Kansatieteellinen Filmi Oy. Finnish Film Archive: www.kansatieteellisetfilmit.fi/videot.htm/. Accessed 16 October 2010.

Villiers, Alan. 1969. *Sons of Sinbad: The great tradition of Arab seamanship in the Indian Ocean*. New York: Charles Scribner's Sons.

Westerdahl, Christer. 2005. Seal on land, elk at sea: Notes on and applications of the ritual landscape at the seaboard. *International Journal of Nautical Archaeology* 34 (1): 2–23.

White, Leslie A. 1949. *The science of culture: A study of man and civilization*. New York: Grove.

White, Luise, Stephan Miescher, and David William Cohen, eds. 2001. *African words, African voices: Critical practices in oral history*. Bloomington: Indiana University Press.

Whittle, Alasdair. 1997. *Sacred mound, holy rings: Silbury Hill and the West Kennet palisade enclosures*. Oxford: Oxbow.

Wilkins, Noël. 2001. *Squires, spalpeens and spats: Oysters and oystering in Galway Bay*. Galway: N. P. Wilkins.

Wilson, Neville Frederick Jarvis. 1909. *The native craft—a general description of the native craft visiting Bombay Harbour and particulars as to their survey, registry, measurement and lighting*. Bombay: Trustees of the Port of Bombay (Bombay Port Trust).

Wobst, Hans Martin. 1978. The archaeo-ethnology of hunter-gatherers, or The tyranny of the ethnographic record in archaeology. *American Antiquity* 43 (2): 303–309.

Wunungmurra, Johnny, and Helen Wunungmurra. 2003. *Djet and Nak Nak: A story from the saltwater country*. Canberra: Australian Studies Press for the Australian Institute of Aboriginal and Torres Strait Islander Studies.

Wylie, Alison. 1985. The reaction against analogy. *Advances in Archaeological Method and Theory* 8: 63–11.

PART V

BEYOND THE SITE

CHAPTER 39

MARITIME HISTORY AND MARITIME ARCHAEOLOGY

FRANCISCO C. DOMINGUES

INTRODUCTION: MARITIME HISTORY

ACCORDING to the editor-in-chief of the *Oxford Encyclopedia of Maritime History*,

> Maritime history embraces naval history; it is the overarching subject that deals
> with the full range of mankind's relationships to the seas and oceans of the world.
> It is a broad theme that cuts across academic boundaries and builds linkages
> between disciplines to form a humanistic understanding of the many dimensions
> involved. Maritime history involves in particular the histories of science,
> technology, cartography, industry, economics, trade, politics, international affairs,
> imperial growth and rivalry, institutional and organizational development,
> communications, migration, law, social affairs, leadership, ethics, art, and
> literature. The range is immense, and the possible vantage points and topics are
> many. (Hattendorf 2003)

Although this definition suitably encompasses all the various aspects of maritime history, it does not fully convey the discipline as one that aggregates multiple understandings and concentrates them into a single domain of knowledge. On the contrary, what John Hattendorf proposes is a comprehensive overview of a field of studies where several specialties intersect and converge into a single purpose: the study of the relationship of human societies with the sea. That is precisely what is reflected in the first sentence, when Hattendorf stresses that "maritime history embraces naval history." This means that a specific subject such as war at sea, a recurring issue in last century's historiography, may no longer be taken into account as a separate branch; rather, it is seen as part of a larger whole. Until the recent past, maritime history has been a subject that only dealt with the economic aspects of maritime life and was oriented toward the understanding of the history of harbors, maritime networks, or fishing activities, for instance, with the study of naval operations, naval artillery, or single battles being topics that belonged to the field of naval history.

Such subdivisions lead to obvious inconveniences, such as the difficulty of disentangling what properly belongs to what, since the analyses commonly tend to be restrained by an excessive compartmentalization imposed by theoretical models. This explains why transdisciplinary approaches are essential, because often the analyses cannot be contained by previously defined boundaries. The seventeenth-century struggle for trade supremacy on the Indian Ocean between newcomers the Netherlands and England and the previously installed Portuguese network is a good example of this concept. The Portuguese Crown directed the commercial affairs through a state monopoly, while the English and the Dutch were organized in commercial companies that operated as such both legally and financially. Nevertheless, these differences in trade organization became blurred in the field of action: the European navies were prepared both for war and for trade, and the ships served commercial and military needs, offensive or defensive ones. Through this example it becomes obvious that there cannot exist a distinction between a maritime history that only deals with subjects as harbors, trade routes, and freights, and a naval history focused on military activities, because the sites where naval action or trade takes place are exactly the same.

Maritime history began to be recognized as a disciplinary field about half a century ago. Its mentors gathered around the *Colloques Internationaux d'Histoire Maritime*, organized in France by Michel Mollat du Jordain in the mid-1950s. The proceedings of the second conference were published in 1959 under the title *Le Navire et l'Economie Maritime du Moyen Age au XVIIIe Siècle* (Mollat 1959). The subsequent gatherings were dedicated to the Mediterranean and North Seas (Mollat and Adam 1961), and it was only in the fourth conference (Paris, May 1959) that issues of methodological nature were addressed: M. F. Benôit presented a paper concerning certain "technical issues," focusing on the methods of underwater archaeology. Mollat and Adam's afterthoughts regarding the colloquiums pertained to the necessity to expand on the principles and methods of underwater archaeology in order to enhance the link between historians and underwater archaeologists (Mollat and Adam 1961: 511).

These statements had no effect, and the following conferences continued to emphasize the economic aspects of maritime history and society's relationship with the sea, such as the study of harbors and maritime commerce in general (i.e., the maritime economy), with less attention given to issues concerning war at sea, either as a standalone subject or in conjunction with the other maritime activities or technical aspects of navigation (i.e., nautical cartography). The same applied when it came to the study of ships, because they were taken into account only as protagonists of navigation, as was emphasized by the title of the first conference. The ship mattered as a transport vehicle and as a means of accomplishing commercial purposes, and this perspective overshadowed the technical aspects of shipbuilding, which in fact are critical to determining shipping efficiency.

The regularity of these meetings led to the creation of the Commission Internationale d'Histoire Maritime (CIHM), which took place on 28 August 1960, during the Congrès Internationale des Sciences Historiques, still under the aegis of Michel Mollat. During that convention, the outlines of future work were defined, mainly focusing on the reissue of Jal's *Glossaire Nautique*, an essential reference work for historians and archaeologists. However, this book would be reprinted with success only much later (NGN 1988). In 1960, the CIHM promoted another conference, the fifth of the series, this time in Lisbon, to coincide with the celebrations of the 500th anniversary of the death of Henry the Navigator. It was this occasion that led to the publication of the *Portugaliae Monumenta Cartographica*, an important reference work in the field of nautical history (Cortesão and Mota 1960). It was also during this conference that the CIHM was formally established, on 14 September, later registered in France on 7 May 1965.

The Lisbon meeting was dedicated to issues concerning navigation at the time of European expansion (fifteenth and sixteenth centuries), mainly focusing on its technical components: the diffusion of new methods regarding the art of navigation; the changes in shipbuilding in Europe and the Iberian influence; and the birth of modern cartography. Nevertheless, this was an unusual meeting if one takes into account the underlying subject, since the CIHM continued to promote studies about maritime economy throughout the 1960s. However, attention to nautical history was spurred on by Portuguese historiography, for which the subject of navigation techniques was prevalent.

Subsequently, the CIHM became mostly known by its English designation, International Commission for Maritime History (ICMH), and developed an affiliation with the International Committee of Historical Sciences (ICHS), which since 1926 has promoted the historical studies by organizing major conferences every five years. The CIHM/ICMH began organizing sessions in the ICHS conferences, but ceased to promote specialized meetings concerning maritime history. This was partly a result of the diminished influence of French historiography, implicit in the fact that Michel Mollat ceased to play a central role in the promotion of these issues, and partly a result of increased organizational efficiency on the part of Anglo-Saxon colleagues (Coutau-Bégarie 1994: 115).

In the 1990s, increased interest led to the creation of the International Maritime Economic History Association (IMEHA), which organizes its major conference every four years and is closely related to the esteemed *International Journal of Maritime History* (IJMH), published since 1989. The papers presented at the IMEHA conferences and the contents of the IJMH follow, if not reinforce, the original trend—the study of maritime economic history, with an emphasis on the period from the eighteenth to the twentieth centuries. More technical matters, namely those related to vessels, tended to be considered secondary, leading to a devaluation of the necessary communication streams between the technical aspects of ship-building and the efficiency of ships as a means of transporting goods (see Unger 2006 and Costa 1997 for exemplary studies on this trend).

These are the underlying grounds that led a group of Portuguese historians to organize the Reunião Internacional de História da Náutica (International Reunion of Nautical History, or IRNH), held in Coimbra in 1968 and organized by Luís de Albuquerque, a specialist in nautical history; Armando Cortesão, at the time one of the recognized experts in the history of cartography; and Avelino Teixeira da Mota. They all agreed that the CIHM/ICMH conferences did not focus enough on such matters, and thanks to Armando Cortesão and Luís de Albuquerque's prestige, the 1968 meeting was able to attract the best experts in the field (Domingues 2004a). The original conference was so successful that others followed, and at the third meeting, held in Greenwich in 1979, it was decided to create the International Committee for the History of Nautical Science.

Fifteen meetings of this organization have been held to date, and the papers presented are evidence that the history of the ship has acquired its own place. Essays on shipbuilding and naval architecture and reports related to underwater archaeology emphasize nautical science, which lies at the core of these meetings.

It was, finally, the publication of *The Oxford Encyclopedia of Maritime History* by John Hattendorf (2007) that represented the consolidation of this varied field, as the approaches adopted during the previous decades were now represented together in one significant volume. The making of this encyclopedia required the collaboration of 33 senior editors and approximately 400 contributors, and its articles cover all the issues that give consistency to maritime history as a unified subfield of the practice of history, without prejudice toward any of diverse components.

ARCHAEOLOGY AND UNDERWATER ARCHAEOLOGY

In the same encyclopedia of maritime history (Hattendorf 2007), archaeology is defined by Staniforth (2007: 124) as "the systematic study of past human life, behaviors, activities, and cultures using material remains (including sites, structures and artifacts) and the relationships among them." In a statement echoing the consolidation of the maritime history, Martín-Bueno (1996: 367) stresses that there is also only one archaeology. However, primarily "due to its principles, methodology and purposes," Martín-Bueno continues, the term "underwater archaeology" was introduced to define archaeological activity carried out under water. The same term was eventually extended to include inland water activities. As the field grew in complexity and scale, underwater archaeology became an inadequate term. What happened, for example, when the subject of research—say, a shipwreck—was located on a beach and not in its native underwater environment?

The archaeologists' theoretical reflections about the exercise of their activity has led, in recent years, to the clarification of thematic subfields according to the environment in which the archaeological practice is developed and the subject of research. Accordingly, Staniforth (2007: 124) put forth the following definitions:

a) *Underwater archaeology* refers to the environment in which archaeology is practiced. It is any site where evidence is found underwater or in a submerged environment;

b) *Marine archaeology* refers to the archaeological study of human material remains submerged in a marine (or salt-water) environment;

c) *Nautical archaeology* refers to the archaeological study of ships and shipbuilding. Like marine archaeology, it can include sites that, though not underwater, are related to ships and shipbuilding, including ship burials, shipwreck remains located on land, and shipbuilding yards.

These definitions are functional but not totally consensual, as expected. Although other authors propose assorted contents for each of these subfields, it is difficult to build a functional grid that only takes into account one criterion, as seems more logical, at least from the point of view of a nonarchaeologist: an *underwater archaeology* defined by the environment in which it is practiced, and a *nautical archaeology* defined by its object of study. One must ask whether a given excavation can or cannot be classified in more than one of those subfields and, above all, whether they are useful at all. The different realities with which archaeologists confront their relation with the maritime environment all somehow are tied to a more broad-spectrum approach, one that covers all forms of relationships between the archaeological work and the maritime environment. Perhaps, then, the term "maritime archaeology" is the most suitable, and one that becomes to archaeology what maritime history is to history.

In recent decades, maritime archaeology has experienced a boost, as seen by the multiplication of specialized publications, such as the *International Journal of Nautical Archaeology* and the recent *Journal of Maritime Archaeology*, which mainly contain relevant articles concerning theoretical and methodological approaches (e.g., Harpster 2009), and the organization of specialized conferences such as the International Symposium on Boat and Ship Archaeology in Europe and the Conference on Historical and Underwater Archaeology in the United States (the latter organized jointly by the Society for Historical Archaeology and the Advisory Council on Underwater Archaeology). Other forums have emerged, centered on specific events—such as the International Symposium on Archaeology of Medieval and Modern Ships of Iberian-Atlantic Tradition: Hull Remains, Manuscripts and Ethnographic Sources: A Comparative Approach (Alves 2001)—that promote encounters among historians and archaeologists in a more open circuit. This allows for the development of a real dialogue between historians and archaeologists and testifies to archaeologists' receptiveness to the contribution of other domains, especially ethnography.

The interconnection between the data of the technical documentation, the results of excavations, and the multidisciplinary perspectives is the way to move forward. Inherent to these aspects is finding a way to articulate the knowledge and the different practices developed by specialists of separate domains that, however, share similar intentions and objects of study.

Maritime historians study, among other things, oceanic voyages, trade routes, ports of call, cargoes shipped to and from different destinations, life at sea, nautical science, and everything else that can aid in the understanding of why and how people interconnect with the maritime environment. Archival documents elucidate all of those details, but archaeology, by revealing material data, is an indispensable complement that can be used to validate or contradict such archival information. Furthermore, archaeology can offer maritime historians information that cannot be obtained in any other way, by revealing the presence of unknown goods on board, such as artifacts, technical instruments and so on. While archival research can be the primary source of information for the location of some shipwrecks, other shipwrecks may, through their physical discovery, identify unknown routes or destinations. Dates can also be clarified by comparing documentary and archaeological data, and certainly an expert on seventeenth-century shipbuilding theory, for instance, will have a much better understanding of the architectural foundation of a certain type of vessel after the discovery of a well-preserved hull; archaeologists, on the other hand, have a lot to learn from existing theoretical information in advance of such shipwreck discoveries.

It is clear by now that both maritime archaeology and maritime history focus on the relationship between human societies and the maritime world in a broad sense, studying the ways people live, work, and travel near or by the sea, at times extending into rivers and lakes. Although the two fields approach their common subject matter with different theoretical and methodological perspectives, it is imperative that they combine approaches and results as, after all, their main focus is essentially the same. The Pepper Wreck is a good example of what can be expected from such an interdisciplinary collaboration.

THE PEPPER WRECK: A CASE STUDY

In September 1606, during the six-month return voyage from India, and after a three-month stop for repairs and victualing in the Azores, the Indiaman *Nossa Senhora dos Mártires* wrecked during a storm only a few miles from its final destination, the port of Lisbon. Its valuable cargo was mainly composed of porcelain, cotton bales, and pepper, which quickly spread along the river, some recovered by the king's officers, other land authorities, and the riverside population (Castro 2005a: 3–4). This was not an extraordinary event, although the ship arrived to Tagus's bar later than expected. It was not even surprising that the wrecking event occurred within sight of the city after a long voyage of thousands of nautical miles: it was not usual, but it had happened before.

The memory of this shipwreck was lost, as with so many others along the Portuguese shores over the centuries. The wreck was rediscovered in the early 1990s, and several archaeological campaigns were organized beginning in 1995. In 2005, Filipe Vieira de Castro published an extensive study of this shipwreck, complemented by several subsequent studies (Castro 2007, 2008a, 2008b; Castro and Fonseca 2006). Given the issues that often plague the preservation, archaeological study, and dissemination of information resulting from shipwrecks, the Pepper Wreck case study is exemplary. Between the original thorough study and the resulting publications, it is the best-researched shipwreck among all those pertaining to the loss of Iberian ships between fifteenth and seventeenth centuries—the same ships that opened up transoceanic routes to European navigators.

Certainly this is not the appropriate place to discuss the results of the studies undertaken so far, but the methodology used by Castro and his collaborators must be emphasized as an example of a multidisciplinary practice, capable of combining outputs of assorted origins, both archaeological and historical.

Maritime archaeology deals with lost materials that, through careful study, allow experts to explore questions such as the construction techniques used in building a ship's hull. However, during the historical period, the theoretical framing of those practical solutions to moving people and goods over the water can be found in the technical documentation developed by the authors of the first Portuguese treatises on naval architecture, such as Fernando Oliveira's *Livro da Fábrica das Naus* (Book on the Fabrication of Naus), dating to around 1580; João Baptista Lavanha's *Livro Primeiro de Architectura Naval* (First Book of Naval Architecture), written sometime around 1600; and Manuel Fernandes's *Livro de Traças de Carpintaria* (Book of Shipwright Drawings), written in 1616. The Pepper Wreck case study was essential to the comprehension of Fernando Oliveira's book, since it proved wrong the assumption that Oliveira addressed shipbuilding-related issues from a strictly theoretical point of view. On the contrary, he knew so well the practice of the shipyards that what he wrote was perfectly consistent with the practical work developed by the shipwrights (Montalvão 2009). Thus, the archaeology served to correct misconceptions regarding the historical record, but the archaeology could not have been as easily understood without the aid of historical documents and methods.

In addition, the archaeologists resorted to construction budgets, lists of materials, and several technical documents that proved to be essential in extending the knowledge of the sixteenth and seventeenth century's Ibero-Atlantic shipbuilding tradition (Domingues 2001, 2004b), thus completing the comparison and clarification process between the contents of the archaeological and historical records.

The excavation's results led to a further study of the ship's characteristics through computer modeling (Castro and Fonseca 2006). The results were far more than expected and allowed the visualization of a plausible reconstruction of the ship's hull and sails in a controlled environment. The current potential of computerized resources enabled the visual re-creation of an Iberian's ship "design" from the early seventeenth century that refers to the configuration of a specific and historically located ship, rather than the reconstitution of a ship-type hull (Castro 2008a).

However, one of the most remarkable aspects of this team's multidisciplinary work was that the archaeological data and the computer modeling results led to the construction of a 1/48-scale plank-on-frame ship model undertaken by Carlos Montalvão (2010), making ship modeling a partner in this multidisciplinary domain. This represents a step forward, since the accurate admeasure of shipwrecks' remains was tested by the construction of a model, which allowed scholars to retrace the ancient procedures that were used by the master shipwrights (Lavery and Stephens 1996). Thus, maritime history and maritime archaeology are also joined by computer science and naval architecture in this study, all to the benefit of our understanding of the past.

The result is a valid reconstruction of one of the mighty ships that systematically rutted the oceans, connecting continents and enabling the interaction between societies and cultures, whose mutual awareness was thereafter fully extended. Therefore, this is the final output of an integrated work between two different philosophies and work methods: maritime history and underwater archaeology, whose paths must be integrated in order to achieve maximum results.

ACKNOWLEDGMENTS

I would like to express my deep gratitude to Joana Marques, who translated this article under unacceptable conditions and gave me invaluable bibliographical information.

REFERENCES

Alves, Francisco, ed. 2001. *International Symposium on Archaeology of Medieval and Modern Ships of Iberian-Atlantic Tradition: Hull Remains, Manuscripts and Ethnographic Sources: A Comparative Approach*. Lisbon: Instituto Português de Arqueologia.

Castro, Filipe Vieira de. 2005a. *The Pepper Wreck: A Portuguese Indiaman at the mouth of the River Tagus*. College Station: Texas A&M University Press.

———. 2005b. Rigging the Pepper Wreck. Part 1: Masts and yards. *International Journal of Nautical Archaeology* 38 (1): 148–154.

———. 2007. Rising and narrowing: 16th-century geometric algorithms used to design the bottom of ships in Portugal. *International Journal of Nautical Archaeology* 36 (1): 148–154.

———. 2008a. In search of unique Iberian ship design concepts. *Historical Archaeology* 42 (2): 63–87.

———. 2008b. Rigging the Pepper Wreck. Part 2: Sails. *International Journal of Nautical Archaeology* 38 (1): 148–154.

Castro, Filipe Vieira de, and Nuno Fonseca. 2006. Sailing the Pepper Wreck: A proposed methodology for understanding an early 17th-century Portuguese Indiaman. *International Journal of Nautical Archaeology* 35 (1): 97–103.

Cortesão, Armando, and Avelino Teixeira da Mota. 1960. *Portugaliae monumenta cartographica.* 6 vols. Lisbon: Comissão para as Comemorações do V Centenário da Morte do infante D. Henrique.

Costa, Leonor. 1997. *Naus e galeões na Ribeira de Lisboa: A construção naval no século XVI para a Rota do Cabo.* Cascais, Portugal: Patrimonia.

Coutau-Bégarie, Hervé. 1994. France. In *Ubi summus? The state of naval and maritime history,* ed. John Hattendorf, 115–136. Newport, RI: Naval War College Press.

Dellino-Musgrave, Virginia E. 2006. *Maritime archaeology and social relations: British action in the Southern Hemisphere.* New York: Springer.

Domingues, Francisco Contente. 2001. Documents on Portuguese naval architecture (late 16th–early 17th centuries)—a general overview. In *Proceedings of the International Symposium on Archaeology of Medieval and Modern Ships of Iberian-Atlantic Tradition: Hull remains, manuscripts and ethnographic sources; A comparative approach,* ed. Francisco Alves, 229–232. Lisbon: Instituto Português de Arqueologia.

———. 2004a. International Commission for the History of Nautical Science and Hydrography. *E-Journal of Portuguese History* 2 (1). Online at www.brown.edu/ Departments/Portuguese_Brazilian_Studies/ejph/. Accessed 10 January 2010.

———. 2004b. *Os navios do mar oceano: Teoria e empiria na arquitectura naval portuguesa dos século XVI e XVII.* Lisbon: Centro de História da Universidade de Lisboa.

Gibbins, David, and Jonathan Adams. 2001. Shipwrecks and maritime archaeology. *World Archaeology* 32 (3): 279–291.

Harpster, Matthew. 2009. Keith Muckelroy: Methods, ideas and maritime archaeology. *Journal of Maritime Archaeology* 4 (1): 67–82.

Hattendorf, John, ed. 2007. *The Oxford encyclopedia of maritime history.* New York: Oxford University Press.

———. 2010. The uses of maritime history in and for the navy. *International Journal of Naval History* 2 (1). Rev. April 2003. Online at www.ijnhonline.org/volume2_ number1_Apr03/article_hattendorf_uses_apr03.htm/. Accessed 28 February 2010.

Lavery, Brian, and Simon Stephens. 1996. *Ship models: Their purpose and development from 1650 to the present.* Greenwich: National Maritime Museum.

Martin-Bueno, Manuel. 1996. Presente y futuro de la arqueología naval y subacuática de época moderna. In *I simposio de historia de las tecnicas: La construccion naval y la navegacion,* ed. Juan José Achútegui et al., 365–376. El Astillero, Spain: Universidad de Cantabria.

Mollat, Michel. 1959. *Le navire et l'économie maritime du Moyen Age au XVIIIe siècle principalement en Méditerranée: Travaux du deuxième colloque international d'histoire maritime.* Paris: SEVPEN.

———. 1962. Les sources de l'histoire maritime en Europe, du Moyen Age au XVIIIe siècle. In *Actes du Quatrième Colloque International d'Histoire Maritime tenu à Paris du 20 au 23 mai 1959,* ed. Michel Mollat, M. M. Paul Adam, Marc Benoist, and Marc Perrichet, 201–203. Paris: SEVPEN.

Mollat, Michel, and Paul Adam. 1961. Le navire et les navires: La Commission d'Histoire Maritime. *Annales: Économies, Sociétés, Civilisations* 16 (3): 511—513.

Montalvão, Carlos. 2009. *O livro da fábrica das naus de Fernando Oliveira: Princípios e procedimentos de construção naval*. MA thesis, University of Lisbon.

———. 2010. *Nau da carreira das Índias—uma história, um projecto*. Online at http://nau-da-india.blogspot.com/. Accessed 15 February 2010.

NGN. 1988. *Nouveau glossaire nautique d'Augustin Jal: Révision de l'édition publiée en 1848; Lettres A–B*. Paris: Centre National de la Recherche Scientifique.

Randles, William G. L. 1998. Luís de Albuquerque and the history of nautical science in Portugal. In *Luís de Albuquerque historiador e matemático, homenagem de amizade a um homem de ciência*, 135–142. Lisbon: Chaves Ferreira—Publicações.

Staniforth, Mark. 2007. Archaeology. In *The Oxford encyclopedia of maritime history*, vol. 1, ed. John Hattendorf, 124–129. New York: Oxford University Press.

Unger, Richard W. 2006. Shipping and western European economic growth in the late Renaissance: Potential connections. *International Journal of Maritime History* 18 (2): 85–104.

CHAPTER 40

ETHICS, UNDERWA∎∎∎∎ CULTURAL HERITAGE, AND INTERNATIONAL LAW

THIJS J. MAARLEVELD

INTRODUCTION: ETHICS AND THE PAST

ETHICS is perhaps one of the most intriguing approaches to human behavior. That is not to belittle archaeology, which of course is an exciting approach as well. But like any science and practice, archaeology is part of a larger whole. It builds on assumptions that define modern research, and it builds on the everyday reality that surrounds us. Ethics is part of both. Ethics is about good and evil. But more importantly, it is about reflection, reflection on what is good and bad, and reflection on what is right and wrong. Such reflection is often seen as defining what it means to be human (Kahn 2007; Renfrew and Morley 2009). In a historical perspective, that is a challenging, but also a problematic proposition. Biologists and archaeologists have a long history in trying to define and redefine the animal-human boundary and the origins of humankind (Corbey 2005). That discussion is highly relevant for humanity's self-definition and there is much to be said for an archaeology that traces how ethics and cognitive processes are reflected in materiality (Renfrew 2008: 107). That is not, however, what this chapter is about. However it started, ethical reflection is a feature, a condition even, of any contemporary human society or self-defined group. That is not to say that such reflection always leads to the same

ome, in every group, in each society, culture, or context. In fact, there is quite a
t of variability. The results of reflection have been codified in written and unwritten codes and rules. And although long traditions of law exist, these are not necessarily compatible. Or aren't they? Not at first sight, perhaps. Different solutions have
been codified for similar problems. New interests and new worldviews arise, and
such ongoing development further complicates the matter, but common ground
can be found. In fact, that is perhaps the core of ethical deliberation: to respect what
others view as important, to be explicit on one's own position, and to figure out what
is negotiable and what is not and thereby find common ground.

Since its beginnings maritime archaeology has given rise to quite a few issues.
It continues to do so. Meanwhile, the meaning of heritage for society has been under
transformation. The role of the archaeologist, the scientist, and the heritage professional changes accordingly. Likewise, the ethical discussion has evolved. That discussion is what this chapter is about. Rather than dealing with the archaeology of
ethics, it deals with ethics in relation to present-day archaeology and thus with
archaeology's role in present-day society. Maritime archaeology is the focus. That is
quite appropriate, as maritime archaeology is the focus of this book. But it is appropriate for another reason as well. In the context of maritime archaeology issues
relating to "ownership" and "identification", "rights" and "responsibilities" seem to
be enlarged in a way that makes them all the more apparent and all the more contentious, almost to the point of caricature. As such, maritime archaeology is a part
of the "heritage field" that is extremely well suited for the fine-tuning of ethical
debate in archaeology. The transnational nature and significance of maritime sites
and the transnational nature of maritime archaeology as a practice contribute to
this. So does the adventurous popular image of recreational and professional diving
and its relationship with excitement and finding things. Resulting practices are not
always consistent. Basic principles are a guide, and codes of practice help to resolve
where one stands. That is what this chapter will address. By extension, it will also
discuss the international development of a body of law specifically concerning
underwater cultural heritage.

ETHICS: A PROFESSION AND PARALLEL TRADITIONS

Ethics aspires to have universal validity as well as to resolve situational dilemmas.
Both aspects are relevant for archaeology. And although they are intricately related,
it is nevertheless useful to distinguish between the two. To do so is, for instance,
highly relevant to the interpretation of the simple phrase "But that is unethical!"
What do people mean when they use it? They give a judgment, a negative judgment,
and they assert that the judgment has universal value. But does it? Sometimes it

does. But interestingly, the phrase is used far more frequently to denote that there are issues that are being resolved in a way that does not comply with the speaker's particular worldview or does not serve his or her interests. That is not the same thing as universal validity. In fact, it is not very helpful either, as it risks blocking dialogue as well as missing the mark. As a reaction, both opponents and supporters retreat into their own little world, harden in their own preconceptions, or ridicule any critical observation. To avoid this is not easy, especially not if one is convinced of always having done the right thing and equally convinced that others should act according to the exact same principles and rules. Ethics, however, is not about asserting one's own viewpoint or stating "the way things have always been done." On the other hand, being clear and transparent about what it means to be a professional, what it means to be an archaeologist, is certainly an important step. It is important in defining the ethics of the profession and in defining the way in which someone who considers oneself as part of that professional group engages in a wider ethical and political debate.

Personal, professional, and public ethics are intricately related. In discussing the ethics of archaeology it is therefore hard to ignore the importance of personal ethics or public ethical traditions. In the present context, however, it is natural to concentrate on the ethics of the profession as such. Is it the ethics of the profession, then, that define whether or not one can rightly consider oneself to be an archaeologist, a scientist, an archaeological practitioner, a heritage professional? I think it is. Others would argue that being an archaeologist comes with the completion of an archaeological education. It is certainly true that a level of knowledge, a level of skills, and the ability to think analytically are very helpful, even essential. But just as in medicine or health care, these skills are of no avail if they are used contrary to the central principles of the profession. A professional education in itself is not enough. One could even argue that professional ethics are more important than a professional education. I would tend to do so, even though I make it my business to educate archaeologists. Regardless, just like in medicine, subscribing to the central principles of the profession is at least as important as holding a degree.

Comparing archaeology and heritage management with medicine and health care seems a bit odd at first sight. But there is more to it than one would suppose. Just like medicine, archaeology has a public function. Both are at least partly publicly funded. Both, also, are subject to some level of public control. Moreover, just like medicine, archaeology is moving into new realms, necessitating fresh or additional debate on newly arising dilemmas. Do solutions of the past still fit the altered scope? They may, but that is not a foregone conclusion. DNA-based genetic research, for instance, is a field into which medicine and archaeology have jointly moved. The ethics of archaeological and medical record-keeping need to be addressed accordingly: the trodden paths of the one profession are not necessarily good enough for the other.

With maritime archaeology, archaeology has literally moved into a new physical realm. The profession is still in the process of accommodating itself to that fact. That seems to be odd after some 50 years of solid experience. George Bass, the eminent author of the introduction to this volume, is by far the most influential propagator of the discipline worldwide. From the very start he has persistently stressed that—practical issues aside—archaeology underwater is in no way different from archaeology on land (Bass 1966, 1975, 2003). It is a tenet—a truism, even—that any archaeologist should and can subscribe to. However, it does not account for the fact that archaeology as such is not as uniform as one would expect it to be. In fact, radically different traditions exist, referring partly to different periods of the past, but also to different regions in the world. As a result, very different ways of thinking defined how to approach heritage; and, more fundamentally, very different ways of thinking defined what heritage actually is or what in practice should be considered as such. An item that is attributed "heritage value" in Australia may not be considered heritage at all in China, the United States, or Greece. Also, very different ways of thinking defined how to approach heritage in the underwater world, even in those subscribing to the idea that it should be approached in the same way as heritage on land. This can only have been confusing for outsiders and those thinking in terms of maritime affairs other than archaeology. Many of the issues that have arisen since the beginnings of maritime archaeology can be traced back to such confusion. It is therefore useful to first look into some general trends in the development of maritime archaeology, before coming back to the professional ethics.

National and International Perspectives

It is obvious that a historical discipline like archaeology is interested in its own history. Many archaeological discourses include a historical review. How data came to be collected and how insights developed, is after all highly relevant for analysis and interpretation. And then there are histories of the discipline as such. Some aim to show to a wider public what archaeology achieved. But histories engaging in self-reflection have also appeared at regular intervals (Daniel 1967; Schnapp 1993; Trigger 1989). The history of maritime archaeology is likewise represented in both genres (Bass 2005; Firth 2002; Flatman 2007; Gianfrotta and Pomey 1981; Silverberg 1963; Throckmorton 1987). More so perhaps than in the past, such histories include reflection on the role of archaeology in contemporary society. That role is far more encompassing than one would expect if one assumes that science, including archaeology, is a "value-free" endeavor. Understandably, the developing role of archaeology attracted the interest of historians of science, historians of culture, and sociopolitical scientists (Gathercole and Lowenthal 1990; Lowenthal 1985; Murray and Evans 2008; Wright 1985).

One of the resulting insights is very relevant here. It is the understanding of the strong relationship between the development of archaeology, the emergence of the nation-state, and the assertion of national politics (Briggs 2005; Kohl and Fawcett 1995) or, alternatively, of colonial rule (Díaz-Andreu 2007; Ray 2008). This comes as no surprise for those who are familiar with the use and abuse of history, ethnography, and archaeology in, for instance, Nazi Germany (Arnold 1990; Kater 1974; Pieper, Maarleveld, and Jull 1992; Müller-Wille 1996), but the tendency is equally strong in ideological opponents of that infamous regime and equally strong in other parts of the world (Kohl, Kozelsky, and Ben-Yehuda 2007; Meskell 1998; van der Waals 1969). It influences research, it influences heritage interpretation, and it influences the attribution of significance in heritage management.

The fact that national biases are presently subject to close scrutiny is in itself of course an expression of a countercurrent. There has been earlier countermotion as well. The "diffusionism" of V. Gordon Childe can be interpreted as an internationalist countercurrent (Rowlands 1994), and so can the development of "World Prehistory" (Clark 1961; Evans 1995). Nevertheless, it is quite clear that the way in which archaeologists and others engage with heritage is generally organized or at least qualified by the state. This even applies to archaeology "abroad," in which support and promotion are closely related to foreign policy (Davis 2008; Howell 2006; Marchand 1996). The level of control varies, in covariance with the way archaeology and heritage management are organized and funded. But some level of control exists everywhere. This control may be in the form of centrally or regionally funded archaeological units, in the form of a central system of providing or withholding of permits, or in the form of a system of guidance and "quality control" on archaeological services that are outsourced or commissioned in the context of spatial planning (Willems and van den Dries 2007). The role of heritage is definitely more prominent in some contexts or states than in others, and in some heritage is more contested than in others, which leads to more political debate. But in any case, public control feeds back into a close relationship between heritage management, archaeology, and national agendas.

For maritime archaeology, this "national" bias has been influential in several ways (Cederlund 1997, 2002). In fact, it continues to be so. For one thing, it has favored the archaeology of periods that are considered particularly important for national identity in the country involved (e.g., Alves Martins 1998; Brøgger and Shetelig 1950; Crumlin-Pedersen 2002; Hoffman 2003; Ucelli 1940). More specific is the emphasis on remains that relate to well-documented episodes in national history. The notorious loss of the great ship *Vasa* on its first sailing trial in 1628 is the *cause célèbre*. Despite its obvious irony, it refers to a period of greatness in Swedish national history, and in a spirit of reassertion of that greatness, the relocation of *Vasa*'s wreck led to a grand national endeavor (Cederlund 2006). Other examples are more ironic still. Well-documented episodes of national history have triggered all sorts of adventures in maritime archaeological exploration. Reference to iconic historical episodes helps to mobilize support. This can ease planning and funding, for well-considered and dilettante actions alike. Although this continues to be case, it was particularly influential in the early days of development of maritime archaeology (Allen 1978; Henderson 1986: 129; Huiskes and de Weerdt 1999; Kiesling 1994;

Lyon 1982; MacInnis 1985; Martin 1975; Marx 1977; McKee 1982; Pickford 1994; Sténuit 1972; Wignall 1982). Sometimes it led to significant results; often it did not.

Ironically, national bias in a competitive international world has frequently inspired officialdom to discreetly cooperate or conspire with specific operators (Maarleveld 2006: 164; Ronquillo 1992; van Duivenvoorde 2006). And it blinded the wider public to negative effects. In other examples, the overall balance has been positive. More often than not, however, exploration that is inspired by iconic stories leads to the destruction of ranges of archaeological sites that have no relationship to the historical episode in question. Preoccupied as explorers are with the identification of what they are specifically looking for, they are frustrated as soon as discovery relates to another period or another kind of vessel—so much so in fact that they fail to report on their many "non"-discoveries in any other than negative terms. This is unfortunate in many ways. It frustrates the assessment of site density and quality in otherwise ill-explored areas. It frustrates the cumulative nature of information gathering. The sites are interfered with and damaged. Some of the sites may in fact be far more significant than the one the explorer is preoccupied with. The urge for identification means that such expeditions focus completely on the collection of significant artifacts. More often than not, this has led to intrusive research strategies without proper or timely consideration of site and context. More often than not, collections have been fully dispersed with at best a short description in an auction catalog (e.g., Christie's 1986, 2004). Sometimes it is backed up by an adventurous coffee-table book (Ball 1995; Hatcher 1987). Occasional donations of artifacts to officials and ill-informed or greedy museums eases procedures for the operators (Alves 2004; Toebosch 2003). Common as the pattern may be, it obviously has ethical ramifications for all those involved.

ARCHAEOLOGIES CONVERGING

By now it is quite clear that archaeology, the cultural landscape, and the distribution of heritage do not stop short at the waterline, or at present-day national borders for that matter (see part III of this volume). Nevertheless, archaeologists, governments, and the wider public are still accommodating themselves to this fact. One reason is that organizationally, if not also conceptually, people are used to defining heritage according to national states and their subdivisions. This translates into rights and responsibilities. In quite a few cases—those instances that have strongly influenced the ethical debate of the last few decades—a specific role is set aside for local communities and for cultural groups that are more indigenous than others (Cooper 2006; Lackey 2006; Zimmermann, Vitelli, and Hollowell-Zimmer 2003: part III). Like any debate on heritage, such debate has an important sociopolitical dimension. It also shows how the ethics of the profession develop in dialogue with the surrounding world. Assertion of such rights, responsibilities, and specific roles is less clear, however, when water and maritime zones are concerned. Unlike towns or residential areas, they have no locally embedded political structure. As a consequence, the level of "identification" and conceptual "ownership" is also far more muddled. Local communities are relevant only if sites are not "too far out"; and what about other stakeholder groups? Well, they certainly exist, but they may not have been identified, and they may not have identified themselves. More so even than with heritage on land, such groups are spread far and wide, possibly centering at the other end of the globe (Maarleveld 2009b).

In looking back at the development of maritime archaeology as a discipline, it is attractive to view it as the initiative of a range of researchers with a vision (Hocker 2003). Such researchers certainly had a role, but hardly a decisive one. It had been possible to explore the sea bottom long before archaeologists embraced SCUBA diving. Objectively, the importance of the underwater area for science had been recognized ever since geologist Charles Lyell (1832: 322) wrote the prophetic words "For it is probable that a greater number of monuments of the skill and industry of man will, in the course of ages, be collected together in the bed of the ocean than will be seen at one time on the surface of the continents." Lyell (1830: 32) even went as far as to ponder that "there can be little doubt, although the reader may, perhaps, smile at the bare suggestion of such an idea, that an amphibious being, who should possess our faculties, would still more easily arrive at sound theoretical opinions." Lyell thus stressed the great potential of underwater observation as a means of understanding the history of the Earth. So from an objective scientific point of view there had been every reason—and a strong exhortation, even—to use the opportunities that diving technology offered, both to understand the development of the Earth and for archaeology. But then, archaeology has hardly ever been guided by objective reasoning alone. Even in inland waters, the use of diving equipment for research remained extremely exceptional. In the 1850s and the beginning of the twentieth century, Adolf von Morlot, Odo Blundell, and Edward Herbert Thompson were visionary researchers or collectors using diving equipment in the exploration of submerged prehistoric lakeside settlements in the Alpine region, artificial prehistoric islands in Scottish lochs, or pre-Columbian offering-sites in sinkholes in Mesoamerica (Dixon 2004; Martos López 2008; Speck 1981). Their efforts were so exceptional that they more or less prove the rule that researchers generally put their effort where others lead them, nationally or otherwise. It was only when the underwater world was opened up for a wider audience that archaeologists really followed suit.

This happened just over 50 years ago, and it happened simultaneously in many places. The world was recovering from the Second World War. The hardest-hit areas were starting to experience an economic boom. Tourism developed and started to include discovery of the underwater world, using the snorkels and SCUBA equipment that had been developed for military purposes during the war (Diolé 1952; Falcon-Barker 1960; Frost 1963; Throckmorton 1987). Interest in underwater archaeology burgeoned as much through the efforts of traveling journalists with a keen eye for exploration and iconic fiction writers such as Arthur C. Clarke, Robert Silverberg, and later Clive Cussler as those of national tourist boards. One could even argue that worldwide their influence on the popular image of maritime archaeology has been greater than that of any visionary archaeologist. Is that of any consequence for the ethics of archaeology? Not really, but it has a bearing on the way the public and governments engaged with ensuing issues. It has influenced the way archaeology and heritage management is organized. It therefore has a bearing on the conditions under which archaeological ethics are relevant and develop.

In this formative period for maritime archaeology we see that some government-sponsored archaeology programs started to include underwater research (Benoît 1961; Goggin 1960; Lamboglia 1952; Olsen and Crumlin-Pedersen 1958; Ruoff 1981). This happened in different ways in different areas. Developments in northern Europe, for instance, have been very different from those in the countries surrounding the Mediterranean. This is not surprising. After all, Mediterranean or "classical" archaeology had followed a completely different trajectory of development than the national archaeologies in northern Europe. Developments in the Americas were different still, with a similar split between approaches that closely resemble "classical" archaeology and "archaeology as anthropology." The management of cultural resources of specific parks, reserves, or landscapes has been a very defining factor (Gould 1983; Lenihan 2002). These different approaches, which also affected the archaeologies of Asia, Africa, and Australia, translated into different approaches to the underwater cultural heritage. On top of that, there is the search for documented wrecks and documented episodes in (national) history. That is a radically different tradition again. More than the other approaches in which it is integrated or with which it is at odds, it builds on traditions of maritime history and maritime salvage.

Despite intensive exchange of personnel, techniques, and ideas and despite considerable overlap and integration, I think it is realistic to distinguish between four different traditions in which maritime archaeology and the management of underwater sites took root: the Mediterranean or "classical" tradition, the northern European or "prehistoric" tradition, the "cultural resource management" tradition, and, finally, the tradition of maritime historical exploration that informed major projects such as those relating to the wrecks of *Vasa*, *Mary Rose*, *H. L. Hunley*, or *La Belle*. Iconic as such projects may be, they are nevertheless exceptional in more than one way. More often than not they originate in initiatives not normally in the sphere of government-sponsored archaeology. Also, they tend to be anomalies in regular policies, so I will say more on this and the other traditions below.

The different traditions have their own ways of traditional thinking. They have their own views on what is important or not. They have their own views on the rights and obligations of archaeologists. They have their own views on such issues as the role of avocationals in archaeology (Maarleveld 1993, 2008). And all that has a bearing on the way in which ethical dilemmas emerge and on the way in which they are addressed. At the same time, it is very clear that the four traditions are converging. Regional and worldwide discussions on the role of archaeology in society and on standards and guidelines contribute to that convergence. I think this is necessary too. Despite national bias, interests in heritage exceed national borders. This is undeniably so for heritage in international maritime zones and for heritage of maritime exchange. Without convergence one cannot hope to find common ground as far as professional ethics are concerned.

DIFFERENCES AND MARITIME LAW

Of the four traditions in which maritime archaeology is rooted, the last one is perhaps the most problematic. In each of the other three, one can relatively easily uphold the tenet that—practical issues aside—archaeology under water is in no way different from archaeology on land. There may be quite a bit of difference between "classical" Mediterranean archaeology, northern European "prehistoric" archaeology, and archaeology based in the cultural resource management tradition, but in each case the maritime manifestation is a logical extension of what happens on land. Practitioners are aware of that and firmly subscribe to the values and ethics of their parent tradition, which is the tradition in which they were trained. For the last of the four, which I call the maritime historical tradition of underwater exploration, this is far less obvious.

More so than in the other traditions, initiators and participants of projects in the maritime historical tradition have come to their interest from widely different backgrounds. And this continues to be so, for minor local initiatives and megaprojects alike. Their dedication and interest is generally very sincere. It may have arisen from a wish to highlight a dramatic story in a museum. It may have arisen from the wish to put one's own town on the map by finding signs of someone who lived there or something produced there that ended up at the other end of the world (Sørensen 2009; Spruit and Manders 2007). It may be inspired by a family history, or it may be inspired by a "scientific problem," a question that arises from written sources for which one wants to find the answer. These are all completely legitimate interests that command loads of appeal. The iconic story is part of this. Everyone, after all, knows about the *Titanic*. Everyone knows about Cleopatra. Everyone knows about the hardship of exploration. And let us not forget the appealing image of the dedicated researcher who wants to adventurously explore a simple question that everyone can understand. Here it coincides best with the popular image and is a role model for many (Flatman 2007; Russell 2002).

Nevertheless, the tradition in all its varieties sits slightly awkwardly in the archaeological spectrum. That is not because it includes dilettante as well as highly accomplished initiatives; that is true in the other traditions as well. Perhaps it is because exploration in this tradition is more markedly and consistently targeted toward a single event and has its starting point in archival research. Initiatives that originate in archival research understandably adopt a mind-set that is related to that type of activity: browsing. It is a mind-set that is shared by many and that has been boosted by the Internet. But it cannot be applied to archaeology. In archival research one browses stacks and stacks of documents without ever bothering about information one is not looking for. One can also get distracted by a sudden surprise. Next time one can look again. Whether the research is well considered or not, it does not affect the archive as such. No need to bother. Someone else can do a better job. It is totally different in archaeology, where "reading" a deposit is possible only once. Many historians and laypeople turned "archaeologist" are fully aware of this and its implications for professional ethics, but others are not. And the same is understandably true for many historians, art historians, ceramics specialists, and museum people who enthusiastically support initiatives that may shed light on issues they are interested in. As a result, underwater exploration in this tradition includes many activities that are different from archaeology on land.

But there are more differences still. As indicated above, the Mediterranean, northern European, or cultural resource management traditions emerged in extension of national approaches. That is not so with maritime historical exploration. In national approaches, it is through government and legislation that archaeology's public role is ascertained. But does such legislation apply at sea at all? Well, the situation is different, to say the least. Traditionally, authority, responsibility, and jurisdiction have not strictly been divided among autonomous states, such as on land. Instead, there exists a body of customary law which is codified in three ways:

- in conventions,
- in private international law governing the relationships between ship operators, and
- in domestic regulations that govern maritime activities.

Conventions such as the comprehensive Law of the Sea Convention of 1982 bind states that are party to them. Private international law and domestic regulations bind individuals, and the ensuing obligations are generally referred to as maritime law. Both the Law of the Sea and maritime law (also called admiralty law) are strongly dominated by the doctrine of the "freedom of the high seas." The concept was given a juridical basis in the early seventeenth century by Hugo Grotius and is still paramount (de Groot 1609). Obviously, such "freedom" does not relieve professionals from their obligations to behave professionally, whether they are mariners, members of the medical profession, or archaeologists. Accordingly, archaeology underwater is in no way different from archaeology on land. But friction between present-day environmental policies, including heritage, and the freedom of the high seas is quite obvious. Consequently, more and more voices are raised in favor of the environment (Soons 2009; Woudenberg and Maarleveld 2002). The matter is complicated, however, by the fact that if governments take responsibilities beyond their own territories, other governments get very upset, even if it is for the most honorable environmental reasons. That is understandable as well. One-sided action is always seen as an assertion of power, and overstepping one's place upsets the balance of power and can thus even lead to war. The concept of the freedom of the high seas was a brilliant solution for this in its time. It was in fact launched in the context of Grotius's larger work on the Law of War and Peace (de Groot 1625).

The Law of the Sea Convention of 1982 reconfirms the principle of the freedom of the high seas while at the same time extending the agreed rights and responsibilities of coastal states for specific purposes. It thus establishes a range of maritime zones (Figure 40.1):

- the Territorial Sea,
- the Contiguous Zone,
- the Continental Shelf,
- the Exclusive Economic Zone (EEZ), and
- the Area.

The width of the Territorial Sea is agreed at 12 nautical miles from the baseline, and in that zone the full jurisdiction of the coastal state applies. The Contiguous Zone exists only if the coastal state has declared itself to have one. Its width is again 12 nautical miles, and it is contiguous to the Territorial Sea in the seaward direction. It thus extends to 24 miles from the baseline. In a way it is a fictional zone. It only applies to the situation in which the authorities reasonably suspect a vessel fleeing from or coming to their territory to be engaged in smuggling. In that case they are allowed to stop the vessel and to assume that the seizure took place within their territory and jurisdiction. Surprisingly (although this can easily be explained in the context of the early 1980s; Maarleveld 2007), the Contiguous Zone also applies to archaeological issues. Some coastal states, such as Denmark, have accordingly declared a heritage protection zone of 24 nautical miles. The Continental Shelf is the

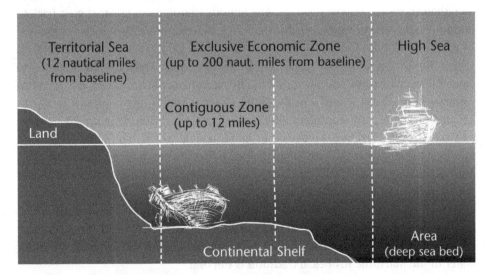

Figure 40.1 Maritime zones according to the Law of the Sea Convention of 1982.
Reproduced with the kind permission of UNESCO.

zone from the territorial waters to the drop-off of the continental shelf, or, in semi-enclosed seas, to the limits of the sector of it that the coastal state agreed with its neighbors. It applies solely to the exploration and exploitation of mineral resources such as oil and gas. The Exclusive Economic Zone (EEZ) gives the coastal state jurisdiction over other economic activities, over the resolution of environmental and planning issues, and over scientific research. Logically, archaeology falls in with the latter two aspects, but the specific rulings of the Contiguous Zone have so far hindered the drawing of that logical conclusion. The EEZ overlaps with other zones and extends to a maximum of 200 nautical miles from the baseline. Finally, there is the Area, the zone beyond all other zones and thus beyond any state jurisdiction. But even there, the "freedom" is no longer as absolute as before. For some aspects, such as the exploration of its deep seabed, it is managed on behalf of all United Nations member states by the International Seabed Authority (ISA) from its base in Jamaica.

Two Lines of Thinking, Two Kinds of Rules

The predominance of long-standing institutions of maritime law has provoked a situation where two lines of thinking compete, especially in relation to wrecks. A wreck, after all, is the result of a mishap. Such accidents continue to happen. An extensive body of maritime law regulates assistance in peril, insurance, fair play among afflicted parties, and compensation for beachcombers and salvors who take possession or are asked to do so. These rules have a long tradition—much longer, in fact, than those addressing heritage. The famous Rhodian sea law that goes back to antiquity is an early example (Ashburner 1909). Related thinking is deeply engrained in maritime minds. Individual loss and individual gain are central to the way in which these rules address fortuitous or deliberate finds. They are not designed to cater for heritage, nor should they be. They are meant for more or less contemporary jetsam, flotsam, and wrecks. Quite understandably, the approach is object-oriented and rife with confidentiality and private allocation. It is meant to serve private interest. Heritage, on the other hand, is qualified by its public dimension and by concepts such as "accessibility" and "public ownership." For archaeological heritage, "context" and "site" are central. For salvage issues they are not. The two approaches imply two lines of thinking that are backed up by two sets of written and unwritten codes and rules (Table 40.1). The two are not necessarily compatible, certainly not at first sight. Confusion and misunderstanding are the result. It is a type of confusion that is completely alien to archaeology on land. But archaeology under water in the maritime historical tradition is full of it.

The principle that "heritage" is a public matter is quite central in the developing ethics of the archaeological profession. Stealth is not really acceptable, partly

Table 40.1 Organizational concepts of archaeology and salvage. The left column lists some central concepts that define the role of heritage in society. These concepts are therefore crucial to the ethics of the archaeological and heritage profession, and they are at the basis of heritage legislation. In the right column the concepts are juxtaposed with those aspects of thinking that dominate the organization of salvage, in line with international private law. Although highly appropriate in that context, such aspects of thinking are not to be stretched to apply to situations in which one deals with "heritage" or cites "heritage" as a reason for interference. When that happens, there occur serious obstacles to clear thinking and the deployment of sound professional ethics.

Heritage	Jetsam, Flotsam, Wreck
Public interest	Private interest
Accessibility	Confidentiality
Public ownership	Private allocation
Site and context	Object

because archaeology serves the public interest, but also because of controllability of "experiments" that cannot be repeated. "Reading" a deposit, after all, is possible only once. In maritime salvage operations, public interests are easily sidestepped for the sake of confidentiality. Another issue is compensation. In maritime salvage, compensation by appropriation in kind is a central issue. In heritage professions, one is not to appropriate the material one is working with. A third reason for confusion is original ownership.

Ownership seems to be a simple issue, but it is not. Some states consider long lost shipwrecks "abandoned" and consequently assume that rights are forfeited and original ownership is lost. Others recognize continuing ownership after a wrecking event, even long after it happened. However, in all likelihood ship, fittings, cargo, and personal belongings (not to speak of contraband) have originally been in several different hands. Recognizing original ownership, therefore, has the consequence that there may be many "heirs" and claimants, unless, of course, a single insurance company has made losses good to everyone and stepped in their place. But even so, an insurance company can hardly claim ownership of sedimentary fill, later contaminants, and intrusively lost objects. In practice original ownership rights are also hard to assert, other than by transferring them "for what they are worth."

Interestingly, in confusing situations it is mostly states that assert their rights by such action. Sometimes these are ownership rights; sometimes they are so-called sovereign rights, which are even more problematic. Such rights are based in the concept of sovereign immunity. This is the concept that makes an embassy immune to the regulations of the host country, and it also applies to warships in operation. On a friendly visit to a foreign port, such a ship will, for instance, be immune from searches by inquisitive customs officials. Some states claim that sovereign immunity extends to long-sunken vessels and make a big issue of it. Others think that the concept applies for reasons connected to intelligence that can influence contemporary national security and contest that it should be applied when such is no longer at issue. They certainly contest that the concept can retrospectively be applied to periods prior to the general acceptance of its application to sunken ships in international law. This happened only during World War I (Maarleveld 2009a).

The transfer of rights in order to assert them is not a problem for heritage issues if the receiver is another state. The 1972 agreement between the Netherlands and Australia concerning Old Dutch shipwrecks (in Australian waters) is an example (Jeffery 2006; Maarleveld 2006). France asserted its rights on *La Belle*, which sank in 1686. When it became apparent that its remains were subject to research, an agreement was struck with the state of Texas (Le Gurun 2006; see Pevny in this volume). When such assertive agreements are struck with private individuals or companies instead of with other states, the friction between the two lines of thinking becomes very visible indeed. The irony is that "research" and "heritage" value are often cited as a central consideration for such contracts in relation to historic ships. We may assume that it is honestly what the authors have in mind. In practice, it works out the other way. Ownership rights and private interest may have been the basis for archaeological collecting in the nineteenth century. In view of the ensuing problems, they have not been the basis on which heritage protection or the approach to site, context, survey, and excavation have since developed in the public interest (Tubb 1995). In short, the maritime historical tradition in archaeology includes many projects that started naively and developed into something that was better considered. Also, it includes many projects that were started very similarly but in which the economics of compensation through retrieved material started to dominate proceedings. Reversing is then difficult or even impossible.

THE SLIDING SCALE AND
SOME IMPLICATIONS

At the far end of the sliding scale we find actions that are undertaken in order to feed the antiquities market. Some operations specifically address "treasure" and say so. A closer look at the economics often reveals that "treasure hunt" is no more than a decoy to attract money from investors, who will not see a return. A good example is the Norwegian diver who claimed to have found the world's richest treasure-ship, a seventeenth-century Spanish galleon, in Ecuadorian waters. An investor supporting him in organizing shares is reported to have said, "It is like walking right into a fairy-tale" (*Daily News* 1997). The news made his shares attractively marketable. Within days, however, someone had calculated that no seventeenth-century ship could ever have carried the weight of the bullion that was claimed as found. More devastating for the fairy tale was the comment of Ecuadorian authorities: the Norwegians had never been there in the first place, let alone done a survey. But this is not where the scoop ended. The wreck would have originated from the Spanish ship *Jesús María de la Limpia Concepción de Nuestra Señora, La Capitana de los Mares del Sur,* which continues to be in the treasure charts. Other companies regularly put its alleged contents up for sale (Salazar 2007).

One could argue that if the "hunt" does not affect archaeological deposits, it should not concern us here. After all, whatever their views on ethics, it is not specifically the business of archaeologists to control capital ventures or the stock market. On the other hand, such operations have created an image of what diving is about that certainly affects public opinion. If the archaeological profession has a public function and responsibility, it cannot ignore the impact of that image. Moreover, "decoy" operations may in fact impact archaeological sites. Most likely these sites have no relationship with the "loss" that is targeted on the basis of historical records, but that will not inspire greater care. Sites are simply sacrificed in a "laundering" process of accounting for exertions. Some activity is, after all, the least investors can expect, even where secrecy rules.

Other operators proclaim that their intentions are not commercial at all. In the tradition of maritime law they strongly assert that "compensation in kind" is perfectly acceptable and legally defendable. They use it as an argument to attract official supporters, sponsors, and investors alike. They insist, however, that it is not the objects but the exciting past, discovery, and research that inspire them. Business plans, promotion, and news items teem with the same language used by other actors in the "heritage industry." They may (try to) hire archaeology students or trained "archaeologists" on their teams. Besides coffee-table books, in which they stress that their activities are purely scientific and that they build on a team of renowned researchers including themselves (Goddio 2002; Mathewson 1986; Stemm and Kingsley 2010), they produce exhibits and documentaries as well as occasional reports and scholarly articles (Cowan, Cowan, and Marsden 1975; Flecker 2003). Dedication and interest can be as sincere as in the instances of the maritime historical tradition cited above, but it sits even more awkwardly. Typically, these operators and their protagonists contrast their dedicated work to the pernicious operations of "treasure hunters" who destroy everything. Frequently, they present themselves as true saviors of heritage that would otherwise have been looted or destroyed (Pope 2007).

What such operators try to do is to assert that they are good and others are bad. That is good for business, I suppose, although it is weak reasoning. They assert that they are in it for the archaeology, for the promotion of archaeological knowledge, and the protection of archaeological objects, if not of archaeological sites. They also try to elude any arguments that what they are doing would not be "archaeology," after all, but salvage or treasure hunting. Such arguments have been brought forward since the early days. They have been used either way: they have been used to dismiss questionable operations (Goggin 1960), and they have been used to plead for the integration of more research in operations following the logic and legislation of salvage operations (Gawronski and Kist 1984; Hildred 2001).

Nevertheless, neither approach has been very helpful. The first reduces the ethical debate to a difference in interest between archaeologists and treasure hunters.

The second explores the possibility of marrying the two. Both start on the wrong footing. After all, it is not to serve the interest of archaeologists (or treasure hunters, for that matter) that concern about heritage has come about. Rather, it is the other way round: the profession has emerged to deal with the interests of society, nationally and internationally. Professional ethics have developed accordingly. Its principles are very simple. In heritage professions, one is not to appropriate the material one is working with. Consequently a professional cannot build up a private collection. Compensation in kind is not an option. If one appropriates or alienates heritage material or helps others to do so, one cannot be considered part of the heritage profession, irrespective of professional training. That is not negotiable.

STEWARDS, OWNERS, AND
ARCHAEOLOGISTS

The issues related to appropriation and sale of "archaeological" artifacts have dominated the debate on maritime archaeology more than is useful. The confusion of mind-sets relating to salvage and heritage has not been helpful. But neither has the fact that during the development of maritime archaeology, the demands of society have changed. The explanations are many. Urbanization and dramatic upscaling of changes in the environment is one (Trotzig and Vahlne 1989). It inspires identification with the past of a place (Ingold 2000). Globalization is another. It inspires a greater need for individuals and groups to identify with their "roots." A third is the economics of marketing heritage (Lowenthal 1996; Rowan and Baram 2004). Moreover, archaeological interest is no longer limited to the long-distant past. Significance varies for different stakeholder groups and in different parts of the world. As a result, the definition of what is considered to be an "archaeological object" is diffuse. What is not diffuse, however, is the intention with which a site or deposit is approached. If that approach includes heritage value or significance, then by definition the approach is "archaeological" in nature. By definition it should follow the basic rules of archaeological engagement. These allow for a range of decisions proportional to the significance that the operation intends to safeguard. Such decisions are subject to the policies of relevant authorities. Fundamentally, however, they are archaeological or heritage decisions, and they should comply with the logic and rules of that domain and profession (Maarleveld 2009a). Are these ethical rules? Not exclusively, but they are not exclusively technical either.

National politics and different traditions of archaeology have influenced the way archaeological sites have been approached. There have been very restrictive policies, limiting access to officials only, and there have been approaches that promote access for all, while only regulating actual excavation. Professional and avocational "archaeologists" have accommodated both approaches. Despite the many inherent differences worldwide, the last 50 years have seen lots of international dialogue, convergence, and integration from which maritime archaeology can profit (Cleere 1984). This is manifest in the scientific debate, with the World Archaeology Congress as an internationalist culmination. But it also shows in the more politically informed debate in international governmental organizations: the Council of Europe, the Caribbean Community (CARICOM), the International Maritime Organisation (IMO), and most prominently UNESCO, the United Nations Educational, Scientific and Cultural Organization. With dedicated professional NGOs such as the International Council of Monuments and Sites (ICOMOS) as sparring partners, these have been instrumental in international policy development and its inscription in international law.

National debates on archaeological ethics follow their own logic. Besides reflecting international concerns, they also feed back into the larger debate. In some countries the practice of archaeology is more or less completely dominated by the state or regional authorities. Interestingly, it is only when the role of those authorities is challenged that extensive debate arises. In systems where the role of an archaeologist depends more on personal authority, there seems to be more need for publicly discussed checks and balances. Discussions addressing these issues go back at least to the 1960s, the very early years of maritime archaeology (McGimsey 2000). But in all contexts debates intensify when authority is under pressure. Since the 1980s, this has been the case in many countries. One reason is the emancipation of eloquent stakeholder groups worldwide. Another has been the successful integration of archaeology in the planning process. Both implied new ways of negotiating and mediating. Decisions with archaeological interest and archaeological consequences explicitly stopped to be the exclusive domain of the specialist (if they ever had been). In many countries this led to a fundamental restructuring of the profession and to reflection on cores values. In fact, it is such changes that prompted the formulation of most of the guidelines and codes of professional ethics that presently govern membership of professional societies. Such codes differ in detail but are remarkably similar at a meta-level, which testifies to (international) convergence. In short, they all revolve around six core concepts: Stewardship, Accountability, Non-commercialization, Public Education, Public Data, and Preservation (Elia 1995). All these concepts are relevant for professionals in maritime archaeology. Archaeology under water is, after all, in no way different from archaeology on land . . .

In passing, all six concepts appeared in the discussion above, with the exception of the first: Stewardship. I feel slightly uncomfortable with the term, although not so much as to refrain from subscribing to a code that uses it to try and describe the specific professional attitude, responsibilities, and obligations that archaeologists should have toward the "archaeological resource" and its integrity. The term as such, however, has two connotations that I do not like. The first is that the archaeologist would be the representative of a "higher authority"; the other is that he or she would be a caretaker of financial affairs. The first is too pretentious for my liking, and the second adds to the confusion in the "ownership" debate on maritime losses rather than helping to resolve it. That, of course, is very specific to the maritime situation. The term, however, inspires confusion between ethical issues and political concerns of control (Groarke and Warrick 2006). This is not necessary. It reduces the archaeological community to an interest group, while in fact it is a profession. No one will contest that heritage interventions should be controlled by professionals, just as everyone agrees that medical interventions are to be controlled by medical professionals. In both professions different interests are combined. Both are research-based, and in both the research interests cannot be pursued without regard to wider responsibilities. That is exactly what professional ethics is about.

INTERNATIONAL DIALOGUE
AND A NEW BODY OF LAW

In 2009 the 2001 UNESCO Convention on the Protection of the Underwater Cultural Heritage (2001 UNESCO Convention) entered into force. For now, it is both the culmination of the international dialogue on heritage and the conciliation of heritage thinking and maritime law. Moreover, it codifies and consolidates the outcome of the debates and convergence discussed above. As such, it is also the basis on which the practice and ethics of maritime archaeology can continue to develop.

Like the United Nations itself, UNESCO was established immediately after the Second World War. It unites states on the basis of intellectual dialogue, with the pragmatic and idealistic motto "Since wars begin in the minds of men, it is in the minds of men that the defences of peace must be constructed." Heritage, with all its complicated connotations, is one of the themes of this dialogue, which by definition is political in nature. Past deprivation of heritage by occupying forces, inequality and decolonization, present usurpation and destruction of heritage in the context of international conflict, and emancipation of the cultural expression of suppressed groups stage the background of its course. So does the role of heritage in defining new or old national and transnational identities.

The 2001 UNESCO Convention fits in a tradition in which states promise ever more respect for each other's heritage, in which the "Hague" Convention for the Protection of Cultural Property in the Event of Armed Conflict of 1954, the "New Delhi" Recommendation on International Principles Applicable to Archaeological Excavations, the 1970 convention on illicit trade, and the World Heritage Convention of 1972 are major stepping-stones. All these instruments build on cooperation and joint public responsibility.

Despite a certain reluctance in justifying public responsibilities at sea, concepts related to heritage were first introduced in maritime law in the United Nations Law of the Sea Convention of 1982. It obligates the nearly 160 states that subscribe to it to protect underwater cultural heritage and to cooperate for that purpose. Also, the International Convention on Salvage of 1989, as negotiated in the context of the International Maritime Organization (IMO), states that maritime cultural property of prehistoric, archaeological, or historic interest can be excluded from its working. Many states made that exception explicitly, thereby indicating that heritage is not subject to a salvage regime. It is only in the 2001 UNESCO Convention, however, that the gap between maritime and heritage thinking is consistently bridged (Carducci 2006). The 2001 convention builds on the obligations that follow from the Law of the Sea Convention and elaborates them in consistency with heritage ethics and legislation (O'Keefe 2002).

The way in which the obligations apply in internal waters and the different maritime zones results in slightly different regimes. From the perspective of heritage, the differences are technical rather than fundamental. They call for conscientious elaboration by the competent authorities of ratifying states, but need not concern us here. It is more important to note that the convention includes 36 operational rules. These are derived from the ICOMOS Charter on the Protection and Management of Underwater Cultural Heritage of 1996. As such, they represent the common denominator of what the profession—in all its traditions—sees as acceptable or not.

The rules address both practice and ethics (Maarleveld 2011). They bind the states who are party to the convention. At present, in the process of gradual implementation, this is only about one-fourth of the states subscribing to the Law of the Sea. Interestingly, however, many other states, including all European states, India, China, the United States, Canada, Australia, and Russia, but also Turkey and Venezuela (two states that do not subscribe to the Law of the Sea Convention), have committed themselves to these operational rules (UNESCO 2002: 156). Also, the 2001 Convention—and especially its operational rules—has had a far more encompassing influence on the development of national laws and policies than would follow from the number of ratifications alone (Dromgoole 2006). The new body of law and its worldwide practical implementation will continue to raise many issues, of a practical, but also of an ethical nature. In the meantime, a range of states continue to make decisions dependable on exclusive rights and admiralty court rulings. Personally, and as an archaeologist, I do not think that is helpful: establishing identity and ownership of individual items in something as interesting and complex as an archaeological deposit is impossible without major intrusion. And it should not be leading in archaeological strategy. On the other hand, perhaps wrongly but for the right reasons, the extensive litigation that accompanies this approach started to embrace the guidance of the 2001 UNESCO Convention (Florida Middle District Court 2009). In summary, it is clear that the entry into force of the UNESCO Convention is a major step, but certainly not the end of the trajectory. The ethical debate will continue, both at the level of professional ethics and on the approaches of heritage in society. And thus it should be, as it is in reflection that we define what we value most.

REFERENCES

Allen, Geoffrey, and David Allen. 1978. *Clive's lost treasure*. London: Robin Gorton.

Alves, Francisco J. S. 2004. *Considerações sobre o recente leilão na Christie's dos espólios de um navio português naufragado na ilha de Moçambique e sobre as opções político culturais do Estado português relativamente ao património cultural subaquático português espalhado pelo mundo*. Lisbon: Instituto Português de Arqueologia.

Alves Martins, António, ed. 1998. Nossa Senhora dos Mártires: *The last voyage*. Lisbon: Expo '98, Verbo.

Arnold, Bettina. 1990. The past as propaganda: Totalitarian archaeology in Nazi Germany. *Antiquity* 64: 464–478.

Ashburner, Walter. 1909. *Nomos Rodiōn nautikos—the Rhodian sea-law; Edited from the manuscripts*. Oxford: Clarendon Press.

Ball, Dorian. 1995. *The Diana adventure*. Kuala Lumpur: Malaysian Historical Salvors.

Bass, George F. 1966. *Archaeology under water*. London: Thames and Hudson.

———. 1975. *Archaeology beneath the sea*. New York: Harper & Row.

———. 2003. The ethics of shipwreck archaeology. In *ethical issues in archaeology*, ed. Larry J. Zimmerman, Karen D. Vitelli, and Julie Hollowell-Zimmer, 57–70. Walnut Creek, CA: AltaMira Press.

———, ed. 2005. *Beneath the seven seas: Adventures with the Institute of Nautical Archaeology*. London: Thames & Hudson.

Benoît, Fernand. 1961. *Fouilles sous-marines: L'épave du Grand Congloué à Marseille*. Gallia, Supplément 14. Paris: CNRS (Centre National de la Recherche Scientifique).

Briggs, C. Stephen. 2005. C. C. Rafn, J. J. A. Worsaae: Archaeology, history and Danish national identity in the Schleswig-Holstein question. *Bulletin of the History of Archaeology* 15 (2): 4–25.

Brøgger, Anton Wilhelm, and Haakon Shetelig. 1950. *Vikingeskipene: Deres forgjengere og etterfølgere*. Oslo: Dreyers Forlag.

———. 1971. *The Viking ships: Their ancestry and evolution*. New York: Twayne.

Carducci, Guido. 2006. The UNESCO Convention 2001: A crucial compromise on salvage law and the law of finds. In *Finishing the interrupted voyage: Papers of the UNESCO Asia-Pacific Workshop on the 2001 Convention on the Protection of the Underwater Cultural*, ed. Lyndel V. Prott, 27–31. Leicester: Institute of Art and Law.

Cederlund, Carl Olof. 1997. *Nationalism eller vetenskap? Svensk marinarkeologi i ideologisk belysning*. Stockholm: Carlssons Forlag.

———. 2002. Archaeology in the marine environment in Sweden. In *International handbook of underwater archaeology*, ed. Carol V. Ruppé and Jan F. Barstad, 333–345. New York: Plenum.

———. 2006. *Vasa I: The archaeology of a Swedish warship of 1628*, ed. Fred Hocker. Stockholm: National Maritime Museums of Sweden.

Christie's. 1986. *"The Bredenhof Bullion": 542 silver bars, most stamped with VOC markings, salvaged this year from the wreck of the "Bredenhof," which went down in 1753 in the Mozambique Channel*. Amsterdam: Christie's.

———. 2004. *The Fort San Sebastian wreck: A 16th century Portuguese porcelain wreck off the island of Mozambique*. Amsterdam: Christie's.

Clark, John Grahame Douglas. 1961. *World prehistory: An outline*. Cambridge: Cambridge University Press.

Cleere, Henry, ed. 1984. *Approaches to the archaeological heritage: A comparative study of world cultural resource management systems.* Cambridge: Cambridge University Press.

Cooper, David E. 2006. Truthfulness and "inclusion" in archaeology. In *The ethics of archaeology: Philosophical perspectives on archaeological practice,* ed. Chris Scarre and Geoffrey Scarre, 131–145. Cambridge: Cambridge University Press.

Corbey, Raymond. 2005. *The metaphysics of apes: Negotiating the animal-human boundary.* Cambridge: Cambridge University Press.

Cowan, Rex, Zelide Cowan, and Peter Marsden. 1975. The Dutch East Indiaman Hollandia wrecked on the Isles of Scilly in 1743. *International Journal of Nautical Archaeology and Underwater Exploration* 4 (2): 267–300.

Crumlin-Pedersen, Ole. 2002. *The Skuldelev Ships.* Ships and boats of the North, Vol. 4. Roskilde: Viking Ship Museum.

Daniel, Glyn. 1967. *The origins and growth of archaeology.* Harmondsworth, UK: Penguin.

Davis, Miriam C. 2008. *Dame Kathleen Kenyon: Digging up the Holy Land.* Walnut Creek, CA: Left Coast Press.

De Groot, Hugo. 1609. *Mare liberum.* Leiden: Elzevier.

———. 1625. *De ivre belli ac pacis libri tres: In quibus ius naturæ et gentium: Item iuris publici præcipua explicantur.* Paris: Nicolavs Bvon.

Díaz-Andreu, Margarita. 2007. *A world history of nineteenth-century archaeology: Nationalism, colonialism, and the past.* Oxford: Oxford University Press.

Diolé, Philippe. 1952. *Promenades d'archéologie sous-marine.* Paris: Albin Michel.

Dixon, Nicholas. 2004. *The Crannogs of Scotland: An underwater archaeology.* Stroud, UK: Tempus.

Dromgoole, Sarah, ed. 2006. *The protection of the underwater cultural heritage: National perspectives in light of the UNESCO Convention 2001.* Leiden: Martinus Nijhoff.

Elia, Ricardo J. 1995. A comment. In *Ethics in American archaeology: Challenges for the 1990s,* ed. Mark J. Lynott and Alison Wylie, 84–86. Washington, DC: Society for American Archaeology.

Evans, Christopher. 1995. Archaeology against the state: Roots of internationalism. In *Theory in archaeology: A world perspective,* ed. Peter Ucko, 312–326. London: Routledge.

Falcon-Barker, Ted. 1960. *1600 years under the sea.* London: Frederick Muller Limited.

Firth, Antony. 2002. *Managing archaeology underwater: A theoretical, historical and comparative perspective on society and its submerged past.* Oxford: Archaeopress.

Flatman, Joe. 2007. The origins and ethics of maritime archaeology. *Public Archaeology* 6 (2): 77–97; (3): 141–154.

Flecker, Michael. 2003. The thirteenth-century Java Sea wreck: A Chinese cargo in an Indonesian ship. *Mariner's Mirror* 89 (4): 388–404.

Florida Middle District Court. 2009. Case Number: 8:2007cv00614. *Odyssey Marine Exploration Inc. v. The Unidentified Shipwrecked Vessel.*

Frost, Honor. 1963. *Under the Mediterranean: Marine antiquities.* London: Routledge and Kegan Paul.

Gathercole, Peter W., and David Lowenthal, eds. 1990. *The politics of the past.* London: Unwin Hyman.

Gawronski, Jerzy, and Bas Kist, 1984. *TVliegend Hart Rapport 1982–1983.* Amsterdam: Rijksmuseum.

Gianfrotta, Piero Alfredo, and Patrice Pomey. 1981. *L'archéologie sous la mer: Histoire, techniques, découvertes et épaves.* Paris: Nathan.

Goddio, Franck. 2002. *Lost at sea: The strange route of the Lena Shoal junk*. London: Periplus.

Goggin, John M. 1960. Underwater archaeology: Its nature and limitations. *American Antiquity* 25: 348–354.

Gould, Richard Allan, ed. 1983. *Shipwreck anthropology*. Albuquerque: University of New Mexico Press.

Groarke, Leo, and Gary Warrick. 2006. Stewardship gone astray? Ethics and the SAA. In *The ethics of archaeology: Philosophical perspectives on archaeological practice*, ed. Chris Scarre and Geoffrey Scarre, 163–177. Cambridge: Cambridge University Press.

Hatcher, Michael. 1987. *The Nanking cargo*. London: Hamilton.

Henderson, Graeme. 1986. *Maritime archaeology in Australia*. Nedlands: University of Western Australia Press.

Hildred, Alex, ed. 2001. *VOC Anniversary Shipwreck Project: Report on the Excavation of the Dutch East Indiaman Vliegent Hart*. N.p.

Hocker, Frederick M. 2003. Maritime archaeology and the ISBSA—where to in the 21st century? In *Boats, ships and shipyards: Proceedings of the Ninth International Symposium on Boat and Ship Archaeology, Venice 2000*, ed. Carlo Beltrame, 1–6. Oxford: Oxbow.

Hoffmann, Gabriele, and Uwe Schnall, eds. 2003. *Die Kogge: Sternstunde der deutschen Schiffsarchäologie*. Hamburg: Convent.

Howell, Georgina. 2006. *Daughter of the desert*. London: Macmillan.

Huiskes, Bert, and Gerald A. de Weerdt. 1999. *De Lutine, 1799–1999: De raadselachtige ondergang van een schip vol goud*. Bussum, the Netherlands: Thoth.

Ingold, Tim. 2000. *The perception of the environment: Essays on livelihood, dwelling and skill*. London: Routledge.

Jeffery, Bill. 2006. Australia. In *The Protection of the Underwater Cultural Heritage: National Perspectives in Light of the UNESCO Convention 2001*, ed. Sarah Dromgoole, 1–15. Leiden: Martinus Nijhoff.

Kahn, Axel. 2007. *L'homme, ce roseau pensant . . .: Essai sur les racines de la nature humaine*. Paris: NiL éditions.

Kater, Michael Hans. 1974. *Das "Ahnenerbe" der SS, 1935–1945: Ein Beitrag zur Kulturpolitik des Dritten Reiches*. Stuttgart: Deutsche Verlags-Anstalt.

Kiesling, Stephen. 1994. *Walking the plank: A true adventure among pirates*. Ashland, OR: Nordic Knight Press.

Kohl, Philip L., and Clare Fawcett, eds. 1995. *Nationalism, politics, and the practice of archaeology*. Cambridge: Cambridge University Press.

Kohl, Philip L., Mara Kozelsky, and Nachman Ben-Yehuda, eds. 2007. *Selective remembrances: Archaeology in the construction, commemoration, and consecration of national pasts*. Chicago: The University of Chicago Press.

Lackey, Douglas P. 2006. Ethics and Native American reburials: A philosopher's view of two decades of NAGPRA. In *The ethics of archaeology: Philosophical perspectives on archaeological practice*, ed. Chris Scarre and Geoffrey Scarre, 146–162. Cambridge: Cambridge University Press.

Lamboglia, Nino. 1952. La Nave Romana de Albenga. *Revue d'études Ligures* 18 (3/4): 131–236.

Le Gurun, Gwénaëlle. 2006. France. In *The Protection of the Underwater Cultural Heritage: National Perspectives in Light of the UNESCO Convention 2001*, ed. Sarah Dromgoole, 59–95. Leiden: Martinus Nijhoff.

Lenihan, Daniel. 2002. *Submerged: Adventures of America's most elite underwater archaeology team*. New York: Newmarket Press.

Lowenthal, David. 1985. *The past is a foreign country*. Cambridge: Cambridge University Press.

———. 1996. *Possessed by the past: The heritage crusade and the spoils of history*. New York: Free Press.

Lyell, Charles. [1830–1833] 1997. *Principles of geology, being an attempt to explain the former changes of the earth's surface*. Harmondsworth, UK: Penguin Classics.

Lyon, Eugene, and Don Kincaid. 1982. Treasure from the Ghost Galleon: "Santa Margarita." *National Geographic* 161: 228.

Maarleveld, Thijs J. 1993. Underwater heritage management: Cultural and legislative perspective. *Analecta Praehistorica Leidensia* 26: 251–265.

———. 2006. The Netherlands. In *The Protection of the Underwater Cultural Heritage: National Perspectives in light of the UNESCO Convention 2001*, ed. Sarah Dromgoole, 161–188. Leiden and Boston: Martinus Nijhoff.

———. 2007. The 2001 UNESCO-Convention on the Protection of the Underwater Cultural Heritage: Origin and consequences. In *Havets kulturarv*, ed. Morten Hahn-Pedersen, 9–32. Esbjerg, Denmark: Fiskeri- og Søfartsmuseet.

———. 2008. Maritime heritage, mutual heritage: Research beats collecting. In *Marine Archaeological Perspective of the Indian Ocean*, ed. Alok Tripathi, 305–329. New Delhi: Sharada Publishing House.

———. 2009a. "Shared heritage: Joint responsibilities in the management of British warship wrecks overseas." International good practice or a few comments upon them. In *shared heritage: Joint responsibilities in the management of British warship wrecks overseas*, ed. Steven Gallagher, 58–74. Swindon, UK: English Heritage.

———. 2009b. Drama, place and verifiable link: Underwater cultural heritage, present experience and contention. In *Spirit of place: Between tangible and intangible heritage*, ed. Laurier Turgeon, 97–108. Quebec: Presses de L`Université Laval.

Maarleveld, Thijs J., ed. 2011. *UNESCO Manual on the Rules Concerning Activities Directed at Underwater Cultural Heritage, Annex to the Convention on the Protection of the Underwater Cultural Heritage*. Paris: UNESCO.

MacInnis, Joe, 1985. *The search for the* Breadalbane. Newton Abbot, UK: David & Charles.

Marchand, Suzanne L. 1996. *Down from Olympus: Archaeology and philhellenism in Germany, 1750–1950*. Princeton, NJ: Princeton University Press.

Martin, Colin. 1975. *Full fathom five: Wrecks of the Spanish Armada*. London: Chatto and Windus.

Martos López, Luis Alberto. 2008. Underwater archaeological exploration of the Mayan cenotes. *Museum International* 240 (60.4): 100–110.

Marx, Robert F. 1977. *The capture of the treasure fleet: The story of Piet Heyn*. New York: McKay.

Mathewson, R. Duncan III. 1986. *Treasure of the* Atocha: *Sixteen dramatic years in search of the historic wreck*. London: Sidgwick & Jackson.

McGimsey, Charles R. III. 2000. Standards, ethics, and archaeology: A brief history. In *Ethics in American archaeology*, 2nd rev. ed., ed. Mark J. Lynott and Alison Wylie, 15–18. Washington, DC: Society for American Archaeology.

McKee, Alexander. 1982. *How we found the "Mary Rose."* London: Souvenir Press.

Meskell, Lynn, ed. 1998. *Archaeology under fire: Nationalism, politics and heritage in the eastern Mediterranean and Middle East*. London: Routledge.

Müller-Wille, Michael. 1996. The political misuse of Scandinavian prehistory in the years
    1933–1945. In *The waking of Angantyr: The Scandinavian past in European culture*, ed.
    Else Roesdahl and Preben Meulengracht Sørensen. Aarhus, Denmark: Aarhus
    University Press.

Murray, Tim, and Christopher Evans, eds. 2008. *Histories of archaeology: A reader in the
    history of archaeology*. Oxford: Oxford University Press.

Daily News (Los Angeles, CA). 1997. Norwegian Expedition Reports Finding Sunken
    Spanish Galleon. 12 March.

O'Keefe, Patrick J. 2002. *Shipwrecked heritage: A commentary on the UNESCO Convention
    on Underwater Cultural Heritage*. Leicester: Institute of Art and Law.

Olsen, Olaf, and Ole Crumlin-Pedersen. 1958. The Skuldelev Ships. *Acta Archaeologica* 29:
    161–175.

Pickford, Nigel. 1994. *The atlas of shipwreck and treasure*. London: Dorling Kindersley.

Pieper, P., Th. J. Maarleveld, and A. J. T. Jull. 1992. Ideology and forgery: The Deventer
    Bones. *Forensic Science International* 54: 93–101.

Pope, Frank. 2007. *Dragon sea: A historical mystery; Buried treasure; An adventure beneath
    the waves*. London: Penguin Books.

Ray, Himanshu Prabha. 2008. *Colonial archaeology in South Asia: The legacy of Sir
    Mortimer Wheeler*. New Delhi: Oxford University Press.

Renfrew, Colin. 2008. *Prehistory: The making of the human mind*. London: Phoenix.

Renfrew, Colin, and Iain Morley. 2009. *Becoming human: Innovation in prehistoric material
    and spiritual culture*. Cambridge: Cambridge University Press.

Ronquillo, Wilfredo P. 1992. Management objectives for Philippine maritime archaeology.
    Bulletin of the Australian Institute for Maritime Archaeology 16 (1): 1–6.

Rowan, Yorke M., and Uzi Baram, eds. 2004. *Marketing heritage: Archaeology and the
    consumption of the past*. Walnut Creek, CA: AltaMira.

Rowlands, Michael. 1994. Childe and the archaeology of freedom. In *The archaeology of
    V. Gordon Childe: Contemporary perspectives*, ed. David R. Harris, 35–54. London:
    University College London Press.

Ruoff, Ulrich. 1981. Die Entwicklung der Unterwasserarchäologie im Kanton Zürich.
    Helvetia Archaeologica 45/48: 62–70.

Russell, Miles. 2002. Digging holes in popular culture: Archaeology and science. Oxford:
    Oxbow.

Salazar, Ernesto. 2007. *La Capitana*. Apachita 4. Online at http://revistas.arqueo-
    ecuatoriana.ec/. Accessed 7 June 2009.

Schnapp, Alain. 1993. *La conquête du passé: Aux origines de l'archéologie*. Paris: Editions
    Carré.

———. 1996. *The discovery of the past: The origins of archaeology*. London: British Museum
    Press.

Silverberg, Robert. 1963. *Sunken history: The story of underwater archaeology*. Chilton, UK:
    Chilton.

Soons, Fred. 2009. Introduction. In *The freedom of the seas revisited: Ocean governance 400
    years after Grotius' Mare Liberum: Current issues in the international law of the sea, in
    light of the thoughts of Hugo De Groot*. Unpublished conference, 11 December, Peace
    Palace, The Hague.

Sørensen, Ove. 2009. Maritime archaeological research at 77° North. *Maritime Archaeology
    Newsletter from Denmark* 24: 14–18.

Speck, Josef. 1981. Pfahlbauten: Dichtung oder Wahrheit? Ein Querschnitt durch 125 Jahre
    Forschungsgeschichte. *Helvetia Archaeologica* 45/48: 98–138.

Spruit, Ruud J., and Martijn Manders. 2007. *De Zoektocht naar de Hoorn: De Wonderbaarlijke Reis van Schouten en Le Maire*. Amsterdam: De Bataafsche Leeuw.

Stemm, Greg, and Sean Kingsley, eds. 2010. *Oceans odyssey: Deep-sea shipwrecks in the English Channel, Straits of Gibraltar and Atlantic Ocean*. Oxford: Oxbow.

Sténuit, Robert. 1971. *Les trésors de l'Armada*. Paris: Albin Michel.

———. 1972. *Treasures of the Armada*. Newton Abbot, UK: David & Charles.

Throckmorton, Peter. 1987. *History from the sea: Shipwrecks and archaeology; From Homer's Odyssey to the Titanic*. London: Beazley.

Toebosch, Theo. 2003. *Grondwerk: 200 jaar archeologie in Nederland*. Amsterdam: SUN.

Trigger, Bruce G. 1989. *A history of archaeological thought*. Cambridge: Cambridge University Press.

Trotzig, Gustav, and Gustav Vahlne, eds. 1989. *Archaeology and society: Large scale rescue operations—their possibilities and problems*. Stockholm: ICAHM Report.

Tubb, Kathryn Walker, ed. 1995. *Antiquities: Trade or betrayed: Legal, ethical and conservation issues*. London: Archetype.

Ucelli, Guido. 1940. *Le navi di Nemi*. Rome: La Libreria Dello Stato.

UNESCO. 2002. *Records of the General Conference*. 31st sess., vol. 1, *Resolutions*. UNESCO, Paris.

van der Waals, Johannes Diderik. 1969. *Praehistorie en Mythevorming*. Groningen, the Netherlands: Wolters-Noordhoff.

van Duivenvoorde, Wendy. 2006. Dutch Ministry of Finance Violates Agreement on Submerged Cultural Heritage. *INA Quarterly* 33 (1): 15–16.

Wignall, Sydney. 1982. *In search of Spanish treasure*. Newton Abbot, UK: David & Charles.

Willems, Willem, and Monique van den Dries. 2007. *Quality management in archaeology*. Oxford: Oxbow.

Woudenberg, Nout, and Thijs Maarleveld. 2002. Hugo de Groot en UNESCO op gespannen voet. *Nederlands Juristenblad* 77 (21): 1025.

Wright, Patrick. 1985. *On living in an old country: The national past in contemporary Britain*. London: Verso.

Zimmerman, Larry J., Karen Donne Vitelli, and Julie Hollowell-Zimmer, eds. 2003. *Ethical issues in archaeology*. Walnut Creek, CA: Altamira.

CHAPTER 41

MANAGEMENT OF MARITIME CULTURAL RESOURCES: AN AMERICAN PERSPECTIVE

TIMOTHY RUNYAN

INTRODUCTION

MANAGEMENT of a cultural resource normally suggests control by either an active or passive manager to provide for the appropriate treatment of the resource. The objectives are usually protection and preservation, though they may also include public education and other goals. Discovered submerged maritime resources can be exploited for their commercial value, left to lie in situ, or investigated to various degrees that may include complete excavation and recovery. Decisions concerning the treatment of a shipwreck or other underwater cultural resources are driven by numerous factors that provide insights into the practice of maritime archaeology and management of underwater cultural heritage (Gould 2000; Kaoru and Hoagland 1994; Satchell and Palma 2007; Silver 2009: 52–84).

Some consider the development of the self-contained underwater breathing apparatus (SCUBA) the key factor in the subsequent efforts to create management regimes for shipwrecks and other submerged cultural resources. Certainly, the development of SCUBA after World War II enabled archaeologists and others to explore the ocean and inland waters. The earlier technology of hard-hat diving could not be utilized by most scientists, including archaeologists, or the public, due to the skills and training required, the physical limitations it imposed on the diver, and the costs involved. But television made underwater archaeology accessible to the public (Bass 1966; Blot 1995; Green 2004: 5; Muckelroy 1978: 10, 1980: 22). Film-makers donned SCUBA gear and went underwater to create programs that opened new worlds to the viewer. Programs by Jacques Cousteau and others inspired the work and careers of many. More refined and reliable SCUBA equipment facilitated the continued efforts to explore more of the ocean and to greater depths. The use of Nitrox, mixed gas, and re-breathers enabled divers to stay underwater at greater depths and for longer periods than ever before. The ability to do sustained work underwater at a site at considerable depth became possible through saturation diving, where divers live in an underwater habitat. Submerged work and living stations, such as the Aquarius habitat in Florida, serve as research stations for conditioning humans to live and work on the seabed.

Driven by technological change, much of it in electronics, humans' ability to work in the corrosive and challenging environment of the ocean has changed dramatically since the 1960s. Much of that change was directed toward putting men and women in the ocean and inland waters, and those efforts continue But to explore the deep ocean, new technology emerged. The development of remotely operated vehicles (ROVs) provided a solution to ocean probing, which was formerly often no more than the lowering of a basket on a line into the deep ocean to recover a sample no larger in scope that the circumference of the basket (Rozwadowski 2005). ROVs equipped with cameras, and today with sophisticated high-definition (HD) cameras, can explore miles of ocean while recording digital images of everything that comes before their lenses. And they are not randomly dropped overboard as the baskets were, but are purposely driven by operators who can direct them to targets using sophisticated global positioning systems guided by satellites. The target was probably identified by the use of side-scan sonar, multibeam sonar, and possibly a magnetometer. The ship is better able to stay on location at sea through the use of thrusters linked to a dynamic positioning system (see Gearhart, Quinn, Tuttle, and Wachsmann, all in this volume).

Clearly, technology is the driver in underwater exploration. And the advances continue. Searching for an object within a grid by towing a side-scan sonar behind a boat ("mowing the grass") can now be done with an autonomous underwater vehicle (AUV) or unmanned underwater vehicle (UUV) that can be programmed to run search patterns in the water. The field of remote sensing was further advanced through the development of sophisticated computer programs and technologies, including differential GPS.

The consequence of this technology as directed toward ocean exploration is that most of the ocean and inland waters of the world can be explored by humans. Furthermore, the results of those explorations can be filmed. Advances in video technology, including HD cameras, and other technologies generate images that reveal more that can be seen by human eyes.

Conservation techniques and technologies have progressed with the application of advances in chemistry and conservation research. Artifacts can be recovered

Figure 41.1 The artifact before the diver, on which *Kad'yak* is inscribed in Cyrillic, identified the wreck of the Russian-American Company bark that sank in 1860. Indicative of the global economy of that age, the "'round the world ship" was built in Germany for use in Alaska and sailed there by way of Cape Horn. The United States purchased Alaska from Russia in 1867. The shipwreck is located in Alaska state waters near Kodiak Island. The expedition took place in 2004. Photograph by Tane Casserley/NOAA.

with greater assurance that a treatment will be available for their preservation. There are conservation textbooks readily available for the student or amateur to employ following the recovery of an object from underwater. The cost of conserving an artifact can be greatly reduced, often with improved results, through the employment of new techniques, such as silicone instead of polyethelene glycol (PEG) (see Hamilton and Smith in this volume).

The advances in the technology of diving, undersea exploration, remote sensing, and conservation have made underwater cultural heritage available not only to archaeologists and other scientists, but also to treasure salvors and the public. A constant flow of television programs and videos explain the techniques of underwater exploration. It should be no surprise that there are now more people looking for heritage resources in the water than ever before. And what the viewer sees is usually the actions of the divers and finders, but little about why or how they are permitted to do what they are doing. They see little about the regulations in place to protect resources that may be of local, national, or international importance. One reason for this is that the laws are resented by those who would like to have free rein in the sea. Restrictions on individuals' right to recover underwater cultural heritage is perceived by some as a violation of their personal freedoms. They may be viewed as laws that contravene customary practices of "finders, keepers" and the perceived neutrality of the ocean as a space owned by no nation or people (Bowens 2009; Dromgoole 1999; Fenwick 1998; King 2004).

These members of society have a voice and are among the most active in the search for historic shipwrecks or other submerged cultural resources, including aircraft (see Fix in this volume). The motive is profit, usually through the discovery of "treasure," which can range from bullion to jewels to simple objects whose value is enhanced due to the notoriety of the sunken vessel or owner. Profit can also come from media rights or agreements for telling the story. Examples of artifacts of value include the recovered possessions of passengers aboard the wrecked liner *Titanic*. The commercial value of underwater resources recovered from shipwrecks has created considerable public interest. It has also encouraged the formation of private enterprises to find and recover items of monetary value from sites. The subsequent interest of the states, and the urging of preservationists and the public, led to the establishment of a number of laws and policies to protect these resources (Ballard 2008; Dromgoole 1999; Gould 1983; Street 2006).

Maritime Preservation Laws and the International Community

Maritime cultural heritage is managed within layers of legal jurisdictions and guidelines. Underwater cultural heritage (UCH) is protected to lesser or greater extents by various laws at the local, regional, state, national, and international levels. Most of the legislation has occurred in the past 50 years, driven by the preservation communities. International law continues to be a major focus of those who wish to see global protection of underwater cultural heritage. Traditional admiralty law provided for claims of salvage and recovery of items from the sea. Early enactments include the seventh century Rhodian sea law, and the laws of Oléron, which date from the twelfth century. Debate during the ensuing centuries primarily focused on the European-centered arguments over the freedom of the seas (*Mare liberum*) espoused by Hugo Grotius of the Netherlands or the closed sea (*Mare clausum*) of Englishman John Selden (Hutt, Zander, and Varmer 1999; Runyan 2010; Workman 2008: 216).

The 1982 Third United Nations Convention on the Law of the Sea (UNCLOS) addressed issues of protection, but it was not very clear, and the procedures were complex. UNCLOS went into force in late 1994. Articles 33, 149, and 303 specifically address UCH. Protections are left to the individual nations concerning inland waters and the territorial seas, extending 12 nautical miles from baselines established ashore, and the exclusive economic zone (EEZ), which extends to 200 nautical miles. Article 33 defines a nation's right to enforce its domestic law out to 24 nautical miles, but makes no reference to underwater cultural heritage. Article 149 is titled "Archaeological and Historical Objects." It states:

> All objects of an archaeological and historical nature found in the Area [beyond the limits of national jurisdiction] shall be preserved or disposed of for the benefit of mankind as a whole, particular regard being paid to the preferential rights of the State or country of origin, or the State of cultural origin, or the State of historical and archaeological origin.

Article 303 recognizes the sovereign authority of coastal states over property, including their vessels, aircraft, and other state-owned vessels that have not been abandoned. The states may prevent the removal of "objects of an archaeological and historical nature" from the contiguous zone, which extends from the limit of the territorial seas (12 nautical miles) to 24 nautical miles. It declares:

1. States have a duty to protect objects of an archaeological and historical nature found at sea and shall cooperate for this purpose.
2. In order to control traffic in such objects the coastal state may, in applying article 33, presume that their removal from the sea-bed in the zone referred to in that article without approval would result in an infringement within its territory or territorial sea of the law and regulations referred to in that article.
3. Nothing in this article affects the rights of identifiable owners, the law of salvage or other rules of admiralty, or laws and practices with respect to cultural exchanges.
4. This article is without prejudice to other international agreements and rules of international law regarding the protection of objects of an archaeological and historical nature. (UNCLOS Article 303: 1–4)

The UN Convention on the Law of the Sea does not directly protect underwater cultural heritage, although it authorizes coastal states to apply their existing domestic preservation laws to the territorial sea and contiguous zone. It also does not address UCH in the "gap" between 24 and 200 nautical miles, the limit of the EEZ. Some have tried to close this gap, while others have directed their attention to alternative proposals (Blanco and Varmer 1996; Blumberg 2005; Strati 1995).

The International Council on Monuments and Sites (ICOMOS) produced the Charter on the Protection and Management of Underwater Cultural Heritage, which was ratified in 1996. It encouraged protection and management of UCH in inland and inshore waters, shallow seas, and the deep oceans. Some of the key elements of the ICOMOS Charter are captured in its introduction:

> Archaeology is concerned with environmental conservation; in the language of resource management, underwater cultural heritage is both finite and non-renewable. If underwater cultural heritage is to contribute to our appreciation of

the environment in the future, then we have to take individual and collective responsibility in the present for ensuring its continued survival.

Archaeology is a public activity; everybody is entitled to draw upon the past in informing their own lives, and every effort to curtail knowledge of the past is an infringement of personal autonomy. Underwater cultural heritage contributes to the formation of identity and can be important to people's sense of community. If managed sensitively, underwater cultural heritage can play a positive role in the promotion of recreation and tourism.

Archaeology is driven by research, it adds to knowledge of the diversity of human culture through the ages and it provides new and challenging ideas about life in the past. Such knowledge and ideas contribute to understanding life today and, thereby, to anticipating future challenges.

Many marine activities, which are beneficial and desirable, can have unfortunate consequences for underwater cultural heritage if their effects are not foreseen.

Underwater cultural heritage may be threatened by construction work that alters the shore and seabed or alters the flow of current, sediment and pollutants. Underwater cultural heritage may also be threatened by insensitive exploitation of living and non-living resources. Furthermore, inappropriate forms of access and the incremental impact of removing "souvenirs" can have a deleterious effect.

Many of the threats can be removed or substantially reduced by consultation with archaeologists and by implementing mitigatory projects. This Charter is intended to assist with bringing a high standard of archaeological expertise to bear on such threats to underwater cultural heritage in a prompt and efficient manner.

Underwater cultural heritage is also threatened by activities that are wholly undesirable because they are intended to profit few at the expense of the many. Commercial exploitation of underwater cultural heritage for trade or speculation is fundamentally incompatible with the protection and management of the heritage. This Charter is intended to ensure that all investigations are explicit in their aims, methodology and anticipated results so that the intention of each project is transparent to all.

In the subsequent statements, the first Fundamental Principle of Article 1 is that the preservation of underwater cultural heritage in situ should be considered as a first option. Furthermore, public access is promoted, nondestructive techniques are encouraged, resources should not be adversely affected, there should be no unnecessary disturbance of human remains or venerated sites, and investigations should be properly documented (Flatman 2009; Prott, Planche, and Roca-Nachem 2000).

The strong and clear statements in the ICOMOS Charter that UCH is by its very character an international resource influenced the language of the 2001 UNESCO Convention for the Protection of Underwater Cultural Heritage. The UNESCO Convention and its Annex Rules were formally adopted by the UNESCO General Conference in November 2001 and were subsequently ratified in 2009. It is the most comprehensive legal instrument to protect UCH beyond territorial waters. Article 1 defines UCH as "all traces of human existence having a cultural, historical or archaeological character which have been partially or totally underwater, periodically or continuously, for at least 100 years such as: Sites, structures, buildings, artefacts and human remains . . .; vessels, aircraft . . . their cargo, together with their archaeological and natural context; and objects of prehistoric character." The Convention supports the protection and conservation of UCH "for the benefit of humanity" as a whole, with a strong emphasis on in situ preservation. Underwater sites, particularly shipwrecks, are often regarded as time capsules. They can be a moment frozen in time, retaining the character, circumstances, and the material culture of that moment in time. The sites, especially deep or buried ones, are often in an exceptional state of preservation. Since the technology for recovery and conservation continue to progress, in situ preservation enables the later use of these advances to examine sites.

The Convention permits excavation when a site is endangered, and such danger includes the possibility of looting. Provisions must be made for the long-term storage and conservation of recovered material. Activities directed at UCH shall "only be undertaken under the direction and control of, and in the regular presence of, a qualified underwater archaeologist with scientific competence appropriate to the project" (UNESCO 2001: Rule 22). The Convention encourages cooperation and the sharing of information and technology among nations while engaging the

Figure 41.2 A useful management strategy is the involvement of volunteer divers in marine protected areas. Divers trained to Nautical Archaeology Society (NAS) standards are qualified to assist in research and monitoring projects for archaeological and environmental purposes within the NOAA national marine sanctuaries. Divers in training shown here are members of the National Association of Black SCUBA Divers. Photograph by Tane Casserley/NOAA.

public. A challenge to resource managers is how to meet the declaration that the public has a right to "enjoy the educational and recreational benefit of responsible, nonintrusive access to in situ cultural heritage." A significant achievement of the Convention was that the law of salvage and the law of finds will not be applicable to underwater cultural heritage. Furthermore, it declares that "the commercial exploitation of underwater cultural heritage for trade or speculation or its irretrievable dispersal is fundamentally incompatible with its protection and proper management. Underwater cultural heritage shall not be traded, sold, bought or bartered as commercial goods" (UNESCO 2001: Preamble).

International laws offer the prospect of shaping states' laws and practices regarding UCH. Debates on content and implementation have been heated and prolonged. The increased activity by treasure salvors, especially in the deep sea, has energized the public and political leadership in a number of states. The results include more active public education programs, more diligent enforcement of existing laws, expanded legal claims, and the creation of bilateral or multilateral agreements. Examples include the RMS *Titanic* agreement among France, the United Kingdom, Canada, and the United States, as well as the bilateral agreements between the United States and France concerning CSS *Alabama* and LaSalle's ship *La Belle*, which was discovered in Matagorda Bay, Texas. There will be continued pressures both for and against the protection of UCH as advancements in technology and the attraction of "treasure" facilitate the discovery of shipwrecks and other cultural resources.

MANAGEMENT OF SHIPWRECKS AND MARITIME HERITAGE RESOURCES IN THE UNITED STATES

The United States has ratified neither UNCLOS nor the 2001 UNESCO Convention. Reasons include concerns over creeping jurisdiction (*horror jurisdictionis*) by coastal states. But it has asserted sovereign rights in its territorial sea and jurisdiction over the contiguous zone, the continental shelf, and the Exclusive Economic Zone (Scovazzi 2002: 152).

Domestically, the United States Abandoned Shipwreck Act (ASA) became law in 1988 as a result of a series of legislative proposals before Congress that began in the late 1970s in response to conflicts over the jurisdiction of historic shipwrecks located in state waters. It asserted federal ownership over abandoned historic shipwrecks and then transferred title to the states. The ASA specified that the law of salvage would not apply to the wrecks covered under the act. Archaeologists supported this bill, arguing for protection and preservation of historic shipwrecks. The act allowed states to control the excavation of submerged lands under their state waters and stem the pillaging of wreck sites by treasure salvors. The states were encouraged to develop multiple-use management plans that accommodated the different interests of historic preservationists, archaeologists, sport divers, and salvors, using voluntary guidelines developed by the National Park Service. The formal guidelines were published in the Federal Register in December 1990 (Carducci 2003; Giesecke 1991; Runyan 1990).

The estimate of the number of historic shipwrecks in U.S. waters drove discussion at some of the hearings. The number of shipwrecks in U.S. waters was believed to be more than 50,000, of which 5–10% might have historical significance. The ASA language specified the categories of shipwrecks that would fall under the control of the act:

   (a) UNITED STATES TITLE. The United States asserts title to any abandoned
       shipwreck that is
       (1) embedded in submerged lands of a State;
       (2) embedded in coralline formations protected by a State on submerged
           lands of a State; or
       (3) on submerged lands of a State and is included in or determined to be
           eligible for inclusion in the National Register of Historic Places.
   (b) The public shall be given adequate notice of the location of any shipwreck
       to which title is asserted under this section. The Secretary of the Interior,
       after consultation with the appropriate State Historic Preservation Officer,
       shall make a written determination that an abandoned shipwreck meets
       the criteria for eligibility for inclusion in the National Register of Historic
       Places under clause (a)(3).
   (c) TRANSFER OF TITLE TO STATES. The title of the United States to any
       abandoned shipwreck asserted under subsection (a) of this section is
       transferred to the State in or on whose submerged lands the shipwreck is
       located.

It should be clear that Congress only intended to transfer to the states the titles of those shipwrecks that were: (l) abandoned; and, (2) either embedded in submerged lands, or embedded in coral formations, or eligible for National Register listing. Normally, under the qualifications for National Register listing, the property (vessel) would need to be at least 50 years old and meet the significance criteria relating to historical and archaeological contexts. Upon passage of the ASA, many states updated or revised their state laws regarding historic shipwrecks. There are now several states that have underwater archaeologists on staff and pursue an active role in resource management, including Maryland, Texas, Florida, Massachusetts, Wisconsin, Georgia, South Carolina, and North Carolina.

But the ASA had some deficiencies. Congress declined to clearly define "abandonment" and "embedded," resulting in ambiguities that have led to lawsuits. With estimates that over 90% of the known historic wrecks were located in state waters, Congress also declined to propose a comprehensive plan for management of underwater cultural heritage beyond state waters. The ASA was designed to be a good first step to provide for preservation and management of historic shipwreck resources.

A number of court cases involving the ASA have impacted states rights under the act, including the *Brother Jonathan*, and the *Juno* and *La Galga* shipwreck cases. *Brother Jonathan* was a 67 m (220 ft) paddle-wheel steamer that sank in over 61 m (200 ft) of water off Crescent City, California, in 1865. The cargo included a shipment of gold and a federal government payroll. Five cargo insurers paid claims within a few months. No insurer or government agency attempted to locate the wreck or recover the ship or cargo. In 1991, Deep Sea Research Inc. initiated an admiralty action *in rem* while equipping for a search effort. The California State Lands Commission intervened and, under the ASA and the California Public Resources Code, asserted title to all abandoned shipwrecks and historic resources on its submerged lands. The state of California then lost a string of district court and appeals court decisions before the case ended up in the Supreme Court.

In April 1998, the U.S. Supreme Court heard *California v. Deep Sea Research, Inc.* The justices held that "abandonment" under the ASA should be similar to the traditional admiralty concept of abandonment. This decision encouraged treasure salvors to locate long-lost owners or insurers as a means of demonstrating that the wreck of interest was not abandoned. The Supreme Court decision did not specify what a state must do to have a "colorable claim," and the Court also did not rule on the validity of state statutes, or whether California's historic preservation statute was preempted by the ASA. The Court also declined to rule on the constitutionality of the ASA.

La Galga and the *Juno* are Spanish warships lost off the coast of Virginia during storms in 1750 and 1802. A claim was made by a treasure salvor, Sea Hunt Inc., as well as the state of Virginia, but the U.S. Department of State intervened on behalf of the Kingdom of Spain, who claimed the vessels as state property that was never abandoned. The U.S. Court of Appeals for the Fourth Circuit decided in favor of Spain. One reason for the decision to intervene was to reinforce the U.S. claim of sovereign immunity over any military vessel or aircraft of the U.S. government; these vessels and aircraft, unless expressly abandoned or transferred, remain property of the U.S. regardless of location or passage of time.

This position was formalized by the Sunken Military Craft Act of 2004. The Naval History and Heritage Command (NHHC) is responsible for managing sunken naval resources in both domestic and foreign territorial waters. For example, a management plan was created in the 1990s for CSS *Alabama*, sunk off Cherbourg, France, during the Civil War, after France recognized the American claim of ownership. Likewise, German World War II submarines lost off the coast of North Carolina are recognized as German sovereign property, and recent efforts have aimed at protecting the sites from looting. The NHHC is also responsible for the management of the Confederate submarine *H. L. Hunley*, raised and conserved in Charleston, South Carolina. Numerous naval aircraft, ships, and other resources fall under its jurisdiction (see Neyland in this volume).

Figure 41.3 The World War II German submarine *U-701* sank off the coast of North Carolina. It remains the property of Germany though it is in U.S. waters. The German government has encouraged efforts to respect and preserve the site. Several U-boats have been looted, although they are grave sites. Sunken military craft are an international issue. Photograph by Tane Casserley/NOAA.

There are other U.S. federal agencies that address underwater cultural heritage, including the National Park Service (NPS). NPS has responsibilities in parks across the United States, ranging from Key Biscayne, Florida, to the USS *Arizona* Memorial in Hawaii. The Bureau of Ocean Energy Management, Regulation and Enforcement (until 2010 known as the Minerals Management Service) manages oil, gas, and other mineral reserves on the outer continental shelf, primarily in the Gulf of Mexico, where there are an estimated 5,000 shipwrecks, among over 30,000 miles of pipelines, and 3,000 platforms. The Bureau manages more seabed than other agencies. Lessees are required to survey their sites for historic cultural resources before pipelines, oil rigs, or other structures are put in place, but there is no authority over third party use or abuse after discovery. The National Oceanic and Atmospheric Administration (NOAA), discussed below, also plays an important role in the preservation, management, and research pertaining to UCH.

There are several historic preservation statutes that, although primarily intended for the preservation of historical sites on land, can under certain circumstances be applied to the protection of UCH. These include the Antiquities Act of 1906, which was used in 2006 to create the nearly 140,000 m² (362,600 km²) Papahānaumokuākea Marine National Monument in the northwestern Hawaiian Islands, extending from Oahu to Midway (U.S. Department of Commerce, NOAA 2009b). The use of the act, however, created issues for the managers. Since it was not created under the

National Marine Sanctuaries Act (see below), NOAA's Office of National Marine Sanctuaries did not have a clear management process and plan to apply. A joint management plan had to be created among the Sanctuaries office, the state of Hawai'i, and the U.S. Fish and Wildlife Service. The state had an interest in all aspects of the monument, but little direct management, while the Fish and Wildlife Service responsibilities focused on the islands, and NOAA assumed responsibility for the waters, including marine life and submerged cultural resources. In the few years since it has been created, several whaling ships and other historic vessels have been discovered. The exhibit, "Lost on a Reef," was created in 2010 to interpret those discoveries to the public at the Mokupāpapa Discovery Center in Hilo, Hawai'i.

The National Historic Preservation Act of 1966 has played a major part in shaping cultural resources management in the United States. The act includes Section 106, which mandates that federal agencies take into account the effects of their actions on historic properties that may be eligible for listing in the National Register of Historic Places, which the act authorized. This includes federally funded undertakings, which are projects, activities, or programs funded in whole or part by a federal agency, and those activities that require a permit review by a federal agency. The act also created the Advisory Council on Historic Preservation, which must be notified of the undertaking and be given an opportunity to respond, as well as encouraged the formation of State Historic Preservation Offices and Tribal Historic

Figure 41.4 The British whaling ships *Pearl* (shown here) and *Hermes* wrecked in 1822 at an atoll that bears their name. They are among the shipwrecks discovered since the creation in 2006 of the Paphānaumokuākea Marine National Monument in the Northwestern Hawaiian Islands. Photograph by Robert Schwemmer/NOAA.

Preservation Offices. Together, these institutions act in consultation with stake-holders to ensure that historic properties are taken into consideration, though not necessarily always preserved. Such properties include maritime heritage resources. In addition, Section 110 of the act requires agencies to inventory, evaluate, and nominate all significant cultural resources under their jurisdiction to the National Register of Historic Places, and to mitigate adverse effects on historically significant cultural resources (King 2004).

The National Environmental Policy Act (NEPA) is a cultural resource management authority, even though its title suggests that it is directed to natural resources. Enacted in 1969, NEPA focuses on the promotion of a healthy environment, but it also emphasizes heritage preservation. It seeks to "preserve important historic, cultural, and natural aspects of our national heritage, and maintain, whenever possible, an environment which supports diversity, and variety of individual choice." This is to be accomplished in part through an interdisciplinary approach that ensures the integrated use of the natural and social sciences.

The Archaeological Resources Protection Act (ARPA) applies to archaeological resources over 100 years of age (in contrast to the 50-year requirement of eligibility for the National Register). ARPA has been used successfully in a case where criminal charges were brought against a salvor of underwater cultural heritage in Florida's Key Biscayne National Park. The act includes a strong statement against trafficking in archaeological resources, which may be applied to underwater cultural heritage (Varmer and Blanco 1999: 219; King 2004: 252–255).

The National Marine Sanctuaries Act of 1972 authorized the Secretary of Commerce, through the National Oceanic and Atmospheric Administration, to designate discrete marine areas, within 200 nautical miles of the coast, which are deemed to be of national importance for a variety of criteria, including an area's historical, cultural, archaeological, or paleontological significance. Following the designation of the first site, the sanctuary to protect the remains of the USS *Monitor*, which sank off Cape Hatteras in 1862, a total of 13 national marine sanctuaries and 1 marine national monument have been created and are administered by NOAA and partners. Together the sanctuaries amount to 150,000 square miles of ocean and Great Lakes; they are located in American Samoa, Hawai'i (2, including the Papahānaumokuākea Marine National Monument), the Pacific coast (4), the Atlantic coast (3), and one each in the Gulf of Mexico, the Florida Keys, and Lake Huron (Terrell 2007).

Within these sanctuaries, NOAA has the authority to regulate activities directed at underwater cultural heritage. Sanctuary sites are committed to use by various user groups, but within a context of resource protection. There is an extensive process for public involvement in the development of management plans for the sanctuaries. They are place-based and address the interests of local communities. Underwater cultural heritage is included in the plans of all sites. Several sites were initially designated as sanctuaries because of their ecological or environmental qualities, but were later found to possess significant cultural heritage resources. Examples include Stellwagen Bank National Marine Sanctuary in Massachusetts Bay and the Monterey Bay National Marine Sanctuary. The NOAA Office of National

Marine Sanctuaries is where the environmental and maritime heritage movements have come together. Its foundation is the National Marine Sanctuaries Act, a strong piece of legislation supporting the preservation of ocean natural resources and of maritime heritage and cultural resources.

Two sites are directed entirely to the preservation of underwater cultural heritage—the Monitor National Marine Sanctuary and the Thunder Bay National Marine Sanctuary and Underwater Preserve. The Thunder Bay sanctuary was created in 2000 and is located off Alpena, Michigan. The sanctuary works in partnership with the state of Michigan. The designation was created to protect a noted repository of shipwrecks—the 80 or more sites that are extremely well preserved in the cold fresh water of Lake Huron. The Thunder Bay management plan incorporates education and public outreach as important components of protection and conservation of the shipwrecks and other cultural resources at the site. Management of the shipwrecks includes an active program of diving, monitoring, and research. The recovery of information, including images, from underwater is shared with the public, and especially schools and educators, in the recently constructed Maritime Heritage Center. All national marine sanctuaries have advisory councils to provide

Figure 41.5 The *F. T. Barney* sank in 1874 but is in remarkable condition in the cold freshwater of Lake Huron at the Thunder Bay National Marine Sanctuary, which includes many other shipwrecks in pristine condition. Exhibits at the Maritime Heritage Center provide public interpretation of the shipwrecks. Other pristine wrecks in the Great Lakes include the *Hamilton* and *Scourge* that sank in 1813 in Lake Ontario. They were transferred from U.S. to Canadian ownership. Photograph by Tane Casserley/NOAA.

guidance and public participation. Councils can be important factors in the management, planning, and growth of sanctuaries. In the case of Thunder Bay, the advisory council took the lead in advocating the expansion of the sanctuary to more than seven times its current size (U.S. Department of Commerce, NOAA 2009a). Other sanctuaries, such as the Olympic Coast, work with several Native American tribes that live along the adjacent coast.

MARINE PROTECTED AREAS
AND PUBLIC ACCESS

Driven by the increasing pressures on the ocean and inland waters from offshore gas and oil extraction, development, overfishing, and other factors, many nations have created various forms of marine protected areas (MPAs). The United States has nearly 1,800 areas in the marine environment that are reserved by federal, state, territorial, tribal, or local laws or regulations. The aim is to provide lasting protection for these areas, not just short-term protection.

Through time, management has taken many forms and is varied and uncoordinated. In May 2000, the president of the United Sates, by Executive Order 13158, called for a national system of MPAs. The National Marine Protected Areas Center was created within NOAA. A Federal Advisory Committee was established to oversee the center's development, and the office created a framework document to provide for direction and guidance (U.S. Department of Commerce, NOAA Framework 2008). The impetus for the creation of the center was to bring some coordination and order to the disparate protected marine areas. Principal issues cited in the framework document produced by the center in 2008 are the "declining fish populations, degradation of coral reefs and other vital habitats, threats to rare or endangered species, and the loss of artifacts and resources that represent the diverse cultural heritage of the United States. The effects of these losses are significant and jeopardize the social and economic fabric of the nation." The integration of marine cultural resources in the executive order is significant. The environmental movement in its global reach is ahead of the maritime heritage movement. A key element in achieving some parity is the incorporation of cultural heritage within the marine environmental protections. This includes submerged cultural resources or those that are part of the maritime landscape. The approach is beneficial to cultural resource managers who can function within the context of an ecosystem-based approach to management. It is important to note that the national system created in the United States is not a federal system, but extends through all levels of government. It requires collaboration among the various agencies and polities that create or manage MPAs. The National Register of Historic Places is cited as the determinant for historical significance of cultural resources (Claesson 2009).

There are Marine Protected Areas across the globe. The 2008 establishment of the Phoenix Islands Protected Area by the Republic of Kiribati was the world's largest, at 408,250 km² (157,626 m²). But in April 2010, the United Kingdom created the Chagos Archipelago Marine Reserve in the Indian Ocean, encompassing 545,000 km² (210,000 m²) (Rincon 2010). The initiative to designate these sites was environmental, but they contain maritime heritage resources.

Not all MPAs incorporate underwater cultural heritage as part of their mandate for conservation and protection. Many are multiuse, including public and commercial activities. Not all are exclusive or, in the case of fishing, "no-take" areas. This corresponds to some degree with the development in the United States of preserves and parks focused on shipwrecks. These include individual wreck sites and also shipwreck trails that have proven popular with the public (Smith 2007). From the Great Lakes and Lake Champlain to Maryland, North Carolina, South Carolina, Florida, and elsewhere, these underwater preserves or parks usually incorporate the interests of sport divers and archaeologists. They tend to generate civic pride and stewardship within adjacent communities. They also promote tourism and economic growth. The challenge is to meet the management requirement to preserve and protect the resources while engaging the public (see Cohn and Dennis in this volume; Jameson and Scott-Ireton 2007; Scott-Ireton 2007). The nondiving public is the largest sector. How are they to be reached? Maritime museums and other heritage sites can provide information to inform the nondiving visitor (see McCarthy in this volume). But it can be difficult to create interactive exhibits, or sites that engage the nondiver. Strategies to address this issue range from Web sites with virtual experience to sophisticated signage to glass-bottomed boats and submersibles. It remains an area in need of further innovation and creative thinking. Advances in technology with maritime heritage resource applications have provided some resolution to the problem of how to connect the visitor with the shipwreck or other resource.

Telepresence, as pertaining to the preservation, research, and management of UCH, is the electronic video presentation to the public of remote sites, often from depths well beyond the range of SCUBA. Through the use of cameras on ROVs or submersibles, the archaeologist can interpret the site to the visitor or viewer. This can be done through a Web cast, podcast, or other communication mode. Early examples that gained international attention were the live broadcasts in 2004 from *Titanic* at a depth of about 12,000 ft (3,650 m). NOAA fitted out the ship *Okeanos Explorer* in 2008 with satellite communication capability, high-definition cameras, and remote-sensing instruments of extremely high quality. This enables live transmission to large audiences from a submerged site, but also allows scientists, including maritime archaeologists, to remotely direct or participate in real-time undersea operations through command centers on shore that can receive the audiovisual transmissions (Ocean Exploration and Research 2010). Monitoring through the use of video at great depths enables some degree of management of deepwater shipwrecks. The future of management of submerged resources will include more deepwater sites that are able to be accessed remotely (Ball, Irion, and

Horrell 2007; Ballard 2008; Irion 2002; Wachsmann in this volume). The issue is complicated by the availability of similar advanced technology to salvagers, and jurisdictional issues in international waters (see Maarleveld in this volume). The proposed *Titanic* Agreement among France, the United Kingdom, Canada, and the United States would control, through permitting, the actions of nationals of each state. It is a collaborative international agreement for the protection of the ship-wreck site through in situ preservation, in accord with the UNESCO convention. A more ambitious proposal is the Siracusa Declaration proposed in 2001 (Scovazzi 2002: 155–156). It calls on the Mediterranean states to endorse a regional agreement to protect the underwater cultural heritage of the Mediterranean Sea. Such regional agreements, if effected, can provide another avenue for protection of underwater cultural heritage.

INTERNATIONAL PERSPECTIVES

The effective management of submerged cultural resources is a challenge to many communities and nations. There are varying approaches. Some adopt the manage-ment strategy that a national authority or responsible party is in control and man-ages the resources for the people. Another approach is that the responsible agency manages with others and partners as an equal in the management decisions. In the United States, the federal or state programs tend to follow the first approach. Other states have developed their own laws and regulations (Bowens 2009; Maarleveld 2007; Street 2007).

New South Wales is a state in eastern Australia with considerable submerged maritime resources. Within the framework of the Australian Historic Shipwrecks Act of 1976, those resources became the responsibility of the New South Wales gov-ernment (Green 2004; Henderson 1994; Nutley 2007; Staniforth 2007). It should be noted that the act does not include other cultural resources, such as aircraft or indigenous sites. Amended in 1993, it does include all shipwrecks sunk more than 75 years ago. Federal involvement continues through the state's Heritage Office, which created an Underwater Cultural Heritage Program. With a small office and an estimated 1,800 shipwrecks, a strategic decision was made for the agency to partner and assist the community in management of the resources rather than managing them for the people of New South Wales. Of course, in such situations funding is often a key issue (Nutley 2007; Spirek and Scott-Ireton 2003).

The United Kingdom's Protection of Wrecks Act 1973 provided the country's initial authority for the protection of historic shipwrecks. The National Heritage Act of 2002 expanded heritage resource protection to include shipwrecks, aircraft, and other cultural resources. Administrative responsibility was transferred from the Department of Culture, Media and Sport to English Heritage. Management of archaeological service in support of the Protection of Wrecks Act is administered by

English Heritage. Since records list more than 30,000 shipwrecks in UK waters, the management task is formidable. English Heritage commissioned in 2003 the United Kingdom's leading organization of archaeologists, the Institute of Field Archaeologists, to assess the state of maritime archaeology by surveying those in the field. The results contained critical observations. These included a lack of funding, too few professionals in the field, the need for a consistent management and research policy, a need for more protection of sites, a closer relationship with terrestrial archaeology, and an admonition to avoid excess regulation of recreational divers. In 2005, English Heritage initiated a five-year plan to address these and other issues. A key point is the effort to increase public understanding of the historical environment and to encourage the public to value it and care for it (Oxley 2007).

The excavation and recovery of Henry VIII's ship *Mary Rose* stimulated international public interest while demonstrating the ability of a maritime archaeological project to generate substantial financial support. An estimated 60 million people viewed on television the raising of the hull of the *Mary Rose* in October 1982, which included the first-ever live underwater broadcast. The Mary Rose Museum opened in 1983 and has averaged about 300,000 visitors per year, and a new museum is being planned. Its Web site was one of the first for a museum in the United Kingdom and receives more than a half a million visits per year (Dobbs 2007).

Ireland has devoted considerable effort to maritime heritage resource protection. The National Monuments Act (1930) was amended in 1987 to include the protection of submerged cultural resources over 100 years old. More than 10,000 shipwrecks are included in the national inventory. An extraordinary and coveted feature of the Irish legislation is the Underwater Heritage Order. This order enables an individual site to be singled out for its exceptional historic or artistic value for state protection. The best-known example of this site-specific authority is the protection extended to the RMS *Lusitania*, which sank off Cork in 1915. The Department of the Environment, Heritage and Local Governments includes the National Monuments Service. It created the Underwater Archaeology unit to manage Irish submerged maritime heritage resources. Among the unit's responsibilities is the review of permits and of plans for harbor developments, piers, pipelines, and dredging operations. Such a survey, conducted in advance of a wind farm constructed on Arklow Bank off the east coast of Ireland, revealed important shipwrecks. Discoveries like these, together with rapid development in Ireland, have resulted in greater pressure to incorporate maritime archaeological surveys in marine spatial planning (Kelleher 2007).

Turkey holds a special place in the preservation of maritime archaeological resources because of its long relationship with the University of Pennsylvania Museum, and later the (American) Institute of Nautical Archaeology and Texas A&M University. The relationship has led to an exceptional number and quality of early shipwrecks that have been excavated, conserved, and exhibited. These extraordinary shipwrecks are on exhibit or under conservation in the Bodrum Museum of Underwater Archaeology, located within the Castle of the Knights of St. John.

In 1983, Turkey extended protection to shipwrecks through the Law Protecting the Cultural and National Heritage. The recent discovery of numerous Byzantine and other early historic shipwrecks along the medieval waterfront of Istanbul opens a new chapter in the management of historic shipwrecks in Turkey (Blake 1999).

Spain has taken an aggressive position in regard to claiming ownership of vessels that belonged to the Crown. *Juno* and *La Galga* are two such cases, but the Spanish government has pursued its claim to ships claimed by salvors in many places. This includes the *Nuestra Señora de las Mercedes*, recently salvaged by an American company. The case is currently pending in the U.S. federal court system (Nogueruela 2000; Phillips 2007).

Neighboring Portugal enacted a law allowing the commercial exploitation of shipwrecks in 1993, but it was replaced by a protective law four years later. The discovery of numerous shipwrecks of historical value resulted in the creation of a national center to manage underwater cultural heritage. Sites include shipwrecks in Portugal, the Azores, Madeira, and foreign waters (Alves 2007).

South Africa provides protection and management of shipwrecks through the National Heritage Resource Act of 1986. Permits are required for investigations of historic sites, which are defined as more than 60 years of age. The South African Heritage Resource Agency is responsible for the management of an estimated 2,700 shipwreck sites, including vessels from more than 20 countries (Staniland 1999).

The Caribbean, long a haunt of treasure hunters, presents many examples of management challenges and responses (see Leshikar-Denton in this volume). The protection of shipwreck sites has not been a priority for many of the region's states. Others, however, have taken a more proactive role. The Cayman Islands has developed a maritime heritage trail and a shipwreck preserve (Leshikar-Denton and Scott-Ireton 2007; Smith 2000). Bermuda replaced its 1959 law for the protection of shipwrecks with a more protectionist Historic Wrecks Act in 2002. The principal driver was the Bermuda Maritime Museum, which has worked to foster professional attitudes toward submerged cultural resources while conserving and exhibiting artifacts recovered from archaeological expeditions.

Canada emerged as a leader in public access to shipwreck sites. Louisburg Harbor was created as a protected site in 1961, and Fathom Five was created within the Province of Ontario and later established as a national marine park. Parks Canada provides management and archaeological guidance for sites and undertakes explorations of important sites such as the Basque whaling ships at Red Bay in Labrador (LaRoche 2003; Grenier 1994). Under the Canada Shipping Act of 2001, responsibility for the development and administration of regulations for the protection of heritage shipwrecks is shared. Transport Canada and Environment Canada through Parks Canada are developing the regulations, expected to be completed in 2010.

China has extensive underwater cultural heritage resources dating to the Neolithic period (see Sasaki in this volume). With thousands of shipwrecks, and what has been a thriving black market in stolen terrestrial archaeological heritage, the government is involved in policy and management issues. The 1989 Regulation on the Protection and Administration of Underwater Cultural Relics claims that such resources are the property of the state. China has extended this protection out to 24 nautical miles and has made statements that it prevails throughout the EEZ. Management is cooperative through the National Museum, the Ocean University at Qingdao, and other agencies and local governments (Hoagland 1997; Zhao 1992).

These selected examples of legislation and management initiatives to protect shipwrecks have much in common. Most of the laws have been enacted in the past few decades, and the trend is toward more protection. This has resulted in more government and community involvement, sometimes generating conflict. The public has become more educated concerning the value of historic shipwrecks, and what they can mean to a society. This includes tourism benefits, which translate into money earned by local communities. More shipwrecks are discovered, or at least brought to the public's attention, through the creation of professional staffs of underwater archaeologists and through the outreach to fishermen and recreational divers concerning the value of shipwrecks and the stories they have to tell. One of the first acts of most newly formed archaeological offices is to inventory the resources under their purview. This follows the maxim that you cannot manage what you cannot measure. Independent of these comprehensive inventories and management activities, high-value shipwrecks continue to be sought by treasure hunters, who must then navigate the local maritime heritage laws.

OBSERVATIONS

More than a century has passed since the passage of the Antiquities Act of 1906. Subsequent acts, including the National Historic Preservation Act, the Abandoned Shipwreck Act, and the Sunken Military Craft Act, have addressed some of the major issues in the protection of underwater cultural heritage. But it should be clear that this is a patchwork and that these acts are targeted toward certain agencies or jurisdictions. There is no omnibus act that addresses issues related to UCH. Some of the acts do not apply to the waters of the Contiguous Zone (12–24 nautical miles). And there is the issue concerning coverage to the 200 nautical mile EEZ. NOAA has produced guidelines for the exploration, research, and salvage of RMS *Titanic* that are very similar to the Annex Rules of the UNESCO Convention. But a *Titanic* bill has not been enacted by the U.S. Congress (Dromgoole 2006).

Some of the major maritime powers appear unlikely to sign the UNESCO Convention on the Protection of the Underwater Cultural Heritage, even as the Convention takes effect. Concerns about sunken military craft and creeping coastal state jurisdiction have not abated. A bright note is the participation of some of those states in the negotiations and adherence to the Annex Rules as guidelines. Acts and regulations shape the management programs of local, state, and federal agencies. One means of protection that is working is the nomination of shipwrecks, and even dirigibles—for example, the 785-foot USS *Macon*, which carried biplanes when it crashed into the Pacific Ocean—to the National Register of Historic Places. Considering submerged maritime heritage as part of a landscape can lead to complementary listing of submerged sites with coastal structures (see Westerdahl in this volume). Maritime regions can incorporate these elements. A maritime regional designation has been proposed in the state of Washington based on Puget Sound (Washington State National Maritime Heritage Area 2009).

The U.S. Commission on Ocean Policy was created to provide advice on a national ocean policy. Its report *An Ocean Blueprint for the 21st Century* (2004) was a major statement on the way forward. It recommended the creation of a National Ocean Council that reports to the president, a nonfederal Council of Advisors on Ocean Policy, and new structures for effecting better governance, science, education, and decision making. The report stated that there were gaps in the management of federal waters—for example, on issues pertaining to cultural resources. An ecosystem-based management approach was called for, along with the creation of a coordinated offshore management regime that

> should incorporate a comprehensive policy on submerged cultural resources including shipwreck sites. The offshore regime will need to balance the historical importance of certain sites with their potential recreational and economic value, preserving the most significant sites for future generations while leaving room for the recreational use and salvage of others. The establishment of national policy will also help in promoting an international regime for the use and protection of submerged cultural resources. (U.S. Commission: 98-102).

The commission was criticized for not providing a clear policy on protection and advocacy of submerged cultural resources. While some of the recommendations of the commission have been implemented, those involving maritime heritage have not. However, a presidential executive order on ocean and Great Lakes stewardship issued in July 2010 called for the "respect and preservation of our nation's maritime heritage, including our social, cultural, recreational, and historical values." Implementation was assigned to a newly created National Ocean Council. Important in these policy initiatives is the recognition that ocean and Great Lakes management includes stewardship of underwater cultural heritage, and that heritage is the legacy of human activity in the marine environment. While the environment itself is a challenge to the archaeologist or manager, securing the protection of underwater cultural heritage remains as great a challenge (Executive Order 2010).

The expansion over the past 50 years of scholarly literature and popular media, primarily for television and the Internet, substantiate the increased public interest in maritime archaeology (Museum of Underwater Archaeology 2009). While much of that media addresses the activities of treasure hunters, advocacy for legal protections and regulations through governmental actions has spurred legislation across the globe. The media is a valuable tool. It generates an audience and can enlist subscribers to best practices if the message is effectively presented.

Contemporary maritime heritage issues and challenges are similar to those facing the environmental community. Making shipwrecks "speak" is a management challenge. Environmental advocates often allow nature to speak—for example, the polar bears, endangered monk seals, or great whales. Giving a voice to underwater heritage is telling the story of that site so that it gains a place in human experience and history (Zarzynski 2007). Few projects succeed without the development of significant partnerships. This "partnering" skill can be employed to build new relationships with those in environmental conservation, legislation, and other areas, who can extend a message or vision.

Effective management strategies are essential to producing positive outcomes. As we move forward with considerations of the place of underwater cultural heritage in marine spatial planning, in developing legislation at the national and international level, and in economic planning, it is fortunate that there are many creative and proven initiatives to consider.

REFERENCES

Ball, David, Jack Irion, and Christopher Horrell. 2007. Outreach beyond the beach: Management of historic shipwrecks on the outer continental shelf. In *Out of the blue: Public interpretation of maritime cultural resources*, ed. J. Jameson and D. Scott-Ireton, 171–181. New York: Springer.

Ballard, Robert, ed. 2008. *Archaeological oceanography*. Princeton, NJ: Princeton University Press.

Bass, George. 1966. *Underwater archaeology*. New York: Penguin.

Blake, Janet. 1999. Turkey. In *Legal protection of the underwater cultural heritage: National and international perspectives*, ed. S. Dromgoole, 160–180. The Hague: Kluwer Law International.

Blot, Jean-Yves. 1996. *Underwater archaeology: Exploring the world beneath the sea*. New York: Abrams.

Blumberg, Robert C. 2006. International protection of underwater cultural heritage. In *Recent developments in the Law of the Sea and China*, ed. Kuen-chen Fu, John Norton Moore, and Myron H. Nordquist, 491–501. Leiden: Martinus Nijhoff.

Bowens, Amanda, ed. 2009. International and national laws relating to archaeology under water. In *Underwater archaeology: The NAS guide to principles and practice*, 2nd ed., ed. Amanda Bowens, 45–52. Oxford: Blackwell.

Carducci, Guido. 2003. The UNESCO Convention 2001: A crucial compromise on salvage law and the law of finds. In *Finishing the uninterrupted voyage: Papers of the UNESCO Asia-Pacific Workshop on the 2001 Convention on the Protection of the Underwater Cultural Heritage*, 27–31. Hong Kong: UNESCO and Institute of Art and Law.

Claesson, Stefan. 2009. An Ecosystem-based framework for the governance and management of maritime cultural heritage in the USA. *Marine Policy* 33: 698–706.

Dobbs, Christopher. 2007. Visitors, funding and museums: Reflecting on the *Mary Rose* experience. In *Managing the marine cultural heritage*, ed. J. Satchell and P. Palma. 69–77. Bootham, UK: Council for British Archaeology.

Dromgoole, Sarah, ed. 1999. *Legal protection of the underwater cultural heritage: National and international perspectives*. The Hague: Kluwer Law International.

———. 2007. The legal framework for the management of the underwater cultural heritage beyond traditional territorial limits: Recent development and future prospects. In *Managing the marine cultural heritage*, ed. J. Satchell and P. Palma, 33–39. Bootham, UK: Council for British Archaeology.

———. 2010. Revisiting the relationship between marine scientific research and the underwater cultural heritage. *International Journal of Marine and Coastal Law* 25: 33–61.

Executive Order 13547: Stewardship of the ocean, our coasts, and the Great Lakes. July 17, 2010. President Barack Obama. Washington, DC.

Fenwick, Valerie, and Alison Gale. 1998. *Historic shipwrecks: Discovered, protected and investigated*. Stroud, UK: Tempus.

Flatman, Joe, ed. 2009. *Conserving marine cultural heritage*. Special issue of *Conservation and Management of Archaeological Sites*, 11 (1).

Giesecke, Anne. 1991. Historic shipwrecks resources and state law: A developmental perspective. PhD diss. Washington, DC: Catholic University.

Gould, Richard. 1983. *Shipwreck anthropology*. Albuquerque: University of New Mexico Press.

———. 2000. *Archaeology and the social history of ships*. Cambridge: Cambridge University Press.

Green, Jeremy. 2004. *Maritime archaeology: A technical handbook*. 2nd ed. London: Elsevier.

Grenier, Robert. 1994. The concept of the Louisburg Underwater Museum. *Northern Mariner* 4 (2): 3–10.

Hoagland, Porter. 1997. Managing the underwater cultural resources of the China Sea: A comparison of political policies in mainland China and Taiwan. *International Journal of Marine and Coastal Law* 12: 265–283.

Hutt, Sherry, M. Zander, and O. Varmer. 1999. *Heritage resources law: Protecting the archaeological and cultural environment*. New York: John Wiley and Sons.

Irion, Jack B. 2002. *Cultural resource management of shipwrecks on the Gulf of Mexico outer continental slope*. Presented at MIT, Cambridge, Mass. 26–28 April, 2002. U.S. Department of the Interior.

Jameson, John H., and Della Scott-Ireton, eds. 2007. *Out of the blue: Public interpretation of maritime cultural resources*. New York: Springer.

Kaoru, Yoshiaki, and Porter Hoagland. 1994. The value of historic shipwrecks: Conflicts and management. *Coastal Management* 22: 194–205.

Kelleher, Connie. 2007. Quantification of the underwater archaeological resource in Ireland as a means to its management and protection. In *Managing the marine cultural heritage*, ed. J. Satchell and P. Palma, 5–16. Bootham, UK: Council for British Archaeology.

King, Thomas. 2004. *Cultural resource laws and practice: An introductory guide*, 2nd ed. Walnut Creek, CA: Alta Mira Press.

La Roche, Daniel. 2003. A review of cultural resource management experiences in presenting Canada's submerged heritage. In *Submerged cultural resource management: Preserving and interpreting our sunken maritime heritage*, ed. James Spirek and Della Scott-Ireton, 29–42. New York: Kluwer Academic/Plenum.

Lenihan, Daniel. 2002. *Submerged: Adventures of America's most elite underwater archaeology team*. New York: Newmarket Press.

Leshikar-Denton, Margaret, and Della A. Scott-Ireton. 2007. A maritime heritage trail and shipwreck preserves for the Cayman Islands. In *Out of the blue: Public interpretation of* maritime cultural resources, ed. J. Jameson and D. Scott-Ireton, 64–84. New York: Springer.

Maarleveld, Thijs. 2007. Maritime management matters. In *Managing the marine cultural heritage*, ed. J. Satchell and P. Palma. Bootham, UK: Council for British Archaeology.

Mastone, V., and David Trubey. 2007. Not just another piece of a boat: Massachusetts' Shoreline Heritage Identification Partnerships Strategy. In *Out of the blue: Public interpretation of maritime cultural resources*, ed. J. Jameson and D. Scott-Ireton, 145–157. New York: Springer: 145–157.

Muckelroy, Keith. 1978. *Maritime archaeology*. Cambridge: Cambridge University Press.

———, ed. 1980. *Archaeology under water*. New York: McGraw-Hill.

Museum of Underwater Archaeology. 2010. Online at http://www.mua.uri.edu/mua. Accessed 6 April.

Nogueruela, Ivan. 2000. Managing the maritime heritage—Spain. *International Journal of Nautical Archaeology* 29 (2): 179–198.

Nutley, David. 2007. Look outwards, reach inwards, pass it on: The three tenures of underwater cultural heritage interpretation. In *Out of the blue: Public interpretation of maritime cultural resources*, ed. J. Jensen and D. Scott-Ireton, 33–51. New York: Springer.

Ocean Exploration and Research. 2010. Online at http://oceanexplorer.noaa.gov/okeanos/welcome.html. Accessed 6 April 2010.

Oxley, Ian. 2007. Making the submerged historic environment accessible—beyond the National Heritage Act (2002). In *Managing the marine cultural heritage*, ed. J. Satchell and P. Palma. Bootham, UK: Council for British Archaeology.

Prott, Lyndell, E. Planche, and R. Roca-Hachem, eds. 2000. *Background materials on the protection of the underwater cultural heritage*, vol. 2. Paris: UNESCO, Ministére de la Culture et Communication.

Rincon, Paul. 2010. *UK sets up Chagos Islands marine reserve*. Rev. 1 April 2010. Online at http://news.bbc.co.uk/2/hi/8599125.stm. Accessed 7 April 2010.

Rozwadowski, Helen. 2005. *Fathoming the ocean: The discovery and exploration of the deep sea*. Cambridge, MA: Belknap Press.

Runyan, Timothy. 1990. Shipwreck legislation and the protection of submerged artifacts. *Journal of International Law* 22 (1): 31–45.

———. 2010. Laws of Oléron. In *The Oxford dictionary of the Middle Ages*, ed. R. Bjork. Oxford: Oxford University Press.

Satchell, Julie, and Paola Palma. 2007. *Managing the marine cultural heritage*. Bootham, UK: Council for British Archaeology.

Scott-Ireton, Della. 2007. The value of public education and interpretation in submerged cultural resource management. In *Out of the blue: Public interpretation of maritime cultural resources*, ed. J. Jameson and D. Scott-Ireton, 19–32. New York: Springer.

Silver, Ewa. 2009. An analysis of management strategies for the protection of shipwrecks in the NOAA National Marine Sanctuaries. PhD diss., East Carolina University.

Smith, Hance D., and A. D. Couper. 2003. The management of the underwater cultural heritage. Journal of Cultural Heritage 4: 25–33.

Smith, Roger. 2000. *The maritime heritage of the Cayman Islands*. Gainesville: University Press of Florida.

———. 2007. Florida's Maritime Heritage Trail. In *Out of the blue: Public interpretation of maritime cultural resources*, ed. J. Jameson and D. Scott-Ireton, 52–63. New York: Springer.

Spirek, James D., and Della Scott-Ireton, eds. 2003. *Submerged cultural resource management: Preserving and interpreting our sunken maritime heritage*. New York: Kluwer Academic.

Staniforth, Mark. 2007. Australian approaches to defining and quantifying underwater
    cultural heritage: learning from our mistakes. In *Managing the marine cultural
    heritage*, ed. J. Satchell and P. Palma, 25–29. Bootham, UK: Council for British
    Archaeology.

Strati, Anastasia. 1995. *The protection of the underwater cultural heritage: An emerging
    objective of the contemporary law of the sea*. The Hague: Kluwer Law International.

Street, Thomas. 2006. Underwater cultural heritage policies of the United States Coastal
    Zone. *Coastal Management* 34: 467–480.

———. 2007. Submerged historical and archaeological resources: A study of the
    conflict and interface between United States cultural resource law and international
    government measures. PhD diss., University of Delaware.

Terrell, Bruce. 2007. *Fathoming our past: Historical contexts of the National Marine
    Sanctuaries*. 2nd ed. Silver Spring, MD: NOAA, Office of National Marine Sanctuaries.

U.S. Commission on Ocean Policy. 2004. *An ocean blueprint for the 21st century*. Final
    report. Washington, DC.

U.S. Department of Commerce, National Oceanic and Atmospheric Administration,
    National Marine Protected Areas Center. 2008. Framework for the National System of
    Marine Protected Areas of the United States of America. Silver Spring, MD.

U.S. Department of Commerce, National Oceanic and Atmospheric Administration, Office
    of National Marine Sanctuaries. 2007. Florida Keys National Marine Sanctuary
    Management Plan. 3 vols. Key West: Florida Keys National Marine Sanctuary.

———. 2009a. Thunder Bay National Marine Sanctuary Management Plan. Alpena:
    Thunder Bay National Marine Sanctuary.

———. 2009b. Papahānaumokuākea Marine National Monument Management Plan.
    Honolulu: Papahānaumokuākea Marine National Monument.

Varmer, Ole. 1999. The case against the "salvage" of the cultural heritage. *Journal of
    Maritime Law and Commerce* 30: 279–293.

Varmer, Ole, and Caroline M. Blanco. 1999. United States of America. In *Legal protection of
    the underwater cultural heritage: National and international perspectives*, ed. S.
    Dromgoole, 205–221. The Hague: Kluwer Law International.

Washington State National Maritime Heritage Area. 2009. Feasibility study prepared
    by Parametrix and Berk and Associates for the Washington State Department of
    Archaeology and Historic Preservation.

Workman, Stephen M. 2008. Preservation, ownership and access: key issues for new U.S.
    underwater cultural heritage legislation beyond state waters. PhD diss., East Carolina
    University.

Zander, Caroline, and Ole Varmer. 1996. Contested waters: Closing the gaps in domestic
    and international law; Achieving comprehensive protection of submerged cultural
    resources. *NPS Common Ground On Line* 1 (3/4).

Zarzynski, Joseph. 2007. Lake George, New York: Making shipwrecks speak. In *Out of the
    blue: Public interpretation of maritime cultural resources*, ed. J. Jameson and D.
    Scott-Ireton, 112–126. New York: Springer.

Zhao, H. 1992. Recent developments in the legal protection of historic shipwrecks in China.
    Ocean Development and International Law 23: 305–333.

....

CHAPTER 42

THE GROWTH OF MARITIME ARCHAEOLOGY IN MEXICO: A CASE STUDY

....

PILAR LUNA ERREGUERENA

INTRODUCTION

....

THE Sea of Cortes on the Pacific coast, the Gulf of Mexico on the east, and the Caribbean on the southeastern tip of the country: Mexico has access to the two largest oceans in the world, with 11,592 km (7,203 miles) of coast and oversight extending seaward up to 200 nautical miles (the Exclusive Economic Zone) in which diverse kinds of jurisdiction regimes apply. Within the country, there are 29,000 km² (11,196 square miles) of rivers, lakes, lagoons, springs, cenotes (sink-holes), and inundated caves. Mexico's underwater cultural heritage represents a vast and splendid universe varying from prehistoric to modern remains. However, one of its main cultural riches is contained in its coastal and open-sea waters, where hundreds of ships have wrecked since the sixteenth century.

In February 1980, the Instituto Nacional de Antropología e Historia (National Institute of Anthropology and History, INAH) created its Underwater Archaeology Department. Most of the underwater archaeological work undertaken since then has been in marine waters, especially the Gulf of Mexico. Since the beginning, it was decided to use the term "underwater archaeology" instead of "maritime" or "nautical archaeology" in order to encompass all possibilities presented by the submerged cultural heritage that can be found in continental and marine waters. Also, since the beginning, all projects have had a multidisciplinary and multi-institutional approach, including international participation.

PRE-COLUMBIAN NAVIGATION

The Maya group centered in the northeast part of the Yucatán Peninsula created a complex trade system that extended throughout much of the region and is often mentioned in codices and colonial manuscripts. Navigation was a skill possessed by the early Mayans of the late Pre-Classic period (300 BCE to 300 CE), and reached its pinnacle by the Post-Classic period (900–1521 CE) due to the influence of the Putun, a Maya Chontal group referred to by Eric Thompson as "the Phoenicians of the New World" (Andrews 1998: 17; Romero 1998: 8). Trade routes extended along a coastline that is more than 600 miles long; navigation was vital not only for communication but also as a way to exchange goods, both for daily use and for prestige. This exchange played a crucial role in the historic development of all the regional groups of the time (Martos 2002: 29).

Between 1984 and 1989, INAH's Underwater Archaeology Department conducted an interesting project along this part of the Yucatán coast. Archaeologists and divers—supported by INAH, a grant from the National Geographic Society, and two North American captains—located and recorded a series of Mayan structures along the coast that might have served as navigational aids before the Spanish arrival. The structures have different sizes and shapes—mainly square and rectangular, from around 2 to 12 m high—but all of them have at least a window or a door facing the sea.

An experiment was conducted in 1985, placing two gaslights at the upper part of El Castillo, the main structure at the archaeological site of the city of Tulum. While two archaeologists remained inside the building controlling the gas lamps, others were in a ship navigating along a south–north orientation, beyond the reef facing Tulum. It was confirmed that when the two lights were visible through the two small windows in the upper part of El Castillo, it was the moment when the ship had to make a turn and navigate toward the beach, passing perfectly through the natural cut of the reef, meaning that the two upper windows of the structure worked as a range light system (Creamer 1985: 85).

The same was observed with other Mayan structures that were utilized to signal, in a very accurate way, the entrance through a reef or the path to safe waters like *caletas* (small inlets). In other cases, the structures served as a warning against a dangerous site (see Westerdahl in this volume for further discussion of seamarks). It was interesting to notice that many of the modern lighthouses along the coast were built very near the ancient pre-Columbian structures; in most cases, cenotes or sinkholes were discovered in the vicinity.

In 2009 we repeated the experiment at Tulum and observed that the two windows of the lower part of El Castillo, which does not have a roof, also work as a range light system with the sunlight.

EUROPEAN NAVIGATION

Mexican waters played an important role during the European exploration, discovery, conquest, and colonization periods. Ships were the only communication between Europe and America. Many of them were lost in these waters, not only due to climatic conditions but also to pirate and corsair attacks, limited cartography, inadequate instruments, damaged ships, and inexperienced pilots.

Fleets were created in 1564 to protect the Spanish Crown's goods as they were transported through the ocean to and from the New World colonies. Fleets were not only a means of transport and communication; they were also, as Trejo Rivera (2003: 21–22) writes, "a sort of continuation of the Spanish empire, a small floating republic, ruled by laws and hierarchies, where all the daily aspects of a society were reproduced on board." The Spanish regularly sent two such fleets: the New Spain Fleet, bound for Veracruz, and the Tierra Firme Fleet, which continued its route to Central and South America.

For the Spanish, the port of Veracruz was the entrance to a new and fantastic reality of pyramids, indigenous peoples, and strange plants and concepts. The Fortress of San Juan de Ulúa in Veracruz became a symbol as the main gateway to America, where ships of different nationalities anchored, during different centuries, to the Wall of Rings (Muro de las Argollas), which still exists. Together with Veracruz, Campeche was crucial to the export of Mexican wealth and materials. Located on the Gulf of Mexico, the city of Campeche is in one of the five Mexican states that form the Mayan world, all located in the southeastern part of the country; the other four are Tabasco, Yucatán, Quintana Roo, and Chiapas. The site's original name, Ah Kin'Pech, or Can Pech, meant "place of serpents and *garrapatas* (chiggers)," and it is among the areas where pre-Columbian navigation has been recorded in codices, ceramics, and architectonic elements, and in a mural painting found inside El Castillo, the main pyramid of Chichén-Itzá. On 22 March 1517, the crew of three Spanish ships on an exploration journey first discovered the Mayan town. The Spanish captain Francisco de Montejo, "El Adelantado," founded the city in 1531, and in 1540 his son, Francisco de Montejo, "El Mozo," named it Villa de San Francisco de Campeche (Luna Erreguerena 1996: 61).

It was through Campeche that all the trade to and from the Yucatán took place, which made it both the best-guarded city in New Spain and the most frequent target of pirates and corsairs. Thus, the Sound of Campeche is one of the places with more remains of maritime accidents, shipwrecks, and isolated materials (Luna Erreguerena 1996: 61). In fact, the last link that led to the creation of the Department of Underwater

Archaeology within INAH was the 1979 discovery of a sixteenth-century bronze cannon in this area by two sport divers from the United States.

On the other side of the newly discovered territory, on the Pacific Ocean, there was another important route from Acapulco to Manila, in the Philippines, navigating through the Kuroshivo current, crossing the Pacific Ocean, touching what is known today as Monterey, California, and then along the Baja California peninsula until reaching the Saint Lucia Bay, in Acapulco (Mejía 2007).

EARLY RECOVERIES IN MEXICAN WATERS

As it happened all around the globe, for many years nobody thought that these submerged traces of people's efforts to know their own universe, to discover new lands, and to communicate among themselves had survived and were important. Human consciousness was far from considering these vestiges a significant part of our own history. However, stories, legends, and traditions passed from generation to generation made mention of valuable offerings to aquatic deities, mainly in the cenotes of the Yucatán Peninsula, and recounted ships sunk while carrying fantastic treasures from the New World to Europe. Local people proudly talked about these events, and others took advantage of this information.

Diego de Landa, one of the first Franciscan friars to arrive in the sixteenth century, wrote about the Sacred Cenote of Chichén-Itzá in Yucatán: "they throw in it many . . . things, like precious gems and valuable things for them. And that if this country had gold, most of it is inside this well" (Folan 1968: 21). The first recoveries from this site date to 1904, when Edward H. Thompson, the first United States consul in Yucatán, used a dredge to recover thousands of pieces, most of which are at the Peabody Museum in Massachusetts; a second extraction took place in 1910–1911. Many of the jade and gold objects that were extracted were punctured or broken, since the Mayans believed that these objects were alive and needed to be "killed" before offering them to Chac, deity of the rain and water (Bush 1972). According to Carrillo Gil (1959: 10–11), thanks to Thompson's recoveries, the Peabody Museum contains one of the richest collections of Mayan exquisite art in the world.

In the 1960s, INAH participated in two field seasons at the Chichén-Itzá cenote, but archaeologists did not dive at that time. As the divers hired to conduct the operation were using a large airlift that damaged several of artifacts, INAH decided to stop the operations. Again, thousands of objects were recovered; some of them are exhibited at the National Museum of Anthropology in Mexico City. The study of human remains recovered from this cenote allowed Dr. Román Piña Chan to conclude that Mayan sacrifices included not only maidens but also men and children (Piña Chan 1970).

Regarding recoveries at sea, in 1957, Robert Marx, who at that time was a diving instructor for tourists in Cozumel, discovered a shipwreck off Punta Matancero, in the state of Quintana Roo. Together with reporter Clay Blair and photographer Walter Bennet, both from the *Saturday Evening Post*, he recovered various objects—including a bottle and some gems that were taken for diamonds. These artifacts were inspected by Mendel Peterson, a historian and curator at the Smithsonian Institution, with experience in examining shipwrecks in the Caribbean. According to Peterson, the bottle had been made in England between 1720 and 1740, and the "diamonds" were nothing but white paste. Marx continued his recovery work, but was stopped by Mexican police after rumors that he was stealing huge amounts of gold (Throckmorton 1969).

Later on, the Club de Exploraciones y Deportes Acuáticos de México (Mexico's Aquatic and Sport Exploration Club, CEDAM) was authorized by the Mexican government to do the recovery; Blair and Marx were allowed to participate. Despite the hard concretion that covered all artifacts, they extracted several cannons, one anchor discovered originally by Marx and Blair, and thousands of diverse objects like spoons, buttons, buckles, religious medals and crucifixes, mosque ammunitions, wine bottles (four of which still contained wine), and a clock with the inscription "Rn. Webster Exchange Alley London"; inside the clock there were two fragments of an eighteenth-century British newspaper (Throckmorton 1969). All of these items were transferred to Cozumel and were then, taken to the CEDAM's museum located first in Akumal, then in Cancun, afterward in Xel-Ha, and currently in Puerto Aventura, in Quintana Roo. However, since no conservation treatment was ever applied, most of this material, especially metals and wood, are quite deteriorated, or completely destroyed. Many of the pieces recovered are lost, and no one knows their final disposition.

Mexican Underwater Archaeology—Stage 1

From 1980 to 1990, INAH's Underwater Archaeology Department undertook several projects, all of them with the invaluable support and guidance of North American colleagues, especially from the Institute of Nautical Archaeology (INA) at Texas A&M University and Ships of Discovery, both based in Texas. Mexican institutions and individuals were also of great help, mainly regarding logistics. Besides the project described above, on Mayan navigation on the eastern coast of Quintana Roo, three other main projects took place during those years: the ones at Cayo Nuevo Reef, Media Luna Spring, and the Bahía de Mujeres wreck.

Cayo Nuevo Reef, Gulf of Mexico

In 1979, two North American sport divers discovered a bronze cannon dated to 1552 CE. Through INA, they contacted INAH in Mexico. In three field seasons—the last one in 1983—two shipwrecks were located; the first one dates from the sixteenth century and is probably Spanish, and a second one dates from the eighteenth century and is believed to be of British or Scottish origin. From the sixteenth-century site, three pieces were recovered: The bronze cannon, one iron cannon, and an iron anchor almost 5 m (15 ft) long. The bronze cannon is the oldest known artillery piece of this type that has been recovered from an underwater context in the Americas. Currently, the bronze cannon and the anchor are exhibited in the city of Campeche (Figure 42.1). The eighteenth-century site was revisited in 2009, and more cannons and other artifacts were found.

Media Luna Spring, San Luis Potosí, Central Mexico

In 1981 and 1982, two INAH field seasons were undertaken in the Media Luna Spring, which was a place of worship in pre-Columbian times between the years 600 and 900 CE. Unfortunately, due to its ideal diving conditions, it is also one of the most looted sites in the country. Even so, archaeologists found bones of Pleistocene fauna, as well as ceramic and lithic artifacts, and two burials belonging to infants. A correlation between 17 land sites near the spring and underwater offerings was made. Findings of the same kind of ceramics, especially figurines, confirmed the hypothesis that the spring had been used as an offering site by the pre-Columbian groups that lived nearby. Some of the recovered material is exhibited at the National Museum of Anthropology.

Figure 42.1 This sixteenth-century bronze cannon was recovered in 1980 in the Gulf of Mexico and is exhibited at the Museum of San Jose El Alto in Campeche City. Reproduced with the kind permission of INAH/SAS.

Bahía de Mujeres Wreck, Chitales Reef, Quintana Roo

According to CEDAM, the sixteenth-century wreck at Bahía de Mujeres was *La Nicolasa*, one of Spanish conqueror Francisco de Montejo's ships. In 1990, a field season was organized with the participation of archaeologists from INAH and Ships of Discovery, and a group of biologists from the Instituto de Ciencias del Mar y Limnología (Institute of Sea Sciences and Limnology) from the Universidad Nacional Autónoma de México (National Autonomous University of Mexico, UNAM). Before archaeologists began the excavation of several sample pits, biologists recorded and moved the living corals that inhabited the site, and when the archaeological work was finished they replanted them and monitored the site during one year, until the corals had recovered and there were no traces of the excavations. The archival research and the archaeological material located confirmed that this site, while a sixteenth-century shipwreck, was not *La Nicolasa*.

In this stage, Mexican underwater archaeologists learned on the go while carrying out these first projects; however, most of them went back to terrestrial archaeology. The outlook was uncertain. In 1994, the first master's-level course in underwater archaeology took place in Mexico City with a field season between Isla Mujeres and Isla Contoy, Quintana Roo, and thus a renewal cycle began for Mexican underwater archaeology.

MEXICAN UNDERWATER ARCHAEOLOGY—STAGE 2

During six months 30 professors from Mexico, Canada, and the United States shared their knowledge and their experience with 20 archaeology and restoration undergraduate students. In 1995, some months after the course was completed, INAH's Underwater Archaeology Department was promoted to a vice-directorate, and remains so to this day. Also in 1995, the Fideicomiso para el Rescate de Pecios (Trust for the Recovery of Shipwrecks) and INAH's Council of Archaeology approved the proposal I presented in order to undertake an important investigation and search for the remains of *Nuestra Señora del Juncal*, one of the two flagships of the New Spain Fleet of 1630. While the fleet successfully navigated to the New World in that year, several of its ships were lost in an October 1631 storm while crossing the Gulf of Mexico to return to Spain. The lost cargo was among the most important of its day.

Immediately, intense archival research began in several cities of Mexico and Spain, which continued on for several years, and later expanded to include Havana, Cuba. The amount of information gathered convinced us to widen the range of our project and to study the whole fleet. The possibility of locating these shipwrecks was a golden opportunity for Mexican underwater archaeology and for the students who had just graduated from the 1994 course. *Nuestra Señora del Juncal* remained the major objective. After the transcription and analysis of the few manuscripts that refer to the accident, among the thousand of documents found, we were able to determine specific areas in the Sound of Campeche to begin our search.

The first field season took place in 1997. In only 16 days, through towing and snorkeling, we located 24 sites with cultural vestiges dating from the sixteenth to the twentieth centuries near the reefs in shallow waters. None of the findings belonged to the fleet under study, but the discoveries led to the creation of a second and parallel project, the Inventory and Diagnosis of Submerged Cultural Resources in the Gulf of Mexico. The purpose of the latter was to document and evaluate cultural heritage resources in these waters in order to adequately protect and investigate them.

AN IMPORTANT STEP

In 1996 INAH began working with archaeologists from the Submerged Cultural Resources Unit (now Submerged Resources Center) of the United States' National Park Service in order to design a remote-sensing system similar to their ADAP (Acquisition Data for the Archaeological Platform). Thanks to their support and guidance, the ESPADAS (Equipos y Sistemas para la Plataforma de Adquisición de Datos Arqueológicos Sumergidos / Equipments and Systems for the Platform of Underwater Archaeological Data Recovery) was created especially to operate in waters with the characteristics of the Gulf of Mexico. It includes a cesium magnetometer, a digital side-scan sonar, an echo sounder, a navigational system, and a GPS unit. Mexican archaeologists have received special training to handle these devices.

This technology was an important step that increased the possibilities of searching in deeper waters for the 1630–1631 New Spain Fleet's remains. Results were evident: during the 1998 field season, 82 anomalies were registered, all of which were verified through diving. A large number, 63 of them, contained cultural vestiges dating from the sixteenth to twentieth centuries. Today, 179 sites with cultural vestiges have been integrated in the Inventory and Diagnosis of Submerged Cultural Resources in the Gulf of Mexico.

Two of the main sites found during these surveys are a shipwreck dating from the sixteenth century, named Pilar, and another dating from the eighteenth century, named Don Pancho after the local fisherman who guided us there. The Pilar site is particularly important not only because it is one of the few shipwrecks dating to the sixteenth century found in Mexican waters, but also because it appears not to have been disturbed by treasure hunters or sport divers (Figure 42.2) (Luna Erreguerena 1999: 111). Therefore, it has the potential to show researchers more about daily life on

Figure 42.2 Sixteenth-century anchor found at the Pilar site, in the Gulf of Mexico, in 1998. Reproduced with the kind permission of INAH/SAS.

board in that particular century and how an accident like this could occur and what consequences it could have had.

As for Don Pancho, the site was discovered through a towing prospection survey in 1997 in the Sound of Campeche. Three anchors, two cannons, and assorted lead elements were recorded in situ; materials include civil-pattern British artillery from the second half of the eighteenth century. In 1998, the site was relocated by INAH using the ESPADAS remote-sensing system (Herrera 2001: 240, 253).

The Pilar and Don Pancho shipwrecks served as thesis topics for two archaeologists who were not present during their location. This is proof of the importance of recording one's actions in the field in the most accurate way possible, and of working as a team, so that when the time comes, future generations of underwater archaeologists may continue past analyses based on original field records.

One of the main challenges encountered by INAH has been to find proper vessels for research campaigns. This was the reason why the 1999 Sound of Campeche field survey did not take place. Instead, the team stayed in Veracruz, where further tests of the ESPADAS system were conducted using a ship lent to us by the Communications and Transport Ministry. Since the ship did not have space for all researchers, a base camp was established in a local hotel near the coast.

After testing the ESPADAS, we conducted some survey work through which the first side-scan digital image of the warship USS *Somers* was obtained. This ship sunk during the 1846 War of Intervention, known in the United States as the Mexican-American War. Also, while surveying in shallow waters around some of the islands and reefs, several shipwrecks were detected, mainly from recent times, and integrated into the inventory.

Due to the lack of financial resources and a proper ship, there were no field seasons between 1999 and 2002. It was not until 2003 that INAH could reinitiate its search for the New Spain Fleet remains in the Sound of Campeche. From 2003 to 2006, we worked aboard a rented vessel that belongs to the Instituto Tecnológico del Mar de Campeche (Campeche Technological Sea Institute, ITMAR). During the 2007 field season, we only worked in coastal waters using small boats and direct diving. In 2008 the Waitt Institute for Discovery (WID), based in La Jolla, California, supported us in a most generous way, allowing INAH's Underwater Archaeology Vice-Directorate to conduct surveys with the assistance of Azulmar Research LLC using WID's ship, *Plan B*. As in other field seasons, meteorological factors prohibited us from profiting from the entire time reserved for survey in the Gulf of Mexico. Nevertheless, we were able to cover a good area and record some anomalies that need to be verified in the near future.

In part, the continuation of fieldwork for the New Spain Fleet and Inventory projects was possible through the creation of five new permanent programs by INAH, introduced in the following section.

PERMANENT PROGRAMS

Underwater archaeological work has never been as intense at INAH as in the last nine years, starting with the new millennium. We focused our efforts in five areas: attention to reports on archaeological findings and their legal protection; training (Figure 42.3); information dissemination; conservation; and national and international collaboration. A new project designed to include all of these aspects was created in 2003: the Special Programs of the Underwater Archaeology Vice-Directorate. These programs helped form a better vision of what work was being done, what the real needs were, and how to optimize human and material resources.

The project operates in several parts of the country. We have verified reports of archaeological findings in at least six states: Baja California, Campeche, Quintana Roo, San Luis Potosí, Veracruz, and Yucatán. However, Campeche is the state in which this project has been applied most systematically and shows the most tangible results.

Figure 42.3 Training session measuring a bronze cannon in Campeche City,
Mexico. Reproduced with the kind permission of INAH/SAS.

An archaeologist was based in Campeche City and put in charge of all issues
regarding regional underwater cultural heritage, including continuous communication with local authorities and natives, especially fishermen. Some of these fishermen are important collaborators, helping researchers to locate cultural remains,
volunteering as guardians of sites along the coast, and helping us to recover artifacts
extracted in the past.

Some field seasons are planned to serve three projects at the same time: the
New Spain Fleet, the Inventory, and Special Programs. While one group of archaeologists works in coastal waters with fishermen and their boats locating and verifying the existence of reported shipwrecks or isolated elements, a second group
looks for remains of the New Spain Fleet in the Sound of Campeche on board a
larger ship carrying the ESPADAS remote-sensing system (Figure 42.4).

Both groups—the one surveying in coastal waters and the one in offshore
waters—work together in areas such as information dissemination, including lectures,
press interviews, and exhibitions. The whole team—together with students from the
Escuela Nacional de Antropología e Historia (National School of Anthropology and
History, ENAH), diving instructors, and fishermen—attend the training courses
given each year by one or two colleagues from the United States, Canada, Spain, or
the Cayman Islands. When possible, we have invited undergraduate students from

Figure 42.4 Shipwreck located with the assistance of local fishermen in the Sound
of Campeche. Reproduced with the kind permission of INAH/SAS.

the official cultural agencies of Argentina, Colombia, Honduras, and Uruguay to
participate in our field seasons. Also, researchers from the vice-directorate teach a
course every other semester, in order to share what we have learned and also to
identify those students interested in underwater archaeology and eventually invite
them to our field seasons or training sessions.

In coastal waters, the majority of recorded shipwrecks are from the nineteenth
and twentieth centuries, especially those of shrimp boats, which represent one of
the main fishing activities in the area (Figure 42.5). Among the most significant
discoveries is a shipwreck known by the local community as "El Pesquero." This
wreck is 20 km (12.5 miles) off the coast of Champotón, a district near the Campeche
City, at a depth of 8 m (25 ft). Archival research and sporadic work at the site from
2004 to 2006, and more formal work in 2007, indicate that this is probably a British
ship dating from the eighteenth century. It was carrying at least six cannon of three
different calibers; four of them were lying on the bottom and two on top of the
mound, very concreted. Given that there are no reefs nearby, the ship probably sank
because of a storm or a fire, or as a consequence of its natural deterioration. Materials retrieved include three cannon shots, four types of ballast, a grinding stone,
brass nails, wood samples, tubular metallic elements, and fragments of lead that
could belong to the hull's sheathing. Metal elements are currently under treatment
at the INAH Center in Campeche and being analyzed at the Centro de Investigación

Figure 42.5 A wooden hull, corresponding to a modern shipwreck in coastal waters of Ciudad del Carmen, Campeche. Reproduced with the kind permission of INAH/SAS.

de Corrosión del Golfo de México (Research Center on Corrosion of the Gulf of Mexico), associated with the Universidad Autónoma de Campeche (State University of Campeche, UAC). Evidence that led to the hypothesis about the date and national origin of the shipwreck includes X-ray diffraction and infrared spectroscopy applied to the ballast that revealed the stones to be from a foreign source; manufacturers' seal and mold lines still visible on some of the cannon balls; and the fact that, according to historical data, it was after 1783 that brass nails started to be used to affix coverings to the hull (Barba Meinecke 2008).

There are plans to create tourist underwater trails along the coast of Campeche, based on the model used in Florida and in the Cayman Islands, along with the first Mexican Maritime Museum. Dissemination of information to the public has always been a permanent program of INAH's Underwater Archaeology Vice-Directorate. Exhibits, lectures, articles, videos, and presentations have been shown not only in Mexico but also in other countries, such as the United States (including Puerto Rico), Canada, Spain, Portugal, Ireland, and several Latin American cities. We have also produced a Web site (www.subacuatica.inah.gob.mx). Our efforts have included presentations on the 2001 UNESCO Convention on the Protection of the Underwater Cultural Heritage. Four books have been published: *Memorias del Congreso Científico de Arqueología Subacuática ICOMOS* (2001), *La Flota de la Nueva*

España 1630–1631: Vicisitudes y naufragios (2003), *Underwater and Maritime Archaeology in Latin America and the Caribbean* (2008), and *Aguas celestiales: El Nevado de Toluca* (2009). Another two books—*Arqueología Marítima en Mexico: Estudios interdisciplinarios en torno al patrimonio cultural sumergido*, and one for children, *En el fondo del mar no sólo hay peces*—will be published in 2010 in Mexico, both by INAH.

Regarding conservation, besides those objects lying on the sea bottom considered key elements for diagnosis, we have only recovered artifacts at risk of being looted or destroyed. We now work closely with INAH's laboratories in Mexico City and UAC's Research Center on Corrosion of the Gulf of Mexico in Campeche. A 2003 collaboration agreement with this center allows us to appropriately treat artifacts recovered in nearby waters.

Earlier on, however, when the sixteenth-century bronze cannon was recovered in 1980 from the aforementioned site located by the two sport divers in the Cayo Nuevo Reef, very little was known in Mexico about how to treat materials recovered from an aquatic environment. Additionally, a second cannon and an anchor, both of iron, were recovered from the same site. The three pieces were taken to INAH's Museum in Mérida, Yucatán, where curators treated them to the best of their abilities, using electrolysis for the iron cannon, which unfortunately had negative effects and damaged the piece. The cleansing used in the bronze cannon and the anchor went well, and both pieces are now exhibited in Campeche City.

In 1999, during an archaeological survey in Veracruz, near a site known as "La Lavandera," INAH discovered several glass bottles dating from the eighteenth, nineteenth, and twentieth centuries, as well as a considerable number of glass fragments dating from the seventeenth century to the present. Most of the bottles were of blown glass. It is known that European glassblowers arrived in New Spain in 1535 and that the first oven to cook glass was built in the city of Puebla in 1542. We recovered some of the bottles, together with diagnostic fragments such as bottoms, mouths, and necks. They were taken to INAH's Escuela Nacional de Conservación, Restauración y Museografía (National School of Conservation, Restoration, and Museography), where they received adequate treatments. Analysis showed that bottles made of dark glass are of British origin and held wine; those with a square shape are from the Netherlands and held gin; and some with amphora necks are of Spanish origin. Other bottles used to contain vinegar and medicines. All recovered bottles are now kept at INAH's Underwater Archaeology Vice-Directorate (Luna Erreguerena 2000: 39).

Another important recovery was that of 40 lead ingots from the site known as Don Pancho in 1998. One year earlier, during the first field season of the New Spain Fleet project, a survey near Triángulos Keys, in the Sound of Campeche, revealed 20 ingots lying on the sea bottom. We only recovered one to conduct laboratory analysis. But when we returned to the site the following year, there were visible traces of a recent looting; at least one ingot was missing. Based on this discovery, it was decided to recover the rest. Besides the visible ingots, others were buried in the sand, resulting in a total of 40 ingots recovered; all were recorded in situ (Figure 42.6).

Figure 42.6 Part of a collection of 40 lead ingots recovered from an eighteenth-century shipwreck in Campeche Bank. Reproduced with the kind permission of INAH/SAS.

The site also contained anchors, artillery pieces, navigation instruments, ballast stones, and parts of a ship. Through preliminary analysis, it was deduced that the site could possibly correspond to the remains of a British ship wrecked in the second half of the eighteenth century (Luna Erreguerena 1998: 111). Part of the ingot collection is exhibited at the Museum of the City of Campeche.

More recently, the vice-directorate has turned its attention to Baja California. After establishing the New Spain Viceroyalty, Spain made several expeditions searching for the ideal route to reach the Spice Islands, now the Philippines. Once they found it, galleons began to travel from Manila to Acapulco loaded with products such as damask, wax, personal fans, furniture, porcelain, silk, cotton, linen, and exotic spices, including cinnamon, nutmeg, ginger, clove, and pepper. Many of the religious images kept in Mexican churches—like the Christ in ivory that can be seen in Mexico City's cathedral—were brought in these ships (Mejía 2007).

As reports of tourists finding remains of porcelain on one of the beaches in Ensenada increased, archaeologists Edward Von der Porten and Jack Hunter, sponsored by the University of Santa Clara, in California, and together with the INAH Center in Baja California, began the Manila Galleon Archaeological Project in 1999. This multidisciplinary project has involved archaeologists, geophysics experts, historians, geologists, and art curators. INAH's Underwater Archaeology Vice-Directorate has codirected the project in four of its five field seasons between 1999 and 2007.

Through surveying with metal detectors, remote-sensing systems, and GPS, archaeologists have found a considerable number of Chinese porcelain fragments, five pieces of terra-cotta, three silver coins, and several blocks of beeswax, among other things. According to the characteristics of these elements and the first analyses, all materials date from the sixteenth century and were probably part of the cargo of one of the Manila galleons (Mejía 2007).

Elsewhere, we have looked inland. The Nevado de Toluca Volcano is located near Mexico City and has two lagoons—known as the Sun and the Moon—in its crater at almost 4,000 m (more than 13,000 feet) of altitude. It served as an offering site for several pre-Columbian groups who inhabited the surrounding lake beginning in the late Post-Classic period (1250–1521 CE). The first combined field season, which included both land and underwater components, took place in May 2007 thanks to the financial support of Mr. Richard Siegel and an additional grant from the Goldsbury Foundation, both received through archaeologist Johan Reinhard, National Geographic Explorer-in-Residence (Junco 2007, 2009).

Among the findings are wooden objects shaped like serpents; cones and spheres of a type of incense known as *copal*, prominent since pre-Hispanic times and still in use today; cactus plants used for self-penitence; and fragments of semiprecious stones, as well as ceramic, lithic, and colonial materials (Junco 2007, 2009).

In order to successfully carry out a number of these projects, the vice-directorate has always fostered close relations and enjoys the support of local authorities and institutions, as well as that of international colleagues, mainly from the United States and Canada. We are convinced that the best way to do underwater archaeology is through the integration of a multidisciplinary team, with the support of academic institutions, authorities, and other sectors of the community where a project is taking place, according to the circumstances of each case. The creation of an international network of support has been vital for the development of Mexican underwater archaeology.

First Experiences with Underwater Cultural Heritage Management

Underwater cultural management has been a significant issue in many forums since the 1990s. In Mexico, effective management of submerged heritage sites has proved difficult. However, in the last six years, we have had the opportunity to participate in two programs regarding underwater cultural heritage management in protected areas: one in Veracruz, in the Gulf of Mexico, and another in the Mexican Caribbean.

As mentioned before, the port of Veracruz played a very important role during colonial times. Its waters contain an immense natural and cultural richness, among which is the National Park of the Reef System, formed of 23 reefs. In 2002, the Ministry of Natural Resources and Environment together with the State University of Veracruz began to form a park management program; INAH was invited to provide proper guidelines regarding activities pertaining to underwater cultural heritage, based on national laws and regulations and meeting international legal instruments as the ICUCH International Charter on the Protection and Management of Underwater Cultural Heritage and the UNESCO 2001 Convention on the Protection of the Underwater Cultural Heritage.

One of the places in Mexico with an impressive ecological diversity is Chinchorro Bank, on the south coast of Quintana Roo. It is part of the Mesoamerican reef, which stretches for almost 1000 km (621 miles) and is considered the second largest barrier reef in the world, after the Great Barrier Reef located in Australia. In 1996, it was declared a Biosphere Reserve; some years later, in 2003, it was nominated as a Ramsar site for the protection of migratory birds and wetlands. In 2004, INAH's Division for World Heritage included this place as both a natural and cultural site in the National Indicative List that was presented to the Mexican Commission before UNESCO in order to start the process to declare the Biosphere Reserve of Chinchorro Bank as a mixed (natural and cultural) world heritage site (Luna Erreguerena and Carrillo Márquez 2005).

To enrich the documentation to be presented before UNESCO by INAH and CONANP, the Underwater Archaeology Vice-Directorate was asked to make an inventory of sites, shipwrecks, and isolated elements located in this area. In 2006, 2007, and 2008, we undertook four field seasons in Chinchorro, locating and recording 66 sites containing submerged cultural remains dating from the sixteenth to the twenty-first centuries (Figure 42.7).

THE PROTECTION OF MEXICAN UNDERWATER CULTURAL HERITAGE

Possibly the first time that Mexican authorities brought a legal action against a looter of underwater archaeological artifacts was in 1926, when former U.S. consul Edward H. Thompson was prosecuted for dredging thousands of pre-Columbian artifacts from the Sacred Cenote of Chichén-Itzá in Yucatán in 1904 and 1910 and taking them to his country. Thompson died in 1935, but a new case was made against Thompson's successors. However, it did not progress until 1944—40 years after the first looting at the cenote—when the case was closed and Thompson family was absolved (Dávalos Hurtado 1965: 34).

Interesting information appears in a book written by Clay Blair, the *Saturday Evening Post* reporter who in 1957 had extracted some pieces with Robert Marx from a shipwreck in Quintana Roo known as *El Matancero*. During the eight pages

Figure 42.7 Archaeologists and local divers measuring an anchor in the Mexican
Caribbean. Reproduced with the kind permission of INAH/SAS.

where Blair discusses his team's attempts to obtain legal permission to excavate the
wreck, he says that Mexico did not have any law that pertained to underwater exploration or underwater archaeology. He adds that very soon a law was approved specifying that all findings should be rendered to the Mexican government and that all
sunken galleons were under the authority of the Antiquities Service (Throckmorton
1969: 50).

Since then, Mexico has gained a better awareness regarding the importance of
preserving its submerged cultural heritage and has signed and ratified diverse international treaties. Even if we do not have a specific law to protect our underwater
cultural heritage, the Ley Federal sobre Monumentos y Zonas Arqueológicos,
Artísticos e Históricos (Federal Law on Archaeological, Artistic, and Historical
Monuments and Zones) (INAH 1972) and the Disposiciones Reglamentarias para la
Investigación Arqueológica en México (Regulations for Archaeological Research in
Mexico) (INAH 1977) have served to protect our heritage, specifying the proper
academic and administrative steps to be fulfilled in order to get an authorization to

perform archaeological work in the country. These laws have also served to control and stop treasure hunters.

The national body in charge of evaluating and authorizing or rejecting any project to be undertaken in Mexican territory is INAH's Council of Archaeology, which constantly receives applications from treasure-hunting groups. One of the most requested permissions has been to exploit *Nuestra Señora del Juncal*, the 1630–1631 New Spain Fleet flagship that has been studied and searched for by INAH's Underwater Archaeology Vice-Directorate since 1995. INAH's Council of Archaeology bases its decisions on the law and regulations mentioned above, as well as on the Reglamento del Consejo de Arqueología (Norms of the Council of Archaeology) (INAH 2005). The council also asks the Underwater Archaeology Vice-Directorate to provide a report on each specific case.

There are other laws that are related in some way to underwater cultural heritage, such as Ley Federal del Mar (Federal Sea Law) (1986), Ley General de Bienes Nacionales (General Law of National Properties) (2004), and Ley de Navegación y Comercio Marítimos (Law of Navigation and Maritime Trade) (2006).

Even if these laws and regulations have been applied successfully so far, the UNESCO Convention on the Protection of Underwater Cultural Heritage, approved in November 2001 and in effect since January 2009, is an important legal instrument that will serve as an enforcement tool.

Mexico's International Presence

In 1982, just two years after INAH had created its Underwater Archaeology Department, we were invited to be part of the Advisory Council on Underwater Archaeology. Ten years later, in 1992, Mexico became a member of ICOMOS's International Committee on Underwater Cultural Heritage (ICUCH). In 1999, ICOMOS held its 12th General Assembly in Mexico, within the framework of the World Congress on the Conservation of Monumental Heritage, and for the first time in its history it included an Underwater Archaeology Scientific Committee. This was regarded as an international recognition of Mexico's position on the defense and preservation of its underwater cultural heritage (Luna Erreguerena 2001).

Mexico also participated in the meetings that took place in Paris to elaborate on the text of the 2001 UNESCO Convention on the Protection of the Underwater Cultural Heritage, and later in UNESCO regional meetings in Kingston, Jamaica (2002), Bogota, Colombia (2004), and Quito, Ecuador (2007). In July 2006, Mexico became the eighth state party to ratify the 2001 Convention and the second country of the Latin American and Caribbean Group (GRULAC) to do so (Luna Erreguerena 2008a). Other countries of the region that have taken this step are Panama (2003), Paraguay (2006), Ecuador (2006), Saint Lucia (2007), Cuba (2008), Barbados

(2008), Grenada (2009), Haiti (2009), and St. Kitts and Nevis (2009) (UNESCO 2010).

The process that led to Mexico's ratification of the 2001 Convention was a delicate and complex one, since once ratified and adopted, this international instrument stands above national laws that deal directly with underwater cultural heritage. It is worth mentioning that, since the first project undertaken in 1979, all Mexican underwater archaeology investigations have followed several of the principles stated in the 2001 Convention, including preservation in situ, nonintrusive work, regional and international cooperation, and, of course, noncommercial exploitation, among others.

Another achievement in the international arena was the participation of researchers from INAH's Underwater Archaeology Vice-Directorate in the Fifth and Sixth World Archaeological Congress (WAC), held in 2003 in Washington, DC, and in 2008 in Dublin, Ireland. In 2003 (WAC-5), for the first time, the theme of underwater archaeology was included. A symposium entitled "Underwater and Maritime Archaeology in Latin America and the Caribbean" was coordinated by Dr. Margaret Leshikar-Denton and MC Pilar Luna Erreguerena, and a book with the same title as the symposium containing the 18 papers presented was published in 2008 by Left Coast Press.

At WAC-6, researchers from INAH presented a whole session entitled "Theory, Methodology and Techniques of Underwater Archaeology Research in Mexico," coordinated by archaeologist Vera Moya Sordo and Dr. Leshikar-Denton. Some of these researchers also presented papers in other sessions, including the plenary about the 2001 UNESCO Convention. One of the resolutions of the Congress reads, "The World Archaeological Congress congratulates Mexico on the preservation and promotion of their underwater cultural heritage. Mexico is leading developments in Latin American underwater archaeology."

WHAT THE FUTURE COULD BRING

Despite the difficult times we are going through in many senses, the future is promising. Hopefully, with the enforcement of the UNESCO 2001 Convention on the Protection of the Underwater Cultural Heritage in January 2009, a new era regarding the preservation of the world's underwater cultural heritage and the role of underwater archaeology will begin. Maybe the time has come to be more aware than ever of our responsibility and commitment toward this legacy, based on the same principles that have been applied to land archaeology and are so well defined in the 2001 Convention. In the same way that the Convention can bring us support to continue with our mission and can make us stronger in our struggle against treasure hunters, we have the opportunity to support and strengthen it through ethical work, a positive attitude, and, most of all, through regional and international cooperation (Luna Erreguerena 2008b).

REFERENCES

Andrews, Anthony P. 1998. El comercio marítimo de los mayas del Posclásico. *Arqueología Mexicana* 33 (September–October): 16–23.

Barba Meinecke, María Elena. 2008. Arqueología subacuática en la costa de Campeche: El caso del pecio "El Pesquero, Champotón." Primeros acercamientos en torno a su investigación. Paper presented at the Sixth World Archaeological Congress, Dublin, Ireland.

Bush Romero, Pablo. 1972. The sacred well of Chichén-Itzá and other freshwater sites in Mexico. In *Underwater archaeology a nascent discipline*, 147–151. Museums and monuments 13. París: UNESCO.

Carrillo Gil, Alvar. 1959. *La verdad sobre el cenote sagrado de Chichén-Itzá*. Mérida: Asociación Cívica Yucatán.

Creamer, Michael A. 1985. Pre-Columbian aids to navigation: A mariner's perspective; Report to the Department of Underwater Archaeology, National Institute of Anthropology and History, Mexico.

Dávalos Hurtado, Eusebio. 1965. El cenote sagrado de Chichén Itzá y su contribución a la arqueología subacuática. In *Memorias del Quinto Congreso Anual de la Sociedad Interamericana de Actividades Subacuáticas, Junio 1964*, 32–36. Mexico City: CEDAM.

Folan, William J. 1968. *El cenote sagrado de Chichén-Itzá*. Mexico City: Departamento de Monumentos Prehispánicos. INAH/SEP.

Instituto Nacional de Antropología e Historia. 1972. Ley Federal sobre Monumentos y Zonas Arqueológicos, Artísticos e Históricos. Mexico City: INAH/SEP.

———. 1977. Disposiciones Reglamentarias para la Investigación Arqueológica en México. Mexico City: INAH/SEP.

———. 2005. Reglamento del Consejo de Arqueología y Disposiciones Reglamentarias para la Investigación Arqueológica en México. Mexico City: INAH/SEP.

Junco, Roberto. 2007. Arqueología Subacuática en el Nevado de Toluca 2007. Online at www.gobiernodigital.inah.gob.mx/mener/index.php?contentPagina=25/. Accessed 22 February 2010.

———. 2009. Arqueología subacuática: Descifrando los misterios del Nevado de Toluca. In *Las aguas celestiales. Nevado de Toluca*, ed. Pilar Luna, Arturo Montero, and Roberto Junco, 23–30. Mexico City: INAH.

Ley de Navegación y Comercio Marítimos. 2006. Ley de Navegación y Comercio Marítimos. Online at www.semar.gob.mx/juridico/ley%20de%20navegacion%20y%20comercio%20%20maritimos.pdf. Accessed 22 February 2010.

Ley Federal del Mar. 1986. Ley Federal del Mar. Online at www.diputados.gob.mx/LeyesBiblio/pdf/124.pdf. Accessed 22 February 2010.

Ley General de Bienes Nacionales. 2004. Ley General de Bienes Nacionales. Online at www.diputados.gob.mx/LeyesBiblio/pdf/267.pdf. Accessed 22 February 2010.

Luna Erreguerena, Pilar. 1996. Navegación colonial en las costas de Campeche. *Arqueología Mexicana* 18 (March–April): 60–63. Report to the Department of Underwater Archaeology, National Institute of Anthropology and History, Mexico.

———. 1999. Proyecto de Investigación Flota de la Nueva España de 1630–1631. Informe de actividades (Marzo 1998 a febrero 1999) y Propuesta de investigación (Marzo-diciembre 1999). 111. Report and proposal to the Council of Archaeology, National Institute of Anthropology and History, Mexico.

———. 2000. Proyecto de Investigación de la Flota de la Nueva España de 1630–1631 e Inventario y Diagnóstico de Recursos Culturales Sumergidos en el Golfo de México (Componente Veracruz). Report to the Council of Archaeology, National Institute of Anthropology and History, Mexico.

———. 2001. Introduction to *Memorias del Congreso Científico de Arqueología Subacuática ICOMOS*, coords. Pilar Luna Erreguerena and Rosa María Roffiel, 11–13. Mexico City: Instituto Nacional de Antropología e Historia.

———. 2008a. Mexico: A leader in ratifications of the UNESCO Convention on the Protection of the Underwater Cultural Heritage. Paper presented at the Sixth World Archaeological Congress, 29 June–4 July, Dublin, Ireland.

———. 2008b. Paper presented at the plenary session. Sixth World Archaeological Congress, 29 June–4 July, Dublin, Ireland.

Luna Erreguerena, Pilar, and Laura Carrillo Márquez. 2005. Banco Chinchorro: Retos en torno a la conservación manejo y disfrute del patrimonio mixto (natural y cultural). *Revista Hereditas* 11 (April): 26–39.

Luna Erreguerena, Pilar, with Arturo Montero and Roberto Junco (coords). 2009. *Las aguas celestiales: Nevado de Toluca*. Mexico City: INAH.

Martos L., Luis Alberto. 2002. La costa oriental de Quintana Roo. *Arqueología Mexicana* 54 (March–April): 26–33.

Mejía, Luz María. 2007. Arqueología Subacuática en Baja California. Online at www. gobiernodigital.inah.gob.mx/mener/index.php?contentPagina=25. Accessed 22 February 2010.

Piña Chán, Román. 1970. Informe preliminar de la reciente exploración del cenote sagrado de Chichén-Itzá. Serie Investigaciones 24. Mexico City: INAH/SEP.

Romero R., María Eugenia. 1998. La navegación maya. *Arqueología Mexicana* 33 (September–October): 6–15.

Throckmorton, Peter. 1969. *Shipwrecks and archaeology: The unharvested sea*. Boston: An Atlantic Monthly Press Book; Littie, Brown.

Trejo Rivera, Flor (coord.). 2003. *La Flota de la Nueva España de 1630–1631: Vicisitudes y naufragios*. Mexico: Colección Obra Varia, INAH.

UNESCO. 2006. Convention on the Protection of the Underwater Cultural Heritage 2001. Online at http://portal.unesco.org/en/ev.php-RL_ID=13520&URL_DO=DO_TOPIC&URL_SECTION=201.html. Accessed 22 February 2010.

———. 2010. Convention on the Protection of the Underwater Cultural Heritage. Paris, 2 November 2001. Online at http://portal.unesco.org/la/convention.asp?KO=13520&language=E&order=alpha. Accessed 22 February 2010.

CHAPTER 43

FROM SKY TO SEA: THE CASE FOR AERONAUTICAL ARCHAEOLOGY

PETER D. FIX

BACKGROUND

UNDERWATER aircraft archaeology may someday become an integral specialty within the theoretical framework of mainstream archaeology. In 2010, however, it remains little more than a disarticulated collective of stakeholder groups that include preservationists, hobbyists, avocational archaeologists, collectors, and professional archaeologists either tasked with the management of submerged cultural resources or interested in investigating individual episodes that helped shape current perceptions of aviation history. Apart from a small number of comprehensive surveys and at least one long-term study, discernable progress associated with the nascent academic discipline has been sporadic and little more than an extension of the time-honored terrestrial aircraft "archaeology." Professional interest in the subject has slowly improved over the last two decades, yet, unlike the archaeological subspecialties of marine, maritime, or nautical archaeology, the study of aircraft in archaeological contexts attracts the attention of a limited number of committed professionals and has no dedicated journal in which to publish research.

Individuals, especially Silvano Jung (2001, 2004, 2007a, 2007b) and Michael McCarthy (1997, 2004) working in Australia, continue to contribute encouraging advancements in methods and theory, particularly regarding site formation processes and site characterization. Archaeological conservators and conservation scientists have contributed greatly to the corpus of knowledge concerning decay processes and methodologies to better stabilize the abundance of dissimilar coupled metal alloys and other materials comprising the aircraft structure and its contents once recovered from both from salt- and freshwater environments. In the last two and a half decades, perhaps the most important step forward has been the recognition by an increasing number of governments that aircraft and aviation-related properties are valuable historic or archaeological resources. Many of these governments have subsequently ratified more stringent cultural resource legislation to protect aviation-related objects. For most, there has been eventual conformity, but it is still possible for others to circumvent regulations by exploiting gaps between nations. It is possible to avoid work in nations with more stringent regulatory efforts in order to plunder the wreck sites of less developed countries with promise of economic compensation or focus on countries that do not feel a direct link to these items of cultural patrimony. Innovations are in place to build on and further strengthen the potential for aircraft archaeology. Nevertheless, only periodic advancements are likely to continue until there are enough interested professionals, and at least one graduate program with a concentration on aircraft in archaeological contexts, to bolster the knowledge base and train subsequent generations of scholars.

The actions of special interest groups that dominate the activity often leads to frustration among professional archaeologists who depend upon the archaeological value of the historical aircraft structure, parts, and context of the crash site to provide additional insight into the history of aviation through archaeological assessment (Figure 43.1) (Ford 2006; Holyoak 2002; Jung 2001, 2004, 2007a, 2007b; McCarthy 1997, 2004; Rodgers, Coble, and Van Tilburg 1998). In this study, by synthesizing concepts of stakeholder groups interested in the bits and pieces of aviation, the hope is that a different portrait of what aviation archaeology could be will develop on the fresh canvas. Only by approaching the subject as a whole with an understanding of the many stakeholders will we be able to parse the individual features, including an explanation as to why there is such a divergence regarding the value of these objects or sites.

DRIVING FORCES: LINKAGES TO HERITAGE, IDENTITY, AND SPECIAL INTEREST COLLECTING

During the early decades of what is commonly referred to as "aircraft archaeology," "aviation archaeology," "wreck hunting," or "wreck chasing," the void left by the limited number of advocates for accepted archaeological practice opened a door for

Figure 43.1 With a concrete ramp of the Japanese seaplane base in the background,
aircraft parts, most likely belonging to Kawanishi H8K "Emily" flying boats or
Mitsubishi A6M2-N "Rufe," the seaplane version of the "Zero" fighter, litter the
shoreline of Emiej (Imeji) Islet, Jaluit Atoll, Republic of Marshall Islands. Photograph
by the author.

special interest groups to determine the direction, attitudes, and approach for the
activity. Despite the potential research value aircraft structures possess, unfortunately a majority of the individual members of these groups believed there was little
advantage in the scientific study of a wreck site. Only the tangible aircraft, or their
component parts, were considered essential trinkets to evoke remembrances of the
past (Hoffman 1998: 42; Holyoak 2002). Their primary mission was, and continues
to be, the reuse of the surviving physical structure or representation through a static
and frequently sterile display of the rebuilt artifact. The rebuild, frequently conducted with only minimal written and photographic documentation, or delineated
drawings, narrowly focuses only on the "newness value," "use value," or "sentimental
value" of the artifact, which degrades the material integrity, "age value," "historical
value," and "research value" through replacement of many critical components,
inaccurate finish coats, or makings (see Reigl 1996). Furthermore, the established

culture continues to permit not only the substantial replacement of principal elements, but also the combination of major components from similar model wrecked aircraft. In 2010, several projects, including the "restoration" of a Messerschmitt Bf 109 and a Bell P-39, are undergoing a sort of Frankenstein fabrication process to form one new aircraft structure from the hulks of several historic planes recovered from Russian territory. If past practice is any indication of the future, the builders will represent these creations as historically accurate restored aircraft composed of original parts. With minimal documentation and new or substituted historic components, it is often impossible to determine without considerable effort what is original to the aircraft. Over time, as those who performed the work retire or pass away, false notions of originality will become more entrenched, and determining the true authenticity of the artifact will be more and more difficult.

The fundamental mission of most aviation heritage groups and museums—to collect and preserve tangible artifacts—developed along parallel lines to early-twentieth-century maritime museums and heritage groups in that the mission positioned a narrowly focused aperture on the aircraft and pilots (versus ships and captains) to reveal individual narratives. The ship is the quintessential marine artifact (White 1995: 179), just as the aircraft is the archetypal artifact of aviation history, and therefore obviously the principal object to save and preserve for posterity. Because such a strong emphasis was placed on re-presentation and display of the artifact, and on tying the planes to the pilots who flew them, little credence was placed on the potential contributions that could be achieved through assessment of the archaeological record.

Perhaps the most significant reason for the slow acceptance or interest in aircraft as a viable field of study is that for many professionals the scientific investigation of material and sites where the date remains within the collective consciousness is senseless. It consumes the limited resources available for the study of older, less-documented periods of human civilization. One of my early professional mentors, a classicist scholar, considered materials or events less than 100 years old a current event and not a subject for archaeological study. Yet it is through remembrances of the shared consciousness that the collecting culture of special interest groups formed heritage linkages to the "newness value" or "commemorative value" of the artifact and ascended to "the modern cult of the monument" (Riegl 1996: 80–83). In his most recent edition of *A Guide to Over 900 Aircraft Museums, USA and Canada*, Michael Blaugher (2009) catalogs over 10,000 aircraft on exhibit or under curation by museums, cities, states, provinces, enthusiast or heritage groups, and businesses. This is an astounding assemblage of aviation artifacts, especially if one considers that it only inventories a portion of aircraft held by organizations on the North American continent. By no means does it include museums and groups from Central America or the other five inhabited continents. Nor does it take into account the significant number of representative historic aircraft held in private collections. The various stakeholder groups have erected aircraft as monuments, marked them as memorial sites, rehabilitated them to flying condition, or represented them as static museum displays.

FROM SKY TO SEA

The intent of aircraft on display is to illustrate the temporal progression of aviation design development in order to disseminate the history of aviation to a broader audience, or to commemorate notable achievements of an individual or significant event. For rebuilt aircraft that are reinstated to flight status, the attraction formed by the tangible objects can act upon the sensatory system in a manner that often promotes deep feelings, inspiring many people to further discovery and exploration of their nation's aviation heritage. The size of the aircraft and unique character generates sufficient allure to draw people to the object and expand the museum educational experience. In the last few decades, perhaps nowhere has the reaction to this effect been better communicated than the *Belmont Report* (AAM 1968). In relating changes to the American museum profession during the 1960s, the authors of the *Belmont Report* recounted the story of the mother of a deaf-mute who wrote an impassioned letter to the director of a major American natural history museum following a visit to the museum. "The child was so impressed by the dinosaurs that he went home and drew a surprisingly accurate picture of the brontosaurus. Wrote the mother . . . 'How could we have explained [in words] the density of the bones, the height, the very existence of the pre-historic animals . . . [or] the environmental difference the dinosaur enjoyed" (AAM 1968: 9). To many people, the rarity or novelty of airplanes, ships, and locomotives brings to mind similar feelings as relayed by the *Belmont Report*.

Historic aircraft create a dramatic narrative, are frequently awe-inspiring, remind us of some spectacular feat, or, to quote the author's preteen nephews, are just "way cool!" They also invoke deeper more profound emotions, and are put on display "for the specific purpose of keeping particular human deeds or destinies . . . alive and present in the consciousness of future generations" (Riegl 1996: 69). History museums and heritage programs help to define a society's collective identity (see McCarthy in this volume). Aircraft museums, like maritime museums, "are popular because of the metaphysical power of [aircraft] which appeal as emblems of memory and identity" (Hicks 2001: 168). In discussing aircraft, it is partly the value placed on this linkage that drives people to go on "obsessive quest[s] for the lost aircraft of World War II" (Hoffman 2001). It drives them to burrow through more than 80 m (270 ft) of the Greenland ice sheet (Hoffman 2004) or to work through 1 km (3,400 ft) of water (Anonymous 2008a) or in swampy tundra kilometers from the nearest town (Côté 2007). In Carl Hoffman's words (2001: 5), his pursuit of aircraft represented the "unique experience of collecting objects that for millions of Americans are icons with profound and deep emotional attachments."

Warships and military aircraft are one of the fastest-growing categories of cherished artifacts set aside for the education of future generations. This is not because the artifacts are emblematic of a warrior or warlike culture; it is only because there is a profound connection originating from a devotion to the structure by those who served on or in them. Those who flew aircraft, especially in combat, have a particular linkage to the structure due to the dependence placed upon it for survival, just as sailors have a particular affinity for the ships on which they served. In 1985, this kinship brought more than 12,000 former B-17 "Flying Fortress" crews to Boeing

Aircraft Corporation's 50th anniversary celebration commemorating rollout of the first model B-17. The organizers anticipated an attendance of perhaps 2,000 people—they stopped counting at 12,000, and some estimates place the total number of attendees at closer to 14,000 (Serling 1992: 52). Retired General Curtis Lemay, USAF, attended the celebration "and [was] watching when the three Forts [Fortresses] did a flyby over Boeing Field. Tears in his eyes, he turned to [organizer Don] Sach and murmured, 'Don, this is one of the most exciting things that ever happened to me'" (Serling 1992: 52). Lemay's reactions were those of a man whose life experiences made him one of the most notable U.S. Air Force generals of the twentieth century, yet the sight of the formation and engine roar evoked that measure of passion and emotion.

In the United States, as in several other countries, a tripoint system of funding exists to pay for cultural and historic preservation work through government appropriation, granting foundations, and individual donors. By far the most consistent and important form of funding is the individual donor. If a particular preservation project requires funding, the groups with the strongest linkage will most readily raise the needed funds to complete the project. One of the most recent examples of an aircraft project funding based on heritage linkage is an F6F-3 "Hellcat" salvaged for the U.S. Navy from Lake Michigan at a depth of approximately 75 m (250 ft). Enterprise CEO Andy Taylor paid for the project through a donation he made in honor of his navy veteran father, Jack Taylor (Pierri 2009).

Along with the notion of the quintessential artifact, this devotion prompts special interest aviation groups to carry out an artifact-centric collecting and preservation mission. To the generation of men and women who built, maintained, and flew these aircraft, conducting an in-depth archaeological investigation on a wrecked plane was, and in some cases remains, tantamount to performing an archaeological investigation on yesterday's car wreck. Aviation archaeology emerged as an avocational pursuit in the United Kingdom and Europe during the 1960s, when the World War II generation was reaching middle age. Those who participated in the first excavations and developed the pursuit were either members of the generation that had first-hand experience with the aircraft, or their immediate descendants. The crash sites, the plane's components, mangled and corroding, simply represented pieces of everyday life. There was no need to keep close control of the site, record associations, understand the site formation processes, or analyze any aspect of the relocated materials. There was no need to develop narrow or broad-based research questions; the pile of twisted wreckage was just the vestiges of youthful remembrances. Unfortunately, the early protractors passed along this attitude to subsequent generations, which perpetuated the culture of artifact-centric collecting. The 1960s and 1970s also witnessed the emergence and rapid growth in the number of aviation museums. Again, this same group of veterans became founding museum members, formed initial board of directors, and served as the principal volunteers needed for the first-hand knowledge and mechanical skills required to "restore" the aircraft that had been located. To them, a shabby-looking, corroded airplane was not the proper image of their past contributions, and the best way to represent the object was to promote its "newness value" just as they remembered it.

Aircraft, like watercraft, hold many literal and metaphoric meanings. They are containers, a means of conveyance, a weapon, a fortress, a vehicle of escape or discovery, and at times a prison. All create doorways to remembrance, discovery, and understanding. With linkage to the artifact, there is some measure of value assigned to that object, and value is what ultimately leads to its preservation. The reprinting of Alois Reigl's seminal work on the value of cultural material (Reigl 1996) listed several types of value transferred to artifacts based on meaning. The list includes "artistic value," "commemorative value," "aesthetic value," "age value," "use value," "newness value," and "historic value." To update the list for present-day cultural interpretations, Barbara Appelbaum (2007: 89–114) recently added to the list "research value" and "educational value." It is easy to determine where a contradiction in values can significantly alter one's approach to the object. If an aircraft is to be airworthy, the restoration program must replace elements weakened during previous use and material degradation in order to avoid potential catastrophe. "Use value" is a very important construct for many stakeholders who believe that planes were intended to fly and that therefore the only correct place for them is in the air. Yet, as in the case of a static but aesthetically pleasing museum display, the greater the percentage of replaced components, the lower the "historic value," "age value," and "research value." The desire to rebuild aircraft to favor "aesthetic value" or "newness value" also diminishes the historic or archaeological significance of the object, especially if only minimal recording and documentation occur while the work is undertaken, or the collection disperses with no associated provenance records (Figure 43.2). On the subject of "newness value" Reigl wrote:

> The masses have always been pleased by everything that appeared new; in works of man they wished to see only the creative triumphant effect of human power and not the destructive force of nature's power, which is hostile to the work of man. According to the masses only the new and complete is beautiful; the old, fragmentary, and discolored is considered ugly. This view of youth being undoubtedly preferable to age has become so deeply rooted over the past millennium that it will be impossible to eradicate in a couple of decades. (Riegl 1996: 80–81)

Over 100 years later, the statement remains true except for the fact that the newness value placed on artifacts was never eradicated, and most modern aircraft museums are held as testament to that fact (Figures 43.3 and 43.4).

A great number of aircraft are required to round out the collections of the 900 museums in North America that include aircraft or aircraft parts in their inventories. Acquisition of the structures has been through purchase, military surplus, or the recovery of viable remains from crash sites. Excluding pockets of World War II aircraft that crashed in remote locations, such as the estimated 800 undisturbed World War II aircraft remaining in the jungles of Papua New Guinea (McDougall 2009), by the 1980s the vast majority of terrestrial crash sites had already provided aircraft for recovery. If no viable structure was available, the focus turned to parts

Figure 43.2 A Douglas Aircraft Co. naval dive bomber, SBD-3 "Dauntless" (U.S. BuNo 06583). The plane crashed during carrier qualifications off the USS *Wolverine* in 1943. Recovered in the early 1990s, the aircraft underwent a passionate and skillful restoration; provenance records are scarce, however, creating confusion as to what material represents the plane's active career and what material is modern. Photograph by the author.

collecting, for use in other rebuilding projects or for sale as memorabilia. In the last two decades, those interested in recovering a museum-quality aircraft "kit" have looked underwater. "'The salvage of underwater aircraft has been unimaginably important" in developing such an impressive collection, says current [National Museum of Naval Aviation] director Robert Rasmussen. "I can point to at least 10 airplanes that are on display right now that have been salvaged, and the only reason we have any airplanes right now that actually took part in World War II is because they came out of Lake Michigan'" (Hoffman 1998: 39). Archaeology, even with adherence to the highest performance standards, is a destructive science. Once disturbed, a certain amount of contextual information is lost. To achieve a high level of success it is imperative that as little disturbance to the site occur, or that changes be recorded so that they can be understood as part of the site formation process. Unfortunately, many terrestrial sites have been plundered or improperly excavated. In 2002, Vince Holyoak (2002: 662) of English Heritage, Monuments Protection Program, noted that early "aircraft archaeological interventions [had] already significantly reduced the resource . . . [and with] little interest among the wider archaeological community in this area of research . . . previous excavations [had] therefore gone unrecorded, the artefacts . . . unavailable for future study, and a mass of materials [left] unprovenanced."

Figure 43.3 Looking forward along the port side of Grumman F6F-5 "Hellcat" (U.S. BuNo 70185) fuselage, undergoing restoration following more than 45 years of immersion in seawater. Photograph by the author.

Figure 43.4 F6F-5 (BuNo 70185) port wing rebuild. In order for the wing to rest with no additional supports, most of the original material will be replaced by new construction. Photograph by the author.

Easier accessibility to terrestrial sites, in some cases scraped clean or scavenged for parts shortly after the crash, has depleted the number of available crash sites for enthusiasts to unearth. In Great Britain, many previously picked-over crash sites are now undergoing a period of reevaluation to recover materials left behind by less attentive excavators (Wotherspoon 2006). With the growing scarcity of terrestrial sites, underwater wrecks likely offer the best opportunity to study historic aircraft without significant human interaction and disturbance. Granted, many recreational SCUBA divers visit shallow underwater aircraft sites, which occasionally results in vandalism, but the frequency of tampering is significantly lower underwater than on land sites. Crashing into, or landing on, water does not necessarily result in a substantially intact aircraft structure. Unlike a crash on land, however, once beneath the waves the aircraft is out of sight and out of mind, or more difficult to locate for salvage purposes. The sites that remain relatively undisturbed offer primary data concerning the rapid technological advances that influenced aircraft design and manufacture in the first half of the twentieth century, adaptations for continued use, wartime (if manufactured during a period of conflict) material selection, and manufacturing processes reflective of the transformation from an "open shop" process to an assembly line. In addition, they offer the potential to gain a better understanding of the individuals who flew in the craft by analysis of personal items that may be uncovered.

AVIATION OR AIRCRAFT ARCHAEOLOGY: THE DEFINITIONS

As mentioned earlier, common names for the subject include "aircraft archaeology," "aviation archaeology," "wreck chasing," and "wreck hunting," and each tends to represent a significantly different practice as applied to a particular stakeholder group. With such a diverse collection of interested parties, pinpointing what the practice actually is can be difficult. Does it focus on aircraft as artifacts, aircraft wrecks, and site preservation, collecting parts and creating new structures, and should support facilities such as buildings, hangars, airfields, and factories be included? With so many descriptions and activities, it is almost impossible for aviation archaeology, both terrestrial and underwater, to move forward as a globally recognized scholastic pursuit within mainstream archaeology.

Undoubtedly, application of the term "archaeology" originated from the physical act of digging and the discovery of unique relics, and conveniently provided the early protractors a respected word with which to communicate their activities. Most stakeholders are not trained archaeologists, and while the basic skill level of avocational archaeologists continues to rise due to special seminars and classes taught by heritage groups, the result of their work seldom advances further than a rudimentary site report, the identification of the wreck, and a vignette of history based on the associated historic record. When asked "Do you think wreck huntings [*sic*] is a form of archaeology?" in an unscientific online poll (63 respondents) conducted on the Warbird Information Exchange between January and May 2006, 71% agreed that it was a form of archaeology, 21% thought that it was not archaeology, and 8% were just not sure (Warbird Information Exchange 2006). Of the 71% who responded in the affirmative, the reason most often provided for their reasoning was that since some photographic documentation and basic recording of the site occurred, this constituted archaeology. The response accentuates the void created by a lack of professional archaeologists. Granted, some level of recording is always better than none; but the application of specific techniques does not elevate the endeavor, and it means very little if the results or artifacts are not available for future study. Not every wreck location amounts to an important archaeological site, but every site has the potential to provide pertinent archaeological data. What often first appears to be an innocuous piece of data actually has greater meaning once associated with similar types of materials. This is one of the greatest weaknesses of aviation archaeology—the focus on the singular, object, or site, while passing over possible associations with other sites or objects, or the larger developments within aviation history. With the infusion of more professionals, it is anticipated that additional work in the subject area will bring about further developments in method and theory and will supply added data, whereby comparisons can be made to the larger body of information derived from previous investigations and analyses.

To find one single appropriate definition of aviation archaeology and make some sense of the diverse traditions held by stakeholder groups, it is possible to apportion each group into one of three separate categories based on their general approach to the subject. The first group represents the established adherence to cultural values inherited from those who were the driving force that developed the pursuit during the 1960s and 1970s. "Aviation archaeology may cover almost any form of research into or collecting of, artefacts connected with the history of aviation" (Wotherspoon 2006: 12). This is the artifact-centric approach, where there is little or nothing additional to learn from a close examination of the aircraft or the material culture found around a crash site. The artifacts are for collection, storage, and visual display and require little or no further analysis. Overall, the intent of such practitioners is not malicious; they are simply stakeholders who have a strong belief that there is nothing of significance to learn from the aircraft or where the plane finally came to rest. For them "archeology has nothing to do with these aircraft. The [archaeologists come up] with stuff that's nonsense. You bring up a plane, look at its information plate and number, and then look at its history. The data is all there" (Hoffman 1998: 42). From the perspective of the professional archaeologist, this is a divergent viewpoint, and what some would consider misguided, but this group's intentions are genuine. The result of this approach has been a double-edged sword. On the one hand, without the work conducted over the last 40 years, the number of available artifacts and interest in the pursuit would be considerably lower. On the other, without associations, proper provenance records, and documentation of restoration processes, these tantalizing objects frequently hold little historic or research value on which to conduct further study.

With antiquarian collecting the focus, a less scrupulous contingent of this first group has been known to hijack the word "archaeology" to lend credence to personal salvage endeavors and mislead their true purpose—to salvage vintage aircraft for personal gain or profit (Public Accounts Committee, The Independent State of Papua New Guinea 2006). These actions reflect poorly on all who participate in the subject regardless of which stakeholder group they represent.

The actions of the second group are less obtrusive than those of the salvors, collectors, or scrappers, preferring instead to focus their efforts on documenting and recording a crash site in order to positively identify the aircraft, preserve an account of the site, and associate the crash episode with the history of pilot and aircraft. Of all the online definitions, the following statements appear to best articulate their view of aviation archaeology:

> Aviation archaeology is primarily the locating and documenting of old aircraft crash sites. It focuses on the preservation of these sites and of the history surrounding the activities that caused them. . . . The goal of aviation archaeology is to record these incidents in historical context rather than record just why it crashed as can (sometimes) be found in government records. (AAIR 2005)

> The main goal of "wreckchasing" is preservation of these historical sites. Aircraft aluminum is suceptible [sic] to corrosion, and suburban development often begins to encroach upon the sites. It is imperative that we record the sites as they exist before they disappear. As it is, a large part of our history as a nation [United States] has vanished under the watchful eyes of developers. (Oklahoma Wreckchasing 2010)

These investigations usually result in little disturbance to the site, but a review of the published literature originating from this group concentrates on the specific aircraft and wreck site as it relates to the history of the individual plane, pilot, crew, and passengers. The publications make little or no attempts to utilize the artifact as an analytical tool in order to understand the broader concepts that make up the history of aviation.

Contrasting the viewpoint of the collectors, diggers, and salvors are professional archaeologists, historic preservationists, and cultural resource managers, who constitute the third group and who would generally assert:

> Aviation archaeology addresses both the archaeology of single airplane wrecks and the archaeology of the support structures of aviation, such as airfields and related structures (air operations centers, flight controls etc.). Research issues focus on the archaeological site formation process of aircraft wrecks and patterns therein; on the study of modern mass transportation systems, and their social and political impacts; as well as on the interpretative uses of such sites for educational and recreational purposes. (Spennemann 1998)

This definition is considerably more comprehensive, covering both the sum and the many discrete elements of aviation archaeology. On the other hand, is it too broad?

Since submerged aircraft are the creation of human enterprise, many professional archaeologists classify the individual structures under the general research umbrella of "marine" or "maritime archaeology" (Delgado and Staniforth 2002; McCarthy 1997; Nutley 2006). The only real qualification for maritime archaeologists to be involved with aircraft is the skill set involved with reaching the site and knowing the logistics of conducting an underwater excavation. Only seaplanes and amphibious planes, by design, are intended to land or navigate on water. All other submerged aircraft came to rest in their current location because of happenstance or because they were on the losing side of aggressive acts or discarded as refuse. Accordingly, an airplane wreck is no different from "The Parking Lot" off Ejit Island, Marshall Islands, where, in 3–36 m (10–120 ft) of water, the U.S. military dumped jeeps and trucks, and sank both a tugboat and a landing craft at the end of World War II. Underwater graduate programs do not prepare professional archaeologists to study the site formation processes of aircraft, aircraft design and material construction, the history of aircraft development and aviation, or aeronautical cultures. The site formation processes for aircraft are different from watercraft structures (Jung 2001, 2004, 2007a, 2007b). The nomenclature for aircraft is different, and construction methods and materials are different from ships, as are materials stabilization requirements if recovery of the artifact is proposed. There is a mountain of potential primary data to be mined in the crash site, the aircraft, and supporting industry structures. Although some excellent contributions have been made to date, there is only so much that a smattering of underwater, warfare, or industrial archaeologists can achieve. The only way to push the subject forward is to create new definitions that divide aviation archaeology into manageable segments that can receive individual attention.

In the course of researching this topic, one observation made through an extensive literature review was the number of times "aviation" and "aircraft" appeared as interchangeable terms or as part of a single definition that was so broad it was difficult to grasp. If the archaeology of aviation is to progress and develop as an academic discipline, there must be a clearly defined set of terms to communicate direction for this branch of archaeology. One possible set of definitions proposed here borrows from concepts put forth by P. J. Capelotti (2004) to anchor the various meanings to the overarching term "aeronautical archaeology":

Aeronautical archaeology—is the umbrella term to describe the archaeological study of humans and their interactions with the atmosphere.

Aviation archaeology—is the archaeological study of humans and their interactions with the atmosphere from sea level to the outer limits of the troposphere, and can include terrestrial sites related to these activities such factories, airports, navigational beacons, docks, and ramps.

Aerospace archaeology—is the archaeological study of humans and their interactions with the atmosphere from the stratosphere to deep space. It can include terrestrial sites as well as space flight and ballistic missile defense.

Aircraft archaeology—is the archaeological study of both heavier- and lighter-than-air aircraft, in both terrestrial and underwater sites.

Those in the archaeological community who are interested in or passionate about the subject of aeronautical archaeology, whether underwater or on land, need to forge stronger alliances by creating networks to share information; in this way the

foothold that has been gained among the other stakeholder groups can be strengthened. No amount of cultural resource legislation can secure an unprotected wreck
site from vandalism or theft if the perpetrator is intent on some sort of malicious
act. Only through continued demonstration of the archaeological potential in sites
and structures will other stakeholders also come to realize the promise held by these
sites. In some areas, better interaction is having a profound effect on the treatment
of the resource. One such example in Great Britain is the formation and adherence
to the mission of the British Aviation Archaeological Council, which promotes ethical standards and preservation of the remnants of historic aircraft. In addition,
while still a small percentage, a growing number of recovered aircraft are being
accepted for their historical value, not just their newness value. Recently, the newly
relocated Wings Museum in West Sussex, UK, opened with numerous exhibits featuring historic aircraft in "as found" condition and not completely rebuilt with
modern materials or parts from other artifact. However, movement that alters the
steadfast culture created by the aforementioned linkages will take considerably
more effort if we are to protect the resource. Advocates for aeronautical archaeology
arrived late to the proverbial table and have been trying to catch up with stakeholders from the other groups for nearly two decades. In reactionary messages,
Gillespie (1992), Foster (1993), Diebold (1993), and Schwarz (1995) all described the
loss of potential archaeological information and damage to the cultural resource
due to the artifact-centric collecting, rebuilding, use, and aesthetic presentation of
aircraft. McCarthy (2004) explained in detail the potential for historic aircraft as an
archaeological site, yet in 2009 three more structures were recovered from the site
where they came to rest over 60 years ago. Two of the structures were from the Lake
Michigan NAS Glenview assemblage (Wills 1997); another one, from off the coast of
Norway, will be dissected for its parts and used in the fabrication of a reconstructed
plane for display (Anonymous 2008b).

THE SITES, THE ARTIFACTS, THE POTENTIAL

The frequent excuse for ignoring aeronautical contexts is the notion there is nothing
to learn from the site or structure that one could not obtain from historic documents. To date, several underwater aircraft sites around the world have been investigated for which the results have been published. I am aware of several other
archaeological surveys that are in some form of preparation, including the results of
an amphibian aircraft in Indonesian waters and two rare navy torpedo bombers in
the Marshall Islands (Figures 43.5, 43.6, and 43.7). Each provides contributions that
enhance perceptions about the events in which the planes were lost, construction
methods, or material selection and quality and/or advance the method and theory

Figure 43.5 Looking aft along the port side of the engine and fuselage of U.S. Navy TBD-1 BuNo 1515–Ex-VT-5 / USS *Yorktown* (CV-5) "5-T-6," resting flat on the bottom of Jaluit Lagoon, Marshall Islands. Photograph by Jerry Ross. Reproduced with the kind permission of TIGHAR.

of aeronautical archaeology. Jung (2001, 2007a, 2007b), studying the 15 flying boats that were lost in Roebuck Bay, Broome, Western Australia, during a Japanese air attack in March 1942, was able to propose viable site formation processes by merging the archaeological data with historic line drawings to illustrate deformation and postdepositional impacts. Through the study of the event and the artifacts in context, Jung developed a theme for a research question involving evacuation, which relates only to aviation archaeology: What does one bring on board an aircraft, knowing that the crisis of an evacuation forces one to leave behind most possessions? On a ship, one can pack a bag or satchel, but the weight restrictions of a plane may preclude the portage of most common items. As part of the study, Jung also assessed the collection of nonprovenienced material removed from multiple aircraft around the site in order to reestablish associations and learn more about the people on board at the time of the wrecking event.

Investigating another Japanese airborne attack, Rodgers, Coble, and Van Tilberg (1998) applied historical archaeology methods to a flying boat wreck in Kaneohe Bay, Hawaiian Islands, that was among the first assets attacked on 7 December 1941. Finally, through the process of studying the lend-lease PBY "Catalina" flying boats scuttled off Rottnest Island, Western Australia, following World War II, Michael McCarthy of the Western Australia Maritime Museum, was able to propose the beginnings of a site characterization format. Based on the individual episode in

Figure 43.6 Using a diagram based on the plane's lines drawings, Robert Neyland
of the Naval History and Heritage Command's Underwater Archaeology Branch
records corrosion details on the top of the starboard wing of U.S. Navy TBD-1,
BuNo 0298–Ex-VT-5 / USS *Yorktown* (CV-5) "5-T-7." The plane ditched in Jaluit
Lagoon, Marshall Islands, on 1 February 1942 during a raid and now lies in shallow
water. The "Devastator" was the first low fixed-wing all-metal aircraft built for the U.S.
Navy by the Douglas Aircraft Co. Photograph by Jerry Ross. Reproduced with the kind
permission of TIGHAR.

which the aircraft came to rest on the bottom of the ocean or lake, the system takes
a hierarchical approach to grouping and classifying wrecked aircraft based on
whether the craft was lost during operational service, abandoned or scuttled, or
abandoned as a hulk. With this assessment tool, McCarthy (1997: 12–13) proposed
an "embryonic" but consistent method to determine sites with decreasing "archeo-
logical/museuological/technological significance."

Aircraft sites have tremendous archaeological possibility for supporting or con-
tradicting the historic record, but the potential value of aeronautical archaeology
must possess an even broader purpose than the individual site. In the past, little
attention has been afforded to the aircraft structure itself. Granted, many restora-
tions have taken place, but with little documentation of their work it is virtually
impossible to know what pertinent data may have been lost. In the rush to reassert
the aircraft's "newness value," frequently ignored are "the pressures of combat

Figure 43.7 The International Group for Historic Aircraft Recovery (TIGHAR)
diver Van Hunn records features of the disarticulated engine from TBD-1,
BuNo 0298. When the plane sank, it slipped down the face of a reef, and the
engine broke free from the fuselage. Photograph by Jerry Ross. Reproduced with the
kind permission of TIGHAR.

[which] meant that much of the aircraft underwent almost continual modification, including airframes, powerplants, armaments, navigational and radio equipment was carried out in the field and little of it was recorded" (Holyoak 2001: 259). Wills (1997) was able to identify evidence of considerable repair in his assessment of the SBD-2 before it was restored. Similarly, the amount of information engineering staff at the Fleet Air Arm Museum (U.K.) were able to learn from KD431 is evidence that aircraft hold considerable research value. The Corsair KD431 had been painted inappropriately following its arrival at the museum in 1963. For three years, starting in 2000, staff from the museum slowly and carefully removed the inaccurate paint layers to reveal the true colors and placement of markings. Enough data were collected to bring into question the model of KD431.

> A great deal of confusion seems to exist regarding what details distinguish an
> FG-1A Corsair from a FG-1D, and from which date either type originated. Many
> books and reference sources seem to vary and conflict. What one would assume
> to be easily established data and details are indeed difficult to pinpoint. To be fair,
> few if any originators of such material had benefit and luxury of an original
> Corsair to study while preparing their information, and they could only act on
> the best information available to them at the time. (Morris 2006: 157)

Although the author of the book about the program referred to the plane as a "time capsule," that is probably not quite accurate. A time capsule is a contrived association of materials intentionally set aside and used as a vehicle to project significance into the future. The painstaking effort by the Fleet Air Arm Museum literally opened a window 65 years into the past. It reflects the nuances of the plane's construction and finish offered by few written documents. Encouraged by their findings with the Corsair, the museum has recently initiated the conservation process on another aircraft in their collection, a Grumman Martlet AL246. The restoration will again attempt to remove the inaccurate paint finish applied during the 1960s in order to reveal the original paintwork from World War II. Some of the information revealed by KD431 is similar to diagnostic features located during the conservation treatment of a Japanese Army Air Force Nakajima Ki 43 "Oscar." Here, the conservators found Japanese characters handwritten in pencil; these are believed to have been part of the manufacturing process (Bailey 2004). Had these three aircraft been rebuilt, all such information would have been lost. Similarly, close metallographic examination of the *Wright Flyer* crankcase showed precipitation hardening of the aluminum copper alloy that predates what was previously accepted as the first known application of precipitation hardened aluminum by seven years (Gayle and Goodway 1994). Had the engine been modified or "restored," much of this information would have been lost.

THE NEED TO BROADEN THE
SCOPE OF INQUIRY

In 1935, the U.S. Bureau of Aeronautics requested designs for a new torpedo plane for the U.S. Navy. The Great Lakes Aircraft Company proposed the XTBG-1, a biplane; the Douglas aircraft Co. presented the XTBD-1, which would ultimately be the navy's first all-metal low-wing aircraft. Within 10 years, jet propulsion on aircraft was in use, and 34 years later Neil Armstrong and "Buzz" Aldren landed on the moon. So dramatic were the technological advancements during this period that one has to wonder how it influenced aircraft construction. Were materials able to keep pace with designers' creativity? Before World War II, labor was managed in "job shops," and low product demand meant that parts could be fabricated in batches, handmade, with a quality based on the skill of the artisan. World War II changed the manufacturing structure, requiring an assembly-line production format. How did the quality of the product change in this period? Were companies scrimping on materials during war? The aeronautical industry in Britain underwent acute shortages of scientists, engineers, and all levels of management at that time (Anonymous 1943). How did this shortage affect the quality of aircraft construction? Were there differences in construction quality between companies building the same model aircraft, or between countries building the same aircraft? While conducting an in situ preservation survey of aircraft in Chuuk Lagoon, Micronesia, Ian McLeod (2006: 135) found sensitive compositional variations between corrosion potentials of examined aluminum alloys, which he accredited in part to supply problems. At what point in the war did a decline in materials begin to affect aircraft quality? Was it a gradual decline, or a sharp one?

Conclusion

The *Wright Flyer*'s first recorded controlled, powered, and sustained heavier-than-air flight was only a little over 100 years ago, and throughout the twentieth century advancements in technology have generated reams of documentation regarding human flight. The mass of photograph, drawing, manuscripts, and manuals should not diminish the possible advantages of applying archaeological methods to aviation sites and aircraft wreckage. There is a mounting body of data that demonstrates the important contributions that aeronautical archaeology can provide to understanding historical perspectives, technological advancements, and period construction practices. In the future, the best available examples of aircraft will be found underwater. Coble lists the U.S. naval losses alone at over 12,000 planes (Coble 2001: 27). Approaches to aeronautical archaeology must continue to evolve, must be held to higher standards, and must be used as tools to better understand the context and times in which these objects were developed and utilized. This will lead to more than could ever be represented by historical documents or heavily rebuilt artifacts on exhibit.

REFERENCES

American Association of Museums (AAM). 1968. *The Belmont Report*. Washington, DC: American Association of Museums.

Anonymous. 1943. Aircraft production in Great Britain. *Science* 98 (2545): 318.

Anonymous. 2008a. Restoring submerged aircraft. *Classic Wings* 15 (1): 34–40.

Anonymous. 2008b. Operation SKUA II. *Classic Wings* 15 (2): 34–37.

Appelbaum, Barbara. 2007. *Conservation treatment methodology*. Amsterdam: Butterworth-Heinemann.

Aviation Archaeological Investigation & Research (AAIR). (2005). *What is aviation archaeology?* Online at www.aviationarchaeology.com /src/aair.htm/. Accessed 15 January 2009.

Bailey, G. 2004. Stabilization of a wrecked and corroded aluminum aircraft. In *Proceedings of Metal 2004*, Canberra, Australia, 4–8 October 2004.

Blaugher, Michael. 2009. *A guide to over 900 aircraft museums, USA and Canada*. 25th ed. Ft. Wayne, IN: Michael Blugher.

Capelotti, P. J. 2004. Space. *Archaeology* 57 (6): 46–51.

Coble, Wendy. 2001. The navy and the protection of Pacific cultural resources. *CRM* 24 (1): 27–29.

Côté, Michel. 2007. Tundra survivor: Recovery of a Canadian historical aircraft, the CF-CPA project. *Warbird Digest* 17: 52–56.

Delgado, James, and Mark Staniforth. 2002. Underwater archaeology. In *The encyclopedia of life support systems*. Paris: UNESCO. Online at www.eolss.co.uk. Accessed 1 February 2010.

Diebold, Paul. 1993. Aircraft as cultural resources. *CRM* 16 (10): 6–7.

Ford, Julie. 2006. *WWII aviation archaeology in Victoria, Australia*. Flinders University Maritime Archaeology Monograph Series No. 1. South Adelaide, Victoria, Australia: Department of Archaeology, Flinders University.

Foster, Kevin. 1993. Cultural resource management and aviation history. *CRM* 16 (10): 13–15.

Gayle, Frank, and Martha Goodway. 1994. Precipitation hardening in the first aerospace aluminum alloy: The Wright Flyer crankcase. *Science* 266 (November): 1015–1017.

Gillespie, Richard. 1992. Aircraft as artifacts: Historic aircraft recovery and movement toward aviation historic preservation. *TIGHAR Tracks* 8 (4): 13–15.

Hicks, R. 2001. What is a maritime museum? *Museum Management and Curatorship* 19 (2): 159–174.

Hoffman, Carl. 1998. Whose planes are they, anyway? *Air & Space/Smithsonian* 13 (4): 37–43.

———. 2001. *Hunting warcraft: The obsessive quest for the lost aircraft of World War II*. New York: Ballantine Books.

———. 2004. Glacier Girl: The Lockheed P-38 saved from an icy tomb is now the star attraction in a previously quiet Kentucky town. *Air & Space/Smithsonian* 18 (6): 20–29.

Holyoak, Vince. 2001. Airfields as battlefields, aircraft as an archaeological resource: British military aviation in the first half of the C20th. In *Fields of conflict: Progress in battlefield archaeology*, ed. Phillip Freeman and A. J. Pollard, 253–264. British Archaeological Reports International Series No. 958. Oxford: Basingstoke Press.

———. 2002. Out of the blue: Assessing military aircraft sites in England, 1912–45. *Antiquity* 76 (293): 657–663.

Jung, Silvano. 2001. Wings beneath the sea: The aviation archaeology of Catalina flying boats in Darwin Harbour, Northern Territory. MA thesis, NTU, Darwin, Australia.

———. 2004. Artefacts from Broome's World War Two flying boat wreck sites: A survey of data collected 1979–2001. *Bulletin of the Australasian Institute for Maritime Archaeology* 28: 63–80.

———. 2007a. A defabrication method for recording submerged aircraft: Observations on sunken flying boat wreck in Roebeck Bay, Broome, Western Australia. *Bulletin of the Australasian Institute for Maritime Archaeology* 31: 26–31.

———. 2007b. Working backwards: Broome's World War II flying boat wreck sites reconstructed from archaeological non-disturbance surveys. *Bulletin of the Australasian Institute for Maritime Archaeology* 31: 32–36.

McCarthy, Michael. 1997. *The "Black Cats": Report into the feasibility of locating, raising and conserving one of the four Catalina Flying Boats scuttled off Rottnest Island in the years 1945–1946*. Report No. 125, Department of Maritime Archaeology, Western Australian Maritime Museum.

———. 2004. Historic aircraft wrecks as archaeological sites. *Bulletin of the Australasian Institute for Maritime Archaeology* 28: 81–90.

McDougall, Bruce. 2009. Plane salver crew craight [*sic*] in crossfire. *Daily Telegraph, Sydney.* 30 May. Online at www.dailytelegraph.com.au/news/plane-salvage-crew-caight-in-crossfire/story-e6freuy9-1225718261343/. Accessed March 2010.

McLeod, Ian. 2006. In-situ corrosion studies on wrecked aircraft of the Imperial Japanese Navy in Chuuk Lagoon, Federated States of Micronesia. *International Journal of Nautical Archaeology* 35 (1): 128–136.

Morris, David. 2006. *The time-capsule fighter: Corsair KD431.* Gloucestershire, UK: Sutton Publishing.

Nutley, David. 2006. Underwater archaeology. In *Maritime archaeology: Australian approaches*, ed. Mark Staniforth and Michael Nash, 83–96. New York: Springer Sciences and Business Media.

Oklahoma Wreckchasing. 2010. What is aviation archaeology? Online at http://okwreckchasing.org/whatis.html. Accessed 26 February 2010.

Pierri, Vincent. 2009. World War II fighter pulled from Lake Michigan. *Chicago Daily Herald.* 30 November. Online at www.dailyherald.com/story/?id=340556. Accessed 28 December 2009.

Public Accounts Committee, The Independent State of Papua New Guinea. 2006. *Final report to the National Parliament: Inquiry into the National Museum and Art Gallery and the sale and export of the Swamp Ghost aircraft.* Port Moresby, PNG: Public Accounts Committee.

Riegl, Alois. 1996. The modern cult of monuments: Its essence and it development. In *Historical and philosophical issues in the conservation of cultural heritage*, ed. Nicolas Stanley Price, M. Kirby Talley Jr., and Alessandra Melluco Vaccaro, 69–83. Los Angeles: Getty Conservation Institute.

Rodgers, B. A., W. M. Coble, and H. K. Van Tilburg. 1998. The lost flying boat of Kaneohe Bay: Archaeology of the first U.S. casualties of Pearl Harbor. *Historical Archaeology* 32 (4): 8–18.

Schwarz, Fredric. 1995. To fly or not to fly. *American Heritage of Invention and Technology* 10 (4): 6–7.

Serling, Robert. 1992. *Legend and legacy: The story of Boeing and its people.* New York: St. Martin's.

Spennemann, Dirk H. R. 1998. *Essays on the Marshallese past: Aviation archaeology in the Marshall Islands.* 2nd ed. Online at http://marshall.csu.edu.au/Marshalls/html/essays/es-ww2-6.html/. Accessed 20 January 2009.

Warbird Information Exchange. 2006. Do you think Wreck Huntings [*sic*] is a form of archaeology? Online forum. Avalable at www.warbirdinformationexchange.org/phpBB3/viewtopic.php?f=3&;t=6216&hilit=aviation+archaeology. Accessed 10 February 2010.

White, Colin. 1995. Too many preserved ships threaten the heritage. In *The archaeology of ships of war*, ed. Mensun Bound, 179–185. International Archaeological Series, Vol. 1. Oswestry, UK: Anthony Nelson.

Wills, Richard. 1997. *Dauntless in peace and war: A preliminary archaeological and historical documentation of Douglas SBD-2 Dauntless BuNo 2106, Midway Madness.* Washington, DC: Naval Historic Center, Underwater Archaeology Branch.

Wotherspoon, Nick. 2006. *North-west aircraft wrecks: New insights into dramatic last flights.* Barnsley, UK: Pen & Sword Aviation.

CHAPTER 44

MARITIME ARCHAEOLOGY AND INDUSTRY

FREDRIK SØREIDE

INTRODUCTION

BECAUSE mankind has traveled the seas since the dawn of time, millions of shipwrecks and other archaeological sites lie undiscovered underwater. Specifically, the United Nations Educational, Scientific and Cultural Organization (UNESCO) has estimated that there are over 3 million shipwrecks in the world; UK Hydrography maintains a comprehensive Wrecks Database containing over 60,000 records, of which approximately 20,000 are named vessels largely in UK territorial waters; the U.S. Office of Coast Survey's database contains information on approximately 10,000 submerged wrecks and obstructions in the coastal waters of the United States; Norway has the longest coastline in Europe, with an estimated 20,000 shipwrecks.

Collectively referred to as "underwater cultural resources," such sites are valuable but finite, nonrenewable assets that incorporate all underwater traces of human existence, including (a) sites, structures, buildings, artifacts, and human remains, together with their archaeological and natural contexts; and (b) wrecks or any part thereof, their cargo or other contents, together with their archaeological and natural context.

Cultural resource management agencies are tasked with the development and maintenance of programs designed to protect, preserve, scientifically study, and otherwise manage these cultural resources, including prehistoric, historic, and more recent sites. Cultural resource managers often work with commercial companies to manage these resources, which leads to complications and opportunities not generally experienced in academic archaeology. In all types of commercial projects, companies naturally try to keep the costs as low as possible. Only the costs necessary for the safe and legally sound completion of a project are covered. Industry has therefore resisted any responsibility for underwater heritage protection. Until recently underwater projects have often also encountered less legal or government involvement than normally land projects usually do.

Several types of industries are involved in activities in the oceans that can potentially be a threat to underwater cultural resources, such as:

- Commercial trawling and fishing
- Offshore constructions, pipelines, cables
- Dredging, sand removal, landfill, harbors, marinas, fish farms
- Unwanted environmental damage as a result of industrial activities
- Salvage and treasure hunting
- Recreational diving

In recent years, increased awareness of marine archaeology by several national authorities responsible for the protection of cultural heritage has led to a requirement that marine archaeological studies be performed as an important part of industry projects. In practice, this varies considerably both from industry to industry and from country to country.

One of the most profound dangers to underwater cultural heritage is the destruction caused by commercial fishing. Since the late 1960s the power and size of commercial fishing boats has greatly increased. This increase in power has resulted in the ability to simply run over and destroy wooden wrecks that used to be avoided. Consequently, wrecks that may be of significant archaeological interest are not safe in areas where commercial fishing is conducted, meaning that leaving wrecks in situ may no longer equal preservation. The most important fishing areas are:

1. The Northwest Pacific—seas bordering central and northern Japan, northern China, Korea, and northeastern Russia.
2. The Northwest Atlantic coast of Newfoundland and New England.
3. The Northeast Atlantic, comprising shallow waters off the European coast extending from the Barents Sea in the north to the Bay of Biscay.
4. The Northeast Pacific from Alaska to California.

However, there are numerous regional fishing activities in almost all areas of the ocean.

The most common and archaeologically destructive commercial fishing method is trawl fishing (Figure 44.1). Trawling works by a vessel dragging a net along the seabed. The mouth of the net is held open by two trawl doors, usually made of steel. A cable connects each door to a winch on the fishing boat. The easiest place to trawl is a flat seafloor, devoid of rocks or other potential snags for the net. However, rocks and other features attract fish, so fishermen are enticed to work near obstructions, such as shipwrecks, which act as artificial reefs. Trawling can affect large areas of the seabed and can reach depths of 500 m or more. While substantial modern wrecks may be able to withstand a few net snagging events before being torn apart, ancient

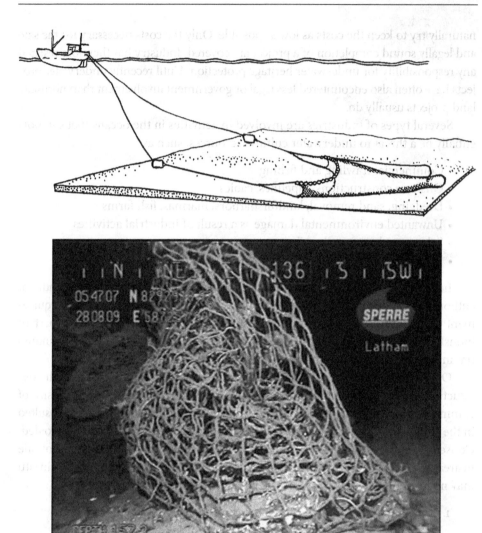

Figure 44.1 (a) Trawl fishing. (b) Trawl bag filled with stones on the seafloor, showing the forces in place during a trawl operation. Images by the author.

shipwrecks are more delicate. Because their exposed wooden hulls are consumed by a variety of animals, ancient shipwrecks typically consist of ceramic or inorganic artifacts lying on the seabed. If a trawl net is dragged through an ancient wreck site, these delicate objects will be smashed and scattered. Repeated trawls may eliminate all traces of a wreck. Based on numerous archaeological examinations of ancient wrecks damaged by fishing activities, it is unlikely that many ancient archaeologically significant sites will survive in areas subjected to trawl fishing. Wreck Watch has analyzed shipwrecks located by Odyssey Marine Exploration in the English Channel. Of some 267 shipwrecks investigated, 115 showed permanent damage

(Kingsley 2009). Another study was also recently carried out in the North Atlantic (Steingimsson 2006).

In recent years, oil companies have been required by various authorities to present more data from their offshore survey work. Based on this data, it seems clear from projects in Norway, the United States, the Baltic, and elsewhere that shipwrecks are under threat from offshore construction work. In Norway, shipwrecks have been located in almost all recently investigated pipeline routes (Søreide and Jasinski 2000; Wickler et al. 1999), and in the Nordstream route, a 1,200 km long gas pipeline route planned from Russia to Germany, more than 40 well-preserved shipwreck sites were located during the pipeline survey (Søreide 2011). It is also well known that the Gulf of Mexico contains many shipwrecks of archaeological and historical significance dating back to the discovery of the New World (see Borgens in this volume). Some have been discovered and documented, yet the majority remain unstudied. The most important discoveries have been made in recent years during the exploration, development, and production of oil and gas resources in the Gulf of Mexico. It is estimated that between 300 and 400 shipwrecks have been discovered during oil- and gas-related activities (Ball, Irion, and Horrell 2007). Historical research conducted for the Bureau of Ocean Energy Management, Regulation and Enforcement (BOEMRE, formerly Minerals Management Service), the federal agency that manages offshore oil and gas development, indicates that over 4,000 ships sank on the Outer Continental Shelf (OCS) between 1625 and 1951 CE; thousands more sank closer to shore in state waters during the same period (Irion 2001).

BOEMRE is required to ensure that oil and gas exploration activities do not adversely affect significant archaeological sites on the OCS. To determine whether there is a potential to affect archaeological resources on the OCS by proposed oil and gas activities, the BOEMRE has funded archaeological studies to ascertain where on the OCS these sites, whether submerged prehistoric Native American sites or historic shipwrecks, are likely to occur. In these areas, the oil and gas industry is required to conduct surveys of the seafloor using remote-sensing instruments. The data collected are reviewed by archaeologists, who write reports on their findings for submittal to BOEMRE. In turn, BOEMRE archaeologists use these reports to review applications from industry to drill wells or construct pipelines. Every year the BOEMRE reviews nearly 2,000 planned wells and pipelines for their potential effect on archaeological sites on the OCS (Ball, Irion, and Horrell 2007; Irion 2001).

Dredging and sand removal can also drastically affect and damage cultural resources underwater. Dredging will most certainly destroy any delicate wooden shipwrecks that are encountered, but dredging is necessary for safe navigation in many areas. To ensure that dredging operations cause as little damage as possible, marine archaeologists are now often present during the operations (Firth 2006). Cultural remains underwater may also be affected by landfills, potentially burying and damaging sites, unless the area is checked and cleared by marine archaeologists prior to construction. Cultural heritage underwater is similarly threatened by an increasing number of marinas and fish farms that are built along the coast.

Unwanted environmental damage from industry such as chemical spills, oil spills, and so on has been studied in very little detail but could also have a negative effect on cultural resources underwater.

Even though many treasure-hunting companies state that the goal of their exploration is to protect the cultural heritage found in shipwrecks, their practical standard for commercial and academic coordination on shipwreck exploration and recovery looks like archaeology but fails in many important senses, since the focus is not on archaeology but on recovery. This is an industry that exploits shipwreck cargo, most of the time with negative effect (Hall 2007; Pickford 1993; Stemm 1992).

Now a major industry, recreational diving poses serious threats to shipwrecks. There are more than 1 million certified SCUBA divers in the world today, many of whom are mainly interested in wreck diving, and there are many examples of diving souvenir collectors who pick wrecks apart item by item. Fortunately, many SCUBA divers are extremely knowledgeable and a resource, both for locating and protecting shipwrecks. Courses in preservation and marine archaeology have been shown to drastically increase awareness among sport divers. Legislation is also an alternative.

LEGAL REFLECTIONS

Because industrial applications underwater are still in their infancy, the extensive rules and regulations for comparable onshore work is still mostly lacking. However, it may be just a matter of decades before the seabed becomes the domain of the general public and all underwater installations and activities become visible to the media. One must therefore take care and introduce sound and defensible standards, similar to those imposed on land—standards to be proud of—rather than fear future judgments on the industrial use of the ocean.

Most European countries insist that underwater cultural heritage belongs to the state, with few rewards to the finder. In the United States, Congress passed the Abandoned Shipwreck Act in 1987. This act holds that all shipwrecks underwater are the property of the federal government and administered by the state in whose waters they are discovered. Some argue that this approach discourages responsible private companies from even looking, while the coastlines are still being clandestinely pillaged by individuals who do not report their discoveries, as they know they will lose what they have found if they do.

In Australia legislation protects shipwrecks and related articles that lie in the waters around the Australian coast that are older than 75 years of age (see Staniforth in this volume). Regulations under this legislation prohibit all kinds of activities (such as trawling or diving) that might damage a historic shipwreck or relic. In some of the developing countries, however, protection of cultural remains is far from acceptable, and it is even possible to buy salvage rights from government authorities (Jasinski 1999).

UNESCO Convention on the Protection of Underwater Cultural Heritage

At present, there is no international legal instrument that adequately protects underwater cultural heritage, which is increasingly threatened by construction work, advanced technology that enhances the identification of and access to wrecks, exploitation of marine resources, and commercialization of efforts to recover underwater cultural heritage. This condition has led to the irretrievable loss of a vast part of our collective cultural heritage. In response, the United Nations Educational, Scientific and Cultural Organization (UNESCO) member states prepared the UNESCO Convention on the Protection of Underwater Cultural Heritage (CPUCH), which provides basic protection beyond the territorial seas of coastal states and aims at avoiding and resolving jurisdictional issues involving underwater cultural heritage (UNESCO 2010).

The convention considers underwater cultural heritage an integral part of the cultural heritage of humanity and a very important element in the history of peoples, nations, and their relations with each other. Thus, exploration, excavation, and protection of underwater cultural heritage must be based on an application of special scientific methods, suitable techniques and equipment, and high degrees of professional specialization. The aim of the convention is to impose these standards on underwater archaeological work and to make sure that the work is approved by the responsible authorities. Some 350 experts from more than 90 countries worked for four years to finalize the draft document, which covers all traces of human existence having a cultural, historical, or archaeological character that have been partially or totally underwater, periodically or continuously, for at least 100 years.

CPUCH was adopted in 2001 by the plenary session of the 31st General Conference by 87 affirmative votes. Four states voted against (Norway, Russian Federation, Turkey, Venezuela), and 15 abstained from voting (Brazil, Colombia, Czech Republic, France, Germany, Greece, Guinea-Bissau, Iceland, Israel, Netherlands, Paraguay, Sweden, Switzerland, United Kingdom, Uruguay). The United States could not vote, of course, because it is not a member of UNESCO. However, as an observer, the United States made a very strong statement against the CPUCH.

Since CPUCH only applies to signatories, and many of the countries that are involved in offshore industries have not signed, the CPUCH will not apply to the nations that possess the vast majority of technological access to the world's oceans, and it is therefore likely that additional efforts are needed to protect heritage in international waters.

Reflections on the Norwegian Law for the Protection of Cultural Heritage

The Norwegian Law for Protection of Cultural Heritage is one of the strictest in the world. In principle, the Norwegian state is the legal owner of all cultural remains found underwater. The original Norwegian Law for the Protection of Cultural Heritage, which dates back to 1963, included protection for shipwreck sites older than 100 years, but did not consider their cargo or single objects. After the discovery of the *Akerendam* treasure wreck in 1972, the law was amended to also include these items. In the latest revision from 1978, the law states that before any construction work can be initiated underwater, it is necessary to carry out marine archaeological investigations in areas that will be influenced by the enterprise. The developer is usually responsible for the costs of these investigations, but if the cost is extraordinarily high, the Norwegian state can pay for the investigations. In addition, Norwegian planning and building regulations state that construction work underwater must consider the protection of cultural remains. The result is that cultural remains on land and underwater are protected in the same way and that, as stated by the Norwegian government (St. Melding No. 46, 1988–1989), the law for the protection of cultural remains is the most important means by which Norway meets the UNESCO recommendations that cultural protection be included in business across all sectors.

Marine archaeological investigations are carried out by five institutions that are responsible for individual sections of Norway's very long (21,000 km) coastline. Every year, these institutions consider several hundred different cases. In the past 15 years, a much stricter practice has been possible due to an increased availability of personnel, experience, and awareness of marine archaeology in general. The result has been that oil companies that operate offshore must also consider protection of cultural remains on the seabed to make sure that archaeological sites are not damaged by their construction work.

INDUSTRY AND ARCHAEOLOGY WORKING TOGETHER—A NORWEGIAN EXAMPLE

In the late 1980s, the Norwegian oil company Statoil started to explore the oil and gas reservoirs on Haltenbanken in the Norwegian Sea. As a result of finding the Heidrun oil and gas field, Statoil and Conoco planned to build a new gas pipeline from the offshore continental shelf to the shore. After having completed several seasons of sonar and topographical seabed surveys, a potential pipeline route, expected to be the route of fewest physical obstacles and the lowest cost, was selected. This pipeline route crosses over a rugged seabed with water depths of over 300 m and has a total length of about 250 km. Because the pipeline route passes close to the Haltenbanken fishing bank, the pipeline project was termed the Haltenpipe Development Project (HDP) (Hovland, Jasinski, and Søreide 1998).

During the initial surveys through the coastal approaches at Ramsøy Fjord, between the islands of Smøla and Hitra, it was discovered that the remnants of an old shipwreck were situated very close to the planned track. Studies of written sources found in Norwegian and Russian archives revealed the tragic events leading to the wrecking of a Russian Navy ship named *Jedinorog* (*Unicorn*) (Søreide and Jasinski 1998).

Jedinorog was built in 1758–1759 CE in Arkhangelsk as a pink, approximately 39.6 m long and carrying 22 cannon. It was on its way from Kronstad in the Baltic Sea to Arkhangelsk loaded with an unknown number of cannon, lead, anchors, and other commodities when a storm off Smøla Island destroyed its three masts on 16 October 1760. Mastless, the ship drifted helplessly in the dangerous waters of Ramsøy Fjord. During the following night, the ship hit the rocky shore of Sæbu Island, broke up, and sank. No one seems to have survived the wrecking apart from 12 sailors who had already been put ashore on Smøla Island some days earlier.

The story of the wrecking was preserved by the inhabitants of the Sæbu, Hitra, and Smøla islands, but over the years some elements were added and some removed until the identity of the ship was no longer certain. In 1877, over 100 cannon were recovered by a salvage company from shallow water at the grounding site. With the introduction of SCUBA diving, a few objects were also recovered by amateur divers and archaeologists from the wreck site in the 1960–1970s (Søreide and Jasinski 1998).

Conflicting Interests

When this incident was brought to Statoil's attention during the initial inspection of the pipeline route, not much was known about the ship; its identity, the purpose of its journey, its cargo, and so on were all unknown. The oil company was interested in completing the pipeline without external interference, while the Norwegian University of Science and Technology (NTNU), which is responsible for the protection of cultural remains in this part of Norway, claimed that remnants of the wreck could potentially be damaged by the pipeline and demanded that special investigations be carried out before the oil company laid the pipeline.

Like most companies, Statoil naturally tries to keep costs as low as possible in all engineering construction projects. In the Haltenpipe project, only the costs necessary for the safe and legally compliant completion of the project were projected. Prior to the HDP, Statoil had already completed several offshore field development projects, including construction of four major offshore oil and gas pipelines, totaling more than 5,000 km of pipe, in water depths up to 540 m. Through this significant experience, the company knew that detailed underwater mapping, inspection, and surveying are crucial to success. For example, during the initial laying of Statoil's first offshore pipeline, Statpipe, between the Statfjord Field and western Norway, the prelay route inspection discovered intact World War I mines. Even though these objects had been detected by a side-scan sonar during the initial pipeline route survey, no intact mines from World War I had been expected to exist, so the objects had been interpreted as boulders. Naturally, the cost of holding up the laying operation for several days of mine clearance far exceeded all survey expenditures for initial pipeline route surveying and inspection. Similarly, unplanned marine archaeological investigations of the HDP pipeline route later in the project would potentially delay the pipelaying operations and increase the cost of the project.

Compared to what is normally the case on land, there has been very little legal or government involvement in most offshore underwater development projects. Only rarely are factors other than fisheries, military, and environmental interests taken into consideration. However, in this particular project NTNU, for the first time ever in an offshore construction project, insisted that Statoil was also responsible for the protection of historic shipwrecks that were discovered during the initial pipeline route surveying and inspection. Because Statoil had no previous experience with similar considerations on previous pipeline projects, the company at first attempted to claim no responsibility for underwater cultural resources.

Traditionally, terrestrial archaeology was treated differently by Statoil. Whereas the claims for marine archaeological investigations came as a surprise to Statoil, onshore archaeology was treated as a routine consideration, which according to Norwegian law had to be taken seriously. However, NTNU maintained that similar law enforcement comes into play offshore if the construction work is in conflict with sites considered by marine archaeologists to be of special heritage interest. Because the pipeline could potentially damage cultural remains, NTNU claimed that Statoil had an obvious responsibility to make sure that proper investigations were undertaken prior to detailed construction planning.

Achieving an Agreement

While NTNU argued that Statoil was responsible for the protection of shipwrecks and other cultural remains that could be damaged by Statoil's construction work, Statoil claimed that the government, including the Ministries of Defense, Nature Conservation, Science, and Education, and the Norwegian Petroleum Directorate had already approved the HDP route and given their consent for the construction. Against this view, NTNU argued that even though Statoil had been given the right to build the pipeline, this could not be done without considering the possible effects on cultural remains on the seabed; Statoil had to accept the added costs of an investigation to establish whether or not the pipeline could damage cultural remains on the seabed. Furthermore, the investigation had to be carried out by the proper authority, namely, NTNU.

Statoil could either choose to ignore NTNU's claim and await a lawsuit, perhaps risking what Statoil considered to be the highly unlikely possibility that the government would halt pipelaying operations, or to cooperate with NTNU. Finally Statoil decided to cooperate.

Creating a Win-Win Situation

From previous experience with academic research institutions in Norway, Statoil had established good relationships, where both Statoil and the institutions gained in knowledge, experience, and public esteem, thus creating a win-win situation. For

Statoil, however, this win-win situation was possible only if the company had an experienced researcher or an enthusiastic in-house engineer who was able and willing to observe the work performed by the institution. Without such a resource on Statoil's side, the expenditure was mainly for the benefit of the academic institution, and a chance for the company to gain experience and first-hand knowledge was lost.

The arguments within Statoil to defend such (academic) expenditure, often considered by seasoned construction engineers to be a waste of money, were rather delicate. However, internal documents and statements on etiquette, the environment, and public relations provide ample scope to assist in measures to protect cultural heritage, in the same way that there is stimulation from top management to protect nature and the environment in any possible way. Therefore, the agreement with NTNU was made not in fear of the authorities holding up the laying operations, but rather in the spirit of sustainable development, research, and basic respect for cultural heritage.

A marine archaeological investigation was financed by Statoil in 1994 and carried out by NTNU between 1994 and 1997 (Hovland, Jasinski, and Søreide 1998). The shallow-water areas were investigated by divers, while ROVs were used to investigate the deepwater areas, up to 280 m in depth. In total, costs for the marine archaeological work on the HDP pipeline added up to about 0.3% of the total construction costs.

In the end, the project was able to reconstruct the events prior to the wrecking and provide significant new knowledge about the site. The project also contributed toward developing a new deepwater marine archaeological methodology. Statoil was able to lay the pipeline without damaging cultural remains on the seabed. Thus, instead of possibly destroying the site, this approach not only made sure that the site was protected, but also resulted in increased knowledge for the oil company, the archaeological institution, and, not least, the public. This project also paved the way for the most advanced industry/archaeology project to date: the Ormen Lange Project.

ORMEN LANGE—THE WORLD'S FIRST DEEPWATER ARCHAEOLOGICAL EXCAVATION

The Ormen Lange gas field is located in the Norwegian Sea, 100 km northwest of the middle Norway coast (Figure 44.2). It is Norway's largest gas field, proven through drilling by Norsk Hydro in 1997. The development of the Ormen Lange field includes installation of a subsea production system, which is linked directly to an onshore processing and export plant. The gas is transported 1,200 km, from Norway to Easington in the United Kingdom, via the world's longest subsea export pipeline. When it reaches full production, the field will meet 20% of the UK demand for gas (Bryn, Jasinski, and Søreide 2007).

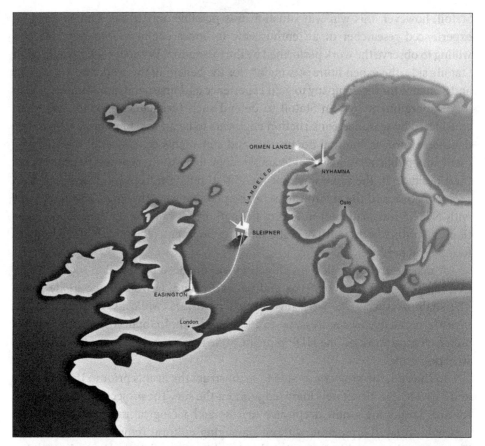

Figure 44.2 (a) Map showing the location of the Ormen Lange and Langeled pipelines and (b) the pipelaying vessel during installation over the wreck site. Reproduced with the kind permission of Norsk Hydro.

In the early stages of the project, Norsk Hydro presented survey data from their proposed pipeline routes to NTNU. Unfortunately, the existing survey data were inadequate to detect, with reasonable certainty, the presence of archaeological material in the proposed pipeline corridors, so NTNU requested that a separate archaeological survey be carried out, utilizing a modern side-scan sonar system and a digital data collection system. The recommended side-scan sonar needed to be of high frequency (i.e., not less than 300 kHz), have high dynamic range, be towed at an altitude no greater than 10 m off the seafloor, and be set to a range of no more than 100 m in order to ensure detection of archaeological material (Bryn, Jasinski, and Søreide 2007; see Quinn in this volume).

Further justifying a separate marine archaeological survey, the pipelines were to pass through an area with a rich maritime history. Due to its geographical location, the area is listed on the Norwegian Directorate for Cultural Heritage's list of areas with special priority for marine archaeology and protection of underwater heritage. The area has been visited by Norwegian and foreign vessels since the Middle Ages in connection with rich herring fisheries, general trade, timber trade, and naval operations. The closest city is Molde, approximately 40 km to the south, which has been a trade center since 1742 CE. The area also bordered directly on Hustadvika, a stretch of water with a reputation as a graveyard of historic and modern ships, mentioned several times in written sources as a place of maritime tragedies caused by storms or poor navigation. Prior to this project there were 20–30 known historical shipwrecks in Hustadvika and surrounding areas (Bryn, Jasinski, and Søreide 2007).

Norsk Hydro and NTNU agreed that NTNU would carry out a new marine archaeological survey in selected areas of the pipeline route, in order to fulfill the requirements of the Law on Protection of Cultural Heritage. During this survey in 2003, the team utilized an ROV to locate cultural resources in the pipeline corridors. The ROV was flown along the centerline of the pipeline routes. High-resolution scanning sonar and side-scan sonar were used as the primary survey instruments. Sonar images were interpreted in real time and used to locate potential targets. When an interesting target was located, the ROV inspected it using video cameras, while the dynamically positioned survey ship held position.

The first survey resulted in the discovery of one modern iron-hulled shipwreck, numerous coils of wire rope, and several large steel objects that posed direct threats to the pipeline installation. The most important discovery, however, was a historic shipwreck situated very close to the planned pipeline routes (Søreide and Jasinski 2005, 2008).

The stern area of the ship was first identified on side-scan sonar due to a dense scatter of glass bottles indicative of the mid- to late eighteenth century. A cursory examination of the bottle scatter revealed that there were probably more than 1,000 bottles of varying morphology visible on the surface and that there were clearly a significant number of bottles partially or completely buried south-southwest of the main site. The bottles were most likely cargo, along with stoneware containers that may have carried wine, beer, champagne, cognac, or brandy. On closer inspection, it was determined that the site was a historically significant wreck, in a state of good preservation. The site contained thousands of artifacts, some exposed on the sea-floor surface, others buried under several centimeters of sandy silt transported across the site by tidal currents.

The visible wooden structure was approximately 30 m long, while the overall shipwreck site was deemed to be more than 40 m in length. It sat on the seafloor along a line running northeast to southwest, from bow to stern, respectively. The natural terrain of the site ranged in depth from approximately 165 m in the bow to 170 m in the stern. The ship was splayed open due to decay of the deck timbers and upper works. The bow of the ship was characterized by the presence of four lead hawse pipes through which anchor cables would have been worked. Clearly visible in the bow were the massive cant-frames and stem-timber, and possibly the remnants of major timbers such as the apron and keelson in a good state of preservation. Abaft there was an expansive area of ship timbers, some exposed and others partially or completely covered with sediment. The stern section of the wreckage contained several classes of artifacts such as porcelain, stoneware, pewter, glass, wood, brass/bronze, and iron.

Alternative Pipeline Routes

The shipwreck was situated in an area with very complex underwater terrain features, in a rocky canyon with limited possibilities to move the pipeline. Norsk Hydro at first attempted to survey an alternative pipeline corridor, but a new side-scan sonar survey revealed another historical shipwreck site in the middle of this alternative route. Consequently, it proved impossible for the oil company to move the pipeline route, and given the complex underwater terrain, the pipeline would have to be installed through the shipwreck site, likely damaging it. Since the shipwreck site is protected under the Law on Protection of Cultural Heritage, additional investigations of the wreck site were necessary prior to installation of the pipeline. During 2004 and 2005, advanced technology and new methods were used to document and excavate the site, making it the most technologically advanced underwater archaeology project ever undertaken at the time.

Documentation and Excavation of the Site

NTNU has been developing marine archaeological methods and performing projects in deep water since the early 1990s. This work has resulted in the discovery and documentation of numerous historic shipwrecks (Jasinski and Søreide 2008; Søreide 2000). When it became clear that extensive documentation and even excavation of the site would be necessary prior to installation of the pipeline, it was decided that this unique experience would be used to design a specially suited marine archaeology ROV with the necessary tooling to document and excavate the site. The ROV is capable of carrying the special tooling needed for deepwater archaeological documentation and excavation. Another smaller ROV system was used as a backup system, for video documentation, and for tasks that required simultaneous use of two ROV systems.

Detailed Inspection

The area surrounding the shipwreck site was initially surveyed with ROV-mounted side-scan sonar and multibeam echo sounder to construct a detailed bathymetric profile of the seafloor in order to determine the extent of the shipwreck site and to minimize the impact of the pipeline installation. A Kongsberg scanning sonar was used to create an even higher-resolution acoustic model of the site and the seafloor. The data was used to produce an x, y, z point representation of the survey area. The x, y, z data were used to form contour charts of the shipwreck site.

The visible parts of the shipwreck and the area surrounding the wreck were then surveyed with video cameras to establish the full extent of the site and to locate artifacts that may have become disassociated from the main wreck site over time. Detailed visual inspection of a 400 by 800 m area surrounding the main hull structure revealed an additional 179 artifacts in the vicinity of the shipwreck, of which the majority were modern. The inspection, however, did reveal a spread of shipwreck-related artifacts to the south and southwest of the wreck, downslope from the main wreck site.

The ROV was equipped with seven high-resolution video cameras, including high-definition and 3CCD broadcast cameras, as well as 1600 W HMI gaslights and 1250 W halogen lights (Figures 44.3 and 44.4). Used in conjunction with flood and wide flood reflectors, these lamps gave remarkable wide-area illumination

Figure 44.3 The specially designed marine archaeology ROV developed for the Ormen Lange project. Image by Fredrik Naumann and Fredrik Søreide.

Figure 44.4 The ROV hovering above the bow section of the Ormen Lange wreck site.
Reproduced with the kind permission of NTNU Vitenskapsmuseet.

compared to traditional lights and enabled the team to document the site with superior quality. Paired lasers were used to introduce a scale in selected video images to obtain measurements in situ. In addition, the ROV was also equipped with a photomosaic camera developed by Woods Hole Oceanographic Institute and used to collect images for photomosaics of the site at various stages of the investigation.

Sub-bottom Survey

In many cases archaeological material will be completely buried underneath the sediments and cannot be located by visual aids. The area surrounding the wreck site was therefore also surveyed with sub-bottom profilers to determine the full extent of the site buried beneath the sediment.

Three different sub-bottom data sets were collected. Targets were only selected if they were single "point-source" or a contiguous series of anomalies and/or diffractions, regardless of amplitude, in the near-surface sediment and not deeper than the glacial sediment boundary. The data was plotted in ArcGIS over the available bathymetry and side-scan sonar mosaic and correlated with cultural material and modern debris to determine the origin of the anomaly in its respective data set.

Based on the sub-bottom results, the extent of the main shipwreck site beneath the sediment with no seafloor expression was postulated to extend south-southwest from the southernmost visible artifact on the seafloor, and the site extent was also enlarged to the west and east.

Pre-excavation Conclusion

The pre-excavation documentation formed the basis for a preliminary site analysis and site plan. The results of the multibeam survey, side-scan survey, detailed visual inspection, and sub-bottom survey, indicated that the spread of material from the shipwreck, visible on the surface and buried beneath the sediments was limited. However, large sections of the main site were believed to be buried beneath a thin layer of sediments. It was therefore decided that the site should be uncovered and partly excavated to establish to what extent it would be damaged by the pipeline construction and to learn more about the shipwreck site itself.

Excavation

An archaeological excavation of sunken historic ships is difficult, even at shallow depths. Doing it at 170 m was extremely complex. An excavation support frame was developed to investigate in detail and excavate the shipwreck with the necessary control and accuracy (Figure 44.5). A 10 by 10 m steel frame was designed and constructed. Suspended on a steel wire from the stern of a support vessel, it was successfully lowered to the seafloor and placed over the shipwreck, its legs resting just outside the wreck site (Søreide, Jasinski, and Sperre 2006).

The ROV then docked onto a movable platform on the frame. The docking platform could be moved in all directions within the frame by motorized cogwheels controlled from the surface. Sitting still on the platform just above the wreck site, the ROV posed no risk to the features and fragile artifacts scattered on the seabed and could be used to document, excavate, and recover artifacts. Positioning of the platform was based on rotation sensors of the cogwheels, backed up by high-resolution directional sonar sensors, with resulting subcentimeter accuracy. Position input from the LBL system was also recorded. The frame allowed the ROV to excavate the seafloor with great precision so that the maximum amount of data could be extracted while carefully handling any artifacts that were recovered. The combination of the specially designed ROV and the excavation frame enabled the team to conduct a systematic excavation, equivalent to a terrestrial excavation, at a greater depth than ever before.

A specially developed marine archaeology dredge was developed to remove the sediment covering the site. It was designed to work together with a water pump that was carried by the ROV. This pump also supplied water to jetting nozzles. The suction force could be adjusted to accommodate to the actual sediment conditions and was successfully used to remove sediment around even small fragile artifacts. An altimeter was used to measure trench depth. Sediments were filtered through a sediment collection basket. Two hundred fifty small artifacts were collected in this device.

When an artifact had been uncovered it was picked up using a seven-function Kraft Raptor force-feedback manipulator arm. While the force-feedback function enabled it to directly pick up fragile artifacts, artifacts were mainly lifted by a specially developed suction picker (Figure 44.6). It picked up artifacts with a small suction cup

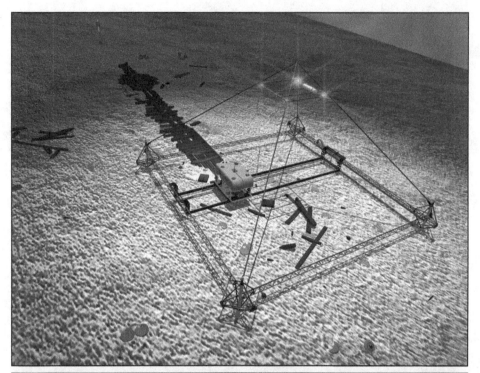

Figure 44.5 The subsea excavation frame on site. This enabled for the
first-time archaeological excavations to be carried out underwater with the same
precision as on land. Reproduced with the kind permission of (a) Brynjar Wiig and
(b) NTNU Vitenskapsmuseet.

Figure 44.6 Recovery of ceramic jar from the Ormen Lange wreck site with a suction device. Reproduced with the kind permission of NTNU Vitenskapsmuseet.

connected to a pump. More than 200 artifacts were recovered without any damage. In addition, some artifacts were lifted by specially developed tooling that was constructed on-site. The artifacts were stored in internal collection baskets in the ROV or lifted in external collection baskets. Artifacts recovered ranged from tiny seeds and buttons to large ceramic vessels in excess of 50 kg.

Ormen Lange Conclusions

The ship's sinking date cannot be determined with precision, since no record regarding its identity or its loss has been discovered so far. There is ongoing research in archives in Norway, England, Netherlands, France, Spain, Portugal, and Russia. It is likely that the vessel sank early in the nineteenth century, as the most modern artifact is a Dutch gold coin dated to 1802. This and the date on the ship's bell are our strongest reference point to determine the date of construction and sinking for this vessel. The bell bears the inscription of its manufacture date: 1745.

Based on the artifacts discovered, it seems most likely that the Ormen Lange shipwreck was a merchantman that navigated along the Norwegian coast to/from Britain or Netherlands with a cargo meant for or originating in Russia. A substantial number of Russian coins and other artifacts point to this. The vessel seems to have been carrying a profitable cargo of spirits, which may have been accompanied by a load of grains, salt, or a similar perishable cargo that did not survive.

Nearly 500 artifacts were recovered from the site, making it the most comprehensive and detailed deepwater excavation ever carried out by an archaeological institution. Research into the material collected from the site will hopefully yield the necessary clues needed to identify the vessel, in combination with the ongoing archival research (Søreide and Jasinski 2008).

Due to the substantial water depth of 170 m, SCUBA diving was impossible and mandated the use of ROVs to conduct all mapping, surveying, sampling, and excavation. The project has successfully developed equipment and methods that enable marine archaeologists to do all tasks that previously could only be done by SCUBA divers. Most notably, the excavation support frame that was developed in combination with the specially modified marine archaeology ROV allows archaeologists to investigate in detail and excavate the seafloor with great precision so that the maximum amount of data can be extracted while carefully handling any artifacts to be recovered. Deepwater excavation was the last frontier for marine archaeology. This new technology enables archaeologists for the first time to investigate and excavate cultural heritage in deep water with the same precision and standards as on land. No longer can industry claim that archaeologists do not have the ability to investigate sites in deep water.

The marine archaeological project, conducted pursuant to the Norwegian Cultural Heritage Act, was financed by Norsk Hydro and other participants in the development. The excavation was completed according to the plan, and in time before the planned pipeline installation in the spring of 2006. The total cost of the project was approximately US$10 million, only 0.1% of the pipeline project's total cost of more than US$10 billion.

DISCUSSION

One of the most complicated problems regarding the social perception and protection of underwater heritage is that it remains unseen for most of society, although sites underwater have become more accessible for the public, largely because SCUBA diving has become a popular sport. The general public can achieve some perception of a site in the form of publications, photographs, films, museum collections, and so on (Bowens 2008).

Still, for the majority of society, including management authorities, something unseen remains something marginal, beyond or on the edge of social practice and not really worth being aware of, and definitely not worth spending funds to preserve or investigate. However much the archaeological world strives to focus some public attention on underwater heritage, only limited results will ensue as long as society does not have the chance to actually see it, get to know it, and enjoy it. Existing beyond everyday perception, this part of the world heritage will often be looked upon by the general public as a curiosity and will remain a preserve of archaeologists and adventurers. In this context, treasure hunting and the earning of private profit from underwater heritage is in fact quite a legitimate activity in the perception of the average person, on the same level as gold or silver mining (see Maarleveld in this volume).

The readers of this book will probably agree that underwater heritage must be protected. But protected against what? Treasure hunters, plunderers, forces of nature, microorganisms, trawlers, construction? Or against anything and anybody, including archaeologists, approaching the sites? Another question is, who should protect monuments in developing countries where such protection is beyond the means of society?

In the last few years, the maritime archaeological community and the salvage industry have used billions of words, megabytes, and tons of paper discussing the UNESCO CPUCH. Unfortunately, most of the participants in this discussion have mainly been concerned with defending their own rights rather than defending something that in fact belongs to all of us as well as to future generations. This time and energy should instead be used to establish clear procedures, work standards, ethical rules, better methods, publishing, and mediating channels.

Thus, even though CPUCH may ensure protection of some sites, it is perhaps not the best solution. As shown, it is possible to search for and investigate archaeological sites underwater, but it will always be an expensive task. It is therefore likely that only a few researchers will have the resources needed to work deep underwater and that only the most spectacular sites will be investigated. One fear, therefore, is that large portions of our heritage will be lost using this approach. Education of and cooperation with industry is probably a better option. Archaeologists must work together with companies that develop projects in the ocean, like the oil companies presented above. This approach will, as discussed, benefit companies, the archaeological institutions, and society at large.

The pressure on underwater cultural heritage will only increase in the years to come, so we can only suggest that more emphasis be placed on the applications of underwater technology in the future and that marine archaeological studies be performed as an important part of industrial projects. Marine archaeologists, companies involved in construction projects underwater, and cultural resource management agencies should start addressing this challenge as soon as possible, creating a win-win situation where our common heritage is protected and projects completed without jeopardizing the reputation of both the project and the company. Since the seabed eventually will become the domain of the general public, it is important to introduce sound and ethical standards, rather than fearing future public judgments.

REFERENCES

Ball, D. A., J. B. Irion, and C. E. Horrell. 2007. Outreach beyond the beach: Management of historic shipwrecks on the Outer Continental Shelf. In *Out of the blue: Public interpretation of maritime cultural resources*, ed. J. H. Jameson Jr. and Della A. Scott-Ireton, 171–181. New York: Springer Press.

Bowens, A., ed. 2008. *Underwater archaeology: The NAS guide to principles and practice.* 2nd ed. Portsmouth: Nautical Archaeology Society.

Bryn, P., M. E. Jasinski, and F. Søreide. 2007. *Ormen Lange—pipelines and shipwrecks.* Oslo: Universitetsforlaget.

Firth, A. 2006. Old shipwrecks and new dredging: An Elizabethan ship in the Thames. In *Underwater cultural heritage at risk: Managing natural and human impacts,* ed. Robert Grenier, David Nutley and Ian Cochran, 35–37. Paris: ICOMOS.

Hall, J. 2007. The *Black Rhino. Journal of Maritime Archaeology* 2 (2): 93–97.

Hovland, M., M. E. Jasinski, and F. Søreide. 1998. Underwater construction projects vs. marine archaeology: How solving conflict saved old shipwreck. *Norwegian Oil Review* 24 (7): 98–102.

Irion, J. 2001. Cultural resource management of shipwrecks on the Gulf of Mexico Outer Continental Slope. Paper presented at the 2nd MIT Conference on Technology, Archaeology, and the Deep Sea, April 2002.

Jasinski M. E. 1999. Which way now? Maritime archaeology and underwater heritage into the 21st century. World Archaeological Congress 4. Cape Town.

Jasinski, M. E., and F. Søreide. 2001. Applications of remote sensing in Norwegian marine archaeology and management of underwater heritage. In *ICOMOS '99—World Congress on Monumental Heritage Conservation, Mexico City, Memorias del Congreso Cientifico de Arqueologia Subacuatica ICOMOS, Serie Arqueologia,* 188–199. Cordoba: Instituto Nacional de Antropologia e Historia.

———. 2008. Seven Seas: Maritime archaeology at the Norwegian University of Science and Technology. In *Collaboration, communication and involvement: Maritime archaeology and education in the 21st century,* 125–146. Toruń, Poland: University Press, Nicolaus Copernicus University.

Jeffery, B. 1999. Australia. In *Legal protection of the underwater cultural heritage: National and international perspectives,* ed. S. Dromgoole, 1–17. The Hague: Kluwer Law International.

Kingsley S. A. 2009. Deep-sea fishing impacts on the shipwrecks of the English Channel and Western Approaches, Odyssey Papers 4. Online at www.shipwreck.net. Accessed November 2010.

Momber, G. 2000. Reflections on the legal standing of underwater archaeology in the UK. *Journal of the Society for Underwater Technology* 24 (3): 115–118.

Pickford, N. 1993. *Atlas of shipwreck and treasure.* London: Dorling Kindersley.

Søreide, F. 2000. Cost-effective deep-water archaeology: Preliminary investigations in Trondheim Harbour. *International Journal of Nautical Archaeology* 29 (2): 284–293.

———. 2011. *Ships from the Depths. Deepwater archaeology.* College Station: Texas A&M University Press.

Søreide, F., and M. E. Jasinski. 1998. The *Unicorn* wreck, central Norway—underwater archaeological investigations of an 18th-century Russian pink, using remotely controlled equipment. *International Journal of Nautical Archaeology* 27 (2): 95–112.

———. 2000. Marine archaeology and protection of heritage in deeper water: Consequences for future offshore construction projects. Paper presented at Oceans 2000, 11–14 September, Providence, RI.

———. 2005. Ormen Lange: Investigation and excavation of a shipwreck in 170m depth. Paper presented at Oceans 2005, 19–23 September, Washington, DC.

———. 2008. Ormen Lange, Norway—the deepest dig. *International Journal of Nautical Archaeology* 37 (2): 380–384.

Søreide, Fredrik, Marek E. Jasinski, and Thor Olav Sperre. 2006. Unique new technology enables archaeology in the deep sea. *Sea Technology* 47 (10): 10–13.

Steingrimsson, S. A., S. A. Ragnarsson, D. Nævestad, and H. P. Haraldsson. 2006. Bottom trawling and scallop dredging in the Arctic: Impacts of fishing on non-target species, vulnerable habitats and cultural heritage. Nordic Council of Ministers Report 206: 529.

Stemm, G. 1992. The future of deep water: Commercial archaeology; A new business? *Treasure Diver* 4 (2): 28–33.

UNESCO. 2010. *The Underwater Cultural Heritage.* Rev. 2010. Online at www.unesco.org/ en/underwater-cultural-heritage/. Accessed February 2010.

Varmer, O., and C. M. Blanco. 1999. United States of America. In *Legal protection of the underwater cultural heritage: National and international perspectives*, ed. S. Dromgoole, 205–221. The Hague: Kluwer Law International.

Wickler, S., M. E. Jasinski, F. Søreide, and O. Grøn. 1999. Remote sensing in marine archaeology: Preliminary results from the Snow White project, Arctic Norway. Paper presented at World Archaeological Congress 4, 10–14 January, Cape Town.

CHAPTER 45

MUSEUMS AND MARITIME ARCHAEOLOGY

MICHAEL McCARTHY

INTRODUCTION

IT seems that with few exceptions a museum with a maritime heritage component is the most common public repository for the range of objects raised in a maritime archaeological, underwater archaeological, or nautical archaeological context. As the following discussion shows, however, those places that are not museums in the accepted sense—for example, universities, institutes, foundations, and conservation laboratories—have tended to provide public access and interpretive materials as well as housing and making available the archaeological and conservation data. In this way, where the public elements are substantial, they are effectively performing functions similar to a museum as defined by the International Council of Museums (ICOM) and accepted by other "umbrella bodies," including the International Council of Maritime Museums (ICMM). As a result, here the term "museum" includes both traditional museums as well as institutions that curate and display archaeological data as part of a broader mission.

Some of our maritime archaeological institutions are independent; some are immensely rich, replete with staff, partners with industry, or with government or philanthropic backing, while others are poor in all respects except the enthusiasm of their people. Still others are part of a far greater whole, with many of the larger institutions serving the museum needs of a region or the nation itself. As their CEOs or directors come and go, as emphases and priorities inevitably change, and as the parent museum itself evolves as a consequence, in some places maritime archaeology (as but one of a host of museum-based activities) will struggle for its survival against a host of equally worthy competing demands. In one period it may be ascendant, in another quiescent, rendering comment on their present phase problematic. Given also that our institutions are so numerous and varied, large and small, and that they are located across the globe in so many nations and from so many cultures, details of any one operation, its holdings, structure, or any specific presentations, will not appear. To provide details of one would be to the exclusion of others; to analyze some would be to ignore many others equally worthy of comment. To mention the works and influence of specific practitioners or personalities, again, would do no justice to those equally worthy. Instead, the reader is referred to some of the recent works analyzing specific museums in transition (e.g., Witcomb 2003) and is invited to examine those places, programs, and personalities of interest to them against the issues raised in what follows.

It is doubly unwarranted to provide detail, for information on the various holdings, staff, philosophical emphasis, and programs, is readily available in printed works and electronically. Many, but certainly not all, places will inevitably be mentioned in other chapters in this work, and some might not appear in what follows. If places are missing from the list provided (Table 45.1), an apology is tendered here, for the institutions presented in the list are intended more to show the range of places carrying the products of our work than to provide an exhaustive account. Finally, we should observe that the categories afforded to each place are intended only as a guide for the same purposes; some institutions clearly have many functions, but will appear only once in the list.

Before reading the list, one should also observe that maritime heritage museums can have maritime archaeological functions beyond the housing, conservation, curation, interpretation, and presentation of materials from a marine or submerged environment. A few museums have also been erected around funerary ships, for example. Many also have libraries that store archaeological reports, some have publication facilities, and many provide their works on Web sites. Some also provide access to their unpublished or in-house working papers, technical reports, or other important unpublished compilations (also called the "gray literature"). These cater to the fundamental obligation of all archaeologists to provide full access to their work, not just via refereed journal articles and the published works.

Some museums are teaching facilities. Some also have a legislated government mandate to act as heritage management agents at the national or regional level. In these circumstances, they are cultural resource managers, protecting, policing, monitoring, and presenting the wrecks and relics under their care, in situ or electronically. Often they do this in association with local communities and avocational divers and enthusiasts. These responsibilities can also result in museums conducting or supervising archaeological programs. These programs range from projects as simple as the recovery of individual relics, to the excavation and recovery of entire wrecks, and in some cases the excavation and interpretation of ancient harbors. In a relatively new development, some actively seek to recover heritage materials and return them to the public domain via amnesties, with surprisingly mixed results (Rodrigues 2009).

Table 45.1 Some places exhibiting maritime archaeological materials

Underwater Archaeology Museums and Places Exhibiting Raised Wrecks (Including Aircraft), Substantial Hull Remains, or Machinery

Ancient Ship Museum, Penglai City, China
Battle of the Restigouche National Historic Site of Canada, Quebec
Bodrum Museum of Underwater Archaeology, Turkey
Brooklands Museum, Weybridge, Surrey
Cape Cod Maritime Museum, Massachusetts
Central Museum, Utrecht
Comacchio Museum, Ravenna
Confederate Naval Museum, Georgia
CSS *Neuse* State Historic Site, North Carolina
De Soto National Wildlife Refuge, Missouri River
Dover Museum, Kent
Egyptian Museum, Cairo
Georgetown Maritime Museum, South Carolina
German Maritime Museum, Bremerhaven
Göteborg City Museum, Sweden
Gottorp Castle Schleswig, Germany
Hull and East Riding Museum, Yorkshire
Kalmar Castle, Sweden
Korean National Maritime Museum, Mokpo
Kyrenia Ship Museum, Cyprus
Ladby Ship Museum, Denmark
Mallorytown Landing, Ontario
Marine Silk Road Museum, Guangdong Province, China
Mariner's Museum, Newport News, Virginia
Marsala Regional Archaeological Museum, Sicily
Mary Rose Museum, Portsmouth
Medieval Museum, Stockholm
Museum of Ancient Navigation, Mainz
Museum of Overseas Communications History, Fujian, China
Museum of Roman Ships, Rome
Museum of Underwater Archaeology Sassnitz, Rügen
National Archaeological Museum of Aquileia, Italy
National Maritime Museum, Chantaburi, Thailand
National Maritime Museum, Haifa
National Museum of American History Smithsonian Institution, Washington, DC
National Museum of Denmark, Copenhagen
National Museum of Naval Aviation, Pensacola, Florida
National Museum of the Pacific War, Fredericksburg, Virginia
National Museum of the Philippines, Manila
National Museum of Underwater Archaeology, Cartagena, Spain
Netherlands Marine (Navy) Museum, Den Helder
Netherlands Museum Kornwerderzand
Netherlands Newland Heritage Center, Lelystad
Norwegian Maritime Museum, Oslo
Pilgrim Hall, Plymouth, Massachusetts
Portland Harbor Museum, South Portland, Maine

RACM, Lelystad Open Depot, the Netherlands
Rahmi M. Koç Museum, Istanbul
Red Bay National Historic Site of Canada, Newfoundland and Labrador
Royal Navy Submarine Museum, Portsmouth
Shipwreck Galleries, Western Australian Museum, Fremantle
South Carolina State Museum
St. Lawrence Islands National Park, Canada
Steamboat *Arabia* Museum, Kansas City
Swedish Aircraft Museum, Linköping
Swedish Naval Museum, Karlskrona
Takashima History and Folklore Museum, Matsuura City, Japan
Turks and Caicos National Museum
University of Haifa, Israel
Vapor Cue Triple Alliance War Museum, Paraguay
Vasa Museum, Stockholm
Vicksburg National Military Park, Mississippi
Viking Ship Museum, Oslo
Viking Ship Museum, Roskilde
Western Canada Aviation Museum, Manitoba
Yigall Alon Museum, Kibbutz Ginosar, Israel

Harbour Museums

Caesaria Maritima, Israel
Haddeby/Haithabu, Schleswig, Germany
Maritime Museum, Rotterdam, Netherlands
Marine (Navy) Museum, Den Helder
Museum of Ancient Shipping, Mainz
Museum of Ancient Ships, Pisa
Yenikapı Byzantine Port (presently excavating), Turkey

Submerged Terrestrial Site Museums

Neuchatel Lake dwellings, Switzerland
Port Royal, Jamaica
Scottish Crannog Centre, Loch Tay
Unteruhidingen, Germany

Burial or Funerary Ship Museums

Aldeburgh Moot Hall Museum, Suffolk
Cheops (Khufu) Pyramid, Egypt
Gokstad Ship, Oslo
Ladby Ship, Kerteminde, Denmark
Oseberg Ship, Norway
Sutton Hoo, Suffolk
Tune Ship, Bygdøy

Museums Managing Wrecks in Their Region

Barbados Museum and Historical Society
Bergen Maritime Museum, Norway
Bermuda Maritime Museum
Bohus County Museum, Västarvet, Sweden

(continued)

Table 45.1 (*continued*)

Cayman Islands National Museum
Estonian State Maritime Museum
Kalmar County Museum, Sweden
Lake Champlain Maritime Museum, Vermont
Langelands Museum, South Denmark
Malmö City Museum, Heritage Skåne, Sweden
Maritime Museum of Finland
Museum of Underwater Archaeology, Raversijde, Belgium
National Maritime Archaeological Museum, Cartagena, Spain
National Maritime Museum, Stockholm
Norwegian National Maritime Museum, Oslo
NTNU Science Museum, Archaeology section, Trondheim, Norway
Rostock Maritime Museum, Germany
St. Augustine Lighthouse Museum, Florida
St. George Shipwreck Museum, Thorsminde
Stavanger Museum, Norway
Swedish National Museum
Trinidad National Museum and Art Gallery, Trinidad and Tobago
Tromsø Museum, Tromsø University, Norway
Western Australian Museum

In Situ Wreck Exhibitions

Bateaux Below Shipwreck Preserve, Lake George, New York
Cape Fear Civil War Shipwreck District, North Carolina
Cayman Islands Shipwreck Preserve
Cooper River Heritage Trail, South Carolina
Falkland Islands–Port Stanley Wrecks
Fathom Five Underwater National Park, Lake Huron, Canada
Florida Underwater Archaeological Preserves
Fortress of Louisbourg National Historic Site of Canada, Nova Scotia
Garden Island Ship's Graveyard, South Australia
Inconstant, Wellington, New Zealand
Isle Royale National Park, Lake Superior, Canada
Kom El Dikka Archaeological Site, Alexandria
Lake Champlain Maritime Museum, Vermont
Lake George Historical Museum, New York
Louisbourg Wrecks, Canada
Mannum Dry Dock, South Australia
Maryland Historic Shipwreck Preserve
Michigan Underwater Preserve
Newport Medieval Ship, Wales
Padre Island National Seashore
Papahānaumokuākea Marine National Monument, Hawaii
Peachman Lake Erie Shipwreck Research Center, Ohio
Purton Hulks, Gloucestershire, England
Shipwreck Heritage Centre, Hastings (visits to *Amsterdam*)
South Carolina Maritime Heritage Trails
SS *Mediator*, Curacao, Netherlands Antilles
Stellwagen Bank National Marine Sanctuary, Massachusetts

Thunder Bay National Marine Sanctuary, Michigan
Truk Lagoon & Bikini Atoll, Micronesia
USS *Arizona* Memorial, Pearl Harbor, Hawaii
Western Australian Shipwreck Trails

Museum Ships Recovered After Being Sunk or Cast Ashore

Edwin Fox Maritime Museum, Picton, New Zealand
Great Britain, Bristol Dry Dock
HMS *Tecumseh*, Discovery Harbour, Penetanguishene, Ontario
James Craig, Australian National Maritime Museum
Kaiyo-Maru, Esashi town, Japan
Polly Woodside, Melbourne Maritime Museum
U534, Birkenhead, England
U.S. Brig *Niagara*, Erie Maritime Museum, Pennsylvania

Conservation Laboratories with Public Facilities

Lake Champlain Maritime Museum
Texas A&M University's Conservation Research Lab (CMAC)
Warren Lasch Conservation Center, Clemson University *HL Hunley*

General Museums (with Some Raised Materials)

Aegean Maritime Museum, Mykonos
Alderney Museum, Alderney, Channel Islands, Britain
Alexandria National Museum, Egypt
Amsterdam Historical Museum
Archaeological Museum, Zadar, Croatia
Archaeological Museum of Campeche, San Miguel Fort, Mexico
Arles Museum, France
Australian National Maritime Museum, Sydney
Australian War Memorial, Canberra
Bayworld Port Elizabeth South Africa
Beachcomber's Museum, Texel
Bermuda Maritime Museum
Bohusläns Museum, Uddevalla, Sweden
Bredasdorp Shipwreck Museum, South Africa
Brunei Maritime Museum, Kota Batu
Bryggen Museum, Bergen
Caen Memorial Museum for Peace, France
Calvert County Maritime Museum, Maryland
Cantabrian Maritime Museum, Cantabria, Spain
Castle Cornet, St Peter Port, Guernsey
Castle of the Royal Force, Havana
Cayman Islands National Museum
Ceuclum Museum, Cuijk, the Netherlands
Cité de la Mer Museum, Cherbourg
Cobh Museum, Ireland
Columbia River Maritime Museum, Astoria, Oregon
Columbus Lighthouse Underwater Archaeology Museum, Santo Domingo
Corpus Christie Museum of Science and History, Texas
East London Museum, East London, South Africa

(*continued*)

Table 45.1 (*continued*)

Flagstaff Hill Maritime Museum, Victoria, Australia
Florida Aquarium, Tampa (Little Salt Spring exhibit)
Florida Museum of Natural History, Gainesville
German Museum of Technology, Berlin
Glasshouse Museum, Kibbutz Nahsholim
Gotland Museum, Sweden
Graeco-Roman Museum of Alexandria, Egypt
Great Lakes Shipwreck Museum, Michigan
Guildhall Museum, London
Guzelyurt Museum of Nature and Archaeology, Cyprus
Hellenic Maritime Museum, Piraeus
Historical Museum of Acapulco, San Diego Fort, Acapulco, Mexico
Hung Yen Province Museum, Vietnam
Israel National Maritime Museum, Haifa
IZIKO National Maritime Museum, Cape Town
Kalmar County Museum, Sweden
Kom El-Dikaa Roman amphitheater, Alexandria
Kota Lukut Museum, Malaysia
La Pérouse Museum, Albi, France
La Pérouse Museum, Sydney
Lake Nemi shipyard, Italy
Lake Vänern Museum, Sweden
Liverpool Maritime Museum
Louisiana State Museum
Maine Maritime Museum, Bath
Malacca Maritime Archaeology Museum
Marine Museum of the Great Lakes at Kingston, Ontario
Mario Brozoski Municipal Museum, Puerto Deseado, Argentina
Maritime and Irish Mossing Museum, Scituate, Massachusetts
Maritime History Museum, New Caledonia
Maritime Museum, Calcutta Port Trust
Maritime Museum, Noumea
Maritime Museum, Rotterdam, the Netherlands
Maritime Museum of Denmark, Helsingør, Denmark
Maritime Museum of Finland, Helsinki
Maritime Museum of Piran Slovenia
Maritime Museum of the Atlantic, Halifax, Nova Scotia
Medieval Museum, Stockholm
Memorial University, Newfoundland
Michinoku Traditional Wooden Boat Museum, Aomori City, Japan
Montevideo National Maritime Museum
Museum of Archaeology and Anthropology Campinas State University, Brazil
Museum of Cadiz, Spain
Museum of London
Museum of Maritime Science, Tokyo
Museum of Mobile, Alabama
Museum of National Antiquities, Stockholm
Museum of San Felipe Bacalar Fort, Quintana Roo, Mexico
Museum of the Plains (Piana delle Orme), Italy
Museum of the Royal Palaces, Santo Domingo

Museum of Tropical Queensland, Australia
Muzium Negara, Kuala Lumpur, Malaysia
Mystic Seaport, Connecticut
Nanjing Municipal Museum
National Archaeological Museum, Athens
National Maritime Museum, Amsterdam
National Maritime Museum, Galle
National Maritime Museum, Gdansk
National Maritime Museum, Greenwich
National Maritime Museum, Paris
National Museum, New Delhi
National Museum of Anthropology, Mexico City
National Museum of Archaeology, Lisbon
National Museum of Cambodia, Phnom Penh
National Museum of China, Beijing
National Museum of Northern Ireland, Belfast
National Museum of the Philippines, Manila
National Museum of Reggio Calabria, Italy
National Museum of Scotland, Edinburgh
National Museum of Vietnamese History, Hanoi
National Museums and Galleries, Liverpool
National Naval Museum of the Nation, Tigre, Argentina
Naval History Museum, Mexico City
Naval History Museum, Veracruz, Mexico
Naval Museum, Montevideo, Uruguay
Naval Museum of Acapulco, Mexico
Naval Museum of Madrid
Navy Museum, Cochin, India
Newfoundland Museum, St. Johns
Norfolk Island Museum, Australia
North Carolina Maritime Museum
Northern Seafaring Museum, Groningen
Oiasso Roman Museum Irun, Spain
Osaka Maritime Museum, Osaka, Japan
Overloon War Museum, Netherlands
Palacio Cantón Museum of Mérida, Yucatán, Mexico
Piraeus Archaeological Museum
Plymouth City Museum and Art Gallery
Polish Maritime Museum, Gdansk
Pompey Museum, Nassau, Bahamas
Poole Museum, Poole, England
Port Natal Maritime Museum
Prince of Wales Museum, Mumbai
The Provincial Museum of Kymenlaakso, Finland
Royal Shipyards Museum, Dominican Republic
Quebec Museum of Civilization
Queen Victoria Museum, Launceston, Tasmania
Queenscliffe Museum, Victoria, Australia
Regional Museum of Campeche, Mexico
Rijksmuseum, Amsterdam

(continued)

Table 45.1 (*continued*)

San Blas Fort, Nayarit, Mexico
San Francisco Maritime National Historical Park
Shihsanhang Museum of Archaeology, Taipei County, Taiwan
Simonstown Museum Cape Town
South Australia Maritime Museum, Port Adelaide
Strandingsmuseum, Jutland, Denmark
Submarine Museum, Gosport
Swedish National Maritime Museum, Stockholm
Swedish Naval Museum, Karlskrona
Swiss National Museum, Zurich
Thalassa Museum, Cyprus
Tobago Museum, Fort King George, Scarborough
Tower Museum Derry, Ireland
Turks and Caicos National Museum, West Indies
Ulster Museum, Ireland
Ushuaia Maritime Museum, Tierra del Fuego, Argentina
U.S. Navy Museum, Washington, DC
Vancouver Maritime Museum
Viborg Historical Museum, St. Petersburg, Russia
Vlissingen Museum, Netherlands
Western Australian Museum, Geraldton

Private and Treasure Ship Museums

Ben Cropp Museum, Queensland, Australia
Bermuda Underwater Exploration Institute, Bermuda Museum
Mel Fisher Maritime Museum, Florida
Whydah Pirate Museum, Cape Cod
Wreck Museum, Terschelling, Netherlands

Children's Museums

Hampshire and White Archaeological Trust

Virtual Museums

AE2 submarine, Gallipoli, Turkey—online exhibition, Submarine Institute of Australia
ARCHEMAR Virtual Museum, Itaparica, Brazil
Collections Search System Maritime Museums, Netherlands
Managing Cultural Heritage Underwater (MACHU)
Maritime Heritage Online, NSW Heritage Branch, Sydney
The Maritime History Virtual Archives
The Memory of the Netherlands
Museums in the Sea, Florida
The Museum of Underwater Archaeology
NSW Department of planning *M24* Wreck Detective
Per Åkesson The Virtual Museum
Queensland Historic Shipwrecks Trail
The SCRAN Trust Scotland
Tour *U-869*
VENUS: Virtual Exploration of Underwater Sites, France, Italy, Portugal

Sometimes these institutions have also proved effective in presenting an in situ "underwater display case" or a "museum without walls" at an excavation, or at a wreck, submerged structure, or dwelling. These are accomplished by the facilitation of field schools, public access programs, and the provision of interpretive materials underwater. Sometimes they are specially designed to cater to people with disabilities. While this is not a new phenomenon (it dates back at least to the early 1980s; see Souter 2006), in the last few years "virtual museums" have filled a similar role (Sanders in this volume). They are invariably produced by maritime heritage or archaeological units taking the visitor down and through wrecks and maritime sites via the Web. These allow visitors to take virtual tours or watch searches take place, view inspections and excavations, read the histories, peruse the data, and sometimes to interact with the archaeologists and other specialists on site. These same experiences have also now found their way via live broadcasts into the museum's auditoriums, onto the exhibition floor, via what are generally termed interactive multimedia, and via other electronic presentations. These devices are the stuff of today and certainly will be far more prominent in the future, not just enabling internal and external public access to a far wider variety of objects, information, and exhibits in a virtual sense, but also to ensure that a collection is better managed. They are also tools with which to develop global networks and interlinks between individuals, groups, and institutions.

In these instances, the museum-based maritime archaeologist is clearly also a "public archaeologist," beholden not just to the site and the objects raised but also to the needs of the general populace with respect to exhibition, publication (in both academic and popular forms), and presentation (Merriman 2004).

Some modern trends also require examination as we look toward our future. One is the commercialization of the museum: financial success or failure is one of the benchmarks presently being applied by some politicians and many financiers and administrators. This is often in place of traditional benchmarks, such as the quality of its exhibitions and collection and the reputation of its curators, visitor service personnel, and exhibition and education staff. There is also a modern tendency to shift collection storage facilities away from the museum's heart to make savings, generate wealth, and create social spaces. Another trend is "new museology" or the "new museum" movement, where museums are promoted as active rather than passive agents for social change and sustainable living. These developments provide both opportunities and threats to our discipline.

Another new development, with few saving graces, has been the rationalizing of collections by deaccessioning objects, a practice fraught with danger and difficulties now and especially for the future. In some societies both maritime archaeology and museology also face the challenge of the stifling overregulation of society now common to most developed Western nations. Again, there is little to recommend this modern malaise.

It is also evident that partly because museums represent one of the main outlets for maritime, underwater, and nautical archaeological materials (here called maritime archaeology for simplicity), museums and our discipline were to an extent allied in their origins and development, their strengths, and their weaknesses. In some cases they might also share a common future. Some of these issues will be examined in more detail in what follows.

Our Early Collection Strategies as a Guide to the Future

In order to understand where institutions carrying maritime archaeological materials to the public might be headed, we need to revisit the past, look at our roots, and see how it all came into being. This could provide some useful insights, for in a period when museums are "in transition, suspended between past practices and future prospects" and as much "repositories for the future as well as the past" (Starn 2005: 96, 98), we need cast our net as widely as possible in the search for future direction.

In our sphere, naval museums are a starting point. They were inadvertently spawned by navies—as one of the first prolific maritime object collectors—seeking to retain touchstones to their past glories. Often they housed multitudinous objects such as weaponry, heraldry, flags, and trophies of war, including captured, destroyed, or surrendered ships, boats, and submarines, in what was once a quiet, little-known repository. Records were invariably scanty, storage and presentation often chaotic, audits unheard of, and conservation little more than an occasional dusting off. Most were in effect private, self-funded museums—laws unto themselves. Clutter, unbridled acquisition, and ad hoc, idiosyncratic presentation—the antithesis of what is generally prescribed as "best practice" in museums—were often the norm (see the "Suggested Reading" section). Yet some collections eventually came to be of such import that they became the foundations of large regional and national institutions of global standing that are now offering the required "best practice." In some cases these collections are now so vast that these museums will forever be able to change, and, more importantly for their visitors and supporters, they will be seen to change, to be alive and worth revisiting—some of the greatest benchmarks for any museum's success. These are the keys to our collective future, for a museum having these attributes will continue to attract funding, private backers, industry, and the public.

Smaller naval holdings often became museums, never to evolve into great or national museums, but now so laden with such regional character that they are highly sought after by tourists willing to leave the beaten path. Again as a pointer to our future, small idiosyncratic museums are an essential counterpoint to those with neat, highly organized exhibitions with prescribed spaces between cabinets, uniform font sizes, set text-to-object ratios, and the other manifestations of "best practice." Experience shows that the public enjoy their clutter and the strange, colorful characters in attendance. As a result, museums, their staff, and their volunteers need be encouraged to maintain their nonconformist individuality. In this context some museums keep an "informal" gallery or set space aside for informal low-budget exhibits that temporarily showcase the products of exciting new work, or to allow their curators and local communities (such as avocational archaeologists, maritime collectors, photographers, and heritage boat builders or repairers) to exhibit their work.

Some navies also retained heritage ships. They were rarely used as exhibits initially; rather, they served as storehouses, as accommodation, or as training facilities. These increasingly rare original hulls were nautical archaeological treasures often held unconsciously for the future. Some navies also retained ships representing past glories, battles, or revolutions, preserving them in service livery as part of the nation or region's overall defense budget. While not part of the maritime archaeological heritage (in that they remained in service and were not abandoned), they are relevant to us as the roots of our shipwreck recoveries. While some retain little of their original fabric, because it was faithfully replaced as each component required renewal, these hulls have also added a great deal to the body of knowledge, serving as comparative studies for those examining ship design, life at sea, fastenings, shipbuilding, and the like.

Another example of a simple yet very effective vision paying great dividends today: in the 1950s and 1960s civilian enthusiasts, imbued with the "romance of sail," similarly and in an equally uncontrolled fashion as their naval predecessors retrieved objects and ephemera of interest and value to them. These were from the whaling, immigrant, colonial, and Gold Rush eras; from the clipper ships; and from the wheat- and guano-carrying trades—the last manifestation of the "great age of sail." These individuals and institutions collected, hoarded, and stored ephemera and objects, enough to form the basis of a nascent museum. Unlike the small naval museum, these were invariably open to a much wider public, often requiring a donation or charging a small fee for entry. They were also administered and staffed mainly by volunteers. Some retired ship's captains and their coterie of retired riggers, riveters, ship's carpenters, and others went a step further to form ship societies or other loose affiliations with an eye to securing the greatest prize of all: an intact ship. Occasionally looking to where they saw their "maritime heritage abroad," they removed once famous ships lying forgotten or unappreciated on far-distant shores. Though often effective in the recovery, transport, conservation, and exhibition of their "prize," in effect they also took from unsuspecting regional societies, thereby shocking them into a belated appreciation of what they once saw as worthless. This caused local societies to resist later incursions and then present their patrimony in situ, sometimes in a very effective manner. Today oceanliners take an increasing number of passengers, mainly retirees, to these sites as part of the overall offering of a region or famous port (see Brouwer 2006 for a list of the world's historic ships).

Convinced of their value, often once-disinterested academics and politicians induced national or regional maritime museums to lobby for the best (or best-known) ships and to enter them into their collections. In many cases the volunteers who saved and then managed these museum ships with their ancient maritime skills, with hands-on style and grubby overalls (often called the "dirty gang" in shipping parlance), returned the ships to a presentable state. For numerous reasons, many of the "dirty gang" left after completion, sometimes midway, often holding the burgeoning bureaucracy in deep disdain and taking much of the "color" and "flavor" that once surrounded the ship and the relics with them. Quickly the situation was reversed when enlightened administrators and curators actively sought to retrieve what remained of the "dirty gang," both as a form of cheap labor and expertise and as an enormous attraction in their own right. They were also a direct link to the "real" world and often liberally pushed the curatorial envelope in thought, knowledge, technique, and expertise. Volunteers in museology and maritime archaeology perform those same functions and bring the same challenges today. Many formed into their own incorporated bodies, with a charter, constitution, and tax status. Most are affiliated with a museum or regional heritage unit. In all respects, though often difficult to manage, they are indispensable, broadening the scope of any museum, helping to keep it relevant, and enhancing its products.

Sometimes, in mirroring the process whereby societies and private enthusiasts were saving abandoned hulks and old ships, equally driven individuals or interest groups—again often with no public funds, few resources, and little academic or political interest—searched for, and often found, long-lost wrecks. Others were found by accident. Either way, after a wreck had been secured and its import became known, professional administrators moved in, rallied by those same formerly disinterested academics and politicians and joined by business interests that provided sponsorship, expertise, or "in kind" logistical support.

In the 1970s, when presented with an unexpected and highly significant find, an archaeologist based in a state or regional museum was occasionally able to emulate these feats and to induce an administration—often blissfully unaware of the magnitude of the task ahead—to agree to a ship or its timbers being raised and to provide the staff and facilities needed to conserve them (much later it was engines, boilers, and the trappings of steam). Once the ship or machine was successfully raised, and then presented to the advantage of the institution, the region, and the nation as a whole, few would question the decision to raise these hulls, timbers, and relics today (see the discussion below on in situ preservation). Nonetheless, a "due diligence" study would lead most directors of large regional maritime museums today to look to the competing demands on their increasingly scarce resources and veto the project (see Delgado 1997 for a list of underwater and maritime archaeological projects up to the end of the twentieth century). One of our challenges for the twenty-first century is how to beat this trend.

As a result of the successes in raising these early remains, the first shipwreck conservators emerged, congregating in places where entire hulls (or substantial portions of them) had been raised. The conservation laboratories of museum and

nonmuseum institutions invariably developed into teaching and then public facilities, and the public flocked in not only to see the unique object, but also to see the
conservators at work. In most cases, the remains taken from a marine environment
in the 1960s and 1970s are still being conserved today (as are many of those recovered in recent decades). This has resulted in conservation staff actually having a
pride of place on the exhibition floor alongside the archaeologists, shipwrights, and
students of shipbuilding doing postgraduate studies. Some see the time taken in
conservation as negative, pointing to the ongoing costs and the resources required
as prohibitive and good reason not to recover submerged objects. On the other
hand, in the very longevity of maritime archaeological projects, and in the decades
of commitment to conservation, research, and presentation, lies one of the acknowledged great strengths of maritime archaeology and its public products (Muckelroy
1978: 249). Research and other benefits aside, from a public perspective conserving,
stabilizing, studying, and exhibiting those relics in a public environment is the stuff
of a living museum of maritime archaeology, and it is evident in a large percentage
of the places on the list provided here. As a result, the 1895 maxim of the famous
museum administrator George Brown Goode (once of the Smithsonian)—"A finished museum is a dead museum, and a dead museum is a useless museum"—rarely
applies in our field (quoted in Kavanagh 1994: 45). This observation can be tested by
examining those institutions in the list provided against this truism.

Mirrored Theoretical Developments
in Archaeology and Museology

Because they are linked by their subject matter, few would be surprised to find that
there have been similar transient philosophical movements within the disciplines of
museology and archaeology.

Many of the best, or most prominent, of the 1960s maritime archaeologists were
lured into universities, forming study collections that they housed on the campus.
In some cases these evolved into private museums and institutions, most often with
ancillary conservation facilities. Then the practitioners of the 1970s began to reach
beyond the classics and prehistory of their predecessors into wrecks from the historical period. There was also a great public interest and widespread support for this
work. To many academics and politicians, especially those in former colonies, well-
publicized wrecks, relics, and survival stories were their "prehistory" in a period
where they mistakenly believed that indigenous maritime history was nonexistent.
As a result, maritime archaeologists excavated, raised, and collected almost without
impediment, so keen were politicians and local and regional museums to accept
what was offered to them during this period. These same practitioners were also
frequently derided by their terrestrial counterparts as mere object collectors, slaves
of acquisitive museums, at worst treasure hunters. As a result, they also looked to

validating their field, developing a theoretical base for underwater, nautical, and maritime archaeology. Initially, nineteenth-century wrecks and relics were not considered as bona fide studies (e.g., Lyon 1974; Muckelroy 1980: 10). As a result, little from this period found its way onto the exhibition floor via a maritime archaeological stream. Nonetheless, as a corollary of these theoretical awakenings, a third wave of archaeologists emerged. Some began studying wooden-hulled steamships, iron sailing ships, and later iron steamers. In this same period, some countries expanded or enacted shipwreck legislation serving to protect these remains, especially warships and ships of state. Nations celebrating the ousting of foreign rulers as the Victorian era came to a close venerated the vessels that brought these successes. So too did the winners of the great internal struggles and revolutions that shaped their modern societies. Thus, by the 1980s and 1990s the study of iron ships, steamships, and steel ships, submarines, and aircraft from the world's great explorations and from early-twentieth-century civil and international wars became accepted as bona fide maritime archaeology. Objects from them then found their way into museums. Inevitably some of the objects studied, raised, collected and exhibited came to be from a time where there are "eyewitness accounts . . . verbal descriptions . . . as well as historical and photographic records" (Renfrew and Bahn 1991: 227).

Attention also moved to survivor's camps, and submerged and above-water settlements and buildings, both ancient and of the recent past. Military installations, harbors, ports, lighthouses, and navigation and port-related structures such as wharves, groynes, jetties, and anchorages came to be examined, and the objects from them readily entered museum collections. Again, there are many examples in the list provided here.

Belatedly, nations began to better understand and more readily appreciate the beauty, complexity, and attractions of their eons-old indigenous maritime history. Thus, we found our museums and other institutions presenting ancient indigenous watercraft and maritime art, sometimes in an archaeological perspective. This caused the world's understanding of what was maritime archaeology and what should be recorded, collected, and exhibited to further evolve.

While most maritime archaeological exhibitions through to the 1980s were object-focused, with treasure, ancient artworks, ceramics, and deepwater finds a major draw, Muckelroy's (1978: 4) observation that the primary object of study for maritime archaeology are people "and not the ships, cargoes, fittings or instruments with which the researcher is immediately confronted" proved a watershed. It was a sentiment echoed and refined by the "shipwreck anthropology" movement in the early 1980s (Gould 1983). At the same time, it was treated with considerable caution by some influential historical particularists (Bass 1983; Green 1990: 235). This produced a useful duality in our field and was reflected in museum exhibits, such that after this time many were found centering as much on the people as on the objects and the technology involved (see below).

In this same period, some of those who did not adhere to the newly espoused archaeological theory slipped out of favor among former friends and colleagues. Those who failed to accept that they were not to keep, sell, or trade their finds were especially ostracized. And so the "great divide" between archaeologist and treasure hunter developed—the divide that is presently severely blighting our collective horizon. As this gulf widened in the late twentieth century, the maritime museum as the chief recipient of these objects intended for exhibition rather than sale found itself in a quandary. Financial administrators were especially vexed when offered exciting exhibitions and "blockbuster" attractions showing "treasure" or objects sometimes wrested from iconic ships in immense depth. Financial ambitions were stymied, either by national and international governing bodies like ICMM or by affiliated directors and archaeologists on staff, primarily because the proposed exhibits contained objects raised in a nonarchaeological fashion. From that time on, maritime museums were forced to line up across the same deep divide between archaeologist and salvor. Notwithstanding the pros and cons of that argument, an opportunity to show both sides of the argument to the hundreds of thousands who would have poured onto the exhibition floor to view the treasures and iconic objects was lost (see discussion in Hosty 1995).

This was also a time when processual archaeology arrived in the mainstream of our discipline and as it became widely accepted, was followed by a stream of passing philosophical fads. These "movements," spawned after the conservative traditions of our parent discipline had been usefully and effectively challenged by the new archaeology, were often based on new or revisited overarching philosophical and sociopolitical theories. Contrary to all the evidence before them, telling them how unimportant they themselves were and how transient society and its underpinnings was, many archaeologists became strangely convinced that the sociopolitical lens through which they were viewing their sites and objects was the only valid lens. Few would be surprised to find that in museology there were similar trends as it too changed over the centuries. These trends are also in evidence as museology itself evolves and as the "new museum" also follows an anthropological path.

THE NEW MUSEUM EXAMINED

"Museums: Agents of social change and development" is the header of a recent edition of the Newsletter of the International Council of Museum and its lead article (Friess 2008), and there is no denying museums' strength, widespread acceptance, and validity as a potent social force. A recent study titled "The Metamorphosis of Museums" references a number of scholars whose research indicates that museums can contribute at an individual level, producing enhanced self-esteem, confidence, and creativity, and at a community level, as a catalyst for social regeneration, to promote tolerance, intercommunity respect, and to challenge stereotypes. In that same study, reference is made to others who go a step further and see museums as having a civic role offering public spaces for people to "learn, exchange views, and balance one perspective against another" (Catsambis n.d.).

The abstracts presented to the recent "Contentious Museum conference" provide a useful opportunity to examine some of these trends and to test the performance of our own museums against them. One very useful presentation was a museum devoted to Mark Twain and the stories of the Mississippi River that, after being roundly criticized for presenting a unidimensional view focusing on white people, with the slaves very much on the periphery, attempted to redress the imbalance and develop exhibits presenting the "the black experience" (Faden 2008). In examining our maritime archaeological museums and institutions against this example, it is pleasing to note that manifestations of this essential change have been visible in many places for some time now. Exhibitions on immigration are now from the immigrant's perspective; those on exploration and subsequent colonization are often from the indigenous perspective; those on slavery, from the perspective of the slaves themselves; and latterly studies of women at sea, including the first female pirates and explorers, have appeared.

Some of these, incidentally, are my own special interests; I have produced exhibitions with both particularist and anthropological emphasis on exploration, treasure ships, former slave ships, warships (including submarines), submerged aircraft, port-related structures, the interaction of indigenous people with shipwrecked mariners, indigenous depictions of watercraft, and the first female circumnavigators. I also produced "Steamships to Suffragettes," an exhibit that combines social and technological themes via the medium of a unique engine raised after over a century underwater. This observation—and that the author also espouses both excavation and in situ preservation (see comments below)—is not intended to be self-serving; rather, it is presented to help diminish perceptions of bias, inexperience, and ignorance that may arise as the various arguments and observations unfold in this chapter. In that context, we must ask how far an institution can, or should, actively use the objects and exhibitions as an overt tool to effect societal change. Certainly a museum can lead by example in its practices. Where facilities are being upgraded or new buildings are being mooted, some are doing so via the "green museum" movement, for example (Brophy and Wylie 2008). Nonetheless, where an existing museum is already struggling with ever-diminishing funds and a plethora of competing demands on its staff, resources, and spaces, one could ask whether the creation of spaces to allow divergent social groups and races to engage and generate useful dialogue (as some presently urge) is more the role of a special-purpose, or purpose-built, "community museum" or "cultural park" (ICOM News 2008).

As one observer has noted in examining the new museum movement, it is the very success of museums that leads some to want them to build on that goodwill to help ameliorate social ills (J. Wood, quoted in Catsambis n.d.). The other reason perhaps lies in the philosophical makeup of museum staff, rendering them willing to make such a change. From experience, it appears that they are generally more socially aware, gender-balanced, multiracial, and willing to help the disadvantaged or the oppressed. It is perhaps for these reasons that activists look to them and their institutions for help.

These examples and the evidence from one recent study showing that visitors tend to "give complex, often contradictory, meanings to museum objects" (Catsambis n.d.) again beg the question whether our institutions can, or should, leave the safe ground of objective collection and presentation to analyze with a social purpose in mind. Certainly they should not refrain from presenting what they hold, but should they comment? And, when they do, who is to provide the social lens? This is a real problem, and as one presenter at the "Contentious Museum conference" noted, in being publicly funded and answerable to society, museums are invariably influenced by the prevailing political climate. As a result, they select issues for contentious discourse that are in line with the prevailing mood (Campbell 2008). This, as we all know, is a cyclic phenomenon.

Threats to Museums and Maritime Archaeology

Staff, with all their authority, color, and eccentricities, are some the greatest draws for museums. In many museums, they and their volunteers are seen at work behind the scenes and in the public galleries and spaces, building, conserving, and developing exhibits.

As indicated in the opening paragraphs, a looming danger for any maritime heritage museum lies in the tendency to rationalize spaces for social or financial purposes. To some administrators, the answer to competing fiscal demands and the need to better manage and house the collection is to move them away into archives far distant from the maritime museum's traditional heart: its exhibition floors, its curators, its central location or waterfront "home." Notwithstanding the advantages, this practice is defensible only where the facility is located close to a transport hub, in a place conducive to visitation, open for people to browse through, and with curators, conservators, and volunteers in attendance—effectively a museum annex with "storage on exhibition" as counterpoint to the formal exhibition gallery.

In turning to the deaccessioning of objects—once a taboo subject—we come to another development of tremendous import for the future of museums and maritime archaeology. This practice is undertaken in order to save costs, free up resources, and open spaces required for the public good. Those objects targeted for deaccession are multiple examples of the same item, or specimens that have deteriorated; are hazardous to other collections, the public, or staff; are not genuine; or are presently considered irrelevant to the museum's mission. While many of these criteria are self-evident and readily justifiable, the question of who decides what is irrelevant now and for the future remains fundamental. As in archaeology and any other of the humanities, museums and their staff often lose sight of the transient nature of it all and are equally prone to passing social, political, economic, and philosophical fashion. Unless totally transparent—externally and independently accountable, with many checks and balances—it is evident that this last reason will

become the most contentious and potentially damaging of all the reasons to deaccession. How many places are now looking again to present, albeit in a different
fashion, that object or that collection deaccessioned in the heat of a former sociopolitical trend?

The phenomenon is visible in maritime heritage museums, with old vessels regularly being disposed of. Here it is argued that the reasons are often as much social—
in that the object is no longer valued by the curators and administrators—as they are
logistical or financial. One particular museum, for example, has "deconstructed"
one of its once famous old iron steamships to provide a skeletal, and to many an
entirely unsatisfactory, representation of its "soul," the engine. "Deconstruction" was
also mooted recently when the hulk of a composite clipper of considerable historical
significance across two nations found itself in the way of some urgent real estate
development. Faced with diminished perceptions of worth (itself a cyclic phenomenon), allied with a mountain of impossibilities and challenges on staff, time, and
resources, it comes as little surprise to find deaccessioning or "deconstruction" occurring—although all the lessons of the past point in the opposite direction.

Deaccessioning and selling collections to raise funds, rather than loaning them to
less-well-off museums, returning them to family, or putting them in the care of groups
or institutions that will cherish and maintain them, is another serious compound blight.
The fundamental breach of trust to the original donors and to the public that is inherent
in the deaccessioning of objects once donated is an institutional low that takes years to
redeem. The practice is spreading in museums, and, as noted by the British Archaeological Trust (2005), "curators of archaeological collections are under increasing pressure
to dispose of all or parts of existing collections as new material accumulates." Some are
even contemplating selling objects (Shanks 2008). For maritime heritage museums this
is an especially pertinent issue given the heat in the present "salvor vs. archaeologist"
debate, where those who sell the heritage for private gain are regularly held up as occupying the lowest rung in our field—if they are to be considered part of our field at all.

Ironically, some museums are deaccessioning and deconstructing objects
because "best practice"—as enunciated by most international, national, and regional bodies overseeing museums (see the reading list below)—requires that if
something is in the collection it must be cataloged, housed, and conserved to a set
standard. If not, accreditation is lost and grants are not forthcoming. In this chapter,
it has been argued that we need look to the legacy of past practices, see their value,
look to what they have given us to choose from now and in the future, and reach a
compromise. Those seeking to dispose of collections, for example, should first seek
secure holding places where the objects, whether large or small, can be stored at
little cost and where the environment, security, and conditions are benign at least.

In maritime archaeology, reburial after excavation is being tested as an alternative, not to deaccessioning, but to accessioning itself (Grenier, Bernier, and Stevens
2007). It is also seen as a means of avoiding what is incorrectly perceived (given the
long-term benefits mentioned above) as maritime archaeology's greatest hidden
cost—conservation. Reburial certainly represents an attempt to find that secure
"holding place," at least buying time in the context of the inevitable cycle.

Allied to reburial, however, is one of the most dangerous recent trends for our maritime archaeological museums and institutions: the slavish uncritical acceptance by some administrators of the "in situ preservation" mantra. Certainly it is the preferred option of the ICOMOS International Committee for the Underwater Cultural Heritage, and none would argue against its being considered as the primary option at any site. It is also one of my own great interests: I have spent well over a decade now in facilitating and participating in these studies at the wreck of a former slave ship.

We should recognize, nonetheless, that many managers and administrators seeking to stifle debate, reject a donation, or avoid the issue currently present in situ preservation as the *only* option open to their institution or staff. What is required when recovery of an object, hull, or machine is being considered is a cold, objective analysis by third parties, including the examination of what would happen if it were to be left on the seabed in situ. This is what my institution did when the recovery of the engine mentioned earlier was mooted (McCarthy 2000). Too often we are given examples of the problems experienced in conservation by those seeking to avoid commitment as the sole reason why similar objects and ship's hulls should not be raised, while the benefits and threats such as passing traffic, looting, natural disintegration, development, and sheer vandalism are given little credence.

Perhaps exacerbating the negative elements of the trends outlined above has been the politicization of public service, in recent decades. Museum directors are often beholden to politicians for tenure. As a result, they are often no longer outspoken, independent thinkers and fierce defenders of their own realm and of the regional and national heritage in general.

Allied and equally dangerous to our collective future are the effects of the overregulation of society in general, as increasingly evident in the last two decades of the twentieth century. We are also in a time when fear of litigation has become an endemic social ill in Western societies. These phenomena now impinge on many museological operations, ranging from collection and exhibition through to diving and boating operations, rendering in the latter case the taking of reasonable risk, once a fundamental and to an extent accepted part of our work, well-nigh impossible. There are many examples (e.g., McCarthy 2006).

Some countries across the globe have yet to be swamped by this debilitating phase in our endeavors and can still maintain a balance between shoddy, dangerous, and sometimes exploitative work practices and the conscious taking of risk by experienced, qualified, and willing practitioners in maritime archaeology. This balance will prove essential for the future.

THE FUTURE

It is evident that as some countries cast off the shackles of a subjugate past, vowing never again to allow their once great maritime heritage to become weak, there will be searches for wrecks and relics reminding the visitor of past maritime glories, their explorers, settlers, traders, and great sailors. Others will look to ancient shoreline cities, once buried under silt as rivers changed their course, or old harbors silted up, still replete with wrecks and relics, to attest to past "golden ages." Some will also seek to present and perhaps recover elements of the now submerged monuments to their greatest religious icons and deities, and, with millions of adherents to these faiths, their future is assured. At these touchstones to past glories, there will be great excavations, recording, and raisings of relics, ships, and structures, burgeoning conservation laboratories, and bold new maritime archaeological museums. This trend is already visible in some countries, and it will continue in the foreseeable future.

Elsewhere, when burdened by the challenges outlined above and the allied diminution in the numbers of practitioners (curation, conservation, education, exhibition, and other front-of-house specialists) in favor of a burgeoning support staff (marketing and PR managers, press secretaries, policy officers, legal advisers, human resource personnel, IT specialists, health and safety officers), what director could allow their hard-pressed institution to be saddled with the demands of a newly raised wreck, its cargo, contents, and/or engine? Perhaps only those independent, special-purpose museums and institutions with a specific focus, assisted by a lean, vibrant, and facilitating bureaucracy, will prove able to attract sponsors and the political backing necessary to enable them to enter into such a large and long-term, but ultimately rewarding, undertaking. The choice of a director or CEO with the ability to buck these trends and resist these forces will also prove crucial.

As one canny director observed in examining the inexorable global drive toward uniform criteria in museology, the end result will inevitably be "a very dull collection," for "it is the idiosyncrasy of our collections which makes them fascinating." That same director's simple recommendation in many ways encapsulates the dilemma facing the heads of many of our large institutions as they wrestle with overweening bureaucracies, debilitating legal strictures, competing demands, and the global trend toward conformity: "Encourage your eccentric curators. But don't tell mine that I have said this" (Anderson 1990: 126).

REFERENCES

Anderson, R. G. W. 1990. Can contemporary collecting be objective? In *The VIIth International Congress of Maritime Museums: Proceedings 1990; Denmark-Sweden-Finland-USSR-Estonia; A Congress in Five Countries*, ed. Anders Björklund, 113–127. Stockholm: Vasa Museum.

Bass, G. F. 1983. A plea for historical particularism in nautical archaeology. In *Shipwreck anthropology*, ed. R. A. Gould, 91–105. Albuquerque: University of New Mexico Press.

British Archaeological Trust. 2005. *Museums in crisis—an outline of the RESCUE position.* Rev. 21 June 2005. Online at www.rescue-archaeology.org.uk/news/museumcrisis. html/. Accessed 13 January 2010.

Brophy, S., and E. Wylie. 2008. *The green museum: A primer on environmental practice*. Lanham, MD: Altamira Press.

Brouwer, N. J. 2006. *International register of historic ships*. London: Anthony, Nelson and World Ship Trust.

Campbell, M. 2008. *The distraction of seeking attention: Re-thinking the values of contention in museums*. Paper presented to The Contentious Museum: Sixth Biennial University Museums in Scotland Conference, 20–21 November, Aberdeen.

Catsambis, A. n.d. When culture became capital: The metamorphosis of museums. Unpublished manuscript.

Delgado, J. P., ed. 1997. *British Museum encyclopaedia of underwater and maritime archaeology*. London: British Museum Press.

Faden, R. 2008. *Mark Twain and Huck Finn at the center of the storm*. Paper intended for presentation to The Contentious Museum: Sixth Biennial University Museums in Scotland Conference, 20–21 November, Aberdeen.

Friess, P. 2008. Museums: Agents of social change and development. *ICOM News. Newsletter of the International Council of Museums* 61 (1): 3.

Gould, R. A., ed. 1983. *Shipwreck anthropology*. Albuquerque: University of New Mexico Press.

Green, J. N. 1990 *Maritime archaeology: A technical handbook*. London: Academic Press.

Grenier, Robert, Marc-André Bernier, and Willis Stevens, eds. 2007. *The underwater archaeology of Red Bay: Basque shipbuilding and whaling in the 16th century*. Ottawa: Parks Canada.

Hosty, K. 1995. A matter of ethics: Shipwrecks, salvage, archaeology and museums. *Bulletin of the Australian Institute for Maritime Archaeology* 19 (1): 33–36.

ICOM News. 2008. *Newsletter of the International Council of Museums* 61 (1).

Kavanagh, G. 1994. *Museum, provision and professionalism*. Leicester: Readers in Museum Studies.

Lyon, D. J. 1974. Documentary sources for the archaeological diver: Ship plans at the National Maritime Museum. *International Journal of Nautical Archaeology* 3 (1): 3–20.

McCarthy, M. 2000. *Iron and steamship archaeology: Success and failure of the SS* Xantho. New York: Kluwer Academic/Plenum.

———. 2006. The Dutch on Australian shores: The Zuytdorp tragedy—unfinished business. In *Dutch connections—400 years of Australian-Dutch maritime links, 1606–2006*, ed. L. Shaw and W. Wilkins, 94–109. Sydney: Australian National Maritime Museum.

Merriman, N. 2004. *Public archaeology*. London: Routledge.

Muckelroy, K. 1978. *Maritime archaeology*. Cambridge: Cambridge University Press.

———, ed. 1980. *Archaeology underwater: An atlas of the world's submerged sites*. New York: McGraw-Hill.

Renfrew, C., and P. Bahn. 1991. *Archaeology: Theories, methods and practice*. New York: Thames and Hudson.

Rodrigues, R. 2009. An amnesty assessed: Human impact on shipwreck sites; The Australian case. *International Journal of Nautical Archaeology* 38 (1): 153–162.

Shanks, H. 2008. A radical proposal: Why don't the archaeologists join the looters? First Person column. *Biblical Archaeology Review* 34 (6): 80.

Souter, C. 2006. Cultural tourism and diver education. In *Maritime archaeology in Australasia: Reviews and overviews*, ed. M. Staniforth, and M. Nash, 163–176. New York: Springer.

Starn, Randolph. 2005. A historian's brief guide to new museum studies. *American Historical Review* 110 (1): 68–98.

Witcomb, A. 2003. *Re-imaging the museum: Beyond the mausoleum*. New York: Routledge.

SUGGESTED READING

Best Practices in Museums

www.aam-us.org/museumresources/accred/standards.cfm/
http://cidoc.ics.forth.gr/docs/guidelines/guideint.htm/
www.chin.gc.ca/English/Standards/metadata_documentation.html/

Museum Regulatory Bodies

International Council of Museums: http://icom.museum/
International Congress of Maritime Museums: www.icmmonline.org/pages/home.htm/
ICOMOS International Committee on the Underwater Cultural Heritage:
    www.icuch.org/artman/publish/about_icuch.shtml/

Making the 'Grey Literature' accessible: an example

http://www.museum.wa.gov.au/research/research-areas/#maritime-archaeology/maritime-
    archaeology-publications

CHAPTER 46

MARITIME ARCHAEOLOGY, THE DIVE COMMUNITY, AND HERITAGE TOURISM

ARTHUR B. COHN AND JOANNE M. DENNIS

INTRODUCTION: MARITIME ARCHAEOLOGY AND THE DIVE COMMUNITY

IN modern times, the development of new survey, navigation, diving, and remotely operated vehicle (ROV) technologies have made the location, exploration, and excavation of historic shipwrecks feasible to the general public. The development and availability of relatively lightweight SCUBA equipment gave a generation of newly minted undersea explorers access to the underwater world. Many of these new divers entered a submerged world whose bottom was literally strewn with artifacts, and this enticed them to become active antiquity collectors. The combined impact of professional treasure hunters and the new army of recreational SCUBA divers who began recovering submerged loot gave rise to new ethical question that focused on these activities.

In time, questions about the ownership, cultural value, and preservation of historic shipwrecks began to conflict with the idea that these "recovery" missions were a triumph of the entrepreneurial explorer's spirit. Because these private enterprises often destroyed the cultural sites they were working on for private enrichment, it became apparent to members of the archaeological and dive communities that these sites and the information they hold about our shared heritage warranted regulations that would protect them from damage for the benefit of few, and instead promote their study and exploration for the public good. A changing ethic emerged that viewed these underwater sites as of cultural importance and information, not as treasure chests of unclaimed wealth but rather as treasured time capsules of our shared past.

During the early era of SCUBA and underwater technology advancement (pre-1970), shipwrecks were the traditional focus of salvage law and the societal system that created incentives to save cargoes, ships, and maritime property in imminent peril on the high seas. Minimizing commercial loss to shippers, merchants, and insurance companies was the goal of an economy dependent on a worldwide maritime transportation system. Much of the world's commerce still uses maritime transport and insurance underwriting systems. However, as society evolved and began to develop concepts and principles about the preservation of historic buildings, archaeological sites, landscapes, and battlefields, the vast, but finite, collection of historic shipwrecks was also brought into consideration. Issues surrounding the value these sites had to society, what techniques should be applied to their study, how to preserve and share them, and who would be allowed access were emerging from the increased accessibility that the new technology allowed. These have become the fundamental questions that drive the modern discussions of historic shipwreck law and the field of maritime archaeology.

In the 1970s and 1980s the debate became even more active as SCUBA equipment became widely available and a new generation of divers began to visit shipwrecks in shallow water. The ethic of the time can best be described as "finders, keepers," and significant historic material from shipwrecks was regularly recovered. These recovery endeavors rarely included a permitting process, or solid planning, and frequently led to the deterioration or destruction of the objects recovered (i.e., *Alvin Clark*).

While discovery of treasure ships helped to fuel public interest, the discussion within the historic preservation and archaeological communities about the state of the world's shipwrecks and how best to preserve and manage them began to accelerate. This debate and concern for the world's finite collection of shipwrecks, for example, gave rise to efforts to change United States law and provide protection and reasonable access to shipwrecks in American waters. The Abandoned Shipwrecks Act (ASA, Public Law 100-298), adopted by the United States in 1987, had significant impacts on individual state policies relating to public access and government protection of shipwreck sites. It is a particularly good example of how a multitude of approaches can be applied to shipwreck protection and the prevention of damage and exploitation of submerged cultural resources.

THE ABANDONED SHIPWRECKS ACT
AND PUBLIC ACCESS

The result of many years of discussion and lobbying came to fruition in 1987 with the passage of the Abandoned Shipwreck Act. This landmark legislation specifically pronounced that the federal government asserted title to any "abandoned shipwreck" included or deemed eligible for inclusion in the National Register of Historic Places and transferred management to states "on whose submerged lands the shipwreck is located." The ASA specifically addressed the law of salvage and the law of finds and declared they "shall not apply to abandoned shipwrecks" as defined in the new law.

One interesting aspect of the ASA is Section 2103, titled "Rights of Access." This section contains several provisions that provide, guarantee, and encourage public access to appropriate shipwrecks. Under this section, the law attempts to define "reasonable access by the public" and to "develop appropriate and consistent policies to ... guarantee recreational exploration of shipwreck sites" (Abandoned Shipwreck Act of 1987 [43 USC 2101 et seq.]). In subsection (b), titled "Parks and Protected Areas," regulators are encouraged to create underwater parks, and the National Park Service is tasked with preparing pertinent guidelines to aid state administrators in accomplishing this goal (National Parks Service 1990: Section 2104). The intent of these guidelines was to

1. Maximize the enhancement of cultural resources.
2. Foster a partnership among sport divers, fisherman, archaeologists, salvors, and other interests.
3. Facilitate access and utilization by recreational interests.
4. Recognize the interests of individuals and groups engaged in shipwreck discovery and salvage.

The broad mandate contained in the ASA suggests that many forces were at play in the legislative process that created it. It recognized the interests of the sport diver community with supportive language for public-diver access in underwater preserves as a way to include them in the process.

The ASA Guidelines (National Parks Service 1990) also called on each state to draft a management protocol for a multiuse approach to underwater resources. Unfortunately, the guidelines are just that—guidelines; they came with no formal authority or funding to help the states implement their management plans. While the ASA transferred title and authority to the states, each state had to determine how to best manage its own underwater cultural heritage. In many jurisdictions, the ASA was perceived by state regulators as defining yet one more class of public resource for which they were responsible and was therefore often met with limited enthusiasm. Frequently the state regulators were already overtasked, and most were unfamiliar with the special techniques and methodologies needed to properly manage submerged cultural resources. It is not surprising that a patchwork of different approaches were developed by the states to meet the spirit of the ASA.

Underwater Preserve Programs in North America

The underwater preserve program that has been established on Lake Champlain serves as a prime example of how the concepts handed down in the ASA can work when the dive community and state officials work together to provide access to submerged cultural resources. Lake Champlain creates a portion of the border between the states of New York and Vermont, and expands into Quebec at its northern terminus. The lake has a long, rich, and continuous human history that make it one of the most historic bodies of water in North America, a fact that is well reflected in its large and well-preserved collection of shipwreck sites (see Kane, Sabick, and Brigadier 2003; Kane et al. 2007; Kane and Sabick 2002; McLaughlin and Lessman 1998; Sabick, Lessmann, and McLaughlin 2000).

Documented recovery of historic shipwrecks on Lake Champlain began as early as the mid-nineteenth century. While these wrecks did not contain treasure in the traditional sense, they did contain historic materials and a connection to the past. Shipwreck salvage began on Lake Champlain not for monetary gain, but out of basic human curiosity and a desire to connect with the past. The recovery of warships from the colonial period, the American Revolution, and the War of 1812, as well as the lake's first steamboat, *Vermont I*, was a common occurrence on Lake Champlain in the first half of the twentieth century. Most of these early recovery efforts unfortunately led to the eventual destruction of the salvaged historic shipwrecks. Two notable exceptions are the Revolutionary War gunboat *Philadelphia*, which was recovered in 1935 and is now displayed at the Smithsonian Institution, and the War of 1812 schooner *Ticonderoga*, which resides in an outdoor shed at the Skenesborough Museum in Whitehall, New York (Bratten 1997; Crisman 1983, Hagglund 1949; Hoffman 1982).

The discovery and study of the wrecks of the sailing canal boat *General Butler*, the early steamboat *Phoenix*, and the canal boat *AR Noyes* in the early 1980s raised the question of who should have access to these historic Lake Champlain shipwrecks. All three sites were located in less than 30.5 m (100 ft) of water and had recreational dive potential. It was also felt that providing divers with reasonable access would help foster an ethic of respect and preservation for these nineteenth-century survivors. The state of Vermont, the Vermont Division for Historic Preservation, local dive shop owners, and history enthusiasts began examining management options. If these sites were "public," as had been advocated, should the public not have access to them? Out of this discussion emerged the concept of "reasonable access to appropriate sites," and it was decided that these three wrecks would be opened to the diving public (see Cohn 2003).

The Vermont Underwater Historic Preserve (VUHP) program opened in 1985 and provided a seasonal mooring system that permitted divers to locate the sites and safely secure their boats without deploying anchors (Figure 46.1). Additionally, the mooring provided a guideline from the surface to the site where an underwater sign welcomed the visitor and asked for their cooperation in minimizing impact on the site. A brochure was also produced that presented each shipwreck's history and offered diving guidelines. The program was deemed an immediate success by both administrators and divers.

One of the most profound benefits of the VUHP was its stimulation of preservation ethics among the diving community. The early program had no site monitors, did not require diver registration, and allowed divers to come and go as they pleased. It simply asked them to respect the sites as underwater museums and

Figure 46.1 Diver next to a Lake Champlain Underwater Historic Preserve mooring buoy. Reproduced with the kind permission of Lake Champlain Maritime Museum.

refrain from any type of impact. Even the program's proponents were surprised at how well this honor system worked. The success of this first phase of the program led to the subsequent opening of two additional preserve sites. The Diamond Island Stone Boat, a late-nineteenth-century canalboat, and the Burlington Bay Horse Ferry (circa 1825), one of the most extraordinary shipwrecks in Lake Champlain, were opened to the public in 1990 (LCUHP 2008).

The Burlington Bay Horse Ferry is a great example of how the inclusion of a shipwreck in an underwater preserve system can be the most effective management option for preserving the wreck site. When this paddle-wheel vessel was first located and analyzed, it was assumed that she was a steamer whose machinery had been removed. However, on further examination, the vessel proved to be the only known archaeological example of a horse-powered watercraft (Figure 46.2; Crisman and Cohn 1998). The discovery of the horse ferry presented a management dilemma; because it was the sole survivor of its class, authorities initially felt that it was better to keep the site out of the VUHP program. While divers had shown tremendous respect for other sites in the preserve system, the delicate nature of the horse ferry site made even minimal diver impact unacceptable. The difficulty with keeping the horse ferry out of the system was that it was about to be the focus of a *National Geographic* magazine article (Shomette 1989). Once a site has been publicized and its location made known, the general experience has been that divers are inclined to find and dive the site. With no mooring to facilitate their activities, it was only a matter of time before an anchor caused irreparable damage to the site. In the end, it

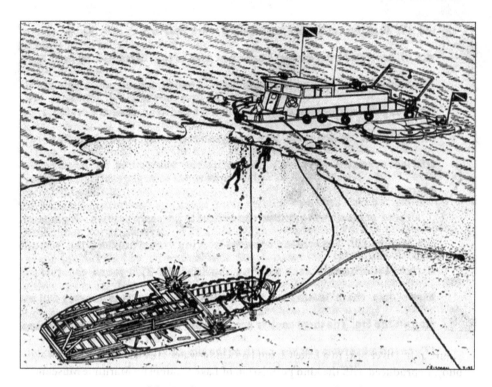

Figure 46.2 Drawing of the Burlington Bay Horse Ferry archaeological investigation. Reproduced with the kind permission of Kevin Crisman.

was decided to incorporate the horse ferry into the VUHP system, in part because there was no other effective strategy for keeping it closed without risking serious damage. Over 15 years later, this has proven to have been a wise decision, as the wreck is still well preserved despite being visited frequently by the dive community.

Over time the VUHP program became more sophisticated. In order to manage the program more effectively, the Underwater Preserve Advisory Committee was created in the early 1990s. This ad hoc committee, composed of members of the dive community, historians, archaeologists, and state officials, meets regularly to discuss issues facing the preserves and makes recommendations to the Vermont Division for Historic Preservation. Additionally, Underwater Preserve Monitors, trained personnel who provide on-site advice, information, and emergency services to visiting divers, were hired. The committee further recommended that because of the fragile nature of some of the wrecks, access should be controlled by a new registration procedure. Today, divers are required to register annually to the system as a whole and to sign up for a specific day and time when they wish to explore particularly sensitive sites. This procedure and a strong "zero impact" diving protocol have worked extremely well at preserving the sites while allowing public access.

In 1997, funding from the federally established Lake Champlain Basin Program resulted in the opening of two additional preserve sites: *O. J. Walker*, a canal boat located in Vermont waters, and the steamer *Champlain II*, which became New York

State's first entry into the system. As the preserve system now spanned two states, this prompted the renaming of the Vermont Underwater Historic Preserves as the Lake Champlain Underwater Historic Preserve (LCUHP) system. Today, the LCUHP system provides divers access to nine sites in both Vermont and New York waters.

Each of the nine wrecks underwent extensive archaeological documentation prior to their addition to the preserve system. This step ensures not only that any unforeseen damage to the wrecks will not result in a loss of information on these archaeological sites, but also that the wrecks are safe for diver visitation. As one of the first fully established preserve systems of its type in North America, the LCUHP system paved the way for addressing such management issues as public access, underwater survey, inventory, documentation, public funding, and complicated underwater cultural resource management situations.

Across the United States and Canada, numerous underwater preserve systems and parks have been established since the 1980s and are managed by either federal, state, local, private nonprofit, or local dive shop entities. Some of these preserve systems involve complex circumstances, such as crossing international boundaries, or involving multistate bottomlands, as in Lake Champlain. Additionally, some of these preserve systems are located on the bottomlands of oceans, rivers, or bays. Some systems only include one site, while others comprise dozens of shipwreck sites and geological features over vast areas. The National Oceanographic and Atmospheric Administration (NOAA) also created three National Marine Sanctuaries that are dedicated specifically to the preservation of historic shipwrecks in North American waters. What follows is a short summary of these underwater dive preserve systems, how they are administered in each community, and what resources they include.

Lake George, New York

In 1993, the Submerged Heritage Preserves system was opened in Lake George, New York. It was a joint collaboration between the New York State Department of Environmental Conservation and the local nonprofit organization Bateaux Below Inc. Lake George's preserve system is currently composed of three primary sites: *Forward*, *Land Tortoise*, and "The Sunken Fleet of 1758" (Zarzynski and Abbass 1997; Zarzynski et al. 1996). The *Forward* preserve is a gasoline-powered wooden launch built in 1906 that rests in 12 to 14 m (40 to 45 ft) of water, and in 1998 it was transformed into "The Forward Underwater Classroom," used as an underwater education facility that focuses on environmental factors, such as water quality (Zarzynski 2002). The Sunken Fleet of 1758 is a cluster of seven British bateaux intentionally sunk in 6 to 12 m (20 to 40 ft) of water, which are listed on the National Register of Historic Places. In 1997, a replica bateaux was sunk in this area to test theories about how the vessels were scuttled in colonial times and to enhance the preserve system (Zarzynski 2002). In 1994, *Land Tortoise*, a 1758 floating gun battery, was added to the system (Zarzynski and Abbass 1997). A year later, this intact British warship that lies in 32.5 m (107 ft) of water was listed on the National Register of Historic Places, and in 1998 the warship was designated a National Historic Landmark, becoming only the sixth shipwreck carrying such recognition. Due to the unique and fragile nature of *Land Tortoise*, the site is encircled by a chained barrier to prevent close contact with the wreck and access to this particular preserve is more restricted, requiring a specific permit (Zarzynski et al. 1996). Since its opening, Lake George's Submerged Heritage Preserves have enjoyed significant popularity, with an estimated 1,000 to 1,500 SCUBA divers visiting annually. Bateaux Below Inc. is in charge of the seasonal maintenance of the preserves (Bateaux Below 2005; New York Department of Education and Conservation 2010).

Florida

The Florida State Underwater Archaeological Preserve system consists of 11 shipwrecks covering a number of different site types located within Florida's inland waters, or offshore within Florida's territorial waters. These wrecks include a galleon of the Spanish treasure fleet of 1715, *Urca de Lima*; a late-nineteenth-century steamboat, *City of Hawkinsville*; and the United States' oldest battleship, USS *Massachusetts* (Scott-Ireton 2003). All 11 sites within the preserve system are listed in the National Register of Historic Places (NRHP), and listing a site in the NRHP is considered an important step in getting a shipwreck included in Florida's system.

The Florida system has grown slowly since its inception in 1987, adding a site every few years through a public nomination process with the Florida Bureau of Archaeological Research (Florida Bureau of Archaeological Research 1992, 2000). The current sites, which rest in 3 to 30.5 m (10 to 100 ft) of water, serve as an opportunity for the education and enjoyment of the tens of thousands of divers who visit them on a yearly basis. Web sites, brochures, and shore-based exhibits complement the underwater diving component of these preserve sites.

Authority and responsibility for all of the preserve sites rest with Florida's Division of Historical Resources; however, the daily operation of the individual preserves falls to local volunteers. The state only staffs four full-time maritime archaeologists and one seasonal intern who inspect the sites once or twice a year and monitor them for deterioration and vandalism. However, the main monitoring falls to the volunteer local dive community, which polices the areas and reports any suspicious activities at or damage to the sites. Furthermore, the local dive shops encourage their patrons to dive responsibly and organize annual clean-up days, which not only remove debris from the sites but also foster a sense of stewardship among local divers (Florida Division of Historical Resources 2010).

Maryland

The Maryland Historic Shipwreck Preserve system currently consists of a single vessel, *U-1105 Black Panther*, and 83.5 m² (900 ft²) of bottom land contiguous with the vessel. *U-1105* is a World War II vintage German submarine located in the Potomac River with its exposed portion (the conning tower and upper hull) resting in roughly 26 m (85 ft) of water (Langley 2003; Pohuski and Shomette 1994). The preserve was established in 1995 through the cooperation of the Maryland Historical Trust, the St. Clement's Island–Potomac River Museum, and the U.S. Naval History and Heritage Command Center. Because the primary goal of the *U-1105* preserve is to safeguard the wreck for future generations, divers are not actively encouraged to visit the site. However, diving on the submarine is permitted, and provisions are made for diver access, as mandated by the Abandoned Shipwreck Act.

The preserve was established due to a grassroots push from the local dive community who feared closure of the wreck due to the implementation of the ASA. The nonprofit Maritime Archaeological and Historical Society, a local maritime history and avocational underwater archaeology group, has taken over the responsibility of deploying and retrieving the site buoy, maintaining it during the season, and storing it during the winter. There are no full-time employees dedicated to the preserve, and on-water enforcement is supplied by the Maryland Department of Natural Resources marine police, the U.S. Coast Guard, and the state police. Safety and liability are considerable concerns in the Maryland preserve due to the depth, limited visibility, current, and proximity to a major boat traffic lane. For this reason the site is described as a Historic Shipwreck Preserve, not a Dive Preserve (Maryland Historic Trust 2009).

Michigan

The Michigan Underwater Preserve system began in the 1980s through legislation supported and drafted by Michigan sport divers and is based on both submerged cultural heritage sites and geological features. It consists of 12 preserve systems and the Thunder Bay National Marine Sanctuary, containing roughly 150 commonly visited wrecks and covering nearly 6,000 km² (2,300 mi²) of bottomlands (Halsey 1990; Halsey and Lindquist 2003). These systems include Alger, De Tour Passage, Isle Royale, Keweenau, Manitou Passage, Marquette, Sanilac Shores, Southwest Michigan, Straits of Mackinac, Thumb Area, Grand Traverse Bay, and Whitefish Point. The promoted wrecks within the systems range from late-nineteenth-century schooners and steamers to a U.S. Coast Guard cutter lost in 1989 and a 1960s packet freighter. The wrecks vary in depth from 3 m to over 60 m (10 ft to over 200 ft), with a large number at or below 21 m (70 ft). Many of the Michigan preserves are run almost entirely by volunteers under the Michigan Underwater Preserve Council (MUPC) and subsumed under the duties of state employees in the Department of Natural Resources, the Department of Environmental Quality, and the State Historic Preservation Office. There are no official means of limiting the number of divers who frequent the sites, as there are no registration procedures and no required scheduling of charters to the preserve wrecks (Michigan Underwater Preserve Council 2004).

South Carolina

The South Carolina Maritime Heritage Trails, administered and maintained by the South Carolina Institute of Archaeology and Anthropology (SCIAA) at the University of South Carolina, is distinct from other dive systems in that it is not a true preserve system. The collection of artifacts is permissible within the trail system under a "hobby license" program, which allows permitted divers to collect up to 10 isolated artifacts per day with the caveat that they report their finds to the state and are willing to furnish photos and drawings upon request. However, since the wrecks included in the trails have undergone extensive archaeological investigations, leaving few if any loose artifacts exposed (Harris, Moss, and Naylor 1993; Spirek and Harris 2003: 170), and the removal of structural features from wrecks is not permitted, the sites are fairly safe from significant damage. There are two trails in the system: a 9.7 km (6 mile) canoeing trail along the Ashley River containing 13 sites along the river banks, and a 4.8 km (3 mile) diving trail along the Cooper River that includes 6 marked wrecks.

The Cooper River diving trail, which consists primarily of vessels associated with the commercial history of the area, serves approximately 200 divers a year. Access to the trails is free except for the cost of interpretive slates and maps, and the fees for charter boat services. Due to the relatively shallow depth (7.5 to 9 m [25 to 30 ft]) of the sites, it is possible for divers to complete the entire trail in a single day of diving. Additionally, many dive shops utilize the trail as a safe place to introduce students to low-visibility diving. The initial funding for this system came from Federal Highway Recreational Trails Program, administered by the South Carolina Parks and Recreation Department, and from Archaeological Research Trust grants.

Like many programs in the United States, the South Carolina program is run by dedicated professionals but has no professionals dedicated solely to it. Consequently, volunteers are an important supplement to the trails' workforce. Due to the lack of a full-time staff, there is no official policing or monitoring of the wrecks. However, it appears that the main reason for the continued preservation of the sites is the goodwill among the diving community and local residents (University of Southern Carolina Maritime Research Division 2010).

North Carolina

The site of the USS *Huron*, located just 230 m (754 ft) off the shore at Nags Head, is the only underwater Historic Shipwreck Preserve hosted by the state of North Carolina. Opened in 1991, this site is technically owned by the U.S. Navy's Naval History and Heritage Command, and a Memorandum of Agreement was established with North Carolina's Underwater Archaeology Branch to help manage this site on a state and local level (Lawrence 2003). The site was fully documented in the 1980s (Friday 1988), and the town of Nags Head has taken on the responsibility of maintaining, managing, monitoring, and interpreting the preserve. The site is accessible from shore, and marker buoys, maintained by the town, indicate the site location.

Designation of the USS *Huron* as North Carolina's first preserve was effective for four primary reasons (Lawrence 2003). First, the wreck was already a popular dive site because it is easily accessible. Second, there was local enthusiasm, involvement, and support for having the site designated. Third, the site has significant history and was already a local attraction. And fourth, the site had been thoroughly documented and listed in the National Register of Historic Places. All of these attributes has made this a successful preserve.

Wisconsin

Wisconsin has established four maritime trails since 1997. One is located in Lake Superior and one each in upper, middle, and lower Lake Michigan. By taking a regional approach to the trail systems, their administration has been simplified and streamlined. The Wisconsin Historical Society Maritime Preservation and Archaeological Program and the University of Wisconsin Sea Grant Institute are the active agents in promoting and maintaining the trail systems, with help from numerous state, federal, and local agencies, chambers of commerce, private businesses, non-profits, and volunteers (University of Wisconsin and Wisconsin Sea Grant Institute 2003). There is no staff dedicated specifically to the maritime trails, but the state underwater archaeologist is responsible for the system. Due to the current lack of official manpower, the trail systems rely heavily on volunteers from a group of roughly 100 members representing the diving community. These individuals are involved in tasks such as conservation, archaeological surveying, mooring maintenance, and historical research (Wisconsin Historical Society 2010).

Lake Erie Coastal Ohio Trail

Multiple volunteer diver groups and research institutions help to support and administer the Lake Erie Coastal Ohio Trail. The Maritime Archaeological Survey Team (MAST), the Peachman Lake Erie Shipwreck Research Center, the Ohio Sea Grant College Program, and Cleveland Underwater Explorers Inc. provide the maintenance and monitoring of the nearly 30 shipwrecks included in this preserve system. Ten of these sites have mooring buoys, which are maintained by MAST and funded through local grant programs (Ohio State University Sea Grant College Program 2010).

California

The California Department of Parks and Recreation opened its first underwater shipwreck park in 1994. The Emerald Bay Historic Barges State Park, located in the California waters of Lake Tahoe, consists of two early-twentieth-century wooden cargo barges (Smith 1991). Full documentation of the barges was carried out by the Los Angeles Maritime Museum, and a mooring buoy and underwater interpretive panel guide divers at the site. In the state of California, over 15 underwater parks have been established since 1968. All of these parks focus on the natural and cultural history of the area, and some of these parks provide access to shipwrecks (e.g., the *Pomona*), but Emerald Bay is the only underwater park dedicated strictly to a shipwreck site.

NOAA National Marine Sanctuaries

Since the passage of the National Marine Sanctuary Act of 1972, NOAA has designated 14 Marine Sanctuaries within the territorial boundaries of the United States, and 3 of these sanctuaries are centered on shipwreck preservation. A marine sanctuary is created to "promote comprehensive management of special ecological, historical, recreational and aesthetic marine resources" within coastal and ocean U.S. waters, as well as in the Great Lakes (Terrell 2003: 151). Though the primary goal of these sanctuaries is to preserve the resources, in the case of two of the three shipwreck sanctuary systems the additional goal is to encourage access to these submerged sites and promote preservation, education, and stewardship (Terrell 2003). These sanctuaries have the benefit of federal funds and full-time staff to carry out the maintenance, administration, and monitoring of the wrecks within the sanctuaries. What follows is a brief description of the *Monitor* National Marine Sanctuary located offshore from North Carolina; Thunder Bay National Marine Sanctuary in Lake Huron; and the Florida Keys National Marine Sanctuary.

USS Monitor

The site of the wreck of the Civil War ironclad USS *Monitor* became a National Marine Sanctuary in 1975. It is also a National Historic Landmark and considered one of the most important submerged cultural resources in America (Broadwater 1996). Technically, the sanctuary is focused on the site of the wreck and encompasses "a column of water extending from the ocean's surface to the seabed and is one nautical mile in diameter" (NOAA 2003a). The sanctuary is run by a staff of four full-time employees who carry out various education, archaeology, conservation, and regulatory programs. People are prohibited from visiting the actual site of the *Monitor* without a NOAA-issued permit. The reason for this is twofold: first, to preserve the site, and second, because the wreck lies in very deep water with a strong current. Despite the difficulty in visiting this site, the USS *Monitor* has extensive educational and public outreach programs that emphasize the importance of this site to the general public and serve as a means of sharing the story of this wreck, and its preservation, without actively promoting visitation to the wreck site itself (Broadwater 1996).

Florida Keys National Marine Sanctuary

Established in November 1990, the NOAA Florida Keys National Marine Sanctuary was executed to protect both biological and cultural resources within the waters around the Florida Keys. Geographically located along colonial period shipping routes, the shipwrecks within this area represent the era of discovery and colonization of the Americas and are rich in artifacts, cargo, and history. It is the goal of the sanctuary to protect and preserve these resources for the public trust while also respecting the federal admiralty rights for wrecks that were arrested by salvagers prior to the designation of the sanctuary. A rigorous permit system that adheres to the Federal Archaeological Program guidelines was established to meet this mission. To date, over 400 underwater archaeological sites have been identified in the sanctuary, and an underwater trail with nine shipwreck sites has been established along the coral reef off the Florida Keys. Each site is accessible via a mooring system, and an informational brochure is provided. Some are relatively easy dives, while others are at 30.5 m (100 ft) or more of water (NOAA 2010; Terrrell 2003).

Thunder Bay National Marine Sanctuary

Beginning in the 1970s, the state of Michigan and NOAA combined forces to work toward the establishment of a national marine sanctuary at the site of the existing Thunder Bay Underwater Preserve, located in Lake Huron (Vrana and Vander Stoep 2003). This was NOAA's first freshwater marine sanctuary dedicated solely to shipwreck sites and was ultimately designated in October 2000. It spans 1,160 km² (448 mi²) and is home to over 100 wrecks. NOAA and the state of Michigan's Historical Center oversee the sanctuary with staff, including a sanctuary superintendent who manages the day-to-day operations of the preserve; a Joint Management Committee that oversees policy, budget, and management issues; and a 15-person Sanctuary Advisory Council (NOAA 2003b). This council allows representatives from the local community to remain involved in this nationally established sanctuary. In 2009 a new final management plan was developed for the sanctuary that outlines the core action plans to implement its overall goals. These include resource protection, education and outreach, research, and sanctuary operations and administration (NOAA 2003b; Thunder Bay National Marine Sanctuary 2009).

Canadian Preserves

Though not mandated by the ASA like its U.S. neighbors, Canada has developed shipwreck preserve systems in a similar fashion. Canada currently lacks "dedicated legislation to protect shipwreck and submerged cultural resources . . . the problem [residing] in the difficulty of harmonizing federal, provincial and territorial levels of jurisdiction without infringing on each level" (La Roche 2003: 29). This is a justifiable struggle for a country as large as Canada; however, there has been some success on various jurisdictional levels. There are currently three established shipwreck preserve systems in Canada, and each represents a different extent of funding and organization. One preserve is administered by Parks Canada, while the other two rely on local entities for management and protection. They serve as a good international comparison of how a country bordering the United States is finding similar ways to address public access and preservation of shipwrecks in similar bodies of water.

ErieQuest and the local chapter of Save Ontario Shipwrecks (SOS) in Leamington, Ontario, work together in a cooperative effort to administer the local dive system in the Canadian waters of Lake Erie. While ErieQuest is dedicated to developing economic activity based on historic shipwrecks, the SOS Windsor chapter is charged with being the conscience of the diving tourism industry on Lake Erie. Both entities work together to administer the 50 known and 15 moored wrecks in the vicinity. SOS also researches and promotes submerged cultural resources on a provincewide basis. Both organizations are stakeholders in the dive area and maintain members on a committee sponsored by the town of Leamington. The wrecks in the area are frequented by approximately 2,000 divers a year. There is no charge to dive any of the wrecks, but the tourism and dive industries of the surrounding community benefit from the large number of divers using the system. The costs incurred to establish a dive system are partially offset because volunteers run the entire program, operating under the ErieQuest Committee. Policing and monitoring of the sites is performed in a similarly unofficial manner. The dive shops and divers themselves monitor the sites and report any suspicious activity, damage to sites, or missing artifacts (ErieQuest 2010; Save Ontario Shipwreck 2010).

Fathom Five National Marine Park, within the Canadian waters of Lake Huron, was established in 1987 and is part of the Parks Canada Agency. This marine park currently serves 6,000 to 8,000 divers a year. It contains 27 buoyed and promoted wrecks in addition to a number of submerged geological features within its 27,606 acres (11,176.5 hectares) of water and islands (LaRoche 2003). The majority of the wrecks date to the mid-nineteenth and early twentieth centuries and consist primarily of schooners, barges, and steamers. The depths range from 3 to over 35 m (10 to over 120 ft), with five wrecks at depths equal to or greater than 27.5 m (90 ft). In addition to the wreck sites, Fathom Five also encompasses a number of geological features that include wall and cave dives. There are eight dive team employees who are responsible for general resource conservation and maintenance, as well as other park duties. Additionally, the park utilizes a large number of volunteers who are involved in diver registration, patrolling the park, and search and rescue duties (Parks Canada 2009).

On a smaller scale, Louisbourg Harbor, Nova Scotia, has a preserve program that has been in effect for over 30 years. The preserve includes eighteenth-century warships like *Celèbre*. This system allows controlled public access to historic shipwrecks that were located and documented by Parks Canada in the 1980s (Stevens 1989). This accessibility is regulated not by Parks Canada staffers, however, but by local dive shops and dive tour operators (La Roche 2003). According to La Roche (2003: 36) this particular preserve, despite past popularity, is not currently successful in terms of management and visitation. Because there is no statistical information from past users of the preserve, the actual reason for this is not certain. LaRoche (2003) suggested that increased Parks Canada involvement, both in terms of promotion and protection, would be of major benefit in reviving this preserve system.

NORTH AMERICAN PRESERVES IN RETROSPECT

While many other states, provinces, and territories in North America are in the process of defining and establishing their underwater cultural resource protection policies (e.g., Puerto Rico and the Caribbean; see Scott-Ireton 2005; Leshikar-Denton in this volume), the main struggle many face is the lack of designated governmental funding for this process. The NOAA Marine Sanctuaries and Parks Canada system discussed in this chapter present what can be seen as a "high-end" model, which has proven effective based on the fact that these preserves have proper funding and full-time staff to help promote, monitor, and protect the wrecks. However, on a local, state, or province level, the preserves described in this chapter also demonstrate that with dedication and cooperation, preserves can be established and can become successful community-maintained entities when they are supported by local divers, nonprofits, state and local agencies, and history enthusiasts. The tricky part is finding a balance between actual protection and promotion of the shipwrecks, as well as the appropriate funds to maintain these preserve systems in a safe and effective manner.

In Lake Champlain, for example, over 25 years of open access to certain sites has caused visible wear and tear on the surface of vessels. Some of the wrecks in the system are not in the same condition they were in when the preserves opened, and it has become evident that even divers diving with good intentions do have an impact. If the concept of public access to appropriate sites is to be successful within the spirit of the ASA, then societies, governments, and jurisdictions need to value these resources from a humanities point of view, value them from a recreational point of view, and invest resources to appropriately establish mooring systems, monitoring protocols, and interpretation systems, along with the genuine goal of protecting the sites. Right now the public access component of the ASA is an underfunded mandate, and the ASA will always be limited in potential until resources are invested to better manage, preserve, and interpret these resources.

The presentation of different preserve systems in this chapter offers a number of scenarios on which we can begin to gauge what constitutes a successful preserve program. Yet the question remains of how the success of these preserves and their different methods of administration and policy should be measured and weighted. Is a successful preserve defined as one that is visited frequently by divers and brings in revenue to the local community through tourism? Should success be measured by how public access and site preservation are balanced? Or does the measurement of success have to do with how many wrecks a system can host, or the amount of attention one wreck receives through educational outreach?

It has not yet been determined by the dive community, the archaeological community, or the historic preservation community how we should measure the success of these efforts to provide "reasonable access to appropriate sites" as mandated in the ASA. However, across the globe other ways to share and still protect submerged cultural resources have been developed, and they demonstrate the utility of technology, public outreach, and museum innovation in this process. With nearly a quarter century of preserve system development in retrospect, alternative means of sharing wreck sites in situ without having to focus strictly on the dive community as the captive audience may become a more practical way of developing a preserve in order to garner more general support and enthusiasm and to protect the wrecks themselves.

Global Preserves, Parks, Museums, and Underwater Heritage Tourism

The logistical issues that revolve around shipwreck preservation and diver access are global in scale. Across the world's oceans and seas there are literally millions of wrecks representing millennia of human maritime activity. These wrecks warrant the same protection and considerations for public access and preservation that the ASA has provided for U.S. submerged cultural resources.

It was not long after the passing of the ASA in 1987 that a global discussion on the world's submerged cultural resources developed. Archaeologists became divers and divers became archaeologists, and there was a push toward the establishment of professional ethical protocols around the world. Academically, this push served to establish the proper research, excavation, and management methods for a new discipline, but it was also a catalyst that promoted the global recognition that the pillage and destruction of shipwrecks for their cargo and wealth was a major issue in the newly established field of nautical archaeology.

It was not until the establishment of the United Nations Educational, Scientific and Cultural Organization (UNESCO) Convention on the Protection of the Underwater Cultural Heritage in 2001 (UNESCO 2001) that an international group of professional underwater archaeologists, delegates, cultural resource managers, and lawyers were brought together to discuss the future of the world's underwater cultural heritage. The UNESCO Convention developed a stance on the accessibility of underwater cultural resources to the public and the promotion of in situ preservation of sites similar to that outlined in the ASA. The 2001 Convention states in Article 2 of the "Objectives and General Principals" (19) that "responsible non-intrusive access to observe or document in situ underwater cultural heritage shall be encouraged to create public awareness, appreciation and protection of the heritage except where such access is incompatible with its protection and management." Below are some examples of underwater parks, museums, and preserves that have been established around the world and are rooted in this philosophy.

Underwater Cultural Heritage Parks

At the ancient port of Caesarea in the Mediterranean Sea, Israel has established an underwater archaeological park at the harbor that was built by King Herod in honor of Caesar Augustus in 10 BCE. Established in 2006 by the Caesarea Development

Corporation and Haifa University, and under the management of the Israel Antiquities Authority, Caesarea currently hosts 36 sites numbered along four trails spread over nearly 8 km² (3.1 mi²). Most sites are close to the shoreline in approximately 7 m (23 ft) of water, while some sites are accessible to expert divers only. Signposts guide the visitors, who are also equipped with a waterproof map of the underwater trail system. The trail system features the ruins of the harbor's ancient lighthouse, breakwater, anchors, and shipwrecks. It is maintained by volunteer divers from local dive shops and universities and is visited by 6,000 to 10,000 divers a year (Caesarea Diving Center 2010; Raban 2003).

Australia hosts an extensive underwater trail system initiated through the Australian Commonwealth Historic Shipwrecks Program; this trail system was founded on the principle that "the nation's underwater heritage is a resource that should be accessible to all, so long as it is respected and maintained for future generations to enjoy" (Smith 2003: 124). Since 1981, five shipwreck trail systems have been established, and two additional ones are in the works (Philippou and Staniforth 2003). Each trail system is administered by an individual state, and in most cases the state maritime museum or Maritime Heritage Unit oversees the trail system. One major pitfall that has been observed in the Australian model is that "there has been no consistency in approach, often even at a state level, nor has the development of new trails been promoted outside the borders of each state" (Smith 2003: 125; see also Strachan 1995). Much like the United States and Canada, Australia has the challenge of being a large country with little consistency in how these preserve systems are created, managed, and monitored. However, many of Australia's trail systems have recently embraced the Internet as a means of sharing information on the shipwrecks in these trails and promoting tourism and educational use of the trails.

Croatia has located over 500 archaeological sites within the crystal-clear waters off its coast in the Adriatic Sea. Many of the known wrecks around Croatia have been damaged due to either antiquity or looting, but the recent discovery of more than 10 untouched and undamaged shipwrecks prompted the Croatian government to take action to protect these resources. With little funding to excavate or remove loose artifacts, the Croatian Institute for the Preservation of Cultural and Natural Monuments (IPCNM) installed metal cages around the most unique wrecks for their protection. That way divers can visit the site, but they cannot come in contact with the vessel or its artifacts. Croatia has become a popular dive destination, and the government has established a system that requires all divers to obtain a Croatian National dive license that is good for an unlimited number of dives within one calendar year (Mesić 2008.)

Established in 1990 around the island of Ustica, in Italy's Tyrrhenian Sea, Ustica National Marine Park helps protect the area's shipwrecks, as well as the unique black coral and turtles of the region. Located off of Sicily, Ustica was once inhabited by the Phoenicians and was a popular pirate destination in the Middle Ages. Divers can visit the now submerged ancient city of Osteodes as well as a number of wrecks around the island (Frost 1990).

Other underwater parks and preserves exist in Portugal (Alves 2006), Finland (Finland National Board of Antiquities 2004), Scotland (Robertson 2003), and the Caribbean (Scott-Ireton 2005), and all are faced with complex management issues in the wake of creating dive preserve systems that are conducive to the dive community's rights to visit these underwater resources. These global examples demonstrate that the struggle to find balance between accessibility, preservation, and management are universal. The most effective programs appear to be in Italy and Israel, where the shipwreck trails are promoted as a dive destination and tourism opportunities are promoted.

While these parks and systems are geared toward SCUBA divers, when it comes to tourism promotion it is crucial to recognize that most of the world's general public does not dive. With this in mind, UNESCO has been tasked with assisting some nations with innovative ways of implementing nondiver access to underwater heritage sites. Underwater museums are currently in the works in China and Egypt that will revolutionize the way we perceive underwater heritage tourism, but as we discuss below, these are multimillion dollar projects that are not feasible for most average underwater heritage projects with limited budgets.

Underwater Cultural Heritage Museums

The submerged royal quarters of Cleopatra, once located on an island that sunk in the fourth century CE, were discovered in the 1990s within the eastern harbor of Alexandria. Widespread remains of the Pharos of Alexandria lighthouse, one of the Seven Wonders of the Ancient World, were also located nearby surrounding the fifteenth-century Fort Quait Bey. The Ministry of Culture of Egypt has partnered with UNESCO to form an International Scientific Committee that will assist in a feasibility study on the establishment of a partial underwater museum in Alexandria featuring these internationally important sites in situ. A museum of this type involves considerable technical challenges with regard to architecture, but the bay itself was man-made and is only 5 to 6 m (15–20 ft) deep (UNESCO 2010).

The Baiheliang Underwater Museum was created as a mediation project to protect China's rare cultural resources that were to become submerged due to the building of the Three Gorges Dam on the Yangtze River. The site is an ancient ridge with hydrological inscriptions that record the changes in the Yangtze River over the past 1,200 years. Additionally, stone carvings along the banks of the river are part of the exhibited sites. Construction began in 2002, with the museum scheduled to open in 2010. The facilities will allow visitors to view the inscriptions and carvings from within submerged tunnels that are up to 30 m (98 ft) below the new water surface (UNESCO 2001).

Both of these examples of underwater museums represent progressive steps in the promotion of in situ preservation, while making submerged cultural resources accessible to the general public. They introduce a new era of heritage tourism for submerged cultural resources where technology and engineering allow new options for sharing these sites with a broader audience. Both of these projects are large in scope and have large budgets, though, and beg the comparison to such high budget projects as the *Vasa*, which have salvaged, conserved, and exhibited shipwrecks. These large scale methods of sharing submerged cultural resources are not attainable to all communities that want to promote their maritime heritage tourism. However, there are other models and programs in effect that allow smaller-scale, less conventional means of expanding the target audience when it comes to learning about and visiting shipwreck sites.

OTHER DIRECTIONS FOR MARITIME HERITAGE TOURISM

Local and national maritime museums, historical societies, and university programs can supplement local preserve systems by creating land-based interpretive venues to help make a connection between submerged shipwrecks and their importance to local and national history. As time capsules that remain untouched and undisturbed on the bottom of bodies of water, shipwrecks are powerful symbols of times past. As much as any other type of archaeological site, shipwrecks excite the general public because they often remain just as they were the day they sank many years ago. Also, to the general public, which does not dive, shipwrecks are considered mysterious and remote. While museums provide a venue to share the story of the wrecks, or the historical contexts in which they existed, there are multiple ways to share this information with the public that will allow them a first-hand experience with a shipwreck that does not have to involve a multimillion-dollar underwater venue or SCUBA gear.

The Lake Champlain Maritime Museum (LCMM), founded in 1985, has strived to continually expand the ways in which shipwrecks can be shared with and presented to the public. To that end, LCMM has developed three innovative programs to help make connections between the public and submerged cultural resources. For the past 15 years, LCMM has operated a full-service archaeological conservation laboratory to support its own fieldwork and to serve as a regional resource for area museums. The lab is integrated into the museum campus and is one of the most popular public exhibits. Here visitors get to see cultural material recovered from shipwrecks in various stages of conservation and learn about the process and reasoning behind recovery or in situ preservation of artifacts. They get to talk with lab staff and often handle real cultural material.

Perhaps the most popular and effective strategy for connecting the public to shipwrecks was the idea of building full-sized operational replica vessels based on the archaeological documentation of the originals (see Ravn et al. in this volume). In 1987, LCMM experimented with the concept by building a working reproduction of a 10.9 m (36 ft) long 1759-era bateau. The original vessel had been recovered from Lake George in the 1960s and is housed at the Adirondack Museum at Blue Mountain

Lake. The building, interpretation, launching, and evaluation of the bateau were such a success that on the project's completion LCMM immediately began planning a second project. This next project was to build an exact replica of the 16.4 m (54 ft) Revolutionary War gunboat *Philadelphia*. The original *Philadelphia* was recovered in 1935 and was eventually acquired and documented by the Smithsonian Institution (Hoffman 1982). The three-year construction project culminated in a dramatic 1991 launching attended by 4,000 people. Since its launching, *Philadelphia II* has hosted more than 250,000 visitors.

The effectiveness of *Philadelphia II* to engage visitors in the history of the American Revolution gave rise to the interest in building a boat to represent the lake's commercial era. In 2000, LCMM initiated the Burlington Schooner Project, which created a replica of an 1862-class canal schooner modeled on *General Butler*. The 28.6 m (88 ft) long replica, which was built within a half-mile of where the original rests on the lake bottom, was launched in 2004 and christened *Lois McClure* (Figure 46.3). Since that time, *Lois McClure* has visited more than 75 ports of call and has hosted more than 100,000 visitors.

Today the visitation trend for many museums is downward and we are challenged to create programs that will be more relevant and creative in the digital age. LCMM's replica programs provide the public with an intimate experience aboard an archaeological reconstruction and have proven to be very effective. However, the

Figure 46.3 Replica canal schooner *Lois McClure* sailing Lake Champlain. Reproduced with the kind permission of Lake Champlain Maritime Museum.

newest program designed to connect the public with shipwrecks is also showing great potential. The new program, entitled Shipwrecks!, involves taking people out on a boat to a shipwreck location. At present the program utilizes the moorings for the LCUHP system, and once the boat is secured, a remotely operated vehicle (ROV) is deployed over the side to find the wreck. The excitement of seeing a real-time image of a shipwreck appear on the vessel's viewing screen is a dynamic new way to make the connection between shipwrecks and the public (Figure 46.4). LCMM received a three-year grant from the Institute of Museum and Library Services to develop this new program, and it has been a complete success, allowing school groups and museum visitors to see a shipwreck without getting wet. In 2009, over 600 viewers logged on to watch footage of the shipwreck *Sarah Ellen* in the deep water of Lake Champlain, Webcasted with live commentary by LCMM archaeologists, allowing this digital outlet to meet the virtual museum world (LCMM 2009).

In a similar vein, in April 2009 the state of Florida launched an interactive Web site entitled Museums in the Sea. This exciting project allows detailed virtual Web tours of the state's 11 underwater preserve sites, with video tours, interactive histories, and information on the marine life that inhabits the sites. It allows anyone with a computer and an Internet connection to explore these underwater sites. The Web site was created by Florida's Bureau of Archaeological Research Underwater

Figure 46.4 LCMM's Shipwrecks! program takes the public out on the water to view a shipwreck using an ROV. Reproduced with the kind permission of Lake Champlain Maritime Museum.

Archaeology Team and the Florida Center for Interactive Media, with funding assistance from the Department of Environmental Protection, Coastal Management Program, and NOAA. It can be visited at www.museumsinthesea.com.

These museum-based options for sharing submerged cultural resources with the public are attainable to local communities that want to bridge the underwater world of shipwrecks with the terrestrial world of local museums and public outreach. Through humanities grants, local funding and support, and volunteer enthusiasm, maritime heritage tourism can become a grassroots way of connecting a community, a state, or a country to the importance of protecting historic sites, both on land and underwater, and to understanding the importance of preserving submerged cultural resources.

Conclusion

On a global level, the debate about the value of underwater cultural heritage has only begun to be appreciated by the public. New concepts about what constitutes a public resource and how that resource should be managed take time to become understood and accepted. The diving community has been engaged in this debate for several decades, and a wide variety of viewpoints have developed (Harris 2002). Many diving instructors now teach preservation of both natural and cultural resources through such diver training institutions as the Professional Association of Dive Instructors (PADI) and the National Association of Underwater Instructors (NAUI). Dive student can take classes and get certification in such areas as underwater archaeology and underwater ecology, which helps to promote diver ethics and stewardship. However, some die-hard wreck divers believe that the past doctrines of "finders, keepers" and free enterprise justify their collecting activities. While the overall position of the dive community seems to be slowly moving toward preservation, for many divers the issue is unclear despite policy changes and changes in public opinion across the globe.

Public venues that focus on underwater cultural heritage, such as museums and underwater preserve systems, can serve as platforms for fostering a discussion of submerged cultural resource protection, reasonable access, and ownership within communities worldwide. When the general public can take advantage of experiential opportunities by way of interactive exhibits, SCUBA and nonSCUBA options to visit submerged cultural resources, and replica vessels, shipwrecks can become more connected to our shared history and appear less remote and mysterious. The ability to share these sites in situ and through museums and other programs, can showcase how these complex sites can invoke lessons of respect. By sharing these sites we promote the idea that the looting and pillaging of shipwrecks is no more sound and justified than the looting and pillaging of prominent archaeological sites on land.

In the past, the underwater world of shipwrecks has been a lawless frontier visited by a relatively small group of underwater adventurers who believed that the ethical laws of preservation did not apply to submerged bottomlands. With global attention to the fact that our world's waters contain some of the most important and well-preserved symbols of our past, the issue of protecting these sites has become an appreciable idea. Although remote, shipwrecks and other submerged cultural resources present opportunities to document and learn from our past and to share in the story of human events. It is the responsibility of policy makers, professionals, the general public, and the diving public to ensure that protections outlined in the ASA and the UNESCO Convention are respected and followed so that these underwater sites can last for future generations.

ACKNOWLEDGMENTS

The LCMM acknowledges and thanks the Institute of Museum and Library Sciences for their support of the Shipwrecks! program.

REFERENCES

Alves, Francisco J. S. 2006. Strategic options with regards to public access—awareness raising in Portugal. In *Underwater cultural heritage at risk: Managing natural and human impacts*, ed. Robert Grenier, David Nutley, and Ian Cochran, 85–87. Heritage at Risk: Special Edition. Paris: International Council on Monuments and Sites.

Bateaux Below. 2005. Online at www.thelostradeau.com. Accessed 10 January 2010.

Bratten, John R. 2002. *The gondola* Philadelphia *and the Battle of Lake Champlain*. Studies in Nautical Archaeology No. 6. College Station: Texas A&M University Press.

Broadwater, John D. 1997. USS *Monitor*. In *Encyclopedia of underwater and maritime archaeology*, ed. James P. Delgado, 281–282. New Haven, CT: Yale University Press.

Caesarea Diving Club. 2010. *Caesarea Diving Club*. Online at www.caesarea-diving.com. Accessed 10 January 2010.

Cohn, Arthur B. 2003. Lake Champlain's Underwater Historic Preserve Program: Reasonable access to appropriate sites. In *Submerged cultural resource management: Preserving and interpreting our sunken maritime heritage*, ed. James D. Spirek and Della A. Scott-Ireton, 85–94. Plenum Series in Underwater Archaeology. New York: Kluwer Academic/Plenum.

Crisman, K. J. 1983. *The history and construction of the United States Schooner* Ticonderoga. Alexandria, VA: Eyrie.

Crisman, Kevin J., and Arthur B. Cohn. 1998. *When horses walked on water: Horse-powered ferries in 19th-century America*. Washington, DC: Smithsonian Institution Press.

Erie Quest. 2010. *Erie Quest*. Online at www.ontarioexplorer.com/Divenet/ErieQuest. html/. Accessed 10 January 2010.

Finland National Board of Antiquities. 2004. *Maritime historical underwater park*. Helsinki: National Board of Antiquities. Online at http://www.nba.fi/en/mmf_park/. Accessed 30 January 2010.

Florida Bureau of Archaeological Research. 1992. A proposal to establish the USS *Massachusetts* as a State Underwater Archaeological Preserve. Florida Bureau of Archaeological Research, Tallahassee.

———. 2000. A proposal to establish the shipwreck *Half Moon* as a State Underwater Archaeological Preserve. Florida Bureau of Archaeological Research, Tallahassee

Florida Division of Historical Resources. 2010. *Florida underwater preserves*. Online at http://www.dhr.dos.state.fl.us/archaeology/underwater/preserves/. Accessed 30 January 2010.

Friday, Joseph D. 1988. A history of the wreck of the USS *Huron*. Master's thesis, Department of History, East Carolina University, Greenville, NC.

Frost, Honor. 1990. Museum report—tourism aids archaeology: The Ustica experiment. *International Journal of Nautical Archaeology* 19 (4): 341–343.

Hagglund, Lorenzo F. 1949. *A page from the past: The story of the continental gondola Philadelphia on Lake Champlain, 1776–1949*. 2nd ed. Lake George, NY: Adirondacks Resorts Press.

Halsey, John R. 1990. *Beneath the inland seas: Michigan's underwater archaeological heritage*. Lansing: Bureau of History, Michigan Department of State.

Halsey, John R., and Peter Lindquist. 2003. Beneath pictured rocks. In *Submerged cultural resource management: Preserving and interpreting our sunken maritime heritage*, ed. James D. Spirek and Della A. Scott-Ireton, 107–118. Plenum Series in Underwater Archaeology. New York: Kluwer Academic/Plenum.

Hannahs, Todd. 2003. Underwater parks versus preserves: Data or access. In *Submerged cultural resource management: Preserving and interpreting our sunken maritime heritage*, ed. James D. Spirek and Della A. Scott-Ireton, 5–16. Plenum Series in Underwater Archaeology. New York: Kluwer Academic/Plenum.

Harris, Lynn. 2002. Underwater heritage and the diving community. In *Public benefits of archaeology*, ed. Barbara J. Little, 59–73. Gainesville: University Press of Florida.

Harris, Lynn, Jimmy Moss, and Carl Naylor. 1993. *The Cooper River Survey: An underwater reconnaissance of the West Branch*. Research Manuscript Series 218. Columbia: South Carolina Institute of Archaeology and Anthropology, University of South Carolina.

Hoffman, Howard P. 1982. *A graphic presentation of the continental gondola Philadelphia: American gunboat of 1776*. Washington, DC: Smithsonian Institute.

Kane, Adam I., A. Peter Barranco, Joanne M. DellaSalla, Sarah E. Lyman, and Christopher R. Sabick. 2007. *Lake Champlain Underwater Cultural Resources Survey*. Vol. 8, *2003 Results*; Vol. 9, *2004 Results*. Ferrisburgh, VT: Lake Champlain Maritime Museum.

Kane, Adam I., and Christopher R. Sabick. 2002. *Lake Champlain Underwater Cultural Resources Survey*. Vol. 4, *1999 Results*; Vol. 5, *2000 Results*. Vergennes, VT: Lake Champlain Maritime Museum.

Kane, Adam I., Christopher R. Sabick, and Sara R. Brigadier. 2003. *Lake Champlain Underwater Cultural Resources Survey*. Vol. 6, *2001 Results*; Vol. 7, *2002 Results*. Vergennes, VT: Lake Champlain Maritime Museum.

La Roche, Daniel. 2003. A Review of Cultural Resource Management Experiences in Presenting Canada's Submerged Heritage. In *Submerged cultural resource management: Preserving and interpreting our sunken maritime heritage*, ed. James D. Spirek and Della A. Scott-Ireton, 29–41. Plenum Series in Underwater Archaeology. New York: Kluwer Academic/Plenum.

Lake Champlain Maritime Museum (LCMM). 2009. *Webcast: Schooner* Sarah Ellen. Online at www.lcmm.org/webcast.html/. Accessed 30 January 2010.

Lake Champlain's Underwater Historic Preserve System. 2008. *Dive historic Lake Champlain.* Ferrisburg, VT: Lake Champlain Maritime Museum.

Langley, Susan B. M. 2003. Historic shipwreck preserves in Maryland. In *Submerged cultural resource management: Preserving and interpreting our sunken maritime heritage,* ed. James D. Spirek and Della A. Scott-Ireton, 45–58. Plenum Series in Underwater Archaeology. New York: Kluwer Academic/Plenum.

Lawrence, Richard W. 2003. From national tragedy to cultural treasure: The USS *Huron* Historic Shipwreck Preserve. In *Submerged cultural resource management: Preserving and interpreting our sunken maritime heritage,* ed. James D. Spirek and Della A. Scott- Ireton, 59–70. Plenum Series in Underwater Archaeology. New York: Kluwer Academic/Plenum.

Maryland Historic Trust. 2009. *U1105.* Online at http://mht.maryland.gov/U1105.html. Accessed 30 January 2010.

McLaughlin, Scott A., and Anne W. Lessmann. 1998. *Lake Champlain Underwater Cultural Resources Survey.* Vol. 1, *Lake survey background and 1996 results.* Ferrisburgh, VT: Lake Champlain Maritime Museum.

Mesić, Jasen. 2008. A resource for sustainable development: The case of Croatia. *Museum International, Underwater Cultural Heritage* 60 (4): 91–99.

Michigan Underwater Preserve Council. 2004. *Michigan underwater preserves.* Online at www.michiganpreserves.org. Accessed 30 January 2010.

Michigan Underwater Preserve Council Inc. (MUPC). 1993. *Diving Michigan's underwater preserves 1993.* St. Ignace, MI: Maritime Press.

National Oceanic and Atmospheric Administration (NOAA). 2003a. *Monitor National Marine Sanctuary.* U.S. Department of Commerce, Washington, DC. Online at http://monitor.nos.noaa.gov/. Accessed 30 January 2010.

———. 2003b. *Thunder Bay National Marine Sanctuary and Underwater Preserve.* U.S. Department of Commerce, Washington, DC. Online at http://thunderbay.noaa.gov/. Accessed 30 January 2010.

———. 2010. *Florida Keys National Marine Sanctuary.* U.S. Department of Commerce, Washington DC. Online at http://floridakeys.noaa.gov/. Accessed 30 January 2010.

National Park Service. 1990. *Abandoned Shipwreck Act Guidelines.* U.S. Department of the Interior, Washington, DC. Online at http://www.cr.nps.gov/aad/submerged/public.htm/. Accessed 30 January 2010.

New York Department of Environmental Conservation. 2010. *Submerged Heritage Preserves Program.* Online at www.dec.ny.gov/lands/315.html/. Accessed 30 January 2010.

Ohio State University Sea Grant College Program. 2010. *Shipwrecks and maritime trails of the Lake Erie coastal Ohio trails.* Online at www.ohioshipwrecks.org. Accessed 30 January 2010.

Parks Canada. 2009. *Fathom five.* Online at www.pc.gc.ca/amnc-nmca/on/fathomfive/index_E.asp/. Accessed 30 January 2010.

Philippou, Cassandra, and Mark Staniforth. 2003. Maritime heritage trails in Australia: An overview and critique of the interpretive programs. In *Submerged cultural resource management: Preserving and interpreting our sunken maritime heritage,* ed. James D. Spirek and Della A. Scott- Ireton, 135–149. Plenum Series in Underwater Archaeology. New York: Kluwer Academic/Plenum.

Pohuski, Michael, and Donald Shomette. 1994. *The U-1105 Survey: A report on the 1993 archaeological survey of 18ST636, a Second World War German submarine in the Potomac River, Maryland.* Crownsville: Maryland Historical Trust.

Raban, Avner. 2003. *Presenting the submerged ancient harbor at Caesarea to the public*. Paper presented at the 5th World Archaeological Congress, 21–26 June, Washington, DC.

Robertson, Philip. 2003. The visitor schemes on the historic shipwrecks of the *Swan* and HMS *Dartmouth*, Sound of Mull, Scotland (UK). In *Submerged cultural resource management: Preserving and interpreting our sunken maritime heritage*, ed. James D. Spirek and Della A. Scott-Ireton, 71–84. Plenum Series in Underwater Archaeology. New York: Kluwer Academic/Plenum.

Sabick, Christopher, Anne Lessmann, and Scott McLaughlin. 2000. *Lake Champlain Underwater Cultural Resources Survey*. Vol. 2, *1997 Results*; Vol. 3, *1998 Results*. Ferrisburgh, VT: Lake Champlain Maritime Museum.

Save Ontario's Shipwrecks. 2010. *Save Ontario's Shipwrecks*. Online at www.saveontarioshipwrecks.on.ca. Accessed 30 January 2010.

Scott-Ireton, Della A. 2003. Florida's underwater archaeological preserves. In *Submerged cultural resource management: Preserving and interpreting our sunken maritime heritage*, ed. James D. Spirek and Della A. Scott-Ireton, 95–105. Plenum Series in Underwater Archaeology. New York: Kluwer Academic/Plenum.

———. 2005. Preserves, parks and trails: Strategy and response in maritime cultural resource management. PhD diss., Florida State University.

Shomette, Donald G. 1989. Heyday of the horse ferry. *National Geographic* 176 (4): 548–556.

Smith, Sheli. 1991. *Emerald Bay Barges Archaeological Survey 1989–1990*. Los Angeles: Los Angeles Maritime Museum.

Smith, Tim. 2003. Shipwreck trails: Public ownership of a unique resource? In *Submerged cultural resource management: Preserving and interpreting our sunken maritime heritage*, ed. James D. Spirek and Della A. Scott-Ireton, 121–133. Plenum Series in Underwater Archaeology. New York: Kluwer Academic/Plenum.

Spirek, James, and Lynn Harris. 2003. Maritime heritage on display: Underwater examples from South Carolina. In *Submerged cultural resource management: Preserving and interpreting our sunken maritime heritage*, ed. James D. Spirek and Della A. Scott-Ireton, 165–175. Plenum Series in Underwater Archaeology. New York: Kluwer Academic/Plenum.

Stevens, E. Willis. 1989. *Louisbourg Submerged Cultural Resource Survey*. Federal Archaeology Office, Parks Canada, Ottawa, Ontario, Canada.

Strachan, Shirley. 1995. Interpreting maritime heritage: Australian historic shipwreck trails. *Historic Environment* 11 (4): 26–35.

Terrell, Bruce G. 2003. Florida Keys National Marine Sanctuary Shipwreck Trail: A model for multiple-use resource management. In *Submerged cultural resource management: Preserving and interpreting our sunken maritime heritage*, ed. James D. Spirek and Della A. Scott-Ireton, 151–163. Plenum Series in Underwater Archaeology. New York: Kluwer Academic/Plenum.

UNESCO. 2001. *The UNESCO Convention on the Protection of the Underwater Cultural Heritage*. Online at http://www.unesco.org/fileadmin/MULTIMEDIA/HQ/CLT/UNDERWATER/pdf/Infokit_en_Final.pdf/. Accessed 30 January 2010.

———. 2010. *The Alexandria Underwater Museum Project*. Online at http://www.unesco.org/en/underwater-cultural-heritage/the-heritage/museums-tourism/alexandria-museum-project/. Accessed 30 January 2010.

University of Southern Carolina Maritime Research Division. 2010. *Maritime heritage trails*. Online at www.cas.sc.edu/sciaa/mrd/sdamp_mht.html/. Accessed 30 January 2010.

Vrana, Kenneth J. and Gail A. Vander Stoep. 2003. The maritime cultural landscape of the Thunder Bay National Marine Sanctuary and Underwater Preserve. In *Submerged cultural resource management: Preserving and interpreting our sunken maritime heritage*, ed. James D. Spirek and Della A. Scott-Ireton, 17–28. Plenum Series in Underwater Archaeology. New York: Kluwer Academic/Plenum.

Wisconsin Historical Society. 2010. *Wisconsin maritime trails*. Online at www.maritimetrails.org. Accessed 30 January 2010.

Zarzynski, Joseph. 2002. Lake George, New York: Recent archaeological investigations at Mountain Waterway. In *International handbook of underwater archaeology*, ed. Carol V. Ruppé and Janet F. Barstad, 75–87. Plenum Series in Underwater Archaeology. New York: Kluwer Academic/Plenum.

Zarzynski, Joseph, and Donna K. Abbass. 1997. Land tortoise. In *Encyclopedia of underwater and maritime archaeology*, ed. James P. Delgado, 237–238. New Haven, CT: Yale University Press.

Zarzynski, Joseph, D. K. Abbass, Bob Benway, and John Farrell. 1996. "Ring-around-a-radeau," or, Fencing in a 1758 shipwreck for public access and preservation. In *Underwater archaeology proceedings from the Society for Historical Archaeology Conference 1996*, ed. Stephen R. James and Camille Stanley, 35–40. Cincinnati: Society for Historical Archaeology.

PART VI

CONCLUSION

CONCLUSION

CONCLUSION: FUTURE DIRECTIONS

PAULA MARTIN

INTRODUCTION

THE chapters in this volume demonstrate the extent to which the subject areas of underwater and maritime archaeology have developed and expanded from the study of shipwrecks and ancient harbors into consideration of the whole maritime cultural landscape, both physical and metaphorical, from prehistory to the twentieth century. The earliest wreck excavated so far is the Uluburun vessel, off the Mediterranean coast of Turkey, dating from the late fourteenth century BCE (Pulak 1998; Pulak 2008), while the location of wrecks from the Second World War has helped to solve mysteries and validate historical accounts (for example, McCarthy 2010; Neyland in this volume). In all periods shipwrecks and other maritime remains are now studied in their wider landscape context (for example, Paddenberg and Hession 2008; Delgado 2009). During the past 50 years, progress has been made not only in diving technology and in underwater archaeological techniques but also, more importantly, in perceptions of the subject and its place in the wider discipline of archaeology. So what might the next 50 years bring?

The assembly of these articles represents much thought and effort. The result is more than the sum of the individual parts and will be of great use to future scholars. The overall effect of 47 chapters summarizing the study of shipwrecks and wider maritime culture in geographical areas throughout the world, for example, is to reinforce the claim that maritime archaeology has much to contribute to the wider history and archaeology of the regions concerned. Wrecked vessels reveal the technological achievements of their day. Warships demonstrate developments in aggressive and defensive technologies. Merchant vessels carry evidence of the range of cargoes traded. All this adds to our understanding of past worlds and their networks of exchange and interaction.

While we have some way to go in convincing all terrestrial archaeologists and historians of the importance of maritime perspectives, seafaring is fundamental to human history. "Without seafarers, there would have been no Minoan civilization. Without river craft the great Egyptian pyramids could not have been built. . . . Without great merchant vessels, neither Greece nor Rome . . . could have prospered" (Bass 2005: 10). And the relevance and contribution of maritime archaeology to archaeology and history more generally goes well beyond the immediate maritime sphere (Domingues in this volume). Trade networks link urban areas with hinterlands. Shipwreck finds can contribute to wider historical knowledge and may lead historians to dig deeper than before among their documentary sources. The discovery of Spanish Armada shipwrecks, for example, stimulated renewed archival research that challenged many accepted theories, often based on secondary or selected published primary sources. Reinforced by the evidence produced by the wrecks, these new discoveries overturned many aspects of the previously accepted discourse from both Spanish and English perspectives (for example, Martin and Parker 1988). The study of American Civil War blockade-runners has similarly helped to redefine the wider historical picture and to emphasize the international dimension of what may appear at first to be a local phenomenon (for example, Block 2007; Graham 2006).

Archaeologists like to create typologies and put their finds into categories. When these typologies are applied to discrete archaeological assemblages, which are often closely dated, such as shipwrecks, these can challenge more theoretical constructs. Life is not so easily compartmentalized. In the early days of the archaeological study of vessel hulls, there was perceived to be a clear regional and chronological distinction between those built "frame-first" and those built "skeleton-first." George Bass (1972: 10) wrote, "Only now are we beginning to see where and when the revolutionary change from Greco-Roman methods of hull-first construction to our modern method of skeleton-first construction took place." The picture today is far more complex, with subtleties and variations within, and overlaps between, these two "traditions" both chronologically and regionally, as well as in their underlying design "philosophies" (see, for example, Hocker, Pomey, and Rieth in this volume). Who knows what may be found in the future and what current theories may be overturned. Objects from shipwrecks are also useful in testing and refining archaeological typologies, and sometimes conflict with sequences built on less secure terrestrial contexts. This has not always been appreciated by land archaeologists, and there is more work to be done in this field for every period and every type of find—particularly, perhaps, in interacting with the wider study of material culture in order to prove the value of shipwrecks and other sealed underwater contexts in helping to refine dating sequences.

SCOPE

Underwater archaeology was carried out sporadically in the nineteenth and early twentieth century in rivers, lakes, and caves, from Mesoamerican cenotes to Scottish crannogs. Modern shipwreck archaeology began with classical shipwrecks in the Mediterranean but has expanded in both geographical and chronological scope and the range of site types. Prehistoric (Bronze Age) wrecks have been found off the coast of Turkey, Greece, Italy, and other places in the Mediterranean. The recent find of Paleolithic axes on Crete demonstrates the use of watercraft at that early date (American School of Classical Studies at Athens). Other Paleolithic tools, as for example in the North Sea, indicate the presence of drowned landscapes (Firth in this volume). The coast is where some of the earliest settlement evidence is being found (for example, see Blue in this volume). In Australia, "some of the earliest terrestrial archaeological sites associated with Australia's indigenous peoples have been inundated and now lie beneath the sea" (Staniforth in this volume). Submerged prehistoric landscapes are a field where land archaeologists are now taking underwater archaeology seriously.

In northwestern Europe, early accidental finds included Viking vessels large and small, warships and merchant ships, and later medieval vessels. The five eleventh-century Skuldelev Ships were found near Roskilde, Denmark, in 1957 and recovered in 1962 (Crumlin-Pedersen and Olsen 2002; Olsen and Crumlin-Pedersen 1968), the same year that the Bremen Cog was discovered (Hoffman and Schnall 2003; Lahn 1992). The vessels of the East India Companies and the Spanish Armada attracted much attention, either for their iconic status and historical interest, or for the riches they often carried. Gradually a wider range of vessels have been identified and studied (for an accessible overview, see Delgado 1997). Whereas many early underwater archaeologists, as well as treasure hunters, searched for specific ships lured by the thrill of discovery, it is now more common to thoroughly investigate shipwrecks as they are located, whether intentionally or unintentionally, whatever their date or vessel type. It is also generally accepted that even a partial shipwreck or one in a poor state of preservation can yield useful information. The result is a greater breadth and depth of knowledge; almost every site, whether named or unidentified, large or small, has evidence to offer the inquiring archaeologist.

In some areas of the world maritime contact has been particularly important. In Australia, for example, "until the twentieth century everyone, or their ancestors, and literally every 'thing' or artifact that was not made there arrived by sea" (Staniforth in this volume). Many seas, such as the North Sea, the Baltic, the Black Sea, the Red Sea, and the Indian Ocean, as well as the Mediterranean and the Caribbean, served as hubs of trade and contact. For the countries around their edges, the sea was a highway, offering direct and relatively inexpensive routes for carrying goods and people.

The validity of archaeology of the relatively recent past has gained wider acceptance, underwater as on land. While many regard it as unimportant to investigate the material remains of subjects for which we have copious documentary evidence, documents rarely cover all aspects of any historical process or event. "Although the world wars are far better known than historical events from earlier periods of human history, professional archaeologists have applied archaeological principles and formulated research questions on the ship and aircraft wrecks of these conflicts. Like other research in historical archaeology, such questioning can confirm, complement, or contradict the historical records" (Neyland in this volume).

The ever-increasing breadth of maritime archaeology leads us, however, to the necessity to target future research in order to use our limited resources most effectively. As Van Tilburg (in this volume) has expressed it so cogently, "The Pacific is so large and the potential archaeological resources there so varied that it is immediately important to address the question of directions in research. . . . What are other major historical themes to which maritime archaeology can make a contribution in the Pacific? What are the gaps in knowledge that can be addressed by this field? Certainly, there is the potential to broaden the focus beyond shipwrecks alone and address indigenous Pacific island resources. . . . And there is the challenge of understanding the significance of shipwreck sites from island or non-Western perspectives."

One of our strengths is our internationality. This started early on, as for example with the work of INA in Turkey. Many projects involve collaboration, for instance in Mexico, where "since the beginning, all projects have had a multidisciplinary and multi-institutional approach, including international participation" (Luna Erreguerena in this volume). This is a strength to be built on. The movement of postgraduate students between institutions, countries, even continents, offers great potential for the sharing of ideas, both theoretical and practical, and the growth of networks of people interested in similar topics. In the future this will, we would hope, serve to stimulate higher standards and new fields of research.

SHIPS AND SHIPWRECKS

Many maritime archaeologists center their work on understanding ships of all periods and all regions, from small vernacular craft to large naval vessels. This is leading to ever greater appreciation of the subtleties of design, of regional variations, and of the complexity of construction methods. There is also a growing willingness to accept that shipbuilding techniques cannot be fitted into simplistic categories. Work on replicas, reconstructions, and "floating hypotheses" is perhaps now being approached with more humility and sensitivity than in the past, as is experimental archaeology more widely (Ravn et al. in this volume). More knowledge derived from whole vessels and partly intact shipwrecks will provide data from which more fragmentary finds of timbers or fittings may be more firmly assigned to dates and types than is the case today. This should lead to a reduced reliance on pictorial or literary evidence as more actual material is found on which hypotheses can be more firmly based. Hopefully the next 50 years will fill some of the gaps and provide an ever wider pool of data. It is also hoped that vessels will more often be seen not as isolated examples of the technology of their period and region, but within the context of their building and use, and as part of the wider cultural landscape. "The study of a shipwreck is not simply a question of providing a description, however precise it may be, of the discovered remains. Rather, the study endeavors, through the understanding of these remains, to reconstitute the original ship and to interpret it within the framework of a well-defined historical context" (Pomey in this volume).

Recently, interest in ships and boats has extended to the sails and rigging without which the hulls could not have moved anywhere, and aspects such as caulking and ballast (for example, Loewen 2005; Polzer 2008; Sanders 2010), but there is much more research to be done in this area. The next 50 years will almost certainly produce more evidence for the complexities of constructing vessels and using them at sea. This is just one example of how our subject, as it grows, is broadening out in its compass and seeing research topics, such as ships or harbors, increasingly as parts of cultural systems rather than as isolated objects. One urgent area for future work is more ethnographic recording, before fiberglass replaces traditional boat-building materials throughout the world. However, in much recent work in this field "boats are addressed as technology rather than as material *culture*, without recognition of human-object intersubjectivity, or the role they play in producing place, identity, and the social world in maritime communities" (Ransley in this volume). So there is a need not only for more recording, but for more recording of whole communities rather than just the boats they build and use.

As a corollary there is a need for collecting oral histories of maritime communities, despite the problems associated with oral history recording. "On the one hand, they are the voices of tradition; on the other, they are by their very nature partial and subjective" (Ransley in this volume). The formality involved, and the need for clarity of copyright, may also make the voices less natural. Folklore is also problematical, relying much on the agenda of the recorder. "Both oral histories and folklore traditions have a particular value as primary sources, but as a direct result they are ambiguous material to analyze for information on maritime traditions and practices" (Ransley in this volume). Even the definition of a "maritime community" raises questions: "Most coastal communities exploit both marine and terrestrial resources; they are not isolated coastal communities facing only toward the sea" (Ransley in this volume). Raising such questions, however, is to be seen not as a criticism, but as an attempt to help focus future studies.

When Keith Muckelroy (1975, 1978) published his observations on site formation processes, and how ships turned into shipwrecks, he tried to categorize the current information in an attempt to "unscramble" shipwrecks and understand better the complete vessels they once represented (see also Gibbs 2006). Once again, finds have demonstrated that there is perhaps greater variety and complexity than he described—indeed, no two shipwrecks are exactly alike. Even those wrecked in the same event may have reacted to different actions of individuals and different surface and seabed conditions to produce a different site type. "No two formations are the same, since the complex and interacting variables that constitute the environmental setting, the nature of the ship, and the circumstances of its loss will combine to create a set of attributes unique to each site" (C. Martin in this volume; see also Wachsmann in this volume for different processes operating in deep water). The definition of site formation processes has gradually expanded. "Human activity, particularly salvage, can also be regarded as a formation process (as can archaeological intervention). The deposition of unrelated material by rubbish dumping, constructional work, or the intrusion of a later wreck are other possibilities to be considered" (C. Martin in this volume). It can include evidence such as survivor camps (for example, Clark and de Biran 2010), or bases for salvage expeditions, as well as the effects of environmental changes, for example alterations in sedimentation patterns caused by sea-level change, sand extraction, or intrusive hard engineering.

Our understanding of the technology involved in building and working wrecked and abandoned vessels has implications well beyond the history of technology. For example, the way vessels were constructed can help explain how they broke up. One held together by metal bolts may fall apart quicker than one constructed using wooden pegs. At the same time, however, we are increasingly coming to appreciate the wide range of individual human actions and reactions involved both during and after the shipwreck process, and how these can be influenced not just by the individual's role, status, and personality but by each individual's wider social and cultural background (for example, Adams 2003).

LEGISLATION AND MANAGEMENT

Underwater archaeology and wider work on the maritime cultural landscape will, we hope, spread to more countries. The regional summaries presented in the preceding chapters have provided a snapshot of what has been achieved so far, and the level of protection provided by different states. Some of the chapters have gone further, as, for example, in suggesting an explanation as to why wrecks are found in some areas and not in others (Werz in this volume). In some areas treasure hunters are a major problem:

> While appreciation of this rich and finite cultural heritage exists in the region, the one dominant problem, especially for Caribbean shipwrecks, is the perceived commercial value of real and imagined treasure cargoes. The quest for treasure endangers all underwater cultural heritage (UCH) sites in the Caribbean. The actions of commercial salvors are a persistent menace to heritage professionals and the UCH they seek to study, manage, and protect. (Leshikar-Denton in this volume)

A key feature of management of the cultural heritage is data gathering and dissemination. Progress in computing has allowed the development of databases now generally known in the United Kingdom as Historic Environment Records, many of which are publicly accessible. It is only such systematic and timely record-keeping that can help to inform other national and regional organizations and reduce the risk of conflict with planners and those working with the natural environment. Hand in hand with management there needs to be public outreach, and several papers in this volume, such as those by Runyan, Staniforth, and Cohn and Dennis, describe what has been done in their areas. Many interesting and imaginative ways of interacting with divers and with the wider nondiving public have been devised. Maturity of the discipline has brought maturity to such systems, which are increasingly allowing not only public access but also public interaction. Much has been achieved, but only time will tell how successful some recent schemes have been (for a range of examples, see Jameson and Scott-Ireton 2007; Spirek and Scott-Ireton 2003).

Many of the chapters in this volume discuss what has been achieved in terms of legal protection of the underwater cultural heritage. The chapter on the Caribbean also highlights how fragile such protection systems can be. A change of government, or even simply of prominent members of a governing group, can lead to changes of attitude, of legislation, or of interpretation or implementation of legislation. While such changes can be positive, they more often seem to tend to undo years of patient work by those interested in the preservation of the underwater cultural heritage. However, "despite the many inherent differences worldwide, the last 50 years have seen lots of international dialogue, convergence and integration of which maritime archaeology can profit" (Maarleveld in this volume). Let us hope that the coming into force in 2009 of the UNESCO Convention on the Protection of the Underwater Cultural Heritage heralds an era of improved appreciation, as well as protection, of our underwater cultural heritage.

THE INTERFACE BETWEEN LAND AND SEA

Ancient harbors have long been a field of interest, especially those within the Mediterranean.

> By at least the Early Bronze Age it had become clear to the inhabitants of the Mediterranean region that travel and the transport of merchandise by sea offered several significant advantages over conveyance by land: ships and rafts could carry very heavy weights; under the right conditions the wind provided powerful, sustained propulsion; and the "pathless ways of the sea" required neither maintenance nor permission for passage. (Oleson and Hohlfelder in this volume)

The symbiotic feedback between the economy and technology is particularly marked in the history of harbor construction, and the study of harbors has now developed into the study of the hinterland that harbors served, the vessels that used them, and how changes were made in reaction to climatic or sea-level changes, to changing political and mercantile networks, and to developments in vessel technology. Interest has spread not only to harbors in other regions and of all periods, but to shipbuilding sites, dockyards, and the infrastructure associated with maritime activities. "Shipyards are interesting because they are intimately linked with both the ships that they built and the cultures that built them" (Moser in this volume). Abandoned vessels are also increasingly appreciated as a useful source of information (Richards in this volume).

But harbors are not the only features to be found along the world's coastlines. For long the coast and intertidal zone had fallen into a gap, both administrative and perceptual, between land and underwater archaeology. Worse, modern archaeologists, seeing the world from a land-based perspective, reinforced by the predominance of land and air travel, tend to perceive coasts as boundaries. It is prehistorians who are leading a change of mind-set. "The role of coastlines has been seriously underestimated in the conventional view of human development," and from the terrestrial viewpoint, "coastlines are seen literally as margins on the edge of continental land masses, rather than as centers of innovation and pathways for movement and communication" (Bailey 2004: 3, 5; see also Firth in this volume). It is heartening to see this argument for the sea as a unifying factor applied to an area as large as the Pacific Ocean (Van Tilburg in this volume).

Within our field, it is now being realized that "the coast links terrestrial and underwater archaeology into a unified maritime archaeology" (Ford in this volume). Wherever serious survey work has been done, a large number and variety of features have been found, some of great significance to the wider archaeological world. Even rapid archaeological assessments of the coastal zone, when carried out sympathetically, can yield a range of new features, sometimes in the most unlikely surroundings (Paddenberg and Hession 2008). Adding a foreshore element to a wider archaeological survey program can produce significant results and serve to open the eyes of the rest of the archaeological community (O'Sullivan 2001). Serious systematic fieldwork can do even more, setting a standard for others to emulate (McErlean, McConkey, and Forsythe 2002). Beyond the basic archaeological survey that is needed to fill long-standing gaps in the record and to provide a basis for analytical work, there has also been a growth in the study of spiritual and cultural aspects of the coast. Place-name evidence, folklore, and evidence for ritual can all inform us about humankind's use of and attitude toward the coast and particular features on that coast (Westerdahl in this volume).

TECHNOLOGY

Remote-sensing techniques have improved tremendously in the last 20 years, as has the computing power necessary to convert the resultant data into a format that can be effectively manipulated and visualized. "Although acoustic systems will never completely replace diver surveys, they do provide baseline data at rates far exceeding those of experienced dive teams" (Quinn in this volume). Recent years have witnessed remarkable "advances in sonar technology, positioning systems, and computer power that have revolutionized the imaging of the seafloor" (Quinn in this volume). The acquisition, processing, and visualization of such data will continue to progress. "Perhaps most importantly for maritime archaeology, every new phase of development in sonar technology brings an increase in sensors' resolving capability and therefore an ability to image smaller and smaller artifacts in greater detail" (Quinn in this volume).

Gearhart, writing about the use of magnetic data, said his chapter is intended to encourage "fresh scientific perspectives on the topic while promoting the complementary goals of increased objectivity in marine magnetic interpretation and improved protection of historic shipwrecks." Both Gearhart's and Quinn's chapters offer realistic ideas about what can and cannot be achieved with current technology. This is an area in which the future may see twofold development. First, there will almost certainly be developments in the equipment available, its range, and the detailed information it can provide. This is closely linked to developments in computing speed and visualization techniques. Second, there may be changes in archaeologists' understanding of the right equipment (or the right combinations of equipment) for the task. Recently much work has been done on how combining information from two different pieces of equipment can help speed up the differentiation between archaeological sites and natural anomalies (for example, Plets et al. 2009; Sakellariou et al. 2007). There is also the potential, now being experimented with, for the extraction of potentially useful archaeological information from existing datasets acquired for other purposes, such as seabed surveys commissioned by the oil industry. The future is open-ended, provided archaeologists and geophysicists continue to interact constructively.

A field with great potential for future development is deepwater archaeology. Although more costly than conventional archaeological projects, deepwater projects carry benefits such as the round-the-clock potential of remote operations (Wachsmann in this volume). Many see the primary objectives of this area of research to be focused on locating and documenting sites, using the information retrieved to help plot trade routes and identify the types of vessels and cargoes visible on the seabed. Others wish to excavate on deepwater sites. The latter should ensure that their enthusiasm for using high-tech equipment does not cloud their judgment as to the quality of work achievable. On the other hand, as Wachsmann has pointed out (in this volume), "technology does not develop on its own: it is purpose-driven and can be improved upon only by initiating actual work." Excavation, however, must always be approached with humility.

While cameras, ROVs, and equipment such as robot arms are becoming both more skillful and less expensive, archaeology is ultimately a subjective discipline, traditionally carried out close-up by individuals. Although remotely operated technology can now provide better images and handle finds with amazing gentleness, we perhaps need a debate as to whether such technology can ever fully replace the diver. A few enthusiasts may suggest that remote-sensing and remotely controlled survey and excavation are the only way forward, to the extent that eventually direct human interaction with underwater sites would be unnecessary. At the same time, a traditional archaeologist when excavating relies on his senses of sight, touch, and even smell; a human being processes information in her brain as she uncovers it with delicate fingers. As Underwood explains (in this volume), "The most sensitive excavation tool is the hand, preferably one without a glove. . . . Some excavators, even in cold water, will cut off the fingertip of at least one finger of their glove to provide additional sensitivity. When excavating delicate material it is often necessary to use a single finger to painstakingly separate an artifact from its surrounding sediment." Excavation using an ROV's robot arm may involve the operator's sense of sight, but not yet that of touch. Perhaps the time is right for a more open discussion about the potential, applications, and limitations of deepwater archaeology.

Progress has also been made in fields beyond the scope of this volume, such as scientific dating methods, perhaps particularly dendrochronology. There has been both an increase in material from which data can be derived, and developments in techniques to source timber ever more specifically (for example, Daly 2007, 2009). The corrosion potential of metals can be more accurately assessed, and some stabilization can be achieved in situ (for example, MacLeod 2006). Modern X-rays and other forms of imaging mean that the interior of concretions can be visualized in much more detail (for example, Troalen et al. 2010). Ways of assessing, conserving, and presenting waterlogged wood have made progress, though one suspects that the conservation of composite objects will never be easy (Hamilton and Smith in this volume).

RECORDING AND DISSEMINATION

Ravn and his colleagues (in this volume) have demonstrated how compiling data for the purposes of "reconstruction" has moved from 1:1 recording on polythene sheets to 3-D digital recording. This is not only faster and more accurate but can also be interrogated more easily. No doubt such technology will develop further in the future. Another field in which technology is advancing is that of computer simulation, virtual reality, and similar technologies. Sanders (in this volume) provides a clear and thorough explanation of what virtual reality can achieve and offers a wide range of examples of how it has helped on an array of sites. He also explains clearly its potential for obtaining further information from sites excavated decades ago: "Re-creations of cultural heritage sites and artifacts can be globally enjoyed in classrooms, museums, excavations, research labs, and living rooms, much the way photography eventually infiltrated those same domains in the late nineteenth century, after decades of wrestling with cumbersome equipment, untrustworthy results, and resistance from the history profession (which utilized some of the same arguments levied against the use of virtual reality by archaeologists)." But this does not mean that all the other aspects of maritime archaeology described in these chapters will not in their own way move forward toward more detail and better means of interpreting that detail, and of providing more context on which better reconstructions can be based.

Computer modeling, simulation, and virtual reality visualizations have become an important part of the maritime archaeologist's interpretive skill set. The increasing use of interactive 3D computer graphics technologies for the study, teaching, and dissemination of maritime archaeology information follows their acceptance by the broader discipline of virtual heritage. The advantages for understanding history and its remains interactively and in three dimensions are that they provide not only new research tools but also the ability to ask new types of questions. These should inevitably lead to new insight into how the past actually happened.

A thoughtful article by McCarthy on maritime museums (in this volume), however, raises several interesting questions, and counteracts some of the arguments in the discussion on virtual archaeology. For example, he supports the view that "small, idiosyncratic museums are an essential counterpoint to neat, highly organized exhibitions with prescribed spaces between cabinets, uniform font sizes, set text-to-object ratios, and the other manifestations of 'best practice.' Experience shows that the public enjoy their clutter and the strange, colorful characters in attendance. As a result museums, their staff, and their volunteers need be encouraged to maintain their nonconformist individuality."

Is Archaeology a Science?

As scientific techniques have progressed, and as we criticize our predecessors for lack of objectivity, there have been those who seek to define archaeology within the sciences rather than the humanities. But total objectivity is impossible. We are fallible humans and cannot totally rid ourselves of our own individual cultural baggage. And, indeed, total objectivity can be sterile. In the words of Charles Darwin in 1861 (quoted in Gould 1992: 393), "About thirty years ago there was much talk that geologists ought only to observe and not theorize; and I well remember someone saying that at this rate a man might as well go into a gravel-pit and count the pebbles and describe the colors. How odd it is that anyone should not see that all observation must be for or against some view to be of any service." Even objective scientific data has to be interpreted: "The success of marine remote-sensing surveys is largely dependent upon the experience of the surveyors and interpreters" (Quinn in this volume).

Human beings in the past are what archaeology is about, and human beings are not always predictable; "we have to assume that the people whose dwelling-places, artifacts, lives even, we are dealing with were rational, integrated, sane and sensible human beings. Then we look at our own contemporaries and wonder how this belief can possibly be sustained" (Flanagan 1998: 5). Or in the words of Flinders Petrie (1904: 177–178), writing over 100 years ago: "The work of the archaeologist is to save lives; to go to some senseless mound of earth, some hidden cemetery, and thence bring into the comradeship of man some portions of the lives of this sculptor, of that artist, of the other scribe; to make their labour familiar to us as a friend; to resuscitate them again, and make them live in the thought . . . of living men and women." We need imagination, enthusiasm, rigor, and humility to do our work, along with an armory of scientific techniques to support them.

ETHICS

"Archaeology is a for-knowledge activity. Treasure-hunting is a for-profit activity. To try to reconcile these two interests is impossible" (Castro 2009). One of the most important chapters in this volume is that on ethics. Thijs Maarleveld explains with great clarity the problems that arise and the subtle shades of argument on both sides of the debate. There is the out-and-out treasure hunter, the treasure hunter who claims to be doing as good a job as an archaeologist but at no cost to the public purse; there are those who "present themselves as true saviors of heritage that would otherwise have been looted or destroyed"; and there are those who encourage archaeologists to work with commercial salvors for the benefit of the archaeological record. But this last argument has no validity, and none of its proponents has produced published results that could confound those who feel that such archaeologists have compromised their integrity. "If one appropriates or alienates heritage material or helps others to do so, one cannot be considered part of the heritage profession, irrespective of professional training. That is not negotiable" (Maarleveld in this volume). He also makes a thought-provoking comparison between archival research, which can be selective because it is nondestructive and can be repeated, and archaeological excavation, which has to be thorough because it cannot be repeated. He is clear about the way some treasure hunters work. "A closer look at the economics often reveals that 'treasure hunt' is no more than a decoy to attract money from investors, who will not see a return. . . . Sites are simply sacrificed in a 'laundering' process."

Maarleveld asks what it is that defines a professional archaeologist: is it educational qualifications, or is it a code of ethics? He provides a considered response by stating that it is "certainly true that a level of knowledge, a level of skills, and the ability to think analytically are very helpful, even essential. But . . . these skills are of no avail if they are used contrary to the central principles of the profession."

The debate about the ethics of treasure hunting and whether or not such people are capable of achieving archaeological standards of survey and excavation, and subsequently of publication, is perhaps the area in which least progress has been made in the past 50 years. Archaeologists still need to convince the rest of the world that archaeology is much more than simply systems of searching and recording, and much more than the sum of the individual objects identified. There is a long way to go before we can hope to win the battle. Søreide (in this volume) has observed that even though many treasure-hunting companies state that the goal for their exploration is protecting the cultural heritage found in shipwrecks, their "practical standard for commercial and academic coordination on shipwreck exploration and recovery" looks like archaeology but fails in many important ways, since the focus is not on archaeology but on recovery.

McCarthy (in this volume) is honest about the dichotomy faced by museums. As the gulf between archaeologists and treasure-hunters widened in the late twentieth century, the maritime museum, as the chief recipient of the objects intended for exhibition, found itself in a quandary.

> Financial administrators were especially vexed when offered exciting exhibitions and "blockbuster" draws showing "treasure" or objects sometimes wrested from iconic ships in immense depth. "Financial ambitions were stymied, . . . primarily because the proposed exhibits contained objects raised in a nonarchaeological fashion. From that time on, maritime museums were forced to line up across the same deep divide between archaeologist and salvor. Notwithstanding the pros and cons of that argument, an opportunity to show both sides of the argument to the hundreds of thousands who would have poured onto the exhibition floor to view the treasures and iconic objects was lost" (McCarthy in this volume).

PUBLICATION

Our main weapon against treasure hunters is good and timely publication, supported by well-informed public outreach presented in a compelling way. Flinders Petrie (1904: 48) described archaeological recording as "the absolute dividing line between plundering and scientific work, between a dealer and a scholar." What he meant was not just basic recording, but interpretation, as is made clear later in the same paragraph: "The unpardonable crime in archaeology is destroying evidence which can never be recovered; and every discovery does destroy evidence unless it is intelligently recorded. Our museums are ghastly charnel-houses of murdered evidence." I have heard otherwise respectable archaeologists argue that an object is doing more good cherished by a collector than languishing in a museum storeroom. Once the collector dies, however, or sells the object, it becomes inaccessible, and often untraceable, while the object in the museum is accessible for scholarly research indefinitely.

Nor is it acceptable to argue that print publication is becoming obsolete and that electronic media are the future. Print publication will not die, and at the moment it is still the safest medium in which to archive material. Film did not destroy the theater, sound recording did not stop live musical performance, and television did not supersede radio. Indeed, advances in technology have made printing less expensive and more flexible, making archaeological publication, with its need for numerous illustrations, easier and less expensive to achieve.

If you look at the chapters in this volume on maritime archaeology by authors from many regions of the world, and then look at their bibliographies, you will see clear evidence that in most areas publication lags behind fieldwork, sometimes by many years. But it gives hope for the future that some of this back-log has recently been published: *The Skuldelev Ships 1: Topography, Archaeology, History, Conservation and Display* (Crumlin-Pedersen and Olsen 2002), for example, and *Serçe Limanı: An Eleventh-Century Shipwreck, Volume 1: The Ship and Its Anchorage, Crew and Passengers* (Bass et al. 2004). The first volume of the report on the raising and excavation of *Vasa* was published in 2006 (Cederlund and Hocker), and more volumes may have appeared by the time you are reading this. Four of the planned five volumes on the excavation and conservation of *Mary Rose* have been published (Jones 2003; Marsden 2003, 2009; Gardiner 2005). The five-volume report on the Red Bay wrecks was published in 2007 (Grenier, Bernier, and Stevens). Furthermore, 2009 saw the second volume of Serçe Limanı, on the glass assemblage (Bass et al. 2009). But the backlog is still extensive.

The resolution of all the authors and readers of this volume should be to set an example to others by high-quality and timely publication. In addition, all media should be exploited in order to persuade the wider public of the importance, indeed the excitement, of what we are finding and what it means. We have to do this to counter the publicity afforded to the more "exciting" message of commercial exploit-ation. But we must achieve outreach without compromising standards. It is too easy for the publicity-seeking archaeologist to "bend" the evidence slightly to satisfy the media's desire for a good story. By taking a bit more time and effort, however, we can produce a better story from the fuller and more reliable material we have, and we should try our best to sell the media the "true" story. The problem lies not with the general public, but with the media's fixed and narrow ideas of what will interest that public. "We should not be afraid to love what we do while simultaneously demanding that more work is done, more money spent, and more attention given by industry, government and the public alike" (Flatman 2009: 78). We must try our best, and keep on trying. If we can demonstrate to the public as much enthusiasm about what we are doing as treasure hunters can, then perhaps we will have better success in getting our arguments across.

"The investigation of ancient harbors will continue to enrich our appreciation of the maritime world of antiquity and the role the sea played in the life and times of the ancient Mediterranean civilizations" (Oleson and Hohlfelder in this volume). These words could be applied to every topic and every period covered in this book. The more you look, the more you find, and the more subtle and complex and inter-active you find things to be. Existing typologies almost always prove too simplistic.

The study of people's interaction with the sea still has a long way to go, and exciting discoveries still await us. Like the sea, the opportunities and the challenges for maritime archaeology are boundless.

ACKNOWLEDGMENTS

I am very grateful to George Bass, Lucy Blue, and Colin Martin for constructive comments on a draft of this chapter, and to the editors, who were a pleasure to work with.

REFERENCES

Adams, Jon. 2003. *Ships, innovation and social change: Aspects of carvel shipbuilding in northern Europe 1450–1850.* Stockholm: Goteborg University Press.

American School of Classical Studies at Athens. 2010. Plakias survey finds Mesolithic and Palaeolithic artifacts on Crete. Rev. 1 February 2010. Online at www.ascsa.edu.gr/index.php/news/newsDetails/plakias-survey-finds-stone-age-tools-on-crete/. Accessed 30 March 2010.

Bailey, Geoffrey N. 2004. The wider significance of submerged archaeological sites and their relevance to world prehistory. In *Submarine prehistoric archaeology of the North Sea: Research priorities and collaboration with industry*, ed. N. C. Flemming, 3–10. London: CBA Research Report 141.

Bass, George. 1972. Introduction to *A history of seafaring based on underwater archaeology*, ed. G. Bass, 9–10. London: Thames and Hudson.

———. 2005. Introduction to *Beneath the Seven Seas: Adventures with the Institute of Nautical Archaeology*, ed. G. Bass, 10–27. London: Thames and Hudson.

Bass, G., R. Brill, B. Lledó, and S. Matthews. 2009. *Serçe Limani.* Vol. 2, *The glass of an eleventh-century shipwreck.* College Station, TX: Texas A&M University Press.

Bass, G. F., S. D. Matthews, J. R. Steffy, and F. H. Van Doorninck. 2004. *Serçe Limanı: An eleventh-century shipwreck, vol. 1: The ship and its anchorage, crew and passengers.* College Station: Texas A&M University Press.

Block, W. T. 2007. *Schooner sail to starboard: The US Navy versus blockade-runners in the western Gulf of Mexico.* Denbigh Shipwreck Project Report Series 3. College Station: Texas A&M University Press.

Castro, Filipe. 2009. Response to *Beyond stone and bone*, a weekly blog by Heather Pringle: Odyssey's never ending quest for treasure. Rev. 6 February 2009. Online at http://archaeology.org/blog/?p=271/. Accessed 28 June 2010.

Cederlund, C. O., and F. Hocker, eds. 2006. *Vasa I: The archaeology of a Swedish warship of 1628.* Oxford: Oxbow.

Clark, G., and A. de Biran. 2010. Geophysical and archaeological investigation of the survivor camp of the *Antelope* (1783) in the Palau Islands, western Pacific. *International Journal of Nautical Archaeology*, doi 10.1111/j.1095-9270.2010.00264/. Online at www3.interscience.wiley.com/journal/120124208/issue/. Accessed 29 March 2010.

Crumlin-Pedersen, O., and O. Olsen, eds. 2002. *The Skuldelev Ships I: Topography, archaeology, history, conservation and display*. Roskilde: Viking Ship Museum.

Daly, Aoife. 2007. The Karschau Ship, Schleswig-Holstein: Dendrochronological results and timber provenance. *International Journal of Nautical Archaeology* 36 (1): 155–166.

———. 2009. The chronology of cogs and their timber origin. In *Between the seas: Transfer and exchange in nautical technology; Proceedings of ISBSA 11, Mainz, 2006*, ed. R. Bockius, 237–248. Mainz: Römisch-Germanisches Zentralmuseum.

Delgado, James P., ed. 1997. *Encyclopaedia of underwater and maritime archaeology*. London: British Museum Press.

———. 2009. Sub marine explorer: A Civil War–era submersible in Panamá. *INA Annual* 2008: 93–99.

Flanagan, Laurence. 1998. *Ancient Ireland: Life before the Celts*. Dublin: Gill & Macmillan.

Flatman, Joe. 2009. Book review. *Conservation and Management and Archaeological Sites* 11 (1): 78–79.

Gardiner, J. 2005. *Before the mast: Life and death aboard the* Mary Rose. Portsmouth, U.K.: Mary Rose Trust.

Gibbs, Martin. 2006. Cultural site formation processes in maritime archaeology: Disaster response, Salvage and Muckelroy 30 years on. *International Journal of Nautical Archaeology* 35 (1): 4–19.

Gould, Stephen J. 1992. Dinosaurs in the haystack. *Natural History* 101 (3): 393–398.

Graham, E. 2006. *Clyde built: Blockade runners, cruisers and armoured rams of the American Civil War*. Edinburgh: Birlinn.

Grenier, R., M.-A. Bernier, and W. Stevens, eds. 2007. *The underwater archaeology of Red Bay: Basque shipbuilding and whaling in the 16th century*. Ottowa: Parks Canada.

Hoffman, G., and U. Schnall. 2003. *Die Kogge*. Steinhagen: Convent Verlag.

Jameson, John H., and Della A. Scott-Ireton, eds. 2007. *Out of the blue: Public interpretation of maritime cultural resources*. New York: Springer.

Jones, M., ed. 2003. *For future generations: Conservation of a Tudor maritime collection*. Portsmouth, U.K.: Mary Rose Trust.

Lahn, W. 1992. *Die Kogge von Bremen: Bauteile und Bauablauf*. Hamburg:Verlag die Hanse.

Loewen, B. 2005. Resinous paying materials in the French Atlantic, CE 1500–1800: History, technology, substances. *International Journal of Nautical Archaeology* 34 (2): 238–252.

MacLeod, I. 2006. In situ corrosion studies on wrecked aircraft of the Imperial Japanese Navy in Chuuk Lagoon, Federated States of Micronesia. *International Journal of Nautical Archaeology* 35 (1): 128–136.

Marsden, P., ed. 2003. *Sealed by time: The loss and recovery of the* Mary Rose. Portsmouth, U.K.: Mary Rose Trust.

———. 2009. Mary Rose: *Your noblest shippe: Anatomy of a Tudor warship*. Portsmouth, U.K.: Mary Rose Trust.

Martin, C. J. M., and N. G. Parker. 1988. *The Spanish Armada*. London: Hamish Hamilton.

McCarthy, Michael. 2010. Australia's greatest maritime mystery solved. *International Journal of Nautical Archaeology* 39 (1): 186–189.

McErlean, Thomas, Rosemary McConkey, and Wes Forsythe. 2002. *Strangford Lough: An archaeological survey of the maritime cultural landscape*. Belfast: Environment and Heritage Service.

Muckelroy, Keith. 1975. A systematic approach to the interpretation of scattered wreck sites. *International Journal of Nautical Archaeology* 4 (2): 173–190.

———. 1978. *Maritime archaeology*. Cambridge: Cambridge University Press.

Olsen, O., and O. Crumlin-Pedersen. 1968. The Skuldelev Ships II: A report on the final underwater excavation in 1959 and the salvaging operation in 1962. *Acta Archaeologica* 38: 95–170.

O'Sullivan, Aidan. 2001. *Foragers, farmers and fishers in a coastal landscape: An intertidal archaeological survey of the Shannon estuary.* Discovery Programme Monograph 5. Dublin: Royal Irish Academy.

Paddenberg, Dietlind, and Brian Hession. 2008. Underwater archaeology on foot: A systematic rapid foreshore survey on the North Kent Coast, England. *International Journal of Nautical Archaeology* 37 (1): 142–152.

Petrie, W. M. Flinders. 1904. *Methods and aims in archaeology.* London: Macmillan.

Plets, R., J. Dix, J. Adams, J. Bull, T. Henstock, M. Gutowski, and A. Best. 2009. The use of a high-resolution 3D Chirp sub-bottom profiler for the reconstruction of the shallow water archaeological site of the Grace Dieu (1439), River Hamble, UK. *Journal of Archaeological Science* 36 (2): 408–418.

Polzer, M. 2008. Toggles and sails in the ancient world: Rigging elements recovered from the Tantura B shipwreck, Israel. *International Journal of Nautical Archaeology* 37 (2): 225–252.

Pulak, C. 1998. The Uluburun shipwreck: An overview. *International Journal of Nautical Archaeology* 27 (3): 188–224.

———. 2008. The Uluburun shipwreck and Late Bronze Age trade. In *Beyond Babylon: Art, trade, and diplomacy in the second millennium BCE*, ed. J. Aruz, K. Bezel, and J. Evans, 288–385. New Haven, CT: Yale University Press and Metropolitan Museum of Art.

Sakellariou, D., P. Georgiou, A. Mallios, V. Kapsimalis, D. Kourkoumelis, P. Micha, T. Theo-doulou, and K. Dellaporta. 2007. Searching for ancient shipwrecks in the Aegean Sea: The discovery of Chios and Kythnos Hellenistic wrecks with the use of marine geological-geophysical methods. *International Journal of Nautical Archaeology* 36 (2): 365–381.

Sanders, D. 2010. Knowing the ropes: The need to record ropes and rigging on wreck-sites and some techniques for doing so. *International Journal of Nautical Archaeology* 39 (1): 2–26.

Spirek, James, and Della Scott-Ireton. 2003. *Submerged cultural resource management: Preserving and interpreting our sunken maritime heritage.* New York: Kluwer/Plenum.

Troalen, L., D. Cox, T. Skinner, A. Ramsey, and D. Bate. 2010. Three-dimensional computed tomography X-radiographic investigation of a 17th-century watch from the wreck of the *Swan*, off Duart Point, Mull, Scotland. *International Journal of Nautical Archaeology* 39 (1): 165–171.

PART VII

GLOSSARY AND
APPENDIX

ILLUSTRATED GLOSSARY OF SHIP AND BOAT TERMS

J. RICHARD STEFFY

[THE following illustrated glossary first appeared in its entirety in *Wooden Ship Building and the Interpretation of Shipwrecks*, by J. Richard Steffy (1994). It is reprinted here by permission of Texas A&M University Press, with minor edits to remove references pertaining to figures and chapters that were incorporated in the original work but do not form part of this volume. The glossary is primarily relevant to the first two sections of this handbook and is not meant to be representative of the entire field of maritime archaeology. As an independent contribution, it is an exquisite source of information on ship construction terminology, but also a testament to the work of the late Mr. Steffy, whose influence has been instrumental to the understanding of wooden ship building and the interpretation of shipwrecks and archival material. —*Eds.*]

Words set in **bold type** are defined elsewhere in the glossary. Entries have been illustrated wherever possible, either within the glossary or in the text. Alternate terms or spellings are listed in brackets after the entry. Alternate definitions for a single entry are commonplace; this is the result of diffusion, varying localities, and technological progress. However, the reader is cautioned that many of the timbers and devices listed here might have had additional identifications, often the invention of the writer or in local slang; some difficulty may be experienced in identifying such entries in various documents. The confusion extends to modern publications. One marine dictionary shows the knee of the head as being located behind the gripe, while most of the others call this timber an apron and properly place the knee of the head just below the bowsprit. I have tried to sort out this confusion where possible.

Ancient ships contained structural arrangements that had disappeared by the medieval period, and therefore they remain unlisted in publications. A few of them have been assigned terms in archaeological publications; the rest I hope I have anticipated and defined accurately.

One more word of caution. Many of the illustrations in the glossary are composite drawings, in some cases including features of several vessels or vessel types in the same drawing. Unless otherwise stated, these illustrations are not intended to represent construction details of specific watercraft.

Adze [Adz] (Fig. G-8). An axe-like tool with its blade at right angles to the handle, used for shaping and dressing wood.

Amidships. The middle of a vessel, either longitudinally or transversely.

Anchor (Figs. G-1 and G-2). A wooden, stone, or metal device that, when connected to a vessel with a cable or chain, was used to secure the vessel to the bed of a waterway to prevent it from drifting.

Anchor bed. A reinforcement or platform, fitted on the side or deck of a vessel, on which an anchor or stack of anchors was stowed.

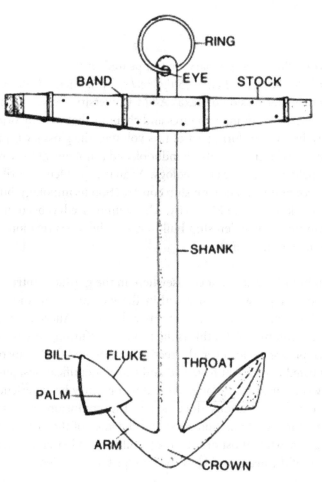

Figure G-1. The parts of an Admiralty anchor.

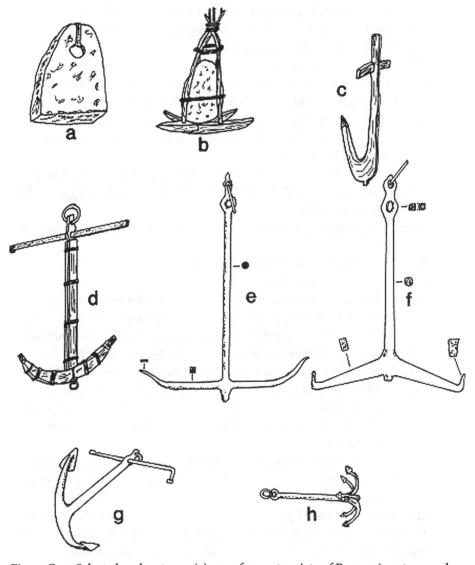

Figure G-2. Selected anchor types: (a) one of a great variety of Bronze Age stone anchor shapes; (b) a primitive stone and wood grapnel; (c) a large, one-armed wooden anchor with a lead-filled stock and copper fluke tip from the Ma'agan Michael wreck, ca. 400 BCE in Israel [after Rosloff, *IJNA* 20.3: 224]; (d) a Roman iron anchor cased in wood, with removable iron stock, from the first-century Nemi excavations [after Ucelli, fig. 270]; (e) a seventh-century Byzantine anchor from Yassi Ada, Turkey [after van Doorninck]; (f) an eleventh-century iron anchor from the wreck at Serçe Limani, Turkey [sketched from a replica by F. H. van Doorninck Jr.]; (g) a nineteenth-century iron anchor most commonly known as a fisherman's anchor; the iron stock could be partially withdrawn and stored adjacent to the shank to save deck space; and (h) an eighteenth-century grapnel with five flukes.

Best bower. One of the principal anchors of a ship, normally the one used first; in the last several centuries, it was usually the second largest anchor and was carried on the starboard bow.

Bill. The tip of the anchor's palm; also called a pea, **peak**, or pick.

Bower. One of the principal anchors of a vessel, permanently attached to a cable or chain and stowed ready for immediate use.

Crown. That portion of an anchor where its arms joined the shank.

Fluke. The pointed or chisel-shaped end of an anchor arm, which was designed to dig into the bottom.

Grapnel (Fig. G-2h). A relatively small anchor, usually fitted with four or five arms, used variously for making fast to other vessels, snagging cables, or anchoring small boats.

Kedge. A light anchor used for moving a vessel or temporarily holding it in a waterway.

Palm. The triangular flat face of an anchor's fluke.

Shank. The shaft of an anchor.

Sheet anchor. The heaviest anchor of a large vessel, shipped in a ready position to be used for any emergency. In the later years of large sailing ships, this was the third bower and was usually carried in the starboard bow next to the best bower. It was also called the sacred anchor.

Shoe. A convex block of wood into which an anchor bill could be fitted to prevent damage to the ship's side when the anchor was hoisted.

Stock. A wooden, stone, or metal crosspiece near the top of and perpendicular to the shank; it was designed to cant one of the arms so that its fluke dug into the bottom.

Stream anchor. A smaller anchor, often about one-third the weight of the best bower, which was carried in the stern and used to prevent a vessel from swinging in narrow waterways.

Anchor stock planking (Fig. G-11a). A form of planking in which the longitudinal shapes of the planks resembled anchor stocks. It was similar to the top and butt method of planking and was intended to prevent shifting and increase the longitudinal strength of wales and other stress-bearing planks.

Apron (Fig. G-3). A curved piece of timber fixed to the after surface of the stem or to the top of the forward end of the keel and the after surface of the stem; an inner stempost.

Athwartships. Across the ship from side to side; perpendicular to the keel.

Auger (Fig. G-8). A tool used for boring holes.

Average frame spacing. *See* **Room and space**.

Back piece (Fig. G-18b). The aftermost piece of a rudder.

Back rabbet (Fig. G-4c). The upper surface of a keel rabbet or the nesting surface of a post rabbet.

Back rabbet line (Fig. G-4d). The line formed by the junction of the inner plank surface and the upper, or inner, rabbet surface.

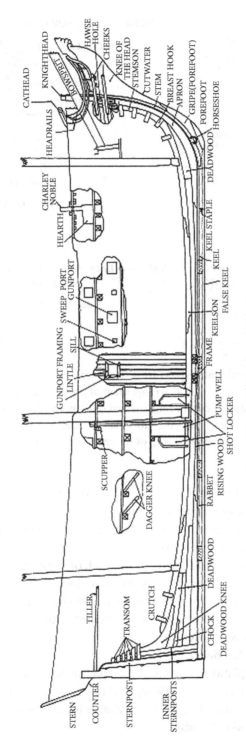

Figure G-3. Hull timbers; side views.

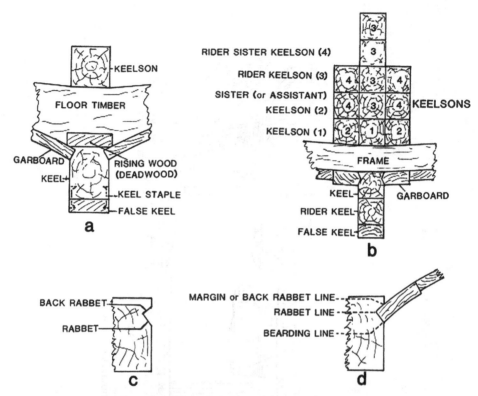

Figure G-4. Principal timbers; sectional views: (a) a popular arrangement for small and medium-sized craft; (b) a typical arrangement of principal timbers for large vessels, this for an early-twentieth-century four-masted schooner with a 200-ft-long double keel; (c) the designations of keel and post rabbet surfaces; and (d) the designations of the lines formed by the junction of the rabbet and garboard surfaces.

Balanced rudder (Fig. G-18a). A rudder whose stock is placed aft of its leading edge so that the water pressure is approximately equal on its forward and after surfaces; balanced rudders require less turning power than conventional rudders.

Ballast. Heavy material, such as iron, lead, or stone, placed low in the hold to lower the center of gravity and improve stability.

Batten. A thin plank or strip of wood used to determine hull curvatures or to temporarily connect timbers during construction.

Batten clamp. *See* **Sintel**.

Baulk [Balk]. *See* **Beam**.

Beakhead. A platform or projecting structure forward of the forecastle.

Beam (Figs. G-5 and G-7a–G-7e). A timber mounted athwartships to support decks and provide lateral strength; large beams were sometimes called baulks. *See also* **Breadth**.

Beam arm [Curved half-beam] (Fig. G-7a). A curved partial beam whose inboard end was scarfed or tenoned into the side of a deck beam and outboard end terminated at the shelf clamp. Beam arms were used to reinforce potentially weak areas adjacent to hatches, bitts, masts, etc. They were essentially long knees laid as half beams.

Bearding line (Fig. G-4d). The line formed by the junction of the outer garboard surface with the keel, or the outer surfaces of planking ends with the posts.

Beetle (Fig. G-8). A heavy wooden mallet used to drive treenails, wedges, etc. *See also* **Mallet**.

Belfry. The structure in which the ship's bell was hung. Belfries were usually mounted in the forecastle, although they sometimes appeared near the helm or mainmast; in some instances they were elaborate and ornate.

Berth deck [Birth deck] (Fig. G-5). The deck immediately below the **gundeck**.

Bevel (Fig. G-12f). The fore-and-aft angle or curvature of an inner or outer frame surface.

Beveled edge. *See* **Chamfer**.

Bevel gauge (Fig. G-8). A tool used to determine frame face bevels.

Beveling. The technique of shaping a frame timber to its correct fore-and-aft curvature.

Bilge. The area of the hull's bottom on which it would rest if grounded; generally, the outer end of the floor. When used in the plural, especially in contemporary documents, **bilges** refers to the various cavities between the frames in the floor of the hold where bilge water tends to collect.

Bilge boards. Loose boards placed over the bilges to protect cargo from bilgewater damage.

Bilge clamp. On ancient ships, a thick strake of ceiling fastened to the inner frame faces at or just above the turn of the bilge; thick ceiling opposite a bilge wale. *See also* **Ceiling**.

Bilge keel. A secondary keel placed beneath the bilge or at the outer end of the floor. Sometimes called a **sister keel**.

Bilge ledge. A rabbeted longitudinal timber fastened over the frames above the bilge to support transverse ceiling planking.

Bilge strake [Bilge plank] (Fig. G-5). A thick strake of planking placed at or below the turn of the bilge; its purpose was to reinforce the area of the bilge or floor heads. Infrequently it is called a bilge wale.

Binding strakes (Fig. G-5). The closest full-length strakes, or belts of strakes, to the middle of the deck. They reinforced the many openings (hatches, mast steps, pumps, etc.) between them. Binding strakes were so named only when they were thicker than the rest of the deck planks, being fitted into notches in the tops of deck beams.

Bite [Bitar (pl.)]. An athwartship beam in a Viking vessel.

Bitt [Bit] (Fig. G-10). A strong upright post used for securing lines and cables. Figure G-10 shows several bitt arrangements.

Boat. An open vessel, usually small and without decks, intended for use in sheltered water. This term is discussed in the introduction.

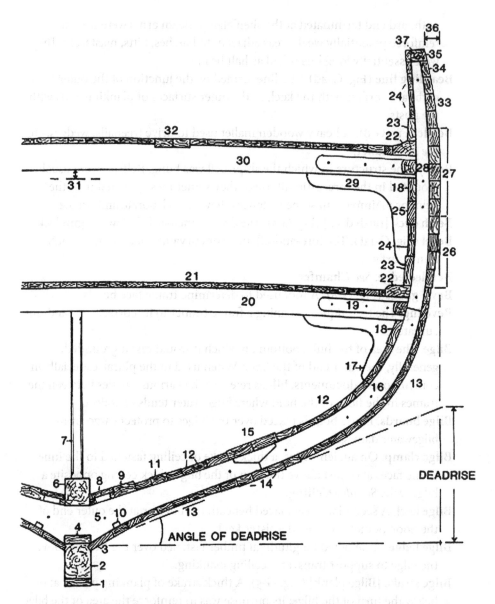

Figure G-5. Hull timbers; a composite sectional view, using the form of the ship-sloop *Peacock*: (1) false keel; (2) keel; (3) garboard; (4) rising wood [deadwood]; (5) floor timber; (6) keelson; (7) stanchion; (8) limber board; (9) limber strake; (10) limber hole; (11) thick stuff [footwaling]; (12) common ceiling; (13) bottom planking; (14) bilge strakes; (15) footwale; (16) second futtock; (17) dagger knee; (18) shelf clamp; (19) lodging knee; (20) lower [or berthing] deck beam; (21) lower deck planking; (22) waterway; (23) spirketting; (24) lining [quickwork]; (25) clamp; (26) diminishing strakes; (27) wale; (28) top timber; (29) hanging knee; (30) upper deck beam; (31) camber; (32) binding strake; (33) bulwark; (34) plansheer; (35) gunwale; (36) tumblehome; and (37) caprail.

Bobstay piece (Fig. G-13d). Part of the knee of the head.

Body lines. *See* **Station lines**.

Bollard timbers. *See* **Knightheads**.

Bolt. A cylindrical metal pin used to fasten ships' timbers together.

Boss. *See* **Wart**.

Bottom. The underwater portion of a fully loaded hull; also used as a general designation for a seagoing vessel.

Bow. The forward part of a hull, specifically, from the point where the sides curve inward to the stem.

Bow drill [Fiddle drill] (Fig. G-8). A device with a hollowed handle in which a spindle rotates; the spindle is connected to a drum, around which a cord is wrapped and run back and forth by means of a bow to rotate the drill bit.

Bowsprit (Figs. G-3, G-15d, G-15e, and G-15f). A spar projecting forward from the bow.

Boxing [Boxing joint] (Fig. G-11b). A type of scarf used primarily to join the keel to the stem or keel timbers to each other.

Brace (Fig. G-18). A metal housing and straps used to secure the stock of a quarter rudder to its blade. Also, the straps of a **pintle** or **gudgeon**.

Bracket. A small brace or knee used to support the gratings in the head of a ship.

Breadth. The width of a hull; sometimes called **beam**, which is technically the length of the main beam.

Breaming. *See* **Graving**.

Breast hook (Figs. G-3 and G-13). A large, horizontal knee fixed to the sides and stem to reinforce and hold them together.

Breastwork. Ballustrades along the upper decks.

Bulkhead. A vertical partition, either fore-and-aft or athwartships.

Bulwark (Fig. G-5). The side of a vessel above its upper deck.

Burden [Burthen]. The cargo capacity of a vessel.

Butt (Fig. G-11b). The lateral end of a hull plank or timber.

Butt joint (Fig. G-11b). The union of two planks or timbers whose ends were cut perpendicularly to their lengths; sometimes called **carvel joint**.

Buttock. The convex part of the hull beneath the stern deck.

Buttock lines. Projections on a lines drawing that reveal vertically oriented longitudinal hull shapes.

Cable locker [Cable tier]. The compartment where the anchor cable was coiled and stored. Large vessels often had elaborate drainage systems for disposing of the seawater that seeped from recently hauled cables, including tier decks with raised beams that allowed the water to pass beneath the coils.

Caboose [Camboose]. A vessel's galley, or kitchen.

Camber [Crown] (Fig. G-5, no. 31). The arch, or convexity, of a timber; decks were usually cambered so that water would run to the sides and out the scuppers.

Cant frame [Cant timber] (Fig. G-13a). A framing member mounted obliquely to the keel centerline in the ends of a vessel; canting provided better frame distribution and permitted more nearly rectangular cross sections of the timbers along the vessel's incurving ends.

Cap [Capping piece]. A block used to cover the exposed ends of timbers and spars.

Caprail [Main rail, Cap] (Fig. G-5). A timber attached to the top of a vessel's frames.

Capstan [Capstern]. A spool-shaped vertical cylinder, mounted on a spindle and bearing, turned by means of levers or bars; used for moving heavy loads, such as hoisting anchors, lifting yards, or careening vessels.

Careen. To deliberately list a vessel so that part of its bottom was exposed for caulking, cleaning, repairing, etc.

Carling [Carline] (Figs. G-7a–G-7d). Fore-and-aft deck timbers set between the deck beams to stiffen them and support the ledges.

Carrick bitt (Fig. G-10). An upright timber supporting the shaft of a windlass; also called a **carrick head** or **windlass bitt**.

Carvel-built (Fig. G-5). Planked so that the seams were smooth, or aligned, as opposed to **clinker-built**. Northern European scholars reserve "carvel-built" for frame-first forms of construction; thus, the flush-laid bottom planks of a cog are not described as "carvel" laid planks.

Carvel joint. *See* **Butt joint**.

Cathead (Fig. G-3). A beam, or crane, projecting from the bow and used for hoisting the anchor clear of the bow after it had surfaced.

Cattail. The inboard end of a cathead.

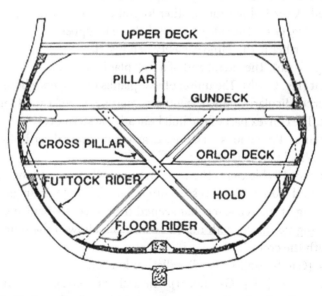

Figure G-6. Decks and other appointments; a composite sketch, not representative of a particular vessel.

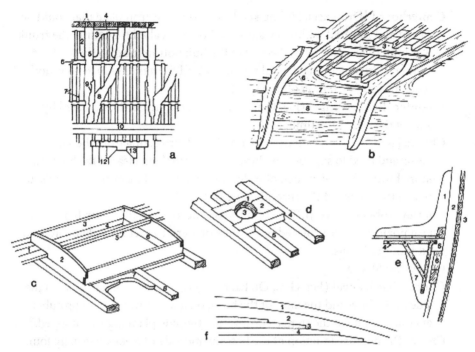

Figure G-7. Deck framing and details. [a] deck framing at the mainmast of a large warship: (1) frames; (2) hanging knee; (3) lodging knee; (4) packing piece; (5) deck beam; (6) carlings; (7) ledges; (8) beam arm; (9) deck beam scarf; (10) binding strake; (11) mast carling; (12) mast partner; and (13) chock; [b] typical deck framing and supporting features (after Stevens 1949: 29): (1) deck beam; (2) ledge; (3) carling; (4) deck planking; (5) hanging knee; (6) lodging knee; (7) shelf clamp; and (8) ceiling [quickwork]; [c] a common form of hatch construction; (1) deck planking; (2) head ledge; (3) hatch coaming; (4) carling; (5) hatch beam; (6) deck beam; (7) lodging knee [only one set shown]; and (8) half beam; [d] a typical mast partner for small merchant ship: the partners are (1) carlings and (2) chocks; (3) mast hole; (4) deck beam; and (5) half beam; [e] standing and plate knees: (1) standing knee; (2) frame; (3) outer planking; (4) plate knee; (5) deck beam; (6) shelf clamp; and (7) chock; [f] a method of terminating deck planks at the incurving sides of ships: (1) waterway; (2) nibbing strake [margin plank]; (3) nibbed end; and (4) deck plank.

Caulk [Calk]. To drive oakum, moss, animal hair, or other fibrous material into the seams of planking and cover it with pitch to make the seams watertight. *See also* **luting**.

Caulking batten [Caulking lath]. A thin wooden strip used to close caulked seams and hold the caulking material in place. *See also* **Ribband carvel**.

Caulking iron (Fig. G-8). A chisel-shaped tool used to drive caulking into seams.

Caulking mallet (Fig. G-8). A short-handled mallet used to strike caulking irons.

Ceiling (Fig. G-5, nos. 9, 11, 12, 15, and 23). The internal planking of a vessel.

Centerboard [Drop keel, Sliding keel]. A wooden or iron plate that could be raised and lowered within a watertight housing called the **trunk**; the trunk was built over a slot in the keel or in the hull bottom next to the keel. Centerboards increased lateral resistance and therefore reduced **leeway** when tacking or sailing off the wind.

Chamfer [Beveled edge] (Fig. G-12f). The flat, sloping surface created by slicing the edge off a timber.

Channel [Chain wale]. A thick, horizontal plank projecting from the side of a vessel and used to support the shrouds and keep them clear of the bulwarks.

Channel wale. A wale, or belt of wales, located at the line of the channels, to which the chains of the shrouds were fastened.

Charley Nobel (Fig. G-3). The chimney, or flue, of the galley hearth or stove.

Chase port. A gunport placed in the bow or stern to accommodate fore-and-aft mounted guns.

Check. *See* **Shake**.

Cheek [Cheek knee] (Fig. G-3). On later vessels, a knee or brace between the side of the bow and the knee of the head; on ancient warships, a protuberance at the side of the stem against which the side planking was stopped.

Chine. The angular junction of the bottom and side of a vessel; usually found on flat-bottomed hulls, or those with little deadrise. Can also refer to a longitudinal timber located just inside the junction, to which athwartships bottom planks are fastened.

Chock (Figs. G-3 and G-13). An angular block or wedge used to fill out areas between timbers or to separate them; chocks were used to fill out deadwoods and head knees, separate frames and futtocks, etc.

Cistern. A term applied variously to pump wells or to collecting basins at the discharge ends of pumps.

Clamp (Fig. G-5, nos. 18 and 25). A thick ceiling strake used to provide longitudinal strength or support deck beams; clamps were often located directly opposite the wales and acted as internal wales; a clamp that supported a deck beam was called a *shelf clamp*.

Clench [Clinch] (Fig. G-9g). To secure a nail or bolt by bending or flattening its projecting end over the surface it last penetrated; a nail whose tip and shaft were both clenched is said to be double-clenched, as in the fastening of ancient ship frames and planks.

Clenched lap [Lapstrake]. *See* **Clinker-built**.

Clinker-built [Clincher-built, Clencher-built]. A vessel constructed so that its outer planking overlaps, and is fastened to, the plank immediately below it. Where planks overlap the ones above them (there have been no European vessel finds to support this alleged method), the procedure is known as *reverse clinker*. The surface of a plank overlapped by a neighbor is called a **land**, and this double thickness is normally held together with closely spaced rivets or nails clenched over metal washers called **roves**. Northern European specialists limit the term "clinker-built" to vessels whose planks are rivetted together; hulls whose overlapping planks are fastened with clenched nails, as in most cog construction, are called *clenched lap* or *lapstrake hulls.*

Coak (Figs. G-9m and G-9n). A rectangular or cylindrical pin let into the ends or seams of timbers about to be joined in order to align or strengthen the union.

Coaming [Combing] (Fig. G-7c). A raised border at the edge of a hatch whose function was to prevent water from entering the space below.

Cockpit. The surgeon's compartment; the sick bay. On yachts, the well from which the vessel is directed.

Common ceiling (Fig. G-5, no. 12). The ordinary ceiling used to prevent cargo and ballast from falling between the frames; common ceiling was usually made from relatively thin planking and seldom contributed longitudinal strength to the hull structure.

Companion. A covering over a cabin hatchway.

Companion way. A stairway or ladder leading from one deck to another.

Compass timber [Compassing]. Naturally curved timbers used for frames and construction in the ends of a hull.

Copper-bottomed [Coppered]. A vessel whose bottom was sheathed in copper to prevent fouling and worm infestation.

Copper fastened. A vessel whose fastenings were made of copper.

Cordage. A general term for ropes and cables.

Counter (Fig. G-14). Technically, the transverse section between the bottom of the stern and the wing transom. However, many documents and drawings refer to the counter as the entire transverse area between the top of the sternpost and the rail or taffrail.

Counter timbers (Figs. G-14a–G-14c). Vertical timbers framing the counter.

Crab. A small capstan, usually portable and lacking a drumhead at the top of its barrel.

Cradle. A structure for supporting a vessel out of water.

Crone. An English translation of an old Norse term denoting the elongated mast steps on Viking vessels.

Crossbeam (Fig. G-10). A substantial timber placed across a pair of bitts.

Cross pillar. *See* **Pillar**.

Crotch [Crotch timber]. A V-shaped or Y-shaped frame or floor timber made from the crotch of a tree; usually mounted on the keel or deadwood in the ends of a vessel.

Crow [Crow bar] (Fig. G-8). A strong iron bar, pointed or chisel-shaped at one end, used for prying or moving heavy timbers.

Crown. *See* **Camber**.

Crutch (Figs. G-3 and G-15a). A bracing timber used to prevent a mast step from shifting laterally; also, a curved or angular timber, similar to a breast hook and used for a similar purpose in the lower part of the stern. On modern vessels, a support for booms at rest.

Cuddy. A cabin or shelter in the forward part of a small vessel.

Curved scarf [Curved butt, S-scarf] (Fig. G-11). The union of two planks or timbers whose ends were canted in the shapes of reverse curves.

Cutting-down line. The elevations of the tops of the floor timbers and deadwoods; in most cases, the curved line formed by the bottom of the keelson, stemson, and sternson.

Cutwater (Fig. G-3). The forwardmost part of the stem; the stem piece or nosing that parts the water.

Dagger knee (Figs. G-3 and G-5). A knee set angularly on the inside of the hull; a knee that is neither vertical or horizontal.

Dagger piece. Any piece of timber, but usually a frame timber, mounted at an angle to the vertical or horizontal planes.

Dead flat. The flat part of the hull in the area of the midship frame; generally, the widest part of the hull, which separated the forward part from the after part.

Deadrise (Fig. G-5). The amount of elevation, or rising, of the floor above the horizontal plane; the difference between the height of the bilge and the height of the keel rabbet.

Deadwood (Fig. G-3). Blocks of timber assembled on top of the keel, usually in the ends of the hull, to fill out the narrow parts of a vessel's body. *See also* **Rising wood**.

Deadwood knee (Fig. G-3). A knee placed within the deadwood to support the sternpost.

Deadwork. The part of the hull above the full-load waterline.

Deal. A thin plank of fir or pine, most commonly used to sheath hulls.

Deck beam. *See* **Beam**.

Deck hook. (Fig. G-13b). A breast hook placed beneath a deck to support it at or near the stem.

Deck transom (Fig. G-14d). A transom that supported the after ends of deck planks.

Depth of hold. The distance between either the bottom of the main deck or the bottom of its beams and the limber boards, measured at the midship frame.

Diagonal braces. Pillars or posts set angularly in the hull to stiffen it; although used in pairs, they differed from cross pillars in that each brace occupied only one side of the hull.

Diagonal framing. Frames or riders placed diagonally over the regular frames or ceiling to provide additional stiffening to a hull.

Diagonals. Lines on a hull drawing representing specific oblique sections of the hull.

Diagonal scarf [Diagonal butt] (Fig. G-11b). An angular junction of two planks or timbers.

Diminishing strakes (Fig. G-5). Belts of outer planking above and below the wales that were successively reduced in thickness, providing a more gradual transition from the protrusion of the wales to the thickness of the side planking.

Double-ender. A vessel whose bow and stern have approximately the same horizontal shape, such as rounded, pointed, or square ends.

Double framing (Fig. G-12). A general term signifying frames composed of two rows of overlapping futtocks.

Dowel [Dowel pin] (Fig. G-9n). A cylindrical piece of wood (of constant diameter) used to align two members by being sunk into each. A cylindrical coak. Unlike treenails and pegs, dowels served an alignment function only, additional fastenings being necessary to prevent separation of the joint.

Draft [Draught]. The depth to which a hull is immersed; also, a drawing or plan.

Draft marks [Draught marks, Load lines]. Figures or lines cut into, or attached to, the stem and sternpost to indicate the depth at which each end of the hull is immersed.

Drag. The difference between the draft of a vessel's stern and its bow.

Drawknife (Fig. G-8). A knife with two handles mounted at right angles to the blade; drawknives are used for shaping and beveling.

Drift. The difference between the diameters of a bored hole and the bolt that is driven into it.

Drift bolt. A cylindrical bolt, headed on one end, that is slightly larger in diameter than the hole into which it is driven.

Drop keel [Sliding keel]. *See* **Centerboard**.

Drop strake (Fig. G-11). A strake of planking that is discontinued near the bow or stern because of decreasing hull surface area. A central stealer.

Dunnage. Brushwood, scrapwood, or other loose material laid in the hold to protect the cargo from water damage or prevent it from shifting, or to protect the ceiling from abrasion.

Ekeing [Lengthening piece] (Fig. G-13b). A timber used to lengthen another timber, such as the extension of a deck hook or knee.

Entrance [Entry]. The foremost underwater part of a vessel.

Eye bolt (Fig. G-9i). A bolt with a circular opening at one end.

Eyes. A name sometimes given to the hawse holes or the areas around them; on ancient ships, ocular decorations at the same locations.

Fair. To shape or adjust a timber or timbers to the correct curvature or location; also, to correct discrepancies in a ship's drawings.

Fair curve [Fair line]. A shape or line whose curvature agrees with the mold loft or that is mechanically acceptable and seaworthy.

Fall home. *See* **Tumblehome**.

False keel [Shoe] (Figs. G-3, G-4a, G-4b, and G-5). A plank, timber, or timbers attached to the bottom of the keel to protect it in the event of grounding or hauling; on large ships, false keels were sometimes made quite thick in order to increase the size and strength of the keel. In North America from the eighteenth century onward, and perhaps in other areas, false keels were called shoes.

False keelson. *See* **Rider keelson**.

False stem. An outer timber fixed to the forward surface of the stem to strengthen or protect it, or to provide better symmetry to the cutwater. Also, a name sometimes given to the apron in English documents.

False sternpost. A member attached to the after surface of the sternpost to reinforce or protect it.

Fashion piece [Fashion timber] (Fig. G-14a). A timber that framed the shape of the stern.

Fay. To fit or join timbers closely together.

Figure piece (G-13d). A name sometimes given to the upper piece of the knee of the head, upon which the figurehead rested.

Filling frame (Fig. G-12e). A frame composed of a single row of timbers, usually scarfed together, that filled the space between the main, or double-rowed, frames of a large ship.

Filling piece [Filler] (Fig. G-12e). A single timber or block used to fill out an area, such as the side of a gunport where it did not coincide with a frame, or in the spaces between frames to maintain rigidity.

Fine lines. A descriptive term applied to a vessel with a sharp entrance and a narrow hull.

Fish. An English term for the modern Norwegian word describing the fishtail-shaped mast partners on Viking vessels.

Fish plate (Fig. G-9). A metal plate used to join two timbers externally.

Flare. The upward and outward curvature of a vessel's bows; a curved outfall.

Flat scarf (Fig. G-11b). The union of two planks or timbers whose diagonal ends were nibbed (cut off) perpendicular to their lengths. When planking is scarfed vertically, the ends are not nibbed.

Floor. The bottom of a vessel between the upward turns of its bilges.

Floor head. The outer extremity of a floor timber.

Floor head line. *See* **Rising line**.

Floor ribband [Floor ribbon]. The floor rising line; specifically, a ribband or batten fastened to the outside of the frames at the heads of the floor timbers; used for fairing and to determine the shapes and lengths of intermediate frames.

Floor timber (Fig. G-12). A frame timber that crossed the keel and spanned the bottom; the central piece of a compound frame.

Flush deck. A deck running continuously from bow to stern, without breaks or raised elements.

Foot wale [Footwaleing] (Fig. G-5, no. 15). Thick longitudinal strakes of ceiling located at or near the floor head line or turn of the bilge. Some eighteenth-century English documents called the thick strakes next to the limber strake, or sometimes all of the ceiling, **footwaleing**, in which case the heavy strakes near the turn of the bilge were known as **thick stuff**.

Forecastle. Variously, a short, raised foredeck, the forward part of the upper deck between the foremast and the stem, or the quarters below the foredeck.

Forefoot (Fig. G-3). A curved piece between the forward end of the keel and the knee of the head; the **gripe**. In some documents describing large ships, it is the name given to the rounded forward portion of the gripe, inserted as a separate piece.

Fore hood. The end of a plank at the stem rabbet.

Forelock bolt (Fig. G-9h). An iron bolt with a head on one end and a narrow slot at the other; secured by placing a washer over its protruding end and driving a flat wedge, called a **forelock**, into the slot. Forelock bolts were one of the most popular of shipbuilding fastenings, being commonly used to secure major timbers from Roman times until the nineteenth century.

Forepeak. The forward extremity of the hold.

Frame (Fig. G-12). A transverse timber, or line or assembly of timbers, that described the body shape of a vessel and to which the planking and ceiling were fastened. Frames were sometimes called **timbers** or, erroneously, ribs (*see* **Rib**). Ancient ships often had frames composed of lines of unconnected timbers; later ships usually had compound frames composed of **floor timbers, futtocks,** and **top timbers. Square frames** were those set perpendicular to the keel; in the bow and stern there were **cant frames,** running obliquely to the keel. Forward of the cant frames and fayed to them, in large round-bowed vessels, were the frames running parallel to the keel and stem, sometimes called **knuckle timbers**; more accurately, these were the **hawse pieces** and **knight heads**, the latter being the frames adjacent to the apron or stem-son that extended above the deck to form bitts and support the bowsprit. The aftermost frames were the **fashion pieces**, which shaped the stern. Frame details are illustrated in Figs. G-3, G-5, G-12, G-13, and G-14.

Frame head. *See* **Timber head**.

Frame heel. *See* **Timber heel**.

Freeboard. The distance between the waterline and upper deck.

Furring. *See* **Sheathing**.

Futtock (Fig. G-12). A frame timber other than a floor timber, half-frame, or top timber; one of the middle pieces of a frame.

Futtock plank. In English shipbuilding, the first ceiling plank next to the limber strake.

Gallery. A balcony projecting from the stern or quarter of a large ship.

Galley. A seagoing vessel propelled primarily by oars, but usually one that also could be sailed when necessary. Also, a name given to a vessel's kitchen.

Gammoning hole [Gammoning slot] (Fig. G-13d). An opening in the knee of the head through which the bowsprit gammoning (lashing) passed.

Gammoning knee. A curved timber attached to the top of a vessel's stem, to which the bowsprit was lashed; sometimes used in lieu of a more elaborate knee of the head.

Gammon piece (Fig. G-13d). The part of the knee of the head containing the gammoning hole.

Garboard strake [Garboard] (Figs. G-4 and G-5). The strake of planking next to the keel; the lowest plank. Also, the lowest side strake of a flat-bottomed hull.

Girdling [Girding]. The practice of adding timber to the sides of ships to increase their breadth and thereby improve stability. The practice was most common on sixteenth- and seventeenth-century British vessels and was employed to overcome design flaws due to inability to calculate metacentric height.

Grating. A latticework hatch cover used for light and ventilation. Also, a term applied to the latticework deck in the heads of large ships.

Graving [Breaming]. The practice of cleaning a hull's bottom by burning barnacles, grass, and other foul material preparatory to recoating it with tar, sulphur, etc. The vessel was careened or drydocked to perform this task.

Graving iron (Fig. G-8). A hook-like tool used for removing old caulking.

Graving piece (Fig. G-11a). A wooden patch, or insert, let into a damaged or rotted plank.

Gripe (Fig. G-3). A curved piece joining the forward end of the keel to the lower end of the knee of the head. Generally, the same as **forefoot**.

Gudgeon (Fig. G-18b). A metal bracket attached to the sternpost into which a rudder **pintle** was hung; the female part of a rudder hinge.

Gundeck (Fig. G-6). The deck where the guns were located; large ships had as many as three gundecks (a three-decker), called the lower, middle, and upper gundecks.

Gunport framing. (Fig. G-3). The **sills, lintles,** and **filling pieces** that shape and reinforce the gunports.

Gunwale [Gunnel] (Fig. G-5, no. 35). The upper edge of a vessel's side. In sixteenth-century vessels, the wale against which the guns rest.

Half beam (Figs. G-7c and G-7d). A beam extending from the side to a hatch or other obstruction. *See also* **Beam arm**.

Half-frame. A frame whose heel began at or near one side of the keel or deadwood and spanned part or all of that side of the hull; half-frames normally were used in pairs.

Hanging knee (Fig. G-5, no. 29). A vertical angular timber used to reinforce the junction of a beam and the side.

Harpins [Harpings]. The forward planks of wales that were strengthened by increased thickness near the stem; usually found on large, round-bowed vessels. Also, a term applied to specially shaped battens fitted to the cant frames or other areas of extreme curvature during construction; used to check and adjust frame bevels.

Hatch [Hatchway] (Fig. G-7c). A rectangular opening in a vessel's deck.

Hatch beam (Fig. G-7c). A removable beam that supported the hatch cover and provided lateral strength when the hatch was not in use.

Hatch coaming. *See* **Coaming**.

Hawse block. A wooden plug used to close a hawse hole in heavy weather.

Hawse bolster. One of the heavy planks fixed around or below the hawse holes to protect the hull planking.

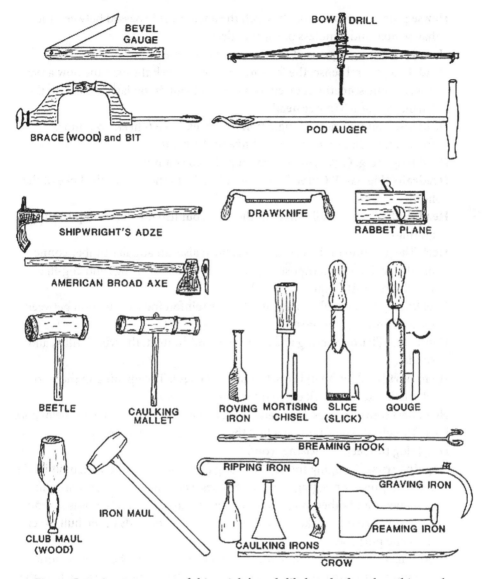

Figure G-8. An assortment of shipwright's tools likely to be found on shipwrecks.

Hawse hole (Fig. G-3). A cylindrical hole in the bow through which the anchor cable passed.

Hawse hook. A breast hook above the upper foredeck; usually, the highest breast hook.

Hawse piece [Hawse timber] (Figs. G-3 and G-13a). A fore-and-aft framing timber whose heel was fayed to the forwardmost cant frame and which reinforced the bow of a large, round-bowed vessel; hawse pieces were so named because the hawse holes were partially cut through them.

Hawse pipe. The tube through which the anchor cable passed between the hawse hole and windlass or capstan deck.

Hawser. A strong rope used to tow or tie up a vessel.

Head. In a general sense, the forward part of a vessel; the extreme bow area; also, a name sometimes given to the **figurehead** or, on later vessels, to the latrine. *See also* **Timber head**.

Head knee. Sometimes a designation for **cheek knee** (cheek), but more frequently an alternate term for **knee of the head**.

Head ledge (Fig. G-7c). An athwartships hatch coaming.

Headrails (Fig. G-3). Curved rails extending from the bow to the knee of the head.

Head timber. Any small timber in the head, but usually those supporting the gratings.

Heel. The junction of the keel and sternpost; also, an angular timber connecting the keel to the sternpost. Separate heel timbers on cogs and cog-like vessels are most frequently called hooks.

Heel knee [Stern knee]. An angular timber reinforcing the junction between the keel and the sternpost.

Helm. The tiller or steering wheel; in a general context, the wheel, tiller, and rudder.

Helm port [Rudder hole] (Figs. G-14a and G-14c). The opening in the stern where the rudder stock entered the hull.

Helm port transom (Figs. G-14a and G-14c). The timber reinforcing the helm port.

Hog [Hogging]. The strain on a hull that causes its ends to droop.

Hog [Hog timber]. *See* **Rising wood**.

Hogging truss [Hogging frame]. A strong fore-and-aft framework built into a vessel to prevent hogging; hogging trusses were most commonly seen in canal boats and other long inland vessels. In ancient vessels, it was a strong cable supported by forked posts and attached to the ends of the hull to serve the same purpose.

Hold (Fig. G-6). In a general sense, the interior of a hull. The term is more commonly used to describe the part of a merchant ship's interior where the cargo and ballast were stowed or, on a warship, the room below the deck where stores and ballast were kept.

Hooding ends [Hoods, Hood ends]. The ends of planks that fit into the stem and sternpost rabbets; hooding ends were sometimes reduced in thickness to permit a better join with the posts.

Hook. A knee-like timber that connected the keel or central plank to the stem or sternpost. A northern European designation, it is used almost exclusively in reference to cogs and cog-like vessels. In later English documents, bow hooks were called **gripes**; stern hooks were called **heels**.

Hook and butt (Fig. G-11a). A method of planking whereby one edge of the plank was straight while its opposite side had sloping edges locked by a hook. Infrequently, the term was also used to denote a hook scarf.

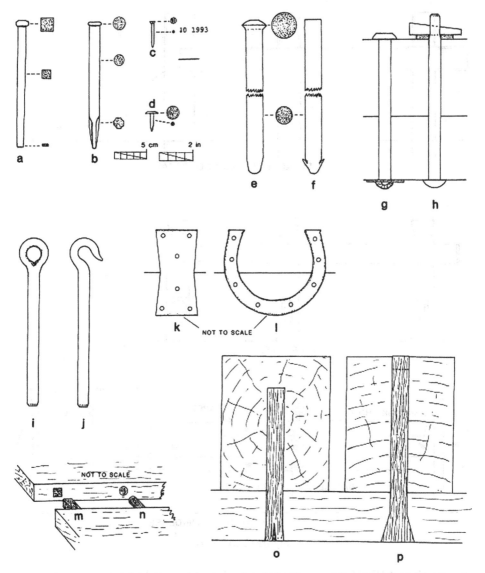

Figure G-9. Typical fastenings: (a) square-headed spike used for planking and general fastening; (b) round-headed dump used for similar fastening; (c) nineteenth-century copper nail used to attach copper sheathing to hull bottoms; (d) fourth-century [BCE] copper nail used to fasten lead sheathing to hull bottoms; (e) a short drift bolt; (f) unheaded rag bolt, barbed with a chisel to deter withdrawal; bolts were sometimes made without heads, the head being formed by pounding; they could be used with or without roves washers); (g) clench bolt, often designated as "bolt" in contemporary documents; (h) forelock bolt; (i) eye bolt; (j) hook bolt; (k) fishplate; (l) horseshoe plate; (m) planks being aligned with a rectangular, or block, coak and (n) with a cylindrical coak dowel; (o) a wedged treenail in a blind hole; and (p) a headed treenail in a through hole; it is wedged at its inner end.

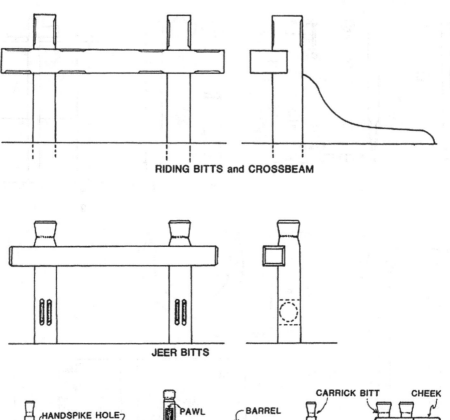

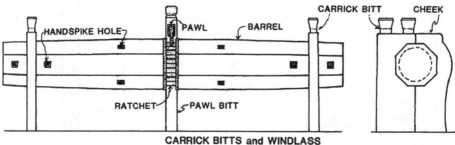

Figure G-10. Bitts.

Hook bolt (Fig. G-9). A bolt with a hook-shaped head used for securing
detachable lines, tackle, and other gear.

Hook scarf (Fig. G-11b). The union of two planks or timbers whose angular
ends are offset to lock the joint. Hook scarfs are sometimes locked with
wedges, or keys.

Horning [To horn]. A process by which frames were aligned to assure that
they were level and exactly perpendicular to the keel. *See* **Horning pole** for
a description of the process.

Horning pole [Horning board, Horning line]. A batten, pole, or line used to
align frames; one end was mounted over the keel centerline, or atop the
stem or sternpost, while the other end was marked and swung across each
frame head to ensure that each side of the frame was equidistant from, and
perpendicular to, the keel centerline.

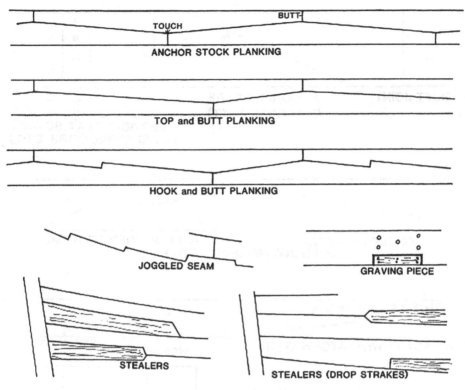

Figure G-11a. Scarfs and seams.

Horseshoe [Horseshoe clamp, Plate] (Figs. G-3 and G-9l). A U-shaped iron plate fastened across the seam of the stem and forefoot to strengthen it.

Horsing. A term used to describe the process of driving caulking into planking seams.

Hypozomata. A cable or assembly of cables installed in ancient galleys to overcome hogging.

Inner stempost. The inner timber or timbers of a double-layered stem; unlike an apron, an inner stempost ends at the keel-stem scarf.

Inner sternpost (Fig. G-14). A vertical timber attached to the forward surface of the sternpost to increase its strength, and in some cases, to support the transoms.

Intermediate timbers. Those individual timbers installed between the sequential frames for additional localized strength. They could span part of the bottom, turn of the bilge, or side. The term applies primarily to ancient ships and inshore craft, where they reinforced the areas around beams, mast steps, bilge sumps, etc., or extended upward as frames for bulkheads and weather screens.

Inverted knee. *See* **Standing knee**.

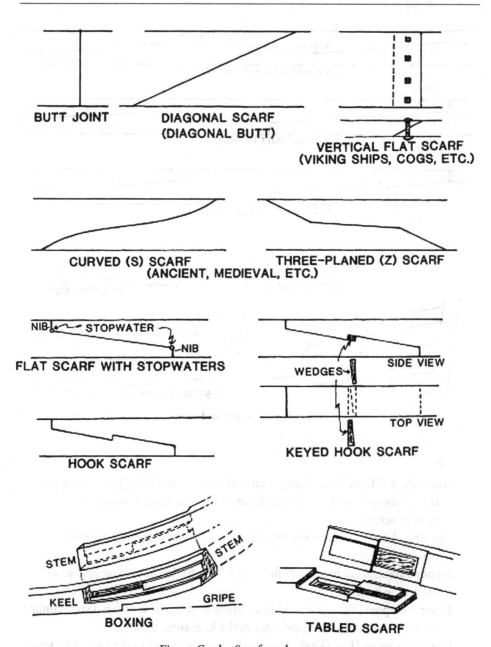

Figure G-11b. Scarfs and seams.

Iron knee. *See* **Plate knee.**

Jeer bitts (Fig. G-10). Upright posts used for staying the various courses or halyards.

Jib-boom. A spar extending the length of the bowsprit.

Joggles. Notches cut into the surface or edge of a timber, as in the exterior frame surfaces of clinker-built hulls or in the edges of some ancient Egyptian hull planks.

Keel (Figs. G-3 and G-4). The main longitudinal timber of most hulls, upon which the frames, deadwoods, and ends of the hull were mounted; the backbone of the hull.

Keel plank [Central plank, Kingplank]. A central hull plank that was substantially thicker than the rest of the bottom planking and whose breadth was at least twice as great as its thickness; a thick bottom plank used in lieu of a **keel**.

Keelson [Kelson] (Figs. G-3, G-4a, and G-4b). An internal longitudinal timber or line of timbers, mounted atop the frames along the centerline of the keel, that provided additional longitudinal strength to the bottom of the hull; an internal keel.Most commonly, a single keelson was installed that was no larger than the keel. On very large vessels, however, various combinations of as many as a dozen keelsons were assembled. Where extra molding was required, one or more additional keelsons, called **rider keelsons** or **false keelsons**, were bolted to the top of the main keelson. They could be of identical size to, or smaller than, the main keelson. Auxiliary keelsons bolted alongside the main keelson were known as *sister* (U.S.), *side, auxiliary,* or *assistant keelsons*. However, care should be exercised in interpreting the various keelsons from contracts. For instance, some nineteenth-century American contracts for large schooners refer to the keelson above the main keelson as the sister, and the one above that as the assistant sister keelson. On occasion, large square timbers were placed at the floor head line or near the bilge, usually above the bilge keels. These were called **bilge keelsons** or, in some British document, **sister keelsons**. Secondary keelsons did not necessarily run the full length of the hull, terminating at the ends of the hold, the last square frames, or some other appropriate location. Figure G-4 illustrates some typical arrangements.

Keel staple [Keel clamp] (Figs. G-3 and G-4a). A large metal staple used to attach the false keel to the keel.

Kevel head. The extension of a frame or top timber above the bulwarks to form a bitt, to which ropes were secured.

Kingplank [Central strake, Kingstrake]. Variously, the central strake of a flush deck or the central strake of a hull without a keel.

Knee [Knee timber] (Figs. G-5, nos. 17, 19, and 29; G-7a, G-7b, G-7c, and G-7e). An angular piece of timber used to reinforce the junction of two surfaces of different planes; usually made from the crotch of a tree where two large branches intersected, or where a branch or root joined the trunk. *See also* **Dagger knee, Hanging knee, Lodging knee,** and **Standing knee**.

Knee of the head [Head knee] (Fig. G-13d). A knee or knee-shaped structure, fixed to the forward surface of the stem, that formed the cutwater at its lower end and supported the headrails and figurehead at its upper end.

Knightheads (Figs. G-3 and G-13a). The forwardmost frame timbers, which ran parallel to the stem, their heels being fayed to the forwardmost cant

frames and their heads extending above deck level to form bitts that
supported the bowsprit between them. Also, a name given to a pair of bitts,
located just aft of the foremast on merchant ships, that supported the ends
of the windlass, or to any bitt whose upper end was carved in the shape of a
human head.

Knuckle. A sharp angle in a frame.

Knuckle timbers (Fig. G-13a). A name sometimes applied to the fore and aft
frames in the bow of a roundbowed ship. The **hawse pieces** and
knightheads.

Land. The portion of a plank that is overlapped by another on a clinker-built vessel.

Lapstrake [Clenched lap]. *See* **Clinker-built**.

Larboard. *See* **Port**.

Ledge (Figs. G-7a and G-7b). A short beam set between and parallel to the
deck beams to provide intermediate support of the deck; the ends of ledges
were supported by **carlings, clamps,** or **lodging knees**.

Leeboard. A large plate, or assembly of timbers, mounted on the side of a hull
and lowered when sailing off the wind to increase lateral resistance and
reduce **leeway**.

Leeway. The sideways drift of a vessel when sailing with the wind abeam.

Lengthening piece. *See* **Ekeing**.

Level lines. Another name for the **waterlines** on hull plans; they described the
horizontal sections of the hull.

Light [Light port]. An opening in a vessel's side or deck, usually glazed, to let
light into a compartment.

Limber boards (Fig. G-5, no. 8). Ceiling planks next to the keelson which could be
removed to clean the limbers; on some ancient vessels, limber boards were laid
transversely above the centerline of the keel. Holes or slots were sometimes cut
into limber boards so that they could be lifted more easily.

Limber holes [Watercourses] (Figs. G-5, no. 10, and G-12). Apertures cut in
the bottom surfaces of frames over, or on either side of, the keel to allow
water to drain into the pump well.

Limber ledges. Rabbeted timbers running parallel to the keel and atop the
floor timbers for the purpose of supporting transverse ceiling planks.

Limbers. Watercourses or channels alongside or central to the keel or keelson,
through which water could drain into the pump well.

Limber strake (Fig. G-5, no. 9). The lowest permanent ceiling strake,
fastened to the tops of the frames next to the limber boards and keelson.

Lines [Hull lines]. The various shapes of a hull; expressed graphically, a set of
geometric projections, usually arranged in three views, that illustrates the
shape of a vessel's hull.

Lining (Fig. G-5). The common ceiling of the orlop, berthing, and gun decks
of ships, set between the spirketting and the clamps. The lining was frequently called **quickwork**, a term more commonly used in British
documents.

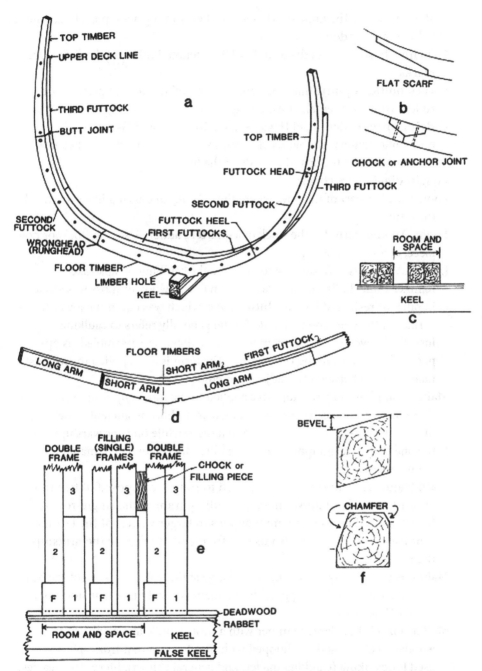

Figure G-12. Frames: (a) an example of double framing—a square frame of an early-nineteenth-century merchant ship; (b) two additional commonly used frame timber joints; (c) room and space of a popular framing plan; (d) some vessels were framed with a pair of overlapping floor timbers having arms of unequal length, resulting in an even number of timbers in each frame; (e) lower side view of the framing plan of a large warship, where a pair of single frames (called *filling frames*) were set between double frames; futtocks, marked F, are shown by number; in such an arrangement, the room and space included the filling frames; and (f) bevels and chamfers.

Lintle (Fig. G-3). The upper horizontal timber framing a gunport, large square light, or gallery door.

Load line. In some cases the term **load line** denoted full-load draft. *See* **Draft marks**.

Locked pintle. A **pintle** that was flanged or keyed in order to prevent the rudder from accidentally unshipping.

Lodging knee [Lodge knee] (Figs. G-5, no. 19, G-7a, and G-7b). A horizontal, angular timber used to reinforce two perpendicular beams or the junction of a beam and the side of the hull.

Longitudinal. *See* **Stringer**.

Loof. The after part of the bow, where the side began curving inward toward the stem.

Loom. Another term for the stock of a quarter rudder. Also, the stock, or pole piece, of an oar or sweep.

Luting. A term used frequently to describe the caulking of lapstrake (clinker-built) hulls. In most cases, animal hair, wool, or moss was soaked in pitch or resin and laid in a **luting cove**, which was cut in the lower inside surface of the overlapping plank. Luting generally refers to caulking inserted between two hull members before they were assembled, as opposed to driven caulking (*see* **Caulk**). The term is also applied to any plastic material used between two adjacent members.

Main. In shipbuilding, the adjective applied to the most important timbers, or those having the greatest cross-sectional area; thus, on ancient vessels the main wale was usually the lowest and largest, while on later warships it was the one below the gunports; also, main breadth, main hatch, main hold, main keelson, etc.

Main frame. A term sometimes applied to frames composed of two rows of futtocks to distinguish them from filling frames, the single-rowed frames placed between them; it applies to larger vessels of the last few centuries. The term was also used infrequently to denote the **midship frame**.

Main piece (Fig. G-13). The longest and largest timber in the knee of the head. Also, a term sometimes applied to the main vertical timber, or stock, of a rudder (Fig. G-18b).

Mallet (Fig. G-8). A large hammer with a short handle and a cylindrical wooden head, sometimes hooped with iron to prevent it from splitting, used for caulking (caulking mallet) and general shipwrightery. The heaviest mallets were also called **beetles**.

Manger. A small compartment, located just inside the hawse hole, whose after bulkhead (called a *manger board*) diverted water entering the hawse hole into the limbers.

Margin plank. *See* **Nibbing strake**.

Mast carlings (Fig. G-7d). Fore-and-aft beams that helped support a mast where it pierced a deck; also called **mast partners**. *See* **Partners**.

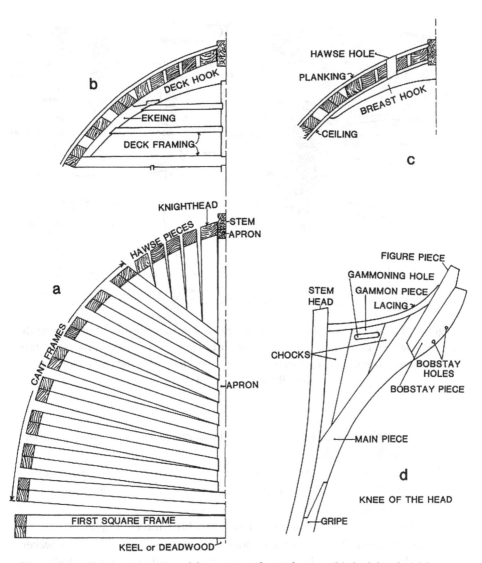

Figure G-13. Bow construction: (a) top view of port frames; (b) deck hook; (c) breast hook and hawse hole; and (d) one of many arrangements used for assembling the knee of the head.

Mast partner (Fig. G-7d). *See* **Partners** and **Mast carlings**.

Mast step (Figs. G-15a–G-15c). A mortise cut into the top of a keelson or large floor timber, or a mortised wooden block or assembly of blocks mounted on the floor timbers or keelson, into which the tenoned heel of a mast was seated. Various types of mast steps are shown in Figure G-15.

Maul (Fig. G-8). A heavy wood or iron hammer, primarily used to drive large bolts.

Meginhufr. A thick plank separating the bottom, or *lower ship*, of a Viking hull from its sides. Either rectangular or L-shaped in cross-section,

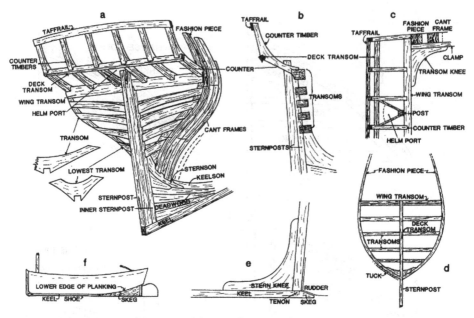

Figure G-14. Stern construction: (a) stern framing of an eighteenth-century brig; (b) partial side view of the same stern near the post; (c) partial top view of the same stern; (d) lower stern framing of a galleon; (e) alternate stern details; and (f) one form of skeg installation on a small sloop.

meginhufrs evolved from the triangular-sectioned sheer strakes of earlier, simpler Norse hulls.

Metacenter. The intersection of a vertical line drawn through the center of gravity of a vessel when it is stable with a vertical line drawn through its center of buoyancy when the vessel is heeled.

Midship [Midships]. A contraction of **amidships** and consequently, in a general sense, it refers to the middle of the ship. In construction, however, it is often used as an adjective referring to the broadest part of the hull, wherever it may be.

Midship beam (Fig. G-5, no. 30). The longest beam in a vessel, located at or near the **midship bend**.

Midship bend (Fig. G-5). The broadest part of the hull; the widest body shape, formed by the centerline of the **midship frame**.

Midship flat [Midship body, Midsection, Midship section]. The extent of the broadest part of the hull, formed by the midship frame and all adjacent frames of the same breadth.

Midship frame (Fig. G-5). The broadest frame in the hull; the frame representing the midship shape on the body plan.

Mold [Mould] (Fig. G-16). A pattern used to determine the shapes of frames and other compass timbers. Molds were usually made from thin, flexible pieces of wood. Convex molds were called *bend molds*, concave molds were

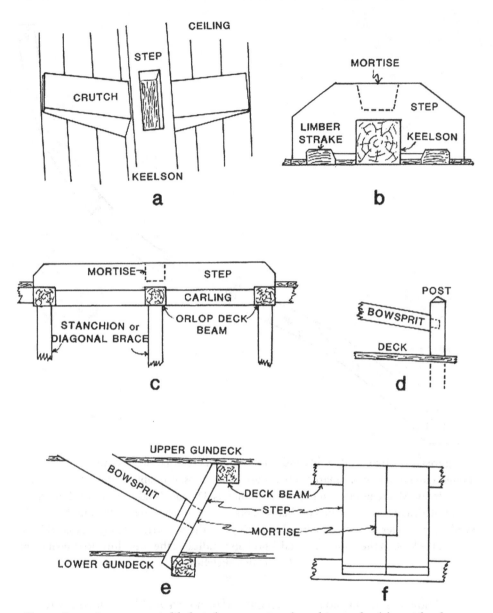

Figure G-15. Arrangements likely to be encountered on shipwrecks: (a) crutches brace the foremast step on the Revolutionary War privateer *Defence*; (b) a mainmast step of the type used on very large eighteenth-century warships; (c) one of a variety of methods for stepping a mizzenmast; (d) bowsprits of smaller vessels were sometimes stepped above deck in a broad sampson post as illustrated, or between pairs of riding bitts just below deck; (e) the bowsprit of a large eighteenth-century warship; and (f) an athwart-ships view of the forward surface of the same step, showing its two-piece construction.

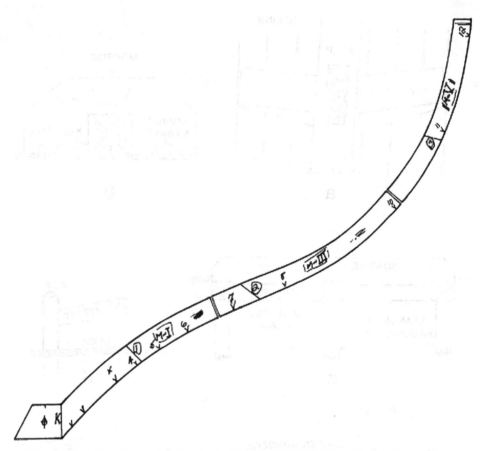

Figure G-16. Two bend molds and a hollow mold are fitted together to form a compound mold or half of a square frame. Individual molds, probably representing futtocks of frame M, are numbered in Roman numerals. Diagonals taken from the loft are indicated, as are carets which probably denote bevel measurements; the numbers and symbols may refer to degrees of bevel or settings on the shipwright's bevel gauge. K is the side of the keel, ⊗ the centerline, and S probably indicates the sheer line. Redrawn from old notebook sketches.

known as *hollow molds*, and *compound* or *reverse molds* included entire frame shapes. The degree of bevel and other pertinent information was written on the molds. The process of shaping outer frame surfaces with molds was known as **beveling**. Figure G-16 illustrates several types of molds. *See also* **Whole molding**.

Molded [Molded dimension]. The various dimensions of timbers as seen from the sheer and body views of construction plans; the dimensions determined by the molds. Thus, the vertical surfaces (the sides) of keels, the fore-and-aft sides of the posts, the vertical or athwartships surfaces of frames, etc. Normally, timbers are expressed in sided and molded dimensions, while planks and wales are listed in thicknesses and widths. Molded and sided dimensions are used because of the changing orientation of timbers, such as frames, where "thick" and "wide" or "height" and "depth" become confusing.

Molded depth. The depth of a hull, measured between the top of the upper deck beams at the side and a line parallel to the top of the keel.

Molding. *See* **Mold** and **Whole molding**.

Mold loft. A protected area or building in a shipyard where the hull lines, from which the molds were produced, were drawn full size on a specially prepared flat surface.

Mortise (Fig. G-17). A cavity cut into a timber to receive a tenon. Large mortises were sometimes referred to as *steps*.

Mortise-and-tenon joint (Fig. G-17). A union of planks or timbers by which a projecting piece (tenon) was fitted into one or more cavities (mortises) of corresponding size. The most common types are:

Fixed tenon and single mortise (Fig. G-17a). A tenon was shaped from the end on one timber and inserted into the mortise of the other. When the tenon of a large vertical timber was left unlocked, as in masts, and sternposts, it was said to be stepped.

Free tenon and two mortises (Fig. G-17b). The most common method of edge-joining planking in ancient and early medieval vessels in the Mediterranean area, it also was used to secure adjoining surfaces of parallel timbers, such as stems and floor timber chocks. Corresponding mortises were cut into each planking edge; a single hardwood tenon was inserted into the lower plank and the adjacent plank fitted over the protruding tenon. In many instances, the joint was locked by driving tapered hardwood pegs into holes drilled near each strake or timber edge.

Free tenon and three or more mortises (Fig. G-17c). Used in superstructure fabrications or places where hull planking was too narrow to provide sufficient seating for the desired tenon length.

Although small planking joints whose tenons are unpegged and contribute no structural strength are essentially **coak joints**, the term mortise-and-tenon joint has become universally accepted for all such forms of edge joinery.

Mortising chisel (Fig. G-8). A specialized chisel used for shaping narrow mortises.

Narrowing line. A curved line on the halfbreadth drawing of a hull, designating the curve of maximum breadth or the ends of the floor timbers throughout the length of the hull. The former was called the *maximum breadth line*; the latter was known as the **breadth of floor line**.

Nib [Nibbing end] (Fig. G-7f). The practice of squaring the ends of deck planks where they terminated at the sides of the hull to avoid fine angles and subsequent splitting and distortion.

Nibbing strake [Margin plank] (Fig. G-7f). A plank running adjacent to the waterways in the ends of a vessel, into which the nibbed ends of deck planks

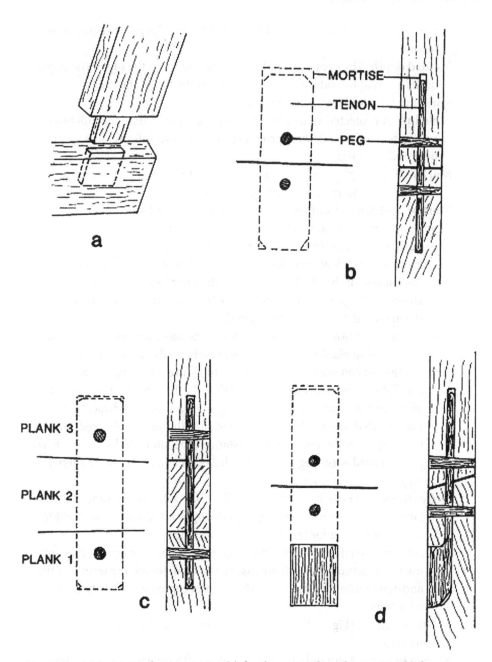

Figure G-17. Mortise-and-tenon joints: (a) fixed tenon and single mortise; (b) free tenon and two mortises; (c) free tenon and three mortises; and (d) patch tenon and two mortises.

were fitted. English documents most frequently referred to this timber as a margin plank; American contracts more commonly called it a nibbing strake.

Oakum [Oakham]. Caulking material made from rope junk, old rope, and rope scraps; it was unwound, picked apart, and the fibers were rolled and soaked in pitch before being driven into planking seams.

Oar port (Fig. G-3). An opening in a vessel's side through which the looms of oars or sweeps passed. *See also* **Sweep port**.

Orlop deck (Fig. G-6). The lowest deck of a large ship.

Outboard. Situated near or on the outer side of a vessel; toward the outer side.

Outer stem. A name sometimes given to the main stempost or to the forward layer of timbers in a double-layered stem.

Outfall. The outward slant of a vessel's sides. *See also* **Flare**.

Overhang. The part of a vessel's stern that projects aft of the rudder stock.

Packing piece (Fig. G-7a). A short piece of timber used to fill open areas between structural timbers; used most frequently at the sides between deck beams or lodging knees.

Parcel. To surround or enclose with strips of flexible material, as in the reinforcement of caulked planking seams (usually lead strips) or between ropes and their servings (usually strips of canvas).

Partners (Fig. G-7d). The timbers surrounding the deck openings for masts, pumps, bitts, and capstans; their primary purpose was to strengthen the deck around the opening and counteract strain. Partners were also used on occasion to steady masts on undecked vessels.

Patch tenon (Fig. G-17d). In ancient vessels, a headed tenon inserted from the exterior or interior surface of a plank. Patch tenons were normally used in the replacement of rotten or damaged planking. The name comes from their installed appearance as square patches in the sides of hulls.

Pay. To coat; to cover a hull bottom with a protective layer of pitch, resin, sulphur, etc.

Peak. The upper portions of the narrow ends of a vessel; cited individually in some documents as **forepeak** and **afterpeak**. Also, a term used to designate the tip of an **anchor palm**.

Peg [Tenon peg] (Fig. G-17b–d). A tapered wooden pin driven into a pre-drilled hole to fasten two members or lock a joint. Pegs came in a variety of sizes and tapers; they could have square, round, or multi-sided cross sections. The important difference between dowels and pegs in ancient construction was that the former were of constant diameter and lightly set, while the latter were tapered and driven with appreciable force. The most common use of pegs in ancient construction was the locking of mortise-and-tenon joints.

Pillar (Fig. G-6). Large vertical stanchion, usually turned or dressed for aesthetic reasons, used to support deck beams or reinforce potentially weak areas. By the seventeenth century, pairs of pillars, called cross pillars, were set diagonally across the hull to provide transverse strength.

Pin rail. A long rack, usually attached to the inside of bulwarks, for holding belaying pins; a short pin rail was called a pin rack.

Pintle (Fig. G-18). A vertical pin at the forward edge of a stern-hung rudder that fit into a gudgeon on the sternpost to form a hinge. On most vessels,

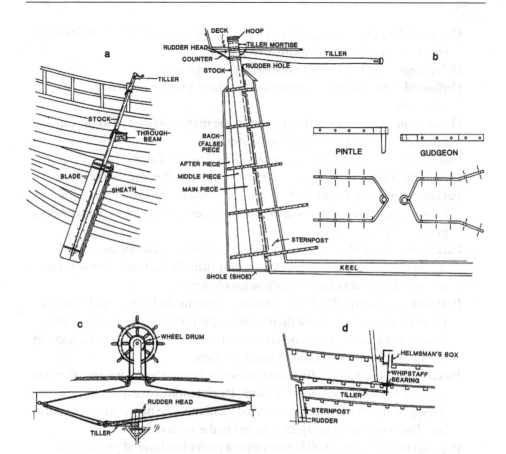

Figure G-18. Steering devices: (a) a Mediterranean balanced quarter-rudder system, ca. fourth century BCE; (b) terminology of an eighteenth-century frigate-sized rudder, which includes a mortise for a manual tiller to be used in [case] the main steering gear failed; details of the hinges—the pintles and gudgeons—are also shown; (c) a common steering wheel rig for medium-sized vessels, eighteenth and nineteenth centuries; and (d) steering with a vertical lever called a whipstaff.

they were welded or cast to a bracket whose arms were fastened to the sides of the rudder.

Pitch [Tar]. A dark, sticky substance used in caulking seams or spread over the inner or outer surfaces of hulls as waterproofing and protection against some forms of marine life. Pitches were variously derived from the resins of certain evergreen trees; from bitumens, such as mineral pitches; or from the distillation of coal tar, wood tar, etc.

Planking (Fig. G-5). The outer lining, or shell, of a hull.

Planking strake [Strake, Streake]. A continuous line of planks, usually running from bow to stern; the sum of a row of planks.

Planksheer [Sheer plank] (Fig. G-5). The strake that described the sheer line of a vessel, attached to the toptimbers from stem to stern at the level of the upper deck. Also, in various times and places, the name given to the uppermost continuous strake of side planking or the upper edge of the uppermost strake. In later English documents, a sheer rail or one of the drift rails.

Plate knee [Plate] (Fig. G-7e). A knee made from iron plate. Normally superimposed over a timber or wooden chock, iron knees were introduced in the latter part of the eighteenth century.

Plug treenail. A piece of straight-grained wood through which metal fastenings were driven. In some cases, pilot holes are said to have been pre-bored through their lengths. They were not driven into the holes of the planks, but fit rather loosely and expanded tightly when the nails were driven through them. Plug treenails were commonly used on the exterior hull surfaces of ancient ships to prevent leakage and splitting of the planks around the fastenings.

Poop [Poopdeck]. The highest and aftermost deck of a ship.

Port [Port side, Larboard]. The left side of a vessel when facing forward.

Pump well [Sump] (Fig. G-3). The cavity or compartment in the bottom of a hull, usually near amidships, where bilgewater collected and from which it was pumped out or bailed. Wells ranged from simple sumps between frames to watertight compartments extending the full height of the hold.

Quarter. The after part of a vessel's side.

Quarterdeck. The after part of the upper deck, from the mainmast to the poop.

Quarter gallery. A small balcony on the side of a ship near its stern.

Quarter rails. Rails, balustrades, or planking running along the quarterdeck.

Quarter rudder. *See* **Rudder**.

Quarter timber. A frame in a vessel's quarter.

Quickwork (Fig. G-5). The common ceiling of the orlop, berthing, and upper decks as well as the gundeck. It was so named because it did not require caulking or precision joinery and therefore could be erected comparatively quickly. *See also* **Lining**.

Rabbet (Figs. G-3 and G-4). A groove or cut made in a piece of timber in such a way that the edges of another piece could be fit into it to make a tight joint. Generally, the term refers to the grooves cut into the sides of the keel, stem, and sternpost, into which the garboards and hooding ends of the outer planking were seated.

Rabbet plane (Fig. G-8). A plane used in smoothing rabbets.

Rag bolt (Fig. G-9). A bolt whose shaft was barbed to prevent it from working out of its hole.

Rail of the head. *See* **Headrails**.

Rake. The inclination of the stem and sternpost beyond the ends of the keel; also, the inclination of the masts from the perpendicular.

Ram. A strong projection on the bow of an ancient warship, usually sheathed in metal, used as a weapon to strike another vessel. Specifically, the ram included the ramming timber, the forward bow timbers configured to reinforce the ramming timber, and a metal sheath; in actual practice, the metal sheath is usually called the ram. Rams were also used, with little success, on iron warships after the middle of the nineteenth century.

Ram bow. Any bow with a projecting forefoot or ram. Ram bows sometimes served non-military functions: a means of reinforcing the bow construction externally, a method of lengthening the waterline to improve lateral resistance and maneuverability, or a decoration or symbol.

Ramming timber. The main timber of an ancient ram, projecting forward from its envelope of bow planks and timbers to reinforce the head of the ram.

Reaming beetle [Reeming beetle] (Fig. G-8). The heaviest caulking mallet, used with a reaming iron for opening seams so that caulking could be driven into them.

Reaming iron [Reeming iron] (Fig. G-8). An iron chisel used for opening planking seams for caulking.

Rib. A small transverse member, often flexible and composed of one or several pieces, that stiffened the outer skin of a hull. Although often a layman's term for **frame**, rib is more properly applied to small craft, such as canoes, small boats, certain heavy frames that run from gunwale to gunwale in clinker-built vessels, or vessels whose skin is made of material other than wood.

Ribband carvel. The designation for a carvel-planked hull whose seams were covered with battens, or ribbands, to prevent the caulking from working out.

Ribbands [Ribbons, Battens]. Long, flexible strips of wood most commonly used as temporary keepers by nailing them across the outside of standing frames while the vessel was being built. When the term *framed on ribbands* was popular in the last few centuries of wooden shipbuilding, the ribbands were sometimes carefully arranged to represent certain rising and narrowing lines, from which planking and intermediate frame shapes were derived.

Rider [Rider frame] (Fig. G-6). An internal frame seated atop the ceiling, to which it was fastened; riders could be single pieces, but more often they were complete frames composed of floor timbers, futtocks, and top timbers. Installed either transversely or diagonally, they provided extra stiffening.

Rider keel (Fig. G-4b). One or more additional keels bolted to the bottom of the main keel to increase its strength. It should not be confused with a false keel, whose primary purpose was to protect the keel's lower surface.

Rider keelson (Fig. G-4b). An additional keelson, or one of several additional keelsons, bolted to the top of the main keelson of a large ship. In some documents, it was called a **False keelson**. *See also* **Keelson**.

Riding bitts (Fig. G-10). Strong, upright timbers in the bow of a ship, to which the anchor cables and hawsers were secured.

Ripping iron (Fig. G-8). A claw-like tool used for removing old copper or wooden sheathing.

Rising line (Fig. 5–19). A curved line on the sheer drawing of a ship, designating the outer ends of the floor timbers or the height of maximum breadth throughout the length of the hull. The former line was called the *rise of floor line* or the *floor head line*; the latter was known as the *height of breadth line. See also* **Narrowing lines**.

Rising wood [Deadwood, Hog] (Figs. G-3 and G-4a). Timbers fastened to the top of the keel and notched into the bottom of the floor timbers to better secure those members to each other and give the proper rising to the floor timbers. Rising wood was located between the apron or forward deadwood and the after deadwood, and was sometimes referred to as the central or keel deadwood.

Rockered keel. A keel that is curved longitudinally so that it is deeper at its middle than at its ends. The term also refers to keels that are molded to a greater dimension amidships than at their ends. *Rocker* should not be confused with **sag**, which is an accidental rocker.

Room and space (Fig. G-12c). The distance from a molded edge of one frame to the corresponding point on an adjoining frame, usually measured at or near the keelson. The part occupied by the frame is called the *room*, while the unoccupied distance between it and the adjacent frame is called the *space*. On large ships of the last few centuries, where filling frames were placed between double frames, the term applied to the distance between the molded edge of one double frame to the corresponding point on the next double frame. Because of the uneven Siding of forward frame faces, irregular spacing, and varying methods of fabrication, **room and space** is often a meaningless term in ancient hull documentation. A more definitive designation for ancient ships is **average frame spacing**, the average of distances between frame centerlines at a common appropriate location, taken throughout the hull or hold.

Round tuck stern. *See* **Tuck**.

Rove [Roove] (Fig. G-9). A small metal washer, used in clinker-built hulls, over which nail or rivet ends are flattened to lock the fastening. The term was also applied to washers used in bolting scarfs, floor timbers, etc.

Roving iron (Fig. G-8). An iron, hollow-ended tool used to drive roves over the ends of nails and bolts before clenching.

Rudder (Fig. G-18). A timber, or assembly of timbers, that could be rotated about an axis to control the direction of a vessel underway. Until the middle of the medieval period, the practice was to mount rudders on one or both stern quarters; these were known as *quarter rudders*. By the late medieval period, however, it appears that most vessels of appreciable size were steered by a single rudder hung at the sternpost; these were known as *stern-hung rudders*. For a brief period, the two types were sometimes used in combination. Rudders were designed for the vessel and type of duty they served. In protected waters they could be made quite broad, while seagoing ships utilized longer, more narrow rudders. For the largest seagoing ships, rudder construction was complex and required huge timbers, the assembly sometimes weighing several tons.

Rudder blade (Fig. G-18). The flat part of the rudder that diverts the water.

Rudder breeching. A strong rope with one end attached to the rudder and the other inside the stern, used to relieve some of the weight on the **gudgeons**.

Rudder chains. Chains or ropes attached to each side of the rudder and to the stern, used to prevent the loss of a rudder if it accidentally became unshipped.

Rudder head (Fig. G-18). The upper part of the rudder stock.

Rudder hole (Fig. G-18). An opening in the stern through which the rudder stock passed.

Rudder post. A term infrequently used to describe either the outer sternpost or the rudder stock.

Rudder sheath (Fig. G-18). A wooden or metal protective covering placed over the leading edge of a quarter rudder blade.

Rudder stock (Fig. G-18). A strong vertical piece to which the tiller was fitted; on large, post-medieval vessels it was the main vertical timber of the rudder, and it was also known as the **mainpiece**.

Rudder trunk. A housing for the rudder stock, usually extending from the counter to the steering deck.

Runghead. *See* **Wronghead**.

Sag [Sagging]. The accidental rocker formed in a keel and bottom due to insufficient timbering or improper loading.

Scantlings. The principal timbers of a vessel.

Scarf [Scarph]. An overlapping joint used to connect two timbers or planks without increasing their dimensions. Figure G-11 illustrates various scarfs used throughout shipbuilding history.

Scroll [Scroll head, Fiddlehead]. Ornamental molding used in place of a figurehead.

Scupper (Fig. G-3). A hole or channel cut in a vessel's side or waterway to drain off deck water.

Scuttle. A small opening, usually covered with a lid, in the side or deck for utilitarian purposes, such as a ballast port.

Seam. The longitudinal joint between two timbers or planks; the term usually refers to planking seams, the longitudinal juxtaposition of the edges of planks in the sides or decks, which were made watertight.

Shake. A longitudinal crack or distortion in a timber, caused by sun, weather, or improper curing. Cracks occurring during curing are also referred to as *checks*.

Sheathing. A thin covering of metal or wood, to protect hulls from marine life or fouling, or to stabilize and protect surface material applied for that purpose. Sheathing was most commonly used in the form of copper, lead, zinc, or alloy sheets, or thin wooden planks known as *furring* or *deals*.

Sheathing nail (Figs. G-9c and G-9d). A small nail or tack used to attach sheathing to a hull.

Sheer. The longitudinal sweep of a vessel's sides or decks.

Sheer line. Specifically, the line of the upper or main deck where it meets the side, but the term is often used to describe the sweep of the bulwarks or weather rail.

Sheer plan. The side view of a vessel's hull plan.

Sheer plank. *See* **Planksheer**.

Shelf [Shelf clamp, Shelf piece]. *See* **Clamp**.

Shelf wale. On ancient and early medieval ships, a thick strake of external planking that supported through-beams and other timbers penetrating the outer planking.

Shell. The external planking of a vessel.

Shell-first construction [Shell-built]. A modern (sometimes misleading) term used to describe the process by which all or part of the outer hull planking was erected before frames were attached to it. In pure shell-built hulls, outer planking was self-supporting and formed the primary structure; the framework fastened to it formed the secondary, or stiffening, structure.

Shift. The act of arranging butts and scarfs so that adjacent joints are not in vertical alignment, thereby avoiding possible hull weaknesses.

Shim. A thin piece of wood used to fill a separation between two timbers or a frame and a plank.

Shipwright. A master craftsman skilled in the construction and repair of ships. In many instances, the person in charge of a ship's construction, including the supervision of carpenters and other personnel, control of expenditures and schedules, and acquisition of materials. Probably in many more areas and periods than have been documented, the term designated a formal title, such as the shipwrights to the English monarchs, or a level of expertise qualifying admission to a guild or association.

Shoe (Figs. G-4 and G-5). A term variously applied to the cover for an anchor fluke or a protecting piece at the bottom of a keel or rudder. *See* **Anchor** and **False keel**.

Shole [Sole, Shoe] (Fig. G-18b). A horizontal piece of wood or metal fixed along the bottom of a rudder to protect the lower ends of the vertical rudder pieces and align the bottom of the rudder with the bottom of the false keel.

Shore. A prop or pole used to brace a vessel in an upright position when not afloat or supported by a cradle.

Shot garland. A rack with hollows cut into it for supporting a row of cannon shot.

Shot locker (Fig. G-3). A small compartment, usually located near the foot of the mainmast, where round shot was stored.

Shroud. A rope or wire support used to steady a mast to the side of a hull.

Side. Described variously as the part of a hull above the waterline or the part above the turn of the bilge.

Sided [Sided dimension]. The dimension of an unmolded surface; the distance across an outer frame surface, the forward or after surface of a stem or sternpost, or the upper surface of a keel or keelson. *See* **Molded** for further information on timber dimensions.

Side keelson. *See* **Keelson**.

Side timbers. In ancient and medieval vessels, one of a series of intermediate framing timbers inserted to provide stiffness along the line of wales. *See also* **intermediate timbers**.

Sill (Fig. G-3). The lower horizontal timber framing a gunport, large square light, or gallery door.

Sintel [Batten clamp]. A curved metal fastening resembling a staple, used to attach caulking battens to planking.

Sister keel. *See* **Bilge keel**.

Sister keelson. *See* **Keelson**.

Skeg (Figs. G-14e and G-14f). A triangular piece, resembling external **deadwood** placed above the after end of the keel; used to reinforce the sternpost and improve sailing qualities of small craft and flat-bottomed vessels. Alternately, the angular after end of the keel, or an extension of the keel, on which the rudder post was mounted or which was used to protect the forward edge of the rudder.

Skeletal construction [Frame-first construction]. A modern (sometimes misleading) term used to describe the procedure in which hulls were constructed by first erecting frames and then attaching the outer skin of planking to them.

Sleeper. A seventeenth-century term for thick ceiling; a bilge stringer or footwale. In eighteenth-century English documents, a transom knee.

Sliding keel. *See* **Centerboard**.

Snelle. A winged, or partition-like, stanchion used to support beams in Viking vessels.

Sny. An archaic term used to describe the upward sweep of bow and stern planking.

Spirketting (Fig. G-5, no. 23). Thick interior planks running between the waterways and the **lining** or **quickwork**.

Square frame. *See* **Frame**.

Square tuck stern. *See* **Tuck**.

Stanchion (Fig. G-5, no. 7). An upright supporting post, including undecorated supports for deck beams and bulkheads.

Standard. *See* **Standing knee**.

Standing knee [Standard] (Figs. G-7e and 5-21). A knee mounted on a deck with its vertical arm pointed upward; most commonly used to reinforce the junction of the deck and side.

Staple (Figs. G-3 and G-4). A metal rod or bar whose sharpened ends were bent at right angles, used to fasten false keels to keels or to secure planking seams that tended to separate. Staples were used from the classical period to the present century.

Starboard. The right side of a vessel when facing forward.

Station lines [Body lines, Section lines]. The projections on a lines drawing that represent the various body shapes of a hull.

Stealer (Fig. G-11a). A short plank inserted between two strakes of planking so that the regular strakes did not have to be made too wide; usually located at the bow or stern ends of bottom or lower side strakes.

Steering gear (Fig. G-18). The mechanism, consisting of chains, ropes, blocks, etc., used to transfer movement of the wheel to the tiller. In more general terms, the various components composing any steering mechanism.

Steering oar. An oar used to steer a small vessel, either from the side or the stern. A steering oar should not be confused with a **quarter rudder**, which is the device commonly used to steer ancient vessels and is permanently mounted and turns about a fixed axis.

Stem [Stempost] (Fig. G-3). A vertical or upward curving timber or assembly of timbers, scarfed to the keel or central plank at its lower end, into which the two sides of the bow were joined.

Stem head (Fig. G-13d). The upper end of the stem.

Stemson (Fig. G-3). A curved timber mounted on the inner surface of the apron; usually, the forward and upward extension of the keelson.

Stern. The after end of a vessel.

Stern framing (Fig. G-14). The assembly of timbers consisting of the sternpost, transoms, and fashion pieces.

Stern knee (Fig. G-14e). An angular timber that reinforced the joint between the keel—or lower deadwoods—and the sternpost or inner sternpost. Also known as the knee of the post.

Stern port. An opening in the stern for guns, cargo loading, or light and ventilation.

Sternpost (Figs. G-14a, b, d). A vertical or upward-curving timber or assembly of timbers stepped into, or scarfed to, the after end of the keel or heel.

Sternson (Fig. G-14a). A curved timber joining the keelson and inner sternpost; usually an extension of the keelson and was mounted on top of the deadwood.

Sternson knee. A knee fitted atop or abaft the sternson to reinforce the upper part of the sternpost.

Stern walk [Stern gallery]. A balcony mounted across the stern.

Stocks. A structure supporting a vessel under construction or repair.

Stopwater (Fig. G-11b). A wooden dowel inserted athwartships in the scarf seams of external timbers to prevent shifting of the joint or to discourage water seepage along the seams.

Strake [Streake]. A continuous line of planks, running from bow to stern.

Stringer [Longitudinal]. A general term describing the longitudinal timbers fixed to the inside surfaces of the frames; the ceiling, other than the common ceiling.

Sump. *See* **Pump well**.

Surmark [Sirmark]. A mark denoting the location or sweep of a ribband or batten.

Sweep port (Fig. G-3). An opening in the bulwarks to accommodate a sweep (large oar).

Tabernacle. A timber assembly or housing that supported a mast or post at deck level. A common support for a hinged mast.

Taffrail [Tafferal] (Figs. G-14a–c). Variously, the upper part of the stern or the rail on top of the stern.

Tenon (Figs. G-14e and G-17). A wooden projection cut from the end of a timber or a separate wooden piece that was shaped to fit into a corresponding mortise. *See* **Mortise-and-tenon joint**.

Tenon-built. A term used to denote vessels whose planking edges were joined by means of **mortise-and-tenon joints**.

Thick stuff (Fig. G-5). A term referring to the thick ceiling of the bottom.

Thole [Tholepin]. A pin, or one of a pair of pins, set vertically in the gunwale to serve as the fulcrum for an oar.

Through-beam (Fig. G-18a). An athwartships timber that extended through and beyond the outer hull planking. Through-beams were most common on ancient and medieval hulls, where they supported the quarter rudders or provided athwartships stiffness to the upper part of the hull.

Thwart. A transverse plank in a boat or galley; used to seat rowers, support masts, or provide lateral stiffness.

Tiller (Fig. G-18). A wooden or metal level fitted into the rudder head, by which the rudder could be moved from side to side.

Timber and room. *See* **Room and space**.

Timber head (Fig. G-12a). The upper extremity of a hull timber.

Timber heel (Fig. G-12a). The lower extremity of a hull timber.

Timbers. In general context, all wooden hull members; specifically, those members that formed the frames of a hull.

Tons burden. *See* **Burden**.

Top and butt (Fig. G-11a). A method of planking whereby one edge of the planks were straight while their opposite sides had two sloping edges of unequal length, reducing the plank widths to half. It was used to increase longitudinal strength and to prevent shifting of wales and other stress-bearing planks.

Top timber (Fig. G-12a). The uppermost member of a frame.

Transom (Figs. G-14a–d). One of the athwartship members, fixed to the sternpost, that shaped and strengthened the stern.

Transom beam. *See* **Transom**.

Transom knee (Fig. G-14c). An angular, horizontal reinforcing timber bolted to a transom and the side.

Treenail [Trunnel, Trennal] (Figs. G-9o and G-9p). A round or multi-sided piece of hardwood, driven through planks and timbers to connect them. Treenails were employed most frequently in attaching planking to frames, attaching knees to ceiling or beams, and in the scarfing of timbers. They were used in a variety of forms: with expanding wedges or nails in their ends, with tapered or square heads on their exterior ends, or completely unwedged and unheaded. When immersed, treenails swelled to make a tight fit.

Tuck (Fig. G-14d). The place where the ends of the bottom planks terminated under the stern or counter. When planks ended in a convex curvature, a vessel was said to have a round tuck; when the stern and counter lay perpendicular to the posts, the vessel was said to have a square tuck.

Tumblehome [Fall home] (Fig. G-5). The inward curvature of a vessel's upper sides as they rose from the point of maximum breadth to the bulwarks. Tumblehome reduced topside weight and improved stability.

Turn of the bilge. The outboard part of the lower hull where the bottom curved toward the side.

Underwater body. The portion of the hull below the waterline.

Upper deck (Fig. G-6). The highest deck extending unbroken from bow to stern.

Upper wale. The highest wale.

Waist. The part of a vessel between the quarterdeck and the forecastle.

Wale. A thick strake of planking, or a belt of thick planking strakes, located along the side of a vessel for the purpose of girding and stiffening the outer hull.

Wart [Boss]. A horizontal hardwood block or projection, attached to the starboard side of a Viking ship's stern, upon which the rudder post rotated.

Waterlines [Level lines]. Lines on a hull drawing representing the horizontal sections of the hull.

Waterway (Fig. G-5). A timber or gutter along the side of a deck whose purpose was to prevent the deck water from running down between the frames and to divert it to the scuppers.

Way. The stocks; a structure on which a vessel was built.

Weather deck. Any exposed deck.

Well. *See* **Pump well**.

Wheel [Steering wheel] (Fig. G-18c). A vertical steering device, fixed to a deck and linked to the tiller by ropes, chains, or gear.

Whipstaff (Fig. G-18d). A vertical steering lever that preceded the wheel; it was connected to the tiller by a toggle arrangement, and it was mounted in a bearing on the deck above the tiller.

Whole molding. A process to determine the transverse shapes of hulls by means of one or more standard molds, which were shifted as necessary to produce fair shapes without the use of compasses and complex drafting methods. The process was not as precise as determining individual hull shapes from lines drawings or with compasses and scales, and it was usually limited to the production of small craft after the seventeenth or early eighteenth century.

Windlass (Fig. G-10). A horizontal cylinder, supported by bitts or brackets, used to haul anchors and hawsers.

Wing transom (Figs. G-14a, c, d). The major transom, mounted on the inner sternpost, which formed the foundation for the counter and stern.

Withy. A flexible twig or root, most frequently worked by hammering to make it more pliable, used for binding the seams of planks and timbers.

Wronghead [Runghead] (Fig. G-12a). The head, or extremity, of a floor timber.

REFERENCES CITED

Rosloff, Jay P. 1991. A one-armed anchor of c. 400 B.C.E. from the Ma'agan Michael vessel, Israel: A preliminary report. *International Journal of Nautical Archaeology* 20 (3): 223–226.

Stevens, John R. 1949. *An account of the construction, and embellishment of old time ships.* Toronto: John R. Stevens.

Ucelli, Guido. 1950. *Le navi de Nemi.* Rome: Istituto Poligrafico e Zecca dello Stato.

van Doorninck, Frederick H., Jr. 1988. The anchors: A limited technology, a sophisticated design. *INA Newsletter* 15 (3): 24–25.

APPENDIX:
SCIENTIFIC ANALYSES
AND DATING TECHNIQUES

The following table is intended to convey the overall breadth and scope of some scientific analyses and dating techniques that can be applied to artifacts and samples recovered from maritime archaeological sites. It is not a comprehensive resource, nor does it reflect the information that can be gleamed from the cultural properties or typological classification of artifacts that often complements the scientific analyses. Given the rapid pace of development in many of the following areas of research, this material is represented in a cursory introductory format, leading the reader to explore current publications that discuss the capabilities and limitations of the analyses and dating techniques mentioned below.

Material	Dating	Identification & Provenience
Ceramics	Fission-track dating	Atomic absorption spectrometry
	Optical classification	Electron probe microanalysis / scanning electron probe microanalysis
	Rehydroxylation dating (limited)	Inductively coupled plasma atomic emission spectrometry
	Thermoluminescence / optically stimulated luminescence	Inductively coupled plasma mass spectrometry
		Mössbauer spectroscopy
		Neutron activation analysis
		Optical classification
		Petrographic analysis
		Scanning electron microscopy
		X-ray fluorescence
Particular Cases		
• Burned clay	Archaeomagnetic dating	

(*continued*)

Material	Dating	Identification & Provenience
Glass/Faience	Fission-track dating	Atomic absorption spectrometry
		Inductively coupled plasma atomic emission spectrometry
		Inductively coupled plasma mass spectrometry
		Neutron activation analysis
		Scanning electron microscopy
		X-ray fluorescence
Metals		Atomic absorption spectrometry
		Electron probe microanalysis / scanning electron probe microanalysis
		Inductively coupled plasma atomic emission spectrometry
		Inductively coupled plasma mass spectrometry
		Metallographic examination
		Neutron activation analysis
		Scanning electron microscopy
		X-ray fluorescence
Particular Cases		
• Archaeometallurgical slag	Optically stimulated luminescence	
• Lead	Magnetic properties	Lead isotope analysis
Organics	Radiocarbon dating	DNA analysis
		Scanning electron microscopy
Particular Cases		
• Bone	Amino-acid racemization	Isotopic analysis
	Uranium-series dating	
• Shell	Amino-acid racemization	Gas chromatography mass spectrometry
		Gas liquid chromatography
		Infrared spectroscopy
		Isotopic analysis
		Optical classification
• Tooth	Electron spin resonance dating	Isotopic analysis
	Uranium-series dating	
• Textiles		Chromatography
		Microwear analysis
• Wood/charcoal	Dendrochronology	

Material	Dating	Identification & Provenience
Sediments	Optically stimulated luminescence	
	Thermoluminescence	
Particular Cases		
• Tephra	Tephrochronology	
Stone	Fission-track dating	Inductively coupled plasma mass spectrometry
		Mass spectrometry
		Microwear analysis
Particular Cases		
• Burnt flint/ stone	Thermoluminescence	Atomic absorption spectrometry
• Calcium-carbonate rich rock	Uranium-series dating	
• Marble		Cathodoluminescence
		Neutron activation analysis
		Isotopic analysis
• Obsidian	Obsidian hydration dating	Fission-track analysis
		Scanning electron microscopy
		Neutron activation analysis
		X-ray fluorescence
		Atomic absorption spectrometry
• Volcanic rock	Argon-Argon dating / Potassium-Argon dating	

INDEX

....